TWELFTH EDITION

# MANAGEMENT

## RICKY W. GRIFFIN

Texas A&M University

CENGAGE
Learning·

Australia • Brazil • Japan • Korea • Mexico • Singapore • Spain • United Kingdom • United States

**Management, Twelfth Edition**
Ricky W. Griffin

Vice President, General Manager, Social
   Science & Qualitative Business: Erin Joyner

Product Director: Jason Fremder

Senior Product Manager: Scott Person

Senior Content Developer: Julia Chase

Product Assistant:  Brian Pierce

Marketing Director: Kristen Hurd

Marketing Manager:  Emily Horowitz

Marketing Coordinator: Christopher Walz

Manufacturing Planner: Ron Montgomery

Art and Cover Direction, Production
   Management, and Composition: Cenveo
   Publisher Services

Cover Image(s): ©Markus Pfaff/Shutterstock
.com

Intellectual Property

   Analyst: Diane Garrity

   Project Manager: Sarah Shainwald

For product information and technology assistance, contact us at
**Cengage Learning Customer & Sales Support, 1-800-354-9706**

For permission to use material from this text or product,
submit all requests online at **cengage.com/permissions**
Further permissions questions can be emailed to
**permissionrequest@cengage.com**

Library of Congress Control Number: 2015950180

ISBN: 978-1-305-50129-4

**Cengage Learning**
20 Channel Center Street
Boston, MA 02210
USA

Cengage Learning is a leading provider of customized learning solutions with
employees residing in nearly 40 different countries and sales in more than
125 countries around the world. Find your local representative at
**www.cengage.com.**

Cengage Learning products are represented in Canada by Nelson
Education, Ltd.

To learn more about Cengage Learning Solutions,
visit **www.cengage.com**

Purchase any of our products at your local college store or at our
preferred online store **www.cengagebrain.com**

Printed in the United States of America
Print Number: 02      Print Year: 2018

# BRIEF CONTENTS

# CONTENTS

## PART TWO Understanding the Environmental Context of Managing

### CHAPTER 3: UNDERSTANDING THE ORGANIZATION'S ENVIRONMENT   64

### CHAPTER 4: RESPONDING TO THE ETHICAL AND SOCIAL ENVIRONMENT   100

## PART SIX  The Controlling Process

Since the publication of its first edition in 1984, over two million students at hundreds of colleges and universities on five continents have used *Management* in preparation for their careers in business. In this twelfth edition, I have retained all the elements that have contributed to the book's success in the past while also taking a clear look toward the future—the future of business, of management, and of learning.

Writing a survey book poses a number of challenges. First, because it is a survey, it has to be comprehensive. Second, it has to be accurate and objective. Third, because management is a real activity, the book has to be relevant. Fourth, it has to be timely and up-to-date. And fifth, it must be as interesting and as engaging as possible. Feedback on previous editions of the text has always suggested that the book meets and exceeds these goals. In this edition, I think these goals have been met even more effectively.

I believe that current and previous users of *Management* will be pleased with how we have retained the essential ingredients of a comprehensive management textbook while adding a variety of new elements and perspectives. I also believe that those new to this edition will be drawn to the solid foundations of management theory and practice combined with new and exciting material.

## Highlights and Improvements in the Twelfth Edition

The twelfth edition of *Management* is a substantial revision of the earlier work. Rather than simply adding the "hot topics" of the moment, I continue to thoroughly revise this book with the long-term view in mind. There are significant revisions of all chapters; an increased emphasis on the service sector, ethics, global management, and information technology; and an integrated organization of chapters. The book has also been streamlined to an economical 20 chapters while maintaining its comprehensive coverage. These changes reflect what I believe, and what reviewers and employers have confirmed, students will need to know as they enter a brand new world of management. In addition, several integrated pedagogical features such as "Manager's Checklist" will also prove to be invaluable.

### Revisions in the Twelfth Edition

While the twelfth edition represents a comprehensive revision of the previous edition, there are also a number of specific changes that have been made. These include:

1. The text has been revised in many places to reflect on and discuss the uncertain fluctuations in the global economy and how those fluctuations affect managers.
2. The text also covers the continued unrest in the Middle East and its implications for business.
3. All data and statistics related to small business, international business, unionization, executive compensation, and other areas of business have been updated to the most current information available.

4. All of the chapter opening cases ("Management in Action") are new.
5. All of the chapter closing cases ("Management at Work") are new.
6. The twelfth edition includes a total of 40 all-new boxed features (two per chapter).
7. There are over 150 new examples in the twelfth edition. In addition, those examples retained from the previous edition have all been checked for currency and continued applicability.
8. The latest research on international business, entrepreneurship, strategic management, decision making, organization design, organization change, individual behavior, leadership, teams, motivation, control, information technology, productivity, and quality management has been cited and integrated throughout the text.
9. All supplements have been updated to match these text changes, including the *CourseMate* website.

## Integrated Coverage

Many textbooks set certain material off from the rest of the text in a separate section at the end of the book or a website called "Emerging Trends," "Special Challenges," or something similar. New and emerging topics, and other material that doesn't easily fit anywhere else, are covered in such a section. Unfortunately, by setting those topics apart in this way, the material often gets ignored or receives low-priority treatment.

But I decided several editions back that if this material was really worth having in the book at all, it needed to be fully merged with the core material. Thus, all material—both traditional and contemporary—is integrated throughout the text in order to provide more uniform and cohesive coverage of the entire field of management. This framework also helps to streamline the book's overall organization into six logical and symmetrical parts. Because reviewers and students have responded so favorably to this approach, it has been retained in the twelfth edition. Furthermore, cross-referencing strengthens the integrated coverage throughout the text.

## Logical Chapter Organization

This integrated approach to management also results in a logical and very effective chapter organization. Part 1 introduces the field of management, while Part 2 focuses on the environment of management. The remaining four parts cover the basic managerial functions of planning and decision making, organizing, leading, and controlling.

# Features of the Book
## Basic Themes

Several key themes are prominent in this edition of *Management*. One critical theme is the ethical scrutiny under which managers work today. While the book has always included substantial coverage of ethics and social responsibility, even more attention has been devoted this time to topics such as corporate governance, ethical leadership, and the proper role of auditing. Another continuing theme is the global character of the field of management, which is reinforced throughout the book by examples and cases. A third key theme, digital technology, is integrated throughout the book. Still another theme is the balance of theory and practice: Managers need to have a sound basis for their decisions, but the theories that provide that basis must be grounded in reality. Throughout the book I explain the theoretical frameworks that guide managerial activities and provide illustrations and examples of how and when those theories do and do not work. A fifth theme is that management is a generic activity not confined to large businesses. I use examples and discuss management in both small and large businesses as well as in not-for-profit organizations.

## A Pedagogical System That Works

The pedagogical elements built into *Management*, Twelfth Edition, continue to be effective learning and teaching aids for students and instructors.

- Learning outcomes preview key themes at the start of every chapter. Key terms and concepts are highlighted in color and defined in the margin near where they are discussed. Effective figures, tables, and photographs with their own detailed captions help bring the material to life.

- A new feature in this edition is "Manager's Checklist." Each major section in every chapter concludes with one to four bullet points that succinctly summarize the major take-aways from that section. These are designed to capture the essential points from that section that are most relevant to current and future managers.

- Three kinds of questions at the end of every chapter are designed to test different levels of student understanding. "Questions for Review" ask students to recall specific information, "Questions for Analysis" ask students to integrate and synthesize material, and "Questions for Application" ask students to apply what they've learned to their own experiences.

- Each chapter also includes useful skill-development exercises. These exercises give students insight into how they approach various management situations and how they can work to improve their management skills in the future. The exercises are derived from the overall managerial skills framework developed in Chapter 1. For this edition, many of the exercises were replaced or substantially revised.

- Finally, and also new to this edition, each chapter also includes a Skill-Building Personal Assessment. These self-assessments give students insights into their individual strengths, weaknesses, and perspectives that are relevant to them as current or future managers.

## Applications That Keep Students Engaged

To fully appreciate the role and scope of management in contemporary society, it is important to see examples and illustrations of how concepts work in the real world. I rely heavily on fully researched examples to illustrate real-world applications. They vary in length, and all were carefully reviewed for their timeliness. To give the broadest view possible, I include examples of both traditional management roles and nontraditional roles; profit-seeking businesses and nonprofits; large corporations and small businesses; manufacturers and services; and international and U.S. situations. Furthermore, in this edition I have developed a better balance of large and established businesses (such as Home Depot, Coca-Cola, Boeing, Intel, and General Electric) and new, emerging businesses (such as Google, Starbucks, Facebook, and Urban Outfitters).

Other applications include:

- Opening incidents at the beginning of every chapter. These vignettes, titled "Management in Action," draw the student into the chapter with a real-world scenario that introduces a particular management theme. Highlights include American Apparel, Harley Davidson in Africa, the *Hunger Games* movies, the Houston Astros baseball team, and many more.

- A companion end-of-chapter feature called "You Make the Call." This feature is tied back to the chapter-opening incident; it requires the student to play the role of a consultant, a manager, or other stakeholder in the organization featured earlier. Students are asked to comment, critique, or make suggestions about how well the business is doing and/or what it needs to do differently.

- Call-out quotations. Spread throughout each chapter, these quotations provide real insights into how managers and other experts see the world of business as it relates to the topic at hand.
- Boxed features. Each chapter includes two boxed features. These boxes are intended to depart briefly from the flow of the chapter to highlight or extend especially interesting or emerging points and issues. There are five types of featured boxes represented throughout the text:

 *A World of Difference* (the role of diversity in organizations)

 *Tech Watch:* (the role and impact of technology in business)

 *Leading the Way* (the role and importance of leadership in business)

 *Doing Business on Plant Earth* (sustainability)

 *Beyond Traditional Business* (management in nonbusiness organizations)

- End-of-chapter cases. Each chapter concludes with a detailed case study, called "Management at Work," written especially for the context of this book. These cases represent companies familiar to students, including Wells Fargo, Starbucks, Blackberry, Uber, Kodak, and many more.

## Instructor Support Materials

- Instructor Companion Website: Instructors can find course support materials, including the Instructor's Resource Manual, Test Bank files, PowerPoint® slides, and DVD guide.
- On the Job DVD: "On the Job" videos provide behind-the-scenes insights into management concepts at work within actual small and large businesses. Corresponding support material can be found in the DVD guide.
- Cengage Learning Testing, powered by Cognero® Instant Access: Cengage Learning Testing powered by Cognero® is a flexible, online system that allows you to import, edit, and manipulate content from the text's test bank or elsewhere, including your own favorite test questions; create multiple test versions in an instant; and deliver tests from your LMS, your classroom, or wherever you want.

## Student Support Materials

- MindTap® Management for Griffin's Management, Twelfth Edition, is the digital learning solution that helps instructors engage students and help them relate management concepts to their lives. Through interactive assignments students connect management concepts to real-world organizations and say how managers should perform in given situations. Finally, all activities are designed to teach students to problem-solve and think like management leaders. Through these activities and real-time course analytics, and an accessible reader, MindTap helps you turn cookie cutter into cutting edge, apathy into engagement, and memorizers into higher-level thinkers.

  Our adaptive learning solution provides customized questions, text, and video resources based on student proficiency. Priced to please students and administrators, this solution will help you develop the next generation of managers.

- The **learning path** is based on our **Engage**, **Connect**, **Perform**, and **Lead** model. Students are drawn into the material with self-assessments. Quizzes and homework assignments help students connect concepts with the real world, and higher-level homework assignments ask students to analyze and manage complex situations.

- **Self-assessments** engage students by helping them make personal connections to the content presented in the chapter.

- **Reading quizzes** assess students' basic comprehension of the reading material to help you gauge their level of engagement and understanding of the content.

- **Homework assignments** for each chapter are presented in our **Aplia** product. Question sets challenge students to think critically and begin to think like managers.

- **Concept videos** present short enrichment clips of information on topics students typically struggle with.

- **Video case activities** engage students by presenting everyday businesses facing managerial challenges, placing concepts in a real-world context and making for great points of discussion.

- **Experiential Exercises powered by YouSeeU** include role play and group projects challenge students to work in teams in our one-of-a-kind collaborative environment to solve real-world managerial problems, develop skills and begin to experience firsthand what it's like to work in management.

- **Branching activities** present challenging problems that cannot be solved with one specific correct answer. Students are presented with a series of decisions to be made based upon information they are given about a company and are scored according to the quality of their decisions.

- **Adaptive study centers** are provided at the unit level and the exam level to help students work toward mastery of course content. Material presented is customized to students' specific needs and serves up questions, feedback, remediation, and instructional content according to how they progress.

- **Writing Activities powered by Write Experience** offers students the opportunity to improve their writing and analytical skills without adding to your workload. Offered through an exclusive agreement with Vantage Learning, creator of the software used for GMAT essay grading, Write Experience evaluates students' answers to a select set of assignments for writing for voice, style, format, and originality.

I would also like to invite your feedback on this book. If you have any questions, suggestions, or issues to discuss, please feel free to contact me. The most efficient way to reach me is through e-mail at *rgriffin@tamu.edu*.

*Ricky W. Griffin*

# ACKNOWLEDGMENTS

I am often asked by my colleagues why I write textbooks, and my answer is always, "Because I enjoy it." I've never enjoyed writing a book more than this one. For me, writing a textbook is a challenging and stimulating activity that brings with it a variety of rewards. My greatest reward continues to be the feedback I get from students and instructors about how much they like this book.

I owe an enormous debt to many different people for helping me create *Management*. My colleagues at Texas A&M University have helped create a wonderful academic climate. The rich and varied culture at Texas A&M makes it a pleasure to go to the office every day.

The fine team of professionals at Cengage Learning has also been instrumental in the success of this book. Erin Joyner, Jason Fremder, Scott Person, Carol Moore, Julia Chase, Brian Pierce, Jennifer Ziegler, Rajachitra Suresh, Sarah Shainwald, and Dianne Garrity were instrumental in the production of this edition. Julia Chase, in particular, played a major role in this edition. Ron Librach also provided valuable assistance with his work on the cases and boxed features in this edition. Many reviewers have played a critical role in the continuous evolution and improvement of this project. They examined my work in detail and with a critical eye. I would like to tip my hat to the following reviewers, whose imprint can be found throughout this text:

Pamela Acuff
*University of Nebraska–Omaha*

Ramon J. Aldag
*University of Wisconsin*

Dr. Raymond E. Alie
*Western Michigan University*

Roanne Angiello
*Bergen Community College*

William P. Anthony
*Florida State University*

Jeanne Aurelio
*Stonehill College*

Jay B. Barney
*Ohio State University*

Richard Bartlett
*Muskingum Area
Technical College*

Michael Bento
*Owens Community College*

John D. Bigelow
*Boise State University*

Bruce Bloom
*DeVry University–Chicago*

Allen Bluedorn
*University of Missouri*

Thomas M. Bock
*The DeVry Institute of Technology*

Henry C. Bohleke
*Tarrant County College*

Marv Borglett
*University of Maryland*

Gunther S. Boroschek
*University of Massachusetts–Boston Harbor
Campus*

Jennifer Bott *Ball
State University*

John Brady
*Indiana Tech*

Paula Brown
*Northern Illinois University*

Dean Bruce
*Northwest College*

Gerald E. Calvasina
*University of North Carolina–Charlotte*

Joseph Cantrell
*DeAnza College*

George R. Carnahan
*Northern Michigan University*

Bruce Charnov
*Hofstra University*

Ron Cheek
*University of New Orleans*

Anwar Chowdhury
*DeVry University*

Thomas G. Christoph
*Clemson University*

Charles W. Cole
*University of Oregon*

Elizabeth Cooper
*University of Rhode Island*

C. Brad Cox
*Midlands Technical College*

Carol Cumber
*South Dakota State University*

Joan Dahl
*California State University–Northridge*

Carol Danehower
*University of Memphis*

Roger Dean
*Washington and Lee University*

Satish Deshpande
*Western Michigan University*

Gregory G. Dess
*University of Kentucky*

Ron DiBattista
*Johnson & Wales University*

Gary N. Dicer
*University of Tennessee*

Nicholas Dietz
*State University of New York—Farmingdale*

Thomas J. Dougherty
*University of Missouri*

Shad Dowlatshahi
*University of Wisconsin—Platteville*

John Drexler Jr.
*Oregon State University*

Joe Eassa
*Palm Beach Atlantic University*

Stan Elsea
*Kansas State University*

Douglas A. Elvers
*University of South Carolina*

Jim Fairbank
*West Virginia University*

Dan Farrell
*Western Michigan University*

Gerald L.Finch
*Universidad Internacional del Ecuador and Universidad San Francisco de Quito*

Charles Flaherty
*University of Minnesota*

Marcy Fusilier
*Northwestern State University*

Ari Ginsberg
*New York University Graduate School of Business*

Norma N. Givens
*Fort Valley State University*

David Glew
*University of North Carolina–Wilmington*

George Goerner
*Mohawk Valley Community College*

Carl Gooding
*Georgia Southern College*

George J. Gore
*University of Cincinnati*

Bill Gray
*San Diego City College*

Jonathan Gueverra
*Lesley College*

Stanley D. Guzell Jr.
*Youngstown State University*

John Hall
*University of Florida*

Mark A. Hammer
*Washington State University*

Barry Hand
*Indiana State University*

Paul Harmon
*University of Utah*

Roxanne Helm
*Azusa Pacific University*

Stephanie Henagan
*Louisiana State University*

Nathan Himelstein
*Essex County College; New Jersey Institute of Technology*

John Hughes
*Texas Tech University*

J. G. Hunt (deceased)
*Texas Tech University*

John H. Jackson
*University of Wyoming*

Neil W. Jacobs
*University of Denver*

Arthur G. Jago
*University of Missouri*

Madge Jenkins
*Lima Technical College*

Kathy Jones
*University of North Dakota*

Gopol Joshi
*Central Missouri State University*

Norman F. Kallaus
*University of Iowa*

Ben L. Kedia
*University of Memphis*

Joan Keeley
*Washington State University*

Thomas L. Keon
*University of Central Florida*

Charles C. Kitzmiller
*Indian River Community College*

Barbara Kovach
*Rutgers University*

William R. LaFollete
*Ball State University*

Kenneth Lawrence
*New Jersey Institute of Technology*

Cynthia Lengnick-Hall
*University of Texas–San Antonio*

Clayton G. Lifto
*Kirkwood Community College*

John E. Mack
*Salem State University*

Elaine Madden
*Anne Arundel Community College*

Myrna P. Mandell
*California State University–Northridge*

Patricia M. Manninen
*North Shore Community College*

Thomas Martin
*University of Nebraska–Omaha*

Barbara J. Marting
*University of Southern Indiana*

Lisa McConnell
*Oklahoma State University*

Melvin McKnight
*Northern Arizona University*

Wayne A. Meinhart
*Oklahoma State University*

Sandy Miles
*Murray State University*

Aratchige Molligoda
*Drexel University*

Behnam Nakhai
*Millersville University of Pennsylvania*

Robert Nale
*Coastal Carolina University*

Linda L. Neider
*University of Miami*

Mary Lippitt Nichols
*University of Minnesota*

Winston Oberg
*Michigan State University*

David Oliver
*Edison College*

Michael Olivette
*Syracuse University*

Eugene Owens
*Western Washington University*

Daewoo Park
*Xavier University*

Sheila Pechinski
*University of Maine*

Monique Pelletier
*San Francisco State University*

E. Leroy Plumlee
*Western Washington University*

Raymond F. Polchow
*Muskingum Area Technical College*

Boris Porkovich
*San Francisco State University*

Paul Preston
*University of Texas–San Antonio*

John M. Purcell
*State University of New York–Farmingdale*

James C. Quick
*University of Texas–Arlington*

Clint Relyea
*Arkansas State University*

Ralph Roberts
*University of West Florida*

Christopher Roe
*DeVry University*

Nick Sarantakas
*Austin Community College*

Khaled Sartawi
*Fort Valley State University*

Gene Schneider
*Austin Community College*

H. Schollhammer
*University of California–Los Angeles*

Diane R. Scott
*Wichita State University*

Mike Shaner
*St. Louis University*

Harvey Shore
*University of Connecticut*

Marc Siegall
*California State University–Chico*

Nicholas Siropolis
*Cuyahoga Community College*

Michael J. Stahl
*University of Tennessee*

Diane Stone
*Ivy Technical State College*

Marc Street
*University of Tulsa*

Charlotte D. Sutton
*Auburn University*

Kambiz Tabibzadeh
*Eastern Kentucky University*

Robert L. Taylor
*University of Louisville*

Mary Thibodeaux
*University of North Texas*

Joe Thomas
*Middle Tennessee State University*

Leslie User
*Concordia University St. Paul*

Sean Valentine
*University of Wyoming*

Robert D. Van Auken
*University of Oklahoma*

Billy Ward
*The University of West Alabama*

Richard Warner
*Lehigh Carbon Community College*

Liesl Wesson
*Texas A&M University*

Fred Williams
*University of North Texas*

Mary Williams
*Community College of Southern Nevada*

James Wilson
*University of Texas–Pan American*

Carl P. Zeithaml
*University of Virginia*

I would also like to make a few personal acknowledgments. The fine work of OneRepublic, Adele, Hozier, Roy Orbison, Lyle Lovett, and Johnny Rivers helped me make it through many late evenings and early mornings of work on the manuscript that became the book you hold in your hands. And Stephen King, Lee Child, James Lee Burke, Peter Straub, and Carl Barks provided me with a respite from my writings with their own.

Finally, there is the most important acknowledgment of all—my feelings for and gratitude to my family. My wife, Glenda, and our children, Dustin, Ashley, Matt, and Lura are the foundation of my professional and personal life. And Griffin, Sutton, and Andrew bring joy to my heart and the occasional tear to my eye, because I love them so much. They help me keep work and play in perspective and give meaning to everything I do. It is with all my love that I dedicate this book to them.

R.W.G.

For Glenda—a survivor, my inspiration, my best friend,
my island, my rock, and the center of my universe
RWG

©Markus Pfaff/Shutterstock.com

# MANAGING AND THE MANAGER'S JOB

**Learning Outcomes**

**After studying this chapter, you should be able to:**

1. Describe the nature of management, define management and managers, and characterize their importance to contemporary organizations.

2. Identify and briefly explain the four basic management functions in organizations.

3. Describe the kinds of managers found at different levels and in different areas of the organization.

4. Identify the basic managerial roles played by managers and the skills they need to be successful.

5. Discuss the science and the art of management, describe how people become managers, and summarize the scope of management in organizations.

6. Characterize the new workplace that is emerging in organizations today.

MANAGEMENT IN ACTION # MANAGEMENT IN ACTION How to Make Mistakes and Influence People

"No one wants to be handed a list from their manager of all the ways they'll inevitably fail."

—ELAINE WHERRY, CO-FOUNDER OF MEEBO

Although she has just a little over fourteen years of management experience under her belt, Elaine Wherry is confident that there's one thing she can teach people about the business of managing a business: MANAGERS MAKE MISTAKES.[1]

Mistakes, as Wherry is quick to point out, come with the territory, especially when the territory that you want to conquer is unfamiliar, whether the wide-open spaces of a brand-new company or the well-defended plot of higher ground occupied by upper-level management. "Everyone," she says, "has to go through the same rites of passage," but "you recover more quickly" when you admit and reflect upon your mistakes. Wherry's specialty is reflecting upon mistakes. In fact, she's made a second career out of reflecting publicly on her own.

In 2005, twenty-something Wherry, who entered Stanford University as a music major and emerged with a degree in symbolic systems, got together with two friends to start up Meebo, a social media platform designed to provide instant messaging to such major network services as Google, Yahoo! Messenger, and Facebook. Like many start-up creators, Wherry soon found herself taking on a variety of jobs, most of which she had to design, develop, and define as she went along. As she moved herself up the company ladder, from code writer to manager, to director, to VP of products and then chief experience officer, Wherry gained first-hand experience at making a broad range of the kinds of mistakes that upwardly mobile managers tend to make.

By 2012, she was on the *CBS Morning Show* explaining how and why she'd kept track of them in a diary in which she dutifully made entries for six years: "I was a typical first-time Silicon Valley entrepreneur," she admitted. "I had no significant managerial experience, and of course I made a ton of mistakes. And so I'd find myself awake at 2:00 or 3:00 a.m., agonizing over the mistakes that I'd made in the daytime. . . . I wanted

Meebo offers chat room services that companies can embed in their web pages. Elaine Wherry, co-founder of Meebo and shown here on the left, has a lot of practical advice for future managers.

Peter DaSilva/The New York Times/Redux

to be able to reflect on them later so I wouldn't beat myself up during the week. It was also a way to get more sleep."

The real value of Wherry's combination of sleep therapy and self-improvement became apparent when she started hiring and managing new employees: "I realized that, being in the unique role of a founder, I was changing hats every six months, and when I started hiring team members to fill my shoes, I saw them make the exact same mistakes that I did."

When Wherry tried to deal with the situation, the first thing she did was make a mistake. "At first, I tried giving new managers and directors my bulleted list. However, that was horribly ineffective. No one wants to be handed a list from their manager of all the ways they'll inevitably fail." After reflecting on her mistake, Wherry hit upon the idea of imparting her experience through stories: "I started focusing on telling stories and setting the scenes for these mistakes. I sketched the scenes of all of the mistakes and started weaving them into a story that showed the professional journey that everyone makes from her first day on the job as a fresh grad to leading the company as a C-level executive." Not surprisingly, Wherry found herself a suitable subject for many of her stories—"the first time I had to scrap a project I loved," for example, "or interviewing disaster stories."

In 2012, as Meebo was being sold to Google for a reported $100 million, Wherry left the company. The next year, she included a "100 Mistakes" feature in her blog at www.ewherry.com, adding whimsical little drawings to underscore the key points made by brief scenarios. "Most mistakes," she says, "happen from good intentions gone astray, lingering habits from previous roles, or not knowing your responsibilities."

So what's a good example of a noteworthy mistake? "Lunch-time conversations," suggests Wherry. "Maybe it's been a frustrating morning, you're surrounded by coworkers, and it's really tempting to say things like, 'I can't believe the company thinks it's going to hit this goal!' Managers don't realize how destructive those conversations really are. The underlying sentiment of a lot of those conversations is, 'Corporate management is clueless.'" The moral of the story? DON'T VENT IN PUBLIC PLACES, which is closely related to IT'S NOT A DEMOCRACY

AND YOU'RE NOT A PAL and DELEGATE AND HOLD YOUR TEAM RESPONSIBLE. For example, Wherry illustrates a relevant story about a new manager at a company like Meebo. Six drawings are accompanied by the following six captions:

1.  *You're ready. Bring it on! You're going to do anything you can to get an A+ and change the world!*
2.  *But what's this? Your codebase and design has hacks.*
3.  *So you send an email to everyone in the company proposing a redesign that scales to billions of people.*

> **3:17 am**
> **To: All**
> **From: You**
>
> **It's come to my attention that we write hacky code.**
>
> **I don't know if that's because you're inept or just lazy.**
>
> **Here's my grand plan to make it perfect.**
>
> **—XOXO**

4.  *But no one is participating. Your meetings feel like you're pulling teeth.*
5.  *Meanwhile, as a manager, you've tried everything—promising go-karts, vacations, parties, beer. Why can't your team deliver?*
6.  *Fine. You'll just have to dig in and do it yourself.**

Wherry has talked about turning "100 Mistakes" into a book, but she's currently busy giving presentations to management and entrepreneurship groups. To demonstrate what she means by telling stories, she relies on narrative as the format of her presentations. Each story consists of original cartoons, usually illustrating a frustrated manager's state of mind, and concludes with Wherry asking participants what mistakes they caught. She's now writing a graphic novel about leadership.

*What's the biggest mistake in this scenario? See *You Make the Call*, question 2 (p. 31).

Elaine Wherry is clearly a manager. So, too, are Phil Knight (chairman of Nike), Ursula Burns (CEO of Xerox), Osamu Kojima (chairman of Mitsubishi), Neil MacGregor (director of the British Museum), Richard Hayne (president and chairman of Urban Outfitters), Jerry Jones (owner and general manager Dallas Cowboys football team), Benedict XVI (pope of the Roman Catholic Church), and Fadi and Hege Kalaouze (co-presidents of Aggieland Outfitters in College Station, Texas). As diverse as they and their organizations are, all of these managers are confronted by many of the same challenges, strive to achieve many of the same goals, and apply many of the same concepts of effective management in their work.

For better or worse, our society is strongly influenced by managers and their organizations. Most people in the United States are born in a hospital (an organization), educated by ... hools (all organizations), depend on organizations for their income, and ... heir consumable products and services from businesses (organizations). ... havior is influenced by various government agencies (also organizations). ... ization as a group of people working together in a structured and coordi... ... hieve a set of goals. The goals may include profit (Starbucks Corporation), ... owledge (University of Missouri), national defense (the U.S. Army), coor... ... local charities (United Way of America), or social satisfaction (a sorority). ... ons play such major roles in our lives, understanding how they operate ... ... managed is important.

... bout managers and the work they do. In Chapter 1, we examine the gen... ... agement, its dimensions, and its challenges. We explain the concepts of ... managers, discuss the management process, present an overview of the ... various kinds of managers. We describe the different roles and skills of ... the nature of managerial work, and examine the scope of management in ... anizations. In Chapter 2, we describe how both the practice and the theory ... ave evolved. As a unit, then, these first two chapters provide an introduction ... roducing both contemporary and historical perspectives on management.

*Handwritten note:* organization: group of people working together in a structured + coordinated fashion to achieve a set of goals → society strongly influenced by managers + organizations so understand them. → uses 4 resources from env: 1. human 3. physical 2. financial 4. information

# An Introduction to Management

**organization**
A group of people working together in structured and coordinated fashion to achieve a set of goals

Although defining the term *organization* is relatively simple, the concept of *management* is a bit more elusive. It is perhaps best understood from a resource-based perspective. As we discuss more completely in Chapter 2, all organizations use four basic kinds of resources from their environment: human, financial, physical, and information. Human resources include managerial talent and labor. Financial resources are the capital used by the organization to finance both ongoing and long-term operations. Physical resources include raw materials, office and production facilities, and equipment. Information resources are usable data needed to make effective decisions. Examples of resources used in four very different kinds of organizations are shown in Table 1.1.

Managers are responsible for combining and coordinating these various resources to achieve the organization's goals. A manager at Royal Dutch/Shell Group, for example, uses the talents of executives and drilling platform workers, profits earmarked for reinvestment, existing refineries and office facilities, and sales forecasts to make decisions regarding the amount of petroleum to be refined and distributed during the next quarter. Similarly, the mayor (manager) of New York City might use police officers, a government grant (perhaps supplemented with surplus tax

Workers negotiate the transport of a company's physical resources. They are moving drilling equipment to another site in order to maximize profits for the entire company.

Â©diyanski/Shutterstock.com

## TABLE 1.1 EXAMPLES OF RESOURCES USED BY ORGANIZ...

All organizations, regardless of whether they are large or small, profit-seekin...
profit, domestic or multinational, use some combination of human, financial,...
information resources to achieve their goals. These resources are generally d...
the organization's environment.

| Organization | Human Resources | Financial Resources | Physical Resources | In... R... |
|---|---|---|---|---|
| Royal Dutch/ Shell Group | Drilling platform workers Corporate executives | Profits Stockholder investments | Refineries Office buildings | Sa... O... proclamations |
| Michigan State University | Faculty Administrative staff | Alumni contributions Government grants | Computers Campus facilities | Research reports Government publications |
| New York City | Police officers Municipal employees | Tax revenue Government grants | Sanitation equipment Municipal buildings | Economic forecasts Crime statistics |
| Susan's Corner Grocery Store | Grocery clerks Bookkeeper | Profits Owner investment | Building Display shelving | Price lists from suppliers Newspaper ads for competitors |

revenues), existing police stations, and detailed crime statistics to launch a major crime prevention program in the city.

How do these and other managers combine and coordinate the various kinds of resources? They do so by carrying out four basic managerial functions or activities: planning and decision making, organizing, leading, and controlling. Management, then, as illustrated in Figure 1.1, can be defined as a set of activities (including planning and decision making, organizing, leading, and controlling) directed at an organization's resources (human, financial, physical, and information), with the aim of achieving organizational goals in an efficient and effective manner.

The last phrase in our definition is especially important because it highlights the basic purpose of management—to ensure that an organization's goals are achieved in an efficient and effective manner. By efficient, we mean using resources wisely and in a cost-effective way. For example, a firm like Toyota Motor Corporation, which produces high-quality products at relatively low costs, is efficient. By effective, we mean making the right decisions and successfully implementing them. Toyota also makes cars with the styling and quality to inspire consumer interest and confidence. A firm could very efficiently produce portable CD players but still not succeed because the market for such devices has largely been supplanted by digital music storage and playbacks such as smartphones. A firm that produces products that no one wants is therefore not effective. In general, successful organizations are both efficient and effective.[2]

**management**
A set of activities (including planning and decision making, organizing, leading, and controlling) directed at an organization's resources (human, financial, physical, and information), with the aim of achieving organizational goals in an efficient and effective manner

**efficient**
Using resources wisely and in a cost-effective way

**effective**
Making the right decisions and successfully implementing them

To be effective businesses must produce products that consumers are willing to buy. A company could very efficiently produce portable cassette tape players like this one but will not be successful.

Axel Bueckert/Shutterstock.com

*[Handwritten margin notes]*
management: a set of activities (inc. planning + decision making, organizing, leading, + controlling) w/ the aim of achieving organizational goals in an efficient + effective manner
→ basic purpose: to ensure that an organization's goals are achieved in an efficient + effective manner
→ mangers → combine + coordinate resources to achieve org's goals

With this basic understanding of management, defining the term *manager* becomes relatively simple: A manager is someone whose primary responsibility is to carry out the management process. In particular, a manager is someone who plans and makes decisions, organizes, leads, and controls human, financial, physical, and information resources. Today's managers face a variety of interesting and challenging situations. The average executive works over 60 hours a week, has enormous demands placed on his or her time, and faces increased complexities posed by globalization, domestic competition, government regulation, shareholder pressure, and Internet-related uncertainties. The job is complicated even more by rapid changes (such as the recession of 2008–2010 and the recovery that began in 2013), unexpected disruptions (including web hacks), and both minor and major crises (such as the Ebola scare in 2014 and terrorists attacks in 2015). The manager's job is unpredictable and fraught with challenges, but it is also filled with opportunities to make a difference. Good managers can propel an organization into unprecedented realms of success, whereas poor managers can devastate even the strongest of organizations.[3]

"Not only can you not plan the impact you're going to have, you often won't recognize it even while you're having it."

—RICHARD COSTOLO, TWITTER CEO[4]

**manager**
Someone whose primary responsibility is to carry out the management process

Many of the characteristics that contribute to the complexity and uncertainty of management stem from the environment in which organizations function. For example, as shown in Figure 1.1, the resources used by organizations to create products and services all come from the environment. Thus it is critical that managers understand this environment. Part 2 of the text discusses the environmental context of management in detail. Chapter 3 provides a general overview and discussion of the organization's environment from a variety of perspectives. Chapter 4 focuses specifically on the ethical and social environment of management, and Chapter 5 explores the global environment of management. After reading these chapters, you will be better prepared to study the essential activities that comprise the management process.

## FIGURE 1.1  MANAGEMENT IN ORGANIZATIONS

Basic managerial activities include planning and decision making, organizing, leading, and controlling. Managers engage in these activities to combine human, financial, physical, and information resources efficiently and effectively and to work toward achieving the goals of the organization.

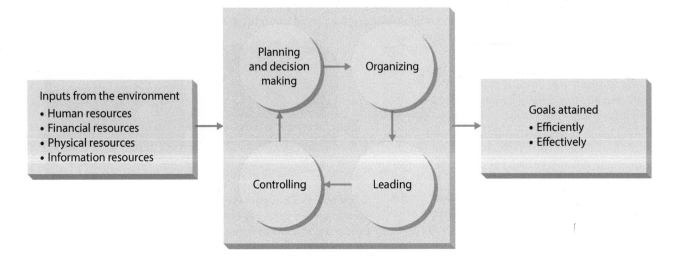

# The Management Process
# (What do Managers do?)

We noted earlier that management involves the four basic functions of planning and decision making, organizing, leading, and controlling. Because these functions represent the framework around which this book is organized, we introduce them here and note where they are discussed more fully. Their basic definitions and interrelationships are shown in Figure 1.2. (Note that Figure 1.2 is an expanded version of the central part of Figure 1.1.)

Consider the management process at Google. Sergey Brin and Larry Page, Google's founders and top managers, must first create goals and plans that articulate what they want the company to become. Then they rely on effective organization to help make those goals and plans reality. Brin and Page also pay close attention to the people who work for the company. And they keep a close eye on how well the company is performing. Each of these activities represents one of the four basic managerial functions illustrated in the figure—setting goals is part of planning, setting up the organization is part of organizing, managing people is part of leading, and monitoring performance is part of controlling.

It is important to note, however, that the functions of management do not usually occur in a tidy, step-by-step fashion. Managers do not plan on Monday, make decisions on Tuesday, organize on Wednesday, lead on Thursday, and control on Friday. At any given time, for example, a manager is likely to be engaged in several different activities simultaneously. Indeed, from one setting to another, managerial tasks are as different as they are similar. The similarities that pervade most settings are the phases in the management process. Important differences include the emphasis, sequencing, and implications of each phase.[5] Thus the solid lines in Figure 1.2 indicate how, in theory, the functions

---

## FIGURE 1.2  THE MANAGEMENT PROCESS

Management involves four basic activities—planning and decision making, organizing, leading, and controlling. Although there is a basic logic for describing these activities in this sequence (as indicated by the solid arrows), most managers engage in more than one activity at a time and often move back and forth between the activities in unpredictable ways (as shown by the dotted arrows).

of management are performed. The dotted lines, however, represent the true reality of management. In the sections that follow, we explore each of these activities.

## Planning and Decision Making: Determining Courses of Action

In its simplest form, planning means setting an organization's goals and deciding how best to achieve them. Decision making, a part of the planning process, involves selecting a course of action from a set of alternatives. Planning and decision making help maintain managerial effectiveness by serving as guides for future activities. In other words, the organization's goals and plans clearly help managers know how to allocate their time and resources. When Alan Mulally took over the ailing Ford Motor Company in 2006, he walked into a business that had low cash reserves, an unpopular product line, a confusing strategy, and a culture that was so resistant to change that one insider said it was "calcified." His first agenda was to set performance goals for all of Ford's top executives and clarify the strategic direction that would guide Ford in the future. He also worked to ensure that decision making was transparent.[6] The four chapters making up Part 3 of this text are devoted to planning and decision making. Chapter 6 examines the basic elements of planning and decision making, including the role and importance of organizational goals. Chapter 7 looks at strategy and strategic planning, which provide overall direction and focus for the organization. Chapter 8 explores managerial decision making and problem solving in detail. Finally, Chapter 9 addresses planning and decision making as they relate to the management of new ventures and entrepreneurial activities, increasingly important parts of managerial work.

## Organizing: Coordinating Activities and Resources

Once a manager has set goals and developed a workable plan, the next management function is to organize people and the other resources necessary to carry out the plan. Specifically, organizing involves determining how activities and resources are to be grouped. After Alan Mulally clarified Ford's strategy, he then overhauled the company's bureaucratic structure in order to facilitate coordination across divisions and promote faster decision making. Organizing is the subject of Part 4. Chapter 10 introduces the basic elements of organizing, such as job design, departmentalization, authority relationships, span of control, and line and staff roles. Chapter 11 explains how managers fit these elements and concepts together to form an overall organization design. Organization change and innovation are the focus of Chapter 12. Finally, processes associated with managing the organization's workforce so as to most effectively carry out organizational roles and perform tasks are described in Chapter 13.

## Leading: Motivating and Managing People

The third basic managerial function is leading. Some people consider leading to be both the most important and the most challenging of all managerial activities. Leading is the set of processes used to get members of the organization to work together to further the interests of the organi-

> "We have good people. They just need a leader who can guide and inspire them."
>
> —BILL FORD, FORMER CEO OF FORD.[7]

zation. Alan Mulally took several steps to change the leadership culture that existed at Ford. During the previous regime the firm had used a directive, top-down approach to management. But Mulally decentralized many activities so as to put the responsibility for making decisions in the hands of those best qualified to make them. He also clarified channels of communication and revamped the incentive system used for senior managers. Finally, he set up a succession plan to ease the transition to the next CEO when he retired in 2014. Leading

**planning**
Setting an organization's goals and deciding how best to achieve them

**decision making**
Part of the planning process that involves selecting a course of action from a set of alternatives

**organizing**
Determining how activities and resources are to be grouped

**leading**
The set of processes used to get members of the organization to work together to further the interests of the organization

involves a number of different processes and activities, which are discussed in Part 5. The starting point is understanding basic individual and interpersonal processes, which we focus on in Chapter 14. Motivating employees is discussed in Chapter 15, and leadership itself and the leader's efforts to influence others are covered in Chapter 16. Managing interpersonal relations and communication is the subject of Chapter 17. Finally, managing work groups and teams, another important part of leading, is addressed in Chapter 18.

## Controlling: Monitoring and Evaluating Activities

The final phase of the management process is controlling, or monitoring the organization's progress toward its goals. As the organization moves toward its goals, managers must monitor progress to ensure that it is performing in such a way as to arrive at its "destination" at the appointed time. A good analogy is that of a space mission to Mars. NASA does not simply shoot a rocket in the general direction of the planet and then look again in four months to see whether the rocket hit its mark. NASA monitors the spacecraft almost continuously and makes whatever course corrections are needed to keep it on track. Controlling similarly helps ensure the effectiveness and efficiency needed for successful management. For example, during a routine quality control inspection of a prototype of Boeing's new 787 Dreamliner aircraft, an inspector discovered that literally thousands of fasteners had been improperly installed. This finding required managers to push the completion schedule for the plane back several months[8] in order to locate and replace all of the questionable fasteners. If control had not worked properly, the subsequent impact could have been disastrous. At Ford, Alan Mulally installed a more rigorous financial reporting system so that he could better assess how various parts of the far-flung Ford empire were performing and get information he needed to make strategic decisions faster and easier than was the case when he first took over.

*ford*

The control function is explored in Part 6. First, Chapter 19 explores the basic elements of the control process, including the increasing importance of strategic control. Managing operations, quality, and productivity is explored in Chapter 20.

☐ Managers use a mix of resources—human, financial, physical, and information—to promote efficiency and effectiveness.

☐ The management process involves a variety of functions. The primary management functions are planning and decision making, organizing, leading, and controlling.

☐ Remember, though, that as a manager your activities will typically not follow a predictable and logical sequence and that the resources you manage may vary in unexpected ways.

**Manager's Checklist** ✓

# Kinds of Managers

Not all managers are the same, of course, nor is the work they perform. Among other things, we can classify managers according to their level in the organization and the area in which they work.

## Managing at Different Levels of the Organization

Managers can be differentiated according to their level in the organization. Although large organizations typically have a number of levels of management, the most common view considers three basic levels: top, middle, and first-line managers, as shown in Figure 1.3.

**controlling**
Monitoring organizational progress toward goal attainment

**levels of management**
The differentiation of managers into three basic categories—top, middle, and first-line

---

### FIGURE 1.3  KINDS OF MANAGERS BY LEVEL AND AREA

Organizations generally have three levels of management, represented by top managers, middle managers, and first-line managers. Regardless of level, managers are also usually associated with a specific area within the organization, such as marketing, finance, operations, human resources, administration, or some other area.

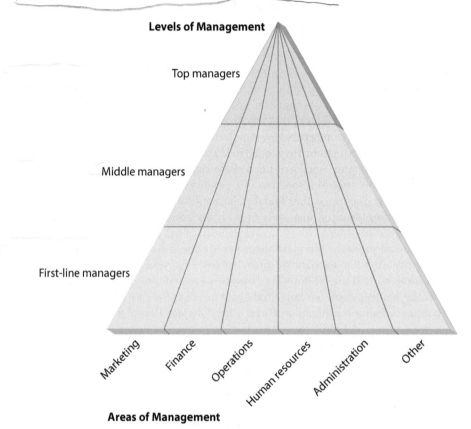

**Top Managers**  Top managers make up the relatively small group of executives who manage the overall organization. Titles found in this group include president, vice president, and chief executive officer (CEO). Top managers create the organization's goals, overall strategy, and operating policies. They also officially represent the organization to the external environment by meeting with government officials, executives of other organizations, and so forth.

Howard Schultz, CEO of Starbucks, is a top manager, as is Sharon Rothstein, the firm's global chief marketing officer. Likewise, Sergey Brin, Larry Page, Tim Cook (CEO of Apple), and Denise Morrison (CEO of Campbell Soup) are also top managers. The job of a top manager is likely to be complex and varied. Top managers make decisions about such activities as acquiring other companies, investing in research and development, entering or abandoning various markets, and building new plants and office facilities. They often work long hours and spend much of their time in meetings or on the telephone. In most cases, top managers are also very well paid. In fact, the elite top managers of very large firms sometimes make several million dollars a year in salary, bonuses, and stock. Starbucks' Howard Schultz received $1,500,000 in salary, $2,250,000 as a bonus, over $13,000,000 in stock and stock options, and $215,933 in other compensation in 2014.

**Middle Managers**  Middle management is probably the largest group of managers in most organizations. Common middle-management titles include plant manager, operations manager, and division head. Middle managers are responsible primarily for implementing the policies and plans developed by top managers and for supervising and coordinating the activities of lower-level managers.[9] Jason Hernandez, a regional manager at Starbucks responsible for the firm's operations in three eastern states, is a middle manager.

Ford plant managers, also middle managers, must meet various production quotas and goals and handle inventory management, quality control, equipment failures, and union problems. They also coordinate the work of supervisors within the plant. In recent years, many organizations have thinned the ranks of middle managers to lower costs and eliminate excess bureaucracy. Still, middle managers are necessary to bridge the upper and lower levels of the organization and to implement the strategies developed at the top. Although many organizations have found that they can indeed survive with fewer middle managers, those who remain play an even more important role in determining how successful the organization will be.

**First-Line Managers** First-line managers supervise and coordinate the activities of operating employees. Common titles for first-line managers are supervisor, coordinator, and office manager. Positions like these are often the first held by employees who enter management from the ranks of operating personnel. Wayne Maxwell and Jenny Wagner, managers of Starbucks coffee shops in Texas, are first-line managers. They oversee the day-to-day operations of their respective stores, hire operating employees to staff them, and handle other routine administrative duties required of them by the parent corporation. Assembly line supervisors at Ford plants are first-line managers. In contrast to top and middle managers, first-line managers typically spend a large proportion of their time supervising the work of subordinates.

Denise Morrison, CEO of Campbell Soup, is a top manager. She makes major decisions about the firm's competitive strategies, research and development investments, and new facilities.

Andrew Toth/Getty Images

## Managing in Different Areas of the Organization

Regardless of their level, managers may work in various areas within an organization. In any given firm, for example, areas of management may include marketing, financial, operations, human resource, administrative, and other areas.

**Marketing Managers** Marketing managers work in areas related to the marketing function—getting consumers and clients to buy the organization's products or services (be they Samsung smartphones, Ford trucks, *Cosmopolitan* magazines, Associated Press news reports, flights on Southwest Airlines, or cups of latte at Starbucks). These areas include new-product development, promotion, and distribution. Given the importance of marketing for virtually all organizations, developing good managers in this area can be critical.

**Financial Managers** Financial managers deal primarily with an organization's financial resources. They are responsible for such activities as accounting, cash management, and investments. In some businesses, such as banking and insurance, financial managers are found in especially large numbers.

**Operations Managers** Operations managers are concerned with creating and managing the systems that create an organization's products and services. Typical responsibilities of operations managers include production control, inventory control, quality control, plant layout, and site selection.

**areas of management**
Managers can be differentiated into marketing, financial, operations, human resource, administration, and other areas

**Human Resource Managers** Human resource managers are responsible for hiring and developing employees. They are typically involved in human resource planning, recruiting and selecting employees, training and development, designing compensation and benefit systems, formulating performance appraisal systems, and discharging low-performing and problem employees.

**Administrative Managers** Administrative, or general, managers are not associated with any particular management specialty. Probably the best example of an administrative management position is that of a hospital or clinic administrator. Administrative managers tend to be generalists; they have some basic familiarity with all functional areas of management rather than specialized training in any one area.[10]

**Other Kinds of Managers** Many organizations have specialized management positions in addition to those already described. Public relations managers, for example, deal with the public and media for firms like Alcoa and the Dow Chemical Company to protect and enhance the image of the organization. Research and development (R&D) managers coordinate the activities of scientists and engineers working on scientific projects in organizations such as Microsoft, NASA, and Boeing. Internal consultants are used in organizations such as Prudential Insurance and Raytheon to provide specialized expert advice to operating managers. International operations are often coordinated by specialized managers in organizations like Disney and Halliburton. The number, nature, and importance of these specialized managers vary tremendously from one organization to another. As contemporary organizations continue to grow in complexity and size, the number and importance of such managers are also likely to increase. For instance the "Tech Watch" feature discusses the emerging need for social media managers.

Sigrid Gombert/Getty Images

Most businesses rely on many different kinds of managers. This facilities manager is checking the calibration settings on an important piece of machinery. One of his employees originally made the calibrations but the manager is now checking them because if the settings are incorrect it could be costly to the business.

**Manager's Checklist**

☐ Organizations need managers at multiple levels. The most common classifications by level are top, middle, and first-line managers. Large organizations usually have multiple levels within each of these broad categories.

☐ Organization also need managers within different areas, such as marketing, finance, operations, human resources, general administration, and other areas.

☐ While it may seem like common sense, you should always have an understanding of the level and area of both your current job and the next job you aspire to have.

# TECH WATCH

# Show Me the ROI (return on investment)

Twenty-thirteen was a big year for *social media*—websites that allow users to create and exchange content. Twitter went public and introduced a video-sharing app called Vine. Facebook responded with Instagram, and YouTube rolled out a new layout feature called One Channel, which allows users to focus on developing bases of followers. Spending on social media advertising reached $4.6 billion, up 35 percent from 2012, and seven out of ten marketers said that they intended to increase social media spending in 2014 (compared to 53 percent who planned to increase email spending and just 9 percent who planned to up TV advertising).

According to Ashley Coombe, social media strategist for All Inclusive Marketing, "2013 was the year social media managers earned legitimacy. . . . Business owners began to realize that they could no longer hire their friend's daughter to do their social media just because she had a lot of friends on Facebook."

Just what do *social media managers* do? Why is your friend's daughter likely to be in over her head? It's a pretty new position, so job descriptions understandably vary. Here, however, is a generic description crafted by a veteran social media executive:

> *The Social Media Manager will implement the Company's Social Media Strategy, developing brand awareness, generating inbound traffic and encouraging product adoption. This role coordinates with the internal marketing and PR teams to support their respective missions, ensuring consistency in voice and cultivating a social media referral network.*

Primarily, social media managers handle information and communications through social media outlets—tracking trends and determining posting rates, creating positive communications, and maintaining a congenial media relationship with a company's community of customers. As you can also see from the job description, a key function of the position is coordination. Typically, social media managers work out of marketing departments and perform a variety of marketing-related tasks—replying to customer inquiries (sales), responding to customer complaints (customer service), handling external communications (public relations). At the same time, however, because they often manage the use of social media among all of a company's employees and communicate information about all of its activities, the scope of responsibilities is companywide.

Even with all of this newfound responsibility, some social media managers aren't quite sure how much "legitimacy" they've earned. "At the last place I was a social manager," reports one brand specialist at a large corporation, "high-level VPs would come over and say I was messing around on the Internet too much." According to another veteran of corporate media management, "the biggest misconception is that, compared to other marketers, we don't understand analytics or don't have the education or background when it comes to the technical side." Old-school executives, charges a third social media strategist, "see [social media] as the warm and fuzzy side of marketing. In reality," he says, "it's a powerful revenue driver when it's given proper funding and attention. . . . When you show them the ROI, people start changing their minds."

*References:* Kelly Clay, "What Social Media Managers Need to Know about Facebook in 2014," *Forbes.com* (December 29, 2014), www.forbes.com, on June 2, 2014; Jennifer Beese, "The Top 7 Social Media Stories of 2013," *SproutSocial* (December 27, 2013), http://sproutsocial.com, on June 2, 2014; Erik Sass, "Most Marketers Will Spend More on Social Media in 2014," *The Social Graf* (November 19, 2013), www.mediapost.com, on June 2, 2014; The CMO Survey, "Social Media Spend Continues to Soar" (March 6, 2012), www.cmosurvey.org, on June 2, 2014; Blaise Grimes-Viort, "Social Media Manager Job Description," *Online Communities and Social Media* (February 9, 2010), http://blaisegv.com, on June 2, 2014; Julian Rio, "Social Media Manager: What Role Does He Really Have?" *JulianRio.com Marketing Solutions* (October 26, 2013), www.julianrio.com, on June 2, 2014; "Confessions of Big Brand Social Media Managers," *Digiday* (February 11, 2014), http://digiday.com, on June 2, 2014.

# Basic Managerial Roles and Skills

Regardless of their levels or areas within an organization, all managers must play certain roles and exhibit certain skills if they are to be successful. The concept of a role, in this sense, is similar to the role an actor plays in a theatrical production. A person does certain things, meets certain needs, and has certain responsibilities in the organization. In the sections that follow, we first highlight the basic roles managers play and then discuss the skills they need to be effective.

## Managerial Roles

One classic study revealed a number of interesting insights into the nature of managerial roles.[11] This study, based on detailed observations of a sample of CEOs, suggested that senior managers generally play ten different roles, and that these roles fall into three basic categories: interpersonal, informational, and decisional.

**Interpersonal Roles** The research noted above suggested that there are three interpersonal roles inherent in the senior manager's job. First, the manager is often expected to serve as a *figurehead*—taking visitors to dinner, attending ribbon-cutting ceremonies, and the like. These activities are typically more ceremonial and symbolic than substantive. The manager is also expected to serve as a *leader*—hiring, training, and motivating employees. A manager who formally or informally shows subordinates how to do things and how to perform under pressure is leading. Finally, managers can have a *liaison* role. This role often involves serving as a coordinator or link among people, groups, or organizations. For example, companies in the computer industry may use liaisons to keep other companies informed about their plans. This enables Microsoft, for example, to create software for interfacing with new Hewlett-Packard printers at the same time those printers are being developed. And, at the same time, managers at Hewlett-Packard can incorporate new Microsoft features into the printers they introduce.

**interpersonal roles**
The roles of figurehead, leader, and liaison, which involve dealing with other people

**informational roles**
The roles of monitor, disseminator, and spokesperson, which involve the processing of information

**Informational Roles** Three informational roles flow naturally from the interpersonal roles just discussed. The process of carrying out the interpersonal roles places the manager at a strategic point to gather and disseminate information. The first informational role is that of *monitor*, one who actively seeks information that may be of value. The manager questions subordinates, is receptive to unsolicited information, and attempts to be as well informed as possible. The manager is also a *disseminator* of information, transmitting relevant information back to others in the workplace. When the roles of monitor and disseminator are viewed together, the manager emerges as a vital link in the organization's chain of communication. The third informational role focuses on external communication. The *spokesperson* formally relays information to people outside the unit or outside the organization. For example, a plant manager at Union Carbide may transmit information to top-level managers so that they will be better informed about the plant's activities. The manager may also represent the organization before a chamber of commerce or consumer group. Although the roles of spokesperson and figurehead are similar, there is one basic difference between them. When a manager acts as a figurehead, the manager's presence as a symbol of the organization is what is of interest. In the spokesperson role, however, the manager carries substantive information and communicates it to others in a formal manner.

One important role that manager's play is that of figurehead. In this role the manager carries out a ceremonial or symbolic function. This manager, for example, is cutting a ribbon to open a new facility.

lovro77/Getty Images

**Decisional Roles** The manager's informational roles typically lead to the decisional roles. The information acquired by the manager as a result of performing the informational roles has a major bearing on important decisions that he or she makes. Research has identified four decisional roles. First, the manager has the role of *entrepreneur*, the voluntary initiator of change. A manager at 3M Company developed the idea for the Post-it note pad but had to "sell" it to other skeptical managers inside the company. A second decisional role is initiated not by the manager but by some other individual or group. The manager responds to her role as *disturbance handler* by handling such problems as strikes, copyright infringements, or problems in public relations or corporate image.

The third decisional role is that of *resource allocator*. As resource allocator, the manager decides how resources are distributed and with whom he or she will work most closely. For example, a manager typically allocates the funds in the unit's operating budget among the unit's members and projects. A fourth decisional role is that of *negotiator*. In this role the manager enters into negotiations with other groups or organizations as a representative of the company. For example, managers may negotiate a union contract, an agreement with a consultant, or a long-term relationship with a supplier. Negotiations may also be internal to the organization. The manager may, for instance, mediate a dispute between two subordinates or negotiate with another department for additional support.

It should also be stressed, of course, that since this pioneering research was conducted several years ago the nature of senior managerial roles may have changed. Some of the roles noted here may be less important, others may be more important, and new roles may have also emerged as a function of globalization, new technology, and so forth. Still, though, there is value in understanding that managers play a variety of different roles. "A World of Difference" illustrates a number of different roles, as well as skills, that were essential in dealing with diversity issues at Sodexo.

Managers often play various informational roles such as disseminating information and serving as a spokesperson. This manager is responding to questions from the press during a press conference. It is obviously important that he be well informed about the questions and that he provide clear and accurate information.

*Dean Mitchell/Getty Images*

**decisional roles**
The roles of entrepreneur, disturbance handler, resource allocator, and negotiator, which relate primarily to making decisions

---

## A WORLD OF DIFFERENCE

# PR and Performance in Diversity Scoring

In 2014, Sodexo came in second on DiversityInc's list of Top 50 Companies for Diversity. Coming on the heels of number-1 finishes in 2010 and 2013 and number-2 finishes in 2011 and 2012, Sodexo's 2014 ranking made it the only company to make DiversityInc's top two for five straight years. The company's press release promised that "sustaining its efforts to engage a diverse workforce and foster an inclusive culture . . . is essential" to its strategy, adding that Sodexo "has a long commitment to diversity in the workplace."

Strictly speaking, that commitment began in earnest in 2005, when Sodexo, a French-based multinational provider of food and facilities-management services, agreed to pay $80 million to settle a lawsuit filed in 2001 by black employees who charged that they weren't being promoted at the same rate as white coworkers. After fighting the case all the way to the U.S. Supreme Court, Sodexo (whose American arm is headquartered in Gaithersburg, MD) also agreed to implement a more structured hiring program and to set up a

*(Continued)*

monitoring panel partly appointed by the plaintiffs. "We are pleased this case has been resolved," said U.S. CEO Richard Macedonia. "We are a stronger and better organization as a result of this process."

"It was a very painful thing for the company," recalls Dr. Rohini Anand, senior VP and global chief diversity officer. Indian-born Anand, whose doctoral degree in Asian Studies from the University of Michigan focused on cross-cultural interactions, was hired in 2003, just over a year after the employee suit had first been filed. A specialist in multicultural issues, she began evaluating the experiences not only of African American employees, but those of Hispanics, Asians, and gays and lesbians. She also instituted a program of metrics to measure the performance of every diversity-related initiative, including a *diversity scorecard* to align the results of such efforts as promotion and retention with organizational strategy.

By 2005—the year of the class-action settlement—Sodexo had pronounced itself "a leader in diversity," but the self-congratulations were a little premature. In fact, complaints about promotion practices—and even about incidents violating basic respect and dignity—continued to surface right up to the time that federal oversight over Sodexo employment practices came to an end. Issued in April 2010, a report entitled "Missing the Mark: Revisiting Sodexo's Record on Diversity" charged that, between 2004 and 2009, the number of African American managers had increased by only 1 percent and that of minority managers as a whole by only 2 percent. Reported one African American employee: "I worked with a chef who would pull down his pants and use the 'n' word and had this thing about 'you people.' I brought it up with Human Resources, but they said since he was part black, it was okay."

As suggested, however, by the run of DiversityInc citations from 2010 to 2014, Anand's efforts may have begun to pay off. Anand likes at least some of the latest scorecard numbers. Today, for example, 10 to 15 percent of total bonuses for about 16,000 managers is tied to the attainment of diversity-related goals, as is 25 percent of upper-management bonuses. "We are trying to drive change," promises Sodexo North America CEO George Chavel. "We're not just pointing to those metrics but using them."

*References*: Sodexo, "Sodexo's Strategic Use of Diversity Metrics to Quantify, Calibrate, and Impact Business Goals Recognized with a Top-Two Spot on DiversityInc's List for Unprecedented 5th Consecutive Year," *Providence* (RI) *Journal* (April 23, 2014), www.providencejournal.com, on May 16, 2014; Annys Shin, "$80 Million Settles Race-Bias Case," *Washington Post* (April 28, 2005), www.washingtonpost.com, on May 16, 2014; Tanya Aquino, "Even After Lawsuit, Report Reveals Food Service Co. Still Struggles with Diversity," Black Radio Network (April 27, 2010), www.blackradionetwork. com, on May 16, 2014; NPR, "Introspection after Allegations of Discrimination," *Listen to the Story* (January 12, 2010), www.npr.org, on May 16, 2013; William Reed, "Diversity Turnaround at Sodexo," *Louisiana Weekly* (March 4, 2013), www.louisianaweekly.com, on May 16, 2014; "Diversity Management: The Chief Diversity Officer's No. 1 Advantage," DiversityInc (n.d.), www.diversityinc.com, on May 16, 2014.

## Managerial Skills

In addition to fulfilling numerous roles, managers also need a number of specific skills if they are to succeed. The most fundamental management skills, summarized in Table 1.2, are technical, interpersonal, conceptual, diagnostic, communication, decision-making, and time-management skills.[12]

**Technical Skills** Technical skills are the skills necessary to accomplish or understand the specific kind of work being done in an organization. Technical skills are especially important for first-line managers. These managers spend much of their time training subordinates and answering questions about work-related problems. They must know how to perform the tasks assigned to those they supervise if they are to be effective managers. Brian Dunn, former director and CEO of Best Buy, began his career in 1985 as a store associate when Best Buy consisted of only twelve stores. He continued to work his way up into various positions, including store manager, district manager, regional manager, regional VP, senior VP, executive VP, and president of retail (North America). Hence, he literally learned the technical aspects of retailing from the ground up. While Sergey Brin and Larry Page spend most of their time now dealing with strategic and management issues, they also keep abreast of new and emerging technologies that may affect Google.

**technical skills**
The skills necessary to accomplish or understand the specific kind of work being done in an organization

---

## TABLE 1.2  BASIC MANAGERIAL SKILLS

---

*Technical Skills*: The skills necessary to accomplish or understand the specific kind of work being done in an organization

- Examples: The manager of a software development company who understands how to write and test relevant code and application; the manager of a restaurant chain knowing the basics of food preparation

*Interpersonal Skills*: The ability to communicate with, understand, and motivate both individuals and groups

- Examples: A manager who establishes a good relationship with an abrasive colleague; a manager who can reprimand someone for poor performance while maintaining a positive working relationship with that person

*Conceptual Skills*: The manager's ability to think in the abstract

- Examples: The manager who first sees a new market for an existing product; a manager who accurately forecasts a next-generation technology

*Diagnostic Skills*: The manager's ability to visualize the most appropriate response to a situation

- Examples: A manager who can understand why customer complaints are increasing; the manager who can quickly assess the impact of a new foreign trade agreement

*Communication Skills*: The abilities both to effectively convey ideas and information to others and to effectively receive ideas and information from others

- Examples: The manager who can write an email that is both informative and inspirational; a manager who can carefully listen to what others are saying and then craft an effective reply

*Decision-Making Skills*: The manager's ability to correctly recognize and define problems and opportunities and to then select an appropriate course of action to solve problems and capitalize on opportunities

- Examples: A manager who can quickly recognize the need for a decision and then frame the nature of the decision that is required; the manager who recognizes that an earlier decision did not result in a good outcome and so starts the decision-making process over again

*Time-Management Skills*: The manager's ability to prioritize work, to work efficiently, and to delegate appropriately

- Examples: The manager who routinely tackles the most pressing and significant tasks and delegates less significant tasks to others; a manager who does not easily get distracted by irrelevant issues

**Interpersonal Skills** Managers spend considerable time interacting with people both inside and outside the organization. For obvious reasons, then, the manager also needs interpersonal skills—the ability to communicate with, understand, and motivate both individuals and groups. As a manager climbs the organizational ladder, he or she must be able to get along with subordinates, peers, and those at higher levels of the organization. Because of the multitude of roles managers must fulfill, a manager must also be able to work with suppliers, customers, investors, and others outside the organization. Although some managers have succeeded with poor interpersonal skills, a manager who has good interpersonal skills is likely to be more successful. Sheryl Sandberg joined Facebook in 2008 as chief operating officer, following careers at the World Bank, the Treasury Department, and Google. Sandberg is renowned for her interpersonal skills and sharp intellect, balancing CEO Mark Zuckerberg's introversion. These skills have helped to cultivate strong relationships with key advertisers and bring continued growth and stability to Facebook.

**interpersonal skills**
The ability to communicate with, understand, and motivate both individuals and groups

**Conceptual Skills**   Conceptual skills depend on the manager's ability to think in the abstract. Managers need the mental capacity to understand the overall workings of the organization and its environment, to grasp how all the parts of the organization fit together, and to view the organization in a holistic manner. This allows them to think strategically, to see the "big picture," and to make broad-based decisions that serve the overall organization.

**Diagnostic Skills**   Successful managers also possess diagnostic skills, or skills that enable a manager to visualize the most appropriate response to a situation. A physician diagnoses a patient's illness by analyzing symptoms and determining their probable cause. Similarly, a manager can diagnose and analyze a problem in the organization by studying its symptoms and then developing a solution.[13] When the original owners of Starbucks failed to make a success of the business, Howard Schultz took over and reoriented the business away from mail order and moved it into retail coffee outlets. His diagnostic skills enabled him to understand both why the current business model was not working and how to construct a better one.

**Communication Skills**   Communication skills refer to the manager's abilities both to effectively convey ideas and information to others and to effectively receive ideas and information from others. These skills enable a manager to transmit ideas to subordinates so that they know what is expected, to coordinate work with peers and colleagues so that they work well together, and to keep higher-level managers informed about what is going on. In addition, communication skills help the manager listen to what others say and to understand the real meaning behind emails, letters, reports, and other written communication. One recent survey found that among corporate recruiters communication skills were very important—70 percent indicated that this was the most important skill set they looked for in new recruits.[14]

**Decision-Making Skills**   Effective managers also have good decision-making skills. Decision-making skills refer to the manager's ability to correctly recognize and define problems and opportunities and to then select an appropriate course of action to solve problems and capitalize on opportunities. No manager makes the right decision *all* the time. However, effective managers make good decisions *most* of the time. And when they do make a bad decision, they usually recognize their mistake quickly and then make good decisions to recover with as little cost or damage to their organization as possible. After joining Gap Inc. in 2007, CEO Glenn Murphy focused his energy on the Gap brand in an effort to revive growth. However, when the company revealed its new logo in 2010, replacing its classic white and navy square logo, customer backlash quickly ensued as its brand identity crumbled. Gap took shoppers' complaints to heart, scrapping the new logo and reverting to its iconic brand. So flawed decision making may have led to the logo change, but more effective decision making quickly allowed the firm to reverse itself.

**Time-Management Skills**   Finally, effective managers usually have good time-management skills. Time-management skills refer to the manager's ability to prioritize work, to work efficiently, and to delegate appropriately. As already noted, managers face many different pressures and challenges. It is too easy for a manager to get bogged down doing work that can easily be postponed or delegated to others.[15] When this happens, unfortunately, more pressing and higher-priority work may get neglected.[16] Jeff Bezos, CEO of Amazon.com, schedules all his meetings on three days a week but insists on keeping the other two days clear so that he can pursue his own ideas and maintain the flexibility to interact with his employees informally.[17]

**conceptual skills**
The manager's ability to think in the abstract

**diagnostic skills**
The manager's ability to visualize the most appropriate response to a situation

**communication skills**
The manager's abilities both to effectively convey ideas and information to others and to effectively receive ideas and information from others

**decision-making skills**
The manager's ability to correctly recognize and define problems and opportunities and to then select an appropriate course of action to solve problems and capitalize on opportunities

**time-management skills**
The manager's ability to prioritize work, to work efficiently, and to delegate appropriately

"The important thing, besides getting up early, is to have a system by which you manage your tasks."

—CHAD DICKERSON, CEO OF ETSY[18]

# The Nature of Managerial Work

We have already noted that managerial work does not follow an orderly, systematic progression through the workweek. Indeed, the manager's job is fraught with uncertainty, change, interruption, and fragmented activities. Numerous studies suggest that in a typical day CEOs are likely to spend their time in both scheduled and unscheduled meetings, doing "desk work," talking on the telephone, reading and responding to email, and reacting to various situations requiring them to make decisions. (The time spent on each activity, of course, varies constantly.) Moreover, the nature of managerial work continues to change in complex and often unpredictable ways.[19]

In addition, managers perform a wide variety of tasks. In the course of a single day, for example, a manager might have to make a decision about the design of a new product, settle a dispute between two subordinates, hire a new assistant, write a report for her boss, coordinate a joint venture with an overseas colleague, form a task force to investigate a problem, search for information on the Internet, and deal with a labor grievance. Moreover, the pace of the manager's job can be relentless. He may feel bombarded by email, telephone calls, and people waiting to see him. Decisions may have to be made quickly and plans formulated with little time for reflection.[20] But, in many ways, these same characteristics of managerial work also contribute to its richness and meaningfulness. Making critical decisions under intense pressure, and making them well, can be a major source of intrinsic satisfaction. And managers are usually well paid for the pressures they bear.

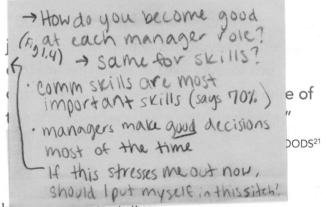

→ How do you become good at each manager role?
(Fig 1.4) → same for skills?
· comm skills are most important skills (says 70%)
· managers make good decisions most of the time
└ If this stresses me out now, should I put myself in this sitch?

## The Science and the Art of Management

Given the complexity inherent in the manager's job, a reasonable question relates to whether management is a science or an art. In fact, <u>effective management is a blend of both science and art.</u> And successful executives recognize the importance of combining both the science and the art of management as they practice their craft.[22]

**The Science of Management**   Many management problems and issues can be approached in ways that are rational, logical, objective, and systematic. Managers can gather data, facts, and objective information. They can use quantitative models and decision-making techniques to arrive at "correct" decisions. And they need to take such a scientific approach to solving problems whenever possible, especially when they are dealing with relatively routine and straightforward issues. When Starbucks considers entering a new market, its managers look closely at a wide variety of objective details as they formulate their plans. Technical, diagnostic, and decision-making skills are especially important when approaching a management task or problem from a scientific perspective.

**The Art of Management**   Even though managers may try to be scientific as often as possible, they must also frequently make decisions and solve problems on the basis of intuition, experience, instinct, and personal insights. Relying heavily on conceptual, communication, interpersonal, and time-management skills, for example, a manager may have to decide among multiple courses of action that look equally attractive. And even "objective facts" may prove to be wrong. When Starbucks was planning its first store in New York City, market research clearly showed that New Yorkers preferred drip coffee to more exotic espresso-style coffees. After first installing more drip coffee makers and fewer espresso makers than in their other stores, managers had to backtrack when New Yorkers lined up, clamoring for espresso. Starbucks now introduces a standard menu and layout in all its stores, regardless of presumed market differences, and then makes necessary adjustments later. Thus managers must blend an element of intuition and personal insight with hard data and objective facts.

> "Business is really an art form. At its best, it's the artistry of how people create things together."
>
> —PETER SENGE, A LEADING BUSINESS EXPERT[23]

Education plays an important role in helping managers develop their skills. These managers are attending a seminar to help them better understand current trends and challenges in their industry.

*Â©Matej Kastelic/Shutterstock.com*

## Becoming a Manager

How does one acquire the skills necessary to blend the science and art of management and to become a successful manager? Although there are as many variations as there are managers, the most common path involves a combination of education and experience.[24] Figure 1.4 illustrates how this generally happens.

**The Role of Education** Many of you reading this book are doing so because you are enrolled in a management course at a college or university. Thus you are acquiring management skills in an educational setting. When you complete the course (and this book), you will have a foundation for developing your management skills in more advanced courses. A college degree has become almost a requirement for career advancement in business, and virtually all CEOs in the United States have a college degree. MBA degrees are also common among successful executives today. More and more foreign universities, especially in Europe, are also beginning to offer academic programs in management.

## FIGURE 1.4 SOURCES OF MANAGEMENT SKILLS

Most managers acquire their skills as a result of education and experience. Though a few CEOs today do not hold college degrees, most students preparing for management careers earn college degrees and may go on to enroll in MBA programs.

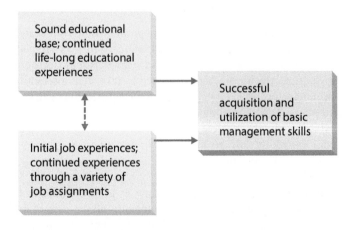

Even after obtaining a degree, most prospective managers have not seen the end of their management education. Many middle and top managers periodically return to campus to participate in executive or management development programs ranging in duration from a few days to several weeks. First-line managers also take advantage of extension and continuing education programs offered by institutions of higher education and/or through online media. A recent innovation in extended management education is the executive MBA program offered by many top business schools, in which middle and top managers with several years of experience complete an accelerated program of study on weekends.[25] Finally, many large companies have in-house training programs for furthering managers' education. Indeed, some firms have even created what are essentially corporate universities to provide the specialized education they feel is required for their managers in order for them to remain successful.[26] General Electric, McDonald's, Shell Oil, and Halliburton are among the leaders in this area. Regardless of the type of training, there is also a distinct trend toward online educational development for managers.[27] The primary advantage of education as a source of management skills is that, as a student, a person can follow a well-developed program of study, becoming familiar with current research and thinking on management. And many college students can devote full-time energy and attention to learning. On the negative side, management education is often very general, to meet the needs of a wide variety of students, and specific know-how may be hard to obtain. Further, many aspects of the manager's job can be discussed in a book but cannot really be appreciated and understood until they are experienced.

**The Role of Experience**   This book will help provide you with a solid foundation for enhancing your management skills. Even if you were to memorize every word in every management book ever written, however, you could not then step into a top management position and immediately be effective. The reason? Management skills must also be learned through experience. Most managers advanced to their present positions from other jobs. Only by experiencing the day-to-day pressures a manager faces and by meeting a variety of managerial challenges can one develop insights into the real nature and character of managerial work.

For this reason, most large companies, and many smaller ones as well, have developed management training programs for their prospective managers. People are hired from college campuses, from other organizations, or from the ranks of the organization's first-line managers and operating employees. These people are systematically assigned to a variety of jobs. Over time, the person is exposed to most, if not all, of the major aspects of the organization. In this way the manager learns by experience. The training programs at some companies, such as Procter & Gamble, General Mills, and Shell Oil, are so good that other companies try to hire people who have graduated from them.[28] Even without formal training programs, managers can achieve success as they profit from varied experiences. For example, Herb Kelleher was a practicing attorney before he took over at Southwest Airlines and led it to become one of the most successful and admired businesses in the United States. Of course, natural ability, drive, and self-motivation also play roles in acquiring experience and developing management skills.

Most effective managers learn their skills through a combination of education and experience. Some type of college degree, even if it is not in business administration, usually provides a foundation for a management career. The person then gets his or her first job and subsequently progresses through a variety of management situations. During the manager's rise in the organization, occasional education "updates," such as management development programs, may supplement on-the-job experience. And, increasingly, managers need to acquire international expertise as part of their personal development. As with general managerial skills, international expertise can be acquired through a combination of education and experience.[29]

## The Scope of Management

When most people think of managers and management, they think of profit-seeking organizations. Throughout this chapter, we use people like Sergey Brin and Larry Page of

Google, Elaine Wherry of Meebo, and Howard Schultz of Starbucks as examples. But we also provide examples from sports, religion, and other fields in which management is essential. Indeed, any group of two or more persons working together to achieve a goal and having human, material, financial, or informational resources at its disposal requires the practice of management.

**Managing in Profit-Seeking Organizations** Most of what we know about management comes from large profit-seeking organizations because their survival has long depended on efficiency and effectiveness. Examples of large businesses include industrial firms such as ExxonMobil, Toyota, BMW, Abercrombie & Fitch, Unilever, and Levi Strauss; commercial banks such as Citicorp, Fuji Bank, and Wells Fargo; insurance companies such as Prudential, State Farm, and Metropolitan Life; retailers such as Urban Outfitters, Kroger, and Target; transportation companies such as United Airlines and Consolidated Freightways; utilities such as Pacific Gas & Electric and Consolidated Edison of New York; communication companies such as CBS and the New York Times Company; and service organizations such as Kelly Services, KinderCare Learning Centers, and Century 21 Real Estate.

Although many people associate management primarily with large businesses, effective management is also essential for small businesses, which play an important role in the country's economy. In fact, most of this nation's businesses are small. In some respects, effective management is more important in a small business than in a large one. A large firm such as ExxonMobil or Apple can recover relatively easily from losing several thousand dollars on an incorrect decision; even losses of millions of dollars would not threaten their long-term survival. But it may be that a small business can ill afford even a much smaller loss. Of course, some small businesses become big ones. Dell Computer, for example, was started by one person—Michael Dell—in 1984. By 2015 it had become one of the largest businesses in the United States, with annual sales of almost $57 billion.

In recent years, the importance of international management has increased dramatically. The list of U.S. firms doing business in other countries is staggering. ExxonMobil, for example, derives around 62 percent of its revenues from foreign markets, and Coca-Cola derives almost half of its sales from foreign markets. Other major U.S. exporters include General Motors, General Electric, Boeing, and Caterpillar. And even numbers like Ford's are deceptive. For example, the automaker has large subsidiaries based in many European countries whose sales are not included as foreign revenue. Moreover, a number of major firms that do business in the United States have their headquarters in other countries. Firms in this category include the Royal Dutch/Shell Group (the Netherlands), Fiat S.p.A. (Italy), Nestlé S.A. (Switzerland), and Four Seasons (Canada). International management is not, however, confined to profit-seeking organizations. Several international sports federations (such as Little League Baseball), branches (embassies) of the federal government, and the Roman Catholic Church are established in most countries as well. In some respects, the military was one of the first multinational organizations. International management is covered in depth in Chapter 5.

A U.S.-based manager meets with his Middle-East based colleagues to strategize their global marketing plans.

Image Source/Getty Images

## Managing in Not-for-Profit Organizations

Intangible goals such as education, social services, public protection, and recreation are often the primary aim of not-for-profit organizations. Examples include United Way of America, the U.S. Postal Service, Girl Scouts of the U.S.A., the International Olympic Committee, art galleries, museums, and the Public Broadcasting System (PBS). Although these and similar organizations may not have to be profitable to attract investors, they must still employ sound management practices if they are to survive and work toward their goals.[30] And they must handle money in an efficient and effective way. If the United Way were to begin to spend larger portions of its contributions on salaries and perks for its top managers, contributors would lose confidence in the organization and make their charitable donations elsewhere.

Marina Park, CEO, Girl Scouts of Northern California speaks at the podium at the ceremony for Girl Scouts of the USA and National Park Service. As head of this non-profit, Park is often called upon for speaking engagements.

The management of government organizations and agencies is often regarded as a separate specialty: public administration. Government organizations include the Federal Trade Commission (FTC), the Environmental Protection Agency (EPA), the National Science Foundation, all branches of the military, state highway departments, and federal and state prison systems. Tax dollars support government organizations, so politicians and citizens' groups are acutely sensitive to the need for efficiency and effectiveness. For instance, the FTC's annual budget is $300 million.

Public and private schools, colleges, and universities all stand to benefit from the efficient use of resources. Growing pressures on state budgets have reduced money available for education. Fewer resources combined with surging costs, in turn, force administrators to make tough decisions about allocating remaining resources.

Managing healthcare facilities such as clinics, hospitals, and HMOs (health maintenance organizations) is now considered a separate field of management. Here, as in other organizations, scarce resources dictate an efficient and effective approach. In recent years some universities have established healthcare administration programs to train managers as specialists in this field.

Good management is also required in nontraditional settings to meet established goals. To one extent or another, management is practiced in religious organizations, terrorist groups, fraternities and sororities, organized crime, street gangs, neighborhood associations, and individual households. In short, as we noted at the beginning of this chapter, management and managers have a profound influence on all of us.

---

☐ Management involves a mix of science (based on logic and objectivity) and art (using intuition and instinct).

☐ Both education and experience play important roles in a manager's career and success.

☐ Management is needed in both profit-seeking and not-for-profit organizations.

☐ Remember that learning is a lifelong process—you should never think that your management education is "finished."

**Manager's Checklist** ☑

# The New Workplace

One of the most interesting characteristics of managerial work is the rapidly changing workplace.[31] Indeed, this new workplace is accompanied by dramatic challenges and amazing opportunities. Among other things, workplace changes relate in part to both workforce reductions and expansion. For example, many firms hired large numbers of new workers during the economic expansion that took place between 2002 and early 2008. But as the recession of 2008–2010 took hold, many of those same firms had to reduce their workforces while others cut hours and pay and suspended all hiring until conditions showed signs of improvement. And as economic growth began anew in 2011, these firms began to cautiously proceed with new hiring. But even more central to the idea of workplace change are such developments as workforce diversity and characteristics of the new workers themselves.

The management of diversity continues to be an important organizational opportunity—and challenge—today. The term *diversity* refers to differences among people. Diversity may be reflected along many dimensions, but most managers tend to focus on age, gender, ethnicity, and physical abilities and disabilities.[32] For example, the average age of workers in the United States is gradually increasing. This is partly because of declining birthrates and partly because people are living and working longer. Some organizations have found retirees to be excellent part-time and temporary employees. McDonald's has hired hundreds of elderly workers in recent years. Apple Computer has used many retired workers for temporary assignments and projects. By hiring retirees, the organization gets the expertise of skilled workers, and the individuals get extra income and an opportunity to continue to use their skills.

An increasing number of women have also entered the U.S. workforce. Fifty years ago only about one-third of U.S. women worked outside their homes; in 2014 over 57 percent of women aged 16 and older are in the workforce. Many occupations traditionally dominated by women—nursing, teaching, secretarial work—continue to be popular with females. But women have also moved increasingly into occupations previously dominated by males, becoming lawyers, physicians, and executives. Further, many blue-collar jobs are increasingly being sought by women, and women are increasingly moving into positions such as business ownership as entrepreneurs and as senior executives in major corporations. Similarly, more and more men are also entering occupations previously dominated by women. For example, there are more male office assistants and nurses today than ever before.

The ethnic composition of the workplace is also changing. One obvious change has been the increasing number of Hispanics and African Americans in the workplace. Further, many of these individuals now hold executive positions. There has also been a dramatic influx of immigrant workers to the United States in the last few years. Immigrants and refugees from Central America and Asia have entered the U.S. workforce in record numbers.

The passage of the Americans with Disabilities Act also brought to the forefront the importance of providing equal employment opportunities for people with various disabilities. As a result, organizations are attracting qualified employees from groups that they may once have ignored. Clearly, then, along just about any dimension imaginable, the workforce is becoming more diverse. Workforce diversity enhances the effectiveness of most organizations, but it also provides special challenges for managers.

Aside from its demographic composition, the workforce today is changing in other ways as well. During the 1980s, many people entering the workforce were what came to be called *yuppies*, slang for "young urban professionals." These individuals were highly motivated by career prospects, sought employment with big corporations, and often were willing to make work their highest priority. Thus, they put in long hours and could be expected to remain loyal to the company, regardless of what happened.

But younger people entering the workforce over the past 20 to 30 years are often quite different from their parents and other older workers. Generation X, Generation Y, and the Millennials, as these groups are called, tend to be less devoted to long-term career prospects and less willing to adapt to a corporate mind-set that stresses conformity and uniformity. Instead, they often seek work in smaller, more entrepreneurial firms that allow flexibility and individuality. They also place a premium on lifestyle preferences, often putting location high on their list of priorities when selecting an employer.

Thus managers are increasingly faced with the challenge of first creating an environment that will be attractive to today's worker. Second, managers must address the challenge of providing new and different incentives to keep people motivated and interested in their work. They must build enough flexibility into the organization to accommodate an ever-changing set of lifestyles and preferences. And, of course, as these generations eventually move into top spots of major corporations, there may even be entirely new paradigms for managing that cannot be foreseen today.[33]

Managers must also be prepared to address organization change.[34] This has always been a concern, but the rapid, constant environmental change faced by businesses today has made change management even more critical. Simply put, an organization that fails to monitor its environment and to change to keep pace with that environment is doomed to failure. But more and more managers are seeing change as an opportunity, not a cause for alarm. Indeed, some managers think that if things get too calm in an organization and people start to become complacent, managers should shake things up to get everyone energized.

New technology, especially as it relates to information, also poses an increasingly important challenge for managers. Communications advances such as smartphones and other wireless communication networks have made it easier than ever for managers to communicate with one another. At the same time, these innovations have increased the pace of work for managers, cut into their time for thoughtful contemplation of decisions, and increased the amount of information they must process. Moreover, as firms come to depend more and more on communication technologies, they also become more vulnerable. Sony's motion picture division, for instance, was hacked in late 2014, apparently in response to its impending release of a new movie.

A final element of the new workplace we will note here is the complex array of new ways of organizing that managers can consider. Many organizations strive for greater flexibility and the ability to respond more quickly to their environments by adopting flatter structures. These flat structures are characterized by fewer levels of management, wider spans of management, and fewer rules and regulations. The increased use of work teams also goes hand in hand with this new approach to organizing. We will examine these new ways of organizing in Chapters 11 and 18.

---

☐ There are a variety of different forces playing a role in defining the new workplace.

☐ Remember to remain vigilant for new trends and issues that will affect managers and organizations in the future.

**Manager's Checklist** ✓

# Summary of Learning Outcomes and Key Points

1. Describe the nature of management, define management and managers, and characterize their importance to contemporary organizations.

   - Management is a set of activities (including planning and decision making, organizing, leading, and controlling) directed at an organization's resources (human, financial, physical, and information) with the aim of achieving organizational goals in an efficient and effective manner.
   - A manager is someone whose primary responsibility is to carry out the management process within an organization.

2. Identify and briefly explain the four basic management functions in organizations.

   - Planning and decision making (determining courses of action)
   - Organizing (coordinating activities and resources)
   - Leading (motivating and managing people)
   - Controlling (monitoring and evaluating activities)
   - These activities are not performed on a systematic and predictable schedule.

3. Describe the kinds of managers found at different levels and in different areas of the organization.

   - By level, we can identify top, middle, and first-line managers.
   - Kinds of managers by area include marketing, financial, operations, human resource, administrative, and specialized managers.

4. Identify the basic managerial roles played by managers and the skills they need to be successful.

   - Interpersonal roles (figurehead, leader, and liaison)
   - Informational roles (monitor, disseminator, and spokesperson)
   - Decisional roles (entrepreneur, disturbance handler, resource allocator, and negotiator)
   - Key management skills are technical, interpersonal, conceptual, diagnostic, communication, decision-making, and time-management skills.

5. Discuss the science and the art of management, describe how people become managers, and summarize the scope of management in organizations.

   - The effective practice of management requires a synthesis of science and art, that is, a blend of rational objectivity and intuitive insight.
   - Most managers attain their skills and positions through a combination of education and experience.
   - Management processes are applicable in a wide variety of settings, including profit-seeking organizations (large, small, and start-up businesses and international businesses) and not-for-profit organizations (government organizations, educational organizations, health-care facilities, and nontraditional organizations).

6. Characterize the new workplace that is emerging in organizations today.

   - The new workplace is characterized by workforce expansion and reduction.
   - Diversity is also a central component, as is the new worker.
   - Organization change is also more common, as are the effects of information technology and new ways of organizing.

# Discussion Questions

## Questions for Review

1. Contrast efficiency and effectiveness. Give an example of a time when an organization was effective but not efficient, efficient but not effective, both efficient and effective, and neither efficient nor effective.

2. What are the four basic activities that comprise the management process? How are they related to one another?

3. Briefly describe the seven basic managerial skills. Give an example of each.

4. Describe a typical manager's day. What are some of the expected consequences of this type of daily experience?

## Questions for Analysis

5. Recall a recent group project or task in which you have participated. Explain how members of the group displayed each of the managerial skills.

6. The text notes that management is both a science and an art. Recall an interaction you have had with a "superior" (manager, teacher, group leader). In that

interaction, how did the superior use science? If he or she did not use science, what could have been done to use science? In that interaction, how did the superior use art? If he or she did not use art, what could have been done to use art?

### Questions for Application

8. Interview a manager from a local organization. Learn about how he or she performs each of the functions of management, the roles he or she plays, and the skills necessary to do the job.

9. Find an organization chart. You can find one in the library or by searching online. Locate top, middle, and first-line managers on the chart. What are some of the job titles held by persons at each level?

7. Visit the websites of at least five large corporations and locate a biography of each CEO. What formal management education do these leaders have? In your opinion, what is the appropriate amount of formal education needed to be a corporate CEO? Why?

10. Watch a movie or television program that involves an organization of some type. Diverse examples include *Draft Day*, *Iron Man*, or one of the newer *Harry Potter* or *James Bond* movies (or perhaps *Citizen Kane* for classic movie buffs). For television, options like *Boardwalk Empire*, *Downton Abbey*, or *The Good Wife* would work. Identify as many management activities, skills, and roles as you can.

# Building Effective Time-Management Skills

### Exercise Overview

Time-management skills refer to the ability to prioritize tasks, to work efficiently, and to delegate appropriately. This exercise allows you to assess your own current time-management skills and to gather some suggestions for how you can improve in this area.

### Exercise Background

As we saw in this chapter, effective managers must be prepared to switch back and forth among the four basic activities in the management process. They must also be able to fulfill a number of different roles in their organizations, and they must exercise a variety of managerial skills in doing so. On top of everything else, their schedules are busy and full of tasks—personal and job-related activities that require them to "switch gears" frequently throughout the workday.

Stephen Covey, a management consultant and author of *The 7 Habits of Highly Effective People*, has developed a system for prioritizing tasks. First, he divides them into two categories—*urgent* and *critical*. *Urgent* tasks, such as those with approaching deadlines, must be performed right away. *Critical* tasks are tasks of high importance—say, those that

will affect significant areas of one's life or work. Next, Covey plots both types of tasks on a grid with four quadrants: A task may be *urgent*, *critical*, *urgent and critical*, or *not urgent and not critical*.

Most managers, says Covey, spend too much time on tasks that are urgent when in fact they should be focused on tasks that are *critical*. He observes, for example, that managers who concentrate on urgent tasks meet their deadlines but tend to neglect such critical areas as long-term planning. (Unfortunately, the same people are also apt to neglect critical areas of their personal lives.) In short, effective managers must learn to balance the demands of urgent tasks with those of critical tasks by redistributing the amount of time devoted to each type.

### Exercise Task

1. Visit the website of FranklinCovey (the firm cofounded by Stephen Covey). Specifically, follow this link: **www. franklincovey.com/urgencyanalysis/ua-prof.html**. Now take the "Urgency Analysis Profile," a brief online survey that should take about 10 minutes.

2. Now look over your profile and examine the assessment of your current use of time and the suggestions for how you can improve your time management. In what ways do you agree and disagree with your personal assessment? Explain your reasons for agreeing or disagreeing.

3. Think of a task that you regularly perform and which, if you were being perfectly honest, you could label *not urgent and not critical*. How much time do you spend on this task? What might be a more appropriate amount of time? To what other tasks could you give some of the time that you spend on this *not-urgent-not-critical* task?

4. What one thing can you do today to make better use of your time? Try it to see if your time management improves.

# Building Effective Conceptual Skills

## Exercise Overview

Your conceptual skills reflect your ability to think in the abstract. This exercise will help you extend your conceptual skills by identifying and analyzing situations that call for different kinds of management functions, roles, and skills in different kinds of organizations.

## Exercise Background

This chapter includes discussions of four management *functions*, ten management *roles*, and seven management *skills*. It also stresses the idea that management activities are necessary in many different kinds of organizations.

Start by identifying five different types of organizations: one large business, one small business, one educational organization, one healthcare organization, and one government organization. You might choose organizations about which you have some personal knowledge or organizations that you simply recognize by name and industry. Next, put yourself in the position of a top manager in each of your five specific organizations.

Write the names of these five organizations across the top of a sheet of paper. Then list the four functions, ten roles, and seven skills down the left side of the sheet. Now put your imagination to work: Think of a situation, a problem, or an opportunity that fits at the intersection of each row and column on the sheet. The dean of your college, for example, must perform a leadership role and apply interpersonal skills. The manager of an all-night diner must perform an organizing function and play the role of monitor.

## Exercise Task

1. Do you notice any patterns of meaningful similarities in functions, roles, or skills across the five columns? Are there, for example, similarities in performing leadership roles or applying communication skills in most or all of the five types of organization? Do you notice any patterns of meaningful differences?

2. Based on your assessment of the patterns of similarities and differences that you identified in task 1, give two or three reasons why managers might find it easy to move from one type of organization to another. Give two or three reasons why managers might find it difficult to move from one type of organization to another.

3. Identify two or three places on your grid where the intersection between a type of organization and a function, role, or skill suggests something at which you might be particularly good. How about something at which, at least right now, you think you wouldn't be very good. Explain your reasoning.

# Skill-Building Personal Assessment

## How Do I Rate as a Manager?

This self-assessment will help you understand your current understanding of the practice of management and your own approach to management. This assessment outlines four important functions of management: planning, organizing, leading, and controlling. You should respond to this in one of three ways:

(a.) respond based on your own managerial experience if you have any;

(b.) respond about effective (or ineffective) managers you have observed in your work experience; or

(c.) respond in terms of how you think an ideal manager should behave.

Instructions: Recall a situation in which you were a member of a group or team that had a specific task or project to complete.

This may have been at work, in a class, or in a church, club, or civic organization. Now assess your behavior in each of the functions. For each question, rate yourself according to the following scale.

Rating scale: Insert your score from one of the following five options for each of the statements that follow:

- *5 Definitely true of me*
- *4 Probably true of me*
- *3 Neither true nor not true, or undecided*
- *2 Probably not true of me*
- *1 Definitely not true of me*

## I.   Planning

_____ 1. I prepare an agenda for meetings.

_____ 2. I try to anticipate what will happen in the future as a result of my current actions and decisions.

_____ 3. I establish clear goals for myself and others.

_____ 4. I carefully analyze the pros and cons involved in situations before reaching decisions.

_____ 5. I am quite willing to try new things, to experiment.

_____ 6. I have a clear vision for accomplishing the task at hand.

_____ 7. I put plans in writing so that others can know exactly what they are.

_____ 8. I try to remain flexible so that I can adapt to changing conditions.

_____ 9. I try to anticipate barriers to goal accomplishment and how to overcome them.

_____ 10. I discuss plans and involve others in arriving at those plans.

_____ Section I Total

## II. Organizing

_____ 1. I try to follow the plan while working on the task.

_____ 2. I try to develop any understanding of the different steps or parts needed to accomplish the task at hand.

_____ 3. I evaluate different ways of working on the task before deciding on which course of action to follow.

_____ 4. I have a clear sense of the priorities necessary to accomplish the task.

_____ 5. I arrange for others to be informed about the degree of progress in accomplishing the task.

_____ 6. I am open to alternative, even novel ways of working on the task.

_____ 7. I adapt the sequence of activities involved if circumstances change.

_____ 8. I have a clear sense of how the steps involved in accomplishing the task should be structured.

_____ 9. I lead or follow where appropriate to see to it that progress is made toward accomplishing the task.

_____ 10. I coordinate with others to assure steady progress on the task.

_____ Section II Total

## III. Leading

_____ 1. I set an example for others to follow.

_____ 2. I am effective at motivating others.

_____ 3. I try to keep a balance between getting the work done and keeping a spirit of teamwork.

_____ 4. I try to handle conflict in nonthreatening, constructive ways.

_____ 5. I help others in the group and provide them with guidance and training to better perform their roles.

_____ 6. I am open to suggestions from others.

_____ 7. I keep everyone informed about the group's activities and progress.

_____ 8. I show a genuine interest in the work of others.

_____ 9. I am considerate when providing constructive suggestions to others.

_____ 10. I understand the needs of others and encourage their initiative in meeting those needs.

_____ Section III Total

## IV. Controlling

_____ 1. I regularly assess the quantity and quality of progress on the task at hand.

_____ 2. I try to assure that the information I have is timely, accurate, complete, and relevant.

_____ 3. I routinely share information with others to help them accomplish their tasks.

_____ 4. I compare progress with plans and take corrective action as warranted.

_____ 5. I manage my time and help others to manage theirs.

_____ 6. I have good sources of information or methods for obtaining information.

_____ 7. I use technology (computers, tablets, smartphones, etc.) to aid in monitoring progress and communicating with others.

_____ 8. I anticipate possible negative reactions and take action to minimize them.

_____ 9. I recognize that fixing problems _before_ they occur is better than fixing problems _after_ they occur.

_____ 10. I try to balance my attention on the many different steps needed to accomplish the task at hand.

_____ Section IV Total

Source: Adapted from D. D. Van Fleet, E. W. Van Fleet, and G. J. Seperich, _Principles of Management for Agribusiness_ (Clifton Park, NY: Cengage Learning, 2013); R. W. Griffin, _Management_ (Mason, OH: Cengage Learning, 2011); and D. D. Van Fleet, _Behavior in Organizations_ (Boston: Houghton Mifflin, 1991) in collaboration with G. Moorhead and R. W. Griffin.

# Management at Work

## Officers and Gentlemen Behaving Badly

Between the fall of 2012 and the spring of 2014, the U.S. military was embarrassed by a series of ethical breaches, mostly incidents involving sexual misbehavior among high-ranking officers. In October 2013, for example, Air Force Maj. Gen. Michael Carey was fired from a job that put him in charge of 450 intercontinental ballistic missiles for getting drunk and carousing with "suspect" women while on an official mission to Moscow. Carey resigned—minus one general's star and at a slightly lower pension—in April 2014.

At least one officer took it upon himself to clamp down on unbecoming conduct in his command. At Fort Jackson, S.C., Army Brig. Gen. Bryan T. Roberts publicly warned his troops that "the Army has zero tolerance for sexual harassment and sexual assault, and so do I. . . . All of us have a shared role in ridding our ranks of this cancerous conduct." Unbeknownst to Roberts, he was under investigation by the Army for charges of assault on a woman who alleged that she'd been having an affair with the married general for 18 months—a relationship that had turned violent on several occasions. The investigation also turned up two other women who admitted to having affairs with Roberts, who was convicted of adultery (a crime under the Uniform Code of Military Justice) and assault. He was fined $5,000 and issued a written reprimand but held on to his general's star. According to his attorney, Roberts will be "retiring soon."

Meanwhile, at Fort Bragg, N.C., Col. Martin P. Schweitzer followed up a meeting with newly elected Congresswoman Renee L. Ellmers with emails to fellow officers in which he described her as "smoking hot" and an apt candidate for a few sexually explicit activities. A year later, Schweitzer was forced to admit to investigators that he'd been "childish" and "truly stupid." Concluding that the colonel had "failed to demonstrate exemplary conduct," the Army inspector general's office cited Schweitzer for misuse of his government email account and placed a "memorandum of concern" in his personnel file. Now a brigadier general, Schweitzer works at the Pentagon for the Joint Chiefs of Staff.

How did Schweitzer's "stupid" email fall into the hands of the inspector general in the first place? Schweitzer, it seems, had copied Brig. Gen. Jeffrey A. Sinclair, deputy commander of Fort Bragg's 82nd Airborne Division. As luck would have it, Sinclair's emails were under surveillance in a search for evidence of misconduct that could have landed him in prison for life, including sexual assault on a female captain with whom he had carried on a three-year affair. Sinclair became only the third Army general to face court-martial in 60 years, but a two-year trial ended in March 2014, when Sinclair pleaded guilty to adultery and a few other minor charges. He was fined $20,000 but got no jail time, and prosecutors recommended that he be allowed to retire with a lieutenant colonel's pension. "It's a terrible outcome," said the attorney for Sinclair's accuser, "and by failing to render justice today, the Army's going to face the reality that this could happen again." California Congresswoman Jackie Speier put the response of critics more bluntly: "This sentence," she said, "is a mockery of military justice. . . . For a sexual predator to gain the rank that [Gen. Sinclair] has gained, go through a court-martial, and be given a slap on the wrist suggests . . . that the system does not work."

A week later, Secretary of Defense Chuck Hagel followed through on a promise that he'd made in February to appoint a Senior Advisor for Military Professionalism—in effect, an ethics officer at the Pentagon. "I want someone," said Hagel, "who understands . . . the pressures of combat, the pressures of curriculums and testing, and who has a well-rounded background in command." The job went to Navy Rear Adm. Margaret D. Klein, who reported directly to Hagel on issues related to military ethics, character, and leadership.

A naval flight officer with a master's degree in education, Klein is a former commandant of midshipmen at the U.S. Naval Academy and chief of staff, U.S. Cyber Command. She's logged more than 4,500 hours in command and control aircraft and held operational positions in an airborne command squadron and an aircraft carrier strike group. Klein "brings to the position a wealth of operational leadership and experience," said Hagel in a written statement. "She also knows that ethics and character are absolute values that must be constantly reinforced. . . .

"An uncompromising culture of accountability," concluded Hagel, "must exist at every level of command." For her part, Klein is convinced that ethics goes hand in hand with professionalism: "When you think about what goes into military professionalism," she says,

> the first word that comes to mind is ethics. . . . We are deeply concerned about the profession. . . . But it's more than that. It's about leadership. That is what we all have in common. We are all leaders, whether in civilian clothes or in the uniform of our country. . . . As a profession, we don't exist because we are a jobs program. We don't exist to perpetuate ourselves. . . . We're an instrument of national power, and we take an oath to the Constitution. . . . We're judged against that special trust and confidence that's placed in us. . . . So

*our actions—good and bad—reflect on the profession, and it's the profession that we're responsible to. . . . We can put all the programs and policies in place to say that we don't condone "X" behavior, but until each* *one of us realizes that it's our responsibility—our duty—to eradicate [certain] behaviors from our profession, they'll continue to exist.*

### Case Questions

1. The text reminds us that the U.S. military is a "government organization" that requires managers. It adds, however, that managing such an organization is often regarded as a "separate specialty." What do you think the "separate specialty" entails in this context? In what respects is Adm. Margaret Klein qualified in the "separate specialty" that's required for success in her job as Senior Advisor for Military Professionalism?

2. The case indicates that the Senior Advisor for Military Professionalism is essentially "an ethics officer at the Pentagon." According to one simple explanation, an *ethics officer* "aligns the practices of a workplace with the stated ethics and beliefs of that workplace, holding people accountable to ethical standards." In what ways must a successful ethics officer play Mintzberg's ten different *managerial roles*? If you were to advise Adm. Klein on the relative importance of these roles, in what order would rank them, from most to least important?

3. According to the text, *not-for-profit organizations* try to meet "intangible goals." What, in the broadest sense,

are the *goals* of the U.S. military? The text also defines *leading* as "the set of processes used to get members of an organization to work together to further the interests of the organization," including meeting its goals. What can and should military leaders do to improve the organization's efforts to meet its goals? Why are ethical standards important in these efforts, and what can military leaders do to improve adherence to ethical standards?

4. A *profession* can be defined as an occupation, practice, or vocation requiring mastery of a complex set of knowledge and skills through formal education and/or practical experience. *Professional ethics* can be defined as professionally accepted standards of personal and occupational behavior, values, and guiding principles. Thus a "profession" is a specific kind of job with certain specific rules for performing job-related activities. How do professional ethics influence job-related activities in ways that don't necessarily apply in "nonprofessional" situations?

### Case References

James Joyner, "The U.S. Military's Ethics Crisis," *The National Interest* (February 13, 2014), http://nationalinterest.org, on May 22, 2014; Craig Whitlock, "Military Brass, Behaving Badly: Files Detail a Spate of Misconduct Dogging Armed Forces," *Washington Post* (January 26, 2014), www.washingtonpost.com, on May 22, 2014; Craig Whitlock, "Disgraced Army General, Jeffrey A. Sinclair, Gets $20,000 Fine, No Jail Time," *Washington Post* (March 20, 2014), www.washingtonpost.com, on May 22, 2014; Gregg Zoroya, "General Avoids Jail Time in Case Involving Affair with Subordinate," *USA Today* (March 20, 2014), www.usatoday.com, on May 22, 2014; Phil Stewart, "As Scandals Swell, U.S. Defense Chief to Install Ethics Officer," Reuters (February 7, 2014), www.reuters.com, on May 22, 2014; Philip Ewing, "Chuck Hagel Preaches 'Professionalism' amid Scandal," *Politico* (March 27, 2014), www.politico.com, on May 22, 2014; Jennifer Hlad, "Hagel Appoints Top Ethics Officer," *Stars and Stripes* (March 25, 2014), www.stripes.com, on May 22, 2014; Tyrone C. Marshall Jr., "Ethics Advisor Equates Professionalism with Leadership," *American Forces Press Service* (May 15, 2014), www.defense.gov, on May 22, 2014

## YOU MAKE THE CALL  How to Make Mistakes and Influence People

1. Wherry organizes her thoughts on managerial mistakes by documenting problems at different levels of an organization's management hierarchy. Here, for example, is the hierarchy at Meebo, along with a few words of advice from Wherry:

   - *Individual code writer* ("Don't turn down anyone offering help")
   - *Manager* ("Stop trying to do your old job")
   - *Director* ("Don't promote someone and then disappear")
   - *Vice president* ("Don't reverse a plan midstream")
   - *CEO* ("Never let your guard down")

   How is this level-by-level approach reflected in the kinds of mistakes that Wherry identifies? Why is this approach effective in identifying mistakes? How can it be effective in avoiding mistakes?

2. Here's one of Wherry's stories:
   *Remember your first job? You were thrilled to join the company but shocked to find less than perfection there—software has bugs and reports have spelling errors. Your response? You send out an email to the whole company telling everyone how to fix these problems. No one responds, but you do get invited to a meeting. You're stoked!*

*(Continued)*

*At the meeting, one participant says his design project is a little behind, so you stick your hand up to offer to help out. Your manager warns you that you have a lot on your plate already, but you assure him you've got it all under control. In reality, you're actually hugely far behind, so you pull an all-nighter—that's always worked before. Unfortunately, the results aren't as amazing as you'd like this time. So you get a two-week extension. Meanwhile, you feel like everything goes too slowly at the company, and all of your friends who are still in school are posting Facebook pictures of themselves on the beach. The result: you decide to make a change and move on to a new company.*

What mistakes is this new employee making? What advice would you offer (be as specific as you can)?

3. Wherry doesn't think that leaving Meebo was a mistake. At the time of the Google sale, she was spending most of her time training new hires and managing her team and less time developing products, which was her strong suit and what she preferred to be doing. Besides, she says, a founder's objective is to "hire oneself out of a role." What does she mean by that statement? Why do many successful founders appear to disagree?

4. What about you? How do you react when faced with the fact that you've made a mistake? Generally speaking . . .

   1) . . . do you reassess the task that you were asked to perform to better grasp why (and how) you were asked to perform it?
   2) . . . what's your emotional response when you realize or are told that you've made a mistake?
   3) . . . how do you respond to any criticism that you receive because of your mistake?
   4) . . . do you reassess your relationships with other people as a result of your mistake?
   5) . . . do you determine to focus more on getting things done particularly well and less on getting along with everyone else?

   These questions are broadly adapted from an article entitled "Five Mistakes Smart People Make at Work," which appeared in *U.S. News & World Report* on February 26, 2014. You might want to check the article itself for the brief discussion accompanying each question. Also, as you may have noticed when you were reading the list, it could have come from a piece on "Five Mistakes Smart People Make in School."

# Endnotes

1 "Why Did a Successful Entrepreneur Keep a Diary of Her Mistakes?" *CBS News* (April 27, 2013) [video], www.cbs.com, on May 13, 2014; Rachel Emma Silverman, "The Manager Who Kept a Six-Year Diary of Her Mistakes," *At Work,* (March 29, 2013), http://blogs.wsj.com, on May 13, 2014; Janet Choi, "Elaine Wherry: Never Let a Good Mistake Go to Waste," *Women 2.0* (September 16, 2013), http://women2.com, on May 13, 2013; Jessica Stillman, "Elaine Wherry: A Visual Guide for First-Time Founders," *Women 2.0* (November 16, 2013), http://women2.com, on May 13, 2014; McKinney, "McKinney's SxSW Journal," *mckinney.com* (March 10, 2013), http://mckinneysxsw.tumblr.com on May 13, 2013; Lynn Dixon, "The Value of Making Mistakes," *Hourly.com* (May 1, 2013), http://blog.hourly.com, May 13, 2014; Katie Morell, "Building an Empire: Meebo's Elaine Wherry," *American Express OPEN Forum* (October 1, 2012), https://www.americanexpress.com, on May 13, 2014.

2 Fred Luthans, "Successful vs. Effective Real Managers," *Academy of Management Executive,* May 1988, pp. 127–132. See also "The Best Performers," *Bloomberg BusinessWeek,* Spring 2015 Special Issue, pp. 57–95.

3 See "The Best (& Worst) Managers of the Year," *Bloomberg BusinessWeek,* January 10-17, 2015, pp. 35–43.

4 "Commencement Advice From the Corner Office," *Bloomberg Businessweek,* May 20-27, 2014, p. 25.

5 Sumantsa Ghospal and Christopher A. Bartlett, "Changing the Role of Top Management: Beyond Structure to Process," *Harvard Business Review,* January–February 1995, pp. 86–96.

6 "Ford's Savior?" *BusinessWeek,* March 16, 2009, pp. 31–34; "Ford's Heir Apparent Set to Take the Wheel," *USA Today,* April 22, 2014, p. 1A.

7 http://www.forbes.com/sites/carminegallo/2012/04/25/alan-mulully-optimism-and-the-power-of-vision/, on April 27, 2015.

8 "Fastener Woes to Delay Flight of First Boeing 787 Jets," *Wall Street Journal,* November 5, 2008, p. B1.

9 Rosemary Stewart, "Middle Managers: Their Jobs and Behaviors," in Jay W. Lorsch (ed.), *Handbook of Organizational Behavior* (Englewood Cliffs, NJ: Prentice-Hall, 1987), pp. 385–391. See also Bill Woolridge, Torsten Schmid, and

Steven W. Floyd, "The Middle Management Perspective on Strategy Process: Contributions, Synthesis, and Future Research," *Journal of Management,* 2008, Vol. 34, No. 6, pp. 1190–1221; and Anneloes Raes, Marielle Heijltjes, Ursula Glunk, and Robert Row, "The Interface of the Top Management Team and Middle Managers: A Process Model," *Academy of Management Review,* January 2011, pp. 102–126.

10 John P. Kotter, "What Effective General Managers Really Do," *Harvard Business Review,* March–April 1999, pp. 145–155. See also Peter Drucker, "What Makes an Effective Executive," *Harvard Business Review,* June 2004, pp. 58–68.

11 Henry Mintzberg, *The Nature of Managerial Work* (Englewood Cliffs, NJ: 1973).

12 See Robert L. Katz, "The Skills of an Effective Administrator," *Harvard Business Review,* September–October 1974, pp. 90–102, for a classic discussion of several of these skills. For a recent perspective, see J. Brian Atwater, Vijay R. Kannan, and Alan A. Stephens, "Cultivating Systemic Thinking in the Next Generation of Business Leaders," *Academy of Management Learning & Education,* 2008, Vol. 7, No. 1, pp. 9–25.

13 See Mark Gottfredson, Steve Schaubert, and Hernan Saenz, "The New Leader's Guide to Diagnosing the Business," *Harvard Business Review,* February 2008, pp. 63–72, for an interesting application.

14 "Brush Up On Your Small Talk," *Bloomberg Businessweek Survey,* January 6, 2015.

15 See "The Real Reasons You're Working So Hard . . . And What You Can Do About It," *BusinessWeek,* October 3, 2005, pp. 60–68; "I'm Late, I'm Late, I'm Late," *USA Today,* November 26, 2002, pp. 1B–2B.

16 For a thorough discussion of the importance of time-management skills, see David Barry, Catherine Durnell Cramton, and Stephen J. Carroll, "Navigating the Garbage Can: How Agendas Help Managers Cope with Job Realities," *Academy of Management Executive,* May 1997, pp. 26–42.

17 "Amazon's Jeff Bezos Keeps the Fires of Growth Burning," *USA Today,* July 1, 2014, p. 4B.

18 http://www.fastcompany.com/3031066/work-smart/etsy-ceo-chad-dickerson-on-having-a-system-any-system, on April 27, 2015.

19 See Michael A. Hitt, "Transformation of Management for the New Millennium," *Organizational Dynamics*, Winter 2000, pp. 7–17.

20 James H. Davis, F. David Schoorman, and Lex Donaldson, "Toward a Stewardship Theory of Management," *Academy of Management Review*, January 1997, pp. 20–47.

21 *Forbes*, February 14, 2005, p. 110.

22 Gary Hamel and C. K. Prahalad, "Competing for the Future," *Harvard Business Review*, July–August 1994, pp. 122–128; see also Joseph M. Hall and M. Eric Johnson, "When Should a Process Be Art, Not Science?" *Harvard Business Review*, March 2009, pp. 58–65.

23 *Biz Ed*, May/June 2010, p. 23.

24 See Steven J. Armstrong and Anis Mahmud, "Experiential Learning and the Acquisition of Managerial Tacit Knowledge," *Academy of Management Learning & Education*, 2008, Vol. 7, No. 2, pp. 189–208.

25 "The Executive MBA Your Way," *BusinessWeek*, October 18, 1999, pp. 88–92.

26 "Despite Cutbacks, Firms Invest in Developing Leaders," *Wall Street Journal*, February 9, 2009, p. B4.

27 "Turning B-School into E-School," *BusinessWeek*, October 18, 1999, p. 94.

28 See "Reunion at P&G University," *Wall Street Journal*, June 7, 2000, pp. B1, B4, for a discussion of Procter & Gamble's training programs.

29 For an interesting discussion of these issues, see Rakesh Khurana, "The Curse of the Superstar CEO," *Harvard Business Review*, September 2002, pp. 60–70.

30 James L. Perry and Hal G. Rainey, "The Public-Private Distinction in Organization Theory: A Critique and Research Strategy," *Academy of Management Review*, April 1988, pp. 182–201. See also Ran Lachman, "Public and Private Sector Differences: CEOs' Perceptions of Their Role Environments," *Academy of Management Journal*, September 1985, pp. 671–680.

31 "The Way We'll Work," *Time*, May 25, 2009, pp. 39–51.

32 Patricia L. Nemetz and Sandra L. Christensen, "The Challenge of Cultural Diversity: Harnessing a Diversity of Views to Understand Multiculturalism," *Academy of Management Review*, 1996, Vol. 21, No. 2, pp. 434–462; Frances J. Milliken and Luis L. Martins, "Searching for Common Threads: Understanding the Multiple Effects of Diversity in Organizational Groups," *Academy of Management Review*, 1996, Vol. 21, No. 2, pp. 402–433.

33 "When Gen X Runs the Show," *Time*, May 25, 2009, p. 48.

34 Craig L. Pearce and Charles P. Osmond, "Metaphors for Change: The ALPS Model of Change Management," *Organizational Dynamics*, Winter 1996, pp. 23–35.

©Markus Pfaff/Shutterstock.com

# 2

# TRADITIONAL AND CONTEMPORARY MANAGEMENT PERSPECTIVES

## MANAGEMENT IN ACTION    The Lighter Side of Sustainability

Did you know that environmental sustainability is good for your circadian rhythm? Sometimes called your "body clock," your *circadian rhythm* is the 24-hour cycle that regulates a number of your physiological processes. When your cycle is out of kilter, you may not eat or sleep the way you should, and you're even more vulnerable to nervous-system disorders, such as depression. So how can taking care of the environment help to keep your circadian rhythm at its optimum tempo? For one thing, even if you're indoors, your circadian rhythm responds to better lighting, whether natural or artificial, and it so happens that the design of interior lighting is one of the most effective ways in which the manager of a building can reduce the amount of energy that's required to maintain its operations.[1]

Take hospitals, for instance, which happen to be among the most resource- and energy-intensive of all industries. If you've ever been hospitalized, you may have noticed that there isn't much natural light in the average hospital. There was probably a window in your double room, but whether you ended up next to it was a 50-50 proposition. Not surprisingly, however, studies show that daylight—and even levels of artificial light designed to approximate daytime light—help to keep circadian rhythms in phase. You'll sleep better at night and you'll be in a better mood during the day, in part because you'll feel less pain if you aren't suffering from fatigue. Because you'll be less stressed, your blood pressure isn't as likely

to go up, your immune system isn't as likely to function poorly, and you'll be less prone to aggressive outbursts. Moreover, your hospital stay will probably be shorter.

Needless to say, all of these conditions lend themselves to better patient outcomes. And because better patient outcomes are consistent with a hospital's *mission*—the organizational purpose that determines how it operates (see Chapter 7)—a hospital's managers have an interest in setting organizational goals that foster conditions for better patient outcomes. Rey Tuazon, for example, who manages gas and electric bills for a midwest hospital system, reasons that because "the mission of the hospital is saving people's lives, I am part of the mission." His thinking? Tuazon has a budget of $6 million, and he figures that "if I can save $1 million, then I'm supporting the mission" of the hospital. After all, "his" $1 million in savings can be used to buy medical equipment and hire clinicians to produce better patient outcomes. In fact, says Cathy Fischer, who manages energy consumption for another midwest system, $1 million in savings is equal in value to $25 million in hospital revenue, "and that's a lot of patients to see" if you want to clear $1 million in patient premiums.

More and more hospital systems are thus committed to *sustainable resource management*—which a report issued by the Northwest Energy Efficiency Alliance (NEEA) defines as the "management of

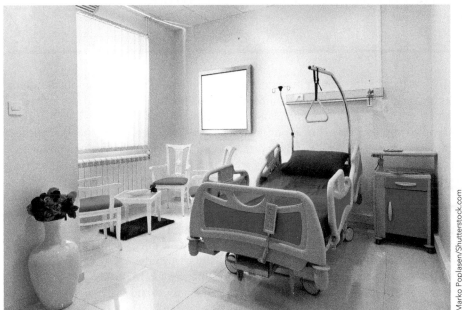

By maximizing natural light, hospitals hope to cut energy usage and costs, while improving patient outcomes. This approach is the result of a variety of management perspectives, some traditional and others very contemporary.

Marko Poplasen/Shutterstock.com

resource-related business practices to reduce consumption, minimize resource intensity, and maximize resource productivity." The gist of the report is that sustainability makes good business sense. In the hospital industry, for example, redesigning a facility to provide natural light will certainly require an initial outlay, but it will eventually cut energy usage and costs—*while improving patient outcomes*. Take Detroit's Beaumont Health System, which, like many hospital operators, includes the health and safety of its community and its employees among its sustainability goals. In 2012, Beaumont installed 1,413 new lighting fixtures, mostly in parking lots and garages, replacing high-intensity discharge (HID) fixtures with lower-watt light-emitting diode (LED) fixtures. The cost amounted to $900,000, but Beaumont's energy savings have ranged from 75 percent to 90 percent—about $300,000 in maintenance costs per year. The initial outlay should be repaid in 2.5 to 3 years.

As you can see, providing better lighting involves the management of material *inputs*, and improving patient outcomes means enhancing service *outputs*. Obviously, then, it makes sense that an organization might approach sustainability management from a *systems perspective*. And according to the authors of the NEEA report, "sustainability is now the touchstone for system-wide innovation" in resource-related business practices. Sustainable resource management, they argue, "requires systemic business change" that cuts across organizational functions—"subsystems"—"to help identify, implement, and measure the performance of the sustainability plan throughout the organization."

The authors single out several "healthcare systems"—organizations in the hospital industry—as innovators who "operate more efficiently by standardizing system-wide resource-management policies."

In particular, they point to PeaceHealth, a ten-hospital system serving Washington, Oregon, and Alaska, which initiated a *strategic energy management plan* (or SEMP) in 2007. The PeaceHealth plan—which covers much more than just lighting—started by benchmarking the system's energy-use practices against those of other systems, setting energy efficiency goals, and identifying projects that would help to meet those goals.

In the first go-round, a systemwide team discovered that incremental efforts could cut energy use by 10 percent and save the organization $800,000 annually. One project, for instance, called for *retrocommissioning* certain energy-use systems, which facilities director Gary Hall describes as "taking existing building systems and putting them back in a fine-tuned operating mode. It's kind of low-hanging fruit," he explains, because "it doesn't take a lot of investment—just some focused time to get systems operating efficiently." Reprogramming a building's air handler to run 10 hours a day instead of 24 doesn't cost anything, and when PeaceHealth decided to spend $500,000 to computerize building controls, it was able to combine $300,000 of its own money with a $200,000 grant from a local utility company. "There's a lot of money available for these projects," advises Hall.

Finally, when PeaceHealth built a new hospital on Washington's San Juan Island, it was able to take advantage of *passive cooling and heating*—systems for both preventing heat from entering a building and removing it as necessary—by simply optimizing the building's orientation to the sun. The facility also uses a *ground-source heat pump*—a central heating/cooling system that transfers heat to and from the ground—as well as low-flow sinks and toilets. The result is one of the most energy-efficient hospitals in North America—one that uses 63 percent less energy than comparable hospitals.

---

Most managers today agree that it's important to focus on how efficiently their organizations use resources and the impact of those resources on the bottom line. They would also agree that it's important to stay abreast of their competitive environment and the ways in which that environment will change tomorrow. But as our story indicates, it's also important that they use the past as context. Managers in a wide array of organizations can learn both effective and ineffective practices and strategies by understanding what managers have done in the past. Indeed, history plays an important role in many businesses today, and more and more managers are recognizing that many lessons of the past are important ingredients in future successes.

This chapter provides an overview of traditional management thought so that you, too, can better appreciate the importance of history in today's business world. We set the stage by establishing the historical context of management. We then discuss the three traditional management perspectives—classical, behavioral, and quantitative. Next we describe the systems and contingency perspectives as approaches that help integrate the three traditional perspectives. Finally, we introduce and discuss a variety of contemporary management issues and challenges.

# The Role of Theory and History in Management

Practicing managers are increasingly seeing the value of theory and history in their work. In this section, we first explain why theory and history are important and then identify important precursors to management theory.

## The Importance of Theory and History

Some people question the value of history and theory. Their arguments are usually based on the assumptions that history is not relevant to contemporary society and that theory is abstract and of no practical use. In reality, however, both theory and history are important to all managers today.

**Why Theory?** A theory is simply a conceptual framework for organizing knowledge and providing a blueprint for action.[2] Although some theories seem abstract and irrelevant, others appear very simple and practical. Management theories, used to build organizations and guide them toward their goals, are grounded in reality.[3] Practically any organization that uses assembly lines (such as Honda, Black & Decker, and Maytag) is drawing on what we describe later in this chapter as "scientific management." Many organizations, including Best Buy, Texas Instruments, and Samsung, use concepts developed from the behavioral perspective (also introduced later) to improve employee satisfaction and motivation. And naming a large company that does not use one or more techniques from the quantitative management perspective would be difficult. For example, retailers like Kroger and Target routinely use operations management to determine how many checkout lines they need to have open at any given time.

In addition, most managers develop and refine their own theories of how they should run their organizations and manage the behavior of their employees. For example, James Sinegal, founder of Costco Wholesale, believes that paying his employees well but otherwise keeping prices as low as possible are the key ingredients in success for his business. This belief is based essentially on his personal theory of competition in the warehouse retailing industry.

**Why History?** Awareness and understanding of important historical developments are also important to contemporary managers.[4] Understanding the historical context of management provides a sense of heritage and can help managers avoid the mistakes of others. Most courses in U.S. history devote time to business and economic developments in this country, including the Industrial Revolution, the early labor movement, and the Great Depression, and to such so-called captains of U.S. industry as Cornelius Vanderbilt (railroads), John D. Rockefeller (oil), and Andrew Carnegie (steel). The contributions of those and other industrialists left a profound imprint on contemporary culture.[5]

Many managers also agree that they can benefit from a greater understanding of history in general. For example, Ian M. Ross, legendary founder of AT&T's Bell Laboratories, often cited *The Second World War* by Winston Churchill as a major influence on his approach to leadership. Other books often mentioned by managers for their relevance to today's business problems include such classics as Plato's *Republic*, Homer's *Iliad*, and Machiavelli's *The Prince*.[6] And new business history books have also been directed at women managers and the lessons they can learn from the past.[7]

Managers at Wells Fargo clearly recognize the value of history. For example, the company maintains an extensive archival library of its old banking documents and records and even employs a full-time corporate historian. As part of their orientation and training, new managers atç Wells Fargo take courses to become acquainted with the bank's history.[8] Similarly, Shell Oil, Levi Strauss, Hershey, Lloyd's of London, Disney, Honda, and Unilever all maintain significant archives about their past and often evoke images from earlier times in their orientation and training programs, advertising campaigns, and other public relations activities.

**theory**
A conceptual framework for organizing knowledge and providing a blueprint for action

"Business history lets us look at what we did right and, more important, it can help us be right the next time."

—ALFRED CHANDLER, NOTED BUSINESS HISTORIAN[9]

## Precursors to Management Theory

Even though large businesses have been around for only a few hundred years, management has been practiced for thousands of years. By examining management in antiquity and identifying some of the first management pioneers, we set the stage for a more detailed look at the emergence of management theory and practice over the last hundred years.

The Egyptians used basic management functions to construct the pyramids.

**Management in Antiquity** The practice of management can be traced back thousands of years. The Egyptians used the management functions of planning, organizing, and controlling when they constructed the pyramids. Alexander the Great employed a staff organization to coordinate activities during his military campaigns. The Roman Empire developed a well-defined organizational structure that greatly facilitated communication and control. Socrates discussed management practices and concepts in 400 B.C., Plato described job specialization in 350 B.C., and Alfarabi listed several leadership traits in A.D. 900.[10] Figure 2.1 is a simple time line showing a few of the most important management breakthroughs and practices over the last 4,000 years.

**Early Management Pioneers** In spite of this history, however, management *per se* was not given serious attention for several centuries. Indeed, the study of management did not begin until the nineteenth century. Robert Owen (1771–1858), a British industrialist and reformer, was one of the first managers to recognize the importance of an organization's human resources. Until his era, factory workers were generally viewed in much the same way that machinery and equipment were. A factory owner himself, Owen believed that workers deserved respect and dignity. He implemented better working conditions, a higher

## FIGURE 2.1 MANAGEMENT IN ANTIQUITY

Management has been practiced for thousands of years. For example, the ancient Babylonians used management in governing their empire, and the ancient Romans used management to facilitate communication and control throughout their far-flung territories. The Egyptians used planning and controlling techniques in the construction of their pyramids.

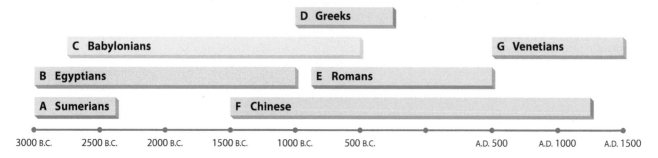

**A** Used written rules and regulations for governance

**B** Used management practices to construct pyramids

**C** Used extensive set of laws and policies for governance

**D** Used different governing systems for cities and state

**E** Used organized structure for communication and control

**F** Used extensive organization structure for government agencies and the arts

**G** Used organization design and planning concepts to control the seas

minimum working age for children, meals for employees, and reduced work hours. He assumed that giving more attention to workers would pay off in increased output.

Whereas Owen was interested primarily in employee welfare, Charles Babbage (1792–1871), an English mathematician, focused his attention on efficiencies of production. His primary contribution was his book *On the Economy of Machinery and Manufactures*.[11] Babbage placed great faith in the division of labor and advocated the application of mathematics to such problems as the efficient use of facilities and materials. In a sense, his work was a forerunner of both the classical and the quantitative management perspectives. Nor did he overlook the human element. He understood that a harmonious relationship between management and labor could serve to benefit both, and he favored such devices as profit-sharing plans. In many ways, then, Babbage was an originator of modern management theory and practice.

---

☐ Don't dismiss theory as something that is too abstract to be relevant—a theory can often be a useful conceptual framework for organizing knowledge and serving as a blueprint for action.

☐ History, too, can serve as a useful tool in today's business world by reminding us of what has and has not worked in the past.

**Manager's Checklist** ☑️

# The Classical Management Perspective

In the early years of the twentieth century, the preliminary ideas and writings of these and other managers and theorists converged with the emergence and evolution of large-scale businesses and management practices to create interest and focus attention on how businesses should be operated. The first important ideas to emerge are now called the classical management perspective. This perspective actually includes two different branches: scientific management and administrative management.

## Scientific Management

Productivity really began to emerge as a serious business challenge during the early 1900s. Business was expanding and capital was readily available, but labor was in short supply. Consequently, managers began to search for ways to use existing labor more efficiently. In response to this need, in turn, experts began to focus on ways to improve the performance of individual workers. Their work led to the development of scientific management. Some of the earliest advocates of scientific management included Frederick W. Taylor (1856–1915), Frank Gilbreth (1868–1924), Lillian Gilbreth (1878–1972), Henry Gantt (1861–1919), and Harrington Emerson (1853–1931).[12] Taylor played the dominant role.

One of Taylor's first jobs was as a foreman at the Midvale Steel Company in Philadelphia. It was there that he observed what he called soldiering—employees deliberately working at a pace slower than their capabilities. Taylor studied and timed each element of the steelworkers' jobs. He determined what each worker should be producing, and then he designed the most efficient way of doing each part of the overall task. Next he implemented a piecework pay system. Rather than paying all employees the same wage, he began increasing the pay of each worker who met and exceeded the target level of output set for his or her job.

"Hardly a competent workman can be found who does not devote a considerable amount of time to sudying just how slowly he can work and still convince his employer that he is going at a good pace."

—FREDERICK W. TAYLOR, EARLY MANAGEMENT PIONEER.[13]

**classical management perspective**
Consists of two distinct branches—scientific management and administrative management

**scientific management**
Concerned with improving the performance of individual workers

**soldiering**
Employees deliberately working at a slow pace

## FIGURE 2.2 STEPS IN SCIENTIFIC MANAGEMENT

Frederick Taylor developed this system of scientific management, which he believed would lead to a more efficient and productive workforce. Bethlehem Steel was among the first organizations to profit from scientific management and still practices some parts of it today.

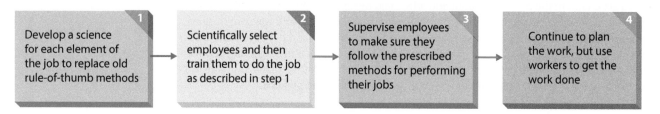

| 1 | 2 | 3 | 4 |
|---|---|---|---|
| Develop a science for each element of the job to replace old rule-of-thumb methods | Scientifically select employees and then train them to do the job as described in step 1 | Supervise employees to make sure they follow the prescribed methods for performing their jobs | Continue to plan the work, but use workers to get the work done |

After Taylor left Midvale, he worked as a consultant for several companies, including Simonds Rolling Machine Company and Bethlehem Steel. At Simonds he studied and redesigned jobs, introduced rest periods to reduce fatigue, and implemented a piecework pay system. The results were higher quality and quantity of output and improved morale. At Bethlehem Steel, Taylor studied efficient ways of loading and unloading railcars and applied his conclusions with equally impressive results. During these experiences, he formulated the basic ideas that he called "scientific management." Figure 2.2 illustrates the basic steps Taylor suggested. He believed that managers who followed his guidelines would improve the efficiency of their workers.[14]

Taylor's work had a major impact on U.S. industry. By applying his principles, many organizations achieved major gains in efficiency. Taylor was not without his detractors, however. Labor argued that scientific management was just a device to get more work from each employee and to reduce the total number of workers needed by a firm. There was a congressional investigation into Taylor's ideas, and evidence suggests that he falsified some of his findings.[15] Nevertheless, Taylor's work left a lasting imprint on business.[16]

Frank and Lillian Gilbreth, contemporaries of Taylor, were a husband-and-wife team of industrial engineers. One of Frank Gilbreth's most interesting contributions was to the craft of bricklaying. After studying bricklayers at work, he developed several procedures for doing the job more efficiently. For example, he specified standard materials and techniques, including the positioning of the bricklayer, the bricks, and the mortar at different levels. The results of these changes were a reduction from 18 separate physical movements to five and an increase in output of about 200 percent. Lillian Gilbreth made equally important contributions to several different areas of work, helped shape the field of industrial psychology, and made substantive contributions to the field of personnel management. Working individually and together, the Gilbreths developed many techniques and strategies for eliminating inefficiency. They applied many of their ideas to their family and documented their experiences raising 12 children in the book and original 1950 movie *Cheaper by the Dozen*.

Henry Gantt, another contributor to scientific management, was an associate of Taylor at Midvale, Simonds, and Bethlehem Steel. Later, working alone, he developed other techniques for improving worker output. One, called the Gantt chart, is still used today. A Gantt chart is essentially a means of scheduling work and can be generated for each worker or for an entire complex project. Gantt also refined Taylor's ideas about piecework pay systems.

Scientific management played a major role in the development of mass-production assembly line technologies. By breaking jobs down into small component tasks and then standardizing how workers perform those tasks managers were able to dramatically increase productivity. Most automobiles, motorcycles and other motorized vehicles today are still produced using assembly lines.

Simon Dawson/Bloomberg/Getty Images

Like Taylor, the Gilbreths, and Gantt, Harrington Emerson was a management consultant. He made quite a stir in 1910 when he appeared before the Interstate Commerce Commission to testify about a rate increase requested by the railroads. As an expert witness, Emerson asserted that the railroads could save $1 million a day by using scientific management. He was also a strong advocate of specialized management roles in organizations, believing that job specialization was as relevant to managerial work as it was to operating jobs.

## Administrative Management

Whereas scientific management deals with the jobs of individual employees, administrative management focuses on managing the total organization. The primary contributors to administrative management were Henri Fayol (1841–1925), Lyndall Urwick (1891–1983), Max Weber (1864–1920), and Chester Barnard (1886–1961).

Henri Fayol was administrative management's most articulate spokesperson. A French industrialist, Fayol was unknown to U.S. managers and scholars until his most important work, *General and Industrial Management*, was translated into English in 1930.[17] Drawing on his own managerial experience, he tried to systematize the practice of management to provide guidance and direction to other managers. Fayol also was the first to identify the managerial functions of planning, organizing, leading, and controlling. He believed that these functions accurately reflect the core of the management process. Most contemporary management books (including this one) still use this framework, and practicing managers agree that these functions are a critical part of their jobs.

After a career as a British army officer, Lyndall Urwick became a noted management theorist and consultant. He integrated scientific management with the work of Fayol and other administrative management theorists. He also advanced modern thinking about the functions of planning, organizing, and controlling. Like Fayol, he developed a list of guidelines for improving managerial effectiveness. Urwick is noted not so much for his own contributions as for his synthesis and integration of the work of others.

Although Max Weber lived and worked at the same time as Fayol and Taylor, his contributions were not recognized until some years had passed. Weber was a German sociologist, and his most important work was not translated into English until 1947.[18] Weber's work on bureaucracy laid the foundation for contemporary organization theory, discussed in detail in Chapter 12. The concept of bureaucracy, as we discuss later, is based on a rational set of guidelines for structuring organizations in the most efficient manner.

Chester Barnard, former president of New Jersey Bell Telephone Company, made notable contributions to management in his book *The Functions of the Executive*.[19] The book proposes a major theory about the acceptance of authority. The theory suggests that subordinates weigh the legitimacy of a supervisor's directives and then decide whether to accept them. An order is accepted if the subordinate understands it, is able to comply with it, and views it as appropriate. The importance of Barnard's work is enhanced by his experience as a top manager.

## The Classical Management Perspective Today

The contributions and limitations of the classical management perspective are summarized in Table 2.1. The classical perspective is the framework from which later theories evolved, and many of its insights still hold true today. For example, many of the job specialization techniques and scientific methods espoused by Taylor and his contemporaries are still reflected in the way that many industrial jobs are designed today.[20] Moreover, many contemporary organizations still use some of the bureaucratic procedures suggested by Weber. Also, these early theorists were the first to focus attention on management as a meaningful field of study. Several aspects of the classical perspective are also relevant to our later discussions of planning, organizing, and controlling. And recent advances in areas such as business-to-business (B2B) digital commerce and the business model used by Amazon.com also have efficiency as their primary goal and directly reflect the premises of the classical perspective.

**administrative management** Focuses on managing the total organization

---

### TABLE 2.1 THE CLASSICAL MANAGEMENT PERSPECTIVE

The limitations of the classical perspective should not be overlooked. These early writers dealt with stable, simple organizations; many organizations today, in contrast, are changing and complex. They also proposed universal guidelines that we now recognize do not fit every organization. A third limitation of the classical management perspective is that it slighted the role of the individual in organizations. This role was much more fully developed by advocates of the behavioral management perspective.

| | |
|---|---|
| **General Summary** | The classical management perspective had two primary thrusts. Scientific management focused on employees within organizations and on ways to improve their productivity. Noted pioneers of scientific management were Frederick Taylor, Frank and Lillian Gilbreth, Henry Gantt, and Harrington Emerson. Administrative management focused on the total organization and on ways to make it more efficient and effective. Prominent administrative management theorists were Henri Fayol, Lyndall Urwick, Max Weber, and Chester Barnard. |
| **Contributions** | Laid the foundation for later developments in management theory. Identified important management processes, functions, and skills that are still recognized today. Focused attention on management as a valid subject of scientific inquiry. |
| **Limitations** | More appropriate for stable and simple organizations than for today's dynamic and complex organizations. Often prescribed universal procedures that are not appropriate in some settings. Even though some writers (such as Lillian Gilbreth and Chester Barnard) were concerned with the human element, many viewed employees as tools rather than resources. |

---

 **Manager's Checklist**

☐ The lessons learned from scientific and administrative management thinking can still play a role in promoting productivity and efficiency today.

☐ However, remember that focusing too much on productivity and efficiency can have a negative impact on other factors that promote overall effectiveness.

## The Behavioral Management Perspective

Early advocates of the classical management perspective viewed organizations and jobs from an essentially mechanistic point of view; that is, they essentially sought to conceptualize organizations as machines and workers as cogs within those machines. Even though many early writers recognized the role of individuals, their focus tended to be on how managers could control and standardize the behavior of their employees. In contrast, the behavioral management perspective placed much more emphasis on individual attitudes and behaviors and on group processes, and it recognized the importance of behavioral processes in the workplace.

The behavioral management perspective was stimulated by a number of writers and theoretical movements. One of those movements was *industrial psychology*, the practice of applying psychological concepts to industrial settings. Hugo Munsterberg (1863–1916), a noted German psychologist, is recognized as the key pioneer of industrial psychology. He established a psychological laboratory at Harvard in 1892, and his pioneering book, *Psychology and Industrial Efficiency*, was translated into English in 1913.[21] Munsterberg suggested that psychologists could make valuable contributions to managers in the areas of employee selection and motivation. Industrial psychology is still a major course of study at many colleges and universities. Another early advocate of the behavioral approach to management was Mary Parker Follett (1868–1933).[22]

**behavioral management perspective**
Emphasizes individual attitudes and behaviors and group processes

Follett worked during the scientific management era, but she quickly came to recognize the human element in the workplace. Indeed, her work clearly anticipated the behavioral management perspective, and she appreciated the need to understand the role of behavior in organizations.

Although Munsterberg and Follett made major contributions to the development of the behavioral approach to management, its primary catalyst was a series of studies conducted near Chicago at Western Electric's Hawthorne plant between 1927 and 1932. The research, originally sponsored by General Electric, was conducted by Elton Mayo and his associates.[23] Mayo was a faculty member and consultant at Harvard. The first study involved manipulating illumination for one group of workers and comparing their subsequent productivity with the productivity of another group whose illumination was not changed. Surprisingly, when illumination was increased for the experimental group, productivity went up in both groups. Produc-

The Hawthorne studies were a series of early experiments that focused on behavior in the workplace. In one experiment involving this group of workers, for example, researchers monitored how productivity changed as a result of changes in working conditions. The Hawthorne studies and subsequent experiments led scientists to the conclusion that the human element is very important in the workplace.

tivity continued to increase in both groups, even when the lighting for the experimental group was decreased. Not until the lighting was reduced to the level of moonlight did productivity begin to decline (and General Electric withdrew its sponsorship).

Another experiment established a piecework incentive pay plan for a group of nine men assembling terminal banks for telephone exchanges. Scientific management would have predicted that each man would try to maximize his pay by producing as many units as possible. Mayo and his associates, however, found that the group itself informally established an acceptable level of output for its members. Workers who overproduced were branded "rate busters," and underproducers were labeled "chiselers." To be accepted by the group, workers produced at the accepted level. As they approached this acceptable level of output, workers slacked off to avoid overproducing.

Other studies, including an interview program involving several thousand workers, led Mayo and his associates to conclude that human behavior was much more important in the workplace than had been previously believed. In the lighting experiment, for example, the results were attributed to the fact that both groups received special attention and sympathetic supervision for perhaps the first time. The incentive pay plans did not work because wage incentives were less important to the individual workers than was social acceptance in determining output. In short, individual and social processes played major roles in shaping worker attitudes and behavior.

## The Human Relations Movement

The human relations movement, which grew from the Hawthorne studies and was a popular approach to management for many years, proposed that workers respond primarily to the social context of the workplace, including social conditioning, group norms, and interpersonal dynamics. A basic assumption of the human relations movement was that the manager's concern for workers would lead to increased satisfaction, which would in turn result in improved performance. Two writers who helped advance the human relations movement were Abraham Maslow (1908–1970) and Douglas McGregor (1906–1964).

In 1943 Maslow advanced a theory suggesting that people are motivated by a hierarchy of needs, including monetary incentives and social acceptance.[24] Maslow's hierarchy, perhaps the

**human relations movement**
Argued that workers respond primarily to the social context of the workplace

*Courtesy of At&T Archives and History Center, Warren, NJ*

### TABLE 2.2  THEORY X AND THEORY Y

Douglas McGregor developed Theory X and Theory Y. He argued that Theory X best represented the views of scientific management and Theory Y represented the human relations approach. McGregor believed that Theory Y was the best philosophy for all managers.

| Theory X Assumptions | 1. People do not like work and try to avoid it. |
|---|---|
| | 2. People do not like work, so managers have to control, direct, coerce, and threaten employees to get them to work toward organizational goals. |
| | 3. People prefer to be directed, to avoid responsibility, and to want security; they have little ambition. |
| Theory Y Assumptions | 1. People do not naturally dislike work; work is a natural part of their lives. |
| | 2. People are internally motivated to reach objectives to which they are committed. |
| | 3. People are committed to goals to the degree that they receive personal rewards when they reach their objectives. |
| | 4. People will both seek and accept responsibility under favorable conditions. |
| | 5. People have the capacity to be innovative in solving organizational problems. |
| | 6. People are bright, but under most organizational conditions their potential is underutilized. |

Source: D. McGregor and W. Bennis, *The Human Side Enterprise: 25th Anniversary Printing*, 1985.

best-known human relations theory, is described in detail in Chapter 15. Meanwhile, Douglas McGregor's Theory X and Theory Y model best represents the essence of the human relations movement (see Table 2.2).[25] According to McGregor, Theory X and Theory Y reflect two extreme belief sets that different managers have about their workers. Theory X is a relatively pessimistic and negative view of workers and is consistent with the views of scientific management. Theory Y is more positive and represents the assumptions that human relations advocates make. In McGregor's view, Theory Y was a more appropriate philosophy for managers to adhere to. Both Maslow and McGregor notably influenced the thinking of many practicing managers.

## The Emergence of Organizational Behavior

Munsterberg, Mayo, Maslow, McGregor, and others have made valuable contributions to management. Contemporary theorists, however, have noted that many assertions of the human relationists were simplistic and provided inadequate descriptions of work behavior. For example, the assumption that worker satisfaction leads to improved performance has been shown to have little, if any, validity. If anything, satisfaction follows good performance rather than precedes it. (These issues are addressed in Chapters 15 and 16.)

Current behavioral perspectives on management, known as organizational behavior, acknowledge that human behavior in organizations is much more complex than the human relationists realized. The field of organizational behavior draws from a broad, interdisciplinary base of psychology, sociology, anthropology, economics, and medicine. Organizational behavior takes a holistic view of behavior and addresses individual, group, and organization processes. These processes are major elements in contemporary management theory.[26] Important topics in this field include job satisfaction, stress, motivation, leadership, group dynamics, organizational politics, interpersonal conflict, and the structure and design of organizations.[27] A contingency orientation also characterizes the field (discussed more fully later in this chapter). Our discussions of organizing (Chapters 10–13) and leading (Chapters 14–18) are heavily influenced by organizational behavior. And, finally, managers need a solid understanding of human behavior as they address such diversity-related issues as ethnicity, gender, and religion in the workplace. Indeed, all of these topics are useful to help managers better deal with fallout from the consequences of layoffs and job cuts, mergers, and outsourcing and to seek better ways to motivate today's workers.

**Theory X**
A pessimistic and negative view of workers consistent with the views of scientific management

**Theory Y**
A positive view of workers; it represents the assumptions that human relations advocates make

**organizational behavior**
Contemporary field focusing on behavioral perspectives on management

## The Behavioral Management Perspective Today

Table 2.3 summarizes the behavioral management perspective and lists its contributions and limitations. The primary contributions relate to ways in which this approach has changed managerial thinking. Managers are now more likely to recognize the importance of behavioral processes and to view employees as valuable resources instead of mere tools. On the other hand, organizational behavior is still relatively imprecise in its ability to predict behavior, especially the behavior of a specific person. It is not always accepted or understood by practicing managers. Hence, the contributions of the behavioral school have yet to be fully realized.

□ Never overlook the importance of the human element in organizations.

□ Avoid making simplistic assumptions about how to affect employee behavior.

**Manager's Checklist** ☑

# The Quantitative Management Perspective

The third major school of management thought began to emerge during World War II. During the war, government officials and scientists in England and the United States worked to help the military deploy its resources more efficiently and effectively. These groups took some of the mathematical approaches to management developed decades earlier by Taylor and Gantt and applied them to logistical problems during the war.[28] They learned that problems with troop, equipment, and submarine deployment, for example, could all be solved through mathematical analysis. After the war, companies such as DuPont and General Electric began to use the same techniques for deploying employees, choosing plant locations, and planning warehouses. Basically, then, this perspective is concerned with applying quantitative techniques to management. More specifically, the quantitative management perspective focuses on decision making, economic effectiveness, mathematical models, and the use of computers. Our *Tech Watch* feature highlights an interesting contemporary perspective on quantitative methods as they relate to social media. There are two branches of the quantitative approach: management science and operations management.

**quantitative management perspective** Applies quantitative techniques to management

### TABLE 2.3  THE BEHAVIORAL MANAGEMENT PERSPECTIVE

| | |
|---|---|
| **General Summary** | The behavioral management perspective focuses on employee behavior in an organizational context. Stimulated by the birth of industrial psychology, the human relations movement supplanted scientific management as the dominant approach to management in the 1930s and 1940s. Prominent contributors to this movement were Elton Mayo, Abraham Maslow, and Douglas McGregor. Organizational behavior, the contemporary outgrowth of the behavioral management perspective, draws from an interdisciplinary base and recognizes the complexities of human behavior in organizational settings. |
| **Contributions** | Provided important insights into motivation, group dynamics, and other interpersonal processes in organizations. |
| | Focused managerial attention on these same processes. |
| | Challenged the view that employees are tools and furthered the belief that employees are valuable resources. |
| **Limitations** | The complexity of individual behavior makes prediction of that behavior difficult. |
| | Many behavioral concepts have not yet been put to use because some managers are reluctant to adopt them. |
| | Contemporary research findings by behavioral scientists are often not communicated to practicing managers in an understandable form. |

# TECH WATCH

# Does ROI Have Redeeming Social Value?

Let's say that you own a local nursery and you're thinking about adding delivery service. It will cost you $45,000 but will add 150 customers who will spend about $250 each, for a total increase in revenue of $62,500. Is delivery service a good investment? It would seem so, but to get a better idea, you might calculate your *ROI—return on investment*. It's a pretty simple formula:

$$ROI = \frac{\$62,500 - \$45,000 = \$17,500}{\$45,000} = 38.8\%$$

Is a 38.8% return on your investment good? It all depends. It is if the same $45,000 could get you an ROI of only 34.9% from the expansion of your lawn furniture department, but it's not if the expansion could get you an ROI of 44.6%.

ROI, then, is relative, but it can come in handy as a mathematical tool for supporting decision making—which is one of the key functions of *quantitative management* tools. It can also be applied to a variety of decisions—say, whether to invest marketing dollars in TV ads or in price rebates.

In fact, the pressure to quantify results is being increasingly felt by today's marketing managers—the middle managers responsible for communicating a firm's value package to, and managing its relationships with, its customers. According to the University of Melbourne's Jody Evans, the marketer's job now entails a sharper "focus on marketing measurement," as marketers are required to measure and demonstrate the effectiveness of their strategies in quantifiable terms. "Return on investment," says Evans, "is the buzzword for marketers today, and it includes such areas as customer satisfaction and brand awareness. It's the marriage of hard numbers and less quantifiable factors."

A study conducted by the research firm MarketingSherpa found that "marketers are under constant pressure to measure everything they do." As a result, they often resort to "tactics that are more easily and accurately measurable, regardless of their effectiveness." The problem is especially acute when it comes to marketing through *social media*—websites that allow users to create and exchange content.

According to the MarketingSherpa study, the difficulty of measuring ROI is the biggest problem in getting top management to allot money for marketing activities undertaken through social media channels.

Marketers can count and collect data on certain aspects of social media usage—*unique visitors, page views, cost per click*, and so forth—but that doesn't necessarily mean that they can quantify that data in terms of a traditional metric such as ROI. In fact, says marketing research executive David Alston, the effort may not be worth the trouble: "The discussion of ROI [and social media]," he argues, "has focused mostly on the search for the holy grail of a metric, but adapting traditional metrics to fit social media would be akin to sticking a square peg in a round hole."

What's the problem? Basically, says Lux Narayan, CEO of the social media research firm Unmetric, ROI isn't useful in analyzing social media campaigns because "it's virtually impossible … to isolate cause and effect"—to attribute a specific dollar of *return* to a specific dollar of *investment*. Did a Facebook user, for example, ultimately buy something from your nursery because he clicked through to your post featuring a fairy tale about a magical green thumb? Did a Twitter user ultimately buy something because she clicked through to your link to an article about gardening and mental health?

Given the business that he's in, Narayan obviously believes that there are effective ways of "thinking outside the ROI box." He does suggest, however, that "the next time you're asked for social media ROI, you should ROFL."*

*Roll On the Floor Laughing

*References:* Angela Haggerty, "Big Data and Multi-Channels Complicating Marketers' Ability to Measure ROI, according to Report," *The Drum*, August 1, 2013, www.thedrum.com, on June 23, 2014; Tia Fisher, "ROI of Social Media: A Look at the Arguments," *Emoderation*, May 13, 2009, www.emoderation.com, on June 23, 2014; MarketingSherpa LLC, "New Chart: How Accurately Can You Gauge the ROI of Social Media Tactics?" May 5, 2009, www.marketingsherpa.com, on June 24, 2014; Giuseppe Crosti, "Truth and Lies of Social Media ROI," *Huffington Post*, November 27, 2013, www.huffingtonpost.com, on June 18, 2014; Christian Arno, "Is It Possible to Measure Social Media ROI?" *ClickZ*, April 15, 2014, www.clickz.com, on June 17, 2014; David Alston, "Social Media ROI—What's the 'Return on Ignoring'?" *MarketingProfs*, January 6, 2009, www.marketingprofs.com, on June 24, 2014; Lux Narayan, "3 Reasons Why There's No Measuring ROI on Social Media," *Forbes.com*, August 28, 2012, www.forbes.com, on June 23, 2014.

## Management Science

Unfortunately, the term *management science* appears to be related to scientific management, the approach developed by Taylor and others early in the twentieth century. But the two have little in common and should not be confused. Management science focuses specifically on the development of mathematical models. A mathematical model is a simplified representation of a system, process, or relationship.

At its most basic level, management science focuses on models, equations, and similar representations of reality. For example, managers at Detroit Edison use mathematical models to determine how best to route repair crews during blackouts. Citizens Bank of New England uses models to figure out how many tellers need to be on duty at each location at various times throughout the day. In recent years, paralleling developments in digital technologies, management science techniques have become increasingly sophisticated. For example, automobile manufacturers Daimler AG and General Motors use realistic computer simulations to study collision damage to cars, and aircraft makers like Boeing and Airbus simulate the effects of crashes and fires to help them improve airplane safety. These simulations give them precise information and lower the costs of crashing as many test cars and airplanes as would have been required in the past.

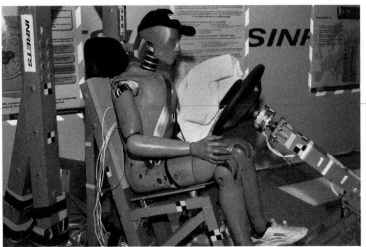

Automobile manufacturers around the world today use crash test dummies like this one to test safety features in their cars. Statistical techniques and methods derived from management science help engineers and managers assess the effectiveness of various safety features. The results include safer vehicles and lower costs for manufacturers.

## Operations Management

Operations management is somewhat less mathematical and statistically sophisticated than management science and can be applied more directly to managerial situations. Indeed, we can think of operations management as a form of applied management science. Operations management techniques are generally concerned with helping the organization produce its products or services more efficiently and can be applied to a wide range of problems.

For example, Rubbermaid and Home Depot each use operations management techniques to manage their inventories. (Inventory management is concerned with specific inventory problems, such as balancing carrying costs and ordering costs, and determining the optimal order quantity.) Linear programming (which involves computing simultaneous solutions to a set of linear equations) helps Delta Airlines plan its flight schedules, Consolidated Freightways develop its shipping routes, and General Instrument Corporation plan what instruments to produce at various times. Other operations management techniques include queuing theory, break-even analysis, and simulation. All of these techniques and procedures apply directly to operations, but they are also helpful in such areas as finance, marketing, and human resource management.[29]

## The Quantitative Management Perspective Today

Like the other management perspectives, the quantitative management perspective has made important contributions and has certain limitations. Both are summarized in Table 2.4. It has provided managers with an abundance of decision-making tools and techniques and has increased understanding of overall organizational processes. It has been particularly useful in the areas of planning and controlling. Relatively new management concepts such as supply chain management and new techniques such as enterprise resource planning, both discussed later in this book, also evolved from the quantitative management perspective.

**management science**
Focuses specifically on the development of mathematical models

**operations management**
Concerned with helping the organization more efficiently produce its products or services

**TABLE 2.4  THE QUANTITATIVE MANAGEMENT PERSPECTIVE**

| | |
|---|---|
| **General Summary** | The quantitative management perspective focuses on applying mathematical models and processes to management situations. Management science deals specifically with the development of mathematical models to aid in decision making and problem solving. Operations management focuses more directly on the application of management science to organizations. Management information systems are developed to provide information to managers. |
| **Contributions** | Developed sophisticated quantitative techniques to assist in decision making. Application of models has increased our awareness and understanding of complex organizational processes and situations. Has been very useful in the planning and controlling processes. |
| **Limitations** | Cannot fully explain or predict the behavior of people in organizations. Mathematical sophistication may come at the expense of other important skills. Models may require unrealistic or unfounded assumptions. |

"Credit cards, bank accounts. Everything is being analyzed 24/7 whether we like it or not. You would be amazed how much data is available."

—SAMER TAKRITI, FINANCIAL ANALYST FOR GOLDMAN SACHS[31]

Even more recently, mathematicians have been using tools and techniques from the quantitative perspective to develop models that might be helpful in the war against terrorism.[30] On the other hand, mathematical models cannot fully account for individual behaviors and attitudes. Some believe that the time needed to develop competence in quantitative techniques retards the development of other managerial skills. Finally, mathematical models typically require a set of assumptions that may not be realistic.

 **Manager's Checklist**

☐ Quantitative perspectives such as management science and operations management are important management tools.

☐ When possible, it is useful to quantify problems and opportunities; however, this is often not possible, and so managers need to also consider other perspectives and approaches.

# Integrating Perspectives for Managers

It is important to recognize that the classical, behavioral, and quantitative approaches to management are not necessarily contradictory or mutually exclusive. Even though each of the three perspectives makes very different assumptions and predictions, each can also complement the others. Indeed, a complete understanding of management requires an appreciation of all three perspectives. The systems and contingency perspectives can help us integrate the earlier approaches and enhance our understanding of all three.

## The Systems Perspective

We briefly introduced the systems perspective in Chapter 1 in our definition of management. A system is an interrelated set of elements functioning as a whole.[32] As shown in Figure 2.3, by viewing an organization as a system, we can identify four basic elements: inputs, transformation processes, outputs, and feedback. First, inputs are the material, human, financial, and information resources the organization gets from its environment. Next, through technological and managerial processes, inputs are transformed into outputs. Outputs include

**system**
An interrelated set of elements functioning as a whole

## FIGURE 2.3  THE SYSTEMS PERSPECTIVE OF ORGANIZATIONS

By viewing organizations as systems, managers can better understand the importance of their environment and the level of interdependence among subsystems within the organization. Managers must also understand how their decisions affect and are affected by other subsystems within the organization.

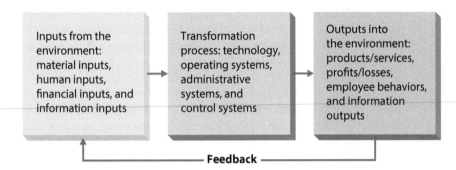

Inputs from the environment: material inputs, human inputs, financial inputs, and information inputs

Transformation process: technology, operating systems, administrative systems, and control systems

Outputs into the environment: products/services, profits/losses, employee behaviors, and information outputs

Feedback

products, services, or both (tangible and intangible); profits, losses, or both (even not-for-profit organizations must operate within their budgets); employee behaviors; and information. Finally, the environment reacts to these outputs and provides feedback to the system.

Thinking of organizations as systems provides us with a variety of important viewpoints on organizations, such as the concepts of open systems, subsystems, synergy, and entropy. Open systems are systems that interact with their environment, whereas closed systems do not interact with their environment. Although organizations are open systems, some make the mistake of ignoring their environment and behaving as though their environment is not important.

The systems perspective also stresses the importance of subsystems—systems within a broader system. For example, the marketing, production, and finance functions within Mattel are systems in their own right but are also subsystems within the overall organization. Because they are interdependent, a change in one subsystem can affect other subsystems as well. If the production department at Mattel lowers the quality of the toys being made (by buying lower-quality materials, for example), the effects are felt in finance (improved cash flow in the short run owing to lower costs) and marketing (decreased sales in the long run because of customer dissatisfaction). Managers must therefore remember that although organizational subsystems can be managed with some degree of autonomy, their interdependence should not be overlooked. For instance, recent research has underscored the interdependence of strategy and operations in businesses.[33]

Synergy suggests that organizational units (or subsystems) may often be more successful working together than working alone. The Walt Disney Company, for example, benefits greatly from synergy. The company's movies, theme parks, television programs, and merchandise-licensing programs all benefit one another. Children who enjoy a Disney movie like *Frozen* want to go to Disney World, see the *Frozen* attractions there, and buy stuffed toys and action

**open system**
A system that interacts with its environment

**closed system**
A system that does not interact with its environment

**subsystem**
A system within another system

**synergy**
Two or more subsystems working together to produce more than the total of what they might produce working alone

Photos 12 / Alamy

Disney is a master of synergy. The firm's movies, theme park attractions, and merchandise, for example, are all linked together so that each enhances the others. For instance, the Disney movie *Frozen* was widely promoted at Disney World and Disneyland before the movie ever opened. And long after the movie left theaters, people could still buy *Frozen* DVDs and merchandise throughout all Disney retail outlets.

figures of the film's characters. Music from the film generates additional revenues for the firm, as do computer games and other licensing arrangements for lunchboxes, clothing, and so forth.

Synergy was also the major objective of the recent merger between United and Continental Airlines. The merger was projected to bring in revenue gains of $800 million to $900 million while also increasing advancement opportunities for employees. The majority of pre-merge United passengers flew in and out of Chicago, Denver, San Francisco, Washington Dulles, and Los Angeles, while Continental's main hubs were Houston, Newark, and Cleveland. Because the two companies had little overlap in their domestic routes and hubs, customers will presumably have more destination options. In terms of international travel, United has long been focused primarily between the United States and Asia, and Continental has long offered more European destinations. So the combined airline will have the opportunity to eventually outperform the combined individual airlines that existed previously.[34]

> "The whole is greater than the sum of its parts"
>
> —ARISTOLE

Finally, entropy is a normal process that leads to system decline. When an organization does not monitor feedback from its environment and make appropriate adjustments, it may fail. For example, witness the problems of Rambler (an automobile manufacturer) and Circuit City (a major retailer). Each of these organizations went bankrupt because it failed to revitalize itself and keep pace with changes in its environment. A primary objective of management, from a systems perspective, is to continually re-energize the organization to avoid entropy.

**entropy**
A normal process leading to system decline

**universal perspective**
An attempt to identify the one best way to do something

**contingency perspective**
Suggests that appropriate managerial behavior in a given situation depends on, or is contingent on, a wide variety of elements

## The Contingency Perspective

Another noteworthy recent addition to management thinking is the contingency perspective. The classical, behavioral, and quantitative approaches are considered universal perspectives because they try to identify the "one best way" to manage organizations. The contingency perspective, in contrast, suggests that universal theories cannot be applied to organizations because each organization is unique. Instead, the contingency perspective suggests that appropriate managerial behavior in a given situation depends on, or is contingent on, unique elements in that situation.[35]

Stated differently, effective managerial behavior in one situation cannot always be generalized to other situations. Recall, for example, that Frederick Taylor assumed that all workers would generate the highest possible level of output to maximize their own personal economic gain. We can imagine some people being motivated primarily by money—but we can just as easily imagine other people being motivated by the desire for leisure time, status, social acceptance, or any combination of these (as Mayo found at the Hawthorne plant). In 2000 Cisco Systems had the largest market capitalization in the world and was growing at a rate of 50 percent per year. A recession and the terrorist attacks in September 2001, however, caused the technology sector to crash, and Cisco's stock dropped in value by 86 percent. Cisco's CEO, John Chambers, had to downsize the company through layoffs and divestitures and transform it into a smaller company. As he did so, he also changed his management style.

> "I'm a command-and-control person. I like being able to say turn right, and we truly have 67,000 people turn right. But that's the style of the past. Today's world requires a different leadership style — more collaboration and teamwork, including using Web 2.0 technologies."
>
> —JOHN CHAMBERS, RECENTLY RETIRED CEO OF CISCO[38]

He had previously been an autocratic manager and led Cisco using a command-and-control hierarchy. As a result of the transformation at Cisco, however, Chambers also decided he needed to change his own management style. He began to adopt a much more democratic approach and to run Cisco using a more democratic organizational structure.[36] Today Cisco has regained its footing as one of the leading technology businesses in the world.[37]

## An Integrating Framework

We noted earlier that the classical, behavioral, and quantitative management perspectives can be complementary and that the systems and contingency perspectives can help integrate them. Our framework for integrating the various approaches to management is shown in Figure 2.4. The initial premise of the framework is that before they try to apply concepts or ideas from the three major perspectives, managers must recognize the interdependence of units within the organization, the effect of environmental influences, and the need to respond to the unique characteristics of each situation. The ideas of subsystem interdependencies and environmental influences are given to us by systems theory, and the situational view of management is derived from a contingency perspective.

With these ideas as basic assumptions, managers can use valid tools, techniques, concepts, and theories of the classical, behavioral, and quantitative management perspectives. For example, managers can still use many of the basic techniques from scientific management. In many contemporary settings, the scientific study of jobs and production techniques can enhance productivity. But managers should not rely only on these techniques, nor should they ignore the human element. The behavioral perspective is also of use to managers today. By drawing on contemporary ideas of organizational behavior, managers can better appreciate the role of employee needs and behaviors in the workplace.

---

**FIGURE 2.4** AN INTEGRATIVE FRAMEWORK OF MANAGEMENT PERSPECTIVES

---

Each of the major perspectives on management can be useful to modern managers. Before using any of them, however, managers should recognize the situational contexts within which they operate. The systems and contingency perspectives serve to integrate the classical, behavioral, and quantitative management perspectives.

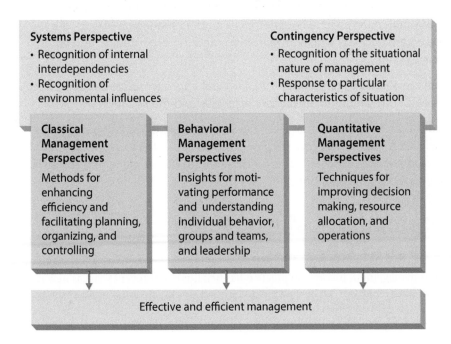

Motivation, leadership, communication, and group processes are especially important. The quantitative perspective provides managers with a set of useful tools and techniques. The development and use of management science models and the application of operations management methods can help managers increase their efficiency and effectiveness.

Consider the new distribution manager of a large wholesale firm whose job is to manage 100 truck drivers and to coordinate standard truck routes in the most efficient fashion. This new manager, with little relevant experience, might try to increase productivity by introducing specialization and close supervision (as suggested by scientific management). But doing so may decrease employee satisfaction and morale and increase turnover (as predicted by organizational behavior). The manager might also develop a statistical formula to use route driver time more efficiently (from management science). But this new system could disrupt existing work groups and social patterns (from organizational behavior). The manager might create even more problems by trying to impose programs and practices derived from her previous job. An incentive program welcomed by retail clerks, for example, might not work for truck drivers.

The manager should soon realize that a broader perspective is needed. Systems and contingency perspectives help provide broader solutions. Also, as the integrative framework in Figure 2.4 illustrates, applying techniques from several schools works better than trying to make one approach solve all problems. To solve a problem of declining productivity, the manager might look to scientific management (perhaps jobs are inefficiently designed or workers improperly trained), organizational behavior (worker motivation may be low, or group norms may be limiting output), or operations management (facilities may be improperly laid out, or material shortages may result from poor inventory management). And before implementing any plans for improvement, the manager should try to assess their effect on other areas of the organization.

Now suppose that the same manager is involved in planning a new warehouse. She will probably consider what type of management structure to create (classical management perspective), what kinds of leaders and work-group arrangements to develop (behavioral management perspective), and how to develop a network model for designing and operating the facility itself (quantitative perspective). As a final example, if employee turnover is too high, the manager might consider an incentive system (classical perspective), plan a motivational enhancement program (behavioral perspective), or use a mathematical model (quantitative perspective) to discover that turnover costs may actually be lower than the cost of making any changes at all.

---

 **Manager's Checklist**

☐ The systems perspective is useful for reminding managers of both the interconnectedness within organizations and the organization and its environment.

☐ Managers need to remember that universal approaches are seldom effective; instead, they should focus on contingencies and the situation.

☐ You should understand that all of the various techniques and perspectives are really tools that managers can draw on to carry out their responsibilities. Just as a carpenter uses different tools for different tasks, the manager's tools will also vary based on the situation.

## Contemporary Management Issues and Challenges

Interest in management theory and practice has heightened in recent years as new issues and challenges have emerged. No new paradigm has been formulated that replaces the traditional views, but managers continue to strive toward a better understanding of how they can compete and lead their organizations to become more effective. Figure 2.5 summarizes the historical

## FIGURE 2.5  THE EMERGENCE OF MODERN MANAGEMENT PERSPECTIVES

Most contemporary management perspectives have emerged and evolved over the last hundred years or so. Beginning with the classical management perspective, first developed toward the end of the nineteenth century, and on through contemporary applied perspectives, managers have an array of useful techniques, methods, and approaches for solving problems and enhancing the effectiveness of their organizations. Of course, managers also need to recognize that not every idea set forth is valid, and that even those that are useful are not applicable in all settings. And new methods and approaches will continue to be developed in the future.

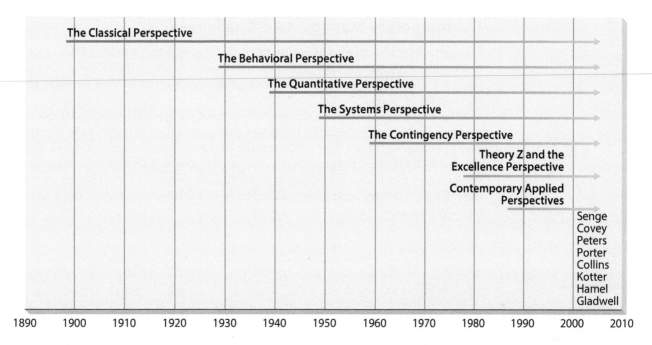

The Classical Perspective
The Behavioral Perspective
The Quantitative Perspective
The Systems Perspective
The Contingency Perspective
Theory Z and the Excellence Perspective
Contemporary Applied Perspectives

Senge
Covey
Peters
Porter
Collins
Kotter
Hamel
Gladwell

1890  1900  1910  1920  1930  1940  1950  1960  1970  1980  1990  2000  2010

development of the major models of management described in the preceding sections, and it puts into historical context the contemporary applied perspectives discussed in the next section.

## Contemporary Applied Perspectives

In recent years, books written for the popular press have also had a major impact on both the field of organizational behavior and the practice of management. This trend first surfaced in the early 1980s with the success of books such as *Theory Z* and *In Search of Excellence*. Each of these books spent time on the *New York Times* best-seller list and was required reading for any manager wanting to at least appear informed. Biographies of business leaders such as Warren Buffett and Jack Welch also have received widespread attention. For instance, the bidding for the publishing rights to the legendary Jack Welch's memoirs, published when he retired as CEO from General Electric, exceeded $7 million.[39]

Other authors have greatly influenced management theory and practice. Among the most popular such authors today are Peter Senge, Stephen Covey, Tom Peters, Jim Collins, Michael Porter, John Kotter, and Gary Hamel.[41] Their books

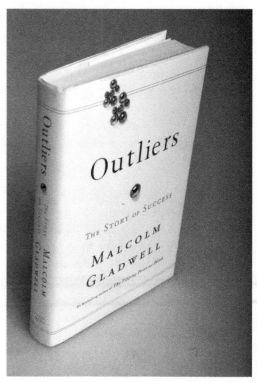

"You are what you read."

—MARTHA FINNEY, BUSINESS WRITER[40]

highlight the management practices of successful firms such as Shell, Ford, IBM, and others, or outline conceptual or theoretical models or frameworks to guide managers as they formulate strategies or motivate their employees. Malcolm Gladwell's books *The Tipping Point*, *Blink*, and *Outliers* have caught the attention of many contemporary managers. Scott Adams, creator of the popular comic strip *Dilbert*, is also immensely popular today. Adams is a former communications industry worker who developed his strip to illustrate some of the absurdities that occasionally afflict contemporary organizational life. The daily strip is routinely posted outside office doors, above copy machines, and beside water coolers in hundreds of offices.

## Contemporary Management Challenges

Managers today also face an imposing set of challenges as they guide and direct the fortunes of their companies. Coverage of each of these is thoroughly integrated throughout this book. In addition, many of them are highlighted or given focused coverage in one or more special ways.

One of the most critical challenges facing managers today is an unpredictable economy that limits growth. A second important challenge is the management of diversity, as noted in Chapter 1. *Leading the Way* features an interesting example of the role of diversity. Another important challenge today is employee privacy. A related issue has to do with the increased capabilities that technology provides for people to work at places other than their offices. The appropriate role of the Internet in business strategy is also a complex topic for managers.

**LEADING THE WAY**

# A Hooters Girl on the Fast Track

Kat Cole started her climb up the corporate ladder in orange shorts. At 16, she took a part-time job serving chicken wings and beer at Hooters, and 19 years later—at the relatively young age of 35—she was president of Cinnabon, a franchise that sells cinnamon-laced concoctions out of 1,100 locations in 56 countries. Cole now leads a team of employees that ranges over four generations in age and includes many men who are much older than she is.

Obviously, it was a fast climb, but Cole didn't skip any rungs (except getting a college degree—she dropped out but eventually earned an MBA). She got started by taking advantage of opportunities that opened up in the Hooters outlet where she was waiting tables. "When the cook quit," Cole reports, "I learned how to run the kitchen, and when the manager quit, I learned how to run a shift." By the time she was 18, her responsibilities included training new employees. "My general manager saw the potential in

me," she recalls, "and my role as a trainer expanded to other stores."

A year later, while still in college, she was asked to join the company's international expansion team, which was headed to Australia. She spent 40 days with the team in Sydney, and within 10 days of her return to the United States, Cole was on her way to open the first Hooters in Central America, "then ones in South America, Asia, Africa, and Canada. By the time I was 20, I'd opened up the first Hooters on most continents outside the U.S. and was failing school. So I quit to become head of Hooters corporate training."

It was worth a 50 percent pay cut, because Cole rose quickly through the ranks, becoming an executive VP at age 26. When she was 29, mentors urged her to go back to school, and so she entered the MBA program at Georgia State. Companies like Cinnabon were already calling, but in 2010, Cole decided to stay at Hooters long enough to take advantage of one more opportunity—helping to manage the sale of the company. She found herself "dealing with analysts, brokers, investors, and the internal team. ... I would go to class one day and learn about transactions, and I would go to work on Monday and be in the middle of the transaction, and I'd think, 'Thank God I went to class that day.'"

Later in 2010, at age 32, Cole took the job as COO of Cinnabon, and two months later, she finished her MBA. She was appointed president of the company in 2011. Under Cole's leadership, Cinnabon has opened 200 new outlets (called "bakeries") and entered licensing programs with such franchises as Burger King and Taco Bell. Cole has also launched a host of branded products, including a cinnamon-scented air freshener, a cinnamon-flavored vodka, and a cinnamon-spiced Keurig coffee blend (although she vetoed a cinnamon-flavored mouthwash). She's also partnered with international packaged-goods companies such as Pillsbury and Kellogg's and such big-box retailers as Costco, Walmart, and Target. Cinnabon now has 50,000 points of distribution around the world and is fast approaching $1 billion in annual sales. "My management style," she says, "is fast and direct. ... We totally celebrate fast failure," adds Cole, who's perfectly willing to launch a product

that's only 75 percent ready for market. "We move as fast as something feels good."

Clearly, speed to market isn't a strategy for the risk averse. Taking risks means making tough calls, but Cole figures that if she has to make a tough call, it's better to make it too soon rather than too late: "If you don't take a risk," she advises, "your competition will." Ironically, Cole regards moving fast and taking risks as good reasons for pausing to get other people's opinions. Her thinking? By the time you get around to making a decision, "there are usually lots of people around you who've known that it's the right thing to do for a long time. The key, in business and in leadership, is staying really close to the other people who kind of know what's going on so that it doesn't take you too long to figure it out."

*References:* Catherine Clifford, "How Kat Cole Went from Hooters Girl to President of Cinnabon by Age 32," *Entrepreneur.com*, August 19, 2013, www.entrepreneur.com, on June 14, 2014; Jenna Goudreau, "From Hooters to Hot Buns: How Kat Cole Turned Cinnabon into a $1 Billion Brand," *Forbes.com*, November 27, 2012, www.forbes.com, on June 14, 2014; Barbara Babbit Kaufman, "Kat Cole: From Hooters Girl to CEO, by Age 35," *Atlanta Business Chronicle*, August 23, 2012, www.bizjournals.com, on June 14, 2014; Laura Dunn, "Women in Business: Q&A with Kat Cole, President of Cinnabon," *Huffington Post*, August 8, 2013, www.huffingtonpost.com, on June 14, 2014; Lydia Dishman, "How Kat Cole Operates Cinnabon Like a Tech Startup," *Fast Company*, April 9, 2014, www.fastcompany.com, on June 14, 2014; Blair Chancey, "Leadership: Kat Cole Style," *QSR Magazine*, September 2011, www.qsrmagazine.com, on June 14, 2014.

Globalization is another significant contemporary challenge for managers. Managing in a global economy poses many different challenges and opportunities. For example, at a macro level, property ownership arrangements vary widely. So does the availability of natural resources and components of the infrastructure, as well as the role of government in business. Moreover, behavioral processes vary widely across cultural and national boundaries. For example, values, symbols, and beliefs differ sharply among cultures. Different work norms and the role that work plays in a person's life, for example, influence patterns of both work-related behavior and attitudes toward work. They also affect the nature of supervisory relationships, decision-making styles and processes, and organizational configurations. Group and intergroup processes, responses to stress, and the nature of political behaviors also differ from culture to culture. Chapter 5 is devoted to these and other global issues.

Another management challenge that has taken on renewed importance in recent years is ethics and social responsibility and their relationship to corporate governance. Unfortunately, business scandals involving unethical conduct have become almost commonplace today. From a social responsibility perspective, increasing attention has been focused on pollution and business's obligation to help clean up our environment, business contributions to social causes, and so forth. The proper framework for corporate governance is often at the center of these debates and discussions.[42] Rising energy costs and growing concerns about climate change have also focused new attention on sustainability. Chapter 4 covers ethics and social responsibility in more detail.

Quality also continues to pose an important management challenge today. Quality is an important issue for several reasons. First, more and more organizations are using quality as a basis for competition. Second, improving quality tends to increase productivity because making higher-quality products generally results in less waste and rework. Third, enhancing quality lowers costs. Managers at Whistler Corporation once realized that the firm was using 100 of its 250 employees to repair defective radar detectors that had been built incorrectly in the first place. Quality is also important because of its relationship to productivity. Quality is highlighted in Chapter 20.

The shift toward a service economy also continues to be important. Traditionally, most U.S. businesses were manufacturers—using tangible resources like raw materials and machinery to create tangible products like automobiles and steel. And manufacturing is indeed still important in the U.S. economy. The United States remains by far the world's largest manufacturer. Between 1990 and 2009, for example, U.S. manufacturing output grew by nearly $800 billion.[43] And in 2014 manufacturers contributed $2.09 trillion to the economy, up from $2.03 trillion in 2012 and $2.08 in 2013.[44]

In the last few decades, however, the service sector of the economy has become much more important. Indeed, services now account for well over half of the gross domestic product in the United States and play a similarly important role in many other industrialized nations. Service technology involves the use of both tangible resources (such as machinery) and intangible resources (such as intellectual property) to create intangible services (such as a haircut, insurance protection, or transportation between two cities). Although there are obviously many similarities between managing in a manufacturing and a service organization, there are also many fundamental differences. We will highlight these similarities and differences at several points in this book.

The role and impact of social media in business also pose unique challenges for business. Few large businesses have grasped how to use social media to compete more effectively, but most would also agree that social media can have a major impact on business. Unfortunately, this impact is often negative. For example, a customer who has a bad experience in a restaurant can use social media to spread the word about that experience, and the story can then get passed along over and over again. Since it seems that many people are more prone to read and react to negative experiences than to positive ones, the ripple effects of poor service (as one example) can be quite damaging. In a similar vein, a disgruntled worker at Target recently used a site called gawker.com to complain about the firm's internal morale. The rant spread so quickly that Target's CEO felt the need to issue a public response.[45]

 **Manager's Checklist**

☐ Many managers remain current by reading leading business books.

☐ You should remain alert for new and emerging management challenges and opportunities.

# Summary of Learning Outcomes and Key Points

1. Justify the importance of history and theory to management and discuss precursors to modern management theory.

   • Theories are important as organizers of knowledge and as road maps for action.
   • Understanding the historical context and precursors of management and organizations provides a sense of

heritage and can also help managers avoid repeating the mistakes of others.

   • Evidence suggests that interest in management dates back thousands of years, but a scientific approach to management has emerged only in the last hundred years.

2. Summarize and evaluate the classical perspective on management, including scientific and administrative management, and note its relevance to contemporary managers.

   - The classical management perspective had two major branches: scientific management and administrative management.
   - Scientific management was concerned with improving efficiency and work methods for individual workers.
   - Administrative management was more concerned with how organizations themselves should be structured and arranged for efficient operations.
   - Both branches paid little attention to the role of the worker as a person.

3. Summarize and evaluate the behavioral perspective on management, including the Hawthorne studies, human relations movement, and organizational behavior, and note its relevance to contemporary managers.

   - The behavioral management perspective, characterized by a concern for individual and group behavior, emerged primarily as a result of the Hawthorne studies.
   - The human relations movement recognized the importance and potential of behavioral processes in organizations but made many overly simplistic assumptions about those processes.
   - Organizational behavior, a more realistic outgrowth of the behavioral perspective, is of interest to many contemporary managers.

4. Summarize and evaluate the quantitative perspective on management, including management science and operations management, and note its relevance to contemporary managers.

   - The quantitative management perspective and its two components, management science and operations management, involve the application of quantitative techniques to decision making and problem solving.
   - Applications of the quantitative perspective have been facilitated by the tremendous increase in the use of personal computers and integrated information networks.

5. Discuss the systems and contingency approaches to management and explain their potential for integrating the other areas of management.

   - The three major perspectives should be viewed in a complementary, not a contradictory, light. Each has something of value to offer.
   - Two relatively recent additions to management theory, the systems and contingency perspectives, appear to have great potential both as approaches to management and as frameworks for integrating the other perspectives.

6. Identify and describe contemporary management issues and challenges.

   - A variety of popular applied perspectives influence management practice today.
   - Important issues and challenges facing managers include employee retention, diversity, the new workforce, organization change, ethics and social responsibility, the importance of quality, and the continued shift toward a service economy.

# Discussion Questions

## Questions for Review

1. Briefly describe the principles of scientific management and administrative management. What assumptions are made about workers?

2. What are the differences between the contingency and the universal perspectives on management? How is the contingency perspective useful in the practice of management today?

## Questions for Analysis

5. Young, innovative, or high-tech firms often adopt the strategy of ignoring history or trying to do something radically new. In what ways might this strategy help them? In what ways might this strategy hinder them?

3. Describe the systems perspective. Why is a business organization considered an open system?

4. For each of the contemporary management challenges, give at least one example, other than the examples found in the text.

6. Can a manager use tools and techniques from several different perspectives at the same time? For example, can a manager use both classical and behavioral perspectives? Give an example of a time when a manager did this, and explain how it enabled him or her to be effective.

7. Visit Amazon.com and find the dropdown box allowing you to "Shop by Department", under "Books and Audible" choose the subcategory of "Books". Next select the link for "Bestsellers," and click on "Business & Money" from the categories listed down the left side of the screen. Look at Amazon's list of best-selling business books. What ideas or themes do you see in the list? Which business leaders do you see?

### Questions for Application

8. Go to the library or go online and locate material about Confucius. Outline his major ideas. Which seem to be applicable to management in the United States today?

9. Find a company that has laid off a significant number of workers in the last year. (Hint: Use the word *layoff* as a search term on the Internet.) Investigate that company. Why did the firm make the layoffs? In your opinion, is the company likely to accomplish its intended goal by laying off so many workers? Why or why not?

10. Read about management pioneer Frederick Taylor at **www.cftech.com/BrainBank/TRIVIABITS/FredWTaylor.html** or another source. Describe Taylor's background and experience. How does an understanding of Taylor's early career help you to better understand his ideas about scientific management?

# Building Effective Decision-Making Skills

### Exercise Overview

Decision-making skills include the ability to recognize and define problems or opportunities and then select the appropriate course of action. This exercise will help you develop your own decision-making skills while also underscoring the importance of subsystem interdependencies in organizations.

### Exercise Background

You're the vice president of a large company that makes outdoor furniture for decks, patios, and pools. Each product line and the firm itself have grown substantially in recent years. Unfortunately, your success has attracted the attention of competitors, and several have entered the market in the last two years. Your CEO wants you to determine how to cut costs by 10 percent so that prices can be cut by the same amount. She's convinced that the move is necessary to retain market share in the face of new competition.

You've examined the situation and decided that you have three options for cutting costs:

- Begin buying slightly lower-grade materials, including hardwood, aluminum, vinyl, and nylon.

- Lay off a portion of your workforce and then try to motivate everyone who's left to work harder; this option also means selecting future hires from a lower-skill labor pool and paying lower wages.
- Replace existing equipment with newer, more efficient equipment; although this option entails substantial up-front investment, you're sure that you can more than make up the difference in lower production costs.

### Exercise Task

With this background in mind, respond to the following questions:

1. Carefully examine each of your three options. In what ways might each option affect other parts of the organization?
2. Which is the most costly option *in terms of impact on other parts of the organization, not in terms of absolute dollars?* Which is the least costly?
3. What are the primary obstacles that you might face in trying to implement each of your three options?
4. Are there any other options for accomplishing your goal of reducing costs?

# Building Effective Interpersonal Skills

### Exercise Overview

Interpersonal skills refer to your ability to communicate with, understand, and motivate both individuals and groups. This exercise asks you to examine your attitudes about how people regard work and how they behave in the workplace.

## Exercise Task

Following is a series of paired statements—that is, each of the eight items consists of *two related statements*. Consider and respond to each pair as follows:

- Ask yourself: How does each statement reflect my attitude about how people regard work and behave in the workplace?
- You have 5 points to divide between each pair of statements. If the first statement, for example, totally reflects your attitude and the other does not, give the first statement 5 points and the second 0. If the first statement usually reflects your attitude, give it 4 points and the second statement 1 point. *The combined score for each pair must always equal 5 points.*

Here's how to determine point values:

*0–5 or 5–0:* One of the statements totally reflects your attitude while the other does not.
*1–4 or 4–1:* One of the statements usually reflects your attitude while the other does not.
*2–3 or 3–2:* Both statements reflect your attitude, though one more than the other.

1. _____ People enjoy working.
   _____ People do not like to work.
2. _____ Employees don't have to be closely watched in order to do their jobs well.
   _____ Employees won't do a good job unless they're closely supervised.
3. _____ Employees will do tasks well if you ask them to.
   _____ If you want something done right, do it yourself.
4. _____ Employees want to be involved in decision making.
   _____ Employees want managers to make decisions.
5. _____ Employees will do their best work when you allow them to do their jobs in their own way.
   _____ Employees do their best work when they're taught the one best way of doing a job.

6. _____ Managers should give employees all information that's not confidential.
   _____ Managers should give employees only the information they need to do their jobs.
7. _____ Employees work just as hard when managers aren't around as they do when managers are around.
   _____ Employees will take things easier when managers aren't around than they will when managers are around.
8. _____ Managers should share managerial responsibilities with members of employee groups.
   _____ Managers should perform managerial functions for employee groups.

Now you can determine your attitude about how people regard work and behave in the workplace. Simply do the following:

- Add up the numbers (0–5) for the first statement in each pair (ignore the numbers for the second statements). Your score should fall somewhere between 0 and 40.
- Place your score on the following continuum:

*Theory* X 0_____5_____10_____15_____20_____
25_____30_____35_____40 *Theory Y*

Generally speaking, the higher your score, the greater your leaning toward Theory Y; the lower your score, the greater your leaning toward Theory X.

Adapted from Robert N. Lussier and Christopher F. Achua, *Leadership: Theory, Application, and Skill Development*, 4th ed. (Mason, OH: Cengage Learning, 2010), p. 48.

# Skill-Building Personal Assessment

## Assessing Your Theory X and Theory Y Tendencies

The following questions are intended to provide insights into your tendencies toward Theory X or Theory Y management styles. Answer each of the following questions on the scales by circling the number that best reflects your feelings. For example, mark a 5 for a statement if you strongly agree with it, or a 2 if you disagree with it.

1. Most employees today are lazy and have to be forced to work hard.

| 5 | 4 | 3 | 2 | 1 |
|---|---|---|---|---|
| Strongly Agree | Agree | Neither Agree Nor Disagree | Disagree | Strongly Disagree |

2. People in organizations are only motivated by extrinsic rewards such as pay and bonuses.

| 5 | 4 | 3 | 2 | 1 |
|---|---|---|---|---|
| Strongly Agree | Agree | Neither Agree Nor Disagree | Disagree | Strongly Disagree |

3. Most people do not like to work.

| 5 | 4 | 3 | 2 | 1 |
|---|---|---|---|---|
| Strongly Agree | Agree | Neither Agree Nor Disagree | Disagree | Strongly Disagree |

4. Most people today generally avoid responsibility.

| 5 | 4 | 3 | 2 | 1 |
|---|---|---|---|---|
| Strongly Agree | Agree | Neither Agree Nor Disagree | Disagree | Strongly Disagree |

5. Many employees in big companies today do not accept the company's goals but instead work only for their own welfare.

| 5 | 4 | 3 | 2 | 1 |
|---|---|---|---|---|
| Strongly Agree | Agree | Neither Agree Nor Disagree | Disagree | Strongly Disagree |

6. Most people are not innovative and are not interested in helping their employer solve problems.

| 5 | 4 | 3 | 2 | 1 |
|---|---|---|---|---|
| Strongly Agree | Agree | Neither Agree Nor Disagree | Disagree | Strongly Disagree |

7. Most people need someone else to tell them how to do their jobs.

| 5 | 4 | 3 | 2 | 1 |
|---|---|---|---|---|
| Strongly Agree | Agree | Neither Agree Nor Disagree | Disagree | Strongly Disagree |

8. Many people today have little ambition, preferring to stay where they are and not work hard for advancement.

| 5 | 4 | 3 | 2 | 1 |
|---|---|---|---|---|
| Strongly Agree | Agree | Neither Agree Nor Disagree | Disagree | Strongly Disagree |

9. Work is not a natural activity for most people and instead is something that they have to do.

| 5 | 4 | 3 | 2 | 1 |
|---|---|---|---|---|
| Strongly Agree | Agree | Neither Agree Nor Disagree | Disagree | Strongly Disagree |

10. Most employees today are not interested in using their full potential and capabilities.

| 5 | 4 | 3 | 2 | 1 |
|---|---|---|---|---|
| Strongly Agree | Agree | Neither Agree Nor Disagree | Disagree | Strongly Disagree |

# Management at Work

## Customer Delight

Wells Fargo emerged from the banking crisis of 2006–2009 in better shape than many of its competitors in the U.S. banking industry. Granted, Wells Fargo lost $31.4 billion, but compare the numbers for Bank of America (BoA) and Citigroup (Citi)—$65.8 billion and $87.2 billion, respectively. In addition, over a 10-year period beginning in 2002 (a tough time for banks everywhere), Wells Fargo's *share price* (the price of a share of the company's stock) gained 25 percent—a modest figure but better than even JPMorgan Chase (14 percent) and *much* better than BoA (–78 percent) and Citi (–92 percent).

Now, because a firm's share price reflects the value of its future cash flows, it's important to investors—buyers of a company's stock—and by this measure, Wells Fargo is obviously rated much more highly than its major competitors. Wells Fargo, however, doesn't care all that much about such strictly financial measures of success as share price—or so says CEO John Stumpf: "This may surprise you," says Stumpf, but "we believe shareholders come last" when management makes decisions about what's best for the bank, especially in the long term.

Stumpf's position flies in the face of the conventional wisdom that firms should strive to *maximize shareholder value*—basically, to enrich shareholders. Stumpf's way of thinking, however, makes sense to Steve Denning, who thinks that the "shareholder value model" of management is "the dumbest idea in the world." Denning, a theorist specializing in leadership and innovation, argues that managers should focus on the "real world" in which products are produced and sold, revenues earned, and real profit entered as dollars on the bottom line. Instead, he says, most managers are required to focus on the "expectations market," where investors buy and sell shares in companies and success is measured in percentages of increases and decreases.

According to Denning, this focus needs to shift, but he's well aware that such a change "means rethinking the very basis of a corporation and the way business is conducted." That's why he calls his program for change "Radical Management," which he defines as "a way of managing organizations that generates at the same time high productivity, continuous innovation, deep job satisfaction, and customer delight."

Let's look more closely at this idea of "customer delight," which is the key to the first of Denning's five "interlocking principles" of Radical Management. "The true bottom line of any business," argues Denning, "—and the key to an enduring future—is whether customers are delighted. Delighting customers means continuously providing new value for customers sooner, so that they are willing to buy the firm's goods and services not just today but also tomorrow." One of the things that Denning likes about Wells Fargo is its commitment to *cross-selling*—designing new products that can be offered to buyers of other bank products. A bank, for example, should be able to service a checking-account customer who wants a mortgage or a small business loan. For Stumpf, cross-selling is a logical means of growing the bank's business: "There are only three ways," he contends, "that a company can grow. First, earn more business from your current customers. Second, attract customers from your competitors. Or third, buy another company. If you can't do the first, what makes you think you can earn more business from your competitors' customers or from customers you buy through acquisition?"

Wells Fargo's attitude—not only toward its customers but toward its products—reflects Denning's conviction that delighting buyers entails a "transition in the power balance between seller and buyer." In today's market, says Denning, "the buyer is in the driver's seat. As a result, a firm's goal has to shift … from inside-out ('You take what we make') to outside-in ('We seek to understand your problems and will surprise you by solving them')."

According to Denning, Wells Fargo has taken a few significant steps toward a model of Radical Management. He believes, however, that the bank's emerging model is still a long way from "radical." On the one hand, the commitment to cross-selling means that Wells Fargo has had to break down a bureaucratic structure composed of different areas of expertise and responsibility. On the other hand, however, the resulting model of teamwork still reflects the conventional concept of the *cross-functional team* (see Chapter 18)—in this case, a "team" composed of "experts" from different product areas (checking accounts, mortgages, small business loans, etc.). Members of such teams, says Denning, tend to function more as representatives of their respective areas and expertise than as members of teams. "The idea that other members of the team might contribute to the expert's area of expertise," he maintains, "is often a strange, practically unthinkable thought."

So far, concludes Denning, "Wells Fargo is satisfying their customers without yet delighting them. To make progress toward actual customer delight, Wells may need to give more explicit attention to shifting the role of managers from controllers to enablers of self-organizing teams and co-ordinating work by dynamic linking rather than traditional bureaucracy."

Members of radically "enabled" teams, argues Denning, will work better as team members because they will make all of their own decisions—how the work will be done, how much time will be needed to meet each self-determined goal—and will be responsible for all of the team's outcomes. The team will also be empowered to identify "impediments" to its progress, even when they issue from "management actions or the organization's policies and practices," and it should be able to count on management to "take action to remove" those impediments. "Everybody and everything in the organization," says Denning, must be committed to providing more value to clients sooner. All work teams and units must have a clear line of sight as to what they are accomplishing in terms of delighting clients. All systems and processes in the organization must be focused on enhancing client delight.

## Case Questions

1. In general, what sorts of criticisms would Denning level at the *behavioral management perspective*? At the *quantitative management perspective*?

2. If your school announced that it was thinking about adopting the management goal of delighting customers, what changes in its current management practices would you recommend? What sort of (reasonable) practices would "delight" rather than merely satisfy you?

3. Consider the following perspectives on management practice: the *quantitative perspective*, the *systems perspective*, and the *contingency perspective*. Let's say that you're asked to develop a plan for shifting your company's management model from one of these models to one in which the company's goal is delighting customers. What recommendations for change would you probably make, given the nature of your company's current management practices? Which current practices might be good springboards for making the shift? Which might be probable impediments to making the shift?

4. Denning likens a manager who manages in the interest of shareholder value to a football coach who coaches to beat the point spread instead of winning the game. Explain the analogy in more detail. In particular, Denning claims that "in such a world, it is hardly surprising that the corporate world is plagued by scandals." Why might the management practice of *maximizing shareholder value* lead to questionable ethical (and even illegal) behavior among top managers?

## Case References

Halah Touryalai, "Wells Fargo: The Bank That Works," *Forbes.com*, January 25, 2012, www.forbes.com, on June 10, 2014; Steve Denning, "Does Wells Fargo Practice Radical Management?" *Forbes.com*, January 30, 2014, www.forbes.com, on June 11, 2014; Denning, "What Is Radical Management?" *SteveDenning.com* (2009), www.stevedenning.com, on June 9, 2014; Denning, "The Death—and Reinvention—of Management: Part 1," *The Leader's Guide to Radical Management*, November 17, 2010, http://stevedenning.typepad.com, on June 9, 2014; Denning, "The Dumbest Idea in the World: Maximizing Shareholder Value," *Forbes.com*, November 28, 2011, www.forbes.com, on June 11, 2014; Denning, "When Cross-Functional Teams Aren't: High-End Knowledge Work," *SteveDenning.com* (2009), www.stevedenning.com, on June 12, 2014; Denning, "Reinventing Management: Part 4: Coordination: From Bureaucracy to Dynamic Linking," *The Leader's Guide to Radical Management*, January 23, 2011, http://stevedenning.typepad.com, on June 12, 2014; Denning, "Reinventing Management: Part 2: How Do You Delight the Client?" *The Leader's Guide to Radical Management*, January 18, 2011, http://stevedenning.typepad.com, on June 11, 2014.

**YOU MAKE THE CALL**     **The Lighter Side of Sustainability**

1. How might an *integrating framework* be used to enhance a *sustainability* strategy in a company whose management perspective is primarily *quantitative*? In one that depends primarily on a *contingency perspective*? Conversely, how might a quantitative perspective lend itself to the development and deployment of a sustainability strategy? How about a contingency perspective?

2. Wisconsin-based Gundersen Health System partners with its local solid waste department to pump enough landfill gas to run a 350,000-square-foot facility. It runs a dairy-digester system (including 2,000 cows) at three local farms in order to produce its own electricity, and because it now produces more electricity than it needs, it sells the surplus to local utilities. In 2014, Gundersen became the nation's first energy-independent health system, producing more fossil fuel than it consumes. Gundersen thus depends on a certain systems-based strategy discussed in the text. What is it? Why isn't it the strategy of choice for more healthcare systems? How might your school take advantage of this strategy?

3. According to the Northwest Energy Efficiency Alliance (NEEA) report on "The Business Imperative for Sustainability,"

   *failure to pursue sustainable business practices has moral, ethical, and business consequences in the face of dire and imminent climate change. Ultimately, sustainability means survival for organizations, the human race, and the planet.*

Leaving aside the debate about the reality of climate change (the evidence for human-based climate change is overwhelming), explain some of the "moral, ethical, and business consequences" to which the NEEA report refers. In what ways can *sustainability* help to avert some of these consequences? Is sustainability enough,

or do you think that additional measures should be explored? What measures?

4. What measures does your school take to practice *sustainable resource management*? Where, specifically, is there room for improvement? Are there any specific recommendations that you'd make to the management of the school?

# Endnotes

1  Anjali Joseph, "The Impact of Light on Outcomes in Healthcare Settings," Center for Health Design, Issue Paper Number 2 (August 2006), www.healthdesign. org, on June 8, 2014; Allison Bond Kotru, "Hospital Room Lighting May Worsen Patients' Mood, Pain," Reuters (November 6, 2013), www.reuters.com, on June 8, 2014; "Better Use of Lighting in Hospital Rooms May Improve Patients' Health," *Science Daily* (October 30, 2013), www.sciencedaily.com, on June 8, 2014; "Hospitals Embrace the Intersection of Patient Outcomes, Sustainable Design," *Healthcare Facilities Today* (August 21, 2013), www.healthcarefacilitiestoday. com, on June 8, 2014; Sharon Graugnard-Fall and David Ray, "The Business Imperative for Sustainability: The Seven Critical Success Factors," Northwest Energy Efficiency Alliance (n.d.), www.betterbricks.com, on June 8, 2014; Lola Butcher, "Harnessing the Power of Sustainability," *Trustee* (March 1, 2014), www. trusteemag.com, on June 8, 2014; Jones Lang LaSalle, "New LED Technology Slashes Electricity Use" (2013), www.leepcampaign.org, on June 8, 2014.

2  Terence Mitchell and Lawrence James, "Building Better Theory: Time and the Specification of When Things Happen," *Academy of Management Review*, 2001, Vol. 26, No. 4, pp. 530–547.

3  Peter F. Drucker, "The Theory of the Business," *Harvard Business Review*, September–October 1994, pp. 95–104. See also Sally Maitlis and Marlys Christianson, "Sensemaking in Organizations: Taking Stock and Moving Forward," in Royston Greenwood, ed., *The Academy of Management Annals Volume 8, No. 1* (Philadelphia: Taylor and Francis, 2014), pp. 57–125.

4  "Why Business History?" *Audacity*, Fall 1992, pp. 7–15. See also Alan L. Wilkins and Nigel J. Bristow, "For Successful Organization Culture, Honor Your Past," *Academy of Management Executive*, August 1987, pp. 221–227 and Matthias Kipping and Behlül Üsdiken, "History in Organization and Management Theory: More Than Meets the Eye," in *The Academy of Management Annals Volume 8, No. 1* (Royston Greenwood, Editor) Taylor and Francis, Philadelphia Pennsylvania, 2014, pp. 535–588.

5  Daniel Wren and Arthur Bedeian, *The Evolution of Management Thought*, 6th ed. (New York: Wiley, 2009); Page Smith, *The Rise of Industrial America* (New York: McGraw-Hill, 1984).

6  Martha I. Finney, "Books That Changed Careers," *HR Magazine*, June 1997, pp. 141–145. See also "Leadership in Literature," *Harvard Business Review*, March 2006, pp. 47–55.

7  See Harriet Rubin, *The Princessa: Machiavelli for Women* (New York: Doubleday/Currency, 1997). See also Nanette Fondas, "Feminization Unveiled: Management Qualities in Contemporary Writings," *Academy of Management Review*, January 1997, pp. 257–282. For one recent example see Sheryl Sandberg, *Lean In: Women, Work, and the Will to Lead* (New York: W.H. Allen, 2013).

8  Alan M. Kantrow (ed.), "Why History Matters to Managers," *Harvard Business Review*, January–February 1986, pp. 81–88.

9  *Audacity*, Fall 1992, p. 15.

10  Wren and Bedeian, *The Evolution of Management Theory*.

11  Charles Babbage, *On the Economy of Machinery and Manufactures* (London: Charles Knight, 1832).

12  Wren and Bedeian, *The Evolution of Management Theory*.

13  http://www.brainyquote.com/quotes/authors/f/frederick_w_taylor.html

14  Frederick W. Taylor, *Principles of Scientific Management* (New York: Harper and Brothers, 1911).

15  Charles D. Wrege and Amedeo G. Perroni, "Taylor's Pig-Tale: A Historical Analysis of Frederick W. Taylor's Pig-Iron Experiment," *Academy of Management Journal*, March 1974, pp. 6–27; Charles D. Wrege and Ann Marie Stoka, "Cooke Creates a Classic: The Story Behind Taylor's Principles of Scientific Management," *Academy of Management Review*, October 1978, pp. 736–749.

16  Robert Kanigel, *The One Best Way* (New York: Viking, 1997); Oliver E. Allen, "'This Great Mental Revolution,'" *Audacity*, Summer 1996, pp. 52–61; Jill Hough and Margaret White, "Using Stories to Create Change: The Object Lesson of Frederick Taylor's 'Pig-Tale,'" *Journal of Management*, 2001, Vol. 27, pp. 585–601.

17  Henri Fayol, *General and Industrial Management*, trans. J. A. Coubrough (Geneva: International Management Institute, 1930).

18  Max Weber, *Theory of Social and Economic Organizations*, trans. T. Parsons (New York: Free Press, 1947); Richard M. Weis, "Weber on Bureaucracy: Management Consultant or Political Theorist?" *Academy of Management Review*, April 1983, pp. 242–248.

19  Chester Barnard, *The Functions of the Executive* (Cambridge, MA: Harvard University Press, 1938).

20  "The Line Starts Here," *Wall Street Journal*, January 11, 1999, pp. R1, R25.

21  Hugo Munsterberg, *Psychology and Industrial Efficiency* (Boston: Houghton Mifflin, 1913).

22  Wren and Bedeian, *The Evolution of Management Theory*, pp. 255–264.

23  Elton Mayo, *The Human Problems of an Industrial Civilization* (New York: Macmillan, 1933); Fritz J. Roethlisberger and William J. Dickson, *Management and the Worker* (Cambridge, MA: Harvard University Press, 1939).

24  Abraham Maslow, "A Theory of Human Motivation," *Psychological Review*, July 1943, pp. 370–396.

25  Douglas McGregor, *The Human Side of Enterprise* (New York: McGraw-Hill, 1960).

26  Sara L. Rynes and Christine Quinn Trank, "Behavioral Science in the Business School Curriculum: Teaching in a Changing Institutional Environment," *Academy of Management Review*, 1999, Vol. 24, No. 4, pp. 808–824.

27  See Ricky W. Griffin and Gregory Moorhead, *Organizational Behavior*, 11th ed. (Cincinnati: Cengage, 2014), for a recent review of current developments in the field of organizational behavior.

28  Wren and Bedeian, *The Evolution of Management Thought*, Chapter 21.

29  "Math Will Rock Your World," *BusinessWeek*, January 23, 2006, pp. 54–61.

30  "Quantitative Analysis Offers Tools to Predict Likely Terrorist Moves," *Wall Street Journal*, February 17, 2006, p. B1.

31  *BusinessWeek*, January 23, 2006, p. 57.

32  For more information on systems theory in general, see Ludwig von Bertalanffy, C. G. Hempel, R. E. Bass, and H. Jonas, "General Systems Theory: A New Approach to Unity of Science," *Human Biology*, Vol. 23, 1951, pp. 302–361. For systems theory as applied to organizations, see Fremont E. Kast and James E. Rosenzweig, "General Systems Theory: Applications for Organizations and Management," *Academy of Management Journal*, December 1972, pp. 447–465. For a recent update, see Donde P. Ashmos and George P. Huber, "The Systems Paradigm in Organization Theory: Correcting the Record and Suggesting the Future," *Academy of Management Review*, October 1987, pp. 607–621. See also Andrew H. Van de Ven, Martin Ganco, and C.R. (Bob) Hinings, "Returning to the Frontier of Contingency Theory of Organizational and Institutional Designs," in Royston Greenwood, ed., *The Academy of Management Annals Volume 7, No. 1* (Philadelphia: Taylor and Francis, 2013), pp. 393–440.

33  See Robert S. Kaplan and David P. Norton, "Mastering the Management System," *Harvard Business Review*, January 2008, pp. 63–72.

34  "United, Continental Merger to Create Synergies, Cut Costs," *International Business Times*, May 3, 2010, pp. 17–19.

35  Fremont E. Kast and James E. Rosenzweig, *Contingency Views of Organization and Management* (Chicago: Science Research Associates, 1973).

36  "There Is No More Normal," *BusinessWeek*, March 23, 2009, pp. 30–34.

37  See "Two Days With a Tech Titan," *USA Today*, January 10, 2013, pp. 1B, 2B.

38  http://www.nytimes.com/2009/08/02/business/02corner.html)

39  "Welch Memoirs Fetch $7.1M," *USA Today*, July 14, 2000, p. 1B.

40  *HR Magazine*, June 1997, p. 141.

41  "The BusinessWeek Best-Seller List," *BusinessWeek*, November 4, 2002, p. 26.

42  See Phanish Puranam and Bart S. Vanneste, "Trust and Governance: Untangling a Tangled Web," *Academy of Management Review*, Vol. 34, No. 1, January 2009, pp. 11–31.

43  "Yes, We'll Still Make Stuff," *Time*, May 25, 2009, p. 49.

44  http://www.nam.org/Statistics-And-Data/Facts-About-Manufacturing/Landing.aspx, accessed on January 4, 2015.

45  "Target Replies to Worker's Rant," *USA Today*, May 15, 2015, p. 3B.

©Markus Pfaff/Shutterstock.com

# 3

# UNDERSTANDING THE ORGANIZATION'S ENVIRONMENT

**After studying this chapter, you should be able to:**

1. Discuss the nature of the organizational environment and identify the environments of interest to most organizations.

2. Describe the components of the general and task environments and discuss their impact on organizations.

3. Identify the components of the internal environment and discuss their impact on organizations.

4. Discuss the importance and determinants of an organization's culture and how the culture can be managed.

5. Describe the multicultural environment of business, and identify major trends and dimensions of diversity and multiculturalism.

6. Identify and describe how the environment affects organizations and how organizations adapt to their environment.

# MANAGEMENT IN ACTION    Putting Miscommunication in Context

"In an age of diversity, cultural differences are just as likely to appear across desks as they are across borders."

—COMMUNICATIONS SPECIALIST BRETT RUTLEDGE

Taking a trip into the international dimension of your business environment doesn't have to make you feel as if you're in the Twilight Zone, but you'll probably want to do a little preparation before you reach for your passport. Even then, however, things can be touch and go. Dana Marlowe, the principal partner in a U.S. IT consulting firm, thought that she'd done her homework before heading to Tunisia to deliver the keynote address at an international conference; after all, she'd read up on cultural differences and even memorized a few well-chosen Arabic phrases. When she got to Tunisia, she was given a reception by a group of local businessmen. Coffee was served all around, but the weather was extremely hot and Marlowe wasn't much of a coffee drinker to start with. The practical and courteous thing to do, she decided, was to accept the cup

of coffee but not to drink it. Fifteen minutes later, she looked up to see that none of her Tunisian hosts had taken sips from their own cups. "I didn't realize," she later admitted, "that they were all waiting for me to take a sip of my coffee first."[1]

Without stumbling over a single word, Marlowe had nevertheless managed to commit a communications faux pas. Fortunately, she didn't cause an international incident, but it wouldn't have been the first time that failure to appreciate differences in cultural norms had led to miscommunication and strained relations between two countries. In 2001, a U.S. Navy submarine struck a Japanese training ship for high school students while surfacing near Hawaii, killing nine people aboard the Japanese vessel. Tension between the two countries arose not simply from the accident itself, but also from differences in cultural norms regarding apologies.

First, the U.S. Navy was slow to make an official apology, issuing only public statements of "sincere regret" while delaying any admission of responsibility. American cultural norms dictated that legal considerations be primary—an investigation had to be

Communicating with people from different cultures can result in unexpected mistakes and create unanticipated problems. When this U.S. Naval submarine struck a Japanese training ship for high school students and killed nine people conflict arose between the two countries because of cultural norms related to apologies.

GEORGE F. LEE/AFP/Getty Images

conducted, and the issues of liability and compensation had to be studied. Eventually, President George W. Bush, Secretary of State Colin Powell, Secretary of Defense Donald Rumsfeld, and U.S. Ambassador to Japan Thomas Foley formally apologized to the Japanese prime minister and the Emperor of Japan. The commander of the Pacific Fleet, Adm. Thomas B. Fargo, personally apologized to the victims' families.

The families, however, rejected all of these apologies out of hand. Why? Japanese cultural norms required a personal apology from the submarine commander, Cmdr. Scott Waddell. Waddell, however, was legally constrained from speaking about the case and prevented by Naval public relations officials from joining Adm. Fargo in his apology to the families, who demanded from Waddell a personal admission of responsibility for his "crime." Some even felt that he should, in keeping with Japanese tradition, kneel before them in order to make it. At that point, they would decide whether or not to accept his apology.*

According to many experts in cross-cultural communications, the problem in such cases results from differences in *cultural context*. In Japan, for example, communication takes place in a *high-context culture*. People in high-context cultures focus their communication efforts on exchanges with members of *in-groups*—longtime friends, family members, and work colleagues. In-group communication tends to be frequent and highly detailed, and members are always kept up-to-date on information that's important to the group. Members of in-groups also depend on certain traditions and ceremonies to define the roles played by individual members.

By contrast, people in *low-context cultures* (such as the United States) are used to directing communications to a variety of groups. They engage in much more *out-group* communication and allow the specific informational requirements of each situation to determine the nature and scope of exchanges. They expect individuals to keep themselves up-to-date and see no reason for discussing absolutely every little thing that's pertinent to a situation.

Not surprisingly, when the two types of cultures come into conflict—as in the episode of the U.S. submarine and the Japanese training vessel—miscommunication is likely to result. The Japanese families, for example, assumed a higher level of mutual understanding than U.S. officials, who assumed that necessary communications could be limited to specific issues, mainly legal.

"In an age of diversity," observes one communications specialist, "cultural differences are just as likely to appear across desks as they are across borders." Or across both at the same time: More and more U.S. businesses have come to realize that the effort to take customers away from competitors in a limited domestic market is less promising than the strategy of seeking new customers in expansive global markets. As companies thus explore opportunities in the global business environment, managers are likely to run into situations like the one encountered by the customer-service manager of a U.S. subsidiary of a Japanese company. He faxed a brief request to the home office in Tokyo for some information needed by a potential customer. When he received no answer, he faxed the request again, this time marking it *urgent*. Again, he received no response. Why? It seems that his request—"Please send this information at once"—was *too* brief: It left out information which, from his low-context perspective, was unnecessary but which, for his Japanese counterparts, was required in order to furnish sufficient context. They wanted to know such basics as who needed the information, why it was so important, and what would happen if it weren't sent at once. Were such details really critical to the exchange of information? Perhaps not, but the communication between the two parties failed and the relationship with a potential customer was jeopardized.

American businesspeople typically don't concern themselves with the dissemination of such detailed information, but Japanese businesspeople consider it important that everyone in the relevant in-group share as much information as possible. So how does such information get disseminated in the high-context culture of a Japanese workplace? A top manager at a U.S. global consulting firm learned about one way from a recently relocated Japanese employee. When the employee complained that he simply could not figure out what was going on in the office, the manager found out that he expected office information to be shared in the same way that it would be in a Japanese workplace. In particular, he missed the Japanese practice of going out with in-group colleagues four or five times a week to drink and chat until the wee hours.

---

*Cmdr. Waddell was reprimanded and allowed to retire with his pension intact. He is now an inspirational speaker who, for $10,000 to $15,000, will speak on such topics as "Failure Is Not Final," "Saying 'I'm Sorry' Works," and "Communicate Effectively! It Doesn't Have to Be Lonely at the Top."

"The fundamental problem," concluded Cornelius Grove,

> is that high-context people are seriously informa-tion deprived in a low-context system. ... Pretty soon, they start to realize that they are not going to be absorbed into a warmly supportive working group. Instead, they have to become self-reliant. That sounds fine to Americans, but to high-context newcomers, it sounds a lot like being isolated.

Employees from high-context cultures, says Grove, need to adapt to the American habit of establishing competitive work relationships and mea-suring achievement according to individual accomplishment.

Grove and business partner Willa Hallowell also recom-mend that employees from low-context cultures adapt cer-tain behaviors of group-oriented coworkers from high-context cultures and learn to present information to them differently, mainly by providing more background about projects as well as more details about workplace processes—that is, about *how* things are done in a specific workplace.

---

Miscommunication can occur in any setting, but it seems to be especially common when managers and decision makers are dealing with people who are different from themselves in one or more important ways. As we noted in Chapter 1, managers must have a deep under-standing and appreciation of the environments in which they and their organizations func-tion. Without this understanding, they are like rudderless ships—moving along, but with no way of maneuvering or changing direction.

This chapter is the first of three devoted to the environmental context of management. After introducing the nature of the organization's environment, we describe first the general and then the task environment in detail. We next discuss key parts of the internal environ-ment of an organization. We then focus on the multicultural environment and then exam-ine organization–environment relationships.

## The Organization's Environments

To illustrate the importance of the environment to an organization, consider the analogy of a swimmer crossing a wide stream. The swimmer must assess the current, obstacles, and distance before setting out. If these elements are properly evaluated, the swimmer will arrive at the ex-pected point on the far bank of the stream. But if these elements are not properly understood, the swimmer might end up too far upstream or downstream. The organization is like the swimmer, and the environment is like the stream. Thus, just as the swimmer needs to understand condi-tions in the water, the organization must understand the basic elements of its environment to properly maneuver among them.[2] More specifically, a key element in the effective management of an organization is determining the ideal alignment between the environment and the organi-zation and then working to achieve and maintain that alignment. To do so, therefore, the man-ager must first thoroughly understand the nature of the organization's environments.[3]

The external environment is everything outside an organization's boundaries that might affect it. As shown in Figure 3.1, there are actually two separate external environments: the general environment and the task environment. An organization's internal environment consists of conditions and forces within the organization. Of course, not all parts of these environments are equally important for all organizations.

A small two-person partnership does not have a board of directors, for example, whereas a large public corporation is required by law to have one. A private university with a large endowment (like Harvard) may be less concerned about general economic conditions than might a state university (like the University of Alabama), which relies on state funding from tax revenues. Still, organizations need to fully understand which environmental forces are important and how the importance of others might increase.

**external environment**
Everything outside an organization's boundaries that might affect it

**internal environment**
The conditions and forces within an organization

## FIGURE 3.1  THE ORGANIZATION AND ITS ENVIRONMENTS

Organizations have both an external and an internal environment. The external environment consists of two layers: the general environment and the task environment.

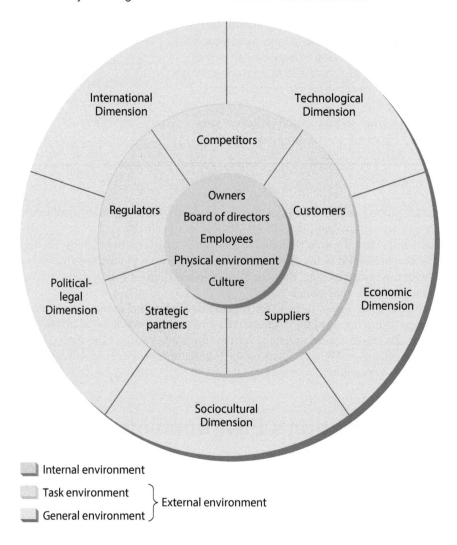

**Manager's Checklist**

☐  Managers need to remember that organizations have multiple environments.

☐  While managers tend to think of the environment as being "outside," their organizations also have internal environments.

# The External Environment

As just noted, an organization's external environment consists of two parts. The general environment of an organization is the set of broad dimensions and forces in its surroundings that create its overall context. These dimensions and forces are not necessarily associated with other specific organizations. The general environment of most organizations has economic, technological, sociocultural, political-legal, and international dimensions. The other significant external environment for an organization is its task environment.

**general environment**
The set of broad dimensions and forces in an organization's surroundings that create its overall context

The task environment consists of specific external organizations or groups that influence an organization.

## The General Environment

Each of these dimensions embodies conditions and events that have the potential to influence the organization in important ways. Some examples to illustrate these dimensions as they relate to McDonald's Corporation are shown in Figure 3.2.

**The Economic Dimension**  The economic dimension of an organization's general environment is the overall health and vitality of the economic system in which the organization operates.[5] Particularly important economic factors for business are general economic growth, inflation, interest rates, and unemployment. After several strong years of growth, the U.S. economy fell into recession during 2008–2010.

> "If you manage the business well throughout the good times, then the bad times are not quite as pronounced or profound. But it's actually more difficult to manage during the good times."
>
> —WILLIAM WELDON,
> FORMER CEO OF JOHNSON & JOHNSON[4]

---

## FIGURE 3.2  MCDONALD'S GENERAL ENVIRONMENT

The general environment of an organization consists of economic, technological, sociocultural, political-legal, and international dimensions. This figure clearly illustrates how these dimensions are relevant to managers at McDonald's.

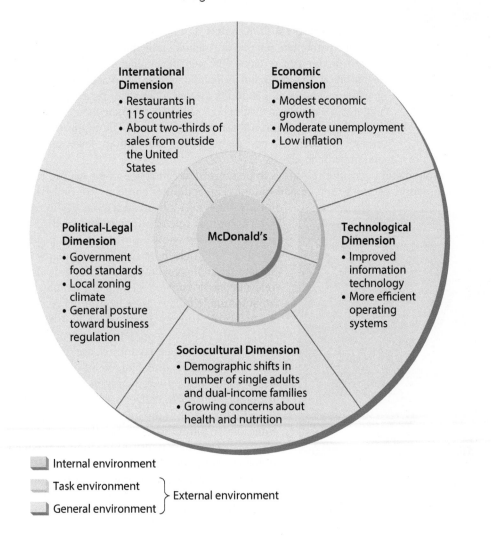

**International Dimension**
- Restaurants in 115 countries
- About two-thirds of sales from outside the United States

**Economic Dimension**
- Modest economic growth
- Moderate unemployment
- Low inflation

**Political-Legal Dimension**
- Government food standards
- Local zoning climate
- General posture toward business regulation

McDonald's

**Technological Dimension**
- Improved information technology
- More efficient operating systems

**Sociocultural Dimension**
- Demographic shifts in number of single adults and dual-income families
- Growing concerns about health and nutrition

Internal environment
Task environment } External environment
General environment

**task environment**
Specific organizations or groups that influence an organization

**economic dimension**
The overall health and vitality of the economic system in which the organization operates

YinYang/Getty Images

Economic growth and prosperity can be a doubled-edged sword for businesses. On the one hand, revenues and profits may grow due to increased consumer demand. On the other hand, though, employees also have more job options and can command higher wages.

**technological dimension**
The methods available for converting resources into products or services

Most people associate the word "technology" with "tangible" products such as airplanes, smartphones, and so forth. But technology also applies to service organizations as well. Take this food service operations, for instance. Workers are preparing and serving food using assembly-line technology pioneered in the manufacturing sector.

Richard Levine / Alamy

During this period, energy and related prices jumped, growth slowed dramatically, and unemployment mushroomed as one struggling business after another made workforce cuts. Since 2011, though, the economy has been slowly improving, with new jobs being created and business profits rebounding.

As noted in Figure 3.2, McDonald's U.S. operation is functioning in an economy characterized by modest growth and unemployment and low inflation. These conditions result in a variety of opportunities and constraints on McDonald's. Economic and job growth suggest that more people are eating out than was the case a few years ago. At the same time, though, fast-food workers who might have had few employment alternatives now have other options, and so McDonald's may have to pay higher wages to retain them. Similarly, low inflation means that the prices McDonald's must pay for its supplies remain relatively constant, but it also is somewhat constrained from increasing the prices it charges consumers for a hamburger or milkshake. The economic dimension is also important to nonbusiness organizations. For example, during weak economic conditions, funding for state universities may drop, and charitable organizations like the Salvation Army are asked to provide greater assistance at the same time that their incoming contributions dwindle. Similarly, hospitals are affected by the availability of government grants and the number of low-income patients they must treat free of charge.

**The Technological Dimension** The technological dimension of the general environment refers to the methods available for converting resources into products or services. Although technology is applied within the organization, the forms and availability of that technology come from the general environment. Computer-assisted manufacturing and design techniques, for example, allow Boeing to simulate the more than three miles of hydraulic tubing that run through a 787 aircraft. The results include decreased warehouse needs, higher-quality tube fittings, fewer employees, and major time savings.

In a roundabout way, the resources to be converted can also come from the technological dimension of the general environment. The computer company Hewlett-Packard, for instance, uses advanced technology to recycle technological refuse—in particular, discarded printer cartridges—into profitable new products. Further, although there may be a tendency to associate technology with manufacturing, it also has relevance to the service sector. For example, just as an automobile follows a predetermined path along an assembly line as it is built, a hamburger at McDonald's follows a predefined path as the meat is cooked, the burger assembled, and the finished product wrapped and bagged for a customer. McDonald's has achieved additional efficiency by using one window to collect payments and another to deliver food at many of its drive-through locations. The rapid infusion of digital technology into all areas of business is also a reflection of the technological dimension. Another recent advancement is the rapid growth of integrated business software systems. The *Doing Business on Planet Earth* illustrates another connection between technology and business.

**DOING BUSINESS ON PLANET EARTH**

# Packaging Sustainability

"The simple truth," says Greg Kishbaugh, an environmentally conscious writer and publisher, "is that *every* company in the packaging market should have begun researching and initiating a sustainability program years ago." Too few of them did, but Kishbaugh, whose main area of interest is the packaging industry, is willing to congratulate Nestlé SA, the Swiss-based global food company, for having "put its sustainability goals into place way back in 1991." In the 20-plus years since, Nestlé has saved as much as 150 million pounds of packaging materials.

"There's no good or bad packaging," says Anne Roulin, global head of packaging and design at Nestlé. The trick is finding "the right packaging material for the specific application." But when you have more than 8,000 brands to package, finding the right material calls for a lot of experimentation. In particular, explains Roulin, "you have to look at it in the broader context of the product life cycle": In other words, designers must assess the impact of packaging from extraction of the raw materials, through manufacture, distribution, and maintenance, to disposal or recycling.

In 2004, Nestlé helped to fund a project undertaken two years earlier by the Sustainable Packaging Alliance (SPA), an Australian organization dedicated to the promotion of sustainable packaging practices. SPA was developing a *life cycle analysis (LCA) tool* called PIQET (*Packaging Impact Quick Evaluation Tool*)—web-based software that would allow food and beverage companies to run scenarios, or models, to evaluate the life-cycle performance of various packaging materials and designs. The prototype was finished in 2006, and Nestlé adopted the web-based version in 2007. "The introduction of the PIQET tool," reports Roulin, "has made a huge difference. We can calculate the impact of different packaging choices at the start of the development cycle, and it also means that we're not focused on just one factor."

In 1991, for example, carbon embedded in the material used for making plastic bottles accounted for 55 percent of the greenhouse gases emitted by Nestlé Waters North America. Over the next 15 years, the company managed to reduce the amount by 40 percent. In 2007, PIQET helped Nestlé to introduce its new EcoShape bottle, which cut the total by another 14 percent while reducing bottle weight from 24 to 9.2 grams.

The process—called *lightweighting*—is a key sustainability strategy in packaging, but as Roulin points out, "lightweighting can go only so far. If you remove so much packaging that damage to the product increases, then the process becomes counterproductive." That's why Nestlé combines its strategy of weight and volume reduction with other strategies that can be modeled with PIQET. "We are also working to increase recycling and recovery rates," says Roulin, "We use recycling materials where appropriate, and we use materials from renewable resources wherever possible." Because PIQET is flexible, Nestlé has been able to align life-cycle goals with compatible corporate sustainability goals, including a three-stage process for managing packaging source materials: from (1) materials derived from food crops (e.g., corn), to (2) materials derived from renewable sources (e.g., sugarcane), to (3) materials derived from nonfood sources (e.g., waste agricultural products).

Naturally, all of these initiatives must be consistent with the company's business objectives. "Our main goal," says Roulin, "is to reinforce our brand identity, but alongside that, we continually reduce the environmental impact of our packaging and our products." She observes that Nestlé can treat both goals "as a whole" because its overall strategy is "about creating shared value. … For some consumers, sustainability is very important." She hastens to add, however, that Nestlé is committed to sustainability "not just because customers want it, but because it's right. … We aren't claiming to save the planet, but we are taking small steps in the right direction."

*References:* Greg Kishbaugh, "Following in the Path of Sustainable Leaders," *Flexo Market News* (February 11, 2013), www.nvpublications.com, on June 8, 2014; Kishbaugh, "A Sustainable Tool," *Flexo Market News* (February 28, 2013), www.flexomarketnews.com, on June 8, 2014; "PIQET. Global Food and Beverage Sustainable Packaging," WSP Digital (2012), www.wspdigital, on June 8, 2014; Bob Sperber, "Nestlé Reveals the Math and Science of Sustainability," *Packaging World* (November 19, 2012), www.packworld.com, on June 8, 2014; "Fresh Thinking," *Packaging-Gateway.com* (April 8, 2010), www.packaging-gateway.com, on June 8, 2014; Nestlé, "Lowering the Impact of Our Packaging with PIQET" (2014), www.nestle.com, on June 8, 2014.

**The Sociocultural Dimension** The sociocultural dimension of the general environment includes the customs, mores, values, and demographic characteristics of the society in which the organization functions. Sociocultural processes are important because they determine the products, services, and standards of conduct that the society is likely to value. In some countries, for example, consumers are willing to pay premium prices for designer clothes, whereas the same clothes have virtually no market in other countries. Consumer tastes also change over time. Preferences for color, style, taste, and so forth change from season to season, for example. Drinking hard liquor and smoking cigarettes are less common in the United States today than they were just a few years ago. And sociocultural factors influence how workers in a society feel about their jobs and organizations.

Appropriate standards of business conduct also vary across cultures. In the United States, accepting bribes and bestowing political favors in return are considered unethical (as well as illegal). In other countries, however, payments to local politicians may be expected in return for a favorable response to such common business transactions as applications for zoning and operating permits. The shape of the market, the ethics of political influence, and attitudes in the workforce are only a few of the many ways in which culture can affect an organization. Figure 3.2 shows that McDonald's is clearly affected by sociocultural factors. For example, in response to concerns about nutrition and health, McDonald's has added salads to its menus and experimented with other low-fat foods. And the firm was among the first fast-food chains to provide customers with information about the ingredients used in its products.

The political-legal dimension of the external environment serves to regulate business activities and the relationship between business and the government. Food nutrition has been a focus of political-legal forces in recent years, resulting in more public information about nutritional content such as this posting in a restaurant.

**sociocultural dimension**
The customs, mores, values, and demographic characteristics of the society in which the organization functions

**political-legal dimension**
The government regulation of business and the relationship between business and government

**The Political-Legal Dimension** The political-legal dimension of the general environment refers to government regulation of business and the relationship between business and government. This dimension is important for three basic reasons. First, the legal system partially defines what an organization can and cannot do. Although the United States is basically a free market economy, there is still major regulation of business activity. McDonald's, for example, is subject to a variety of political and legal forces, including food preparation standards and local zoning requirements.

Second, pro- or antibusiness sentiment in government influences business activity. For example, during periods of pro-business sentiment, firms find it easier to compete and have fewer concerns about antitrust issues. On the other hand, during a period of antibusiness sentiment, firms may find their competitive strategies more restricted and have fewer opportunities for mergers and acquisitions because of antitrust concerns. During the prolonged period of economic growth that ended in 2008, the U.S. government had adopted a very hands-off approach to business, letting market forces determine business successes and failures. However, as the economy ground to a halt in 2008 and first one and then another industry began to stumble, critics began to point to lack of regulation and oversight as contributing factors. As a result, lawmakers began to take a much more pronounced interest in adopting new and stricter regulations for business.[6]

Finally, political stability has ramifications for planning. No business wants to set up shop in another country unless trade relationships with that country are relatively well defined and stable. Hence, U.S. firms are more likely to do business with England, Mexico, and Canada than with Haiti and Afghanistan. The political upheavals in the Middle East that began in 2011 and continue today create complications for many businesses with operations in the region. Similar issues are relevant to assessments of local and state governments.

A new mayor or governor can affect many organizations, especially small firms that do business in only one location and are susceptible to deed and zoning restrictions, property and school taxes, and the like.

**The International Dimension** Yet another component of the general environment for many organizations is the international dimension, or the extent to which an organization is involved in or affected by businesses in other countries.[7] As we discuss more fully in Chapter 5, multinational firms such as General Electric, Boeing, Nestlé, Sony, Siemens, and Hyundai clearly affect and are affected by international conditions and markets. For example, as noted in Figure 3.2, McDonald's operates restaurants in 118 countries and derives about two-thirds of its total sales from outside the United States. When the United States and Cuba began to re-establish relations in 2015, many businesses expressed interest in potential trade opportunities.[8]

Even firms that do business in only one country may face foreign competition at home, and they may use materials or production equipment imported from abroad. The international dimension also has implications for not-for-profit organizations. For example, the Peace Corps sends representatives to underdeveloped countries. As a result of advances in transportation and information technology in the past century, almost no part of the world is cut off from the rest. As a result, virtually every organization is affected by the international dimension of its general environment.

## The Task Environment

Because the impact of the general environment is often vague, imprecise, and long term, most organizations tend to focus their attention on their task environments. These environments include competitors, customers, suppliers, strategic partners, and regulators. Although the task environment is also quite complex, it provides useful information more readily than does the general environment because the manager can identify environmental factors of specific interest to the organization, rather than having to deal with the more abstract dimensions of the general environment.[9] Figure 3.3 depicts the task environment of McDonald's.

**Competitors** An organization's competitors are other organizations that compete with it for resources. The most obvious resources that competitors vie for are customer dollars. Adidas, Under Armour, and Nike are competitors, as are Albertson's, Safeway, and Kroger. McDonald's competes with other fast-food operations, such as Burger King, Starbucks, Subway, and Dairy Queen. But competition also occurs between substitute products. Thus Ford competes with Yamaha (motorcycles) and Schwinn (bicycles) for your transportation dollars; and Walt Disney World, Marriott Resorts, and Carnival Cruise Lines compete for your vacation dollars. And ironically, sometimes a business suffers because of problems that beset its competition. The economic recession of 2008–2010 hit many retailers just as the holiday season was gearing up. As some retailers such as KB Toys, Circuit City, and Linens 'n Things were closing their doors for good, they launched major "going out of business" or "inventory reduction" sales to generate cash. But these same sales hurt other retailers, such as Toys 'R' Us, Best Buy, and Bed, Bath, and Beyond, who were otherwise in a good position to weather the economic storm.[10]

Nor is competition limited to business firms. Universities compete with trade schools, the military, other universities, and the external labor market to attract good students; art galleries and museums compete with each other to attract the best exhibits; and state governments compete for federal grants and tax dollars. Our *Beyond Traditional Business* feature explores this perspective. Organizations may also compete for different kinds of resources besides consumer dollars. For example, two totally unrelated organizations might compete to acquire a loan from a bank that has only limited funds to lend. Two retailers might compete for the right to purchase a prime piece of real estate in a

**international dimension**
The extent to which an organization is involved in or affected by business in other countries

**competitor**
An organization that competes with other organizations for resources

## FIGURE 3.3  MCDONALD'S TASK ENVIRONMENT

An organization's task environment includes its competitors, customers, suppliers, strategic partners, and regulators. This figure clearly highlights how managers at McDonald's can use this framework to identify and understand their key constituents.

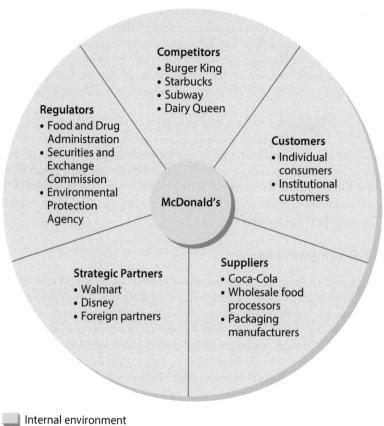

**Competitors**
- Burger King
- Starbucks
- Subway
- Dairy Queen

**Regulators**
- Food and Drug Administration
- Securities and Exchange Commission
- Environmental Protection Agency

**Customers**
- Individual consumers
- Institutional customers

McDonald's

**Strategic Partners**
- Walmart
- Disney
- Foreign partners

**Suppliers**
- Coca-Cola
- Wholesale food processors
- Packaging manufacturers

☐ Internal environment

☐ Task environment

**customer**
Whoever pays money to acquire an organization's products or services

Competitors include businesses that compete for consumer dollars. Burger King, McDonald's Taco Bell, and Arby's each try to attract people in search of fast-food.

growing community. In a large city, the police and fire departments might compete for the same tax dollars. And businesses also compete for quality labor, technological breakthroughs and patents, and scarce raw materials.

**Customers**  A second dimension of the task environment is customers, or whoever pays money to acquire an organization's products or services. Most of McDonald's customers are people who walk into a restaurant to buy food. But customers need not be individuals. Schools, hospitals, government agencies, wholesalers, retailers, and manufacturers are just a few of the many kinds of organizations that may be major customers of other organizations. Some institutional customers, such as schools, prisons, and hospitals, also buy food in bulk from restaurants like McDonald's.

Dealing with customers has become increasingly complex in recent years. New products and services, new methods of marketing, and more discriminating customers have all added uncertainty to how businesses relate to their customers, as has lower brand loyalty. McDonald's has announced plans to allow customers to skip the traditional queue and instead use kiosks where customers can customize everything about their order. The company believes that

# How to Make a Cause Effective

Two days before her first birthday, Alexandra Scott was diagnosed with pediatric cancer. In July 2000, when "Alex" was four and a half, she and her brother set up "Alex's Lemonade Stand for Cancer" on the front lawn of their West Hartford, CT, home. They made $2,000 and decided to make the event an annual tradition. When Alex died at the age of eight, her parents founded Alex's Lemonade Stand Foundation (ALSF) to promote fund-raising, education, and research in the area of pediatric cancer. Now a registered 501(c)3 charity, ALSF has raised $100 million and funded 475 research projects.

The foundation's cause is obviously a worthy one, but so are those of, say, Save the Children, St. Jude's Children's Research Hospital, and hundreds of other charities, and like most not-for-profit organizations, ALSF has to compete for every dollar that it raises. Naturally, the organization takes advantage of as many fundraising sources as it can, including contributions, membership dues, special events, and private and government grants. Like many organizations for whom communications with a community of individuals, groups, and other organizations are essential, ALSF maintains a strong online presence. The foundation has had particular success in using social media—websites which, like Facebook, Twitter, and YouTube, allow users to create and share content—to broaden and strengthen its connections with supporters. Public-service announcements, for example, go out over YouTube, while regular postings on Facebook and Twitter keep potential supporters supplied with information about ongoing events and initiatives.

This is where Melissa Jones comes in. Jones joined ALSF as a volunteer while still in college, served a summer internship, and because of her success in expanding the foundation's social media network, was soon a full-time employee. As a social media specialist, Jones (who has since left ALSF to pursue her education) communicated the organization's message and generated donations through online channels and helped supporters use social media to promote fundraising events. Her watchword was *simplicity*: "In social media," she says, "distractions fly a mile a minute, so you want to make it as easy as possible for people to participate." Her "Connect with Us Today" webpage, for example, is not a control panel with a bewildering array of buttons, but rather a billboard featuring reader-friendly introductions to ALSF's programs and opportunities that are accessible to younger as well as adult users.

Perhaps most importantly, Jones saw the organization's website not simply as a forum for sending out messages, but also as a convenient tool for helping supporters get involved. "Most nonprofits," she explains, "are now focusing their efforts on ways not only to engage their online supporters, but also to offer them the resources they need to be online advocates and/or fundraisers." The ALSF site, for instance, provides easy-to-use guides for setting up lemonade stands (which still account for more than a third of the foundation's revenues) as well as templates for fundraising and media communications.

Don Martelli, VP and director of digital integration at the marketing firm Schneider Associates, helped his own children organize Alex's Lemonade Stands in 2012 and 2013. In the first year, he reports, they raised $1,001, and the following year, they topped that figure with $1,500. A lot of lemonade, you say. Not exactly. In each year, the sale of lemonade accounted for only about $300 of the total. The rest, says Martelli, came through "social media and online community building": Following ALSF guidelines, the Martellis coordinated a variety of postings on Facebook and Twitter, telling Alex's story, talking about the children's efforts to raise money for her cause, and engaging the attention of potential supporters not only in their own city but across the country. Of the $2,600 that they raised, $2,000 came in as a result of these additional social media activities.

*References:* Stanford Graduate School of Business, "Alex's Lemonade Stand Foundation: Eradicating Cancer, One Cup at a Time," Case: M-331 (August 25, 2010), http://faculty-gsb.stanford.edu, on June 30, 2014; Charity Navigator, "Alex's Lemonade Stand Foundation," Non-Profit Startup Center (2014), www.charitynavigator.com, on June 30, 2014; "Melissa Jones: From Volunteer to Social Media Manager for Alex's Lemonade Stand Foundation," *Pay It Forward, Philly!* (November 29, 2011), http://payitforwardphilly.wordpress.com, on June 30, 2014; Bernard Shimkus, "Outlook 2012: Young Professionals' Perspectives," *Philly Ad News Digital Edition* (January-February 2012), http://mobile.phillyadnews.com, on June 30, 2014; Joanne Fritz, "How Alex's Lemonade Stand Invites Supporters to Engage through Social Media," *About.com* (2014), http://nonprofit.about.com, on June 30, 2014; Meaghan Edelstein, "Eight Tips for a Successful Social Media Cause Campaign," *Mashable* (May 10, 2010), http://mashable.com, on June 30, 2014; Don Martelli, "Building Online Communities and Selling Lemonade," *Schneider Associates Blog* (August 1, 2013), www.schneiderpr.com, on June 30, 2014.

today's younger customers are willing to trade quick service for more variety and will be comfortable in using digital ordering stations.[11]

Companies face especially critical differences among customers as they expand internationally. McDonald's sells beer in its German restaurants, for example, and wine in its French restaurants. Customers in those countries see those particular beverages as normal parts of a meal, much as customers in the United States routinely drink water, tea, or soft drinks with their meals. The firm has even opened restaurants with no beef on the menu! Those restaurants are in India, where beef is not a popular menu option. Instead, the local McDonald's restaurants in that country use lamb in their sandwiches.

**Suppliers** Suppliers are organizations that provide resources for other organizations. McDonald's buys soft-drink products from Coca-Cola; individually packaged servings of ketchup from various suppliers; ingredients from wholesale food processors; and napkins, sacks, and wrappers from packaging manufacturers. Common wisdom in the United States used to be that a business should try to avoid depending exclusively on particular suppliers because a firm that buys all of a certain resource from one supplier may be vulnerable if that supplier raises its prices, goes out of business, or is shut down by a labor strike. This practice can also help maintain a competitive relationship among suppliers, keeping costs down. But firms eager to emulate successful Japanese firms have started changing their approach. Japanese firms have a history of building major ties with only one or two major suppliers. This enables them to work together better for their mutual benefit and makes the supplier more responsive to the customer's needs.

Honda picked Donnelly Corporation to make all the mirrors for its U.S.-manufactured cars. Honda chose Donnelly because it learned enough about the firm to know that it did high-quality work and that its corporate culture and values were consistent with those endorsed by Honda. Recognizing the value of Honda as a customer, Donnelly built an entirely new plant to make the mirrors. And all this was accomplished with only a handshake. Motorola goes even further, providing its principal suppliers with access to its own renowned quality training program and evaluating the performance of each supplier as a way of helping that firm boost its own quality. On the other hand, auto manufacturers around the world experienced production interruptions following the earthquake and tsunami that struck Japan in 2011 as parts suppliers in that country were forced to suspend production and shipping for weeks.

**Strategic Partners** Another dimension of the task environment is strategic partners (also called *strategic allies*)—two or more companies that work together in joint ventures or other partnerships.[12] For instance, Disney and Steven Spielberg's Dreamworks film studio formed a partnership that calls for Disney to provide investment capital to Dreamworks and to distribute four to six Dreamworks films each year. In return, Disney gets 10 percent of the box office revenue from each film, as well as additional revenue from the distribution of DVDs.[13] As shown in Figure 3.3, McDonald's has several strategic partners. For example, it has one arrangement with Walmart whereby small McDonald's restaurants are built into some Walmart stores. The firm also has a long-term deal with Disney: McDonald's promotes Disney movies in its stores, and Disney has built McDonald's restaurants and kiosks at some of its resorts. And many of the firm's foreign stores are built in collaboration with local investors. Strategic partnerships help companies get from other companies the expertise they lack. They also help spread risk and open new market opportunities. Indeed, most strategic partnerships are actually among international firms. For example, Sony (a Japanese firm) and Samsung (a South Korean company) are fierce competitors in many sectors of the electronics industry, but they partnered to open a $2 billion factory that makes flat panel televisions and computer monitors.[14]

**supplier**
An organization that provides resources for other organizations

**strategic partners (strategic allies)**
Organizations that work together with one or more other organizations in a joint venture or similar arrangement

**Regulators** Regulators are elements of the task environment that have the potential to control, legislate, or otherwise influence an organization's policies and practices. There are two important kinds of regulators. The first, regulatory agencies, are created by the government to protect the public from certain business practices or to protect organizations from one another. The second, interest groups, are organized by their members to try to influence organizations.

Powerful federal regulatory agencies include the Environmental Protection Agency (EPA), the Securities and Exchange Commission (SEC), the Food and Drug Administration (FDA), and the Equal Employment Opportunity Commission (EEOC). Many of these agencies play important roles in protecting the rights of individuals. The FDA, for example, helps ensure that the food we eat is free from contaminants and thus is an important regulator for McDonald's. At the same time, many managers complain that there is too much government regulation. Most large companies must dedicate thousands of

McDonald's has relationships with a number of strategic partners. For instance, this Happy Meal was used to promote Disney's *Finding Nemo* animated movie.

labor hours and hundreds of thousands of dollars a year to complying with government regulations. An interesting example of emerging regulations involves the drone industry. The Federal Aviation Administration is taking an active role in developing rules and regulations governing how commercial drones can be used.[15]

To complicate the lives of managers even more, unfortunately, different regulatory agencies sometimes provide inconsistent—even contradictory—mandates. For example, in one of the worst environmental disasters in history, the *Exxon Valdez* tanker ran aground, spilling 11 million gallons of crude oil off the coast of Alaska. The EPA forced ExxonMobil to cover the costs of the ensuing cleanup. Because an investigation suggested that the ship's captain was drunk at the time, the EPA also mandated that ExxonMobil impose stricter hiring standards for employees in high-risk jobs. To comply with this mandate, ExxonMobil adopted a policy of not assigning anyone with a history of alcohol or substance abuse to certain jobs such as tanker captain. However, another regulatory agency, the EEOC, then sued ExxonMobil on the grounds that restricting people who have been rehabilitated from alcohol abuse from any job violates their rights under the Americans with Disabilities Act. ExxonMobil was thus forced to change its policy, but was then again sanctioned by the EPA.

The regulatory environment in other countries, however, is even more stringent. When U.S. retailer Walmart wants to open a new store, its regulatory requirements are actually quite low, and the procedures it must follow are clearly spelled out. In a sense, within reason and general basic ground rules, the firm can open a store just about anywhere it wants and operate it in just about any manner it wants. But conditions in Germany are quite different. That country's largest retailer, Allkauf, tried for over 15 years to open a store in one town— on land that it already owned. But the city government did not allow it because it feared that local competitors would suffer. And, by German law, all retailers—including Allkauf—can only be open between the hours of 6:00 A.M. and 8:00 P.M. Monday through Saturday and must remain closed on Sunday (gasoline retailers and tourist shops may open on Sunday, and bakeries can open for a few hours to provide bread and pastries after church services). They can also hold large sales only twice a year and can never discount food items.

**regulator**
A unit that has the potential to control, legislate, or otherwise influence the organization's policies and practices

**regulatory agency**
An agency created by the government to regulate business activities

**interest group**
A group organized by its members to attempt to influence business

Alex Lentati / Associated Newspapers / Rex FeaturesDaily Mail/Rex / Alamy

The other basic form of regulator is the interest group. Prominent interest groups include the National Organization for Women (NOW), Mothers Against Drunk Drivers (MADD), the National Rifle Association (NRA), the League of Women Voters, the Sierra Club, the Center for the Study of Responsive Law, Consumers Union, and industry self-regulation groups like the Council of Better Business Bureaus. Although interest groups lack the official power of government agencies, they can exert considerable influence by using the media to call attention to their positions. MADD, for example, puts considerable pressure on alcoholic-beverage producers (to put warning labels on their products), automobile companies (to make it more difficult for intoxicated people to start their cars), local governments (to stiffen drinking ordinances), and bars and restaurants (to refuse to sell alcohol to people who are drinking too much). An interesting new interest group is the Basel Action Network (BAN), a three-person environmental nonprofit that serves as a watchdog over the rapidly growing electronics recycling industry. Among other things, BAN keeps an eye on shipments of discarded televisions, computer parts, and so forth to developing nations for dumping. While this practice is legal under narrow and controlled circumstances, there have been many reports of businesses trying to circumvent both international and local regulations in their efforts to dump electronic components, some containing toxic components, as inexpensively as possible.[16] Similarly, several interest groups have been lobbying the FDA to require soft drink distributors to add a label to their products indicating that the caramel coloring used in colas may cause cancer.[17]

**Manager's Checklist**

☐ Managers need to understand the general environment in which their business operates and how elements of that environment affect their business.

☐ Managers also need to know the core elements of their task environment and be able to assess their impact.

☐ If managers can not only understand their general and task environments but also be able to anticipate changes, they can use their insights for competitive advantage.

# The Internal Environment

As we showed earlier in Figure 3.1, organizations also have internal environments that consist of their owners, boards of directors, employees, physical work environments, and cultures.

## Owners

The owners of a business are, of course, the people who have legal property rights to that business. Owners can be a single individual who establishes and runs a small business, partners who jointly own the business, individual investors who buy stock in a corporation, or other organizations. McDonald's has 959.13 million shares of stock, each of which represents one unit of ownership in the firm. The family of McDonald's founder Ray Kroc stills owns a large block of this stock, as do several large institutional investors. In addition, there are thousands of people who own just a few shares each. McDonald's, in turn, owns other businesses. For example, it owns several large regional bakeries that supply its restaurants with buns. Each of these is incorporated as a separate legal entity and managed as a wholly or partially owned subsidiary by the parent company. McDonald's is also a partner in some Russian farms that grow potatoes to supply regional restaurants with French fries.

**owner**
Whoever can claim property rights to an organization

## Board of Directors

A corporate board of directors is a governing body elected by the stockholders and charged with overseeing the general management of the firm to ensure that it is being run in a way that best serves the stockholders' interests. Some boards are relatively passive. They perform a general oversight function but seldom get actively involved in how the company is really being run. But this trend is changing, as more and more boards are carefully scrutinizing the firms they oversee and exerting more influence over how they are being managed. This trend has in part been spurred by numerous recent business scandals. In some cases, board members have been accused of wrongdoing. In other cases, boards have been found negligent for failing to monitor the actions of firm executives.[18] At issue is the concept of *corporate governance*—who is responsible (and accountable) for governing the actions of a business.

This board of directors holds a meeting to review the proposed CEO salary increase for the upcoming fiscal year. An increasing number of boards are carefully scrutinizing the firms they oversee, especially when it comes to CEO pay.

## Employees

An organization's employees are also a major element of its internal environment. Of particular interest to managers today (as discussed later) is the changing nature of the workforce, as it becomes increasingly diverse in terms of gender, ethnicity, age, and other dimensions. Workers are also calling for more job ownership—either partial ownership in the company or at least more say in how they perform their jobs.[19] Another trend in many firms is increased reliance on temporary workers—individuals hired for short periods of time with no expectation of permanent employment. Employers often prefer to use "temps" because they provide greater flexibility, earn lower wages, and often do not participate in benefits programs. But these managers also have to deal with what often amounts to a two-class workforce and with a growing number of employees who feel no loyalty to the organization where they work because they may be working for a different one tomorrow.[20]

The permanent employees of many organizations are organized into labor unions, representing yet another layer of complexity for managers. The National Labor Relations Act of 1935 requires organizations to recognize and bargain with a union if that union has been legally established by the organization's employees. At present, around 11.1 percent of the U.S. labor force is represented by unions. Some large firms, such as Ford, Exxon, and General Motors, have several different unions. Even when an organization's labor force is not unionized, its managers do not ignore unions. For example, Honda of America, Walmart, and Delta Air Lines all actively work to minimize the presence of unions in their organizations. And even though people think primarily of blue-collar workers as union members, many white-collar workers, such as government employees and teachers, as well as many professional athletes, are also represented by unions.

## Physical Work Environment

A final part of the internal environment is the actual physical environment of the organization and the work that people do. Some firms have their facilities in downtown skyscrapers, usually spread across several floors. Others locate in suburban or rural settings

**board of directors**
Governing body elected by a corporation's stockholders and charged with overseeing the general management of the firm to ensure that it is being run in a way that best serves the stockholders' interests

The physical work environment of a business plays an important role in setting a "tone" for a company. Many businesses today use shared work spaces such as these work stations clustered together in one large room.

and may have facilities more closely resembling a college campus. Some facilities have long halls lined with traditional offices. Others have modular cubicles with partial walls and no doors. The top hundred managers at Mars, makers of Snickers and Milky Way, all work in a single vast room. The president's desk is located in the very center of the room, while others are arrayed in concentric circles around it. Increasingly, newer facilities have an even more open arrangement, where people work in large rooms, moving among different tables to interact with different people on different projects. Freestanding computer workstations are available for those who need them, and a few small rooms might be off to the side for private business.[21]

---

 **Manager's Checklist**

☐ Managers need to understand the main parts of their organization's internal environment, as well as how it affects the organization's success.

☐ Regardless of their level, managers should have a clear knowledge of their organization's governance structure.

---

"It's creating a sense [in your employees] that 'If I want to make a difference, I can make a difference.' Freedom is only one part of the Netflix culture; the other is responsibility. [Netflix] has created a culture of high performance. 'Adequate performance gets a generous severance package.'"

—REED HASTINGS, FOUNDER AND CEO OF NETFLIX[23]

# The Organization's Culture

An especially important part of the internal environment of an organization is its culture. Organization culture is the set of values, beliefs, behaviors, customs, and attitudes that helps the members of the organization understand what it stands for, how it does things, and what it considers important.[22] Culture is an amorphous concept that defies objective measurement or observation. Nevertheless, because it is the foundation of the organization's internal environment, it plays a major role in shaping managerial behavior.

## The Importance of Organization Culture

Culture determines the "feel" of the organization. The stereotypic image of Microsoft, for example, is a workplace where people dress very casually and work very long hours. In contrast, the image of Bank of America for some observers is a formal setting with rigid work rules and people dressed in conservative business attire. And Texas Instruments employees talk about its "shirtsleeve" culture, in which ties are avoided and few managers ever wear jackets. Southwest Airlines maintains a culture that stresses fun and excitement.

Of course, the same culture is not necessarily found throughout an entire organization. For example, the sales and marketing department may have a culture quite different from that of the operations and manufacturing department. Regardless of its nature, however, culture is a powerful force in organizations, one that can shape the firm's overall effectiveness and long-term success. Companies that can develop and maintain a strong culture, such as

**organization culture**
The set of values, beliefs, behaviors, customs, and attitudes that helps the members of the organization understand what it stands for, how it does things, and what it considers important

Apple, Starbucks, and Procter & Gamble, tend to be more effective than companies that have trouble developing and maintaining a strong culture, such as Kmart.[24]

## Determinants of Organization Culture

Where does an organization's culture come from? Typically, it develops and blossoms over a long period of time. Its starting point is often the organization's founder. For example, James Cash Penney believed in treating employees and customers with respect and dignity. Employees at J. C. Penney are still called "associates" rather than "employees" (to reflect partnership), and customer satisfaction is of paramount importance. The impact of Sam Walton, Ross Perot, and Walt Disney is still felt in the organizations they founded.[25] As an organization grows, its culture is modified, shaped, and refined by symbols, stories, heroes, slogans, and ceremonies. For example, an important value at Hewlett-Packard is the avoidance of bank debt. A popular story still told at the company involves a new project that was being considered for several years. All objective criteria indicated that HP should borrow money from a bank to finance it, yet Bill Hewlett and David Packard rejected it out of hand simply because "HP avoids bank debt." This story, involving two corporate heroes and based on a slogan, dictates corporate culture today. And many decisions at Walt Disney Company today are still framed by asking, "What would Walt have done?"

Corporate success and shared experiences also shape culture. For example, Hallmark Cards has a strong culture derived from its years of success in the greeting card industry. Employees speak of "the Hallmark family" and care deeply about the company; many of them have worked at the company for years. At Kmart, in contrast, the culture is quite weak, the management team has changed rapidly, and few people sense any direction or purpose in the company. The differences in culture at Hallmark and Kmart are in part attributable to past successes and shared experiences.

## Managing Organization Culture

How can managers deal with culture, given its clear importance but intangible nature? Essentially, the manager must understand the current culture and then decide whether it should be maintained or changed. By understanding the organization's current culture, managers can take appropriate actions. At Hewlett-Packard, the values represented by "the HP way" still exist, guiding and directing most important activities undertaken by the firm. Culture can also be maintained by rewarding and promoting people whose behaviors are consistent with the existing culture and by articulating the culture through slogans, ceremonies, and so forth.

But managers must walk a fine line between maintaining a culture that still works effectively and changing a culture that has become dysfunctional. For example, many of the firms already noted, as well as numerous others, take pride in perpetuating their culture. Shell Oil, for example, has an elaborate display in the lobby of its Houston headquarters that tells the story of the firm's past. But other companies may face situations in which their culture is no longer a strength. For example, some critics feel that General Motors' culture places too much emphasis on product development and internal competition among divisions, and not enough on marketing and competition with other firms. They even argue that this culture was a major contributing factor in the business crisis GM faced during the recent recession.

Culture problems sometimes arise from mergers or the growth of rival factions within an organization. For example, Continental and United merged in recent years to form one of the world's largest airlines. Combining the two companies led to many cases of conflict and operational difficulties because the cultures of the merging firms were so different.[26] To change culture, managers must have a clear idea of what they want to create. While focusing on three key areas for improvement within the company's restaurants, Yum! Brands' executive chairman Dave Novak realized that its lack of a single corporate culture was standing in his way. (Yum! Owns Pizza Hut, KFC, and Taco Bell.) In order to provide healthier items and more variety across brands, Novak had to tackle the fact that the various brands and operations across countries had little to do with one another. By adopting an innovative focus and creating specialized courses for employees, the new culture spread down from senior executives to restaurant employees across the world.[27]

One major way to shape culture is by bringing outsiders into important managerial positions. The choice of a new CEO from outside the organization is often a clear signal that things will be changing. Adopting new slogans, telling new stories, staging new ceremonies, and breaking with tradition can also alter culture. Culture can also be changed by methods discussed in Chapter 12.[28]

---

 **Manager's Checklist**

☐  All members of an organization should understand its culture.

☐  Managers need to help create, communicate, and sustain a strong organization culture.

# The Multicultural Environment

In addition to the external and internal environments (including organization culture) there are also other important elements in the environment that relate to multiculturalism and diversity. We choose to discuss these elements separately because in many ways they connect and overlap with other aspects of the environment. In particular, the people comprising an organization, as well as other organizations with which it interacts, come from different backgrounds and locations and reflect different values, beliefs, customs, viewpoints, attitudes, and experiences. These and other differences, in turn, pose unique opportunities and challenges for managers. These broad issues are generally referred to as multiculturalism.

A related area of interest is diversity. Diversity exists in a community of people when its members differ from one another along one or more important dimensions. These differences can obviously reflect the multicultural composition of a community. In the business world, however, the term *diversity per se* is more generally used to refer to demographic differences among people within a culture—differences in gender, age, ethnicity, and so forth. Of course, diversity is not an absolute phenomenon that specifies that a group or organization is or is not diverse. Instead, diversity can be conceptualized as a continuum and should be thought of in terms of degree or level of diversity along relevant dimensions. Beyond their strict definitions, of course, diversity and multiculturalism essentially relate to differences among people. Therefore, because organizations today are becoming more diverse and multicultural, it is important that all managers understand the major trends and dimensions of diversity and multiculturalism.

## Trends in Diversity and Multiculturalism

The most fundamental trend in diversity and multiculturalism is that virtually all organizations, simply put, are becoming more diverse and multicultural. The composition of their workforces is changing in many different ways. The basic reasons for this trend are illustrated in Figure 3.4.

One factor contributing to increased diversity is changing demographics in the labor force. As more women and minorities have entered the labor force, for example, the available pool of talent from which organizations hire employees has changed in both size and composition. In 1955, for example, only 26.6 percent of adult women in the United States worked outside the home. By 2013, however, that figure had grown to 57.2 percent.[29]

If talent within each segment of the labor pool is evenly distributed (for example, if the number of very talented men in the workforce as a percentage of all men in the workforce is

**multiculturalism**
The broad issues associated with differences in values, beliefs, behaviors, customs, and attitudes held by people in different cultures.

**diversity**
Exists in a group or organization when its members differ from one another along one or more important dimensions, such as age, gender, or ethnicity

## FIGURE 3.4 REASONS FOR INCREASING DIVERSITY AND MULTICULTURALISM

Diversity and multiculturalism are increasing in most organizations today for four basic reasons. These reasons promise to make diversity even greater in the future.

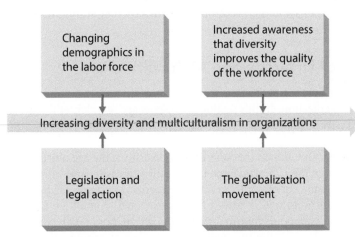

the same as the number of very talented women in the labor force as a percentage of all women in the workforce), it follows logically that, over time, proportionately more women and proportionately fewer men will be hired by an organization. For example, suppose that a firm's top management team is 90 percent men and only 10 percent women. If the relevant labor pool is, say, 40 percent female, then women are clearly underrepresented in this firm. Over time, though, as men leave and are replaced by women at a percentage close to their representation in the labor pool, the composition of the top management team will gradually move closer to reflecting that labor pool.

A related factor contributing to diversity is the recognition that organizations can improve the overall quality of their workforce by hiring and promoting the most talented people available. By casting a broader net in recruiting and looking beyond traditional sources for new employees, organizations are finding more broadly qualified and better-qualified employees from many different segments of society. Thus these organizations are finding that diversity can be a source of competitive advantage.[30]

Another reason for the increase in diversity is that both legislation and judicial decisions have forced organizations to hire more broadly. In earlier times, organizations in the United States were essentially free to discriminate against women, African Americans, and other minorities. Although not all organizations consciously or openly engaged in these practices, many firms nevertheless came to be dominated by white males. But starting with the passage of the Civil Rights Act in 1964, numerous laws have outlawed discrimination against these and most other groups. As we detail in Chapter 13, organizations must hire and promote people today solely on the basis of their qualifications.

This chemical plant embraces its diverse workforce by providing safety regulation signage in two languages, English & Malay.

A final factor contributing to increased multiculturalism in particular is the globalization movement. Organizations that have opened offices and related facilities in other countries have had to learn to deal with different customs, social norms, and mores. Strategic alliances and foreign ownership also contribute, as managers today are more likely to have job assignments in other countries or to work with foreign managers within their own countries. As employees and managers move from assignment to assignment across national boundaries, organizations and their subsidiaries within each country thus become more diverse and multicultural.

## Dimensions of Diversity and Multiculturalism

As we indicated earlier, many different dimensions of diversity and multiculturalism can characterize an organization. In this section we discuss age, gender, ethnicity, and other dimensions of diversity.

**Age Distributions**  One important dimension of diversity is the age distribution of its workers. The average age of the U.S. workforce is gradually increasing and will continue to do so for the next several years. For example, in 2000 the median age among U.S. workers was 35.5 years. By 2014 it had risen to 42.3 years, and it is expected to continue to rise for the next several years. Several factors are contributing to this pattern. For one, the baby boom generation (a term used to describe the unusually large number of people who were born in the 20-year period after World War II) continues to age. Declining birthrates among the post–baby boom generations simultaneously account for smaller percentages of new entrants into the labor force. Another factor that contributes to the aging workforce is improved health and medical care. As a result of these improvements, people can remain productive and active for longer periods of time. Finally, and unfortunately, many people approaching traditional retirement ages do not have enough savings to pay for retirement and so must work longer. These factors combine to result in more and more people working beyond the age at which they might have retired just a few years ago.

How does this trend affect organizations? Older workers tend to have more experience, to be more stable, and to make greater contributions to productivity than younger workers. On the other hand, despite the improvements in health and medical care, older workers are nevertheless likely to require higher levels of insurance coverage and medical benefits. And the declining labor pool of younger workers will continue to pose problems for organizations as they find fewer potential new entrants into the labor force.[31]

"[Many younger workers] believe workers in the older generations have been too slow to adopt social media and other tools, and place too much value on tenure rather than knowledge and performance."

—ADRIENNE FOX, HR CONSULTANT[32]

**Gender**  Organizations have also experienced changes in the relative proportions of male and female employees. In the United States, for example, the workforce in 1964 was 66 percent male and 34 percent female. By 2012 the proportions were around 53 percent male and 47 percent female. Moreover, around 52 percent of all workers engaged in management, professional, and related occupations in the United States are now women. These trends aside, one gender-related problem that many organizations face today is the so-called glass ceiling. The glass ceiling describes a barrier that keeps women from advancing to top management positions in many organizations. This ceiling is a real barrier that is difficult to break, but it is also so subtle as to be hard to see. Indeed, whereas women comprise a significant percentage of all managers, there are still only a small proportion that make it into upper management. Further, their distribution across functional areas is uneven, with relatively more of them holding marketing and human resource positions and relatively fewer of them holding finance and operations positions.[33] Similarly, the average pay of women in organizations is lower than that of men. Although the pay gap is gradually shrinking, inequalities are present nonetheless.

**glass ceiling**
A perceived barrier in some organizations that keeps women from advancing to top management positions

Why does the glass ceiling still seem to exist? One reason may be that real obstacles to advancement for women, such as subtle discrimination, may still exist in some organizations. Another is that many talented women choose to leave jobs in large organizations and start their own businesses. Still another factor is that some women choose to suspend or slow their career progression to have children. But there are also many talented women continuing to work their way up the corporate ladder and getting closer and closer to a corporate "top spot."[34]

**Ethnicity**    A third major dimension of cultural diversity in organizations is ethnicity. Ethnicity refers to the ethnic composition of a group or organization. Within the United States, most organizations reflect varying degrees of ethnicity, comprising Whites, African Americans, Latinos, and Asians. Figure 3.5 shows the ethnic composition of the U.S. population in 2012 and as projected by the U.S. Census Bureau for the year 2060 in terms of various ethnic groups.[35]

The biggest projected changes involve Whites and individuals of Hispanic origin. In particular, the percentage of Whites in the United States is expected to drop from 63 percent to 43 percent. At the same time, the percentage of Hispanic origin is expected to climb from 17 percent to 31 percent. The percentage of African Americans, Asians, and others is also expected to climb, but at lower rates. As with women, members of the African American, Latino, and Asian groups are generally underrepresented in the executive ranks of most organizations today. And their pay is similarly lower than might be expected. But, as is also the case for women, the differences are gradually disappearing as organizations fully embrace equal employment opportunity and recognize the higher overall level of talent available to them.[36]

**ethnicity**
The ethnic composition of a group or organization

## FIGURE 3.5  ETHNICITY DISTRIBUTION TRENDS IN THE UNITED STATES

Ethnic diversity in the United States is increasing. For example, the percentage of the U.S. population that is White will gradually decline. Meanwhile, other ethnic groups will experience percentage growth, with the largest increase coming from people of Hispanic origin.

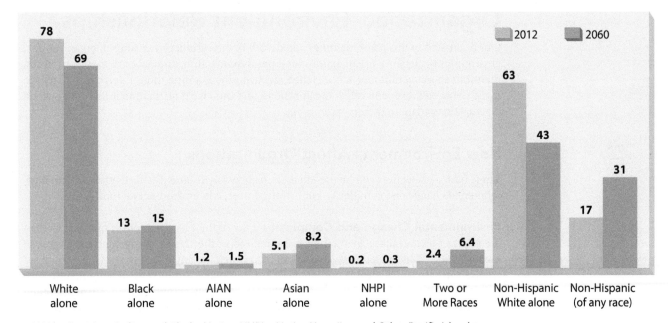

AIAN = American Indian and Alaska Native; NHPI = Native Hawaiian and Other Pacific Islander

Source: http://www.census.gov/newsroom/releases/archives/population/cb12-243.html

**Other Dimensions of Diversity** In addition to age, gender, and ethnicity, organizations are confronting other dimensions of diversity. Different religious beliefs, for example, constitute an important dimension of diversity. Single parents, dual-career couples, gays and lesbians, people with special dietary preferences (such as vegetarians), and people with different political ideologies and viewpoints also represent major dimensions of diversity in today's organizations. And of course handicapped and physically challenged employees are increasingly important in many organizations, especially since the 1990 passage of the Americans with Disabilities Act.

**Multicultural Differences** In addition to these various diversity-related dimensions, organizations are increasingly being characterized by multicultural differences as well. Some organizations, especially international businesses, are actively seeking to enhance the multiculturalism of their workforces. But even organizations that are more passive in this regard may still become more multicultural because of changes in the external labor market.

Immigration into the United States is at its highest rate since 1910, for example. Between 2000 and 2010, 12.3 million immigrants arrived in the United States. This is the highest seven-year period of immigration in the country's history. (An estimated 6 million of these immigrants are illegal aliens.)

> "… we are determined to build a community and a culture that is inclusive."
>
> —DREW HUDSON, DROPBOX CEO[37]

---

 **Manager's Checklist**

☐ Managers need a clear understanding of multiculturalism and diversity.

☐ Managers should be able to identify core dimensions of diversity that are most relevant to organizations and be knowledgeable about their trends.

☐ It is also important to remember that these dimensions might be related to one another.

# Organization–Environment Relationships

Our discussion to this point identifies and describes the various dimensions of organizational environments. Because organizations are open systems, they interact with these various dimensions in many different ways. Hence, we will now examine those interactions. First we discuss how environments affect organizations, and then we note a number of ways in which organizations adapt to their environments.

## How Environments Affect Organizations

Three basic perspectives can be used to describe how environments affect organizations: environmental change and complexity, competitive forces, and environmental turbulence.[38]

**Environmental Change and Complexity** One of the first perspectives on how environments affect organizations focused on two dimensions: the rate of change and the degree of homogeneity.[39] The rate of change is the extent to which the environment is relatively stable or relatively dynamic. The degree of homogeneity is the extent to which the environment is relatively simple (few elements, little segmentation) or relatively complex (many elements, much segmentation). These two dimensions interact to determine the level of uncertainty faced by the organization. Uncertainty, in turn, is a driving force that influences many organizational decisions. Figure 3.6 illustrates a simple view of the four levels of uncertainty defined by different degrees of homogeneity and change.

**uncertainty**
Unpredictability created by environmental change and complexity

## FIGURE 3.6 ENVIRONMENTAL CHANGE, COMPLEXITY, AND UNCERTAINTY

The degree of homogeneity and the degree of change combine to create uncertainty for organizations. For example, a simple and stable environment creates the least uncertainty, and a complex and dynamic environment creates the most uncertainty.

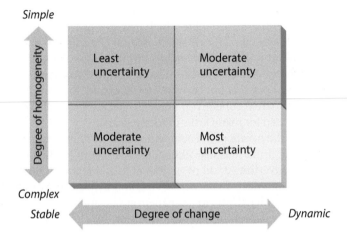

Source: From J. D. Thompson, *Organizations in Action,* 1967

The least environmental uncertainty is faced by organizations with stable and simple environments. Although no environment is totally without uncertainty, some entrenched franchised food operations (such as Subway and Taco Bell) and many container manufacturers (like Ball Corporation and Federal Paper Board) have relatively low levels of uncertainty to contend with. Subway, for example, focuses on a certain segment of the consumer market, produces a limited product line, has a stable network of suppliers, and faces relatively consistent competition.

Organizations with dynamic but simple environments generally face a moderate degree of uncertainty. Examples of organizations functioning in such environments include clothing manufacturers (targeting a certain kind of clothing buyer but sensitive to fashion-induced changes) and music producers (catering to certain kinds of music buyers but alert to changing tastes in music). Levi Strauss faces relatively few competitors (Diesel, Wrangler, and Lee), has few suppliers and few regulators, and uses limited distribution channels. This relatively simple task environment, however, also changes quite rapidly as competitors adjust prices and styles, consumer tastes change, and new fabrics become available.

Another combination of factors is one of stability and complexity. Again, a moderate amount of uncertainty results. Ford, Nissan, and BMW face these basic conditions. Overall, they must interact with myriad suppliers, regulators, consumer groups, and competitors. Change, however, occurs quite slowly in the automobile industry. Despite many stylistic changes, cars of today still have four wheels, a steering wheel, an engine, a glass windshield, and many of the other basic features that have characterized cars for decades.

Finally, very dynamic and complex environmental conditions yield a high degree of uncertainty. The environment has a large number of elements, and the nature of those elements is constantly changing. Intel, Apple, Samsung, Sony, and other firms in the electronics field face these conditions because of the rapid rate of technological innovation and change in consumer markets that characterize their industry, their suppliers, and their competitors. Web-based firms like eBay and Amazon face similarly high levels of uncertainty.

**Competitive Forces** Although these general classifications are useful and provide some basic insights into organization–environment interactions, in many ways they lack the precision and specificity needed by managers who must deal with their environments on a day-to-day basis. Michael E. Porter, a Harvard professor and expert in strategic management, has proposed a more refined way to assess environments. In particular, he suggests that managers view the environments of their organizations in terms of five competitive forces: the threat of new entrants, competitive rivalry, the threat of substitute products, the power of buyers, and the power of suppliers.[40]

*The threat of new entrants* is the extent to which new competitors can easily enter a market or market segment. It takes a relatively small amount of capital to open a dry-cleaning service or a pizza parlor, but it takes a tremendous investment in plant, equipment, and distribution systems to enter the automobile business. Thus the threat of new entrants is fairly high for a local sub shop or pizzeria but fairly low for Ford and Toyota. The Internet has reduced the costs and other barriers of entry in many market segments, however, so the threat of new entrants has increased for many firms in recent years.

*Competitive rivalry* is the nature of the competitive relationship between dominant firms in the industry. In the soft-drink industry, Coca-Cola and PepsiCo often engage in intense price wars, comparative advertising, and new-product introductions. Other firms that have intense rivalries include American Express and Visa, and British Airways and Virgin Atlantic. And auto companies continually try to outmaneuver one another with warranty improvements and rebates. Local car-washing establishments or dry cleaners, in contrast, seldom engage in such practices.

*The threat of substitute products* is the extent to which alternative products or services may supplant or diminish the need for existing products or services. The electronic calculator eliminated the need for slide rules. The advent of personal computers, in turn, reduced the demand for calculators as well as for typewriters and large mainframe computers. And now digital tablets like the iPad are cutting demand for personal computers. DVD players have rendered VCRs obsolete, but high-definition DVD technology and streaming video services are now replacing today's conventional DVD players. Also on the way out may be mass-market TV programming (or a lot of it, anyway) as other providers such as NetFlix and Amazon.com continue to develop and provide their own original content.

*The power of buyers* is the extent to which buyers of the products or services in an industry can influence the suppliers. For example, a Boeing 777 has relatively few potential buyers. Only companies such as Delta, Emirates, and KLM Royal Dutch Airlines can purchase them. Hence, these buyers may have considerable influence over the price they are willing to pay, the delivery date for the order, and so forth. United Airlines attempted to exploit this power recently by requesting that Boeing and Airbus bid on a massive single order of up to 150 new planes. United felt that since the global recession had hurt sales at both manufacturers, and the costs of parts, labor, and credit were dropping, it would be able to get more favorable terms than might otherwise be the case.[41] On the other hand, during times of shortage, individual buyers have little power; if one buyer will not pay the asking price, others are waiting in line. For instance, if global airline traffic is booming and many carriers are buying new planes, manufacturers like Boeing and Airbus can negotiate from strength and make few price concessions.

*The power of suppliers* is the extent to which suppliers can influence potential buyers. The local electric company may be the only source of electricity in your community. Subject to local or state regulation (or both), it can therefore charge what it wants for its product, provide service at its convenience, and so forth. Likewise, even though Boeing has few potential customers, those same customers have only two suppliers that can sell them a 300-passenger jet (Boeing and Airbus, a European firm). So Boeing and Airbus, too, have power. On the other hand, a small vegetable wholesaler has little power in selling to restaurants because if they do not like the produce, they can likely find an alternative supplier.

**five competitive forces**
The threat of new entrants, competitive rivalry, the threat of substitute products, the power of buyers, and the power of suppliers

**Environmental Turbulence** Although always subject to unexpected changes and upheavals, the five competitive forces can nevertheless be studied and assessed systematically, and plans can be developed for dealing with them. At the same time, though, organizations face the possibility of environmental change or turbulence, occasionally with no warning at all. The most common form of organizational turbulence is a crisis of some sort.

The terrorist attacks on September 11, 2001, are, of course, one obvious illustration of environmental turbulence. Beyond the human and social costs, these events profoundly affected myriad businesses ranging from airlines to New York's entertainment industry to those firms with operations in the World Trade Center.[42] Natural disasters (like the 2011 earthquake and tsunami in Japan and resultant nuclear power plant crisis), industrial accidents (like the chemical explosion in West, Texas, in 2014), political unrest (like that in the Middle East and Russia), digital hacking (like Sony experienced in 2014), and health-care crises (such as the 2014 Ebola scare) all lead to higher levels of uncertainty and potential resource scarcity.[43] Another type of crisis that has captured the attention of managers in recent years is workplace violence—situations in which disgruntled workers or former workers assault other employees, often resulting in injury and sometimes in death.

Environmental turbulence can disrupt any organization. Take this industrial accident, for example. People have died, and others have been injured. The company will need to deal with the human side of this tragedy as quickly as possible. The accident will also disrupt production for an extended period of time.

BRAM VAN DE BIEZEN/EPA/Newscom

Such crises affect organizations in different ways, and some organizations have developed crisis plans and teams.[44] When a US Airways plane made an emergency landing in the Hudson River, rescue boats were on their way to the disabled plane within minutes. Their preparedness came from crisis plans developed after the September 11 terrorist attacks. Similarly, a grocery store in Boston once received a threat that someone had poisoned cans of its Campbell's tomato juice. Within six hours, a crisis team from Campbell Soup Company removed two truckloads of juice from all 84 stores in the grocery chain. Still, far too few companies in the United States have a plan for dealing with major crises. For example, during the H1N1 virus scare in 2009, one survey reported that only 27 percent of all U.S. employers had plans for dealing with such a potential health crisis.[45] Similarly, even though General Motors had a contingency plan for disruptions in its supply chain, the firm was still not adequately prepared to deal with parts shortages caused by the Japanese earthquake and tsunami.[46]

## How Organizations Adapt to Their Environments

Given the myriad issues, problems, and opportunities in an organization's environments, how should the organization adapt? Obviously, each organization must assess its own unique situation and then adapt according to the wisdom of its senior management.[47] Figure 3.7 illustrates the six basic mechanisms through which organizations adapt to their environments. One of these, social responsibility, is given special consideration in Chapter 4.

**Information Management** One way organizations adapt to their environments is through information management. Information management is especially important when forming an initial understanding of the environments and when monitoring the environments for signs of change. One technique for managing information is relying on boundary spanners. A *boundary spanner* is an employee, such as a sales representative or a purchasing agent, who spends much of his or her time in contact with others outside the organization. Such people

---

### FIGURE 3.7 HOW ORGANIZATIONS ADAPT TO THEIR ENVIRONMENTS

Organizations try to adapt to their environments. The most common methods are information management; strategic response; mergers, acquisitions, and alliances; organization design and flexibility; direct influence; and social responsibility.

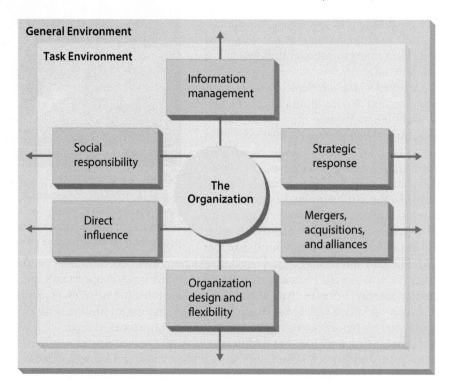

are in a good position to learn what other organizations are doing. All effective managers engage in *environmental scanning*, the process of actively monitoring the environments through activities such as observation and reading. Within the organization, most firms have also established computer-based *information systems* to gather and organize relevant information for managers and to assist in summarizing that information in the form most pertinent to each manager's needs. Enterprise resource planning techniques are also useful methods for improving information management.

**Strategic Response** Another way that an organization adapts to its environments is through a strategic response. Options include maintaining the status quo (for example, if its management believes that it is doing very well with its current approach), altering strategy a bit, or adopting an entirely new strategy. If the market that a company currently serves is growing rapidly, the firm might decide to invest even more heavily in products and services for that market. Likewise, if a market is shrinking or does not provide reasonable possibilities for growth, the company may decide to cut back. For example, a few years ago managers at Starbucks recognized that the firm's growth opportunities in the United States were slowing simply because there already were so many Starbucks shops. Accordingly, they devised a new plan to expand aggressively into international markets, thus providing an avenue for continued growth.

"I've long held to a view of innovation that says the role of the CEO is essentially to figure out where the world is going and to ensure his or her company is there when that world unfolds."

—RON SHAICH, FOUNDER, PANERA BREAD[48]

**Mergers, Acquisitions, and Alliances** A related strategic approach that some organizations use to adapt to their environments involves mergers, acquisitions, and alliances. A *merger* occurs when two or more firms combine to form a new firm. For example, Delta merged with Northwest Airlines. Part of the logic behind this merger was that the two firms had strength in different but complementary markets, and so by merging, a much stronger airline would result. Meanwhile, Continental and United believed that the Delta–Northwest merger threatened their markets, so they subsequently decided to merge as well. An *acquisition* occurs when one firm buys another, sometimes against its will (usually called a "hostile takeover"). The firm taken over may cease to exist and becomes part of the other company. For example, as part of its international expansion, Starbucks bought a British coffee shop chain called the Seattle Coffee Company. Starbucks subsequently changed many Seattle Coffee outlets into Starbucks shops.

In other situations, the acquired firm may continue to operate as a subsidiary of the acquiring company. Royal Caribbean Cruise Lines bought a controlling interest in Celebrity Cruise Lines, but maintains it as a separate cruise line. And, as already discussed, in a *partnership* or *alliance* the firm undertakes a new venture with another firm. A company engages in these kinds of strategies for a variety of reasons, such as easing entry into new markets or expanding its presence in a current market. In a somewhat unusual case, SBC Communications acquired AT&T. But even though SBC was the acquiring company, it adopted the AT&T name for the combined enterprise. Why? Because its managers felt that AT&T had more national brand recognition and the name would better enable the firm to gain market share. They felt it would be especially helpful in attracting new corporate clients.[49]

**Organization Design and Flexibility** An organization may also adapt to environmental conditions by incorporating flexibility in its structural design. For example, a firm that operates in an environment with relatively low levels of uncertainty might choose to use a design with many basic rules, regulations, and standard operating procedures. Alternatively, a firm that faces a great deal of uncertainty might choose a design with relatively few standard operating procedures, instead allowing managers considerable discretion and flexibility with decisions. The former type, sometimes called a "mechanistic organization design," is characterized by formal and rigid rules and relationships. The latter, sometimes called an "organic design," is considerably more flexible and permits the organization to respond quickly to environmental change. We learn much more about these and related issues in Chapter 11.

**Direct Influence** Organizations are not necessarily helpless in the face of their environments. Indeed, many organizations can directly influence their environments in many different ways. For example, firms can influence their suppliers by signing long-term contracts with fixed prices as a hedge against inflation. Or a firm might become its own supplier. Sears, for example, owns some of the firms that produce the goods it sells, and Campbell Soup Company makes its own soup cans. Similarly, almost any major activity in which a firm engages affects its competitors. When Mitsubishi lowers the prices of its DVD players, Sony may be forced to follow suit. Organizations also influence their customers by creating new uses for a product, finding entirely new customers, taking customers away from competitors, and convincing customers that they need something new. Automobile manufacturers use this last strategy in their advertising to convince people that they need a new car every two or three years.

Organizations influence their regulators through lobbying and bargaining.[50] Lobbying involves sending a company or industry representative to Washington in an effort to influence relevant agencies, groups, and committees. For example, the U.S. Chamber of Commerce lobby, the nation's largest business lobby, has an annual budget of around $75 million. The automobile companies have been successful on several occasions in bargaining with the EPA to extend deadlines for compliance with pollution control and mileage standards.

✓ **Manager's Checklist**

☐ The environment clearly influences organizations, so it is important to understand the nature and impact of these influences.

☐ Managers should also remember that they can affect their environment.

☐ Remember, though, there are limits to how much managers can influence their environment, and they should guard against crossing legal or ethical boundaries.

# Summary of Learning Outcomes and Key Points

1. Discuss the nature of the organizational environment and identify the environments of interest to most organizations.

   - Environmental factors play a major role in determining an organization's success or failure.
   - Managers should strive to maintain the proper alignment between their organization and its environments.
   - All organizations have both external and internal environments.

2. Describe the components of the general and task environments and discuss their impact on organizations.

   - The external environment is composed of general and task environment layers.
   - The general environment consists of five dimensions: economic, technological, sociocultural, political-legal, and international.
   - The task environment consists of five elements: competitors, customers, suppliers, strategic partners, and regulators.

3. Identify the components of the internal environment and discuss their impact on organizations.

   - The internal environment consists of the organization's owners, board of directors, employees, physical environment, and culture.

4. Discuss the importance and determinants of an organization's culture and how the culture can be managed.

   - Organization culture is the set of values, beliefs, behaviors, customs, and attitudes that helps the members of the organization understand what it stands for, how it does things, and what it considers important.

   - Managers must understand that culture is an important determinant of how well their organization will perform.
   - Culture can be determined and managed in a number of different ways.

5. Describe the multicultural environment of business, and identify major trends and dimensions of diversity and multiculturalism.

   - Diversity exists in a community of people when its members differ from one another along one or more important dimensions.
   - Multiculturalism is reflected when the people comprising an organization represent different cultures and have different values, beliefs, behaviors, customs, and attitudes.
   - Diversity and multiculturalism are increasing in organizations today because of changing demographics, the desire of organizations to improve their workforces, legal pressures, and increased globalization.
   - There are several important dimensions of diversity, including age, gender, and ethnicity. The overall age of the workforce is increasing.

6. Identify and describe how the environment affects organizations and how organizations adapt to their environment.

   - Environmental influences on the organization can occur through uncertainty, competitive forces, and turbulence.
   - Organizations use information management; strategic response; mergers, acquisitions, and alliances; organization design and flexibility; direct influence; and social responsibility to adapt to their environments.

# Discussion Questions

### Questions for Review

1. Consider the three environments of a firm. Which of the environments has the most direct and immediate impact on the firm? Which of the environments has a more diffuse and delayed impact? Explain.

2. Describe the organization's general environment. For each dimension, give at least one specific example, other than the examples mentioned in your text.

3. What is diversity? Why is it increasing?

4. What are the major forces that affect organization–environment relationships? Describe those factors.

### Questions for Analysis

5. Elements from the general environment affect all organizations, but they may not affect all organizations in the same way. Choose an industry and discuss the impact of at least two different elements from the general environment on firms in that industry. Are all firms affected equally? Explain.

6. Which of the firm's environments is most readily changed by the firm? Which of the firm's environments is least amenable to change by the firm? How does this influence the actions that firms take?

### Questions for Application

7. Go to Hoover's Online at **www.hoovers.com**. Enter a company name in the Search boxes. When that company's profile is shown, go to "Top Competitors." Here you can learn who the firm's top competitors are. Were you surprised by the list? How do you think Hoover's determines the list?

8. Attention has recently been focused on the lack of diversity in many high-tech companies. Select one such company, such as Google, Facebook, Yahoo!, or a similar firm, and research what that company is doing to promote diversity.

9. Interview a manager from a local organization about his or her organization's internal environment, including owners, directors, employees, the physical work environment, and the organization culture. How do these various elements interact?

10. Consider an organization with which you are familiar. Outline its environments in detail. Then provide specific examples to illustrate how each dimension affects your organization.

# Building Effective Time-Management Skills

### Exercise Overview

Time-management skills refer to the ability to prioritize tasks, to work efficiently, and to delegate appropriately. This exercise gives you an opportunity to apply your time-management skills to your understanding of the tasks that managers typically perform.

### Exercise Background

A key problem faced by all managers is the fact that time is a finite resource: There are only so many hours in a day and only so many tasks that you can take on in a given period of time. As a result, managers are constantly making choices about how they spend their time. Obviously, they must use it wisely, and as any veteran manager will tell you, spending time on trivial matters and neglecting more pressing concerns is not only a mistake but a surprisingly easy trap to fall into. Using your time wisely means dividing it appropriately among the various tasks that you have to perform on a daily basis.

Many time-management experts suggest that managers begin each day by listing what they need to accomplish before the workday is done. After they've compiled this list, they can then sort their daily tasks into three groups: (1) those that must be addressed today, (2) those that should be addressed today but can be postponed if necessary, and (3) those that can easily be postponed. The next step is a matter of common sense: Perform the tasks in order of priority.

You can use the organization of the material in this chapter to get a better understanding of managerial tasks and how to prioritize them. As we saw in this chapter, for example, both managers and organizations must be sensitive to a variety of forces at work in a firm's *external* and *internal* environments. We then divided the external environment into two categories—the *general* and *task* environments. For the purpose of this exercise, you can focus on the *task environment*, which includes competitors, customers, suppliers, strategic partners, and regulators. You also need to remember that the *internal environment* consists of a firm's owners, board of directors, employees, physical work environment, and organization culture.

### Exercise Task

This exercise consists of the following steps:

1. Across the top of a sheet of paper, write the three priority levels that we described above (tasks that need to be done today, etc.).

2. Down the left side of the same sheet of paper, list the elements of the *task environment* plus the elements of a firm's *internal environment*.

3. At the intersection of each row and column, provide an appropriate example of a task that a manager might face:

When you come to *Customers*, for example, think of three hypothetical tasks—one that's of high priority (do today), one that's of moderate priority (postpone if necessary), and one that's of lower priority (postpone).

4. When you've finished, your instructor will divide the class into small groups of three or four people. Once your group is assembled, share the examples that you came up with. Focus on whether the group agrees or disagrees about the way that each person has prioritized his or her tasks.

# Building Effective Communication Skills

### Exercise Overview

Communication skills refer to the ability not only to convey information and ideas to others but also to handle information and ideas received from them. This exercise will help you develop your skills in conveying certain information that you've received during your study of business—namely, information about customer segments as an element in an organization's task environment.

### Exercise Background

You're a newly hired middle manager in the marketing department of a large food manufacturer. Having just completed your formal study of marketing management, you're excited about the opportunity to apply some of the theories that you've read about to real situations faced by a real business. As luck would have it, you haven't been on the job very long when you're confronted by an intriguing problem. Your boss, the VP for marketing, has developed a survey to solicit customer feedback about the company's products. Unfortunately, the feedback varies considerably, with responses typically ranging from 2 to 5 on a scale of 1 to 5. Even you can see that such a wide range of data isn't very helpful in drawing conclusions about customer opinions. Moreover, sales have been slowly but steadily declining over time, and upper management has been putting pressure on the marketing department to figure out why.

Suspecting that the survey results are so broad because they reflect a broad range of customers, you make a suggestion to your boss: "To get a better idea of what their needs are, why don't we gather some information about our customers themselves? For example, our customers include individual consumers, schools, restaurants, and other organizations. Maybe each type of customer wants something different from our products." Your boss gives you a patronizing look and says, "Our products have been best-sellers for years, and do you want to know why? Because good quality is good quality—always has been and always will be. Show me a 'customer' and I'll show you somebody who just wants good quality."

### Exercise Task

1. Go back to your office (or your dorm room, the library, or your kitchen table) and compose a written proposal for your boss in which you outline your position on developing a customer-needs survey. Be sure that your proposal accomplishes two goals: (1) It emphasizes your fundamental concern—namely, that in order to provide products that meet customer needs, the marketing department must better understand what those needs are. (2) It communicates some good reasons why the marketing department should follow through on your proposal. (*Hint*: Telling your boss bluntly that he's wrong probably won't get the job done.)

2. Now review what you've written. Do you think that your boss will change his mind? If yes, which of your reasons is most likely to persuade him? If no, what might be your next move in trying to get your proposal a fair hearing from management?

# Skill-Building Personal Assessment

## Refining Your Sense of Culture

This exercise is designed to help you assess what you now know about organization culture. The 10 statements in the following table reflect certain opinions about the nature of work performed in the context of organization culture. Indicate the extent to which you agree or disagree with each opinion by circling the number in the appropriate column.

| Statement of Opinion | Strongly Agree | | | | Strongly Disagree |
|---|---|---|---|---|---|
| 1. If a person can do well in one organization, he or she can do well in any organization. | 1 | 2 | 3 | 4 | 5 |
| 2. Skills and experience are all that really matter; how a job candidate will "fit in" is not an important factor in hiring. | 1 | 2 | 3 | 4 | 5 |
| 3. Members of an organization explicitly tell people how to adhere to its culture. | 1 | 2 | 3 | 4 | 5 |
| 4. After appropriate study, astute managers can fairly quickly change a corporate culture. | 1 | 2 | 3 | 4 | 5 |
| 5. A common culture is important for unifying employees but does not necessarily affect the firm's financial health. | 1 | 2 | 3 | 4 | 5 |
| 6. Conscientious workers are not really influenced by an organization's culture. | 1 | 2 | 3 | 4 | 5 |
| 7. Strong organization cultures are not necessarily associated with high organization performance. | 1 | 2 | 3 | 4 | 5 |
| 8. Members of a subculture share the common values of the subculture but not those of the dominant organization culture. | 1 | 2 | 3 | 4 | 5 |
| 9. Job candidates seeking to understand a prospective employer's culture can do so by just asking the people who interview them. | 1 | 2 | 3 | 4 | 5 |

Source: Hunsaker, Phillip L., Management: *A Skills Approach*, 2nd Edition, © 2005. Reprinted by permission of Pearson Education, Inc., Upper Saddle River, NJ.

# Management at Work

## The Canary in the Coal Mine

"If the only reason you're invested in sustainability is because it's the 'right thing to do,' you're in trouble."

—JIM HANNA, DIRECTOR OF ENVIRONMENTAL
AFFAIRS, STARBUCKS

According to Starbucks VP of Global Responsibility Ben Packard, the company's efforts to establish itself as a leading sustainable brand start with its *mission* — the statement of its organizational purpose (see Chapter 6). "We aim to take care of the communities that we depend on for our retail business by ... finding meaningful ways to be engaged with those communities," says Packard. "And we aim to take care of those communities where we source our core products, like coffee, tea, and cocoa." It's a matter of "nurturing the human spirit," explains Packard, who adds that incorporating that value into the firm's *culture* has allowed Starbucks to set and meet "very bold standards" in sustainability.

Starbucks sells hot and cold beverages out of more than 23,000 stores in 64 countries, and those stores account for about 80 percent of the company's *carbon footprint* — the total of its greenhouse gas emissions (primarily carbon dioxide). In order to reduce its footprint, Starbucks has set a series of realistic goals to be met by 2015, including the widespread recycling of the disposable cups that it hands out with almost every beverage sold — about 4 billion per year. Actually, those cups constitute only a miniscule fraction of Starbucks' carbon footprint,* but according to Jim Hanna, the company's director of environmental affairs, "perception is reality" when it comes to disposable cups: What most people see is the litter strewn about the streets or tumbling out of overflowing trash cans. By 2015, Starbucks intends to have front-of-store recycling bins in every North American store.

Before we go any further, we should point out that although Starbucks has incorporated sustainability practices into its operations since 1990, it hasn't always been as sensitive to environmental issues as some people would like. If you were hooked on your daily Starbucks latte or cappuccino before 2008, you might have noticed, next to the giant espresso machine, a sink called a "dipper well." Baristas used it to quick-rinse equipment, and the water was kept running to ensure that pipes stayed clean. Unfortunately, leaving the water running in 10,000 stores worldwide used up more than 6 million gallons of water per day — enough to fill an Olympic-size swimming pool every 83 minutes. The company had been warned that the dipper-well system wasn't good for its environmental reputation, but only after a blitz of bad PR in the global press did Starbucks finally turn off the water. Today, says Ben Packard, "we look at water on the supply side of coffee" — as a resource to be protected — and Starbucks has plans to cut in-store water consumption by 25 percent.

That goal is part of the company's Shared Planet Program, which was launched in 2008. A year later, Starbucks announced that, as part of the same initiative, all of its new stores would satisfy certification requirements for LEED (Leadership in Energy & Environmental Design), a rating system for the construction and operation of environment-friendly buildings. Because the guidelines were developed for office buildings, Starbucks helped to create programs for both new and renovated retail spaces, and 75 percent of all Starbucks locations opening in 2014 attained LEED certification. "My dream," says Jim Hanna, "is that we solve the cup issue and a customer walks into a store and says, 'Look at that ultra-efficient air conditioning unit.'"

By 2015, Starbucks also plans to "ethically source" 100 percent of the coffee that it buys from producers. Over the past 40 years, Starbucks has invested more than $70 million in programs to support sustainable and socially sound agricultural practices among the roughly 1 million people — most of them in Latin America — who represent its coffee supply chain. Programs include loans to help farmers develop not only sustainable growing practices but forest-conservation practices as well.

Since 2008, Starbucks has partnered with Conservation International (CI), a U.S.-based nonprofit environmental organization, to implement C.A.F.E. (Coffee and Farmer Equity) Practices — a set of independently developed guidelines for monitoring the economic, social, and environmental impact of coffee-production programs and practices. By 2012, 98 percent of the small coffee farms operating according to Starbucks-promoted C.A.F.E. practices had managed to improve soil fertility, and 100 percent of the school-age children on those farms were able to attend school.

CI chairman and CEO Peter Seligmann points out that Starbucks' sustainability efforts are motivated in large part by the need to deal with a major issue in the company's environment, both business and natural: namely, *climate change* — "figuring out how to ensure that coffee farming can be a part of the climate solution," as Ben Packard puts it. "The convergence of climate change and ecosystem deterioration," explains Seligmann, "is what creates stress on the ability of coffee farmers to produce crops." The coffee bean grows only in specific climates, and those climates are particularly vulnerable

---

* The nitrous oxide that puts the foam in whipped cream accounts for more of Starbucks' carbon footprint than all of its U.S. roasting operations combined.

to rising global temperatures. Thus if Starbucks intends to survive over the long term, it makes good business sense to ensure that it has access to its most important ingredient. "We're the canary in the coal mine," quips Hanna, likening the fate of the first victim of unbreathable air to the company's potential fate as one of the first victims of climate change.

Starbucks, then, sees sustainability as a matter of business survival, and if *business* isn't *the* operative word, at least it's at the top of the list. "If the only reason you're invested in sustainability is because it's the 'right thing to do,'" says Hanna,

"you're in trouble." A business enterprise needs to see some *return on investment*, and as Clarice Turner, Starbucks VP of U.S. business, puts it, that return "can manifest itself in many ways." Front-of-store recycling, for example, saves thousands of dollars annually in trash-hauling costs." Of course, says Turner, working to reduce the company's environmental impact "is the right thing to do," but she hastens to add that highly visible sustainability efforts also "put a halo on your brand and business, which is very real to both consumers and employees. If done right, those efforts have a tangible bottom-line impact."

## Case Questions

1. The term *sustainability* refers generally to the maintenance and preservation of systems and processes. At what types of systems and processes are Starbucks' sustainability efforts directed?

2. In what ways might Starbucks' sustainability efforts be affected by events in each dimension of its general *external environment—economic, technological, sociocultural, political-legal,* and *international*? In which dimensions can the company be most *proactive* in taking steps toward its sustainability goals? In which dimensions are events most likely to necessitate *reactive* steps?

3. In what ways might each group in Starbucks' *task environment—competitors, customers, suppliers, strategic*

*partners,* and *regulators*—be involved in its sustainability efforts? Be sure to include *competitors* in your answer. List each group in order of its importance to Starbucks' sustainability efforts; explain your ranking.

4. According to Ben Packard, "One of the strengths of Starbucks' culture is treating the people and places where our products come from and are served in a better way. Not delivering on that vision and mission would be a problem in the culture of this company."

Why is the management of its *culture* important to the success of the company's sustainability efforts? In what ways can Starbucks work to ensure that the values reflected in its sustainability commitment are embraced by members of the organization?

## Case References

Andrew Nusca, "In Sustainability, Starbucks Takes a Leading Role," *Smart Planet* (November 9, 2010), www.smartplanet.com, on June 26, 2014; Charley Cameron, "Interview: Eight Questions with Starbucks Global Responsibility VP Ben Packard," *Inhabitat* (May 12, 2014), http://inhabitat. com, on June 26, 2014; Christina Williams, "Starbucks Sustainability Leader Urges Others to Make the Business Case," *Portland* (OR) *Business Journal* (December 5, 2012), www.bizjournals.com, on June 26, 2014; Philip Victor, "Starbucks Wasting More Than 6 Million Gallons of Water a Day," ABC News (October 6, 2008), http://abcnews.go.com, on June 28, 2014;

Claudia Girrbach, "How Starbucks Took the Lead on LEED," *GreenBiz.com* (October 28, 2010), www.greenbiz.com, on June 26, 2014; Conservation International, "CI and Starbucks Recognize That Forests and Coffee Farmers Can Be Solutions to Climate Change" (2014), www.conservation. org, on June 26, 2014; Jennifer Elks, "Starbucks Expands Ethical Sourcing Efforts with New Global Agronomy Center," *Sustainable Brands* (March 20, 2013), www.sustainablebrands.com, on June 27, 2014; National Restaurant Association, "Starbucks: Sustainability Pays Off in Dollars and Sense" (March 12, 2014), www.restaurant.org, on June 26, 2014.

## YOU MAKE THE CALL    Putting Miscommunication in Context

1. Think of the categories of the *task environment— competitors, customers, suppliers, strategic partners, regulators*—as groups of people with whom you might need to carry on some form of cross-cultural communication. First, rank the five categories in order of *importance* when it comes to ensuring effective communications. What factors did you consider when ranking the groups in order of importance? Next, rank them in order of *difficulty.* What factors did you consider when ranking them in order of difficulty? How did the issue of *cultural context* affect both of your rankings?

2. In what ways—both positive and negative—might an *organization's culture* reinforce the role of interpersonal and communications norms among its members? Under what circumstances might an organization find it advantageous to adjust the effects of cultural context on communications, both with people inside the organization and with people outside of it? What practical steps might an organization take to adjust the effects of cultural context on its communications practices?

3. Log on to the front page of Facebook—the one intended for Americans. Look it over and then log on to

*(Continued)*

the front page of Weibo, the Chinese version of Facebook. Needless to say, each is designed for an audience with cultural norms that favor different types of communication. Leaving aside the fact that you probably can't read anything on the Weibo page, what sorts of generalizations can you make about the difference in communications norms between the American and Chinese audiences targeted by the ads?

4. For each of the five items in the table below, check *1, 2, 3, 4,* or *5* to indicate your tendencies and preferences in a work situation.* The questionnaire is abbreviated, and you don't have to worry about scoring. Once you've finished, give some thought to your responses and try to draw some broad conclusions about the *cultural context* in which you're most comfortable—*high* or *low.*

| CULTURAL CONTEXT INVENTORY | | Hardly ever | Sometimes | | | Almost always |
|---|---|---|---|---|---|---|
| | | 1 | 2 | 3 | 4 | 5 |
| 1. | When communicating, I tend to use a lot of facial expressions, hand gestures, and body movements rather than relying mostly on words. | | | | | |
| 2. | When communicating, I tend to spell things out quickly and directly rather than talking around and adding to the point. | | | | | |
| 3. | I describe myself in terms of my accomplishments rather than in terms of my family relationships. | | | | | |
| 4. | I prefer working on one thing at a time to working on a variety of things at once. | | | | | |
| 5. | In figuring out problems, I prefer focusing on the whole situation to focusing on specific parts or taking one step at a time. | | | | | |

*Questionnaire by Claire B. Halverson. Adapted from Bruce La Back, ed., "What's Up with Culture?" *On-Line Cultural Resource for Training Abroad* (University of the Pacific, 2014), www2.pacific.edu, on July 16, 2014.

# Endnotes

1  "Avoid Miscommunication When Conducting International Business," *Western Union* (2013), http://onlinefx.westernunion.com, on July 11, 2014; Darren Lingley, "Apologies Across Cultures: An Analysis of Intercultural Communication Problems Raised in the *Ehime Maru* Incident," *The Asian EFL Journal,* 2006, Vol. 8, No. 1, www.asian-efl-journal.com, on July 11, 2014; Mike Lambert, "Ten Years Later—Japanese Continue to Mourn Their Loss—*Ehime Maru* Sinking," *I Like the Cut of His Jib!!* (February 10, 2011), http://navycaptain-therealnavy.blogspot.com, on July 12, 2014; Anita Stokes Thomas, "One Message, Many Cultures: Best Practices for Global Communication," *Cross-Cultural Internal Communication* 2008, Vol. 6, No. 4, www.iabc.com, on July 14, 2014; Brett Rutledge, "Cultural Differences—High Context versus Low Context," *The Articulate CEO* (August 21, 2011), http://thearticulateceo.typepad.com, on July 14, 2014; Cornelius Grove and Willa Hallowell, "Expats from Abroad in the U.S.A.: Six Steps to Effective Integration" (1999) (Grovewell LLC: Professional Knowledge Center, 2014), www.grovewell.com, on July 11, 2014.

2  Arie de Geus, *The Living Company—Habits for Surviving in a Turbulent Business Environment* (Boston: Harvard Business School Press, 1997). See also John G. Sifonis and Beverly Goldberg, *Corporation on a Tightrope* (New York: Oxford University Press, 1996), for an interesting discussion of how organizations must navigate through the environment.

3  Eric D. Beinhocker, "Robust Adaptive Strategies," *Sloan Management Review* (Spring 1999), pp. 95–105; see also John Crotts, Duncan Dickson, and Robert Ford, "Aligning Organizational Processes with Mission: The Case of Service Excellence," *Academy of Management Executive,* 2005, Vol. 19, No. 3,

pp. 54–63; Sebastian Raisch and Julian Birkinshaw, "Organizational Ambidexterity: Antecedents, Outcomes, and Moderators," *Journal of Management,* 2008, Vol. 34, No. 3, pp. 375–409.

4  *Fortune,* March 16, 2009, p. 111.

5  See Jay B. Barney and William G. Ouchi (eds.), *Organizational Economics* (San Francisco: Jossey-Bass, 1986), for a detailed analysis of linkages between economics and organizations.

6  See, for example, "Political Pendulum Swings Toward Stricter Regulation," *Wall Street Journal,* March 24, 2008, pp. A1, A11; see also "Changing Safety Rules Perplex and Polarize," *USA Today,* February 5, 2009, pp. 1B, 2B; Nina Easton and Telis Demos, "The Business Guide to Congress," *Fortune,* May 11, 2009, pp. 72–75.

7  See Ricky Griffin and Michael Pustay, *International Business: A Managerial Perspective,* 8th ed. (Upper Saddle River, NJ: Prentice Hall, 2015), for an overview.

8  See "U.S. Firms Eager for More Access to Cuba" *USA Today,* January 13, 2015, p. 5B.

9  For example, see Susanne G. Scott and Vicki R. Lane, "A Stakeholder Approach to Organizational Identity," *Academy of Management Review,* 2000, Vol. 25, No. 1, pp. 43–62.

10  "Rising Retailer Threat: Liquidations," *Wall Street Journal,* December 12, 2008, p. B1.

11  "McDonald's Slows its Roll," *USA Today,* December 8, 2014, p. 1B.

12  Richard N. Osborn and John Hagedoorn, "The Institutionalization and Evolutionary Dynamics of Interorganizational Alliances and Networks," *Academy*

*of Management Journal*, April 1997, pp. 261–278. See also "More Companies Cut Risk by Collaborating with Their 'Enemies,'" *Wall Street Journal*, January 31, 2000, pp. A1, A10.

13  "Disney, Spielberg to Team Up," *Wall Street Journal*, January 10, 2009, p. B7.

14  "Behind Sony-Samsung Rivalry, An Unlikely Alliance Develops," *Wall Street Journal*, January 13, 2006, p. A1.

15  "Drone Limits Don't Deter Firms," *USA Today*, February 17, 2015, p. 1B.

16  "Watchdogs Hound E-Waste Exports," *USA Today*, December 30, 2008, pp. 1B, 2B.

17  "Group Urges Caramel Coloring in Colas be Banned," *USA Today*, February 21, 2011, p. 1B.

18  "The Best & Worst Boards," *BusinessWeek*, October 7, 2002, pp. 104–114. See also Amy Hillman and Thomas Dalziel, "Boards of Directors and Firm Performance: Integrating Agency and Resource Dependence Perspectives," *Academy of Management Review*, 2003, Vol. 23, No. 3, pp. 383–396.

19  "The Wild New Workforce," *BusinessWeek*, December 6, 1999, pp. 38–44.

20  "Temporary Workers Getting Short Shrift," *USA Today*, April 11, 1997, pp. 1B, 2B.

21  "Don't Get Too Cozy," *Bloomberg Businessweek*, September 22–28, 2014, pp. 51–52.

22  Terrence E. Deal and Allan A. Kennedy, *Corporate Cultures: The Rights and Rituals of Corporate Life* (Reading, MA: Addison-Wesley, 1982).

23  http://www.gsb.stanford.edu/insights/netflix-founder-reed-hastings-make-few-decisions-possible

24  Jay B. Barney, "Organizational Culture: Can It Be a Source of Sustained Competitive Advantage?" *Academy of Management Review*, July 1986, pp. 656–665.

25  For example, see Carol J. Loomis, "Sam Would Be Proud," *Fortune*, April 17, 2000, pp. 131–144. See also Yair Berson, Shaul Oreg, and Taly Dvir, "CEO Values, Organizational Culture, and Firm Outcomes," *Journal of Organizational Behavior*, 2008, Vol. 29, pp. 615–633.

26  "United Continental: How the Mega-Carrier Works," *Fortune*, May 2, 2011, pp. 50–57.

27  "Taking the Hill Less Climbed," *The Economist*, October 29, 2010.

28  See Tomothy Galpin, "Connecting Culture to Organizational Change," *HR Magazine*, March 1996, pp. 84–94.

29  "Employment and Earnings, 2013 Annual Averages and the Monthly Labor Review," U.S. Department of Labor, Bureau of Labor Statistics, April 2014.

30  Gail Robinson and Kathleen Dechant, "Building a Business Case for Diversity," *Academy of Management Executive*, August 1997, pp. 21–31. See also Orlando C. Richard, "Racial Diversity, Business Strategy, and Firm Performance: A Resource-Based View," *Academy of Management Journal*, 2000, Vol. 43, No. 2, pp. 164–177.

31  "How to Manage an Aging Workforce," *The Economist*, February 18, 2006, p. 11.

32  *HR Magazine*, May 2011, pp. 24–25. See also Sean Lyons and Lisa Kuron, "Generational Differences in the Workplace: A Review of the Evidence and Directions for Future Research," *Journal of Organizational Behavior*, 2014, Vol. 35, No. S1, pp. S139–S157.

33  "Number of Women Managers Barely Grows," *CNN Money*, September 28, 2010. See also "Boardrooms Globally Are Heavily Male," *USA Today*, January 13, 2015, p. 6B.

34  Patricia Sellers, "The 50 Most Powerful Women in Business," *Fortune*, November 14, 2014, pp. 125–170.

35  http://www.census.gov/newsroom/releases/archives/population/cb12-243.html (accessed on January 6, 2015).

36  "The Power of Diversity: Who's Got the Clout?" *Fortune*, August 22, 2005, special issue.

37  *USA Today*, November 6, 2014, p. 1B.

38  For a recent review, see Allen C. Bluedorn, "Pilgrim's Progress: Trends and Convergence in Research on Organizational Size and Environments," *Journal of Management*, 1993, Vol. 19, No. 2, pp. 163–191.

39  James D. Thompson, *Organizations in Action* (New York: McGraw-Hill, 1967).

40  Michael E. Porter, *Competitive Strategy: Techniques for Analyzing Industries and Competitors* (New York: Free Press, 1980). See also Joel A. C. Baum and Helaine J. Korn, "Competitive Dynamics of Interfirm Rivalry," *Academy of Management Journal*, April 1996, pp. 255–291.

41  "United Plans Huge Jet Order," *Wall Street Journal*, June 4, 2009, pp. A1, A10.

42  "Starting Over," *Fortune*, January 21, 2002, pp. 50–68.

43  "Toyota Rations Japanese Parts; Honda to Cut Hours," *USA Today*, March 30, 2011, p. 1B.

44  Bala Chakravarthy, "A New Strategy Framework for Coping with Turbulence," *Sloan Management Review*, Winter 1997, pp. 69–82.

45  "Companies Devise Strategies for Flu Interruptions," *Wall Street Journal*, May 4, 2009, p. B4.

46  "G.M. Pieces Together Japanese Supply Chain," *New York Times*, May 13, 2011, p. 5.

47  See Magali A. Delmas and Michael W. Toffel, "Organizational Responses to Environmental Demands: Opening the Black Box," *Strategic Management Journal*, 2008, Vol. 29, pp. 1027–1055.

48  http://www.fastcompany.com/3034022/hit-the-ground-running/panera-breads-ceo-attempts-to-innovate-the-way-we-order-sandwiches)

49  "In Wooing AT&T, SBC Has Eye on Business Customers," *Wall Street Journal*, January 28, 2005, pp. A1, A2.

50  Sean Lux, T. Russell Crook, and David Woehr, "Mixing Business with Politics: A Meta-Analysis of the Antecedents and Outcomes of Corporate Political Activity," *Journal of Management*, January 2011, pp. 223–247.

©Markus Pfaff/Shutterstock.com

# 4

# RESPONDING TO THE ETHICAL AND SOCIAL ENVIRONMENT

**Learning Outcomes**

**After studying this chapter, you should be able to:**

1. Discuss managerial ethics, three areas of special ethical concern for managers, and how organizations manage ethical behavior.

2. Identify and summarize key emerging ethical issues in organizations today.

3. Discuss the concept of social responsibility, specify to whom or what an organization might be considered responsible, and describe four types of organizational approaches to social responsibility.

4. Explain the relationship between the government and organizations regarding social responsibility.

5. Describe some of the activities organizations may engage in to manage social responsibility.

## MANAGEMENT IN ACTION   Management by Objectionable Behavior

### "I'm a bit of a dirty guy, but people like that right now."

—AMERICAN APPAREL FOUNDER AND FORMER
CEO DOV CHARNEY

On June 17, 2014, American Apparel's then-CEO Dov Charney took a red-eye from Los Angeles to New York for the annual meeting with his handpicked board of directors. Shortly after the meeting convened, things took an unexpected turn, at least from Charney's perspective. He was fired for misconduct. Or, to put it more precisely, he was given an ultimatum: resign (with a multimillion-dollar severance package and a four-year consulting contract) or be fired. Charney's termination letter charged, in part:

> Your conduct has required the Company to incur significant and unwarranted expenses, including expenses associated with litigation and defense costs, significant settlement payments, and substantial severance packages. … The resources American Apparel had to dedicate to defend the numerous lawsuits resulting from your conduct,

> and the loss of critical, qualified Company employees as a result of your misconduct cannot be overlooked.[1]

Just what sort of "misconduct" had Charney engaged in? For one thing, the CEO who kept a makeshift boudoir at the company distribution facility and was known to run around headquarters in his underwear made no secret of his idiosyncratic attitudes toward sex both in and out of the office. In one well-publicized incident, Charney invited an interviewer from *Jane* magazine to spectate multiple sexual activities, at least one of which didn't require a partner. "I'm a bit of a dirty guy," he informed Claudine Ko, "but people like that right now."

More to the point of his firing, Charney, as the board charged, had obligated the company to defend "numerous lawsuits," most (but not all) of them revolving around similarly libertine behavior. In one, a former female employee accused Charney of using her as a sex slave and sought damages of $260 million. Charney responded that he had photos showing that Irene Morales was not a victim in any of the activities she

Dov Charney, former CEO of American Apparel, was accused of several instances of poor judgment and questionable conduct. His alleged transgressions finally reached the point at which the firm's board of directors felt they had no choice but to push him out.

Keith Bedford/Bloomberg/Getty Images

cited. The American Apparel (APP) board did not object to Charney's using the photos in his defense, and they were sent to several newspapers and websites. An arbitrator dismissed Morales's claims but ruled that APP was responsible for the actions of an employee who had brought the photos to light in the first place by creating a false blog under Morales's name. To settle the charge of allowing an employee to set up what the Washington *Post* called "a revenge porn blog," APP reportedly paid Morales $700,000.

In another case, the manager of an APP outlet in Malibu accused Charney of assault, claiming that the CEO had rubbed dirt in his face because he didn't like the store's appearance or performance. The company responded that Michael Bumblis's story was "entirely contrived or wildly exaggerated." Bumblis, however, had access to the store's security cameras and brought his case before a Los Angeles court. American Apparel defended the case by citing the company's employee agreement, which forbids workers from filing claims against the firm or revealing anything about the personal life of its CEO. The document also stipulates that anyone who breaks the agreement can be sued for $1 million. The judge called the contract "unconscionable" and denied the company's request to take the case to confidential arbitration.

APP is currently appealing the ruling, which is a potential blow not only to Charney but to the firm itself, which has routinely responded to allegations against its CEO by citing the employee agreement and forcing plaintiffs into arbitration. In the wake of the Morales case, for example, four more former employees had filed suits against Charney and APP, with one young woman charging that Charney had sexually assaulted her during an ostensible hiring interview. APP argued that the four plaintiffs had conspired to "shake down" the company and its CEO, who called the accusations "frivolous." All four cases were either dismissed or settled out of court by an arbitrator.

By the time Charney was fired, however, APP was facing no fewer than nine lawsuits charging him with various degrees of sexual harassment. Charney argued that the board's new charges of misconduct referred to old charges of misconduct and reminded them that he hadn't been sued in nearly two years. Besides, he said, business was picking up. The board stood its ground, but so did Charney, who refused to resign. Instead, he consulted his lawyer, who claimed that the board's

decision hinged on "activities that occurred long ago (if at all) and about which the Board and Company have had knowledge for years."

Indeed, as Charney engaged in stock and loan maneuvers to hold on to the company that he'd founded in 1998 and taken public in 2007, many people in the industry were asking "Why now?" Why had the board waited so long to unload its controversial CEO? There's no doubt that Charney, who had turned APP into a manufacturer-wholesaler-retailer with 249 stores in 20 countries, had once been APP's most valuable asset. By 2012, however, the company had failed to turn a profit for four years. Losses for the period totaled $270 million, and the company twice teetered on the brink of bankruptcy—all despite increasing revenues. The problem was debt: APP was persistently burdened with increasingly heavy payments on borrowed money.

Charney admitted that "the largest of all expenses is interest" but was convinced that "we can pay that down in cash." He also maintained that "we can refinance our debt when we're earning more money." As of 2013, however, APP still needed additional financing, and the board apparently felt that the CEO's financial strategy was failing. In finally deciding to fire Charney, the board thus drew a connection between his conduct and the company's financial struggles: "The Company," said Charney's letter of termination, "has had a very difficult time raising capital and securing debt financing … because of your actions. Indeed, many financing sources have refused to become involved with American Apparel as long as you remain involved with the company."

Board member Allan Mayer, a Hollywood crisis-management expert whom Charney had installed on the board in 2007, explained that the board's timing was a matter of finding the right opportunity to risk removing Charney. He was, of course, an increasingly embarrassing (and expensive) CEO, but as the company's largest individual stockholder, Charney was also in a position to challenge the board's effectiveness in implementing its decision. As one expert in corporate governance put it, "Terminating a founder with a lot of stock is dangerous." In APP's case, the board's efforts to deal with the company's financial problems might have been seriously hampered by Charney's challenge, resulting in further lack of confidence on the part of potential lenders. "I know there's a lot of people who have criticized us for not taking action earlier than we did," said Mayer. "But you don't want to embark on a course of action that will bring down the whole house."

Why did the board finally consider the time right? According to Thomas White, a professor of business ethics at Loyola Marymount University, the answer is fairly straightforward: "All along," he says, "the APP board was thinking that anything goes in Charneyville. They only started to worry when they looked up and saw financial disaster."

As of October 1, 2014, Dov Charney was still employed by APP as a consultant. He was last spotted visiting stores and yelling instructions to employees. APP had no comment.

---

Managers, executives, and entrepreneurs are all unique, and their behaviors run the gamut from prim-and-proper to wild-and-crazy. Most fall somewhere in between, though, and generally engage in behaviors that are appropriate for prevailing social and business norms. When people behave in ways that violate those norms in ways that are damaging to their businesses, however, their employers likely need to take some form of action ranging from a reprimand to outright termination. The conduct of individual managers is often assessed in terms of ethical standards and organizational activity in terms of social responsibility.

This chapter explores the basic issues of ethics and social responsibility in detail. We first look at individual ethics and their organizational context and then note several emerging ethical issues in organizations today. Next, we expand our discussion to the more general subject of social responsibility. After we explore the relationships between businesses and the government regarding socially responsible behavior, we examine the activities organizations sometimes undertake to be more socially responsible.

## Individual Ethics in Organizations

We define ethics as one's personal beliefs about whether a behavior, action, or decision is right or wrong.[2] Note that we define ethics in the context of the individual—people have ethics; organizations do not. Likewise, what constitutes ethical behavior varies from one person to another. For example, one person who finds a 20-dollar bill on the floor of an empty room believes that it is okay to keep it, whereas another feels compelled to turn it in to the lost-and-found department. Further, although ethical behavior is in the eye of the beholder, it usually refers to behavior that conforms to generally accepted social norms. Unethical behavior, then, is behavior that does not conform to generally accepted social norms.

A society generally adopts formal laws that reflect the prevailing ethical standards—the social norms—of its citizens. For example, because most people consider theft to be unethical, laws have been passed to make such behaviors illegal and to prescribe ways of punishing those who do steal. But although laws are designed to be clear and unambiguous, their application and interpretation still lead to ethical ambiguities. For example, almost everyone would agree that forcing employees to

**ethics**
One's personal beliefs about whether a behavior, action, or decision is right or wrong

**ethical behavior**
Behavior that conforms to generally accepted social norms

**unethical behavior**
Behavior that does not conform to generally accepted social norms

Ethical conduct is becoming increasingly important in today's dynamic business world. But how are our ethics formed? One early context that influences our personal ethics is what we see others do. This child, for example, is watching his mother work from home. How she conducts herself and what she says and does in front of him may play a role in his own ethical standards later in life.

"I just think that if you're going to try to run an organization that's very cost-conscious, then you can't have those disparities. Having an individual who is making 100 or 200 or 300 times more than the average person working on the floor is wrong."

—JIM SENEGAL, COSTCO CEO[4]

work excessive hours, especially for no extra compensation, is unethical. Accordingly, laws have been established to define work and pay standards. But applying the law to organizational settings can still result in ambiguous situations, which can be interpreted in different ways.

A person's ethics are determined by a combination of factors. People start to form ethical standards as children, in response to their perceptions of their parents' and other adults' behaviors and in response to the behaviors they are allowed to choose. As children grow and enter school, they are also influenced by peers with whom they interact every day. Myriad important individual events shape people's lives and contribute to their ethical beliefs and behavior as they grow into adulthood. Values and morals also contribute to ethical standards, as do religious beliefs. People who place financial gain and personal advancement at the top of their list of priorities, for example, will adopt personal codes of ethics that promote the pursuit of wealth. Thus they may be ruthless in their efforts to gain these rewards, regardless of the costs to others. In contrast, people who clearly establish their family and friends as their top priorities will adopt different ethical standards.

## Managerial Ethics

Managerial ethics are the standards of behavior that guide individual managers in their work.[3] Although ethics can affect managerial work in any number of ways, three areas of special concern for managers are shown in Figure 4.1.

**How an Organization Treats Its Employees** One important area of managerial ethics is the treatment of employees by the organization. This area includes policies such as hiring and firing, wages and working conditions, and employee privacy and respect. For example, both ethical and legal guidelines suggest that hiring and firing decisions should be based solely on one's ability to perform the job. A manager who discriminates against women in hiring is exhibiting both unethical and illegal behavior. But consider the case of a manager who does not discriminate in general, but who hires a family friend when other applicants might be just as qualified. Although this and similar hiring decisions may not be illegal, they may be objectionable on ethical grounds.

Wages and working conditions, although tightly regulated, are also areas for potential controversy. For example, a manager paying an employee less than he deserves, simply because the manager knows the employee cannot afford to quit or risk losing his job by complaining, might be considered unethical. The same goes for his benefits, especially if an organization takes action that affects the compensation packages—and welfare—of an entire workforce.

"[The alleged theft of corporate documents is] the clearest imaginable case of corporate espionage, theft of trade secrets, unfair competition, and computer fraud."

—STARWOOD LEGAL FILINGS AGAINST HILTON[5]

Our *Leading the Way* feature illustrates some innovative ways that a leader can foster a company culture centered around trust and ethical behavior.

Finally, most observers would also agree that an organization is obligated to protect the privacy of its employees. If a manager gossips to others at work that one of their coworkers has an STD or is having an affair, most people would see that as an unethical breach of privacy. Likewise, the manner in which an organization addresses issues associated with sexual harassment involves employee privacy and related rights.

**managerial ethics**
Standards of behavior that guide individual managers in their work

**How Employees Treat the Organization** Many ethical issues also stem from how employees treat the organization, especially in regard to conflicts of interest, secrecy and confidentiality, and honesty. A conflict of interest occurs when a decision potentially benefits the individual to the possible detriment of the organization. To guard against such

## FIGURE 4.1  MANAGERIAL ETHICS

The three basic areas of concern for managerial ethics are the relationships of the firm to the employee, the employee to the firm, and the firm to other economic agents. Managers need to approach each set of relationships from an ethical and moral perspective.

practices, most companies have policies that forbid their buyers to accept gifts from suppliers. Divulging company secrets is also clearly unethical. Employees who work for businesses in highly competitive industries—electronics, software, and fashion apparel, for example—might be tempted to sell information about company plans to competitors. A third area of concern is honesty in general. Relatively common problems in this area include such activities as using a business telephone to make personal long-distance calls, stealing supplies, and padding expense accounts.

In recent years, new issues regarding such behaviors as personal Internet use at work have also become more pervasive. Another disturbing trend is that more workers are calling in sick simply to get extra time off. One survey, for instance, found that the number of workers who reported taking more time off for personal needs was increasing substantially. A recent CareerBuilder survey found that 32 percent of workers surveyed admitted to having called in sick when they were actually well.[6] And yet another survey found that two-thirds of U.S. workers who call in sick do so for reasons other than illness. On a different front, 30 percent of the companies sampled in another study reported that they had found fake references on the resumes of job seekers. Although most employees are basically honest, organizations must nevertheless be vigilant to avoid problems resulting from such behaviors.

**LEADING THE WAY**

# Happy Fit

Tony Hsieh (pronounced *Shay*), the son of Taiwanese immigrants, started his first company in 1996, just after he graduated from Harvard. LinkExchange was an ingenious Internet advertising network that permitted members to exchange ad space on their own sites for space on other members' sites. Two and a half years later, Hsieh and his partner sold their company to Microsoft for $265 million. It wasn't the money, says Hsieh; LinkExchange just wasn't a fun place to work at anymore.

"It worked great," he recalls, "until we got to about 15 or 20 people, and then we ran out of friends to hire. So then we started hiring people who had all the right skill sets but weren't necessarily great for the company culture. By the time we got to 100 people, I myself dreaded getting out of bed in the morning." He knew it was time to move on, recalls Hsieh, when "the culture just went completely downhill."

What does Hsieh want in a company culture? "For me," he says, "the initial motivation was what would make me happy. … If I was going to go to an office, I wanted it to be with people I would choose to be around even if we didn't have to work together." Fortunately, Hsieh had a choice of the office he worked in and the people he worked with. He originally joined an online shoe retailer as an investor and advisor but soon became co-CEO, and the company, now known as Zappos, reached two of his chief goals by 2008: It topped $1 billion in sales (two years early) and made *Fortune* magazine's list (at #23) of the "Top 100 Companies to Work For."

In November 2009, Hsieh and his partners sold Zappos to Amazon for $1.2 billion. Amazon agreed to let its new acquisition operate independently, and Hsieh agreed to stay on as CEO—for a salary of $36,000. "That's my way of making sure that I'm actually there for my own happiness," explains Hsieh, "not for the money." This time, he was determined to foster the kind of company culture that he deemed optimum for both personal satisfaction and business success:

"I didn't want to repeat the same mistake I'd made at" LinkExchange, where, he admits, we hadn't "paid any attention to company culture [because] we just didn't know any better."

As far as Hsieh is concerned, "company culture is all about making employees happy," and Zappos is certainly an employee-friendly workplace: cafeteria food is free, for instance, and the company covers all medical benefits. In November 2013, however, Hsieh unveiled plans to take his concept of "company culture" a giant step further: By the end of 2014, he announced, Zappos would be a full-fledged *holacracy*. It's one of the latest concepts in radical management, and, basically, it calls for two things that should make employees happy: Bosses quit being bosses, and all employees are authorized to do whatever they want (especially to experiment with innovative ideas) until they entirely screw up. The CEO gives up his centralized authority, and the whole company is reorganized into decentralized teams, usually called "circles," that choose their own goals and assign their own roles in order to perform whatever organizational task needs to be done.

According to Hsieh, holacracy holds out the possibility of turning the bureaucratic model of organization into one that reflects the model of a city. He points out that when cities double in size, innovation and productivity per citizen go up by 15 percent, whereas corporations that double in size typically decline on both measures. Why? "In a city," says Hsieh, "people are self-organizing." He wants Zappos to "function more like a city and less like an organization" because self-organized employees "actually increase the innovation and productivity of an organization." In theory, everyone should be happier.

*References:* Rob Wallace and Marc Dorian, "More Than Money: Surprising Stories of the Superrich and How They Gave Back," ABC News (October 28, 2011), http://abcnews.go.com, on July 21, 2014; Peter Hopkins, "*Big Think* Interview with Tony Hsieh," *Big Think* (October, 11, 2010), http://bigthink.com, on July 22, 2014; Gregory Ferenstein, "Zappos Just Abolished Bosses: Inside Tech's Latest Management Craze," *Vox* (July 11, 2014), www.vox.com, on July 21, 2014; Nicole Leinbach-Reyhle, "Shedding Hierarchy: Could Zappos Be Setting an Innovative Trend?" *Forbes* (July 15, 2014), forbes.com on July 21, 2014.

**How Employees and the Organization Treat Other Economic Agents** Managerial ethics also come into play in the relationship between the firm and its employees with other economic agents. As shown in Figure 4.1, the primary agents of interest include customers, competitors, stockholders, suppliers, dealers, and unions. The interactions between the organization and these agents that may be subject to ethical ambiguity include advertising and promotions, financial disclosures, ordering and purchasing, shipping and solicitations, bargaining and negotiation, and other business relationships.

For example, state pharmacy boards are charged with overseeing prescription drug safety in the United States. All told, there are almost 300 pharmacists who serve on such boards. It was recently reported that 72 of these pharmacists were employees of major drugstore chains and supermarket pharmacies. These arrangements, while legal, could create the potential for conflicts of interest, because they might give the pharmacist's employers influence over the regulatory system designed to monitor their own business practices.[7]

An ethical issue of growing concern today is the increase in the number of prospective employees who falsify or exaggerate their accomplishments on their resumes. In one recent study, for example, nearly one-third of the companies in the study reported finding fake references on the resumes of job seekers.

Another area of concern in recent years involves financial reporting by some e-commerce firms. Because of the complexities inherent in valuing the assets and revenues of these firms, some of them have been very aggressive in presenting their financial positions in a highly positive light. In at least a few cases, some firms have substantially overstated their earnings projections to entice more investment. After Time-Warner merged with AOL, it discovered that its new online partner had overstated its value through various inappropriate accounting methods. Some of today's accounting scandals in traditional firms have stemmed from similarly questionable practices.[8]

Hilton Hotels hired two senior executives away from rival Starwood Hotels. It was later determined that the executives took eight boxes of electronic and paper documents with them; much of the material in the boxes related to Starwood's plans and details for starting a new luxury hotel brand. When Hilton subsequently announced plans to start a similar chain itself, to be called Denizen Hotels, officials at Starwood became suspicious and investigated. When they learned about the theft of confidential materials, which Hilton subsequently returned, Starwood filed a lawsuit against the two executives and Hilton.[9]

Additional complexities faced by many firms today include the variations in ethical business practices in different countries. In some countries, bribes and side payments are a normal and customary part of doing business. However, U.S. laws forbid these practices, even if a firm's rivals from other countries are paying them. For example, a U.S. power-generating company lost a $320 million contract in the Middle East because government officials demanded a $3 million bribe. A Japanese firm paid the bribe and won the contract. Another major American company had a big project in India cancelled because newly elected officials demanded bribes. Although such payments are illegal under U.S. law, other situations are more ambiguous. In China, for example, local journalists expect their cab fare to be paid if they are covering a business-sponsored news conference. In Indonesia, it normally takes more than a year for a foreigner to get a driver's license, but the process can be "expedited" for an extra $100. In Romania, building inspectors routinely expect a "tip" for a favorable review.[10] And in 2009 the government of

"[Enron] took on the monopolies. I believe we were on the side of consumers. I was proud walking into the lobby.... By making things happen, we were making the world better."

—JEFFREY SKILLING, FORMER ENRON CEO[12]

Bahrain charged Alcoa with involvement in a 15-year conspiracy involving overcharging, fraud, and bribery. Bahrain and Alcoa subsequently agreed to a $384 million settlement.[11]

## Ethics in an Organizational Context

Of course, although ethics are an individual phenomenon, ethical or unethical actions by particular managers do not occur in a vacuum. Indeed, they most often occur in an organizational context that is conducive to them. Actions of peer managers and top managers, as well as the organization's culture, all contribute to the ethical context of the organization.[13]

The starting point in understanding the ethical context of management is, of course, the person's own ethical standards. Some people, for example, would risk personal embarrassment or lose their jobs before they would do something unethical. Other people are much more easily swayed by the unethical behavior they see around them and by other situational factors, and they may even be willing to commit major crimes to further their own careers or for financial gains. Organizational practices may strongly influence the ethical standards of employees. Some organizations openly permit unethical business practices as long as they are in the firm's best interests.

If managers become aware of unethical practices and allow them to continue, they contribute to an organization culture that says such activity is permitted. For example, Equinox Payments (formerly Hypercom Corporation), a Phoenix company that makes card-swiping machines for retailers, came under fire because of the actions and alleged wrongdoing of a senior marketing executive named Jairo Gonzalez. Gonzalez was accused of rape by his former secretary (she was paid a $100,000 settlement by the firm), and three other women accused him of sexual harassment. He also set up his own outside business—run by his father—to charge Hypercom for handling overseas shipping. Gonzalez got a job for his girlfriend at a video production firm used by Hypercom in Miami; when she moved to Phoenix, the firm switched its account to the video production firm she joined there. But the firm's CEO, George Wallner, defended his decision to retain Gonzalez because of the huge revenues Gonzalez generated. In Wallner's words, "He [is] bringing in $70 million a year. Do you fire your number one rock star because he's difficult?" Regarding the payment to Gonzalez's former secretary, Wallner asserted, "On a moral level this is confusing. But if you think of only the business decision, it was dead right." Perhaps it is not surprising, then, that another Hypercom manager married a temp and then got her a job at the firm, or that Wallner and his brother borrowed $4.5 million from the firm, some of it interest free.

The organization's environment also contributes to the context for ethical behavior. In a highly competitive or regulated industry, for example, a manager may feel more pressure to achieve high performance. When managers feel pressure to meet goals or lower costs, they may explore a variety of alternatives to help achieve these ends. And, in some cases, the alternative they choose may be unethical or even illegal.

## Managing Ethical Behavior

Spurred partially by increased awareness of ethics scandals in business and partially by a sense of enhanced corporate consciousness about the importance of ethical and unethical behaviors, many organizations have reemphasized ethical behavior on the part of employees. This emphasis takes many forms, but any effort to enhance ethical behavior must begin with top management. It is top managers, for example, who establish the organization's culture and define what will and will not be acceptable behavior. Some companies also offer employees training in how to cope with ethical dilemmas. At Boeing, for example, line managers lead training sessions for other employees, and the company also has an ethics committee that reports directly to the board of directors. The training sessions involve discussions of different ethical dilemmas that employees might face and how managers might handle those dilemmas. Citibank and Xerox also have ethics training programs for their managers.[14]

**Creating Ethics Codes** Some organizations also go to even greater lengths to formalize their ethical standards. Some, such as General Mills and Johnson & Johnson, have guidelines that detail how employees are to treat suppliers, customers, competitors, and other constituents. Others, such as Whirlpool, Texas Instruments, and Hewlett-Packard, have formal codes of ethics—written statements of the values and ethical standards that guide the firms' actions. Of course, firms must adhere to such codes if they are to be of value. In one now-infamous case, Enron's board of directors voted to set aside the firm's code of ethics to implement a business plan that violated the code.[15]

Codes of ethics guide the firms' actions by outlining its values and ethical standards.

And, of course, no code, guideline, or training program can truly make up for the quality of one's personal judgment about what are right and what are wrong behaviors in a particular situation. Such devices may prescribe what people should do, but they often fail to help people understand and live with the consequences of their choices. Making ethical choices, for instance, may lead to very unpleasant outcomes—firing, rejection by colleagues, and forfeiture of monetary gain, to name a few. Thus managers must be prepared to confront their own consciences and weigh the options available when making difficult ethical decisions.[16]

**Applying Moral Judgment** Unfortunately, what distinguishes ethical from unethical behavior is often subjective and subject to differences of opinion. So how does one go about deciding whether a particular action or decision is ethical? Traditionally, experts have suggested a three-step model for applying ethical judgments to situations that may arise during the course of business activities. These steps are: (1) Gather the relevant factual information, (2) determine the most appropriate moral values, and (3) make an ethical judgment based on the rightness or wrongness of the proposed activity or policy.

**code of ethics**
A formal, written statement of the values and ethical standards that guide a firm's actions

But the analysis is seldom as simple as these steps might imply. For instance, what if the facts are not clear-cut? What if there are no agreed-upon moral values? Nevertheless, a judgment and a decision must be made. Experts point out that, otherwise, trust is impossible, and trust, they add, is indispensable to any business transaction. Thus, to more completely assess the ethics of a particular behavior, a more complete perspective is necessary. To illustrate this perspective, consider the following common dilemma faced by managers who are given expense accounts.[17]

Companies routinely provide their managers with accounts to cover their work-related expenses when they are traveling on company business or entertaining clients for business purposes. Common examples of such expenses include hotel bills, meals, rental cars or taxis, and so forth.

Corporate expense accounts are sometimes the subject of ethical lapses. For instance, these two colleagues are having lunch together and discussing business. In theory, it may be easy for one of them to "pad" the lunch expense so as to be reimbursed for more money than was actually spent.

But employees, of course, are expected to claim only expenses that are accurate and work related. For example, if a manager takes a client out to dinner while traveling on business and spends $200 for dinner, submitting a receipt for reimbursement for that $200 dinner is clearly accurate and appropriate. Suppose, however, that the manager has a $200 dinner the next night in that same city with a good friend for purely social purposes. Submitting that receipt for full reimbursement would be unethical. A few managers, however, might rationalize that it would be okay to submit a receipt for dinner with a friend. They might argue, for example, that they are underpaid, so this is just a way for them to increase their income. (In reality, most companies would agree that the manager should be reimbursed for her own meal but not for the friend's meal.)

Other principles that come into play in a case like this include various ethical norms. Four such norms involve utility, rights, justice, and caring. By utility, we mean whether a particular act optimizes what is best for the organization's constituencies. By rights, we mean whether the act respects the rights of the people involved. By justice, we mean whether the act is consistent with what most people would see as fair. And by caring, we mean whether the act is consistent with people's responsibilities to one another. Figure 4.2 illustrates a model that incorporates these ethical norms.

Now, reconsider the case of the inflated expense account. Although the utility norm would acknowledge that the manager benefits from padding an expense account, others, such as coworkers and owners, would not. Similarly, most experts would agree that such an action does not respect the rights of others. Moreover, it is clearly unfair and compromises responsibilities to others. Thus this particular act would appear to be clearly unethical. However, the figure also provides mechanisms for considering unique circumstances that might fit only in certain limited situations. For example, suppose the manager loses the receipt for the legitimate dinner but has the receipt for the same amount for the social dinner. Some people would now argue that it is okay to submit the social dinner receipt because the manager is only doing so to get what he or she is entitled to. Others, however, would still argue that submitting the social receipt is wrong under any circumstances. The point, simply, is that changes in the situation can make things more or less clear-cut.

> I must stand with anybody that stands right, and stand with him while he is right, and part with him when he is wrong.
>
> ABRAHAM LINCOLN[18]

**Maintaining Organizational Justice** Another important consideration in managing ethical behavior in organizations is ensuring that people perceive decisions as being made in a fair and just manner. Organizational justice refers to the perceptions of people in an organization regarding fairness.[19] There are four basic forms of organizational justice.

*Distributive justice* refers to people's perceptions of the fairness with which rewards and other valued outcomes are distributed within the organization. Distributive justice takes a more holistic view of reward distribution than simply a comparison between one person and another. For instance, the compensation paid to top managers (especially the CEO), to peers and colleagues at the same level in an organization, and even to entry-level hourly workers can all be assessed in terms of their relative fairness vis-à-vis anyone else in the organization. Perceptions of distributive justice affect individual satisfaction with various work-related outcomes such as pay, work assignments, recognition, and opportunities for advancement. Specifically, the more people see rewards being distributed in a just and ethical manner, the more satisfied they will be with those rewards; the more unjustly they see rewards being distributed, the less satisfied they will be. Moreover, people who feel that rewards are not distributed justly may be inclined to attribute such injustice to a breach of ethical conduct.

Another important form of organizational justice is *procedural justice*—individual perceptions of the fairness used to determine various outcomes. For instance, suppose an employee's performance is evaluated by someone very familiar with the job being performed. Moreover, the evaluator clearly explains the basis for the evaluation and then discusses how that evaluation will translate in other outcomes such as promotions and pay increases.

**organizational justice**
The perceptions of people in an organization regarding fairness

## FIGURE 4.2  A GUIDE FOR ETHICAL DECISION MAKING

Managers should try to apply ethical judgment to the decisions they make. For example, this useful framework for guiding ethical decision making suggests that managers apply a set of four criteria based on utility, rights, justice, and caring when assessing decision options. The resulting analysis allows a manager to make a clear assessment of whether a decision or policy is ethical.

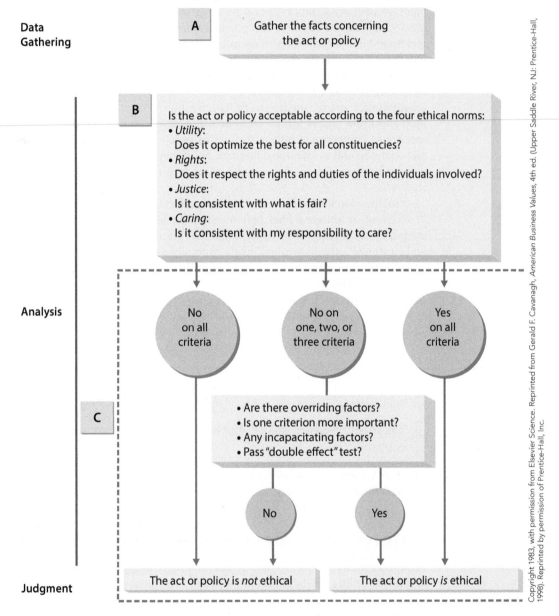

Source: Adapted from Gerald F. Cavanagh, Dennis J. Moberg, and Manuel Velasquez, "Making Business Ethics Practical," *Business Ethics Quarterly*, 1995, Vol. 5, No. 3, pp. 399–418; Manuel Velasquez, Gerald F. Cavanagh, and Dennis Moberg, "Organizational Statesmanship and Dirty Politics," *Organizational Dynamics*, Autumn 1983, p. 84.

The employee will probably see this set of procedures as being ethical, fair, and just. But if the evaluation is conducted by someone unfamiliar with the job and who provides no explanation as to how the evaluation is being done or what it will mean, the employee is likely to see the process as unethical, less fair, and unjust.

When workers perceive a high level of procedural justice, they are somewhat more likely to be motivated to participate in activities, to follow rules, to accept relevant outcomes as being fair, and to view the organization in an ethical light. But if workers perceive more procedural injustice, they will tend to withdraw from opportunities to participate, to pay less attention to rules and policies, to see relevant outcomes as being unfair, and to assess the organization in a less ethical light. In addition, perceptions of procedural injustice may be accompanied by interpretations based on the ethical conduct of others.

*Interpersonal justice* relates to the degree of fairness people see in how they are treated by others in their organizations. For instance, suppose an employee is treated by his boss with dignity and respect. The boss also provides information on a timely basis and is always open and honest in her dealings with the subordinate. The subordinate will express high levels of interpersonal justice and see the boss as an ethical leader. But if the boss treats her subordinate with disdain and a clear lack of respect, and withholds important information and is often ambiguous or dishonest in her dealings with the subordinate, he will experience more interpersonal injustice and see the boss as being less ethical. Perceptions of interpersonal justice will most affect how people feel about those with whom they interact and communicate. If they experience interpersonal justice, they are likely to reciprocate by treating others with respect and openness and in an ethical manner. But if they experience interpersonal injustice, they may be less respectful in turn, and may be less inclined to follow the directives of their leaders.

Finally, *informational justice* refers to the perceived fairness of information used to arrive at decisions. If someone feels that another manager made a decision based on relatively complete and accurate information, and that the information was appropriately processed and considered, the person will likely experience informational justice even if they don't completely agree with the decision. That is, they will see the decision as having been made in an ethical manner. But if the person feels that the decision was based on incomplete and inaccurate information and/or that important information was ignored, he or she will experience less informational justice and may see the decision as having been made in a less ethical manner.

**Manager's Checklist**

☐ Managers should strive to have a clear understanding of their own ethical standards.

☐ You should develop the habit of assessing all decisions in terms of their ethical context.

☐ When assessing the ethical context of decisions, be sure to consider everyone who might be affected.

# Emerging Ethical Issues in Organizations

Ethical scandals have become almost commonplace in today's world. Ranging from business to sports to politics to the entertainment industry, these scandals have rocked stakeholder confidence and called into question the moral integrity of our society. But, at the same time, it is important to remember that most women and men today conduct themselves and their affairs with high ethical standards. Hence, as we summarize several emerging ethical issues in organizations, it is important to remember that one cannot judge everyone by the transgressions of a few.

## Ethical Leadership

For every unethical senior manager, there are many highly ethical ones. But over the past decade the actions of such high-profile deposed executives as Bernard Madoff, Dennis Kozlowski (Tyco), Kenneth Lay (Enron), and Bernard Ebbers (WorldCom) have substantially increased the scrutiny directed at all executives. As a direct result, executives everywhere are being expected to exhibit nothing but the strongest ethical conduct. This leadership, in turn, is expected to help set the tone for the rest of the organization and to help establish both norms and a culture that reinforce the importance of ethical behavior.

The basic premise behind ethical leadership is that because leaders serve as role models for others, their every action is subject to scrutiny. If a senior executive exercises questionable judgment, this sends a signal to others that such actions are acceptable. This signal may, in turn, be remembered by others when they face similar situations. As a result, CEOs like Aramark's Eric Foss and Costco's W. Craig Jelinek are sometimes held up as the standard against which others are being measured. The basic premise is that a CEO must set the company's moral tone by being honest and straightforward and by taking responsibility for any identified shortcomings. And, to support this view, Congress passed the Sarbanes-Oxley Act, requiring CEOs and CFOs to personally vouch for the truthfulness and fairness of their firms' financial disclosures. The law also imposes tough new measures to deter and punish corporate and accounting fraud and corruption.

## Ethical Issues in Corporate Governance

A related area of emerging concern relates to ethical issues in corporate governance. As discussed in Chapter 3, the board of directors of a public corporation is expected to ensure that the business is being properly managed and that the decisions made by its senior management are in the best interests of shareholders and other stakeholders. But in far too many cases, ethical scandals such as those previously mentioned have actually started with a breakdown in the corporate governance structure. For instance, WorldCom's board approved a personal loan to the firm's CEO, Bernard Ebbers, for $366 million, when there was little evidence that he could repay it. Likewise, Tyco's board approved a $20 million bonus for one of its own members for helping with the acquisition of another firm.

But boards of directors are also increasingly being criticized even when they are not directly implicated in wrongdoing. The Swiss company Panalpina World Transport Ltd. and its U.S. subsidiary Panalpina Inc. admitted to paying $27 million in bribes to various foreign officials on behalf of their oil and gas customers to avoid local rules and regulations regarding the import of goods to foreign countries. The firm agreed to pay $156 million in criminal fines and forfeited profits of $80 million. Part of the problem, critics charge, was that some members of Panalpina's board were not sufficiently knowledgeable about the industry and other board members were close friends with senior management.[20] Although board members need to have some familiarity with both the firm and its industry to function effectively, they also need to have enough independence to carry out their oversight function. And increasingly, corporate boards are creating strict rules dictating governance standards that provide a clear separation of authority between the board and the CEO.[21]

**Sarbanes-Oxley Act**
A law passed in 2002 that requires CEOs and CFOs to personally vouch for the truthfulness and fairness of their firms' financial disclosures

## Ethical Issues in Information Technology

A final set of issues that has emerged in recent times involves information technology. Among the specific questions in this area are individual rights to privacy and the potential abuse of information technology by individuals. Indeed, online privacy has become a hot topic as companies sort out the ethical and management issues. DoubleClick, an online advertising network, is one of the firms at the eye of the privacy storm. The company has collected data on the habits of millions of web surfers, recording which sites they visit and which ads they click on. DoubleClick insists the profiles are anonymous

"Consumers should be in the driver's seat when it comes to their data. They don't want to be left in the dark and they don't want to be surprised at how it's used."

—EDITH RAMIREZ, CHAIRWOMAN OF FEDERAL TRADE COMMISSION[22]

and are used to better match surfers with appropriate ads. However, after the company announced a plan to add names and addresses to its database, it was forced to back down because of public concerns over invasion of online privacy.

DoubleClick is not the only firm gathering personal data about people's Internet activities. People who register at Yahoo! are asked to list date of birth, among other details. Amazon.com, eBay, Facebook, and other sites also ask for personal information. As Internet usage increases, however, surveys show that people are troubled by the amount of information being collected and who gets to see it.

One way management can address these concerns is to post a privacy policy on their website. The policy should explain exactly what data the company collects and who gets to see the data. It should also allow people a choice about having their information shared with others and indicate how people can opt out of data collection. Disney, IBM, and other companies support this position by refusing to advertise on websites that have no posted privacy policies.

> "We should be concerned about things like accidental social oversharing, purposeful but unwanted social sharing, government overreaching and security breaches."
>
> —JONATHAN MAYER,
> CYBERSECURITY FELLOW AT THE CENTER FOR INTERNATIONAL
> SECURITY AND COOPERATION AT STANFORD UNIVERSITY[24]

In addition, companies can offer web surfers the opportunity to review and correct information that has been collected, especially medical and financial data. In the offline world, consumers are legally allowed to inspect credit and medical records. In the online world, this kind of access can be costly and cumbersome because data are often spread across several computer systems. Despite the technical difficulties, government agencies are already working on Internet privacy guidelines, which means that companies will need internal guidelines, training, and leadership to ensure compliance.[23]

---

 **Manager's Checklist**

☐ Remember that while you think you will make ethical decisions, until you face hard choices you may not know for sure.

☐ Know that your subordinates and employees will look to you for ethical leadership.

☐ Keep abreast of the latest thinking about ethical issues that relate to information privacy and information technology.

# Social Responsibility and Organizations

As we have seen, ethics relate to individuals and their decisions and behaviors. Organizations themselves do not have ethics, but they do relate to their environment in ways that often involve ethical dilemmas and decisions. These situations are generally referred to within the context of the organization's social responsibility. Specifically, social responsibility is the set of obligations an organization has to protect and enhance the societal context in which it functions.

## Areas of Social Responsibility

Organizations may exercise social responsibility toward their stakeholders, toward the natural environment, and toward general social welfare. Some organizations acknowledge their responsibilities in all three areas and strive diligently to meet each of them, whereas others emphasize only one or two areas of social responsibility. And a few acknowledge no social responsibility at all. Moreover, views of social responsibility vary between countries.[25]

**social responsibility**
The set of obligations an organization has to protect and enhance the societal context in which it functions

**Organizational Stakeholders** In Chapter 3 we described the task environment as comprising those elements in an organization's external environment that directly affect the organization in one or more ways. Another way to describe these same elements is from the perspective of organizational stakeholders, or those people and organizations who are directly affected by the practices of an organization and have a stake in its performance.[26] Major stakeholders are depicted in Figure 4.3.

Most companies that strive to be responsible to their stakeholders concentrate first and foremost on three main groups: customers, employees, and investors. They then select other stakeholders that are particularly relevant or important to the organization and try to address their needs and expectations as well.

Organizations that are responsible to their customers strive to treat them fairly and honestly. They also seek to charge fair prices, to honor warranties, to meet delivery commitments, and to stand behind the quality of the products they sell. Companies that have established excellent reputations in this area include L.L. Bean, Lands' End, Dell Computer, and Johnson & Johnson.

Organizations that are socially responsible in their dealings with employees treat their workers fairly, make them a part of the team, and respect their dignity and basic human needs. Organizations such as Four Seasons Hotels, 3M Company, SAS Institute, and Southwest Airlines have all established strong reputations in this area. In addition, they go to great lengths to find, hire, train, and promote qualified minorities.

To maintain a socially responsible stance toward investors, managers should follow proper accounting procedures, provide appropriate information to shareholders about the

**organizational stakeholder**
Person or organization who is directly affected by the practices of an organization and has a stake in its performance

## FIGURE 4.3 ORGANIZATIONAL STAKEHOLDERS

All organizations have a variety of stakeholders who are directly affected by the organization and who have a stake in its performance. These are people and organizations to whom an organization should be responsible.

How businesses interact with the natural environment plays a complex role in social responsibility. This scene alone, for example, shows a wind farm set near an industrial site spewing black some into the environment.

financial performance of the firm, and manage the organization to protect shareholder rights and investments. Moreover, they should be accurate and candid in their assessment of future growth and profitability, and should avoid even the appearance of improprieties involving such sensitive areas as insider trading, stock price manipulation, and the withholding of financial data.[27]

**The Natural Environment** A second critical area of social responsibility relates to the natural environment.[28] Not that long ago, many organizations indiscriminately dumped sewage, waste products from production, and trash into streams and rivers, into the air, and on vacant land. When Shell Oil first explored the Amazon River Basin for potential drilling sites in the late 1980s, its crews ripped down trees and left a trail of garbage in their wake. Now, however, many laws regulate the disposal of waste materials. In many cases, companies themselves have become more socially responsible in their release of pollutants and general treatment of the environment. For example, when Shell launched its next exploratory expedition into another area of the Amazon Basin, the group included a biologist to oversee environmental protection and an anthropologist to help the team interact more effectively with native tribes.[29]

Still, much remains to be done. Companies need to develop economically feasible ways to lessen their impact on climate change and, instead, to promote sustainable business practices and develop less damaging methods for handling sewage, hazardous wastes, and ordinary garbage.[30] Procter & Gamble, for example, is an industry leader in using recycled materials for containers. Hyatt Corporation established a new company to help recycle waste products from its hotels. Monsanto launched an entire new product line aimed at improving the environment with genetically engineered crops. Ford and other automakers are working to create low-pollution and electrically powered vehicles. *Doing Business on Planet Earth* discusses how Clif Bar & Co. is also promoting earth-friendly business practices. The Internet is also seen as having the potential to play an important role in resource conservation, as many e-commerce businesses and transactions are reducing both energy costs and pollution.

Companies also need to develop safety policies that cut down on accidents that may have potentially disastrous environmental results. When one of Ashland Oil's storage tanks ruptured, spilling more than 500,000 gallons of diesel fuel into Pennsylvania's Monongahela River, the company moved quickly to clean up the spill but was still indicted for violating U.S. environmental laws. After the oil tanker *Exxon Valdez* spilled millions of gallons of oil off the coast of Alaska, the tanker's owner, ExxonMobil, adopted new and more stringent procedures to keep another disaster from happening. Similarly, after the disastrous oil spill in the Gulf of Mexico in 2010, BP also adopted new procedures to help avoid other problems in the future.

One of today's more contentious business practices related to the natural environment is fracking. Fracking involves injecting water and chemical compounds into underground rock formations in order to break them apart. After this has been done, oil companies can then extract petroleum more easily and in areas where drilling was previously impossible. Fracking has led to a dramatic increase in the supply of oil and has resulted in lower energy prices. At the same time, though, environmentalists have expressed concerns that the chemical compounds used in fracking may be polluting underground water sources and causing instability in nearby towns and residential areas.[31]

**DOING BUSINESS ON PLANET EARTH**

# Raising the CSR Bar

To celebrate its twentieth anniversary, Clif Bar & Co., a maker of organic nutrition foods and beverages, gave all of its employees—more than 250 of them—new bicycles. It may not be the workplace perk for everyone, but it caught the eye of Leon Kaye, a consultant specializing in corporate social responsibility (CSR). Kaye put the company's bicycle giveaway on his list of the year's "Top 10 Employee Engagement Strategies."

As a matter of fact, bicycles figure prominently in Clif Bar's "Cool Commute" program: Employees can take advantage of financial incentives for riding their bicycles to work, and those who missed out on a free bike can still get a $500 stipend toward the purchase of one. Other programs provide incentives for buying fuel-efficient cars and making eco-friendly home improvements. In turn, the "Cool Commute" program reflects two of Clif Bar's five core values—"Sustaining Our Planet" and "Sustaining Our People." The company is also committed to sustaining its community, business, and brands, and taken together, these five values constitute its "Five Aspirations."

Kit Crawford, who co-owns Clif Bar with husband Gary Erickson, stresses "the interconnectivity of the Five Aspirations," which, as she's also quick to point out, serve as the company's "five bottom lines." "Gary and I," she says, "use these bottom lines … as a measurement of our return on investment," and all five are "of equal importance" in determining how well the company is using its resources to achieve its goals. In addition, says Crawford, the five commitments ensure that "our people have a clear understanding of Clif Bar's values." By providing a clear "decision-making framework," they also guide employees in "exploring, creating, and launching ideas that are in tune with the company's priorities." Finally, they figure into each employee's annual review: "Our people," explains Crawford, "receive specific feedback on their contributions to each of the Five Aspirations. … These assessments determine each employee's bonus for the year."

The company itself works out of a state-of-the-art solar-powered facility in Emeryville, CA, where 80 percent of the waste is reused or recycled. There's even a staff ecologist on the payroll. For founder Gary Erickson, the goals of sustaining the planet and sustaining his company's people are inseparable threads in a single fabric of socially responsible leadership: "We want to sustain a business," he says, "where people can live, not just make a living. We believe that if we provide meaningful work as well as something beyond work, people will do their jobs well and lead healthier, more balanced lives."

Clif Bar thus maintains an elaborate wellness program that encourages employees to get out and enjoy the natural environment that they're working to sustain. Employees who've been with the company for seven years, for instance, can take six to eight weeks of paid sabbatical, and the Emeryville facility boasts an in-house fitness center where employees can get paid time off to work out under the guidance of full-time personal trainers.

How has all of this socially responsible conduct affected the bottom line—that is, the bottom line which is typically defined as how much money a company makes? In 1992, its first year of business, Clif Bar had $700,000 in sales. That figure doubled every year up to 1997, when sales hit $20 million. Since then, the company has grown rapidly ("stratospherically," as Leon Kaye would have it), achieving a remarkable compounded annual growth rate of 23 percent in the 10 years from 2002 to 2011, when sales reached $340 million. A year later, sales topped $500 million.

*References:* Leon Kaye, "Top 10 Employment Engagement Strategies," *TriplePundit* (April 15, 2013), www.triplepundit.com, on July 28, 2014; Susan McPherson, "The Most Dynamic Social Innovation Initiatives of 2012," *Forbes.com* (December 17, 2012), www.forbes.com, on July 28, 2014; Bob Vanourek and Gregg Vanourek, "Sustainable Leadership': Interview with Kit Crawford," *Triple Crown Leadership* (October 18, 2012), www.triplecrown-leadership.com, on July 28, 2014; Robert Girling, "Good Companies Like Clif Bar: How They Do It," *TriplePundit* (July 17, 2012), www.triplepundit.com, on July 28, 2014; Great Place to Work, "Clif Bar & Company," *Great Rated* (2014), http://us.greatrated.com, on July 28, 2014; Lauren Drell, "Six Companies with Awesome Employee Perks," *Mashable* (August 7, 2011), http://mashable.com, on July 28, 2014.

**General Social Welfare**   Some people believe that, in addition to treating constituents and the environment responsibly, business organizations also should promote the general welfare of society. Examples include contributing financially to charities, philanthropic organizations, and not-for-profit foundations and associations; providing other support (such as buying advertising space in programs) to museums, symphonies, and public radio and television; and taking a role in improving public health and education. Some people also believe that organizations should act even more broadly to correct the political inequities that exist in the world. For example, these observers would argue that businesses should not conduct operations in countries with a record of human rights violations. Thus they stand in opposition to companies doing business in China, Vietnam, and some areas of the Middle East.

## Arguments For and Against Social Responsibility

On the surface, there seems to be little disagreement about the need for organizations to be socially responsible. In truth, though, those who oppose broad interpretations of social responsibility use several convincing arguments.[32] Some of the more salient arguments on both sides of this contemporary debate are summarized in Figure 4.4 and further explained in the following sections.

**Arguments For Social Responsibility**   People who argue in favor of social responsibility claim that because organizations create many of the problems that need to be addressed, such as air and water pollution and resource depletion, they should play a major role in solving them. They also argue that because corporations are legally defined entities with most of the same privileges as private citizens, businesses should not try to avoid their obligations as citizens. Advocates of social responsibility point out that whereas governmental organizations have stretched their budgets to the limit, many large businesses often have surplus revenues that could be used to help solve social problems. For example, Hewlett-Packard routinely donates surplus computers to schools, and many restaurants give leftover food to homeless shelters.

---

## FIGURE 4.4   ARGUMENTS FOR AND AGAINST SOCIAL RESPONSIBILITY

While many people want everyone to see social responsibility as a desirable aim, there are several strong arguments that can be used both for and against social responsibility. Hence, organizations and their managers should carefully assess their own values, beliefs, and priorities when deciding which stance and approach to take regarding social responsibility.

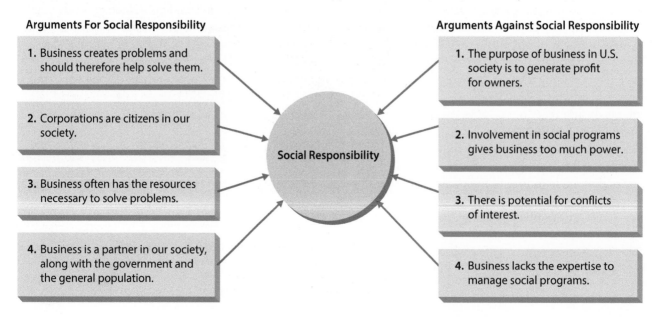

**Arguments For Social Responsibility**

1. Business creates problems and should therefore help solve them.

2. Corporations are citizens in our society.

3. Business often has the resources necessary to solve problems.

4. Business is a partner in our society, along with the government and the general population.

**Social Responsibility**

**Arguments Against Social Responsibility**

1. The purpose of business in U.S. society is to generate profit for owners.

2. Involvement in social programs gives business too much power.

3. There is potential for conflicts of interest.

4. Business lacks the expertise to manage social programs.

Although each of the arguments just summarized is a distinct justification for socially responsible behaviors on the part of organizations, another more general reason for social responsibility is profit itself. For example, organizations that make clear and visible contributions to society can achieve an enhanced reputation and garner greater market share for their products. Although claims of socially responsible activities can haunt a company if they are exaggerated or untrue, they can also work to the benefit of both the organization and society if the advertised benefits are true and accurate.

Products from a mid-sized tech company are loaded into a cargo truck. This company, as part of its social mission, donates excess inventory to impoverished areas abroad. By providing technology to an underserved communality they are connecting populations across the globe.

### Arguments Against Social Responsibility

Some people, however, including the famous economist Milton Friedman, argue that widening the interpretation of social responsibility will undermine the U.S. economy by detracting from the basic mission of business: to earn profits for owners. For example, money that Chevron or General Electric contributes to social causes or charities is money that could otherwise be distributed to owners as a dividend. Shareholders of Ben & Jerry's Homemade Holdings once expressed outrage when the firm refused to accept a lucrative exporting deal to Japan simply because the Japanese distributor did not have a strong social agenda.

Another objection to deepening the social responsibility of businesses points out that corporations already wield enormous power and that their activity in social programs gives them even more power. Still another argument against social responsibility focuses on the potential for conflicts of interest. Suppose, for example, that one manager is in charge of deciding which local social program or charity will receive a large grant from her business. The local civic opera company (a not-for-profit organization that relies on contributions for its existence) might offer her front-row tickets for the upcoming season in exchange for her support. If opera is her favorite form of music, she might be tempted to direct the money toward the local company, when it might actually be needed more in other areas.[33]

Finally, critics argue that organizations lack the expertise to understand how to assess and make decisions about worthy social programs. How can a company truly know, they ask, which cause or program is most deserving of its support or how money might best be spent? For example, ExxonMobil donates about $1 million each year to help save the Bengal tiger, an endangered species that happens also to serve as the firm's corporate symbol. ExxonMobil gives most of the money to support breeding programs in zoos and to help educate people about the tiger. But conservationists criticize the firm and its activities, arguing that the money might be better spent

These Bengal tiger pelts are the product of poaching and illegal trading of tiger fur. ExxonMobil donates $1 million to helps save the endangered species by supporting zoo breeding programs. Critics argue, however, that this social program does not go far enough.

instead on eliminating poaching, the illegal trade of tiger fur, and the destruction of the tiger's natural habitat.

## Organizational Approaches to Social Responsibility

As we have seen, some people advocate a larger social role for organizations, and others argue that their role is already too large. Not surprisingly, organizations themselves adopt a wide range of positions on social responsibility. As Figure 4.5 illustrates, the four stances that an organization can take concerning its obligations to society fall along a continuum ranging from the lowest to the highest degree of socially responsible practices.

**Obstructionist Stance** The few organizations that take what might be called an obstructionist stance to social responsibility usually do as little as possible to solve social or environmental problems. When they cross the ethical or legal line that separates acceptable from unacceptable practices, their typical response is to deny or avoid accepting responsibility for their actions. A Georgia peanut processing plant owned by Peanut Corporation of America shipped products that were contaminated with salmonella. Preliminary tests of the products were positive for salmonella. But when a retest came back negative, rather than investigate further, the firm simply ignored the first results and shipped anyway. The company's president and three other senior managers were subsequently indicted on 76 counts of criminal behavior.[34] Similarly, UBS, Switzerland's largest bank, admitted that it had helped about 19,000 wealthy U.S. citizens evade income taxes by refusing to disclose their identities or report income earned on accounts maintained by the bank.[35] GlaxoSmithKline, a major British pharmaceutical company, came under fire in 2010 when its former vice president and associate general counsel, Lauren Stevens, denied initial claims that the company had been unlawfully marketing an antidepressant drug for use as a weight-loss aid.[36] Similarly, several automobile rental firms, including Enterprise, Hertz, and Avis, have been criticized for being slow to respond to recall notices from automobile manufacturers and continue to rent vehicles that may have known safety defects.[37]

> "We are shocked at what's been going on in [Peanut Corporation of America]."
>
> —REPRESENTATIVE HENRY WAXMAN, DURING CONGRESSIONAL PROBE OF SALMONELLA OUTBREAK[38]

**obstructionist stance**
An approach to social responsibility in which firms do as little as possible to solve social or environmental problems

**defensive stance**
A social responsibility stance in which an organization does everything that is required of it legally, but nothing more

**Defensive Stance** One step removed from the obstructionist stance is the defensive stance, whereby the organization does everything that is required of it legally, but nothing more. This approach is most consistent with the arguments used against social responsibility. Managers in organizations that take a defensive stance insist that their job is to generate profits. For example, such a firm would install pollution control equipment dictated by law, but would not install higher-quality but slightly more expensive equipment even though it might limit pollution further.

## FIGURE 4.5 APPROACHES TO SOCIAL RESPONSIBILITY

Organizations can adopt a variety of approaches to social responsibility. For example, a firm that never considers the consequences of its decisions and tries to hide its transgressions is taking an obstructionist stance. At the other extreme, a firm that actively seeks to identify areas where it can help society is pursuing a proactive stance toward social responsibility.

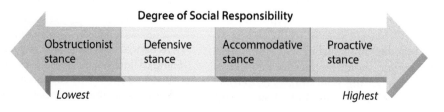

Tobacco companies like Philip Morris take this position in their marketing efforts. In the United States, they are legally required to include warnings to smokers on their products and to limit their advertising to prescribed media. Domestically they follow these rules to the letter of the law, but they often use stronger marketing methods in countries that have no such rules. In many African countries, for example, cigarettes are heavily promoted, contain higher levels of tar and nicotine than those sold in the United States, and carry few or no health warning labels. Philip Morris is also aggressively trying to gain market share in Russia, where over 60 percent of all men smoke, and in China, where over 53 percent of all men smoke.[39] Firms that take this position are, however, unlikely to cover up wrongdoing, and will generally admit their mistakes and take appropriate corrective actions.

> "[We're] being very socially responsible in a rather controversial industry."
> —LOUIS CAMILLERI, FORMER CEO OF PHILIP MORRIS INTERNATIONAL[40]

> "If we find evidence of systematic [worker abuse], we're not going to do business with you."
> —JIM WALTER, MATTEL SENIOR VICE PRESIDENT OF GLOBAL PRODUCT INTEGRITY[41]

**Accommodative Stance** A firm that adopts an accommodative stance meets its legal and ethical obligations but will also go beyond these obligations in selected cases. Such firms voluntarily agree to participate in social programs, but solicitors have to convince the organization that the programs are worthy of its support. Both ExxonMobil and Halliburton, for example, will match contributions made by their employees to selected charitable causes. And many organizations will respond to requests for donations to Little League, Girl Scouts, youth soccer programs, and so forth. The point, though, is that someone has to knock on the door and ask—the organizations do not proactively seek such avenues for contributing.

**Proactive Stance** The highest degree of social responsibility that a firm can exhibit is the proactive stance. Firms that adopt this approach take to heart the arguments in favor of social responsibility. They view themselves as citizens in a society and proactively seek opportunities to contribute. An excellent example of a proactive stance is the Ronald McDonald House program underwritten by McDonald's. These houses, located close to major medical centers, can be used by families for minimal cost while their sick children are receiving medical treatment nearby. Target stopped selling guns in its stores, and Toys "R" Us stopped selling realistic toy guns, both due to concerns about escalating violence. Increasingly, some firms, such as Mattel, Nike, and Home Depot, have on occasion severed relationships with foreign suppliers found not to be treating their employees fairly.[42]

**accommodative stance**
A social responsibility stance in which an organization meets its legal and ethical obligations but will also go beyond these obligations in selected cases

**proactive stance**
A social responsibility stance in which an organization views itself as a citizen in a society and proactively seeks opportunities to contribute

When the founder of L'Occitane en Provence, a French bath-and-body firm, noticed a blind woman having difficulty while shopping for perfume in one of his stores, he launched an initiative to have Braille labels applied to most L'Occitane products.[43] Peet's Coffee, a Seattle-based coffee business, works with TechnoServe, a nonprofit organization funded by the Bill & Melinda Gates Foundation, to help develop coffee farming in Rwanda.[44] Drug maker Pfizer donated prescription medicines to people who lost their jobs during the 2008–2010 recession and did not have prescription drug insurance.[45] Subway, the world's largest fast-food company (based on number of outlets), in 2011 announced a voluntary measure to reduce the sodium content of most of its sandwiches.[46] Each year Apple sponsors a two-week global fundraising campaign to support AIDS research.[47] During the 2015 drought in

A proactive stance regarding social responsibility exists when a business seeks opportunities to contribute to society. McDonald's support of the Ronald McDonald House program represents proactive social responsibility.

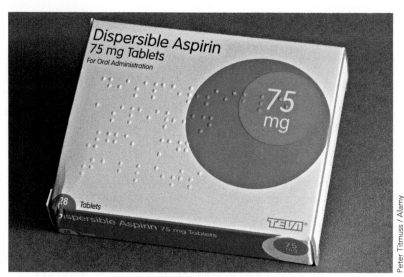

Peter Titmuss / Alamy

Some firms take a proactive stance in their product labeling. This pharmaceutical company provides Braille raised writing on their prescriptions.

California, Starbucks proactively decided to stop using sources in that state for its bottled water while other bottled firms took no such action. These and related activities and programs exceed the accommodative stance — they indicate a sincere and potent commitment to improving the general social welfare and thus represent a proactive stance to social responsibility.

Remember, too, that these categories are not discrete but merely define stages along a continuum of approaches. Organizations do not always fit neatly into one category. The Ronald McDonald House program has been widely applauded, for example, but McDonald's also has come under fire for allegedly misleading consumers about the nutritional value of its food products. Nestlé, along with others, created the World Cocoa Foundation, focused on increasing farmer income, educating cocoa farmers on sustainable farming techniques, and encouraging social and environmental programs. At the same time, though, Nestlé has been criticized for its heavy use of palm oil in its products. This is contributing to deforestation in Indonesia for the creation of palm oil plantations, which is harming various species.[48] And even though the unethical conduct of a small number of people at an organization might tarnish the firm's reputation, other employees at the same organization may be highly ethical people who would never consider an unethical action.

**Manager's Checklist**

☐ Remember that the views of others about social responsibility may not necessarily be the same as your views.

☐ Develop a clear understanding of your own personal views of social responsibility as well as the views of your employer.

# The Government and Social Responsibility

An especially important element of social responsibility is the relationship between business and government. For example, in planned economies the government heavily regulates business activities, ostensibly to ensure that business supports some overarching set of social ideals. And even in market economies there is still considerable government control of business, much of it again directed at making sure that social interests are not damaged by business interests. On the other side of the coin, business also tries to influence the government. Such efforts are usually undertaken in an effort to offset or reverse government restrictions. As Figure 4.6 shows, organizations and the government use several methods in their attempts to influence each other.

## How Government Influences Organizations

The government tries to shape social responsibility practices through both direct and indirect channels. Direct influence usually involves regulation, whereas indirect influence can take a number of forms, most notably taxation policies.[49]

## FIGURE 4.6 HOW BUSINESS AND THE GOVERNMENT INFLUENCE EACH OTHER

Business and the government influence each other in a variety of ways. Government influence can be direct or indirect. Business influence relies on personal contacts, lobbying, political action committees (PACs), and favors. Federal Express, for example, has a very active PAC.

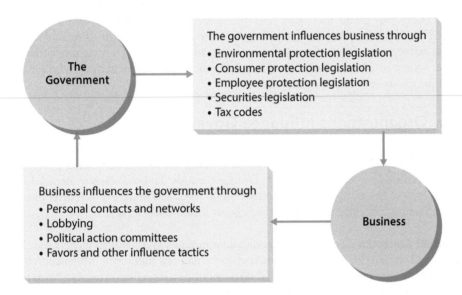

The Government

The government influences business through
- Environmental protection legislation
- Consumer protection legislation
- Employee protection legislation
- Securities legislation
- Tax codes

Business influences the government through
- Personal contacts and networks
- Lobbying
- Political action committees
- Favors and other influence tactics

Business

**Direct Regulation** The government most often directly influences organizations through regulation, or the establishment of laws and rules that dictate what organizations can and cannot do. As noted earlier in this chapter, such regulation usually evolves from societal beliefs about what businesses should or should not be allowed to do. To implement the laws, the government generally creates special agencies to monitor and control certain aspects of business activity. For example, the Environmental Protection Agency handles environmental issues; the Federal Trade Commission and the Food and Drug Administration focus on consumer-related concerns; the Equal Employee Opportunity Commission, the National Labor Relations Board, and the Department of Labor help protect employees; and the Securities and Exchange Commission handles investor-related issues. These agencies have the power to levy fines or bring charges against organizations that violate regulations.

Another approach that governments can use to regulate business practices is through legislation. For instance, among other things the U.S. Foreign Corrupt Practices Act provides for financial sanctions against businesses or business officials who engage in bribery. Siemens AG, a large German engineering firm, has been investigated for practices that include routine bribery of foreign officials to win infrastructure construction projects. All told, the firm is alleged to have spent over $1 billion in bribing officials in at least 10 different countries. Siemens agreed to pay the U.S. government a fine of $800 million. (The U.S. government had the authority to fine Siemens because the German firm has a class of stock listed on the New York Stock Exchange and was thus subject to the Foreign Corrupt Practices Act.)[50] Similarly, another German firm, Daimler AG, has been charged with bribery in 22 countries, helping the company earn over $50 million in profit. The company was alleged to have given millions of dollars in bribes to foreign officials in order to win contracts supplying their governments with vehicles. Charges include conspiracy and falsifying records. Daimler agreed to pay $185 million in its settlement.[51] An American entrepreneur named Joseph Sigelman launched a successful oilfield service company in the Columbian

**regulation**
Government's attempts to influence business by establishing laws and rules that dictate what businesses can and cannot do

rainforest called PetroTiger but was recently charged with six counts of bribery, accepting kickbacks, and laundering money.[52]

**Indirect Regulation**   Other forms of regulation are indirect. For example, the government can indirectly influence the social responsibility of organizations through its tax codes. In effect, the government can influence how organizations spend their social responsibility dollars by providing greater or lesser tax incentives. For instance, suppose that the government wanted organizations to spend more on training the hard-core unemployed. Congress could then pass laws that provided tax incentives to companies that opened new training facilities. As a result, more businesses would probably do so. Of course, some critics argue that regulation is already excessive. They maintain that a free market system would eventually accomplish the same goals as regulation, with lower costs to both organizations and the government.

## How Organizations Influence Government

As we mentioned in Chapter 3, organizations can influence their environment in many different ways. In particular, businesses have four main methods of addressing governmental pressures for more social responsibility. During the early days of President Barack Obama's administration, however, he implemented several measures designed to restrict or regulate business influence on the government, especially through lobbying.[53]

**Personal Contacts**   Because many corporate executives and political leaders travel in the same social circles, personal contacts and networks offer one method of influence. A business executive, for example, may be able to contact a politician directly and present his or her case regarding a piece of legislation being considered.

**Lobbying**   Lobbying, or the use of persons or groups to formally represent an organization or group of organizations before political bodies, is also an effective way to influence the government. The National Rifle Association (NRA), for example, has a staff of lobbyists in Washington, with a substantial annual budget. These lobbyists work to represent the NRA's position on gun control and to potentially influence members of Congress when they vote on legislation that affects the firearms industry and the rights of gun owners. As noted above, President Obama took many steps to control or limit lobbying. For instance, any discussion between a lobbyist and a member of Congress that goes beyond general conversation has to be written in the form of a letter and posted online.

**lobbying**
The use of persons or groups to formally represent an organization or group of organizations before political bodies to influence the government

**political action committee (PAC)**
An organization created to solicit and distribute money to political candidates

The National Rifle Association (NRA) has a very effective lobbying arm. NRA lobbyists actively work to influence government legislation away from any measures that might restrict the rights of gun owners in the United States. The NRA has over 5 million members and an annual budget of over $200 million.

Kelly Nigro/Getty Images

**Political Action Committees**   Companies themselves cannot legally make direct donations to political campaigns, so they influence the government through political action committees. Political action committees (PACs) are special organizations created to solicit money and then distribute it to political candidates. Employees of a firm may be encouraged to make donations to a particular PAC because managers know that it will support candidates with political views similar to their own. PACs, in turn, make the contributions themselves, usually to a broad slate of state and national candidates. For example, Federal Express's PAC is called FedExpac. FedExpac makes regular contributions to the campaign funds of political candidates who are most likely to work in the firm's best interests. As with lobbying, President Obama implemented measures to limit the influence of PACs.

**Favors**  Finally, organizations sometimes rely on favors and other influence tactics to gain support. Although these favors may be legal, they are still subject to criticism. A few years back, for example, two influential members of a House committee attending a fundraising function in Miami were needed in Washington to finish work on a piece of legislation that Federal Express wanted passed. The law being drafted would allow the company and its competitors to give their employees standby seats on airlines as a tax-free benefit. As a favor, Federal Express provided one of its corporate jets to fly the committee members back to Washington. Federal Express was eventually reimbursed for its expenses, so its assistance was not illegal, but some people argue that such actions are dangerous because of how they might be perceived.

☐  Understand how the government affects social responsibility as it relates to your organization.

☐  Be aware of how your organization influences (or tries to influence) the government in terms of social responsibility.

**Manager's Checklist**

# Managing Social Responsibility

The demands for social responsibility placed on contemporary organizations by an increasingly sophisticated and educated public are probably stronger than ever. As we have seen, there are pitfalls for managers who fail to adhere to high ethical standards and for companies that try to circumvent their legal obligations. Organizations therefore need to fashion an approach to social responsibility in the same way that they develop any other business strategy. In other words, they should view social responsibility as a major challenge that requires careful planning, decision making, consideration, and evaluation. They may accomplish this through both formal and informal dimensions of managing social responsibility.

## Formal Organizational Actions

Some actions for managing social responsibility involve a formal and planned activity on the part of the organization. Indeed, some businesses approach social responsibility from a strategic perspective.[54] Formal organizational dimensions that can help manage social responsibility are legal compliance, ethical compliance, and philanthropic giving.

**Legal Compliance**  Legal compliance is the extent to which the organization conforms to local, state, federal, and international laws. The task of managing legal compliance is generally assigned to the appropriate functional managers. For example, the organization's top human resource executive is responsible for ensuring compliance with regulations concerning hiring, pay, and workplace safety and health. Likewise, the top financial executive generally oversees compliance with securities and banking regulations. The organization's legal department is also likely to contribute to this effort by providing general oversight and answering queries from managers about the appropriate interpretation of laws and regulations.

**legal compliance**
The extent to which an organization complies with local, state, federal, and international laws

Unfortunately, though, legal compliance may not be enough—in some cases, for instance, perfectly legal accounting practices have still resulted in deception and other problems.[55]

**Ethical Compliance** Ethical compliance is the extent to which the members of the organization follow basic ethical (and legal) standards of behavior. We noted earlier that organizations have increased their efforts in this area—providing training in ethics and developing guidelines and codes of conduct, for example. These activities serve as vehicles for enhancing ethical compliance. Many organizations also establish formal ethics committees, which may be asked to review proposals for new projects, help evaluate new hiring strategies, or assess a new environmental protection plan. They might also serve as peer review panels to evaluate alleged ethical misconduct by employees.[56]

**Philanthropic Giving** Finally, philanthropic giving is the awarding of funds or gifts to charities or other worthy causes. Target Corporation routinely gives 5 percent of its taxable income to charity and social programs. Omaha Steaks gives more than $100,000 per year to support the arts.[57] Giving across national boundaries is also becoming more common. For example, Alcoa gave $112,000 to a small town in Brazil to build a sewage treatment plant. And Japanese firms like Sony and Mitsubishi make contributions to a number of social programs in the United States. However, in the current climate of cutbacks, many corporations have also had to limit their charitable gifts over the past several years as they continue to trim their own budgets.[58] And many firms that continue to make contributions are increasingly targeting them to programs or areas where the firm will get something in return. For example, firms today are more likely to give money to job training programs than to the arts. The logic is that they get more direct payoff from the former type of contribution—in this instance, a better-trained workforce from which to hire new employees.[59] And indeed, corporate donations to arts programs declined 5 percent between 2003 and 2009.[60]

> "When the economy is struggling, the arts help people move forward. We take a long-term view of our business and a long-term view of our community."
>
> —TODD SIMON, SENIOR VICE PRESIDENT OF FAMILY-OWNED OMAHA STEAKS[61]

## Informal Organizational Actions

In addition to these formal dimensions for managing social responsibility, there are also informal ones. Leadership, organization culture, and how the organization responds to whistleblowers all help shape and define people's perceptions of the organization's stance on social responsibility.

**Organization Leadership and Culture** Leadership practices and organization culture can go a long way toward defining the social responsibility stance an organization and its members will adopt.[62] As described earlier, ethical leadership often sets the tone for the entire organization. For example, Johnson & Johnson executives for years provided a consistent message to employees that customers, employees, communities where the company did business, and shareholders were all important—and primarily in that order. Thus, when packages of poisoned Tylenol showed up on store shelves in the 1980s, Johnson & Johnson employees did not wait for orders from headquarters about how to respond because they already knew what to do: They immediately pulled all the packages from shelves before any other customers could buy them.[63] By contrast, the message sent to Equinox employees by the actions of their top managers communicated much less regard for social responsibility.

**Whistle-Blowing** Whistle-blowing is the disclosure by an employee of illegal or unethical conduct on the part of others within the organization.[64] How an organization responds to this practice often indicates its stance on social responsibility. Whistle-blowers may have to proceed through a number of channels to be heard, and they may even get fired for their efforts.[65] Many organizations, however, welcome their contributions. A person who observes

**ethical compliance**
The extent to which an organization and its members follow basic ethical standards of behavior

**philanthropic giving**
Awarding funds or gifts to charities or other worthy causes

**whistle-blowing**
The disclosure by an employee of illegal or unethical conduct on the part of others within the organization

questionable behavior typically first reports the incident to his or her boss. If nothing is done, the whistle-blower may then inform higher-level managers or an ethics committee, if one exists. Eventually, the person may have to go to a regulatory agency or even the media to be heard. For example, Charles W. Robinson, Jr., worked as a director of a SmithKline lab in San Antonio. One day he noticed a suspicious billing pattern that the firm was using to collect lab fees from Medicare: The bills were considerably higher than the firm's normal charges for the same tests. He pointed out the problem to higher-level managers, but his concerns were ignored. He subsequently took his findings to the U.S. government, which sued Smith-Kline and eventually reached a settlement of $325 million.[66]

More recently, David Magee, a former employee of Mississippi's Stennis Space Center, reported to superiors and federal agents that government employees conspired with Lockheed Martin and Science Applications International Corp. to ensure they would win the contract to work on the Naval Oceanographic Office Major Shared Resource Center, violating the False Claims Act. Allegedly, the defendants shared secret information about the bidding process, ensuring a successful bid. For providing the information to the government that led to legal action Magee received $560,000 of the $2 million settlement against Lockheed.[67] Harry Markopolos, a portfolio manager at Rampart Investments, spent nine years trying to convince the Securities and Exchange Commission that a money-management firm run by Bernard Madoff was falsifying the results it was reporting to investors. Only when the U.S. economy went into recession in 2008 did the truth about Madoff come out.[68] In response, the SEC announced plans to overhaul its whistle-blowing system.[69]

## Evaluating Social Responsibility

Any organization that is serious about social responsibility must ensure that its efforts are producing the desired benefits. Essentially this requires applying the concept of control to social responsibility. Many organizations now require current and new employees to read their guidelines or code of ethics and then sign a statement agreeing to abide by it. An organization should also evaluate how it responds to instances of questionable legal or ethical conduct. Does it follow up immediately? Does it punish those involved? Or does it use delay and coverup tactics? Answers to these questions can help an organization form a picture of its approach to social responsibility.

More formally, an organization may sometimes evaluate the effectiveness of its social responsibility efforts. For example, when BP Amoco established a job-training program in Chicago, it allocated additional funds to evaluate how well the program was meeting its goals. Some organizations occasionally conduct corporate social audits. A corporate social audit is a formal and thorough analysis of the effectiveness of a firm's social performance. The audit is usually conducted by a task force of high-level managers from within the firm. It requires that the organization clearly define all of its social goals, analyze the resources it devotes to each goal, determine how well it is achieving the various goals, and make recommendations about which areas need additional attention. Recent estimates suggest that around 95 percent of the world's 250 largest firms now issue annual reports summarizing their efforts in the areas of environmental and social responsibility.

**corporate social audit**
A formal and thorough analysis of the effectiveness of a firm's social performance

---

☐ Remember that what is legal and what is ethical may not always be the same.

☐ If someone in your organization becomes a whistle-blower, try to understand their point of view and why they took action as they did.

☐ Managers should always understand how the organization's culture affects social responsibility within the organization.

**Manager's Checklist** ☑

# Summary of Learning Outcomes and Key Points

1. Discuss managerial ethics, three areas of special ethical concern for managers, and how organizations manage ethical behavior.

   - Ethics are an individual's personal beliefs about what constitutes right and wrong behavior.
   - Important areas of ethical concern for managers are how the organization treats its employees, how employees treat the organization, and how the organization and its employees treat other economic agents.
   - The ethical context of organizations consists of each manager's individual ethics and messages sent by organizational practices.
   - Organizations use leadership, culture, training, codes, guidelines, and justice to help them manage ethical behavior.

2. Identify and summarize key emerging ethical issues in organizations today.

   - One emerging ethical issue is ethical leadership and its key role in shaping ethical norms and the culture of the organization.
   - Another involves corporate governance and focuses on the need for the board of directors to maintain appropriate oversight of senior management.
   - Third, ethical issues in information technology relate to issues such as individual privacy and the potential abuse of an organization's information technology resources.

3. Discuss the concept of social responsibility, specify to whom or what an organization might be considered responsible, and describe four types of organizational approaches to social responsibility.

   - Social responsibility is the set of obligations an organization has to protect and enhance the society in which it functions.
   - Organizations may be considered responsible to their stakeholders, to the natural environment, and to the general social welfare.
   - There are strong arguments both for and against social responsibility.
   - The approach an organization adopts toward social responsibility falls along a continuum of lesser to greater commitment: the obstructionist stance, the defensive stance, the accommodative stance, and the proactive stance.

4. Explain the relationship between the government and organizations regarding social responsibility.

   - Government influences organizations through regulation, which is the establishment of laws and rules that dictate what businesses can and cannot do in prescribed areas.
   - Organizations rely on personal contacts, lobbying, political action committees, and favors to influence the government.

5. Describe some of the activities organizations may engage in to manage social responsibility.

   - Organizations use three types of activities to formally manage social responsibility: legal compliance, ethical compliance, and philanthropic giving.
   - Leadership, culture, and allowing for whistle-blowing are informal means of managing social responsibility.
   - Organizations should evaluate the effectiveness of their socially responsible practices as they would any other strategy.

# Discussion Questions

## Questions for Review

1. Define ethical and unethical behavior. Give three specific examples of ethical behavior and three specific examples of unethical behavior.

2. Summarize the basic stances that an organization can take regarding social responsibility.

## Questions for Analysis

5. What is the relationship between the law and ethical behavior? Can illegal behavior possibly be ethical?

3. Who are the important stakeholders of your college or university? What does each stakeholder group get from the school? What does each give to the school?

4. Describe the formal and informal dimensions of social responsibility.

6. Where do organizational ethics come from? Describe the contributions made by the organization's

founder, managers, and workers, as well as laws and social norms. Which do you think is most influential? Why?

7. There are many worthy causes or programs that deserve support from socially responsible companies. In your opinion, which types of causes or programs are the most deserving? Explain your reasoning.

## Questions for Application

8. In the last several years a number of corporate scandals have been brought to light. Many organizations have responded by, for example, appointing a chief ethics officer, beginning an ethics training program for workers, writing a formal code of ethics, or setting up a hotline for whistle-blowers. In your opinion, are these measures likely to increase organizational ethics in the long run? If so, why? If not, what would be effective in improving organizational ethics?

9. Review the arguments for and against social responsibility. On a scale of 1 to 10, rate the validity and importance of each point. Use these ratings to develop a position on how socially responsible an organization should be. Now compare your ratings and position with those of two of your classmates. Discuss your respective positions, focusing primarily on disagreements.

10. Give three specific examples of a way in which the government has influenced an organization. Then give three specific examples of a way in which an organization has influenced the government. Do you think the government's actions were ethical? Were the company's actions ethical? Why or why not?

# Building Effective Diagnostic and Decision-Making Skills

## Exercise Overview

Diagnostic and decision-making skills are closely related. Diagnostic skills enable a manager to visualize the most appropriate response to a situation, thereby providing a foundation for effective decision making. Decision-making skills refer to the ability to recognize and define problems and opportunities correctly and then to select an appropriate course of action for solving problems or capitalizing on opportunities. This exercise will help you develop your diagnostic and decision-making skills by applying them to the kind of ethical dilemma with which you might be confronted during your business career.

## Exercise Background

As businesses, industries, and technologies—not to mention societies—become more complex, ethical dilemmas also tend to become more complicated. Consider, for example, the business of publishing music online, in which a variety of factors—the advent of split-second cyber connections, the desire of many businesses to bypass intermediaries, new definitions of *theft*—conspire to contribute to a number of potential ethical dilemmas. In this exercise, we'll use the Internet to collect some up-to-date information about online music publishing and then answer a few ethics-oriented questions.

## Exercise Task

1. Start by considering each of the stakeholders in the online music publishing industry—recording artists, recording companies, online file-sharing companies such as Napster, and consumers. Consider the kinds of ethical problems faced by the industry and explain how each stakeholder is affected by each problem.

2. For each problem, determine the best outcome for each stakeholder.

3. For each problem, do you see any way to satisfy the needs of every stakeholder? If yes, explain how this outcome can be brought about. If no, explain why no mutually beneficial solution is possible.

4. In what ways did your own code of ethics influence your various answers to question 2 and your reasoning in question 3?

# Building Effective Interpersonal Skills

## Exercise Overview

Interpersonal skills refer to the ability to communicate with, understand, and motivate individuals and groups. Because they may prove especially important in situations involving issues of ethics and social responsibility, we'll use this exercise to help you apply interpersonal skills to a situation in which you're called upon to make an ethical decision.

## Exercise Background

You're a department manager in a large retail store, and your work group has had a brush with allegations of sexual harassment. Specifically, one of your female employees reported that a male colleague was in the habit of telling off-color jokes and making mildly suggestive comments. When you asked the accused employee about the charges, he didn't deny them but rather attributed them to a misunderstanding.

You passed along the allegations to the HR department, which suspended the male employee, with pay, pending an investigation. When the process was completed, the HR manager who interviewed both parties and other employees concluded that the male employee should be placed on six months' probation. Any further substantiated charges during this period would be cause for immediate dismissal.

HR's decision was based on the following factors: (1) The employee had worked in the store for over 10 years, with a good performance record and without any previous problems. (2) The female who made the charges believed that he was guilty of general insensitivity and hadn't targeted her directly. (3) She didn't think that his behaviors were sufficient to warrant dismissal but simply wanted him to stop them.

Tomorrow will be the accused employee's first day back at work since the HR decision was handed down. You're satisfied with the ruling, but you're a bit worried about potential tension in your work group. You intend to meet with the female today and the male tomorrow morning and try to head off as much tension as possible.

## Exercise Task

In preparing for these two meetings, do the following:

1. Jot down some general notes for your conversation with the male employee.

2. Jot down some general notes for your conversation with the female employee.

3. Make sure that you have a handle on the ethical issues in this situation. Precisely what are they?

4. Consider the options of having the two employees work closely together or keeping them separated. Which will you choose? Why?

# Skill-Building Personal Assessment

Instructions: Read each of the following statements. Select the three statements that best reflect your feelings and beliefs about corporate social responsibility.

1. _____ I think businesses should voluntarily contribute a percentage of their annual profits to social causes.

2. _____ Any time a business is asked to contribute to a social cause the manager should do so.

3. _____ Businesses should never do more than they have to in contributing to social causes.

4. _____ If a manager can cut corners on pollution control to earn more profits she or he should do so.

5. _____ There is nothing wrong with bending the rules to earn more profits if no one will be hurt.

6. _____ All business profits should be distributed to owners or reinvested for future growth.

7. _____ Managers and business owners should try to support local social programs whenever asked.

8. _____ Business owners and managers should make contributions to social programs a normal part of their operations.

9. _____ In the United States you are innocent until proven guilty, so any business accused of unethical conduct should claim innocence.

10. _____ In terms of social responsibility, managers should always avoid unethical or illegal decisions but are obligated to do nothing more.

11. _____ If I owned a business and a local charity asked for a contribution I would be inclined to donate.

12. _____ If I owned a business I would set aside a certain percentage of my annual profits to support social causes.

# Management at Work

## All the News That's Fit to Repeat

*"As the* New York Post *will tell you, any brown people in the vicinity of a bombing are suspect."*

—JOURNALIST ADRIAN CHEN

At 2:49 P.M. on Monday, April 15, 2013, bombs exploded near the finish line of the Boston Marathon. Just before 5:00 P.M., the *New York Post* reported "at least 12 dead," and about half an hour later, the *Post* updated its story to add that a "suspect"—a "Saudi Arabian national"—was under guard at a Boston hospital.

The *Post* had done what every journalistic organization strives to do with any major news event: It reported the story early and grabbed the attention of information seekers in its market. Unfortunately, both of the details in its story were wrong: The death toll was three, and the Saudi Arabian "suspect" was a victim and possible witness. Indeed, rumors and misinformation were rampant in news coverage of the Marathon bombing. By most accounts, questionable reports—especially early-breaking accounts—circulated more rapidly and widely than they had in the wake of the New York Trade Center attacks in 2001. Why? In 2001, cable news was basically the only source of continuous information about such events. Today, however, "news" can be gathered and disseminated almost instantaneously by 24-hour online channels, cellphones, and social media technologies.

Within hours of the Marathon bombings, for example, radio host Alex Jones was telling his 180,000 Twitter followers that "this thing stinks to high heaven" of a government operation designed to frame an unspecified foreign enemy for an act of terrorism. The next day, the governor of Massachusetts was asked to confirm the "report." Similarly, when a college student uploaded a photo of a blurred figure on a nearby rooftop, the image—and reports of a "suspect" captured on camera—rapidly went viral in social media. The "Twittersphere" was soon abuzz with speculations about the mystery man on the roof, and although the person in the photo was far more likely to be a spectator, maintenance worker, or security officer, the image—and the speculation—were soon picked up by CNN, ABC, and CBS.

A few days after the "mystery man" photo first showed up on TV and computer screens, MSN (which is itself a supplier of online information) observed that members of Reddit and 4Chan, two user-controlled websites, were "leading the charge to find the Boston Marathon bombers." Reddit, one of the world's largest websites, even set up a special forum—a *subreddit*—called "findbostonbombers," where members were soon poring over the possible clues contained in a second "crowdsourced" photo. It depicted two men—one wearing a back pack, the other holding a tote bag—among a throng of Marathon spectators near the bomb site, and they looked … well, suspicious.

Another photo of the two men revealed that one was dark skinned, and Reddit identified him as one Sunil Tripathi, a Pakistani-American college student. With further contributions from Facebook, Twitter, BuzzFeed, @YourAnonNews, and celebrity blogger Perez Hilton, who passed on the "information" to six million followers, Tripathi became suspect number one. When the Tripathi lead failed to get satisfactory results, Reddit proceeded to identify the dark-skinned man as Salah Barhoum, a 17-year-old Moroccan-American high school student. The other man turned out to be Barhoum's friend Yassine Zaime, a 24-year-old Moroccan college student. "A lot of people have bags," said the stunned Barhoum. "I thought, 'Why me?' The only thing they looked at was my skin color. Last night, I couldn't sleep, just thinking about the consequences—what people are going to say and what the result is going to be."

And that was before the *New York Post* picked up the photo. On Thursday, April 18, the *Post* emblazoned its front page with the photo of the two men with suspicious baggage and ran a story under the heading: "BAG MEN: Feds seek these two pictured at Boston Marathon." "As the *New York Post* will tell you," quipped New York journalist Adrian Chen, "any brown people in the vicinity of a bombing are suspect." Later that day, the FBI identified two suspects as Chechen brothers Dzhokhar and Tamerlan Tsarnaev. Tamerlan Tsarnaev was killed by police on the same day and Dzhokhar Tsarnaev captured the following day.

Barhoum and Zaimi have sued the *Post* for libel, negligent infliction of emotional distress, and invasion of privacy. Ryan Chittum, an editor at the *Columbia Journalism Review*, thinks that Barhoum and Zaimi will be getting "a very large check from [*Post* owner] Rupert Murdoch in the not-too-distant future." Chittum also thinks that the *Post's* coverage of early events in the Marathon bombing "exhibited reckless and appalling journalistic judgment."

*Post* editor Col Allen defended his paper by maintaining that "we did not identify [Barhoum and Zaimi] as suspects." Perhaps, replies Chittum, but "the *Post* did everything *but* call them suspects." Needless to say, the plaintiffs make the same point in their lawsuit: "The [*Post's*] front page," charges the complaint, "would lead a reasonable reader to believe that plaintiffs had bombs in their bags and were involved in the bombing." Moreover, a lawyer for the two men maintains that the *Post* engaged in racial profiling: "What kind of stereotyping … led the *Post* to think this was okay?" asks Max Stern. "Would they ever have done this if it was just some white kid from the suburbs who was standing there with a backpack?"

Chittum was also critical of "the keyboard crimefighters at Reddit" for compounding the confusion over the identity of the dark-skinned man in the photo that eventually hit the front page of the *New York Post*. Reddit, Chittum charged, dismissed "the backlash to their amateur sleuthing" by falling back on such user plaudits as "This is historic Internet sleuthing!" and "Good job Reddit, we caught him!" Tech blogger Matthew Ingram admits that

*Reddit made mistakes—plenty of them, including identifying the wrong person as a suspect a second time. … But the Post made plenty of mistakes as well—something that Chittum … doesn't mention in his post about how brilliant the traditional media was and how wrong Reddit has been. The larger point is that this isn't an either/or situation—*

*crowdsourcing is valuable for journalism and will continue to be.*

Erroneous reporting is hardly new, but according to Sara Morrison, a colleague of Chittum at the *Columbia Journalism Review*, social media technologies increase both the likelihood of errors and the likelihood of error contagion: "When news gets out and it's wrong," says Morrison, "it gets spread around much faster than it ever did before." The problem is heightened in social media reporting, which puts an even greater premium on immediacy than do traditional media: After all, observes Morrison, "if you're the first to have something notable, you'll get all the attention and all the hits." Conversely, social media technologies tend to put less of a premium on verification than do traditional media. Readers, Morrison observes, assume that social media reporters have done their homework before tweeting or retweeting whatever information they're anxious to pass on. Unfortunately, she says, that is "less and less often" the case.

## Case Questions

1. Since 1897, the motto "All the News That's Fit to Print" has appeared on the front page of the *New York Times*. It was coined by new owner-publisher Adolph Ochs to distinguish his newspaper from its more sensationalistic competitors. What makes news "fit to print" in today's news media? In your opinion, is there any category of contemporary news reporting that tends to encourage *unethical* journalistic behavior? Give at least one example of a story that fits into your category.

2. According to writing specialist Roy Peter Clark, "Immediacy is a value, and it's a positive value. And verification is a positive value. However, the two don't always go together." Clark suggests an ethical *conundrum*—a problem that doesn't necessarily have a satisfactory solution. Explain Clark's conundrum in your own words. How, for example, do you interpret the phrase "don't always go together"? How might this conundrum lead to specifically *ethical* uncertainty on the part of a news reporter? Give at least one example of a newsworthy event in which the conflict between immediacy and verification might lead to a legitimate ethical conundrum for a news reporter.

3. According to one critic, the *New York Post*'s coverage of the Marathon bombing added to "a long history of not exactly getting things right" and confirmed its reputation as "a 'print-first-ask-questions-later' tabloid." In what sense does this criticism suggest problems not only in *ethics*, but in *social responsibility* as well? Specifically, in which *areas of social responsibility* can the *Post* be criticized for failing in its obligations to constituents?

4. The *New York Post* was not the only journalistic organization to be criticized for its coverage of the Marathon bombing. CNN's John King, for example, had repeatedly told viewers that a "dark-skinned male" was being sought by authorities. A fellow journalist criticized King for his description: "Just explain to me what news value exists in the adjective 'dark-skinned.' What exactly is newsworthy that is communicated in that phrase?" Does this criticism indicate any *ethical* lapse on King's part, or just poor journalistic judgment? Should King's description even be regarded as a matter of poor journalistic judgment? If you were King, how would you reply to this criticism?

## Case References

Tommy Christopher, "The *New York Post* Reports Boston Marathon Bombing Suspect in Custody," *Mediaite* (April 15, 2013), www.mediaite.com, on July 30, 2014; "Rumor: Police Detain Saudi National as Person of Interest in Boston Bombing," *MSN News* (April 16, 2013), http://news.msn.com, on July 30, 2014; "Rumor: Boston Marathon Bomber Spotted in Photos?" *MSN News* (April 17, 2013), http://news.msn.com, on July 30, 2014; Katherine Fung, "Media Criticize *New York Post*, CNN for Boston Marathon Bombings Coverage," *Huffington Post* (April 21, 2013), www.huffingtonpost.com, on July 30, 2014; Ryan Chittum, "The *New York Post*'s Disgrace," *Columbia Journalism Review* (April 19, 2013), www.cjr.org, on July 30, 2014; Maria Sacchetti, "Mass. Pair Sues *New York Post* over Marathon Bombing Portrayal," *The Boston Globe* (June 6, 2013), www.bostonglobe.com, on July 31, 2014; Jack Mirkinson, "Al Sharpton: John King's 'Dark-Skinned Male' Comments 'Shameful,'" *Huffington Post* (April 18, 2013), www.huffingtonpost.com, on August 1, 2014; Chittum, "On a Wild Night of News, A Remarkable Press Performance," *Columbia Journalism Review* (April 19, 2013), www.cjr.org, on August 1, 2014.

**YOU MAKE THE CALL** Management by Objectionable Behavior

1. Let's say that, back in 1999, Dov Charney had helped you get an entry-level executive job that you badly wanted. You flourished at the company and by 2010 had risen to CEO. In 2012, Charney handpicked you for the board of directors of American Apparel. On June 15, 2014, you get a call from fellow board member Allan Mayer, who informs you that a certain number of board members are prepared to fire Charney. He wants to know what your vote would be and asks for a response in 36 hours. When the time comes, what will you tell Mayer?

2. In 2009, American Apparel avoided bankruptcy when Lion Capital, an English investment firm, loaned it $80 million. A provision in the agreement allows Lion to recall the loan in case of a CEO change. Early in 2014 (before the announcement of Charney's firing), a Swiss firm called FiveT Capital enabled APP to meet its debt payment by buying a 13 percent share in the company's stock. When Charney was fired, the CEO of FiveT said, "I wonder about the timing of this because I think Dov did a pretty good job turning around the company."

   If you were an APP board member, how might such considerations affect your decision on whether to fire Charney?

3. American Apparel employs 5,000 workers, mostly immigrants, who are paid an average $12 an hour—twice the California minimum wage. "Dov, for all of his misbehavior," says one industry analyst, "was trying to do the right thing. He wasn't paying workers in Bangladesh $2 a day. He was paying $10, $15 an hour in Los Angeles." Even Allan Mayer says that it's "the idealistic component of the brand—our commitment to a sweatshop-free, made-in-the-USA philosophy—that gives it its special place in the culture." Again, put yourself in the position of an APP board member: How might this consideration enter into your decision on whether to fire Charney?

4. Let's go back to Question 1. The circumstances are the same except for one thing: Mayer wants to know how you'd vote at a board meeting scheduled for one week later. What would you do in that week? What factors would you consider? How would you rank those factors in order of importance? Who, for example, are your *constituencies*—the groups for whose interests you're responsible? How would you rank them? How would you vote?

# Endnotes

1 Susan Berfield, "Dov Charney's Sleazy Struggle for Control of American Apparel," *BloombergBusinessweek* (July 9, 2014), www.businessweek.com, on July 17, 2014; Jim Edwards and Charlie Minato, "The Full Story of the Amazing Rise and Predictable Fall of American Apparel CEO Dov Charney," *Business Insider* (June 19, 2014), www.businessinsider.com, on July 20, 2014; Kyle Stock, "American Apparel Founder Dov Charney Finally Gets Fired," *BloombergBusinessweek* (June 19, 2014), www.businessweek.com, on July 17, 2014; Suzanne Kapner et al., "Inside the American Apparel Revolt," *Wall Street Journal* (June 20, 2014), http://online.wsj.com, on July 20, 2014; Claudine Ko, "Meet Your New Boss," *Jane* (June/July 2004), www.claudineko.com, on July 17, 2014; Berfield, "American Apparel: Charney's Bad Behavior Was Very, Very Expensive," *BloombergBusinessweek* (June 23, 2014), www.businessweek.com, on July 17, 2014; Shan Li et al., "CEO Dov Charney's Ouster Could Be Ruinous for American Apparel," *Los Angeles Times* (June 19, 2014), www.latimes.com, on July 14, 2014; Berfield, "Allan Mayer Helped Take Down American Apparel Founder Dov Charney. Who's Allan Mayer?" *BloombergBusinessweek* (June 23, 2014), www.businessweek.com, on July 14, 2014; Kim Bhasin, "Somehow, Dov Charney Still Has a Job at American Apparel," *Huffington Post* (October 1, 2014), www.huffingtonpost.com, on November 30, 2014.

2 See Norman Barry, *Business Ethics* (West Lafayette, IN: Purdue University Press, 1999).

3 Thomas Donaldson and Thomas W. Dunfee, "Toward a Unified Conception of Business Ethics: An Integrative Social Contracts Theory," *Academy of Management Review*, 1994, Vol. 19, No. 2, pp. 252–284.

4 http://www.nytimes.com/2005/07/17/business/yourmoney/17costco.html?pagewanted=all

5 *Wall Street Journal*, April 22, 2009, p. B1.

6 "CareerBuilder Releases Annual List of the Most Unusual Excuses for Calling in Sick, According to U.S. Employers," *CareerBuilder*.com, accessed on January 18, 2015.

7 "Chains' Ties Run Deep on Pharmacy Boards," *USA Today*.com, accessed on January 18, 2015.

8 Jeremy Kahn, "Presto Chango! Sales Are Huge," *Fortune*, March 20, 2000, pp. 90–96; "More Firms Falsify Revenue to Boost Stocks," *USA Today*, March 29, 2000, p. 1B.

9 "U.S. Probes Hilton Over Theft Claims," *Wall Street Journal*, April 22, 2009, accessed on January 18, 2015.

10 "How U.S. Concerns Compete in Countries Where Bribes Flourish," *Wall Street Journal*, September 29, 1995, pp. A1, A14; Patricia Digh, "Shades of Gray in the Global Marketplace," *HR Magazine*, April 1997, pp. 90–98.

11 "Alcoa Faces Allegation by Bahrain of Bribery," *Wall Street Journal*, February 28, 2009, p. A2.

12 *USA Today*, April 11, 2006, p. 1B.

13 Patricia H. Werhane, *Moral Imagination and Management Decision Making* (New York: Oxford University Press, 1999).

14 "Training Managers to Behave," *Time*, May 25, 2009, p. 41.

15 William Dill, "Beyond Codes and Courses," *Selections*, Fall 2002, pp. 21–23.

16 See Donald Lange, "A Multidimensional Conceptualization of Organizational Corruption Control," *Academy of Management Review*, 2008, Vol. 33, No. 3, pp. 710–729, for a recent discussion of these perspectives.

17 Gerald F. Cavanagh, *American Business Values*, 2nd ed. (Upper Saddle River, NJ: Prentice-Hall, 1998).

18 https://surenrajdotcom.wordpress.com/2013/01/27/my-top-10-good-governance-quotes/

19 See Jerald Greenberg and Jason Colquitt, *Handbook of Organizational Justice* (Mahwah, NJ: Lawrence Erlbaum Associates, 2004) for a comprehensive discussion and review of the literature on justice in organization. See also James Lavelle, Deborah Rupp, and Joel Brockner, "Taking a Multifoci Approach to the Study of Justice, Social Exchange, and Citizenship Behavior," *Journal of*

*Management*, 2007, Vol. 33, No. 6, pp. 841–866; and Russell Cropanzano, David Bowen, and Stephen Gilliland, "The Management of Organizational Justice," *Academy of Management Perspectives*, November 2008, pp. 34–44, for recent updates.

20  "U.S. Announces Settlement in Global Bribery Scandal," *Washington Times*, November 4, 2010.

21  "How to Fix Corporate Governance," *BusinessWeek*, May 6, 2002, pp. 68–78. See also Catherine Daily, Dan Dalton, and Albert Cannella, "Corporate Governance: Decades of Dialogue and Data," *Academy of Management Review*, 2003, Vol. 28, No. 3, pp. 371–382; "CEOs Report Stricter Rules," *USA Today*, March 20, 2006, p. 1B.

22  http://www.nytimes.com/2014/08/13/technology/the-boon-of-online-data-puts-social-science-in-a-quandary.html

23  "Hello, Big Brother: Digital Sensors Are Watching Us," *USA Today*, January 26, 2011, pp. 1A, 2A.

24  Ibid, p. 2A.

25  Dirk Matten and Jeremy Moon, "'Implicit' and 'Explicit' CSR: A Conceptual Framework for a Comparative Understanding of Corporate Social Responsibility," *Academy of Management Review*, 2008, Vol. 33, No. 2, pp. 404–424.

26  Thomas Donaldson and Lee E. Preston, "The Stakeholder Theory of the Corporation: Concepts, Evidence, and Implications," *Academy of Management Review*, 1995, Vol. 20, No. 1, pp. 65–91. See also Jeffrey S. Harrison and R. Edward Freeman, "Stakeholders, Social Responsibility, and Performance: Empirical Evidence and Theoretical Perspectives," *Academy of Management Journal*, 1999, Vol. 42, No. 5, pp. 479–495; André O. Laplume, Karan Sonpar, and Reginald A. Litz, "Stakeholder Theory: Reviewing a Theory That Moves Us," *Journal of Management*, 2008, Vol. 34, No. 6, pp. 1152–1189.

27  See Douglas A. Bosse, Robert A. Phillips, and Jeffrey S. Harrison, "Stakeholders, Reciprocity, and Firm Performance," *Strategic Management Journal*, 2009, Vol. 30, pp. 447–456.

28  Aseem Prakash, *Greening the Firm* (Cambridge, UK: Cambridge University Press, 2000); Forest L. Reinhardt, *Down to Earth* (Cambridge, MA: Harvard Business School Press, 2000).

29  "Oil Companies Strive to Turn a New Leaf to Save Rain Forest," *Wall Street Journal*, July 17, 1997, pp. A1, A8.

30  See J. Alberto Aragon-Correa and Sanjay Sharma, "A Contingent Resource-Based View of Proactive Corporate Environmental Strategy," *Academy of Management Review*, 2003, Vol. 28, No. 1, pp. 71–88.

31  See "Frack Fluid Tracer," *Bloomberg Businessweek*, December 1–7, 2014, p. 37.

32  For discussions of this debate, see Jean B. McGuire, Alison Sundgren, and Thomas Schneeweis, "Corporate Social Responsibility and Firm Financial Performance," *Academy of Management Journal*, December 1988, pp. 854–872; Margaret A. Stroup, Ralph L. Neubert, and Jerry W. Anderson, Jr., "Doing Good, Doing Better: Two Views of Social Responsibility," *Business Horizons*, March–April 1987, pp. 22–25.

33  Andrew Singer, "Can a Company Be Too Ethical?" *Across the Board*, April 1993, pp. 17–22.

34  "Peanut Plant's Practices Not 'Rampant,'" *USA Today*, February 6, 2009, p. 4B.

35  "UBS Admits to Helping U.S. Tax Evaders," *USA Today*, February 10, 2009, p. 1B.

36  "Former Glaxo Lawyer Indicted," *New York Times*, November 9, 2010.

37  "Rent-a-Car Companies Putting Recalled Autos on the Road," *ABC News*, July 7, 2010.

38  *USA Today*, February 12, 2009, p.1B.

39  "Philip Morris Unbound," *BusinessWeek*, May 4, 2009, pp. 38–42. See also global.tobaccofreekids.org, accessed on January 20, 2015.

40  *BusinessWeek*, May 4, 2009, p. 41.

41  *USA Today*, March 27, 2006, p. 1B.

42  See "The Good Business Issue," *Bloomberg Businessweek*, December 29, 2014-January 11, 2015 for several other examples of proactive social responsibility.

43  "L'Occitane Leading the Blind," *Fortune*, November 13, 2006, p. 55.

44  "Into Africa: Capitalism From the Ground Up," *BusinessWeek*, May 4, 2009, pp. 60–61.

45  "Over 70 Pfizer Drugs Could Be Free for Laid-Off Workers," *USA Today*, May 15, 2009, p. 6B.

46  "Subway Reduces Sodium Content in Sandwiches," *USA Today*, April 18, 2011, p. 1B.

47  "Apple Once Again Seeing (RED) Over AIDS," *USA Today*, November 24, 2014, p. 1B.

48  Nestle's Palm Oil Woes," *Green Living Tips*, March 21, 2010.

49  Nina Easton and Telis Demos, "The Business Guide to Congress," *Fortune*, May 11, 2009, pp. 72–75.

50  "Siemens to Pay Huge Fine in Bribery Inquiry," *Wall Street Journal*, December 15, 2008, pp. B1, B5.

51  "Daimler Pleads Guilty to Bribing Foreign Governments," *Business Pundit*, April 5, 2010; "Daimler Charged with Bribing Government Officials," *Motor Trend*, March 23, 2010.

52  "Felon or Mark?" *Bloomberg Businessweek*, January 19–25, 2015, pp. 64-69.

53  Nina Easton and Telis Demos, "The Business Guide to Congress," *Fortune*, May 11, 2009, pp. 72–75.

54  Peter A. Heslin and Jenna Ochoa, "Understanding and Developing Strategic Corporate Social Responsibility," *Organizational Dynamics*, 2008, Vol. 37, No. 2, pp. 125–144.

55  "Legal—But Lousy," *Fortune*, September 2, 2002, p. 192.

56  Lynn Sharp Paine, "Managing for Organizational Integrity," *Harvard Business Review*, March–April 1994, pp. 106–115.

57  "To Give, or Not to Give," *Time*, May 11, 2009, p. 10.

58  "Battling 'Donor Dropsy,'" *Wall Street Journal*, July 19, 2002, pp. B1, B4.

59  "A New Way of Giving," *Time*, July 24, 2000, pp. 48–51. See also Michael Porter and Mark Kramwe, "The Competitive Advantage of Corporate Philanthropy," *Harvard Business Review*, December 2002, pp. 57–66.

60  "To Give, or Not to Give," *Time*, May 11, 2009, p. 10.

61  *Time*, May 11, 2009, p. 10.

62  David M. Messick and Max H. Bazerman, "Ethical Leadership and the Psychology of Decision Making," *Sloan Management Review*, Winter 1996, pp. 9–22; see also Muel Kaptein, "Developing and Testing a Measure for the Ethical Culture of Organizations," *Journal of Organizational Behavior*, 2008, Vol. 29, pp. 923–947.

63  "Ethics in Action: Getting It Right," *Selections*, Fall 2002, pp. 24–27.

64  For a thorough review of the literature on whistle-blowing, see Janet P. Near and Marcia P. Miceli, "Whistle-Blowing: Myth and Reality," *Journal of Management*, 1996, Vol. 22, No. 3, pp. 507–526. See also Michael Gundlach, Scott Douglas, and Mark Martinko, "The Decision to Blow the Whistle: A Social Information Processing Framework," *Academy of Management Review*, 2003, Vol. 28, No.1, pp. 107–123.

65  For instance, see "The Complex Goals and Unseen Costs of Whistle-Blowing," *Wall Street Journal*, November 25, 2002, pp. A1, A10.

66  "A Whistle-Blower Rocks an Industry," *BusinessWeek*, June 24, 2002, pp. 126–130.

67  "Lockheed to Pay $2 Million to Settle Lawsuit," *Washington Post*, January 25, 2011; "Feds Intervening in Mississippi Bid-Rigging Lawsuit at Stennis Space Center," *Associated Press*, July 3, 2009.

68  "He Blew a Whistle for 9 Years," *USA Today*, February 13, 2009, pp. 1B, 2B.

69  "SEC Announces a Whistle-Blower Overhaul Plan," *USA Today*, March 6, 2009, p. 1B.

©Markus Pfaff/Shutterstock.com

# 5

# NAVIGATING THE GLOBAL ENVIRONMENT

**Learning Outcomes**

**After studying this chapter, you should be able to:**

1. Describe the nature of international business, including its meaning, recent trends, management of globalization, and competition in a global market.

2. Discuss the structure of the global economy, and describe the GATT and the WTO.

3. Identify and discuss the environmental challenges inherent in international management.

4. Describe the basic issues involved in competing in a global economy, including organization size and the management challenges in a global economy.

## MANAGEMENT IN ACTION    Into Africa

"Africa is one of the few bright spots on the gloomy global economic horizon."

—AMERICAN INVESTOR GEORGE SOROS

With engines thundering, a pack of some 30 chrome-girded Harleys descends like a squad of nomadic storm troopers on the sleepy town of San Pedro. The riders are garbed in bandanas, ripped jeans, studded boots, and black leather bedecked with emblems of an anarchic motorcycle culture. You can tell, however, that it's not your ordinary gang of Hells Angels by the group's logo—an elephant in cowboy boots. They call themselves the Elephant's Bikers, and they ride the poorly maintained highways and dusty byways of the West African nation of Côte d'Ivoire (aka Ivory Coast).[1]

The Elephant's Bikers club was founded in 2003 to celebrate the 100th birthday of the iconic American motorcycle maker Harley-Davidson. The members, of course, ride Harleys, even though they tend to be rather pricey: Taking import costs into account, the club's preferred models run from US$8,200 (the cheapest) to US$52,000. Obviously, club members are fairly affluent, and they include the son of a former president and a current cabinet official. "You'll often see a big boss show up with ripped jeans and skulls even though he's in charge of a highly rated company," reports one member. "That's the

paradox among Harley-Davidson lovers" in Côte d'Ivoire. In San Pedro, a port town of about 150,000 in which a few residents get around on rickety mopeds, a contingent of men, women, and children turns out to greet the riders and snap pictures from aging cellphones.

In May 2014, a similar scene played out in Margate, South Africa—multiplied by a hundred times. The coastal town of Margate is home to Africa Bike Week, an annual Harley-sponsored event catering to riders and enthusiasts. The 2014 version—held a year after Harley had hosted a worldwide 110th anniversary celebration—attracted some 3,000 bikers and a throng of 110,000 enthusiasts. Located on the southern tip of the continent some 3,000 miles from Côte d'Ivoire, South Africa boasts Africa's second-largest economy (behind Nigeria) and is one of only four African countries ranked as upper-middle-income by the World Bank.

Harley launched in South Africa in 1996—two years after the country abandoned the notorious policies of racial segregation known as *apartheid*. It was a well-timed move: With the end of apartheid, the South African economy was finally liberated from 12 years of international sanctions. Since 1996, South Africa's *gross domestic product* (the value of all goods and services produced annually) has tripled, and a sizable middle class has emerged.

SIA KAMBOU/Getty Images

Harley-Davidson has done an excellent job of extending its brand and products to foreign markets. The Elephant's Bikers club in West Africa, formed in 2003, is but one result of the Harley brand name. Harley sees even stronger potential for expansion in South Africa and has been making major marketing investments there to spur sales. For example, the Harley-sponsored Africa Bike Week in South Africa draws over 100,000 enthusiasts each year.

It's this growing middle class that interests Harley, particularly because it includes so many black consumers. According to Michael Carney, who's in charge of the company's African marketing efforts, Harley's African strategy calls for bypassing its traditional core market—41-year-old-plus white males—in favor of "an emerging middle-class black market hungry for the lifestyle of Harley-Davidson. … We foresee this market becoming our main market in the not too distant future in Africa." Harley opened a subsidiary office in Cape Town in 2008, and of 11 authorized dealerships in sub-Saharan Africa, nine are located in South Africa.

South Africa was a logical point of entry into the African market. Along with Nigeria, South Africa accounts for more than half of all spending in sub-Saharan Africa. Perhaps more importantly, the black middle class grew from 1.7 million in 2004 to 4.2 million in 2013, and its spending power has also increased significantly: In 2013, black middle-class South Africans spent US$3.7 billion, compared to US$3.0 billion by their white counterparts. The label "middle class," however, can be misleading in South Africa, where the distribution of wealth along racial lines is extremely unequal. A so-called "*actual* middle class," for instance, falls in the "actual middle" of the spread of household incomes. According to one recent study, this segment consists of households with monthly income between US$142 and US$426. It is overwhelmingly black. Some economists also identify an "*affluent* middle class" consisting of households with monthly income ranging from US$523 to US$3,733. Blacks make up 52 percent of this group and whites 29 percent. (Only 4 percent of South Africans enjoy higher incomes than this "affluent middle class," and this group is 60 percent white and 20 percent black.)

Now consider these numbers in light of the fact that nearly 80 percent of the total South African population is black and less than 9 percent white. Blacks, therefore, are significantly underrepresented in both categories of middle class. In reality, concludes one South African economist, "the 'middle class' is not in the middle of the income distribution, and those who are in the middle are not 'middle class' in the sense of being above some minimum level of affluence. … It follows," he adds, "that the differences between the two groups go beyond income and can be expected to reflect aspects of poverty and deprivation." In fact, South Africa has an extremely high rate of unemployment—about 25 percent. Among blacks, the unemployment rate is 41 percent; among whites, it's 6.3 percent.

So why is Harley so bullish on South Africa? Indeed, why does it have such high expectations for sub-Saharan Africa as a whole, especially among middle-class consumers? After all, the sub-Saharan middle class is typically defined as households with US$2 to US$20 to spend per day. Given the fact that the cheapest model currently sells in South Africa for US$9,166, Harleys are clearly out of reach even for "middle-class" sub-Saharan consumers. Why, then, do so many people flock around the Elephant's Bikers club whenever it makes a pit stop in a town where a run-down moped is a luxury? "We're sharing a pleasure, a dream," explains one club member. "People identify with that. They see that it's accessible, that it's not just on television."

Michael Carney sees a similar dynamic at work in the attraction of Africa Bike Week. The success of the event, he believes, is due in large part to Harley's brand image: "Owning and riding a Harley-Davidson motorcycle," he says, "is a unique experience and lifestyle that unites people from all walks of life. As a brand, we've been fulfilling dreams of personal freedom for 110 years." According to Carney, the Harley image thus appeals to a key psychographic dimension of the company's target market—namely, aspirations of upward social mobility.

Nick Blazquez, head of African operations for the European beverage company Diageo, agrees that well-known brands benefit from the personal and social aspirations of middle-class African consumers: "The African middle class," he says, "aspires to improve their lot. … In that regard, they aspire to brands in the same way as consumers around the world aspire to brands. I'm just not sure," Blazquez admits, "what the middle class is in the context of Africa."

The influential American investor George Soros, however, is sure about one thing: The African middle class is the fastest-growing middle class in the world. That US$2 to US$20 in per diem spending power, for example, represents an increase of more than 100 percent in less than 20 years. It also represents 123 million people, or 13 percent of the population, and will include 1.1 billion by 2060 (42 percent). African consumers spent US$860 billion in 2008 (the most recent year for which official numbers are available) and will spend US$1.4 trillion in 2020. This trajectory, according to the World Bank, is "unstoppable," and Soros calls Africa "one of the few bright spots on the gloomy global economic horizon."

Every business is unique. Likewise, every market is also unique. And when an iconic business like Harley-Davidson invests heavily in an emerging and dynamic market like the African middle class, things can get complicated very quickly. But at the same time, the challenges and opportunities posed by an increasingly global business environment are much the same for any firm with international aspirations. In particular, businesses must make critical decisions about allocating their resources in different markets and about the best means of gaining a competitive advantage in those markets. To be successful today, managers like Harley's Michael Carney need a clear understanding of the global context in which they intend to carry out their plans.

This chapter explores the global context of management. We start by describing the nature of international business. We then discuss the structure of the global market in terms of different economies and economic systems. The basic environmental challenges of management are introduced and discussed next. We then focus on issues of competition in a global economy. Finally, we conclude by characterizing the managerial functions of planning and decision making, organizing, leading, and controlling as management challenges in a global economy.

It is also important to remember, though, that it is no longer feasible to segregate a discussion of "international" management from a discussion of "domestic" management as if they were unrelated activities. Hence, although we highlight the central issues of international management in this chapter, we also integrate international issues, examples, opportunities, and challenges throughout the rest of this book. This treatment provides the most realistic possible survey and discussion of the international environment of management.

## The Nature of International Business

As you prepared breakfast this morning, you may have plugged in a coffee pot manufactured in China and perhaps ironed a shirt or blouse made in Taiwan with an iron made in Mexico. The coffee you drank was probably made from beans grown in South America or Africa. To get to campus, you may have driven a Japanese car. Even if you drove a Ford or a Chevrolet, some of its parts were engineered or manufactured abroad. Perhaps you did not drive a car to school but rode a bus (manufactured by Daimler AG, a German company) or a motorcycle (manufactured by Honda, Kawasaki, Suzuki, or Yamaha—all Japanese firms).

Our daily lives are strongly influenced by businesses from around the world. But no country is unique in this respect. For instance, people drive Fords in Germany, use Apple computers in China, eat McDonald's hamburgers in France, and snack on Mars candy bars in England. They drink Pepsi, drive Harley motorcycles, and wear Levi Strauss jeans in China and South Africa. The Japanese line up to see Disney movies and pay with Visa credit cards. People around the world fly on United Airlines in planes made by Boeing. Their buildings are constructed with Caterpillar machinery, their factories are powered by General Electric engines, and they buy Chevron oil.

In truth, we have become part of a global village and have a global economy where no organization is insulated from the effects of foreign markets and competition.[2] Indeed, more and more firms are reshaping themselves for international competition and discovering new ways to exploit markets in every corner of the world. Failure to take a global perspective is one of the biggest mistakes managers can

McDonald's competes with other restaurants and fast food outlets in over 115 countries. This McDonald's has a prime location at the Dubai International Airport.

make.[3] Thus we start laying the foundation for our discussion by introducing and describing the basics of international business.

## The Meaning of International Business

There are many different forms and levels of international business. Although the lines that distinguish one from another may be arbitrary, we can identify four general levels of international activity that differentiate organizations.[4] These are illustrated in Figure 5.1. A domestic business acquires essentially all of its resources and sells all of its products or services within a single country. Most small businesses are essentially domestic in nature; this category includes local retailers and restaurants, agricultural enterprises, and small service firms such as dry cleaners and hair salons. However, there are very few large domestic businesses left in the world today.

Indeed, most large firms today are either international or multinational companies. An international business is one that is based primarily in a single country but acquires some meaningful share of its resources or revenues (or both) from other countries. Lowe's, the home improvement retailer, fits this description. The firm has more than 1,800 stores in the United States plus another 40 in Canada and Mexico. Lowe's earns around 90 percent of its revenues from its U.S. operations and has no current plans to expand outside of North America. At the same time, however, many of the products it sells, such as tools and appliances, are made abroad.[5]

A multinational business has a worldwide marketplace from which it buys raw materials, borrows money, where it manufactures its products, and to which it subsequently sells its products. Coca-Cola, long considered the quintessential American business, derives more than half of its revenues and profits from outside of the United States. Coke promotes global advertising campaigns but also dozens of local campaigns. The firm markets hundreds of beverages in other countries that have never been sold in the United States. It also formally sponsors over 50 different national Olympic teams and provides support for more than 100 others.[6] Multinational businesses like Coca-Cola are often called *multinational corporations*, or *MNCs*.[7]

The final form of international business is the global business. A global business is one that transcends national boundaries and is not committed to a single home country. Although no business has truly achieved this level of internationalization, a few are edging closer and closer. For example, Hoechst AG, a large German chemical company, portrays itself as a "non-national company." Similarly, Unocal Corporation is legally headquartered in California, but in its company literature, Unocal says it "no longer considers itself as a U.S. company" but is, instead, a "global energy company." Firms that take this approach often have senior leadership that is well grounded in global thinking. For instance, Philip Morris International (PMI) is headed by an executive who was born in Egypt, raised in England, educated in Switzerland, and spent most of his career in New York.

**domestic business**
A business that acquires all of its resources and sells all of its products or services within a single country

**international business**
A business that is based primarily in a single country but acquires some meaningful share of its resources or revenues (or both) from other countries

**multinational business**
A business that has a worldwide marketplace from which it buys raw materials, borrows money, where it manufactures its products, and to which it subsequently sells its products

**global business**
A business that transcends national boundaries and is not committed to a single home country

## FIGURE 5.1 LEVELS OF INTERNATIONAL BUSINESS ACTIVITY

There are four levels of international business activity. These range from domestic business (the lowest level of international activity) to global business (the highest level).

PMI is incorporated in New York, is run out of an operations center in Geneva, Switzerland, and represents itself purely as a global corporation.[8]

Some businesses have attracted unwanted attention in recent years as they sought to relocate their corporate headquarters to other countries. Halliburton, for example, is headquartered in Houston. But the company made waves when it opened a second "headquarters" location in Dubai. All the company was really doing was raising its profile in the Middle East among potential customers and partners. More substantively, Burger King considered moving its headquarters from Miami to Canada as part of its acquisition of a Canadian fast food company, and Walgreen's contemplated moving from Illinois to Switzerland when it bought a Swiss drugstore chain. In both cases, though, it became clear that the motivation for moving would be to escape high U.S. business taxes, and the companies eventually succumbed to public and government pressures to maintain their U.S. headquarters.[9]

## Trends in International Business

To understand why and how these different levels of international business have emerged, we must look briefly to the past. Most of the industrialized countries in Europe were devastated during World War II. Many Asian countries, especially Japan, fared no better. There were few passable roads, few standing bridges, and even fewer factories dedicated to the manufacture of peacetime products. And those regions less affected by wartime destruction—Canada, Latin America, and Africa—had not yet developed the economic muscle to threaten the economic preeminence of the United States.

Businesses in war-torn countries like Germany and Japan had no choice but to rebuild from scratch. Because of this position, they essentially had to rethink every facet of their operations, including technology, production, finance, and marketing. Although it took many years for these countries to recover, they eventually did so, and their economic systems were subsequently poised for growth. During the same era, many U.S. companies grew somewhat complacent. Their customer base was growing rapidly. Increased population spurred by the baby boom and increased affluence resulting from the postwar economic boom greatly raised the average person's standard of living and expectations. The U.S. public continually wanted new and better products and services. Many U.S. companies profited greatly from this pattern, but most were also perhaps guilty of taking the status quo for granted.

> "We regard ourselves as having a home base in each of the 23 countries where we operate."
>
> —MARC BECKER, FORMER EXECUTIVE AT UNICREDIT, A LARGE LENDER INCORPORATED IN ITALY WORKING TO PRESENT A GLOBAL IMAGE[10]

But U.S. firms are no longer isolated from global competition or the global market. A few simple numbers help tell the full story of international trade and industry. First of all, the volume of international trade increased more than 4,000 percent between 1960 and 2010. Further, although 139 of the world's largest corporations are headquartered in the United States, there are also 71 in Japan, 39 in France, 37 in Germany, and 46 in China.[11] Within certain industries, the preeminence of non-U.S. firms is even more striking. For example, only one of the world's 10 largest banks and none of the largest electronics companies are based in the United States. Only three of the 10 largest chemical companies are U.S. firms. On the other hand, U.S. firms comprise seven of the 10 largest aerospace companies, three of the six largest airlines, and three of the nine largest computer companies.

U.S. firms are also finding that international operations are an increasingly important element of their sales and profits. For example, in 2013 Yum! Brands (owners of Pizza Hut, Taco Bell, and KFC) realized 70 percent of its profits abroad.[12] Similarly, General Electric generated more than half of its 2014 profits from foreign markets.[13] From any perspective, then, it is clear that we live in a truly global economy. Virtually all businesses today must be concerned with the competitive situations they face in lands far from home and with how companies from distant lands are competing in their homelands.

## Managing the Process of Globalization

Managers should also recognize that their global context dictates two related but distinct sets of challenges. One set of challenges must be confronted when an organization chooses to change its level of international involvement. For example, a firm that wants to move from being an international to a multinational business has to manage that transition.[14] The other set of challenges occurs when the organization has achieved its desired level of international involvement and must then function effectively within that environment. This section highlights the first set of challenges, and the next section introduces the second set of challenges. When an organization makes the decision to increase its level of international activity, there are several alternative strategies that can be adopted.

Importing and exporting are common forms of international business. Exporters load their products into cargo containers such as these. The containers are shipped to foreign markets and unloaded for distribution and sale there.

**Importing and Exporting** Importing or exporting (or both) is usually the first type of international business in which a firm gets involved. Exporting, or making the product in the firm's domestic marketplace and selling it in another country, can involve both merchandise and services. Importing is bringing a good, service, or capital into a firm's home country from abroad. For example, automobiles (Mazda, Ford, Volkswagen, Mercedes-Benz, Ferrari) and stereo equipment (Sony, Bang & Olufsen, Sanyo) are routinely exported by their manufacturers to other countries. Likewise, many wine distributors buy products from vineyards in France, Italy, or California and import them into their own countries for resale.

An import/export operation has several advantages. For example, it is the easiest way of entering a market with a small outlay of capital. Because the products are usually sold "as is," there is no need to adapt the product to the local conditions, and little risk is involved. Nevertheless, there are also disadvantages. For example, imports and exports are subject to taxes, tariffs, and higher transportation expenses. Furthermore, because the products are not adapted to local conditions, they may miss the needs of a large segment of the market. Finally, some products may be restricted and thus can be neither imported nor exported.

**Licensing** A company may prefer to arrange for a foreign company to manufacture or market its products under a licensing agreement. Factors that may lead to this decision include excessive transportation costs, government regulations, and home production costs. Licensing is an arrangement whereby a firm allows another company to use its brand name, trademark, technology, patent, copyright, or other assets. In return, the licensee pays a royalty, usually based on sales. For example, Kirin Brewery, Japan's largest producer of beer, wanted to expand its international operations but feared that the time involved in shipping it from Japan would cause the beer to lose its freshness. Thus it has entered into a number of licensing arrangements with breweries in other markets. These brewers make beer according to strict guidelines provided by the Japanese firm and then package and market it as Kirin Beer. They then pay a royalty back to Kirin for each case sold. Molson produces Kirin in Canada under such an agreement, while the Charles Wells Brewery does the same in England.

Two advantages of licensing are increased profitability and extended profitability. This strategy is often used for entry into less-developed countries where older technology is still acceptable and, in fact, may be state of the art. For instance, in countries with little or no

**exporting**
Making a product in the firm's domestic marketplace and selling it in another country

**importing**
Bringing a good, service, or capital into the home country from abroad

**licensing**
An arrangement whereby one company allows another company to use its brand name, trademark, technology, patent, copyright, or other assets in exchange for a royalty based on sales

Licensing can allow a company to extend the life of its technology. For instance, older versions of computer hardware and software that have limited markets in industrialized countries may still be widely used in less-developed parts of the world. This Egyptian library, for example, uses computers that have little market value in the United States.

wireless Internet access, dial-up modems are still the norm. A primary disadvantage of licensing is inflexibility. A firm can tie up control of its product or expertise for a long period of time. And, if the licensee does not develop the market effectively, the licensing firm can lose profits. A second disadvantage is that licensees can take the knowledge and skill to which they have been given access for a foreign market and exploit them in the licensing firm's home market. When this happens, what used to be a business partner becomes a business competitor.

**Strategic Alliances** In a strategic alliance, two or more firms jointly cooperate for mutual gain.[15] FedEx subsidiary FedEx Trade Networks recently joined with Fritz Companies Israel to make the company its only regional service provider in the area. The alliance is expected to increase FedEx Trade Networks' global presence by offering customers greater international ocean and air freight services and will provide Fritz Companies Israel clients with the strength of the FedEx brand. The move is also intended to show customers that both companies are hearing and acting on their desires for more reliable global reach and supply chain solutions.[16] Starbucks recently announced a partnership with India-based Tata Coffee to purchase its coffee beans. They plan on also working with the company to open stores in hotels and other retail stores.[17] Most airline alliances also fit this category. For instance, American Airlines and British Air have a code-sharing alliance. International agreements allow British Air (BA) to fly passengers from London to Dallas. However, it cannot board new passengers in Dallas and fly them on to Los Angeles. But passengers can buy a single ticket that allows them to fly from London to Dallas on BA and then change to an American Airlines flight to continue their journey.

A joint venture is a special type of strategic alliance in which the partners actually share ownership of a new enterprise. General Mills and Nestlé formed a separate company called Cereal Partners Worldwide (CPW) to produce and market cereals. General Mills supplies the technology and proven formulas, while Nestlé provides its international distribution network. The two partners share equally in ownership and profits from CPW. Strategic alliances have enjoyed a tremendous upsurge in the past few years. In most cases, each party provides a portion of the equity or the equivalent in physical plant, raw materials, cash, or other assets. The proportion of the investment then determines the percentage of ownership in the venture.[18]

Strategic alliances have both advantages and disadvantages.[19] For example, they can allow quick entry into a market by taking advantage of the existing strengths of participants. Japanese automobile manufacturers employed this strategy to their advantage to enter the U.S. market by using the already-established distribution systems of U.S. automobile manufacturers. Strategic alliances are also an effective way to gain access to technology or raw materials. And they allow the firms to share the risk and cost of the new venture. One major disadvantage lies with the shared ownership of joint ventures. Although it reduces the risk for each participant, it also limits the control and return that each firm can enjoy.[20] Another is political interference or intrusion in countries where the government plays an active role in international joint ventures. For example, BP recently lost control of a long-standing and highly lucrative joint venture in Russia when its senior management misread the wishes and intentions of some key government officials about how a new venture was to be structured.[21] Blending disparate corporate cultures can also be a challenge.[22]

**strategic alliance**
A cooperative arrangement between two or more firms for mutual gain

**joint venture**
A special type of strategic alliance in which the partners share in the ownership of an operation on an equity basis

**Direct Investment** Another level of commitment to internationalization is direct investment. Direct investment occurs when a firm headquartered in one country builds or purchases operating facilities or subsidiaries in a foreign country. For instance, Disney is investing approximately $4 billion to construct a new Disney theme park and resort near Shanghai, China. Similarly, Coca-Cola spent $150 million to build a new bottling and distribution network in India. Harley-Davidson recently constructed an assembly plant in India to better serve that country's market.[23] And in 2015 Swedish automaker Volvo, owned by a Chinese company, announced plans to increase its market share in the United States and started construction on a $500 million factory in South Carolina to support its plans.[24]

Disney is making a significant direct investment in constructing a major new theme park and resort near Shanghai, China. This building, for example, is just one part of a huge entertainment complex Disney has built at the resort. The Disney park opened in Spring 2016 and represented the fourth Disney park outside of the United States.

One major reason many firms make direct investments is to capitalize on lower labor costs. In other words, the goal is often to transfer production to locations where labor is cheap. Japanese businesses have moved some of their production facilities to Thailand because labor costs are much lower there than in Japan. Many U.S. firms have been using maquiladoras for the same purpose. Maquiladoras are light assembly plants built in northern Mexico close to the U.S. border. The plants are given special tax breaks by the Mexican government, and the area is populated with workers willing to work for very low wages. More than 3,000 plants in the region employ about 1.2 million workers. The plants are owned by major corporations, primarily from the United States, Japan, South Korea, and major European industrial countries. This concentrated form of direct investment benefits Mexico, the companies themselves, and workers who might otherwise be without jobs. Some critics argue, however, that the low wages paid by the maquiladoras amount to little more than slave labor.[25] Some of the production in this area has been shifted to China, where there is also a large pool of talented workers, most of whom will work for even lower wages. But in recent years some overseas production has been moved back to the United States because labor costs in both Mexico and China have increased to the point that when travel and shipping costs are factored in, it is almost as cheap to produce in the United States. This trend has been most pronounced in the garment industry.[26]

**direct investment**
When a firm headquartered in one country builds or purchases operating facilities or subsidiaries in a foreign country

**maquiladoras**
Light assembly plants built in northern Mexico close to the U.S. border that are given special tax breaks by the Mexican government

Like the other approaches for increasing a firm's level of internationalization, direct investment carries with it a number of benefits and liabilities. Managerial control is more complete, and profits do not have to be shared as they do in joint ventures. Purchasing an existing organization provides additional benefits in that the human resources and organizational infrastructure (administrative facilities, plants, warehouses, and so forth) are already in place. Acquisition is also a way to purchase the brand-name identification of a product. This could be particularly important if the cost of introducing a new brand is high. When Nestlé bought the U.S. firm Carnation Company, it retained the firm's brand names for all of its products sold in the United States. Likewise, when Ford bought Volvo it retained that brand name; and when Ford later sold Volvo to a

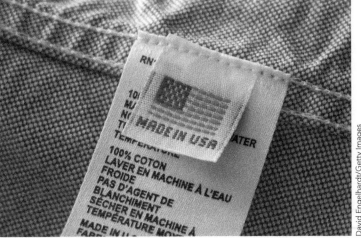

For years manufacturers moved production to overseas factories to capitalize on cheaper labor. But as foreign wages have increased and U.S. workers have become more productive some manufacturers, like this jeans company, have relocated production back to the United States.

Chinese company, the name was again retained by its new owners. These advantages notwithstanding, a company that does this is now operating a part of itself entirely within the borders of a foreign country. The additional complexity in the decision making, the economic and political risks, and other challenges may outweigh the advantages that can be obtained by international expansion.

Of course, we should also note that these approaches to internationalization are not mutually exclusive. Indeed, most large firms use all of them simultaneously. MNCs have a global orientation and worldwide approach to foreign markets and production. They search for opportunities all over the world and select the best strategy to serve each market. In some settings, they may use direct investment, in others licensing, in others strategic alliances; in still others they might limit their involvement to exporting and importing. The advantages and disadvantages of each approach are summarized in Table 5.1.

## Competing in a Global Market

Even when a firm is not actively seeking to increase its desired level of internationalization, its managers are still responsible for seeing that it functions effectively within whatever level of international involvement the organization has achieved. Moreover, local firms must be prepared to compete with multinationals with aggressive globalization goals.[27] In one sense, the job of a manager in an international business may not be that much different from the job of a manager in a domestic business. Each may be responsible for acquiring resources and materials, making products, providing services, developing human resources, advertising, or monitoring cash flow.

In another sense, however, the complexity associated with each of these activities may be much greater for managers in international firms. Rather than buying raw materials from sources in California, Texas, and Missouri, an international purchasing manager may buy materials from sources in Peru, India, and Spain. Rather than training managers for new plants in Michigan, Florida, and Oregon, the international human resources executive may be training new plant managers for facilities in China, Mexico, and Scotland. And instead of developing a single marketing campaign for the United States, an advertising director may be working on promotional efforts in France, Brazil, and Japan.

---

## TABLE 5.1 ADVANTAGES AND DISADVANTAGES OF DIFFERENT APPROACHES TO INTERNATIONALIZATION

When organizations decide to increase their level of internationalization, they can adopt several strategies. Each strategy is a matter of degree, as opposed to being a discrete and mutually exclusive category. And each has unique advantages and disadvantages that must be considered.

| Approach to Internationalization | Advantages | Disadvantages |
|---|---|---|
| Importing or Exporting | • Small cash outlay<br>• Little risk<br>• No adaptation necessary | • Tariffs and taxes<br>• High transportation costs<br>• Government restrictions |
| Licensing | • Increased profitability<br>• Extended profitability | • Inflexibility<br>• Competition |
| Strategic Alliances/ Joint Ventures | • Quick market entry<br>• Access to materials and technology | • Shared ownership (limits control and profits) |
| Direct Investment | • Enhanced control<br>• Existing infrastructure | • Complexity<br>• Greater economic and political risk<br>• Greater uncertainty |

Finally, the key question that must be addressed by any manager trying to be effective in an international market is whether to focus on globalization or on regionalism. A global thrust requires that activities be managed from an overall global perspective as part of an integrated system. Regionalism, on the other hand, involves managing within each region with less regard for the overall organization. In reality, most larger MNCs manage some activities globally (for example, finance and manufacturing are commonly addressed globally) and others locally (human resource management and advertising are frequently handled this way).

☐ Managers need to have a clear understand how of global forces and markets affect their business.

☐ You should also have a clear understanding of both the current and projected level of internationalization of your business.

**Manager's Checklist** ☑

# The Structure of the Global Economy

One thing that can be helpful to managers seeking to operate in a global environment is to better understand the structure of the global economy. Although each country and indeed many regions within any given country are unique, we can still note some basic similarities and differences. We describe three different elements of the global economy: mature market economies and systems, high-potential/high-growth economies, and other economies.[28]

## Mature Market Economies and Systems

A market economy is based on the private ownership of business, and it allows market factors such as supply and demand to determine business strategy. Mature market economies include the United States, Canada, Japan, the United Kingdom, France, Germany, and Sweden. These countries have several things in common. For example, they tend to employ market forces in the allocation of resources. They also tend to be characterized by private ownership of property, although there is some variance along this dimension. France, for example, has a relatively high level of government ownership among the market economies.

U.S. managers have relatively few problems operating in market economies. Many of the basic business "rules of the game" that apply in the United States also apply, for example, in Germany or England. And consumers there often tend to buy the same kinds of products. For these reasons, it is not unusual for U.S. firms seeking to expand geographically to begin operations in other market economies. Although the task of managing an international business in an industrial market economy is somewhat less complicated than operating in some other type of economy, it still poses some challenges. Perhaps foremost among them is that the markets in these economies are typically quite mature. Many industries, for example, are already dominated by large and successful companies. Thus, competing in these economies poses a major challenge.

Figure 5.2 highlights three relatively mature market systems. Market systems are clusters of countries that engage in high levels of trade with one another. One mature market system is North America. The United States, Canada, and Mexico are major trading partners with one another; more than 80 percent of Mexico's exports go to the United States, and more than 51 percent of what Mexico imports comes from the United States.[29] These countries have also negotiated a variety of agreements to make trade even easier. The most important of these, the North American Free Trade Agreement (NAFTA), eliminates many of the trade barriers—quotas and tariffs, for example—that existed previously.

**market economy**
An economy based on the private ownership of business that allows market factors such as supply and demand to determine business strategy

**market systems**
Clusters of countries that engage in high levels of trade with one another

**North American Free Trade Agreement (NAFTA)**
An agreement made by the United States, Canada, and Mexico to promote trade with one another

## FIGURE 5.2 THE GLOBAL ECONOMY

The global economy is dominated by three relatively mature market systems. As illustrated here, these market systems consist of North America, Europe (especially those nations in the European Union), and Pacific Asia (parts of which are high-potential/ high-growth economies). Other areas of Asia, as well as Africa and South America, have the potential for future growth but currently play only a relatively small role in the global economy. The Middle East region plays a major role in the global petroleum market.

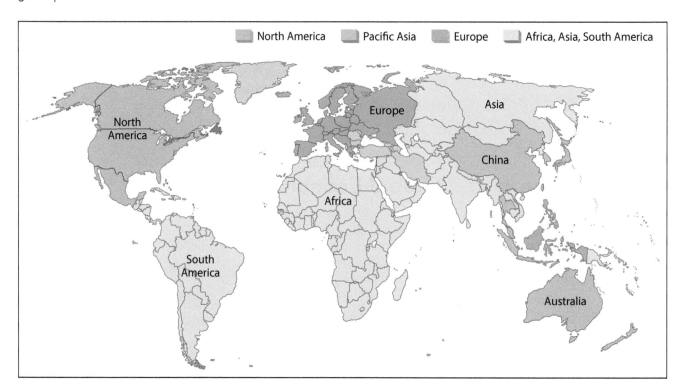

Another mature market system is Europe. For most of the twentieth century, Europe was really two distinct economic areas. The eastern region consisted of communist countries such as Poland, Czechoslovakia, and Romania. These countries relied on government ownership of business and greatly restricted trade. In contrast, Western European countries with traditional market economies have been working together to promote international trade for decades. In particular, the European Union (or *EU*, as it is often called), currently comprised of 28 members, has long been a formidable market system. The EU's origins can be traced to 1957 when Belgium, France, Luxembourg, Germany, Italy, and the Netherlands signed the Treaty of Rome to promote economic integration. Between 1973 and 1986, these countries were joined by Denmark, Ireland, the United Kingdom, Greece, Spain, and Portugal, and the group became known first as the European Community and then the European Union. Austria, Finland, and Sweden joined the EU in 1995. Ten other countries, including Poland, Estonia, and Hungary, joined in 2004; Romania and Bulgaria became members in 2007. For years these countries have followed a basic plan that led to the systematic elimination of most trade barriers. The new market system achieved significantly more potential in 2002 when 11 of the EU members eliminated their home currencies (such as French francs and Italian lira) and adopted a new common currency called the *euro*. The euro is now widely accepted throughout Europe and, like the dollar, is also traded in most global financial markets.

The European situation remains complex, however. With the collapse of communism, the market economies adopted by the Eastern countries are not as developed as those in Western Europe, for instance. These countries also want greater participation in trade with

**European Union (EU)**
The first and most important international market system

the Western European countries and more voice in the EU. Indeed, in some ways the emergence of the East has slowed and complicated business activities in the West. Most members agree that the governance structure created for a six-member alliance needs revision since the EU has become so big, but there is little agreement on how to approach such a revision. Sharp divisions among EU members regarding U.S. policies in the Middle East has strained relations among such key nations as Spain and the United Kingdom (which supported the war in Iraq) and France and Germany (which opposed the war in Iraq). And economic turmoil in some EU countries—such as Greece—has created even more difficulties. In the long term, however, the EU is likely to remain an important force in the global economy.

Yet another mature market system is Pacific Asia. As shown in Figure 5.2, this market system includes Japan, China, Thailand, Malaysia, Singapore, Indonesia, South Korea, Taiwan, the Philippines, and Australia. Indeed, Japan, Taiwan, Singapore, Thailand, and South Korea were major economic powerhouses until a regional currency crisis slowed their growth in the late 1990s. Although that crisis has passed, the global effects of the 2008–2010 recession continue to affect all parts of the global economy, including Pacific Asia. The earthquake and tsunami that struck Japan in 2011 have also had disastrous effects on that country in particular.

## High-Potential/High-Growth Economies

In contrast to the highly developed and mature market economies just described, other countries have what can be termed *high-potential/high-growth economies*. These economies have been relatively underdeveloped and immature and, until recently, were characterized by weak industry, weak currency, and relatively poor consumers.[30] The governments in these countries, however, have been actively working to strengthen their economies by opening their doors to foreign investment and by promoting international trade. Some of these countries have only recently adopted market economies, while others still use a command economy.

Even though it is technically part of Pacific Asia and is rapidly becoming a major economic force, the People's Republic of China remains largely underdeveloped. But its market potential is enormous. For example, it is already the world's second-largest automobile market (mostly for smaller cars, though) and has recently become the world's second-largest economy. The transfer of control of Hong Kong from Great Britain to China focused even more attention on the market potential in the world's most populous country. This fact is the primary reason that Disney chose to build its newest theme park in China. India is also emerging as a major force in the global economy. Marvel Comics launched an Indian version of its popular Spider-Man comic book in India.[31] And Walmart launched a joint venture in India under the brand name Best Price Modern Wholesale.[32] Vietnam has become a potentially important market, and Brazil is becoming more important as well.[33] Likewise, Russia and the other states and republics that previously made up the Commonwealth of Independent States are being closely watched by many companies for emerging market opportunities.[34] South Africa also holds considerable promise.

The primary challenges presented by the developing economies to those interested in conducting international business there are potential consumers' lack of wealth and an underdeveloped infrastructure. Developing economies have enormous economic potential, but much of it remains untapped. Thus international firms entering these markets often have to invest heavily in distribution systems, in training consumers how to use their products, and even in providing living facilities for their workers. They also run the risk of major policy changes that can greatly distort the value of their investments.[35]

> "China is big, but it is hard…[other] places are equally big, but they are not quite as hard."
>
> —JEFFREY IMMELT, CEO OF GENERAL ELECTRIC[36]

## Other Economies

There are some economic systems around the world that defy classification as either mature markets or high-potential/high-growth economies. One major area that falls outside of these

**Pacific Asia**
A market system located in Southeast Asia

The United States and Cuba are taking steps to normalize their relationship after decades of restrictions and embargoes. For years Cuban coffee and cigars could not be brought into the United States, but these restrictions may soon be lifted. And if this does happen, Cuban retailers like this one should see an increase in their sales.

categories is the oil-exporting region generally called the Middle East. The oil-exporting countries present mixed models of resource allocation, property ownership, and infrastructure development. These countries all have access to major amounts of crude oil, however, and thus are important players in the global economy.

These countries include Iran, Iraq, Kuwait, Saudi Arabia, Libya, Syria, and the United Arab Emirates. High oil prices in the last four decades have created enormous wealth in these countries. Many of them invested heavily in their infrastructures. Whole new cities were built, airports were constructed, and the population was educated. The per capita incomes of the United Arab Emirates and Qatar, for example, are among the highest in the world. Although there is great wealth in the oil-producing nations, they provide great challenges to managers. Political instability (as evidenced by the Persian Gulf War in 1991, the U.S.-led war in Iraq starting in 2003, and the political turmoil that swept the region in 2011 and continued into 2015) and tremendous cultural differences, for example, combine to make doing business in many parts of the Middle East both very risky and very difficult.

Other countries pose risks of a different sort to business. Politically and ethnically motivated violence, for example, still characterizes some countries. Foremost among these are Peru, El Salvador, Turkey, Colombia, and Northern Ireland. Cuba presents special challenges because it has been so insulated from the outside world. With the demise of other communist regimes, some experts believe that Cuba will eventually join the ranks of the market economies. And in 2015 the United States began to lift longstanding trade embargoes, and the two countries took steps to normalize their relationship. Assuming this trend continues, Cuba's strategic location 90 miles from Florida will quickly make it an important business center.[38]

> "The dominant logic holds that innovation comes from the U.S., goes to Europe and Japan, and then gravitates to poor countries. But now we're starting to see a reversal of that flow."
>
> —C. K. PRAHALAD, LEADING STRATEGY EXPERT[37]

### The Role of the GATT and the WTO

The global economy is also increasingly being influenced by the General Agreement on Tariffs and Trade (GATT) and the World Trade Organization (WTO).

**General Agreement on Tariffs and Trade (GATT)** The General Agreement on Tariffs and Trade, or GATT, was first negotiated following World War II in an effort to avoid trade wars that would benefit rich nations and harm poorer ones. Essentially, the GATT is a trade agreement intended to promote international trade by reducing trade barriers and making it easier for all nations to compete in international markets. The GATT was a major stimulus to international trade after it was first ratified in 1948 by 23 countries.

One key component of the GATT was the identification of the so-called *most favored nation* (MFN) principle. This provision stipulates that if a country extends preferential treatment to any other nation that has signed the agreement, the same preferential treatment must be extended to all signatories of the agreement. Members can extend such treatment to nonsignatories as well, but are not required to do so.

**GATT**
A trade agreement intended to promote international trade by reducing trade barriers and making it easier for all nations to compete in international markets

**World Trade Organization (WTO)** The World Trade Organization, or WTO, came into existence on January 1, 1995. The WTO replaced the GATT and absorbed its mission. The WTO is headquartered in Geneva, Switzerland, and currently includes 161 member nations. Members are required to open their markets to international trade and follow WTO rules. The WTO has three basic goals:

1. To promote trade flows by encouraging nations to adopt nondiscriminatory and predictable trade policies
2. To reduce remaining trade barriers through multilateral negotiations
3. To establish impartial procedures for resolving trade disputes among its members

The World Trade Organization is certain to continue to play a major role in the evolution of the global economy. At the same time, it has also become a lightning rod for protesters and other activists who argue that the WTO focuses too narrowly on globalization issues to the detriment of human rights and the environment.

World Trade
Organization (WTO)
An organization, which
currently includes 161
member nations and 23
observer countries, that
requires members to open
their markets to international
trade and follow WTO rules

---

☐ Managers should know the current economic conditions in all relevant marketplaces.

☐ Managers should also understand the GATT and WTO and how they affect their business.

☐ You should have a clear understanding of possible international assignments your firm may have in mind for you and the role of those assignments in your career progression.

**Manager's Checklist**

# Environmental Challenges of International Management

We noted earlier that managing in a global context creates additional challenges for the manager. As illustrated in Figure 5.3, three environmental challenges in particular warrant additional exploration at this point—the economic environment, the political-legal environment, and the cultural environment of international management.[39]

## The Economic Environment

Every country is unique and creates a unique set of challenges for managers trying to do business there. However, there are three aspects of the economic environment in particular that can help managers anticipate the kinds of economic challenges they are likely to face in working abroad.

**Economic System** The first of these is the economic system used in the country. As we described earlier, most countries today are moving toward a market economy. In a mature market economy, the key element for managers is freedom of choice. Consumers are free to make decisions about which products they prefer to purchase, and firms are free to decide what products and services to provide. As long as both the consumer and the firm are free to decide to be in the market, then supply and demand determine which firms and which products will be available.

A related characteristic of market economies that is relevant to managers concerns the nature of property ownership. There are two pure types—complete private ownership and complete public ownership. In systems with private ownership, individuals and

### FIGURE 5.3 ENVIRONMENTAL CHALLENGES OF INTERNATIONAL MANAGEMENT

Managers functioning in a global context must be aware of several environmental challenges. Three of the most important include economic, political-legal, and cultural challenges.

organizations—not the government—own and operate the companies that conduct business. In systems with public ownership, the government directly owns the companies that manufacture and sell products. Few countries have pure systems of private ownership or pure systems of public ownership. Most countries tend toward one extreme or the other, but usually a mix of public and private ownership exists.

**Natural Resources** Another important aspect of the economic environment in different countries is the availability of natural resources. A very broad range of resources is available in different countries. Some countries, like Japan, have relatively few natural resources of their own. Japan is thus forced to import most of the oil, iron ore, and other natural resources it needs to manufacture products for its domestic and overseas markets. The United States, in contrast, has enormous natural resources and is a major producer of oil, natural gas, coal, iron ore, copper, uranium, and other metals and materials that are vital to the development of a modern economy.

One natural resource that is particularly important in the modern global economy is oil. As we noted earlier, a small set of countries in the Middle East, including Saudi Arabia, Iraq, Iran, and Kuwait, controls a very large percentage of the world's total known reserves of crude oil. Access to this single natural resource has given these oil-producing countries enormous clout in the international economy. One of the more controversial global issues today involving natural resources is the South American rain forest. Developers and farmers in Brazil, Peru, and other countries are clearing vast areas of rain forest, arguing that it is their land and that they can do what they want with it. Many environmentalists, however, fear the deforestation is wiping out entire species of animals and may so alter the environment as to affect weather patterns around the world.[40] The *Doing Business on Planet Earth* feature illustrates another international situation today that involves (potential) natural resources in Antarctica.

**infrastructure**
The schools, hospitals, power plants, railroads, highways, ports, communication systems, airfields, and commercial distribution systems of a country

"For more than a year it has been particularly difficult to get to and from work. The minimal space has meant cars have been mounting the pavement and pushing cyclists and pedestrians into each other. The new road is a big relief!"

—MA CUNLIN, NANJING, CHINA, RESIDENT[41]

**Infrastructure** Yet another important aspect of the economic environment of relevance to international management is infrastructure. A country's infrastructure consists of its schools, hospitals, power plants, railroads, highways, shipping ports, communication systems, airfields, commercial distribution systems, and so forth. The United States has a highly developed infrastructure. For example, its educational system is modern, roads and bridges are well developed, and

**DOING BUSINESS ON PLANET EARTH**

# Cold Calling

Australia says that it owns a good chunk of Antarctica, the ice-bound continent at the bottom of the world. Established in 1933, the Australian Antarctic Territory (ATT) covers 3 million square miles, or 42 percent of the continent. Australia maintains four permanent research stations in the ATT, in which the government prohibits claims made by other nations. Australia also refuses to accept any reduction in the scope of its own claims by international treaty or other means.

As it happens, however, China, which is a relative newcomer to Antarctica, has built two of its five research stations within the ATT. Russia and India have also located stations within the Australian claim, and no one has yet to ask Australia's permission. Nor has Australia taken any action to enforce the terms of its claim. Why has there been such a notable absence of geopolitical tension? For one thing, despite the claims of Australia, there is no international agreement on sovereignty over any part of Antarctica. The Antarctic Treaty of 1959, which was originally signed by 12 countries, laid the groundwork for a pattern of consensual dealings that has so far prevailed among nations with an active interest in the continent. The treaty froze all territorial claims but did not otherwise interfere with them, and it also ensured the right of nations to decline to recognize such claims. Since 1959, 38 other nations have signed the treaty.

So how does a country assert its right to be active in Antarctica? According to one expert on the geopolitics of the continent, you build a research station and "put a huge flag on a flagpole close to the station." So far, 29 nations have run up a total of 82 flags. The United States has six stations in Antarctica, and China's five give it one more than Great Britain and Australia. China, which signed the Antarctic Treaty in 1983, has called it "a rich man's club" but has also used its membership as a means of asserting its prestige in the international scientific community.

Perhaps more importantly, the presence of its facilities in Antarctica gives China more clout in international decision making about activities on the continent. Currently, the Madrid Protocol, which was adopted in 1991, provides strict environmental protections for Antarctica, including prohibitions against mining. Signatories have played by the rules for more than 20 years now, despite Antarctica's significant deposits of oil and gas, coal, lead, iron, copper, nickel, gold, silver, platinum, and uranium. The absence of mining, however, may be less a matter of self-restraint than one of practical constraint: "The landmass," says José Retamales of the Chilean Antarctic Institute, "is protected by up to two miles of ice. So far, this has been a barrier against the exploitation of mineral resources because it's almost impossible to drill through the ice with current technology."

China, however, has made no secret of its objectives in Antarctica. It's certainly looking for a little scientific respect, but "also we're here about the potential of the resources," admits Qu Tanzhou, director of the country's polar programs. The Madrid Protocol does not expire until 2048, but at that time, it's scheduled for review by the "consultative parties" among its members—a select group to which China now belongs because of its recent Antarctic buildup. In a little more than 30 years, ice melt (driven by climate change) may combine with advanced technology to make resource extraction much more feasible in Antarctica. If that happens, says Antonio José Teixeira of Brazil's Antarctic program, "it's likely that countries will be discussing a convention on exploitation."

*References:* Anthony Bergin and Tony Press, "Action Needed to Cement Role in Antarctica," *Sydney* (Australia) *Morning Herald* (December 1, 2011), www.smh.com.au, on August 20, 2014; Andrew Darby, "China Flags Its Antarctic Intent," *Sydney* (Australia) *Morning Herald* (January 11, 2010), www.smh.com.au, on August 19, 2014; Paula Leighton, "Developing Nations Seek a Share of Antarctica's Spoils," *SciDev.Net* (February 10, 2014), www.scidev.net, on August 19, 2014; "Polar Power Play," *The Economist* (UK) (November 7, 2013), www.economist.com, on August 18, 2014; Bruce Einhorn, "As China Goes Exploring, Antarctica Becomes Another Frontier," *BloombergBusinessweek* (January 3, 2014), www.businessweek.com, on August 19, 2014.

A country's infrastructure plays a role in its ability to promote international trade. Burma's Mandalay airport, for example, is not on par with other major international airports. This makes it harder for companies to ship their products into or out of Burma by air and also creates a poor image for international business travelers.

most people have access to medical care. Overall, the United States has a relatively complete infrastructure sufficient to support most forms of economic development and activity.

Some countries, on the other hand, lack a well-developed infrastructure. Some countries do not have enough electrical generating capacity to meet demand. Such countries—Kenya, for example—often schedule periods of time during which power is turned off or reduced. These planned power failures reduce power demands but can be an enormous inconvenience to business. In the extreme, when a country's infrastructure is greatly underdeveloped, firms interested in beginning businesses may have to build an entire township, including housing, schools, hospitals, and perhaps even recreational facilities, to attract a sufficient overseas workforce.

As this section indicates, a country's economic *environment* involves much more than its economic system. Its economic environment is linked not only to the state of its infrastructure and to its supply of natural resources, but also to the conditions of its natural environment.

## The Political-Legal Environment

A second environmental challenge facing the international manager is the political-legal environment in which he or she will do business. Four especially important aspects of the political-legal environment of international management are government stability, incentives for multinational trade, controls on international trade, and the influence of economic communities on international trade.

**Government Stability**   Stability can be viewed in two ways—as the ability of a given government to stay in power against opposing factions in the country and as the permanence of government policies toward business. A country that is stable in both respects is preferable because managers have a higher probability of successfully predicting how government will affect their businesses. Civil war in countries such as Syria has made it virtually impossible for international managers to predict what government policies are likely to be and whether the government will be able to guarantee the safety of international workers. Consequently, international firms are very reluctant to invest in Syria.

> "Europe in many ways is the global regulatory superpower."
>
> —JEFFREY IMMELT, CEO OF GENERAL ELECTRIC[42]

In many countries—the United States, Great Britain, and Japan, for example—changes in government occur with very little disruption. In other countries—India, Argentina, and Greece, for example—changes are likely to be somewhat chaotic. Even if a country's government remains stable, the risk remains that the policies adopted by that government might change. In some countries, foreign businesses may be nationalized (taken over by the government) with little or no warning. For example, the government of Peru once nationalized Perulac, a domestic milk producer owned by Nestlé at the time, because of a local milk shortage.

**nationalized**
Taken over by a national government

**Incentives for International Trade**   Another facet of the political environment is incentives to attract foreign business. For example, the state of Alabama offered Mercedes-Benz huge tax breaks and other incentives to entice the German firm to select a location for a new factory in that state. Similarly, Texas offered substantial incentives to Toyota to convince the Japanese company to consolidate all of its U.S. operations outside of Dallas. In like fashion, the French government sold land to the Walt Disney Company far below its market value and agreed to build a connecting freeway in exchange for the company's agreeing to build a European theme park outside of Paris.

Such incentives can take a variety of forms. Some of the most common include reduced interest rates on loans, construction subsidies, and tax incentives. Less-developed countries tend to offer different packages of incentives. In addition to lucrative tax breaks, for example, they can also attract investors with duty-fee entry of raw materials and equipment, market protection through limitations on other importers, and the right to take profits out of the country. They may also have to correct deficiencies in their infrastructures, as noted previously, to satisfy the requirements of foreign firms.

**Controls on International Trade** A third element of the political environment that managers need to consider is the extent to which there are controls on international trade. In some instances, a country's government might decide that foreign competition is hurting domestic trade. To protect domestic business, such governments may enact barriers to international trade. These barriers include tariffs, quotas, export restraint agreements, and "buy national" laws. During the recent global economic recession, many countries began to raise tariffs on imports from other countries and/or subsidize their own exports in order to protect domestic businesses, despite the opinions of experts who argue that such practices, over the long run, tend to make things worse instead of better.[44]

A tariff is a tax collected on goods shipped across national boundaries. Tariffs can be collected by the exporting country, countries through which goods pass, and the importing country. Import tariffs, which are the most common, can be levied to protect domestic companies by increasing the cost of foreign goods. Japan charges U.S. tobacco producers a tariff on cigarettes imported into Japan as a way to keep their prices higher than the prices charged by domestic firms. Tariffs can also be levied, usually by less-developed countries, to raise money for the government.

In the United States, the Byrd Amendment (named after West Virginia Senator Robert Byrd) stipulates that, if a domestic firm successfully demonstrates that a foreign company is dumping (selling for less than fair-market value) its products in the U.S. market, those products will be hit with a tariff and the proceeds given to the domestic company filing the complaint. U.S. ball-bearing maker Torrington received $63 million under provisions of this statute.[45]

Quotas are the most common form of trade restriction. A *quota* is a limit on the number or value of goods that can be traded. The quota amount is typically designed to ensure that domestic competitors will be able to maintain a certain market share. Honda is allowed to import 425,000 autos each year into the United States. This quota applies to cars imported into the United States, but the company can produce as many cars within U.S. borders as it wants because those cars are not considered imports. (Indeed, that is one major reason that Honda and other foreign automakers have built factories in the United States.)

Megapress / Alamy

Government stability is a major factor businesses consider before entering a foreign market. This building, for example, was once a major government office building in Cairo, Egypt. During the overthrow of President Hosni MuBarak a few years ago protesters set fire to the building, rendering it unusable. Businesses are cautious about establishing operations in certain African and Middle Eastern countries due to potential uprisings and regime changes.

"[Russian Prime Minister Vladimir] Putin visits a combine harvester factory and decides on the spot he will raise tariffs [on European imports]."

—UNNAMED EU TRADE OFFICIAL[43]

**tariff**
A tax collected on goods shipped across national boundaries

**quota**
A limit on the number or value of goods that can be traded

Export restraint agreements are designed to persuade other governments to voluntarily limit the volume or value of goods exported to or imported from a particular country. They are, in effect, export quotas. Japanese steel producers voluntarily limit the amount of steel they send to the United States each year to avoid the possibility that the United States might impose quotas or charge tariffs to protect U.S. steel producers.

"Buy national" legislation gives preference to domestic producers through content or price restrictions. Several countries have this type of legislation. Brazil requires that Brazilian companies purchase only Brazilian-made computers. Indeed, Brazil's bureaucratic control of foreign investment remains a major obstacle to doing business in that country.[46] The United States requires that the Department of Defense purchase only military uniforms manufactured in the United States, even though the price of foreign uniforms would be half as much. Mexico requires that 50 percent of the car parts sold in Mexico be manufactured inside its own borders.

**Economic Communities** Just as government policies can either increase or decrease the political risk facing international managers, trade relations between countries can either help or hinder international business. Relations dictated by quotas, tariffs, and so forth can hurt international trade. There is currently a strong movement around the world to reduce many of these barriers. This movement takes its most obvious form in international economic communities.

An international economic community is a set of countries that agree to markedly reduce or eliminate trade barriers among member nations. The first and in many ways still the most important of these economic communities is the European Union (EU), discussed earlier. The passage of NAFTA, as also noted earlier, represents perhaps the first step toward the formation of a North American economic community. Other important economic communities include the Latin American Integration Association (Bolivia, Brazil, Colombia, Chile, Argentina, and other South American countries) and the Caribbean Common Market (15 members including the Bahamas, Belize, Jamaica, Antigua, and Barbados, and five associate members).

## The Cultural Environment

Another environmental challenge for the international manager is the cultural environment and how it affects business. Disney's Hong Kong theme park struggled after it first opened, in large part because Disney made the mistake of minimizing all elements of Chinese culture in the park—essentially, making it a generic miniature reproduction of the original Disneyland in California. Disney also confused potential visitors with ads showing a father, mother, and two children walking hand-in-hand toward the theme park—overlooking China's laws that restrict many families to a single child. Only after a refurbishment to make the park more Chinese and a revised ad campaign did attendance begin to improve.[47] A country's culture includes all the values, symbols, beliefs, and language that guide behavior.

**Values, Symbols, Beliefs, and Language** Cultural values and beliefs are often unspoken; they may even be taken for granted by those who live in a particular country. Cultural factors do not necessarily cause problems for managers when the cultures of two countries are similar. Difficulties can arise, however, when there is little overlap between the home culture of a manager and the culture of the country in which business is to be conducted. For example, most U.S. managers find the culture and traditions of England relatively familiar. The people of both countries speak the same language and share strong historical roots, and there is a history of strong commerce between the two countries. When U.S. managers begin operations in Japan or the People's Republic of China, however, most of those commonalities disappear.

In Japanese, the word *hai* (pronounced "hi") means "yes." In conversation, however, this word is used much like people in the United States use "uh-huh"; it moves a conversation

**export restraint agreements**
Accords reached by governments in which countries voluntarily limit the volume or value of goods they export to or import from one another

**economic community**
A set of countries that agree to markedly reduce or eliminate trade barriers among member nations (a formalized market system)

along or shows the person with whom you are talking that you are paying attention. So when does *hai* mean "yes" and when does it mean "uh-huh"? This turns out to be difficult to answer. If a U.S. manager asks a Japanese manager if he agrees to some trade arrangement, the Japanese manager is likely to say, "Hai"—but this may mean "Yes, I agree," "Yes, I understand," or "Yes, I am listening." Many U.S. managers become frustrated in negotiations with the Japanese because they believe that the Japanese continue to raise issues that have already been settled (because the Japanese managers said "Yes"). What many of these managers fail to recognize is that "yes" does not always mean "yes" in Japan.

Cultural differences between countries can have a direct impact on business practice. For example, the Islam teaches that people should not make a living by exploiting the misfortune of others; charging

Cultural differences can affect business meetings involving people from different countries. These American and Japanese colleagues, for example, seem to be communicating effectively. But in reality they may or may not be in full agreement with each other.

interest payments, for example, is seen as immoral. This means that in Saudi Arabia there are few businesses that provide auto wrecker services to tow stalled cars to the garage (because that would be capitalizing on misfortune), and in the Sudan banks cannot pay or charge interest. Given these cultural and religious constraints, those two businesses—automobile towing and banking—do not seem to hold great promise for international managers in those countries!

Some cultural differences between countries can be even more subtle and yet have a major impact on business activities. For example, in the United States, most managers clearly agree about the value of time. Most U.S. managers schedule their activities very tightly and then try to adhere to their schedules. Other cultures do not put such a premium on time. In the Middle East, managers do not like to set appointments, and they rarely keep appointments set too far into the future. U.S. managers interacting with managers from the Middle East might misinterpret the late arrival of a potential business partner as a negotiation ploy or an insult, when it is rather a simple reflection of different views of time and its value.[48] The *World of Difference* feature discusses another set of issues facing international businesses today that relates to cultural forces.

Language itself can be an important factor. Indeed, many major companies are working to better connect with non-English speakers. India, for example, has the second most Internet users in the world, but over half of those Internet users are not proficient in English. This makes it difficult for them to use the Google search engine or to order from Amazon.com. Google in particular is investing heavily in translation platforms that enable web content to be accurately translated back and forth between English and other languages.[49]

Beyond the obvious and clear barriers posed by people who speak different languages, subtle differences in meaning can also play a major role. For example, Imperial Oil of Canada markets gasoline under the brand name Esso. When the firm tried to sell its gasoline in Japan, it learned that *esso* means "stalled car" in Japanese. Likewise, when Chevrolet first introduced a U.S. model called the Nova in Latin America, General Motors executives could not understand why the car sold poorly. They eventually learned, though, that, in Spanish, *no va* means "it doesn't go." The color green is used extensively in Muslim countries, but it signifies death in some other countries. The color associated with femininity in the United States is pink, but in many other countries, yellow is the most feminine color.

# Competing with Local Headhunters

Responsible for the Greater China and North Asia region, Kent Kedl is managing director of the British-based management consulting firm Control Risks LLC. During his first six months at his new job, no fewer than four top managers came into his Shanghai office to tell him that they'd been offered three times their salaries from local competitors. Was it a ploy to take advantage of a foreign manager new to the job in an alien business culture? No, says Kedl, all four managers soon left the company for the higher-paying jobs that they'd told him about. "These guys are getting calls every week from headhunters," explains Kedl. "It's problem number one around here."

Edward Mermelstein, a partner in the New York law firm Rheem Bell & Mermelstein, had similar problems in Russia. When the firm opened an office in Moscow, Mermelstein spent six months training top-level managers to run it. In the last two years, two of his highest-ranking executives have been poached by local competitors who doubled their salaries. "The competition is cutthroat," reports Mermelstein, "and they don't even give you two-week notices. They just leave."

Like most companies with operations in emerging markets, Control Risks and Rheem Bell & Mermelstein prefer to place *expatriate managers*—managers from the home country—in charge of overseas operations while filling management-level positions below them with local hires. Expatriates are generally much more expensive than local hires, but—at least until recently—most multinationals have preferred them in top positions on the grounds that they have greater knowledge of the company's business and industry and more experience in strategic leadership. In the past decade or so, however, many companies have been reevaluating the advantages of expat executives. Cost is the major consideration, but a growing number of multinationals is starting to factor in the advantages of such "softer-side" managerial assets as cultural sensitivity and the ability to forge relationships with local business organizations and government bodies.

"Expat managers," says Jeffrey A. Joerres, executive chairman of the multinational human resources firm Manpower, "are notoriously bad at adapting to local culture. What's more," adds Joerres, "the presence of these foreigners often fuels a belief among local employees that there is a ceiling on their own potential in the company." Joerres is well aware of the situation that Kedl and Mermelstein encountered firsthand—namely, the fact that "the war for managerial talent is heating up in the developing world." He also points out that more and more local companies in developing markets are emerging as "tougher competitors for multinational companies, for which a dearth of intimate local knowledge is increasingly costly."

For his part, Kent Kedl has decided to tackle the problem by revisiting some basic strategies in human resource management. He lays out clear career paths for new management hires, including specific steps toward greater pay and leadership opportunities, and offers raises and promotions even before managers ask. For companies in the position of Control Risks, says Kedl, "The whole 'people-are-the-most-important-assets' thing is not corporate baloney. That's the hard-core truth … in a market like China."

*References:* Jennifer Alsever, "The Great Expatriate Hiring Boom," *Fortune* (May 15, 2013), http://fortune.com, on August 25, 2014; Jeffrey A. Joerres, "Beyond Expats: Better Managers for Emerging Markets," *McKinsey Quarterly* (May 2011), www.mckinsey.com, on August 25, 2014; E. Michael Norman, "What Does the Future Hold for Expatriate Talent Management?" Sibson Consulting *Perspectives* 18:1 (2010), www.sibson.com, on August 25, 2014; Sibson Consulting, "Expatriate Talent Market Trends Survey" (Fall 2009), www.sibson.com, on August 25, 2014.

**Individual Behaviors Across Cultures** There also appear to be clear differences in individual behaviors and attitudes across different cultures. For example, Geert Hofstede, a Dutch researcher, studied 116,000 people working in dozens of different countries and found several interesting differences.[50] Hofstede's initial work identified four important dimensions along which people seem to differ across cultures. More recently, he has added a fifth dimension. These dimensions are illustrated in Figure 5.4.

# FIGURE 5.4  INDIVIDUAL DIFFERENCES ACROSS CULTURES

Hofstede identified five fundamental differences that can be used to characterize people in different cultures. These dimensions are social orientation, power orientation, uncertainty orientation, goal orientation, and time orientation. Different levels of each dimension affect the perceptions, attitudes, values, motivations, and behaviors of people in different cultures.

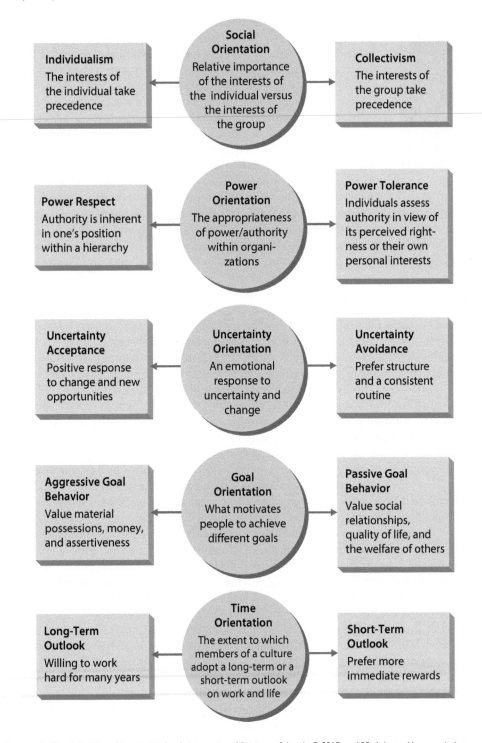

Source: Griffin, Ricky W. and Pustay, Michael, *International Business*, 8th ed., © 2015, p. 105. Adapted by permission of Pearson Education, Inc., Upper Saddle River, NJ.

John Lund/Getty Images

This team has just received an award for outstanding performance. If they are from collectivist cultures the team recognition will likely be very rewarding and meaningful to them. On the other hand, if they are from individualistic cultures they may have preferred some form of individual recognition.

**social orientation**
A person's beliefs about the relative importance of the individual versus the groups to which that person belongs

**power orientation**
The beliefs that people in a culture hold about the appropriateness of power and authority differences in hierarchies such as business organizations

**uncertainty orientation**
The feeling people have about uncertain and ambiguous situations

**goal orientation**
The manner in which people are motivated to work toward different kinds of goals

**time orientation**
The extent to which members of a culture adopt a long-term versus a short-term outlook on work, life, and other elements of society

The first dimension identified by Hofstede is social orientation.[51] Social orientation is a person's beliefs about the relative importance of the individual versus the groups to which that person belongs. The two extremes of social orientation are individualism and collectivism. *Individualism* is the cultural belief that the person comes first. Hofstede's research suggested that people in the United States, the United Kingdom, Australia, Canada, New Zealand, and the Netherlands tend to be relatively individualistic. *Collectivism*, the opposite of individualism, is the belief that the group comes first. Hofstede found that people from Mexico, Greece, Hong Kong, Taiwan, Peru, Singapore, Colombia, and Pakistan tend to be relatively collectivistic in their values. In countries with higher levels of individualism, many workers may prefer reward systems that link pay with the performance of individual employees. In a more collectivistic culture, such a reward system may in fact be counterproductive.

A second important dimension is power orientation, the beliefs that people in a culture hold about the appropriateness of power and authority differences in hierarchies such as business organizations. Some cultures are characterized by *power respect*. This means that people tend to accept the power and authority of their superiors simply on the basis of their position in the hierarchy and to respect their right to hold that power. Hofstede found that people in France, Spain, Mexico, Japan, Brazil, Indonesia, and Singapore are relatively power accepting. In contrast, people in cultures with a *power tolerance* orientation attach much less significance to a person's position in the hierarchy. These people are more willing to question a decision or mandate from someone at a higher level or perhaps even refuse to accept it. Hofstede's work suggested that people in the United States, Israel, Austria, Denmark, Ireland, Norway, Germany, and New Zealand tend to be more power tolerant.

The third basic dimension of individual differences studied by Hofstede was uncertainty orientation. Uncertainty orientation is the feeling people have about uncertain and ambiguous situations. People in cultures with *uncertainty acceptance* are stimulated by change and thrive on new opportunities. Hofstede suggested that many people in the United States, Denmark, Sweden, Canada, Singapore, Hong Kong, and Australia are among those in this category. In contrast, people with *uncertainty avoidance* tendencies dislike and will avoid ambiguity whenever possible. Hofstede found that many people in Israel, Austria, Japan, Italy, Colombia, France, Peru, and Germany tend to avoid uncertainty whenever possible.

The fourth dimension of cultural values measured by Hofstede is goal orientation. In this context, goal orientation is the manner in which people are motivated to work toward different kinds of goals. One extreme on the goal orientation continuum is *aggressive goal behavior*. People who exhibit aggressive goal behaviors tend to place a high premium on material possessions, money, and assertiveness. On the other hand, people who adopt *passive goal behavior* place a higher value on social relationships, quality of life, and concern for others. According to Hofstede's research, many people in Japan tend to exhibit relatively aggressive goal behaviors, whereas many people in Germany, Mexico, Italy, and the United States reflect moderately aggressive goal behaviors. People from the Netherlands and the Scandinavian countries of Norway, Sweden, Denmark, and Finland all tend to exhibit relatively passive goal behaviors.

A fifth dimension, called time orientation, was recently added to the framework.[52] Time orientation is the extent to which members of a culture adopt a long-term versus a short-term outlook on work, life, and other elements of society. Some cultures, such as Japan, Hong Kong, Taiwan, and South Korea, have a longer-term orientation. One implication of this orientation is that people from these cultures are willing to accept that they may have to work hard for many years before achieving their goals. Other cultures, like Pakistan and West Africa, are more likely to have a short-term orientation. As a result, people from these cultures may prefer jobs that provide more immediate rewards. Hofstede's work suggests that the United States and Germany tend to have an intermediate time orientation.

# Competing in a Global Economy

Competing in a global economy is both a major challenge and an opportunity for businesses today. The nature of these challenges depends on a variety of factors, including the size of the organization. In addition, international management has implications for the basic functions of planning and decision making, organizing, leading, and controlling.

## Globalization and Organization Size

Although organizations of any size may compete in international markets, there are some basic differences in the challenges and opportunities faced by MNCs, medium-size organizations, and small organizations.

**Multinational Corporations** The large MNCs have long since made the choice to compete in a global marketplace. In general, these firms take a global perspective. They transfer capital, technology, human resources, inventory, and information from one market to another. They actively seek new expansion opportunities wherever feasible. MNCs tend to allow local managers a great deal of discretion in addressing local and regional issues. At the same time, each operation is ultimately accountable to a central authority. Managers at this central authority (headquarters, a central office) are responsible for setting the overall strategic direction for the firm, making major policy decisions, and so forth. MNCs need senior managers who understand the global economy and who are comfortable dealing with executives and government officials from a variety of cultures. Table 5.2 lists the world's largest multinational enterprises based on annual revenues.

**Medium-Size Organizations** Many medium-size businesses remain primarily domestic organizations, but they still may buy and sell products made abroad and compete with businesses from other countries in their own domestic markets. Increasingly, however, medium-size organizations are expanding into foreign markets as well. For example, Gold's Gym, a U.S. fitness chain, has successfully opened facilities in a few foreign locations, including Moscow. In contrast to MNCs, medium-size organizations doing business abroad are much more selective about the markets they enter. They also depend more on a few international specialists to help them manage their foreign operations.

**Small Organizations** More and more small organizations are also finding that they can benefit from the global economy. Some, for example, serve as local suppliers for MNCs. A dairy farmer who sells milk to Carnation Company, for example, is actually transacting business with Nestlé. Local parts suppliers also have been successfully selling products to the Toyota and Honda plants in the United States. Beyond serving as local suppliers, some small businesses buy and sell products and services abroad. For example, the Collin Street Bakery, based in Corsicana, Texas, ships fruitcakes around the world. In 2014 the firm shipped fruitcakes to customers in 196 countries, including over 150,000 pounds of fruitcakes to Japan alone. Most small businesses rely on simple importing or exporting operations (or both) for their international sales. Thus only a few specialized management positions are needed. Collin Street Bakery, for example, has one local manager who

---

**TABLE 5.2** THE WORLD'S LARGEST BUSINESSES BY REVENUE (2014)

| Rank | Company | Revenue ($ Millions) | Profits ($ Millions) |
|---|---|---|---|
| 1 | Wal-Mart Stores | 476,294 | 16,022 |
| 2 | Royal Dutch Shell | 459,599 | 16,371 |
| 3 | Sinopec Group | 457,201 | 8,932 |
| 4 | China National Petroleum | 432,007 | 18,504 |
| 5 | Exxon Mobil | 407,666 | 32,580 |
| 6 | BP | 396,217 | 23,451 |
| 7 | State Grid | 333,386 | 7,982 |
| 8 | Volkswagen | 261,539 | 12,071 |
| 9 | Toyota Motors | 256,454 | 18,198 |
| 10 | Glencore | 232,694 | −7,402 |
| 11 | Total | 227,882 | 11,204 |
| 12 | Chevron | 220,356 | 21,423 |
| 13 | Samsung Electronics | 208,938 | 27,245 |
| 14 | Berkshire Hathaway | 182,150 | 19,476 |
| 15 | Apple | 170,910 | 37,037 |
| 16 | AXA | 165,893 | 5,950 |
| 17 | Gazprom | 165,016 | 35,769 |
| 18 | E.ON | 162,560 | 2,843 |
| 19 | Phillips 66 | 161,175 | 3,726 |
| 20 | Daimler | 156,628 | 9,083 |
| 21 | General Motors | 155,427 | 5,346 |
| 22 | ENI | 154,108 | 6,850 |
| 23 | Japan Post Holdings | 152,125 | 4,782 |
| 24 | EXOR Group | 150,996 | 2,768 |
| 25 | Industrial & Commerce Bank of China | 148,802 | 42,718 |

Source: fortune.com, accessed 12 May 2015

handles international activities. Mail-order activities within each country are subcontracted to local firms in each market.

## Management Challenges in a Global Economy

The management functions that constitute the framework for this book—planning and decision making, organizing, leading, and controlling—are just as relevant to international managers as to domestic managers. International managers need to have a clear view of where they want their firm to be in the future; they have to organize to implement their plans; they have to motivate those who work for them; and they have to develop appropriate control mechanisms.[53]

**Planning and Decision Making in a Global Economy** To effectively plan and make decisions in a global economy, managers must have a broad-based understanding of both environmental issues and competitive issues. They need to understand local market conditions and technological factors that will affect their operations. At the corporate level, executives need a great deal of information to function effectively. Which markets are growing? Which markets are shrinking? What are our domestic and foreign competitors doing in each market? They must also make a variety of strategic decisions about their organizations. For example, if a firm wishes to enter the market in France, should it buy a local firm there, start a new operation, or seek a strategic alliance? Critical issues include understanding environmental circumstances, the role of goals and planning in a global organization, and how decision making affects the global organization. We note special implications for global managers as we discuss planning and decision making in Chapters 6 through 9.

**Organizing in a Global Economy** Managers in international businesses must also attend to a variety of organizing issues. For example, General Electric has operations scattered around the globe. The firm has made the decision to give local managers a great deal of responsibility for how they run their business. In contrast, many Japanese firms give managers of their foreign operations relatively little responsibility. As a result, those managers must frequently travel back to Japan to present problems or get decisions approved. Managers in an international business must address the basic issues of organization structure and design, managing change, and dealing with human resources. Strategically, too, organizing decisions can be used to help promote everything from organizational flexibility to the development of expatriate managers.[54] We address the special issues of organizing the international organization in Chapters 10 through 13.

**Leading in a Global Economy** We noted earlier some of the cultural factors that affect international organizations. Individual managers must be prepared to deal with these and other factors as they interact with people from different cultural backgrounds. Supervising a group of five managers, each of whom is from a different state in the United States, is likely to be much simpler than supervising a group of five managers, each of whom is from a different culture. Managers must understand how cultural factors affect individuals, how motivational processes vary across cultures, how the role of leadership changes in different cultures, how communication varies across cultures, and how interpersonal and group processes depend on cultural background. In Chapters 14 through 18, we note special implications for international managers that relate to leading and interacting with others.

**Controlling in a Global Economy** Finally, managers in international organizations must also be concerned with control. Distances, time zone differences, and cultural factors also play a role in control. For example, in some cultures close supervision is seen as being appropriate, whereas in other cultures it is not. Likewise, executives in the United States and China may find it difficult to communicate vital information to one another because of the time zone differences. Basic control issues for the international manager revolve around operations management, productivity, quality, technology, and information systems. These issues are integrated throughout our discussion of control in Chapters 19 and 20.

---

☐ Managers should understand how the four basic management functions relate to international business.

☐ Small business owners should carefully assess possible international markets and competitors.

**Manager's Checklist** ☑

# Summary of Learning Outcomes and Key Points

1. Describe the nature of international business, including its meaning, recent trends, management of globalization, and competition in a global market.

   - Learning to operate in a global economy is an important challenge facing many managers today.
   - Businesses can be primarily domestic, international, multinational, or global in scope.
   - Managers need to understand both the process of internationalization and how to manage within a given level of international activity.

2. Discuss the structure of the global economy, and describe the GATT and the WTO.

   - Mature market economies and systems dominate the global economy today.
   - North America, the European Union, and Pacific Asia are especially important.
   - High-potential/high-growth economies in Eastern Europe, Latin America, the People's Republic of China, India, and Vietnam are increasingly important to managers.
   - The oil-exporting economies in the Middle East are also important.

   - The GATT and the WTO play critical roles in the evolution of the global economy.

3. Identify and discuss the environmental challenges inherent in international management.

   - Many of the challenges of management in a global context are unique issues associated with the international environmental context.
   - These challenges reflect the economic, political-legal, and cultural environments of international management.

4. Describe the basic issues involved in competing in a global economy, including organization size and the management challenges in a global economy.

   - Basic issues of competing in a global economy vary according to whether the organization is an MNC, a medium-size organization, or a small organization.
   - In addition, the basic managerial functions of planning and decision making, organizing, leading, and controlling must all be addressed in international organizations.

# Discussion Questions

### Questions for Review

1. Describe the four basic levels of international business activity. Do you think any organization will achieve the fourth level? Why or why not?

2. For each of the four globalization strategies, describe the risks associated with that strategy and the potential returns from that strategy.

### Questions for Analysis

5. What are the advantages and disadvantages for a U.S.-based multinational firm entering a mature market economy? What are the advantages and disadvantages for such a firm entering a high-potential/high-growth economy?

6. Choose an industry that interests you. Describe the impact that international business has had on firms in that industry. Are there any industries that

### Questions for Application

8. Use the Internet to locate information about a company that is using a global strategic alliance or global joint

3. Describe the various types of political controls on international trade. Be sure to highlight the differences between the types.

4. Explain the relationship between organizational size and globalization. Are large firms the only ones that are global?

might not be affected by the trend toward international business? If so, what are they? If not, why are there none?

7. You are the CEO of an up-and-coming toy company and have plans to go international soon. What steps would you take to carry out that strategy? What areas would you stress in your decision-making process? How would you organize your company?

venture. (*Hint:* Almost any large multinational firm will be involved in these ventures, and you can find information at corporate home pages.) What do you think are the major goals for the venture? Do you expect that the firm will accomplish its goals? If so, why? If not, what stands in its way?

9. Assume that you are the CEO of Walmart. What are the basic environmental challenges you face as your com-

pany continues its globalization efforts? Give some specific examples that relate to Walmart.

10. Review the following chart of Hofstede's cultural dimensions. Based on the chart, tell which country you would most like to work in and why. Tell which country you would like least to work in and why.

| | Power Distance Range: 11–104 | Individualism Range: 6–91 | Uncertainty Avoidance Range: 8–112 | Aggressiveness Range: 5–95 |
|---|---|---|---|---|
| Germany | 35 | 67 | 65 | 66 |
| India | 77 | 48 | 40 | 56 |
| Israel | 13 | 54 | 81 | 47 |
| United Kingdom | 35 | 89 | 35 | 66 |
| United States | 40 | 91 | 46 | 62 |

Adapted from: Geert Hofstede, *Cultures and Organizations: Software of the Mind: Intercultural Cooperation and Its Importance for Survival* (London: HarperCollins, 1994), pp. 26, 55, 84, 113.

# Building Effective Technical Skills

## Exercise Overview

Technical skills are necessary to understand or perform the specific kind of work that an organization does. At some companies, the work involves analyzing data in order to develop effective

international strategies. This exercise will help you develop certain technical skills related to the tasks of collecting information and determining its possible effects on a firm's activities.

## Exercise Background

Five of the largest countries in the world, in terms of population, are China, India, the United States, Indonesia, and Brazil. As the manager of a large U.S.-based multinational firm, you need some information about trade and population in each of these countries. You can isolate the information that you need by reviewing the six items that constitute the following Exercise Task. Here are a few helpful hints for using the Internet to find the information that you need. You can get

import/export data from the U.S. Census Bureau; go to **www.census.gov/foreign-trade/aip/index.html#profile** and, working from this main page, locate the most recent figures. You can also get estimates of future population from the Census Bureau at **www.census.gov/ipc/www/idb/rank.php**. You can gather the rest of the data you need from the *World Factbook*, which is published by the U.S. Central Intelligence Agency at **www.cia.gov/cia/publications/factbook/index.html**.

## Exercise Task

To compile the information you need, do the following:

1. List the five countries in the world projected to have the largest populations in 2050.

2. List the five countries that currently export the most products to the United States.

3. List the five countries that currently import the most products from the United States.

4. Life span is a measure of individual prosperity in a country. What is the average life span in each of the five largest countries in the world? In each of the five largest exporters to the United States? In each of the five largest importers from the United States?

5. Gross domestic product (GDP) per capita is a measure of a country's economic health. What is the GDP per capita, in U.S. dollars, of each of the world's five largest countries? Of each of the five largest exporters to the United States? Of each of the five largest importers from the United States?

6. What are the implications for your firm? What, for example, do the data suggest about the desirability of various countries as current trading partners? What do the data suggest about the desirability of the same countries as future trading partners?

# Building Effective Communication Skills

## Exercise Overview

Communication skills refer not only to the ability to convey information and ideas to others but to handle information and ideas received from them. Obviously, differences in language and a whole array of cultural differences mean that international managers face additional communication adjustments. This exercise focuses on communication skills in a context to which you probably haven't given much thought—differences in time zones.

## Exercise Background

You're a manager in a large multinational firm headquartered in San Francisco. You need to arrange a conference call with several other managers to discuss an upcoming strategic change. The other managers are located in New York, London, Rome, Moscow, Tokyo, Singapore, and Sydney.

## Exercise Task

To arrange your conference call, do the following:

1. Determine the time zone differences in each of the cities involved.

2. Assuming that people in each city have a typical workday of 8:00 A.M. to 5:00 P.M., determine the optimal time for your conference call. At what time, in other words, can you schedule the call so that the fewest people are inconvenienced?

3. Now assume that, as a result of the call, you need to visit each office in person, spending one full day in each office. Using the Internet, review airline schedules and develop an efficient itinerary.

# Skill-Building Personal Assessment

## Global Awareness

**Introduction**: As we have noted, the environment of business is becoming more global. The following assessment is designed to help you assess your readiness to respond to managing in a global context.

**Instructions**: You will agree with some of the following statements and disagree with others. In some cases you may find it difficult to make a decision, but you should force yourself to make a choice. Record your answers next to each statement according to the following scale:

4 Strongly agree
3 Somewhat agree
2 Somewhat disagree
1 Strongly disagree

1. _____ Some areas of Switzerland are very much like Italy.

2. _____ Although aspects of behavior such as motivation and attitudes within organizational settings remain quite diverse across cultures, organizations themselves appear to be increasingly similar in terms of design and technology.

3. _____ Spain, France, Japan, Singapore, Mexico, Brazil, and Indonesia have cultures with a strong orientation toward authority.

4. _____ Japan and Austria define male and female roles more rigidly and value qualities such as forcefulness and achievement more than do Norway, Sweden, Denmark, and Finland.

5. _____ Some areas of Switzerland are very much like France.

6. _____ Australia, Great Britain, the Netherlands, Canada, and New Zealand have cultures that view people first as individuals and place a high priority on their own interests and values, whereas Colombia, Pakistan, Taiwan, Peru, Singapore, Mexico, Greece, and Hong Kong have cultures in which the good of the group or of society is considered of greatest importance.

7. _____ The United States, Israel, Austria, Denmark, Ireland, Norway, Germany, and New Zealand have cultures with a low orientation toward authority.

8. _____ The same manager may behave differently in different cultural settings.

9. _____ Denmark, Canada, Norway, Singapore, Hong Kong, and Australia have cultures in which employees tolerate a great deal of uncertainty, but such high levels of uncertainty are not well tolerated in Israel, Austria, Japan, Italy, Argentina, Peru, France, and Belgium.

10. _____ Some areas of Switzerland are very much like Germany.

# Management at Work

## Nano Technology and Other Innovations

*"That is what disruptive technology is all about: extending the user base to reach new types of customers."*

—JANE CHEN, COFOUNDER OF EMBRACE GLOBAL

The business model of Mitra Biotech, which specializes in personalized cancer treatment, revolves around a principle known as *rational drug design*—the selection of specific biologically active compounds to treat particular cancerous tumors. Scientists put tumor cultures in an incubator that mimics the micro-environment of the human body and test different drugs on the samples. An algorithm then ranks the drugs according to their suitability for the specific patient. A drug selection process that can take months is thus reduced to about seven days, and the savings in the cost of expensive cancer drugs alone is significant.

Mitra's CANScript model earned it a spot on *Fast Company* magazine's 2014 list of "The Top Ten Most Innovative Companies in India." Not surprisingly, high tech also figures in the innovations of most of the companies on the list. Eram Scientific Solutions' Delight public toilet system, for example, addresses a fairly obvious urban problem by flushing automatically—not only when people come in and go out but at regular intervals as well. Motion-sensor lights and fans also save energy.

Many Indian innovations reflect a phenomenon known as *reverse innovation*—innovation that appears first in the developing world and then spreads to more developed markets. Mitra's cancer-care process, for example, is currently available to Indian patients for about US$600. The company's founders, however, are currently working with Cancer Treatment Centers of America, a for-profit chain of cancer-treatment hospitals, to bring CANScript technology to the United States. "The business potential," says cofounder Pradip K. Majumder, "is much higher outside India. For the same technology, we can bill patients at $4,000" in the United States.

Unlike CANScript, however, most reverse-innovation products are inexpensive versions of more sophisticated technology designed to meet the specific needs of people in developing nations. In fact, says Rishikesha T. Krishnan of the Indian Institute of Management, the country's commitment to innovation is in large part a response to India's immense social challenges. With the second-largest population in the world, the world's largest number of poor people, a literacy rate of only 70 percent, inadequate healthcare, and poor nutrition levels, India's economic and geopolitical aspirations will have meaning only if they can raise their performance on social indicators.

It was in India, for instance, which has one of the highest heart attack rates in the world, that GE developed a portable, battery-operated, easy-to-use, easy-to-repair electrocardiograph machine that sells for US$800 (compared to $50,000 for models sold in the industrialized world). Likewise, Philips India, a division of the giant Dutch technology company, developed the ClearVue ultrasound scanner, a lightweight, modular, energy-efficient alternative to conventional models that's also easier to service and less expensive to operate.

Also noteworthy is a blood monitor made from an old alarm clock. Some skeptics call such devices *juggad*—a Hindi word for "improvised arrangement"—but Navi Radjou, a faculty member at the World Economic Forum, is quick to explain that "*juggad* innovation is creative improvisation in the face of adversity." An Indian inventor's idea of "hacking" an old alarm clock showed promise to Frugal Digital, a research group run by the Copenhagen Institute of Interaction Design, which partners with Indian investors to promote an approach to product design known as *frugal innovation*. So Frugal Digital attached an old-fashioned clock to two LEDs and a simple light sensor (both available from an old TV remote) and called it Clock Sense, which measures the amount of hemoglobin in the blood. It's merely a screening tool designed for low-level healthcare, but frugal innovation, says Kirsten Bound, the author of a study on the phenomenon, "is not simply about making things cheaper, but also more appropriate and scalable. It involves leveraging available resources and reducing or reusing waste."

Above all, frugal innovation begins with a fundamental knowledge of people's needs. In 2009, for example, the four founders of Embrace, a nonprofit inspired by a class in Design for Extreme Affordability at Stanford University, moved their company and the prototype of a portable infant warmer to Bangalore, in southern India. "Learning how to make things locally appropriate," explains cofounder Jane Chen, "doesn't come from a couple of visits. It comes from living and breathing the environment it's intended for." Designed for village clinics, the Nest Infant Warmer launched in 2011 and costs US$100 (compared to $20,000 for a traditional incubator). It was designed for village clinics, and it's already been credited with helping 50,000 babies. The objective, says Chen, was not simply "developing a cheaper incubator, but saving babies' lives with the new product. And that," she adds, "is what disruptive technology is all about: extending the user base to reach new types of customers."

Many frugal innovations actually come from the very people who need the products. Inventors in rural India, for example, have produced a number of eminently practical devices. One recent exhibition of such inventions featured the Solar Mosquito Destroyer, which makes use of both the sun and odors from the user's septic tank, and the Bamboo Lathe Machine, which can perform all the operations necessary for making raw bamboo a suitable substitute for plastics in bottles and cans.

Rishikesha Krishnan points out that many large Indian companies have also initiated their own "innovation projects of increasing complexity and risk." The business models of companies like Mitra and Embrace, for instance, are inherently *disruptive* — that is, they create new markets and value networks by disrupting existing markets and networks. Krishnan, however, points to companies like Tata Motors, India's largest industrial company, as pioneers in disruptive technology. Tata builds the world's least expensive car — the Nano, which is targeted at Indian buyers with a retail price of US$2,500.

How did Tata manage to build such an inexpensive car? According to Krishnan, Tata disrupted its business model. To begin with, engineers approached the project by imposing a market-driven constraint — namely, the goal of doing more with less. In order to be sufficiently frugal, they challenged conventional engineering wisdom by substituting materials (the Nano has very little steel, and even the engine is aluminum) and conventional marketing wisdom by adjusting the car's design to the needs of targeted buyers (there are no such features as air conditioning, power brakes, or a radio). Most disruptive to conventional car-building practices, however, is the Nano's modular design, which has allowed Tata to completely reconfigure its value network by revamping its distribution system: The car's components are shipped separately for assembly by local entrepreneurs in multiple locations. Tata supplies both the know-how and the tools.

"We will create entrepreneurs across the country," explains Tata chairman Ratan Tata, "who will produce the car. We will produce mass items and ship them to entrepreneurs as kits. That is my idea of dispersing the wealth."

## Case Questions

1. Let's say that you're the CEO of a publicly owned company in the United States and you're interested in getting involved in the Indian market. You've found an innovative Indian company whose success stems from its willingness to prioritize longer-term innovation goals over shorter-term financial goals. The company would make a good partner on some level, and you need to decide which sort of globalization strategy would work best for you: *exporting*, *joint venture* (or some other form of *strategic alliance*), or *direct investment*. Generally speaking, what are the pros and cons of each option?

2. Here are a few facts about work and management in India, each of which naturally reflects elements of the country's *cultural environment* — attitudes, values, beliefs, and so forth:

   - Each employee has a well-defined role to play in the organization.
   - Failure may cause an Indian employee to suffer long-term loss of confidence.
   - Indian employees are quite careful about such time guidelines as schedules and deadlines.
   - Indian employees are highly relationship and group oriented.

   - Honor and reputation are very important to Indian employees.

   Where do you see noteworthy differences between attitudes, values, and beliefs in the Indian workplace and those in the "typical" U.S. workplace? If you were an American manager who's been posted to an office in India, what changes would you probably have to make in your approach to management? How about you *personally*? Do you think that you'd have more or less difficulty in making the transition than the "typical" American manager?

3. Rishikesha Krishnan says that innovation in India can grow only if Indian business develops "a complete and reinforcing innovation ecosystem." Among other things, such an "ecosystem" requires companies to adopt "well-developed and well-executed innovation strategies" and to be prepared to "ride one technology wave after another." Can you think of any U.S. industry in which companies have developed an "innovation ecosystem" like the one recommended by Krishnan? Explain how Krishnan's criteria can be used to describe business practices in this industry.

4. Where does the precept "value for the money" fit into your business philosophy? How about the precept "value for the many"?

## Case References

"The Top Ten Most Innovative Companies in India," *Fast Company* (February 10, 2014), www.fastcompany.com, on August 9, 2014; Goutam Das, "For Your Treatment Only," *Business Today* (India) (February 3, 2014), http://businesstoday.intoday.in, on August 9, 2014; Arundhati Ramanathan and P.R. Sanjai, "Innovation Has Improved Living Standards in India," *Livemint* (India) (July 28, 2014), www.livemint.com, on August 10, 2014; William Shaw, "Frugal Innovation: Adapting Local Tech Where Top-of-the-Range Is Out of Reach," *Wired* (UK) (April 4, 2013), www.wired.co.uk, on August 11, 2014; Arion McNicoll, "Enter India's Amazing World of Frugal Innovation," *CNN.com* (June 25, 2013), on August 5, 2013; Rishikesha T. Krishnan, "Silicon Valley to India: Build an Innovation Ecosystem and Good Things Will Come," *Ivey Business Journal* (September/October 2011), on August 9, 2014; Anirudha Dutta, "Embrace: Where Philanthropy, Innovation and Entrepreneurship Meet," *Forbes India* (August 9, 2012), http://forbesindia.com, on August 11, 2014; John Hagel and John Seely Brown, "Learning from Tata's Nano," *Businessweek* (February 27, 2008), www.businessweek.com, on August 12, 2014.

**YOU MAKE THE CALL** | Into Africa

1. According to Harley-Davidson's Africa country manager Celine Gruizinga, "No one who comes here is going to make a quick buck. It's no small feat. It's a type of commitment that takes decades." Let's say that you're the CEO of a publicly owned U.S. company that manufactures fashion footwear. You're interested in getting involved in the sub-Saharan Africa market, which will eventually total 1.1 billion middle-class consumers—50 years from now. You need to decide which sort of globalization strategy would work best for you: *exporting, licensing, joint venture* (or some other form of *strategic alliance*), or *direct investment*. Generally speaking—and given Gruizinga's warning—what are the pros and cons of each option?

2. As it happens, Celine Gruizinga is also Harley's first-ever female country manager. She's also an avid Harley rider. The company is targeting women buyers in sub-Saharan Africa, who already account for 26 percent of Harley riders in a region where the company reports "a significant increase in the number of both white and black women riders." Interestingly, Harley is also targeting women in the United States. What kinds of marketing appeals might Harley make to female consumers in both markets? What kinds of appeals will probably have to be distinctive for each market? Why do you think more women are interested in buying Harleys?

3. Nigeria has the largest economy in Africa. It's oil rich, and the economy is growing rapidly, driven by agriculture, telecommunications, and services. The banking sector is strong.* Unfortunately, Nigeria is also a serious security risk. The government has been unable to recover 233 schoolgirls abducted in April 2014 by a radical Islamic group, and in May a car bomb—the second in a month—killed 19 people in the capital of Abuja on the eve of a World Economic Forum meeting in the city. "There's a good-news story and a bad-news story here," said a USAID official. "The good news is that Nigeria is thriving economically. But the bad news is that the incident [with the schoolgirls] cuts to the heart of the continuing problem with safety and security" in Nigeria.†

    How should Harley-Davidson proceed with any plans to do business in Nigeria? ("Cautiously" is a good answer, but try to be more thorough in analyzing the situation.)

*"Abuja Blast: Car Bomb Attack Rocks Nigerian Capital," BBC News (May 2, 2014), www.bbc.com, on August 17, 2014.

†Rana Foroohar, "Africa's Middle Class Is at the Crossroads," *Time* (May 7, 2014), http://time.com, on August 17, 2014.

# Endnotes

1 Joris Fioriti, "Meet the Elephant's Bikers, Côte d'Ivoire's Version of Hells Angels," *Voices of Africa* (South Africa) (November 27, 2013), www.voicesofafrica.co.za, on August 5, 2014; Anthony Volastro, "Harleys, Hogs and Hells Angels Ride on Africa," CNBC (December 5, 2013), www.cnbc.com, on August 4, 2014; Elaine King, "Motorcycling: Harley-Davidson Rides Into Africa," *Financial Mail* (South Africa) (May 22, 2014), www.financialmail.co.za, on August 4, 2014; Zwelakhe Shangase, "Mike Rides In for Harley," *The New Age* (South Africa) (March 21, 2013), www.thenewage.co.za, on August 7, 2014; Sulaiman Philip, "South Africa's Black Middle Class on the Rise," Media Club South Africa (November 22, 2013), www.mediaclubsouthafrica.com, on August 6, 2014; "The World's Fastest-Growing Middle Class," UHY International (July 12, 2012), www.uhy.com, on August 6, 2014.

2 See Ricky W. Griffin and Michael Pustay, *International Business*, 8th ed. (Upper Saddle River, NJ: Prentice-Hall, 2015), for an overview of international business.

3 See Thomas Begley and David Boyd, "The Need for a Global Mind-Set," *Sloan Management Review*, Winter 2003, pp. 25–36.

4 For a more complete discussion of forms of international business, see Griffin and Pustay, *International Business*.

5 *Hoover's Handbook of American Business 2015* (Austin, TX: Hoover's Business Press, 2015), pp. 726–727.

6 See "Coke Bets on Russia for Sales Even as Economy Falls Flat," *Wall Street Journal*, January 28, 2009, pp. A1, A12.

7 John H. Dunning, *Multinational Enterprises and the Global Economy* (Wokingham, UK: Addison-Wesley, 1993); Christopher Bartlett and Sumantra Ghoshal, *Transnational Management* (Homewood, IL: Irwin, 1992).

8 "Philip Morris Unbound," *BusinessWeek*, May 4, 2009, pp. 38–42; businessweek.com accessed on January 20, 2015.

9 See "In Dixon, an Uproar Over Walgreens Going Swiss," *USA Today*, July 30, 2014, p. 5B.

10 *Wall Street Journal*, November 19, 2008 p. B1.

11 "The Fortune Global 500—World's Largest Corporations," *Fortune*, July 25, 2011.

12 "Taco Bell Parent Yum Brands to Continue Global Growth," *Los Angeles Business*, January 11, 2011.

13 "GE to Increase Focus on Chinese Market," *China Daily*, March 15, 2011.

14 "Going Global—Lessons from Late Movers," *Harvard Business Review*, March–April 2000, pp. 132–142.

15 Kenichi Ohmae, "The Global Logic of Strategic Alliances," *Harvard Business Review*, March–April 1989, pp. 143–154.

16 "Global Logistics: FedEx Trade Networks Forms Strategic Alliance with Fritz Companies Israel," *Logistics Management*, July 7, 2010.

17 "A Starbucks Venture in Tea-Drinking India," *The New York Times*, January 13, 2011.

18 See Balaji R. Koka and John E. Prescott, "Designing Alliance Networks: The Influence of Network Position, Environmental Change, and Strategy on Firm Performance," *Strategic Management Journal*, 2008, Vol. 29, pp. 639–661.

19 Dovev Lavie, "Capturing Value from Alliance Portfolios," *Organizational Dynamics*, January–March 2009, pp. 26–36; see also Paul Beamish and Nathaniel Lupton, "Managing Joint Ventures," *Academy of Management Perspectives*, 2009, Vol. 23, No. 2, pp. 75–84.

20 Hans Mjoen and Stephen Tallman, "Control and Performance in International Joint Ventures," *Organization Science*, May–June 1997, pp. 257–274; see also Hemant Merchant, "International Joint Venture Configurations in Big Emerging Markets," *The Multinational Business Review*, Vol. 16, No. 3, 2008, pp. 93–120.

21 "Misreading the Kremlin Costs BP Control in Russia Venture," *Wall Street Journal*, December 16, 2008, pp. A1, A6.

22 See "Corporate Culture Shock is a Big Deal," *Financial Times*, July 31, 2008, p. 9.

23 "Harley-Davidson to Build Bikes in India," CNN, November 4, 2010, cnn.com accessed on January 18, 2015.

24 "Volvo Goes USA With South Carolina Plant," *USA Today*, May 12, 2015, p. 1B.

25   Mike Westfall, "Maquiladoras—American Industry Creates Modern-Day Mexican Slaves," *The Cutting Edge*, June 8, 2009.

26   "Sewn In the USA," *USA TODAY*, July 3, 2014, page 1B.

27   Arindam K. Bhattacharya and David C. Michael, "How Local Companies Keep Multinationals at Bay," *Harvard Business Review*, March 2008, pp. 85–94.

28   Griffin and Pustay, *International Business*.

29   "Background Note: Mexico," Bureau of Western Hemisphere Affairs, U.S. Department of State, April 15, 2014.

30   Eileen P. Gunn, "Emerging Markets," *Fortune*, August 18, 1997, pp. 168–173; See also Tarun Khanna, "China + India—The Power of Two," *Harvard Business Review*, December 2007, pp. 60–70.

31   "Cartoon Characters Get a Big Makeover for Overseas Fans," *Wall Street Journal*, October 16, 2007, p. A1.

32   "Wal-Mart Exports Bog-Box Concept to India," *Wall Street Journal*, May 28, 2009, p. B1.

33   "Argentina Cries Foul as Choice Employers Beat a Path Next Door," *Wall Street Journal*, May 2, 2000, pp. A1, A8.

34   "GM Is Building Plants in Developing Nations to Woo New Markets," *Wall Street Journal*, August 4, 1997, pp. A1, A4.

35   For example, see "China Weighs Lifting Curbs on Foreign Firms," *Wall Street Journal*, January 1, 2000, p. A17.

36   http://www.economist.com/news/leaders/21595001-life-getting-tougher-foreign-companies-those-want-stay-will-have-adjust-china

37   *BusinessWeek*, March 23/30, 2009, p. 38.

38   "U.S. Firms Eager for More Access to Cuba" *USA Today*, January 13, 2015, p. 5B.

39   Griffin and Pustay, *International Business*.

40   "Oil Companies Strive to Turn a New Leaf to Save Rain Forest," *Wall Street Journal*, July 17, 1997, pp. A1, A8.

41   https://www.megaprojects.co.ke/articles/251/highway-construction-in-densely-populated-areas-what-kenya-can-learn-from-china/#.VRLk1vl4rYg

42   *Fortune*, June 27, 2010, p. 160.

43   *Wall Street Journal*, February 6, 2009, p. A1.

44   "Nations Rush to Establish New Barriers to Trade," *Wall Street Journal*, February 6, 2009, pp. A1, A6.

45   "Host of Companies Pocket Windfalls from Tariff Law," *Wall Street Journal*, December 5, 2002, pp. A1, A14.

46   "Brazil Still An Elusive Target for Investors," *USA Today*, June 30, 2014, p. 1B; "Why Wal-Mart Hasn't Conquered Brazil," *Bloomberg Businessweek*, May 12–18, 2014, pp. 24–25.

47   "Main Street, H.K.—Disney Localizes Mickey to Boost Its Hong Kong Theme Park," *Wall Street Journal*, January 23, 2008, pp. B1, B2.

48   "What if There Weren't Any Clocks to Watch?" *Newsweek*, June 30, 1997, p. 14.

49   "Imagine How it Would Be To Use the Internet if You Could Read Only One-Third Of It," *Bloomberg Businessweek*, January 19–25, 2015, pp. 37–38.

50   Geert Hofstede, *Culture's Consequences: International Differences in Work-Related Values* (Beverly Hills, CA: Sage, 1980).

51   I have taken the liberty of changing the actual labels applied to each dimension for several reasons. The terms I have chosen are more descriptive, simpler, and more self-evident in their meanings.

52   Geert Hofstede, "The Business of International Business Is Culture," *International Business Review*, 1994, Vol. 3, No. 1, pp. 1–14.

53   Stratford Sherman, "Are You as Good as the Best in the World?" *Fortune*, December 13, 1993, pp. 95–96.

54   Riki Takeuchi, Jeffrey P. Shay, and Jiatao Li, "When Does Decision Autonomy Increase Expatriate Managers' Adjustment? An Empirical Test," *Academy of Management Journal*, 2008, Vol. 51, No. 1, pp. 45–60.

©Markus Pfaff/Shutterstock.com

# BASIC ELEMENTS OF PLANNING AND DECISION MAKING

## 6

**Learning Outcomes**

After studying this chapter, you should be able to:

1. Summarize the essential functions of decision making and the planning process.

2. Discuss the purpose of organizational goals, identify different kinds of goals, discuss who sets goals, and describe how to manage multiple goals.

3. Identify different kinds of organizational plans, note the time frames for planning, discuss who plans, and describe contingency planning.

4. Discuss how tactical plans are developed and executed.

5. Describe the basic types of operational plans used by organizations.

6. Identify the major barriers to goal setting and planning, how organizations overcome those barriers, and how to use goals to implement plans.

## MANAGEMENT IN ACTION    Cruise Control

"Is this really smart crisis communications—to get into a p------g contest with 3,000 angry customers with full bladders?"

—CRISIS MANAGEMENT EXPERT STEVEN FINK

In February 2013, passengers aboard the Carnival cruise ship *Triumph* were busy texting, tweeting, and posting digital photographs to document their latest vacation adventures. Most of the photographs showed overflowing toilets and bags of human waste lined up in the hallways. "Just on our deck alone," reported one passenger, "there were biohazard bags lined up across the floor. We're talking about raw sewage. It was repulsive."[1]

Not exactly what the travel brochure promised.

It all started with a fire in one of the engine rooms, which caused the ship to lose power, including propulsion, and the *Triumph* was left adrift in the Gulf of Mexico for five days. As passengers took to their cellphones to provide family and friends with a constant flow of updates, reports and pictures were quickly relayed to the media, and the public was soon getting news of the so-called "poop cruise" in virtual real time. Carnival president Gerry Cahill responded by stating publicly that passenger reports weren't entirely accurate: In truth, said Cahill, toilet facilities, running water, and air conditioning had been partially restored. True enough, admits crisis management expert Steven Fink, "but is this really smart crisis communications—to get into a p——g contest with 3,000 angry customers with full bladders?"

The fuel-hose leak that caused the *Triumph* fire was similar to the problem that set fire to Carnival's *Costa Allegra* one year earlier. The *Costa Allegra* drifted for three days in pirate-infested waters in the Indian Ocean. The propulsion-unit issues that canceled the cruises of both the Carnival *Legend* and the Carnival *Elation* on the same weekend in March 2013 were described by the company as "minor." The generator problem that stalled the Carnival *Dream* during the same week was unrelated.

Fink, who's president of Lexicon Communications, the country's oldest crisis management firm, was reminded of Carnival's response to the *Costa Concordia* disaster of January 2012. The *Costa*

Carnival Cruise Lines has had a number of problems in recent years, most notably with the Carnival Triumph (in the Gulf of Mexico) and the Costa Concordia (shown here off the coast of Italy). In both cases Carnival was widely criticized for its poor approach to crisis management.

ANDREAS SOLARO/Getty Images

*Concordia* hit a rock off the western coast of Italy, tearing a 160-foot gash through which water rushed into the engine room, cutting off power to the ship's electrical and propulsion systems. The *Costa Concordia* was eventually grounded with most of her starboard side under water. After a chaotic six-hour evacuation effort, 32 people were left dead.

Fink recalls (correctly) that Carnival CEO Micky Arison's crisis communications from company headquarters in Miami consisted of "a handful of tweets on his Twitter account as … the ship's personnel and captain pointed fingers of blame at each other." Meanwhile, *Cruise Law News* was reporting that "some Carnival executives have been gallivanting around town at black-tie gala parties and Miami Heat basketball games." Arison, who owns the Heat, apparently did not participate in the gallivanting, but neither did he consider it necessary to leave the comfort of his 200-foot yacht, where, *five days later*, he tweeted his condolences and "my personal assurance that we will take care of each & every one of our guests, crew and their families."

A week after the accident, Carnival vice chairman and COO Howard Frank arrived at the crash site with CEO Pier Luigi Foschi of Costa Cruises, the Carnival subsidiary that operated the *Costa Concordia*. It was bad enough that Foschi's compensation offer to *Concordia* passengers was a mere 30 percent off their next Costa cruise. The press and public were locked on the question posed in a *Wall Street Journal* headline: "Where's Micky?" "Who is this mysterious boss," wondered the Italian newspaper *La Repubblica*, "and how has he managed to remain like a ghost since the tragedy?" "When the Heat won the NBA championship," recalled Jim Walker, a maritime lawyer and publisher of *Cruise Law News*, "Arison was photographed everywhere and with everyone. … He even took his trophy on a worldwide tour … on Costa cruise ships. But now, with 30 dead or missing from the *Concordia* wreck, Arison is nowhere to be seen." Walker even took the opportunity to remind readers that "Arison has never stepped up to the plate to address unpleasant issues, like sexual assaults on his fleet of cruise ships, Carnival's avoidance of taxes, or exploitation of foreign crewmembers."

You'd think that Carnival management would have learned something about crisis management from its more effective handling of the Carnival *Splendor* incident in 2010. When the *Splendor* was disabled by an engine-room fire (if you're counting, that's three fires in four years), company executives rushed to the site, held

a highly publicized press conference, and offered generous compensation, reimbursing fares, waiving onboard purchases, and promising a future cruise to all passengers willing to give the company another try. Instead, its handling of the *Costa Concordia* disaster suggested that Carnival's crisis management skills had deteriorated. (The decline continued with the *Triumph* episode, as "poop cruise" passengers were offered a future cruise and a paltry $500.)

To Walker, it looked as if Arison and Foschi were trying to keep up with the disgraced captain of the *Concordia* "in trying to ruin their reputations." Granted, Captain Francesco Schettino had put Carnival and Costa in a deep PR hole. After wrecking his ship, says Walker, Schettino violated "the 'three A's' of cruise line crisis management": First, "his *attitude* was defiant. And his *appearance*? None. He abandoned ship in dereliction of traditional maritime duty. … His *actions*? Self-preservation. He disregarded orders by the Italian Coast Guard to return to his ship and assist in the evacuation."

Carnival and Costa officials wasted no time in trying to foist all the blame onto Schettino, who, according to Foschi, was guilty of "serious errors of judgment" in trying to maneuver for a "salute" to the nearby island of Giglo. The decision, declared Foschi, was "unauthorized, unapproved, and unknown to Costa. The captain has the authority to make decisions on board. In this case, he decided to change the route and went into waters that he did not know in advance." The conduct of Schettino, who claimed that he left the ship because he accidentally fell into a lifeboat, wasn't exactly commendable, but according to Judy Brennan of Ogilvy PR, blaming one employee isn't very good crisis management: "Generally speaking," says Brennan, "companies should not place blame squarely on one or more individuals. … A company needs to go beyond placing blame. The focal point should be what changes it will take to ensure that the problem doesn't arise again."

Adds David Bartlett, senior VP of the crisis management firm Levick: "Crisis management experts know that customers and the general public are more likely to judge an organization by how it handles a problem than how it got into the problem in the first place." Executing the crisis management plan, says Bartlett, means being fast as well as effective—"aggressively and clearly delivering [the company's] message *now*." The CEO, says Larry Berg of the media and marketing company Valassis, should both act with a sense of urgency and focus on the company's long-term reputation: "Rebuilding after a crisis," he explains, "is all about how you handle the situation as it occurred. Did you communicate openly to consumers, or were you evasive and not directly involved. People sense this."

"No plan survives first contact with the enemy"—historians are not sure who said this first—Dwight Eisenhower, Napoleon, Patton, or (most likely) a nineteenth century Prussian field marshal named Helmuth Von Moltke. The sentiment, however, is undeniable. No matter how effectively leaders make decisions, plan, and strategize, it is impossible to predict with certainty exactly how well those decisions, plans, and strategies will work once they are set in motion. Unexpected responses by other businesses, faulty assumptions, human error, or simple luck can all cause business plans to fail or to succeed far better than expected. Nevertheless, when leaders do work to make good decisions and develop effective plans and strategies, they substantially increase their chances of success. Similarly, though, when leaders like top managers at Carnival make bad decisions and execute plans poorly when things do go wrong, they will likely make matters far worse.

As we noted in Chapter 1, planning and decision making comprise the first managerial functions that organizations must address. This chapter is the first of four that explore the planning process in detail. We begin by briefly relating decision making and planning, and then explaining the planning process that most organizations follow. We then discuss the nature of organizational goals and introduce the basic concepts of planning. Next we discuss tactical and operational planning more fully. Finally, we conclude with a discussion of how to manage the goal-setting and planning processes.

## Decision Making and the Planning Process

Decision making is the cornerstone of planning. For instance, consider that several years ago Procter & Gamble (P&G) set a goal of doubling its revenues over a 10-year period. At the time the firm's top managers could have adopted an array of options, including increasing revenues by only 25 percent or increasing revenues threefold. The time frame for the projected revenue growth could also have been somewhat shorter or longer than the 10-year period that was actually specified. Alternatively, the goal could have included diversifying into new markets, cutting costs, or buying competing businesses. Thus P&G's exact mix of goals and plans for growth rate and time frame reflected choices—or decisions—from among a variety of alternatives. (Not surprisingly, of course, over the course of the 10-year period P&G refined its goals and plans several times.) More recently, Ford Motor Company announced a goal of tripling global sales of its luxury brand Lincoln by the year 2020. This goal, in turns, will now drive investments in new production facilities, sales and marketing initiatives, factory hiring, financial planning, and other areas within the firm.[2] Ford's goal, while different and more focused than P&G's in several ways,

Kevin Hagen/Getty Images

Ford recently announced a goal of tripling sales of its luxury brand Lincoln by the year 2020. The forthcoming relaunch of the venerable Lincoln Continental plays a key role in the firm's plans to meeting this goal.

nevertheless reflects the same mix of decisions regarding area, level, and time frame.

Clearly, then, decision making is the catalyst that drives the planning process. An organization's goals follow from decisions made by various managers. Likewise, deciding on the best plan for achieving particular goals also reflects a decision to adopt one course of action as opposed to others. We discuss decision making *per se* in Chapter 8. Our focus here is on the planning process itself, of which decision making is one part. As we discuss goal setting and planning, however, keep in mind that decision making underlies every aspect of setting goals and formulating plans.[3]

The planning process itself can best be thought of as a generic activity. All organizations engage in planning activities, but no two organizations plan in exactly the same fashion. Figure 6.1 is a general representation of the planning process that many organizations try to follow. But, although most firms follow this general framework, each also has its own nuances and variations.[5]

As Figure 6.1 shows, all planning occurs within an environmental context. If managers do not understand this context, they will be unable to develop effective plans. Thus understanding the environment is essentially the first step in planning. The three previous chapters cover many of the basic environmental issues that affect organizations and how they plan. With this understanding as a foundation, managers must then establish the organization's mission. The mission outlines the organization's purpose, premises, values, and directions. Flowing from the mission are parallel streams of goals and plans. Directly following the mission are strategic goals. These goals and the mission help determine strategic plans. Strategic goals and plans are primary inputs for developing tactical goals. Tactical goals and the original strategic plans help shape tactical plans. Tactical plans, in turn, combine with the tactical goals to shape operational goals. These goals and the appropriate tactical plans

> "Policy making could go on and on endlessly, and there are always resources to be allocated. 'Decision' implies the end of deliberation and the beginning of action."
>
> —WILLIAM STARBUCK, LEADING MANAGEMENT THEORIST[4]

## FIGURE 6.1  THE PLANNING PROCESS

The planning process takes place within an environmental context. Managers must develop a complete and thorough understanding of this context to determine the organization's mission and to develop its strategic, tactical, and operational goals and plans.

determine operational plans. Finally, goals and plans at each level can also be used as input for future activities at all levels. This chapter discusses goals and tactical and operational plans. Chapter 7 covers strategic plans.

---

☑️ **Manager's Checklist**

☐ Managers need to remember that decision making and planning are critical parts of their jobs.

☐ Managers should also keep in mind that even if their decisions and plans are not perfect, trying to make effective decisions and plans increases their chances for success.

# Organizational Goals

Goals are critical to organizational effectiveness, and they serve a number of purposes. Organizations can also have several different kinds of goals, all of which must be appropriately managed. And a number of different kinds of managers must be involved in setting goals.

## Purposes of Goals

Goals serve four important purposes.[6] First, they provide guidance and a unified direction for people in the organization. Goals can help everyone understand where the organization is going and why getting there is important.[7] Top managers at General Electric have a long-standing goal that every business owned by the firm will be either number one or number two in its industry (or have a reasonable chance of achieving that ranking). This goal helps set the tone for decisions made by GE managers as it competes with other firms like Whirlpool and Electrolux (appliances), Rolls Royce (jet engines), and numerous financial services firms.[8] Likewise, P&G's goal of doubling revenues helps everyone in the firm recognize the strong emphasis on growth and expansion that is driving the firm, while Ford's goal reflects a clear focus on product diversification. Intel recently announced a goal that the diversity of its workforce should mirror the talent available in the United States by the year 2020.[9]

Second, goal-setting practices strongly affect other aspects of planning. Effective goal setting promotes good planning, and good planning facilitates future goal setting. For example, the ambitious revenue goal set for P&G demonstrates how setting goals and developing plans to reach them should be seen as complementary activities. The strong growth goal should encourage managers to plan for expansion by looking for new market opportunities, for example. Similarly, they must also always be alert for competitive threats and new ideas that will help facilitate future expansion. Ford, meanwhile, is focusing on increasing revenues from a particular product line.

Third, goals can serve as a source of motivation for employees of the organization. Goals that are specific and moderately difficult can motivate people to work harder, especially if attaining the goal is likely to result in rewards.[10] The Italian furniture manufacturer Natuzzi uses goals to motivate its workers. Each craftsperson has a goal for how long it should take to perform her or his job, such as sewing leather sheets together to make a sofa cushion or building wooden frames for chair arms. At the completion of assigned tasks, workers enter their ID numbers and job numbers into the firm's computer system. If they get a job done faster than their goal, a bonus is automatically added to their paycheck.[11] Intel has tied compensation of its top managers to their achievement of the firm's diversity goal.

"If you don't invest in the future and don't plan for the future, there won't be one."

—GEORGE BUCKLEY,
FORMER PRESIDENT, CHAIRMAN AND CEO OF 3M[12]

Finally, goals provide an effective mechanism for evaluation and control. This means that performance can be assessed in the future in terms of how successfully today's goals are accomplished. For example, suppose that officials of the United Way of America set a goal of collecting $250,000 from a particular small community. If, midway through the campaign, they have raised only $50,000, they know that they need to change or intensify their efforts. If they raise only $100,000 by the end of their drive, they will need to carefully study why they did not reach their goal and what they need to do differently next year. On the other hand, if they succeed in raising $265,000, evaluations of their efforts will take on an entirely different character. The Food and Drug Administration (FDA) recently revealed that it was not meeting the goals it had set for itself for auditing food safety inspection programs. To address the issue, the FDA also announced plans to overhaul its inspection program and to tie individual performance ratings to food safety audits.[13] And in 2015 the agency completely overhauled its organization structure to perform at an even higher level.

The United Way of America sets annual fund raising goals for each community where it solicits donations. United Way also uses signs such as this one to indicate both the local goal ($4.13 million in this case) and progress toward that goal (90 percent).

## Kinds of Goals

Organizations establish many different kinds of goals. In general, these goals vary by level, area, and time frame.[14] Figure 6.2 provides examples of each type of goal for a fast-food chain.

**Level**  Goals are set for and by different levels within an organization. As we noted earlier, the four basic levels of goals are the mission and strategic, tactical, and operational goals. An organization's *mission* is a statement of its "fundamental, unique purpose that sets a business apart from other firms of its type and identifies the scope of the business's operations in product and market terms."[15] For instance, Starbucks' mission statement is "To inspire and nurture the human spirit—one person, one cup, and one neighborhood at a time." Starbucks also espouses these principles[16]:

- *Our Coffee* It has always been, and will always be, about quality. We're passionate about ethically sourcing the finest coffee beans, roasting them with great care, and improving the lives of people who grow them. We care deeply about all of this; our work is never done.
- *Our Partners* We're called partners, because it's not just a job, it's our passion. Together, we embrace diversity to create a place where each of us can be ourselves. We always treat each other with respect and dignity. And we hold each other to that standard.
- *Our Customers* When we are fully engaged, we connect with, laugh with, and uplift the lives of our customers—even if just for a few moments. Sure, it starts with the promise of a perfectly made beverage, but our work goes far beyond that. It's really about human connection.
- *Our Stores* When our customers feel this sense of belonging, our stores become a haven, a break from the worries outside, a place where you can meet with friends. It's about enjoyment at the speed of life—sometimes slow and savored, sometimes faster. Always full of humanity.
- *Our Neighborhood* Every store is part of a community, and we take our responsibility to be good neighbors seriously. We want to be invited in wherever we do business. We can be a force for positive action—bringing together our partners, customers, and the community to contribute every day. Now we see that our responsibility—and our potential for good—is even larger. The world is looking to Starbucks to set the new standard, yet again. We will lead.
- *Our Shareholders* We know that as we deliver in each of these areas, we enjoy the kind of success that rewards our shareholders. We are fully accountable to get each of these elements right so that Starbucks—and everyone it touches—can endure and thrive.

**mission**
A statement of an organization's fundamental purpose

An organization's mission is a statement of purpose. This mission statement, for example, clearly indicates that this organization (eBay) views itself as a service organization dedicated to building an engaged and loyal community (of buyers and sellers).

Hence, the mission statement and basic principles help managers at Starbucks make decisions and direct resources in clear and specific ways.

Strategic goals are goals set by and for top management of the organization. They focus on broad, general issues. For example, Starbucks has a strategic goal of increasing the profitability of each of its coffee stores by 25 percent over the next five years. Tactical goals are set by and for middle managers. Their focus is on how to operationalize actions necessary to achieve the strategic goals. To achieve Starbucks' goal of increasing its per-store profitability, managers are working on tactical goals related to company-owned versus licensed stores and the global distribution of stores in different countries.

Operational goals are set by and for lower-level managers. Their concern is with shorter-term issues associated with the tactical goals. An operational goal for Starbucks might be to boost the profitability of a certain number of stores in each of the next five years. (Some managers use the words *objective* and *goal* interchangeably. When they are differentiated, however, the term *objective* is usually used instead of *operational goal*.)

**Area** Organizations also set goals for different areas. The restaurant chain shown in Figure 6.2 has goals for operations, marketing, and finance. Hewlett-Packard (HP) routinely sets production goals for quality, productivity, and so forth. By keeping activities focused on these important areas, HP has managed to remain competitive against organizations from around the world. Human resource goals might be set for employee turnover and absenteeism. 3M and Rubbermaid set goals for product innovation. Similarly, Bath & Body Works has a goal that 30 percent of the products sold in its retail outlets each year will be new. In addition to its profit growth goals, Starbucks also has financial goals related to return on investment and return on assets.

**Time Frame** Organizations also set goals across different time frames. In Figure 6.2, three goals are listed at the strategic, tactical, and operational levels. The first is a long-term goal, the second an intermediate-term goal, and the third a short-term goal. Some goals have an explicit time frame (open 150 new restaurants during the next 10 years), and others have an open-ended time horizon (maintain 10 percent annual growth). Finally, we should also note that the meaning of different time frames varies by level. For example, at the strategic level, "long term" often means 10 years or longer, "intermediate term" around five years or so, and "short term" around one year. But two or three years may be long term at the operational level, while short term may mean a matter of weeks or even days.

## Responsibilities for Setting Goals

Who sets goals? The answer is actually quite simple: All managers should be involved in the goal-setting process. Each manager, however, generally has responsibilities for setting goals that correspond to his or her level in the organization. The mission and strategic goals are generally determined by the board of directors and top managers. Top and middle managers then work together to establish tactical goals. Finally, middle and lower-level managers are jointly responsible for operational goals. Many managers also set individual goals for

**strategic goal**
A goal set by and for top management of the organization

**tactical goal**
A goal set by and for middle managers of the organization

**operational goal**
A goal set by and for lower-level managers of the organization

## FIGURE 6.2  KINDS OF ORGANIZATIONAL GOALS FOR A REGIONAL FAST-FOOD CHAIN

Organizations develop many different types of goals. A regional fast-food chain, for example, might develop goals at several different levels and for several different areas.

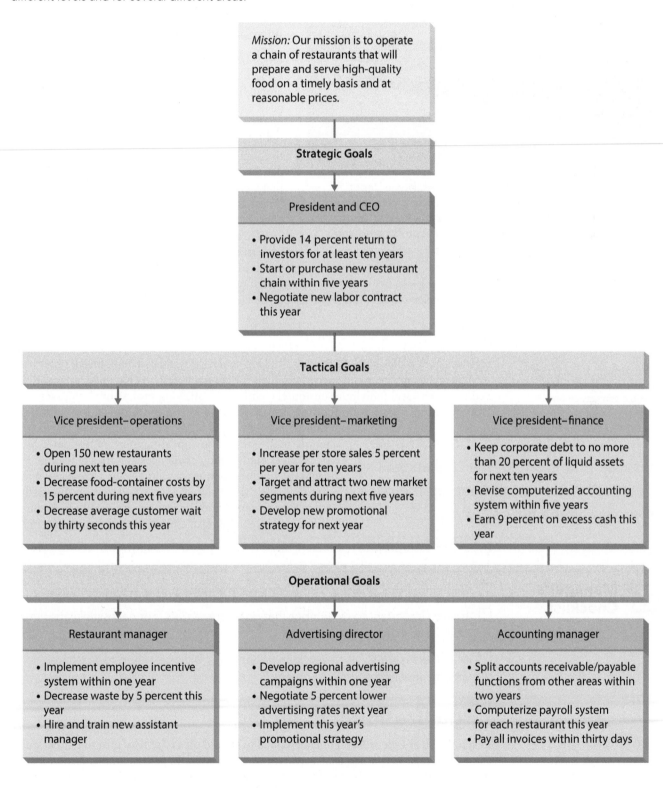

Bloomberg/Getty Images

Most firms have to work toward multiple goals. Home Depot, for example, strives to meet the needs of home owners and other do-it-yourselfers. But the retailer also wants to appeal to contractors and other professionals who expect a different product mix and approach to service.

themselves. These goals may involve career paths, informal work-related goals outside the normal array of official goals, or just about anything of interest or concern to the manager.

## Managing Multiple Goals

Organizations set many different kinds of goals and sometimes experience conflicts or contradictions among goals. Nike had problems with inconsistent goals a few years ago. The firm was producing high-quality shoes (a manufacturing goal), but they were not particularly stylish (a marketing goal). As a result, the company lost substantial market share when Adidas, Reebok, and New Balance started making shoes that were both high quality and fashionable. When Nike management recognized and corrected the inconsistencies, Nike regained its industry standing.

To address such problems, managers must understand the concept of optimizing. Optimizing involves balancing and reconciling possible conflicts among goals. Because goals may conflict with one another, the manager must look for inconsistencies and decide whether to pursue one goal to the exclusion of another or to find a midrange target between the extremes. For example, Home Depot first achieved success in the retailing industry by offering do-it-yourselfers high-quality home improvement products at low prices and with good service. The firm then added an additional goal of doubling its revenues from professional contractors. To help achieve this, many Home Depot stores have separate checkout areas and special products for contractors. The challenge, however, has been to keep loyal individual customers while also satisfying professional contractors.[17] Home Depot's biggest competitor, Lowe's, is also optimizing, but among different alternatives—trying to retain its core customer group (primarily male) while also appealing more to women.[18] Starbucks faces optimization challenges as it tries to maintain its cachet as an upscale purveyor of fine coffees while also opening roadside drive-through stores and adding non-coffee drinks to its menu. And the airlines almost always seem to face a classic optimizing question—carrying more passengers for lower prices or fewer passengers for higher prices.[19]

**optimizing**
Balancing and reconciling possible conflicts among goals

"We have always grown at a rapid pace because that is one of the challenges I set for myself. We hope to keep up the pace of growth in the future."

—JIN CHANG, CEO FOREVER 21 CLOTHING[20]

**Manager's Checklist**

☐ Remember that goals and goal setting are a major part of a manager's job.

☐ It's also important to remember that goals are targets, not necessarily absolute objectives that must be attained.

☐ Managers need to also keep in mind that they will often need to optimize among and across multiple goals.

## Organizational Planning

Given the clear link between organizational goals and plans, we now turn our attention to various concepts and issues associated with planning itself. In particular, this section identifies kinds of plans, time frames for planning, who is responsible for planning, and contingency planning.

## Kinds of Organizational Plans

Organizations establish many different kinds of plans. At a general level, these include strategic, tactical, and operational plans.

**Strategic Plans** Strategic plans are the plans developed to achieve strategic goals. More precisely, a strategic plan is a general plan outlining decisions of resource allocation, priorities, and action steps necessary to reach strategic goals. These plans are set by the board of directors and top management, generally have an extended time horizon, and address questions of scope, resource deployment, competitive advantage, and synergy. *Tech Watch* discusses an emerging area of importance for many businesses, the need for a social media strategy. We discuss strategic planning further in Chapter 7.

**Tactical Plans** A tactical plan, aimed at achieving tactical goals, is developed to implement specific parts of a strategic plan. Tactical plans typically involve upper and middle management and, compared with strategic plans, have a somewhat shorter time horizon and a more specific and concrete focus. Thus tactical plans are concerned more with actually getting things done than with deciding what to do. Tactical planning is covered in detail in a later section.

**Operational Plans** An operational plan focuses on carrying out tactical plans to achieve operational goals. Developed by middle and lower-level managers, operational plans have a short-term focus and are relatively narrow in scope. Each one deals with a fairly small set of activities. We also cover operational planning in more detail later.

## Time Frames for Planning

As we noted previously, strategic plans tend to have a long-term focus, tactical plans an intermediate-term focus, and operational plans a short-term focus. The sections that follow address these time frames in more detail. Of course, we should also remember that time frames vary widely from industry to industry.

**Long-Range Plans** A long-range plan covers many years, perhaps even decades. The founder of Matsushita Electric (maker of Panasonic and JVC electronic products), Konosuke Matsushita, once wrote a 250-year plan for his company![21] Today, however, most managers recognize that environmental change makes it unfeasible to plan too far ahead, but large firms like Ford Motor Company and ExxonMobil still routinely develop plans for five- to 10-year intervals. Ford executives, for example, have a pretty good idea today about new car models that they plan to introduce during the next decade. Recall, for instance, the earlier example of Ford announcing a five-year plan for growing revenues from the Lincoln brand. The time span for long-range planning, of course, varies from one organization to another. For our purposes, we regard any plan that extends beyond five years as long range. Managers of organizations in complex, volatile environments face a special dilemma. These organizations probably need a longer time horizon than do organizations in less dynamic environments, yet the complexity of their environment makes long-range planning difficult. Managers at these companies therefore develop long-range plans but also must constantly monitor their environment for possible changes.

**strategic plan**
A general plan outlining decisions of resource allocation, priorities, and action steps necessary to reach strategic goals

**tactical plan**
A plan aimed at achieving tactical goals, developed to implement parts of a strategic plan

**operational plan**
Focuses on carrying out tactical plans to achieve operational goals

**long-range plan**
A plan that covers many years, perhaps even decades; common long-range plans are for five years or more

"Our goal is to ensure that we are adapting to keep pace with the changing marketplace. We are intent on strengthening our brand by running even better restaurants and delivering the best food and beverage offerings. We will accomplish this by accentuating our key brand attributes, modernizing our connection with the more than 69 million customers who visit McDonald's each day, and optimizing our globally diversified restaurant portfolio."

—DON THOMPSON,
CEO MCDONALD'S ON THEIR LONG-TERM GOALS[22]

# Starting Conversations

If you run a business and are aware of the fact that 73 percent of all American adults have a social media account, then you have undoubtedly arrived at an inescapable conclusion: *Your business needs a social media strategy.* What you need, in other words, is a set of goals and objectives for your social media marketing efforts, as well as a set of marketing tools and a set of metrics to figure out if those tools are getting the job done.

Fortunately, there's no shortage of specialized consultancies out there ready to help you maximize your social media strategy. Many of them have even prepared step-by-step procedures for developing or massaging strategies. The plan of one agency, for example, promises that you can develop a "Social Media Strategy in 8 Steps." Here are a few highlights:

- *Build an Ark.* "Your social media strategy should be more like air (everywhere) than like water (you have to go get it)."
- *What's Your One Thing?* "How will your company appeal to the heart of your audience rather than the head?"
- *How Will You Be Human?* "Your company has to act like a person, not an entity."

To be fair, some of the plan's recommendations make common sense and have obvious practical value. For example: *Analyze Your Audiences:* "**What are the characteristics of your current or prospective customers?** How does the answer to that question affect what you can and should attempt in social media?" Jess Collins, of Type Communications, a full-service ad agency in Britain, offers an increasingly common answer to these questions: "It's not quantity," she says. "It's quality. It's about attracting fans/followers that are your target market, and so you need to make sure you're speaking to real fans rather than looking popular but not being seen by the people who matter most."

"Fans and follower counts are over," adds Jan Rezab, CEO of the social media metrics company Socialbakers. "Now it's about what is social doing for you and your real business objectives." Take, for example, the Ritz-Carlton Hotel Co., which operates luxury hotels and resorts in 26 countries. In May 2013, the company bought a series of Facebook ads to promote its brand page. The ads attracted a large number of fans—too many, as far as Ritz-Carlton was concerned. "We were fearful that our engagement and connection with our community was dropping," explains VP of global public relations Allison Sitch. Rather than amassing fans and followers, Ritz-Carlton's strategy calls for analyzing its social media *conversations*—the networks of connections built and sustained by the most "passionate" users of a company's social media—in order to determine what real customers really do and don't like about the company's products.

Today, even social networking services admit that companies should start rethinking their social media strategies. Not surprisingly, for example, Twitter maintains that it's a good thing for companies to have big followings, but director of brand strategy Ross Hoffman hastens to add that "engagement is the key and … can in turn further grow your audience." A spokesman for Facebook agrees: "Fans," he says, "should be a means to positive business outcomes, not the end in themselves."

*References:* Lisa Parkin, "Why Businesses Don't Need a Social Media Strategy," *Huffington Post* (August 6, 2014), www.huffingtonpost.com, on August 30, 2014; Jay Baer, "Social Media Strategy in Eight Steps," Convince & Convert LLC (July 17, 2014), www.convinceandconvert.com, on August 30, 2014; Jess Collins, "Social Media Strategy: Seven Lessons for Engaging Your Fanbase," *The Guardian* (UK) (August 8, 2014), www.the guardian.com, on August 30, 2014; Jeff Elder, "Social Media Fail to Live Up to Early Marketing Hype," *Wall Street Journal* (June 23, 2014), http://online.wsj.com, on August 29, 2014; John Rampton, "Why Most Social Media Strategies Fail," *Forbes* (April 22, 2014), www.forbes.com, on August 29, 2014.

**Intermediate Plans** An intermediate plan is somewhat less tentative and subject to change than is a long-range plan. Intermediate plans usually cover periods from one to five years and are especially important for middle and first-line managers. Thus they generally parallel tactical plans. For many organizations, intermediate planning has become the central focus of planning activities. Nissan, for example, fell behind its domestic rivals Toyota and Honda in profitability and productivity. To turn things around, the firm developed several plans ranging in duration from two to four years, each intended to improve some part of the company's operations. One plan (three years in duration) involved updating the manufacturing technology used in each Nissan assembly factory. Another (four years in duration) called for shifting more production to foreign plants to lower labor costs. And the successful implementation of these plans helped turn things around for Nissan.

**Short-Range Plans** Managers also develop short-range plans, which have a time frame of one year or less. Short-range plans greatly affect the manager's day-to-day activities. There are two basic kinds of short-range plans. An action plan operationalizes any other kind of plan. When a specific Nissan plant was ready to have its technology overhauled, its managers focused their attention on replacing the existing equipment with new equipment as quickly and as efficiently as possible, to minimize lost production time. In most cases, this was done in a matter of a few months, with actual production halted for only a few weeks. An action plan thus coordinates the actual changes at a given factory. A reaction plan, in turn, is a plan designed to allow the company to react to an unforeseen circumstance. At one Nissan factory, the new equipment arrived earlier than expected, and plant managers had to shut down production more quickly than expected. These managers thus had to react to events beyond their control in ways that still allowed their goals to be achieved. In fact, reacting to any form of environmental turbulence, as described in Chapter 3, is a form of reaction planning.

## Responsibilities for Planning

Earlier we noted briefly who is responsible for setting goals. We can now expand that initial perspective and examine more fully how different parts of the organization participate in the overall planning process. All managers engage in planning to some degree. Marketing sales managers develop plans for target markets, market penetration, and sales increases. Operations managers plan cost-cutting programs and better inventory control methods. As a general rule, however, the larger an organization becomes, the more the primary planning activities become associated with groups of managers rather than with individual managers.

**Planning Staff** Some large organizations maintain a professional planning staff. General Motors, Caterpillar, Raytheon, Ford, and Boeing all have planning staffs. And although the planning staff was pioneered in the United States, foreign firms like Nippon Telegraph and Telephone have also started using them. Organizations might use a planning staff for a variety of reasons. In particular, a planning staff can reduce the workload of individual managers, help coordinate the planning activities of individual managers, bring to a particular problem many different tools and techniques, take a broader view than individual managers, and go beyond pet projects and particular departments. In recent years, though, some businesses have realized that they can plan more effectively by diffusing planning responsibility throughout their organization and/or by using planning task forces. For instance, Disney and Shell Oil have eliminated or downsized their centralized planning units.[23]

**Planning Task Force** Organizations sometimes use a planning task force to help develop plans. Such a task force often comprises line managers with a special interest in the relevant area of planning. The task force may also have members from the planning staff if the organization has one. A planning task force is most often created when the organization wants to address a special circumstance. For example, when Electronic Data Systems (EDS) decided to expand its information management services to Europe, managers knew that the firm's

**intermediate plan**
A plan that generally covers from one to five years

**short-range plan**
A plan that generally covers a span of one year or less

**action plan**
A plan used to operationalize any other kind of plan

**reaction plan**
A plan developed to react to an unforeseen circumstance

Taylor Hill/Getty Images

Kenneth Chenault has served as CEO of American Express for several years. He works with the Amex board of directors, executive committee, and other top managers to develop and implement strategies and plans for the financial services giant.

normal planning approach would not suffice, and top management created a special planning task force. The task force included representatives from each of the major units within the company, the corporate planning staff, and the management team that would run the European operation. Once the plan for entering the European market was formulated and implemented, the task force was eliminated.

**Board of Directors** Among its other responsibilities, the board of directors establishes the corporate mission and strategy. In some companies the board takes an active role in the planning process.[24] At CBS, for example, the board of directors has traditionally played a major role in planning. In other companies the board selects a competent chief executive and delegates planning to that person.

**Chief Executive Officer** The chief executive officer (CEO) is usually the president or the chair of the board of directors. The CEO is probably the single most important person in any organization's planning process. The CEO plays a major role in the complete planning process and is responsible for implementing the strategy. The board and CEO, then, assume direct roles in planning. The other organizational players involved in the planning process have more of an advisory or a consulting role.

**Executive Committee** The executive committee is usually composed of the top executives in the organization working together as a group. Committee members usually meet regularly to provide input to the CEO on the proposals that affect their own units and to review the strategic plans that develop from this input. Members of the executive committee are often assigned to various staff committees, subcommittees, and task forces to concentrate on specific projects or problems that might confront the entire organization at some time in the future.

**Line Management** The final component of most organizations' planning activities is line management. Line managers are those persons with formal authority and responsibility for the management of the organization. They play an important role in an organization's planning process for two reasons. First, they are a valuable source of inside information for other managers as plans are formulated and implemented. Second, the line managers at the middle and lower levels of the organization usually must execute the plans developed by top management. Line management identifies, analyzes, and recommends program alternatives, develops budgets and submits them for approval, and finally sets the plans in motion.

## Contingency Planning and Crisis Management

**contingency planning**
The determination of alternative courses of action to be taken if an intended plan is unexpectedly disrupted or rendered inappropriate

Another important type of planning is contingency planning—the determination of alternative courses of action to be taken if an intended plan of action is unexpectedly disrupted or rendered inappropriate (Figure 6.3).[25] Crisis management, a related concept, is the set of procedures the organization uses in the event of a disaster or other unexpected calamity. Some elements of crisis management may be orderly and systematic, whereas others may be more ad hoc and develop as events unfold.

**crisis management**
The set of procedures the organization uses in the event of a disaster or other unexpected calamity

A classic example of widespread contingency planning occurred during the late 1990s in anticipation of what was popularly known as the "Y2K bug." Concerns about the impact of technical glitches in computers stemming from their internal clocks' changing from 1999 to 2000 resulted in contingency planning for most organizations. Many banks and hospitals, for example, had extra staff available; some organizations created backup computer systems;

and some even stockpiled inventory in case they could not purchase new products or materials.[26] Today, more firms have contingency plans in place to deal with events such as terrorism, Internet security breaches, pandemics, and so forth. However, given the uncertainty of when and how crises may unfold, it is actually very difficult to know in advance how to respond.[27]

The devastating hurricanes that hit the Gulf Coast of the United States in 2005—Katrina and Rita—dramatically underscored the importance of effective crisis management. For example, inadequate and ineffective responses by the Federal Emergency Management Agency (FEMA) illustrated to many people that organization's weaknesses in coping with crisis situations. On the other hand, some organizations responded much more effectively. Walmart began ramping up its emergency preparedness on the same day that Katrina was upgraded from a tropical depression to a tropical storm. In the days before the storm struck, Walmart stores in the region were supplied with powerful generators and large supplies of dry ice so they could reopen as quickly as possible after the storm had passed. In neighboring states, the firm also had scores of trucks standing by crammed with both emergency-related inventory for its stores and emergency supplies it was prepared to donate—bottled water, medical supplies, and so forth. And Walmart often beat FEMA by several days in getting those supplies delivered.[29]

Seeing the consequences of poor crisis management after the terrorist attacks of September 11, 2001, and the 2005 hurricanes, many firms today are actively working to create new and better crisis management plans and procedures. For example, both Reliant Energy and Duke Energy rely on computer trading centers where trading managers actively buy and sell energy-related commodities. If a terrorist attack or natural disaster such as a hurricane were to strike their trading centers, they would essentially be out of business. Prior to September 11, each firm had relatively vague and superficial crisis plans. But now they and most other companies have much more detailed and comprehensive plans in the event of another crisis. Both Reliant and Duke, for example, have created secondary trading centers at other locations. In the event of a shutdown at their main trading centers, these firms can quickly transfer virtually all their core trading activities to their secondary centers within 30 minutes or less.[30] Of course, as illustrated in our "Management in Action" case that opened this chapter, some businesses handle this better than do others!

Unfortunately, however, because it is impossible to forecast the future precisely, no organization can ever be perfectly prepared for all crises. For example, due to 2011's disastrous earthquake and tsunami in Japan, many U.S. companies faced shortages of goods and materials imported from that country. General Motors was the first automaker forced to temporarily shut down one of its truck plants because it could not get enough Japanese-made parts. Two months after the disaster, Toyota's facilities in the United States were operating at less than 30 percent of capacity, and they did not return to full production until several months later.[31]

The mechanics of contingency planning are shown in Figure 6.3. In relation to an organization's other plans, contingency planning comes into play at four action points. At action point 1, management develops the basic plans of the organization. These may include strategic, tactical, and operational plans. As part of this development process, managers usually

"This fight [against terrorism] will not be decided on the battlefield, but in the classrooms, workplaces, and places of worship of the world."

—JOHN KERRY, U.S. SECRETARY OF STATE[28]

Natural disasters like hurricanes and earthquakes can have a devastating impact on business. Large companies often have crisis management plans in place to provide at least partial direction and support for those affected by such a disaster. But smaller businesses like this one are likely to suffer long-term financial consequences and many do not survive.

"[G.M. has contingency plans for supply disruptions] but nothing on this kind of scale or scope."

—STEPHEN GIRSKY, GENERAL MOTORS VICE CHAIRMAN[32]

## FIGURE 6.3   CONTINGENCY PLANNING

Most organizations develop contingency plans. These plans specify alternative courses of action to be taken if an intended plan is unexpectedly disrupted or rendered inappropriate.

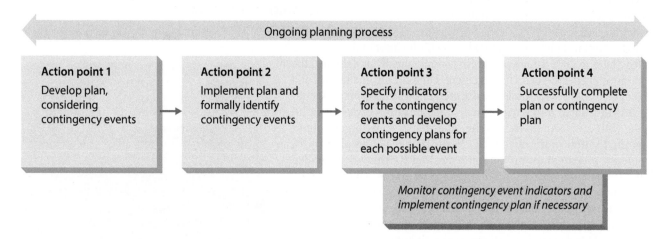

consider various contingency events. Some management groups even assign someone the role of devil's advocate to ask, "But what if …" about each course of action. A variety of contingencies are usually considered.

At action point 2, the plan that management chooses is put into effect. The most important contingency events are also defined. Only the events that are likely to occur and whose effects will have a substantial impact on the organization are considered in the contingency planning process. Next, at action point 3, the company specifies certain indicators or signs that suggest that a contingency event is about to take place. A bank might decide that a 2 percent drop in interest rates should be considered a contingency event. An indicator might be two consecutive months with a drop of 0.5 percent in each. As indicators of contingency events are being defined, the contingency plans themselves should also be developed. Examples of contingency plans for various situations are delaying plant construction, developing a new manufacturing process, and cutting prices.

After this stage, the managers of the organization monitor the indicators identified at action point 3. If the situation dictates, a contingency plan is implemented. Otherwise, the primary plan of action continues in force. Finally, action point 4 marks the successful completion of either the original or a contingency plan.

Contingency planning is becoming increasingly important for most organizations, especially for those operating in particularly complex or dynamic environments. Few managers have such an accurate view of the future that they can anticipate and plan for everything. Contingency planning is a useful technique for helping managers cope with uncertainty and change. Crisis management, by its very nature, however, is more difficult to anticipate. But organizations that have a strong culture, strong leadership, and a capacity to deal with the unexpected stand a better chance of successfully weathering a crisis than do other organizations.[33]

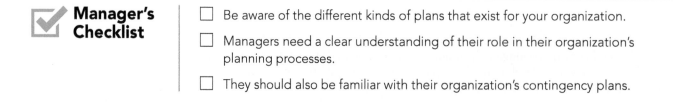

**Manager's Checklist**

☐ Be aware of the different kinds of plans that exist for your organization.

☐ Managers need a clear understanding of their role in their organization's planning processes.

☐ They should also be familiar with their organization's contingency plans.

# Tactical Planning

As we noted earlier, tactical plans are developed to implement specific parts of a strategic plan. You have probably heard the saying about winning the battle but losing the war. Tactical plans are to battles what strategy is to a war: an organized sequence of steps designed to execute strategic plans. Strategy focuses on resources, environment, and mission, whereas tactics focus primarily on people and action.[34] Figure 6.4 identifies the major elements in developing and executing tactical plans.

## Developing Tactical Plans

Although effective tactical planning depends on many factors, which vary from one situation to another, we can identify some basic guidelines. First, the manager needs to recognize that tactical planning must address a number of tactical goals derived from a broader strategic goal.[35] An occasional situation may call for a stand-alone tactical plan, but most of the time tactical plans flow from and must be consistent with a strategic plan.

For example, top managers at Coca-Cola once developed a strategic plan for cementing the firm's dominance of the soft-drink industry. As part of developing the plan, they identified a critical environmental threat—considerable unrest and uncertainty among the independent bottlers that packaged and distributed Coca-Cola's products. To simultaneously counter this threat and strengthen the company's position, Coca-Cola bought several large independent bottlers and combined them into one new organization called "Coca-Cola Enterprises." Selling half of the new company's stock reaped millions in profits while effectively keeping control of the enterprise in Coca-Cola's hands. Thus the creation of the new business was a tactical plan developed to contribute to the achievement of an overarching strategic goal.[36]

> "We reinvested in our people, we reinvested in innovation, and we reinvested in the values of the company."
>
> —HOWARD SCHULTZ, CEO STARBUCKS ON REINVIGORATING HIS WORKFORCE AND COMPANY[37]

Second, although strategies are often stated in general terms, tactics must specify resources and time frames. A strategy can call for being number one in a particular market or industry, but a tactical plan must specify precisely what activities will be undertaken to achieve that goal. Consider the Coca-Cola example again. Another element of its strategic plan involves increased worldwide market share. To facilitate additional sales in Europe, managers developed tactical plans for building a new plant in the

## FIGURE 6.4  DEVELOPING AND EXECUTING TACTICAL PLANS

Tactical plans are used to accomplish specific parts of a strategic plan. Each strategic plan is generally implemented through several tactical plans. Effective tactical planning involves both development and execution.

**Developing tactical plans**
- Recognize and understand overarching strategic plans and tactical goals
- Specify relevant resource and time issues
- Recognize and identify human resource commitments

**Executing tactical plans**
- Evaluate each course of action in light of its goal
- Obtain and distribute information and resources
- Monitor horizontal and vertical communication and integration of activities
- Monitor ongoing activities for goal achievement

south of France to make soft-drink concentrate and for building another canning plant in Dunkirk. The firm has also invested heavily in India.[38] Building these plants represents a concrete action involving measurable resources (funds to build the plants) and a clear time horizon (a target date for completion).

Finally, tactical planning requires the use of human resources. Managers involved in tactical planning spend a great deal of time working with other people. They must be in a position to receive information from others within and outside the organization, process that information in the most effective way, and then pass it on to others who might make use of it. Coca-Cola executives have been intensively involved in planning the new plants, setting up the new bottling venture noted earlier, and exploring a joint venture with Cadbury Schweppes in the United Kingdom. Each activity has required considerable time and effort from dozens of managers. One manager, for example, crossed the Atlantic 12 times while negotiating the Cadbury deal, although it was never finalized.

## Executing Tactical Plans

Regardless of how well a tactical plan is formulated, its ultimate success depends on the way it is carried out. Successful implementation, in turn, depends on the astute use of resources, effective decision making, and insightful steps to ensure that the right things are done at the right times and in the right ways. A manager can see an absolutely brilliant idea fail because of improper execution.

Proper execution depends on a number of important factors. First, the manager needs to evaluate every possible course of action in light of the goal it is intended to reach. Next, he or she needs to make sure that each decision maker has the information and resources necessary to get the job done. Vertical and horizontal communication and integration of activities must be present to minimize conflict and inconsistent activities. And, finally, the manager must monitor ongoing activities derived from the plan to make sure they are achieving the desired results. This monitoring typically takes place within the context of the organization's ongoing control systems.

For example, managers at Walt Disney Company recently developed a new strategic plan aimed at spurring growth in and profits from foreign markets. One tactical plan developed to stimulate growth involves expanding the cable Disney Channel into more and more foreign markets; another involved expanding the relatively small Disney theme park near Hong Kong that opened in 2006 into a much larger park. Yet another involved buying George Lucas's Star Wars properties and then exploiting them with new movies, video games, and books. Although expanding cable television, expanding a theme park, and planning new movies are big undertakings in their own right, they are still tactical plans within the overall strategic plan focusing on international growth.[39]

LI SU/FEATURECHINA/News.com

As part of Disney's strategy the firm is extending its products and services into international markets. Underneath this strategic umbrella Disney is also pursuing a number of tactical plans as well. A recent major initiative was the construction of a new Disney theme park outside of Shanghai, China. The centerpiece of the new park is the Enchanted Storybook Castle, shown here being finished in May 2015. Within any major investment such as this businesses develop and execute myriad tactical and operational plans.

**Manager's Checklist**

☐ You need to clearly understand how to both develop and then execute tactical plans.

☐ Remember that tactical plans need to be consistent with overarching strategic plans.

# Operational Planning

Another critical element in effective organizational planning is the development and implementation of operational plans. Operational plans are derived from tactical plans and are aimed at achieving operational goals. Thus operational plans tend to be narrowly focused, have relatively short time horizons, and involve lower-level managers. The two most basic forms of operational plans and specific types of each are summarized in Table 6.1.

It remains to be seen if American Airlines will retain the same look, feel, and branding in their Ambassador Lounges, given their merger with US Airways. Passengers at this New York JFK American Airlines Ambassador Lounge may or may not see changes next time they visit.

## Single-Use Plans

A single-use plan is developed to carry out a course of action that is not likely to be repeated in the future. As Disney plans the expansion of its theme park in Hong Kong, it will develop many single-use plans for individual rides, attractions, and hotels. Similarly, Disney is also expanding its Animal Kingdom theme park in Florida and has multiple single-use plans for those new rides, shows, and attractions as well. The two most common forms of single-use plans are programs and projects.

**Programs** A program is a single-use plan for a large set of activities. It might consist of identifying procedures for introducing a new product line, opening a new facility, or changing the organization's mission. American Airlines and US Airways are currently merging to create a single airline. As part of the merger, the new firm must make decisions about harmonizing frequent flyer programs, airport lounge facilities, in-flight services such as coffee and meal services, work schedules and benefits for pilots and flight crews, route

**single-use plan**
Developed to carry out a course of action that is not likely to be repeated in the future

**program**
A single-use plan for a large set of activities

## TABLE 6.1  TYPES OF OPERATIONAL PLANS

Organizations develop various operational plans to help achieve operational goals. In general, there are two types of single-use plans and three types of standing plans.

| Plan | Description |
| --- | --- |
| **Single-use plan** | Developed to carry out a course of action not likely to be repeated in the future |
| Program | Single-use plan for a large set of activities |
| Project | Single-use plan of less scope and complexity than a program |
| **Standing plan** | Developed for activities that recur regularly over a period of time |
| Policy | Standing plan specifying the organization's general response to a designated problem or situation |
| Standard operating procedure | Standing plan outlining steps to be followed in particular circumstances |
| Rules and regulations | Standing plans describing exactly how specific activities are to be carried out |

structures, and myriad other things. The total integration of the two airlines can be thought of as a program.

**Projects**    A project is similar to a program but is generally of less scope and complexity. A project may be a part of a broader program, or it may be a self-contained single-use plan. Consider the airline merger just mentioned. Airlines generally offer their passengers an inflight magazine. The company has decided to scrap both of the two existing magazines and create a new one from scratch. The plan for developing and launching this new magazine is one project among several that are part of the overall merger program. In other settings, projects may also be used to introduce a new product within an existing product line or to add a new benefit option to an existing salary package.

## Standing Plans

Whereas single-use plans are developed for nonrecurring situations, a standing plan is used for activities that recur regularly over a period of time. Standing plans can greatly enhance efficiency by making decision making routine. Policies, standard operating procedures, and rules and regulations are three kinds of standing plans.

**Policies**    As a general guide for action, a policy is the most general form of standing plan. A policy specifies the organization's general response to a designated problem or situation. For example, McDonald's has a policy that it will not grant a franchise to an individual who already owns a competing fast-food restaurant. Similarly, Starbucks has a policy that it will not franchise at all, instead retaining ownership of all Starbucks coffee shops. Likewise, a university admissions office might establish a policy that admission will be granted only to applicants with a minimum SAT score of 1,200 and a ranking in the top quarter of their high school class. Admissions officers may routinely deny admission to applicants who fail to reach these minimums. A policy is also likely to describe how exceptions are to be handled.

The university's policy statement, for example, might create an admissions appeals committee to evaluate applicants who do not meet minimum requirements but may warrant special consideration.

**Standard Operating Procedures**    Another type of standing plan is the standard operating procedure, or SOP. An SOP is more specific than a policy, in that it outlines the steps to be followed in particular circumstances. The admissions clerk at the university, for example, might be told that, when an application is received, he or she should (1) set up an electronic file for the applicant; (2) merge test-score records, transcripts, and letters of reference to the electronic file as they are received; and (3) forward the electronic file to the appropriate admissions director when it is complete. Gallo Vineyards in California has a 300-page manual of SOPs. This planning manual is credited with making Gallo one of the most efficient wine operations in the United States. McDonald's has SOPs explaining exactly how Big Macs are to be cooked, how long they can stay in the warming rack, and so forth. Our *Beyond Traditional Business* feature discusses another interesting take on standard operating procedures.

**project**
A single-use plan of less scope and complexity than a program

**standing plan**
Developed for activities that recur regularly over a period of time

**policy**
A standing plan that specifies the organization's general response to a designated problem or situation

**standard operating procedure (SOP)**
A standard plan that outlines the steps to be followed in particular circumstances

ZUMA Press, Inc./ Alamy

Wine making is a complex process that involves many different steps that take place over an extended period of time. Most larger wineries have detailed standard operating procedures that winemakers follow in order to achieve consistency. Gallo Vineyards, for instance, has a 300 page manual detailing its standard operating procedures.

# Secret Operating Procedure 303

After two bombs exploded during the Boston Marathon on April 15, 2013, the Associated Press (AP) reported that cellphone service in the Boston area had been shut down "to prevent any potential remote detonations of explosives." As we saw in the *Management at Work* case in Chapter 4, much of the early reporting about the Marathon bombing was unreliable, and the AP story was no exception. The news agency referred to "a law enforcement official" who cited "an intelligence briefing" but was later told by wireless providers that no such shutdown had been requested.

But it could have been.

"No one in Washington or in any statehouse or bunker anywhere can press a button and shut down phone service," says Harold Feld of the advocacy group Public Knowledge, but federal law enforcement officials can in fact request the deactivation of cellphone service in particular neighborhoods or across an entire metropolitan area. They just have to follow *standard operating procedure*—in this case, the "Emergency Wireless Protocols" known in government circles as "SOP 303." Originally conceived to deter the deployment of radio-activated bombs or IEDs (improvised explosive devices), SOP 303 is also known as the "Internet kill switch" because wireless networks are also used to provide Internet service.

So far, details of SOP 303 are pretty much limited to information disclosed in a 2007 report issued by the National Security Telecommunications Advisory Committee, a group of government officials and telecom company executives. According to the report, SOP 303 specifies a "shutdown process" to be activated "during national crisis." How would the process work? The National Coordinating Center for Telecommunications—which includes representatives from the CIA, National Security Agency, and major telecom and defense companies—would field shutdown requests from Homeland Security officials and, depending upon the answers to a "series of questions," pass them on to wireless carriers.

Naturally, SOP 303 has raised concerns about potential abuses. Because of the secrecy surrounding it, for example, no one can even be sure that it's constitutional. At the very least, says Amie Stepanovich, a lawyer with the Electronic Privacy Information Center (EPIC), "whenever you have secret procedures, there's the question of transparency and accountability." The controversy came to a head in July 2013, when the shooting of a homeless man by a San Francisco Bay Area Rapid Transit (BART) officer sparked protests at several transit stations. A second series of planned demonstrations was frustrated when BART officials shut down all cellular service inside four stations for three hours. Some critics likened BART's action to the Chinese government's policy of cutting off cellular service to quell protests. "The context is important," says Harold Feld. "If the shutdown is because we're concerned about protesters, that raises much more fundamental First Amendment concerns than [if the government says] 'we're afraid there's a bomb in the area.'"

As it happens, EPIC had already filed a Freedom of Information Act request with the Department of Homeland Security (DHS) asking for the full text of SOP 303. The DHS replied that it was "unable to locate or identify any responsive records." The agency also argued that it didn't have to release the document because it detailed a "law enforcement technique." A federal judge rejected the DHS argument and ordered the disclosure of SP 303 pending appeal. That's where the case stands as of this writing.

*References:* Timothy B. Lee, "Gov't Didn't Shut Down Cell Networks in Boston—But It Could Have," *Ars Technica* (April 16, 2013), http://arstechnica.com, on September 9, 2014; Adam Serwer and Nick Baumann, "The Government Didn't Shut Down Cell Service in Boston. But with SOP 303, It Could Have," *Mother Jones* (April 17, 2013), www.motherjones.com, on September 9, 2014; Eric Saferstein, "The Problem with Standard Operating Procedure 303," AGSAF (Artificially Generated Stampede Awareness Foundation) (November 22, 2013), www.agsaf.org, on September 9, 2014; David Jacobs, "The Government Might Finally Have to Explain Its 'Internet Kill Switch' Policy," *Future Tense* (May 25, 2013), www.slate.com, on September 9, 2014; EPIC—Electronic Privacy Information Center, "EPIC v. DHS—SOP 303," *Epic.org* (February 21, 2014), https://epic.org, on September 9, 2014.

**Rules and Regulations** The narrowest of the standing plans, rules and regulations, describe exactly how specific activities are to be carried out. Rather than guiding decision making, rules and regulations actually take the place of decision making in various situations. Each McDonald's restaurant has a rule prohibiting customers from using its telephones, for example. The university admissions office might have a rule stipulating that if an applicant's file is not complete two months before the beginning of a semester, the student cannot be admitted until the next semester. Of course, in most organizations a manager at a higher level can suspend or bend the rules. If the high school transcript of the child of a prominent university alumnus and donor arrives a few days late, the director of admissions might waive the two-month rule. Indeed, rules and regulations can become problematic if they are excessive or enforced too rigidly.

Rules and regulations and SOPs are similar in many ways. They are both relatively narrow in scope, and each can serve as a substitute for decision making. An SOP typically describes a sequence of activities, however, whereas rules and regulations focus on one activity. Recall our examples: The admissions SOP consisted of three activities, whereas the two-month rule related to only one activity. In an industrial setting, the SOP for orienting a new employee could involve enrolling the person in various benefit options, introducing him or her to coworkers and supervisors, and providing a tour of the facilities. A pertinent rule for the new employee might involve when to come to work each day.

**Manager's Checklist**

- [ ] As a manager, keep in mind that single-use and standing plans are a common and necessary part of doing business.

- [ ] At the same time, though, it can become dysfunctional to fall back on rules, SOPs, and so forth without understanding their intended purpose.

## Managing Goal-Setting and Planning Processes

Obviously, all of the elements of goal setting and planning discussed to this point involve managing these processes in some way or another. In addition, however, because major barriers sometimes impede effective goal setting and planning, knowing how to overcome some of the barriers is important.

### Barriers to Goal Setting and Planning

Several circumstances can serve as barriers to effective goal setting and planning; the more common ones are listed in Table 6.2.

**Inappropriate Goals** Inappropriate goals come in many forms. Paying a large dividend to stockholders may be inappropriate if it comes at the expense of research and development. Goals may also be inappropriate if they are unattainable. If Kmart were to set a goal of earning more revenues than Walmart next year, people at the company would probably be embarrassed because achieving such a goal would be impossible. Goals may also be inappropriate if they place too much emphasis on either quantitative or qualitative measures of success. Some goals, especially those relating to financial areas, are quantifiable, objective, and verifiable. Other goals, such as employee satisfaction and development, are difficult, if not impossible, to quantify. Organizations are asking for trouble if they put too much emphasis on one type of goal to the exclusion of the other. A few years ago Starbucks set an ambitious goal of having 40,000 locations globally. But in its zeal to meet this target, the company made

**rules and regulations** Describe exactly how specific activities are to be carried out

## TABLE 6.2  BARRIERS TO GOAL SETTING AND PLANNING

As part of managing the goal-setting and planning processes, managers must understand the barriers that can disrupt them. Managers must also know how to overcome the barriers.

| Major barriers | Inappropriate goals |
| --- | --- |
| | Improper reward system |
| | Dynamic and complex environment |
| | Reluctance to establish goals |
| | Resistance to change |
| | Constraints |
| Overcoming the barriers | Understanding the purposes of goals and planning |
| | Communication and participation |
| | Consistency, revision, and updating |
| | Effective reward system |

numerous poor decisions for new sites, cluttered its stores with too much merchandise, and lost its focus on coffee. As a result, when the global recession hit in 2009, Starbucks was forced to postpone new openings, close several hundred underperforming stores, and eliminate several thousand jobs.[40] This also stimulated its current focus on improving profitability for individual stores as opposed to simply adding new stores.

**Improper Reward System**  In some settings, an improper reward system acts as a barrier to goal setting and planning. For example, people may inadvertently be rewarded for poor goal-setting behavior or go unrewarded or even be punished for proper goal-setting behavior. Suppose that a manager sets a goal of decreasing turnover next year. If turnover is decreased by even a fraction, the manager can claim success and perhaps be rewarded for the accomplishment. In contrast, a manager who tries to decrease turnover by 5 percent but actually achieves a decrease of only 4 percent may receive a smaller reward because of her or his failure to reach the established goal. And if an organization places too much emphasis on short-term performance and results, managers may ignore longer-term issues as they set goals and formulate plans to achieve higher profits in the short term.

**Dynamic and Complex Environment**  The nature of an organization's environment is also a barrier to effective goal setting and planning. Rapid change, technological innovation, and intense competition can all increase the difficulty of an organization's accurately assessing future opportunities and threats. For example, when an electronics firm like Dell develops a long-range plan, it tries to take into account how much technological innovation is likely to occur during that interval. But forecasting such events is extremely difficult. During the early boom years of personal computers, data were stored primarily on floppy disks. Because these disks had a limited storage capacity, hard disks were developed. Whereas the typical floppy disk can hold hundreds of pages of information, a hard disk can store thousands of pages. Today, computers increasingly store information on shared servers or virtual storage facilities (known

Technological breakthroughs and developments add complexity and uncertainty to the environment. So-called "virtual keyboards" like this one, for example, may become commonplace in the future. But for now they are not widely available. As a result, computer makers like Dell and Hewlett-Packard must be ready to quickly adjust their plans as new technological innovations become available.

"My advice … is to be ready to revise any system, scrap any methods, abandon any theory if the success of the job demands it."

—HENRY FORD[41]

as clouds) capable of holding vast quantities of information. The manager who tries to set goals and plan in this rapidly changing environment faces a truly formidable task.

**Reluctance to Establish Goals** Another barrier to effective planning is some managers' reluctance to establish goals for themselves and their units of responsibility. The reason for this reluctance may be lack of confidence or fear of failure. If a manager sets a goal that is specific, concise, and time related, then whether he or she attains it is obvious. Managers who consciously or unconsciously try to avoid this degree of accountability are likely to hinder the organization's planning efforts. Pfizer, a large pharmaceutical company, ran into problems because its managers did not set goals for research and development. Consequently, the organization fell further and further behind because managers had no way of knowing how effective their R&D efforts actually were.

**Resistance to Change** Another barrier to goal setting and planning is resistance to change. Planning essentially involves changing something about the organization. As we will see in Chapter 12, people tend to resist change. Avon Products almost drove itself into bankruptcy several years ago because it insisted on continuing a policy of large dividend payments to its stockholders. When profits started to fall, managers resisted cutting the dividends and started borrowing to pay them. The company's debt grew from $3 million to $1.1 billion in eight years. Eventually, managers were forced to confront the problem and cut dividends.

**Constraints** Constraints that limit what an organization can do are another major obstacle. Common constraints include a lack of resources, government restrictions, and strong competition. For example, Owens-Corning Fiberglass took on an enormous debt burden as part of its fight to avoid a takeover by Wickes Ltd. The company then had such a large debt that it was forced to cut back on capital expenditures and research and development. And those cutbacks greatly constrained what the firm could plan for the future. Time constraints are also a factor. It is easy to say, "I'm too busy to plan today; I'll do it tomorrow." Effective planning takes time, energy, and an unwavering belief in its importance.

## Overcoming the Barriers

Fortunately, there are several guidelines for making goal setting and planning effective. Some of the guidelines are listed in Table 6.2.

**Understand the Purposes of Goals and Planning** One of the best ways to facilitate goal-setting and planning processes is to recognize their basic purposes. Managers should also recognize that there are limits to the effectiveness of setting goals and making plans. Planning is not a panacea that will solve all of an organization's problems, nor is it an ironclad set of procedures to be followed at any cost. And effective goals and planning do not necessarily ensure success; adjustments and exceptions are to be expected as time passes. For example, Coca-Cola followed a logical and rational approach to setting goals and planning a few years ago when it introduced a new formula to combat Pepsi's increasing market share. But all the plans proved to be wrong as consumers rejected the new version of Coca-Cola. Managers quickly reversed the decision and reintroduced the old formula as Coca-Cola Classic. Thus, even though careful planning resulted in a big mistake, the company was able to recover from its blunder.

**Communication and Participation** Although goals and plans may be initiated at high levels in the organization, they must also be communicated to others in the organization. Everyone involved in the planning process should know what the overriding organizational strategy is, what the various functional strategies are, and how they are all to be integrated and coordinated. People responsible for achieving goals and implementing plans must have a voice in developing them from the outset. These individuals almost always have valuable information to contribute, and because they will be implementing the plans, their involvement is critical: People are usually more committed to plans that they have helped shape. Even when an organization is somewhat centralized or uses a planning staff, managers from a variety of levels in the organization should be involved in the planning process.

**Consistency, Revision, and Updating** Goals should be consistent both horizontally and vertically. Horizontal consistency means that goals should be consistent across the organization, from one department to the next. Vertical consistency means that goals should be consistent up and down the organization—strategic, tactical, and operational goals must agree with one another. Because goal setting and planning are dynamic processes, they must also be revised and updated regularly. Many organizations are seeing the need to revise and update on an increasingly frequent basis. Citigroup, for example, once used a three-year planning horizon for developing and providing new financial services. That cycle was subsequently cut to two years, and the bank now often uses a one-year horizon.

**Effective Reward Systems** In general, people should be rewarded both for establishing effective goals and plans and for successfully achieving them. Because failure sometimes results from factors outside the manager's control, however, people should also be assured that failure to reach a goal will not necessarily bring punitive consequences. Frederick Smith, founder and CEO of Federal Express, has a stated goal of encouraging risk. Thus, when Federal Express lost $233 million on an unsuccessful service called ZapMail, no one was punished. Smith believed that the original idea was a good one but was unsuccessful for reasons beyond the company's control.

## Using Goals to Implement Plans

Goals are often used to implement plans. Formal goal-setting programs represent one widely used method for managing the goal-setting and planning processes concurrently to ensure that both are done effectively. Some firms call this approach management by objectives, or MBO. We should also note, however, that although many firms use this basic approach, they often tailor it to their own special circumstances and use a special term or name for it.[43] For example, Raytheon uses an MBO-type system but calls it the "Performance Agreement System," or PAS.

**The Nature and Purpose of Formal Goal Setting** The purpose of formal goal setting is generally to give subordinates a voice in the goal-setting and planning processes and to clarify for them exactly what they are expected to accomplish in a given time span. Thus formal goal setting is often concerned with goal setting and planning for individual managers and their units or work groups.

**The Formal Goal-Setting Process** The basic mechanics of the formal goal-setting process are shown in Figure 6.5. This process is described here from an ideal perspective. In any given organization, the steps of the process are likely to vary in importance and may even take a different sequence. As a starting point, however, most managers believe that, if a formal goal-setting program is to be successful, it must start at the top of the organization. Top managers must communicate why they have adopted the program, what they think it will do, and that they have accepted and are committed to formal goal setting. Employees must also be educated about what goal setting is and what their roles in it will be. Having committed to

> "Everybody should know what everybody's goals and controls are, and everybody should understand their individual ones relative to their department, and their department's goals relative to the company's."
>
> —KRIS DUGGAN, COFOUNDER OF BADGEVILLE (DESIGNER OF GAME-BASED PROGRAMS FOR BUSINESSES[42]

**management by objectives (MBO)**
A formal goal-setting process involving collaboration between managers and subordinates; the extent to which goals are accomplished is a major factor in evaluating and rewarding subordinates' performance

## FIGURE 6.5  THE FORMAL GOAL-SETTING PROCESS

Formal goal setting is an effective technique for integrating goal setting and planning. This figure portrays the general steps that most organizations use when they adopt formal goal setting. Of course, most organizations adapt this general process to fit their own unique needs and circumstances.

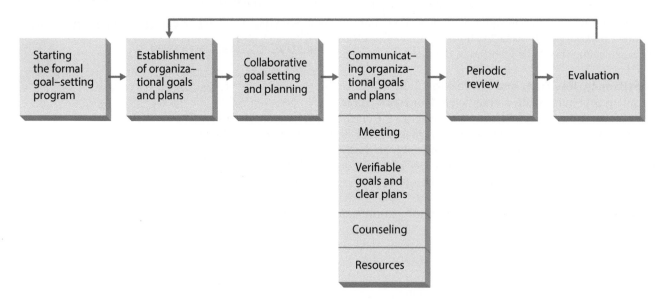

formal goal setting, managers must implement it in a way that is consistent with overall organizational goals and plans. The idea is that goals set at the top will systematically cascade down throughout the organization.

Although establishing the organization's basic goals and plans is extremely important, collaborative goal setting and planning are the essence of formal goal setting. The collaboration involves a series of distinct steps. First, managers tell their subordinates what organizational and unit goals and plans top management has established. Then managers meet with their subordinates on a one-to-one basis to arrive at a set of goals and plans for each subordinate that both the subordinate and the manager have helped develop and to which both are committed. Next, the goals are refined to be as verifiable (quantitative) as possible and to specify a time frame for their accomplishment. They should also be written. Further, the plans developed to achieve the goals need to be as clearly stated as possible and directly relate to each goal. Managers must play the role of counselors in the goal-setting and planning meeting. For example, they must ensure that the subordinates' goals and plans are attainable and workable and that they will facilitate both the unit's and the organization's goals and plans. Finally, the meeting should spell out the resources that the subordinate will need to implement his or her plans and work effectively toward goal attainment.

Conducting periodic reviews as subordinates are working toward their goals is advisable. If the goals and plans are for a one-year period, meeting quarterly to discuss progress may be a good idea. At the end of the period, the manager meets with each subordinate again to review the degree of goal attainment. They discuss which goals were met and which were not met in the context of the original plans. The reasons for both success and failure are explored, and the employee is rewarded on the basis of goal attainment. In an ongoing goal-setting program, the evaluation meeting may also serve as the collaborative goal-setting and planning meeting for the next time period.

**The Effectiveness of Formal Goal Setting**   A large number of organizations, including Alcoa, Urban Outfitters, DuPont, General Motors, Zara, Boeing, and Caterpillar all use some form of goal setting. As might be expected, goal setting has both strengths and weaknesses. A primary benefit of goal setting is improved employee motivation. By clarifying exactly what is expected, by allowing the employee a voice in determining expectations, and by basing rewards on the achievement of those expectations, organizations create a powerful motivational system for their employees.

Communication is also enhanced through the process of discussion and collaboration. And performance appraisals may be done more objectively, with less reliance on arbitrary or subjective assessment. Goal setting focuses attention on appropriate goals and plans, helps identify superior managerial talent for future promotion, and provides a systematic management philosophy that can have a positive effect on the overall organization. Goal setting also facilitates control. The periodic development and subsequent evaluation of individual goals and plans helps keep the organization on course toward its own long-run goals and plans.

On the other hand, goal setting occasionally fails because of poor implementation. Perhaps the major problem that can derail a goal-setting program is lack of top-management support. Some organizations decide to use goal setting, but then its implementation is delegated to lower management. This limits the program's effectiveness because the goals and plans cascading throughout the organization may not actually be the goals and plans of top management and because others in the organization are not motivated to accept and become committed to them. Another problem with goal setting is that some firms overemphasize quantitative goals and plans and burden their systems with too much paperwork and record keeping. Some managers will not or cannot sit down to work out goals and plans with their subordinates. Rather, they "suggest" or even "assign" goals and plans to people. The result is resentment and a lack of commitment to the goal-setting program.

---

☐ As a manager you need to know the primary barriers to goal setting and planning and how to overcome those barriers.

☐ You should also understand how to use goals to implement plans.

**Manager's Checklist**

---

# Summary of Learning Outcomes and Key Points

1. Summarize the essential functions of decision making and the planning process.

   - The planning process is the first basic managerial function that organizations must address.
   - With an understanding of the environmental context, managers develop a number of different types of goals and plans.
   - Decision making is the underlying framework of all planning because every step of the planning process involves a decision.

2. Discuss the purpose of organizational goals, identify different kinds of goals, discuss who sets goals, and describe how to manage multiple goals.

   - Goals serve four basic purposes:
     o provide guidance and direction
     o facilitate planning
     o inspire motivation and commitment
     o promote evaluation and control

   - Goals can be differentiated by level, area, and time frame.
   - All managers within an organization need to be involved in the goal-setting process.
   - Managers need to pay special attention to the importance of managing multiple goals through optimizing and other approaches.

3. Identify different kinds of organizational plans, note the time frames for planning, discuss who plans, and describe contingency planning.

   - The major types of plans are strategic, tactical, and operational.
   - Plans are developed across a variety of time horizons, including long-range, intermediate, and short-range time frames.
   - Essential people in an organization responsible for effective planning are the planning staff, planning

task forces, the board of directors, the CEO, the executive committee, and line management.

- Contingency planning helps managers anticipate and plan for unexpected changes.

4. Discuss how tactical plans are developed and executed.

- Tactical plans are at the middle of the organization, have an intermediate time horizon, and are of moderate scope.
- Tactical plans are developed to implement specific parts of a strategic plan.
- Tactical plans must flow from strategy, specify resource and time issues, and commit human resources.
- Tactical plans must be effectively executed.

5. Describe the basic types of operational plans used by organizations.

- Operational plans are at the lower levels of the organization, have a shorter time horizon, and are narrower in scope.
- Operational plans are derived from a tactical plan and are aimed at achieving one or more operational goals.
- Two major types of operational plans are single-use and standing plans.
  - o Single-use plans are designed to carry out a course of action that is not likely to be repeated in the future. Programs and projects are examples of single-use plans.
  - o Standing plans are designed to carry out a course of action that is likely to be repeated several times. Policies, standard operating procedures, and rules and regulations are all standing plans.

6. Identify the major barriers to goal setting and planning, how organizations overcome those barriers, and how to use goals to implement plans.

- Several barriers exist to effective goal setting and planning:
  - o improper reward system
  - o dynamic and complex environment
  - o reluctance to establish goals
  - o resistance to change
  - o various constraints
- Methods for overcoming these barriers include:
  - o understanding the purposes of goals and plans
  - o communication and participation
  - o consistency, revision, and updating
  - o an effective reward system
- One particularly useful technique for managing goal setting and planning is formal goal setting, a process of collaborative goal setting and planning.

# Discussion Questions

## Questions for Review

1. Describe the nature of organizational goals. Be certain to include both the purposes and the kinds of goals.

2. Describe the scope, responsible personnel, and time frames for each kind of organizational plan. How are plans of different kinds related?

## Questions for Analysis

5. Managers are often criticized for focusing too much attention on the achievement of short-term goals. In your opinion, how much attention should be given to long-term versus short-term goals? In the event of a conflict, which should be given priority? Explain your answers.

6. What types of plans and decisions most likely require board of director involvement, and why? What types of

## Questions for Application

8. Interview the head of the department in which you are majoring. What kinds of goals exist for the department

3. Explain the various types of operational plans. Give a real or hypothetical business example for each type. Do not use examples from the text.

4. List the steps in the formal goal-setting process. What are some of the advantages for companies that use this approach? What are some of the problems that may arise from the use of this approach?

decisions and plans are not appropriate for board involvement, and why?

7. Standing plans help make an organization more effective. However, they may inhibit experimentation and organizational learning. Under what conditions, if any, should organizations ignore their own standing plans? In the area of planning, how can an organization balance the need for effectiveness against the need for creativity?

and for the members of the department? Share your findings with the rest of the class.

9. Tell about a time when an organization was not able to fully achieve all of its goals simultaneously. Why did this occur? Is complete realization of all goals impossible for an organization? Why or why not?

10. From your library or the Internet, find information about a company's mission statement and goals. List its mission and some of its strategic, tactical, and operational goals. Explain the relationship you see among the goals at different levels.

# Building Effective Decision-Making Skills

### Exercise Overview

Decision-making skills refer to the ability to recognize and define problems and opportunities correctly and then to select an appropriate course of action for solving problems or capitalizing on opportunities. In this exercise, you're asked to apply your decision-making skills to a situation calling for both good business sense and a sense of personal values.

### Exercise Background

You're the owner of a company that makes dress and casual shoes at two small factories, each with a workforce of 40 people. One is located in Smallville, Illinois, and the other in Modesto, Texas, both small towns. You've been in business for 40 years, and both factories have long been profitable. Unfortunately, however, competitive conditions in the industry have changed in recent years. In particular, you're now facing stiff competition from Italian firms whose shoes not only sell for less money but boast higher quality.

You're confident that you can close the quality gap with new high-tech equipment, but your overhead is still 30 percent higher than that of your Italian competitors. At the moment, you feel that your best option is to close the Smallville factory and lay off the workers, but you're a little reluctant to do so. You're the major employer in Smallville, which is dependent on your factory and has just spent a good deal of money to improve utility service and highway access. In addition, most of your employees are older people who have lived most of their lives in Smallville.

### Exercise Task

1. Your instructor will divide the class into groups of three or four people each. Each group will meet as a management team responsible for deciding the fate of the Smallville plant.

2. The team may decide to close the plant or to keep it open, but the goal of the decision-making process is twofold: (1) to keep the company viable and (2) to reflect the team's individual and group values.

3. If the team decides to close the plant, it must draw up a list of the factors on which it based its decision and be prepared to justify it.

4. If the team decides to keep the plant open, it must draw up a plan explaining how the company can still remain competitive.

5. Each member of each team should be prepared to explain the choices that he or she made in helping the group reach its decision.

# Building Effective Time-Management Skills

### Exercise Overview

Time-management skills refer to the ability to prioritize tasks, to work efficiently, and to delegate appropriately. This exercise asks you to apply your time-management skills to the process of goal optimization.

### Exercise Background

All managers face a variety of goals, challenges, opportunities, and, of course, demands on their time. Juggling all these demands successfully requires a clear understanding of priorities, scheduling, and a number of related factors. You're about to learn just how difficult this task is because you're about to open your own business—a retail store in a local shopping mall. You're starting from scratch, with no prior business connections, but you do have a strong business plan and you're sure that it will work.

In getting ready to open your business, you know that you need to meet and draw up plans with each of the following parties:

1. The mall manager, to negotiate a lease

2. A local banker, to arrange partial financing

3. An attorney, to incorporate your business

4. An accountant, to set up a bookkeeping system

5. Suppliers, to arrange credit terms and delivery schedules

6. An advertising agency, to start promoting your business

7. A staffing agency, to hire employees

8. A design firm, to plan the physical layout of the store

## Exercise Task

Review all the preceding information and then do the following:

1. Develop a schedule listing the sequence in which you need to meet with the eight parties that you've listed. Do the best that you can to minimize backtracking (seeing one party and then having to see him again after seeing someone else).

2. Compare your schedule with that of a classmate and discuss the differences.

3. Do you find that it's possible to draw up different schedules which are nevertheless equally valid? If so, why? If not, why not?

# Skill-Building Personal Assessment

## Goal-Setting Questionnaire

This personal assessment will help you understand how to conceptualize the elements of goal setting and your own goal-setting tendencies. Your score will give you insights into how effectively you set goals.

**Instructions:** Indicate your concepts of your goal-setting behaviors and feelings by circling the appropriate number on the scale for each statement.

| Statements | Strongly Agree | Slightly Agree | Not Sure | Slightly Disagree | Strongly Disagree |
|---|---|---|---|---|---|
| 1. Rewards should be allocated based on goal achievement. | 5 | 4 | 3 | 2 | 1 |
| 2. I set goals for all key results areas. | 5 | 4 | 3 | 2 | 1 |
| 3. Goals should have clear deadlines. | 5 | 4 | 3 | 2 | 1 |
| 4. I work hard to give others feedback on how they're doing. | 5 | 4 | 3 | 2 | 1 |
| 5. I tend to set goals that I can't quite achieve to force me to try harder. | 1 | 2 | 3 | 4 | 5 |
| 6. Sometimes when I think maybe I'm not doing so well, I don't want feedback from others. | 1 | 2 | 3 | 4 | 5 |
| 7. My goals are always clearly stated. | 1 | 2 | 3 | 4 | 5 |
| 8. My goals are stated in quantifiable terms. | 5 | 4 | 3 | 2 | 1 |
| 9. Achieving goals is the way to promotion and success. | 5 | 4 | 3 | 2 | 1 |
| 10. My boss (parent, etc.) will not get on my case if I don't achieve my goals. | 1 | 2 | 3 | 4 | 5 |
| 11. My boss (parent, etc.) usually sets my goals. | 1 | 2 | 3 | 4 | 5 |

*(Continued)*

| | | | | | | |
|---|---|---|---|---|---|---|
| 12. | I don't always know what the key result areas are. | 1 | 2 | 3 | 4 | 5 |
| 13. | I work better without specific deadlines. | 1 | 2 | 3 | 4 | 5 |
| 14. | Others allow me to take part in setting my goals. | 5 | 4 | 3 | 2 | 1 |
| 15. | The more challenging my goals, the better I work | 5 | 4 | 3 | 2 | 1 |
| 16. | If I'm not on target to achieve my goals, my boss (parent, etc.) should get on my case. | 5 | 4 | 3 | 2 | 1 |
| 17. | When I'm working on my goals, my boss (parent, etc.) doesn't always give me the support I need. | 1 | 2 | 3 | 4 | 5 |
| 18. | Specific goals make me nervous, so I prefer general goals. | 1 | 2 | 3 | 4 | 5 |
| 19. | My goals state exactly what results I plan to achieve. | 5 | 4 | 3 | 2 | 1 |
| 20. | I challenge myself by setting goals that are just out of my reach. | 1 | 2 | 3 | 4 | 5 |

# Management at Work

### The Ingredients of a Sustainability Plan

## "We can have real impact on the ground."

—ROLAND WEENING, PRESIDENT OF COFFEE, MONDELEZ INTERNATIONAL

As one of the world's largest snack food companies, Mondelez International operates in more than 80 countries, sourcing ingredients for coffee products from Vietnam, Indonesia, and Brazil and cocoa for chocolate from Côte d'Ivoire, Ghana, India, and the Dominican Republic. Mondelez, which is headquartered in the Chicago suburb of Deerfield, Illinois, is committed to promoting sustainability throughout its supply chain, and such initiatives as its Cocoa Life and Coffee Made Happy programs are designed to ensure that agricultural supplies are sustainably sourced.

In its "2013 Call for Well-Being Progress Report," for instance, Mondelez announced that with 10 percent of its cocoa supply sustainably sourced, the company is on target to reach its longer-term goals. In order to reach those goals, Mondelez plans to spend $400 million over 10 years to train cocoa farmers in better agricultural and business practices and to provide them with access to planting materials. "We're investing in much more than farming," explains Bharat Puri, president of global chocolate and candy. "It's about empowering cocoa communities as a whole so cocoa-farming villages become places where people want to live."

Coffee division president Roland Weening agrees: "Together with our partners," he says, "we can help farmers solve challenges and secure a more sustainable coffee supply." For Mondelez, then, working closely with communities of growers is not simply a matter of improving supply-chain efficiency: It also reflects the principle that the power of a big company to contribute to global sustainability can be harnessed most effectively when it's extended to the activities of the smaller organizations with which it does business. "We can have real impact on the ground," says Weening.

As of 2013, Weening's division was sustainably sourcing 56 percent of its coffee and was well on its way to its goal of 70 percent by 2015. As a matter of fact, Mondelez is big on *goal setting* in all of its sustainability initiatives. In wheat, for example, which is a core ingredient in the company's line of biscuits, Mondelez established the Harmony Charter, a partnership with members of its wheat supply chain designed to encourage "more respectful agricultural practices, which include wheat variety selection, soil management, limiting fertilizers and pesticides, and smart water use." The company has set a goal of using Harmony wheat in 75 percent of its total biscuit volume by 2015. According to its 2013 report, it has reached a volume of 44 percent and is on target to meet that goal.

Mondelez is also a member of the Roundtable on Sustainable Palm Oil (RSPO), which was established in 2004 to promote the production of sustainable palm oil products through the certification of industry practices. The company set a goal of having 100 percent of its palm oil supply RSPO certified by 2015, and in 2013, Mondelez announced that the goal had been reached two years ahead of schedule. Now that the goal has been attained, says Dave Brown, VP of global commodities and strategic sourcing,

> *we recognize the need to go further, so we also challenged our palm oil suppliers to provide transparency on the levels of traceability in their palm oil supply chains. Knowing the sources of palm oil supplies is an essential first step to enable scrutiny and promote improvements in practice on the ground.*

Not surprisingly, Mondelez set a goal for ensuring acceptable levels of supply-chain *traceability*—the ability to trace an ingredient through every stage of production and distribution. The company plans to review suppliers' traceability practices and then publish an action plan for giving priority to suppliers whose practices are consistent with companywide sustainability principles. The goal is to eliminate all supplies that don't meet standards by 2020.

To understand how Mondelez wants to coordinate the entire range of its sustainability efforts, we might take a look at one of its most recent initiatives. In 2014, Mondelez Ireland announced a partnership with Bord Bia Origin Green, a nationwide Irish food-related sustainability program, to promote sustainability throughout the country's food sector. "We have already achieved significant positive change in Ireland," explains Patrick Miskelly, manufacturing director of Mondelez Ireland, "but we have a lot more goals to achieve," and the company sees the Origin Green partnership as the means of taking its sustainability plans to the next level.

These plans revolve around the three manufacturing plants that Mondelez operates in Ireland, and the immediate

focus will be on the supply chain—in particular, the sourcing of raw materials. The company is already committed to local sourcing. At one plant, for example, 37 percent of all raw materials originate locally; another plant uses 21 million gallons of milk from local cooperatives that have adopted sustainable farming practices. Origin Green will add independent verification of farmers' and food suppliers' success in setting and achieving measurable sustainability goals.

Sustainable sourcing, however, is only one aspect of Mondelez Ireland's sustainability strategy. In terms of *organizational planning*, sustainable-sourcing programs reflect a set of carefully developed *tactical plans* designed to further a larger *strategic plan*. Sustainability goals, for example, also include the protection of Ireland's rich natural resources and a reduction of the company's overall environmental impact. Between 2005 and 2010, the company reduced waste at all three Irish plants by 42 percent, and the largest of the three has already met its goal of diverting all of its waste from Irish landfills by 2014.

Mondelez Ireland also plans to reduce carbon emissions from natural gas consumption by 15 percent by 2016, and like most sustainability-conscious organizations, Mondelez International regards its various sustainability plans as part of an overarching strategy to reduce its *carbon footprint*—the total of greenhouse-gas (GHG) emissions for which it is responsible. Between 2005 and 2010, the company reduced GHG emissions by 18 percent and then set a goal of another 15 percent reduction by 2015. As of 2013, it had attained a 9 percent reduction and considered itself on target. As for reducing energy use, Mondelez admits that "more improvement is needed" if it is to meet its goal of a 15 percent reduction by 2015; as of 2013, it had cut energy use by only 6 percent. On the upside, the company has exceeded its 2015 goal of reducing manufacturing waste by 15 percent, having achieved a 46 percent reduction by 2013.

## Case Questions

1.  Here are a series of Mondelez's publicly announced objectives for enhancing sustainability:

    -   reducing production waste to landfill sites by 60 percent
    -   reducing our energy and GHS in manufacturing
    -   educating employees to reuse water and improve processes
    -   reducing the impact of our operations
    -   addressing child labor in the cocoa supply chain
    -   reducing packaging material
    -   eliminating 50 million pounds of packaging material
    -   buying certified commodities

    Which of these are BEST considered *strategic plans*? *Tactical plans*? *Operational plans*? Which ones might qualify as *programs*? *Projects*? *Policies*? Be sure to explain your reasoning for each item.

2.  "Our business success," says Mondelez chairman and CEO Irene Rosenfeld, "is directly linked to enhancing the well-being of the people who make and enjoy our products and to supporting the communities where we grow our ingredients."

    Assume that you're a Mondelez representative who's been asked to give a presentation to students in an introductory management class. Explain Rosenfeld's reasoning or her "philosophy" of "business success." Be sure to give some examples of how and why this approach works at Mondelez (which, remember, is a global snack food company).

3.  Explain—hypothetically—how the following might emerge as *barriers to sustainability planning* at Mondolez:

    -   inappropriate goals
    -   an improper reward system
    -   a dynamic and complex environment

- resistance to change
- constraints

4. According to a 2014 McKinsey & Co. survey of executives, 36 percent included *reputation management*—building, maintaining, or improving corporate reputation—among the top three reasons for addressing sustainability.*

Explain how the following management strategies can help to enhance both sustainability and reputation:

- setting aggressive internal goals for sustainability initiatives
- adopting a unified sustainability strategy with clearly articulated priorities
- building a broad leadership coalition in shaping sustainability strategy
- ensuring that everyone in the organization understands the financial benefits of sustainability

*Sheila Bonini and Anne-Titia Bové, "Sustainability's Strategic Worth: McKinsey Global Survey Results," McKinsey & Co., July 2014, www.mckinsey.com, on September 15, 2014.

## Case References

Mondelez International, "Environmental Footprint," "Sustainable Resources and Agriculture," "Agricultural Supply Chain," "Cocoa" (2014), www.mondelezinternational.com, on September 12, 2014; "Mondelez International Releases First Well-Being Progress Report," *Market Watch* (PR Newswire) (September 9, 2014), www.marketwatch.com, on September 12, 2014; "Mondelez 'On Target' to Meet Sustainability Goals," *Environmental Leader* (September 10, 2014), www.environmentalleader. com, on September 11, 2014; Max Sosland, "Mondelez on Pace toward Wellness, Sustainability Goals," *Food Business News* (September 10, 2014), www.foodbusinessnews.net, on September 11, 2014; Eric Schroeder, "Mondelez Reaches Palm Oil Goal Two Years Early," *Food Business News* (January 16, 2014), www.foodbusinessnews.net, on September 11, 2014; Sorcha Corcoran, "Mondelez Ireland Partners with Origin Green to Promote Sustainability," *Business & Leadership* (May 9, 2014), www.businessandleadership.com, on September 11, 2014.

**YOU MAKE THE CALL**   **Cruise Control**

1. As a consumer, how has your attitude toward Carnival been affected by your understanding of this case? How about your attitude toward the cruise industry as a whole?

2. Says one specialist in digital strategy:

    *In the online era, it becomes critical for the business of any size to have a social media crisis management plan—or even better, a crisis prevention plan—in place for those times when things go wrong. And it is truly the matter of "when" vs. "if."*\*

    Social media played a big role in both the Carnival *Triumph* and *Costa Concordia* crises. In what ways did the availability of social media undoubtedly make the crises more difficult for Carnival management to deal with? In what ways could Carnival have used social media as a tool in its crisis management strategy?

3. Maritime lawyer Jim Walker believes that companies should be forgiven for such episodes as the grounding of the *Costa Concordia*—**if** they apply what he calls "the 'three A's' of cruise line crisis management":

    *Companies should be forgiven if they demonstrate a humble and respectful attitude; if they appear on the scene to take stock of the*

    *problems they caused; and if they take prompt action to help those injured by their conduct.*†

    In what ways did Carnival fail to apply Walker's "three A's"? What should the company have done in order to apply Walker's "three A's"? Had you been a passenger on either the Carnival *Triumph* or *Costa Concordia*, what would it have taken for you to "forgive" the company?

4. "After a crisis," says Andrew Griffin, CEO of the crisis management company Regester Larkin,

    *stakeholders will be re-evaluating their opinions of the organization, which in turn affects its wider reputation. Reputations that have been built over many years can be severely challenged or destroyed in a small number of days. … This means that reaching out to stakeholders becomes even more important.*‡

    Recall our discussion of "Organizational Stakeholders" in Chapter 4. Who are the *stakeholders* of Carnival Cruise Lines? How is each group of stakeholders affected by such crises as the *Triumph* and *Costa Concordia*? How might each group affect the company's reputation? How can the company deal with each group as part of its crisis management strategy?

*Ekaterina Walter, "Ten Tips for Reputation and Crisis Management in the Digital World," *Forbes* (November 12, 2013), www.forbes.com, on September 8, 2014.
†"Cruise Crisis Management FAIL—How Carnival Is Ruining Its Reputation Following the *Costa Concordia* Disaster," *Cruise Law News* (January 22, 2012), www.cruiselawnews.com, on September 3, 2014.
‡ "Reputation Recovery: What Next after the Crisis Subsides?" *The Holmes Report* (February 21, 2014), www.holmesreport.com, on September 3, 2014.

# Endnotes

1  Molly Hennssey-Fiske, "*Triumph, Elation, Dream* and *Legend*: Carnival Ship Woes Continue," *Los Angeles Times* (March 15, 2013), http://articles.latimes.com, on September 4, 2014; Steven Fink, "Important Crisis Communications Lessons from Carnival Cruise Lines' 'Ship of Fools,'" *CommPRO.biz* (April 18, 2013), www.commpro.biz, on September 3, 2014; Kim Bhasin, "Carnival Is Failing Spectacularly in the Handling of Its *Costa Concordia* Crisis," *Business Insider* (January 24, 2012), www.businessinsider.com, on September 3, 2014; Jim Walker, "Cruise Crisis Management FAIL—How Carnival Is Ruining Its Reputation Following the *Costa Concordia* Disaster," *Cruise Law News* (January 22, 2012), www.cruiselawnews.com, on September 3, 2014; Walker, "Costa Cruise Disaster: Spotlight Shifts to Carnival—Where's Micky?" *Cruise Law News* (January 25, 2012), www.cruiselawnews.com, on September 5, 2014; Scott Van Camp, "PR Lessons to Be Learned from the *Costa Concordia* Tragedy," *PRNews* (January 23, 2012), on September 3, 2014; David Bartlett, "How Carnival Can Clean Up the PR Mess," *CNN.com* (February 15, 2013), on September 3, 2014.

2  "The Lap of Luxury," *USA Today*, March 30, 2015, p. 3B.

3  Patrick R. Rogers, Alex Miller, and William Q. Judge, "Using Information-Processing Theory to Understand Planning/Performance Relationships in the Context of Strategy," *Strategic Management Journal*, 1999, Vol. 20, pp. 567–577.

4  https://hbr.org/2006/01/a-brief-history-of-decision-making

5  See Peter J. Brews and Michelle R. Hunt, "Learning to Plan and Planning to Learn: Resolving the Planning School/Learning School Debate," *Strategic Management Journal*, 1999, Vol. 20, pp. 889–913.

6  Max D. Richards, *Setting Strategic Goals and Objectives*, 2nd ed. (St. Paul, MN: West, 1986).

7  Jim Collins, "Turning Goals into Results: The Power of Catalytic Mechanisms," *Harvard Business Review*, July–August 1999, pp. 71–81.

8  "GE, No. 2 in Appliances, Is Agitating to Grab Share from Whirlpool," *Wall Street Journal*, July 2, 1997, pp. A1, A6. See also "A Talk with Jeff Immelt," *BusinessWeek*, January 28, 2002, pp. 102–104.

9  "Intel Pledges Diversity by 2020," *USA Today*, January 7, 2015, p. 3B.

10  Kenneth R. Thompson, Wayne A. Hochwarter, and Nicholas J. Mathys, "Stretch Targets: What Makes Them Effective?" *Academy of Management Executive*, August 1997, pp. 48–58.

11  "A Methodical Man," *Forbes*, August 11, 1997, pp. 70–72.

12  http://www.mckinsey.com/insights/leading_in_the_21st_century/leadership_lessons_for_hard_times

13  "FDA Not Meeting Its Audit Goals," *USA Today*, May 7, 2009, p. 1B.

14  See Thomas Bateman, Hugh O'Neill, and Amy Kenworthy-U'Ren, "A Hierarchical Taxonomy of Top Managers' Goals," *Journal of Applied Psychology*, 2002, Vol. 87, No. 6, pp. 1134–1148.

15  John A. Pearce II and Fred David, "Corporate Mission Statements: The Bottom Line," *Academy of Management Executive*, May 1987, p. 109.

16  http://www.starbucks.com/about-us/company-information/mission-statement (accessed May 10, 2015).

17  "Renovating Home Depot," *BusinessWeek*, March 6, 2006, pp. 50–58; see also Ram Charan, "Home Depot's Blueprint for Culture Change," *Harvard Business Review*, April 2006, pp. 60–71.

18  "Lowe's Is Sprucing Up Its House," *BusinessWeek*, June 3, 2002, pp. 56–58.

19  "Airlines Try Cutting Business Fares, Find They Don't Lose Revenue," *Wall Street Journal*, November 22, 2002, pp. A1, A6.

20  http://www.forbes.com/2009/04/29/billionaire-retail-forever21-korea-rich-09-wealth.html

21  *Hoover's Handbook of World Business 2015* (Austin, TX: Hoover's Business Press, 2015), pp. 351–352.

22  http://news.mcdonalds.com/Corporate/Press-Releases/Financial-Release?xmlreleaseid=123040

23  See "Disney Cuts Strategic-Planning Unit," *Wall Street Journal*, March 28, 2005, pp. A1, A12.

24  See Jeffrey L. Kerr and William B. Werther, Jr., "Engaging the Board in Strategy," *Organizational Dynamics*, 2008, Vol. 37, No. 2, pp. 112–124.

25  K. A. Froot, D. S. Scharfstein, and J. C. Stein, "A Framework for Risk Management," *Harvard Business Review*, November–December 1994, pp. 91–102.

26  "How the Fixers Fended off Big Disasters," *Wall Street Journal*, December 23, 1999, pp. B1, B4.

27  "Business World Must be 'Watchful'," *USA Today*, January 24, 2015, p. 5T.

28  Ibid.

29  "At Wal-Mart, Emergence Plan Has Big Payoff," *Wall Street Journal*, September 12, 2005, pp. B1, B3.

30  "Next Time," *USA Today*, October 4, 2005, pp. 1B, 2B; see also Judith A. Clair and Ronald L. Dufresne, "How Companies Can Experience Positive Transformation from a Crisis," *Organizational Dynamics*, 2007, Vol. 36, No. 1, pp. 63–77.

31  "Lacking Parts, G.M. Will Close Plant," *New York Times*, March 17, 2011.

32  G.M. Pieces Together Japanese Supply Chain," *New York Times*, May 13, 2011, p. 5.

33  Michael Watkins and Max Bazerman, "Predictable Surprises: The Disasters You Should Have Seen Coming," *Harvard Business Review*, March 2003, pp. 72–81.

34  James Brian Quinn, Henry Mintzberg, and Robert M. James, *The Strategy Process* (Englewood Cliffs, NJ: Prentice-Hall, 1988).

35  Vasudevan Ramanujam and N. Venkatraman, "Planning System Characteristics and Planning Effectiveness," *Strategic Management Journal*, 1987, Vol. 8, No. 2, pp. 453–468.

36  "Coca-Cola May Need to Slash Its Growth Targets," *Wall Street Journal*, January 28, 2000, p. B2. See also "Pepsi and Coke Roll Out Flavors to Boost Sales," *Wall Street Journal*, May 7, 2002, pp. B1, B4.

37  https://hbr.org/2010/07/the-hbr-interview-we-had-to-own-the-mistakes

38  "Finally, Coke Gets It Right," *BusinessWeek*, February 10, 2003, p. 47.

39  "Disney, Revisited," *USA Today*, December 14, 1999, pp. 1B, 2B.

40  "At Starbucks, a Tall Order for New Cuts, Store Closures," *Wall Street Journal*, January 29, 2009, pp. B1, B4.

41  Quoted in *Fortune*, June 27, 2005, p. 98.

42  http://www.nytimes.com/2013/03/10/business/kris-duggan-of-badgeville-on-the-getting-stuff-done-index.html

43  Andrew Campbell, "Tailored, Not Benchmarked," *Harvard Business Review*, March–April 1999, pp. 41–48.

©Markus Pfaff/Shutterstock.com

# MANAGING STRATEGY AND STRATEGIC PLANNING

**7**

## Learning Outcomes

**After studying this chapter, you should be able to:**

1. Discuss the components of strategy, types of strategic alternatives, and the distinction between strategy formulation and strategy implementation.

2. Describe how to use SWOT (**S**trengths, **W**eaknesses, **O**pportunities, and **T**hreats) analysis in formulating strategy.

3. Identify and describe various alternative approaches to business-level strategy formulation.

4. Describe how business-level strategies are implemented.

5. Identify and describe various alternative approaches to corporate-level strategy formulation.

6. Describe how corporate-level strategies are implemented.

7. Discuss international and global strategies.

203

## MANAGEMENT IN ACTION    Stay Hungry

"I mean, that's what Facebook and Twitter are. It's like your way of identifying who you are and sharing that with your friends."

—DANIELLE DEPALMA, SOCIAL MEDIA STRATEGIST

In the spring of 2013, fans of the *Hunger Games* movie franchise, especially veterans of the 2012 marketing run-up to the first installment, had good reason to be suspicious when billboards started popping up to advertise the futuristic fashion line of a company called Capitol Couture and a brand-new fragrance entitled "L'Essence D'un Champion." Those who realized that they were being contacted in code from the Cloud knew what to do

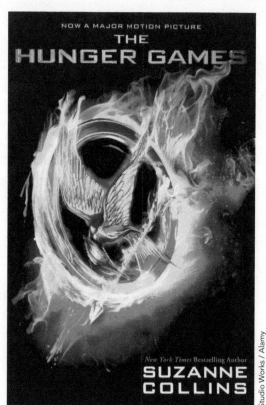

Facebook, Twitter, and other social media platforms are playing an increasingly important role in strategy and strategic planning. Distributors of the *Hunger Game* movies used social media very effectively to help launch each of the four movie blockbusters based on the popular young adult series.

next: They googled "Capitol Couture" and, sure enough, they were directed to a Tumblr site, where they found themselves perusing a clandestine online magazine targeted at citizens of "the Capitol."[1]

Although little of the content directly referenced the ongoing narrative of *The Hunger Games* (*THG*), it was unquestionably related: Fashion and make-up articles from high-end brands provided the distinctive *THG* feel, and, besides, the Tumblr site provided access to the Capitol's Facebook and Instagram pages, Twitter account, and YouTube channel—all of which made it amply clear that exciting events were brewing in the Capitol. Most of these previews of upcoming Capitol events were furnished by the New York trans-media agency Campfire. Steve Coulson, the company's creative director, suspected that the Capitol Couture element of the campaign "might be a little highbrow," but he was confident that

> *Tumblr skews younger. The system is built from the ground up to distribute and share this material. Most people will see this content on their own Tumblr dashboards instead of going to a Tumblr website. That's how high school kids use the web. They're not destination visitors. They're social visitors.*

In case you're still a preapocalyptic entertainment seeker, *THG* is a franchise built around three young-adult novels published by Suzanne Collins between 2008 and 2010. Set in a postapocalyptic dystopia, the story is centered on the ultra-wealthy, fashion-obsessed Capitol of Panem, which holds periodic games in which young participants are forced to fight to the death. Film adaptations of the first two novels, *The Hunger Games* and *The Hunger Games: Catching Fire*, were released by producer-distributor Lionsgate in 2012 and 2013, respectively. The first installment of the third novel was released as *The Hunger Games: Mockingjay—Part 1* in 2014, with the second installment scheduled for late 2015. Produced on budgets of $80 million and $130 million, respectively, *The Hunger Games* and *The Hunger Games: Catching Fire* have each generated nearly a $1 billion in revenue.

The groundwork for Campfire's *Catching Fire* campaign, including Capitol Couture, was laid by the

Lionsgate marketing department. Led by chief marketing officer Tim Palen and social media strategist Danielle DePalma, the team pioneered a multiplatform campaign designed to engage *THG* fans, and for a number of marketing experts, the original *THG* campaign became a "case study" in how to market a movie through social media.

"Our first mission," reports DePalma, "was to start connecting with the fans of the books by utilizing Facebook and Twitter." Thus the team created not one but 13 Facebook pages—one each for the 13 districts under the Capitol's dominion—thereby establishing a central site for fan gatherings. "It was really our way of developing a direct connection and direct dialogue" with fans, says DePalma, who also created a Twitter account—@TheCapitolPN—where fans could not only register for preferred districts but could also be assigned roles in *THG*'s fictional world. "I mean, that's what Facebook and Twitter are," explains DePalma. "It's like your way of identifying who you are and sharing that with your friends. So by giving them occupations within their districts, we gave them identities."

Overlapping the *THG* fictional world inhabited by Collins' characters with the real world inhabited by fans also anchored the *tactical plan* (see Chapter 6) of appealing first to core fans and then broadening the campaign's reach to those not yet invested in the world of *THG*. It worked: "People started sharing it," says DePalma, "and it really took on a life of its own." The same tactic enabled the team to gather fan feedback, which told them, among other things, that *THG* fans weren't interested in a soapy love triangle like the one in the *Twilight* series. In particular, male fans reminded them that "romance is part of the story but not the core of the story," as Palen puts it.

"We established early on," recalls DePalma, "that the fans really became this self-policing system. They'd say, 'Don't do that, this film is much more.' So we learned the do's and don't's from them." Fan comments also helped the marketing team get a sharper focus on their prospective audience.

The romance plot of *Twilight*, says DePalma, was "definitely much more teen and young-girl focused," while *The Hunger Games* "appeals to all four quads"—namely, men under 25; men over 25; women under 25; and women over 25.

Further use of fan feedback was made possible by a partnership between Lionsgate and Microsoft, which launched "The Hunger Games Explorer," a browser that pulled fan-created content from Twitter, Tumblr, Instagram, and other sources, thus generating a constant stream of fan-generated conversation. Noticing that fans tended to sprinkle their conversations with quotes from *THG* books, Palen started using them as poster taglines. "It was a way for us to talk to them the way they talk to each other," he says.

Other facets of the Lionsgate campaign also called for synergies between traditional and online media. Separate hashtags, for example, were assigned to a variety of online events designed to launch with the release of TV spots or trailers. Thus "#HungerGames24" invited fans to tweet the candidacies of their hometowns as early-screening venues. "In less than a week," reports DePalma, "we saw 100,000 tweets. It was amazing to see the results of something … that was simply the fans expressing their excitement. It gave them the opportunity to get involved just by tweeting."

"#HungerGames100" (launched 100 days before the film's release) was a viral campaign featuring an elaborate puzzle: Fans were urged to visit 100 different websites (including MTV, E! Online, and *People*) in order to collect 100 pieces of a puzzle which, when completed, would reveal the latest poster for the film. As it turns out, this particular social media activity was a little too time-consuming for even some of the franchise's most ardent fans ("If I didn't have a job," tweeted one, "I would absolutely be trying to solve the #HungerGames100 puzzle"), but there was no doubt about its ability to set hearts (and stomachs) a-twitter ("This #HungerGames100 is making me too excited," tweeted another. "I think I'm gonna throw up!")

---

The competitive environment of business is becoming increasingly complex. And nowhere is this more apparent than the complexities of rolling out new products and using social media effectively. Devising successful strategies is a complex task affected by a lot of factors. As our opening story shows, when managers can develop and implement effective strategies integrating product rollouts and social media, they can achieve considerable success.

This chapter discusses how organizations manage strategy and strategic planning. We begin by examining the nature of strategic management, including its components and alternatives. We then describe the kinds of analysis needed for firms to formulate their strategies. Next we examine how organizations first formulate and then implement business-level strategies, followed by a parallel discussion at the corporate strategy level. We conclude with a discussion of international and global strategies.

# The Nature of Strategic Management

A strategy is a comprehensive plan for accomplishing an organization's goals. Strategic management, in turn, is a way of approaching business opportunities and challenges—it is a comprehensive and ongoing management process aimed at formulating and implementing effective strategies. Finally, effective strategies are those that promote a superior alignment between the organization and its environment and the achievement of strategic goals.[2]

## The Components of Strategy

In general, a well-conceived strategy addresses three areas: distinctive competence, scope, and resource deployment. A distinctive competence is something the organization does exceptionally well. (We discuss distinctive competencies more fully later.) A distinctive competence of Abercrombie & Fitch is its ability to manage its supply chain more effectively than most of its competitors. It tracks consumer preferences daily with real-time point-of-sale data, digitally transmitting orders to suppliers in Hong Kong and other Asian manufacturing centers, chartering 747s to fly products to the United States, and having products in stores 48 hours later. Because other retailers generally have needed weeks or sometimes months to accomplish the same things, Abercrombie & Fitch has used this distinctive competence to remain competitive.[3] But A&F also continues to innovate. Abercrombie & Fitch recently implemented what it calls Management Dynamics' Supply Chain Visibility to streamline its supply chain process and provide real-time visibility. The system provides one detailed view of shipments to track, display any in-transit delays, and respond to potential crises across A&F's 30 trading partners and international business units. A&F has found that the new system further decreases cycle time and increases availability through improvements in stores' inventory allocations.[4]

The scope of a strategy specifies the range of markets in which an organization will compete. Hershey Foods has essentially restricted its scope to the confectionery business, with a few related activities in other food-processing areas. In contrast, its biggest competitor, Mars, has adopted a broader scope by competing in the pet food business and the electronics industry, among others. Some organizations, called conglomerates, compete in dozens or even hundreds of markets.

A strategy should also include an outline of the organization's projected resource deployment—how it will distribute its resources across the areas in which it competes. General Electric, for example, uses profits from its U.S. operations to invest in new businesses in Europe and Asia. Alternatively, the firm might have chosen to invest in different industries in its domestic market or to invest more heavily in Latin America. The choices it makes as to where and how much to invest reflect issues of resource deployment.

**strategy**
A comprehensive plan for accomplishing an organization's goals

**strategic management**
A comprehensive and ongoing management process aimed at formulating and implementing effective strategies; a way of approaching business opportunities and challenges

**effective strategy**
A strategy that promotes a superior alignment between the organization and its environment and the achievement of strategic goals

**distinctive competence**
An organizational strength possessed by only a small number of competing firms

**scope**
When applied to strategy, it specifies the range of markets in which an organization will compete

**resource deployment**
How an organization distributes its resources across the areas in which it competes

Abercrombie and Fitch's Management Dynamics' Supply Chain Visibility makes it possible to manage their 30 trading partners and international business units, including off shore factories like this one.

SCPhotos / Alamy

## Levels of Strategy

Most businesses today also develop strategies at two distinct levels. These levels provide a rich combination of strategic alternatives for organizations. The two general levels are business-level strategies and corporate-level strategies. Business-level strategy is the set of strategic alternatives from which an organization chooses as it conducts business in a particular industry or market. Such alternatives help the organization focus its competitive efforts for each industry or market in a targeted and focused manner.

Corporate-level strategy is the set of strategic alternatives from which an organization chooses as it manages its operations simultaneously across several industries and several markets. As we discuss later, most large companies today compete in a variety of industries and markets. Thus, although they develop business-level strategies for each industry or market, they also develop an overall strategy that helps define the mix of industries and markets that are of interest to the firm.

Resource deployment is an essential element of strategic planning. General Electric is using profits from its U.S. operations to invest in new business opportunities in Europe and Asia.

**business-level strategy**
The set of strategic alternatives from which an organization chooses as it conducts business in a particular industry or market

**corporate-level strategy**
The set of strategic alternatives from which an organization chooses as it manages its operations simultaneously across several industries and several markets

## Strategy Formulation and Implementation

Drawing a distinction between strategy formulation and strategy implementation is also instructive. Strategy formulation is the set of processes involved in creating or determining the strategies of the organization, whereas strategy implementation is the methods by which strategies are operationalized or executed within the organization. The primary distinction is along the lines of content versus process: The formulation stage determines what the strategy is, and the implementation stage focuses on how the strategy is achieved.

Sometimes the processes of formulating and implementing strategies are rational, systematic, and planned. This is often referred to as a deliberate strategy—a plan chosen and implemented to support specific goals.[5] Texas Instruments (TI) excels at formulating and implementing deliberate strategies. TI uses a planning process that assigns most senior managers two distinct responsibilities: an operational, short-term responsibility and a strategic, long-term responsibility. Thus, one manager may be responsible for both increasing the efficiency of semiconductor operations over the next year (operational, short term) and investigating new materials for semiconductor manufacturing in the twenty-first century (strategic, long term). TI's objective is to help managers make short-term operational decisions while keeping in mind longer-term goals and objectives. Our *Beyond Traditional Business* feature highlights another example of using a deliberate strategy to promote social activism.

Other times, however, organizations use an emergent strategy—a pattern of action that develops over time in an organization in the absence of mission and goals or despite mission and goals.[6] Implementing emergent strategies involves allocating resources even though an organization has not explicitly chosen its strategies. 3M has at times benefited from emergent strategies. The invention of invisible tape, for instance, provides a good example. Entrepreneurial engineers working independently took the invention to their boss, who concluded that it did not have major market potential because it was not part of an approved research and development plan. Only when the product was evaluated at the highest levels in the organization was it accepted and made part of 3M's product mix. Of course, 3M's Scotch tape became a major success despite the fact that

**strategy formulation**
The set of processes involved in creating or determining the strategies of the organization; it focuses on the content of strategies

**strategy implementation**
The methods by which strategies are operationalized or executed within the organization; it focuses on the processes through which strategies are achieved

**deliberate strategy**
A plan of action that an organization chooses and implements to support specific goals

**emergent strategy**
A pattern of action that develops over time in an organization in the absence of mission and goals or despite mission and goals

# Like It or Not

From inside a third-world hovel, a 10-year-old orphan speaks directly to the camera. His little brother is playing in the background:

> My name is Rahim. I'm 10 years old. I live here with my younger brother. Sometimes I worry that I will get sick, like my mom got sick. Then who will look after my brother? But I think everything will be alright. Today UNICEF Sweden has 177,000 likes on Facebook. Maybe they will reach 200,000 by summer. Then we should be alright.

A message then appears on the screen: "Likes don't save lives. Money does."

The video spot is sponsored by UNICEF Sweden, a branch of the United Nations program created to provide long-term humanitarian and developmental assistance to children and mothers in developing countries. "We like likes," says Petra Hallebrant, UNICEF Sweden's director of communications, "and social media could be a good first step to get involved, but it cannot stop there. Likes don't save children's lives. We need money to buy vaccines."

The point is made more directly (though not without a dash of harsh irony) on a poster that was also created by the ad agency Forsman & Bodenfors for a campaign that includes material for TV, radio, and print. Above a photo of a young girl receiving a polio shot, big blue letters make a promise: "Like us on Facebook, and we will vaccinate zero children against polio." In smaller print, UNICEF Sweden explains, "We have nothing against likes, but vaccine costs money."

Naturally, we'd all like a world in which children get medical attention and enough to eat, but the campaign is designed to question whether the mere virtual support of organizations like UNICEF amounts to much more than wishful thinking, "like everyone in the theater clapping to revive Tinker Bell," as one social media critic puts it. Hallebrandt admits that the campaign is designed to encourage people to consider more active engagement in charitable programs: "We hope people discuss the value of a like," she says, "how you look upon the possibilities of getting involved in charities, and also what role social media has in society today."

At the same time, however, the UNICEF Sweden campaign can't help but reflect a stance in the debate about social media *slacktivism*—doing something to support an issue or cause that has little practical effect except making doers feel good about themselves. In an era in which organizations are turning increasingly to social media to attract support, research has begun to explore the role of slacktivism in contemporary attitudes toward social activism and advocacy. In fact, UNICEF Sweden's "likes-don't-save-lives" campaign was launched after the organization saw the results of a poll that it had commissioned from YouGov, a British-based market research firm. "One in five," reported Petra Hallebrant, "thinks that a like on Facebook is a good way of supporting an organization … and one in seven thinks that liking an organization on Facebook is as good as donating money."

Zeynep Tufecki, a sociologist at the University of North Carolina, insists that the relationship between slacktivism and actual activism needs clarification: "What is commonly called "slacktivism," she writes,

> is not at all about "slacking activists"; rather, it is about non-activists taking symbolic action—often in spheres traditionally engaged in only by activists or professionals. … Since so-called "slacktivists" were never activists to begin with, they are not in dereliction of their activist duties. On the contrary, they are acting, symbolically and in a small way, in a sphere that has traditionally been closed off to "the masses" in any meaningful fashion.

Ironically, if Tufecki is right, then UNICEF may be targeting the wrong people: If slacktivists are people who have never been in a position to make practical contributions in the past, there's no reason to believe that social media will turn them into viable activists today.

*References:* Olga Khazan, "UNICEF Tells Slacktivists: Give Money, Not Facebook Likes," *The Atlantic* (April 30, 2013), www.theatlantic.com, on October 2,

2014; Emma Grummas, "Likes Don't Save Lives—Lessons from a Social Media Campaign," *The Guardian* (UK) (February 28, 2014), www.theguardian.com, on September 30, 2014; Tom Murphy, "UNICEF Asks People to Stop 'Liking' Things on Facebook and Send Money," *Humanosphere* (April 29, 2013), www.humanosphere.org, on October 2, 2014; Amar Toor, "UNICEF Says Facebook 'Likes' Won't Save Children's Lives," *The Verge* (May 3, 2013), www.theverge.com, on September 30, 2014; Kate Bennion, "The Age of 'Slacktivism': Online Advocacy Has Many Supporters and Detractors," *Deseret News* (May 28, 2013), www.deseretnews.com, on October 2, 2014; Zeynep Tufecki, "#Kony2012, Understanding Networked Symbolic Action and Why Slacktivism Is Conceptually Misleading," *Technosociology* (March 10, 2012), http://technosociology.org, on October 2, 2014.

it arose outside of the firm's established practices. 3M now counts on emergent strategies to help expand its numerous businesses.

What are the basic components of strategy?

---

☐ Managers need to understand the differences between corporate and business strategies.

☐ Managers need to also remember the distinctions between strategy formulation and strategy implementation.

**Manager's Checklist** ☑

# Using SWOT Analysis to Formulate Strategy

The starting point in formulating strategy is usually SWOT analysis. SWOT is an acronym that stands for strengths, weaknesses, opportunities, and threats. As shown in Figure 7.1, SWOT analysis is a careful evaluation of an organization's internal strengths and weaknesses as well as its environmental opportunities and threats. In SWOT analysis, the best strategies accomplish an organization's mission by (1) exploiting an organization's opportunities and strengths while (2) neutralizing its threats and (3) avoiding (or correcting) its weaknesses.

## Evaluating an Organization's Strengths

Organizational strengths are skills and capabilities that enable an organization to conceive of and implement its strategies. Strengths may include such things as a deep pool of managerial talent, surplus capital, a unique reputation and/or brand name, and well-established distribution channels.[7] Sears, for example, has a nationwide network of trained service employees who repair Sears appliances. Jane Thompson, a Sears executive at the time, conceived of a plan to consolidate repair and home improvement services nationwide under the well-known Sears brand name and to promote them as a general repair operation for all appliances, not just those purchased from Sears. Thus the firm capitalized on existing capabilities and the strength of its name to launch a new operation. Different strategies call on different skills and capabilities. For example, Matsushita Electric has demonstrated strengths in manufacturing and selling consumer electronics under the brand name Panasonic. Matsushita's strength in electronics does not ensure success, however, if the firm expands into insurance, swimming pool manufacturing, or retail. Different strategies like these require

**SWOT**
An acronym that stands for strengths, weaknesses, opportunities, and threats

**organizational strength**
A skill or capability that enables an organization to conceive of and implement its strategies

**FIGURE 7.1  SWOT ANALYSIS**

SWOT analysis is one of the most important steps in formulating strategy. Using the organization's mission as a context, managers assess internal strengths (distinctive competencies) and weaknesses as well as external opportunities and threats. The goal is then to develop good strategies that exploit opportunities and strengths, neutralize threats, and avoid weaknesses.

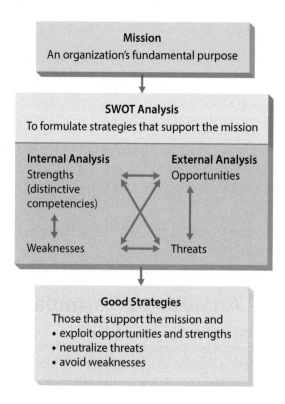

different organizational strengths. SWOT analysis divides organizational strengths into two categories: common strengths and distinctive competencies.

**Common Organizational Strengths**  A common strength is an organizational capability possessed by a large number of competing firms. For example, all the major Hollywood film studios possess common strengths in lighting, sound recording, set and costume design, and makeup. *Competitive parity* exists when large numbers of competing firms are able to implement the same strategy. In this situation, organizations generally attain only average levels of performance. Thus a film company that exploits only its common strengths in choosing and implementing strategies is not likely to go beyond average performance.

**Distinctive Competencies**  A *distinctive competence* is a strength possessed by only a small number of competing firms. Distinctive competencies are rare among a set of competitors. George Lucas's Industrial Light & Magic (ILM), for example, brought the cinematic art of special effects to new heights. Some of ILM's special effects can be produced by no other organization; these rare special effects are thus ILM's distinctive competencies. Organizations that exploit their distinctive competencies often obtain a *competitive advantage* and attain above-normal economic performance.[8] Indeed, a main purpose of SWOT analysis is to discover an organization's distinctive competencies so that the organization can choose and implement strategies that exploit its unique organizational strengths.

**common strength**
A skill or capability held by numerous competing firms

## Imitation of Distinctive Competencies

An organization that possesses distinctive competencies and exploits them in the strategies it chooses can expect to obtain a competitive advantage and above-normal economic performance. However, its success will lead other organizations to duplicate these advantages. Strategic imitation is the practice of duplicating another firm's distinctive competence and thereby implementing a valuable strategy. Although some distinctive competencies can be imitated, others cannot be. When a distinctive competence cannot be imitated, strategies that exploit these competencies generate sustained competitive advantage. A sustained competitive advantage is a competitive advantage that exists after all attempts at strategic imitation have ceased.[9]

A distinctive competence might not be imitated for three reasons. First, the acquisition or development of the distinctive competence may depend on unique historical circumstances that other organizations cannot replicate. Caterpillar, for example, obtained a sustained competitive advantage when the U.S. Army granted it a long-term contract during World War II. The army felt obligated to offer this contract because of the acute international construction requirements necessary to meet the army's needs. Caterpillar's current competitors, including Komatsu and John Deere & Company, cannot re-create these circumstances.

Second, a distinctive competence might be difficult to imitate because its nature and character might not be known or understood by competing firms. Procter & Gamble, for example, considers that its sustained competitive advantage is based on its manufacturing practices. Large sections of Procter & Gamble's plants are screened off to keep this information secure. Industrial Light & Magic also refuses to disclose how it creates some of its special effects.

Finally, a distinctive competence can be difficult to imitate if it is based on complex social phenomena, like organizational teamwork or culture. Competing organizations may know, for example, that a firm's success is directly traceable to the teamwork among its managers but, because teamwork is a difficult thing to create, may not be able to imitate this distinctive competence. Southwest Airlines is successful in part because of the unique culture that has existed within the company for decades.

A distinctive competence is a strength possessed by only a small number of competing firms. Industrial Lights & Magic, founded by George Lucas in 1975, remains a leading provider of special visual effects for major movies due to its patented technologies. In addition to all of the Star Wars movies, IL&M has also contributed to such recent blockbusters as *The Great Gatsby* (2013), *Noah* and *Captain America: The Winter Solder* (2014), *Avengers: The Age of Ultron* and *Jurassic World* (2015), and *Captain America: Civil War* (2016).

## Evaluating an Organization's Weaknesses

Organizational weaknesses are skills and capabilities that do not enable (and may limit) an organization to choose and implement strategies that support its mission. An organization has essentially two ways of addressing weaknesses. First, it may need to make investments to obtain the strengths required to implement strategies that support its mission. Second, it may need to modify its mission so that it can be achieved with the skills and capabilities that the organization already has.

In practice, organizations have a hard time focusing on weaknesses, in part because organization members are often reluctant to admit that they do not have all the skills and capabilities needed. Evaluating weaknesses also calls into question the judgment of managers who chose the organization's mission in the first place and who failed to invest in the skills and capabilities needed to accomplish it.

**strategic imitation**
The practice of duplicating another organization's distinctive competence and thereby implementing a valuable strategy

**sustained competitive advantage**
A competitive advantage that exists after all attempts at strategic imitation have ceased

**organizational weakness**
A skill or capability that does not enable (and may limit) an organization to choose and implement strategies that support its mission

Bill Pugliano/Getty Images

Kmart has suffered for years due to several organizational weaknesses. One of the pioneers of big-store discounting, the firm grew complacent based on its early success and fell behind Walmart. Kmart then failed to invest in new technologies, allowed its stores to become run down and poorly maintained, did not adequately develop new managers, and has not been able to develop a unique identity and focus. As a result of these weaknesses the retailer has continued to struggle.

Organizations that fail either to recognize or to overcome their weaknesses are likely to suffer from competitive disadvantages. An organization has a competitive disadvantage when it is not implementing valuable strategies that are being implemented by competing organizations. Organizations with a competitive disadvantage can expect to attain below-average levels of performance.

## Evaluating an Organization's Opportunities and Threats

Whereas evaluating strengths and weaknesses focuses attention on the internal workings of an organization, evaluating opportunities and threats requires analyzing an organization's environment. Organizational opportunities are areas that may generate higher performance. Organizational threats are areas that increase the difficulty of an organization's performing at a high level.

Porter's "five forces" model of the competitive environment, as discussed in Chapter 3, can be used to characterize the extent of opportunity and threat in an organization's environment. Re-

**competitive disadvantage**
A situation in which an organization is not implementing valuable strategies that are being implemented by competing organizations

call that Porter's five forces are level of competitive rivalry, power of suppliers, power of buyers, threat of substitutes, and threat of new entrants. In general, when the level of competitive rivalry, the power of suppliers and buyers, and the threat of substitutes and new entrants are all high, an industry has relatively few opportunities and many threats. Firms in these types of industries typically can achieve only normal economic performance. On the other hand, when the level of rivalry, the power of suppliers and buyers, and the threat of substitutes and new entrants are all low, then an industry has many opportunities and relatively few threats. Firms in these industries hold the potential for above-normal performance.[10]

**Manager's Checklist**

☐ Managers need a clear understanding of SWOT analysis as they go about formulating strategy.

☐ At the same time, managers should also recognize that SWOT analysis is partially based on perceptions and subjective assessment and may, therefore, not lead to expected options.

**organizational opportunity**
An area in the environment that, if exploited, may generate higher performance

**organizational threat**
An area in the environment that increases the difficulty of an organization's achieving high performance

# Formulating Business-Level Strategies

A number of frameworks have been developed for identifying the major strategic alternatives that organizations should consider when choosing their business-level strategies. Three important classification schemes are Porter's generic strategies, the Miles and Snow typology, and strategies based on the product life cycle.

## Porter's Generic Strategies

According to Michael Porter, organizations may pursue a differentiation, overall cost leadership, or focus strategy at the business level.[11] Table 7.1 summarizes each of these strategies.

An organization that pursues a differentiation strategy seeks to distinguish itself from competitors through the quality (broadly defined) of its products or services. Firms that successfully implement a differentiation strategy can charge more than competitors because customers are willing to pay more to obtain the extra value they perceive.[12] Rolex pursues a differentiation strategy. Rolex watches are handmade of precious metals like gold or platinum and stainless steel, and they are subjected to strenuous tests of quality and reliability. The firm's reputation enables it to charge thousands of dollars for its watches. Coca-Cola and Pepsi compete in the market for bottled water on the basis of differentiation. Coke touts its Dasani brand on the basis of its fresh taste, whereas Pepsi promotes its Aquafina brand on the basis of its purity.[13] Other firms that use differentiation strategies are Lexus, Godiva, Nikon, Mont Blanc, and Ralph Lauren.

Rolex has been very successful in using a a differentiation strategy based on product quality. Its differentiated image, in turn, allows Rolex to charge premium prices for its watches. Rolex also maintains its differentiated image through exclusive partnerships with high-end retailers, celebrity endorsements, and not offering discounted prices.

An organization implementing an overall cost leadership strategy tries to gain a competitive advantage by reducing its costs below the costs of competing firms. By keeping costs low, the organization can sell its products at low prices and still make a profit. Timex uses an overall cost leadership strategy. For decades, this firm has specialized in manufacturing relatively simple, low-cost watches for the mass market. The price of Timex watches, starting around $39.95, is low because of the company's efficient high-volume manufacturing

## TABLE 7.1   PORTER'S GENERIC STRATEGIES

Michael Porter has proposed three generic strategies. Each of these strategies—differentiation, overall cost leadership, and focus—is presumed to be widely applicable to many different competitive situations.

| Strategy Type | Definition | Examples |
| --- | --- | --- |
| Differentiation | Distinguish products or services | Rolex (watches)<br>Godiva (chocolate)<br>Mercedes-Benz (automobiles)<br>Nikon (cameras)<br>Cross (writing instruments) |
| Overall cost leadership | Reduce manufacturing and other costs | Timex (watches)<br>Hershey (chocolate)<br>Kia (automobiles)<br>Kodak (cameras)<br>BIC (writing instruments) |
| Focus | Concentrate on specific regional market, product market, or group of buyers | Tag Heuer (watches)<br>Vosges (chocolate)<br>Ferrari, Alfa Romeo (automobiles)<br>Hasselblad (cameras)<br>Waterman (writing instruments) |

**differentiation strategy**
A strategy in which an organization seeks to distinguish itself from competitors through the quality of its products or services

**overall cost leadership strategy**
A strategy in which an organization tries to gain a competitive advantage by reducing its costs below the costs of competing firms

Gistimages / Alamy

The venerable Tropicana casino in Las Vegas lost much of its market share to newer and glitzier casinos like Winn and The Mirage. Two savvy investors, however, have rejuvenated the Tropicana by focusing on middle-aged and older gamblers who are not interested in high-stakes gambling but instead are drawn to smaller stakes games.

**focus strategy**
A strategy in which an organization concentrates on a specific regional market, product line, or group of buyers

**prospector strategy**
A strategy in which the firm encourages creativity and flexibility and is often decentralized

**defender strategy**
A strategy in which the firm focuses on lowering costs and improving the performance of current products

**analyzer strategy**
A strategy in which the firm tries to maintain its current businesses and to be somewhat innovative in new businesses

capacity. Poland Springs and Crystal Geyser bottled waters are also promoted on the basis of their low cost. Other firms that implement overall cost leadership strategies are Hyundai, BIC, Old Navy, and Hershey.

A firm pursuing a focus strategy concentrates on a specific regional market, product line, or group of buyers. This strategy may have either a differentiation focus, whereby the firm differentiates its products in the focus market, or an overall cost leadership focus, whereby the firm manufactures and sells its products at low cost in the focus market. In the watch industry, Tag Heuer follows a focus differentiation strategy by selling only rugged waterproof watches to active consumers. Hasselblad makes expensive cameras targeted at professional photographers, as opposed to recreational or casual photographers. Fisher-Price uses focus differentiation to sell electronic calculators with large, brightly colored buttons to the parents of preschoolers; stockbroker Edward Jones focuses on small-town markets. General Mills focuses one part of its new-product development on consumers who eat meals while driving—their watchword is "Can we make it 'one-handed'?" so that drivers can safely eat or drink it. Two investors realized that most Las Vegas casinos were targeting either high-end big spenders or the young hip market. So, they bought the venerable old Tropicana casino, renovated it, and began marketing it to so-called "Middle America"—middle-aged or older gamblers who aren't into big-dollar wagering. Their occupancy rates have soared, as have their profits.[14]

## The Miles and Snow Typology

A second classification of strategic options was developed by Raymond Miles and Charles Snow.[15] These authors suggested that business-level strategies generally fall into one of four categories: prospector, defender, analyzer, and reactor. Table 7.2 summarizes each of these strategies. Of course, different businesses within the same company might pursue different strategies.

A firm that follows a prospector strategy is a highly innovative firm that is constantly seeking out new markets and new opportunities and is oriented toward growth and risk taking. Over the years, 3M has prided itself on being one of the most innovative major corporations in the world. Employees at 3M are constantly encouraged to develop new products and ideas in a creative and entrepreneurial way. This focus on innovation has led 3M to develop a wide range of new products and markets, including invisible tape and anti-stain fabric treatments. Amazon.com also follows a prospector strategy as it constantly seeks new market opportunities for selling different kinds of products through its websites and by offering a growing array of delivery options.[16] Similarly, Apple is also using a prospector strategy and helped create markets for MP3 players (with its iPod), smartphones (the iPhone), and tablets (the iPad).

Rather than seeking new growth opportunities and innovation, a company that follows a defender strategy concentrates on protecting its current markets, maintaining stable growth, and serving current customers, generally by lowering its costs and improving the performance of its existing products. With the maturity of the market for writing instruments, BIC has used this approach—it has adopted a less aggressive, less entrepreneurial style of management and has chosen to defend its substantial market share in the industry. It has done this by emphasizing efficient manufacturing and customer satisfaction. Although eBay is expanding into foreign markets, the online auctioneer is still pursuing what amounts to a defender strategy, in that it is keeping its focus primarily on the auction business. Thus, while it is prospecting for new markets, it is defending its core business focus.

A business that uses an analyzer strategy, in which it tries to maintain its current businesses and to be somewhat innovative in new businesses, combines elements of prospectors

## TABLE 7.2  THE MILES AND SNOW TYPOLOGY

The Miles and Snow typology identifies four strategic types of organizations. Three of these—the prospector, the defender, and the analyzer—can all be effective in certain circumstances. The fourth type—the reactor—represents an ineffective approach to strategy.

| Strategy Type | Definition | Examples |
| --- | --- | --- |
| Prospector | Is innovative and growth oriented, searches for new markets and new growth opportunities, encourages risk taking | Amazon.com<br>3M<br>Rubbermaid |
| Defender | Protects current markets, maintains stable growth, serves current customers | BIC<br>eBay<br>Mrs. Fields |
| Analyzer | Maintains current markets and current customer satisfaction with moderate emphasis on innovation | DuPont<br>IBM<br>Yahoo! |
| Reactor | No clear strategy, reacts to changes in the environment, drifts with events | International Harvester<br>Joseph Schlitz Brewing Co.<br>Kmart<br>Montgomery Ward |

and defenders. Most large companies use this approach because they want to both protect their base of operations and create new market opportunities. IBM uses analyzer strategies. DuPont is currently using an analyzer strategy; the firm is relying heavily on its existing chemical and fiber operations to fuel its earnings for the foreseeable future. At the same time, though, DuPont is moving systematically into new business areas such as biotech agriculture and pharmaceuticals. Yahoo! is also using this strategy by keeping its primary focus on its role as an Internet portal while simultaneously seeking to extend that portal into more and more applications.

Finally, a business that follows a reactor strategy has no consistent strategic approach; it drifts with environmental events, reacting to but failing to anticipate or influence those events. Not surprisingly, these firms usually do not perform as well as organizations that implement other strategies. Although most organizations would deny using reactor strategies, a firm called International Harvester Company (IH) was clearly a reactor. At a time when IH's market for trucks, construction equipment, and agricultural equipment was booming, the company failed to keep pace with its competitors. By the time a recession cut demand for its products, it was too late for IH to respond, and the company lost millions of dollars. The firm was forced to sell off virtually all of its businesses, except its truck-manufacturing business. IH, now renamed Navistar, moved from being a dominant firm in trucking, agriculture, and construction to a smaller truck and bus manufacturer because it failed to anticipate changes in its environment. Kmart, Eddie Bauer, and Chrysler have all

**reactor strategy**
A strategy in which a firm has no consistent approach to strategy

International Harvester was once a dominate competitor in the truck, construction, and agricultural equipment industries. However, the firm began to employ a reactor strategy, failed to anticipate changes in its environment, and today operates as a much smaller company rebranded as Navistar.

Dziewul/Shutterstock.com

shown signs of being reactors in recent years. The lack of a consistent strategy is also the primary reason that RadioShack collapsed.[17]

## Strategies Based on the Product Life Cycle

The product life cycle is a model that shows how sales volume changes over the life of products. Understanding the four stages in the product life cycle helps managers recognize that strategies need to evolve over time. As Figure 7.2 shows, the cycle begins when a new product or technology is first introduced. In this *introduction stage*, demand may be very high, sometimes outpacing the firm's ability to supply the product. At this stage, managers need to focus their efforts on "getting product out the door" without sacrificing quality. Managing growth by hiring new employees and managing inventories and cash flow are also concerns during this stage.

During the *growth stage*, more firms begin producing the product, and sales continue to grow. Important management issues include ensuring quality and delivery and beginning to differentiate an organization's product from competitors' products. Entry into the industry during the growth stage may threaten an organization's competitive advantage; thus, strategies to slow the entry of competitors are important.

After a period of growth, products enter a third phase. During this *maturity stage*, overall demand growth for a product begins to slow down, and the number of new firms producing the product begins to decline. The number of established firms producing the product may also begin to decline. This period of maturity is essential if an organization is going to survive in the long run. Product differentiation concerns are still important during this stage, but keeping costs low and beginning the search for new products or services are also important strategic considerations.

In the *decline stage*, demand for the product or technology decreases, the number of organizations producing the product drops, and total sales drop. Demand often declines because all those who were interested in purchasing a particular product have already done so. Organizations that fail to anticipate the decline stage in earlier stages of the life cycle may go

**product life cycle**
A model that portrays how sales volume for products changes over the life of products

---

### FIGURE 7.2 THE PRODUCT LIFE CYCLE

Managers can use the framework of the product life cycle—introduction, growth, maturity, and decline—to plot strategy. For example, management may decide on a differentiation strategy for a product in the introduction stage and a prospector approach for a product in the growth stage. By understanding this cycle and where a particular product falls within it, managers can develop more effective strategies for extending product life.

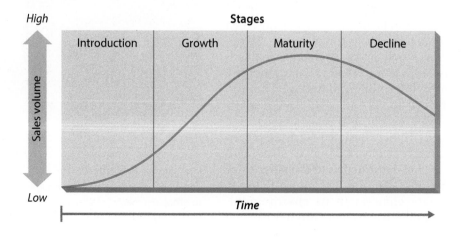

out of business. Those that differentiate their product, keep their costs low, or develop new products or services may do well during this stage.

---

☐ Regardless of the business-level strategy being pursued, managers need to be sure their decisions are consistent with that strategy.

☐ Managers should strive to develop a logical business-level strategy based on their SWOT analysis.

**Manager's Checklist**

---

# Implementing Business-Level Strategies

As we noted earlier, after business strategies are formulated, they must then be implemented. To do this effectively, managers must integrate the activities of several different functions. *Marketing* and *sales*, for example, are used to promote products or services and the overall public image of the organization (often through various types of advertising), price products or services, directly contact customers, and make sales. *Accounting* and *finance* control the flow of money both within the organization and from outside sources to the organization, and *manufacturing* creates the organization's products or services.[18] Organizational *culture*, as discussed in Chapter 3, also helps firms implement their strategies.[19] Indeed, one of the biggest challenges facing managers is how to integrate all of these functions and culture as part of successful implementation.[20]

## Implementing Porter's Generic Strategies

Differentiation and cost leadership can each be implemented through these basic organizational functions. (Focus is implemented through the same approaches, depending on which one it is based on.)

**Differentiation Strategy**   In general, to support differentiation, marketing and sales must emphasize the high-quality, high-value image of the organization's products or services. Neiman Marcus, a department store for financially secure consumers, has excelled at using marketing to support its differentiation strategy. People do not go to Neiman Marcus just to buy clothes or to shop for home electronics. Instead, a trip to Neiman Marcus is advertised as a "total shopping experience." Customers who want to shop for $3,000 pet houses, $50,000 mink coats, and $7,000 exercise machines recognize that the store caters to their needs. Other organizations that have used their marketing function to implement a differentiation strategy include Chanel, Calvin Klein, and Bloomingdale's.

The function of accounting and finance in a business that is implementing a differentiation strategy is to control the flow of funds without discouraging the creativity needed to constantly develop new products and services to meet customer needs. If keeping track of and controlling the flow of money become more important than determining how money and resources are best spent to meet customer needs, then no organization, whether high-tech firm or fashion designer, will be able to implement a differentiation strategy effectively. In manufacturing, a firm implementing a differentiation strategy must emphasize quality and meeting specific customer needs, rather than simply reducing costs. Manufacturing may sometimes have to keep inventory on hand so that customers will have access to products when they want them. Manufacturing also may have to engage in costly customization to meet customer needs.

The culture of a firm implementing a differentiation strategy, like the firm's other functions, must also emphasize creativity, innovation, and response to customer needs.

Lands' End's culture puts the needs of customers ahead of all other considerations. This firm, which sells men's and women's leisure clothing through a catalog service, offers a complete guarantee on merchandise. Dissatisfied customers may return clothes for a full refund or exchange, with no questions asked. Lands' End takes orders 24 hours a day and will ship most orders within 24 hours. Items with lost buttons and broken zippers are replaced immediately. The priority given to customer needs is typical of an organization that is successfully implementing a differentiation strategy.

**Overall Cost Leadership Strategy** To support cost leadership, marketing and sales are likely to focus on simple product attributes and how these product attributes meet customer needs in a low-cost and effective manner. These organizations are very likely to engage in advertising. Throughout this effort, however, emphasis is on the value that an organization's products provide for the price, rather than on the special features of the product or service. Advertising for BIC pens ("Writes first time, every time"), Timex watches ("Takes a licking and keeps on ticking"), and Walmart stores ("Save Money. Live Better") helps these firms implement cost leadership strategies.

Proper emphasis in accounting and finance is also pivotal. Because the success of the organization depends on having costs lower than the competitors, management must take care to reduce costs wherever possible. Tight financial and accounting controls at Walmart, Costco, and Wells Fargo have helped these organizations implement cost leadership strategies. Manufacturing typically helps, with large runs of highly standardized products. Products are designed both to meet customer needs and to be easily manufactured. Manufacturing emphasizes increased volume of production to reduce the per-unit costs of manufacturing. Organizations such as Toshiba (a Japanese semiconductor firm) and Texas Instruments have used this type of manufacturing to implement cost leadership strategies.

> "… in the absence of sufficient product differentiation or innovation, it's harder to create consumer value and shareholder value."
>
> —A. G. LAFLEY, FORMER CEO OF PROCTER & GAMBLE[21]

The culture of organizations implementing cost leadership strategies tends to focus on improving the efficiency of manufacturing, sales, and other business functions. Managers in these organizations are almost fanatical about keeping their costs low. Walmart appeals to its customers to leave shopping carts in designated areas in its parking lots with signs that read, "Please—help us keep *your* costs low." Fujitsu Electronics, in its Tokyo manufacturing facilities, operates in plain, unpainted, cinderblock and cement facilities to keep its costs as low as possible. Family Dollar, a thriving low-cost retailer, concentrates on second- and third-tier brands, which cost less but have higher profit margins than do first-tier brands (Gain detergent rather than Tide, for example) and locates its stores in low-rent strip centers in unglamorous locations.[22]

## Implementing Miles and Snow's Strategies

Similarly, a variety of issues must be considered when implementing any of Miles and Snow's strategic options. (Of course, no organization would purposefully choose to implement a reactor strategy.)

**Prospector Strategy** An organization implementing a prospector strategy is innovative, seeks new market opportunities, and takes many risks. To implement this strategy, organizations need to encourage creativity and flexibility.[23] Creativity helps an organization perceive, or even create, new opportunities in its environment; flexibility enables it to change quickly to take advantage of these new opportunities. Organizations often increase creativity and flexibility by adopting a decentralized organization structure. (An organization is decentralized when major decision-making responsibility is delegated to middle- and lower-level managers.) Johnson & Johnson links decentralization with a prospector strategy. Each of the firm's different businesses is organized into a separate unit, and the managers of these units hold full decision-making responsibility and authority. Often these businesses develop new products for new markets. As the new products develop and sales grow, Johnson & Johnson reorganizes so that each new product is managed in a separate unit.

**Defender Strategy**  An organization implementing a defender strategy tries to protect its market from new competitors. It tends to downplay creativity and innovation in bringing out new products or services and to focus its efforts instead on lowering costs or improving the performance of current products. Often a firm implementing a prospector strategy will switch to a defender strategy. This happens when the firm successfully creates a new market or business and then tries to protect its market from competition. A good example is Mrs. Fields Cookies. One of the first firms to introduce high-quality, high-priced cookies, Mrs. Fields sold its product in special cookie stores and grew very rapidly. This success, however, encouraged many other companies to enter the market. Increased competition, plus reduced demand for high-priced cookies, threatened Mrs. Fields's market position and eventually forced the firm to scale back its operations and defend its current market share rather than seeking additional growth.

**Analyzer Strategy**  An organization implementing an analyzer strategy tries to maintain its current business and to be somewhat innovative in new businesses. Because the analyzer strategy falls somewhere between the prospector strategy (with focus on innovation) and the defender strategy (with focus on maintaining and improving current businesses), the attributes of organizations implementing the analyzer strategy tend to be similar to both of these other types of organizations. They have tight accounting and financial controls as well as high flexibility, efficient production as well as customized products, and creativity along with low costs. Organizations maintain these multiple and contradictory processes with difficulty.

Starbucks uses an analyzer strategy. Although the firm is growing rapidly, its fundamental business is still coffee. At the same time, however, the firm is cautiously branching out into music and ice cream and other food products, and is experimenting with restaurants with more comprehensive menu selections such as truffle mac and cheese, grilled vegetables, and flatbreads. This approach is allowing Starbucks to remain focused on its core coffee business but to explore new business opportunities at the same time. Similarly, Procter & Gamble has also revised some of its business strategies in an attempt to both protect its core businesses and also expand into new ones.[24]

☐ It is important for managers to carefully align their formulation and implementation of business-level strategies.

☐ Don't underestimate the challenges in successfully implementing strategy.

☐ Managers should also be aware that if they intend to alter their business strategy (that is, formulate new ones) they should also consider the implications for implementation issues.

**Manager's Checklist** ☑

# Formulating Corporate-Level Strategies

Most large organizations are engaged in several businesses, industries, and markets. Each business or set of businesses within such an organization is often referred to as a *strategic business unit*, or *SBU*. An organization such as General Electric operates hundreds of different businesses, making and selling products as diverse as jet engines, nuclear power plants, and light bulbs. GE organizes these businesses into approximately 49 SBUs. Even organizations that sell only one product may operate in several distinct markets.

Decisions about which businesses, industries, and markets an organization will enter, and how to manage these different businesses, are based on an organization's corporate strategy. The most important strategic issue at the corporate level concerns the extent and nature of organizational diversification. Diversification describes the number of different businesses that an organization is engaged in and the extent to which these businesses are related to one another. There are three types of diversification strategies: single-product strategy, related diversification, and unrelated diversification.[25]

## Single-Product Strategy

An organization that pursues a single-product strategy manufactures or provides just one product or service; this product is also often sold in a single market. Red Bull GmbH, an Austrian company, produces and markets only the energy drink that bears its name. While there are a few variations, such as a low-calorie formulation, Red Bull is essentially one product. The firm sells no other energy products and does not retail its own products, instead focusing on astute marketing and promotions to drive sales.

The single-product strategy has one major strength and one major weakness. By concentrating its efforts so completely on one product and market, a firm is likely to be very successful manufacturing and marketing the product. Because it has staked its survival on a single product, the organization works very hard to make sure that the product is a success. Of course, if the product is not accepted by the market or is replaced by a new one, the firm will suffer. This happened to slide-rule manufacturers when electronic calculators became widely available and to companies that manufactured only black-and-white televisions when low-priced color televisions were first mass-marketed. Similarly, Wrigley long practiced what amounted to a single-product strategy with its line of chewing gums. But, because younger consumers are buying less gum than earlier generations, Wrigley experienced declining revenues and lower profits. As a result, the Wrigley family eventually sold their business to Mars.[26]

## Related Diversification

Given the disadvantage of the single-product strategy, most large businesses today operate in several different businesses, industries, or markets.[27] If the businesses are somehow linked, that organization is implementing a strategy of related diversification. Virtually all larger businesses in the United States practice related diversification.

**Bases of Relatedness**  Organizations link their different businesses, industries, or markets in different ways. Table 7.3 gives some typical bases of relatedness. In companies such as Philips, a European consumer electronics company, a similar type of electronics technology underlies all the businesses. A common technology in aircraft design links Boeing's commercial and military aircraft divisions, and a common computer design technology links Dell's various computer products and peripherals.

Organizations such as Philip Morris, Kraft Foods, and Procter & Gamble operate multiple businesses related by a common distribution network (grocery stores) and common marketing skills (advertising). Disney and Universal rely on strong brand names and reputations to link their diverse businesses, which include movie studios and theme parks. Pharmaceutical firms such as Merck sell numerous products to a single set of customers: hospitals, doctors, patients, and drugstores. Similarly, AMF-Head sells snow skis, tennis rackets, and sportswear to active, athletic customers.

**Advantages of Related Diversification**  Pursuing a strategy of related diversification has three primary advantages. First, it reduces an organization's dependence on any one of its business activities and thus reduces economic risk. Even if one or two of a firm's businesses lose money, the organization as a whole may still survive because the healthy businesses will

---

**diversification**
The number of different businesses that an organization is engaged in and the extent to which these businesses are related to one another

**single-product strategy**
A strategy in which an organization manufactures just one product or service and sells it in a single geographic market

**related diversification**
A strategy in which an organization operates in several businesses that are somehow linked with one another

## TABLE 7.3  BASES OF RELATEDNESS IN IMPLEMENTING RELATED DIVERSIFICATION

Firms that implement related diversification can do so using any number of bases of relatedness. Four often-used bases of related uses for diversification are similar technology, common distribution and marketing skills, common brand name and reputation, and common customers.

| Basis of Relatedness | Examples |
| --- | --- |
| Similar technology | Philips, Boeing, Westinghouse |
| Common distribution and marketing skills | Kraft Foods, Philip Morris, Procter & Gamble |
| Common brand name and reputation | Disney, Universal |
| Common customers | Merck, IBM, AMF-Head |

generate enough cash to support the others.[28] At Disney, a decline in theme park attendance may be offset by an increase in box office and DVD sales for Disney movies.

Second, by managing several businesses at the same time, an organization can reduce the overhead costs associated with managing any one business. In other words, if the normal administrative costs required to operate any business, such as legal services and accounting, can be spread over a large number of businesses, then the overhead costs *per business* will be lower than they would be if each business had to absorb all costs itself. Thus the overhead costs of businesses in a firm that pursues related diversification are usually lower than those of similar businesses that are not part of a larger corporation.[29]

Third, related diversification allows an organization to exploit its strengths and capabilities in more than one business. When organizations do this successfully, they capitalize on synergies, which are complementary effects that exist among their businesses. *Synergy* exists among a set of businesses when the businesses' economic value together is greater than their economic value separately. McDonald's is using synergy as it diversifies into other restaurant and food businesses. For example, its McCafe premium coffee stands in some McDonald's restaurants allow the firm to create new revenue opportunities while using the firm's existing strengths in food-product purchasing and distribution. Similarly, Starbucks is experimenting with an evening menu featuring wine and cheese in a select number of stores. Our *Leading the Way* feature discusses another example of related diversification.

**unrelated diversification**
A strategy in which an organization operates multiple businesses that are not logically associated with one another

## Unrelated Diversification

Firms that implement a strategy of unrelated diversification operate multiple businesses that are not logically associated with one another. At one time, for example, Quaker Oats owned clothing chains, toy companies, and a restaurant business. Unrelated diversification was a very popular strategy in the 1970s. During that time, several conglomerates like ITT and Transamerica grew by acquiring literally hundreds of other organizations and then running these numerous businesses as

Gustavo Caballero/Getty Images

Disney has thrived by using related diversification. It's movie, theme park, video, and retail operations are all centered around the common base of family-oriented entertainment. Retailers such as this carry Disney merchandise tied to Disney movies and characters, thereby extending the revenue stream from those movies and characters for years.

# The Beauty of Differentiation

One day back in the late 1990s, an urbane Englishman stopped two Chinese women on a street in Shanghai. He wanted to know if they used L'Oréal products to color their hair. No, they replied, they had it done in a salon. The gentleman promptly escorted them to the nearest department store, where a couple of models in shimmering lycra were dancing in front of a huge backdrop of the New York City skyline. "This brand comes from America," intoned a Chinese sales-woman. "It's very trendy." The Englishman offered the two women that he'd brought with him free hair-color kits.

The L'Oréal front man was actually the company's CEO, Lindsay Owen-Jones, and the hair color was from Maybelline, which L'Oréal had acquired a few years earlier. "We have made a conscious effort to diversify the cultural origins of our brands," said Owen-Jones at the time. The giant French cosmetics and beauty company had given Maybelline a radical makeover, promoting it as "urban American chic" to underscore both its bold new product line and its U.S. origins.

When he took over L'Oréal in 1988, Owen-Jones (who stepped down in 2006) was faced with a problem confronting many global companies—how to resolve the tension between "global integration" and "local responsiveness." Owen-Jones saw the issue as a question of how far to optimize the mass-market appeal of L'Oréal's product lines or how far to diversify them in an effort to appeal to a range of multicultural markets. He chose multiculturalism, especially in light of emerging markets in the Asia Pacific region, Africa, and the Middle East.

The strategy is called "global branding," and Owen-Jones' version called for a two-pronged approach: diversifying L'Oréal's brands according to countries of origin (which include France, Britain, Germany, Italy, and Japan) and then calling upon the company's marketing expertise to cultivate the allure of different cultures and exotic brand offerings in markets from China to Mexico. Once dominated by French executives, the company's management team now features a staff of professionals with multicultural backgrounds in new-product design. "We like to try stuff," explains Stéphane Bérubé, chief marketing officer of L'Oréal Canada since 2014, "and we're not afraid to go first into testing and new adventures." When it expanded in India, for example, L'Oréal was the first company to offer any hair-color alternatives to black.

Bérubé reports that the company has recently done a lot of research into three global-market segments: "the South Asian consumer, the Chinese consumer, and the baby boomers, which are three booming markets in terms of both growth and buying power. ... We have products from most of our brands," he adds, "that are targeted to these three segments," but he admits that the company can still do better in two areas that reflect Owen-Jones' original two-pronged marketing strategy: "One, to have more offerings and, two, to better target" selected consumers.

"The name of the game right now," says Bérubé, "is to have the right product at the right time in front of the consumer. And that," he states, "can be done through digital or in-store." Thus in 2014, L'Oréal signed on with Sitecore, a marketing-technology firm whose platform can be used to connect across media and electronic consumer touch points with thousands of stores and millions of customers, potentially on a one-to-one basis. "The goal," says Sitecore chief strategy officer Darren Guarnaccia, "is understanding the person behind the keyboard and then delivering experiences that matter."

References: Hae-Jung Hong and Yves Doz, "L'Oréal Masters Multiculturalism," *Harvard Business Review* (June 2013), http://hbr.org, on September 15, 2014; Gail Edmondson et al., "L'Oréal: The Beauty of Global Branding," *Bloomberg Businessweek* (June 28, 1999), www.businessweek.com, on September 15, 2014; Tanya Kostiw, "L'Oréal Homes In On a One-on-One Approach with Shoppers," *Strategy* (May 28, 2014), http://strategy online. ca, on September 15, 2014; John Koetsier, "One-to-One Marketing, Global Scale: Sitecore Lands L'Oréal to Personalize Beauty," *VentureBeat* (April 16, 2014), http://venturebeat.com, on September 15, 2014.

independent entities. Even if there are important potential synergies among their different businesses, organizations implementing a strategy of unrelated diversification do not try to exploit them.

In theory, unrelated diversification has two advantages. First, a business that uses this strategy should have stable performance over time. During any given period, if some businesses owned by the organization are in a cycle of decline, others may be in a cycle of growth. Unrelated diversification is also thought to have resource allocation advantages. Every year, when a corporation allocates capital, people, and other resources among its various businesses, it must evaluate information about the future of those businesses so that it can place its resources where they have the highest potential for return. Given that it owns the businesses in question and thus has full access to information about the future of those businesses, a firm implementing unrelated diversification should be able to allocate capital to maximize corporate performance.

Despite these presumed advantages, research suggests that unrelated diversification usually does not lead to high performance. First, corporate-level managers in such a company usually do not know enough about the unrelated businesses to provide helpful strategic guidance or to allocate capital appropriately. To make strategic decisions, managers must have complete and subtle understanding of a business and its environment. Because corporate managers often have difficulty fully evaluating the economic importance of investments for all the businesses under their wing, they tend to concentrate only on a business's current performance. This narrow attention at the expense of broader planning eventually hobbles the entire organization. Many of International Harvester's problems noted earlier grew from an emphasis on current performance at the expense of investments for the future success of the firm.

Second, because organizations that implement unrelated diversification fail to exploit important synergies, they are at a competitive disadvantage compared to organizations that use related diversification. Universal Studios has been at a competitive disadvantage relative to Disney because its theme parks, movie studios, and licensing divisions are less integrated and therefore achieve less synergy.

For these reasons, almost all organizations have abandoned unrelated diversification as a corporate-level strategy. Transamerica sold off many businesses and now concentrates on a core set of related businesses and markets. Large corporations that have not concentrated on a core set of businesses have eventually been acquired by other companies and then broken up. Research suggests that these organizations are actually worth more when broken up into smaller pieces than when joined.[30]

---

☐ Managers should be aware of the different ways to formulate corporate-level strategies and know the advantages and disadvantages of each.

☐ Managers who pursue a single-product strategy need to be aware that potential threats can affect them very dramatically.

☐ If managers pursue a diversification strategy, they need to clearly understand what they hope to achieve and make sure their decisions support these goals.

**Manager's Checklist** ☑

## Implementing Corporate-Level Strategies

In implementing a diversification strategy, organizations face two important questions. First, how will the organization move from a single-product strategy to some form of diversification? Second, once the organization diversifies, how will it manage diversification effectively?

Honda has successfully become a diversified company by developing new products and product lines based on its expertise in engine design and manufacturing. Most people associate Honda with motorcycles (like these) and high-quality automobiles. But the firm also sells portable electric generators, lawn mowers, snow blowers, and all-terrain vehicles.

## Becoming a Diversified Firm

Most organizations do not start out completely diversified. Rather, they begin operations in a single business, pursuing a particular business-level strategy. Success in this strategy then creates resources and strengths that the organization can use in related businesses.[31]

**Development of New Products** Some firms diversify by developing their own new products and services within the boundaries of their traditional business operations. Honda followed this path to diversification. Relying on its traditional strength in the motorcycle market, over the years Honda learned how to make fuel-efficient, highly reliable small engines. Honda began to apply its strengths in a new business: manufacturing small, fuel-efficient cars for the Japanese domestic market. These vehicles were first sold in the United States in the late 1960s. Honda's success in the U.S. market led the company to increase the size and improve the performance of its cars. Over the years, Honda has introduced automobiles of increasing quality, culminating in the Acura line of luxury cars. While diversifying into the market for automobiles, Honda also applied its engine-building strengths to produce a line of all-terrain vehicles, portable electric generators, and lawn mowers. In each case, Honda was able to parlay its strengths and resources into successful new businesses.

**backward vertical integration**
An organization's beginning the business activities formerly conducted by its suppliers

**forward vertical integration**
An organization's beginning the business activities formerly conducted by its customers

**merger**
The purchase of one firm by another firm of approximately the same size

**acquisition**
The purchase of a firm by a firm that is considerably larger

**Replacement of Suppliers and Customers** Firms can also become diversified by replacing their former suppliers and customers. A company that stops buying supplies (either manufactured goods or raw materials) from other companies and begins to provide its own supplies has diversified through backward vertical integration. Campbell Soup once bought soup cans from several different manufacturers but later began manufacturing its own cans. In fact, Campbell is currently one of the largest can-manufacturing companies in the world, although almost all the cans it makes are used in its own soup operations.

An organization that stops selling to one customer and sells instead to that customer's customers has diversified through forward vertical integration. G.H. Bass used forward vertical integration to diversify its operations. Bass once sold its shoes and other products only to retail outlets. More recently, however, Bass opened numerous factory outlet stores, which now sell products directly to consumers. Nevertheless, Bass has not abandoned its former customers, retail outlets. Many firms are also employing forward vertical integration today, as they use the Internet and social media to market their products and services directly to consumers.

**Mergers and Acquisitions** Another common way for businesses to diversify is through mergers and acquisitions—that is, through purchasing another organization. Such a purchase is called a merger when the two organizations being combined are approximately the same size. United and Continental airlines merged to create a new airline. The firm kept United's name but Continental's logo and livery. An acquisition, in contrast, occurs when one of the organizations involved is larger than the other. In most cases, the acquired firm's "identity" disappears altogether. When Delta bought Northwest Airlines, Northwest was simply folded into Delta. Organizations engage

"The key to making acquisitions is being ready because you really never know when the right big one is going to come along."

—JAMES MCNERNEY, CEO BOEING COMPANY[33]

in mergers and acquisitions to diversify through vertical integration by acquiring former suppliers or former customers. Mergers and acquisitions are also becoming more common in other countries, such as Germany and China.[32]

Most organizations use mergers and acquisitions to acquire complementary products or complementary services, which are products or services linked by a common technology and common customers. The objective of most mergers and acquisitions is the creation or exploitation of synergies.[34] Synergy can reduce the combined organizations' costs of doing business; it can increase revenues; and it may open the way to entirely new businesses for the organization to enter. For example, Procter & Gamble made a decision to launch a nationwide chain of car washes under the widely recognized brand name of Mr. Clean, one of its leading brands of cleaning products. To jump-start the Mr. Clean Car Wash venture, the firm acquired the assets of Atlanta-based Carnett's Car Wash and its 14 locations.[35]

G.H. Bass has effectively implemented forward vertical integration. While Bass once distributed its shoes only through other retailers, the firm has now successfully launched its own chain of retail stores to serve customers directly. This has resulted in higher revenues and profits for the firm, as well as greater control over its product and merchandising mix.

## Managing Diversification

However an organization implements diversification—whether through internal development, vertical integration, or mergers and acquisitions—it must monitor and manage its strategy. The two major tools for managing diversification are (1) organization structure and (2) portfolio management techniques. We discuss how organization structure can be used to manage a diversification strategy in detail in Chapter 10.[36] Portfolio management techniques are methods that diversified organizations use to determine which businesses to engage in and how to manage these businesses to maximize corporate performance. Two important portfolio management techniques are the BCG matrix and the GE Business Screen.

**BCG Matrix**   The BCG (for Boston Consulting Group) matrix provides a framework for evaluating the relative performance of businesses in which a diversified organization operates. It also prescribes the preferred distribution of cash and other resources among these businesses.[37] The BCG matrix uses two factors to evaluate an organization's set of businesses: the growth rate of a particular market and the organization's share of that market. The matrix suggests that fast-growing markets in which an organization has the highest market share are more attractive business opportunities than slow-growing markets in which an organization has a small market share. Dividing market growth and market share into two categories (low and high) creates the simple matrix shown in Figure 7.3.

The matrix classifies the types of businesses in which a diversified organization can engage as dogs, cash cows, question marks, and stars. *Dogs* are businesses that have a very small share of a market that is not expected to grow. Because these businesses do not hold much economic promise, the BCG matrix suggests that organizations either should not invest in them or should consider selling them as soon as possible. *Cash cows* are businesses that have a large share of a market that is not expected to grow substantially. These businesses characteristically generate high profits that the organization should use to support question marks and stars. (Cash cows are "milked" for cash to support businesses in markets that have greater growth potential.) *Question marks* are businesses that have only a small share of a quickly growing market. The future performance of these businesses is uncertain. A question mark that can capture increasing amounts of this growing market

**portfolio management technique**
A method of determining which businesses to engage in and how to manage these businesses to maximize corporate performance

**BCG matrix**
A method of evaluating businesses relative to the growth rate of their market and the organization's share of the market

---

### FIGURE 7.3  THE BCG MATRIX

The BCG matrix helps managers develop a better understanding of how different strategic business units contribute to the organization. By assessing each SBU on the basis of its market growth rate and relative market share, managers can make decisions about whether to commit further financial resources to the SBU or to sell or liquidate it.

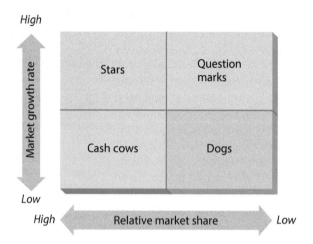

Source: Adapted from the BCG Portfolio Matrix from the "Product Portfolio Matrix," © 1970, The Boston Consulting Group.

may be very profitable. On the other hand, a question mark unable to keep up with market growth is likely to have low profits. The BCG matrix suggests that organizations should invest carefully in question marks. If their performance does not live up to expectations, question marks should be reclassified as dogs and divested. *Stars* are businesses that have the largest share of a rapidly growing market. Cash generated by cash cows should be invested in stars to ensure their preeminent position. For example, BMW bought Rover a few years ago, thinking that its products would help the German automaker reach new consumers. But the company was not able to capitalize on this opportunity, so it ended up selling Rover's car business to a British firm and Land Rover to Ford. Ford couldn't get leverage out of Rover either and ended up selling it (along with Jaguar) to India's up-and-coming Tata Motors.

More recently, Yum Brands has also made significant decisions based on the BCG matrix approach. For several years Yum owned and operated five restaurant chains—KFC, Pizza Hut, Taco Bell, A&W, and Long John Silver's. As the U.S. fast-food market approached saturation, Yum managers started to expand aggressively into foreign markets. The firm's three flagship brands, KFC, Pizza Hut, and Taco Bell, had been successfully launched in many foreign markets several years ago, and now overseas profits account for around 70 percent of Yum's total profits. But A&W and Long John Silver's had few foreign outlets, and managers decided there was little potential for overseas growth. Consequently Yum sold those two businesses in order to more effectively concentrate on the other three. Then the firm bought WingStreet and added it to the Yum portfolio.[38] WingStreet, like the other chains, has had success in foreign markets, and managers project significant growth potential abroad.

**GE Business Screen**
A method of evaluating businesses along two dimensions: (1) industry attractiveness and (2) competitive position; in general, the more attractive the industry and the more competitive the position, the more an organization should invest in a business

**GE Business Screen**  Because the BCG matrix is relatively narrow and overly simplistic, General Electric (GE) developed the GE Business Screen, a more sophisticated approach to managing diversified business units. The Business Screen is a portfolio management technique that can also be represented in the form of a matrix. Rather than focusing solely on market growth and market share, however, the GE Business Screen considers industry attractiveness and competitive position. These two factors are divided into three categories each, to make the nine-cell matrix shown in Figure 7.4.[39] These cells, in turn, classify business units as winners, losers, question marks, average businesses, or profit producers.

As Figure 7.4 shows, both market growth and market share appear in a broad list of factors that determine the overall attractiveness of an industry and the overall quality of a firm's competitive position. Other determinants of an industry's attractiveness (in addition to market growth) include market size, capital requirements, and competitive intensity. In general, the greater the market growth, the larger the market, the smaller the capital requirements, and the less the competitive intensity, the more attractive an industry will be. Other determinants of an organization's competitive position in an industry (besides market share) include technological know-how, product quality, service network, price competitiveness, and operating costs. In general, businesses with large market share, technological know-how, high product quality, a quality service network, competitive prices, and low operating costs are in a favorable competitive position.

Think of the GE Business Screen as a way of applying SWOT analysis to the implementation and management of a diversification strategy. The determinants of industry attractiveness are similar to the environmental opportunities and threats in SWOT analysis, and the determinants of competitive position are similar to organizational strengths and weaknesses. By conducting this type of SWOT analysis across several businesses, a diversified organization

## FIGURE 7.4 THE GE BUSINESS SCREEN

The GE Business Screen is a more sophisticated approach to portfolio management than the BCG matrix. As shown here, several factors combine to determine a business's competitive position and the attractiveness of its industry. These two dimensions, in turn, can be used to classify businesses as winners, question marks, average businesses, losers, or profit producers. Such a classification enables managers to allocate the organization's resources more effectively across various business opportunities.

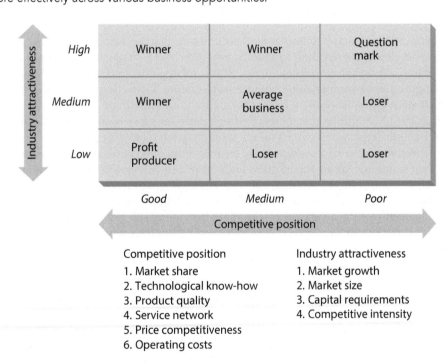

| Competitive position | Industry attractiveness |
|---|---|
| 1. Market share | 1. Market growth |
| 2. Technological know-how | 2. Market size |
| 3. Product quality | 3. Capital requirements |
| 4. Service network | 4. Competitive intensity |
| 5. Price competitiveness | |
| 6. Operating costs | |

can decide how to invest its resources to maximize corporate performance. In general, organizations should invest in winners and in question marks (where industry attractiveness and competitive position are both favorable); should maintain the market position of average businesses and profit producers (where industry attractiveness and competitive position are average); and should sell losers. For example, Unilever once assessed its business portfolio using a similar framework and, as a result, decided to sell off several specialty chemical units that were not contributing to the firm's profitability as much as other businesses. The firm then used the revenues from these divestitures and bought more related businesses such as Ben & Jerry's Homemade and Slim-Fast.[40] During the recent economic recession, many diversified businesses took an especially aggressive approach to selling or closing underperforming businesses. For instance, Japan's Pioneer electronics business sold its television business, Home Depot shut down its Expo home-design stores, and Textron closed a business unit that financed real estate deals.[41]

 **Manager's Checklist**

☐ If a business decides to diversify managers need to know their various options and the advantages and disadvantages of each.

☐ When acquiring other businesses, managers need to have a clear understanding of how the acquisitions fit its corporate-level strategy.

# International and Global Strategies

Strategic management is in many ways a continuing challenge for managers. But an increasingly important and special set of challenges confronting today's managers relates to international and global strategies.

## Developing International and Global Strategies

Developing an international strategy is far more complex than developing a domestic one.[42] Managers developing a strategy for a domestic firm must deal with one national government, one currency, one accounting system, one political system, one legal system, and usually a single language and a comparatively homogeneous culture. Conversely, managers responsible for developing a strategy for an international firm must understand and deal with multiple governments, multiple currencies, multiple accounting systems, multiple political systems, multiple legal systems, and a variety of languages and cultures.

Moreover, managers in an international business must also coordinate the implementation of their firm's strategy among business units located in different parts of the world, with different time zones, different cultural contexts, and different economic conditions, as well as monitor and control their performance. Managers usually consider these complexities acceptable trade-offs for the additional opportunities that come with global expansion. Indeed, international businesses can exploit three sources of competitive advantage unavailable to domestic firms.

**Global Efficiencies** International firms can improve their efficiency through several means not accessible to a domestic firm. They can capture *location efficiencies* by locating their facilities anywhere in the world that yields them the lowest production or distribution costs or that best improves the quality of service they offer their customers. Production of athletic shoes, for example, is very labor intensive, and Nike, like many of its competitors, centers its manufacturing in countries where labor costs are especially low.[43] Similarly, by building factories to serve more than one country, international firms may also lower their production costs by capturing *economies of scale*. By broadening their product lines in each of the countries they enter, international firms may enjoy *economies of scope*, lowering their production and marketing costs and enhancing their bottom line. Finally, firms can take action to centralize operations in order to increase control over far-flung activities.

**Multimarket Flexibility** As we discussed in earlier chapters, there are wide variations in the political, economic, legal, and cultural environments of countries. Moreover, these environments are constantly changing: New laws are passed, new governments are elected, economic policies are changed, new competitors may enter (or leave) the national market, and so on. International businesses thus face the challenge of responding to these multiple diverse and changing environments. Often firms find it beneficial to empower local managers to respond quickly to such changes. However, unlike domestic firms, which operate in and respond to changes in the context of a single domestic environment, international businesses may also respond to a change in one country by implementing a

Tyson Foods has capitalized on multimarket flexibility to boost sales of packaged chicken. Health-conscious consumers in the United States have driven up demand for chicken breasts but are not as interested in dark meat such as legs, thighs, and other parts of the chicken. However, these same chicken parts are very desirable in some other areas of the world such as Russia and China. These workers, for example, are packing Tyson chicken legs and thighs for Chinese consumers. The plant itself is a joint venture between Tyson and Chinese investors in China's Shandong province.

change in another country. Chicken processor Tyson Foods, for example, has benefited from the increased demand by health-conscious U.S. consumers for chicken breasts. In producing more chicken breasts, Tyson also produced more chicken legs and thighs, which are considered less desirable by U.S. consumers. Tyson capitalized on its surplus by targeting the Russian market, where dark meat is preferred over light, and the Chinese market, where chicken feet are considered a tasty delicacy. So, Tyson now successfully exports most of its chicken thighs and legs to Russia and China.

**Worldwide Learning** The diverse operating environments of multinational corporations (MNCs) may also contribute to organizational learning.[44] Differences in these operating environments may cause the firm to operate differently in one country than in another. An astute firm may learn from these differences and transfer this learning to its operations in other countries.[45] For example, McDonald's U.S. managers once believed that its restaurants should be freestanding entities located in suburbs and small towns. A Japanese franchisee convinced McDonald's to allow it to open a restaurant in an inner-city office building. That restaurant's success caused McDonald's executives to rethink their store location criteria. Nontraditional locations—office buildings, Walmart superstores, even airplanes—are now an important source of new growth for the firm.

> "It was hard, but we knew enough not to try to do it all ourselves. Every country has its own culture; it's best to let the local people run the stores."
>
> —FRANK TOSKAN, COFOUNDER, MAC COSMETICS[46]

Unfortunately, it is difficult to exploit these three factors simultaneously. Global efficiencies can be more easily obtained when a single unit of a firm is given worldwide responsibility for the task at hand. BMW's engineering staff at headquarters in Munich, for example, is responsible for the research and design of the company's new automobiles. By focusing its research and development (R&D) efforts at one location, BMW engineers designing new transmissions are better able to coordinate their activities with their counterparts designing new engines. However, centralizing control of its R&D operations also hinders BMW's ability to customize its product to meet the differing needs of customers in different countries. Consider the simple question of whether to include cup holders in its cars. In designing cars to be driven safely at the

*Corbis Wire/Corbis*

prevailing high speeds of Germany's autobahn, the company's engineers decided that cup holders were both irrelevant and dangerous. Driving speeds in the United States, however, are much lower, and cup holders are an important comfort feature in autos sold to U.S. consumers. Lengthy battles were fought between BMW's German engineers and its U.S. marketing managers over this seemingly trivial issue. Only after years of debate did cup holders finally become a standard feature in the firm's automobiles sold in North America.

As this example illustrates, if too much power is centralized in one unit of a firm, the unit may ignore the needs of consumers in other markets. Conversely, multimarket flexibility is enhanced when a firm delegates responsibility to the managers of local subsidiaries. Vesting power in local managers allows each subsidiary to tailor its products, personnel policies, marketing techniques, and other business practices to meet the specific needs and wants of potential customers in each market the firm serves. However, this increased flexibility will reduce the firm's ability to obtain global efficiencies in such areas as production, marketing, and R&D.

Furthermore, the unbridled pursuit of global efficiencies or multimarket flexibility may stifle the firm's attempts to promote worldwide learning. Centralizing power in a single unit of the firm to capture global efficiencies may cause the unit to ignore lessons and information acquired by other units of the firm. Moreover, the other units may have little incentive or ability to acquire such information if they know that the "experts" at headquarters will ignore them. Decentralizing power in the hands of local subsidiary managers may create similar problems. A decentralized structure may make it difficult to transfer learning from one subsidiary to another. Local subsidiaries may be disposed to automatically reject outside information as not being germane to the local situation. Firms wishing to promote worldwide learning must use an organizational structure that promotes knowledge transfer among its subsidiaries and corporate headquarters. The firms must also create incentive structures that motivate managers at headquarters and in subsidiaries to acquire, disseminate, and act on worldwide learning opportunities.

## Strategic Alternatives for International Business

International businesses typically adopt one of four strategic alternatives in their attempt to balance the three goals of global efficiencies, multimarket flexibility, and worldwide learning. The first of these strategic alternatives is the home replication strategy. In this approach, a firm uses the core competency or firm-specific advantage it developed at home as its main competitive weapon in the foreign markets that it enters. In other words, the firm takes what it does exceptionally well in its home market and tries to duplicate it in foreign markets. Mercedes-Benz's home replication strategy, for example, relies on its well-known brand name and its reputation for building well-engineered, luxurious cars capable of traveling safely at very high speeds. It is this market segment that Mercedes-Benz has chosen to exploit internationally, despite the fact that only a very few countries have both the high income levels and the high speed limits appropriate for its products. But consumers in Asia, the rest of Europe, and the Americas are nevertheless attracted by the car's mystique.

The multidomestic strategy is a second alternative available to international firms. A multidomestic corporation manages itself as a collection of relatively independent operating subsidiaries, each of which focuses on a specific domestic market. In addition, each of these subsidiaries is free to customize its products, its marketing campaigns, and its operating techniques to best meet the needs of its local customers. The multidomestic approach is particularly effective when there are clear differences among national markets; when economies of scale for production, distribution, and marketing are low; and when the cost of coordination between the parent corporation and its various foreign subsidiaries is high. Because each subsidiary must be responsive to the local market, the parent company usually delegates considerable power and authority to managers of its subsidiaries in various host countries. International businesses operating before World War II often adopted this approach because

**home replication strategy**
International strategy in which a company uses the core competency or firm-specific advantage it developed at home as its main competitive weapon in the foreign markets that it enters

**multidomestic strategy**
International strategy in which a company manages itself as a collection of relatively independent operating subsidiaries, each of which focuses on a specific domestic market

of the difficulties in controlling distant foreign subsidiaries, given the communication and transportation technologies of that time.

The global strategy is the third alternative philosophy available for international firms. A global corporation views the world as a single marketplace and has as its primary goal the creation of standardized goods and services that will address the needs of customers worldwide. The global strategy is almost the exact opposite of the multidomestic strategy. Whereas the multidomestic firm believes that its customers in every country are fundamentally different and must be approached from that perspective, a global corporation assumes that customers are fundamentally the same regardless of nationality. Thus the global corporation views the world market as a single entity as the corporation develops, produces, and sells its products. It tries to capture economies of scale in production and marketing by concentrating its production activities in a handful of highly efficient factories and then creating global advertising and marketing campaigns to sell the goods produced in those factories. Because the global corporation must coordinate its worldwide production and marketing strategies, it usually concentrates power and decision-making responsibility at a central headquarters.

The home replication strategy and the global strategy share an important similarity: Under either approach, a firm conducts business the same way anywhere in the world. There is also an important difference between the two approaches. A firm using the home replication strategy takes its domestic way of doing business and uses that approach in foreign markets as well. In essence, a firm using this strategy believes that if its business practices work in its domestic market, then they should also work in foreign markets. Conversely, the starting point for a firm adopting a global strategy has no such home-country bias. In fact, the concept of a home market is irrelevant because the global firm thinks of its market as a global one, not one divided into domestic and foreign segments. The global firm tries to figure out the best way to serve all of its customers in the global market and then does so.

A fourth approach available to international firms is the transnational strategy. The transnational corporation tries to combine the benefits of global scale efficiencies, such as those pursued by a global corporation, with the benefits and advantages of local responsiveness, which is the goal of a multidomestic corporation. To do so, the transnational corporation does not automatically centralize or decentralize authority. Rather, it carefully assigns responsibility for various organizational tasks to the unit of the organization best able to achieve the dual goals of efficiency and flexibility.

A transnational corporation may choose to centralize certain management functions and decision making, such as R&D and financial operations, at corporate headquarters. Other management functions, such as human resource management and marketing, may be decentralized, allowing managers of local subsidiaries to customize their business activities to better respond to the local culture and business environment. Microsoft, for example, locates most of its product development efforts in the United States, whereas responsibility for marketing is delegated to its foreign subsidiaries. Often, transnational corporations locate responsibility for one product line in one country and responsibility for a second product line in another country. To achieve an interdependent network of operations, transnational corporations focus considerable attention on integration and coordination among their various subsidiaries.

**global strategy**
International strategy in which a company views the world as a single marketplace and has as its primary goal the creation of standardized goods and services that will address the needs of customers worldwide

**transnational strategy**
International strategy in which a company tries to combine the benefits of global scale efficiencies with the benefits and advantages of local responsiveness

---

☐ Managers should be aware of the basic strategic options available to multinational businesses.

☐ Managers should also remember that international strategic planning is similar to but also different from domestic strategic planning.

**Manager's Checklist**

# Summary of Learning Outcomes and Key Points

1. Discuss the components of strategy, types of strategic alternatives, and the distinction between strategy formulation and strategy implementation.

   - A strategy is a comprehensive plan for accomplishing the organization's goals.
   - Effective strategies address three organizational issues: distinctive competence, scope, and resource deployment.
   - Most large companies have both business-level and corporate-level strategies.
   - Strategy formulation is the set of processes involved in creating or determining the strategies of an organization.
   - Strategy implementation is the process of executing strategies.

2. Describe how to use SWOT (**S**trengths, **W**eaknesses, **O**pportunities, and **T**hreats) analysis in formulating strategy.

   - SWOT analysis considers an organization's strengths, weaknesses, opportunities, and threats.
   - Using SWOT analysis, an organization chooses strategies that support its mission and
     o exploit its opportunities and strengths.
     o neutralize its threats.
     o avoid its weaknesses.
   - Common strengths cannot be ignored, but distinctive competencies hold the greatest promise for superior performance.

3. Identify and describe various alternative approaches to business-level strategy formulation.

   - A business-level strategy is the plan an organization uses to conduct business in a particular industry or market.
   - Porter suggests that businesses may formulate:
     o a differentiation strategy
     o an overall cost leadership strategy
     o a focus strategy
   - According to Miles and Snow, organizations may choose one of four business-level strategies:
     o prospector
     o defender
     o analyzer
     o reactor
   - Business-level strategies may also take into account the stages in the product life cycle.

4. Describe how business-level strategies are implemented.

   - Strategy implementation at the business level takes place in the areas of marketing, sales, accounting and finance, and manufacturing.

   - Culture also influences strategy implementation.
   - Implementation of Porter's generic strategies requires different emphases in each of these organizational areas.
   - Implementation of Miles and Snow's strategies affects organization structure and practices.

5. Identify and describe various alternative approaches to corporate-level strategy formulation.

   - A corporate-level strategy is the plan an organization uses to manage its operations across several businesses.
   - A firm that does not diversify is implementing a single-product strategy.
   - An organization pursues a strategy of related diversification when it operates a set of businesses that are somehow linked.
   - An organization pursues a strategy of unrelated diversification when it operates a set of businesses that are not logically associated with one another.

6. Describe how corporate-level strategies are implemented.

   - Strategy implementation at the corporate level addresses two issues:
     o how the organization will go about its diversification
     o the way an organization is managed once it has diversified
   - Businesses accomplish this in three ways:
     o developing new products internally
     o replacing suppliers (backward vertical integration) or customers (forward vertical integration)
     o engaging in mergers and acquisitions
   - Organizations manage diversification through the organization structure that they adopt and through portfolio management techniques.
   - The BCG matrix classifies an organization's diversified businesses as dogs, cash cows, question marks, or stars according to market share and market growth rate.
   - The GE Business Screen classifies businesses as winners, losers, question marks, average businesses, or profit producers according to industry attractiveness and competitive position.

7. Discuss international and global strategies.

   - Although there are many similarities in developing domestic and international strategies, international firms have three additional sources of competitive advantage unavailable to domestic firms. These are:
     o global efficiencies
     o multimarket flexibility
     o worldwide learning

- Firms participating in international business usually adopt one of four strategic alternatives:
  - the home replication strategy
  - the multidomestic strategy
  - the global strategy
  - the transnational strategy

- Each of these strategies has advantages and disadvantages in terms of its ability to help firms be responsive to local circumstances and to achieve the benefits of global efficiencies.

# Discussion Questions

### Questions for Review

1. Define the four parts of a SWOT analysis.

2. Describe the relationship between a distinctive competency, a competitive advantage, and a sustained competitive advantage.

3. List and describe Porter's generic strategies and the Miles and Snow typology of strategies.

4. What are the characteristics of businesses in each of the four cells of the BCG matrix?

### Questions for Analysis

5. Describe the process that an organization follows when using a deliberate strategy. How does this process differ when an organization implements an emergent strategy?

6. Which strategy should a firm develop first—its business-level or its corporate-level strategy? Describe the relationship between a firm's business- and corporate-level strategies.

7. Volkswagen sold its original Beetle automobile in the United States until the 1970s. The original Beetle was made of inexpensive materials, was built using an efficient mass-production technology, and offered few options. Then, in the 1990s Volkswagen introduced its new Beetle, which has a distinctive style, provides more optional features, and is priced for upscale buyers. What was Volkswagen's strategy with the original Beetle—product differentiation, low cost, or focus? Which strategy did Volkswagen implement with its new Beetle? Explain your answers.

### Questions for Application

8. Assume that you are the owner and manager of a small business. Write a strategy for your business. Be sure to include each of the three primary strategic components.

9. Interview a manager and categorize the business- and corporate-level strategies of his or her organization according to Porter's generic strategies, the Miles and Snow typology, and extent of diversification.

10. Give an example of a corporation following a single-product strategy, a related diversification strategy, and an unrelated diversification strategy. What level of performance would you expect from each firm, based on its strategy? Examine the firm's profitability to see whether your expectations were accurate.

# Building Effective Decision-Making Skills

### Exercise Overview

Decision-making skills refer to the ability to recognize and define problems and opportunities correctly and then to select an appropriate course of action for solving problems or capitalizing on opportunities. As we noted in this chapter, many organizations use SWOT analysis as part of the strategy-formulation process. This exercise will help you better understand both how managers obtain the information they need to perform such an analysis and how they use it as a framework for making decisions.

## Exercise Background

SWOT is an acronym for *Strengths*, *Weaknesses*, *Opportunities*, and *Threats*. The idea behind SWOT is that a good strategy exploits an organization's opportunities and strengths while neutralizing threats and avoiding or correcting weaknesses.

You've just been hired to run a medium-size company that manufactures electric motors, circuit breakers, and similar electronic components for industrial use. In recent years, the firm's financial performance has gradually eroded, and your job is to turn things around.

At one time, the firm was successful in part because it was able to charge premium prices for top-quality products. In recent years, however, management has tried cutting costs as a means of bringing prices in line with those of new competitors in the market. Unfortunately, the strategy hasn't worked very well, with the effect of cost cutting being primarily a fall-off in product quality. Convinced that a new strategy is called for, you've decided to begin with a SWOT analysis.

## Exercise Task

Reviewing the situation, you take the following steps:

1. List the sources that you'll use to gather information about the firm's strengths, weaknesses, opportunities, and threats.

2. Then ask yourself: For what types of information are data readily available on the Internet? What categories of data are difficult or impossible to find on the Internet?

(*Note*: When using the Internet, be sure to provide specific websites or URLs.)

3. Next, rate each source that you consult in terms of probable reliability.

4. Finally, ask yourself how confident you'd be in basing decisions on the information that you've obtained.

# Building Effective Conceptual Skills

## Exercise Overview

Conceptual skills require you to think in the abstract, and they're particularly important to top managers who are responsible for managing a firm's strategy. Because strategic management is a process of pursuing goals in a competitive environment, it naturally invites metaphors involving war or sports. And that's one reason why people tend to forget that cooperation is often a viable strategic alternative to competition. Indeed, cooperation has been a popular business strategy in many countries for years, and the choice of cooperative alternatives—such as strategic alliances and joint ventures—is also on the rise in the United States. The game that we'll play in this exercise is designed to illustrate the advantages of cooperative strategy as an alternative to competitive strategy.

## Exercise Background

Needless to say, both competitive and cooperative strategies can be quite complex when you're trying to implement them in an organizational context. Perhaps, however, we can simplify matters by playing a simple game.

The game we have in mind reflects a classic situation that has proved quite useful in demonstrating some basic concepts in game theory. Here's the original "Prisoner's Dilemma" scenario:

*Authorities suspect two criminals of a crime but don't have enough evidence to convict either of them. So they separate the two and offer each prisoner a deal:*

- *If one rats on the other and the other refuses to rat, the rat goes free and the other prisoner gets a full 10-year sentence.*

- *If both refuse to rat, then both get lesser six-month sentences.*
- *If each rats on the other, both get reduced five-year sentences.*

*The prisoners must choose one of the two options—to rat or not to rat.*

*Assuming that the lowest possible sentence is of optimal value to the prisoners, what's the optimal outcome—that is, the outcome that's most beneficial to both prisoners?*

The optimal outcome for *both* prisoners occurs when they cooperate and neither rats on the other: Each gets the lowest possible sentence (six months). The most common outcome, however, is mutual ratting: Both rat and both get five-year sentences.

Game theorists use the "Prisoner's Dilemma" scenario as a hypothetical situation in which people are obliged to make a decision about whether to act cooperatively or competitively. Although real life presents us with many "competitive" situations in which cooperation would be more beneficial for both parties, people often gravitate toward competition—an option that often leads to less-than-optimal outcomes. The game that you're about to play should be a good illustration of the point.

### Exercise Task

1. Break into small groups and play the board game according to the instructions you receive from your professor.

2. Present your group's results to the class.

3. Analyze the results reported by every group and be prepared to share your thoughts about the outcomes.

## Skill-Building Personal Assessment

Effective strategic management requires strong conceptual skills. Effective conceptual skills, in turn, often rely on our abilities to solve problems. This personal assessment will give you insights into your preferred problem solving style.

For each of the following questions, indicate the response that usually describes your concerns and behaviors. There are no right or wrong answers to the questions. For each question, indicate which of the two alternative statements is more characteristic of you. Some statements may seem to be equally characteristic or uncharacteristic of you. While that may be true, try to choose the statement that is relatively more characteristic of what you do or feel in your everyday life. You will be working with pairs of statements and will have 5 points to distribute among the statements. Points may be divided between each A and B statement in any of the following combination pairs.

- If A is completely characteristic of you and B is completely uncharacteristic,

  | A | B |
  |---|---|
  | 5 | 0 |

  write a 5 on your answer sheet under A and a 0 under B.
- If A is considerably more characteristic of you and B is somewhat characteristic,

  | A | B |
  |---|---|
  | 4 | 1 |

  write a 4 on your answer sheet under A and a 1 under B.
- If A is only slightly more characteristic of you than B, write a 3 on your answer

  | A | B |
  |---|---|
  | 3 | 2 |

  sheet under A and a 2 under B.
- Each of the above three combinations may be used in reverse under. For example,

  | A | B |
  |---|---|
  | 2 | 3 |

  should you feel that B is slightly more characteristic of you than A, write a 2 on your answer sheet under A and a 3 under B (and so on, for A = 1, B = 4; or A = 0 and B = 5).

Be sure that the numbers you assign to each pair sum to 5 points. Relate each question in the index to your own behavior. Remember, there is no right or wrong answer. Attempts to give a "correct" response merely distort the meaning of your answers and render the inventory's results valueless.

| Questions | Score |
|---|---|
| 1. Are you more<br>(A) pragmatic<br>(B) idealistic | A \| B |
| 2. Are you more impressed by<br>(A) standards<br>(B) sentiments | A \| B |
| 3. Are you more interested in that which<br>(A) convinces you by facts<br>(B) emotionally moves you | A \| B |
| 4. It is worse to<br>(A) be practical<br>(B) have a boring routine | A \| B |
| 5. Are you more attracted to<br>(A) a person with common sense<br>(B) a creative person | A \| B |
| 6. In judging others, are you more swayed by<br>(A) the rules<br>(B) the situation | A \| B |
| 7. Are you more interested in<br>(A) what has happened<br>(B) what can happen | A \| B |
| 8. Do you more often have<br>(A) presence of mind<br>(B) warm emotions | A \| B |
| 9. Are you more frequently<br>(A) a realistic sort of person<br>(B) an imaginative sort of person | A \| B |
| 10. Are you more<br>(A) faithful<br>(B) logical | A \| B |

| Questions | Score |
|---|---|
| 11. Are you more<br>(A) action oriented<br>(B) creation oriented | A \| B |
| 12. Which guides you more,<br>(A) your brain<br>(B) your heart | A \| B |
| 13. Do you take pride in your<br>(A) realistic outlook<br>(B) imaginative ability | A \| B |
| 14. Which is more of a personal compliment:<br>(A) you are consistent in reasoning<br>(B) you are considerate of others | A \| B |
| 15. Are you more drawn to<br>(A) basics<br>(B) implications | A \| B |
| 16. It is better to be<br>(A) fair<br>(B) sentimental | A \| B |
| 17. Would you rather spend time with<br>(A) realistic people<br>(B) idealistic people | A \| B |
| 18. Would you describe yourself as<br>(A) hard<br>(B) soft | A \| B |
| 19. Would your friends say that you are<br>(A) someone who is filled by new ideas<br>(B) someone who is a realist | A \| B |
| 20. It is better to be called a person who shows<br>(A) feelings<br>(B) reasonable consistency | A \| B |

# Management at Work

## The Most Admired Strategist of the Twentieth Century

> "We must be prepared for [dangers and difficulties] like men in business who do not waste energy in vain talk and idle action."
>
> —NELSON MANDELA

As a leader of the African National Congress (ANC), Nelson Mandela played a significant role in planning the strategy of the organization, which was dedicated to the overthrow of the apartheid regime in South Africa. *Apartheid*—a systematic policy of racial segregation—was enforced in South Africa from 1948 to 1994 through legislation, policing, and the often violent suppression of resistance, and Mandela was prominent among the leaders who called for strikes, boycotts, and other acts of defiance, including violence, as a legitimate defense against the increasing violence of government repression.

Given that he was sentenced to life in prison in 1964, Mandela was forced to embrace a long-term strategy in contributing to the cause of ANC. Fortunately, he never doubted the eventual collapse of apartheid, and because he regarded himself and his fellow political prisoners as leaders of a government in waiting, he never ceased pursuing strategies designed to ensure not only the fall of the current regime but the success of the new one in which he hoped to play a part.

Norman Chorn, founder of the Australia-based Centre for Strategic Development, considers Mandela (who died in 2013) a prime example of a strategist who understood the relationship between long-term thinking and flexible tactics. Over time, says Chorn, leaders find themselves caught up in cycles of opportunities and challenges, but "the more worthwhile the goal," the easier it is to accept the need to adjust one's strategy. It helps, Chorn adds, if you can explain how every step you take ultimately gets you closer to your final objective.

Consider, for example, Mandela's evolving stance toward the role of violence as a tactic in civil resistance. In the early 1950s, the ANC espoused a program of nonviolence, consisting mostly of strikes and protests, but by 1953, Mandela had concluded that the strategy wasn't working. In September of that year, he delivered a speech that was to become famous as his "No Easy Walk to Freedom" address: "Dangers and difficulties," he declared, "have not deterred us in the past. They will not frighten us now. But we must be prepared for them like men in business who do not waste energy in vain talk and idle action."

By 1961, he had helped to form an underground military wing of the ANC, which carried out its first missions—bomb attacks on government installations—in December of that year. Mandela embraced violence as a tactic for two reasons. First, he deemed it the only effective response to escalating government violence against peaceful resistance. Second, he was convinced that more radical young people outside the ANC were ready to take up arms; if the ANC failed to provide them with leadership, it risked becoming irrelevant and forfeiting any claim to leadership in post-apartheid South African society.

Mandela was arrested on charges of treason in 1962 and imprisoned in 1964. In 1985, after nearly two decades of hard labor and confinement in an eight-foot-by-eight-foot cell, Mandela made a decision that Paul Schoemaker, professor of strategic decision making at the University of Pennsylvania's Wharton School of Business, regards as one of several "crucial judgments that cemented his greatness." In August of that year, South African president P.W. Botha offered to release Mandela from prison on the condition that he renounce violence as a tactic of resistance. "Let *him* renounce violence," replied Mandela. "… I am not prepared to sell the birthright of the people to be free." In refusing the government's offer of freedom, Mandela not only underscored his commitment to the long-term objective that justified the use of violence, but also established himself as a leader who placed the long-term objective of reforming South African society above his own personal sacrifice. "Mandela's remarkable story," contends Schoemaker,

> *holds valuable lessons for other leaders involved in deep struggles, foremost among which are the importance of holding firm to a morally just vision and the ability to influence a sequence of key strategic decisions over time … in order to bring about truly remarkable results.*

Schoemaker hastens to add that Mandela's strategic decision to decline release from prison reflected his "keen situational awareness"—namely, his conviction that political change was both inevitable and imminent. And in this, Madela was right: In the same year, Botha, under intense international political and economic pressure, indicated a willingness to seek a resolution to the decades-long conflict. Between 1985 and 1989, Mandela was shuttled back and forth from prison to a series of secret meetings designed to lay the groundwork for future negotiations between the government and anti-apartheid organizations. In 1990, Botha's successor, F.W. de Klerk, lifted the ban on the ANC and announced Mandela's unconditional release after 27 years in prison. Representatives of the ANC and the South African government continued to meet through 1993, when an interim constitution was ratified. On April 27, 1994, the ANC won 62 percent of the votes in the country's first election in which members of all races were allowed to vote. Under the newly formed Government of National Unity, the National Assembly elected Nelson Mandela president.

As it happens, the negotiations were almost sabotaged in June 1993, when a popular black activist was murdered by a white extremist. Chris Hani, former head of the armed wing of the ANC, was the charismatic spokesman for the young and more radical faction of the anti-apartheid movement and thus an important player in the ongoing negotiations between the ANC and the government. At his trial, Hani's assassin admitted that the murder was intended to spark a race war that would derail negotiations and the process of ending white rule in South Africa. The plot had nearly worked, as violence broke out around the country amid calls for revenge.

Warning the government that there could be no further delays in reaching an agreement on a new constitution, Mandela made what Schoemaker identifies as another significant strategic decision. At great risk to his own credibility, he went on TV to call for calm and national unity. In the process, he not only solidified his own image as a forceful leader, but demonstrated to white South Africans that, under ANC leadership, a new postapartheid government would be committed to holding the country together.

The address was a risky decision: Had Mandela failed to quell the violence, he would have demonstrated that neither he nor his organization could control their own partisans, much less provide leadership for the entire country. For Norman Chorn, the decision reflected Mandela's understanding that "the system drives behavior"—that such behavior as resistance to change and the desire for retaliation have been "shaped by the system" under which people are obliged to live. White South Africans, for example, were "driven by a fear of losing privilege" and black South Africans by a long and "systematic denial of rights." As usual, says Chorn, the pragmatic Mandela understood that "addressing the situation through systems and structures can offer better outcomes for the leader seeking to create meaningful change."

## Case Questions

1. In what ways can the strategies of an organization like the African National Congress (ANC) be compared to those of a business organization? In order to respond to this question, focus on the chapter sections entitled "The Nature of Strategic Management" and "Using SWOT Analysis to Formulate Strategy."

2. "Always keep your eye on the long-term goal," advises Norman Chorn:

   *[A]t every set-back and obstacle, [Nelson Mandela] kept his sights fixed on his objective and did not get distracted. He recognized that he would have to adjust his approach as the circumstances changed, but he never wavered in his goal. Strategic leadership is about having a longer term, big-picture view of your goal. It means that you have to be flexible in the particular tactics that you use. … [W]ith every step you take, you should be able to explain how it gets you closer to your final objective.*

   First, explain in your own words what Nelson Mandela's long-term goal was. Then show (as precisely as possible) how one or two of his strategic decisions was aimed directly at that long-term goal.

   How might he (or you) have been distracted in each case by the appeal of a shorter-term tactic?

3. According to Paul H. Schoemaker,

   *What Nelson Mandela offers aspiring strategic leaders is a living example of how complex societal forces, uncompromising values, and key moments of decision can be woven together over time, and across political, legal and economic domains, into a compelling vision.*

   In what ways might the contemporary CEO of a large organization put these lessons to use? To approach this question, first imagine a scenario in which such a CEO is faced with opportunities and challenges analogous to those faced by Mandela. Then offer a series of suggestions (as concrete as possible) on how he or she might apply lessons learned from Mandela's experience.

4. A former anti-apartheid leader recalls that Mandela did not try to lead the movement away from armed resistance. He was, however, "a great leader because he recognized that the movement had become a civil insurrection, a largely nonviolent struggle. A great leader

is one who recognizes where the movement is and leads it accordingly, not one who says, 'Do it my way!'"

First, explain in your own words what Nelson Mandela's long-term goal was. Then explain why, as a strategic tactic, nonviolence was ultimately more consistent than violence with Mandela's long-term goal. What features in the ANC's social and political environment dictated that nonviolence would ultimately be necessary for Mandela to reach his long-term goal?

## Case References

Paul H. Schoemaker, "Lasting Legacy: Nelson Mandela's Evolution as a Strategic Leader," *Knowledge@Wharton* (July 9, 2013), http://knowledge.wharton.upenn.edu, on September 19, 2014; Norman Chorn, "Leadership Lessons from Nelson Mandela," *Innovatum* (January 2010), www.centstrat.com, on September 19, 2014; Ta-Nehisi Coates, "Mandela and the Question of Violence," *The Atlantic* (December 11, 2013), www.theatlantic.com, on September 21, 2014; Stephen Zunes, "Mandela's Utilitarianism and the Struggle for Liberation," *openDemocracy* (December 13, 2013), www.opendemocracy.net, on September 19, 2014; Robyn Dixon, "Nelson Mandela's Legacy: As a Leader, He Was Willing to Use Violence," *Los Angeles Times* (December 6, 2013), www.latimes.com, on September 22, 2014; Stefan Semanowitz, "Chris Hani's Assassination Put South Africa on the Brink of Civil War," *Vice* (April 11, 2013), www.vice.com, on September 22, 2014; Allan Little, "How Mandela Responded to the Assassination of Chris Hani" [video], *BBC Newsnight* (December 9, 2013), www.youtube.com, on September 23, 2014.

## YOU MAKE THE CALL  Stay Hungry

1. A few definitions:

   - *Marketing strategy*: comprehensive plan for increasing sales and achieving a sustainable competitive advantage
   - *Marketing plan:* plan for satisfying market needs and reaching measurable marketing goals
   - *Tactical marketing plan*: marketing plan detailing specific actions to be accomplished in the current year

   Technically speaking, which of these three categories *best* describes the *THG* and *THG: Catching Fire* campaigns described in the case? Judging from the details provided by the case, what can you tell about Lionsgate's objectives for the two categories that you did not choose in answering the first part of the question?

2. Lionsgate is a Canadian-American film production and distribution company. It's the largest and most successful "mini-major" film company in North America—meaning that it's not quite as big as the diversified media conglomerates that command approximately 90 percent of U.S. and Canadian box office revenues. Although it has traditionally focused on foreign and independent films, it has also had a hand in a few commercially successful series such as *The Hunger Games.*

   Judging from the *THG* case, what would you say are Lionsgate's *organizational strengths*? Besides some fairly obvious *common strengths*, does it appear to be able to call upon any *distinctive competencies*? Still judging from the *THG* case, what can you say about Lionsgate's *corporate-level strategies*? To what extent, for example, does it practice a *single-product strategy*? How about *related diversification*?

3. In addition to *The Hunger Games* and *The Hunger Games: Catching Fire* websites (www.thehungergames.co.uk/ and www.catchingfiremovie.com/), Lionsgate marketers made use of such social media channels as Facebook, Twitter, YouTube, and Instagram. What are the distinctive features of each of these channels? In what ways did Lionsgate marketers gear different aspects of their campaign to the different features of the channels available to them?

4. What about you? What are your social media habits and preferences? Which channels do you use, and what, primarily, do you use them for? Are you a "destination visitor" or a "social visitor"? Are you a "core fan" of anything? Do you feel that social media "empower" you by letting you express your opinion, choose what content to pay attention to, or help you "identify who you are"?

# Endnotes

1  Adam B. Vary, "Five Things You Should Know about the Curious New Marketing Campaign for 'The Hunger Games: Catching Fire,'" *Buzzfeed* (August 23, 2013), www.buzzfeed.com, on September 27, 2014; John Furrier, "How a Startup Powered *Hunger Games* into a Global Social Phenomenon—A Money Machine," *Forbes* (March 25, 2012), www.forbes.com, on September 26, 2014; Ari Karpel, "Inside 'The Hunger Games' Social Media Machine," *Fast Company* (April 9, 2012), www.fastcocreate, on September 26, 2014; Taylor Smith, *"The Hunger Games* Isn't Hungry for Social Media," *prSPEAK* (April 13, 2012), www.pancommunications.com, on September 29, 2014; Mike Girard, *"The Hunger Games'* Social Media Campaign: A Case Study in Content Marketing," *exacttarget* (March 26, 2012), www.exacttarget.com, on September 26, 2014; Marc Graser, "Lionsgate's Tim Palen Crafts Stylish Universe for 'Hunger Games: Catching Fire,'" *Variety* (October 29, 2013), http://variety.com, on September 27, 2014; Amy Wilkinson, "'Hunger Games' Goes Viral for 100-Day Countdown," *MTV News* (December 15, 2011), www.mtv.com, on September 28, 2014.

2  For early discussions of strategic management, see Kenneth Andrews, *The Concept of Corporate Strategy*, rev. ed. (Homewood, IL: Dow Jones–Irwin, 1980); and Igor Ansoff, *Corporate Strategy* (New York: McGraw-Hill, 1965). For more recent perspectives, see Michael E. Porter, "What Is Strategy?" *Harvard Business Review*, November–December 1996, pp. 61–78; Kathleen M. Eisenhardt, "Strategy as Strategic Decision Making," *Sloan Management Review*, Spring 1999, pp. 65–74; Sarah Kaplan and Eric Beinhocker, "The Real Value of Strategic Planning," *Sloan Management Review*, Winter 2003, pp. 71–80.

3  *Hoover's Handbook of American Business 2015* (Austin, TX: Hoover's Business Press, 2015), pp. 32–33.

4  "Abercrombie & Fitch Improves Supply Chain with Management Dynamics," *Retail Technology Review*, April 13, 2010.

5  See Gary Hamel, "Strategy as Revolution," *Harvard Business Review*, July–August 1996, pp. 69–82.

6  See Henry Mintzberg, "Patterns in Strategy Formulation," *Management Science*, October 1978, pp. 934–948; Henry Mintzberg, "Strategy Making in Three Modes," *California Management Review*, 1973, pp. 44–53.

7  T. R. Holcomb, R. M. Holmes, Jr., and B. L. Connelly, "Making the Most of What You Have: Managerial Ability as a Source of Resource Value Creation," *Strategic Management Journal*, Vol. 32, No. 5, 2011, pp. 457–486.

8  Jay Barney, "Firm Resources and Sustained Competitive Advantage," *Journal of Management*, June 1991, pp. 99–120; see also T. Russell Crook, David J. Ketchen Jr., James G. Combs, and Samuel Y. Todd, "Strategic Resources and Performance: A Meta-Analysis," *Strategic Management Journal*, 2008, Vol. 29, pp. 1141–1154.

9  Jay Barney, "Strategic Factor Markets," *Management Science*, December 1986, pp. 1231–1241. See also Constantinos C. Markides, "A Dynamic View of Strategy," *Sloan Management Review*, Spring 1999, pp. 55–64.

10  See Michael Porter, *Competitive Strategy* (New York: Free Press, 1980).

11  Porter, *Competitive Strategy*. See also Colin Campbell-Hunt, "What Have We Learned about Generic Competitive Strategy? A Meta-Analysis," *Strategic Management Journal*, 2000, Vol. 21, pp. 127–154. See also Michael E. Porter, "The Five Competitive Forces that Shape Strategy," *Harvard Business Review*, January 2008, pp. 79–90 for a recent update.

12  Ian C. MacMillan and Rita Gunther McGrath, "Discovering New Points of Differentiation," *Harvard Business Review*, July–August 1997, pp. 133–136.

13  "In a Water Fight, Coke and Pepsi Try Opposite Tacks," *Wall Street Journal*, April 18, 2009, pp. A1, A8.

14  "It Ain't the Bellagio…" *Business Week*, June 20–26, 2011, pp. 84–85.

15  Raymond E. Miles and Charles C. Snow, *Organizational Strategy, Structure, and Process* (New York: McGraw-Hill, 1978); see also Wayne DeSarbo, C. Anthony Benedetto, Michael Song, and Indrajit Sinha, "Revisiting the Miles and Snow Strategic Framework: Uncovering the Interrelationships Between Strategic Types, Capabilities, Environmental Uncertainty, and Firm Performance," *Strategic Management Journal*, 2005, Vol. 26, pp. 47–74.

16  See Donald L. Laurie, Yves L. Doz, and Claude P. Sheer, "Creating New Growth Platforms," *Harvard Business Review*, May 2006, pp. 80–91.

17  "Inside RadioShack's Collapse," *Bloomberg Businessweek*, February 9–February 15, 2015, pp. 54–59.

18  See Lawrence G. Hrebiniak, "Obstacles to Effective Strategy Implementation," *Organizational Dynamics*, February 2006, pp. 12–21.

19  Robert Kaplan and David Norton, "How to Implement a New Strategy Without Disrupting Your Organization," *Harvard Business Review*, March 2006, pp. 100–109.

20  Donald Sull, Rebecca Homkes, and Charles Sull, "Why Strategy Execution Unravels—And What to Do About It," *Harvard Business Review*, March 2015, pp. 58–66.

21  *Fortune*, February 21, 2005, p. 100.

22  Suzanne Kapner, "The Almighty Dollar," *Fortune*, April 27, 2009, pp. 64–66.

23  See Scott D. Anthony, Matt Eyring, and Lib Gibson, "Mapping Your Innovation Strategy," *Harvard Business Review*, May 2011, pp. 104–113.

24  Larry Huston and Nabil Sakkab, "Connect and Develop: Inside Procter & Gamble's New Model for Innovation," *Harvard Business Review*, March 2006, pp. 58–67.

25  Alfred Chandler, *Strategy and Structure: Chapters in the History of the American Industrial Enterprise* (Cambridge, MA: MIT Press, 1962); Richard Rumelt, *Strategy, Structure, and Economic Performance* (Cambridge, MA: Division of Research, Graduate School of Business Administration, Harvard University, 1974); Oliver Williamson, *Markets and Hierarchies* (New York: Free Press, 1975).

26  "Mars's Takeover of Wrigley Creates a Global Powerhouse," *Wall Street Journal*, April 29, 2010, p. 1A.

27  K. L. Stimpert and Irene M. Duhaime, "Seeing the Big Picture: The Influence of Industry, Diversification, and Business Strategy on Performance," *Academy of Management Journal*, 1997, Vol. 40, No. 3, pp. 560–583.

28  See Chandler, *Strategy and Structure*; Yakov Amihud and Baruch Lev, "Risk Reduction as a Managerial Motive for Conglomerate Mergers," *Bell Journal of Economics*, 1981, pp. 605–617.

29  Chandler, *Strategy and Structure*; Williamson, *Markets and Hierarchies*.

30  For a discussion of the limitations of unrelated diversification, see Jay Barney and William G. Ouchi, *Organizational Economics* (San Francisco: Jossey-Bass, 1986).

31  See Belen Villalonga and Anita McGahan, "The Choice among Acquisitions, Alliances, and Divestitures," *Strategic Management Journal*, 2005, Vol. 26, pp. 1183–1208; see also Xiaoli Yin and Mark Shanley, "Industry Determinants of the 'Merger Versus Alliance' Decision," *Academy of Management Review*, 2008, Vol. 33, No. 2, pp. 473–491.

32  "Latest Merger Boom Is Happening in China, and Bears Watching," *Wall Street Journal*, July 30, 1997, pp. A1, A9; "A Breakthrough in Bavaria," *BusinessWeek*, August 4, 1997, p. 54.

33  http://www.brainyquote.com/quotes/keywords/acquisitions.html

34  Kathleen M. Eisenhardt and D. Charles Galunic, "Coevolving—At Last: A Way to Make Synergies Work," *Harvard Business Review*, January–February 2000, pp. 91–100; see also Harry G. Barkema and Mario Schijven, "How Do Firms Learn to Make Acquisitions? A Review of Past Research and an Agenda for the Future," *Journal of Management*, 2008, Vol. 34, No. 3, pp. 594–634.

35  "Mr. Clean Takes Car-Wash Gig," *Wall Street Journal*, February 5, 2011, p. B1.

36  See Constantinoes C. Markides and Peter J. Williamson, "Corporate Diversification and Organizational Structure: A Resource-Based View," *Academy of Management Journal*, April 1996, pp. 340–367; see also Harry Bowen and Margarethe Wiersema, "Foreign-Based Competition and Corporate Diversification Strategy," *Strategic Management Journal*, 2005, Vol. 26, pp. 1153–1171.

37  See Barry Hedley, "A Fundamental Approach to Strategy Development," *Long Range Planning*, December 1976, pp. 2–11; Bruce Henderson, "The Experience Curve—Reviewed. IV: The Growth Share Matrix of the Product Portfolio," *Perspectives*, No. 135 (Boston: Boston Consulting Group, 1973).

38  "Yum Brands Will Sell A&W, Long John Silver's," *USA Today*, January 18, 2011, p. B3.

39  Michael G. Allen, "Diagramming G.E.'s Planning for What's WATT," in Robert J. Allio and Malcolm W. Pennington (eds.), *Corporate Planning: Techniques and Applications* (New York: AMACOM, 1979). Limits of this approach are discussed in R. A. Bettis and W. K. Hall, "The Business Portfolio Approach: Where It Falls Down in Practice," *Long Range Planning*, March 1983, pp. 95–105.

40  "Unilever to Sell Specialty-Chemical Unit to ICI of the U.K. for About $8 Billion," *Wall Street Journal*, May 7, 1997, pp. A3, A12; "For Unilever, It's Sweetness and Light," *Wall Street Journal*, April 13, 2000, pp. B1, B4.

41  "Unprofitable Businesses Getting Axed More Often," *Wall Street Journal*, February 17, 2010, pp. B1, B2.

42  Howard Thomas, Timothy Pollock, and Philip Gorman, "Global Strategic Analyses: Frameworks and Approaches," *Academy of Management Executive*, 1999, Vol. 13, No. 1, pp. 70–80.

43  Kasra Ferdows, "Making the Most of Foreign Factories," *Harvard Business Review*, March–April 1997, pp. 73–88.

44  Anil K. Gupta and Vijay Govindarajan, "Knowledge Flows Within Multinational Corporations," *Strategic Management Journal*, 2000, Vol. 21, No. 4, pp. 473–496; see also Jane Lu and Paul Beamish, "International Diversification and Firm Performance: The S-Curve Hypothesis," *Academy of Management Journal*, 2004, Vol. 47, pp. 598–609.

45  Christopher A. Bartlett and Sumantra Ghoshal, *Transnational Management*, 2nd ed. (Chicago: Irwin, 1995), pp. 237–242. See also Tatiana Kostova, "Transnational Transfer of Strategic Organizational Practices: A Contextual Perspective," *Academy of Management Review*, 1999, Vol. 24, No. 2, pp. 308–324.

46  http://www.huffingtonpost.com/rana-florida/mac-cosmetics-frank-toskan_b_1905808.html

©Markus Pfaff/Shutterstock.com

# 8

# MANAGING DECISION MAKING AND PROBLEM SOLVING

**Learning Outcomes**

After studying this chapter, you should be able to:

1. Define decision making and discuss types of decisions and decision-making conditions.

2. Discuss rational perspectives on decision making, including the steps in rational decision making.

3. Describe the behavioral aspects of decision making.

4. Discuss group and team decision making, including the advantages and disadvantages of group and team decision making and how it can be more effectively managed.

## MANAGEMENT IN ACTION    Moneyball on Steroids

"All we can really control is the process and the decision making that comes from that."

—SIG MEJDAL,
HOUSTON ASTROS DIRECTOR OF DECISION SCIENCES

Back in 1989, during the pre-Internet days of fantasy baseball, Northwestern University MBA candidate Jeff Luhnow was commissioner of a pioneer Rotisserie league. Once a week, he'd enter *USA Today* statistics into a personal spreadsheet and fax copies to team owners. He was also a team owner himself and reports that he was pretty successful at drafting the right Major League players to fill out his fantasy roster: "I probably won the league about four times in the ten years I did it," Luhnow recalls. "If you had to punch in every player in the National League by hand, you got to know them pretty well."[1]

It should perhaps come as no surprise, then, that when the World Series got underway in 2013, Luhnow,

as head of the team's scouting department, had drafted 16 of the 25 players on the roster of the National League representative, the St. Louis Cardinals. Actually, it does qualify as *something* of a surprise. Luhnow, who'd graduated from the University of Pennsylvania with dual degrees in economics and engineering and had finished his MBA at Northwestern's Kellogg School of Management, was not a baseball man. He was—among other things—a management consultant at McKinsey and Co., one of the world's premier consulting agencies. Luhnow's specialty was the application of advanced analytics to business decision making. In other words, he collected massive amounts of data and made sense—and use—of it.

And that's the skill that paved Luhnow's way from fantasy league baseball to Major League Baseball. His first job was with the Cardinals, where owner Bill DeWitt Jr. hired him in 2003 to design a better system for evaluating players. The challenge, as Luhnow

The Houston Astros pair their algorithm-oriented management team, along with the quantitative information that their scouts and coaches amass. This combination may prove to be a winner in seasons to come.

Eric Christian Smith/Getty Images

understood it, was "creating and sustaining a scouting and player-development pipeline that can consistently produce Major League players." One of the first things that he did was hire former NASA engineer Sig Mejdal to design a system for organizing all the new data sources that were becoming available to baseball analysts and executives. "These sorts of skills," admits Luhnow, "weren't valued 10 or 15 years ago—or really valuable—because the data that you can use today to help you makes decisions wasn't available."

That data is not only more useful—there's a lot more of it. In fact, says Luhnow, "it's overload for any human being." He hastens to point out that, however, human beings have to make decisions at critical points in the process—who to draft, who to promote, who to re-sign, who to release. Baseball decision makers, adds Mejdal, whose NASA research was designed to uncover the limits of human intuition in making predictions, must deal with an "overwhelming amount of information from different sources with different degrees of certainty associated with each." Technically speaking, it's his responsibility, explains Mejdal, to "identify the attributes that lead to an understanding of the expectancies and variabilities relevant to a particular decision. … That's my job: Creating decision aids based on the analysis in order to assist our decision makers."

In 2006, the Cardinals promoted Luhnow to VP of scouting and player development, and while he oversaw the team's amateur draft, no team in baseball selected more players who would make it to the majors. In 2009, Luhnow, the onetime baseball outsider, was hired as general manager of the Houston Astros. He immediately hired Mejdal as "Director of Decision Sciences." New owner Jim Crane had made his fortune in the logistics business and attributed his success to better data: "If you have better information," he says, "you can run your competitors ragged." He wanted to turn the Astros into the Cardinals, and, fortunately, he also brought a wealth of patience to the task. When Luhnow and Mejdal got their first look at the numbers, they knew what their strategy had to be: They would have to be ruthlessly efficient in stripping down the organization in order to rebuild it. That meant that Crane would have to put up with a few years of losing both baseball games and money.

In Luhnow's first two years, the Astros won 106 games and lost 218. They drew a total of 3.3 million fans—about the same number as they drew in 2007 alone—and local TV ratings occasionally came in at 0.0. Perhaps more importantly, help was hardly on the way from the team's minor league system: In 2010, *Baseball America* declared it the worst in baseball. Luhnow, however, was thinking ahead: "When you're in 2017," he hypothesized, "you don't really care that much about whether you lost 98 or 107 games in 2012. You care about how close you are to winning a championship in 2017."

The Astros lost 107 games in 2012—and 111 in 2013—but things started to look up in 2014, when they lost only 92. Attendance started to pick up, and, more importantly, ESPN ranked the Houston farm system the best in baseball. Like the benchmark Cardinals, the Astros want to build a perennial mid-market contender from within, and 2014 witnessed the first fruits of that strategy, as young talent from the minor league system began taking the field with the Major League team. Mejdal admits, of course, that the Astros' algorithm-oriented management team can't guarantee results over which it has no control. "All we can really control," he says, 'is the process and the decision making that comes from that. … Our attention and energies are focused on the process. There are no guarantees in baseball, but we feel that if we have a good process, as time goes on, we will have good results."

What is that process? "The basis of all our decisions," explains Luhnow, "is the reports we get from our scouts." All of those reports then go into the team's proprietary system—dubbed Ground Control—where they're collated with scouting reports from previous years. Some of the data is "hard"—how fast is a pitcher's fastball, how fast can a player get to first base; a lot of it is "soft"—what's a player's work ethic, how likely is he to get injured. An algorithm-driven system translates every piece of information into a single language and runs regressions against a database stretching back to the mid-1990s. If a young pitcher's mechanics don't conform to a model described by reports, the system tells Luhnow and Mejdal how often previous pitchers with the same variation got hurt. If a young hitter's power stroke is similar to that of past players at his age, it tells them how his swing is likely to develop. The final result is a numerical projection that gives a quantitative answer to a single bottom-line question: How many runs is a player likely to produce (or prevent) compared with what the team will probably have to pay him?

Astro scouts, most of them longtime baseball men, are apparently comfortable with the system: "They're not asking us to be sabermetricians," says one veteran scout. "They're asking us to do what we've always done." The difference is the analytics-driven approach of Luhnow's front-office team to the synthesis of quantitative and qualitative information. "How do you combine the soft information with the hard information," asks Luhnow, "in a way that allows you to make the best decisions? That's the crux of what we're trying to do here." The question, in other words, is how do you make decision making more reliable, and the answer—at least for ex-blackjack dealer Sig Mejdal—is to produce a metric that will make decisions about baseball players as simple as *hit or stay.*

Regardless of their industry—banking, retailing, manufacturing, transportation, health care, or professional sports—all managers have to make decisions about resource allocations, goals, options, and strategies. Indeed, making effective decisions, as well as recognizing when bad decisions have been made and quickly responding to mistakes, is a key ingredient in organizational effectiveness. Indeed, some experts believe that decision making is the most basic and fundamental of all managerial activities.[2] Thus we discuss it here in the context of the first management function, planning. Keep in mind, however, that although decision making is perhaps most closely linked to the planning function, it is also part of organizing, leading, and controlling.

We begin our discussion by exploring the nature of decision making. We then describe rational perspectives on decision making. Behavioral aspects of decision making are then introduced and described. We conclude with a discussion of group and team decision making.

**decision making**
The act of choosing one alternative from among a set of alternatives

**decision-making process**
Recognizing and defining the nature of a decision situation, identifying alternatives, choosing the "best" alternative, and putting it into practice

# The Nature of Decision Making

Managers at Disney made the decision to buy Marvel Comics for $4.3 billion. At about the same time, the general manager of the Ford dealership in Bryan, Texas, made a decision to sponsor a local youth soccer team for $250. Each of these examples reflects a decision, but the decisions differ in many ways. Thus, as a starting point in understanding decision making, we must first explore the meaning of decision making as well as types of decisions and conditions under which decisions are made.[3]

### Decision Making Defined

Decision making can refer to either a specific act or a general process. Decision making *per se* is the act of choosing one alternative from among a set of alternatives. The decision-making process, however, is much more than this. One step of the process, for example, is that the person making the decision must both recognize that a decision is necessary and identify the set of feasible alternatives before selecting one. Hence, the decision-making process includes recognizing and defining the nature of a decision situation, identifying alternatives, choosing the "best" alternative, and putting it into practice.[4]

The word *best*, of course, implies effectiveness. Effective decision making requires that the decision maker understand the situation driving the decision. Most people would consider an effective decision to be one that optimizes some set of factors, such as profits, sales, employee welfare, and market share. In some situations, though, an effective decision may be one that minimizes losses, expenses, or employee

A great deal of information gathering and discussion occurred at high levels of Disney before they made the decision to buy Marvel Comics for $4.3 billion.

> "Too many think inaction is the least risky path. Sometimes action is the most conservative and safest path. Not doing anything is exceedingly dangerous."
>
> —FREDERICK SMITH, CEO OF FEDEX[5]

turnover. It may even mean selecting the best method for going out of business, laying off employees, or terminating a strategic alliance.

We should also note that managers make decisions about both problems and opportunities. For example, making decisions about how to cut costs by 10 percent reflects a problem—an undesirable situation that requires a solution. But decisions are also necessary in situations of opportunity. Learning that the firm is earning higher-than-projected profits, for example, requires a subsequent decision. Should the extra funds be used to increase shareholder dividends, reinvest in current operations, or expand into new markets?

Of course, it may take a long time before a manager can know if the right decision was made. For example, in 2009 government leaders made the decision to invest billions of dollars in failing financial institutions and other businesses. It will be years—or perhaps decades—before economists and other experts will know if those were sound decisions or if the United States would have been better off allowing those businesses to fail.

**programmed decision**
A decision that is fairly structured or recurs with some frequency (or both)

**nonprogrammed decision**
A decision that is relatively unstructured and occurs much less often than a programmed decision

## Types of Decisions

Managers must make many different types of decisions. In general, however, most decisions fall into one of two categories: programmed and nonprogrammed.[6] A programmed decision is one that is relatively structured or recurs with some frequency (or both). Starbucks uses programmed decisions to purchase new supplies of coffee beans, cups, and napkins, and Starbucks employees are trained in exact procedures for brewing coffee. Likewise, the Bryan Ford dealer made a decision that he will sponsor a youth soccer team each year. Thus, when the soccer club president calls, the dealer already knows what he will do. Many decisions about basic operating systems and procedures and standard organizational transactions are of this variety and can therefore be programmed.[7]

Nonprogrammed decisions, on the other hand, are relatively unstructured and occur much less often. Disney's decision to buy Pixar was a nonprogrammed decision. Managers faced with such decisions must treat each one as unique, investing enormous amounts of time, energy, and resources into exploring the situation from all perspectives. Intuition and experience are major factors in nonprogrammed decisions. Most of the decisions made by top managers involving strategy (including mergers, acquisitions, and takeovers) and organization design are nonprogrammed. So are decisions about new facilities, new products, labor contracts, and legal issues.

When the general manager of the Ford dealership in Bryan, Texas, made a decision to sponsor a local youth soccer team for $250, he was making a programmed decision. Each year he will make this same contribution.

*Monkey Business Images/Shutterstock.com*

## Decision-Making Conditions

Just as there are different kinds of decisions, there are also different conditions in which decisions must be made. Managers sometimes have an

## FIGURE 8.1 DECISION-MAKING CONDITIONS

Most major decisions in organizations today are made under a state of uncertainty. Managers making decisions in these circumstances must be sure to learn as much as possible about the situation and approach the decision from a logical and rational perspective.

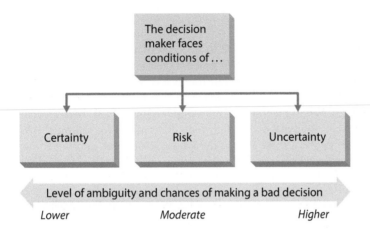

almost perfect understanding of conditions surrounding a decision, but at other times they have few clues about those conditions. In general, as shown in Figure 8.1, the circumstances that exist for the decision maker are conditions of certainty, risk, or uncertainty.[8]

**Decision Making under Certainty** When the decision maker knows with reasonable certainty what the alternatives are and what conditions are associated with each alternative, a state of certainty exists. Suppose, for example, that managers at Singapore Airlines make a decision to buy five new jumbo jets. Their next decision is from whom to buy them. Because there are only two companies in the world that make jumbo jets, Boeing and Airbus, Singapore Airlines knows its options exactly. Each has proven products and

**state of certainty**
A condition in which the decision maker knows with reasonable certainty what the alternatives are and what conditions are associated with each alternative

will guarantee prices and delivery dates. The airline thus knows the alternative conditions associated with each. There is little ambiguity and relatively little chance of making a bad decision.

Few organizational decisions, however, are made under conditions of true certainty. The complexity and turbulence of the contemporary business world make such situations rare. Even the airplane purchase decision we just considered has less certainty than it appears. The aircraft companies may not be able to really guarantee delivery dates, so they may write cost-increase or inflation clauses into contracts. Thus the airline may be only partially certain of the conditions surrounding each alternative.

**Decision Making under Risk** A more common decision-making condition is a state of

Singapore Airlines engages in decision making under certainty when deciding from whom to purchase jumbo jets. Only 2 manufacturers make them, Boeing and Airbus, thus reducing the risk of Singapore Airlines making a bad decision.

risk. Under a state of risk, the availability of each alternative and its potential payoffs and costs are all associated with probability estimates.[9] Suppose, for example, that a labor contract negotiator for a company receives a "final" offer from the union right before a strike deadline. The negotiator has two alternatives: to accept or to reject the offer. The risk centers on whether the union representatives are bluffing. If the company negotiator accepts the offer, she avoids a strike but commits to a relatively costly labor contract. If she rejects the contract, she may get a more favorable contract if the union is bluffing, but she may provoke a strike if it is not.

On the basis of past experience, relevant information, the advice of others, and her own judgment, she may conclude that there is about a 75 percent chance that union representatives are bluffing and about a 25 percent chance that they will back up their threats. Thus she can b unstructured and occur much less often. Disney's ase a calculated decision on the two alternatives (accept or reject the contract demands) and the probable consequences of each. When making decisions under a state of risk, managers must reasonably estimate the probabilities associated with each alternative. For example, if the union negotiators are committed to a strike if their demands are not met, and the company negotiator rejects their demands because she guesses they will not strike, her miscalculation will prove costly.

> "What's served me very well, which is easy to say for me now that I'm as successful as I am, is being patient, is not getting impatient and making stupid career decisions."
>
> —ROBERT IGER, DISNEY CEO[10]

**state of risk**
A condition in which the availability of each alternative and its potential payoffs and costs are all associated with probability estimates

**state of uncertainty**
A condition in which the decision maker does not know all the alternatives, the risks associated with each, or the consequences each alternative is likely to have

As indicated in Figure 8.1, decision making under conditions of risk is accompanied by moderate ambiguity and chances of a bad decision. For instance, Ford made the decision to redesign its F-150 pickup, the firm's best-selling and most profitable vehicle. The key element in the new design was to replace the typical steel pickup bed with one made from aluminum. The firm's logic was that aluminum is much lighter than steel, so the F-150 could get better gas mileage with no loss of functionality. The risk was that if buyers rejected the concept of an aluminum pickup, or if the vehicle's quality was compromised by the redesign, then Ford would have done perhaps irreparable harm to the image and reputation of its most important vehicle.

**Decision Making under Uncertainty** Most of the major decision making in contemporary organizations is done under a state of uncertainty. The decision maker does not know all the alternatives, the risks associated with each, or the likely consequences of each alternative. This uncertainty stems from the complexity and dynamism of contemporary organizations and their environments. The emergence of the Internet as a significant force in today's competitive environment has served to increase both revenue potential and uncertainty for most managers.

To make effective decisions in these circumstances, managers must acquire as much relevant information as possible and approach the situation from a logical and rational perspective. Intuition, judgment, and experience always play

The all new 2015 Ford F-150 is made of aluminum instead of the typical steel. This decision was made under a state of risk.

Zoran Karapancev/Shutterstock.com

major roles in the decision-making process under conditions of uncertainty. Even so, uncertainty is the most ambiguous condition for managers and the one most prone to error.[11] Lorraine Brennan O'Neil is the founder and CEO of 10 Minute Manicure, a quick-service salon located in airports. The company found quick success and experienced rapid growth from its start in 2006, but the economic downturn in 2009 required O'Neil to rethink her plans in an attempt to stay afloat through a rocky and unknown future. Knowing that the company no longer had the time to wait and monitor new stores' success, she opted to focus solely on existing stores with profits, shutting down those with losses. Aside from this, she restructured her business plan, seeking nontraditional locations, reducing corporate overhead, cutting products, and developing an online product line as a second source of income.[12]

☐ Managers should seek to program routine decisions but to also recognize when decisions are not programmable.

☐ Managers also need to understand the conditions under which they make decisions.

**Manager's Checklist**

# Rational Perspectives on Decision Making

Most managers like to think of themselves as rational decision makers. And, indeed, many experts argue that managers should try to be as rational as possible in making decisions.[13] This section highlights the fundamental and rational perspectives on decision making.

"Nothing is more difficult, and therefore more precious, than to be able to decide."

—NAPOLEON BONAPARTE[14]

## The Classical Model of Decision Making

The classical decision model is a prescriptive approach that tells managers how they should make decisions. It rests on the assumptions that managers are logical and rational and that they make decisions that are in the best interests of the organization. Figure 8.2 shows how the classical model views the decision-making process.

1. Decision makers have complete information about the decision situation and possible alternatives.
2. They can effectively eliminate uncertainty to achieve a decision condition of certainty.
3. They evaluate all aspects of the decision situation logically and rationally.

As we will see later, these conditions rarely, if ever, actually exist.

**classical decision model**
A prescriptive approach to decision making that tells managers how they should make decisions; assumes that managers are logical and rational and that their decisions will be in the best interests of the organization

---

**FIGURE 8.2  THE CLASSICAL MODEL OF DECISION MAKING**

The classical model of decision making assumes that managers are rational and logical. It tries to prescribe how managers should approach decision situations.

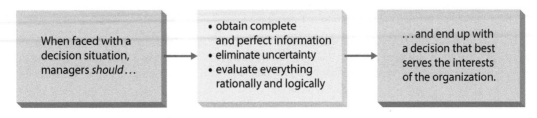

## Steps in Rational Decision Making

A manager who really wants to approach a decision rationally and logically should try to follow the steps in rational decision making, listed in Table 8.1. These steps in rational decision making help keep the decision maker focused on facts and logic and help guard against inappropriate assumptions and pitfalls.

**Recognizing and Defining the Decision Situation** The first step in rational decision making is recognizing that a decision is necessary—that is, there must be some stimulus or spark to initiate the process. For many decisions and problem situations, the stimulus may occur without any prior warning. When equipment malfunctions, the manager must decide whether to repair or replace it. Or, when a major crisis erupts, as described in Chapter 3, the manager must quickly decide how to deal with it. As we already noted, the stimulus for a decision may be either positive or negative. A manager who must decide how to invest surplus funds, for example, faces a positive decision situation. A negative financial stimulus could involve having to trim budgets because of cost overruns.

Inherent in problem recognition is the need to define precisely what the problem is. The manager must develop a complete understanding of the problem, its causes, and its relationship to other factors. This understanding comes from careful analysis and thoughtful consideration of the situation. Consider the situation faced in the international air travel industry. Because of the growth of international travel related to business, education, and tourism, global carriers like Singapore Airlines, KLM, JAL, British Airways, American Airlines, and others need to increase their capacity for international travel. Because most

**steps in rational decision making**
Recognize and define the decision situation; identify appropriate alternatives; evaluate each alternative in terms of its feasibility, satisfactoriness, and consequences; select the best alternative; implement the chosen alternative; follow up and evaluate the results of the chosen alternative

## TABLE 8.1 STEPS IN THE RATIONAL DECISION-MAKING PROCESS

Although the presumptions of the classical decision model rarely exist, managers can still approach decision making with rationality. By following the steps of rational decision making, managers ensure that they are learning as much as possible about the decision situation and its alternatives.

| Step | Detail | Example |
|---|---|---|
| 1. Recognizing and defining the decision situation | Some stimulus indicates that a decision must be made. The stimulus may be positive or negative. | A plant manager sees that employee turnover has increased by 5 percent. |
| 2. Identifying alternatives | Both obvious and creative alternatives are desired. In general, the more important the decision, the more alternatives should be generated. | The plant manager can increase wages, increase benefits, or change hiring standards. |
| 3. Evaluating alternatives | Each alternative is evaluated to determine its feasibility, its satisfactoriness, and its consequences. | Increasing benefits may not be feasible. Increasing wages and changing hiring standards may satisfy all conditions. |
| 4. Selecting the best alternative | Consider all situational factors and choose the alternative that best fits the manager's situation. | Changing hiring standards will take an extended period of time to cut turnover, so increase wages. |
| 5. Implementing the chosen alternative | The chosen alternative is implemented into the organizational system. | The plant manager may need permission from corporate headquarters. The human resource department establishes a new wage structure. |
| 6. Following up and evaluating the results | At some time in the future, the manager should ascertain the extent to which the alternative chosen in step 4 and implemented in step 5 has worked. | The plant manager notes that, six months later, turnover dropped to its previous level. |

major international airports are already operating at or near capacity, adding a significant number of new flights to existing schedules is not feasible. As a result, the most logical alternative is to increase capacity on existing flights. Thus Boeing and Airbus, the world's only manufacturers of large commercial aircraft, recognized an important opportunity and defined their decision situation as how to best respond to the need for increased global travel capacity.[15]

**Identifying Alternatives** Once the decision situation has been recognized and defined, the second step is to identify alternative courses of effective action. Developing both obvious, standard alternatives and creative, innovative alternatives is generally useful.[16] In general, the more important the decision, the more attention is directed to developing alternatives.[17] If the decision involves a multimillion-dollar relocation, a great deal of time and expertise will be devoted to identifying the best locations. JetBlue announced in 2009 that it would be seeking a new location for its corporate offices. After a year of searching and analyzing incentives to relocate to Orlando, the airline decided it would keep its headquarters in Queens, New York.[18] If the problem is to choose a color for the company softball team uniforms, less time and expertise will be brought to bear.

Although managers should seek creative solutions, they must also recognize that various constraints often limit their alternatives. Common constraints include legal restrictions, moral and ethical norms, authority constraints, and constraints imposed by the power and authority of the manager, available technology, economic considerations, and unofficial social norms. Boeing and Airbus identified three different alternatives to address the decision situation of increasing international airline travel capacity: They could independently develop new large planes, they could collaborate in a joint venture to create a single new large plane, or they could modify their largest existing planes to increase their capacity.

**Evaluating Alternatives** The third step in the decision-making process is evaluating each of the alternatives. Figure 8.3 presents a decision tree that can be used to judge different alternatives. The figure suggests that each alternative be evaluated in terms of its *feasibility*, its *satisfactoriness*, and its *consequences*. The first question to ask is whether an alternative is feasible. Is it within the realm of probability and practicality? For a small, struggling firm, an alternative requiring a huge financial outlay is probably out of the question. Other alternatives may not be feasible because of legal barriers. And limited human, material, and information resources may make other alternatives impractical.

When an alternative has passed the test of feasibility, it must next be examined to see how well it satisfies the conditions of the decision situation. For example, a manager searching for

This overcrowded airport departure terminal highlights the number of customers trying to fly the international friendly skies. There are simply not enough commercial aircrafts to meet the demand. Boeing and Airbus continue to work on new products to help airlines meet growing demand.

In 2009, JetBlue announced that it would relocate it corporate offices. After identifying all of the alternatives to their current Queen, New York offices, the decision was made to not relocate but instead to remain in their original location.

## FIGURE 8.3 EVALUATING ALTERNATIVES IN THE DECISION-MAKING PROCESS

Managers must thoroughly evaluate all the alternatives, which increases the chances that the alternative finally chosen will be successful. Failure to evaluate an alternative's feasibility, satisfactoriness, and consequences can lead to a wrong decision.

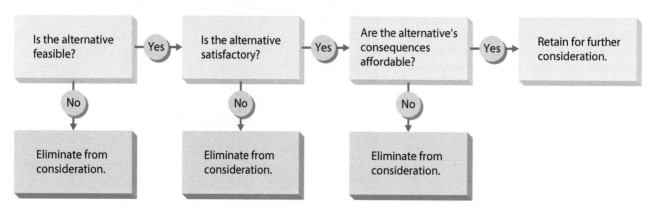

ways to double production capacity might initially consider purchasing an existing plant from another company. If more detailed analysis reveals that the new plant would increase production capacity by only 35 percent, this alternative may not be satisfactory. Finally, when an alternative has proven both feasible and satisfactory, its probable consequences must still be assessed. To what extent will a particular alternative influence other parts of the organization? What financial and nonfinancial costs will be associated with such influences? For example, a plan to boost sales by cutting prices may disrupt cash flows, require a new advertising program, and alter the behavior of sales representatives because it requires a different commission structure. The manager, then, must put "price tags" on the consequences of each alternative. Even an alternative that is both feasible and satisfactory must be eliminated if its consequences are too expensive for the total system. Airbus felt it would be at a disadvantage if it tried to simply enlarge its existing planes, because the Boeing 747 was already the largest aircraft being made and could readily be expanded to remain the largest. Boeing, meanwhile, was seriously concerned about the risk inherent in building a new and even larger plane, even if it shared the risk with Airbus as a joint venture.

**Selecting an Alternative** Even though many alternatives fail to pass the triple tests of feasibility, satisfactoriness, and affordable consequences, two or more alternatives may remain. Choosing the best of these is the real crux of decision making. One approach is to choose the alternative with the optimal combination of feasibility, satisfactoriness, and affordable consequences. Even though most situations do not lend themselves to objective, mathematical analysis, the manager can often develop subjective estimates and weights for choosing an alternative.

Optimization is also a frequent goal. Because a decision is likely to affect several individuals or units, any feasible alternative will probably not maximize all of the relevant goals. Suppose that the manager of the Kansas City Royals needs to select a new outfielder for the upcoming baseball season. Bill hits .350 but has difficulty catching fly balls; Joe hits only .175 but is outstanding in the field; and Sam hits .290 and is a solid but not outstanding fielder. The manager probably would select Sam because of the optimal balance of hitting and fielding. Decision makers should also remember that finding multiple acceptable alternatives may be possible; selecting just one alternative and rejecting all the others might not be necessary. For example, the Royals' manager might decide that Sam will start each game, Bill will be retained as a pinch hitter, and Joe will be retained as a defensive substitute. In many hiring decisions, the candidates remaining after evaluation are ranked. If the top candidate rejects the offer, it may be automatically extended to the number-two candidate and, if necessary, to the remaining candidates in order. For the reasons noted earlier, Airbus proposed a joint venture with Boeing. Boeing, meanwhile, decided that its best course of action was to modify its existing 747 to increase its capacity. As a result, Airbus then decided to proceed on its own to develop and manufacture a new jumbo jet. Boeing, however, also decided that in addition to modifying its 747 it would also develop a new plane to offer as an alternative, albeit one not as large as the 747 or the proposed new Airbus plane.

**Implementing the Chosen Alternative** After an alternative has been selected, the manager must put it into effect. In some decision situations, implementation is fairly easy; in others, it is more difficult. In the case of an acquisition, for example, managers must decide how to integrate all the activities of the new business, including purchasing, human resource practices, and distribution, into an ongoing organizational framework. For example, when Halliburton made the decision to buy Baker Hughes in 2015, managers estimated that it would take at least a year to integrate the two firms into a single one. Operational plans, which we discussed in Chapter 6, are useful in implementing alternatives.

Managers must also consider people's resistance to change when implementing decisions. The reasons for such resistance include insecurity, inconvenience, and fear of the unknown. When JC Penney decided to move its headquarters from New York to Texas, many employees resigned rather than relocate. Managers should anticipate potential resistance at various stages of the implementation process. (Resistance to change is covered in Chapter 12.) Managers should also recognize that even when all alternatives have been evaluated as precisely as possible and the consequences of each alternative weighed, unanticipated consequences are still likely. Any number of factors—unexpected cost increases, a less-than-perfect fit with existing organizational subsystems, or unpredicted effects on cash flow or operating expenses, for example—could develop after implementation has begun. Boeing set its engineers to work expanding the capacity of its 747 from 416 passengers to as many as 520 passengers by adding 30 feet to the plane's body. The company also started its new plane intended for international travel, the Boeing 787 Dreamliner. Airbus engineers, meanwhile, spent years developing and constructing its new jumbo jet, the A380. The A380 has a capacity of 525 passengers in a three-cabin configuration. And if an airline chose to outfit an A380 with only economy-class seats the plane could hold up to 853 tightly packed passengers (although no airline has ordered such a configuration). Airbus's development costs alone have exceeded $15 billion.

**Following Up and Evaluating the Results** The final step in the decision-making process requires that managers evaluate the effectiveness of their decision—that is, they should make sure that the chosen alternative has served its original purpose. If an implemented alternative appears not to be working, the manager can respond in several ways. Another previously identified alternative (the original second or third choice, for instance) could be adopted. Or the manager might recognize that the situation was not correctly defined to begin with and start the process all over again. Finally, the manager might decide that the original alternative is in fact appropriate but has not yet had time to work or should be implemented in a different way.[19]

Failure to evaluate decision effectiveness may have serious consequences. The Pentagon once spent $1.8 billion and eight years developing the Sergeant York anti-aircraft gun. From the beginning, tests revealed major problems with the weapon system, but not until it was in its final stages, when it was demonstrated to be completely ineffective, was the project scrapped.

At this point, both Boeing and Airbus are still learning about the consequences of their decisions. Airbus's A380 was placed in commercial service but was quickly found to suffer from numerous mechanical problems. Moreover, just as Airbus corrected these problems the global recession hit and several international airlines, some of them—such as Qantas Airways and Emirates Airlines—deferred or cancelled orders for the plane. Airbus estimated that it needs to sell 420 A380s before it starts making a profit. Thus far there are 135 in service, and at this writing the firm had current orders for 324 more. Projections suggest that sales of the plane may not hit the target of 420 planes until at least 2020.[20] Meanwhile, Boeing's 787 had a rough launch. Delivery of the first orders was delayed multiple times, and shortly after the 787 was placed in service it had to be grounded again while Boeing corrected a problem with the plane's batteries. But things seem to be going much more smoothly now for the 787. The plane uses 20 percent less fuel than comparable planes and Boeing has orders for over 1,000 new 787s. The company has also introduced a new longer version of the 787 than can carry up to 323 passengers.

When managers realize that they have made a poor decision, of course, they should take steps to set things right. In 2015 Intuit, maker of the popular income tax preparation software Turbo-Tax, made a bad decision that required users to pay an upgrade fee for services they had previously offered free when customers bought the software. The firm's biggest competitor, H&R Block, jumped on the mistake and quickly began to offer price cuts for Turbo-Tax users who switched to their service. Turbo-Tax then responded by dropping the service charge and refunding to users who had already paid.[21]

## Evidence-Based Management

Setting your mind to making rational decisions may seem like a no-brainer, but some researchers worry that managers tend all too often to slip into bad decision-making habits. As a result, some experts have recently reminded managers of the need to use rationality and evidence when making decisions. This reminder has been called evidence-based management, or EBM.[22] "Management decisions," they argue, "[should] be based on the best evidence, managers [should] systematically learn from experience, and organizational practices [should] reflect sound principles of thought and analysis." They define evidence-based management as "a commitment to finding and using the best theory and data available at the time to make decisions," but their "Five Principles of Evidence-Based Management" make it clear that EBM means more than just sifting through data and crunching numbers. Here's what they recommend:

1. Face the hard facts and build a culture in which people are encouraged to tell the truth, even if it's unpleasant.
2. Be committed to "fact-based" decision making—which means being committed to getting the best evidence and using it to guide actions.
3. Treat your organization as an unfinished prototype—encourage experimentation and learning by doing.
4. Look for the risks and drawbacks in what people recommend (even the best medicine has side effects).
5. Avoid basing decisions on untested but strongly held beliefs, what you have done in the past, or on uncritical "benchmarking" of what winners do.

This perspective is particularly persuasive when EBM is used to question the outcomes of decisions based on "untested but strongly held beliefs" or on "uncritical benchmarking." For instance, consider the popular policy of paying high performers significantly more than low performers. EBM research shows that pay-for-performance policies get good results when employees work solo or independently. But it's another matter altogether when it comes to collaborative teams—the kind of team that makes so many organizational decisions today. Under these circumstances, the greater the gap between highest- and lowest-paid executives, the weaker the firm's financial performance. Why? According to the experts, wide disparities in pay often weaken both trust among team members and the social connectivity that contributes to strong team-based decision making.[23]

Or consider another increasingly prevalent policy for evaluating and rewarding talent. Pioneered at General Electric by the legendary Jack Welch, the practice of "forced ranking" divides employees into three groups based on performance—the top 20 percent, middle 70 percent, and bottom 10 percent—and terminates those at the bottom. EBM research suggests that, according to many HR managers, forced ranking impaired morale and collaboration and ultimately reduced productivity. The researchers also concluded that automatically firing the bottom 10 percent resulted too often in the unnecessary disruption of otherwise effective teamwork. That's how they found out that 73 percent of the errors committed by commercial airline pilots occur on the first day that reconfigured crews work together.

---

☐ Whenever possible, managers should engage in rational decision making, applying logic and evidence to the decision-making process.

☐ At the same time, you should understand that some decisions do not lend themselves to rational analysis, and some do not allow time to follow all of the rational steps.

**Manager's Checklist** ✅

---

# Behavioral Elements in Decision Making

If all decision situations were approached as logically as described in the previous section, more decisions might prove to be successful. Yet decisions are often made with little consideration for logic and rationality. Some experts have estimated that U.S. companies use rational decision-making techniques less than 20 percent of the time.[24] And even when organizations try to be logical, they sometimes fail. For example, when Starbucks opened its first coffee shops in New York, it relied on scientific marketing research, taste tests, and rational deliberation in making a decision to emphasize drip over espresso coffee. However, that decision still proved wrong, as New Yorkers strongly preferred the same espresso-style coffees that were Starbucks mainstays in the West. Hence, the firm had to hastily reconfigure its stores to better meet customer preferences.

On the other hand, sometimes when a decision is made with little regard for logic, it can still turn out to be correct.[25] An important ingredient in how these forces work is the behavioral aspect of decision making. The administrative model better reflects these subjective considerations. Other behavioral aspects include political forces, intuition and escalation of commitment, risk propensity, and ethics.

> "... I'm a bit of a maverick. I listen, but I've got the final say. Then it's up to me to make it work so I don't lose my credibility."
>
> —RICHARD BRANSON, FOUNDER, OWNER, AND CEO OF VIRGIN GROUP[26]

## The Administrative Model

Herbert A. Simon was one of the first experts to recognize that decisions are not always made with rationality and logic.[27] Simon was subsequently awarded the Nobel Prize in economics. Rather than prescribing how decisions should be made, his view of decision making, now called the administrative model, describes how decisions often actually are made. As illustrated in Figure 8.4, the model holds that managers (1) use incomplete and imperfect information, (2) are constrained by bounded rationality, and (3) tend to "satisfice" when making decisions.

Bounded rationality suggests that decision makers are limited by their values and unconscious reflexes, skills, and habits. They are also limited by less-than-complete information and knowledge. Bounded rationality partially explains how U.S. auto executives allowed Japanese automakers to get such a strong foothold in the U.S. domestic market. For years, executives at GM, Ford, and Chrysler compared their companies' performance only to one another's and ignored foreign imports. The foreign "threat" was not acknowledged until the domestic auto market had been changed forever. If managers had gathered complete information from the beginning, they might have been better able to thwart foreign competitors.

**administrative model**
A decision-making model that argues that decision makers (1) use incomplete and imperfect information, (2) are constrained by bounded rationality, and (3) tend to "satisfice" when making decisions

**bounded rationality**
A concept suggesting that decision makers are limited by their values and unconscious reflexes, skills, and habits

## FIGURE 8.4  THE ADMINISTRATIVE MODEL OF DECISION MAKING

The administrative model is based on behavioral processes that affect how managers make decisions. Rather than prescribing how decisions should be made, it focuses more on describing how they are made.

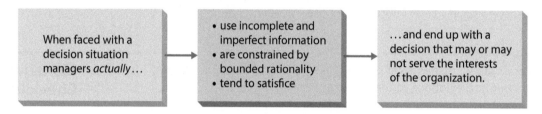

Essentially, then, the concept of bounded rationality suggests that although people try to be rational decision makers, their rationality has limits. This point is vividly illustrated in our *A World of Difference* feature.

Another important part of the administrative model is satisficing. This concept suggests that rather than conducting an exhaustive search for the best possible alternative, decision makers tend to search only until they identify an alternative that meets some minimum standard of sufficiency. A manager looking for a site for a new plant, for example, may select the first site she finds that meets basic requirements for transportation, utilities, and price, even though further search might yield a better location. People satisfice for a variety of reasons. Managers may simply be unwilling to ignore their own motives (such as reluctance to spend time making a decision) and therefore may not be able to continue searching after a minimally acceptable alternative is identified. The decision maker may be unable to weigh and evaluate large numbers of alternatives and criteria. Also, subjective and personal considerations often intervene in decision situations.

Because of the inherent imperfection of information, bounded rationality, and satisficing, the decisions made by a manager may or may not actually be in the best interests of the organization. A manager may choose a particular location for the new plant because it offers the lowest price and best availability of utilities and transportation. Or she may choose the site because it is located in a community where she wants to live.

In summary, then, the classical and administrative models paint quite different pictures of decision making. Which is more correct? Actually, each can be used to better understand how managers make decisions. The classical model is prescriptive: It explains how managers can at least try to be more rational and logical in their approaches to decisions. The administrative model can be used by managers to develop a better understanding of their inherent biases and limitations.[28] In the following sections, we describe more fully other behavioral forces that can influence decisions.

## Political Forces in Decision Making

**satisficing**
The tendency to search for alternatives only until one is found that meets some minimum standard of sufficiency

**coalition**
An informal alliance of individuals or groups formed to achieve a common goal

Political forces are another major element that contributes to the behavioral nature of decision making. Organizational politics is covered in Chapter 16, but one major element of politics, coalitions, is especially relevant to decision making. A coalition is an informal alliance of individuals or groups formed to achieve a common goal. This common goal is often a preferred decision alternative. For example, coalitions of stockholders often band together to force a board of directors to make a certain decision.

The impact of coalitions can be either positive or negative. They can help astute managers get the organization on a path toward effectiveness and profitability, or they can strangle well-conceived strategies and decisions. Managers must recognize when to use coalitions,

# The Verdict on Diversity

On the night of February 26, 2012, George Zimmerman, a watch volunteer at a white gated community in Sanford, Florida, spotted a young black man in his neighborhood. His suspicions aroused, he called police, referring to "f—ing punks," and despite the warning of the police dispatcher, continued to follow the "suspect." The details of what happened next are murky, but shortly thereafter, 17-year-old Trayvon Martin was dead. Zimmerman had shot him, explaining that Martin had jumped out of some bushes and begun punching him and slamming his head on the concrete sidewalk.

Zimmerman was indicted for second-degree murder and tried in July 2013. His lawyers argued that Zimmerman acted in self-defense, while the prosecution contended that he "didn't shoot Trayvon Martin because he had to. He shot him because he wanted to." A jury of six women—five of them white and one of them a minority—found Zimmerman not guilty of either second-degree murder or manslaughter.

"We'd be intellectually dishonest," said a lawyer for Martin's family, "if we didn't acknowledge racial undertones in this case." One of the prosecution witnesses was Rachel Jeantel, whom Martin had phoned, complaining about being followed by "a creepy-a– cracker," shortly before he was killed. Speaking after the trial, one jury member, identified only as Juror B37, admitted that she found Jeantel's speech "hard to understand"; her testimony, said Juror B37, was peppered with "phrases I had never understood before."

Jeantel, a 19-year-old black woman, comes from a Haitian-Dominican background, and her English tends to be inflected by Creole and Spanish. Juror B37, says Richard Gabriel, "could more easily relate to Zimmerman as the watch volunteer trying to protect his neighborhood." Gabriel, president of the American Society of Trial Consultants, believes that

Juror B37's decision to vote for Zimmerman's acquittal was less a matter of racial bias than of "ingroup-outgroup bias, which is the tendency to judge members of your own group more favorably and others more harshly." The effect of such "implicit bias," warns Gabriel, is "a pernicious form of decay in our justice system."

Gabriel's recommendation? "The courts and local communities," he says, "would benefit from greater diversity." Studies show, he argues, "that diverse juries make better decisions because the different perspectives make them more thorough and less likely to make factual errors." As a matter of fact, those studies show that racially diverse juries are more conscientious in their efforts to process information presented at trials: They engage in deeper analysis of the facts, participate in lengthier deliberations, and make fewer inaccurate statements. When issues of race are directly involved, they're more likely to discuss relevant race-related topics and entertain relevant race-related factors.

According to Kathleen Nalty, executive director of the Denver-based Center for Legal Inclusiveness, studies also demonstrate that "interacting with people who are different helps interrupt and reduce unconscious bias." "Generally speaking," explains Katherine Phillips of the Kellogg School for Management, "people would prefer to spend time with others who agree with them rather than disagree with them. But diversity often comes with more cognitive processing and more exchange of information and more perceptions of conflict."

*References:* Greg Botelho, "George Zimmerman Found Not Guilty of Murder in Trayvon Martin's Death," *CNN.com* (July 14, 2014), www.cnn.com, on October 20, 2014; Richard Gabriel, "Race, Bias and the Zimmerman Jury," *CNN.com* (July 16, 2013), www.cnn.com, on October 20, 2014; Sonia Chopra, "Preserving Jury Diversity by Preventing Illegal Peremptory Challenges," *The Trial Lawyer* (Summer 2014), www.njp.com, on October 20, 2014; Kathleen Nalty and Andrea Juarez, "Diversity Really Does Matter," *NALP Bulletin* (September 2012), www.legalinclusiveness.org, on October 20, 2014; Bunkhuon Chhun, "Better Decisions through Diversity," *Kellogg Insight* (October 1, 2010), http://insight.kellogg.northwestern.edu, on October 20, 2014.

**A WORLD OF DIFFERENCE**

This coalition appears to be one of 2 co-conspirators. Their secretive stance and body language do not appear to be beneficial to group decision making.

how to assess whether coalitions are acting in the best interests of the organization, and how to constrain their dysfunctional effects.[29]

## Intuition and Escalation of Commitment

Two other important decision processes that go beyond logic and rationality are intuition and escalation of commitment to a chosen course of action.

**Intuition** Intuition is an innate belief about something, without conscious consideration. Managers sometimes decide to do something because it "feels right" or they have a "hunch." This feeling usually is not arbitrary, however. Rather, it is based on years of experience and practice in making decisions in similar situations.[30] An inner sense may help managers make an occasional decision without going through a full-blown rational sequence of steps. For example, Kip Tindell, CEO of The Container Store, emphasizes the use of intuition throughout his company and urges employees to believe that it is critical in the workplace. He is quoted as saying, "Intuition is only the sum total of your life experiences. So why would you want to leave it at home when you come to work in the morning?"[31] Of course, all managers, but most especially inexperienced ones, should be careful not to rely too heavily on intuition. If rationality and logic are continually flouted in favor of "what feels right," the odds are that disaster will strike one day.

> "Intuition is a very powerful thing—more powerful than intellect, in my opinion."
>
> —STEVE JOBS, COFOUNDER AND LONGTIME CEO OF APPLE[32]

**Escalation of Commitment** Another important behavioral process that influences decision making is escalation of commitment to a chosen course of action. In particular, decision makers sometimes make decisions and then become so committed to the courses of action suggested by those decisions that they stay with them even when the decisions appear to have been wrong.[33] For example, when people buy stock in a company, they sometimes refuse to sell it even after repeated drops in price. They choose a course of action—buying the stock in anticipation of making a profit—and then stay with it even in the face of increasing losses. Moreover, after the value drops, they rationalize that they can't sell now because they will lose money.

For years Pan American World Airways ruled the skies and used its profits to diversify into real estate and other businesses. But with the advent of deregulation, Pan Am began to struggle and lose market share to other carriers. When Pan Am managers finally realized how ineffective their airline operations had become, experts today point out, the "rational" decision would have been to sell off the remaining airline operations and concentrate on the firm's more profitable businesses. But because they still saw the company as being first and foremost an airline, they instead began to slowly sell off the firm's profitable holdings to keep the airline flying. Eventually, the company was left with nothing but an ineffective and inefficient airline, and then had to sell off its more profitable routes before eventually being taken over by Delta. Had Pan Am managers made the more rational decision years earlier, chances are the firm could still be a profitable enterprise today, albeit one with no involvement in the airline industry.[34]

**intuition**
An innate belief about something, without conscious consideration

**escalation of commitment**
A decision maker's staying with a decision even when it appears to be wrong

In contrast, a group of investors licensed the use of Hard Rock logos and trademarks for a theme park—Hard Rock Park—to be built in South Carolina. After six years of planning and construction and an investment of over $400 million, the park opened in Myrtle Beach to dismal reviews and poor attendance. Rather than increasing their investment and trying to increase attendance, owners decided after only nine months to shut the park down and sell off its assets.[35]

Thus decision makers must walk a fine line. On the one hand, they must guard against sticking too long with an incorrect decision. To do so can bring about financial decline. On the other hand, managers should not bail out of a seemingly incorrect decision too soon, as Adidas once did. Adidas had dominated the market for professional athletic shoes. It subsequently entered the market for amateur sports shoes and did well there also. But managers interpreted a sales slowdown as a sign that the boom in athletic shoes was over. They thought that they had made the wrong decision and ordered drastic cutbacks. The market took off again with Nike at the head of the pack, and Adidas never recovered. Fortunately, a new management team has changed the way Adidas makes decisions, and the firm is again on its way to becoming a force in the athletic shoe and apparel markets.

Few business decisions are made under a condition of certainty. When a major international airline decides to buy new jumbo jets, however, there are only two alternatives--Boeing and Airbus. Consequently, there is relatively little ambiguity, especially when the airline is buying an existing plane such as a Boeing 777 or an Airbus A340. On the other hand, if the airline is placing an order for a plane not yet in production then its risk increases substantially.

## Risk Propensity and Decision Making

The behavioral element of **risk propensity** is the extent to which a decision maker is willing to gamble when making a decision. Some managers are cautious about every decision they make. They try to adhere to the rational model and are extremely conservative in what they do. Such managers are more likely to avoid mistakes, and they infrequently make decisions that lead to big losses. Other managers are extremely aggressive in making decisions and are willing to take risks.[36] They rely heavily on intuition, reach decisions quickly, and often risk big investments on their decisions. As in gambling, these managers are more likely than their conservative counterparts to achieve big successes with their decisions; they are also more likely to incur greater losses.[37] The organization's culture is a prime ingredient in fostering different levels of risk propensity.

## Ethics and Decision Making

As we introduced in Chapter 4, individual ethics are personal beliefs about right and wrong behavior. Ethics are clearly related to decision making in a number of ways. For example, suppose that, after careful analysis, a manager realizes that his company could save money by closing his department and subcontracting with a supplier for the same services. But to recommend this course of action would result in the loss of several jobs, including his own. His own ethical standards will clearly shape how he proceeds.[38] Indeed, each component of managerial ethics (relationships of the firm to its employees, of employees to the firm, and of the firm to other economic agents) involves a wide variety of decisions, all of which are likely to have an ethical component. A manager must remember, then, that just as behavioral processes such as politics

**risk propensity**
The extent to which a decision maker is willing to gamble when making a decision

**DOING BUSINESS ON PLANET EARTH**

# Sealing the Deal

Let's say that you're out to dinner with an old high school friend—we'll call him Vinny Devine. Vinny has become a connoisseur of fine wines, so you invite him to make a selection. After carefully perusing the wine list, he asks the waiter for a Rodney Strong Pinot Noir 2011, a wine from Sonoma County, California. "It has a nice toasty vanilla flavor," he promises.

When the wine arrives, he shows you the label on the back of the bottle, which features an array of certification seals. Vinny explains them one at a time. The first one says "USDA Organic." "It means that the grapes are grown without synthetic pesticides or fertilizers," says Vinny. Another seal says "Demeter," which, according to Vinny, "means Demeter Certified Biodynamic—the winemaker maintains a healthy ecosystem." Then there's a rectangular seal featuring a smiling fish in a clear blue stream. "Fish Friendly Farming," says Vinny, "means that the winegrower conserves natural creek banks to protect native species."

The pinot noir is very good, but you're thinking that perhaps Vinny knows more about the winery than he needs to know in order to enjoy drinking the wine. A recent survey, however, found that 34 percent of all U.S. wine consumers consider a winemaker's sustainability practices when selecting a purchase. Among consumers who identify themselves as buyers of eco-friendly, environmentally responsible products, 52 percent look for evidence of sustainable growing and processing practices. Bottles like the Rodney Strong pinot noir that you're drinking feature certification seals because that's how 66 percent of environmentally conscious consumers find out what they want to know about a wine. And that, in turn, is why 70 to 80 percent of wine distributors, retailers, and restaurant buyers rely on certification organizations and the seals they authorize. "Customers care about sustainability," says the aptly named Emily Wines of Kimpton Hotels & Restaurants, "and they look to retailers and restaurateurs to do the research and make those wines available."

It should come as no surprise, then, that the wine industry recognizes consumer and trade demand for sustainability as a stimulus for some rational decision making. "Many consumers and the trade are showing interest in sustainably grown and produced

wines," says Robert P. Koch, president of the Wine Institute, an association of California winemakers. "With 1,800 California winegrape growers and winemakers participating in the California Sustainable Winegrowing Alliance program," adds Koch, "it's clear that we're committed to sustainable practices."

In evaluating the alternatives for meeting its sustainability goals, Rodney Strong is guided by the "three E's" of the California Sustainable Winegrowing Alliance (CSWA): The vineyard strives to be environmentally sound, socially equitable, and economically feasible. "Considering the environment," says director of winegrowing Douglas McIlroy, "is part of the core company values and has always been part of our business practices. ... As far as Sonoma County goes, we're the poster child for sustainability. We're not just here supporting the county since our winemaking business is here—we also care about the longevity of the community."

In 2003, for example, Rodney Strong completed construction of a 4,032-panel solar array and made the transition to 100 percent solar power. About half the cost of $980,000 was defrayed by a state grant, and the almost maintenance-free system has already paid for the rest. By 2020, Rodney Strong will have reduced its carbon emissions by nearly 90,000 tons—the equivalent of planting 2,500 acres of trees or not driving 22 million miles. "Sustainable farming," says CEO Tom Klein, "led us to us to install solar panels to conserve energy, audit our whole winery's green practices for immediate and ongoing environmental progress, and hold ourselves accountable for our carbon footprint. Global warming is real and one of today's biggest threats to our future. This is something we had to do. The whole world needs to get involved in solving this problem."

*References:* Rodney Strong Vineyards, "Sustainable Practices: Our Unwavering Commitment" (2014), www.rodneystrong.com, on October 14, 2014; California Sustainable Winegrowing Alliance, "CCSW—Certified Participants" (2006–2014), www.sustainablewinegrowing.org, on October 15, 2014; Wine Institute, "New Research on Sustainability's Impact on Wine Buying Decisions" (May 7, 2013), www.wineinstitute.org, on October 14, 2014; Amy Payne, "Sustainable Sonoma," *FSR Magazine* (February 6, 2013), www.frsmagazine.com, on October 15, 2014; Kara DiCarrillo, "California Wineries Switch to Solar Power," *TreeHugger* (June 15, 2005), www.treehugger.com, on October 17, 2014; "Rodney Strong Vineyards First Carbon Neutral Winery," *Wine Country This Week* (November 13, 2009), www.winecountrythisweek.com, on October 15, 2014.

and risk propensity affect the decisions he makes, so, too, do his ethical beliefs.[39] The *Doing Business on Planet Earth* provides a detailed example of how ethics and decision making are intertwined.

---

☐ Managers should remember that even though they think they are rational and logical, in fact several different behavioral forces might influence their decisions.

☐ You should also understand, though, that deviating from rationality will not necessarily lead to bad decisions. Intuition, for example, can often help improve decision making effectiveness.

**Manager's Checklist**

---

# Group and Team Decision Making in Organizations

In more and more organizations today, important decisions are made by groups and teams rather than by individuals. Examples include the executive committee of The Walt Disney Company, product design teams at Texas Instruments, and marketing planning groups at Olive Garden. Managers can typically choose whether to have individuals or groups and teams make a particular decision. Thus knowing about forms of group and team decision making and their advantages and disadvantages is important.[40]

## Forms of Group and Team Decision Making

The most common methods of group and team decision making are interacting groups, Delphi groups, and nominal groups. Increasingly, these methods of group decision making are being conducted online.[41]

**Interacting Groups and Teams**  Interacting groups and teams are the most common form of decision-making group. The format is simple—either an existing or a newly designated group or team is asked to make a decision. Existing groups or teams might be functional departments, regular work teams, or standing committees. Newly designated groups or teams can be ad hoc committees, task forces, or newly constituted work teams. The group or team members talk among themselves, argue, agree, argue some more, form internal coalitions, and so forth. Finally, after some period of deliberation, the group or team makes its decision. An advantage of this method is that the interaction among people often sparks new ideas and promotes understanding. A major disadvantage, though, is that political processes can play too big a role.

**Delphi Groups**  A Delphi group is sometimes used to develop a consensus of expert opinion. Developed by the Rand Corporation, the Delphi procedure solicits input from a panel of experts who contribute individually. Their opinions are combined and, in effect, averaged. Assume, for example, that the problem is to establish an expected date for a major technological breakthrough in converting coal into usable energy. The first step in using the Delphi procedure is to obtain the cooperation of a panel of experts. For this situation, experts might include various research scientists, university researchers, and executives in a relevant energy industry. At first, the experts are asked to anonymously predict a time frame for the expected breakthrough. The persons coordinating the Delphi group collect the responses, average them, and ask the experts for another prediction. In this round, the experts who provided unusual or extreme predictions may be asked to justify them. These explanations may then be relayed to the other experts. When the predictions stabilize, the average prediction is taken to represent the decision of the group of experts. The time, expense, and logistics of the Delphi technique rule out its use for routine, everyday decisions, but it has been successfully used for forecasting

**interacting group and team**
A decision-making group or team in which members openly discuss, argue about, and agree on the best alternative

**Delphi group**
A form of group decision making in which a group is used to achieve a consensus of expert opinion

technological breakthroughs at Boeing, market potential for new products at General Motors, research and development patterns at Eli Lilly, and future economic conditions by the U.S. government.[42] Moreover, the Delphi method originally relied on paper-and-pencil responses obtained and shared through the mail; modern communication technologies such as e-mail and the Internet have enabled Delphi users to get answers much more quickly than in the past.

**Nominal Groups** Another useful group and team decision-making technique that is occasionally used is the nominal group. Unlike the Delphi method, in which group members do not see one another, nominal group members are brought together in a face-to-face setting. The members represent a group in name only, however; they do not talk to one another freely like the members of interacting groups. Nominal groups are used most often to generate creative and innovative alternatives or ideas. To begin, the manager assembles a group of knowledgeable experts and outlines the problem to them. The group members are then asked to individually write down as many alternatives as they can think of. The members then take turns stating their ideas, which are recorded on a flip chart or board at the front of the room. Discussion is limited to simple clarification. After all alternatives have been listed, more open discussion takes place. Group members then vote, usually by rank-ordering the various alternatives. The highest-ranking alternative represents the decision of the group. Of course, the manager in charge may retain the authority to accept or reject the group decision.[43]

## Advantages of Group and Team Decision Making

The advantages and disadvantages of group and team decision making relative to individual decision making are summarized in Table 8.2. One advantage is simply that more information is available in a group or team setting—as suggested by the old axiom, "Two heads are better than one." A group or team represents a variety of education, experience, and perspective. Partly as a result of this increased information, groups and teams typically can identify and evaluate more alternatives than can one person.[44] The people involved in a group or team decision understand the logic and rationale behind it, are more likely to accept it, and are equipped to communicate the decision to their work group or department.[45]

**nominal group**
A structured technique used to generate creative and innovative alternatives or ideas

---

### TABLE 8.2 ADVANTAGES AND DISADVANTAGES OF GROUP AND TEAM DECISION MAKING

To increase the chances that a group or team decision will be successful, managers must learn how to manage the process of group and team decision making. Federal Express and IBM are increasingly using groups and teams in the decision-making process.

| Advantages | Disadvantages |
| --- | --- |
| More information and knowledge are available. | The process takes longer than individual decision making, so it is costlier. |
| More alternatives are likely to be generated. | |
| More acceptance of the final decision is likely. | Compromise decisions resulting from indecisiveness may emerge. |
| Enhanced communication of the decision may result. | One person may dominate the group. |
| Better decisions generally emerge. | Groupthink may occur. |

## Disadvantages of Group and Team Decision Making

Perhaps the biggest drawback of group and team decision making is the additional time and hence the greater expense entailed. The increased time stems from interaction and discussion among group or team members. If a given manager's time is worth $50 an hour, and if the manager spends two hours making a decision, the decision "costs" the organization $100. For the same decision, a group of five managers might require three hours of time. At the same $50-an-hour rate, the decision "costs" the organization $750. Assuming the group or team decision is better, the additional expense may be justified, but the fact remains that group and team decision making is more costly.

Group or team decisions may also represent undesirable compromises.[46] For example, hiring a compromise top manager may be a bad decision in the long run because he or she may not be able to respond adequately to various subunits in the organization nor have everyone's complete support. Sometimes one person dominates the group process to the point where others cannot make a full contribution. This dominance may stem from a desire for power or from a naturally dominant personality. The problem is that what appears to emerge as a group decision may actually be the decision of one person.

Finally, a group or team may succumb to a phenomenon known as "groupthink." Groupthink occurs when the desire for consensus and cohesiveness overwhelms the goal of reaching the best possible decision.[47] Under the influence of groupthink, the group may arrive at decisions that are made not in the best interests of either the group or the organization, but rather to avoid conflict among group members. One of the most clearly documented examples of groupthink involved the space shuttle *Challenger* disaster. As NASA was preparing to launch the shuttle, many problems and questions arose. At each step of the way, however, decision makers argued that there was no reason to delay and that everything would be fine. Shortly after its launch, the shuttle exploded, killing all seven crew members.

## Managing Group and Team Decision-Making Processes

Managers can do several things to help promote the effectiveness of group and team decision making. One is simply being aware of the pros and cons of having a group or team make a decision to start with. Time and cost can be managed by setting a deadline by which the decision must be made final. Dominance can be at least partially avoided if a special group is formed just to make the decision. An astute manager, for example, should know who in the organization may try to dominate and can either avoid putting that person in the group or put several strong-willed people together.

To avoid groupthink, each member of the group or team should critically evaluate all alternatives. So that members present divergent viewpoints, the leader should not make his or her own position known too early. At least one member of the group or team might be assigned the role of devil's advocate. And after reaching a preliminary decision, the group or team should hold a follow-up meeting wherein divergent viewpoints can be raised again if any group members wish to do so.[48] Gould Paper Corporation used these methods by assigning managers to two different teams. The teams then spent an entire day in a structured debate, presenting the pros and cons of each side of an issue to ensure the best possible decision.

**groupthink**
A situation that occurs when a group or team's desire for consensus and cohesiveness overwhelms its desire to reach the best possible decision

---

☐ Managers should be familiar with the advantages and disadvantages of group versus individual decision making and try to use the best approach for each situation.

☐ You should also be aware different formats for group decision making.

**Manager's Checklist**

# Summary of Learning Outcomes and Key Points

1. Define decision making and discuss types of decisions and decision-making conditions.

   - Decision making is the act of choosing one alternative from among a set of alternatives.
   - The decision-making process includes recognizing and defining the nature of a decision situation, identifying alternatives, choosing the "best" alternative, and putting it into practice.
   - Two common types of decisions are programmed and nonprogrammed.
   - Decisions may be made under states of certainty, risk, or uncertainty.

2. Discuss rational perspectives on decision making, including the steps in rational decision making.

   - Rational perspectives on decision making rest on the classical model.
   - This model assumes that managers have complete information and that they will behave rationally. The primary steps in rational decision making are
     o recognizing and defining the situation.
     o identifying alternatives.
     o evaluating alternatives.
     o selecting the best alternative.
     o implementing the chosen alternative.
     o following up and evaluating the effectiveness of the alternative after it is implemented.

3. Describe the behavioral aspects of decision making.

   - Behavioral aspects of decision making rely on the administrative model.
   - This model recognizes that managers use incomplete information and that they do not always behave rationally.
   - The administrative model also recognizes the concepts of bounded rationality and satisficing.
   - Political activities by coalitions, managerial intuition, and the tendency to become increasingly committed to a chosen course of action are all important.
   - Risk propensity is also an important behavioral perspective on decision making.
   - Ethics also affect how managers make decisions.

4. Discuss group and team decision making, including the advantages and disadvantages of group and team decision making and how it can be more effectively managed.

   - To help enhance decision-making effectiveness, managers often use interacting, Delphi, or nominal groups or teams.
   - Group and team decision making in general has both advantages and disadvantages compared to individual decision making.
   - Managers can adopt a number of strategies to help groups and teams make better decisions.

# Discussion Questions

## Questions for Review

1. Describe the differences between programmed and nonprogrammed decisions. What are the implications of these differences for decision makers?

2. Describe the behavioral nature of decision making. Be certain to provide some detail about political forces, risk propensity, ethics, and commitment in your description.

## Questions for Analysis

5. Was your decision about what college or university to attend a rational decision? Did you go through each step in rational decision making? If not, why not?

6. Most business decisions are made under conditions of either risk or uncertainty. In your opinion, is it easier to

3. What is meant by the term *escalation of commitment*? In your opinion, under what conditions is escalation of commitment likely to occur?

4. Explain the differences between three common methods of group decision making—interacting groups, Delphi groups, and nominal groups.

make a decision under a condition of risk or a condition of uncertainty? Why?

7. Consider the following list of business decisions. Which decisions would be handled most effectively by group or team decision making? Which would be handled most

effectively by individual decision making? Explain your answers.

- A decision about switching pencil suppliers
- A decision about hiring a new CEO

- A decision about firing an employee for stealing
- A decision about calling 911 to report a fire in the warehouse
- A decision about introducing a brand-new product

## Questions for Application

8. Interview a local business manager about a major decision that he or she made recently. Try to determine whether the manager used a rational decision-making process or whether behavioral elements were also present. If the process was wholly rational, why do you think there was no behavioral component? If the process contained behavioral components, why were these components present?

9. Describe a recent decision you made that relied on intuition. In your opinion, what experiences formed the source of your intuition? Did the decision lead to attainment of the desired outcomes? Did your intuition play a positive or negative role in goal attainment? Explain.

10. Interview a department head at your college or university to determine whether group or team decision making is used. If it is, how does the head try to overcome the disadvantages of group decision making? Are the attempts successful? Why or why not?

# Building Effective Conceptual Skills

## Exercise Overview

Conceptual skills require you to think in the abstract—an area that's fraught with the risk of error (or at least mistakes in judgment). This exercise is designed to show you how certain pitfalls in abstract thinking—namely, nonrational biases and risk propensity—can lead to faulty decision making.

## Exercise Background

Psychologists Amos Tversky and Daniel Kahneman conducted much of the research contributing to the current state of our knowledge about decision-making biases. Tversky and Kahneman tested tendencies in people's real-life choices by presenting experimental subjects with laboratory-simulated decision-making situations. From the results they developed a set of principles called *prospect theory* to explain why people tend to be nonrational in making economic decisions.

Tversky and Kahneman's most important finding was that an individual's *perception* of gain or loss in a situation is more important than an objective measure of gain or loss. In this respect, they're being *nonrational*—that is, they aren't making decisions based purely on rational criteria. Similarly, they found that different people think differently about gains and losses—a phenomenon they call *framing*. Not surprisingly, people also tend to allow their perceptions to be skewed (positively or negatively) by the information they receive about a

situation. Unfortunately, when new information later becomes available, they have a hard time letting go of their initial perceptions, even if the new information contradicts their original impressions. Tversky and Kahneman refer to this process as *anchoring and adjustment*.

In this exercise, we're going to ask you to answer a few questions. To answer them, however, you must know how to calculate an *expected value*. To do this, you multiply each possible outcome value of a situation by the probability of its occurrence and then sum all the results. Here's a simple example: Let's say you have a 50 percent chance of earning 80 points on an exam and a 50 percent chance of earning 70 points. You can calculate the expected value as

$$(.5*80) + (.5*70) = 75$$

In other words, a .5 chance of 80 points equals 40 points and a .5 chance of 70 points equals 35 points. Therefore, the expected value of your exam is 40 + 35 = 75 points.

## Exercise Task

1. Respond to the list of brief questions that your professor provides to you. Remember: No answer is correct or incorrect; simply choose *your most likely response*. Then, when your instructor tells you to, share your answers with the class.

2. Discuss the answers given by the class. Why do students' answers differ?

3. What have you learned from this exercise about decision-making biases and risk propensity?

# Building Effective Decision-Making Skills

## Exercise Overview

Decision-making skills refer to the ability to recognize and define problems and opportunities correctly and then to select an appropriate course of action for solving problems or capitalizing on opportunities. This exercise allows you to compare the results of individual decision making with the results of decision making conducted by nominal groups.

## Exercise Background

Individual decision making, of course, has its advantages—speed, simplicity, lack of conflict. At times, however, these advantages are outweighed by other considerations. In particular, solitary decision making isn't conducive to innovation. Groups are better at innovating because they benefit from the input of diverse individuals, which, in turn, generates greater variety in alternative courses of action.

Nominal groups—so called because they exist *in name only*—are especially well suited for fostering creativity. They provide the freedom to develop as many creative options as possible without risk of criticism or political pressure. Nominal groups also pool input from many individuals and encourage creative responses to the pooled input. In short, nominal groups foster creativity because they combine techniques for improving both individual and group creativity.

## Exercise Task

Listen as your professor describes a problem situation and then do the following:

1. Write down as many creative responses to the problem as you can. Don't worry about whether or not they're practical. In fact, try to come up with as many unexpected—even "far-out"—responses as you can.

2. When your instructor calls on you, share your list with the class.

3. Query other students about their suggestions for clarification only. *Do not, under any circumstances, reveal whether you think any idea is "good" or "bad."*

4. After all individual ideas have been listed and clarified, add to the list any other ideas that you've developed while participating in the in-class part of the exercise.

5. Vote on the list, focusing on the "creativity" of individual items: Which suggestion does the class regard as the "best" solution to the problem at hand?

6. Did the nominal-group technique generate more creative alternatives than those that you generated on your own?

7. In your opinion, is the alternative voted "best" by the class a "better" solution than anything you thought of on your own? Explain your answer.

8. Give some suggestions about the types of organizational decisions that could be more effective if made by nominal groups. When should nominal groups *not* be used?

# Skill-Building Personal Assessment

## Decision-Making Styles

Decision making is clearly important. However, individuals differ in their decision-making styles, or the way they approach decisions. The following assessment is designed to help you understand your decision-making style. Respond to the following statements by indicating the extent to which they describe you. Circle the response that best represents your self-evaluation.

1. Overall, I'm _____ to act.
   1. quick   2. moderately fast   3. slow

2. I spend _____ amount of time making important decisions as/than I do making less important ones.
   1. about the same   2. a greater   3. a much greater

3. When making decisions, I _____ go with my first thought.
   1. usually   2. occasionally   3. rarely

4. When making decisions, I'm _____ concerned about making errors.
   1. rarely   2. occasionally   3. often

5. When making decisions, I _____ check my work more than once.
   1. rarely   2. occasionally   3. usually

6. When making decisions, I gather_____ information.
   1. little   2. some   3. lots of

7. When making decisions, I consider_____ alternatives.
   1. few   2. some   3. lots of

8. I usually make decisions_____ before the deadline.
   1. way   2. somewhat   3. just

9. After making a decision, I_____ look for other alternatives, wishing I had waited.
   1. rarely   2. occasionally   3. usually

10. I _____ regret having made a decision.
    1. rarely   2. occasionally   3. often

Source: Adapted from Robert N. Lussier, *Supervision: A Skill-Building Approach*, 2nd ed., 1994, pp. 122–123, © 1994 by Richard D. Irwin, Inc. Reproduced with permission of The McGraw-Hill Companies.

# Management at Work

### The Not-So-Smart Phone Company

## "We would say, 'We know better, and they'll eventually figure it out.'"

—FORMER BLACKBERRY EXECUTIVE ON CUSTOMER RELATIONS AT RIM

During the runup to his first inauguration, in 2009, President-elect Barack Obama was informed by security advisors that his beloved BlackBerry smartphone was a potential security risk. Hackers and spy agencies, they warned him, might figure out how to get into his e-mail. "They're going to pry it out of my hands," joked Obama, but he was adamant about his phone privileges, and security officials ultimately gave in. For one thing, BlackBerry was already known for such features as Secure Work Space and was the phone of choice for business leaders in security-sensitive positions. In addition, it was possible to modify the BlackBerry with enhanced encryption, and Obama soon became the first president to be connected by e-mail.

In 2014, however, the White House Communications Agency announced that it was testing smartphones from Samsung and LG for future use by administration officials. President Obama would be holding onto his BlackBerry, but the announcement was bad news for the Canadian maker of BlackBerrys, especially coming on the heels of a $423 million loss for the quarter ending on March 1. The company's U.S. market share had also plunged to 3 percent—down from 43 percent just four years earlier. What had happened to the corporate inventor of the smartphone and one of the world's most influential technology companies?

Arguably, bad decision making.

In 1999, Research in Motion (RIM), as the company was originally known, released the first version of its mobile e-mail device. The RIM 5810, with a tactile keyboard and preinstalled app for e-mail, became an instant hit—indeed, a cultural icon—and in the next decade, RIM would become the global leader in mobile e-mail communications. The BlackBerry was designed for and marketed to business customers—the executives who ran corporate IT programs and selected devices for use by all of the company's employees who needed to stay in constant touch. RIM management assumed that mobile e-mail adoption would follow the same pattern as so much previous technology: Like the typewriter and the computer, the BlackBerry would win over business users and then extend its reach to individual consumers.

Unfortunately, the world was on the verge of a revolution in technological diffusion: It's commonly called the *consumerization of IT*, and it means that the adoption process started to flow in the opposite direction—from consumers to corporate buyers. New products like the iPhone (which was introduced in 2007) and Androids (2008) caught on with consumers, and although they came with a lot of extraneous apps, businesses began to consider them because employees were so attached to them.

When it was first introduced, RIM co-CEOs Mike Lazaridis and Jim Balsillie publicly dismissed the iPhone as a potential threat to their product line. Said Balsillie: "It's kind of one more entrant into an already busy space with lots of choice for consumers. … But in terms of a sea-change for BlackBerry, I think that's overstating it." According to some insiders, BlackBerry management suspected that iPhone technology was superior, but Lazaridis and Balsillie continued to express confidence in the BlackBerry's security features and, especially, its tactile QWERTY keyboard: "Try typing a web key on an iPhone touchscreen," suggested Lazaridis. "It's a real challenge—you can't see what you type." As late as 2012, Lazaridis would hold up a BlackBerry for his board to see: "I get this," he'd say. "It's clearly differentiated." Then he'd hold up a touchscreen phone: "I *don't get this*," he would declare. Lazaridis saw no reason to abandon RIM's core corporate customers in order to cater to the perceived needs of consumers in a rapidly crowding market.

It's important to point out that the Apple iPhone had been developed in collaboration with Internet provider AT&T. Its touchscreen was more responsive, its browser was faster, and it was loaded with more apps, and it wasn't long before it was being touted as a "BlackBerry killer." As early as July 2007, RIM had been approached by AT&T competitor Verizon with a plan to develop an "iPhone killer" (which would feature a touchscreen and no keyboard). When the BlackBerry Storm was released in November 2008, however, customers didn't like it. The touchscreen was awkward and the processor was slow. "The technology," admitted one RIM executive, "was cobbled together quickly and wasn't quite ready." RIM abandoned the Storm, and Verizon turned to Motorola, which succeeded in adapting Google's new Android operating system to its Droid phone, which came out in 2009 with a user-friendly interface.

Not only was the Droid itself immensely successful, but Android quickly became the most popular mobile OS,

with Android devices now outselling those with Windows, iOS, and Mac OS combined. Within 14 months, Android's market share had climbed from 5.2 percent to 23.5 percent, while RIM's share dropped 10 points, to 31.6 percent. A year later, Android commanded a 47.3 percent share and RIM a mere 16 percent.

Back in 2007, when he first opened up an iPhone to have a look inside, Lazaridis, an engineer who'd founded RIM in 1984, was surprised to find that the device broke most of the rules that he'd helped to write. For one thing, the iPhone had a fully Internet capable browser—one of two—and its Android OS took up 700 megabytes. RIM's OS, which had been designed in the 1990s, ran on one processor and used 32 megabytes. "I said, 'How did they get AT&T to allow that?'" Lazaridis later recalled. He was certain that the iPhone would overstrain the network of its wireless partner. AT&T, however, was preparing to ride the consumerization wave. "There was a time," says former RIM executive VP Patrick Spence, "when wireless carriers tried to keep data usage predictable. Then, when the iPhone became compelling, they shifted to … trying to drive much more usage in different packages."

BlackBerry users told RIM that they wanted features like those on the iPhone, but RIM held onto the business rationale that it had pioneered—the one that operated on the assumption that the value of a smartphone lay in its hardware rather than in its software applications. Says a former company insider:

*We believed we knew better what customers needed long term than they did. Consumers would say, "I want a faster browser." We might say, "You might think you want a faster browser, but you don't want to pay overage on your bill." "Well, I want a super-big very responsive touchscreen." "Well, you might think you want that, but you don't want your phone to die at 2:00 P.M." We would say, "We know better, and they'll eventually figure it out."*

## Case Questions

1. Once the iPhone and Androids had penetrated the market, RIM faced a serious challenge: It had two distinct groups of customers to which it had to market its products. What were those two groups, and why were their needs and wants incompatible? Explain how this situation put RIM in a *state of uncertainty*. What *risks* did it face in making decisions to respond to this situation?

2. When RIM decided to incorporate personal apps into the BlackBerry, developers were required to use the company's Java-based operating system, which had been

created in the 1990s. In addition, they were required to submit apps for prior approval. Several apps—including Instagram and Tumblr—went elsewhere. Explain this problem as a problem in *bounded rationality*. Judging from what you know about RIM from the case, in what other ways would you say that RIM decision makers were hampered by bounded rationality?

3. Hersh Schefrin,* a pioneer in the behavioral aspects of financial decision making, studies how a specific set of psychological traps snare decision makers, causing them

to make inferior decisions. [Two] of the most common are excessive optimism [and] overconfidence. People learn to be excessively optimistic and overconfident. This means that successful people overestimate their past successes, which feeds these biases.

Judging from the details of the case, show how these two forms of "bias" affected decision making at RIM. How might RIM's "inferior decisions" have been avoided if executives like Lazaridis and Balsillie had applied the *steps in rational decision making*?

4. According to one industry observer,[†] the workplace is changing. The barrier between work and home has been eroded, and if people are going to have to be constantly connected, they at least want to use their own phones. Companies have quickly come to love consumerization, too: A recent study found that executives like the way it keeps workers plugged in all day long. And since workers often end up paying for their own devices, it can also help businesses cut costs. What about you? Do you ever use your own phone for work-related activities? If so, what kinds of activities? Do you sometimes feel that your employer is taking advantage of the fact that you're "plugged in all day long"? Or do you feel that the trade-off—at least you're allowed to use your own phone—is worth it? Do you sometimes take advantage of your employer—do you use your phone for personal business when you're at work?

*"Psychological Traps Snare BlackBerry Decision Makers," *Forbes* (November 7, 2013), www.forbes.com, on October 9, 2014.

[†]James. Surowiecki, "BlackBerry Season," *The New Yorker* (February 13, 2012), www.newyorker.com, on October 8, 2014.

## Case References

Jeff Zeleny, "Is Obama Planning to Ditch His BlackBerry?" *ABC News* (May 21, 2014), http://abcnews.go.com, on October 11, 2014; Sean Silcoff et al., "Inside the Fall of BlackBerry: How the Smartphone Inventor Failed to Adapt," *The* (Toronto) *Globe and Mail* (September 27, 2013), www.theglobeandmail.com, on October 13, 2014; Jeff de Cagna, "BlackBerry Breakdown: How a Smartphone Lost Its Way," *Associations* *Now* (August 1, 2014), http://associationsnow.com, on October 9, 2014; James Surowiecki, "BlackBerry Season," *The New Yorker* (February 13, 2012), www.newyorker.com, on October 8, 2014; Jay Yarrow, "All the Dumb Things RIM's CEOs Said While Apple and Android Ate Their Lunch," *Business Insider* (September 16, 2011), www.businessinsider.com, on October 13, 2014.

## YOU MAKE THE CALL  Moneyball on Steroids

1. As general manager of the Astros, Jeff Luhnow is responsible for player-related operations. Owner Jim Crane is responsible for organizational strategy. Describe a few circumstances under which *nonprogrammed decisions* made by Crane might affect Luhnow's system of highly *programmed decision making*.

2. What conditions contribute to the *state of certainty* under which Luhnow does his job? What conditions contribute to the *state of risk* under which he does his job? What conditions might contribute to the *state of uncertainty* under which he does his job? (Remember: *risk* and *uncertainty* are not the same thing.) Be as specific as you can in giving examples of each set of conditions.

3. According to Luhnow, "it's our job in player development to turn the raw material that the scouts provide into Major League players. The more efficient and effective we can be at doing this, the bigger the edge we might have over other teams." Recall the distinction that we make between *efficiency* and *effectiveness* in Chapter 1. What must Luhnow do in order to make sure that his system is as *efficient* as possible? What must he do in order to make sure that it's as *effective* as possible?

4. What about you? Is your decision making susceptible to any of the following behavioral tendencies— *bounded rationality, intuition, escalation of commitment*? Do you prefer to gather information or to accept recommendations? Have you ever made a decision that you'd like to undo and reconsider? What steps might you take to improve your overall decision making?

# Endnotes

1 Dave Zeitlin, "When Fantasy Baseball Gets Real," *Penn Gazette* (March-April 2013), www.upenn.edu, on October 7, 2014; Ben Reiter, "Astro-Matic Baseball," *Sports Illustrated* (June 27, 2014), www.si.com, on October 7, 2014; Joshua Green, "Extreme Moneyball," *BloombergBusinessweek* (August 28, 2014), www.businessweek.com, on October 5, 2014; Erik Manning, "BtB Jeff Luhnow Interview," *Beyond the Box Score* (December 8, 2011), www.beyondtheboxscore.com, on October 6, 2014; Jose de Jesus Ortiz, "Thumbprints of Astros GM All Over Cardinals," *Houston Chronicle* (October 23, 2013), www.houstonchronicle.com, on October 6, 2014; Brian McTaggart, "Analyze This: Astros' Mejdal Takes On Unique Role," *MLB.com* (January 31, 2012), http://m.astros.mlb.com, on October 6, 2014; David Laurila, "Q&A: Sig Mejdal, Astros Director of Decision Sciences," *FanGraphs* (March 11, 2013), www.fangraphs.com, on October 7, 2014.

2 Richard Priem, "Executive Judgment, Organizational Congruence, and Firm Performance," *Organization Science* (August 1994), pp. 421–432. See also R. Duane Ireland and C. Chet Miller, "Decision-Making and Firm Success," *Academy of Management Executive*, 2004, Vol. 18, No. 4, pp. 8–12.

3 Paul Nutt, "The Formulation Processes and Tactics Used in Organizational Decision Making," *Organization Science* (May 1993), pp. 226–240.

4 For a review of decision making, see E. Frank Harrison, *The Managerial Decision Making Process*, 5th ed. (Boston: Houghton Mifflin, 1999). See also Elke U. Weber and Eric J. Johnson, "Mindful Judgment and Decision Making," in Susan T. Fiske, Daniel L. Schacter, and Robert Sternberg, eds., *Annual Review of Psychology 2009* (Palo Alto, CA: Annual Reviews, 2009), pp. 53–86; Gerd Gigerenzer and Wolfgang Gaissmaier, "Heuristic Decision Making," in Susan T. Fiske, Daniel L. Schacter, and Shelley Taylor, eds., *Annual Review of Psychology 2011* (Palo Alto, CA: Annual Reviews, 2011), pp. 451–482.

5 http://usatoday30.usatoday.com/money/companies/management/2005-06-19-fedex-advice_x.htm, accessed May 12, 2015.

6 George P. Huber, *Managerial Decision Making* (Glenview, IL: Scott, Foresman, 1980).

7 For an example, see Paul D. Collins, Lori V. Ryan, and Sharon F. Matusik, "Programmable Automation and the Locus of Decision-Making Power," *Journal of Management*, 1999, Vol. 25, pp. 29–53.

8 Huber, *Managerial Decision Making*. See also David W. Miller and Martin K. Starr, *The Structure of Human Decisions* (Englewood Cliffs, NJ: Prentice-Hall, 1976); Alvar Elbing, *Behavioral Decisions in Organizations*, 2nd ed. (Glenview, IL: Scott, Foresman, 1978).

9 Rene M. Stulz, "Six Ways Companies Mismanage Risk," *Harvard Business Review*, March 2009, pp. 86–94.

10 http://www.bloomberg.com/bw/articles/2014-10-30/disney-ceo-bob-iger-gives-advice-to-college-students-over-skype

11 Gerard P. Hodgkinson, Nicola J. Bown, A. John Maule, Keith W. Glaister, and Alan D. Pearman, "Breaking the Frame: An Analysis of Strategic Cognition and Decision Making under Uncertainty," *Strategic Management Journal*, 1999, Vol. 20, pp. 977–985.

12 "Using Intuition in Your Business Plan," *Forbes*, September 20, 2010.

13 Glen Whyte, "Decision Failures: Why They Occur and How to Prevent Them," *Academy of Management Executive*, August 1991, pp. 23–31. See also Jerry Useem, "Decisions, Decisions," *Fortune*, June 27, 2005, pp. 55–154.

14 Quoted in *Fortune*, June 27, 2005, p. 55.

15 Jerry Useem, "Boeing vs. Boeing," *Fortune*, October 2, 2000, pp. 148–160; "Airbus Prepares to 'Bet the Company' as It Builds a Huge New Jet," *Wall Street Journal*, November 3, 1999, pp. A1, A10.

16 Robert C. Litchfield, "Brainstorming Reconsidered: A Goal-Based View," *Academy of Management Review*, 2008, Vol. 33, No. 3, pp. 649–668.

17 Paul Nutt, "Expanding the Search for Alternatives During Strategic Decision-Making," *Academy of Management Executive*, 2004, Vol. 18, No. 4, pp. 13–22.

18 "Queens-Based JetBlue Is Seeking New Corporate Office Site," *New York Daily News*, April 8, 2009; "JetBlue Headquarters to Stay in New York," *The New York Times*, March 22, 2010.

19 See Paul J. H. Schoemaker and Robert E. Gunther, "The Wisdom of Deliberate Mistakes," *Harvard Business Review*, June 2006, pp. 108–115.

20 "Airbus Clips Superjumbo Production," *Wall Street Journal*, May 7, 2009, p. B1.

21 "Turbo-Tax 'Mess Up,' Refunding Customers," *USA Today*, January 24, 2015, p. 5T.

22 Jeffrey Pfeffer and Robert I. Sutton, *Hard Facts, Dangerous Half-Truths, and Total Nonsense: Profiting from Evidence-Based Management* (Cambridge, MA: Harvard Business School Press, 2006).

23 Jack Soll, Katherine Milkman, and John Payne, "Outsmart Your Own Biases," *Harvard Business Review*, May 2015, pp. 64–71.

24 "The Wisdom of Solomon," *Newsweek*, August 17, 1987, pp. 62–63.

25 "Making Decisions in Real Time," *Fortune*, June 26, 2000, pp. 332–334. See also Eugene Sadler-Smith and Erella Shefy, "The Intuitive Executive: Understanding and Applying 'Gut Feel' in Decision-Making," *Academy of Management Executive*, 2004, Vol. 18, No. 4, pp. 76–91; Don A. Moore and Francis J. Flynn, "The Case of Behavioral Decision Research in Organizational Behavior," in James P. Walsh and Arthur P. Brief, *The Academy of Management Annals*, Vol. 2 (London: Routledge, 2008), pp. 399–432.

26 "Hard Choices," *Business Week*, November 22–28, 2010, p. 92.

27 Herbert A. Simon, *Administrative Behavior* (New York: Free Press, 1945). Simon's ideas have been refined and updated in Herbert A. Simon, *Administrative Behavior*, 3rd ed. (New York: Free Press, 1976), and Herbert A. Simon, "Making Management Decisions: The Role of Intuition and Emotion," *Academy of Management Executive*, February 1987, pp. 57–63.

28 Patricia Corner, Angelo Kinicki, and Barbara Keats, "Integrating Organizational and Individual Information Processing Perspectives on Choice," *Organization Science*, August 1994, pp. 294–302.

29 Kimberly D. Elsbach and Greg Elofson, "How the Packaging of Decision Explanations Affects Perceptions of Trustworthiness," *Academy of Management Journal*, 2000, Vol. 43, pp. 80–88.

30 Kenneth Brousseau, Michael Driver, Gary Hourihan, and Rikard Larsson, "The Seasoned Executive's Decision-Making Style," *Harvard Business Review*, February 2006, pp. 111–112; see also Erik Dane and Michael G. Pratt, "Exploring Intuition and Its Role in Managerial Decision Making," *Academy of Management Review*, 2007, Vol. 32, No. 1, pp. 33–54.

31 "Three Good Hires? He'll Pay More for One Who's Great," *New York Times*, March 13, 2010.

32 https://hbr.org/2012/04/the-real-leadership-lessons-of-steve-jobs

33 Barry M. Staw and Jerry Ross, "Good Money after Bad," *Psychology Today*, February 1988, pp. 30–33; D. Ramona Bobocel and John Meyer, "Escalating Commitment to a Failing Course of Action: Separating the Roles of Choice and Justification," *Journal of Applied Psychology*, 1994, Vol. 79, pp. 360–363.

34 Mark Keil and Ramiro Montealegre, "Cutting Your Losses: Extricating Your Organization When a Big Project Goes Awry," *Sloan Management Review*, Spring 2000, pp. 55–64.

35 "Closing Time for a Rock Theme Park," *Wall Street Journal*, January 7, 2009, p. B1.

36 Gerry McNamara and Philip Bromiley, "Risk and Return in Organizational Decision Making," *Academy of Management Journal*, 1999, Vol. 42, pp. 330–338.

37 For an example, see Brian O'Reilly, "What It Takes to Start a Startup," *Fortune*, June 7, 1999, pp. 135–140.

38 Martha I. Finney, "The Catbert Dilemma—The Human Side of Tough Decisions," *HR Magazine*, February 1997, pp. 70–78.

39 See Ann E. Tenbrunsel and Kristen Smith-Crowe, "Ethical Decision Making: Where We've Been and Where We're Going," in James P. Walsh and Arthur P. Brief, *The Academy of Management Annals*, Vol. 2 (London: Routledge, 2008), pp. 545–607.

40 Edwin A. Locke, David M. Schweiger, and Gary P. Latham, "Participation in Decision Making: When Should It Be Used?" *Organizational Dynamics*, Winter 1986, pp. 65–79; Nicholas Baloff and Elizabeth M. Doherty, "Potential

Pitfalls in Employee Participation," *Organizational Dynamics*, Winter 1989, pp. 51–62.

41  "The Art of Brainstorming," *BusinessWeek*, August 26, 2002, pp. 168–168.

42  Andre L. Delbecq, Andrew H. Van de Ven, and David H. Gustafson, *Group Techniques for Program Planning* (Glenview, IL: Scott, Foresman, 1975); Michael J. Prietula and Herbert A. Simon, "The Experts in Your Midst," *Harvard Business Review*, January–February 1989, pp. 120–124.

43  See Kevin P. Coyne, Patricia Gorman Clifford, and Renee Dye, "Breakthrough Thinking from Inside the Box," *Harvard Business Review*, December 2007, pp. 71–80, for an extension of the nominal group method.

44  Norman P. R. Maier, "Assets and Liabilities in Group Problem Solving: The Need for an Integrative Function," in J. Richard Hackman, Edward E. Lawler III, and Lyman W. Porter, eds., *Perspectives on Business in Organizations*, 2nd ed. (New York: McGraw-Hill, 1983), pp. 385–392.

45  Anthony L. Iaquinto and James W. Fredrickson, "Top Management Team Agreement about the Strategic Decision Process: A Test of Some of Its Determinants and Consequences," *Strategic Management Journal*, 1997, Vol. 18, pp. 63–75.

46  Richard A. Cosier and Charles R. Schwenk, "Agreement and Thinking Alike: Ingredients for Poor Decisions," *Academy of Management Executive*, February 1990, pp. 69–78.

47  Irving L. Janis, *Groupthink*, 2nd ed. (Boston: Houghton Mifflin, 1982).

48  Ibid.

# 9

©Markus Pfaff/Shutterstock.com

# MANAGING START-UPS AND NEW VENTURES

**Learning Outcomes**

**After studying this chapter, you should be able to:**

1. Discuss the meaning of entrepreneur-ship, start-ups, and new ventures.

2. Describe the role of entrepreneur-ships, start-ups and new ventures in society.

3. Understand the major issues involved in choosing strategies for small businesses and the role

of international management in start-ups and new ventures.

4. Discuss the structural challenges unique to start-ups and new ventures.

5. Understand the determinants of the performance of entrepreneurs, start-ups, and new ventures.

## MANAGEMENT IN ACTION   Leaping to Constructions

"You would look at construction and say that nothing much had changed in a thousand years."

—ANN HAND, CEO OF PROJECT FROG

How much does it cost to build a school? As a rule, between $280 and $310 per square foot. Ash Notaney, however, told officials in Santa Ana, California, that he could build one for $200 to $210 per square foot, and Santa Ana's El Sol Academy gave him a chance to make good on his sales pitch in the summer of 2013. As of May, demolition of the old El Sol structure hadn't yet begun, and work on the new building couldn't begin until July, but Notaney was undeterred by the daunting schedule: He promised to finish construction by December. The two-story, 12-classroom building was finished when Notaney said it would be, and on top of everything else, it's 40 to 50 percent more energy efficient than buildings erected by conventional means. When a second phase of construction is completed, the total price tag will be $15 million—about 20 to

25 percent cheaper per square foot than that of traditional permanent structures.[1]

Ash Notaney is VP of product and innovation at Project Frog, a San Francisco–based builder of component structures designed for on-site assembly. "We design a common chassis or platform for different types of building that people can reprogram according to their needs," explains CEO Ann Hand, who thinks of her company as more of a tech firm than a construction company. Project Frog (which stands for *Flexible Response to Ongoing Growth*) was founded in 2006, and Hand, who'd been an executive at BP for 20 years, was brought in as CEO in 2009, just after RockPort Capital had invested $8 million in the company.

RockPort thought of Project Frog as a "smart building start-up," and Hand realized that its industry "space" was located in the vicinity of the construction industry, if not necessarily within its traditional perimeters. "You would look at construction," she recalls, "and say that nothing much had changed in a thousand years. It was an industry just waiting to be disrupted." Hand thus benchmarked companies like

In many ways the basic procedures used in building construction have not changed for years. A group of entrepreneurs saw business opportunity if they could develop new concepts for construction. Their start-up firm, Project Frog, developed new approaches and methods for building schools faster, cheaper, and in a more energy efficient manner than traditional firms.

Justin Sullivan/Getty Images

Toyota and Boeing—manufacturers noted for process efficiency—and from the beginning, her approach to industrywide disruption has involved both product and process. Like Boeing, she insists, "we are a product manufacturer, but if Boeing can assemble a 747 in eight days, why does it take 24 months to design and construct a building?" According to Project Frog president Adam Tibbs,

> we focus on smart manufacturing techniques rather than merely shifting construction from on-site to off-site. By doing this, we can bring the same efficiencies as really smart, highly efficient industries. ... This is about being smarter and building a process that can be replicated easily in order to both stay efficient and maintain quality.

How does "smart manufacturing" work at Project Frog? The company manufactures building components, ships them in flat packs to the construction site, and partners with local contractors to assemble the finished building. The process begins at the design stage, which, as Notaney puts it, "we see as an opportunity to rethink everything." In a traditional building, for example, one contractor will put up the ceiling, another will add insulation, and then an electrician will come in to install the wiring and the lighting. A Project Frog ceiling, on the other hand, already includes insulation and energy-efficient LED light fixtures. Likewise, other components include such features as motorized blinds and temperature-control systems—items that might get engineered out of a conventional building when the architect estimates the cost of heating, ventilating, and air conditioning. Thus a Project Frog building is not merely "prefab" or "modular"; the company prefers the term "componentized" in order to underscore the fact that its buildings are highly customizable. El Sol Academy, for example, features plasma-TV-screen "learning" walls.

In designing a componentized building, says Ash Notaney, "you have to get all the details right up front, as it's all about sequencing and assembly." The process thus begins with a detailed 3D software rendering. "It's complicated and time-consuming to develop a 3D model," admits Adam Tibbs, but he hastens to add that Project Frog developed "a proprietary 3D design tool" in 2008. In fact, that's just about the only thing that the company did in 2008: "We spent a lot of 2008 taking the time to learn from initial prototypes and to lock in a solution that we really feel delivers value," explains Tibbs.

The company's software, for example, will create models of all the pieces of steel needed for a particular building. According to Tibbs, the program then applies special algorithms

> to determine the most efficient way to cut as little steel as possible from a sheet. ... Then we look at all the pieces of steel we need and the order in which we'll need to assemble them. ... By spending 2008 building our software, we've been able to drastically cut the cost of steel per project and also to speed up the amount of time it takes to build a Project Frog building.

Equally important, adds Tibbs, its software program allows Project Frog to incorporate component features that make its buildings "greener—50 percent more energy efficient than code. ... When you buy a Project Frog structure, you get performance-monitoring software and embedded sensors that automatically monitor energy performance and maintenance." Combined with designs that maximize the use of daylight, componentized LED lighting-control systems can cut lighting demand by 85 percent. Some Project Frog buildings use zero energy, and some even export energy to the electrical power grid.

Then there's the matter of waste. Tibbs points out that "more than one-fifth of all materials brought to [a conventional] building site are thrown away. ... If you can get to a near zero-waste facility, that's a huge savings ... from using less material and eliminating the need for waste removal." Besides, waste is a special item on Ann Hand's disruption agenda: "I won't rest," she says, "until we shake up the industry and attach some guilt to wasteful construction."

Hand's number-one goal, however, reflects the sort of aspiration that you more often hear from CEOs: She's working toward "a sales volume north of nine digits." How does she plan to get there? "With a few school districts alone," she says, "we can be a $100 million company." That's why Project Frog's current focus is on small to medium-sized commercial buildings like the 19,000-square-foot El Sol Academy building.

The competition, says Tibbs, comes mostly from "portables" (think double-wide trailers), which "do not have to pass code. They're very energy inefficient and not made to last, and the biggest problem is mold." Back in 2009, Hand admitted that "we can't compete with portables on price" because the "only objective in the school world is to hit a cost number when there's no spec for quality or energy efficiency." Four years later, however, she was able to announce that "we now have a price point affordable to the masses." Project Frog's mission, says Education VP Marijke Smit, "is to democratize school buildings that work to service the kids that inhabit them. By making them affordable, we've now created access to a whole new market."

Project Frog is betting that, in addition to being eco-friendly, its innovative classroom designs will improve student performance. More and more school systems think it's a good bet. As of this writing, Project Frog is filling its largest contract to date: more than 250,000 square feet of educational facilities for the South San Francisco United School District. All of the buildings are designed to perform 40 percent better than California's strict energy-code standards.

---

Just like Project Frog, thousands of new businesses are started every year. Some of them succeed but many, unfortunately, fail. Some of those entrepreneurs who fail in a new business try again, and sometimes it takes two or more failures before a successful business gets under way. Henry Ford, for example, went bankrupt twice before succeeding with Ford Motor Company. On the other hand, of course, there are also those who succeed. This process of starting a new business or business venture, sometimes failing and sometimes succeeding, is part of what is called "entrepreneurship," the subject of this chapter. The new businesses themselves are often referred to as start-ups or new ventures. We begin by exploring the nature of start-ups and new ventures. We then examine the role of start-ups and new ventures in the business world and discuss strategies for start-ups and new ventures organizations. We then describe the structure and performance of start-ups and new ventures. First, though, we will look more closely at entrepreneurship, the underlying ingredient of all new businesses.

**entrepreneurship**
The process of planning, organizing, operating, and assuming the risk of a start-up or new venture

**entrepreneur**
Someone who engages in entrepreneurship

**small business**
A business that is privately owned by one individual or a small group of individuals and has revenues and assets that are not large enough to influence its environment

## The Meaning of Entrepreneurship

Entrepreneurship is the process of planning, organizing, operating, and assuming the risk of a start-up or new venture. An entrepreneur, in turn, is someone who engages in entrepreneurship. Reed Hastings, who launched and still runs NetFlix, is an entrepreneur. He put his own resources on the line and took a personal stake in the success or failure of NetFlix. On the other hand, business owners who hire professional managers to run their businesses and then turn their attention to other interests are not true entrepreneurs. Although they are assuming the risk of the venture, they are not actively involved in organizing or operating it. Likewise, professional managers whose job is running someone else's business are not entrepreneurs, because they assume less than total personal risk for the success or failure of the business.

Entrepreneurs start new businesses, usually small ones. We define a small business as one that is privately owned by one individual or a small group of individuals and has revenues and assets that are not large enough to influence

A small business is one that is privately owned and whose assets and revenues are not large enough to influence its environment. This flower grower, a small business, is checking a shipment destined for a local garden center.

its environment. A small, two-person software development company with annual sales of $100,000 would clearly be a small business, whereas Microsoft Corporation is just as clearly a large business. But the boundaries are not always this clear-cut. For example, a regional retailing chain with 20 stores and annual revenues of $30 million may sound large but is really very small when compared to such giants as Walmart and Target. We will also define a start-up or new venture as a relatively new small business. Any start-up or new venture may succeed and grow to become a large business, succeed but remain small, fail and shut down, or be bought by an existing business.

# The Role of Entrepreneurs, Start-Ups and New Ventures in Society

The history of entrepreneurship and of the development of new businesses is in many ways the history of great wealth and of great failure. Some entrepreneurs have been very successful and have accumulated vast fortunes from their entrepreneurial efforts. For example, when Microsoft Corporation first sold its stock to the public in 1986, Bill Gates, then just 30 years old, received $350 million for his share of Microsoft.[2] Today his holdings—valued at over $80 billion—make him one of the richest persons not only in the United States but also in the entire world.[3] Many more entrepreneurs, however, have lost a great deal of money. Research suggests that the majority of new businesses fail within the first few years after founding.[4] Many that last longer do so only because the entrepreneurs themselves work long hours for very little income.

As Figure 9.1 shows, most U.S. businesses employ fewer than 100 people, and most U.S. workers are employed by small firms. For example, Figure 9.1(a) shows that approximately 85 percent of all U.S. businesses employ fewer than 20 people; another 12 percent employ between 20 and 99 people. In contrast, only about 2.5 percent employ between 100 and 499 workers and another .5 percent employ 500 or more. Figure 9.1(b) shows that about 25 percent of all U.S. workers are employed by firms with fewer than 20 people; another 30 percent work in firms that employ between 20 and 99 people. The vast majority of these companies are owner-operated.[5] Figure 9.1(b) also shows that 25.5 percent of U.S. workers are employed by firms with 100 to 499 employees and another 19.5 percent work for businesses that employ 500 or more total employees.

On the basis of numbers alone, then, small business is a strong presence in the economy, which is also true in virtually all of the world's mature economies. In Germany, for example, companies with fewer than 500 employees generate over 99 percent of the country's sales tax revenue and two-thirds of the nation's gross national product, train nine of 10 apprentices, and employ four of every five workers. Small businesses also play major roles in the economies of Italy, France, and Brazil. In addition, experts agree that small businesses will be quite important in the emerging economies of countries such as Russia and Vietnam. The contribution of start-ups and new ventures can be measured in terms of their effects on key aspects of an economic system. In the United States, these aspects include job creation, innovation, and importance to big business.

**start-up or new venture**
A relatively new small business

dotshock/Shutterstock.com

A start-up or new venture refers to a relatively new small business. This computer retailer, for example, has just opened its doors. The firm may one day grow into a giant international chain. Or, it may remain small and focused on its local market or eventually fail.

## FIGURE 9.1 THE IMPORTANCE OF SMALL BUSINESS IN THE UNITED STATES

(a) Approximately 85 percent of all U.S. businesses employ fewer than 20 people; another 12 percent employ between 20 and 99 people. In contrast, only about 2.5 percent employ between 100 and 400 workers, and another .5 percent employ 500 or more. (b) 25 percent of all U.S. workers are employed by firms with fewer than 20 people; another 30 percent work in firms that employ between 20 and 99 people. 25.5 percent of U.S. workers are employed by firms with 100–499 employees, and another 19.5 percent work for businesses that employ 500 or more total employees.

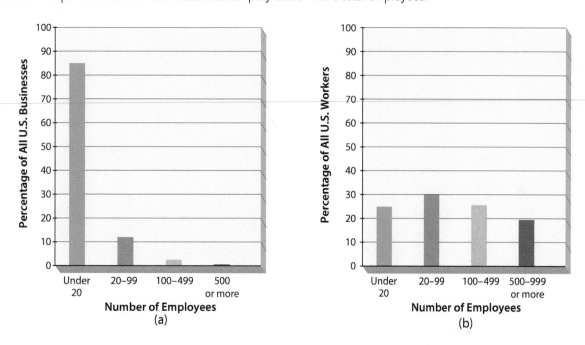

Source: U.S. Census Bureau, *Statistical Abstract of the United States*, 2014 (Washington, DC: Government Printing Office, 2015), www.census.gov/, accessed on May 14, 2015.

## Job Creation

In the early 1980s, a widely cited study suggested that start-ups and new ventures are responsible for creating eight of every 10 new jobs in the United States. This contention touched off considerable interest in the fostering of small business as a matter of public policy. As we will see, though, relative job growth among businesses of different sizes is not easy to determine. But it is clear that start-ups and new ventures—especially in certain industries—are an important source of new (and often well-paid) jobs in the United States. According to the Small Business Administration (SBA), for example, seven of the 10 industries that added the most new jobs in 2014 were in sectors dominated by small businesses. Moreover, start-ups and new ventures currently account for 37 percent of all jobs in high-technology sectors of the economy.[6]

Note that new jobs are also being created by small firms specializing in international business. For example, Bob Knosp operates a small business in Bellevue, Washington, that makes computerized sign-making systems. Knosp gets over half his sales from abroad and has dedicated almost 75 percent of his workforce to handling international sales. Indeed, according to the SBA, small businesses account for 98 percent of all U.S. exporters.[7]

It is important to note, though, that tracking job gains and losses is very complicated and somewhat imprecise. For instance, suppose a business eliminates one full-time job but later replaces it with two part-time jobs. Some statistics would count this as a loss of one job followed by a gain of two jobs. Similarly, the jobs within a company can fluctuate when it acquires or sells a business unit. For instance, media outlets once reported that Halliburton

## TABLE 9.1  JOB CREATION BY RECENT SUCCESSFUL START-UPS AND NEW VENTURES

All businesses create and eliminate jobs. Because of their size, the magnitude of job creation and elimination is especially pronounced in bigger businesses. But successful start-ups and new ventures add jobs, sometimes slowly and sometimes very rapidly.

| Firm | Year Started | Number of Jobs 2015 |
| --- | --- | --- |
| Amazon.com | 1994 | 117,300 |
| Buffalo Wild Wings | 1982 | 25,500 |
| Cinemark | 1985 | 22,500 |
| Dell Computer | 1984 | 111,300 |
| eBay | 1997 | 33,500 |
| Facebook | 2004 | 6,337 |
| GameStop | 1994 | 65,000 |
| Google | 1997 | 47,756 |
| JetBlue | 2000 | 14,347 |
| LinkedIn | 2003 | 3,458 |
| NetFlix | 1997 | 2,237 |
| Starbucks | 1971 | 182,000 |
| Twitter | 2007 | 3,900 |
| Whole Foods | 1978 | 78,400 |
| Yahoo! | 1994 | 11,700 |

had "cut" 53,000 jobs in the previous year. But in reality, those "losses" actually came when the firm sold its largest subsidiary, KBR. Only a handful of jobs were actually eliminated; instead, over 50,000 jobs were simply moved to a new firm.

At least one message is clear: Entrepreneurial business success, more than business size, accounts for most new job creation. Whereas successful retailers like Walmart and Best Buy have been growing and adding thousands of new jobs, struggling chains like Kmart have been eliminating thousands. Hence, most firms, especially those in complex and dynamic

Some start-ups and new ventures grow and expand, some remain the same size, and others fail. The business on the left is growing and needs to hire new employees. However, the one on the right is shutting down and its workers are losing their jobs.

environments, go through periods of growth when they add new jobs but also have periods when they cut jobs.

The reality, then, is that jobs are created by entrepreneurial companies of all sizes, all of which hire workers and all of which lay them off. Although small firms often hire at a faster rate than large ones, they are also likely to eliminate jobs at a far higher rate. Small firms are also usually the first to hire in times of economic recovery, whereas large firms are generally the last. Conversely, however, big companies are also the last to lay off workers during economic downswings.

## Innovation

History has shown that major innovations are as likely to come from start-ups and new ventures as from big businesses. For example, small firms and individuals invented the personal computer and the stainless-steel razor blade, the transistor radio and the photocopying machine, the jet engine and the self-developing photograph. They also gave us the helicopter and power steering, automatic transmissions and air conditioning, cellophane and the disposable ballpoint pen. Today, says the SBA, start-ups and new ventures consistently supply over half of all "innovations" introduced into the U.S. marketplace each year. In particular, of all businesses that produce 15 or more patents during the most recent four-year period, start-ups and new ventures produce 16 times more patents per employee than large firms.[8]

Not surprisingly, history is repeating itself with increasing rapidity in the age of high-tech communication and social media. For example, much of today's most innovative software is being written at relatively new start-up companies. Yahoo! and Netscape brought the Internet into the average U.S. living room, and online companies such as Amazon.com, eBay, and Google are using it to redefine our shopping habits. Instagram, Facebook, and Twitter have changed how we interact with one another.[9] Each of these firms started out as a small business.

Of course, not all successful new start-ups are leading-edge dot-com enterprises. Take Sacha White, for example. He moved to Oregon a few years ago and got a job as a bicycle messenger. He began to tinker with his bike, and eventually built himself a custom one from scratch. Other riders took note, and started wanting him to build bikes for them as well. White eventually started his own business called Vanilla Bicycles. He handcrafts each one and has a waiting list of five years. All told, he makes around 50 bikes per year; about 40 percent of these bikes are sold domestically, the rest to international customers. The custom bikes range in price from $5,000 to $12,000.[11] Entrepreneurs have also achieved success in such diverse fields as specialized dog training, hand-crafted musical instruments, and finely balanced fly fishing reels.

> "[Twitter's founders] created a new way for people to communicate publicly and instantaneously."
>
> —FRED WILSON, VENTURE CAPITALIST[10]

Many small businesses provide valuable services to larger businesses. This delivery van, for example, is bringing office supplies to a large business headquarters. Both the office supply company and the business headquarters are large enterprises but they reply on the small local delivery company to pick up the supplies and then deliver them.

## Importance to Big Business

Most of the products made by big manufacturers are sold to consumers by small businesses.

For example, the majority of dealerships selling Fords, Chevrolets, Toyotas, and Kias are independently owned and operated. Moreover, small businesses provide big businesses with many of the services, supplies, and raw materials they need. Likewise, Microsoft (once a start-up business) relies heavily on small businesses in the course of its routine business operations. For example, the software giant outsources much of its routine code-writing function to hundreds of sole proprietorships and other small firms. It also outsources much of its packaging, delivery, and distribution to smaller companies. Dell Computer (also a former new venture) uses this same strategy, buying most of the parts and components used in its computers from small suppliers around the world.

---

**Manager's Checklist**

☐ Managers should understand the complexities of assessing and comparing job creation and job elimination.

☐ You should also remember the key role that start-ups and new ventures play in both innovation and their contributions to big business.

## Strategy for Start-Ups and New Ventures

One of the most basic challenges facing a start-up operation is choosing a strategy. The three strategic challenges facing small firms are choosing an industry in which to compete, emphasizing distinctive competencies, and writing a business plan.[12]

### Choosing an Industry

Not surprisingly, start-ups and new ventures are more common in some industries than in others. The major industry groups that include successful new ventures and small businesses are services, retailing, construction, financial and insurance, wholesaling, transportation, and manufacturing. Obviously, each group differs in its requirements for employees, money, materials, and machines. In general, the more resources an industry requires, the harder it is to start a business and the less likely that the industry is dominated by small firms. Remember, too, that *small* is a relative term: The criteria (number of employees and total annual sales) differ from industry to industry and are often meaningful only when compared with businesses that are truly large. Figure 9.2 shows the distribution of all U.S. businesses employing fewer than 20 people across industry groups.

> "Entrepreneurship is certainly not the exclusive province of business. It can mushroom anywhere."
>
> —BARRON HARVEY,
> DEAN OF HOWARD UNIVERSITY'S BUSINESS SCHOOL[13]

**Services** Primarily because they require few resources, service businesses are the fastest-growing segment of small-business enterprise. In addition, no other industry group offers a higher return on time invested for start-ups and new ventures. Finally, services appeal to the talent for innovation typified by many new enterprises. As Figure 9.3 shows, around 35.5 percent of all businesses with fewer than 20 employees are services.

Small-business services range from shoeshine parlors to car rental agencies, from marriage counseling to computer software, from accounting and management consulting to professional dog walking. In Dallas, for example, Jani-King has prospered by selling commercial cleaning services to local companies. In Virginia Beach, Virginia, Jackson Hewitt Tax Services has found a profitable niche in providing computerized tax preparation and electronic tax-filing services. Great Clips, Inc. is a fast-growing family-run chain of hair salons headquartered in Minneapolis.

## FIGURE 9.2  SMALL BUSINESSES (BUSINESSES WITH FEWER THAN 20 EMPLOYEES) BY INDUSTRY

Small businesses are especially strong in certain industries, such as retailing and services. On the other hand, there are relatively fewer small businesses in industries such as transportation and manufacturing. The differences are affected primarily by factors such as the investment costs necessary to enter markets in these industries. For example, starting a new airline would require the purchase of large passenger aircraft and airport gates, and hiring an expensive set of employees.

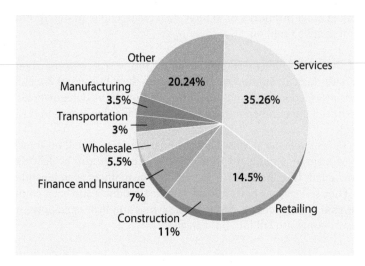

Source: U.S. Census Bureau, *Statistical Abstract of the United States*, 2014

**Retailing** A retail business sells directly to consumers products manufactured by other firms. There are hundreds of different kinds of retailers, ranging from wig shops and frozen yogurt stands to automobile dealerships and department stores. Usually, however, people who start small businesses favor specialty shops—for example, big-men's clothing or gourmet coffees—which let them focus limited resources on narrow market segments. Retailing accounts for around 14.5 percent of all businesses with fewer than 20 employees.

John Mackey, for example, launched Whole Foods out of his own frustration at being unable to find a full range of natural foods at other stores. He soon found, however, that he had tapped a lucrative market and started an ambitious expansion program. Today, with more than 410 outlets scattered across the United States, Canada, and the United Kingdom, Whole Foods is the world's leader in natural and organic foods supermarkets.[14] Likewise, when Olga Tereshko found it difficult to locate just the right cloth diapers and breast-feeding supplies for her newborn son, she decided to start selling them herself. Instead of taking the conventional retailing route, however, Tereshko set up shop on the Internet. Her business, called Little Koala, has established a customer base of over 10,000 loyal customers.

Retailing is a common industry for start-ups and new ventures. About 14.5 percent of all businesses with fewer than 20 employers compete in the retail industry.

**Construction**    About 11 percent of businesses with fewer than 20 employees are involved in construction. Because many construction jobs are relatively small local projects, local construction firms are often ideally suited as contractors. Many such firms are begun by skilled craftspeople who start out working for someone else and subsequently decide to work for themselves. Common examples of small construction firms include home builders, wood finishers, roofers, painters, and plumbing, electrical, and roofing contractors.

For example, Marek Brothers Construction in College Station, Texas, was started by two brothers, Pat and Joe Marek. They originally worked for other contractors but started their own partnership in 1980. Their only employee is a receptionist. They manage various construction projects, including new-home construction and remodeling, subcontracting out the actual work to other businesses or to individual craftspeople. Marek Brothers has annual gross income of about $5 million.

**Finance and Insurance**    Financial and insurance businesses comprise about 7 percent of all firms with fewer than 20 employees. In most cases, these businesses are either affiliates of or sell products provided by larger national firms. Although the deregulation of the banking industry has reduced the number of small local banks, other businesses in this sector are still doing quite well.

Typically, for example, local State Farm Mutual offices are small businesses. State Farm itself is a major insurance company, but its local offices are run by 18,000 independent agents. In turn, agents hire their own staff, run their own offices as independent businesses, and so forth. They sell various State Farm insurance products and earn commissions from the premiums paid by their clients. Some local savings and loan operations, mortgage companies, and pawn shops also fall into this category.

**Wholesaling**    Small-business owners often do very well in wholesaling, too; about 5.5 percent of businesses with fewer than 20 employees are wholesalers. A wholesale business buys products from manufacturers or other producers and then sells them to retailers. Wholesalers usually buy goods in bulk and store them in quantity at locations that are convenient for retailers. For a given volume of business, therefore, they need fewer employees than manufacturers, retailers, or service providers.

They also serve fewer customers than other providers—usually those who repeatedly order large volumes of goods. Wholesalers in the grocery industry, for instance, buy packaged food in bulk from companies like Del Monte and Campbell and then sell it to both large grocery chains and smaller independent grocers. Luis Espinoza found a promising niche for Inca Quality Foods, a midwestern wholesaler that imports and distributes Latino foods for consumers from Mexico, the Caribbean, and Central America. Partnered with the large grocery-store chain Kroger, Espinoza's firm continues to grow steadily.[15]

**Transportation**    Some small firms—about 3 percent of all companies with fewer than 20 employees—do well in transportation and transportation-related businesses. Such firms include local taxi and limousine companies in smaller markets, charter airplane services, and tour operators. In addition, in many smaller markets, bus companies, and regional airlines subcontract local equipment maintenance to small businesses.

Consider, for example, some of the transportation-related small businesses at a ski resort like Steamboat Springs, Colorado. Most visitors fly to the town of Hayden, about 15 miles from Steamboat Springs. Although some visitors rent vehicles, many others use the services of Alpine Taxi, a small local operation, to transport them to their destinations in Steamboat Springs. While on vacation, they also rely on the local bus service, which is subcontracted by the town to another small business, to get to and from the ski slopes each day. Other small businesses offer van tours of the region, hot-air balloon rides, and helicopter lifts to remote areas for extreme skiers. Still others provide maintenance support at Hayden for the American and United aircraft that serve the area during ski season.

**Manufacturing** More than any other industry, manufacturing lends itself more to big businesses than smaller businesses—and for good reason. Because of the investment normally required in equipment, energy, and raw materials, a good deal of money is usually needed to start a manufacturing business. Automobile manufacturing, for example, calls for billions of dollars of investment and thousands of workers before the first automobile rolls off the assembly line. Obviously, such requirements shut out most individuals. Although Henry Ford began with $28,000, it would take a much larger sum today to create a new car company from scratch.

Research has shown that manufacturing costs often fall as the number of units produced by an organization increases. This relationship between cost and production is called an *economy of scale*.[16] Small organizations usually cannot compete effectively on the basis of economies of scale. As depicted in Figure 9.3(a), organizations with higher levels of production have a major cost advantage over those with lower levels of production. Given the cost positions of small and large firms when there are strong economies of scale in manufacturing, it is not surprising that small manufacturing organizations generally do not do as well as large ones.

Interestingly, when technology in an industry changes, it often shifts the economies-of-scale curve, thereby creating opportunities for smaller organizations. For example, steel manufacturing was historically dominated by a few large companies, which owned several huge facilities. With the development of mini-mill technology, however, extracting

Manufacturing tends to be a more favorable industry for larger businesses rather than smaller ones. This is due in large part to large initial investment required to build and outfit a factory or other production facility. Still, some start-ups and new ventures manage to succeed in manufacturing.

## FIGURE 9.3 ECONOMIES OF SCALE IN SMALL-BUSINESS ORGANIZATIONS

Small businesses sometimes find it difficult to compete in manufacturing-related industries because of the economies of scale associated with plant, equipment, and technology. As shown in (a), firms that produce a large number of units (that is, larger businesses) can do so at a lower per-unit cost. At the same time, however, new forms of technology occasionally cause the economies-of-scale curve to shift, as illustrated in (b). In this case, smaller firms may be able to compete more effectively with larger ones because of the drop in per-unit manufacturing cost.

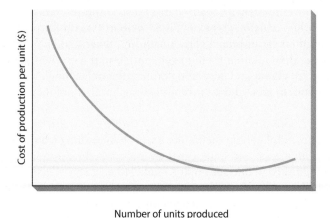

**(a) Standard economies-of-scale curve**

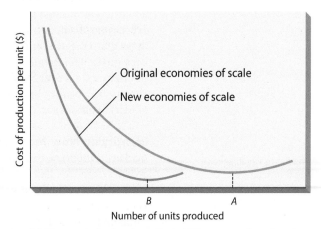

**(b) Change in technology that shifts economies of scale and may make small-business manufacturing possible**

economies of scale at a much smaller level of production became possible. This type of shift is depicted in Figure 9.3(b). Point A in this panel is the low-cost point with the original economies of scale. Point B is the low-cost point with the economies of scale brought on by the new technology. Notice that the number of units needed for low costs is considerably lower for the new technology. This has allowed the entry of many smaller firms into the steel industry. Such entry would not have been possible with the older technology.

This is not to say that there are no small-business owners who do well in manufacturing—about 3.5 percent of businesses with fewer than 20 employees are involved in some aspect of manufacturing. Indeed, it is not uncommon for small manufacturers to outperform big business in such innovation-driven industries as chemistry, electronics, toys, and computer software. Some small manufacturers prosper by serving as suppliers to large manufacturers. Our *Leading the Way* feature highlights a high-profile start-up manufacturer that, so far at least, seems to be doing very well.

## Emphasizing Distinctive Competencies

As we defined in Chapter 7, an organization's distinctive competencies are the aspects of business that the firm performs better than its competitors. The distinctive competencies of small business usually fall into three areas: the ability to identify new niches in established markets, the ability to identify new markets, and the ability to move quickly to take advantage of new opportunities.

**Identifying Niches in Established Markets** An established market is one in which several large firms compete according to relatively well-defined criteria. For example, for years the cellular telephone market was dominated by firms like Nokia and Motorola. These firms competed on the bases of size, design, and price. Meanwhile, so-called PDAs like the BlackBerry prospered by providing remote e-mail service. But then Apple introduced the iPhone and everything changed. The iPhone served as a telephone, an e-mail device, and also provided web browsing service.

Apple's approach to competition has actually long been to identify a new niche in an established market. The first Apple computers, for example, used parts from other computer manufacturers. It was user friendliness that separated Apple from the rest of the pack. A niche is simply a segment of a market that is not currently being exploited. In general, start-ups and new ventures are better at discovering these niches than are larger organizations. Large organizations usually have so many resources committed to older, established business practices that they are less vigilant about new opportunities. Entrepreneurs can see these opportunities and move quickly to take advantage of them.[17]

Dave Gilboa and Neil Blumenthal founded Warby Parker, a business that sells prescription eyewear through the mail. The entrepreneurs realized that most consumers disliked the experience of going to an optical shop to try on glasses and then were irritated at the price of those glasses. So, Warby Parker offers lower-priced glasses with hip designs and a money-back guarantee. Astute marketing then allowed them to get a quick start with their niche business, selling over 50,000 pairs of glasses and generating profits after only a single year of operation.[18] Warby Parker continues to grow and is currently selling hundreds of thousands of pairs of glasses each year.

**Identifying New Markets** Successful entrepreneurs also excel at discovering whole new markets. Discovery can happen in at least two ways. First, an entrepreneur can transfer a product or service that is well established in one geographic market to a second market. This is what Marcel Bich did with ballpoint pens, which occupied a well-established market in Europe before Bich introduced them to this country. Bich's company, Société Bic, eventually came to dominate the U.S. market for low-priced pens.

Second, entrepreneurs can sometimes create entire industries. Entrepreneurial inventions of the dry paper copying process and the semiconductor have created vast new industries.

**established market**
A market in which several large firms compete according to relatively well-defined criteria

**niche**
A segment of a market not currently being exploited

# Current Affairs in the Electric Vehicle Business

On June 12, 2014, Tesla Motors CEO Elon Musk informed the high-tech world that "Tesla will not initiate patent lawsuits against anyone who, in good faith, wants to use our technology." Musk's unexpected open-source initiative was no mere token of technological outreach: Tesla holds more than 300 valuable patents—with many more pending—on the technology behind mass-produced fully electric cars.

Even so, Musk says that his patent-sharing overture is "a modest thing." In order to reach the kind of goals that he's set for Tesla, Musk feels that he can't be satisfied with the usual pace of technological advancement, whether in his own company or among other organizations that share his goals. If there's a certain sense of urgency in Musk's gambit, it's because his ultimate goal isn't merely to sell more electric cars than anybody else: What he really wants to do is to disrupt the global automotive infrastructure in order to make the planet safe for automotive transportation. "I don't think people quite appreciate the gravity of what's going on [with regard to global warming]," says Musk. "We really need to do something. It would be shortsighted if we try to hold these things close to the vest."

As drastic as it may seem, Musk's strategy isn't unheard of in Silicon Valley, where firms that rely heavily on innovative technology must often be more concerned with developing a market for innovative ideas than with protecting them. Musk has done the math. There are about 2 billion cars on the road worldwide, with new-vehicle production approaching 100 million units per year. Unfortunately, zero-emission vehicles like Tesla's latest Model S account for less than 1 percent of those 100 million vehicles, and neither Musk nor anyone else can do much for the planet at that rate. At the same time, however, there are potential customers for electric cars—literally billions, in fact, and Tesla sees his biggest challenge as persuading a significant number of them to switch from gasoline-powered vehicles. He reasons that if competitors share Tesla's vested interest in electric-car technology, then they'll contribute not only to the technology but to the effort to develop a market for it. In short, Musk is convinced that "Tesla, other companies making electric cars, and the world would all benefit from a common, rapidly evolving technological platform. ...

"It's the velocity of innovation that matters," says Musk. "You want to be innovating so fast that you invalidate your prior patents, in terms of what really matters." Musk, for whom staying ahead of the competition and leading the way to the car of the future are the same thing, isn't worried about either the pace at which other companies can make use of Tesla technology or about Tesla's ability to pick up its own pace in improving in-house technology. Right now, Tesla has a comfortable lead in the all-important areas of battery-pack and power-management technology, including the circuitry in its large battery pack, the process by which it cools the batteries in the pack, and the software that regulates the power flow between battery pack and motor.

Tesla has already cut the cost of the battery back—a flat slab of densely packed lithium-ion cells tucked inconspicuously between the rear wheels of the Model S—from half the car's total cost to less than a fourth. It also gives the Model S a range of 265 miles between charges—about triple that of Nissan's Leaf and Chevy's Volt—and it's supported by a (currently modest) network of "supercharger" stations that deliver a 200-mile charge in 30 minutes, compared to several hours at ordinary stations. Finally, Tesla has plans to build a massive $5 billion "Gigafactory" to manufacture both cars and batteries.

*References:* Ashlee Vance, "Why Elon Musk Just Opened Tesla's Patents to His Biggest Rivals," *BloombergBusinessweek* (June 12, 2014), www.businessweek.com, on October 31, 2014; William J. Watkins Jr., "Rethinking Patent Enforcement: Tesla Did What?" *Forbes* (July 17, 2014), www.forbes.com, on November 1, 2014; Elmira Mateva, "Tesla Motors Inc. Share Price Down, Musk Opens Patents Vault to Speed Up Electric Car Development," *Binary Tribune* (June 13, 2014), www.binarytribune, on November 1, 2014; Kevin Bullis, "How Tesla Is Driving Electric Car Innovation," *MIT Technology Review* (August 7, 2013), wwwtechnologyreview.com, on October 31, 2014; John Gertner, "Why Tesla Motors Is Betting on the Model S," *Fast Company* (March 19, 2012), www.fastcompany.com, on October 31, 2014; Kyle Stock, "With Big Obstacles Ahead, Tesla Still Isn't Checking Its Rear View Mirror," *BloombergBusinessweek* (May 8, 2014), www.businessweek.com, on October 31, 2014.

Not only have the first companies into these markets been very successful (Xerox and National Semiconductor, respectively), but their entrepreneurial activity has spawned the development of hundreds of other companies and hundreds of thousands of jobs. Again, because entrepreneurs are not encumbered with a history of doing business in a particular way, they are usually better at discovering new markets than are larger, more mature organizations.

**First-Mover Advantages** A first-mover advantage is any advantage that comes to a firm because it exploits an opportunity before any other firm does. Sometimes large firms discover niches within existing markets or new markets at just about the same time as start-ups or new ventures, but they cannot move as quickly as these smaller companies to take advantage of these opportunities.

There are many reasons for this difference. For example, many large organizations make decisions slowly because each of their many layers of hierarchy has to approve an action before it can be implemented. Also, large organizations may sometimes put a great deal of their assets at risk when they take advantage of new opportunities. Every time Boeing decides to build a new model of a commercial jet, it is making a decision that could literally bankrupt the company if it does not turn out well. The size of the risk may make large organizations cautious. The dollar value of the assets at risk in a small organization, in contrast, is quite small. Managers may be willing to "bet the company" when the value of the company is only $100,000. They might be unwilling to "bet the company" when the value of the company is $1 billion.

## Writing a Business Plan

Once an entrepreneur has chosen an industry to compete in and determined which distinctive competencies to emphasize, these choices are usually included in a document called a business plan. In a business plan the entrepreneur summarizes the business strategy and how that strategy is to be implemented. The very act of preparing a business plan forces prospective entrepreneurs to crystallize their thinking about what they must do to launch their business successfully and obliges them to develop their business on paper before investing time and money in it. The idea of a business plan is not new. What is new is the growing use of specialized business plans by entrepreneurs, mostly because creditors and investors demand them for use in deciding whether to help finance a small business.[19]

The plan should describe the match between the entrepreneur's abilities and the requirements for producing and marketing a particular product or service. It should define strategies for production and marketing, legal aspects and organization, and accounting and finance. In particular, it should answer three questions: (1) What are the entrepreneur's goals and objectives? (2) What strategies will the entrepreneur use to obtain these goals and objectives? (3) How will the entrepreneur implement these strategies?

Business plans should also account for the sequential nature of much strategic decision making in start-ups and new ventures. For example, entrepreneurs cannot forecast sales revenues without first researching markets. The sales forecast itself is one of the most important elements in the business plan. Without such forecasts, it is all but impossible to estimate intelligently the size of a plant, store, or office, or to determine how much inventory to carry or how many employees to hire.

Another important component of the overall business plan is financial planning, which translates all other activities into dollars. Generally, the financial plan is made up of a cash budget, an income statement, balance sheets, and a breakeven chart. The most important of these statements is the cash budget because it tells entrepreneurs how much money they need before they open for business and how much money they need to keep the business operating.

**first-mover advantage**
Any advantage that comes to a firm because it exploits an opportunity before any other firm does

**business plan**
A document that summarizes the business strategy and structure

## Entrepreneurship and International Markets

Finally, although many people associate international management with big business, many smaller companies are also finding expansion and growth opportunities in foreign countries. For example, California-based Gold's Gym is expanding into foreign countries and has been especially successful in Russia. And Markel Corporation, a small Philadelphia-based firm that manufactures tubing and insulated wiring, derives 42 percent of its annual revenues (currently around $52 million) from international sales. Although such ventures are accompanied by considerable risks, they also give entrepreneurs new opportunities and can be a real catalyst for success.

California-based Gold's Gym has enjoyed considerable success in international markets, especially Russia.

Pavel L Photo and Video/Shutterstock.com

☐ Would-be entrepreneurs need to carefully assess industries and be fully aware of distinctive competencies when launching a start-up or new venture.

☐ Entrepreneurs should also not underestimate the importance of a well-constructed business plan.

**Manager's Checklist**

# Structure of Start-Ups and New Ventures

With a strategy in place and a business plan in hand, the entrepreneur can then proceed to devise a structure that turns the vision of the business plan into a reality. Many of the same concerns in structuring any business, which are described in the next five chapters of this book, are also relevant to small businesses. For example, entrepreneurs need to consider organization design and develop job descriptions, organization charts, and management control systems.

Getting into business today is easier and faster than ever before, there are many more potential opportunities than at any other time in history, and the ability to gather and assimilate information is at an all-time high. Even so, would-be entrepreneurs must still make the right decisions when they start. They must decide, for example, precisely how to get into business. Should they buy an existing business or build from the ground up? In addition, would-be entrepreneurs must find appropriate sources of financing and decide when and how to seek the advice of experts.

## Starting the New Business

The first step in launching a start-up or new venture is the individual's commitment to becoming a business owner. Next comes choosing the goods or services to be offered—a process that means investigating one's chosen industry and market. Making this choice also requires would-be entrepreneurs to assess not only industry trends but also their own skills. Like the managers of existing businesses, new business owners must also be sure that they understand the true nature of the enterprise in which they are engaged.

**Buying an Existing Business** After choosing a product and making sure that the choice fits their own skills and interests, entrepreneurs must decide whether to buy an existing business or to start from scratch. Consultants often recommend the first approach. Quite simply, the odds are better: If successful, an existing business has already proved its ability to draw customers at a profit. It has also established working relationships with lenders, suppliers, and the community. Moreover, the track record of an existing business gives potential buyers a much clearer picture of what to expect than any estimate of a new business's prospects. Around 30 percent of the new businesses started each year are bought from someone else. The McDonald's empire, for example, was started when Ray Kroc bought an existing hamburger business and then turned it into a global phenomenon. Likewise, Starbucks was a struggling mail-order business when Howard Schultz bought it and turned his attention to retail expansion.

> "It never really feels like, 'I have arrived,' or we are where we want to be. I am never surprised. I am happy, I am pleased, but we have so much to do."
>
> —SUSAN PETERSON, FOUNDER OF HERBALIFE[20]

**Starting from Scratch** Some people, however, prefer the satisfaction that comes from planting an idea, nurturing it, and making it grow into a strong and sturdy business. There are also practical reasons to start a business from scratch. A new business does not suffer the ill effects of a prior owner's errors. The start-up owner is also free to choose lenders, equipment, inventories, locations, suppliers, and workers, unbound by a predecessor's commitments and policies. Around 70 of the start-ups and new ventures launched each year are started from scratch.

Not surprisingly, though, the risks of starting a business from scratch are greater than those of buying an existing firm. Founders of start-ups and new ventures can only make predictions and projections about their prospects. Success or failure thus depends heavily on identifying a genuine business opportunity—a product for which many customers will pay well but which is currently unavailable to them. To find openings, entrepreneurs must study markets and answer the following questions: (1) Who are my customers? (2) Where are they? (3) At what price will they buy my product? (4) In what quantities will they buy? (5) Who are my competitors? (6) How will my product differ from those of my competitors?

Finding answers to these questions is a difficult task even for large, well-established firms. But where can the new business owner get the necessary information? Other sources of assistance are discussed later in this chapter, but we briefly describe three of the most accessible here. For example, the best way to gain knowledge about a market is to work in it before going into business in it. If you once worked in a bookstore and now plan to open one of your own, you probably already have some idea about the kinds of books people request and buy. Second, a quick web scan will reveal many potential competitors, as will advertisements in trade journals. Personal visits to these establishments and websites can give you insights into their strengths and weaknesses. And, third, studying magazines, books, and websites aimed specifically at start-ups and new ventures can also be of help, as can hiring professionals to survey the market for you.

## Financing the New Business

Although the choice of how to start is obviously important, it is meaningless unless a new business owner can obtain the money to set up shop. Among the more common sources for funding are family and friends, personal savings, banks and similar lending institutions, investors, and government agencies. Lending institutions are more likely to help finance the purchase of an existing business than a new business because the risks are better understood. Individuals launching a start-up or new venture are more likely to have to rely on their personal resources.

**Personal Resources** According to research by the National Federation of Independent Business, an owner's personal resources, not loans, are the most important source of money. Including money borrowed from friends and relatives, personal resources account for over two-thirds of all money invested in start-ups and new ventures and one-half of that invested in the purchase of existing businesses. John Mackey started Whole Foods with a $10,000 loan from his father. Fred Smith used $4 million he had inherited from his father to launch FedEx. And Rebecca Boenigk started Neutral Posture, an ergonomic chair company, with personal savings and loans from several family members.

**Strategic Alliances**  Strategic alliances are also becoming a popular method for financing business growth. When Steven and Andrew Grundy decided to launch an Internet CD-exchange business called Spun.com, they had very little capital and thus made extensive use of alliances with other firms. They partnered, for example, with wholesaler Alliance Entertainment Corporation as a CD

Fred Smith, founder of FedEx, saw a need for efficient and fast delivery of goods. He used a $4 million inheritance to realize his entrepreneurial dream.

supplier. Orders to Spun.com actually go to Alliance, which ships products to customers and bills Spun.com directly. This setup allowed Spun.com to promote a vast inventory of labels without actually having to tie up its own resources in inventory. All told, the firm quickly created an alliance network that provided the equivalent of $40 million in capital.[21] Today Spun.com has expanded into offering an online exchange market not only for CDs but also for vinyl records, DVDs, and games.

**Traditional Lenders**  Although banks, independent investors, and government loans all provide much smaller portions of start-up funds than the personal resources of owners, they are important in many cases. Getting money from these sources, however, requires some extra effort. Banks and private investors usually want to see formal business plans—detailed outlines of proposed businesses and markets, owners' backgrounds, and other sources of funding. Government loans have strict eligibility guidelines.

**Venture Capital Companies**  Venture capital companies are groups of small investors seeking to make profits on companies with rapid growth potential. Most of these firms do not lend money: They invest it, supplying capital in return for stock. The venture capital company may also demand a representative on the board of directors. In some cases, managers may even need approval from the venture capital company before making major decisions. Of all venture capital currently committed in the United States, around 25 percent comes from pure venture capital firms.[22] In 2014, venture capital firms invested $30 billion in new start-ups in the United States.

As noted earlier, Fred Smith used his inheritance to launch FedEx. Once he got his business plan developed and started service, though, he needed an infusion of substantial additional capital. All told, he raised about $80 million in venture capital to buy his first small fleet of planes. Venture capital was also important in the launch of both Facebook and Twitter.

**Small-Business Investment Companies**  Taking a more balanced approach in their choices than venture capital companies, small-business investment companies (SBICs) seek profits by investing in companies with potential for rapid growth. Created by the Small Business Investment Act of 1958, SBICs are federally licensed to borrow money from the SBA and to invest it in or lend it to start-ups and new ventures. They are themselves investments for their shareholders. Past beneficiaries of SBIC capital include Apple, Intel, and FedEx. In addition, the government has recently begun to sponsor *minority enterprise small-business*

**venture capital company**
A group of small investors seeking to make profits on companies with rapid growth potential

*investment companies* (MESBICs) under a separate program. As the name suggests, MESBICs specialize in financing businesses that are owned and operated by minorities.

**SBA Financial Programs** Since its founding in 1953, the SBA has offered more than 20 financing programs to small businesses (both new and ongoing) that meet certain standards of size and independence. Eligible firms must also be unable to get private financing at reasonable terms. Because of these and other restrictions, SBA loans have never been a major source of small-business financing. In addition, budget cutbacks at the SBA have reduced the number of firms benefiting from loans. Nevertheless, several SBA programs currently offer funds to qualified applicants.

For example, under the SBA's guaranteed loans program, small businesses can borrow from commercial lenders. The SBA guarantees to repay 75 to 85 percent of the loan amount, not to exceed $5 million. Under a related program, small companies engaged in international trade can also borrow up to $5 million. Such loans may be made for as long as 15 years for machinery and equipment and up to 25 years for real estate. Most SBA lending activity flows through this program.

Sometimes, however, both desired bank and SBA-guaranteed loans are unavailable (perhaps because the business cannot meet stringent requirements). In such cases, the SBA may help finance the entrepreneur through its immediate participation loan program. Under this arrangement, the SBA and the bank each puts up a share of the money, with the SBA's share not to exceed $150,000. Under the local development companies (LDCs) program, the SBA works with a corporation (either for-profit or nonprofit) founded by local citizens who want to boost the local economy. The SBA can lend up to $500,000 for each small business to be helped by an LDC.

**Crowdfunding** In the last few years new sources of funding for start-ups and new ventures have also emerged. The most common ones are a form of crowdfunding. This is done through several different online services. Essentially, entrepreneurs post details of their ideas for a start-up or new venture, along with other key information. Would-be investors then peruse the ideas that are posted and decide if they want to help fund the start-up or new venture. Some services limit investments to ownership stakes (i.e., invest a certain number of dollars for a certain percentage of ownership in the business). Other services focus more on loans with agreed-upon repayment terms.

## Sources of Management Advice

Financing is not the only area in which start-ups and new ventures may need help. Until World War II, for example, the business world involved few regulations, few taxes, few records, few big competitors, and no computers. Since then, simplicity has given way to complexity. Today, few entrepreneurs are equipped with all the business skills they need to survive. New business owners can no longer be their own troubleshooters, lawyers, bookkeepers, financiers, and tax experts. For these jobs, they rely on professional help. To survive and grow, however, start-ups and new ventures may also need advice about management. This advice is usually available from four sources: advisory boards, management consultants, the SBA, and the process of networking.

**Advisory Boards** All companies, even those that do not legally need boards of directors, can benefit from the problem-solving abilities of advisory boards. Thus some start-ups and new ventures create boards to provide advice and assistance. For example, an advisory board might help an entrepreneur determine the best way to finance a plant expansion or to start exporting products to foreign markets.

**Management Consultants** Opinions vary widely about the value of management consultants—experts who charge fees to help managers solve problems. They often specialize in one area, such as international business, start-ups and new ventures, on-going small businesses, or manufacturing. Thus they can bring an objective and trained outlook to problems and provide logical recommendations. They can be quite expensive, however, as some consultants charge $1,000 or more for a day of assistance.

Like other professionals, consultants should be chosen with care. They can be found through major corporations that have used their services and can provide references and reports on their work. Not surprisingly, they are most effective when the client helps (for instance, by providing schedules and written proposals for work to be done).

**The Small Business Administration**  Even more important than its financing role is the SBA's role in helping new business owners improve their management skills. It is easy for entrepreneurs to spend money; SBA programs are designed to show them how to spend it wisely. The SBA offers small businesses a variety of advisory programs at little or no cost.

An entrepreneur who needs help in starting a new business can get it free through the Service Corps of Retired Executives (SCORE). All SCORE members are retired executives, and all are volunteers. Under this program, the SBA tries to match the expert to the need. For example, if a new business owner needs help putting together a marketing plan, the SBA will link the business owner with a SCORE counselor with marketing expertise. SCORE currently includes more than 11,000 counselors.

The talents and skills of students and instructors at colleges and universities are fundamental to the Small Business Institute (SBI). Under the guidance of seasoned professors of business administration, students seeking advanced degrees work closely with small-business owners to help solve specific problems, such as sagging sales or rising costs. Students earn credit toward their degree, with their grades depending on how well they handle a client's problems. Several hundred colleges and universities counsel thousands of small-business owners through this program every year.

The Small Business Administration (SBA) plays an important role in the success of many new businesses. This speaker, for example, is sharing advice and information with small business owners at an SBA-sponsored conference.

Finally, another SBA management counseling project is its Small Business Development Center (SBDC) program. SBDCs are designed to consolidate information from various disciplines and institutions, including technical and professional schools. Then they make this knowledge available to new and existing small businesses. Currently, universities in 36 states take part in the program.

**Networking**  More and more, entrepreneurs and new business owners are discovering the value of networking—meeting regularly with one another to discuss common problems and opportunities and, perhaps most important, to pool resources. Businesspeople have long joined organizations such as the local chamber of commerce and the National Federation of Independent Businesses (NFIB) to make such contacts.

Today, organizations are springing up all over the United States to facilitate small-business networking. One such organization, the Council of Smaller Enterprises of Cleveland, boasts a total membership of nearly 14,000 small-business owners, the largest number in the country. This organization offers its members not only networking possibilities but also educational programs and services tailored to their needs. In a typical year, its 85 educational programs draw more than 8,500 small-business owners.

In particular, women and minorities have found networking to be an effective problem-solving tool. The National Association of Women Business Owners (NAWBO), for example, provides a variety of networking forums. The NAWBO also has chapters in most major cities, where its members can meet regularly. Increasingly, women are relying more

Networking is playing an increasingly important role in new ventures and start-ups. These people, for example, either own a new business or are in the process of launching one. This networking event will help them make important contacts and share advise.

on other women to help locate venture capital, establish relationships with customers, and provide such essential services as accounting and legal advice. According to Patty Abramson of the Women's Growth Capital Fund, all of these tasks have traditionally been harder for women because, until now, they have never had friends in the right places. "I wouldn't say this is about discrimination," adds Abramson. "It's about not having the relationships, and business is about relationships."

## Franchising

The next time you drive or walk around town, be on the alert for a McDonald's, Taco Bell, Subway, Denny's, or KFC restaurant; a 7-Eleven or Circle K convenience store; a RE/MAX or Coldwell Banker real estate office; a Holiday Inn or Ramada Inn motel; a Sylvan Learning Center or Mathnaseum educational center; an Express Oil Change or Precision Auto Wash service center; or a Supercuts hair salon. What do these businesses have in common? In most cases, they are franchised operations, operating under licenses issued by parent companies to local entrepreneurs who own and manage them.

As many would-be businesspeople have discovered, franchising agreements are an accessible doorway to entrepreneurship. A franchise is an arrangement that permits the *franchisee* (buyer) to sell the product of the *franchiser* (seller, or parent company). Franchisees can thus benefit from the selling corporation's experience and expertise. They can also consult the franchiser for managerial and financial help.[23]

For example, the franchiser may supply financing. It may pick the store location, negotiate the lease, design the store, and purchase necessary equipment. It may train the first set of employees and managers and provide standardized policies and procedures. Once the business is open, the franchiser may offer franchisees savings by allowing them to purchase from a central location. Marketing strategy (especially advertising) may also be handled by the franchiser. Finally, franchisees may benefit from continued management counseling. In short, franchisees receive—that is, invest in—not only their own ready-made business but also expert help in running it.

Franchises offer many advantages to both sellers and buyers. For example, franchisers benefit from the ability to grow rapidly by using the investment money provided by franchisees. This strategy has enabled giant franchisers such as McDonald's and Subway to mushroom into billion-dollar concerns in a brief time.

For the franchisee, the arrangement combines the incentive of owning a business with the advantage of access to big-business management skills. Unlike the person who starts from scratch, the franchisee does not have to build a business step by step. Instead, the business is established virtually overnight. Moreover, because each franchise outlet is probably a carbon copy of every other outlet, the chances of failure are reduced. McDonald's, for example, is a model of consistency—Big Macs taste the same everywhere.

Of course, owning a franchise also involves certain disadvantages. Perhaps the most significant is the start-up cost. Franchise prices vary widely. Fantastic Sams hair salon franchise costs are $185,000. Extremely profitable or hard-to-get franchises are much more expensive, though. A McDonald's franchise costs $750,000 plus the costs of building the restaurant itself. Franchisees may also have continued obligations to contribute percentages of sales to the parent corporation.

**franchising agreement**
A contract between an entrepreneur (the franchisee) and a parent company (the franchiser); the entrepreneur pays the parent company for the use of its trademarks, products, formulas, and business plans

Buying a franchise also entails less-tangible costs. For one thing, the small-business owner sacrifices some independence. A McDonald's franchisee cannot change the way its hamburgers or milkshakes are made. Nor can franchisees create an individual identity in their community; for all practical purposes, the McDonald's owner is anonymous. In addition, many franchise agreements are difficult to terminate. *Beyond Traditional Business* highlights legal problems facing one new franchising operation.

Finally, although franchises minimize risks, they do not guarantee success. Many franchisees have seen their investments—and their dreams—disappear because of poor location, rising costs, or lack of continued franchiser commitment. Moreover, figures on failure rates are artificially low because they do not include failing franchisees bought out by their franchising parent companies. An additional risk is that the chain itself could collapse. In any given year, dozens—sometimes hundreds—of franchisers close shop or stop selling franchises.

---

☐ Would-be new business owners need a clear understanding of the pros and cons of starting a new business versus buying an existing one.

☐ Entrepreneurs need a clear financial plan in order to finance their start-up or new venture in the most effective manner possible. What are the pros and cons of starting a new business from scratch versus buying an existing business?

☐ Regardless of the size of their enterprise, managers should be aware of the various sources to which they may turn for advice and information.

**Manager's Checklist** ☑

---

**BEYOND TRADITIONAL BUSINESS**

## The Dating Service with a Date in Court

An article in *Minnesota Monthly*, a guide to arts and leisure in the Minneapolis-St. Paul area, recently touted the local franchise of It's Just Lunch (IJL) as "a fun solution to the age-old problem that many busy professionals face—finding the time to date." Franchise owner Sara Darling assured readers that IJL was "like hiring a personal assistant to help with your love life. … It's an intelligent approach to dating," she explained, "for those who want to be selective in their search." The local Better Business Bureau (BBB) gave Darling's franchise agency a *B+* rating, citing 18 client complaints on the downside but balancing that figure against 14 successful resolutions.

Granted, the one negative review received by the BBB was *very* negative: "If you're looking for a dating service that will lie, cheat, and steal from you," wrote a woman who signed herself "JC," "then please look no further than It's Just Lunch.

… The experience I had was unprofessional, unethical, and downright disgusting." The BBB doesn't typically go easy on small local businesses just because they're small and local. An IJL franchise in Florida, for instance, earned an *F* rating for failing to resolve 17 out of a barrage of 90 client complaints.

Founded in 1991, IJL International bills itself as "the world's #1 personal matchmaking service" and claimed in 2012 that it "offers dating services in over 150 cities in the U.S. and around the world and has matched tens of thousands of single professionals and arranged over 2 million first dates." Its services are pricier than the industry average, with a six-month contract guaranteeing one date per month for $1,500. "JC" says that she paid $2,200 for six dates, and when she complained about the company's failure to deliver the six rendezvous, she was told that "the contract terms only state six

*(Continued)*

introductions and an introduction is not an actual date; it's just us telling you about someone to see if you are interested."

The stipulated IJL process begins with an interview with "an experienced IJL director." "IM" from New York City paid $1,000 for a three-month contract during which, as she understood it, "the service was to set up dates from its database, take feedback from each person after the fact, and use the feedback to refine selections for subsequent rendezvous." The agency, however, failed to provide "IM," an affluent, well-educated woman who's typical of IJL's clientele, with suitable matches. "You expect some rejection when you sign up with a dating service," she admits, "but hearing 'Sorry, this isn't working' from a CVS employee" wasn't what she bargained for. When another New York professional woman asked for "a well-traveled New York City professional," she was matched with a 38-year-old man who still lived with his parents. "One of the dating coordinators," reported a San Diego woman, "set me up with her brother."

After Sarah Dunphy, who paid $2,700 for her membership, had been introduced to a series of "married, unemployed, or otherwise unsuitable partners" in 2007, she got a lawyer, and in May 2014, she was listed as lead plaintiff in a class-action lawsuit against IJL. According to the suit, IJL claims that its services are "tailored to the needs and desires of successful professionals" while representatives are in reality forced to meet "monthly quota requirements which … disregard customers' stated interests and preferences." The owner of the IJL franchise in San Diego admits that there are indeed quotas. If reps bring in $15,000 worth of business, explains Lisa Purdum, they get a bonus. Otherwise, they get just a base salary which, according to one San Diego ex-employee, "was so low it didn't make sense to work there."

*References:* "Sara Darling, Owner, It's Just Lunch," *Minnesota Monthly* (n.d.), www.minnesotamonthly.com, on November 5, 2014; Joel Waldman, "Complaints about Dating Service," *myfoxny.com* (February 14, 2012), www.myfoxny.com, on November 5, 2014; David Segal, "In Search of Romance, and Maybe a Refund," *New York Times* (July 27, 2013), www.nytimes.com, on November 5, 2014; Chris Francescani, "Cupid Shook Me Down: Top-Tier Dating Service Sued," ABC News (October 22, 2007), http://abcnews.go.com, on November 5, 2014; "Ex-Employee: Dating Service Forced Questionable Matches," ABC 10 News (San Diego) (February 8, 2011), www.10news.com, on November 6, 2014; Jonathan Stempel, "It's Just Lunch to Face U.S. Class-Action Lawsuit over Matchmaking Claims," Reuters (May 14, 2014), www.reuters.com, on November 5, 2014; Christina Davis, "Matchmaking Service 'It's Just Lunch!' Hit with Class-Action Lawsuit," *Top Class Actions* (September 15, 2014), http://topclassactions.com, on November 5, 2014.

# The Performance of Start-Ups and New Ventures

The formulation and implementation of an effective strategy plays a major role in determining the overall performance of a start-up or new venture. This section examines how start-ups and new ventures evolve over time and the attributes of these firms that enhance their chances of success. For every Henry Ford, Walt Disney, Mary Kay Ash, or Bill Gates—people who transformed fledgling small businesses into major corporations—there are many small-business owners and entrepreneurs who fail.

Exact numbers of start-ups and failures are surprisingly difficult to determine, however. For instance, a business may shut down because it is out of money (a failure) or simply because the owner decides to do something else; or the business may be sold to another business and cease to exist as an independent entity. Likewise, an ongoing sole proprietorship that becomes a partnership or corporation is not really a new business but may be counted as such in some statistics; similarly, a large corporation might launch a new enterprise as a new wholly owned but separately incorporated enterprise.

In general, though, experts believe that new business start-ups generally run between 400,000 and 450,000 per year and that business failures generally run between 425,000 and

475,000 per year. In this section, we look first at a few key trends in small-business start-ups. Then we examine some of the main reasons for success and failure in small-business undertakings.

## Trends in Start-Ups and New Ventures

Thousands of new businesses are started in the United States every year. Several factors account for this trend, and in this section we focus on four of them.

**Emergence of E-Commerce** Clearly, one of the most significant recent trends in start-ups and new ventures is the rapid emergence of electronic commerce. Because the Internet has provided fundamentally new ways of doing business, savvy entrepreneurs have been able to create and expand new businesses faster and more easily than ever before. Such leading-edge firms as Google, Amazon, eBay, and Facebook, for example, owe their very existence to the Internet. At the same time, however, many would-be Internet entrepreneurs have also gone under. Still, in 2014, online retail sales exceeded $835 billion, and they are projected to top $1 trillion by 2020.

Indeed, it seems as if new ideas emerge virtually every day. Andrew Beebe, for example, is scoring big with Bigstep, a web business that essentially creates, hosts, and maintains websites for other small businesses. Bigstep has signed up over 100,000 small-business clients. Beebe actually provides his basic services for free but earns money by charging for such so-called premium services as customer billing and data analytics. Karl Jacob's Keen.com is a web business that matches people looking for advice with experts who have the answers. Keen got the idea when he and his father were struggling to fix a boat motor and did not know where to turn for help. Keen.com attracted 100,000 subscribers in just three months.

**Crossovers from Big Business** It is interesting to note that increasing numbers of businesses are being started by people who have opted to leave big corporations and put their experience and know-how to work for themselves. In some cases, these individuals see great new ideas they want to develop. Often, they get burned out working for a big corporation. Sometimes they have lost their jobs, only to discover that working for themselves was a better idea anyway.

Cisco Systems founder and long-time CEO John Chambers is acknowledged as one of the best entrepreneurs around. But he spent several years working first at IBM and then at Wang Laboratories before he set out on his own. Under his leadership, Cisco became one of the most important technology companies in the world. In a more unusual case, Gilman Louie left an executive position at Hasbro toy company's online group to head up a CIA-backed venture capital firm called In-Q-It. The firm's mission is to help nurture high-tech companies making products of interest to the nation's intelligence community.

**Opportunities for Minorities and Women** In addition to big-business expatriates, minorities and women are starting more small businesses. For example, the number of African American–owned businesses totals about 1.9 million, an increase of 60.5 percent since 2002. These businesses account for around 7.1 percent of all U.S. businesses, generate $137.5 billion in revenue, and employ 921,032 people. African American purchasing power is expected to soon hit $1.2 trillion, an increase of 35 percent since 2008.[24]

Latino-owned businesses have grown at a rate of 43.6 percent and now number about 2.3 million. Other ethnic groups are also making their presence felt among U.S. business owners. Business ownership among Asians and Pacific Islanders has increased 34.3 percent, to over 1.6 million. Although the number of businesses owned by American Indians and Alaska Natives is still somewhat small, at slightly over 235,000, the total nevertheless represents a five-year increase of 17.9 percent.

The number of women entrepreneurs is also growing rapidly. There are now around 8 million businesses owned by women—about 28.7 percent of all businesses in the

"Attitudes about women in the workplace, period, have changed, let alone women running their own businesses."

—ERIN FULLER, FORMER DIRECTOR OF THE NATIONAL ASSOCIATION OF WOMEN BUSINESS OWNERS[25]

United States and an increase of 20.1 percent since 2002. Combined, they generate nearly $1.2 trillion in revenue a year and employ 7.6 million people. Celeste Johnson, for example, left a management position at Pitney Bowes to launch Obex, Inc., which makes gardening and landscaping products from mixed recycled plastics. Katrina Garnett gave up a lucrative job at Oracle to start her own software company, Crossworlds Software. Laila Rubenstein closed her management-consulting practice to create Greeting Cards.com, Inc., an Internet-based business selling customizable electronic greetings. "Women-owned business," says Teresa Cavanaugh, director of the Women Entrepreneurs' Connection at BankBoston, "is the largest emerging segment of the small- business market. Women-owned businesses are an economic force that no bank can afford to overlook."

**Better Survival Rates** Finally, more people are encouraged to test their skills as entrepreneurs because the failure rate among small businesses has been declining in recent years. About half of start-ups and new ventures survive at least five years today. About a third survive at least 10 years, and over a quarter are still in operation after 15 years. For reasons discussed in the next section, start-ups and new ventures do suffer a higher mortality rate than larger concerns. Even so, however, survival rates are better now than at any time in the last 50 years.

## Reasons for Failure

Why do some businesses succeed and others fail? Although no set pattern has been established, four general factors contribute to new business failure. One factor is managerial incompetence or inexperience. Some would-be entrepreneurs assume that they can succeed through common sense, overestimate their own managerial acumen, or think that hard work alone will lead to success. But if managers do not know how to make basic business decisions or understand the basic concepts and principles of management, they are unlikely to be successful in the long run.

Neglect can also contribute to failure. Some entrepreneurs try either to launch their ventures in their spare time or to devote only a limited amount of time to a new business. But starting a new business requires an overwhelming time commitment. Entrepreneurs who are not willing to put in the time and effort that a business requires are unlikely to survive.

Third, weak control systems can lead to serious problems. Effective control systems are needed to keep a business on track and to help alert entrepreneurs to potential trouble. If control systems do not signal impending problems, managers may be in serious trouble before more visible difficulties alert them.

"I consider your rejection a lucky charm, because everything that ever happened in my life came on the heels of failure."

—BARBARA CORCORAN, *SHARK TANK* INVESTOR/REAL ESTATE MOGUL/SERIAL ENTREPRENEUR[27]

Finally, insufficient capital can contribute to new business failure. Some entrepreneurs are overly optimistic about how soon they will start earning profits. In most cases, however, it takes months or years before a business is likely to start turning a profit. Amazon.com, for example, has only recently started to generate profits. Most experts say that a new business should have enough capital to operate for at least six months without earning a profit; some recommend enough to last a year.[26]

## Reasons for Success

Similarly, four basic factors are typically cited to explain new business success. One factor is hard work, drive, and dedication. New business owners must be committed to succeeding and be willing to put in the time and effort to make it happen. Having positive feelings and a good outlook on life may also play an important role.[28]Kendra Scott started making unique jewelry with $500 in her pocket. Hard work, long hours, drive, and an innate sense of optimism kept her going. Today her jewelry is sold in Nordstrom, Bloomingdales, and Neiman-Marcus.

Careful analysis of market conditions can help new business owners assess the probable reception of their products in the marketplace. This will provide insights about market demand for proposed products and services. Whereas attempts to expand local restaurants specializing in baked potatoes, muffins, and gelato have been largely unsuccessful, hamburger and pizza chains continue to have an easier time expanding into new markets.

Managerial competence also contributes to success. Successful new business owners may acquire competence through training or experience or by using the expertise of others. Few successful entrepreneurs succeed alone or straight out of college. Most spend time working in successful companies or partner with others in order to bring more expertise to a new business.

Finally, luck also plays a role in the success of some firms. For example, after Alan McKim started Clean Harbors, an environmental cleanup firm based in New England, he struggled to keep his business afloat. Then the U.S. government committed $1.6 billion to toxic waste cleanup—McKim's specialty. He was able to get several large government contracts and put his business on solid financial footing. Had the government fund not been created at just the right time, McKim may well have failed.

---

□ Any would-be entrepreneur needs to understand important trends that may affect his or her business.

□ Managers of start-ups and new ventures should also candidly assess the factors that may lead to failure or success for their business.

---

# Summary of Learning Outcomes and Key Points

1. Discuss the nature of entrepreneurship, start-ups, and new ventures.

   - Entrepreneurship is the process of planning, organizing, operating, and assuming the risk of a business venture.
   - An entrepreneur is someone who engages in entrepreneurship. In general, entrepreneurs start new businesses.

2. Describe the role of entrepreneurships, starts-ups, and new ventures in society.

   - Start-ups and new ventures are an important source of innovation.
   - Start-ups and new ventures create many jobs.
   - Start-ups and new ventures contribute to the success of large businesses.

3. Understand the major issues involved in choosing strategies for small businesses and the role of international management in start-ups and new ventures.

   - In choosing strategies, entrepreneurs have to consider the characteristics of the industry in which they are going to conduct business.
   - Start-ups and new ventures generally have several distinctive competencies that they should exploit in choosing their strategy. Start-ups and new ventures are usually skilled at identifying niches in established markets, identifying new markets, and acting quickly to obtain first-mover advantages.
   - Start-ups and new ventures are usually not skilled at exploiting economies of scale.
   - Once an entrepreneur has chosen a strategy, the strategy is normally written down in a business plan. Writing a business plan forces an entrepreneur to plan thoroughly and to anticipate problems that might occur.

4. Discuss the structural challenges unique to start-ups and new ventures.

   - With a strategy and business plan in place, entrepreneurs must choose a structure to implement them.

All of the structural issues summarized in the next five chapters of this book are relevant to the entrepreneur.

- In addition, the entrepreneur has some unique structural choices to make. For example, the entrepreneur can buy an existing business or start a new one.
- In determining financial structure, an entrepreneur has to decide how much personal capital to invest in an organization, how much bank and government support to obtain, and whether to encourage venture capital firms to invest.

- Entrepreneurs can also rely on various sources of advice.

5. Understand the determinants of the performance of entrepreneurs, start-ups, and new ventures.

- Several interesting trends characterize new business start-ups today.
- There are several reasons why some new businesses fail and others succeed.

# Discussion Questions

## Questions for Review

1. Describe the similarities and differences between entrepreneurial firms and large firms in terms of their job creation and innovation.

2. What characteristics make an industry attractive to entrepreneurs? Based on these characteristics, which industries are most attractive to entrepreneurs?

## Questions for Analysis

5. Entrepreneurs and start-ups and new ventures play a variety of important roles in society. If these roles are so important, do you think that the government should do more to encourage the development of start-ups and new ventures? Why or why not?

6. Consider the four major reasons for new business failure. What actions can entrepreneurs take to minimize or avoid each cause of failure?

## Questions for Application

8. Assume that you are opening a new business in your town. What are your financing options? Which option or options are you likely to choose, and why?

9. List five entrepreneur-owned businesses in your community. In which industry does each business compete? Based on the industry, how do you rate each business's long-term chances for success? Explain your answers.

3. Describe recent trends in new business start-ups.

4. What are the different sources of advice for entrepreneurs? What type of information would an entrepreneur be likely to get from each source? What are the drawbacks or limitations of each source?

7. The U.S. automotive industry is well established, with several large and many small competitors. Describe the unexploited niches in the U.S. auto industry and tell how entrepreneurs could offer products that fill those niches.

10. Using the information about managing start-ups and new ventures presented in this chapter, analyze whether you would like to work in a start-up or new venture, either as an employee or as a founder. Given your personality, background, and experience, does working in or starting a new business appeal to you? What are the reasons for your opinion?

# Building Effective Interpersonal Skills

## Exercise Overview

Interpersonal skills refer to your ability to communicate with, understand, and motivate both individuals and groups. Needless to say, such skills are extremely important to the manager of a new or small business who wants to improve his or her chances of survival and success through the process of *networking*—getting together with other managers to discuss common problems and opportunities. This exercise asks you to take stock of your networking skills, whether well developed already or likely to be developed as you embark on your work life.

### Exercise Task

Consider each of the following statements. How accurately does each describe your current attitudes or behavior? Rate each item on a scale of 1–5 according to how well it describes you: If it describes you very well, give it a 5; if it doesn't describe you, rate it *1*.

1. _____ When I start something (taking on a new project, making a major purchase, making a career move), I seek help from people whom I know and look for new contacts who may be helpful.

2. _____ I view networking as a way to create win–win situations.

3. _____ I like meeting new people; I don't have trouble striking up conversations with people whom I don't know.

4. _____ I can quickly explain two or three of my most significant accomplishments.

5. _____ Before contacting businesspeople who may be of help to me in my career (say, by providing me with career information), I set goals that I want to achieve through the interaction.

6. _____ Before contacting businesspeople who may be of help to me, I plan out a short opening statement.

7. _____ Before contacting businesspeople who may be of help to me, I draw up a set of questions to ask.

8. _____ When I contact businesspeople who may be of help to me, I make sure to praise their accomplishments.

9. _____ I have contact information for at least 10 people who may be of help to me.

10. _____ I maintain a file or database of people who may be of help to me; I keep it updated and continually add new names.

11. _____ During communications with people who may be of help to me, I ask them for the names of other people whom I can contact for further information.

12. _____ When seeking help from other people, I ask them how I might be of help to them.

13. _____ When people help me, I thank them at the time, and when someone does me an especially important favor, I follow up with thanks.

14. _____ I keep in touch with people who have helped me or may help me at least once a year and update them on my career progress.

15. _____ I maintain regular communications with people who work in other organizations related to my line of business, such as members of trade or professional organizations.

16. _____ I attend trade, professional, and career meetings in order to maintain relationships and make new contacts.

Now add up your total score and place it on the following continuum:

*Effective networking 80—70—60—50—40—30—16
Ineffective networking*

Adapted from Robert N. Lussier and Christopher F. Achua, *Leadership: Theory, Application, and Skill Development*, 4th ed. (Mason, OH: Cengage Learning, 2010), pp. 127–128.

# Building Effective Conceptual Skills

### Exercise Overview

Conceptual skills require you to think in the abstract. This exercise will help you apply your conceptual skills to an analysis of certain criteria for successful entrepreneurship.

### Exercise Background

Now that you're about to graduate, you've decided to open a new business in the local community where you've been attending college. We won't ask where you got them, but we'll assume that you have enough funds to start a business without having to worry about finding investors.

*Based solely on your personal interests*, list five businesses that you might want to open and operate. For the moment, forget about such technicalities as market potential or profitability. If, for example, you like riding your bicycle, think about opening a shop that caters to cyclists.

Next, *without regard to any personal interest you might have in them*, list five businesses that you might want to open and operate. In this case, your only criteria are market opportunity and profitability. What types of businesses might be profitable in your chosen community? Use the Internet to gather information on such factors as population, local economic conditions, local competition, franchising opportunities, and so on.

Finally, evaluate the prospects for success of each of the 10 businesses that you've listed and jot down some notes to summarize your conclusions.

## Exercise Task

Reviewing your lists, the information that you've gathered, and the conclusions that you've drawn, do the following:

1. Form a small group of four or five classmates and discuss your respective lists. Look for instances in which the same type of business appears either on (1) both of your lists or (2) on one of your lists and one of a classmate's lists. Also look for cases in which the same business appears on more than one list with either similar or dissimilar prospects for success.

2. At this point, how important do you regard personal interest as a factor in small-business success?

3. How important do you regard market potential as a factor in small-business success?

# Skill-Building Personal Assessment

## An Entrepreneurial Quiz

**Introduction:** Entrepreneurs are starting ventures all the time. These new businesses are vital to the economy. The following assessment is designed to help you understand your readiness to start your own business—to be an entrepreneur.

**Instructions:** Place a checkmark or an X in the box next to the response that best represents your self-evaluation.

1. Are you a self-starter?
   - ☐ I do things on my own. Nobody has to tell me to get going.
   - ☐ If someone gets me started, I keep going all right.
   - ☐ Easy does it. I don't push myself until I have to.

2. How do you feel about other people?
   - ☐ I like people. I can get along with just about anybody.
   - ☐ I have plenty of friends—I don't need anybody else.
   - ☐ Most people irritate me.

3. Can you lead others?
   - ☐ I can get most people to go along when I start something.
   - ☐ I can give orders if someone tells me what we should do.
   - ☐ I let someone else get things moving. Then I go along if I feel like it.

4. Can you take responsibility?
   - ☐ I like to take charge of things and see them through.
   - ☐ I'll take over if I have to, but I'd rather let someone else be responsible.
   - ☐ There are always eager beavers around wanting to show how smart they are. I let them.

5. How good an organizer are you?
   - ☐ I like to have a plan before I start. I'm usually the one to get things lined up when the group wants to do something.
   - ☐ I do all right unless things get too confused. Then I quit.

   - ☐ You get all set and then something comes along and presents too many problems. So I just take things as they come.

6. How good a worker are you?
   - ☐ I can keep going as long as I need to. I don't mind working hard for something I want.
   - ☐ I'll work hard for a while, but when I've had enough, that's it.
   - ☐ I can't see that hard work gets you anywhere.

7. Can you make decisions?
   - ☐ I can make up my mind in a hurry if I have to. It usually turns out OK, too.
   - ☐ I can if I have plenty of time. If I have to make up my mind fast, I think later I should have decided the other way.
   - ☐ I don't like to be the one who has to decide things.

8. Can people trust what you say?
   - ☐ You bet they can. I don't say things I don't mean.
   - ☐ I try to be on the level most of the time, but sometimes I just say what's easiest.
   - ☐ Why bother if the other person doesn't know the difference?

9. Can you stick with it?
   - ☐ If I make up my mind to do something, I don't let anything stop me.
   - ☐ I usually finish what I start—if it goes well.
   - ☐ If it doesn't go well right away, I quit. Why beat your brains out?

10. How good is your health?
    - ☐ I never run down!
    - ☐ I have enough energy for most things I want to do.
    - ☐ I run out of energy sooner than most of my friends.

    Total the checks or Xs in each column here ___.

Source: DIBLE, DONALD, BUSINESS STARTUP BASICS, 1st Edition, © 1978, pp. 9–10. Reprinted by permission of Pearson Education, Inc., Upper Saddle River, NJ.

# Management at Work

### Taxi Dancing around the Question of Regulation

> "Uber may be the next Amazon, but Amazon doesn't have the same potential to leave a trail of bodies in the street."
>
> —TREVOR JOHNSON,
> SAN FRANCISCO CAB DRIVERS ASSOCIATION

One day, Larry Downes, project director at the Georgetown University Center for Business and Public Policy, had to catch a cab from a San Francisco train station:

> As the law requires, I could only choose the first cab in line, which was filthy. The driver begrudgingly popped the trunk, which was full of garbage, so I had to stow my own suitcase inside. Throughout the ride, he never stopped talking on a headset connected to his cell phone, blasting the radio in the back seat so I couldn't overhear his private conversation.
>
> The driver had no idea where he was going … and asked me repeatedly to tell him how to get there—directions he ignored, nearly missing every turn. He said nothing when I paid him and sped off before I'd made it to the curb.

According to Downes, the incident is typical of "the bizarro world of licensed taxicabs and limousines." What the industry needs, said Downes, coauthor of *Big Bang Disruption: Strategy in the Age of Devastating Innovation*, is "the sudden arrival of disruptive technologies that could vastly improve quality, efficiency, and profitability while also introducing new competitors."

As Downes well knew, the taxi and limousine industry was already experiencing *disruption*—the displacement of an existing market, industry, or technology by something new and more efficient. It had arrived in 2009 in the form of Uber, a San Francisco–based ridesharing service that matches people who need rides with privately owned vehicles that can take them where they want to go. It's sort of the eBay of taxi services, and Benchmark, a venture capitalist firm that invested in both start-ups, points out that Uber is growing even faster than eBay did. By the end of 2014, Uber, with operations in 290 cities and 50 countries, was valued at $40 billion. "Uber is probably the fastest-growing company that we've ever had," says Benchmark partner Bill Gurley.

How does Uber go about the business of disruption? The so-called "e-hail" process begins when you create an account by logging in with your credit card information. Then you can download an app to your smartphone. When you need

a ride, you fire up your app, and between your phone's GPS and Uber's ultra-sophisticated traffic-modeling technology, you'll find out how long it will be until the nearest car can reach you (usually within 10 minutes). If you're satisfied with the ETA, you push a button and wait (from whatever comfy location you happen to be in) for a text message telling you when your ride is waiting. Then you get in and go. Billing (including tip) is automatic.

"It's an elegant use of technology to hack the legal system," says journalist Matthew Yglesias. "Through the magic of computer power, a sedan becomes a cab without changing its legal status." Yet Yglesias also admits that Uber "arguably shouldn't exist at all. It's [nothing more] than a solution to a ridiculous problem created by [taxi] cartels and overregulation." Downes agrees: "There's nothing especially novel or proprietary about the platform Uber has built—at least nothing that couldn't or shouldn't have already been implemented by existing taxi and limo services." Downes, however, is not surprised by the way that the industry has reacted to the advent of Uber: "Instead of responding to a new kind of virtual competitor with better products and services," charges Downes, "highly regulated taxi and limousine companies have instead gone the route of trying to ban Uber."

Uber isn't allowed to operate in Miami, for example, where regulation openly protects taxis from competition, and it's also banned in Las Vegas and the Belgian capital of Brussels. In many cities, however, Uber has successfully battled regulatory resistance. In 2012, for instance, a transportation bill in Washington, D.C. proposed a floor under car-service prices that would have made Uber five times more expensive than a taxi ride. Uber reached out to its clientele, who responded with 50,000 emails and 37,000 tweets to local policymakers. Before the year was out, the proposed bill had been turned on its head: When finally passed, it had not only lost its minimum-price provisions, but also provided a legal framework for the concept of "digital dispatch" at the heart of Uber's business model. Uber riders, says cofounder and CEO Travis Kalanick, "are the most affluent, influential people in their cities. When we get to critical mass, it's impossible to shut us down."

Fortified by $50 million in venture capital, Uber may be reconciled to the short-term necessity of combating regulatory resistance, but that doesn't mean that Kalanick is resigned to what he calls "corruption and cronyism and *regulatory capture*"—the process whereby regulators and regulated industries eventually develop a mutual vested interest in maintaining the regulatory system. In the taxi and limousine industry, regulation covers such factors as insurance, fare structure, vehicle condition, and background screening for drivers, and such regulations could interfere with the Uber business model.

The company's opponents, however, scoff at Uber's claim that it can't be regulated like a taxi or limo provider because it doesn't own any cars or directly employ any drivers. Kalanick also asserts that Uber hasn't introduced anything other than the software that enables its transactions, but opponents reply that there's a big difference between Uber and other innovative ventures in the tech-facilitated "sharing economy": Uber, says Trevor Johnson of the San Francisco Cab Drivers Association, "may be the next Amazon, but Amazon doesn't have the same potential to leave a trail of bodies in the street."

Larry Downes agrees that such "public-interest goals" as safety can be served only by regulation. "Watch what happens," he wrote in early 2013, "the first time a shared-ride vehicle gets into a serious accident." He didn't have long to wait. On New Year's Eve, an Uber driver ran into a San Francisco family, killing six-year-old Sofia Liu. Syed Muzzafar was charged with vehicular manslaughter. "We have deactivated his Uber account," said a company statement, and when the family filed suit against the company for wrongful death, Uber defended itself by arguing that Muzzafar "was not transporting a rider who requested transportation services through the Uber App. He was not en route to pick up a rider who requested transportation services though the Uber App. He was not receiving a request for transportation services through the Uber App."

A month earlier, an Uber driver had allegedly assaulted a passenger when they got into an argument. Although Uber claims a zero-tolerance policy on drug-related offenses, the driver had two felony convictions for selling drugs and was on probation for a charge of battery. He had, however, received good reviews from other passengers, and in challenging the ruling of the California Public Utilities Commission that it should be regulated as a taxi company, Uber had argued that its system of gathering customer feedback meant that it was self-regulating.

## Case Questions

1. What are Uber's *distinctive competencies*—the aspects of the business of transporting passengers that it appears to perform better than its competitors? In what ways has Uber successfully exploited its distinctive competencies?

2. Uber operates specifically in the taxi and limousine industry, in which cars transport passengers according to various dispatch and fare systems. In a broader sense, however, it also participates in certain "major industry groups" (see the chapter section on "Choosing an Industry"). What are the relevant "industry groups"? In what ways do the demands of competing within these groups overlap with or affect the demands of competing in the taxi and limousine industry? In particular, how might these demands influence Uber's entrepreneurial strategies?

3. "Innovation and regulation simply don't work together." So says Larry Downes, the victim of the cab ride described at the outset of the case and formerly of the Northwestern University School of Law and the University of California-Berkeley's Haas School of Business. Assuming that he's right, why is this so? Why is regulation often incompatible with innovation? Why do we regulate most industries in the first place? In your opinion, what sort of trade-offs should we seek when we try to balance the opposing advantages of regulation and innovation?

4. The case defines *regulatory capture* as the process whereby regulators and regulated industries eventually develop a mutual vested interest in maintaining the regulatory system. The regulator, as Downes puts it, "becomes the industry's cheerleader, and regulations shift subtly from protecting the public interest to protecting the status quo." Think of a couple of industries with which you do business. Does the process of regulatory capture appear to be at work in these industries? In what ways do you think the system of regulatory capture adversely affects the relationship between a given industry and its customers?

## Case References

Larry Downes, "Lessons from Uber: Why Innovation and Regulation Don't Mix," *Forbes* (February 6, 2013), www.forbes.com, on October 27, 2014; Matthew Yglesias, "When Is a Taxi Not a Taxi?" *Slate* (December 15, 2011), www.slate.com, on October 28, 2014; "2014 CNBC's Disruptor 50: 10. Uber," CNBC (June 17, 2014), www.cnbc.com, on October 27, 2014; Romain Dillet, "Benchmark's Bill Gurley: 'Uber Is Growing Faster Than eBay Did,'" *TechCrunch* (April 29, 2013), http://techcrunch.com, on October 29, 2014; Katie Lobosco, "Uber Cheaper Than New York City Taxi—For Now," *CNN Money* (July 7, 2014), http://money.cnn.com, on October 27, 2014; L. Gordon Crovitz, "Uber Shocks the Regulators," *Wall Street Journal* (June 15, 2014), http://online.wsj.com, on October 30, 2014; Christine Lagorio-Chafkin, ""Resistance Is Futile," *Inc.* (July 2013), www.inc.com, on October 30, 2014; David Streitfeld, "Rough Patch for Uber Service's Challenge to Taxis," *New York Times* (January 26, 2014), www.nytimes.com, on October 27, 2014; Kate Conger, "Uber Files Defense in Sofia Liu Wrongful Death Lawsuit," *San Francisco Examiner* (May 6, 2014), www.sfexaminer.com, on October 30, 2014.

1. In the section entitled "Strategy for Start-Ups and New Ventures," the text identifies three "strategic challenges" facing small or start-up firms. Focus on the first two: (1) choosing an *industry* and (2) emphasizing *distinctive competencies*. How would you characterize the main industry in which Project Frog has chosen to compete? Are there overlaps with other industries? If so, explain how the company's activities in those industries are related but subordinate to its activities in its main industry. What are Project Frog's *distinctive competencies*? In what ways has it succeeded in emphasizing them?

2. Now that it has a foothold in school construction, Project Frog has set its sights on an even more promising sector—healthcare construction. Why is the construction of healthcare facilities consistent with Project Frog's *distinctive competencies*? Why does the company see this sector as such a promising area of growth? Why, for example, was there $23 billion worth of healthcare construction in the United States in 2012?

3. The Center for Green Schools reports that students' ability to learn can be enhanced by improvements in indoor air, acoustics, thermal comfort, and daylighting. Former president Bill Clinton says that "we should be right now engaged in retrofitting every school in America for sustainability."* What about you? Judging from your own experience—whether positive, negative, or somewhere in between—do you think that the environmental quality of school facilities is an important factor in helping students learn? How did the schools that you attended measure up on environmental support for learning? How about the classroom that you're sitting in now?

4. As the vignette informs us, RockPort Capital played a crucial role in providing Project Frog with financing at an early stage of its development ($8 million in 2008). In 2011, GE Energy Financial Services led a second round of funding totaling $22 million. A third round, in 2013, netted $20 million, mostly from Convergent Capital Management (CCM), bringing the total to $50 million. All three investment firms are *venture capital companies*. Check out each of these companies on the Internet (you probably don't have to go much farther than the home page). You'll find that each company has different investment criteria. It should also be clear that Project Frog was a good investment match for each one. Why? *Note:* Be sure to take the company's early life cycle into account in evaluating each company's decision to invest.

*The Center for Green Schools, "Green Schools Enhance Learning," U.S. Green Building Council (2014), www.centerforgreenschools.org, on October 27, 2014.

# Endnotes

1 Todd Woody, "Meet the Startup Making Snap-Together Office Buildings, Schools and 7-Elevens," *Forbes* (January 2, 2013), www.forbes.com, on October 22, 2014; Alex Salkever, "Project Frog Seeks to Make Pre-Fab School Buildings Fab—and Green," *Daily Finance* (December 2, 2009), www.dailyfinance.com, on October 22, 2014; Nathan Hurst, "The 'Componetized' School of the Future, Built in 90 Days," *Wired* (May 2013), www.wired.com, on October 22, 2014; Elise Craig, "Project Frog Rethinks Construction with Smart Component Buildings," *Xconomy* (December 17, 2013), www.xconomy.com, on October 22, 2014; Annie Sciacca, "Ann Hand: CEO, Project Frog," *San Francisco Business Times* (September 27, 2013), www.bizjournals.com, on October 23, 2014; Eliza Brooke, "Raising $20M, Project Frog Ramps Up Production on Its Energy Efficient Buildings," *TechCrunch* (November 7, 2013), http://techcrunch.com, on October 23, 2014; Project Frog, "Project Frog + El Sol Science and Arts Academy of Santa Ana" [video], YouTube (March 13, 2014), www.youtube.com, on October 22, 2014; Joann Gonchar, "Modular Classroom Makeover," *Architectural Record* (January 2014), http://archrecord.construction.com, on October 24, 2014.

2 Bro Uttal, "Inside the Deal that Made Bill Gates $350,000,000," *Fortune*, July 21, 1986, pp. 23–33.

3 "The World's Billionaires," *Forbes*, March 14, 2015.

4 Murray B. Low and Ian MacMillan, "Entrepreneurship: Past Research and Future Challenges," *Journal of Management*, June 1988, pp. 139–159.

5 U.S. Bureau of the Census, *Statistical Abstract of the United States*, 2009 (Washington, DC: Government Printing Office, 2009).

6 http://www.sba.gov/sites/default/files/advocacy/FAQ_March_2014_0.pdf. Accessed on May 14, 2015.

7 http://www.sba.gov/sites/default/files/advocacy/FAQ_March_2014_0.pdf. Accessed on May 14, 2015.

8 http://www.sba.gov/sites/default/files/advocacy/FAQ_March_2014_0.pdf. Accessed on May 14, 2015.

9 "A World that's All A-Twitter," *USA Today*, May 26, 2009, pp. 1B, 2B.

10 *USA Today*, May 26, 2009, p. 1B.

11 "Heaven on Wheels," *Forbes*, April 13, 2009, pp. 74–75.

12 Amar Bhide, "How Entrepreneurs Craft Strategies that Work," *Harvard Business Review*, March–April 1994, pp. 150–163.

13 *USA Today*, April 7, 2004, p. 8B.

14 *Hoover's Handbook of American Business 2015* (Austin, TX: Hoover's Business Press, 2015), pp. 896–897; *Whole Foods Market 2014 Annual Report*, Wholefoodsmarket.com.

15 Nancy J. Lyons, "Moonlight over Indiana," *Inc.*, January 2000, pp. 71–74.

16 F. M. Scherer, *Industrial Market Structure and Economic Performance*, 2nd ed. (Boston: Houghton Mifflin, 1980).

17 The importance of discovering niches is emphasized in Charles Hill and Gareth Jones, *Strategic Management: An Integrative Approach*, 7th ed. (Boston: Houghton Mifflin, 2007).

18 "A Startup's New Prescription for Eyewear," *Business Week*, July 4–10, 2011, pp. 49–51.

19 D. Kirsch, B. Goldfarb, and A. Gera, "Form or Substance: The Role of Business Plans in Venture Capital Decision Making," *Strategic Management Journal*, Vol. 30, No. 5, 2009, pp. 487–516.

20 http://www.entrepreneur.com/article/244282. Accessed May 16, 2015.

21 "Cheap Tricks," *Forbes*, February 21, 2000, p. 116.

22 U.S. Bureau of the Census, *Statistical Abstract of the United States*, 2014.

23 James Combs, David Ketchen, Christopher Shook, and Jeremy Short, "Antecedents and Consequences of Franchising: Past Accomplishments and Future Challenges," *Journal of Management*, January 2011, pp. 99–126.

24 "BET: African-Americans Grow in Numbers, Buying Power," *Multichannel News*, January 26, 209.

25 AP wire story, January 29, 2006.

26 Norman M. Scarborough and Thomas W. Zimmerer, *Effective Small Business Management: An Entrepreneurial Approach*, 6th ed. (Upper Saddle River, NJ: Prentice Hall, 2000), pp. 412–413.

27 http://www.entrepreneur.com/article/242631, Accessed May 16, 2015.

28 See Robert A. Baron, "The Role of Affect in the Entrepreneurial Process," *Academy of Management Review*, 2008, Vol. 33, No. 2, pp. 328–340; see also Keith M. Hmieleski and Robert A. Baron, "Entrepreneurs' Optimism and New Venture Performance: A Social Cognition Perspective," *Academy of Management Journal*, 2009, Vol. 52, No. 3, pp. 540–572.

©Markus Pfaff/Shutterstock.com

# 10

# BASIC ELEMENTS OF ORGANIZING

## Learning Outcomes

**After studying this chapter, you should be able to:**

1. Identify the basic elements of organizations.

2. Describe the basic alternative approaches to designing jobs.

3. Discuss the rationale and the most common bases for grouping jobs into departments.

4. Describe the basic elements involved in establishing reporting relationships.

5. Discuss how authority is distributed in organizations.

6. Discuss the basic coordinating activities undertaken by organizations.

7. Describe basic ways in which positions within an organization can be differentiated.

## MANAGEMENT IN ACTION  Who's the Boss?

"This is what people do when you put managers over them. The managers start acting like parents, and the people they're managing start acting like children."

—RYAN CARSON, CEO OF TREEHOUSE

Ryan Carson and Alan Johnson founded Treehouse in 2011 as an online interactive education platform. Officially known as Treehouse Island Inc., the company produces courses in web development and programming and business education, using such tools as videos and interactive code challenges to teach students a range of technology-related skills. Or, as one business journalist puts it, Treehouse is "an online trade school whose mission is to get students jobs" without having to spend years pursuing expensive college degrees.[1]

Fueled by $12.6 million in venture capital, Treehouse had become the largest computer science school in the world within less than three years. It wasn't long, however, before Carson and Johnson were

hearing rumblings of discontent. "By 2013," recalls Carson, "we had grown to 60 people with seven managers and four executives. As we added more people to the team, we noticed something disconcerting: rumors, politics, and complaints started appearing." Putting their joint ears to the ground, the cofounders learned that some front-line employees felt that their input was being ignored. The news was disturbing because Carson and Johnson believed that it was important for employees to be involved in the decision-making process.

"If they're feeling disempowered at the bottom," suggested Carson, "maybe we have too many managers." Seven managers didn't exactly seem like an army of overseers, but it did amount to more than 10 percent of the workforce. According to Carson,

*Alan and I started exploring possible solutions and considered removing the lowest layer of managers and asking them to go back into producing. ... Then we went up the chain and asked hard questions about the value of the mid-tier managers. Then we kept going all the way to the executives at the top.*

Ryan Carson, chief executive officer of Treehouse, runs a "no-manager company." While this format has its challenges, he feels that this structure works the best for his company of 70 people.

Bloomberg/Getty Images

Eventually, the conversation reached a certain logical plateau: "What if we removed all management and simply empowered everyone to choose what they do every day? We laughed at first and then the conversation turned serious. We had hired talented and motivated people. Did they *need* managers?"

The company's predicament—"the normal political stuff," as Carson puts it, with "people complaining or feeling disempowered"—led Carson and Johnson to a general conclusion about manager-employee relations: "We realized," says Carson, "that this is what people do when you put managers over them. The managers start acting like parents, and the people they're managing start acting like children." Carson hastens to add that this principle has a practical corollary: "In my experience," he explains, "managers started off as workers and then moved up the ladder, getting farther and farther from the front line. They gained power but slowly lost touch with day-to-day realities. ... Their teams lost respect for them because they could no longer produce, which means they would set unrealistic deadlines."

As Carson saw it, people at Treehouse were thinking too much about organizational structure and too little about organizational activity:

> *Everyone was getting abstracted away from actually doing and instead focused all their attention on structuring. As our team grew, we spent more and more time talking about priorities, aligning everyone, and checking on progress. The whole structure was taking power and responsibility away from people on the front lines.*

Having reached a logical jumping-off point in their meditations about management, Carson and Johnson took the next logical step: They wrote up a "manifesto" about how the company would work without managers, posted it on an internal forum, and invited everyone to "discuss" the matter. "The company ground to a halt for two days," reports Carson, while the workforce generated 447 comments. When the proposal was put to a vote, 90 percent of Treehouse employees endorsed a bossless workplace.

So, on June 20, 2013, says Carson, "we removed all managers. ... We changed the way the company operated and gave all employees 100 percent control of their time and let them decide what they work on each day. From then on, no one would tell anyone what to do, not even the CEO." The result?

At first, Carson admits, "it was total chaos," but Carson and Johnson quickly realized what we'll find out in Chapter 17—namely, that much of a manager's job involves *communication* and that subordinates mostly need managers because they need *information*.

In short, even if you've addressed the problem of overmanaging, running an organization is basically a matter of *coordination*. "The chaos," contends Carson, came from the fact that "nonmanagers aren't used to the level of communication needed to coordinate with other teams and projects, so there's often not enough proactive communication and coordination. We don't have managers to coordinate across projects, so it's up to individuals to take time to communicate what's happening on their projects and how it affects other people."

Thus, one of the first corrective measures taken by the two (former) top managers was building a new internal information tool called Canopy, a sort of open-source Gmail account that gives everyone the capability to access and contribute to companywide communications.

Not surprisingly, shared information is also crucial to the process of getting along without bosses. Projects are proposed by employees, who use Canopy to circulate the information needed to get other employees interested. If a proposal attracts sufficient interest, it moves forward, with the employees who've chosen to get involved selecting a manager for the project. "There are still going to be managers at Treehouse," explains Carson. "There just aren't titles. The only way you can be a leader is if you lead and people want to follow."

The system, of course, has its drawbacks. For one thing, says Carson, "I can't make people do things. ... I've even had people tell me they don't have time or aren't interested in my ideas. It sucks, but it's part of running a no-manager company." Needless to say, Carson is also frustrated by the fact that "I can't make things happen very fast. There are many times I just want to say, 'Do this right now,' but I can't. It's basically against the rules." More importantly, it can often take quite a while to get projects off the ground. According to Treehouse rules, "you have to propose a project, explain it thoroughly, and convince people to join. The process," Carson admits, "can take weeks or months."

Perhaps the biggest problem, however, is still ahead. "We have 70 employees now," says Carson, "and for a company our size, this model works. However, it's probably going to start showing serious signs of trouble at around 150 people."

"But then again, we'll figure it out."

All managers need the assistance of others to succeed and so must trust the members of their team to do their jobs and carry out their responsibilities. And the team members themselves need the support of their boss and a clear understanding of their role in the organization. This mutual dependence may be especially important when, as in the case of Treehouse, the company is both new and small but begins to grow and add structure. In any case, the working relationship between managers and their subordinates is one of the most critical elements comprising an organization.[2] As you will see in this chapter, managing the basic frameworks that organizations use to get their work done—structure—is a fundamental part of the management process.

This chapter discusses many of the critical elements of organization structure that managers can control and is the first of four devoted to organizing, the second basic managerial function identified in Chapter 1. In Part 3, we describe managerial planning—deciding what to do. Organizing, the subject of Part 4, focuses on how to do it. We first elaborate on the meaning of organization structure. Subsequent sections explore the basic elements that managers use to create an organization.

# The Elements of Organizing

Imagine asking a child to build a castle with a set of building blocks. She selects a few small blocks and other larger ones. She uses some square ones, some round ones, and some triangular ones. When she finishes, she has her own castle, unlike any other. Another child, presented with the same task, constructs a different castle. He selects different blocks, for example, and combines them in different ways. The children's activities—choosing certain combinations of blocks and then putting them together in unique ways—are in many ways analogous to the manager's job of organizing.[3]

Organizing is deciding how best to group organizational elements. Just as children select different kinds of building blocks, managers can choose a variety of structural possibilities. And just as the children can assemble the blocks in any number of ways, so, too, can managers put the organization together in many different ways. Understanding the nature of these building blocks and the different ways in which they can be configured can have a powerful impact on a firm's competitiveness.[4] In this chapter, our focus is on the building blocks themselves—organization structure. In Chapter 11 we focus on how the blocks can be put together—organization design.

There are six basic building blocks that managers can use in constructing an organization: designing jobs, grouping jobs, establishing reporting relationships between jobs, distributing authority among jobs, coordinating activities among jobs, and differentiating among positions. The logical starting point is the first building block—designing jobs for people within the organization.

# Designing Jobs

The first building block of organization structure is job design. Job design is the determination of a person's work-related responsibilities.[5] For a machinist at Caterpillar, job design might specify what machines are to be operated during the construction of a new piece of equipment, how those machines are to be operated, and what performance standards are expected. For a manager at Caterpillar, job design might involve defining areas of decision-making responsibility, identifying goals and expectations, and establishing appropriate indicators of success. The natural starting point for designing jobs is determining the level of desired specialization.

## Job Specialization

Job specialization is the degree to which the overall task of the organization is broken down and divided into smaller component parts. Job specialization evolved from the concept of

**organizing**
Deciding how best to group organizational activities and resources

**organization structure**
The set of elements that can be used to configure an organization

**job design**
The determination of a person's work-related responsibilities

**job specialization**
The degree to which the overall task of the organization is broken down and divided into smaller component parts

*division of labor.* Adam Smith, an eighteenth-century economist, first discussed division of labor in his case study about how a pin factory used it to improve productivity.[6] He described how "one man pulled the wire from a spool, another straightened it, a third cut it, a fourth ground the point," and so on. Smith claimed that 10 men working in this fashion were able to produce 48,000 pins in a day, whereas each man working alone could have produced only about 20 pins per day.

The first examples of the impact of specialization came from the automobile assembly line pioneered by Henry Ford and his contemporaries. Mass-production capabilities stemming from job specialization techniques have had a profound impact throughout the world. During the twentieth century, high levels of low-cost production transformed U.S. society into one of the strongest economies in the history of the world.[7]

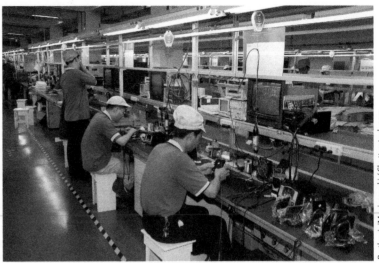

Job specialization is the basis for mass-production assembly lines such as this one. Tasks are broken down into small component elements. Partially assembled products move along the assembly line as each worker adds to the product by attaching or building new parts of the product.

Job specialization in its purest form is simply a normal extension of organizational growth. For example, when Walt Disney started his company, he did everything himself—wrote cartoons, drew them, added character voices, and then marketed them to theaters. As the business grew, though, he eventually hired others to perform many of these same functions. As growth continued, so, too, did specialization. For example, as animation artists work on Disney movies today, they may specialize in generating computer images of a single character or doing only background scenery. Others provide voices, and marketing specialists develop promotional campaigns. And today, the Walt Disney Company has literally thousands of different specialized jobs. Clearly, no one person could perform them all.

## Benefits and Limitations of Specialization

Job specialization provides four benefits to organizations.[8] First, workers performing small, simple tasks will become very proficient at each task. Second, transfer time between tasks decreases. If employees perform several different tasks, some time is lost as they stop doing the first task and start doing the next. Third, the more narrowly defined a job is, the easier it is to develop specialized equipment to assist with that job. Fourth, when an employee who performs a highly specialized job is absent or resigns, the manager can train someone new at relatively low cost. Although specialization is generally thought of in terms of operating jobs, many organizations have extended the basic elements of specialization to managerial and professional levels.[9]

On the other hand, job specialization can have negative consequences. The foremost criticism is that workers who perform highly specialized jobs may become bored and dissatisfied. The job may be so specialized that it offers no challenge or stimulation. Boredom and monotony set in, absenteeism rises, and the quality of the work may suffer. Furthermore, the anticipated benefits of specialization do not always occur. For example, a classic study conducted at Maytag found that the time spent moving work in process from one worker to another was greater than the time needed for the same person to change from job to job.[10] Thus, although some degree of specialization is necessary, it should not be carried to extremes, because of the possible

"The best [Tour de France] teams have specialists to help position leaders for a win."

—PAUL HOCHMAN, BUSINESS WRITER[11]

negative consequences. Managers must be sensitive to situations in which extreme specialization should be avoided. And indeed, several approaches to designing jobs have been developed in recent years.

## Alternatives to Specialization

To counter the problems associated with specialization, managers have sought other approaches to job design that achieve a better balance between organizational demands for efficiency and productivity and individual needs for creativity and autonomy. Five alternative approaches are job rotation, job enlargement, job enrichment, the job characteristics approach, and work teams.[12]

**job rotation**
An alternative to job specialization that involves systematically moving employees from one job to another

**job enlargement**
An alternative to job specialization that involves giving the employee more tasks to perform

**Job Rotation**  Job rotation involves systematically moving employees from one job to another. A worker in a warehouse might unload trucks on Monday, carry incoming inventory to storage on Tuesday, verify invoices on Wednesday, pull outgoing inventory from storage on Thursday, and load trucks on Friday. Thus the jobs do not change; instead, workers move from job to job. Unfortunately, for this very reason, job rotation has not been very successful in enhancing employee motivation or satisfaction. Jobs that are amenable to rotation tend to be relatively standard and routine. Workers who are rotated to a "new" job may be more satisfied at first, but satisfaction soon wanes. Although many companies (among them American Cyanamid, Bethlehem Steel, Ford, Prudential Insurance, and Western Electric) have tried job rotation, it is most often used today as a training device to improve worker skills and flexibility. Job rotation is also being used more to increase flexibility and lower costs. That is, because workers who can perform multiple jobs can be moved around to different jobs when demand shifts, the business can often get by with fewer workers. Transportation Security Administration (TSA) security screeners rotate jobs every 15 minutes in order to maintain proficiency at all tasks and maintain focus.

> "[rotating jobs]…makes the day go by. You don't get bored doing the same thing over and over."
>
> —RICK RUSH, GENERAL MOTORS ASSEMBLY LINE WORKER[13]

Wally Skalij/Getty Images

By utilizing job rotation, the Transportation Security Administration (TSA) security can employ less workers. The screener below, rotating jobs every 15 minutes, will head to the entryway checkpoint entrance next. Rotation also helps offset monotony and keeps screeners focused on their tasks.

**Job Enlargement**  On the assumption that doing the same basic task over and over is the primary cause of worker dissatisfaction, job enlargement was developed to increase the total number of tasks workers perform. As a result, all workers perform a wide variety of tasks, which presumably reduces the level of job dissatisfaction. Many organizations have used job enlargement, including IBM, Detroit Edison, AT&T, the U.S. Civil Service, and Maytag. At Maytag, for example, the assembly line for producing washing-machine water pumps was systematically changed so that work that had originally been performed by six workers, who passed the work sequentially from one person to another, was performed by four workers, each of whom assembled a complete pump.[14] Unfortunately, although job enlargement does have some positive consequences, these are often offset by some disadvantages: (1) Training costs usually increase, (2) unions have argued that pay should increase because the worker is doing more tasks, and (3) in many cases the work remains boring and routine even after job enlargement.

**Job Enrichment** A more comprehensive approach, job enrichment, assumes that increasing the range and variety of tasks is not sufficient by itself to improve employee motivation.[15] Thus job enrichment is an attempt to increase both the number of tasks a worker does and the control the worker has over the job. To implement job enrichment, managers remove some controls from the job, delegate more authority to employees, and structure the work in complete, natural units. These changes increase subordinates' sense of responsibility. Another part of job enrichment is to continually assign new and challenging tasks, thereby increasing employees' opportunity for growth and advancement.

AT&T was one of the earliest companies to try job enrichment. In one experiment, eight data entry clerks in a service unit prepared customer service orders. Faced with low output and high turnover, management determined that the data entry clerks felt little responsibility to clients and received little feedback. The unit was changed to create a data entry team. Data entry specialists were matched with designated service representatives, the task was changed from 10 specific steps to three more general steps, and job titles were upgraded. As a result, the frequency of order processing increased from 27 percent to 90 percent, the need for messenger service was eliminated, accuracy improved, and turnover became practically nil.[16] Other organizations that have tried job enrichment include Texas Instruments, IBM, and General Foods. Job enrichment is also being used in some banks today, with employees in branches being trained to work as tellers, open new accounts, and accept loan applications. By training all of its employees to perform multiple tasks, Orlando-based Anderen Bank has been able to reduce the average number of employees at each of its branches from 10 to four.[17] This approach, however, also has disadvantages. For example, work systems need to be analyzed before enrichment, but this seldom happens, and managers rarely ask for employee preferences when enriching jobs. And note that while Anderen Bank employees get to do more tasks and have greater responsibility, the firm's goal was to lower labor cost by employing fewer people. The impact of the changes on employee morale, performance, and turnover have also not been assessed.

**Job Characteristics Approach** The job characteristics approach is an alternative to job specialization that does take into account the work system and employee preferences.[18] As illustrated in Figure 10.1, the job characteristics approach suggests that jobs should be diagnosed and improved along five core dimensions:

1. *Skill variety*, the number of things a person does in a job
2. *Task identity*, the extent to which the worker does a complete or identifiable portion of the total job
3. *Task significance*, the perceived importance of the task
4. *Autonomy*, the degree of control the worker has over how the work is performed
5. *Feedback*, the extent to which the worker knows how well the job is being performed

The higher a job rates on those dimensions, the more employees will experience various psychological states. Experiencing these states, in turn, presumably leads to high motivation, high-quality performance, high satisfaction, and low absenteeism and turnover. Finally, a concept called *growth-need strength* is presumed to affect how the model works for different people. People with a strong desire to grow, develop, and expand their capabilities (indicative of high growth-need strength) are expected to respond strongly to the presence or absence of the basic job characteristics; those with low growth-need strength are expected not to respond as strongly or consistently.

Many studies have been conducted to test the usefulness of the job characteristics approach. The Southwestern Division of Prudential Insurance, for example, used this approach in its claims division. Results included moderate declines in turnover and a small but measurable improvement in work quality. Other research findings have not supported this approach as strongly. Thus, although the job characteristics approach is one of the most promising alternatives to job specialization, it is probably not the final answer.

**job enrichment**
An alternative to job specialization that involves increasing both the number of tasks the worker does and the control the worker has over the job

**job characteristics approach**
An alternative to job specialization that suggests that jobs should be diagnosed and improved along five core dimensions, taking into account both the work system and employee preferences

## FIGURE 10.1  THE JOB CHARACTERISTICS APPROACH

The job characteristics approach to job design provides a viable alternative to job specialization. Five core job dimensions may lead to critical psychological states that, in turn, may enhance motivation, performance, and satisfaction while also reducing absenteeism and turnover.

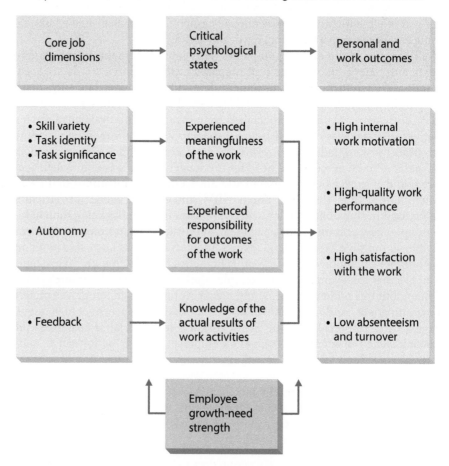

Source: J. R. Hackman and G. R. Oldham, "Motivation Through the Design of Work: Test of a Theory," *Organizational Behavior and Human Performance*, Vol. 16 (1976), pp. 250–279. Copyright © Academic Press, Inc. Reprinted by permission of Academic Press and the authors.

**Work Teams** Another alternative to job specialization is work teams. Under this arrangement, a group is given responsibility for designing the work system to be used in performing an interrelated set of tasks. In the typical assembly-line system, the work flows from one worker to the next, and each worker has a specified job to perform. In a work team, however, the group itself decides how jobs will be allocated. For example, the work team assigns specific tasks to members, monitors and controls its own performance, and has autonomy over work scheduling.[19] We discuss work teams more fully in Chapter 18.

**work team**
An alternative to job specialization that allows an entire group to design the work system it will use to perform an interrelated set of tasks

 **Manager's Checklist**

☐ Managers need to understand the advantages and disadvantages of each approach to job design.

☐ At the same time, managers need to also realize that there is no one perfect way to design jobs.

☐ You should also be aware of how your own job is designed and how that design affects you.

# Grouping Jobs: Departmentalization

The second building block of organization structure is the grouping of jobs according to some logical arrangement. The process of grouping jobs is called departmentalization. After establishing the basic rationale for departmentalization, we identify some common bases along which departments are created.[20]

## Rationale for Departmentalization

When organizations are small, the owner–manager can personally oversee everyone who works there. As an organization grows, however, personally supervising all the employees becomes more and more difficult for the owner–manager. Consequently, new managerial positions are created to supervise the work

Departmentalization involves grouping jobs according to a logical arrangement. Individuals needing out-patient services at this hospital know to follow the directional markers on this sign, as do patients coming for x-ray services. The hospital will also have multiple other departments such as emergency, surgery, physical therapy, and so forth.

of others. Employees are not assigned to particular managers randomly. Rather, jobs are grouped according to some plan. The logic embodied in such a plan is the basis for all departmentalization.[21]

## Common Bases for Departmentalization

Figure 10.2 presents a partial organizational chart for Apex Computers, a hypothetical firm that manufactures and sells computers and software. The chart shows that Apex uses each of the four most common bases for departmentalization: function, product, customer, and location.

**Functional Departmentalization**   The most common base for departmentalization, especially among smaller organizations, is by function. Functional departmentalization groups together those jobs involving the same or similar activities. (The word *function* is used here to mean organizational functions such as finance and production, rather than the basic managerial functions, such as planning or controlling.) The computer department at Apex has manufacturing, finance, and marketing departments, each an organizational function.

This approach, which is most common in smaller organizations, has three primary advantages. First, each department can be staffed by experts in that functional area. Marketing experts can be hired to run the marketing function, for example. Second, supervision is facilitated because an individual manager needs to be familiar with only a relatively narrow set of skills. And, third, coordinating activities inside each department is easier.

On the other hand, as an organization begins to grow in size, several disadvantages of this approach may emerge. For one, decision making tends to become slower and more bureaucratic. Employees may also begin to concentrate too narrowly on their own unit and lose sight of the total organizational system. Finally, accountability and performance become increasingly difficult to monitor. For example, determining whether a new product fails because of production deficiencies or a poor marketing campaign may not be possible.

**Product Departmentalization**   Product departmentalization, a second common approach, involves grouping and arranging activities around products or product groups. Apex Computers has two product-based departments at the highest level of the firm.

**departmentalization**
The process of grouping jobs according to some logical arrangement

**functional departmentalization**
Grouping jobs involving the same or similar activities

**product departmentalization**
Grouping activities around products or product groups

---

## FIGURE 10.2  BASES FOR DEPARTMENTALIZATION

Organizations group jobs into departments. Apex, a hypothetical organization, uses all four of the primary bases of departmentalization—function, product, customer, and location. Like Apex, most large organizations use more than one type of departmentalization.

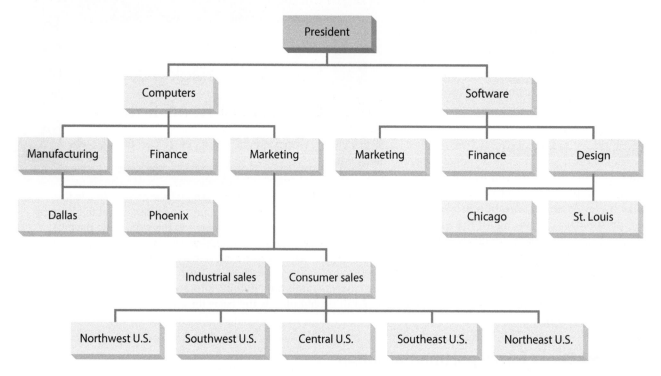

One is responsible for all activities associated with Apex's personal computer business, and the other handles the software business. Most larger businesses adopt this form of departmentalization for grouping activities at the business or corporate level.

Product departmentalization has three major advantages. First, all activities associated with one product or product group can be easily integrated and coordinated. Second, the speed and effectiveness of decision making are enhanced. Third, the performance of individual products or product groups can be assessed more easily and objectively, thereby improving the accountability of departments for the results of their activities.

Product departmentalization also has two major disadvantages. For one, managers in each department may focus on their own product or product group to the exclusion of the rest of the organization. For example, a marketing manager may see her or his primary duty as helping the group rather than helping the overall organization. For another, administrative costs rise because each department must have its own functional specialists for areas such as market research and financial analysis.

**Customer Departmentalization**   Under customer departmentalization, the organization structures its activities to respond to and interact with specific customers or customer groups. The lending activities in most banks, for example, are usually tailored to meet the needs of different kinds of customers (business, consumer, mortgage, and agricultural loans). Figure 10.2 shows that the marketing branch of Apex's computer business has two distinct departments—industrial sales and consumer sales. The industrial sales department handles marketing activities aimed at business customers, whereas the consumer sales department is responsible for wholesaling computers to retail stores catering to individual purchasers.

The basic advantage of this approach is that the organization can use skilled specialists to deal with unique customers or customer groups. It takes one set of skills to evaluate a balance

**customer departmentalization**
Grouping activities to respond to and interact with specific customers or customer groups

sheet and lend a business $500,000 for operating capital, and a different set of skills to evaluate a person's creditworthiness and lend $20,000 for a new car. However, a fairly large administrative staff is required to integrate the activities of the various departments. In banks, for example, coordination is necessary to make sure that the organization does not over-commit itself in any one area and to handle collections on delinquent accounts from a diverse set of customers.

**Location Departmentalization** Location departmentalization groups jobs on the basis of defined geographic sites or areas. The defined sites or areas may range in size from a hemisphere to only a few blocks of a large city. The manufacturing branch of Apex's computer business has two plants—one in Dallas and another in Phoenix. Similarly, the design division of its software design unit has two labs—one in Chicago and the other in St. Louis. Apex's consumer sales group has five sales territories corresponding to different regions of the United States. Transportation companies, police departments (precincts represent geographic areas of a city), and the Federal Reserve Bank all use location departmentalization.

The primary advantage of location departmentalization is that it enables the organization to respond easily to unique customer and environmental characteristics in the various regions. On the negative side, a larger administrative staff may be required if the organization must keep track of units in scattered locations.

**Other Forms of Departmentalization** Although most organizations are departmentalized by function, product, customer, or location, other forms are occasionally used. Some organizations group certain activities by time. One of the machine shops of Baker Hughes in Houston, for example, operates on three shifts. Each shift has a superintendent who reports to the plant manager, and each shift has its own functional departments. Time is thus the framework for many organizational activities. Other organizations that use time as a basis for grouping jobs include some hospitals and many airlines. In other situations, departmentalization by sequence is appropriate. Many college students, for instance, must register in sequence: seniors on Monday, juniors on Tuesday, and so on. Other areas that may be organized in sequence include credit departments (specific employees run credit checks according to customer name) and insurance claims divisions (by policy number).

**location departmentalization**
Grouping jobs on the basis of defined geographic sites or areas

**Other Considerations** Two final points about job grouping remain to be made. First, departments are often called something entirely different—*divisions*, *units*, *sections*, and *bureaus* are all common synonyms. The higher we look in an organization, the more likely we are to find departments referred to as divisions. H. J. Heinz, for example, is organized into five major divisions. Nevertheless, the underlying logic behind all the labels is the same: They represent groups of jobs that have been yoked together according to some unifying principle. Second, almost any organization is likely to employ multiple bases of departmentalization, depending on level. Although Apex Computer is a hypothetical firm that we created to explain departmentalization, it is quite similar to many real organizations in that it uses a variety of bases of departmentalization for different levels and different sets of activities. Finally, as illustrated in our *Tech Watch* feature, the role of social media in departmentalization is just now beginning to have an impact.

This shift of factory workers is leaving the plant floor. They have just been relieved by the second shift crew.

**TECH WATCH**

# A Disturbance in the Twelpforce

In June 2013, Conversocial Ltd., which helps businesses manage large-scale customer-service operations on social media, issued the results of a study of the way in which the top 100 online retailers handled customer-service issues on Facebook and Twitter. According to the report, the average response time to questions and concerns was over 11 hours. In addition, the study found that merchants responded to an average of only 13.8 percent of customer inquiries.

Conversocial CEO Joshua March thinks that the results reflect a serious disconnect between retailers' and customers' conceptions of social media: "While retailers see social as a marketing platform, they also have to realize that their customers are using it for customer service." March also notes that retailers manage to deal with only 50 percent of social media inquiries within the Facebook or Twitter channel: The other half are redirected to other channels, usually email or phone. "Redirecting customers," says March, "is a terrible customer experience, particularly because many people turn to social as a last resort after already trying to get a response over email or from the call center."

There was, however, one clear winner in the Conversocial report: The study found that Best Buy not only responded to 42.1 percent of its social media inquiries, but managed to do so in an average of 14 minutes. The study credited Twelpforce, Best Buy's Twitter and Facebook handle for its online community. The consumer-electronics giant had launched @Twelpforce (for *tweet help*) in 2009 as a means of boosting its online visibility, but it soon became a widely applauded innovation in customer service. As the company's Social and Emerging Media Manager, John Bernier oversaw the development of Twelpforce, which he envisioned as a way of "keeping one of our brand promises, which was to help the customer know what we know as fast as we know it." From the beginning, Bernier saw Twelpforce as a team open to *all* Best Buy employees: In addition to having people constantly available to respond to inquiries, a team assembled from companywide human resources ensured that no electronics-related inquiry would go unanswered.

Bernier credits top management, under CEO Brian Dunn, for taking one of the biggest risks you could ask an organization to take, which is ask your employees to do and say the right thing consistently. "What we came back to is this: We trust our employees to say and do the right thing every day in the store, so the only difference with Twelpforce is we're doing and saying things in a public platform that's available for all time."

By 2013, more than 3,000 registered Best Buy employees had sent more than 65,000 tweets. Customer complaints had dropped by 20 percent. In May 2013, however, Best Buy, under new CEO Hubert Joly, announced that it was discontinuing Twelpforce, which would be folded into the online accounts of its Geek Squad subsidiary and other customer-service units. The reasons weren't clear, but many inquiries that would have been handled through online channels would now be redirected to a call center accessed through the company's website. There, as of July 2013, customers were engaged in a rigidly scripted "conversation" from which agents could deviate only at the risk of their jobs. Customers, reported one such agent, are "mostly mystified" at employees' stubborn refusal to have normal conversations: "It can make us come across like crazy people," says the agent. "Normal human conversation doesn't happen like this. And, yes, some callers do get angry."

*References:* Zak Stambor, "Best Buy Is Best at Resolving Shoppers' Complaints on Social Media," *Internet Retailer* (July 2, 2013), www.internetretailer.com, on November 21, 2014; Drew Neisser, "Twelpforce: Marketing That Isn't Marketing," *Fast Company* (May 18, 2010), www.fastcompany.com, on November 21, 2014; "Best Buy's John Bernier on the Challenges of Adopting Social Media," *Sell or Else* (November 8, 2010), https://sellorelse.ogilvy.com, on November 23, 2014; Corey Padveen, "The Best Buy Twelpforce Program Has Taken the Brand from a Major Force in Local Retail to an Industry Leader on Social Media," *t2Marketing International* (May 2, 2013), http://t2marketinginternational, on November 21, 2014; John Vomhof Jr., "Best Buy Scraps Twelpforce, Shifts Twitter Support to Geek Squad," *Minneapolis/St. Paul Business Journal* (May 7, 2013), www.bizjournals.com, on November 21, 2014; Chris Morran, "Some Best Buy Customer Service Reps Not Thrilled with Having to Stick to Script," *Consumerist* (July 1, 2013), http://consumerist.com, on November 24, 2014.

**Manager's Checklist**

# Establishing Reporting Relationships

The third basic element of organizing is the establishment of reporting relationships among positions. Suppose, for example, that the owner–manager of a small business has just hired two new employees, one to handle marketing and one to handle production. Will the marketing manager report to the production manager, will the production manager report to the marketing manager, or will each report directly to the owner–manager? These questions reflect the basic issues involved in establishing reporting relationships: clarifying the chain of command and the span of management. We should also note before proceeding, though, that in addition to formal departmental arrangements (as described earlier) and prescribed reporting relationships (as discussed below), there is also considerable informal interaction that takes place among people in any organization.

## Chain of Command

Chain of command is an old concept, first popularized in the early years of the twentieth century. For example, early writers on the chain of command argued that clear and distinct lines of authority need to be established among all positions in an organization. The chain of command actually has two components. The first, called *unity of command*, suggests that each person within an organization must have a clear reporting relationship to one and only one boss (as we see in Chapter 11, newer models of organization design routinely—and successfully—violate this premise). The second, called the *scalar principle*, suggests that there must be a clear and unbroken line of authority that extends from the lowest to the highest position in the organization. The popular saying "The buck stops here" is derived from this idea—someone in the organization must ultimately be responsible for every decision.

## Narrow Versus Wide Spans

Another part of establishing reporting relationships is determining how many people will report to each manager. This defines the span of management (sometimes called the *span of control*). For years, managers and researchers sought to determine the optimal span of management. For example, should it be relatively narrow (with few subordinates per manager) or relatively wide (with many subordinates)? One early writer, A. V. Graicunas, went so far as to quantify span of management issues.[22] Graicunas noted that a manager must deal with three kinds of interactions with and among subordinates: direct (the manager's one-to-one relationship with each subordinate), cross (among the subordinates themselves), and group (between groups of subordinates). The number of possible interactions of all types between a manager and subordinates can be determined by the following formula:

$$I = N \left( 2^N/2 + N - 1 \right)$$

where $I$ is the total number of interactions with and among subordinates and $N$ is the number of subordinates.

If a manager has only two subordinates, six potential interactions exist. If the number of subordinates increases to three, the possible interactions total 18. With five subordinates, there are 100 possible interactions. Although Graicunas offers no prescription for what $N$ should be, his ideas demonstrate how complex the relationships become when more

**chain of command**
A clear and distinct line of authority among the positions in an organization

**span of management**
The number of people who report to a particular manager

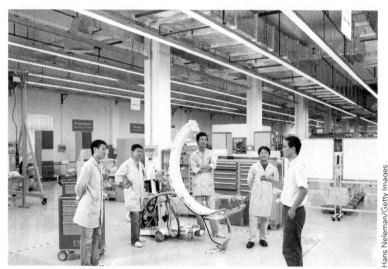

Hans Neleman/Getty Images

In the firm pictured above, there are 5 managers working on a new product. The tall structure of this organization leads to longer lead times on product innovation because communication must filter down to the people that report to these managers.

subordinates are added. The important point is that each additional subordinate adds more complexity than the previous one did. Going from nine to ten subordinates is very different from going from three to four.

Another early writer, Ralph C. Davis, described two kinds of spans: an operative span for lower-level managers and an executive span for middle and top managers. He argued that operative spans could approach 30 subordinates, whereas executive spans should be limited to between three and nine (depending on the nature of the managers' jobs, the growth rate of the company, and similar factors). Lyndall F. Urwick suggested that an executive span should never exceed six subordinates, and General Ian Hamilton reached the same conclusion.[23] Today we recognize that the span of management is a crucial factor in structuring organizations but that there are no universal, cut-and-dried prescriptions for an ideal or optimal span.[24] Later we summarize some important variables that influence the appropriate span of management in a particular situation. First, however, we describe how the span of management affects the overall structure of an organization.

## Tall Versus Flat Organizations

Imagine an organization with 31 managers and a narrow span of management. As shown in Figure 10.3, the result is a relatively tall organization with five layers of management. With a somewhat wider span of management, however, the flat organization shown in Figure 10.3 emerges. This configuration has only three layers of management.

What difference does it make whether the organization is tall or flat? One classic study at Sears found that a flat structure led to higher levels of employee morale and productivity.[25] Researchers have also argued that a tall structure is more expensive (because of the larger number of managers involved) and that it fosters more communication problems (because of the increased number of people through whom information must pass). On the other hand, a wide span of management in a flat organization may result in a manager's having more administrative responsibility (because there are fewer managers) and more supervisory responsibility (because there are more subordinates reporting to each manager). If these additional responsibilities become excessive, the flat organization may suffer.[26]

Many experts agree that businesses can function effectively with fewer layers of organization than they currently have. The Franklin Mint, for example, reduced its number of management layers from six to four. At the same time, the CEO increased his span of management from six to 12. In similar fashion, IBM has eliminated several layers of management. The British firm Cadbury PLC, maker of Cadbury Dairy chocolates, Trident gum, and other confectionary products, eliminated a layer of management separating the CEO and the firm's operating units. Anglo American PLC, a large global mining company, also cut a layer of management. And Allergan announced that a major reorganization will result in the elimination of an organizational layer to maintain the company's lean and efficient business model.[27] The specific reasons for the change were to improve communication between the CEO and the operating unit heads and to speed up decision making.[28] One additional reason for this trend is that improved communication technologies such as e-mail and text messaging allow managers to stay in touch with a larger number of subordinates than was possible even just a few years ago.[29]

"We must build a corporate lattice, not a corporate ladder."

—UNNAMED PARTNER, DELOITTE LLP[30]

## FIGURE 10.3  TALL VERSUS FLAT ORGANIZATIONS

(Wide spans of management result in flat organizations, which may lead to improved employee morale and productivity as well as increased managerial responsibility. Many organizations today, including IBM and General Electric, are moving toward flat structures to improve communication and flexibility.

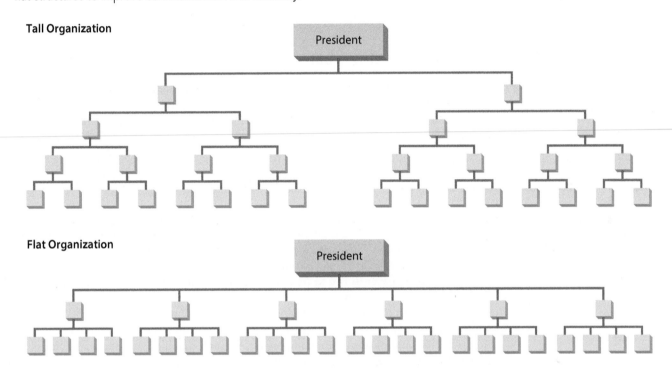

**Tall Organization**

President

**Flat Organization**

President

## Determining the Appropriate Span

Of course, the initial question remains: How do managers determine the appropriate span for their unique situation? Although no perfect formula exists, researchers have identified a set of factors that influence the span for a particular circumstance.[31] Some of these factors are listed in Table 10.1. For example, if the manager and subordinates are competent and well trained, a wide span may be effective. Physical dispersion is also important. The more widely subordinates are scattered, the narrower the span should be. On the other hand, if all the subordinates are in one location, the span can be somewhat wider. The amount of nonsupervisory work expected of the manager is also important. Some managers, especially at the lower levels of an organization, spend most or all of their time supervising subordinates. Other managers spend a lot of time doing paperwork, planning, and engaging in other managerial activities. Thus these managers may need a narrower span.

Some job situations also require a great deal of interaction between supervisor and subordinates. In general, the more interaction that is required, the narrower the span should be. Similarly, if there is a fairly comprehensive set of standard procedures, a relatively wide span is possible. If only a few standard procedures exist, however, the supervisor usually has to play a larger role in overseeing day-to-day activities and may find a narrower span more efficient. Task similarity is also important. If most of the jobs being supervised are similar, a supervisor can handle a wider span. When each employee is performing a different task, more of the supervisor's time is spent on individual supervision. Likewise, if new problems that require supervisory assistance arise often, a narrower span may be called for. If new problems are relatively rare, though, a wider span can be established. Finally, the preferences of both supervisor and subordinates may affect the optimal span. Some managers prefer to spend

---

### TABLE 10.1 FACTORS INFLUENCING THE SPAN OF MANAGEMENT

Although researchers have found advantages to the flat organization (less expensive and with fewer communication problems than a tall organization, for example), a number of factors may favor a tall organization.

1. Competence of supervisor and subordinates (the greater the competence, the wider the potential span)
2. Physical dispersion of subordinates (the greater the dispersion, the narrower the potential span)
3. Extent of nonsupervisory work in manager's job (the more nonsupervisory work, the narrower the potential span)
4. Degree of required interaction (the less required interaction, the wider the potential span)
5. Extent of standardized procedures (the more procedures, the wider the potential span)
6. Similarity of tasks being supervised (the more similar the tasks, the wider the potential span)
7. Frequency of new problems (the higher the frequency, the narrower the potential span)
8. Preferences of supervisors and subordinates

less time actively supervising their employees, and many employees prefer to be more self-directed in their jobs. A wider span may be possible in these situations.

For example, the Case Corporation factory in Racine, Wisconsin, makes farm tractors exclusively to order in five to six weeks. Farmers can select from among a wide array of options, including engines, tires, power trains, and music systems with USB ports. A wide assortment of machines and processes is used to construct each tractor. Although workers are highly skilled operators of their particular machines, each machine is different. In this kind of setup, the complexities of each machine and the advanced skills needed by each operator mean that one supervisor can oversee only a small number of employees.[32]

In some organizational settings, other factors may influence the optimal span of management. The relative importance of each factor also varies in different settings. It is unlikely that all eight factors will suggest the same span; some may suggest a wider span, and others may indicate a need for a narrow span. Hence, managers must assess the relative weight of each factor or set of factors when deciding the optimal span of management for their unique situation.

---

 **Manager's Checklist**

☐ Managers need to have a clear understanding of the factors that should be considered when determining the appropriate span of management for a particular setting.

☐ You should know both your own span of management and the span of management of your manager.

☐ You should also have a clear understanding of how both your span and the span of your manager affect you and your work.

## Distributing Authority

**authority**
Power that has been legitimized by the organization

Another important building block in structuring organizations is the determination of how authority is to be distributed among positions. Authority is power that has been legitimized by the organization.[33] Distributing authority is another normal outgrowth of increasing organizational size. For example, when an owner–manager hires a sales representative to market his products, he needs to give the new employee appropriate authority to make decisions about delivery dates, discounts, and so forth. If every decision requires the approval of the owner–manager, he is no better off than he was before he hired the sales representative. The power given to the sales representative to make certain kinds of decisions, then, represents the establishment of a pattern of authority—the sales representative can make some decisions alone and others in consultation with coworkers, and the sales representative must defer some decisions to the boss. Two specific issues that managers must address when distributing authority are delegation and decentralization.[34]

Authority is power that has been legitimized by the organization. This supply chain manager is using her authority to instruct one of her subordinates on how to complete a project at one of the firm's distribution centers.

## The Delegation Process

Delegation is the establishment of a pattern of authority between a superior and one or more subordinates. Specifically, delegation is the process by which managers assign a portion of their total workload to others.[35]

**Reasons for Delegation** The primary reason for delegation is to enable the manager to get more work done. Subordinates help ease the manager's burden by doing major portions of the organization's work. In some instances, a subordinate may have more expertise in addressing a particular problem than the manager does. For example, the subordinate may have had special training in developing information systems or may be more familiar with a particular product line or geographic area. Delegation also helps develop subordinates. By participating in decision making and problem solving, subordinates learn about overall operations and improve their managerial skills.

**Parts of the Delegation Process** In theory, as shown in Figure 10.4, the delegation process involves three steps. First, the manager assigns responsibility or gives the subordinate a job to do. The assignment of responsibility might range from telling a subordinate to prepare a report to placing the person in charge of a task force. Along with the assignment, the person is also given the authority to do the job. The manager may give the subordinate the power to requisition needed information from confidential files or to direct a group of other workers. Finally, the manager establishes the subordinate's accountability—that is, the subordinate accepts an obligation to carry out the task assigned by the manager. For instance, the CEO of AutoZone will sign off for the company on financial performance only when the individual manager responsible for each unit has certified his or her own results as being accurate. The firm believes that this high level of accountability will help it avoid the kind of accounting scandal that has hit many businesses in recent times.[36]

These three steps do not occur mechanically, however. Indeed, when a manager and a subordinate have developed a good working relationship, the major parts of the process may be implied and understood rather than stated. The manager may simply mention that a particular job must be done. A perceptive subordinate may realize that the manager is actually assigning the job to her. From past experience with the boss, she may also know, without being told, that she has the necessary authority to do the job and that she is accountable to the boss for finishing the job as "agreed."

**delegation**
The process by which managers assign work to subordinates

## FIGURE 10.4 STEPS IN THE DELEGATION PROCESS

Good communication skills can help a manager successfully delegate responsibility to subordinates. A manager must not be reluctant to delegate, nor should he or she fear that the subordinate will do the job so well that the manager's advancement is threatened.

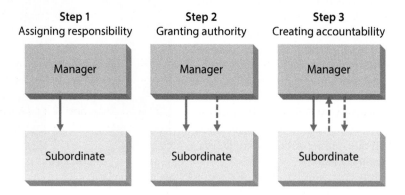

**Problems in Delegation** Unfortunately, problems often arise in the delegation process. For example, a manager may be reluctant to delegate. Some managers are so disorganized that they cannot plan work in advance and, as a result, cannot delegate appropriately. Similarly, some managers may worry that subordinates will do too well and pose a threat to their own advancement. And, finally, managers may not trust the subordinate to do the job well. Similarly, some subordinates are reluctant to accept delegation. They may be afraid that failure will result in a reprimand. They may also perceive that there are no rewards for accepting additional responsibility. Or they may simply prefer to avoid risk and therefore want their boss to take all responsibility.

There are no quick fixes for these problems. The basic issue is communication. Subordinates must understand their own responsibility, authority, and accountability, and the manager must come to recognize the value of effective delegation. With the passage of time, subordinates should develop to the point at which they can make substantial contributions to the organization. At the same time, managers should recognize that a subordinate's satisfactory performance is not a threat to their own career, but an accomplishment by both the subordinate who did the job and the manager who trained the subordinate and was astute enough to entrust the subordinate with the project. Ultimate responsibility for the outcome, however, continues to reside with the manager.

Richard Branson, the founder of Virgin Records and now the owner of over 400 companies within the Virgin Group, learned the importance of delegation early in his career. When Virgin Records first began, employees had the freedom to take charge of any responsibilities they had the ability and desire to do. However, as the employee count reached 100, Branson feared the company was becoming too slow. To maintain employee flexibility but prevent slowdown, he split the company in half and pinpointed talented employees from Virgin Records to run it. Branson has continued this strategy as his empire has grown, identifying employees with management potential and fostering employee empowerment through systematic delegation.[37]

**decentralization**
The process of systematically delegating power and authority throughout the organization to middle and lower-level managers

## Decentralization and Centralization

Just as authority can be delegated from one person to another, organizations also develop patterns of authority across a wide variety of positions and departments. Decentralization is the process of systematically delegating power and authority throughout the organization to middle and lower-level managers. It is important to remember that decentralization is actually one end of a continuum anchored at the other end by centralization, the process of systematically retaining power and authority in the hands of higher-level managers. Hence, a decentralized organization is one in which decision-making power and authority are delegated as far down the chain of command as possible. Conversely, in a centralized organization, decision-making power and authority are retained at the higher levels of management. When H. Ross Perot started EDS, he practiced centralization; his successors have used decentralization. No organization is ever completely decentralized or completely centralized; some firms position themselves toward one end of the continuum, and some lean the other way.[38]

What factors determine an organization's position on the decentralization–centralization continuum? One common determinant is the organization's external environment. Usually, the greater the complexity and uncertainty of the environment, the greater is the tendency to decentralize. Another crucial factor is the history of the organization. Firms have a tendency to do what they have done in the past, so there is likely to be some relationship between what an organization did in its early history and what it chooses to do today in terms of centralization or decentralization. The nature of the decisions being made is also considered. The costlier and riskier the decisions, the more pressure there is to centralize. Organizations also consider the abilities of lower-level managers. If lower-level managers do not have the ability to make high-quality decisions, there is likely to be a high level of centralization. If lower-level managers are well qualified, top management can take advantage of their talents by decentralizing; in fact, if top management does not, talented lower-level managers may leave the organization.[39]

A manager has no clear-cut guidelines for determining whether to centralize or decentralize. Many successful organizations, such as General Electric and Johnson & Johnson, are quite decentralized. Equally successful firms, such as McDonald's and Walmart, have remained centralized. And some firms move from one to the other. Royal Dutch Shell, long operated in a highly decentralized manner, has recently gone through several major changes, all intended to make the firm more centralized. The firm's CEO went so far as to note that "fewer people will make strategic decisions."[40] Yahoo Inc. has also initiated a change to become more centralized.[41] In contrast, Toyota, traditionally run in a highly centralized fashion with all major decisions made in Japan by top managers, has become more decentralized and given country managers more decision-making authority.[42]

**centralization**
The process of systematically retaining power and authority in the hands of higher-level managers

"When you have command and control by the top 10 people, you can only do one or two things at a time. The future is about collaboration and teamwork and making decisions with a process that offers scale, speed, and flexibility."

—JOHN CHAMBERS, FORMER CISCO CEO[43]

Ken Wolter/Shutterstock.com

Walmart is a centralized organization. Managers at the firm's headquarters in Arkansas have established an extensive set of rules, regulations, and standard operating procedures to be followed by store managers. Store managers also have little discretion over how their store is laid out, how products are displayed, and the prices they will charge for different items.

---

☐ Managers should understand their own tendencies, as well as the tendencies of their managers, if those tendencies relate to delegation.

☐ You should be aware of the extent to which your organization is relatively more centralized or relatively more decentralized.

**Manager's Checklist** ☑

# Coordinating Activities

A fifth major element of organizing is coordination. As we discuss earlier, job specialization and departmentalization involve breaking jobs down into small units and then combining those jobs into departments. Once this has been accomplished, the activities of the departments must be linked—systems must be put into place to keep the activities of each department focused on the attainment of organizational goals. This is accomplished by coordination—the process of linking the activities of the various departments of the organization.[44]

## The Need for Coordination

The primary reason for coordination is that departments and work groups are interdependent—they depend on one another for information and resources to perform their respective activities. The greater the interdependence between departments, the more coordination the organization requires if departments are to be able to perform effectively. There are three major forms of interdependence: pooled, sequential, and reciprocal.[45]

Pooled interdependence represents the lowest level of interdependence. Units with pooled interdependence operate with little interaction—the output of the units is pooled at the organizational level. Old Navy clothing stores operate with pooled interdependence. Each store is considered a "department" by the parent corporation. Each has its own operating budget, staff, and so forth. The profits or losses from each store are "added together" at the organizational level. The stores are interdependent to the extent that the final success or failure of one store affects the others, but they do not generally interact on a day-to-day basis.

In sequential interdependence, the output of one unit becomes the input for another in a sequential fashion. This creates a moderate level of interdependence. At Nissan, for example, one plant assembles engines and then ships them to a final assembly site at another plant, where the cars are completed. The plants are interdependent in that the final assembly plant must have the engines from engine assembly before it can perform its primary function of producing finished automobiles. But the level of interdependence is generally one way—the engine plant is not necessarily dependent on the final assembly plant.

Reciprocal interdependence exists when activities flow both ways between units. This form is clearly the most complex. Within a Marriott hotel, for example, the reservations department, front-desk check-in, and housekeeping are all reciprocally interdependent. Reservations has to provide front-desk employees with information about how many guests to expect each day, and housekeeping needs to know which rooms require priority cleaning. If any of the three units does not do its job properly, all the others will be affected.

**coordination**
The process of linking the activities of the various departments of the organization

**pooled interdependence**
When units operate with little interaction; their output is simply pooled

**sequential interdependence**
When the output of one unit becomes the input for another in sequential fashion

**reciprocal interdependence**
When activities flow both ways between units

A warehouse facility like this one often requires considerable coordination. At any given time shipments are coming in while other shipments are going out. Boxes and crates are also being moved from one location to another at the same time that merchandise is being packed for shipment.

wavebreakmedia/Shutterstock.com

## Structural Coordination Techniques

Because of the obvious coordination requirements that characterize most organizations, many techniques for achieving coordination have been developed. Some of the most useful devices for maintaining coordination among interdependent units are the managerial hierarchy, rules and procedures, liaison roles, task forces, and integrating departments.[46]

**The Managerial Hierarchy** Organizations that use the hierarchy to achieve coordination place one manager in charge of interdependent departments or units. In Walmart distribution centers, major activities include receiving and unloading bulk shipments from railroad cars and loading other shipments onto trucks for distribution to retail outlets. The two groups (receiving and shipping) are interdependent in that they share the loading docks and some equipment. To ensure coordination and minimize conflict, one manager is in charge of the whole operation.

**Rules and Procedures** Routine coordination activities can be handled via rules and standard procedures. In the Walmart distribution center, an outgoing truck shipment has priority over an incoming rail shipment. Thus, when trucks are to be loaded, the shipping unit is given access to all of the center's auxiliary forklifts. This priority is specifically stated in a rule. But, as useful as rules and procedures often are in routine situations, they are not particularly effective when coordination problems are complex or unusual.

**Liaison Roles** We introduced the liaison role of management in Chapter 1. As a device for coordination, a manager in a liaison role coordinates interdependent units by acting as a common point of contact. This person may not have any formal authority over the groups but instead simply facilitates the flow of information between units. Two engineering groups working on component systems for a large project might interact through a liaison. The liaison maintains familiarity with each group as well as with the overall project. She can answer questions and otherwise serve to integrate the activities of all the groups.

**Task Forces** A task force may be created when the need for coordination is acute. When interdependence is complex and several units are involved, a single liaison person may not be sufficient. Instead, a task force might be assembled by drawing one representative from each group. The coordination function is thus spread across several individuals, each of whom has special information about one of the groups involved. When the project is completed, task force members return to their original positions. For example, a college overhauling its degree requirements might establish a task force made up of representatives from each department affected by the change. Each person retains her or his regular departmental affiliation and duties but also serves on the special task force. After the new requirements are agreed on, the task force is dissolved.

**Integrating Departments** Integrating departments are occasionally used for coordination. These are somewhat similar to task forces but are more permanent. An integrating department generally has some permanent members as well as members who are assigned temporarily from units that are particularly in need of coordination. One study found that successful firms in the plastics industry, which is characterized by complex and dynamic environments, used integrating departments to maintain internal integration and coordination.[47] An integrating department usually has more authority than a task force and may even be given some budgetary control by the organization.

In general, the greater the degree of interdependence, the more attention the organization must devote to coordination. When interdependence is pooled or simple sequential, the managerial hierarchy or rules and procedures are often sufficient. When more complex forms of sequential or simpler forms of reciprocal interdependence exist, liaisons or task forces may be more useful. When reciprocal interdependence is complex, task forces or integrating departments are needed. Of course, the manager must also rely on her or his own experience and insights when choosing coordination techniques for the organization. Moreover, informal interactions among people throughout the organization can also serve to effectively coordinate activities. The *Doing Business on Planet Earth* feature describes an especially complex set of interdependent activities that require coordination.

# Collaboration, Connection, and Chromosomal Configuration

Kathrin Winkler is chief sustainability officer (CSO) and senior VP of EMC Corporation, a worldwide leader in data storage. She's been at the job (originally as senior director of corporate sustainability) since 2008, but she was passionate about the possibilities of corporate sustainability even before the CSO job opened up. When the position was announced, recalls Winkler, "I told my boss I absolutely had to apply for this job," and she's still excited today by "those amazing moments of satisfaction when … an employee shows pride over a process redesign or the lights go on in a middle manager's eyes." Besides, as she likes to remind herself, "someone is paying me to try to make the world a better place."

Winkler admits, however, that there are "some things I don't love so much about my job." One pet peeve is having to deal with surveys. "We get lots of surveys from analysts and self-appointed rating systems," she explains, most of which

> have some really annoying questions that have no regard for the core purpose of our business. … For example, we're often docked points because we don't have a line of "green" products. But whenever we find a way to reduce the negative impact or improve the positive impact of our products, we try to put it across the entire product line. Isn't that a good thing?

Likewise—and this may come as a bit of a surprise—Winkler doesn't like getting sponsorship requests. Once in a while, she says, "it's useful for our customers to know what's important to us," but EMC customers—whether money-center banks, telecommunications providers, airlines, or educational institutions—"aren't often primary audiences for these events." In any case, she adds, "I'm not convinced that the best use of our money is putting our logo on things. Mostly, I try to use the majority of my budget to fulfill the mission of embedding sustainability into how we conduct business."

Clearly, Winkler is a little skeptical when it comes to how much people know about the job responsibilities of a CSO, especially at a company like EMC. So,

when asked exactly what they are, Winkler answers with a statement like the following:

> I'm responsible for making sure that the interdependencies between our business, the environment, and society are identified and explicit in our strategy, and that the opportunities and risks from environmental and social developments are integrated into our day-to-day decision making.

The goal at EMC is to make sure that sustainability is considered in every aspect of the company's business, and Winkler's job is ensuring that sustainability goes hand in hand with company growth. "We want sustainability to be a core value—like quality and customer responsiveness. It requires a culture change," she admits, "and that's always the hardest thing to do." That's why the reach of EMC's Office of Sustainability is designed to embrace the entire organization. "I have a virtual cross-functional team," explains Winkler. "There are many people whose job titles do not include 'sustainability' but whose jobs could be framed as sustainable development roles, such as those who are managing marketing and communications."

It's all about "collaboration and connection," she says, and she suspects that

> women's leadership styles tend to be especially open to consultation and collaboration. While I believe that my chromosomal configuration doesn't make me any better at my job or any more attracted to it, there are a number of characteristics—often considered more prevalent in women than in men—that are beneficial to the role.

For the record, one of the things that Winkler likes about her job is "collaborating rather than competing with my counterparts."

*References:* Kathrin Winkler, "Ten Challenges of Being the CSO," *GreenBiz* (July 9, 2013), www.greenbiz.com, on November 13, 2014; Weinreb Group, *CSO Backstory: How Chief Sustainability Officers Reached the C-Suite* (September 2011), www.weinrebgroup.com, on November 14, 2014; Winkler, "Building a Green Company Culture, One Day at a Time," *GreenBiz* (October 29, 2009), www.greenbiz.com, on November 13, 2014; Kyle Alspach, "EMC Goes Green," *Boston Business Journal* (July 15, 2011), www.bizjournals.com, on November 14, 2014; Maya Albanese, "How She Leads: Kathrin Winkler of EMC Corporation," *GreenBiz* (July 11, 2011), www.greenbiz.com, on November 14, 2014; Winkler, "Do Women Make Better Sustainability Leaders?" *The Guardian* (May 5, 2015), www.theguardian.com, on November 13, 2014.

## Electronic Coordination

Recent advances in electronic information technology are also providing useful mechanisms for coordination. E-mail, for example, makes it easier for people to communicate with one another. This communication, in turn, enhances coordination. Similarly, many people in organizations today use electronic scheduling, at least some of which is accessible to others. Hence, if someone needs to set up a meeting with two colleagues, he can often check their electronic schedules to determine their availability, making it easier to coordinate their activities.

Local networks, increasingly managed by handheld electronic devices, are also making it easier to coordinate activities. Bechtel, for example, now requires its contractors, subcontractors, and suppliers to use a common web-based communication system to improve coordination among their myriad activities. The firm estimates that this improved coordination technology routinely saves it thousands of dollars on every big construction project it undertakes.

---

☐ Managers need to be aware of the three kinds of interdependence that necessitate coordination.

☐ You should understand the coordination mechanisms used in your organization.

**Manager's Checklist**

# Differentiating Between Positions

The last building block of organization structure is differentiating between line and staff positions in the organization. A line position is a position in the direct chain of command that is responsible for the achievement of an organization's goals. A staff position is intended to provide expertise, advice, and support for line positions. In many modern organizations these differences are beginning to disappear, and in a few the difference has been eliminated altogether. However, there are still sufficient meaningful differences to warrant discussion.

## Differences Between Line and Staff

The most obvious difference between line and staff is purpose—line managers work directly toward organizational goals, whereas staff managers advise and assist. But other distinctions exist as well. One important difference is authority. Line authority is generally thought of as the formal or legitimate authority created by the organizational hierarchy. Staff authority is less concrete and may take a variety of forms. One form is *advise authority*. In this instance, the line manager can choose whether to seek or to avoid input from staff; and even when advice is sought, the line manager might still choose to ignore it.

Another form of staff authority is called *compulsory advice*. In this case, the line manager must consider the advice but can choose to heed it or ignore it. For example, the pope is expected to listen to the advice of the Sacred College of Cardinals when dealing with church doctrine, but he may follow his own beliefs when making decisions. Perhaps the most important form of staff authority is called *functional authority*—formal or legitimate authority over activities related to the staff member's specialty. For example, a human resource staff manager may have functional authority when there is a question of discrimination in hiring. Conferring functional authority is probably the most effective way to use staff positions because the organization can take advantage of specialized expertise while also maintaining a chain of command.

**line position**
A position in the direct chain of command that is responsible for the achievement of an organization's goals

**staff position**
A position intended to provide expertise, advice, and support for line positions

## Administrative Intensity

Organizations sometimes try to balance their emphasis on line versus staff positions in terms of administrative intensity. Administrative intensity is the degree to which managerial positions are concentrated in staff positions. An organization with high administrative intensity is one with many staff positions relative to the number of line positions; low administrative intensity reflects relatively more line positions. Although staff positions are important in many different areas, they tend to proliferate unnecessarily. All else being equal, organizations would like to devote most of their human resource investment to line managers because, by definition, they contribute to the organization's basic goals. A surplus of staff positions represents a drain on an organization's cash and an inefficient use of resources.

Many organizations have taken steps over the past few years to reduce their administrative intensity by eliminating staff positions. CBS cut hundreds of staff positions at its New York headquarters, and IBM cut its corporate staff workforce from 7,000 to 2,300. Burlington Northern generates almost $22 billion in annual sales and manages a workforce of 43,000 with a corporate staff of only 77 managers. Ford and General Motors have both downsized dramatically through job cuts and plant closings.

**administrative intensity**
The degree to which managerial positions are concentrated in staff positions

**Manager's Checklist**

☐ Managers should understand the basic difference between line and staff positions.

☐ You should have a clear understanding of whether your job is a line or staff position and how that affects your job.

# Summary of learning Outcomes and Key Points

1. Identify the basic elements of organizations.

   - Organizations are made up of a series of elements:
     o designing jobs
     o grouping jobs
     o establishing reporting relationships
     o distributing authority
     o coordinating activities
     o differentiating between positions.

2. Describe the basic alternative approaches to designing jobs.

   - Job design is the determination of a person's work-related responsibilities.
   - The most common form is job specialization.
   - Other alternatives include job rotation, job enlargement, job enrichment, the job characteristics approach, and work teams.

3. Discuss the rationale and the most common bases for grouping jobs into departments.

   - The most common bases for departmentalization are:
     o function
     o product

   o customer
   o location
   - large organizations employ multiple bases of departmentalization at different levels.

4. Describe the basic elements involved in establishing reporting relationships.

   - Establishing reporting relationships starts with clarifying the chain of command.
   - The span of management partially dictates whether the organization is relatively tall or flat.
   - In recent years there has been a trend toward flatter organizations.
   - Several situational factors influence the ideal span.

5. Discuss how authority is distributed in organizations.

   - Distributing authority starts with delegation.
   - Delegation is the process by which the manager assigns a portion of his or her total workload to others.
   - Systematic delegation throughout the organization is decentralization.
   - Centralization involves keeping power and authority at the top of the organization.
   - Several factors influence the appropriate degree of decentralization.

6. Discuss the basic coordinating activities undertaken by organizations.

   - Coordination is the process of linking the activities of the various departments of the organization.
   - Pooled, sequential, or reciprocal interdependence among departments is a primary reason for coordination.
   - Managers can draw on several techniques to help achieve coordination.
   - Electronic coordination is becoming increasingly important.

7. Describe basic ways in which positions within an organization can be differentiated.

   - A line position is a position in the direct chain of command that is responsible for the achievement of an organization's goals.
   - A staff position provides expertise, advice, and support for line positions.
   - Administrative intensity is the degree to which managerial positions are concentrated in staff positions.

# Discussion Questions

## Questions for Review

1. Describe the five alternatives to job specialization. What is the advantage of each, as compared to specialization?

2. What is meant by unity of command? By the scalar principle? Can an organization have one without the other? Explain.

3. Describe the organizational structure that results from each of the different bases of departmentalization.

What implications does each of these structures have with regard to the distribution of authority within the organization?

4. Explain the differences between line and staff positions. What are the advantages and disadvantages of high versus low administrative intensity?

## Questions for Analysis

5. Some people have claimed that the increasing technological sophistication required by many of today's corporations has led to a return to job specialization. In your opinion, what would be the consequences of a sharp increase in job specialization? Consider both positive and negative outcomes in your answer.

6. Try to develop a different way to departmentalize your college or university, a local fast-food restaurant, a manufacturing firm, or some other organization. What might be the advantages of your form of organization?

7. Consider the following list of jobs. In your opinion, what is the appropriate span of management for each?

Describe the factors you considered in reaching your conclusion.

   - A physician practices medicine in a privately owned clinic while also supervising a number of professional nurses and office staff.
   - An owner–manager of an auto body shop deals with customers, directs several experienced mechanics, and also trains and oversees the work of some unskilled laborers.
   - A manager in an international advertising agency directs a team of professionals who are located in offices around the world.

## Questions for Application

8. Consider a job you have held. (Or, if you have not held a job, interview a worker.) Using the job characteristics approach, assess that job's core dimensions. Then describe how the core dimensions led to critical psychological states and, ultimately, to personal and work outcomes.

9. Use the Internet to locate organization charts for five different organizations. (Or use data from the Internet to draw the organization charts yourself.) Look for similarities and differences among them and try to account for what you find.

10. Contact two very different local organizations (retailing firm, manufacturing firm, church, civic club, and so on) and interview top managers to develop organization charts for each organization. How do you account for the similarities and differences between them?

# Building Effective Conceptual Skills

### Exercise Overview

Conceptual skills require you to think in the abstract. This exercise calls on your conceptual skills to address questions about span of management.

### Exercise Background

Finding an optimal span of management is as important as it's always been in trying to ensure a level of supervision that provides adequate control but which doesn't stifle workplace flexibility. The process of finding the right level, however, has changed fairly dramatically. Early management scholars, for instance, believed that there was one optimal span of management or that, at the very least, analysts could determine an optimal span by examining just one or a very few variables. Today, however, most experts agree that identifying an optimal span of management depends on the answers to a number of complex questions.

### Exercise Task

With this change in expert opinion in mind, do the following:

1. First, survey 10 workers and managers about the span of management in their respective workplaces.

2. Now choose one of these individuals for further investigation. Interview this person to get a better idea about the type of work that he or she does, the amount of required interaction with supervisors, the skill levels expected of workers, and other factors that may enter into the determination of optimal span of management. (See Table 10.1 for guidance.)

3. Given the information that you gathered in performing task 2, does the span of management in the workplace make sense? Why or why not?

4. If the span of management seems to be appropriate, what are some of the likely outcomes that the organization can expect? What are some likely outcomes if it seems inappropriate?

# Building Effective Diagnostic Skills

### Exercise Overview

Diagnostic skills enable a manager to visualize the most appropriate response to a situation. In this exercise, you're asked to apply your diagnostic skills to the question of centralization versus decentralization in an organization.

### Exercise Background

Managers often find it necessary to change an organization's degree of centralization or decentralization. Begin this exercise by reflecting on two very different scenarios in which this issue has arisen:

*Scenario* A. You're the top manager in a large organization with a long and successful history of centralized operations.

For valid reasons beyond the scope of this exercise, however, you've decided to make the firm much more decentralized.

*Scenario B.* Assume the exact opposite of the situation in Scenario A. You still occupy the top spot in your firm, but this time you're going to centralize operations in an organization that's always been decentralized.

### Exercise Task

Now do the following:

1. For Scenario A, list the major barriers to decentralization that you foresee.

2. For Scenario B, list the major barriers to centralization that you foresee.

3. In your opinion, which scenario would be easier to implement in reality? In other words, is it probably easier to move from centralization to decentralization or vice versa? Whatever your opinion in the matter, be ready to explain it.

4. Given a choice of starting your career in a firm that's either highly centralized or highly decentralized, which would you prefer? Why?

# Skill-Building Personal Assessment

### Delegation Aptitude Survey

**Purpose:** To help students gain insight into the process of and the attitudes important to delegation.

**Introduction:** Delegation has a number of advantages for managers, workers, and organizations, but it also presents challenges. Managers who understand the benefits of delegation, who trust their subordinates, and who have the emotional maturity to allow others to succeed are more likely to be effective delegators.

**Instructions:**

1. Complete the following Delegation Aptitude Survey. You should think of work-related or group situations in which you have had the opportunity to delegate responsibility to others. If you have not had such experiences, try to imagine how you would respond in such a situation. Circle the response that best typifies your attitude or behavior.

2. Score the survey according to the directions that follow. Calculate your overall score.

3. Working with a small group, compare individual scores and prepare group responses to the discussion questions.

4. Calculate a class-average score. Have one member of the group present the group's responses to the discussion questions.

## Delegation Aptitude Survey

| Statement | Strongly Agree | Slightly Agree | Not Sure | Slightly Disagree | Strongly Disagree |
|---|---|---|---|---|---|
| 1. I don't think others can do the work as well as I can. | 1 | 2 | 3 | 4 | 5 |
| 2. I often take work home with me. | 1 | 2 | 3 | 4 | 5 |
| 3. Employees who can make their own decisions tend to be more efficient. | 5 | 4 | 3 | 2 | 1 |
| 4. I often have to rush to meet deadlines. | 1 | 2 | 3 | 4 | 5 |
| 5. Employees with more responsibility tend to have more commitment to group goals. | 5 | 4 | 3 | 2 | 1 |
| 6. When I delegate, I always explain precisely how the task is to be done. | 1 | 2 | 3 | 4 | 5 |
| 7. I always seem to have too much to do and too little time to do it in. | 1 | 2 | 3 | 4 | 5 |
| 8. When employees have the responsibility to do a job, they usually do it well. | 5 | 4 | 3 | 2 | 1 |
| 9. When I delegate, I make clear the end results I expect. | 5 | 4 | 3 | 2 | 1 |
| 10. I usually only delegate simple, routine tasks. | 1 | 2 | 3 | 4 | 5 |
| 11. When I delegate, I always make sure everyone concerned is so informed. | 5 | 4 | 3 | 2 | 1 |
| 12. If I delegate, I usually wind up doing the job over again to get it right. | 1 | 2 | 3 | 4 | 5 |
| 13. I become irritated watching others doing a job I can do better. | 1 | 2 | 3 | 4 | 5 |
| 14. When I delegate, I feel I am losing the control I need. | 1 | 2 | 3 | 4 | 5 |

*(Continued)*

| | | | | | |
|---|---|---|---|---|---|
| 15. | When I delegate, I always set specific dates for progress reports. | 5 | 4 | 3 | 2 | 1 |
| 16. | When I do a job, I do it to perfection. | 1 | 2 | 3 | 4 | 5 |
| 17. | I honestly feel that I can do most jobs better than my subordinates can. | 1 | 2 | 3 | 4 | 5 |
| 18. | When employees make their own decisions, it tends to cause confusion. | 1 | 2 | 3 | 4 | 5 |
| 19. | It's difficult for subordinates to make decisions because they don't know the organization's goals. | 1 | 2 | 3 | 4 | 5 |
| 20. | When employees are given responsibility, they usually do what is asked of them. | 5 | 4 | 3 | 2 | 1 |

## Discussion Questions

1. In what respects do the survey responses agree or disagree?

2. What might account for some of the differences in individual scores?

3. How can you make constructive use of the survey results?

Source: Linda Morable, *Exercises in Management*, 8th ed., pp. 82–84. © 2005.

# Management at Work

### From Pyramid Schemes to Mutual Fun

## "If it's not fun, it's work; and if it's work, it sucks."

—JIM LAVOIE, CEO OF RITE-SOLUTIONS

Jim Lavoie boasts an impressive résumé as an executive manager, especially in manufacturing and operations. In addition to directing test manufacturing at Xerox, he served as senior industrial engineer at Hughes Aircraft and director of operations at Emerson Technologies. With partner Joe Marino, he cofounded Analysis & Technology, a provider of engineering and information technology and technology-based training systems for the military, and he served as CEO until he and Marino sold the firm for $100 million in 1999.

Looking back in 2011, Lavoie declared that "for my whole career, I did it wrong." What aspect of a distinguished career had left him unsatisfied? Generally speaking, organizational structure and, in particular, the kind of organizational behavior that was encouraged by the pyramid model of both manager-to-manager and manager-to-employee relations (recall the *levels of management pyramid* from Chapter 1). "The hierarchical pyramid," contends Lavoie, "is a relic of command-and-control conventional wisdom—more suited to controlling information flow than fostering innovation."

Over the years, Lavoie experienced firsthand the rapidly increasing importance of innovation to organiza-

tional survival, especially in a Web 2.0 world. All too often, however, he found that companies "specialized in innovative ways of saying 'no' to innovation." Take, for instance, the "murder board"—Lavoie and Marino's epithet for the innovation committee at a company where they once worked. Anyone with a promising idea took it before the committee, where members would bombard the hopeful intrapreneur with questions about market size and cost projections. In the end, reports Lavoie, "you're standing in front of six fat white guys who say that they're there to help with your idea, but what they're doing is shooting down your relevance."

Ironically, adds Lavoie, he prospered under the very same system: In one firm, he reports, "I made it to executive VP not by being bright; but by being theatrical." And that, he realized, was a widespread problem with the system: "Most people," says Lavoie, "make innovation a contact sport. Which automatically leaves out the introverts. ... Innovation offsites, jams, and 'war rooms' have the same effect: the idea with the most theater wins and the people with the most charisma suck all of the oxygen out of the room."

Again, Lavoie found himself calling on personal experience as an executive manager: "I had spent 30 years in highly structured organizations where good ideas could only flow from the top down. ... The relationship I had with people was transactional—'I pay you, you work. You behave, you stay.'... In the old world, your relevance to the organization was defined more by the level of your box in the pyramid than by your actual insight. …

"The best thing for an idea," says Lavoie, "is air, and the more air you give it, and the more people who breathe the air, the better it will become." So Lavoie and Marino decided to start up another company, and this time they would commit themselves to "two fundamental beliefs." The first was the conviction that the pyramid was a relic, and the second held that "nobody is as smart as everybody—good ideas are not bounded by organizational structure, but can come from anyone, in any place, at any time. … So we scrapped the pyramid and the power politics that go along with it," explains Lavoie, "to rethink the company as a community."

The company, called Rite-Solutions, builds advanced software for the military and defense contractors as well as consumer-gaming platforms for casinos. It employs approximately 175 engineers, programmers, and analysts and is 100 percent employee owned. Community building begins on Day 1, when new employees are given a birthday party—to show, says Lavoie, "that you've arrived at a new place where you belong, you were expected, and you're important."

It's on Day 2, however, that you're invited to "buy in" to the Rite-Solutions way of doing things. You're given $10,000 in virtual money with which you can invest in portfolios of ideas proposed by Rite-Solutions employees. You can also volunteer time to any project that you deem promising. Most importantly, you can float your own idea on one of three indices: "Savings Bonds" (for efficiency measures), "Bow Jones" (for extensions of current company capabilities), or "Spazdaq" (for ventures into new businesses or technologies). You begin by drawing up an "Expect-Us" (as opposed to *prospectus*), whereupon you're assigned a ticker symbol and an offering price of $10. An algorithm then determines the daily value of your idea, which is derived from the level of interest expressed by your fellow employees.

If yours is among the top ideas on the board, management will help you flesh out an official proposal, and when it's ready, company employees can invest money in or volunteer

an "assist" with your project. If your project attracts sufficient employee-investor interest, you get a project manager who may take your idea all the way through production. In that case, your name will go on the patent filing, and you—and everyone who invested in your idea—will share in the financial rewards that your product generates.

The game, which is called "Mutual Fun," was launched in 2005 "with the aim," as Lavoie explains it, "of making our people feel relevant to the success of the business … and tapping their amazing intellectual bandwidth far beyond assigned 'job tasks.' We wanted to entrust them with the future of the company." Besides, adds Lavoie, "if it's not fun, it's work; and if it's work, it sucks."

Does Mutual Fun produce results? One of the very first ideas on the board (ticker symbol: VIEW) proposed an application of the company's three-dimensional visualization technology to a program for teaching naval and security-industry personnel to practice decision making in emergency situations. In its first year, the resulting product, called Rite-View, accounted for 30 percent of the company's total sales. "Would this have happened if it were just up to the guys at the top?" asks Marino. "Absolutely not. But we could not ignore the fact that so many people were rallying around the idea. This system removes the terrible burden of us always having to be right."

To date, Mutual Fun has generated more than 50 innovative product and process ideas. Fifteen have been launched and currently account for 20 percent of Rite-Solutions's total revenue. Interestingly, Mutual Fun itself has turned into one of the company's biggest revenue producers: By building in appropriate variations, Rite-Solutions has turned its in-house game into a cloud-based application for such customers as major universities, defense-industry clients, and large corporations. In its first year on the market, 2006, Mutual Fun accounted for 50 percent of the company's new-business growth, and it has since certified Rite-Solutions as a pioneer in the growing trend toward *gamification*—the incorporation of competition, reward, and other game mechanics and techniques into business applications.

## Case Questions

1. Obviously, Jim Lavoie and Joe Marino have little confidence in the *chain of command* principle as a means of fostering success in today's business world. Explain why, referring to shortcomings in the concepts of *unity of command* and the *scalar principle*. How would Lavoie and Marino respond to the criticism that, under their system, "the buck doesn't stop anywhere in particular"?

2. Says Jim Lavoie: "Being acknowledged as part of an organization's future is all it takes for an employee to grow deeper roots in it." First of all, explain what Lavoie means. Then consider the following questions: Do you

basically agree or disagree with Lavoie? Do you think that it's important to "grow roots" in an organization that you work for? What might it take for you to feel that you're "part of an organization's future"—that it's worth it to sink "deeper roots"? What other factors might be important to you in feeling that you're something more than a mere cog in some organizational machine?

3. According to Lavoie, Mutual Fun is Rite-Solutions's "Innovation Engine". Its function, he says, is twofold: (1) It generates the good ideas that "fuel a Web 2.0 environment," and (2) it "engages the Y Generation to strive for the betterment of the organization." What is a *Web 2.0*

*environment?* What is the Y *Generation?* Do you work, or are you likely to be working, in a Web 2.0 environment? What do you think you need to learn in order to succeed in such an environment? Are you a member of the Y Generation? What values do you have that reflect Y Generation values?

4. According to one researcher on the role of *gamification* in business,*

> *the difference between a product created in a factory and one that is crowdsourced is that in the former case, coordination is supplied by managers. In the*

*latter case, it is provided by a structure that emerges spontaneously through the actions of the crowd.*

What about you? Are you more comfortable working *with other people* when the requirements of the work are handed down by someone in "authority" or more comfortable when they "emerge spontaneously" from the interactions of a group? Under which circumstances are you more "creative"? Has your experience with social media influenced your attitude toward game playing as a way of connecting or even collaborating with other people?

*Neil B. Niman, *The Gamification of Higher Education: Developing a Game-Based Business Strategy in a Disrupted Marketplace* (Palgrave Macmillan, 2014), pp. 58–59.

## Case References

Polly LaBarre, "Provoking the Future to Arrive—Constructive Disruption and Collective Genius," *MIX Mashup* (July 18, 2011), www.mixmashup.org, on November 7, 2014; William C. Taylor, "Here's an Idea: Let Everyone Have Ideas," *NYTimes.com* (March 26, 2006), www.nytimes.com, on November 7, 2014; Jim Lavoie, "Nobody's as Smart as Everybody—Unleashing Individual Brilliance and Aligning Collective Genius," *Management Innovation eXchange* (April 8, 2010), www.managementexchange.com, on November 7, 2014; "How to Kickstart Your Company's Idea Market," *Inc.* (September 16, 2014), www.inc.com, on November 10, 2014; Emily Greenhaigh, "No Longer Taboo in the Workplace, Games Tap Creativity," *PBN.com* (February 4, 2013), www.pbn.com, on November 10, 2014; Brandon Butler, "Competition, Games Can Bring About Enterprise App Advances," *Network World* (June 6, 2012), www.networkworld.com, on November 10, 2014.

## YOU MAKE THE CALL   Who's the Boss?

1. Treehouse is closed on Fridays. Employees work four eight-hour days, and "so far it's gone really well for us," says cofounder Alan Johnson. Ryan Carson says that the company is productive on such a schedule because its structure allows people to stay focused on what they're doing. Treehouse, he says, has "a culture of non-interruption." What aspects of a no-manager structure probably contribute to the development of "a culture of non-interruption"? Under a no-manager structure, what daily activities have probably changed so that "a culture of non-interruption" has taken hold?

2. Recalling that Treehouse first experienced "morale problems" back when it had 60 employees and seven managers, Carson projects that if the company grew to 500 employees, "we'd need at least 50 managers. What would that be like?" he shudders. On a more serious note, Johnson reports that "we're really keeping an eye on how things scale for us as we grow. We're not sure what'll happen there, but so far all signs point to [removing managers] as the right decision." What sorts of problems will Treehouse face as it grows? What kinds of steps will Carson and Johnson probably have to take?

3. "A lot of people think they want to work without managers," says Carson, "but actually they like the security of someone telling them what to do every day. This means working at a no-manager company isn't right for everyone." Among other things, he adds, the need to find people for whom a no-manager company is a good fit "cuts down the potential number of people we can hire."

   What about you? Would you be comfortable working in a no-manager company? Or would you prefer a more conventional organizational structure in which you perform assigned tasks? Under which type of system do you think that you would ultimately prosper, both as a member of the workforce and as a human being? If you wanted to try working at Treehouse, how would you present yourself at an interview held today? Why might you be more interested in, say, five years?

4. Treehouse attributes its success to the fact that it "employs a full-time teaching staff made up of experienced professionals who develop high-quality instructional content" for students wanting to learn high-tech skills.

"Students are able to access a variety of compelling educational offerings, including virtual video teaching, coding live in the web browser with Treehouse Code Challenges, and learning by doing with Treehouse Console."

These "experienced professionals" make up Treehouse's "front lines," and products such as Treehouse Code Challenges and Treehouse Console result from the kinds of projects that drive operations at Treehouse. In what ways is Treehouse a logical company in which to experiment with a no-manager, project-based structure? Why, for example, is a high reliance on workplace collaboration appropriate in the development of products for the contemporary education industry?

# Endnotes

1  Mike Rogoway, "Portland Startup Treehouse Eliminates the Boss, Tells Workers to Manage Themselves," *OregonLive* (December 2013), www.oregonlive.com, on November 17, 2014; Ryan Carson, "No Managers: Why We Removed Managers at Treehouse," *The Naive Optimist* (September 17, 2013), http://ryancarson.com, on November 17, 2014; Treehouse Island Inc., "Treehouse Receives $7 Million in Series B Financing Led by Kaplan Ventures" (press release) (April 9, 2013), www.marketwired.com, on November 18, 2014; Adam Bryant, "Ryan Carson of Treehouse, on When Titles Get in the Way," *NYTimes.com* (June 5, 2014), www.nytimes.com, on November 17, 2014; Malia Spencer, "Five Things I Learned from One of Portland's Most Bustling Startups," *Portland* (Oregon) *Business Journal* (October 29, 2014), www.bizjournals.com, on November 17, 2017; Carson, "The Negative Side of #NoManager Companies," *The Naive Optimist* (January17, 2014), http://ryancarson.com, on November 17, 2014.

2  See David Lei and John Slocum, "Organization Designs to Renew Competitive Advantage," *Organizational Dynamics*, 2002, Vol. 31, No. 1, pp. 1–18.

3  For a related discussion, see Kathleen M. Eisenhardt and Shona L. Brown, "Patching—Restitching Business Portfolios in Dynamic Markets," *Harvard Business Review*, May–June 1999, pp. 106–105.

4  David A. Nadler and Michael L. Tushman, *Competing by Design: The Power of Organizational Architecture* (New York: Oxford University Press, 1997).

5  Ricky W. Griffin and Gary McMahan, "Motivation Through Job Design," in Jerald Greenberg (ed.), *Organizational Behavior: The State of the Science* (Hillsdale, NJ: Lawrence Erlbaum Associates, 1994), pp. 23–44. See also Adam M. Grant, Yitzhak Fried, and Tina Juillerat, "Work Matters: Job Design in Classic and Contemporary Perspectives," in Sheldon Zedeck (ed.), *Handbook of Industrial and Organizational Psychology* (Washington, DC: American Psychological Association, 2010), pp. 190–225.

6  Adam Smith, *Wealth of Nations* (New York: Modern Library, 1937; originally published in 1776).

7  Andrea Gabor, *The Capitalist Philosophers* (New York: Times Business, 2000).

8  Ricky W. Griffin, *Task Design* (Glenview, IL: Scott Foresman, 1982).

9  Anne S. Miner, "Idiosyncratic Jobs in Formal Organizations," *Administrative Science Quarterly*, September 1987, pp. 327–351.

10  M. D. Kilbridge, "Reduced Costs Through Job Enlargement: A Case," *Journal of Business*, Vol. 33, 1960, pp. 357–362.

11  *Fortune*, June 12, 2006, p. 150.

12  Griffin and McMahan, "Motivation Through Job Design."

13  "Jacks of All Trades, and Masters of All," *USA Today*, July 6, 2010, p. 1B.

14  Kilbridge, "Reduced Costs Through Job Enlargement: A Case."

15  Frederick Herzberg, *Work and the Nature of Man* (Cleveland: World Press, 1966).

16  Robert Ford, "Job Enrichment Lessons from AT&T," *Harvard Business Review*, January–February 1973, pp. 96–106.

17  "Companies Do More with Fewer Workers," *USA Today*, February 23, 2010, p. 1B.

18  J. Richard Hackman and Greg R. Oldham, *Work Redesign* (Reading, MA: Addison-Wesley, 1980).

19  Jerry Useem, "What's That Spell? Teamwork!" *Fortune*, June 12, 2006, pp. 64–66.

20  For a related discussion, see Etienne C. Wenger and William M. Snyder, "Communities of Practice: The Organizational Frontier," *Harvard Business Review*, January–February 2000, pp. 139–148.

21  George P. Huber, "Organizations: Theory, Design, Future," in Sheldon Zedeck (ed.), *Handbook of Industrial and Organizational Psychology* (Washington, DC: American Psychological Association, 2010), pp. 80–105.

22  A. V. Graicunas, "Relationships in Organizations," *Bulletin of the International Management Institute*, March 7, 1933, pp. 39–42.

23  Ralph C. Davis, *Fundamentals of Top Management* (New York: Harper & Row, 1951); Lyndall F. Urwick, *Scientific Principles and Organization* (New York: American Management Association, 1938), p. 8; Ian Hamilton, *The Soul and Body of an Army* (London: Edward Arnold, 1921), pp. 229–230.

24  David D. Van Fleet and Arthur G. Bedeian, "A History of the Span of Management," *Academy of Management Review*, 1977, pp. 356–372.

25  James C. Worthy, "Factors Influencing Employee Morale," *Harvard Business Review*, January 1950, pp. 61–73.

26  Dan R. Dalton, William D. Todor, Michael J. Spendolini, Gordon J. Fielding, and Lyman W. Porter, "Organization Structure and Performance: A Critical Review," *Academy of Management Review*, January 1980, pp. 49–64.

27  "Allergan Board of Directors Announces Departure of President F. Michael Ball; Chairman of the Board and Chief Executive Officer David E. I. Pyott Resumes Role as President," *CNBC*, March 7, 2010.

28  "Cadbury Gives Its CEO More Control," *Wall Street Journal*, October 15, 2008, p. B2.

29  See Jerry Useem, "Welcome to the New Company Town," *Fortune*, January 10, 2000, pp. 62–70, for a related discussion. See also "Wherever You Go, You're on the Job," *BusinessWeek*, June 20, 2005, pp. 87–90.

30  http://www.forbes.com/sites/joshbersin/2013/09/12/millenials-will-soon-rule-the-world-but-how-will-they-lead/

31  David Van Fleet, "Span of Management Research and Issues," *Academy of Management Journal*, September 1983, pp. 546–552.

32  Philip Siekman, "Where 'Build to Order' Works Best," *Fortune*, April 26, 1999, pp. 160C–160V.

33  Richard L. Daft, *Organization Theory and Design*, 11$^{th}$ed. (Mason, OH: Cengage Learning, 2013).

34  William Kahn and Kathy Kram, "Authority at Work: Internal Models and Their Organizational Consequences," *Academy of Management Review*, 1994, Vol. 19, No. 1, pp. 17–50.

35  Carrie R. Leana, "Predictors and Consequences of Delegation," *Academy of Management Journal*, December 1986, pp. 754–774.

36  Jerry Useem, "In Corporate America It's Cleanup Time," *Fortune*, September 16, 2002, pp. 62–70.

37  "Delegate, Step Back, and Let Go," *livemint.com*, March 8, 2010.

38  "Remote Control," *HR Magazine*, August 1997, pp. 82–90.

39  "Toppling the Pyramids," *Canadian Business*, May 1993, pp. 61–65.

40  "New Shell CEO Begins Shake-Up," *Wall Street Journal*, May 28, 2009, p. B4.

41  "Yahoo CEO to Install Top-Down Management," *Wall Street Journal*, February 23, 2009, p. B1.

42  "Toyota Overhauls Management, Gives More Autonomy to North America," *L.A. Times*, March 6, 2015, p. 1B.

43  *BusinessWeek*, March 23/30, 2009, p. 33.

44 Kevin Crowston, "A Coordination Theory Approach to Organizational Process Design," *Organization Science*, March–April 1997, pp. 157–166.

45 James Thompson, *Organizations in Action* (New York: McGraw-Hill, 1967). For a more recent discussion, see Bart Victor and Richard S. Blackburn, "Interdependence: An Alternative Conceptualization," *Academy of Management Review*, July 1987, pp. 486–498.

46 Jay R. Galbraith, *Designing Complex Organizations* (Reading, MA: Addison-Wesley, 1973) and *Organizational Design* (Reading, MA: Addison-Wesley, 1977).

47 Paul R. Lawrence and Jay W. Lorsch, "Differentiation and Integration in Complex Organizations," *Administrative Science Quarterly*, March 1967, pp. 1–47.

©Markus Pfaff/Shutterstock.com

# 11

# MANAGING ORGANIZATION DESIGN

## Learning Outcomes

**After studying this chapter, you should be able to:**

1. Describe the basic nature of organization design.

2. Identify and explain the two basic universal perspectives on organization design.

3. Identify and explain several situational influences on organization design.

4. Discuss how an organization's strategy and its design are interrelated.

5. Describe the basic forms of organization design.

6. Describe emerging issues in organization design.

## MANAGEMENT IN ACTION   The First Axiom of New Law

### "The model seemed broken to me."

—MARK HARRIS, CEO, AXIOM LAW

When Kraft Foods decided in 2011 to sell its North American grocery chain and rechristen itself Mondelez International, there was a lot of legal work to be done—nearly 40,000 contracts had to be drawn up in order to finalize negotiations with several thousand counterparties. When the monumental task had been completed, the Association of Corporate Counsel (ACC) named Mondelez and its legal firm, Axiom Law, winners of its annual Value Challenge. According to *Bloomberg Law*, the ACC awards this distinction "to in-house legal departments and law firms recognized for implementing client-service models that deliver results while keeping efficiency high and legal costs low."[1]

Pam Woldow of Edge International, a consultant on law firm management, says that the Mondelez-Axiom partnership reflects "a real sea change in the legal profession. … When Kraft retained Axiom to handle such a large amount of its work," says Woldow (who is apparently fond of oceanic metaphors), "it created a legal tsunami." Why such seismic upheaval? "We are not technically a law firm," admits Thomas Finke, general manager of Axiom's Chicago office, which took on the Mondelez workload. Axiom, explains Finke, can't handle litigation or certain other legal specialties, "but we can do commercial contract work, intellectual property, compliance, and mergers and acquisitions"—precisely the sort of legal work that

Mondelez needed done. What's more, says Finke, Axiom can do what it does "on a very cost-effective basis."

So, if it's not a law firm, what *is* Axiom Legal? Axiom is obviously engaged in the business of law, but unlike a *law firm*, it's not a business entity owned by and composed of lawyers who work together under a specific organizational name. Axiom is usually characterized as an *alternative legal service provider*—an innovative legal business model that Eric Chin, an analyst at Beaton Capital, assigns to the category "NewLaw": "These firms," explains Chin,

> are designed around virtual work spaces and rely on the rise of supertemps—lawyers who have been trained by traditional BigLaw firms who are now looking for flexible work arrangements. … Legal service providers are able to provide service at the same or similar levels as BigLaw—but at or below incumbents' break-even points.

Axiom was founded in 2000 by Mark Harris, who'd spent a couple of years in the late 1990s as an associate at a prestigious New York law firm. One day in February 1999, Harris realized that he'd already billed enough hours for the firm to pay his entire annual salary— meaning that every dollar he earned for the rest of the year would be used to pay for overhead or to fill the pockets of the firm's partner/owners. "The model seemed broken to me," says Harris, who'd also learned firsthand that law firm associates were typically overworked and underappreciated. He was also aware that

sergign/Shutterstock.com

Large businesses require an enormous amount of legal work. Some of this work is handled in-house by a corporate legal staff while other work is outsourced to different vendors depending on the nature of the legal services required. Axiom is a major new vendor for outsourced legal services. Axiom is actually a virtual law firm staffed by independent lawyers seeking flexible work arrangements.

firms employed a lot of so-called "contract lawyers"—registered lawyers hired through temp agencies to work on specific assignments for limited periods of time.

Harris started thinking about ways to integrate the resources represented by disillusioned associates and disenfranchised contract layers into a new legal-business model that would address some of the flaws in the traditional model that he himself had decided to abandon. When it first opened for business, Axiom was regarded as a high-end temp service for in-house legal departments. "An obvious mischaracterization," says Harris, who conceived of Axiom not as a refuge for lawyers with miscellaneous skills, but rather as a pool of specialist *teams*. Axiom assembles teams of well-trained lawyers designed to meet each client's particular needs. When an assignment has been completed, the team disbands, although it may re-form, perhaps with other lawyers, to contribute to the range of complementary specialties needed by the next client.

Axiom was soon able to bill clients at about half the $450 hourly rate charged by traditional law firms. The company first turned a profit in 2003, and by 2007, Axiom had experienced a 1,000-plus percent annual growth rate over a period of three years. Between 2002 and 2011, revenue grew at 72 percent annually—compared to 13 percent for the nation's largest law firm, DLA Piper. With revenues growing tenfold through 2013, Axiom is on a theoretical pace to surpass DLA Piper as the largest firm in the U.S. legal industry by 2018.

"We are right in the middle of helping transform the way the legal industry operates," says Harris, who hastens to point out that a new model is "fundamentally transformative" only if it changes "how the work gets done. ... So much of the work that goes to law firms can be done a better way. ... The problem," Harris contends, "is that law firms aren't actually oriented toward managing the *effective delivery* of complex processes."

That's where Axiom's Managed Services unit comes in. Launched in 2010, it's the company's fastest-growing division, propelled by a 300 percent growth spurt in its first fiscal year, and it now accounts for about 25 percent of Axiom's revenue. Harris calls managed services "Phase 2" in the evolution of the company's product line. Axiom's Managed Services package goes beyond the basic *outsourcing* phase, in which Axiom lawyers and managers work offsite from the client's premises to oversee such processes as drawing up contracts and procuring patents. The concept of managed services takes what Harris calls a "multidisciplinary view" of service delivery: Teams include not only lawyers, but project managers, technology specialists, and consultants who provide legal services, technology applications, business analysis, and long-term solutions to management-related problems. As a function of "Phase 2," explains Harris, "we lead the solutions design, working with our clients to apply process innovation and technology to reduce both risk and cost. The intent is for Axiom to assume the burden of creating efficiencies."

It was Phase 2 that Mondelez bought into when it chose Axiom over a traditional law firm, and Gerhard Pleuhs, head of Mondelez's legal department, is pleased not only with the results but with the lessons learned from working with an innovative model:

> Axiom was proactive in learning all about our company upfront, such as our business model and our culture, and they used these insights to train everyone at Axiom involved in the project. [Their] up-front work made it much easier for everyone to work even better together. [We] pulled together a joint team that delivered flawless execution … in 10 months, on time and with a substantial cost savings. … Neither of us could have done this alone—this was continuous cooperation and teamwork.

In addition to the efficiencies made possible by collaboration, Pleuhs is enthusiastic about the long-term benefits derived from the project: "We now have better ways of working and better systems in place," he says. "Beyond completing the project, we created a cost-effective system to separate, organize, and perform due diligence on our contracts on an ongoing basis."

As for Axiom, Tom Finke reports that the success of the Mondelez project has made other potential clients "comfortable with non-traditional approaches to large-scale commercial projects." Axiom's revenues had already ballooned from $80 million in 2010 to $130 million in 2011, before topping $150 million in 2012. "Developing a better understanding of Axiom Law," advises attorney Brian Peterson, "will give law firm managers a new perspective on the current state of the legal-services industry and help them re-evaluate their firm's place in it. I have no doubt that Axiom will accomplish its mission of becoming the largest and most innovative provider of legal services in the world within the next ten years."

One of the major ingredients in managing any business is the creation of an organization design to link the various elements that comprise the organization. There is a wide array of alternatives that managers in any organization might select for its design, including newly emerging virtual designs like Axiom Law, as profiled in our opening case. In Chapter 10, we identified the basic elements that go into creating an organization. In this chapter, we explore how those elements can be combined to create an overall design for the organization. We first discuss the nature of organization design. We then describe early approaches aimed at identifying universal models of organization design. Situational factors, such as technology, environment, size, and life cycle, are then introduced. Next we discuss the relationship between an organization's strategy and its structure. Basic forms of organization design are described next. We conclude by presenting four emerging issues in organization design.

# The Nature of Organization Design

What is organization design? In Chapter 10, we noted that job specialization and span of management are among the common elements of organization structure. We also described how the appropriate degree of specialization can vary, as can the appropriate span of management. Not really addressed, however, were questions of how specialization and span might be related to each other. For example, should a high level of specialization be matched with a certain span? And will different combinations of each work best with different bases of departmentalization? These and related issues are associated with questions of organization design.[2]

Organization design is the overall set of structural elements and the relationships among those elements used to manage the total organization. Thus organization design is a means to implement strategies and plans to achieve organizational goals.[3] As we discuss organization design, keep in mind two important points. First, organizations are not designed and then left intact. Most organizations change almost continuously as a result of factors such as situations and people. (The processes of organization change are discussed in Chapter 12.) Second, organization design for larger organizations is extremely complex, with so many nuances and variations that no description of it can ever be a full and complete explanation.

# Universal Perspectives on Organization Design

In Chapter 2, we made the distinction between *contingency* and *universal* approaches to solving management problems. Recall, for example, that universal perspectives try to identify the "one best way" to manage organizations, whereas contingency perspectives suggest that appropriate managerial behavior in a given situation depends on, or is contingent on, unique elements in that situation. The foundation of contemporary thinking about organization design can be traced back to two early universal perspectives: the bureaucratic model and the behavioral model.

**organization design**
The overall set of structural elements and the relationships among those elements used to manage the total organization

## Bureaucratic Model

We also noted in Chapter 2 that Max Weber, an influential German sociologist, was a pioneer of classical organization theory. At the core of Weber's writings was the bureaucratic model of organizations.[4] The Weberian perspective suggests that a bureaucracy is a model of organization design based on a legitimate and formal system of authority. Many people associate bureaucracy with "red tape," rigidity, and passing the buck. For example, how many times have you heard people refer disparagingly to "the federal bureaucracy"? And many U.S. managers believe that bureaucracy in the Chinese government is a major impediment to U.S. firms' ability to do business there.

Weber viewed the bureaucratic form of organization as logical, rational, and efficient. He offered the model as a framework to which all organizations should aspire—the "one best way" of doing things. According to Weber, the ideal bureaucracy exhibits five basic characteristics:

1.  The organization should adopt a distinct division of labor, and each position should be filled by an expert.
2.  The organization should develop a consistent set of rules to ensure that task performance is uniform.
3.  The organization should establish a hierarchy of positions or offices that creates a chain of command from the top of the organization to the bottom.
4.  Managers should conduct business in an impersonal way and maintain an appropriate social distance between themselves and their subordinates.
5.  Employment and advancement in the organization should be based on technical expertise, and employees should be protected from arbitrary dismissal.

Perhaps the best examples of bureaucracies today are government agencies and universities. Consider, for example, the steps you must go through and the forms you must fill out to apply for admission to college, request housing, register each semester, change majors, submit a degree plan, substitute a course, and file for graduation. Even when paper is replaced with electronic media, the steps are often the same. The reason these procedures are necessary is that universities deal with large numbers of people who must be treated equally and fairly. Hence, rules, regulations, and standard operating procedures are needed. Large labor unions are also usually organized as bureaucracies.[5]

**bureaucracy**
A model of organization design based on a legitimate and formal system of authority

Some bureaucracies, such as the U.S. Postal Service, have been trying to portray themselves as less mechanistic and impersonal. The strategy of the Postal Service is to become more service oriented as a way to fight back against business competitors like FedEx and UPS.

A primary strength of the bureaucratic model is that several of its elements (such as reliance on rules and employment based on expertise) do, in fact, often improve efficiency. Bureaucracies also help prevent favoritism (because everyone must follow the same rules) and make procedures and practices very clear to everyone. Unfortunately, however, this approach also has several disadvantages. One major disadvantage is that the bureaucratic model results in inflexibility and rigidity. Once rules are created and put in place, making exceptions or changing them is often difficult. In addition, the bureaucracy often results in neglect of human and social processes within the organization.

This woman pulls a number while at the Department of Motor Vehicles. She is in line to renew her license. Many drivers often complain about the DMV's bureaucratic and archaic processes.

## Behavioral Model

Another important universal model of organization design was the behavioral model, which paralleled the emergence of the human relations school of management thought. Rensis Likert, a management researcher, studied several large organizations to determine what made some more effective than others.[6] He found that the organizations in his sample that used the bureaucratic model of design tended to be less effective than those that used a more behaviorally oriented model consistent with the emerging human relations movement—in other words, organizations that paid more attention to developing work groups and were more concerned with interpersonal processes.

Likert developed a framework that characterized organizations in terms of eight important processes: leadership, motivation, communication, interactions, decision making, goal setting, control, and performance goals. Likert believed that all organizations could be measured and categorized along a continuum associated with each of these dimensions. He argued that the basic bureaucratic form of organization, which he called a System 1 design, anchored one end of each dimension. The characteristics of the System 1 organization in Likert's framework are summarized in the left column of Table 11.1.

Also summarized in the right column of this table are characteristics of Likert's other extreme form of organization design, called System 4 design, based on the behavioral model. For example, a System 4 organization uses a wide array of motivational processes, and its interaction processes are open and extensive. Other distinctions between System 1 and System 4 organizations are equally obvious. Between the System 1 and System 4 extremes lie the System 2 and System 3 organizations. Likert argued that System 4 should be adopted by all organizations. He suggested that managers should emphasize supportive relationships, establish high performance goals, and practice group decision making to achieve a System 4 organization. Many organizations tried to adopt the System 4 design during its period of peak popularity. General Motors, for instance, once converted a plant in the Atlanta area from a System 2 to a System 4 organization. Over a period of three years, direct and indirect labor efficiency improved, as did tool breakage rates, scrap costs, and quality.[7]

Like the bureaucratic model, the behavioral approach has both strengths and weaknesses. Its major strength is that it emphasizes human behavior by stressing the value of an organization's employees. Likert and his associates thus paved the way for a more humanistic approach to designing organizations. Unfortunately, the behavioral approach also argues that there is one best way to design an organization—as a System 4. As we see, however, evidence is strong that there is no one best approach to organization design.[8] What works for one organization may not work for another, and what works for one organization may change as that organization's situation changes. Hence, universal models like bureaucracy and System 4 have been largely supplanted by newer models that take contingency factors into account. In the next section, we identify a number of factors that help determine the best organization design for a particular situation.

**behavioral model**
A model of organization design consistent with the human relations movement, stressing attention to developing work groups and concern with interpersonal processes

**System 1 design**
Similar to the bureaucratic model

**System 4 design**
Similar to behavioral model

Monkey Business Images/Shutterstock.com

The behavioral model of organization design acknowledges the importance of work groups and interpersonal processes. This workplace is very casual and people can freely interact with each other. The organization itself, therefore, is using an organization design consistent with the behavioral model.

## TABLE 11.1 SYSTEM 1 AND SYSTEM 4 ORGANIZATIONS

The behavioral model identifies two extreme types of organization design called System 1 and System 4. The two designs vary in eight fundamental processes. The System 1 design is considered to be somewhat rigid and inflexible.

| System 1 Organization | System 4 Organization |
|---|---|
| 1. Leadership process includes no perceived confidence and trust. Subordinates do not feel free to discuss job problems with their superiors, who in turn do not solicit their ideas and opinions. | 1. Leadership process includes perceived confidence and trust between superiors and subordinates in all matters. Subordinates feel free to discuss job problems with their superiors, who in turn solicit their ideas and opinions. |
| 2. Motivational process taps only physical, security, and economic motives through the use of fear and sanctions. Unfavorable attitudes toward the organization prevail among employees. | 2. Motivational process taps a full range of motives through participatory methods. Attitudes are favorable toward the organization and its goals. |
| 3. Communication process is such that information flows downward and tends to be distorted, inaccurate, and viewed with suspicion by subordinates. | 3. Communication process is such that information flows freely throughout the organization—upward, downward, and laterally. The information is accurate and undistorted. |
| 4. Interaction process is closed and restricted. Subordinates have little effect on departmental goals, methods, and activities. | 4. Interaction process is open and extensive. Both superiors and subordinates can affect departmental goals, methods, and activities. |
| 5. Decision process occurs only at the top of the organization; it is relatively centralized. | 5. Decision process occurs at all levels through group processes; it is relatively decentralized. |
| 6. Goal-setting process is located at the top of the organization; discourages group participation. | 6. Goal-setting process encourages group participation in setting high, realistic objectives. |
| 7. Control process is centralized and emphasizes fixing of blame for mistakes. | 7. Control process is dispersed throughout the organization and emphasizes self-control and problem solving. |
| 8. Performance goals are low and passively sought by managers who make no commitment to developing the human resources of the organization. | 8. Performance goals are high and actively sought by superiors who recognize the necessity for making a full commitment to developing, through training, the human resources of the organization. |

Source: Adapted from Rensis Likert, *The Human Organization*, 1967. Copyright © 1967 The McGraw-Hill Companies, Inc. Reprinted with permission.

☐ Managers should avoid the mistake of assuming there is one best way to design an organization.

☐ You should not automatically assume an organization that uses the bureaucratic model is ineffective.

**Manager's Checklist**

# Situational Influences on Organization Design

The situational view of organization design is based on the assumption that the optimal design for any given organization depends on a set of relevant situational factors. In other words, situational factors play a role in determining the best organization design for any

**situational view of organization design** Based on the assumption that the optimal design for any given organization depends on a set of relevant situational factors

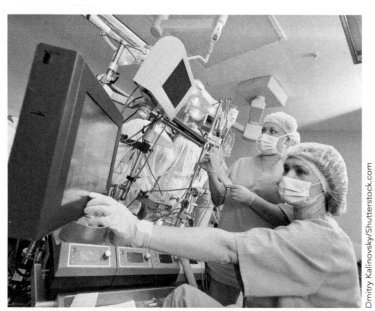

Dmitry Kalinovsky/Shutterstock.com

An organization's core technology can play an important role in organization design. A hospital, for example, uses many different kinds of equipment, and this equipment is often assigned to specific departments.

particular circumstance.[9] Four basic situational factors—technology, environment, size, and organizational life cycle—are discussed here. Another factor, strategy, is described in the next section.

## Core Technology

Technology consists of the conversion processes used to transform inputs (such as materials or information) into outputs (such as products or services). Most organizations use multiple technologies, but an organization's most important one is called its *core technology*. Although most people visualize assembly lines and machinery when they think of technology, the term can also be applied to service organizations. For example, an investment firm like Fidelity uses technology to transform investment dollars into income in much the same way that Union Carbide uses natural resources to manufacture chemical products.

The link between technology and organization design was first recognized by Joan Woodward.[10] Woodward studied 100 manufacturing firms in southern England, collecting information about such aspects as the history of each organization, its manufacturing processes, its forms and procedures, and its financial performance. Woodward expected to find a relationship between the size of an organization and its design, but no such relationship emerged. As a result, she began to seek other explanations for differences. Close scrutiny of the firms in her sample led her to recognize a potential relationship between technology and organization design. This follow-up analysis led Woodward to first classify the organizations according to their technology. Three basic forms of technology were identified by Woodward:

1. *Unit or small-batch technology.* The product is custom-made to customer specifications or produced in small quantities. Organizations using this form of technology include a tailor's shop specializing in custom suits, a print shop that produces business cards and company stationery, and a photography studio.
2. *Large-batch or mass-production technology.* The product is manufactured in assembly-line fashion by combining component parts into another part or finished product. Examples include automobile manufacturers like Subaru, appliance makers like Whirlpool Corporation, and electronics firms like Philips.
3. *Continuous-process technology.* Raw materials are transformed into a finished product by a series of machine or process transformations. The composition of the materials themselves is changed. Examples include petroleum refineries like ExxonMobil and Shell, and chemical refineries like Dow Chemical and Hoechst AG.

These forms of technology are listed in order of their assumed levels of complexity. In other words, unit or small-batch technology is presumed to be the least complex and continuous-process technology the most complex. Woodward found that different configurations of organization design were associated with each technology.

As technology became more complex in Woodward's sample, the number of levels of management increased (that is, the organization became taller). The executive span of management also increased, as did the relative size of its staff component. The supervisory span of management, however, first increased and then decreased as technology became more complex, primarily because much of the work in continuous-process technologies is automated. Fewer workers are needed, but the skills necessary to do the job increase.

**technology**
Conversion processes used to transform inputs into outputs

These findings are consistent with the discussion of the span of management in Chapter 10—the more complex the job, the narrower the span should be.

At a more general level of analysis, Woodward found that the two extremes (unit or small-batch and continuous-process) tended to be very similar to Likert's System 4 organization, whereas the middle-range organizations (large-batch or mass-production) were much more like bureaucracies or System 1. The large-batch and mass-production organizations also had a higher level of specialization.[11] Finally, she found that organizational success was related to the extent to which organizations followed the typical pattern. For example, successful continuous-process organizations tended to be more like System 4 organizations, whereas less successful firms with the same technology were less like System 4 organizations.

Thus technology clearly appears to play an important role in determining organization design. As future technologies become more diverse and complex, managers will have to be even more aware of different technologies' impact on the design of organizations. For example, the increased use of robotics may necessitate alterations in organization design to better accommodate different assembly methods. Likewise, increased usage of new forms of information technology, including social media, will almost certainly cause organizations to redefine the nature of work and the reporting relationships among individuals.[12]

## Environment

In addition to the various relationships described in Chapter 3, environmental elements and organization design are specifically linked in a number of ways.[13] The first widely recognized analysis of environment–organization design linkages was provided by Tom Burns and G. M. Stalker.[14] Like Woodward, Burns and Stalker worked in England. Their first step was identifying two extreme forms of organizational environment: stable (one that remains relatively constant over time) and unstable (subject to uncertainty and rapid change). Next they studied the designs of organizations in each type of environment. Not surprisingly, they found that organizations in stable environments tended to have a different kind of design than did organizations in unstable environments. The two kinds of design that emerged were called mechanistic and organic organizations.

A mechanistic organization, quite similar to the bureaucratic or System 1 model, was most often found in stable environments. Free from uncertainty, organizations structured their activities in rather predictable ways by means of rules, specialized jobs, and centralized authority. Mechanistic organizations are also quite similar to bureaucracies. Although no environment is completely stable, Abercrombie & Fitch and Wendy's use mechanistic designs. Each A&F store, for example, has prescribed methods for store design and merchandise-ordering processes. Little or no deviation is allowed from these methods. An organic organization, on the other hand, was most often found in unstable and unpredictable environments, in which constant change and uncertainty usually dictate a much higher level of fluidity and flexibility. Microsoft (facing rapid technological change) and Apple (facing both technological change and constant change in consumer tastes) both use organic designs. *A World of Difference* explores some of these ideas in more detail.

These ideas were extended in the United States by Paul R. Lawrence and Jay W. Lorsch.[16] They agreed that environmental factors influence organization design but

**mechanistic organization**
Similar to the bureaucratic or System 1 model, most often found in stable environments

**organic organization**
Very flexible and informal model of organization design, most often found in unstable and unpredictable environments

"Networks are becoming the locus for innovation. Firms ... are more porous and decentralized."

—WALTER POWELL, STANFORD PROFESSOR[15]

Abercrombie & Fitch uses a mechanistic form of organization design. The firm uses prescribed methods for store layout and product displays, and individual managers have little discretion over merchandise ordering procedures.

## A WORLD OF DIFFERENCE

# Attitude Adjustments

Today more than ever, an international company operates in an unstable environment—"a turbulent and contradictory world, where there are few certainties and change is constant," as one team of researchers reminds us. Uncertainty, report the authors of *Management across Cultures: Developing Global Competencies*, results primarily from economic forces and technological change that "resist pressures for stability and predictability," but Nardon, Steers, and Sanchez-Runde also argue that a good deal of uncertainty "results from individual and corporate failure to understand the realities on the ground when they pit themselves against local institutions, competitors, and cultures."

Ephraim Okoro, a specialist in intercultural communication and workforce diversity at Howard University, agrees: Among "the major causes of the demise of global business ventures," Okoro cites "managers' lack of intercultural skills, failure to engage in cross-cultural exchange, inability to communicate effectively in the global marketplace, and unacceptable practices in business ethics and etiquette." On the other hand, reports Okoro, global corporations that have "embraced appropriate acculturation strategies, employed effective cultural-awareness models, and avoided ethnocentric management styles … have been successful."

Okoro recommends that expanding multinationals adopt a strategy that encourages managers to develop and apply skills in "cross-cultural management, communication, and negotiation. … Success or failure in managing a diverse or multicultural workforce," says Okoro, "largely depends on the ability of managers at all levels to communicate effectively with people from different backgrounds and nationalities and show respect for cultural differences."

The skills that Okoro describes comprise what many experts call *multicultural competence* (MCC)—the ability to deal with differences in cultural assumptions and expectations, behaviors, and communication styles in ways that are both appropriate

and effective. Nardon, Steers, and Sanchez-Runde observe that "business knowledge is transmitted through interpersonal interactions," and they emphasize that the successful development of multicultural competence among a company's managers involves both organizational and personal commitments.

According to Joseph Santana, who designed a highly successful diversity program for Siemens USA, the development of multicultural competence must begin at the top: "Top leadership behavior," says Santana, "drives what people perceive as the company's 'real values' and the way 'things are done around here.'" How can leaders jumpstart an organization's drive toward multicultural competence? "When an organization's top leadership wants to change its current results relative to diversity by changing how the organization behaves, its leaders need to start with their own personal self-development."

Psychologist Silvia Dutchevici points out that our attitudes toward people who are different from us "run deep into our conscious process and influence the way we view the world." Self-awareness, she suggests, is necessary if one is to change those attitudes and the behaviors that go along with them—and thus to develop the kind of multicultural competence that will improve one's chances of dealing successfully with people in other cultures: "Self-reflection," she says, "plays a big part in identifying biases and changing them. Examining one's own biases and prejudicial attitudes, particularly when one is learning about and working with different identity groups, facilitates the process of change."

*References:* Luciara Nardon, Richard M. Steers, and Carlos J. Sanchez-Runde, "Developing Multicultural Competence," *European Business Review* (May 9, 2013), www.europeanbusinessreview.com, on December 8, 2013; Ephraim Okoro, "International Organizations and Operations: An Analysis of Cross-Cultural Communication Effectiveness and Management Orientation" [abstract], *Journal of Business & Management*, 2013, Vol. 1, No. 1, http://econpapers.repec.org, on December 9, 2014; Robin Maddell, "Developing Multicultural Competence," *The Glass Hammer* (February 21, 2013), www.theglasshammer.com, on December 9, 2014.

believed that this influence varies between different units of the same organization. In fact, they said that each organizational unit has its own unique environment and responds by developing unique attributes. Lawrence and Lorsch suggested that organizations could be characterized along two primary dimensions.

One of these dimensions, differentiation, is the extent to which the organization is broken down into subunits. A firm with many subunits is highly differentiated; one with few subunits has a low level of differentiation. The second dimension, integration, is the degree to which the various subunits must work together in a coordinated fashion. For example, if each unit competes in a different market and has its own production facilities, they may need little integration. Lawrence and Lorsch reasoned that the degree of differentiation and integration needed by an organization depends on the stability of the environments that its subunits face.

## Organizational Size

The size of an organization is yet another factor that affects its design.[17] Although several definitions of size exist, we define organizational size as the total number of full-time or full-time-equivalent employees. A team of researchers at the University of Aston in Birmingham, England, believed that Woodward had failed to find a size–structure relationship (which was her original expectation) because almost all of the organizations she studied were relatively small (three-fourths had fewer than 500 employees).[18] Thus they decided to undertake a study of a wider array of organizations to determine how size and technology both individually and jointly affect an organization's design.

Their primary finding was that technology did in fact influence structural variables in small firms, probably because all of their activities tend to be centered on their core technologies. In large firms, however, the strong technology–design link broke down, most likely because technology is not as central to ongoing activities in large organizations. The Aston studies yielded a number of basic generalizations: When compared to small organizations, large organizations tend to be characterized by higher levels of job specialization, more standard operating procedures, more rules, more regulations, and a greater degree of decentralization. Walmart is a good case in point. The firm expects to continue its dramatic growth for the foreseeable future, adding several thousand new jobs in the next few years. But, as it grows, the firm acknowledges that it will have to become more decentralized for its first-line managers to stay in tune with their customers.[19] Marathon Oil, meanwhile, announced in early 2011 that it would be spinning off its downstream business, creating two independent businesses and significantly reducing the size of its business.[20] Consequently, Marathon is becoming a much smaller organization.

## Organizational Life Cycle

Of course, size is not constant. As we noted in Chapter 9, for example, some small businesses are formed but soon disappear. Others remain as small, independently operated enterprises as long as their owner–manager lives. A few, like Dell Computer, JetBlue, and Starbucks, skyrocket to become organizational giants. And occasionally large organizations reduce their size through layoffs or divestitures. For example, Navistar is today far smaller than was its previous incarnation as International Harvester Company. And as noted above, Marathon Oil is making a strategic decision to reduce its size by splitting itself into two businesses.

Although no clear pattern explains changes in size, many organizations progress through a four-stage organizational life cycle.[22] The first stage is the *birth* of the organization. The second stage, *youth*, is characterized by growth and the expansion of organizational resources. *Midlife* is a period of gradual growth evolving eventually into stability. Finally, *maturity* is a period of stability, perhaps eventually evolving

**differentiation**
Extent to which the organization is broken down into subunits

**integration**
Degree to which the various subunits must work together in a coordinated fashion

**organizational size**
Total number of full-time or full-time-equivalent employees

**organizational life cycle**
Progression through which organizations evolve as they grow and mature

"Managerial problems and practices are rooted in time. They do not last throughout the life of an organization."

—LARRY GREINER, ORGANIZATION DESIGN EXPERT[21]

Organizational life cycle affects organization design. New and modern firms such as this one are often designed in ways that are very different from older, more traditional companies.

into decline. Firms like NetFlix and Starbucks, for instance, are still in their youth stage; Halliburton and Chevron are in midlife, and Ford and Boeing are in maturity. (A key challenge for managers, of course, is to avoid allowing a mature organization to begin to decline. Hence, they must be alert for opportunities to re-energize the organization with new products and new markets.)

Managers must confront a number of organization design issues as the organization progresses through these stages. In general, as an organization passes from one stage to the next, it becomes bigger, more mechanistic, and more decentralized. It also becomes more specialized, devotes more attention to planning, and takes on an increasingly large staff component. Finally, coordination demands increase, formalization increases, organizational units become geographically more dispersed, and control systems become more extensive. Thus an organization's size and design are clearly linked, and this link is dynamic because of the organizational life cycle.[23]

**Manager's Checklist**

☐ Managers need to understand how technology, the environment, organization size, and organizational life cycle all affect organization design.

☐ You should also have a clear understanding of your own organization's technology, environment, size, and life cycle.

## Strategy and Organization Design

Another important determinant of an organization's design is the strategy adopted by its top managers. In general, corporate and business strategies both affect organization design. Basic organizational functions such as finance and marketing can also affect organization design in some cases.[24]

### Corporate-Level Strategy

As we noted in Chapter 7, an organization can adopt a variety of corporate-level strategies. Its choice will partially determine what type of design will be most effective. For example, a firm that pursues a single-product strategy likely relies on functional departmentalization and can use a mechanistic design. If either unrelated or related diversification is used to spur growth, managers need to decide how to arrange the various units within the organizational umbrella. For example, if the firm is using related diversification, there must be a high level of coordination among the various units to capitalize on the presumed synergistic opportunities inherent in this strategy. On the other hand, firms using unrelated diversification more likely rely on a strong hierarchical reporting system, so that corporate managers can better monitor the performance of individual units with the firm.

An organization that adopts the portfolio approach to implement its corporate-level strategies must also ensure that its design fits its strategy. For example, each strategic business unit may remain a relatively autonomous unit within the organization. But managers at the corporate level need to decide how much decision-making latitude to give the head of each unit (a question of decentralization), how many corporate-level executives are needed to oversee the operations of various units (a question of span of management), and what information, if any, is shared among the units (a question of coordination).[25]

### Business-Level Strategy

Business-level strategies affect the design of individual businesses within the organization as well as the organization itself. An organization pursuing a defender strategy, for example, is likely to be somewhat tall and centralized, have narrow spans of management, and perhaps take a functional approach to departmentalization. Thus it may generally follow the bureaucratic approach to organization design.

In contrast, a prospecting type of organization is more likely to be flatter and decentralized. With wider spans of management, it tries to be very flexible and adaptable in its approach to doing business. A business that uses an analyzer strategy is likely to have an organization design somewhere between these two extremes (perhaps being a System 2 or 3 organization). Given that a reactor is essentially a strategic failure, its presumed strategy is probably not logically connected to its design.

Generic competitive strategies can also affect organization design. A firm using a differentiation strategy, for example, may structure departments around whatever it is using as a basis for differentiating its products (such as marketing in the case of image or manufacturing in the case of quality). A cost leadership strategy requires a strong commitment to efficiency and control. Thus such a firm is more centralized as it tries to control costs. And a firm using a focus strategy may design itself around the direction of its focus (location departmentalization if its focus is geographic region, customer departmentalization if its focus is customer groups).

### Organizational Functions

The relationship between an organization's functional strategies and its design is less obvious and may be subsumed under corporate or business-level concerns. If the firm's marketing strategy calls for aggressive marketing and promotion, separate departments may be needed for advertising, direct sales, and promotion. If its financial strategy calls for low debt, it may need only a small finance department. If production strategy calls for manufacturing in diverse locations, organization design arrangements need to account for this geographic dispersion. Human resource strategy may call for greater or lesser degrees of decentralization as a way to develop skills of new managers at lower levels in the organization. And research and development strategy may dictate various designs for managing the R&D function itself. A heavy commitment to R&D, for example, may require a separate unit with a vice president in charge. A lesser commitment to R&D may be achieved with a director and a small staff.[26]

☐ Managers need to know how organization design relates to strategy.

☐ You should be fully aware of your organization's corporate, business, and functional strategies and how they affect the design of your organization.

**Manager's Checklist**

# Basic Forms of Organization Design

Because technology, environment, size, life cycle, and strategy can all influence organization design, it should come as no surprise that organizations adopt many different kinds of designs. Most designs, however, fall into one of four basic categories. Others are hybrids based on two or more of the basic forms.

This employee of the McIlhenny Company, famous makers of TABASCO sauce, is part of the production team. Her company uses the U-form design, where members and units are grouped into functional departments.

OMAR TORRES/AFP/Getty Images

## Functional (U-Form) Design

The functional design is an arrangement based on the functional approach to departmentalization, as detailed in Chapter 10. This design has been termed the *U form* (for unitary) by the noted economist Oliver E. Williamson.[27] Under the U-form arrangement, the members and units in the organization are grouped into functional departments such as marketing and production.

For the organization to operate efficiently in this design, there must be considerable coordination across departments. This integration and coordination are most commonly the responsibility of the CEO and members of senior management. Figure 11.1 shows the U-form design applied to the corporate level of a small manufacturing company. In a U-form organization, none of the functional areas can survive without the others. Marketing, for example, needs products from operations to sell and funds from finance to pay for advertising. The WD-40 Company, which makes a popular lubricating oil, and the McIlhenny Company, which makes TABASCO sauce, are both examples of firms that use the U-form design. Abercrombie & Fitch also uses the U-form design.

In general, this approach shares the basic advantages and disadvantages of functional departmentalization. Thus it allows the organization to staff all important positions with functional experts and facilitates coordination and integration. On the other hand, it also promotes a functional, rather than an organizational, focus and tends to promote centralization. And, as we noted in Chapter 10, functionally based designs are most commonly used in small organizations because

---

## FIGURE 11.1 FUNCTIONAL OR U-FORM DESIGN FOR A SMALL MANUFACTURING COMPANY

The U-form design is based on functional departmentalization. This small manufacturing firm uses managers at the vice presidential level to coordinate activities within each functional area of the organization. Note that each functional area is dependent on the others.

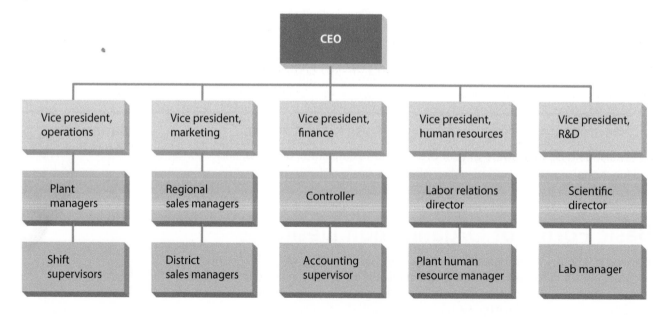

an individual CEO can easily oversee and coordinate the entire organization. As an organization grows, the CEO finds staying on top of all functional areas increasingly difficult.

## Conglomerate (H-Form) Design

Another common form of organization design is the conglomerate, or H-form, approach.[28] The conglomerate design is used by an organization made up of a set of unrelated businesses. Thus the H-form design is essentially a holding company that results from unrelated diversification. (The *H* in this term thus stands for holding.)

This approach is based loosely on the product form of departmentalization (see Chapter 10). Each business or set of businesses is operated by a general manager who is responsible for its profits or losses, and each general manager functions independently of the others. Samsung Electronics Company, a South Korean firm, uses the H-form design. As illustrated in Figure 11.2, Samsung consists of four basic business groups. Other firms that use the H-form design include General Electric (power and water, oil and gas, energy management, aviation, healthcare, transportation, and other unrelated businesses) and Tenneco (pipelines, auto parts, financial services, and other unrelated businesses).

In an H-form organization, a corporate staff usually evaluates the performance of each business, allocates corporate resources across companies, and shapes decisions about buying and selling businesses. The basic shortcoming of the H-form design is the complexity associated with holding diverse and unrelated businesses. Managers usually find comparing and integrating activities across a large number of diverse operations difficult. Research by Michael Porter suggests that many organizations following this approach achieve only average to weak financial performance.[29] Thus, although some U.S. firms are still using the H-form design, many others have abandoned it for other approaches.

## Divisional (M-Form) Design

In the divisional design, which is becoming increasingly popular, a product form of organization is also used; in contrast to the H-form, however, the divisions are related. Thus the divisional design, or M-form (for multidivisional), is based on multiple businesses in related areas operating within a larger organizational framework. This design results from a strategy of related diversification.

**functional (U-form) design**
Based on the functional approach to departmentalization

**conglomerate (H-form) design**
Used by an organization made up of a set of unrelated businesses

**divisional (M-form) design**
Based on multiple businesses in related areas operating within a larger organizational framework

---

### FIGURE 11.2  CONGLOMERATE (H-FORM) DESIGN AT SAMSUNG

Samsung Electronics Company, a South Korean firm, uses the conglomerate form of organization design. This design, which results from a strategy of unrelated diversification, is a complex one to manage. Managers find that comparing and integrating activities among the dissimilar operations are difficult. Companies may abandon this design for another approach, such as the M-form design.

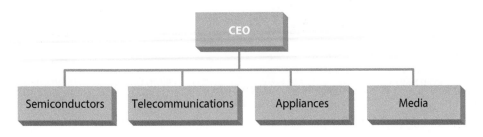

Hilton uses a divisional (M-form) organization design. Each of the hotel's brands, such as Garden Inn, Hampton Inn, Doubletree, and Hilton, are run as separate divisions.

Some activities are extremely decentralized down to the divisional level; others are centralized at the corporate level.[30] For example, as shown in Figure 11.3, Hilton Hotels uses this approach. Each of its divisions is headed by a president or executive vice president and operates with reasonable autonomy, but the divisions also coordinate their activities as appropriate. Other firms that use this approach include the Walt Disney Company (theme parks, movies, and merchandising units, all interrelated) and Hewlett-Packard (computers, printers, scanners, electronic medical equipment, and other electronic instrumentation).

The opportunities for coordination and shared resources represent one of the biggest advantages of the M-form design. Hilton's market research and purchasing departments are centralized. Thus a site selector can visit a city and look for possible locations for different Hilton brands, and a buyer can purchase bed linens for multiple Hilton brands from the same supplier. The M-form design's basic objective is to optimize internal competition and cooperation. Healthy competition for resources among divisions can enhance effectiveness, but cooperation should also be promoted. Research suggests that the M-form organization that can achieve and maintain this balance will outperform large U-form and all H-form organizations.[31]

## Matrix Design

**matrix design**
Based on two overlapping bases of departmentalization

The matrix design, another common approach to organization design, is based on two overlapping bases of departmentalization.[32] The foundation of a matrix is a set of functional departments. A set of product groups, or temporary departments, is then superimposed across the functional departments. Employees in a matrix are simultaneously members of a functional department (such as engineering) and of a project team.

Figure 11.4 shows a basic matrix design. At the top of the organization are functional units headed by vice presidents of engineering, production, finance, and marketing. Each of these managers has several subordinates. Along the side of the organization are a number of positions called *project manager*. Each project manager heads a project group composed

## FIGURE 11.3  MULTIDIVISIONAL (M-FORM) DESIGN AT HILTON HOTELS

Hilton Hotels uses the multidivisional approach to organization design. Although each unit operates with relative autonomy, all units function in the same general market. This design resulted from a strategy of related diversification. Other firms that use M-form designs include PepsiCo and the Walt Disney Company.

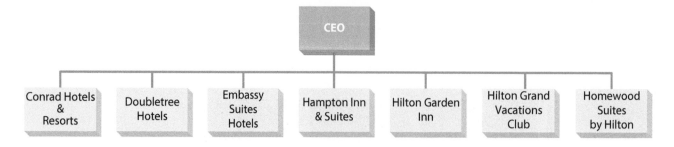

## FIGURE 11.4 A MATRIX ORGANIZATION

A matrix organization design is created by superimposing a product form of departmentalization on an existing functional organization. Project managers coordinate teams of employees drawn from different functional departments. Thus a matrix relies on a multiple-command structure.

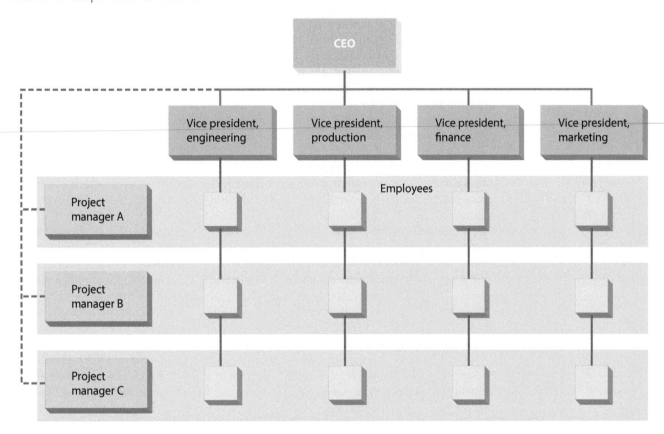

of representatives or workers from the functional departments. Note from the figure that a matrix reflects a *multiple-command structure*—any given person reports to both a functional manager and one or more project managers.

The project groups, or teams, are assigned to designated projects or programs. For example, the company might be developing a new product. Representatives are chosen from each functional area to work as a team on the new product. They also retain membership in the original functional group. At any given time, a person may be a member of several teams as well as a member of a functional group. Ford used this approach in creating its popular Focus automobile. It formed a group called "Team Focus" made up of designers, engineers, production specialists, marketing specialists, and other experts from different areas of the company. This group facilitated getting a very successful product to the market at least a year earlier than would have been possible using Ford's previous approaches.

Martha Stewart also uses a matrix organization for her lifestyle business. The company was first organized broadly into media and merchandising groups, each of which has specific products and product groups. Layered on top of this structure are teams of lifestyle experts organized into groups such as cooking, crafts, weddings, and so forth. Each of these groups is targeted toward specific customer needs, but they work as necessary across all of the product groups. For example, a wedding expert might contribute to an article on wedding planning for a *Martha Stewart Living* magazine, contribute a story idea for a cable television program, and supply content for a Martha Stewart website. This same person might also help select fabrics suitable for wedding gowns for retailing.[33]

Many other organizations have also used the matrix design. Notable among them are American Cyanamid, Monsanto, NCR, Chase Manhattan Bank, Prudential, General Motors, and several state and federal government agencies. Some organizations, however, such as Citibank and the Dutch firm Philips, adopted and then dropped the matrix design. Thus it is important to recognize that a matrix design is not always appropriate.

The matrix form of organization design is most often used in one of three situations.[34] First, a matrix may work when there is strong pressure from the environment. For example, intense external competition may dictate the sort of strong marketing thrust that is best spearheaded by a functional department, but the diversity of a company's products may argue for product departments. Second, a matrix may be appropriate when large amounts of information need to be processed. For example, creating lateral relationships by means of a matrix is one effective way to increase the organization's capacity for processing information. Third, the matrix design may work when there is pressure for shared resources. For example, a company with 10 product departments may have resources for only three marketing specialists. A matrix design would allow all the departments to share the company's scarce marketing resources.

Both advantages and disadvantages are associated with the matrix design. Researchers have observed six primary advantages of matrix designs. First, they enhance flexibility because teams can be created, redefined, and dissolved as needed. Second, because they assume a major role in decision making, team members are likely to be highly motivated and committed to the organization. Third, employees in a matrix organization have considerable opportunity to learn new skills. A fourth advantage of a matrix design is that it provides an efficient way for the organization to take full advantage of its human resources. Fifth, team members retain membership in their functional units so that each person can serve as a bridge between the functional unit and the team, enhancing cooperation. Sixth, the matrix design gives top management a useful vehicle for decentralization. Once the day-to-day operations have been delegated, top management can devote more attention to areas such as long-range planning.

On the other hand, the matrix design also has some major disadvantages. Employees may be uncertain about reporting relationships, especially if they are simultaneously assigned to a functional manager and to several project managers. To complicate matters, some managers see the matrix as a form of anarchy in which they have unlimited freedom. Another set of problems is associated with the dynamics of group behavior. Groups take longer than individuals to make decisions, may be dominated by one individual, and may compromise too much. They may also get bogged down in discussion and not focus on their primary objectives. Finally, in a matrix, more time may be required for coordinating task-related activities.[35]

## Hybrid Designs

Some organizations use a design that represents a hybrid of two or more of the common forms of organization design.[36] For example, an organization may have five related divisions and one unrelated division, making its design a cross between an M form and an H form. Indeed, few companies use a design in its pure form; most firms have one basic organization design as a foundation for managing the business but maintain sufficient flexibility so that temporary or permanent modifications can be made for strategic purposes. Ford, for example, used the matrix approach to design the Focus and the newest Mustang, but the company is basically a U-form organization showing signs of moving to an M-form design. As we noted earlier, any combination of factors may dictate the appropriate form of design for any particular company.

---

**Manager's Checklist**

☐  Managers need to understand the basic forms of organization design.

☐  You should know your organization's corporate, business, and functional strategies and how they relate to the organization's design.

# Emerging Issues in Organization Design

In today's complex and ever-changing environment, it should come as no surprise that managers continue to explore and experiment with new forms of organization design. Many organizations today are creating designs for themselves that maximize their ability to adapt to changing circumstances and to a changing environment. They try to accomplish this by not becoming too compartmentalized or too rigid. As we noted earlier, bureaucratic organizations are hard to change, slow, and inflexible. To avoid these problems, then, organizations can try to be as different from bureaucracies as possible—relatively few rules, general job descriptions, and so forth. This final section highlights some of the more important emerging issues.[37]

> "As we scaled, we noticed that the bureaucracy we were all used to was getting in the way of adaptability."
>
> —JOHN BUNCH, ZAPPOS EXECUTIVE ON TRANSITIONING TO A NEW MANAGEMENT STRUCTURE[38]

## The Team Organization

Some organizations today are using the team organization, an approach to organization design that relies almost exclusively on project-type teams, with little or no underlying functional hierarchy. Within such an organization, people float from project to project as necessitated by their skills and the demands of those projects. At Cypress Semiconductor, founder and CEO T. J. Rodgers refuses to allow the organization to grow so large that it cannot function this way. Whenever a unit or group starts getting too large, he simply splits it into smaller units. Consequently, all units within the organization are small. This allows them to change direction, explore new ideas, and try new methods without dealing with a rigid bureaucratic organizational context. Although few organizations have actually reached this level of adaptability, Apple Computer and Xerox are among those moving toward it.[39]

## The Virtual Organization

Closely related to the team organization is the virtual organization. A virtual organization is one that has little or no formal structure. Such an organization typically has only a handful of permanent employees and a very small staff and administrative headquarters facility. As the needs of the organization change, its managers bring in temporary workers, lease facilities, and outsource basic support services to meet the demands of each unique situation. As the situation changes, the temporary workforce changes in parallel, with some people leaving the organization and others entering. Facilities and the services subcontracted to others change as well. Thus the organization exists only in response to its needs. And, increasingly, virtual organizations are conducting most—if not all—of their businesses online.[40]

For example, TLG Research Inc. was founded as a virtual organization focused on marketing research for automotive, aviation, marine, and industrial markets for original equipment and replacement parts. Currently, the company consists of an in-house project management staff of 10 people and a virtual network of industry professionals. It also has a global business and research sources in Europe, Latin America, and Asia–Pacific to refer to for consulting and research services as needed.

## The Learning Organization

Another recent approach to organization design is the so-called learning organization. Organizations that adopt this approach work to integrate continuous improvement with continuous employee learning and development. Specifically, a learning organization is one that works to facilitate the lifelong learning and personal development of all of its employees

**team organization**
An approach to organization design that relies almost exclusively on project-type teams, with little or no underlying functional hierarchy

**virtual organization**
One that has little or no formal structure

**learning organization**
One that works to facilitate the lifelong learning and personal development of all of its employees while continually transforming itself to respond to changing demands and needs

while continually transforming itself to respond to changing demands and needs.[41] Our *Leading the Way* feature highlights one such organization.

Although managers might approach the concept of a learning organization from a variety of perspectives, improved quality, continuous improvement, and performance measurement are frequent goals. The idea is that the most consistent and logical strategy for achieving continuous improvement is by constantly upgrading employee talent, skill, and knowledge. For example, if each employee in an organization learns one new thing each day and can translate that knowledge into work-related practice, continuous improvement will logically follow. Indeed, organizations that wholeheartedly embrace this approach believe that only through constant learning by employees can continuous improvement really occur.[42]

In recent years, many different organizations have implemented this approach. For example, Royal Dutch Shell owns and operates a conference center in RijsWijk, Norway, which it calls the Learning Centre for Technical Courses. The center boasts state-of-the-art classrooms with instructional technology and drilling simulators, lodging facilities, a restaurant and a sandwich shop, a prayer room, and quiet spaces where people can go to reflect and meditate. The Learning Centre can accommodate 270 students per day and more than 5,000 per year. Line managers at the firm rotate through the Shell Learning Centre and serve as teaching faculty. Such teaching assignments last anywhere from a few days to several months. At the same time, all Shell employees routinely attend training programs, seminars, and related activities, all the while learning the latest information that they need to contribute more effectively to the firm. Recent seminar topics have ranged from time management, to the latest oil drilling techniques, to balancing work and family demands, to international trade theory. The idea is that by continuously immersing people in shared learning experiences the firm will promote an organic design populated by people with common knowledge, goals, and expectations.

## Special Issues in International Organization Design

Another emerging issue in organization design is the trend toward the internationalization of business. As we discussed in Chapter 5, most businesses today interact with suppliers, customers, or competitors (or all three) from other countries. The relevant issue for organization design is how to design the firm to most effectively deal with international forces and compete in global markets. For example, consider a moderate-sized company that has just decided to "go international." Should it set up an international division, retain its current structure and establish an international operating group, or make its international operations an autonomous subunit?[43] Whatever the case, managers need to recognize that when they approach international organization design from a strategic perspective rather than simply allowing it to evolve haphazardly and without forethought, they can reap important advantages, including the development of expatriate managers and enhanced organizational flexibility.[44]

Figure 11.5 illustrates four of the most common approaches to organization design used for international purposes. The design shown in A is the simplest, relying on a separate international division. Levi Strauss & Company uses this approach. The design shown in B, used by Ford Motor Company, is an extension of location departmentalization to international settings. An extension of product departmentalization, with each product manager being responsible for all product-related activities regardless of location, is shown in C. Finally, the design shown in D, most typical of larger multinational corporations, is an extension of the multidivisional structure with branches located in various foreign markets. Nestlé and Unilever use this type of design.

# Feeding the Chicken

Jessica Webb started working at Zaxby's, a Georgia-based franchise chain of fast-casual restaurants, when she was still in high school. "I didn't like cleaning up after people," she admits, and when she was assigned to the kitchen, she found that she didn't like to cook either. "But," she hastens to add, "it was all a part of getting more on-the-job training." Today, she confesses that "nothing can replace the experience I got in the kitchen. … I kept trying to improve myself because I was young, and I needed to learn all I could as fast as I could." Now 25, Webb has been general manager of the outlet for six years. When it comes to training new managers (many of whom are older than she is), "I tell them that it doesn't make any difference how long any of us work, there will still be things to learn."

It's an ideal attitude for getting ahead at Zaxby's, which puts a premium on employee learning and companywide continuous improvement. "We want someone who wants to get better every day," says COO Robert Baxley. "Success is the development of people." Zaxby's share of success—it's grown to 640 outlets in just over two decades—derives in large part from its conviction that employee training reduces turnover, improves standards of performance, and, in the process, helps it meet such business goals as maintaining brand consistency and preserving the company's Southern culture. "Our mission," explains Richard Fletcher, VP of Talent Management, "is to attract and retain a talented workforce and provide them with a supportive learning environment that enhances performance in alignment with the company's vision and values."

Much of Zaxby's learning and training program is designed for franchisees, who own 80 percent of those 640 restaurants. Originally, CEO Zach McLeroy believed that centralized training was essential to maintaining brand consistency, so a franchisee's management candidates traveled to corporate classrooms and certified training restaurants at the franchisee's

expense (an average of $6,000 per student). Unfortunately, trainees were absent from their home restaurants for six weeks. Many quit during training, while others failed to attain certification and others were deemed unsuitable. As a result, certified managers were running only 25 percent of Zaxby's outlets, where turnover was a robust 100 percent.

As a matter of fact, those numbers were about par for the industry, but corporate leadership was unhappy, and so were franchisees, who wanted more control over training. "We had to find a way," recalls Fletcher, "to balance the need for consistent training with franchisee demand for control over training." So in 2012, Zaxby's unveiled its Licensee Managed Training Program. It begins with an online *licensed management system* (*LMS*) that allows trainees to customize their learning plans within a basic modular structure. The company also provides material pegged to such specific managerial roles as "front of the house," "back of the house," "manager," and even "owner." Franchisees are free to alter materials to suit their own needs. Finally, the program tracks progress through both conventional and hands-on tests that allow trainees to demonstrate the skills that they've learned.

A trainee's success is acknowledged by a program called "feeding the chicken." Each individual's learning plan features Zaxby's learning logo—a cartoon chicken sporting a mortarboard—and as he or she meets a customized goal, the chicken turns increasingly gold, culminating in a solid-gold image when training has been completed.

*References:* Dwight Dana, "Worker Sticks with Zaxby's for Nine Years," *SCNow* (January 2, 2013), www.scnow.com, on December 5, 2014; Christine LaFave Grace, "Chasing Improvement, Not Trends," *Technomic* (December 19, 2013), http://blogs.technomic.com, on December 5, 2014; Terry Mayhew, "Zaxby's Appoints a New VP of Talent Management," *QSR* (November 19, 2012), www.qsrmagazine.com, on December 5, 2014; Lisa Goldstein, "Meet Richard Fletcher of Zaxby's Franchising," *L&D Global Events* (December 7, 2012), http://ldglobalevents.com, on December 5, 2014; John Tabellione, "Zaxby's CEO McLeroy Drums Up Decades of Growth," *Savannah CEO* (November 2014), http://savannahceo.com, on December 5, 2014; Paul Harris, "'The Chicken' Rules Zaxby's Learning Roost," *T&D* (October 8, 2013), www.astd.org, on December 5, 2014.

---

## FIGURE 11.5  COMMON ORGANIZATION DESIGNS FOR INTERNATIONAL ORGANIZATIONS

Companies that compete in international markets must create an organization design that fits their own unique circumstances. These four general designs are representative of what many international organizations use. Each is derived from one of the basic forms of organization design.

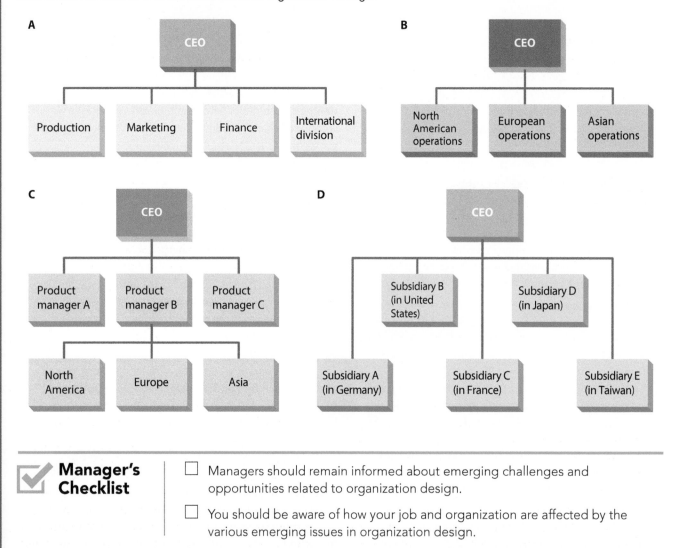

---

**Manager's Checklist**

☐ Managers should remain informed about emerging challenges and opportunities related to organization design.

☐ You should be aware of how your job and organization are affected by the various emerging issues in organization design.

# Summary of Learning Outcomes and Key Points

1. Describe the basic nature of organization design.

   - Organization design is the overall set of structural elements and the relationships among those elements used to manage the total organization.

2. Identify and explain the two basic universal perspectives on organization design.

   - Two early universal models of organization design were the bureaucratic model and the behavioral model.

   - These models tried to prescribe how all organizations should be designed.

3. Identify and explain several situational influences on organization design.

   - The situational view of organization design is based on the assumption that the optimal organization design is a function of situational factors.

   - Four important situational factors are:
     o technology
     o environment

o size
o organizational life cycle

4. Discuss how an organization's strategy and its design are interrelated.

- An organization's strategy also helps shape its design.
- In various ways, corporate- and business-level strategies both affect organization design.
- Basic organizational functions like marketing and finance also play a role in shaping design.

5. Describe the basic forms of organization design.

- Many organizations today adopt one of four basic organization designs:

o functional (U form)
o conglomerate (H form)
o divisional (M form)
o matrix

- Other organizations use a hybrid design derived from two or more of these basic designs.

6. Describe emerging issues in organization design.

- Four emerging issues in organization design are:
o team organization
o virtual organization
o learning organization
o international business organization

# Discussion Questions

### Questions for Review

1. Describe the three forms of core technology. Tell about the differences in organizational structure that occur in firms with each of the three types.

2. List the changes that occur as an organization grows in size. List the changes that occur as an organization ages over time. Are the two lists the same? Explain any differences you find.

3. Describe the basic forms of organization design. What are the advantages and disadvantages of each?

4. Compare and contrast the matrix organization and the team organization, describing any similarities and differences.

### Questions for Analysis

5. The business world today is increasingly complex and variable, in virtually every country and industry. Thus organizations must become more organic. What are some of the outcomes that companies will experience as they become more organic and less mechanistic? Be sure to include both positive and negative outcomes.

6. Each of the organization designs is appropriate for some firms but not for others. Describe the characteristics that a firm using the U form should have. Then do the same for the H form, the M form, and the matrix designs. For

each item, explain the relationship between that set of characteristics and the choice of organization design.

7. What are the benefits of using the learning organization approach to design? Now consider that, in order to learn, organizations must be willing to tolerate many mistakes because it is only through the effort of understanding mistakes that learning can occur. With this statement in mind, what are some of the potential problems with the use of the learning organization approach?

### Questions for Application

8. Consider an organization (such as your workplace, a club or society, a sorority or fraternity, a church, and so on) of which you are a member. Describe some structural elements of that organization that reflect the bureaucratic model. Describe some elements that reflect the behavioral model. In your opinion, is that organization more bureaucratic or more behavioral in its structure? Why?

9. Use the Internet or library to investigate a corporation's strategy. Then use the Internet or library to obtain a

description of the firm's organization design. Can you identify any links between the company's strategy and structure? Share your findings with the class.

10. What form of organization does your university or college use? What form does your city or town government use? What form do other organizations with which you are familiar use? What similarities and differences do you see? Explain your answers.

# Building Effective Conceptual Skills

## Exercise Overview

Conceptual skills require you to think in the abstract. In this exercise, you'll use your conceptual skills in analyzing organizational structure.

## Exercise Background

Looking at its organization chart allows you to understand a company's structure, including its distribution of authority, its divisional breakdown, its levels of hierarchy, and its reporting relationships. The reverse is also true: When you understand the elements of a company's structure, you can draw up an organization chart to reflect it. In this exercise, that's just what you'll do: You'll use the Internet to research a firm's structure and then draw an appropriate organization chart.

## Exercise Task

1. Alone or with a partner, go online to research a publicly traded U.S. firm in which you're interested. Focus on information that will help you understand the company's structure. If you research Ford Motor Company, for example, you should look for information about different types of vehicles, different regions in which Ford products are sold, and different functions that the company performs. (*Hint:* The firm's annual report is usually available online and typically contains a great deal of helpful information. In particular, take a look at the section containing an editorial message from the chairman or CEO and the section summarizing financial information. *Note:* In many cases, "segment" data reveal a lot about divisional structure.)

2. Draw an organization chart based on your research.

3. Share your results with another group or with the class as a whole. Be prepared to explain and justify the decisions that you made in determining the firm's structure.

# Building Effective Technical Skills

## Exercise Overview

Technical skills are necessary to understand or perform the specific kind of work that an organization does. This exercise asks you to use your technical skills to understand the impact of an organization's strategy on its structure.

## Exercise Background

You're a manager in a firm that's developed an innovative new system of personal transportation, much like the Segway HT but different enough to get you a patent. (If you're not familiar with Segway products, go to the website at www.segway.com.)

## Exercise Task

Each of the following items provides you with a hypothetical direction for your firm's corporate-level strategy. Combining this information about your strategy with your knowledge of your Segway-like product, choose an appropriate form of organization structure for your company.

1. Your corporate-level strategy calls for continued production of a limited line of similar products for sale in the United States. What would be the most appropriate organization structure for your firm?

2. Your corporate-level strategy calls for continued production of your core product only, but you intend to sell it in Asia and Europe as well as North America. What would be the most appropriate organization structure for your firm?

3. Your corporate-level strategy calls for you to move into areas related to your core product, integrating the design innovations that you developed for that product into several other products. What would be the most appropriate organization structure for your firm?

4. Your corporate-level strategy calls for you to exploit your expertise in personal ground transportation in order to move into other areas, such as personal air or personal

water transport. What would be the most appropriate organization structure for your firm?

5. Your corporate-level strategy calls for you to invest the revenue generated by core-product sales in industries unrelated to that product. What would be the most appropriate organization structure for your firm?

6. Review your responses to each of the five preceding strategies. Explain precisely how a given strategy influenced your choice of a given organizational design.

# Skill-Building Personal Assessment

### Finding Your Comfort Level

This exercise is designed to help you determine whether you are more comfortable working in an organization with a mechanistic structure or one with an organic structure. The 15 statements below reflect preferences that people can have in workplace structure and environment. Using the following scale, indicate the extent to which each statement accurately describes your preference:

5 Strongly agree
4 Agree somewhat
3 Undecided
2 Disagree somewhat
1 Strongly disagree

I prefer to work in an organization in which:

1. _____ Goals are defined by those at higher levels.

2. _____ Work methods and procedures are specified.

3. _____ Top management makes important decisions.

4. _____ My loyalty counts as much as my ability to do the job.

5. _____ Clear lines of authority and responsibility are established.

6. _____ Top management is decisive and firm.

7. _____ My career is pretty well planned out for me.

8. _____ I can specialize.

9. _____ My length of service is almost as important as my level of performance.

10. _____ Management is able to provide the information I need to do my job well.

11. _____ The chain of command is well established.

12. _____ Rules and procedures are adhered to equally by everyone.

13. _____ People accept the authority of a leader's position.

14. _____ People do as they've been instructed.

15. _____ People clear things with their bosses before going over their heads.

How to score: Find your score by adding the numbers that you assigned to the 15 statements. Interpret your score as follows:

- The higher your score above 64, the more comfortable you are with a mechanistic structure.
- The lower your score *below* 48, the more comfortable you are with an organic structure.
- Scores between 48 and 64 can go either way.

*Reference*: John F. Veiga and John N. Yanousa, *The Dynamics of Organization Theory: Gaining a Macro Perspective* (St. Paul, MN: West, 1979).

# Management at Work

### Dealing a Rigged Game

## "Anything mechanical wears out. So it wasn't exactly rocket science."

—PETE MILLER, FORMER CEO OF NATIONAL OILWELL VARCO

In June 2014, Houston-based National Oilwell Varco (NOV), a manufacturer of equipment and components for oil and gas drilling operations, completed the spinoff of one of its three main divisions—its distribution business.

The new company, called DistributionNOW (or NOW), is separately traded and operates out of 415 locations in 26 countries. It's a big company but "something you could very easily break off from what we had," according to Pete Miller, the longtime CEO of NOV who now serves as executive chairman of NOW. The spinoff was both feasible and advantageous, says Miller, because NOV's distribution arm had attained "the market size and scale to operate as a stand-alone, world-class distribution company."

How had it gotten so big? Acquisitions. According to Barron's, Miller, who became CEO of National Oilwell in 2001, always had "a penchant for deals." In May 2012, for example, Miller had paid $233 million for C.E. Franklin, a Canadian energy services provider and products distributor. Less than two weeks later, he spent $800 million for Wilson International, a distributor of pipes, valves, fittings, and other products to the international energy industry and other industrial customers. Both acquisitions were folded into NOV's Distribution and Transmission Division, which, as we've seen, was ready for a spinoff two years later.

The financial services firm Edward T. Jones figures that Miller made about 200 acquisitions in the decade between 2004 and 2014. Miller himself puts the number at closer to 300, "but every one," he hastens to add, "had a specific purpose, and every one was part of a strategy to become *the* manufacturer for the oilfield." Miller's most important deal—"the game changer"—came in 2005, when he engineered the merger of National Oilwell with Varco International. Varco, which was also based in Houston, did pretty much the same thing as National Oilwell—providing drilling and well-servicing equipment and other products and services to the oil and gas industry. Strategically, then, the merger was a matter of scale: With an augmented workforce of 25,000, the new company was soon making more than half of the world's new drilling rigs, not to mention a significant share of such auxiliary equipment as cranes, mud pumps, and blowout preventers.

Within two years of the merger, Miller had acquired 20 smaller companies for a total of $800 million, as he continued to plow profits into acquisitions. "We had a vision," he explains, "and that vision goes back to 1996. … We could see what was going to happen in the future." From the early 1980s to the mid-1990s, the oil and gas industry was in a recession, and many companies in National Oilwell's end of the business—equipment making—were in straitened circumstances. "We started buying distressed companies," says Miller, as a means of acquiring the increased production capacity that would eventually strengthen the company's position as a supplier of both new and replacement equipment. And Miller was confident that demand for equipment would increase sooner rather than later: "Anything mechanical," he explains, "wears out. So it wasn't exactly rocket science."

Since 2005, NOV's net income has grown from $287 million to $2.3 billion. Over the same 10-year timeframe, its stock has increased by 500 percent, compared to a "mere" 350 percent for its most successful rival, Halliburton. NOV now employs 64,000 people at 1,200 locations in 63 countries, and while Halliburton boasts 100,000 employees in more than 80 countries, NOV enjoys a 60 percent share of the key market for offshore-drilling gear. Its inventory consists of more than 11 million stock-keeping units, and as a result of Miller's confidence in the growth of the market for repair parts, NOV is better positioned to profit from the demand for

replacement parts for aging drill fleets. "If you buy a rig for 30 years," promises Miller, "I can deliver it on time, and I'll have parts in inventory. And down the road, if you want to move it to Brazil or West Africa or India, we'll be there."

Although scale is crucial to NOV's strategy, Miller stresses that "the biggest issue is, does it fit strategically? Do we need the product? Does it give us something that we don't currently have? If it does, good. Let's go get it." In 2007, for instance, when NOV bought drilling-products maker Grant Prideco for $7.37 billion, it consolidated its position in the drilling sector by acquiring a maker of drill bits and pipe. With Robbins & Myers, for which NOV paid $2.5 billion in 2012, it landed a producer of valve controls and energy systems for both industrial and chemical markets.

How does NOV manage all of its new businesses? Miller admits that acquisitions weren't always placed where they belonged on the organization chart. Constantly altering the contours of internal divisions tended to push them further out of alignment, and customers sometimes found that they had to navigate multiple channels to get parts for the same project. The spinoff of NOW, however, has facilitated a reorganization of NOV's core units, and it's now divided into three segments:

- *Rig Systems*, which provides capital equipment for drilling gas and oil wells (e.g., land and offshore rigs)
- *Wellbore Technologies*, which supplies products and services to improve drilling performance (e.g., drilling fluid, drill pipes)
- *Completion & Production Solutions*, which provides equipment to complete wells (e.g., pumping equipment, piping, tubing)

Analysts at Motley Fool (who admit that NOV is "a fan favorite" at the investment-services company) maintain that NOV "is poised to profit in a big way." Why? Primarily because of its dominant share of the market for offshore drilling equipment—a segment of the industry that reported the most orders ever in 2013. Again, Miller's forecasts of future demand in the oil and gas industry have proved prescient: More than half of the world's fleet of jack-up rigs—mobile platforms that extend to the seabed in shallow waters—are nearly 30 years old and will soon be retired. In addition, older rigs are increasingly noncompliant with newer technology requirements aimed at improving safety.

Today, with most of the world's onshore oil having been exploited, offshore drilling is the next big frontier in oil and gas production. Offshore, says Miller, energy companies are "looking for the Big Kahuna, that big oil field," and are prepared to spend big money on the equipment needed to find it. NOV, he says, is poised to capitalize on the segment of its business that "our investors [already] know best—the actual building of the drilling rigs, jack-ups, and ships that have to go offshore and do the drilling."

## Case Questions

1. Recall our definition of *strategy* in Chapter 7 as "a comprehensive plan for accomplishing an organization's goals." Explain why NOV's approach to acquisitions qualifies as *corporate-level strategy*. Be specific by discussing the company's moves, the nature and state of the industry that it's in (drilling equipment and services), the nature and state of the industry to which it's closely related (oil and gas drilling), and, most importantly, its *goals*. What *are* NOV's goals?

2. How does each of the following *situational influences on organizational design* affect organizational design (and strategy) at NOV—*core technology*, *environment*, and *organizational size*? How about *organizational life cycle*? At what stage in that cycle would you put NOV? Which of NOV's actions give an indication of the company's life-cycle stage as management sees it? (*Note:* NOV intends to spend $100 billion in the next 10 years.)

3. Wall Street has a surprisingly uneasy relationship with NOV. Stock price, for example, hasn't nearly kept pace with increase in earnings over the past decade. For one thing, some sectors of the company's business make its overall performance somewhat volatile, and analysts at Motley Fool observe that "NOV's volatility isn't its best feature." Asked about the spinoff of DistributionNOW and the subsequent reorganization, Pete Miller replied: "We think it's going to give the analysts a better opportunity to be able to look at the company and say, 'OK,

I understand this part of it, and I understand this part of it,' and probably get a better valuation."

Strategically speaking, how would you characterize the message that the combination spinoff and organizational redesign are supposed to send to investors and analysts? Why do you suppose NOV management felt the need to send it? Why do you suppose it was sent when it was sent?

4. An investment analyst asked Pete Miller how his acquisitions strategy affects the company "from the top down in your company culture." How does the company culture "allow your employees to buy into these new companies coming into the fold?" Miller replied, "I don't think a company like ours can have a culture. We're too spread out. In 63 countries, you've got all different cultures." But he also added that employees understand how a strategy of acquisition provides opportunity. "I tell everybody in this company, I'm not sure what a CEO is supposed to do, but one of the things that I do try to do is provide opportunity to our employees. You provide that opportunity by growing. As you continue to grow and people actually see the opportunity, then they see what it affords to employees as well as customers."

What about you? Would this theory of company culture, along with its theory about employee appreciation of opportunity, appeal to you? Would it be relevant to you in deciding whether to take a job at NOV? Would you want to work for a company with 64,000 employees in 63 countries?

## Case References

Jack Hough, "Drilling for Value at National Oilwell Varco," *Barron's* (January 4, 2014), http://online.barrons.com, on December 14, 2014; Deon Daugherty, "National Oilwell Varco's Recent Acquisitions Set the Stage for Spinoff," *Houston Business Journal* (September 24, 2013), www.bizjournals. com, on December 15, 2014; Taylor Muckerman, "An Interview with Pete Miller, CEO of National Oilwell Varco," *The Motley Fool* (December 13, 2013), www.fool.com, on December 15, 2014; Christopher Helman, "National Oilwell Varco: The Rig Game," *Forbes* (December 20, 2007),

www.forbes.com, on December 16, 2014; Ryan Holeywell, "Changes in Leadership, Structure Herald New Day at NOV," *Houston Chronicle* (September 19, 2014), www.houstonchronicle.com, on December 14, 2014; Magnus Tchekhov, "Introducing National Oilwell Varco, a 'Warren Buffett Stock,'" *Market Realist* (October 21, 2014), http://marketrealist. com, on December 14, 2014; Alex Planes, "Is National Oilwell Varco Destined for Greatness?" *The Motley Fool* (January 12, 2013), www.fool.com, on December 14, 2014.

---

**YOU MAKE THE CALL** ## The First Axiom of New Law

1. In what sense is Axiom a *team organization*? A *virtual organization*? Judging from the case, explain why it makes sense for Axiom to develop along both lines at the same time.

2. In considering the *environment* as a *situational factor* in Axiom's organizational design, what type of organization

is Axiom? Why? When it comes to *business-level strategy*, what type of firm is Axiom? Why?

3. Axiom has 13 offices in eight foreign countries, ranging from the United Kingdom and Poland to Singapore and Hong Kong. What, if any, kinds of strategic decisions about organizational design is the company likely to

*(Continued)*

face when it comes to competing in global legal markets?

4. Bill Henderson, professor of law at Indiana University, says that "part of Axiom's Managed Services practice is analyzing and redesigning workflows"—that is, *the series of activities that are necessary to complete a task.*\* As a result,

> *in-house lawyers have the cost and quality information needed to make better sourcing decisions. Because Axiom is helping to redesign the workflows, including the specifications for sourcing decisions, it is well positioned to do much of the resulting work. ... What is the goal of the workflow redesigns? To reduce legal risk and legal cost at the same time, primarily through process, measurement, and feedback loops.*

Henderson adds that a Managed Services team may include "systems engineers, information technologists, and project managers" and observes that "much of the key design and execution work ... is done by nonlawyers who formerly worked for global consulting businesses."

Judging from the case, explain some of the ways that an Axiom Managed Services team can contribute to the analysis and design of workflows in an in-house legal department, where the tasks generally involve work on taxes, mergers and acquisitions, labor law, and intellectual property? How can an Axiom Managed Services team make the performance of such tasks "better, faster, cheaper," as Henderson contends they can?

\*"Is Axiom the Bellweather for Disruption in the Legal Industry?" *The Legal Whiteboard* (November 10, 2013), http://lawprofessors.typepad.com, on November 25, 2014.

# Endnotes

1  "Q&A with ACC Value Champions 2013: Axiom Law and Mondelez International," *Bloomberg Law* (August 22, 2013), www.bna.com, on November 28, 2014; Sherry Karabin, "A New Way of Doing Business," *Chicago Lawyer* (April 2013), http://chicagolawyermagazine.com, on November 28, 2014; Eric Chin, "2018: The Year Axiom Becomes the World's Largest Legal Services Firm," *Beaton Capital* (September 13, 2013), www.beatoncapital.com, on November 28, 2014; Dan Slater, "'The Model Seemed Broken to Me'—Looking at a Law Firm Alternative," *Wall Street Journal* (July 3, 2008), http://blogs.wsj.com, on December 2, 2014; Bruce MacEwan, "A Conversation with Mark Harris of Axiom," *Adam Smith, Esq.* (August 6, 2012), www.adamsmithesq.com, on November 25, 2014; Bill Henderson, "Is Axiom the Bellwether for Disruption in the Legal Industry?" *The Legal Whiteboard* (November 10, 2013), http://lawprofessors.typepad.com, on November 25, 2014; Brian Peterson, "Axiom Law Uses Ethics to Innovate," *Disruptive Legal Innovations* (December 4, 2013), http://disruptivelegal.wordpress.com, on November 25, 2014; Peterson, "Axiom Law Is Not an LPO. But It Is One of the Most Important Companies in the Legal Services Industry," *Disruptive Legal Innovations* (July 19, 2013), http://disruptivelegal.wordpress.com, on May 20, 2015.

2  See George P. Huber, "Organizations: Theory, Design, Future," in Sheldon Zedeck (ed.), *Handbook of Industrial and Organizational Psychology*, Vol. 1: *Building and Developing the Organization* (Washington, DC: American Psychological Association, 2010), pp. 117–160.

3  See Royston Greenwood and Danny Miller, "Tackling Design Anew: Getting Back to the Heart of Organizational theory," *Academy of Management Perspectives*, November 2010, pp. 78–88.

4  Max Weber, *Theory of Social and Economic Organizations*, trans. T. Parsons (New York: Free Press, 1947).

5  Paul Jarley, Jack Fiorito, and John Thomas Delany, "A Structural Contingency Approach to Bureaucracy and Democracy in U.S. National Unions," *Academy of Management Journal*, 1997, Vol. 40, No. 4, pp. 831–861.

6  Rensis Likert, *New Patterns in Management* (New York: McGraw-Hill, 1961), and *The Human Organization* (New York: McGraw-Hill, 1967).

7  William F. Dowling, "At General Motors: System 4 Builds Performance and Profits," *Organizational Dynamics*, Winter 1975, pp. 23–28.

8  Gareth Jones, *Organizational Theory, Design, and Change*, 7th ed. (Upper Saddle River, NJ: Prentice Hall, 2014). See also "The Great Transformation," *BusinessWeek*, August 28, 2000, pp. 84–99.

9  See N. Anand and Richard L. Daft, "What Is the Right Organization Design?" *Organizational Dynamics*, 2007, Vol. 36, No. 4, pp. 329–344 for a recent review.

10  Joan Woodward, *Industrial Organization: Theory and Practice* (London: Oxford University Press, 1965).

11  Joan Woodward, *Management and Technology, Problems of Progress Industry*, No. 3 (London: Her Majesty's Stationery Office, 1958).

12  William Bridges, "The End of the Job," *Fortune*, September 19, 1994, pp. 62–74.

13  For example, see Michael Russo and Niran Harrison, "Organizational Design and Environmental Performance: Clues from the Electronics Industry," *Academy of Management Journal*, 2005, Vol. 48, No. 4, pp. 582–593; see also Sebastian Raisch and Julian Birkinshaw, "Organizational Ambidexterity: Antecedents, Outcomes, and Moderators," *Journal of Management*, 2008, Vol. 34, No. 3, pp. 375–409.

14  Tom Burns and G. M. Stalker, *The Management of Innovation* (London: Tavistock, 1961).

15  *BusinessWeek*, June 20, 2005, p. 81.

16  Paul R. Lawrence and Jay W. Lorsch, *Organization and Environment* (Homewood, IL: Irwin, 1967).

17  Edward E. Lawler III, "Rethinking Organization Size," *Organizational Dynamics*, Autumn 1997, pp. 24–33. See also Henrich R. Greve, "A Behavioral Theory of Firm Growth: Sequential Attention to Size and Performance Goals," *Academy of Management Journal*, 2008, Vol. 51, No. 3, pp. 476–494.

18  Derek S. Pugh and David J. Hickson, *Organization Structure in Its Context: The Aston Program* I (Lexington, MA: D. C. Heath, 1976).

19  "Can Wal-Mart Get Any Bigger?" *Time*, January 13, 2003, pp. 38–43.

20  "Marathon Oil to Split in Two," *New York Times*, January 13, 2011.

21  https://hbr.org/search?term=larry+e.+greiner

22  Robert H. Miles and Associates, *The Organizational Life Cycle* (San Francisco: Jossey-Bass, 1980). See also "Is Your Company Too Big?" *BusinessWeek*, March 27, 1989, pp. 84–94.

23  Douglas Baker and John Cullen, "Administrative Reorganization and Configurational Context: The Contingent Effects of Age, Size, and Change in Size," *Academy of Management Journal*, 1993, Vol. 36, No. 6, pp. 1151–1177. See also Kevin Crowston, "A Coordination Theory Approach to Organizational Process Design," *Organization Science*, March–April 1997, pp. 157–168.

24 See "The Corporate Ecosystem," *BusinessWeek*, August 28, 2000, pp. 166–197.

25 Richard D'Aveni and David Ravenscraft, "Economies of Integration Versus Bureaucratic Costs: Does Vertical Integration Improve Performance?" *Academy of Management Journal*, 1994, Vol. 37, No. 5, pp. 1167–1106.

26 Gerardine DeSanctis, Jeffrey Glass, and Ingrid Morris Ensing, "Organizational Designs for R&D," *Academy of Management Executive*, 2002, Vol. 16, No. 2, pp. 55–64.

27 Oliver E. Williamson, *Markets and Hierarchies* (New York: Free Press, 1975).

28 Ibid.

29 Michael E. Porter, "From Competitive Advantage to Corporate Strategy," *Harvard Business Review*, May–June 1987, pp. 43–59.

30 Williamson, *Markets and Hierarchies*.

31 Jay B. Barney and William G. Ouchi (eds.), *Organizational Economics* (San Francisco: Jossey-Bass, 1986); Robert E. Hoskisson, "Multidivisional Structure and Performance: The Contingency of Diversification Strategy," *Academy of Management Journal*, December 1987, pp. 625–644. See also Bruce Lamont, Robert Williams, and James Hoffman, "Performance During 'M-Form' Reorganization and Recovery Time: The Effects of Prior Strategy and Implementation Speed," *Academy of Management Journal*, 1994, Vol. 37, No. 1, pp. 153–166.

32 Stanley M. Davis and Paul R. Lawrence, *Matrix* (Reading, MA: Addison-Wesley, 1977).

33 "Martha, Inc.," *BusinessWeek*, January 17, 2000, pp. 63–72.

34 Davis and Lawrence, *Matrix*.

35 See Lawton Burns and Douglas Wholey, "Adoption and Abandonment of Matrix Management Programs: Effects of Organizational Characteristics and Interorganizational Networks," *Academy of Management Journal*, 1993, Vol. 36, No. 1, pp. 106–138.

36 See Michael Hammer and Steven Stanton, "How Process Enterprises Really Work," *Harvard Business Review*, November–December 1999, pp. 108–118.

37 Raymond E. Miles, Charles C. Snow, John A. Mathews, Grant Miles, and Henry J. Coleman, Jr., "Organizing in the Knowledge Age: Anticipating the Cellular Form," *Academy of Management Executive*, November 1997, pp. 7–24.

38 http://www.washingtonpost.com/blogs/on-leadership/wp/2014/01/03/zappos-gets-rid-of-all-managers/

39 John Mathieu, M. Travis Maynard, Tammy Rapp, and Lucy Gibson, "Team Effectiveness 1997–2007: A Review of Recent Advancements and a Glimpse into the Future," *Journal of Management*, 2008, Vol. 34, No. 3, pp. 410–476.

40 "Management by Web," *BusinessWeek*, August 28, 2000, pp. 84–96.

41 Peter Senge, *The Fifth Discipline* (New York: Free Press, 1993). See also David Lei, John W. Slocum, and Robert A. Pitts, "Designing Organizations for Competitive Advantage: The Power of Unlearning and Learning," *Organizational Dynamics*, Winter 1999, pp. 24–35.

42 Amy C. Edmondson, "The Competitive Imperative of Learning," *Harvard Business Review*, July–August 2008, pp. 60–70.

43 See William G. Egelhoff, "Strategy and Structure in Multinational Corporations: A Revision of the Stopford and Wells Model," *Strategic Management Journal*, 1988, Vol. 9, pp. 1–14, for a discussion of these issues. See also Ricky W. Griffin and Michael Pustay, *International Business: A Managerial Perspective*, 8th ed. (Upper Saddle River, NJ: Prentice-Hall, 2015).

44 Riki Takeuchi, Jeffrey P. Shay, and Jiatao Li, "When Does Decision Autonomy Increase Expatriate Managers' Adjustment? An Empirical Test," *Academy of Management Journal*, 2008, Vol. 51, No. 1, pp. 45–60.

©Markus Pfaff/Shutterstock.com

# 12

# MANAGING ORGANIZATION CHANGE AND INNOVATION

# MANAGEMENT IN ACTION   Accenturate the Positive

## "Tails sometimes can wag dogs."

—GIB BULLOCH, MANAGING DIRECTOR,
ACCENTURE DEVELOPMENT PARTNERSHIPS

In 1999, Gib Bulloch was, as he himself puts it, living "the gilt-edged lifestyle of business-class flights, expensive hotels, and fancy restaurants." He was, after all, a senior manager at Accenture, the world's largest management-consulting firm, specializing as a strategist in the energy sector. A year later, Bulloch was living in an apartment in the town of Gostivar, in the central European country of Macedonia, which was ravaged by poverty, unemployment, and ethnic conflict. He was helping to teach business skills to the staff of the local support center for small and medium enterprises at a salary reduction of 95 percent.[1]

Why the apparent change in Bulloch's fortunes?

Actually, it was Bulloch's idea: He wanted to do some good while he was in his 30s instead of his 60s. "I was very happy at Accenture," he hastens to point out, "but there was something missing." It was in the late 1990s, and Bulloch found himself in the midst of a "quest to understand the broader role of business in society." As luck would have it, he had an "epiphany" one day in March 1999: He read an article about an international nongovernmental organization (NGO) called Voluntary Service Overseas (VSO), which was trying to recruit volunteers. What caught Bulloch's attention was the organization's request for accountants and business managers rather than monetary donations. "Prior to this," he recalls, "I didn't realize that my business-consulting experience could be applied in the development area."

So Bulloch talked senior Accenture executives into backing a pilot program that allowed him and several other company volunteers to heed the VSO call. "I had never been more motivated in my life," says Bulloch of his one-year assignment. "The business context was radically different. … I questioned my role and the impact I was or wasn't having on issues that were complex and systemic." Before long,

This scene shows the main square in Gostivar, Macedonia. Gib Bulloch, senior manager at Accenture, lived in this central European country, teaching business skills to local managers, in a 'quest to understand the broader role of business in society.' This experience proved to be life-changing for him.

Robert Atanasovski/Getty Images

he reports, he was pondering a more ambitious question:

> How much more could I get done if I had my normal team of consultants working with me? … Surely Accenture could and should … go beyond the industry-default pro bono model which produces piecemeal services and creates good stories in annual reports but doesn't add up to much in terms of scalable impact. Could we create a nonprofit business within a for-profit business?

On a still more practical level, of course, the question came down to: "Would Accenture give up profit in lieu of other tangible business benefits?" Bulloch was convinced that the company would support an intrapreneurial nonprofit venture if he could make a case for compelling "tangible benefits." So he and a group of like-minded colleagues drew up a proposal that focused on the benefit of "retaining and developing top performers." In pitching this intrapreneurial model to Accenture, Bulloch focused on the benefits of "employee engagement, retention, leadership development, and recruitment" to be gained from offering employees the same kind of opportunity that he had crafted for himself with VSO in Macedonia.

Bulloch was well aware, however, that he was proposing "a new hybrid business that would effectively turn the classical management-consultancy model upside down." What he wanted to test was the feasibility of a "tripartite business model": "Accenture provides access to its high performers free of profit and corporate overhead; these employees voluntarily give up a substantial percentage of their salary; and nonprofits cut a check to Accenture for consulting and technology services at significantly reduced rates."

By 2002, Bulloch had convinced upper management at Accenture—tentatively, at any rate—and he quickly found that not only were a lot of employees eager to participate, but they were essentially "the people we wanted to attract, retain, and develop in the business." In short, there were more than enough qualified staff "willing to walk the talk on the salary cut." As for prospective nonprofit clients, reports Bulloch, initial reactions were "mixed." After all, he was challenging "the deeply entrenched view that large businesses give money to charities," not the other way around. Bulloch stressed the fairness and sensibleness of his model of three-way contributions: Accenture, he would tell nonprofit financial officers, "is investing, our employees

are investing, and we expect you to invest, too." Fortunately, a few of them "took a leap of faith."

Since 2003, Accenture Development Partnerships (ADP) has operated as a business unit inside Accenture, with Bulloch as managing director. It identifies itself as a *corporate social enterprise* whose mission is to channel the company's strategic-business, technology, and project-management expertise into the *international development sector*—the area in which both public and private organizations address the problems, such as disease and poverty, that hinder economic growth in developing countries. The ADP model is based on what Bulloch calls *cross-sector convergence*, by which "business, government, and civil society … create markets and innovative solutions that tackle development challenges."

Among ADP's longest and most productive convergence relationships is its collaboration with UNICEF, a United Nations program that provides long-term assistance to children and mothers in developing countries. "We can't tell UNICEF about maternal health," explains Bulloch, "but we can tell UNICEF how supply chain expertise can improve the logistics of delivering medicines and vaccines." ADP can also show UNICEF how to apply new technologies and new models of business thinking to fundamental problems in development—how to train nurses more quickly on an eLearning platform or how to track the spread of diseases by using cellphones.

Today, reports Bulloch, ADP operates according to the "self-sustaining and scalable business model" that he envisioned just over a decade ago. "When something works," he explains, "we scale it," and scalable success now comes not just from long-standing collaborations with nonprofits, but from commercial clients who have called upon Accenture to help them in their own efforts to get involved in development projects. Accenture itself has also experienced measurable success not only in attracting the best talent, but in getting the best out of them once they're on the payroll. This facet of the "not-for-profit" business-within-a-business model should not be underestimated: After 12 years, reports Bulloch, internal surveys "point to a direct correlation between staff who volunteered through ADP and the ability of employees to grow and learn, the likeliness for higher levels of employee engagement, and the ability to take on more responsibility and autonomy. Moreover, some highly recruited job candidates are attracted to Accenture just to take part in ADP."

Finally, Bulloch emphasizes that ADP is not simply a "not-for-profit" enterprise, but a "not-for-loss" proposition as well. Accenture absorbs the overhead for ADP and accepts zero profit margins (as measured by clients' fees), and as long as this "cost-neutral" balance is maintained, ADP is "sustainable from the standpoint of the company." The success of ADP, Bulloch concludes, shows that companies can profit from identifying and nurturing "the latent socially minded innovators or 'intrapreneurs' in their midst. … Tails sometimes can wag dogs."

Managers like Gib Bulloch and his colleagues at Accenture are keenly aware of the changing environment of business and its role in the global society. They also understand when and how to implement change as a vital part of management. This chapter describes how organizations manage change. We first examine the nature of organization change and identify the basic issues of managing change. We then identify and describe major areas of change, including business process change, a major type of change undertaken by many firms recently. We then examine organization development and conclude by discussing organizational innovation as a vital form of change.

# The Nature of Organization Change

Organization change is any substantive modification to some part of the organization.[2] Thus change can involve virtually any aspect of an organization: work schedules, bases for departmentalization, span of management, machinery, organization design, people themselves, and so on. It is important to keep in mind that any change in an organization may have effects extending beyond the actual area where the change is implemented. For example, when Boeing recently installed a new automated production system at one of its plants, employees were trained to operate new equipment, the compensation system was adjusted to reflect new skill levels, the span of management for supervisors was altered, and several related jobs were redesigned. Selection criteria for new employees were also changed, and a new quality-control system was installed.[3] In addition, it is quite common for multiple organization change activities to be going on simultaneously.[4]

**organization change**
Any substantive modification to some part of the organization

## Forces for Change

Why do organizations find change necessary? The basic reason is that something relevant to the organization either has changed or is likely to change in the foreseeable future. The organization therefore may have little choice but to change as well. Indeed, a primary reason for the problems that organizations often face is failure to anticipate or respond properly to changing circumstances. The forces that compel change may be external or internal to the organization.[5]

**External Forces** External forces for change derive from the organization's general and task environments. For example, two energy crises, an aggressive Japanese automobile industry, floating currency exchange rates, and floating international interest rates—all manifestations

Boeing simultaneously underwent many organization change activities when it installed a new automated production system at one of its plants.

The task environment is a force for change in this shopping area. Often when one clothing store advertises a sale, others on the block follow suit.

of the international dimension of the general environment—profoundly changed U.S. automobile companies. New rules of production and competition forced them to dramatically alter the way they do business. In the political arena, new laws, court decisions, and regulations affect organizations. The technological dimension may yield new production techniques that the organization needs to explore. The economic dimension is affected by inflation, the cost of living, and money supplies. The sociocultural dimension, reflecting societal values, determines what kinds of products or services will be accepted in the market.

Because of its proximity to the organization, the task environment is an even more powerful force for change. Competitors influence an organization through their price structures and product lines. When Hewlett-Packard lowers computer prices, Dell may have little choice but to follow suit. Because customers determine what products can be sold at what prices, organizations must be concerned with consumer tastes and preferences. Suppliers affect organizations by raising or lowering prices or changing product lines. Regulators can have dramatic effects on an organization. For example, if OSHA rules that a particular production process is dangerous to workers, it can force a firm to close a plant that uses that process until it meets stricter safety standards. Unions can force change when they have the clout to negotiate for higher wages or if they go on strike.[6]

> "The things that an organization stands for should remain firm and fixed, but how it does things should be adjusted constantly."
>
> —JIM COLLINS, MANAGEMENT CONSULTANT[7]

**Internal Forces** A variety of forces inside the organization may cause change. If top management revises the organization's strategy, organization change is likely to result. A decision by an electronics company to enter the home computer market or a decision to increase a 10-year product sales goal by 3 percent would occasion many organization changes. Other internal forces for change may be reflections of external forces. As sociocultural values shift, for example, workers' attitudes toward their jobs may also shift—and workers may demand a change in working hours or working conditions. In such a case, even though the force is rooted in the external environment, the organization must respond directly to the internal pressure it generates.[8]

## Planned Versus Reactive Change

Some change is planned well in advance; other change comes about as a reaction to unexpected events. Planned change is change that is designed and implemented in an orderly and timely fashion in anticipation of future events. Reactive change is a piecemeal response to circumstances as they develop. Because reactive change may be hurried, the potential for poorly conceived and executed change is increased. Planned change is almost always preferable to reactive change.[9]

Georgia-Pacific, a large forest products business, is an excellent example of a firm that went through a planned and well-managed change process. When A. D. Correll became CEO, he quickly became alarmed at the firm's high accident rate—nine serious injuries per 100 employees each year, and 26 deaths during the most recent five-year period.

**planned change**
Change that is designed and implemented in an orderly and timely fashion in anticipation of future events

**reactive change**
A piecemeal response to circumstances as they develop

Although the forest products business is inherently dangerous, Correll believed that the accident rate was far too high and set out on a major change effort to improve things. He and other top managers developed a multistage change program intended to educate workers about safety, improve safety equipment in the plant, and eliminate a long-standing part of the firm's culture that made injuries almost a badge of courage. As a result, Georgia-Pacific soon achieved the best safety record in the industry, with relatively few injuries.[10]

On the other hand, Caterpillar was caught flat-footed by a worldwide recession in the construction industry, suffered enormous losses, and took several years to recover. Had managers at Caterpillar anticipated the need for change earlier, they might have been able to respond more quickly. Similarly, Kodak had to cut 12,000 jobs and then thousands more in reaction to sluggish sales and profits.[11] Again, better anticipation might have forestalled those

Accident rates in saw mills and other forest product businesses are often high. One company, Georgia-Pacific, initiated a multi stage change process to educate workers, improve safety equipment and adjust corporate culture.

job cuts. The importance of approaching change from a planned perspective is reinforced by the frequency of organization change. Most companies or divisions of large companies implement some form of moderate change at least every year and one or more major changes every four to five years.[12] Managers who sit back and respond only when they have to are likely to spend a lot of time hastily changing and rechanging things. A more effective approach is to anticipate forces urging change and plan ahead to deal with them.[13]

☐ Managers should understand the primary forces for change that might affect their organization.

☐ You should also remember, though, that no amount of foresight or awareness will totally eliminate the chances that reactive change may be necessary.

**Manager's Checklist** ✓

# Managing Change in Organizations

Organization change is a complex phenomenon. A manager cannot simply wave a wand and implement a planned change like magic. Instead, any change must be systematic and logical to have a realistic opportunity to succeed.[14] To carry this off, the manager needs to understand the steps of effective change and how to counter employee resistance to change.[15]

## Steps in the Change Process

Researchers have over the years developed a number of models or frameworks outlining steps for change.[16] The Lewin model was one of the first, although a more comprehensive approach is usually more useful in today's complex business environment.

**The Lewin Model**   Kurt Lewin, a noted organizational theorist, suggested that every change requires three steps.[17] The first step is *unfreezing*—individuals who will be affected by the impending change must be led to recognize why the change is necessary. Next, the *change* *itself* is implemented. Finally, *refreezing* involves reinforcing and supporting the change so that it becomes a part of the system.[18] For example, one of the changes Caterpillar faced in response to the recession noted earlier involved a massive workforce reduction. The first step (unfreezing) was convincing the United Auto Workers to support the reduction because of its importance to long-term effectiveness. After this unfreezing was accomplished, 30,000 jobs were eliminated (implementation). Then Caterpillar worked to improve its damaged relationship with its workers (refreezing) by guaranteeing future pay hikes and promising no more cutbacks. As interesting as Lewin's model is, however, it unfortunately lacks operational specificity. Thus a more comprehensive perspective is often needed.

**A Comprehensive Approach to Change**   The comprehensive approach to change takes a systems view and delineates a series of specific steps that often lead to successful change. This expanded model is illustrated in Figure 12.1. The first step is recognizing the need for change. Reactive change might be triggered by employee complaints, declines in productivity or turnover, court injunctions, sales slumps, or labor strikes. Recognition may simply be managers' awareness that change in a certain area is inevitable. For example, managers may be aware of the general frequency of organizational change undertaken by most organizations and recognize that their organization should probably follow the same pattern. The immediate stimulus might be the result of a forecast indicating new market potential, the accumulation of a cash surplus for possible investment, or an opportunity to achieve and

## FIGURE 12.1  STEPS IN THE CHANGE PROCESS

Managers must understand how and why to implement change. A manager who, when implementing change, follows a logical and orderly sequence like the one shown here is more likely to succeed than a manager whose change process is haphazard and poorly conceived.

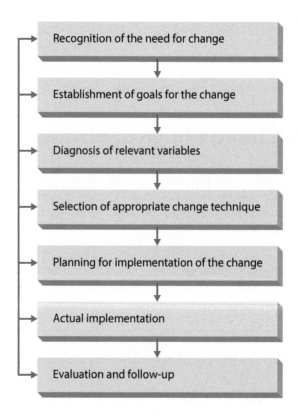

capitalize on a major technological breakthrough. Managers might also initiate change today because indicators suggest that it will be necessary in the near future.[19]

Managers must next set goals for the change. To increase market share, to enter new markets, to restore employee morale, to settle a strike, and to identify investment opportunities all might be goals for change. Third, managers must diagnose what brought on the need for change. Turnover, for example, might be caused by low pay, poor working conditions, poor supervisors, or employee dissatisfaction. Thus, although turnover may be the immediate stimulus for change, managers must understand its causes to make the right changes.

The next step is to select a change technique that will accomplish the intended goals. If turnover is caused by low pay, a new reward system may be needed. If the cause is poor supervision, interpersonal skills training may be called for. (Various change techniques are summarized later in this chapter.) After the appropriate technique has been chosen, its implementation must be planned. Issues to consider include the costs of the change, its effects on other areas of the organization, and the degree of employee participation appropriate for the situation. If the change is implemented as planned, the results should then be evaluated. If the change was intended to reduce turnover, managers must check turnover after the change has been in effect for a while. If turnover is still too high, other changes may be necessary.[20]

## Understanding Resistance to Change

Another element in the effective management of change is understanding the resistance that often accompanies change.[21] Managers need to know why people resist change and what can be done about their resistance. Resistance is common for a variety of reasons.[22]

**Uncertainty** Perhaps the biggest cause of employee resistance to change is uncertainty. In the face of impending change, employees may become anxious and nervous. They may worry about their ability to meet new job demands, they may think that their job security is threatened, or they may simply dislike ambiguity. Nabisco was once the target of an extended and confusing takeover battle, and during the entire time, employees were nervous about the impending change. The *Wall Street Journal* described them this way: "Many are angry at their leaders and fearful for their jobs. They are swapping rumors and spinning scenarios for the ultimate outcome of the battle for the tobacco and food giant. Headquarters staffers in Atlanta know so little about what's happening in New York that some call their office 'the mushroom complex,' where they are kept in the dark."[23] In another example, 12,500 British Airways cabin crew members voted to participate in a strike over the heavily traveled holiday season. The action against the airline was spurred by high levels of uncertainty as British Airways planned to merge with Iberia Airlines and proposed cutting 1,700 jobs and freezing employee wages in the process.[24]

**Threatened Self-Interests** Many impending changes threaten the self-interests of some managers within the organization. A change might diminish their power or influence within the company, so they fight it. Managers at Sears once developed a plan calling for a new type of store. The new stores would be somewhat smaller than a typical Sears store and would not be located in large shopping malls. Instead, they would be located in smaller strip centers. They would carry clothes and other "soft goods," but not hardware, appliances, furniture, or automotive products. When executives

When companies such as Iberia Airlines and British Airways plan to merge this can leave existing employees of both firms uncertain and resistant to change. Threats of layoffs and frozen wages ofter circulate among workers.

in charge of the excluded product lines heard about the plan, they raised such strong objections that the plan was cancelled.

**Different Perceptions**   A third reason that people resist change is due to different perceptions. A manager may make a decision and recommend a plan for change on the basis of her own assessment of a situation. Others in the organization may resist the change because they do not agree with the manager's assessment or they perceive the situation differently.[25] Executives at 7-Eleven battled this problem as they tried to enact a major organizational change. The corporation wanted to take its convenience stores a bit "upscale" and begin selling fancy fresh foods to go, the newest hardcover novels, some gourmet products, and higher-quality coffee. But many franchisees balked because they saw this move as taking the firm away from its core blue-collar customers.

**Feelings of Loss**   Many changes involve altering work arrangements in ways that disrupt existing social networks. Because social relationships are important, most people resist any change that might adversely affect those relationships. Other intangibles threatened by change include power, status, security, familiarity with existing procedures, and self-confidence.

## Overcoming Resistance to Change

Of course, a manager should not give up in the face of resistance to change. Although there are no sure-fire cures, there are several techniques that at least have the potential to overcome resistance.[26]

**Participation**   Participation is often the most effective technique for overcoming resistance to change. Employees who participate in planning and implementing a change are better able to understand the reasons for the change. Uncertainty is reduced, and self-interests and social relationships are less threatened. Having had an opportunity to express their ideas and assume the perspectives of others, employees are more likely to accept the change gracefully. A classic study of participation monitored the introduction of a change in production methods among four groups in a Virginia pajama factory.[27] The two groups that were allowed to fully participate in planning and implementing the change improved significantly in their productivity and satisfaction relative to the two groups that did not participate. Allstate Technology created the Allstate Change Agent Network to involve employees in change by fostering their understanding and input. Those involved spend about four hours per month for one year taking part in task forces to develop ideas for change which go directly to leadership.

> "People often resent change when they have no involvement in how it should be implemented. So, contrary to popular belief, people do not resist change, they resist being controlled."
>
> —KEN BLANCHARD, MANAGEMENT CONSULTANT AND LEADERSHIP EXPERT[28]

**Education and Communication**   Educating employees about the need for and the expected results of an impending change should reduce their resistance. If open communication is established and maintained during the change process, uncertainty can be minimized. Caterpillar used these methods to reduce resistance during many of its cutbacks. First, it educated UAW representatives about the need for and potential value of the planned changes. Then management told all employees what was happening, when it would happen, and how it would affect them individually.

**Facilitation**   Several facilitation procedures are also advisable. For instance, making only necessary changes, announcing those changes well in advance, and allowing time for people to adjust to new ways of doing things can help reduce resistance to change.[29] One manager at a Prudential regional office spent several months systematically planning a change in work

## FIGURE 12.2 FORCE-FIELD ANALYSIS FOR PLANT CLOSING AT GENERAL MOTORS

A force-field analysis can help a manager facilitate change. A manager able to identify forces acting both for and against a change can see where to focus efforts to remove barriers to change (such as offering training and relocation to displaced workers). Removing the forces against the change can at least partially overcome resistance.

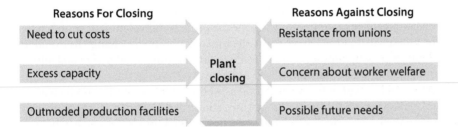

| Reasons For Closing | Plant closing | Reasons Against Closing |
|---|---|---|
| Need to cut costs | | Resistance from unions |
| Excess capacity | | Concern about worker welfare |
| Outmoded production facilities | | Possible future needs |

procedures and job design. He then became too impatient, coming in over the weekend with a work crew and rearranging the office layout. When employees walked in on Monday morning and saw what he had done, they were hostile, anxious, and resentful. What was a promising change became a disaster, and the manager had to scrap the entire plan.

**Force-Field Analysis**  Although force-field analysis may sound like something out of a *Star Trek* movie, it can help overcome resistance to change. In almost any change situation, forces are acting for and against the change. To facilitate the change, managers start by listing each set of forces and then trying to tip the balance so that the forces facilitating the change outweigh those hindering the change. It is especially important to try to remove or at least minimize some of the forces acting against the change. Suppose, for example, that General Motors is considering a plant closing as part of a change. As shown in Figure 12.2, three factors are reinforcing the change: GM needs to cut costs, it has excess capacity, and the plant has outmoded production facilities. At the same time, there is resistance from the UAW, concern for workers being put out of their jobs, and a feeling that the plant might be needed again in the future. GM might start by convincing the UAW that the closing is necessary by presenting profit and loss figures. It could then offer relocation and retraining to displaced workers. And it might shut down the plant and put it in "mothballs" so that it can be renovated later. The three major factors hindering the change are thus eliminated or reduced in importance.[30]

---

☐ Managers need to understand the importance of implementing change as systematically and logically as possible.

☐ Managers must be aware that people resist change and why this resistance is likely to occur.

☐ They should also know the most effective ways to address resistance to change.

☐ You should have an appreciation of your own tolerance for change.

**Manager's Checklist**

## Areas of Organization Change

We noted earlier that change can involve virtually any part of an organization. In general, however, most change interventions involve organization structure and design, technology and operations, or people. The most common areas of change within each of these broad categories are listed in Table 12.1. In addition, many organizations have gone through massive and comprehensive business process change programs.

## Changing Organization Structure and Design

Organization change might be focused on any of the basic components of organization structure or on the organization's overall design. Thus the organization might change the way it designs its jobs or its bases of departmentalization. Likewise, it might change reporting relationships or the distribution of authority. For example, we noted in Chapter 11 the trend toward flatter organizations. Coordination mechanisms and line-and-staff configurations are also subject to change. On a larger scale, the organization might change its overall design. For example, a growing business could decide to drop its functional design and adopt a divisional design. Or it might transform itself into a matrix. Changes in culture usually involve the structure and design of the organization as well (recall that we discussed changing culture back in Chapter 3). Finally, the organization might change any part of its human resource management system, such as its selection criteria, its performance appraisal methods, or its compensation package.[31]

## Changing Technology and Operations

Technology is the conversion process used by an organization to transform inputs into outputs. Because of the rapid rate of all technological innovation, technological changes are becoming increasingly important to many organizations. Table 12.1 lists several areas where technological change is likely to be experienced. One important area of change today revolves around information technology. The adoption and institutionalization of information technology innovations is almost constant in most firms today. Sun Microsystems, for example, adopted a very short-range planning cycle to be best prepared for environmental changes.[32] Another important form of technological change involves equipment. To keep pace with competitors, firms periodically find that replacing existing machinery and equipment with newer models is necessary.

---

### TABLE 12.1  AREAS OF ORGANIZATION CHANGE

Organization change can affect any part, area, or component of an organization. Most change, however, fits into one of three general areas: organization structure and design, technology and operations, and people.

| Organization Structure and Design | Technology and Operations | People |
|---|---|---|
| Job design | Information technology | Abilities and skills |
| Departmentalization | Equipment | Performance |
| Reporting relationships | Work processes | Perceptions |
| Authority distribution | Work sequences | Expectations |
| Coordination mechanisms | Control systems | Attitudes |
| Line–staff structure | Enterprise resource planning (ERP) | Values |
| Overall design | | |
| Culture | | |
| Human resource management | | |

A change in work processes or work activities may be necessary if new equipment is introduced or new products are manufactured. In manufacturing industries, the major reason for changing a work process is to accommodate a change in the materials used to produce a finished product. Consider a firm that manufactures battery-operated flashlights. For many years flashlights were made of metal, but now most are made of plastic. A firm might decide to move from metal to plastic flashlights because of consumer preferences, raw materials costs, or other reasons. Whatever the reason, the technology necessary to make flashlights from plastic differs importantly from that used to make flashlights from metal. Work process changes may occur in service organizations as well as in manufacturing firms. As traditional barbershops and beauty parlors are replaced by hair salons catering to both sexes, for example, the hybrid organizations have to develop new methods for handling appointments and setting prices.

A change in work sequence may or may not accompany a change in equipment or a change in work processes. Making a change in work sequence means altering the order or sequence of the workstations involved in a particular manufacturing process. For example, a manufacturer might have two parallel assembly lines producing two similar sets of machine parts. The lines might converge at one central quality-control unit, where inspectors verify tolerances. The manager, however, might decide to change to periodic rather than final inspection. Under this arrangement, one or more inspections are established farther up the line. Work sequence changes can also be made in service organizations. The processing of insurance claims, for example, could be changed. The sequence of logging and verifying claims, requesting checks, getting countersignatures, and mailing checks could be altered in several ways, such as combining the first two steps or routing the claims through one person while another handles checks. Organizational control systems may also be targets of change.[33] For example, a firm trying to improve the quality of its products might develop and implement a set of more rigorous and comprehensive quality-control procedures.

Finally, many businesses have been working to implement technological and operations change by installing and using complex and integrated software systems. Such systems—called *enterprise resource planning*—link virtually all facets of the business, making it easier for managers to keep abreast of related developments. Enterprise resource planning, or ERP, is a large-scale information system for integrating and synchronizing the many activities in the extended enterprise. In most cases these systems are purchased from external vendors who then tailor their products to the client's unique needs and requirements. Companywide processes—such as materials management, production planning, order management, and financial reporting—can all be managed via ERP. In effect, these are the processes that cut across product lines, departments, and geographic locations.

Developing the ERP system starts by identifying the key processes that need critical attention, such as supplier relationships, materials flows, or customer order fulfillment. The system could result, for instance, in sales processes being integrated with production planning and then integrating both of these into the firm's financial accounting system. For example, a customer in Rome can place an order that is to be produced in Ireland, schedule it to be shipped via air cargo to Rome, and then have it picked up by a truck at the airport and delivered to the customer's warehouse by a specified date. All of these activities are synchronized by activities linkages in one massive database.

The ERP integrates all activities and information flows that relate to the firm's critical processes. It also keeps updated real-time information on their current status, reports recent past transactions and upcoming planned transactions, and provides electronic notices that action is required on some items if planned schedules are to be met. It coordinates internal operations with activities by outside suppliers and notifies business partners and customers of current status and upcoming deliveries and billings. It can integrate financial flows among the firm, its suppliers, its customers, and commercial bank deposits for up-to-the-minute status reports that can be used to create real-time financial reports at a moment's notice, rather than in the traditional one-month (or longer) time span for producing a financial statement. ERP's multilanguage capabilities also allow real-time correspondence in various languages to facilitate international transactions.

**enterprise resource planning (ERP)**
A large-scale information system for integrating and synchronizing the many activities in the extended enterprise

## Changing People, Attitudes, and Behaviors

A third area of organization change has to do with human resources. For example, an organization might decide to change the skill level of its workforce. This change might be prompted by changes in technology or by a general desire to upgrade the quality of the workforce. Thus training programs and new selection criteria might be needed. The organization might also decide to improve its workers' performance level. In this case, a new incentive system or performance-based training might be in order. Due to intense competition for talent from competitors, Microsoft has increased its employees' compensation by shifting a portion of their stock awards to their base salaries, as well as boosting funding for bonuses and stock awards to reward its top performers.[34] Volvo Construction Equipment laid off roughly 25 percent of its workforce globally, leaving the company with employees who are focused and understand the urgency necessary to facilitate change.[35]

Perceptions and expectations are also a common focus of organization change. Workers in an organization might believe that their wages and benefits are not as high as they should be. Management, however, might have evidence that shows the firm is paying a competitive wage and providing a superior benefit package. The change, then, would be centered on informing and educating the workforce about the comparative value of its compensation package. A common way to do this is to publish a statement that places an actual dollar value on each benefit provided and compares that amount to what other local organizations are providing their workers. Change might also be directed at employee attitudes and values. In many organizations today, managers are trying to eliminate adversarial relationships with workers and to adopt a more collaborative relationship. In many ways, changing attitudes and values is perhaps the hardest thing to do.[36]

## Changing Business Processes

**business process change (reengineering)**
The radical redesign of all aspects of a business to achieve major gains in cost, service, or time

Many organizations today have also gone through massive and comprehensive change programs involving all aspects of organization design, technology, and people. Although various descriptions are used, the terms currently in vogue for these changes are *business process change* or *reengineering*. Specifically, business process change, or reengineering, is the radical redesign of all aspects of a business to achieve major gains in cost, service, or time.[37] ERP, as described previously, is a common platform for changing business processes. However, business process change is a more comprehensive set of changes that goes beyond software and information systems.

Corning, for example, has undergone major reengineering over the last several years. Whereas the 150-year-old business once manufactured cookware and other durable consumer goods, it has transformed itself into a high-tech powerhouse making such products as the ultra-thin screens used in products like smartphones and laptop computers.[38] Similarly, the dramatic overhauls of Apple to shift away from personal computers to other digital devices, of Yellow Roadway Corporation into a sophisticated freight delivery firm, and of UPS into a major international delivery giant all required business process changes throughout these organizations.

Yellow Roadway Corporation has used business process change and cutting edge technology to transform itself from on old-line trucking company into a modern and competitive freight delivery firm. This Yellow Roadway truck is awaiting a customs inspection as it crosses the border into Finland.

**The Need for Business Process Change** Why are so many organizations finding it necessary to undergo business process change? We note in

Chapter 2 that all systems, including organizations, are subject to entropy—a normal process leading to system decline. An organization is behaving most typically when it maintains the status quo, does not change in sync with its environment, and starts consuming its own resources to survive. In a sense, that is what happened to Kmart. In the early and mid-1970s, Kmart was in such a high-flying growth mode that it passed first JCPenney and then Sears to become the world's largest retailer. But then the firm's managers grew complacent and assumed that the discount retailer's prosperity would continue and that they need not worry about environmental shifts, the growth of Walmart, and so forth—and entropy set in. The key is to recognize the beginning of the decline and immediately move toward changing relevant business processes. For instance, Netflix required business process changes throughout the organization as it shifted its focus to delivering movies and TV over the Internet rather than through the mail. But these changes were approached in a planned and strategic fashion.[39] Major problems occur when managers either do not recognize the onset of entropy until it is well advanced or are complacent about taking steps to correct it.[40]

**Approaches to Business Process Change** Figure 12.3 shows general steps in changing business processes, or reengineering. The first step is setting goals and developing a strategy for the changes. The organization must know in advance what new business processes are supposed to accomplish and how those accomplishments will be achieved. Next, top managers must begin and direct the reengineering effort. If a CEO simply announces that business process change is to occur but does nothing else, the program is unlikely to be successful. But if the CEO is constantly involved in the process, underscoring its importance and taking the lead, business process change stands a much better chance of success.

Most experts also agree that successful business process change is usually accompanied by a sense of urgency. People in the organization must see the clear and present need for the changes being implemented and appreciate their importance. In addition, most successful

---

## FIGURE 12.3 THE REENGINEERING PROCESS

Reengineering is a major redesign of all areas of an organization. To be successful, reengineering requires a systematic and comprehensive assessment of the entire organization. Goals, top management support, and a sense of urgency help the organization re-create itself and blend both top-level and bottom-up perspectives.

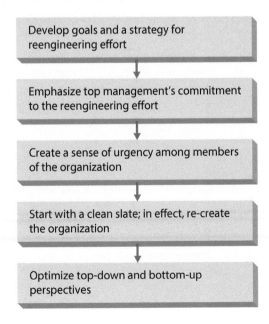

Develop goals and a strategy for reengineering effort

Emphasize top management's commitment to the reengineering effort

Create a sense of urgency among members of the organization

Start with a clean slate; in effect, re-create the organization

Optimize top-down and bottom-up perspectives

## BEYOND TRADITIONAL BUSINESS

# Am(ortizing) Ex(penses)

In January 2013, American Express (Amex) announced that it was cutting 5,400 jobs—about 8.5 percent of its total workforce of 63,500. The cuts were scheduled to take place through the year, and CFO Dan Henry announced that they would be "spread proportionally between U.S. and international markets and occur primarily among positions that do not directly generate revenues."

Amex had last cut its workforce as a response to the financial crisis of 2007–2008, eliminating 7,000 jobs in October 2008 and, as part of the same cost-cutting measure, another 4,000 in May 2009. CEO Kenneth Chenault referred to the plan as a "reengineering program" designed to "help us manage through one of the most challenging economic environments we've seen in many decades."

The "reengineering program" that Amex initiated in late 2008 is an example of *restructuring*—generally speaking, a modification in a firm's operations or structure, usually as a result of financial pressure. As part of the process, Amex took a *restructuring charge* of $240 million to $290 million in the fourth quarter of 2008 to cover severance pay and other costs related to the workforce reduction. The second round of cuts entailed a restructuring charge of $180 million to $250 million in the second quarter of 2009. A restructuring charge, however, is a one-time expense—a short-term loss meant to save money in the long run. At the end of 2009, Chenault reported that operating costs had been cut by 14 percent: "We took a long-term approach," he told shareholders in the company's annual report. "We didn't just want to reduce expenses for 2009; we wanted to prepare our expense base for the conditions we saw ahead, a period of relatively weak economic growth after the recession."

The spending cuts eventually saved Amex approximately $2.6 billion.

And what about the round of job reductions in 2013?

Amex is not only the country's largest credit card issuer by client purchases, but also the biggest U.S.-based travel agency. In this sector, it competes not with Visa and MasterCard, but with the online travel agencies Priceline and Expedia. "We've delivered strong results coming out of the recession," said Chenault in January 2013, but in the five years leading up to the latest round of job cuts, as more and more customers turned to online companies for travel booking and advisory services, the Corporate Travel division had seen a decline in billings of $6 billion. "The economics of business travel," said Chenault, "has changed more dramatically … than any part of the business." Thus "the biggest impact" of the 4,500 job cuts, he explained, would be felt in "global business travel, where we are reengineering the business model to reduce its cost structure and invest in capabilities that will help us better align with the shift of customer volumes to online channels and automated servicing areas." For the fourth quarter of 2012, Amex took a $400 million restructuring charge for the job cuts, resulting in a 47 percent decline in net income from the previous year.

Theresa Jameson, an analyst at marketing-intelligence provider Datamonitor, called the Amex measures "drastic" but saw them as part of "a conscious move … to address the growing popularity of online and mobile-service use among consumers." Throughout 2012, she points out, Amex had unveiled "a number of products and services across the mobile and online spaces geared at a more youthful and technologically savvy audience. … The company," she concluded, "is strategically adapting to the digital age."

In March 2014, Amex sold half of its business travel unit to an investor group for $900 million. The company plans to spend the proceeds on new technology for its remaining share of the travel business.

*References:* Mary Ann McNulty, "Amex to Trim 5,400 Jobs amid Changing Business Travel Economics," *Business Travel News* (January 11, 2013), www.businesstravelnews.com, on December 21, 2014; Jennifer Booton, "American Express to Slice Up to 6% of Workforce in '13," *Fox Business* (January 10, 2013), www.foxbusiness.com, on December 21, 2014; Andrew Clark, "American Express Sheds 7,000 Jobs," *The Guardian* (October 30, 2008), www.theguardian.com, on December 23, 2014; Dawn Kopecki, "AmEx Cuts Jobs as Digital Age Transforms Travel Business," Bloomberg (January 11, 2013), www.bloomberg.com, on December 23, 2014; Theresa Jameson, "Amex to Restructure Business with a Renewed Focus on Digital," Datamonitor (January 17, 2013), www.datamonitorfinancial.com, on December 23, 2014; Michael J. de la Merced, "American Express to Sell Half of Its Business Travel Arm for $900 Million," *New York Times* (May 17, 2014), http://dealbook.nytimes.com, on December 24, 2017.

reengineering efforts start with a new, clean slate. In other words, rather than assuming that the existing organization is a starting point and then trying to modify it, business process change usually starts by asking questions such as how customers are best served and competitors best neutralized. New approaches and systems are then created and imposed in place of existing ones.

Finally, business process change requires a careful blend of top-down and bottom-up involvement. On the one hand, strong leadership is necessary, but too much involvement by top management can make the changes seem autocratic. Similarly, employee participation is also important, but too little involvement by leaders can undermine the program's importance and create a sense that top managers do not care. Thus care must be taken to carefully balance these two countervailing forces. This chapter's *Beyond Traditional Business* explores how American Express has gone through a reengineering process to help it remain competitive. Our next section explores more fully one related but distinct approach called *organization development*.

## Organization Development

We have noted in several places the importance of people and change. Beyond those change interests discussed previously, a special area of interest that focuses almost exclusively on people is organization development (OD).

**OD Assumptions**  Organization development is concerned with changing attitudes, perceptions, behaviors, and expectations. More precisely, organization development (OD) is a planned effort that is organization-wide and managed from the top, intended to increase organizational effectiveness and health through planned interventions in the organization's process, using behavioral science knowledge.[41] The theory and practice of OD are based on several very important assumptions. The first is that employees have a desire to grow and develop. Another is that employees have a strong need to be accepted by others within the organization. Still another critical assumption of OD is that the total organization and the way it is designed will influence the way individuals and groups within the organization behave. Thus some form of collaboration between managers and their employees is necessary to (1) take advantage of the skills and abilities of the employees and (2) eliminate aspects of the organization that retard employee growth, development, and group acceptance. Because of the intensely personal nature of many OD activities, many large organizations rely on one or more OD consultants (either full-time employees assigned to this function or outside experts hired specifically for OD purposes) to implement and manage their OD programs.[42]

**OD Techniques**  Several kinds of interventions or activities are generally considered part of organization development.[43] Some OD programs may use only one or a few of these; other programs use several of them at once.

- *Diagnostic activities.* Just as a physician examines patients to diagnose their current condition, an OD diagnosis analyzes the current condition of an organization. To carry out this diagnosis, managers use questionnaires, opinion or attitude surveys, interviews, archival data, and meetings to assess various characteristics of the organization. The results of this diagnosis may generate profiles of the organization's activities, which can then be used to identify problem areas in need of correction.
- *Team building.* Team-building activities are intended to enhance the effectiveness and satisfaction of individuals who work in groups or teams and to promote overall group effectiveness. Given the widespread use of teams today, these activities have taken on increased importance. An OD consultant might interview team members to determine how they feel about the group; then an off-site meeting could be held to discuss the issues that surfaced and iron out any problem areas or member concerns. Caterpillar used team

**organization development (OD)**
An effort that is planned, organization-wide, and managed from the top, intended to increase organizational effectiveness and health through planned interventions in the organization's process, using behavioral science knowledge

Andresr/Shutterstock.com

These two functional groups are involved in an intergroup activity. As part of a company-wide initiative to improve dialogue between all facets of the company, retreats such as this one filled with team-building exercises, are occurring on a quarterly basis.

building as one method for changing the working relationships between workers and supervisors from confrontational to cooperative. An interesting new approach to team building involves having executive teams participate in group cooking classes to teach them the importance of interdependence and coordination.[44]

- *Survey feedback.* In survey feedback, each employee responds to a questionnaire intended to measure perceptions and attitudes (for example, satisfaction and supervisory style). Everyone involved, including the supervisor, receives the results of the survey. The aim of this approach is usually to change the behavior of supervisors by showing them how their subordinates view them. After the feedback has been provided, workshops may be conducted to evaluate results and suggest constructive changes.

- *Education.* Educational activities focus on classroom training. Although such activities can be used for technical or skill-related purposes, an OD educational activity typically focuses on "sensitivity skills"—that is, it teaches people to be more considerate and understanding of the people they work with. Participants often go through a series of experiential or role-playing exercises to learn better how others in the organization feel.[45]

- *Intergroup activities.* The focus of intergroup activities is on improving the relationships between two or more groups. We noted in Chapter 11 that, as group interdependence increases, so do coordination difficulties. Intergroup OD activities are designed to promote cooperation or resolve conflicts that arose as a result of interdependence. Experiential or role-playing activities are often used to bring this about.

- *Third-party peacemaking.* Another approach to OD is through third-party peacemaking, which is most often used when substantial conflict exists within the organization. Third-party peacemaking can be appropriate on the individual, group, or organizational level. The third party, usually an OD consultant, uses a variety of mediation or negotiation techniques to resolve any problems or conflicts among individuals or groups.

- *Technostructural activities.* Technostructural activities are concerned with the design of the organization, the technology of the organization, and the interrelationship of design and technology with people on the job. A structural change such as an increase in decentralization, a job design change such as an increase in the use of automation, and a technological change involving a modification in work flow all qualify as technostructural OD activities if their objective is to improve group and interpersonal relationships within the organization.

- *Process consultation.* In process consultation, an OD consultant observes groups in the organization to develop an understanding of their communication patterns, decision-making and leadership processes, and methods of cooperation and conflict resolution. The consultant then provides feedback to the involved parties about the processes he or she has observed. The goal of this form of intervention is to improve the observed processes. A leader who is presented with feedback outlining deficiencies in his or her leadership style, for example, might be expected to change to overcome them.

- *Life and career planning.* Life and career planning helps employees formulate their personal goals and evaluate strategies for integrating their goals with the goals of the organization. Such activities might include specification of training needs and plotting a career map. General Electric has a reputation for doing an outstanding job in this area.

- *Coaching and counseling.* Coaching and counseling provide nonevaluative feedback to individuals. The purpose is to help people develop a better sense of how others see them and learn behaviors that will assist others in achieving their work-related goals. The focus is not on how the person is performing today; instead, it is on how the person can perform better in the future.

- *Planning and goal setting.* More pragmatic than many other interventions are activities designed to help managers improve their planning and goal setting. Emphasis still falls on the individual, however, because the intent is to help individuals and groups integrate themselves into the overall planning process. The OD consultant might use the same approach as in process consultation, but the focus is more technically oriented on the mechanics of planning and goal setting.

**The Effectiveness of OD**   Given the diversity of activities encompassed by OD, it is not surprising that managers report mixed results from various OD interventions. Organizations that actively practice some form of OD include American Airlines, Texas Instruments, Procter & Gamble, and BFGoodrich. Goodrich, for example, has trained 60 people in OD processes and techniques. These trained experts have subsequently become internal OD consultants to assist other managers in applying the techniques.[46] Many other managers, in contrast, report that they have tried OD but discarded it.[47]

OD will probably remain an important part of management theory and practice. Of course, there are no sure things when dealing with social systems such as organizations, and the effectiveness of many OD techniques is difficult to evaluate. Because all organizations are open systems interacting with their environments, an improvement in an organization after an OD intervention may be attributable to the intervention, but it may also be attributable to changes in economic conditions, luck, or other factors.[48]

---

☐ All managers need to be aware of the different areas of change that may be necessary in their organizations.

☐ When planning and implementing change in one area you should be aware that changes may then be necessary in other areas as well.

**Manager's Checklist**

# Organizational Innovation

A final element of organization change that we address is innovation. Innovation is the managed effort of an organization to develop new products or services, or new uses for existing products or services. Innovation is clearly important because, without new products or services, any organization will fall behind its competition.[49]

## The Innovation Process

The organizational innovation process consists of developing, applying, launching, growing, and managing the maturity and decline of creative ideas.[50] This process is depicted in Figure 12.4.

**Innovation Development**   Innovation development involves the evaluation, modification, and improvement of creative ideas. Innovation development can transform a product or service with only modest potential into a product or service with significant potential. Parker Brothers, for example, decided during innovation development not to market an indoor volleyball game but instead to sell separately the appealing little foam ball designed for the game. The firm will never know how well the volleyball game would have sold, but the Nerf ball and numerous related products generated millions of dollars in revenues for Parker Brothers.

**innovation**
The managed effort of an organization to develop new products or services or new uses for existing products or services

## FIGURE 12.4 THE INNOVATION PROCESS

Organizations actively seek to manage the innovation process. These steps illustrate the general life cycle that characterizes most innovations. Of course, as with creativity, the innovation process will suffer if it is approached too mechanically and rigidly.

| **Development** Organization evaluates, modifies, and improves on a creative idea. | → | **Application** Organization uses developed idea in design, manufacturing, or delivery of new products, services, or processes. | → | **Launch** Organization introduces new products or services to the marketplace. |

| **Decline** Demand for an innovation decreases, and substitute innovations are developed and applied. | ← | **Maturity** Most competing organizations have access to the idea. | ← | **Growth** Demand for new products or services grows. |

**Innovation Application** Innovation application is the stage in which an organization takes a developed idea and uses it in the design, manufacturing, or delivery of new products, services, or processes. At this point the innovation emerges from the laboratory and is transformed into tangible goods or services. One example of innovation application is the use of radar-based focusing systems in Polaroid's instant cameras. The idea of using radio waves to discover the location, speed, and direction of moving objects was first applied extensively by Allied forces during World War II. As radar technology developed during the following years, the electrical components needed became smaller and more streamlined. Researchers at Polaroid applied this well-developed technology in a new way.[51]

**Application Launch** Application launch is the stage at which an organization introduces new products or services to the marketplace. The important question is not "Does the innovation work?" but "Will customers want to buy the innovative product or service?" History is full of creative ideas that did not generate enough interest among customers to be successful. Some notable innovation failures include a portable seat warmer from Sony, "New" Coke, Polaroid's SX-70 instant camera (which cost $3 billion to develop, but never sold more than 100,000 units in a year), and the flip video recorder. Thus, despite development and application, new products and services can still fail at the launch phase.

**Application Growth** Once an innovation has been successfully launched, it then enters the stage of application growth. This is a period of high economic performance for an organization because demand for the product or service is often greater than supply. Organizations that fail to anticipate this stage may unintentionally limit their growth, as Apple did by not anticipating demand for its iMac computer.[52] At the same time, overestimating demand for a new product can be just as detrimental to performance. Unsold products can sit in warehouses for years.

Application launch is a critical element in the success or failure of a new product. Polaroid spent over $3 billion in developing this camera but only recouped a small fraction of its investment.

fotografos/Shutterstock.com

**Innovation Maturity**   After a period of growing demand, an innovative product or service often enters a period of maturity. Innovation maturity is the stage at which most organizations in an industry have access to an innovation and are applying it in approximately the same way. The technological application of an innovation during this stage of the innovation process can be very sophisticated. Because most firms have access to the innovation, however, either as a result of their developing the innovation on their own or copying the innovation of others, it does not provide competitive advantage to any one of them. The time that elapses between innovation development and innovation maturity varies notably depending on the particular product or service. Whenever an innovation involves the use of complex skills (such as a complicated manufacturing process or highly sophisticated teamwork), moving from the growth phase to the maturity phase will take longer. In addition, if the skills needed to implement these innovations are rare and difficult to imitate, then strategic imitation may be delayed, and the organization may enjoy a period of sustained competitive advantage.

**Innovation Decline**   Every successful innovation bears the seeds of its own decline. Because an organization does not gain a competitive advantage from an innovation at maturity, it must encourage its creative scientists, engineers, and managers to begin looking for new innovations. This continued search for competitive advantage usually leads new products and services to move from the creative process through innovation maturity, and finally to innovation decline. Innovation decline is the stage during which demand for an innovation decreases and substitute innovations are developed and applied.

## Forms of Innovation

Each creative idea that an organization develops poses a different challenge for the innovation process. Innovations can be radical or incremental, technical or managerial, and product or process.

**Radical Versus Incremental Innovations**   Radical innovations are new products, services, or technologies developed by an organization that completely replace the existing products, services, or technologies in an industry.[53] Incremental innovations are new products or processes that modify existing ones. Firms that implement radical innovations fundamentally shift the nature of competition and the interaction of firms within their environments. Firms that implement incremental innovations alter, but do not fundamentally change, competitive interaction in an industry.

Over the last several years, organizations have introduced many radical innovations. For example, compact disc technology replaced long-playing vinyl records in the recording industry, digital downloading is supplanting CD, and digital downloading is already being replaced by Spotify and SoundCloud; DVDs have replaced videocassettes but are now being supplanted by Blu-ray DVDs and streaming video; and high-definition television is replacing regular television technology. Whereas radical innovations like these tend to be very visible and public, incremental innovations actually are more numerous. For instance, each new generation of the iPhone and the iPod represent relatively minor changes over previous versions.

**radical innovation**
A new product, service, or technology that completely replaces an existing one

**incremental innovation**
A new product, service, or technology that modifies an existing one

Amazon has pioneered several new processes for selling and distributing products. One of its most recent experiments involves the potential use of drones such as this one to deliver products to customers the same day as their order.

**Technical Versus Managerial Innovations** Technical innovations are changes in the physical appearance or performance of a product or service, or of the physical processes through which a product or service is manufactured. Many of the most important innovations over the last 50 years have been technical. For example, the serial replacement of the vacuum tube with the transistor, the transistor with the integrated circuit, and the integrated circuit with the microchip has greatly enhanced the power, ease of use, and speed of operation of a wide variety of electronic products. Not all innovations developed by organizations are technical, however. Managerial innovations are changes in the management process by which products and services are conceived, built, and delivered to customers.[54] Managerial innovations do not necessarily affect the physical appearance or performance of products or services directly. In effect, business process change or reengineering, as we discuss earlier, represents a managerial innovation.

**Product Versus Process Innovations** Perhaps the two most important types of technical innovations are product innovations and process innovations. Product innovations are changes in the physical characteristics or performance of existing products or services or the creation of brand-new products or services. Process innovations are changes in the way products or services are manufactured, created, or distributed. Whereas managerial innovations generally affect the broader context of development, process innovations directly affect manufacturing.

The implementation of robotics, as we discussed earlier, is a process innovation. As Figure 12.5 shows, the effect of product and process innovations on economic return depends on the stage of the innovation process that a new product or service occupies. At first, during development, application, and launch, the physical attributes and capabilities of an innovation most affect organizational performance. Thus product innovations are particularly important during these beginning phases. Later, as an innovation enters the phases of growth, maturity, and decline, an organization's ability to develop process innovations, such as fine-tuning manufacturing, increasing product quality, and improving product distribution, becomes important to maintaining economic return.

Japanese organizations have often excelled at process innovation. The market for 35 mm cameras was dominated by German and other European manufacturers when, in the early 1960s, Japanese camera companies such as Canon and Nikon began an aggressive push to increase their global market shares. Some of the early Japanese products were not very successful, but these companies continued to invest in their process technology and eventually were able to increase quality and decrease manufacturing costs.[55] The Japanese organizations eventually came to dominate the worldwide market for 35 mm cameras, and the German companies, because they were not able to maintain the same pace of process innovation, struggled to maintain market share and profitability. And as film technology gave way to digital photography, the same Japanese firms have effectively transitioned to leadership in this market as well.

**technical innovation**
A change in the appearance or performance of products or services, or of the physical processes through which a product or service passes

**managerial innovation**
A change in the management process in an organization

**product innovation**
A change in the physical characteristics or performance of an existing product or service or the creation of new ones

**process innovation**
A change in the way a product or service is manufactured, created, or distributed

Nixki/Shutterstock.com

This Nikon camera is an example of Japan's ability to innovate in a speedy manner. Other camera manufacturers were not able to keep up with customer's changing desires and technological advances.

## The Failure to Innovate

To remain competitive in today's economy, organizations must be innovative. And yet many organizations that should be innovative are not successful at bringing out new products or services or do so only after innovations created by others are very mature. Organizations may fail to innovate for at least three reasons.

## FIGURE 12.5  EFFECTS OF PRODUCT AND PROCESS INNOVATION ON ECONOMIC RETURN

As the innovation process moves from development to decline, the economic return from product innovations gradually declines. In contrast, the economic return from process innovations increases during this same process.

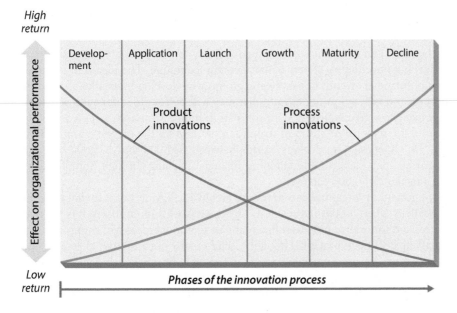

**Lack of Resources** Innovation is expensive in terms of dollars, time, and energy. If a firm does not have enough money to fund a program of innovation or does not currently employ the kinds of employees it needs in order to be innovative, it may lag behind in innovation. Even highly innovative organizations cannot become involved in every new product or service its employees think up. For example, numerous other commitments in the electronic instruments and computer industry forestalled Hewlett-Packard from investing in Steve Jobs and Steve Wozniak's original idea for a personal computer. With infinite resources of money, time, and technical and managerial expertise, HP might have entered this market early. Because the firm did not have this flexibility, however, it had to make some difficult choices about which innovations to invest in.[56]

**Failure to Recognize Opportunities** Because firms cannot pursue all innovations, they need to develop the ability to carefully evaluate innovations and to select the ones that hold the greatest potential. To obtain a competitive advantage, an organization usually must make investment decisions before the innovation process reaches the mature stage. The earlier the investment, however, the greater the risk. If organizations are not skilled at recognizing and evaluating opportunities, they may be overly cautious and fail to invest in innovations that later turn out to be successful for other firms.

**Resistance to Change** As we discuss earlier, many organizations tend to resist change. Innovation means giving up old products and old ways of doing things in favor of new products and new ways of doing things. These kinds of changes can be personally difficult for managers and other members of an organization. Thus resistance to change can slow the innovation process.

"Dynamic corporations of the future should simultaneously be trying alternative ways of doing things in competition within themselves."

—NORMAN MACRAE, ECONOMIST[58]

## Promoting Innovation in Organizations

A wide variety of ideas for promoting innovation in organizations have been developed over the years. Three specific ways for promoting innovation are through the reward system, through the organizational culture, and through a process called *intrapreneurship*.[57]

**The Reward System** A firm's reward system is the means by which it encourages and discourages certain behaviors by employees. Major components of the reward system include salaries, bonuses, and perquisites. Using the reward system to promote innovation is a fairly mechanical but nevertheless effective management technique. The idea is to provide financial and nonfinancial rewards to people and groups who develop innovative ideas. Once the members of an organization understand that they will be rewarded for such activities, they are more likely to work creatively. With this end in mind, Monsanto gives a $50,000 award each year to the scientist or group of scientists who develop the biggest commercial breakthrough. 3M's Genesis Grant offers awards between $35,000 and $75,000 to innovators whose projects may have trouble attaining financial backing through normal means and provides a total of $750,000 each year.

It is important for organizations to reward creative behavior, but it is vital to avoid punishing creativity when it does not result in highly successful innovations. It is the nature of the creative and innovative processes that many new product ideas will simply not work out in the marketplace. Each process is fraught with too many uncertainties to generate positive results every time. A person may have prepared herself to be creative, but an insight may not be forthcoming. Or managers may try to apply a developed innovation, only to recognize that it does not work. Indeed, some organizations operate according to the assumption that, if all their innovative efforts succeed, then they are probably not taking enough risks in research and development. At 3M, nearly 60 percent of the creative ideas suggested each year do not succeed in the marketplace.

Managers need to be very careful in responding to innovative failure. If innovative failure is due to incompetence, systematic errors, or managerial sloppiness, then a firm should respond appropriately, for example, by withholding raises or reducing promotion opportunities. People who act in good faith to develop an innovation that simply does not work out, however, should not be punished for failure. If they are, they will probably not be creative in the future. A punitive reward system will discourage people from taking risks and therefore reduce the organization's ability to obtain competitive advantages.

**Organization Culture** As we discussed in Chapter 3, an organization's culture is the set of values, beliefs, and symbols that help guide behavior. A strong, appropriately focused organizational culture can be used to support innovative activity. A well-managed culture can communicate a sense that innovation is valued and will be rewarded and that occasional failure in the pursuit of new ideas is not only acceptable but even expected. In addition to reward systems and intrapreneurial activities, firms such as Apple, Google, Nintendo, Nokia, Sony, Walt Disney, Vodafone, and Hewlett-Packard are all known to have strong, innovation-oriented cultures that value individual creativity, risk taking, and inventiveness.[59] Google, for instance, allows employees to use 20 percent of their time (one day per week) to work on their own side projects in order to foster innovation. Our *Tech Watch* feature illustrates the importance of organization culture in innovation.

**Intrapreneurship in Larger Organizations** In recent years, many large businesses have realized that the entrepreneurial spirit that propelled their growth becomes stagnant after they transform themselves from a small but growing concern into a larger one.[60] To help revitalize this spirit, some firms today encourage what they call "intrapreneurship." Intrapreneurs are similar to entrepreneurs except that they develop a new business in the

**intrapreneurs**
Similar to entrepreneurs except that they develop new businesses in the context of a large organization

# Breaking the Mold

Jeff Applegate, CEO of Texas Injection Molding (TIM), appreciates flexibility: "The thing I love about this business," he says, "is the fact that everyday I'm working with a different industry, a different company, a different entrepreneur."

Applegate purchased TIM, a Houston company that manufactures products and parts by injecting thermoplastic and thermosetting polymers into specially designed molds, in 2014, but he's no novice in the industry: For 10 years, he'd been president of Blackwell Plastics, a leader in Houston's thriving plastics-injection industry. Applegate had just left Blackwell to run his own company when Manufacturing. Net named Blackwell one of its "Most Innovative Industrial Companies for 2013." What Manufacturing.Net liked about Blackwell was its flexibility—its ability to make plastics products with applications ranging from the kitchen to aerospace.

Companies like Blackwell and TIM, explains Applegate, "own no tools; we make no products. We're contract manufacturers for other people who bring their ideas to us." Obviously, it helps to be responsive to innovative product designs and to have an open mind about untried manufacturing techniques. Back in 1971, for instance, an inventor named George Ballas brought founder L.D. Blackwell the crude prototype of a product for use around residential lawns—a set of handlebars and a small motor fixed to one end of a wooden pole and a string-laced tin can attached to the other. Blackwell bought a stake in Ballas' invention and figured out how to turn his demonstration model into a commercial appliance featuring molded plastic components. Within five years, sales had topped $40 million, and the next year Ballas sold the Weed Eater to Emerson Electric for an undisclosed sum (widely understood to be a fortune).

Blackwell has since transformed product designs into product realities for such clients as renowned cardiac surgeon Michael DeBakey (the first disposable tools for open-heart surgery) and NASA (parts for sensors worn by astronauts on America's first manned spaceflights). Along the

way, it's also produced such smaller-margin products as the screw-pull wine opener, nylon slides for venetian blinds, liners for water coolers, and holders for iPads. Today, Blackwell's top 10 customers are in 10 different industries, and no single client accounts for more than 10 percent of the firm's revenues.

"We don't target" industries or markets, says Applegate. The injection molder's turn to innovate comes when the company buys into the vision of an entrepreneur and takes on the task of turning a concept into a molded-plastic reality. Thus its customer diversity is reflected in the flexibility of its manufacturing machines, which range in size from 20 to 550 tons and have over the years been modified to turn out everything from automotive parts to toothbrushes.

According to Applegate, managerial flexibility is also a good thing to cultivate. "We're a pretty small company," he explains, "and I don't have teams of people to go out and solve problems. So my solution is finding ways to cross disciplines and cross industries to solve problems." In 2009, for example, when "we were at the end of our rope" in seeking the right material for a faceplate on a frozen drink dispenser, Applegate turned to Eastman Chemical, whose new copolymer was being used to produce pitchers that kept drinks chilled without ice and coffee makers that could go in the dishwasher. With a little modification on Blackwell's part, the same resin produced a faceplate that performed at the required heat ranges while resisting chemical and impact damage and magnifying visuals displayed by the dispenser.

*References:* "Most Innovative Industrial Companies for 2013," Manufacturing. Net (January 17, 2014), www.manufacturing.net, on December 14, 2014; Frank Esposito, "Texas Injection Molding Sees Rapid Growth after Recent Sale," *Plastics News* (August 4, 2014), www.plasticsnews.com, on December 16, 2014; Tony Deligio, "Plant Tour: Seven Decades of Custom Molding and Counting," *Plastics Today* (June 9, 2010), www.plasticstoday.com, on December 16, 2014; Rachel Leisemann Immel, "Dream, Build, Create," *IMPO* (August 12, 2013), www.impomag.com, on December 16, 2014; "Jeff Applegate" [video], *Plastics News* (February 27, 2012), www.plasticsnews. com, on December 20, 2014; Rhoda Miel, "Eastman's Tritan Shines at Housewares Show," *Plastics News* (March 30, 2009), www.eastman.com, on December 20, 2014.

context of a large organization. There are three intrapreneurial roles in large organizations.[61] To successfully use intrapreneurship to encourage creativity and innovation, the organization must find one or more individuals to perform these roles.

The *inventor* is the person who actually conceives of and develops the new idea, product, or service by means of the creative process. Because the inventor may lack the expertise or motivation to oversee the transformation of the product or service from an idea into a marketable entity, however, a second role comes into play. A *product champion* is usually a middle manager who learns about the project and becomes committed to it. He or she helps overcome organizational resistance and convinces others to take the innovation seriously. The product champion may have only limited understanding of the technological aspects of the innovation. Nevertheless, product champions are skilled at knowing how the organization works, whose support is needed to push the project forward, and where to go to secure the resources necessary for successful development. A *sponsor* is a top-level manager who approves of and supports a project. This person may fight for the budget needed to develop an idea, overcome arguments against a project, and use organizational politics to ensure the project's survival. With a sponsor in place, the inventor's idea has a much better chance of being successfully developed.

Several firms have embraced intrapreneurship as a way to encourage creativity and innovation. Colgate-Palmolive has created a separate unit, Colgate Venture Company, staffed with intrapreneurs who develop new products. SC Johnson & Son established a $250,000 fund to support new product ideas. Texas Instruments refuses to approve a new innovative project unless it has an acknowledged inventor, champion, and sponsor. Lockheed Martin's Advanced Development Programs, also known as Skunk Works, focuses on innovative aerospace technologies and aircraft.[62]

---

 **Manager's Checklist**

☐ Managers should be knowledgeable about the basic forms of innovation.

☐ Managers should also have a clear understanding of their organization's approach to innovation.

---

# Summary of Learning Outcomes and Key Points

1. Describe the nature of organization change, including forces for change and planned versus reactive change.

   - Organization change is any substantive modification to some part of the organization.
   - Change may be prompted by forces internal or external to the organization.
   - In general, planned change is preferable to reactive change.

2. Discuss the steps in organization change and how to manage resistance to change.

   - The Lewin model provides a general perspective on the steps involved in change.
   - A comprehensive model is usually more effective.
   - People tend to resist change because of uncertainty, threatened self-interests, different perceptions, and feelings of loss.

   - Participation, education and communication, facilitation, and force-field analysis are methods for overcoming this resistance.

3. Identify and describe major areas of organization change and discuss the assumptions, techniques, and effectiveness of organization development.

   - The most common areas of change involve changing organizational structure and design, technology, and people.
   - Business process change is a more massive and comprehensive change.
   - Organization development is concerned with changing attitudes, perceptions, behaviors, and expectations. Its effective use relies on an important set of assumptions.
   - There are conflicting opinions about the effectiveness of several OD techniques.

4. Describe the innovation process, forms of innovation, failure to innovate, and how organizations can promote innovation.

   - The innovation process has six steps: development, application, launch, growth, maturity, and decline.
   - Basic categories of innovation include radical, incremental, technical, managerial, product, and process innovations.

- Despite the importance of innovation, many organizations fail to innovate because they lack the required creative individuals or are committed to too many other creative activities, fail to recognize opportunities, or resist the change that innovation requires.
- Organizations can use a variety of tools to overcome these problems, including the reward system, organizational culture, and intrapreneurship.

# Discussion Questions

## Questions for Review

1. What forces or kinds of events lead to organization change? Identify each force or event as a planned or a reactive change.

2. Compare planned and reactive change. What are the advantages of planned change, as compared to reactive change?

3. In a brief sentence or just a phrase, describe each of the organizational development (OD) techniques.

4. Consider the following list of products. Categorize each along all three dimensions of innovation, if possible (radical versus incremental, technical versus managerial, and product versus process). Explain your answers.

- Teaching college courses by videotaping the instructor and sending the image over the Internet
- The rise in popularity of virtual organizations (discussed in Chapter 11)
- Checking the security of packages on airlines with the type of MRI scanning devices that are common in health care
- A device combining features of a cellphone and a handheld computer with Internet capability
- Robotic arms that can perform surgery that is too precise for a human surgeon's hands
- Hybrid automobiles, which run on both batteries and gasoline
- Using video games to teach soldiers how to plan and execute battles

## Questions for Analysis

5. What are the symptoms that a manager should look for in determining whether an organization needs to change? What are the symptoms that indicate that an organization has been through too much change?

6. Assume that you are the manager of an organization that has a routine way of performing a task and now faces a major change in how it performs that task. Using Lewin's model, tell what steps you would take to implement the change. Using the comprehensive approach, tell what steps you would take. For each step, give specific examples of actions you would take at that step.

7. Think back to a time when a professor announced a change that you, the student, did not want to adopt. What were the reasons for your resistance to change? Was the professor able to overcome your resistance? If so, tell what he or she did. If not, tell what he or she could have done that might have been successful.

## Questions for Application

8. Some people resist change, whereas others welcome it enthusiastically. To deal with the first group, one needs to overcome resistance to change; to deal with the second, one needs to overcome resistance to stability. What advice can you give a manager facing the latter situation?

9. Can a change made in one area of an organization—in technology, for instance—not lead to change in other areas? If you think that change in one area must lead to change in other areas, describe an example of an organization change to illustrate your point. If you think that change can occur in just one area without causing change in other areas, describe an example of an organization change that illustrates your point.

10. Research an innovation change that occurred in a real organization, by either interviewing an employee, reading the business press, or using the Internet. Describe the process by which the innovation was developed. Did the actual process follow the ideal process described in the chapter? Why or why not?

# Building Effective Decision-Making Skills

## Exercise Overview

Decision-making skills include the ability to recognize and define problems or opportunities and then select the proper course of action. This exercise provides a format for analyzing the phases in a decision-making process. As you'll see, the condition prompting the decision can be characterized as either a problem or an opportunity.

## Exercise Task

At the risk of oversimplifying, let's begin by supplementing our discussion of "Force-Field Analysis" on page 375 by dividing the process of change making—both personal and organizational—into three broad phases:

1. *Unfreezing:* Recognizing the need for change—identifying the problem(s) that make change necessary

2. *Changing:* Making the change—designing and implementing a plan for a new way of doing things

3. *Refreezing:* Locking in the change—replacing old attitudes and behaviors with new ones that become just as habitual

### Step 1: Individual Preparation

This step should be done in writing. Think of a change at work or in your personal life that you would like to make. Now develop a plan for making it, using the three phases of the change process:

1. *Unfreezing:* Briefly describe the change and explain why you think it's needed.

2. *Changing:* Decide upon a date on which you intend to initiate the change and a date by which you want to feel that you've accomplished your goal. Describe your plan for making the change.

3. *Refreezing:* Describe your plans for *maintaining* the change.

### Step 2: In-Class Exercise (10–30 minutes)

Your instructor will choose an in-class procedure from among these two options:

- *Option A:* Break the class into three to six groups in which members share their plans and offer suggestions for improvement.

- *Option B:* Break the class into three to six groups in which members share their plans. The group selects its best plan to be shared with the class. Each group shares its best plan with the class.

Your instructor may offer some concluding remarks.

### Step 3: Application (2–4 minutes)

This step should be done in writing. Respond to the following questions:

- What did I learn from this experience?
- How will I use the knowledge that I gained in the future?

You may also want to restate the dates in your original plan.

Adapted from Robert N. Lussier and Christopher F. Achua, *Leadership: Theory, Application, and Skill Development*, 4th ed. (Mason, OH: South-Western Cengage Learning, 2010), pp. 435–438, 448.

# Building Effective Diagnostic Skills

## Exercise Overview

Diagnostic skills, which enable a manager to visualize the most appropriate response to a situation, are especially important during periods of organizational change.

## Exercise Background

You're the general manager of a hotel situated along a beautiful stretch of beach on a tropical island. One of the oldest of six large resorts in the immediate area, your hotel is owned by a group of foreign investors. For several years, it's been operated as a franchise unit of a large international hotel chain, as have all the other hotels on the island.

For the past few years, the hotel's franchisee-owners have been taking most of the profits for themselves and putting relatively little back into the hotel. They've also let you know that their business is not in good financial health and that the revenue from the hotel is being used to offset losses incurred elsewhere. In contrast, most of the other hotels on the island have recently been refurbished, and plans for two brand-new hotels have been announced for the near future.

A team of executives from franchise headquarters has just visited your hotel. They're quite disappointed in the property, particularly because it's failed to keep pace with other resorts on the island. They've informed you that if the property isn't brought up to standards, the franchise agreement, which is up for review in a year, will be revoked. You realize that this move would be a potential disaster because you can ill afford to lose the franchisor's brand name, access to its reservation system, or any other benefits of the franchise arrangement.

Sitting alone in your office, you've identified several seemingly viable courses of action:

1. Convince the franchisee-owners to remodel the hotel. You estimate that it will take $7 million to meet the franchisor's minimum standards and another $8 million to bring the hotel up to the standards of the island's top resort.

2. Convince the franchisor to give you more time and more options for upgrading the facility.

3. Allow the franchise agreement to terminate and try to succeed as an independent hotel.

4. Assume that the hotel will fail and start looking for another job. You have a pretty good reputation, but you're not terribly happy about the possibility of having to accept a lower-level position (say, as an assistant manager) with another firm.

### Exercise Task

Having mulled over your options, do the following:

1. Rank-order your four alternatives in terms of probable success. Make any necessary assumptions.

2. Identify alternatives other than the four that you identified above.

3. Can more than one alternative be pursued simultaneously? Which ones?

4. Develop an overall strategy for trying to save the hotel while protecting your own interests.

# Skill-Building Personal Assessment

## Innovation and Learning Styles

**Introduction:** David Kolb, a professor at Case Western University, has described a learning model that tells about different learning styles. While individuals move through all four activities, most express a preference for either hands-on learning or learning by indirect observation, and most express a preference for either learning about abstract concepts or learning about concrete experience. When these two dimensions are combined, the following learning styles are created.

|  | Active Experimentation | Reflective Observation |
|---|---|---|
| Concrete Experience | Accommodator | Diverger |
| Abstract Conceptualization | Converger | Assimilator |

Individuals with any of these styles can be creative and their learning innovative, although the way they will approach creativity and the contribution they can make to the innovation process differ. If you understand style, you'll be better equipped to participate in innovation.

Rank from 1 to 4
(1 = least like you,
4 = most like you)

1.    a.   I want to try something out first.
      b.   I need to feel personally involved with things.
      c.   I focus on useful practical applications.
      d.   I look for differences and distinctions.

---

Rank from 1 to 4
(1 = least like you,
4 = most like you)

2.   a.   I work mainly by intuition.

b.   I tend to ask myself questions.

c.   I always try to think logically.

d.   I am very result oriented.

---

Rank from 1 to 4
(1 = least like you,
4 = most like you)

3.   a.   I let everything filter through my head and think about it.

b.   I am interested in the here and now.

c.   I mainly have a practical nature.

d.   I am mostly interested in the future.

---

Rank from 1 to 4
(1 = least like you,
4 = most like you)

4.   a.   I consider the facts, and then I act.

b.   I act.

c.   I ponder until I have evaluated every option, and then I act.

d.   I would rather dream or imagine than think about the facts.

---

# Management at Work

## Kodak Fails to Focus on the Big Picture

### "Mama, don't take my Kodachrome away."

—PAUL SIMON

As recently as 1994—just 20 short years ago as of this writing—Eastman Kodak was among the top 20 companies in the *Fortune 500*. In 1996, the renowned manufacturer of photographic film and equipment employed 145,000 workers and enjoyed revenues of more than $13 billion. As of 2005, the workforce had been trimmed to 51,000 but revenues topped $14 billion. By fiscal 2013, Kodak was reporting revenues of $2.5 billion; the workforce had been reduced to 13,000.

What had happened to the onetime corporate giant? Among other things, bankruptcy. Kodak filed for Chapter 11 protection in January 2012, citing "restructuring costs and recessionary forces" and claiming $5.1 billion in assets against $6.8 billion in debts. Since 2004, the company had posted only one full year of profit. Former Kodak executive Larry Matteson says that the company was hit by a perfect storm: "I can't think of another major company in the U.S. that has undergone as tough a transformation as Kodak. When IBM changed," explains Matteson, "its core capabilities remained essentially the same; at Kodak, everything changed, right through research, to marketing, to sales."

So—more to the point—what changed everything and reduced a blue-chip corporation to a shadow of itself in just a couple of decades? Most analysts approach this question by citing the advent of *digital technology*—the capacity to store and process data as computerized bits and bytes rather than as streams of electronic signals loaded onto such physical materials as magnetic tape or silver halide film (known as *analog technology*). The so-called *Digital Revolution*—the widespread transition from analog to digital—took off in the 1980s and 1990s, as cellphones became ubiquitous and the Internet became a fixture in business operations.

According to Harvard's John Kotter, a widely acknowledged authority on organizational change, "Kodak's problem … is that it did not move into the digital world well enough and fast enough." It's pretty much a consensus opinion, but Kotter is careful to add the qualifier "on the surface." Below the surface, suggests Kotter, where Kodak made the business decisions that led to bankruptcy, it's an opinion that needs further investigation. Kodak, for example, pioneered digital technologies throughout the 1970s and 1980s, including innovations in color digital cameras, digital print kiosks, and digital image compression. Kodak, says Bill Fischer, CEO of the private equity firm Manzanita Capital, "played along the entire 'imaging' value chain and was certainly in an excellent position to be intimately familiar with whatever was going on within and around the imaging business."

Unfortunately, says Fischer, top Kodak managers "failed to take advantage of their unique perspective." Fischer concludes that Kodak ultimately succumbed to "creeping disruption by digital imaging." As for Kotter, he argues that Kodak was facing a "technological discontinuities challenge," which occurs when a new technology features "low margins and cannibalizes your high-margin core business." In Kotter's estimation, "Kodak did not take decisive action to combat the inevitable challenges" posed by such technologies.

The challenge can be particularly difficult when the discontinuity comes from an unexpected source. The first "smartphone" was rolled out in 1994 and the first camera-equipped smartphone in 2000. By 2010, smartphone manufacturers were shipping more units (100.9 million) than PC makers (92.1 million). A year later, the iPad 2 hit the market. Says Bill Fischer: "We can suspect that Kodak, while recognizing the impending threat of a digital 'something,' probably did not immediately imagine that it would be a 'telephone' that would ultimately be the most damaging agent of disruption" to its core film- and camera-making businesses.

Some of the company's critics charge that, even on the brink of bankruptcy, Kodak managers failed—or refused—to acknowledge that many of the company's products had been marginalized by digital substitutions. According to George T. Conboy, chairman of Brighton Securities, Kodak "made a big mistake of riding the cash cow—film—to the point that there was simply no more milk coming from it." During the bankruptcy process, for example, Kodak management hoped to sell one of the firm's prized assets—a package of 1,100 digital-imaging patents—for as much as $2.6 billion. Ultimately, the portfolio brought in only $527 million. Says Jay T. Westbrook, a bankruptcy specialist at the University of Texas law school: "What that situation signified—which was part of the problem with the whole business model—is that they thought their technology and their patents were more valuable than they really were. They clung to that belief right until the end."

Kotter agrees with the consensus opinion that Kodak's demise was a result of "strategic decisions either avoided or made poorly." He reminds us, however, that there's still an underlying question to be answered: "*Why* did Kodak managers make the poor strategic decisions they made?" His own answer is fairly simple—on the surface: "The organization," he charges, "overflowed with complacency." In particular, says Kotter, Kodak failed to recognize that digital was a "huge opportunity" only if the company acted with equally "huge urgency." As a matter of fact, Kodak had developed the first electronic photographic camera in 1975, and as of 2005, it was the number-one seller of digital cameras in the U.S. Within two years, however, it had slipped to fourth, and by 2010 it had plummeted to number seven.

Kodak, it seems, was too slow in realizing that in order to make the transition to digital, it would have to give up the comfort of dominance in an analog technology which was facing a rapidly diminishing market. In 1976, for instance, Kodak commanded 90 percent of film sales and 85 percent of camera sales in the U.S. As of 1996, it controlled over two-thirds of global market share in both categories. According to Andrew Salzman, former Kodak VP for worldwide marketing, top managers at the company were well aware that its markets were "being reinvented" but failed to commit themselves to

> *its next generation of revenue drivers. … Kodak had tomes of research on how digital would develop, how the whole notion of image capture, storage, manipulation, and retrieval would reinvent the category. But from a go-to-market point of view, from an organizational prioritization vantage point, it was tethered to the 95 percent of revenue coming from paper and film.*

Or, as Kotter puts it, although "there were people who saw the problem coming," they were "buried in the organization." Says one former executive who was hired in the 1990s to help bring the company into the digital era: "I couldn't get anywhere without running into the consumer product or professional division selling film or paper. Every time I wanted to make a move, they would argue that I was destroying margin and value."

Kodak, concludes Allen Adamson of Landor Associates, a global consultant on branding research and design,

> *was built on a manufacturing mindset, a business model in which you build something, put it in front of consumers, and they come. … Despite an abundance of superior technology, it was this intransigent culture that was among the reasons Kodak failed to move forward. The world is moving so much faster that no matter how strong or powerful your brand name may be, you have to think in terms of revolution, not evolution.*

## Case Questions

1. Explain how—theoretically, anyway—making "change innovations" in each of the following *Areas of Organizational Change* might have helped Kodak ease the severity of both the conditions that led it to bankruptcy and the challenges facing it now that it's emerged from bankruptcy: *changing organization structure and design, changing people and attitudes,* and *changing processes.*

2. Judging from the case, explain how, at one point or another, each of the following reasons for *Failure to Innovate* played a role in the process that brought Kodak to bankruptcy: *lack of resources, failure to recognize opportunities, resistance to change.*

3. You can still buy a digital camera with the Kodak name on it, and you can still print pictures at digital kiosks in your local drugstore. These businesses, however, are no longer owned by Kodak. In addition, Kodak no longer publishes photos online or makes pocket video cameras, camera film, or photographic paper. Having emerged from bankruptcy, Kodak intends to focus on the commercial side of the imaging business, such as packaging labels and graphics and printing solutions to client businesses. It also plans to make components and products that other companies can sell under their own brands.

   In what ways does each of the following *Forms of Innovation* figure to play a role in Kodak's efforts to rebuild itself after bankruptcy: *radical innovations, incremental innovations, technical innovations, product innovations,* and *process innovations?*

4. How about you? How surprised are you to learn how fast a blue-chip corporation with a line of household-name products can collapse? Do you think that we live in times that make such stories as Kodak's more or less likely? In your opinion, what's the most important downside of the demise of a company such as Kodak? What's the most important upside?

## Case References

John Kotter, "Barriers to Change: The Real Reason behind the Kodak Downfall," *Forbes* (May 2, 2012), www.forbes.com, on December 30, 2014; David DiSalvo, "The Fall of Kodak: A Tale of Disruptive Technology and Bad Business," *Forbes* (October 2, 2011), www.forbes.com, on December 30, 2014; Bill Fischer, "There Are No 'Kodak Moments,'" *Forbes* (July 4, 2014), www.forbes.com, on December 29, 2014; Julie Creswell, "Kodak's Fuzzy Future," *New York Times* (May 3, 2013), http://dealbook.nytimes.com, on December 29, 2014; Jim Riley, "Organisational Culture: When Culture Needs to Change," Tutor2u (June 6, 2013), www.tutor2u.net, on December 29, 2014; Andrew Hill, "Kodak—A Victim of Its Own Success," *Financial Times* (April 5, 2012), http://professorjickblog.com, on December 29, 2014; Allen Adamson, "For BlackBerry, For All Brands: Three Lessons Learned from the Demise of Kodak," *Digital Imaging Reporter* (October 2013), www.app.com, on December 29, 2014.

## YOU MAKE THE CALL  Accenturate the Positive

1. In what ways has Gib Bulloch performed all three *intrapreneurial roles—inventor, product champion,* and *sponsor*—in the development of Accenture Development Partnerships (ADP)?

2. Show how ADP is a good example of an *incremental innovation.* Of a *technical innovation.* Of a combination *product* and *process innovation.*

3. In Bulloch's experience, people typically face a "binary choice" when they graduate from college:

   *Either you join a public-sector organization and do good, or you join a business and do well. If it's the latter, you make a great deal of money and then as retirement looms, the desire to "give back" kicks in—the philanthropy gene comes to the fore and you start donating hard-earned cash to so-called good causes. But what if you don't want to wait until you're 60 to do good? What if you feel you have the most to give in your 20s or 30s?*

   *ADP started, says Bulloch, when he and a number of relatively young colleagues "started thinking in terms of a 'hybrid career' that blends all the attractive benefits of training and remuneration found in the private sector with opportunities to apply core skills to social challenges."\**

   How about you? Let's say for the sake of argument that Bulloch's characterization of this decision-making point isn't overly simplified. Do you think that you might find the prospect of a "hybrid career" attractive when you graduate from college? Why or why not? Do you think

\*"Inside-Out Transformation: A Hybrid Business Model for a Converging World," Management Innovation eXchange (May 10, 2012), www.managementexchange.com, on January 2, 2015.

that you might find the prospect more attractive 20 years later, when (with a little luck) you've carved out a "standard" career for yourself? Why or why not?

4. Here's how Bulloch describes people who do what he's done:

> *To operate as a social entrepreneur within an established profit-making organization often requires getting management to treat you, and your definition of success, differently. Not only that, but the job description for the role that you want simply doesn't exist: You have to create your own job. It's not easy*

> *and it takes a degree of chutzpah bordering on the disruptive. Not for nothing are such people sometimes referred to as "troublemakers." But I prefer to call them "changemakers." They're social intrapreneurs.*[†]

Again, what about you? Do you find the prospect of such a professional life appealing? Why or why not? Do you think that you have some of the qualities that probably characterize "social entrepreneurs" as Bulloch describes them? Which qualities would you personally have to focus on and develop further?

[†] "Social Intrapreneurs: The Changemakers Working inside Companies," *The Guardian* (UK) (April 17, 2013), www.theguardian.com, on January 2, 2015.

# Endnotes

1  Gib Bulloch, "Inside-Out Transformation: A Hybrid Business Model for a Converging World," Management Innovation eXchange (May 10, 2012), www.managementexchange.com, on January 2, 2015; "Meet a Private Sector Focal Point: Gib Bulloch, Accenture Development Partnerships," *UN—Business Focal Point Newsletter*, Issue 15 (June 2011), http://business.un.org, on January 2, 2015; Bulloch, Peter Lacy, and Chris Jurgens, *Convergence Economy: International Development in a Converging World* (Accenture, 2011), www.accenture.com, on January 6, 2014; Bulloch, "The Rise of a Fourth Sector Skills Set," *Stanford Social Innovation Review* (November 26, 2014), www.ssireview.org, on January 6, 2015; Cate O'kane, "People + Technology as a Best Investment," *Impact* (March 6, 2014), http://psiimpact.com, on January 8, 2015; Bulloch, "Social Intrapreneurs: The Changemakers Working inside Companies," *The Guardian* (UK) (April 17, 2013), www.theguardian.com, on January 2, 2015.

2  For an excellent review of this area, see Achilles A. Armenakis and Arthur G. Bedeian, "Organizational Change: A Review of Theory and Research in the 1990s," *Journal of Management*, 1999, Vol. 25, No. 3, pp. 293–315. For a more recent review, see Luis L. Martins, "Organizational Change and Development," in Sheldon Zedeck (ed.), *Handbook of Industrial and Organizational Psychology*, Vol. 3: *Maintaining, Expanding, and Contracting the Organization* (Washington, DC: American Psychological Association, 2010), pp. 691–728.

3  For additional insights into how technological change affects other parts of the organization, see P. Robert Duimering, Frank Safayeni, and Lyn Purdy, "Integrated Manufacturing: Redesign the Organization Before Implementing Flexible Technology," *Sloan Management Review*, Summer 1993, pp. 47–56.

4  Joel Cutcher-Gershenfeld, Ellen Ernst Kossek, and Heidi Sandling, "Managing Concurrent Change Initiatives," *Organizational Dynamics*, Winter 1997, pp. 21–38.

5  Michael A. Hitt, "The New Frontier: Transformation of Management for the New Millennium," *Organizational Dynamics*, Winter 2000, pp. 7–15. See also Michael Beer and Nitin Nohria, "Cracking the Code of Change," *Harvard Business Review*, May–June 2000, pp. 123–144; Clark Gilbert, "The Disruption Opportunity," *MIT Sloan Management Review*, Summer 2003, pp. 27–32.

6  See Warren Boeker, "Strategic Change: The Influence of Managerial Characteristics and Organizational Growth," *Academy of Management Journal*, 1997, Vol. 40, No. 1, pp. 152–170.

7  http://www.bloomberg.com/bw/management/how-to-change-and-stay-the-same-01272012.html

8  Alan L. Frohman, "Igniting Organizational Change from Below: The Power of Personal Initiative," *Organizational Dynamics*, Winter 1997, pp. 39–53.

9  Nandini Rajagopalan and Gretchen M. Spreitzer, "Toward a Theory of Strategic Change: A Multi-Lens Perspective and Integrative Framework," *Academy of Management Review*, 1997, Vol. 22, No. 1, pp. 48–79.

10  Anne Fisher, "Danger Zone," *Fortune*, September 8, 1997, pp. 165–167.

11  "Kodak to Cut Staff up to 21% amid Digital Push," *Wall Street Journal*, January 22, 2005, pp. A1, A7.

12  John P. Kotter and Leonard A. Schlesinger, "Choosing Strategies for Change," *Harvard Business Review*, March–April 1979, p. 106.

13  Clayton M. Christensen and Michael Overdorf, "Meeting the Challenge of Disruptive Change," *Harvard Business Review*, March–April 2000, pp. 67–77.

14  "To Maintain Success, Managers Must Learn How to Direct Change," *Wall Street Journal*, August 12, 2002, p. B1. See also Andrew Van de Ven and Kangyong Sun, "Breakdowns in Implementing Models of Organization Change," *Academy of Management Perspectives*, August 2011, pp. 58–68.

15  See Eric Abrahamson, "Change Without Pain," *Harvard Business Review*, July–August 2000, pp. 75–85. See also Gib Akin and Ian Palmer, "Putting Metaphors to Work for Change in Organizations," *Organizational Dynamics*, Winter 2000, pp. 67–76.

16  Erik Brynjolfsson, Amy Austin Renshaw, and Marshall Van Alstyne, "The Matrix of Change," *Sloan Management Review*, Winter 1997, pp. 37–54.

17  Kurt Lewin, "Frontiers in Group Dynamics: Concept, Method, and Reality in Social Science," *Human Relations*, June 1947, pp. 5–41.

18  Michael Roberto and Lynne Levesque, "The Art of Making Change Initiatives Stick," *MIT Sloan Management Review*, Summer 2005, pp. 53–62.

19  "Time for a Turnaround," *Fast Company*, January 2003, pp. 55–61.

20  See Connie J. G. Gersick, "Revolutionary Change Theories: A Multilevel Exploration of the Punctuated Equilibrium Paradigm," *Academy of Management Review*, January 1991, pp. 10–36; see also John P. Kotter and Leonard A. Schlesinger, "Choosing Strategies for Change," *Harvard Business Review*, July–August 2008, pp. 120–141.

21  See Mel Fugate, Angelo J. Kinicki, and Gregory E. Prussia, "Employee Coping with Organizational Change: An Examination of Alternative Theoretical Perspectives and Models," *Personnel Psychology*, 2008, Vol. 61, pp. 1–36. See also Jeffrey D. Ford and Laurie W. Ford, "Decoding Resistance to Change," *Harvard Business Review*, April 2009, pp. 99–104.

22  See Clark Gilbert and Joseph Bower, "Disruptive Change," *Harvard Business Review*, May 2002, pp. 95–104.

23  "RJR Employees Fight Distraction amid Buy-Out Talks," *Wall Street Journal*, November 1, 1988, p. A8.

24  "Flight Chaos Looms as BA Staff Vow to Strike," *Sydney Morning Herald*, December 16, 2010.

25  Arnon E. Reichers, John P. Wanous, and James T. Austin, "Understanding and Managing Cynicism about Organizational Change," *Academy of Management Executive*, February 1997, pp. 48–59.

26  For a classic discussion, see Paul R. Lawrence, "How to Deal with Resistance to Change," *Harvard Business Review*, January–February 1969, pp. 4–12, 166–176; for a more recent discussion, see Jeffrey D. Ford, Laurie W. Ford, and Angelo D'Amelio, "Resistance to Change: The Rest of the Story," *Academy of Management Review*, 2008, Vol. 33, No. 2, pp. 362–377.

27  Lester Coch and John R. P. French, Jr., "Overcoming Resistance to Change," *Human Relations*, August 1948, pp. 512–532.

28  "9 Keys to Driving Cultural Change," *Business Insider*, April 19, 2011.

29  Benjamin Schneider, Arthur P. Brief, and Richard A. Guzzo, "Creating a Climate and Culture for Sustainable Organizational Change," *Organizational Dynamics*, Spring 1996, pp. 7–19.

30  "Troubled GM Plans Major Tuneup," *USA Today*, June 6, 2005, pp. 1B, 2B.

31  Paul Bate, Raza Khan, and Annie Pye, "Towards a Culturally Sensitive Approach to Organization Structuring: Where Organization Design Meets Organization Development," *Organization Science*, March–April 2000, pp. 197–211.

32 David Kirkpatrick, "The New Player," *Fortune*, April 17, 2000, pp. 162–168.

33 Jeffrey A. Alexander, "Adaptive Change in Corporate Control Practices," *Academy of Management Journal*, March 1991, pp. 162–193.

34 "Microsoft to Boost Cash Pay for Employees," *Wall Street Journal*, April 22, 2011.

35 "CIO Innovator on Creative Destruction: Getting Out of the Comfort Zone," *SearchCIO.com*, April 21, 2011.

36 Gerd Bohner and Nina Dickel, "Attitudes and Attitude Change," in Susan T. Fiske, Daniel L. Schacter, and Shelley Taylor (eds.), *Annual Review of Psychology 2011* (Palo Alto, CA: Annual Reviews, 2011), pp. 391–418.

37 Thomas A. Stewart, "Reengineering—The Hot New Managing Tool," *Fortune*, August 23, 1993, pp. 41–48.

38 "Old Company Learns New Tricks," *USA Today*, April 10, 2000, pp. 1B, 2B.

39 "10 Practices of Fortune's 2010 Top 10 Business People," *Brian Dodd on Leadership*, December 25, 2010; see also "How Netflix Reinvented Itself," Forbes.com, accessed June 3, 2015.

40 Paul Nunes and Tim Breen, "Reinvent Your Business Before It's Too Late," *Harvard Business Review*, January–February 2011, pp. 80–87.

41 Richard Beckhard, *Organization Development: Strategies and Models* (Reading, MA: Addison-Wesley, 1969), p. 9.

42 W. Warner Burke, "The New Agenda for Organization Development," *Organizational Dynamics*, Summer 1997, pp. 7–20.

43 Wendell L. French and Cecil H. Bell, Jr., *Organization Development: Behavioral Science Interventions for Organization Improvement*, 2nd ed. (Englewood Cliffs, NJ: Prentice-Hall, 1978).

44 "Memo to the Team: This Needs Salt!" *Wall Street Journal*, April 4, 2000, pp. B1, B14.

45 Raymond A. Noe, Michael J. Tews, and Alison McConnell Dachner, "Learner Engagement: A New Perspective for Enhancing Our Understanding of Learner Motivation and Workplace Learning," in James P. Walsh and Arthur P. Brief (eds.), *The Academy of Management Annals 2010* (Philadelphia: Taylor and Francis, 2010), pp. 279–316.

46 Roger J. Hower, Mark G. Mindell, and Donna L. Simmons, "Introducing Innovation Through OD," *Management Review*, February 1978, pp. 52–56.

47 "Is Organization Development Catching On? A Personnel Symposium," *Personnel*, November–December 1977, pp. 10–22.

48 For a recent discussion on the effectiveness of various OD techniques in different organizations, see John M. Nicholas, "The Comparative Impact of Organization Development Interventions on Hard Criteria Measures," *Academy of Management Review*, October 1982, pp. 531–542.

49 Constantinos Markides, "Strategic Innovation," *Sloan Management Review*, Spring 1997, pp. 9–24. See also James Brian Quinn, "Outsourcing Innovation: The New Engine of Growth," *Sloan Management Review*, Summer 2000, pp. 12–21.

50 L. B. Mohr, "Determinants of Innovation in Organizations," *American Political Science Review*, 1969, pp. 111–126; G. A. Steiner, *The Creative Organization* (Chicago: University of Chicago Press, 1965); R. Duncan and A. Weiss, "Organizational Learning: Implications for Organizational Design," in B. M. Staw (ed.), *Research in Organizational Behavior*, Vol. 1 (Greenwich, CT: JAI Press, 1979), pp. 75–123; J. E. Ettlie, "Adequacy of Stage Models for Decisions on Adoption of Innovation," *Psychological Reports*, 1980, pp. 991–995.

51 See Alan Patz, "Managing Innovation in High Technology Industries," *New Management*, September 1986, pp. 54–59.

52 "Apple Can't Keep Up with Demand for Newest iMac," *USA Today*, August 26, 2002, p. 3B.

53 See Willow A. Sheremata, "Centrifugal and Centripetal Forces in Radical New Product Development under Time Pressure," *Academy of Management Review*, 2000, Vol. 25, No. 2, pp. 389–408. See also Richard Leifer, Gina Colarelli O'Connor, and Mark Rice, "Implementing Radical Innovation in Mature Firms: The Role of Hobs," *Academy of Management Executive*, 2001, Vol. 15, No. 3, pp. 102–112.

54 See Julian Birkinshaw, Gary Hamel, and Michael J. Mol, "Management Innovation," *Academy of Management Review*, 2008, Vol. 33, No. 4, pp. 825–845.

55 See "Amid Japan's Gloom, Corporate Overhauls Offer Hints of Revival," *Wall Street Journal*, February 21, 2002, pp. A1, A11.

56 See Clayton M. Christensen, Stephen P. Kaufman, and Willy C. Shih, "Innovation Killers," *Harvard Business Review*, January 2008, pp. 98–107.

57 Dorothy Leonard and Jeffrey F. Rayport, "Spark Innovation Through Empathic Design," *Harvard Business Review*, November–December 1997, pp. 102–115.

58 http://www.huffingtonpost.com/tom-lowery/how-to-leap-from-employee_b_4138577.html

59 "The 25 Most Innovative Companies," *Bloomberg BusinessWeek*, April 20–April 27, 2015, pp. 46–47.

60 Geoffrey Moore, "Innovating Within Established Enterprises," *Harvard Business Review*, July–August 2004, pp. 87–96. See also David A. Garvin and Lynne C. Levesque, "Meeting the Challenge of Corporate Entrepreneurship," *Harvard Business Review*, October 2006, pp. 102–112.

61 See Gifford Pinchot III, *Intrapreneuring* (New York: Harper & Row, 1985).

62 "What Is Intrapreneurship?" *Entrepreneurship*, June 3, 2009.

©Markus Pfaff/Shutterstock.com

# 13

# MANAGING HUMAN RESOURCES IN ORGANIZATIONS

**After studying this chapter, you should be able to:**

1. Describe the environmental context of human resource management, including its strategic importance and its relationship with legal and social factors.

2. Discuss how organizations attract human resources, including human resource planning, recruiting, and selection.

3. Describe how organizations develop human resources, including training and development, performance appraisal, and performance feedback.

4. Discuss how organizations maintain human resources, including the determination of compensation and benefits and career planning.

5. Discuss labor relations, including how employees form unions and the mechanics of collective bargaining.

6. Describe the key issues associated with managing knowledge and contingent and temporary workers.

## MANAGEMENT IN ACTION    Elementary, Watson

"Twenty years from now, labor demand for lots of skill sets will be substantially lower. I don't think people have that in their mental model"

—MICROSOFT FOUNDER BILL GATES

In January 2012, Geoff Colvin, a longtime editor at *Fortune* magazine and a respected commentator on economics and infotech, agreed to play a special game of *Jeopardy*. The occasion was the annual convention of the National Retail Federation in New York, and Colvin's opponents were a woman named Vicki and an empty podium with the name tag "Watson." Watson's sponsors at IBM wanted to show retailers how smart Watson is. "I wasn't expecting this to go well," recalls Colvin, who knew that Watson had already defeated *Jeopardy*'s two greatest champions. As it turned out, it was even worse than he had expected. "I don't remember the score," says Colvin, "but at the end of our one round I had been shellacked."[1]

Obviously, Watson isn't your average *Jeopardy* savant. It's a *cognitive computing system* that can handle complex problems in which there is ambiguity and uncertainty and draw inferences from data in a way that mimics the human brain. In short, it can deal with the kinds of problems faced by real people. Watson, explains Colvin, "is not connected to the Internet. It's a freestanding machine just like me, relying only on what it knows. … So let's confront reality: Watson is smarter than I am."

Watson is also smarter than anyone who's ever been on *Jeopardy*, but it's not going to replace human game show contestants any time soon. Watson, however, has quite an impressive skill set beyond its game-playing prowess. For example, it has a lot to offer medical science. At the University of Texas, Watson is employed by the M.D. Anderson Cancer Center's "Moon Shots" program, whose stated goal is the elimination of cancer. This version of Watson, says John Kelly, who oversees the development of IBM's micro-electronics technologies, including Watson, is already "dramatically faster" than the one that was introduced

IBM's Watson is a cognitive computing system that can mimic human thought processes. Watson has participated in several versions of the popular game show *Jeopardy* against a variety of highly regarded opponents and defeated them all. Effectively integrating cognitive computing systems like Watson into the workplace will pose an interesting and compelling challenge for human resource managers in the future.

Ben Hider/Getty Images

on *Jeopardy* back in February 2011 (about three times as fast).

Already, reports Kelly, "Watson has ingested a large portion of the world's medical information," and it's currently "in the final stages of learning the details of cancer." Then what? "Then Watson has to be trained," explains Kelly. Here's how it works:

> *Watson is presented with complex healthcare problems where the treatment and outcome are known. So you literally have Watson try to the best diagnosis or therapy. And then you look to see whether that was the proper outcome. You do this several times, and* the learning engines in Watson begin to make connections between pieces of information. *The system learns patterns, it learns outcomes, it learns what sources to trust (emphasis added).*

Working with Watson, doctors at the Anderson Center, who are especially interested in leukemia, have made significant headway in their efforts to understand and treat the disease. Watson's role in this process has been twofold:

1. *Expanding capacity:* It helps to make sense out of so-called *big data*—the mountain of text, images, and statistics which, according to Kelly, "is so large that traditional databases and query systems can't deal with it." Moreover, says Kelley, big data is "unstructured" and flows "at incredible speeds. … With big data, we're not always looking for precise answers; we're looking for information that will help us make decisions."

2. *Increasing speed:* Kelley also points out that "Watson can do in seconds what would take people years." The system can, for example, process 500 GB of information—the equivalent of a million books—per second. When it comes to making sense out of the enormous amount of data concerning the genetic factors in cancer, says Kelly, "Watson is like big data on steroids."

Clearly, however, Watson is not replacing "knowledge workers" (doctors) at the Anderson Center. Rather, it's being used to facilitate their knowledge work. In this respect, argues Thomas H. Davenport, a widely recognized specialist in knowledge management, Watson is confirming "one of the great clichés of cognitive business technology—that it should be used not to replace knowledge workers, but rather to augment them." On the one hand, even Davenport admits

that some jobs have been lost to cognitive technology. In the field of financial services, for instance, "many lower-level" decision makers—loan and insurance-policy originators, credit-fraud detectors—have been replaced by automated systems. At the same time, however, Davenport observes that "experts" typically retain the jobs that call for "reviewing and refining the rules and algorithms [generated by] automated decision systems."

Likewise, human data analysts can create only a few statistical models per week, while machines can churn out a couple of thousand. Even so, observes Davenport, "there are still hundreds of thousands of jobs open for quantitative analysts and big data specialists." Why? "Even though machine learning systems can do a lot of the grunt work," suggests Davenport, "data modeling is complex enough that humans still have to train the systems in the first place and check on them occasionally to see if they're making sense."

Colvin, however, isn't sure that these trends will hold true for much longer. Two years after he competed against Watson, Colvin reported that "Watson is [now] 240 percent faster. I am not." He adds that by 2034—when Watson will probably be an antiquated curiosity—its successors will be another 32 times more powerful. "For over two centuries," says Colvin, "practically every advance in technology has sparked worries that it would destroy jobs, and it did. … But it also created even more new jobs, and the improved technology made those jobs more productive and higher paying. … Technology has lifted living standards spectacularly."

Today, however, Colvin is among many experts who question the assumption that the newest generations of technologies will conform to the same pattern. "Until a few years ago," acknowledges former Treasury Secretary Larry Summers, "I didn't think [technological job loss] was a very complicated subject. I'm not so completely certain now." Microsoft founder Bill Gates, on the other hand, is not quite so ambivalent: "Twenty years from now," predicts Gates, "labor demand for lots of skill sets will be substantially lower. I don't think people have that in their mental model."

According to Colvin, today's technology already reflects a different pattern in job displacement: It's "advancing steadily into both ends of the spectrum" occupied by knowledge workers, replacing both low- and high-level positions and "threatening workers who thought they didn't have to worry." Take lawyers, for instance. In the legal-discovery process of gathering information for a trial, computers are already performing the document-sorting process that can otherwise require small armies of attorneys. They can scan legal literature for precedents much more thoroughly and will soon be able to identify relevant matters of law without human help. Before long, says Colvin, they "will move nearer to the heart of what lawyers do" by offering better advice on such critical decisions as whether to sue or settle or go to trial.

So what appears to be the long-term fate of high-end knowledge workers? Davenport thinks that the picture is "still unclear," but he suggests that, in order to be on the safe side, would-be knowledge workers should consider reversing the cliché about technology as a means of augmenting human activity: "If there is any overall lesson" to be learned from current trends, "it is to make sure you are capable of augmenting an automated system. If the decisions and actions that you make at work are remarkably similar to those made by a computer, that computer will probably be taking your paycheck before long."

This chapter is about how organizations manage the people who comprise them. But as our opening story vividly illustrates, the kinds of jobs people have and how they perform those jobs continues to change rapidly. It is critical, therefore, that managers understand the jobs in their organizations, who is available to perform those jobs, and how both jobs and workers will change in the future. The set of processes by which companies manage their people is called "human resource management," or HRM. We start by describing the environmental context of HRM. We then discuss how organizations attract human resources. Next we describe how organizations seek to further develop the capacities of their human resources. We also examine how high-quality human resources are maintained by organizations. We conclude by discussing labor relations.

# The Environmental Context of Human Resource Management

Human resource management (HRM) is the set of organizational activities directed at attracting, developing, and maintaining an effective workforce.[2] Human resource management takes place within a complex and ever-changing environmental context. Three particularly vital components of this context are HRM's strategic importance and the legal and social environments of HRM.

## The Strategic Importance of HRM

Human resources—the people who comprise an organization—are critical for both effectiveness and competitiveness. HRM (or "personnel," as it is sometimes called) was once relegated to second-class status in many organizations, but its importance has grown dramatically in the last several years. Its growing importance stems from increased legal complexities, the recognition that human resources are a valuable means for improving productivity, and the increased awareness of the costs associated with poor human resource management.[3] For example, Microsoft announced that it was laying off 5,000 people in parts of its business expected to shrink. At the same time, though, the firm also announced plans for hiring highly talented people in parts of its business targeted as important growth areas for the company.[4] This careful and systematic approach, reducing human resources in areas where they are no longer needed and adding new human resources to key growth areas, reflects a strategic approach to human resource management.

**human resource management (HRM)**
The set of organizational activities directed at attracting, developing, and maintaining an effective workforce

Indeed, managers now realize that the effectiveness of their HR function has a substantial impact on the bottom-line performance of the firm. Poor human resource planning can result in spurts of hiring followed by layoffs—costly in terms of unemployment compensation payments, training expenses, and morale. Haphazard compensation systems do not attract, keep, and motivate good employees, and outmoded recruitment practices can expose the firm to expensive and embarrassing discrimination lawsuits. Consequently, the chief human resource executive of most large businesses is a vice president directly accountable to the CEO, and many firms are developing strategic HR plans and integrating those plans with other strategic planning activities.[5]

Even organizations with as few as 200 employees usually have a human resource manager and a human resource department charged with overseeing these activities. Responsibility for HR activities, however, is shared between the HR department and line managers. The HR department may recruit and initially screen candidates, but the final selection is usually made by managers in the department where the new employee will work. Similarly, although the HR department may establish performance appraisal policies and procedures, the actual evaluation and coaching of employees is done by their immediate superiors.

The growing awareness of the strategic significance of human resource management has even led to new terminology to reflect a firm's commitment to people. Human capital reflects the organization's investment in attracting, retaining, and motivating an effective workforce. Hence, just as the phrase *financial capital* is an indicator of a firm's financial resources and reserves, so, too, does *human capital* serve as a tangible indicator of the value of the people who comprise an organization.[6] *Talent management* is also a term that is growing in popularity.

Human Resource functions have an enormous impact on most aspects of an organization. Ineffective human resource management can lead to high rates of employee turnover, layoffs, and reduced revenue and profits.

Nattapol Sritongcom/Shutterstock.com

"Most HR people derive their influence through knowledge of rules and regulations. Our power comes from influence, from the roles we play in helping the business succeed."

—ALLISON HOPKINS, VP OF HUMAN RESOURCES, NETFLIX[7]

## The Legal Environment of HRM

A number of laws regulate various aspects of employee–employer relations, especially in the areas of equal employment opportunity, compensation and benefits, labor relations, and occupational safety and health. Several major ones are summarized in Table 13.1.

**Equal Employment Opportunity** Title VII of the Civil Rights Act of 1964 forbids discrimination in all areas of the employment relationship. The intent of Title VII is to ensure that employment decisions are made on the basis of a person's qualifications rather than on the basis of personal biases. The law has reduced direct forms of discrimination (refusing to promote African Americans into management, failing to hire men as flight attendants, refusing to hire women as construction workers) as well as indirect forms of discrimination (using employment tests that whites pass at a higher rate than African Americans).

**human capital**
Reflects the organization's investment in attracting, retaining, and motivating an effective workforce

**Title VII of the Civil Rights Act of 1964**
Forbids discrimination on the basis of sex, race, color, religion, or national origin in all areas of the employment relationship

**adverse impact**
When minority group members pass a selection standard at a rate less than 80 percent of the pass rate of majority group members

---

## TABLE 13.1   THE LEGAL ENVIRONMENT OF HUMAN RESOURCE MANAGEMENT

As much as any area of management, HRM is subject to wide-ranging laws and court decisions. These laws and decisions affect the human resource function in many areas. For example, AT&T was once fined several million dollars for violating Title VII of the Civil Rights Act of 1964.

### Equal Employment Opportunity

*Title VII of the Civil Rights Act of 1964 (as amended by the Equal Employment Opportunity Act of 1972).* Forbids discrimination in all areas of the employment relationship.

*Age Discrimination in Employment Act.* Outlaws discrimination against people older than 40 years.

*Various executive orders, especially Executive Order 11246 in 1965.* Requires employers with government contracts to engage in affirmative action.

*Pregnancy Discrimination Act.* Specifically outlaws discrimination on the basis of pregnancy.

*Vietnam Era Veterans Readjustment Assistance Act.* Extends affirmative action mandate to military veterans who served during the Vietnam War.

*Americans with Disabilities Act.* Specifically outlaws discrimination against disabled persons.

*Civil Rights Act of 1991.* Makes it easier for employees to sue an organization for discrimination but limits punitive damage awards if they win.

### Compensation and Benefits

*Fair Labor Standards Act.* Establishes minimum wage and mandated overtime pay for work in excess of 40 hours per week.

*Equal Pay Act of 1963.* Requires that men and women be paid the same amount for doing the same job.

*Employee Retirement Income Security Act of 1974 (ERISA).* Regulates how organizations manage their pension funds.

*Family and Medical Leave Act of 1993.* Requires employers to provide up to 12 weeks of unpaid leave for family and medical emergencies.

### Labor Relations

*National Labor Relations Act.* Spells out procedures by which employees can establish labor unions and requires organizations to bargain collectively with legally formed unions; also known as the Wagner Act.

*Labor-Management Relations Act.* Limits union power and specifies management rights during a union-organizing campaign; also known as the Taft-Hartley Act.

### Health and Safety

*Occupational Safety and Health Act of 1970 (OSHA).* Mandates the provision of safe working conditions.

---

**Equal Employment Opportunity Commission**
Federal agency charged with enforcing Title VII of the Civil Rights Act of 1964

**Age Discrimination in Employment Act**
Outlaws discrimination against people older than 40 years; passed in 1967, amended in 1978 and 1986

Employment requirements such as test scores and other qualifications are legally defined as having an adverse impact on minorities and women when such individuals meet or pass the requirement at a rate less than 80 percent of the rate of majority group members. Criteria that have an adverse impact on protected groups can be used only when there is solid evidence that they effectively identify those who are better able than others to do the job. The Equal Employment Opportunity Commission is charged with enforcing Title VII as well as several other employment-related laws.

The Age Discrimination in Employment Act, passed in 1967, amended in 1978, and amended again in 1986, is an attempt to prevent organizations from discriminating against older workers. In its current form, it outlaws discrimination against people older than 40 years. Both the Age Discrimination in Employment Act and Title VII require passive nondiscrimination, or equal employment opportunity. Employers are not required to seek out and hire minorities, but they must treat all who apply fairly.

Several executive orders, however, require that employers holding government contracts engage in affirmative action—intentionally seeking and hiring employees from groups that are underrepresented in the organization. These organizations must have a written affirmative action plan that spells out employment goals for underutilized groups and how those goals will be met. These employers are also required to act affirmatively in hiring Vietnam-era veterans (as a result of the Vietnam Era Veterans Readjustment Assistance Act) and qualified handicapped individuals. Finally, the Pregnancy Discrimination Act forbids discrimination against women who are pregnant.

In 1990 Congress passed the Americans with Disabilities Act, which forbids discrimination on the basis of disabilities and requires employers to provide reasonable accommodations for disabled employees.

Contrary to popular belief, discrimination *per se* is not illegal. Businesses routinely discriminate on the basis of performance, experience, education, seniority, and other job-related criteria. That is, they hire a person with more experience rather than someone with less experience or give a salary increase to high performers but not low performers. However, several laws and executive orders make it illegal to discriminate on the basis of non-job-related criteria such as sex, race, color, religion, or national origin.

More recently, the Civil Rights Act of 1991 amended the original Civil Rights Act as well as other related laws by both making it easier to bring discrimination lawsuits (which partially explains the aforementioned backlog of cases) and simultaneously limiting the amount of punitive damages that can be awarded in those lawsuits.

**Compensation and Benefits** Laws also regulate compensation and benefits. The Fair Labor Standards Act, passed in 1938 and amended frequently since then, sets a minimum wage and requires the payment of overtime rates for work in excess of 40 hours per week. Salaried professional, executive, and administrative employees are exempt from the minimum hourly wage and overtime provisions. The Equal Pay Act of 1963 requires that men and women be paid the same amount for doing the same job. Attempts to circumvent the law by having different job titles and pay rates for men and women who perform the same work are also illegal. Basing an employee's pay on seniority or performance is legal, however, even if it means that a man and woman are paid different amounts for doing the same job.

The provision of benefits is also regulated in some ways by state and federal laws. Certain benefits are mandatory—for example, workers' compensation insurance for employees who are injured on the job. Employers who provide a pension plan for their employees are regulated by the Employee Retirement Income Security Act of 1974 (ERISA). The purpose of this act is to help ensure the financial security of pension funds by regulating how they can be invested. The Family and Medical Leave Act of 1993 requires employers to provide up to 12 weeks of unpaid leave for family and medical emergencies.

In the last few years some large employers, most notably Walmart, have come under fire because they do not provide healthcare for all of their employees. In response to this, the state of Maryland passed a law, informally called the "Walmart bill," that requires employers with more than 10,000 workers to spend at least 8 percent of their payrolls on healthcare or else pay a comparable amount into a general fund for uninsured workers.

**affirmative action**
Intentionally seeking and hiring qualified or qualifiable employees from racial, sexual, and ethnic groups that are underrepresented in the organization

**Americans with Disabilities Act**
Prohibits discrimination against people with disabilities

**Civil Rights Act of 1991**
Amends the original Civil Rights Act, making it easier to bring discrimination lawsuits while also limiting punitive damages

**Fair Labor Standards Act**
Sets a minimum wage and requires overtime pay for work in excess of 40 hours per week; passed in 1938 and amended frequently since then

**Equal Pay Act of 1963**
Requires that men and women be paid the same amount for doing the same job

**Employee Retirement Income Security Act of 1974 (ERISA)**
Regulates how organizations manage their pension funds

Lisa S./Shutterstock.com

This employee heads her company's labor union. This firm provides security services for a major city's railway system. As such, it falls under the National Emergency Strike provision, as part of the Tart-Hartley Act.

**Labor Relations** Union activities and management's behavior toward unions constitute another heavily regulated area. The National Labor Relations Act (also known as the Wagner Act), passed in 1935, sets up a procedure for employees to vote on whether to have a union. If they vote for a union, management is required to bargain collectively with the union. The National Labor Relations Board (NLRB) was established by the Wagner Act to enforce its provisions. Following a series of severe strikes in 1946, the Labor-Management Relations Act (also known as the Taft-Hartley Act) was passed in 1947 to limit union power. The law increases management's rights during an organizing campaign. The Taft-Hartley Act also contains the National Emergency Strike provision, which allows the president of the United States to prevent or end a strike that endangers national security. Taken together, these laws balance union and management power. Employees can be represented by a legally created and managed union, but the business can make nonemployee-related business decisions without interference.

**Health and Safety** The Occupational Safety and Health Act of 1970 (OSHA) directly mandates the provision of safe working conditions. It requires that employers (1) provide a place of employment that is free from hazards that may cause death or serious physical harm and (2) obey the safety and health standards established by the Department of Labor. Safety standards are intended to prevent accidents, whereas occupational health standards are concerned with preventing occupational disease. For example, standards limit the concentration of cotton dust in the air because this contaminant has been associated with lung disease in textile workers. The standards are enforced by OSHA inspections, which are conducted when an employee files a complaint of unsafe conditions or when a serious accident occurs.

Spot inspections of plants in especially hazardous industries such as mining and chemicals are also made. Employers who fail to meet OSHA standards may be fined. A Miami-based company, Lead Enterprises Inc., was cited by OSHA as knowingly failing to protect employees from lead exposure despite knowing the potential hazards (brain damage, kidney disease, and reproductive system damage). The company, which produces various lead products, including fish tackles and lead diving weights, was cited for 32 safety and health violations after multiple inspections and fined more than $307,000 in penalties.[8]

**Emerging Legal Issues** Several other areas of legal concern have emerged during the past few years. One is sexual harassment. Although sexual harassment is forbidden under Title VII, it has received additional attention in the courts recently, as more and more victims have decided to publicly confront the problem. Another emerging human resource management issue is alcohol and drug abuse. Both alcoholism and drug dependence are major problems today. Recent court rulings have tended to define alcoholics and drug addicts as disabled, protecting them under the same laws that protect other handicapped people. AIDS is an important legal issue as well. AIDS victims, too, are most often protected

**Family and Medical Leave Act of 1993**
Requires employers to provide up to 12 weeks of unpaid leave for family and medical emergencies

**National Labor Relations Act**
Passed in 1935 to set up procedures for employees to vote on whether to have a union; also known as the Wagner Act

**National Labor Relations Board (NLRB)**
Established by the Wagner Act to enforce its provisions

**Labor-Management Relations Act**
Passed in 1947 to limit union power; also known as the Taft-Hartley Act

**Occupational Safety and Health Act of 1970 (OSHA)**
Directly mandates the provision of safe working conditions

under various laws protecting the disabled. Finally, employee privacy is also becoming a controversial issue in the HR arena. For instance, can employers refuse to hire an otherwise qualified applicant because of information that person posts on social networking sites?

## Social Change and HRM

Beyond the objective legal context of HRM, various social changes are also affecting how organizations interact with their employees. First, many organizations are using more and more temporary workers today. This trend, discussed more fully later, allows them to add workers as necessary without the risk that they may have to eliminate their jobs in the future. Second, dual-career families are much more common today than just a few years ago. Organizations are finding that they must make accommodations for employees who are dual-career partners. These accommodations may include delaying transfers, offering employment to the spouses of current employees to retain them, and providing more flexible work schedules and benefits packages.

The Occupational Safety and Health Act (OSHA), passed in 1970, mandates that organizations provide their employees with a workplace that is free from hazards, provide necessary safety equipment, and follow guidelines to minimize potential occupational diseases. This worker, for instance, is using several forms of safety equipment while performing a potentially hazardous job. All of this equipment meets OSHA requirements.

Employment-at-will is also becoming an important issue. Although employment-at-will has legal implications, its emergence as an issue is socially driven. Employment-at-will is a traditional view of the workplace that says organizations can fire an employee for any reason. Increasingly, however, people are arguing that organizations should be able to fire only people who are poor performers or who violate rules and, conversely, should not be able to fire people who report safety violations to OSHA or refuse to perform unethical activities. Several court cases in recent years have upheld this view and have limited many organizations' ability to terminate employees to those cases where there is clear and just cause or there is an organization-wide cutback. Further, in the wake of massive layoffs during the recession that began in 2008, several ex-workers sued their former employers, citing alleged violations of various severance laws.[9]

**employment-at-will**
A traditional view of the workplace that says organizations can fire their employees for whatever reason they want; recent court judgments are limiting employment-at-will

---

☐ Managers need a clear understanding of the strategic role human resource management plays in their organization.

☐ All managers should be able to identify and briefly summarize the key laws that affect human resource management.

☐ To the extent that you are involved in human resource management activities, such as interviewing potential new employees, you should be very familiar with laws and regulations that affect those activities.

**Manager's Checklist** ✓

# Attracting Human Resources

With an understanding of the environmental context of human resource management as a foundation, we are now ready to address its first substantive concern—attracting qualified people who are interested in employment with the organization.

> "We are in the midst of a major structural shift in manufacturing.... The number of good-paying, middle-class jobs that have been the bulk of manufacturing is likely going to be less in the future."
>
> —HARLEY SHAIKEN, PROFESSOR OF LABOR RELATIONS, UNIVERSITY OF CALIFORNIA, BERKELEY[10]

## Human Resource Planning

The starting point in attracting qualified human resources is planning. HR planning, in turn, involves job analysis and forecasting the demand and supply of labor.

**Job Analysis** Job analysis is a systematic analysis of jobs within an organization. A job analysis is made up of two parts. The job description lists the duties of a job, the job's working conditions, and the tools, materials, and equipment used to perform it. The job specification lists the skills, abilities, and other credentials needed to do the job. Job analysis information is used in many human resource activities. For instance, knowing about job content and job requirements is necessary to develop appropriate selection methods and job-relevant performance appraisal systems and to set equitable compensation rates.

**Forecasting Human Resource Demand and Supply** After managers fully understand the jobs to be performed within the organization, they can start planning for the organization's future human resource needs. Figure 13.1 summarizes the steps most often followed. The manager starts by assessing trends in past human resources usage, future organizational plans, and general economic trends. A good sales forecast is often the foundation, especially for smaller organizations. Historical ratios can then be used to predict demand for such employees as operating employees and sales representatives. Of course, large organizations use much more complicated models to predict their future human resource needs. About 10 years ago Walmart went through an exhaustive planning process that projected that the firm would need to hire 1 million people over the next decade. Of this projected total, 800,000 would be new positions created as the firm grew, and the other 200,000 would replace current workers who were expected to leave for various reasons.[11] As time passed, of course, Walmart adjusted these figures both up and down. But as the decade drew to its close, Walmart did indeed employ about 800,000 more people than it did when the plan was completed.

Forecasting the supply of labor is really two tasks: forecasting the internal supply (the number and types of employees who will be in the firm at some future date) and forecasting the external supply (the number and types of people who will be available for hiring in the labor market at large).[12] The simplest approach merely adjusts present staffing levels for anticipated turnover and promotions. Again, though, large organizations use extremely sophisticated models to make these forecasts. Union Oil Company of California, for example, has a complex forecasting system for keeping track of the present and future distributions of professionals and managers. The Union Oil system can spot areas where there will eventually be too many qualified professionals competing for too few promotions or, conversely, too few good people available to fill important positions.[13]

At higher levels of the organization, managers plan for specific people and positions. The technique most commonly used is the replacement chart, which lists each important managerial position, who occupies it, how long he or she will probably stay in it before moving on, and who (by name) is now qualified or soon will be qualified to move into the position. This technique allows ample time to plan developmental experiences for persons identified as potential successors to critical managerial jobs.[14] Xerox CEO Anne Mulcahy essentially identified her eventual successor when she appointed Ursula Burns as president. And sure

**job analysis**
A systematized procedure for collecting and recording information about jobs within an organization

**replacement chart**
Lists each important managerial position in the organization, who occupies it, how long he or she will probably remain in the position, and who is or will be a qualified replacement

## FIGURE 13.1   HUMAN RESOURCE PLANNING

Attracting human resources cannot be left to chance if an organization expects to function at peak efficiency. Human resource planning involves assessing trends, forecasting supply and demand of labor, and then developing appropriate strategies for addressing any differences.

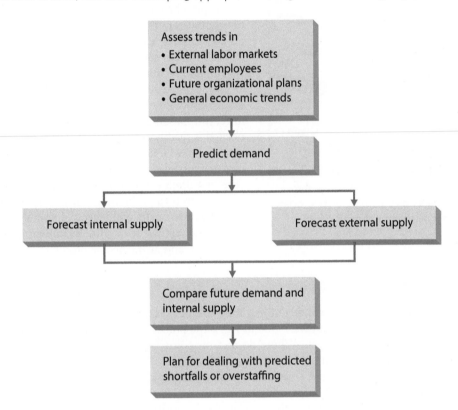

enough, when Mulcahy decided to retire, Burns was quickly appointed as the new CEO. This well-managed process made the transition easy and efficient.[15] Similarly, when Morgan Stanley's CEO John Mack announced he would like to step back from the CEO role, the company's board created a succession plan, announcing that Co-President James Gorman would take over as CEO when Mack retired.

To facilitate both planning and identifying persons for current transfer or promotion, some organizations also have an employee information system, or skills inventory. Such systems are usually computerized and contain information on each employee's education, skills, work experience, and career aspirations. Such a system can quickly locate all the employees in the organization who are qualified to fill a position requiring, for instance, a degree in chemical engineering, three years of experience in an oil refinery, and fluency in Spanish. Enterprise resource planning (ERP) systems, as described in Chapter 12, generally include capabilities for measuring and managing the internal supply of labor in ways that best fit the needs of the organization.

**employee information system (skills inventory)** Contains information on each employee's education, skills, experience, and career aspirations; usually computerized

Forecasting the external supply of labor is a different problem altogether. How does a manager, for example, predict how many electrical engineers will be seeking work in Georgia three years from now? To get an idea of the future availability of labor, planners must rely on information from such outside sources as state employment commissions, government reports, and figures supplied by colleges on the number of students in major fields.

"We overlooked our own people. It was easier to go to the outside. [But insiders] know our firm and in some cases they already know the client."

—LUCY SORRENTINI, PRINCIPAL IN PEOPLE SERVICES AT BOOZ ALLEN HAMILTON CONSULTING FIRM ON SWITCHING HIRING PRACTICES[16]

There are many methods for recruiting employees. At one time, the "Help Wanted" section in daily newspapers was the only way but today recruiters have many different methods available for attracting job applicants.

**Matching Human Resource Supply and Demand** After comparing future demand and internal supply, managers can make plans to manage predicted shortfalls or overstaffing. If a shortfall is predicted, new employees can be hired, present employees can be retrained and transferred into the understaffed area, individuals approaching retirement can be convinced to stay on, or labor-saving or productivity-enhancing systems can be installed.

If the organization needs to hire, the external labor supply forecast helps managers plan how to recruit, based on whether the type of person needed is readily available or scarce in the labor market. As we noted earlier, the trend in temporary workers also helps managers in staffing by affording them extra flexibility. If overstaffing is expected to be a problem, the main options are transferring the extra employees, choosing not to replace individuals who quit, encouraging early retirement, and laying people off.

## Recruiting Employees

Once an organization has an idea of its future human resource needs, the next phase is usually recruiting new employees.[17] Recruiting is the process of attracting qualified persons to apply for jobs that are open. Where do recruits come from? Some recruits are found internally; others come from outside the organization.

Internal recruiting means considering present employees as candidates for openings. Promotion from within can help build morale and keep high-quality employees from leaving the firm. In unionized firms, the procedures for notifying employees of internal job change opportunities are usually spelled out in the union contract. For higher-level positions, a skills inventory system may be used to identify internal candidates, or managers may be asked to recommend people who should be considered. Most businesses today routinely post job openings on their internal communication network, or intranet. One disadvantage of internal recruiting is its ripple effect. When an employee moves to a different job, someone else must be found to take his or her old job. In one organization, 454 job movements were necessary as a result of filling 195 initial openings!

External recruiting involves attracting persons outside the organization to apply for jobs. External recruiting methods include advertising, campus interviews, employment agencies or executive search firms, union hiring halls, referrals by present employees, and hiring "walk-ins" or "gate-hires" (people who show up without being solicited). Increasingly, firms are using the Internet to post job openings and to solicit applicants. Of course, a manager must select the most appropriate methods—using the state employment service to find maintenance workers but not a nuclear physicist, for example. Private employment agencies can be a good source of clerical and technical employees, and executive search firms specialize in locating top-management talent. Newspaper ads are often used because they reach a wide audience and thus allow minorities equal opportunity to find out about and apply for job openings.

The organization must also keep in mind that recruiting decisions often go both ways—the organization is recruiting an employee, but the prospective employee is also selecting a job.[18] For instance, when unemployment is low (meaning there are fewer people seeking work), businesses may have to work harder to attract new employees. During the late 1990s, when unemployment dropped to a 25-year low, some recruiters at

**recruiting**
The process of attracting individuals to apply for jobs that are open

**internal recruiting**
Considering current employees as applicants for higher-level jobs in the organization

**external recruiting**
Getting people from outside the organization to apply for jobs

firms such as Sprint, PeopleSoft, and Cognex stressed how much "fun" it was to work for them, reinforcing this message with ice cream socials, karaoke contests, softball leagues, and free movie nights.[19] But when unemployment is higher (meaning there are more people looking for work), organizations may find it easier to recruit prospective employees without having to resort to expensive hiring incentives. For example, during the economic recession that began in 2008, many firms reduced jobs and/or cut back on labor hours. As a result, firms that needed to hire new workers found it much easier to do so. Avon, for instance, used this period to substantially increase the size and effectiveness of its sales force by hiring talented people who would not otherwise have had much interest in direct sales.[20]

Nevertheless, even if a firm can take its pick of the best potential employees, it still should put its best foot forward, treat all applicants with dignity, and strive for a good person–job fit. Hiring the wrong employee can cost the company about half of a low-skilled worker's annual wages or three to five times upper-level employees' annual wages. Therefore, hiring the "wrong" employee for $40,000 per year could cost the company at least $20,000. These costs stem from training, counseling, low productivity, termination, and recruiting and hiring a replacement.

One generally successful method for facilitating a good person–job fit is the so-called realistic job preview (RJP). As the term suggests, the RJP involves providing the applicant with a real picture of what performing the job that the organization is trying to fill would be like.[21] For example, it would not make sense for a firm to tell an applicant that the job is exciting and challenging when in fact it is routine and straightforward, yet some managers do this to hire the best people. The likely outcome will be a dissatisfied employee who will quickly be looking for a better job. If the company is more realistic about a job, though, the person hired will be more likely to remain in the job for a longer period of time.

## Selecting Employees

Once the recruiting process has attracted a pool of applicants, the next step is to select whom to hire. The intent of the selection process is to gather from applicants information that will predict their job success and then to hire the candidates likely to be most successful.[22] Of course, the organization can only gather information about factors that are predictive of future performance. The process of determining the predictive value of information is called validation.

Two basic approaches to validation are predictive validation and content validation. *Predictive validation* involves collecting the scores of employees or applicants on the device to be validated and correlating their scores with actual job performance. A significant correlation means that the selection device is a valid predictor of job performance. *Content validation* uses logic and job analysis data to establish that the selection device measures the exact skills needed for successful job performance. The most critical part of content validation is a careful job analysis showing exactly what duties are to be performed. The test is then developed to measure the applicant's ability to perform those duties.

**Application Blanks** The first step in selection is usually asking the candidate to fill out an application blank. Application blanks are an efficient method of gathering information about the applicant's previous work history, educational background, and other job-related demographic data. They should not contain questions about areas not related to the job, such as gender, religion, or national origin. Application blank data are generally used informally to decide whether a candidate merits further evaluation, and interviewers use application blanks to familiarize themselves with candidates before interviewing them. Unfortunately, in recent years there has been a trend toward job applicants either falsifying or inflating their credentials to stand a better chance of getting a job. Indeed, one survey of 2.6 million job applications found that an astounding 44 percent of them contained some false information.[23] Another survey conducted by Accu-Screen found that 53 percent of resumes and job applications have false information and 78 percent have misleading information.[24]

**realistic job preview (RJP)**
Provides the applicant with a real picture of what performing the job that the organization is trying to fill would be like

**validation**
Determining the extent to which a selection device is really predictive of future job performance

In this interview, the HR representative is explaining to the candidate how to perform a test. All candidates have been asked to perform the same test. The test requires them to analyze sales data and research to propose a marketing plan for a new product. Their performance on this test will be used as one measure to determine the best candidate for the job.

**Tests** Tests of ability, skill, aptitude, or knowledge that is relevant to the particular job are usually the best predictors of job success, although tests of general intelligence or personality are occasionally useful as well. In addition to being validated, tests should be administered and scored consistently. All candidates should be given the same directions, should be allowed the same amount of time, and should experience the same testing environment (temperature, lighting, distractions).[25]

**Interviews** Although a popular selection device, interviews are sometimes poor predictors of job success. For example, biases inherent in the way people perceive and judge others at a first meeting affect subsequent evaluations by the interviewer. Interview validity can be improved by training interviewers to be aware of potential biases and by increasing the structure of the interview. In a structured interview, questions are written in advance, and all interviewers follow the same question list with each candidate they interview. This procedure introduces consistency into the interview procedure and allows the organization to validate the content of the questions to be asked.[26]

For interviewing managerial or professional candidates, a somewhat less structured approach can be used. Question areas and information-gathering objectives are still planned in advance, but the specific questions vary with the candidates' backgrounds. Trammell Crow Real Estate Investors uses a novel approach in hiring managers. Each applicant is interviewed not only by two or three other managers but also by a secretary or young leasing agent. This provides information about how the prospective manager relates to nonmanagers.[27]

**Assessment Centers** Assessment centers are a popular method used to select managers and are particularly good for selecting current employees for promotion.[28] The assessment center is a content-valid simulation of major parts of the managerial job. A typical center lasts two to three days, with groups of 6 to 12 persons participating in a variety of managerial exercises. Centers may also include interviews, public speaking, and standardized ability tests. Candidates are assessed by several trained observers, usually managers several levels above the job for which the candidates are being considered. Assessment centers are quite valid if properly designed and are fair to members of minority groups and women.[29] For some firms, the assessment center is a permanent facility created for these activities. For other firms, the assessment activities are performed in a multipurpose location such as a conference room. AT&T pioneered the assessment center concept. For years the firm has used assessment centers to make virtually all of its selection decisions for management positions.

**Other Techniques** Organizations also use other selection techniques depending on the circumstances. Polygraph tests, once popular, are declining in popularity. On the other hand, more and more organizations are requiring that applicants in whom they are interested take physical exams. Organizations are also increasingly using drug tests, especially in situations in which drug-related performance problems could create serious safety hazards. For example, applicants for jobs in a nuclear power plant would likely be tested for drug use. And some organizations today even run credit checks on prospective employees.

**Manager's Checklist ☑**

☐ Managers should be familiar with the processes of human resource planning, recruiting, and selection.

☐ Managers should also understand that selection techniques provide useful information but none is perfect.

☐ You should also remember that recruiting and selection are two-way streets: just as you are trying to find the best employee, prospective employees are also looking for the best jobs.

# Developing Human Resources

Regardless of how effective a selection system is, however, most employees need additional training if they are to grow and develop in their jobs. Evaluating their performance and providing feedback are also necessary.

## Training and Development

In HRM, training usually refers to teaching operational or technical employees how to do the job for which they were hired. Development refers to teaching managers and professionals the skills needed for both present and future jobs.[30] Most organizations provide regular training and development programs for managers and employees. For example, IBM spends more than $750 million annually on programs and has a vice president in charge of employee education. The FBI recently conducted a large-scale training program to help 30,000 agents better prepare themselves for confronting active shooters in schools, businesses, and public places.[31] U.S. businesses spend more than $70 billion annually on training and development programs away from the workplace. And this figure does not include wages and benefits paid to employees while they are participating in such programs.

> "Whether you have 30 employees or 300, creating a culture of opportunity at your business will make a huge difference for your staff. Learning won't be restricted to set training periods, but will happen in all areas of your business, all day long."
>
> —RICHARD BRANSON, FOUNDER VIRGIN GROUP[32]

**Assessing Training Needs** The first step in developing a training plan is to determine what needs exist. For example, if employees do not know how to operate the machinery necessary to do their jobs, a training program on how to operate the machinery is clearly needed. On the other hand, when a group of office workers is performing poorly, training may not be the answer. The problem could be motivation, aging equipment, poor supervision, inefficient work design, or a deficiency of skills and knowledge. Only the last could be remedied by training. As training programs are being developed, the manager should set specific and measurable goals specifying what participants are to learn. Managers should also plan to evaluate the training program after employees complete it. The training process from start to finish is diagrammed in Figure 13.2.

**Common Training Methods** Many different training and development methods are available. Selection of methods depends on many considerations, but perhaps the most important is training content. When the training content is factual material (such as company rules or explanations of how to fill out forms), assigned reading, programmed learning, and lecture methods work well. When the content is interpersonal relations or group decision making, however, firms must use a method that allows interpersonal contact, such as role-playing or case discussion groups. When employees must learn a physical skill, methods allowing practice and the actual use of tools and materials are needed, as in on-the-job training

**training**
Teaching operational or technical employees how to do the job for which they were hired

**development**
Teaching managers and professionals the skills needed for both present and future jobs

## FIGURE 13.2 THE TRAINING PROCESS

Managing the training process can go a long way toward enhancing its effectiveness. If training programs are well conceived and well executed, both the organization and its employees benefit. Following a comprehensive process helps managers meet the objectives of the training program.

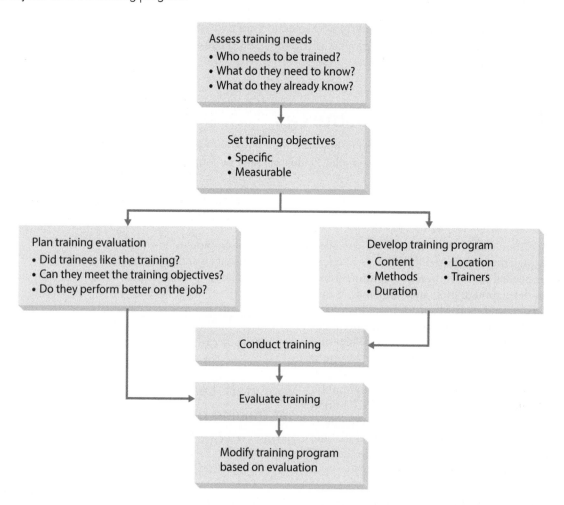

or vestibule training. (Vestibule training enables participants to focus on safety, learning, and feedback rather than on productivity.)

Web-based and other electronic media–based training are becoming very popular. Such methods allow a mix of training content, are relatively easy to update and revise, let participants use a variable schedule, and lower travel costs.[33] On the other hand, they are limited in their capacity to simulate real activities and facilitate face-to-face interaction. Xerox, Massachusetts Mutual Life Insurance, and Ford have all reported tremendous success with these methods. In addition, most training programs actually rely on a mix of methods. Boeing, for example, sends managers to an intensive two-week training seminar involving tests, simulations, role-playing exercises, and flight simulation exercises.[34]

Finally, some larger businesses have started creating their own self-contained training facilities, often called *corporate universities*. McDonald's was among the first to start this practice with its so-called Hamburger University in Illinois. All management trainees for the firm attend training programs there to learn exactly how long to grill a burger, how to maintain good customer service, and so on. The cult hamburger chain In-N-Out Burger also has a similar training venue it calls In-N-Out University. Other firms that use this approach include Shell Oil and General Electric.[35] Our *Tech Watch* feature highlights other new perspectives on learning and training.

**Evaluation of Training** Training and development programs should always be evaluated. Typical evaluation approaches include measuring one or more relevant criteria (such as attitudes or performance) before and after the training, and determining whether the criteria changed. Evaluation measures collected at the end of training are easy to get, but actual performance measures collected when the trainee is on the job are more important. Trainees may say that they enjoyed the training and learned a lot, but the true test is whether their job performance improves after their training.

Training refers to teaching operational or technical employees how to better perform the jobs for which they were hired. This manager is showing two new employees how to monitor a complex production system and what steps to take in the event of a system malfunction.

## Performance Appraisal

Once employees are trained and settled into their jobs, one of management's next concerns is performance appraisal.[37] Performance appraisal is a formal assessment of how well employees are doing their jobs. Employees' performance should be evaluated regularly for many reasons. One reason is that performance appraisal may be necessary for validating selection devices or assessing the impact of training programs. A second reason is administrative—to aid in making decisions about pay raises, promotions, and training. Still another reason is to provide feedback to employees to help them improve their present performance and plan their future careers.[38]

"Certainly times are tough, but we recognize that employee development needs to continue."

—DAVID METZGER, CANON USA'S DIRECTOR OF MANAGEMENT DEVELOPMENT[36]

Because performance evaluations often help determine wages and promotions, they must be fair and nondiscriminatory. In the case of appraisals, content validation is used to show that the appraisal system accurately measures performance on important job elements and does not measure traits or behavior that are irrelevant to job performance.

**Common Appraisal Methods** Two basic categories of appraisal methods commonly used in organizations are objective methods and judgmental methods. Objective measures of performance include actual output (that is, number of units produced), scrap rate, dollar volume of sales, and number of claims processed. Objective performance measures may be contaminated by "opportunity bias" if some persons have a better chance to perform than others. For example, a sales representative selling snow blowers in Michigan has a greater opportunity than does a colleague selling the same product in Alabama. Fortunately, adjusting raw performance figures for the effect of opportunity bias and thereby arriving at figures that accurately represent each individual's performance is often possible.

Another type of objective measure, the special performance test, is a method by which each employee is assessed under standardized conditions. This kind of appraisal also eliminates opportunity bias. For example, Dell Computer call centers record telephone conversations between technical support employees and customers who call with questions or problems. The technical support employees are periodically graded on speed, accuracy, and courtesy in handling the calls. Performance tests measure ability but do not measure the extent to which one is motivated to use that ability on a daily basis. (A high-ability person may be a lazy performer except when being tested.) Special performance tests must therefore be supplemented by other appraisal methods to provide a complete picture of performance.

**performance appraisal**
A formal assessment of how well an employee is doing his or her job

# TECH WATCH

# What You Can Learn from Math Media

Matthew Carpenter peers at the screen of his laptop, which presents him with an inverse trigonometric function: $\cos^{-1}(1) = ?$. A few seconds later, he clicks on "0 degrees" and is immediately informed by the computer that he's correct. "It took a while for me to get it," he admits, but that's understandable. After all, Matthew is only 10 years old, and as his fifth-grade math teacher is quick to point out, most students don't get around to inverse trig until they're in high school (if even then).

Is Matthew a math prodigy? Not necessarily. And he might not end up with an appointment at, say, the Center for Computational Relativity and Gravitation, but he will probably be prepared for a lot of jobs that other people won't be. "Math is the killer," says Microsoft founder Bill Gates, whose foundation has conducted studies on unemployment. "If you ask people, 'Hey, why don't you get one of these nursing jobs?' math is often the reason they give for not applying. 'Why didn't you pass the police exam?' Math."

Matthew Carpenter and Bill Gates have more in common than a positive attitude toward math: They're both excited by a certain way of learning it. Matthew's math class in Los Altos, California, is a test classroom for a system devised by former hedge-fund manager Sal Khan, whose nonprofit Khan Academy consists of about 6,000 mini-lectures and tutorials accessible as videos on YouTube. Most of these videos are pretty low tech, consisting of handwritten visuals and voiceovers recorded by Khan from a closet in his office. Following an educational strategy known as *flipping* the classroom model, students like Matthew Carpenter sit through lectures (watch videos) at home and do their homework (work problems) in the classroom, where teachers are available to help out. Students work at their own pace, advancing and winning badges when the computer recognizes certain achievements. Considerably more high tech than Khan's

videos are the *dashboards*—user interfaces that organize information in easy-to-read format—on which teachers can track students' individual efforts (how many videos they've watched and problems they've worked). Everything from Khan Academy is free.

As the organization has grown—it now reaches 6 million students in 23 languages in some 200 countries—it has expanded its software platform to accommodate such features as rigorous online diagnostic and assessment tools. Khan's growth strategy also involves the expansion of MOOC (*massive open online course*) technology into the world of professional training and development (T&D). "When they do training," says Khan, "a lot of corporations mimic the classroom. They create corporate universities at which people have to take time off and listen to lectures. … But the whole self-paced model makes a lot more sense. If you're sitting at your desk and you want to improve your skills at something, you can do it at your own time and pace."

In 2013, the Association for Talent Development (ADT), a nonprofit organization of workplace learning and performance professionals, awarded Khan its Champion of Learning award for "his revolutionary work at the intersection of technology and learning." According to the ADT, "the Khan Academy model that leverages today's technology to create educational tools and resources that are accessible and customizable to the individual has spurred the T&D profession to reimagine the possibilities available for adult learners."

*References:* Clive Thompson, "How Khan Academy Is Changing the Rules of Education," *Wired* (July 15, 2011), www.wired.com, on February 2, 2015; Candace Walters, "Re-evaluate Approach to Training, Reap Benefits from Technology," *Rochester Business Journal* (October 26, 2012), www.hrworks-inc.com, on February 2, 2015; edSurge, "Khan Academy," *EdTech Index* (2011–2015), www.edsurge.com, on February 3, 2015; Tracy M. Flynn, "What Can Khan Academy Teach Corporate Training?" *eLearning Industry* (October 7, 2013), http://elearningindustry.com, on February 3, 2015; "Salman Khan on *Charlie Rose* 2013" (video), Khan Academy (2015), www.khanacademy.org, on February 3, 2015; "ASTD Presents Lifetime Achievement Award, Honors Others for Contributions to the Training and Development Profession," Association for Talent Development (2014), www.td.org, on February 3, 2015.

*Judgmental methods*, including ranking and rating techniques, are the most common way to measure performance. Ranking compares employees directly with one another and orders them from best to worst. Ranking has a number of drawbacks. Ranking is difficult for large groups, because the individuals in the middle of the distribution may be hard to distinguish from one another accurately. Comparisons of people in different work groups are also difficult. For example, an employee ranked third in a strong group may be more valuable than an employee ranked first in a weak group. Another criticism of ranking is that the manager must rank people on the basis of overall performance, even though each person likely has both strengths and weaknesses. Furthermore, rankings do not provide useful information for feedback. To be told that one is ranked third is not nearly as helpful as to be told that the quality of one's work is outstanding, its quantity is satisfactory, one's punctuality could use improvement, or one's paperwork is seriously deficient.

Rating differs from ranking in that it compares each employee with a fixed standard rather than with other employees. A rating scale provides the standard. Figure 13.3 gives examples of three graphic rating scales for a bank teller. Each consists of a performance dimension to be rated (punctuality, congeniality, and accuracy) followed by a scale on which to make the rating. In constructing graphic rating scales, performance dimensions that are relevant to job performance must be selected. In particular, they should focus on job behaviors and results rather than on personality traits or attitudes.

## FIGURE 13.3 GRAPHIC RATING SCALES FOR A BANK TELLER

Graphic rating scales are very common methods for evaluating employee performance. The manager who is doing the rating circles the point on each scale that best reflects her or his assessment of the employee on that scale. Graphic rating scales are widely used for many different kinds of jobs.

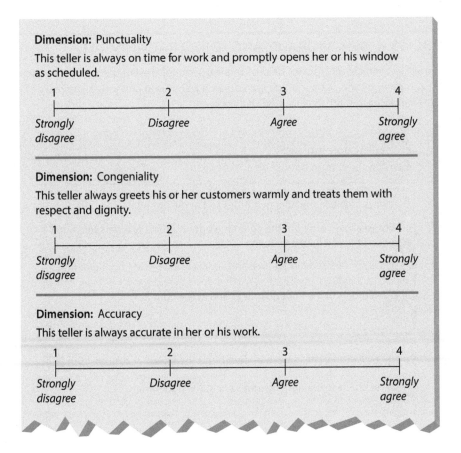

The behaviorally anchored rating scale (BARS) is a sophisticated and useful rating method. Supervisors construct rating scales with associated behavioral anchors. They first identify relevant performance dimensions and then generate anchors—specific, observable behaviors typical of each performance level. Figure 13.4 shows an example of a behaviorally anchored rating scale for the dimension "Inventory control."

The other scales in this set, developed for the job of department manager in a chain of specialty stores, include "Handling customer complaints," "Planning special promotions," "Following company procedures," "Supervising sales personnel," and "Diagnosing and solving special problems." BARS can be effective because they require that management take proper care in constructing the scales, and they provide useful anchors for supervisors to use in evaluating people. They are costly, however, because outside expertise is usually needed and because scales must be developed for each job within the organization.

**Errors in Performance Appraisal** Errors or biases can occur in any kind of rating or ranking system.[39] One common problem is *recency error*—the tendency to base judgments on the subordinate's most recent performance because it is most easily recalled. Often a rating or ranking is intended to evaluate performance over an entire time period, such as six months or a year, so the recency error does introduce error into the judgment. Other errors include overuse of one part of the scale—being too lenient, being too severe, or giving everyone a rating of "average."

*Halo error* is allowing the assessment of an employee on one dimension to "spread" to ratings of that employee on other dimensions. For instance, if an employee is outstanding on quality of output, a rater might tend to give her or him higher marks than deserved on other dimensions. Errors can also occur because of race, sex, or age discrimination, intentionally or unintentionally. The best way to offset these errors is to

**behaviorally anchored rating scale (BARS)**
A sophisticated rating method in which supervisors construct a rating scale associated with behavioral anchors

---

## FIGURE 13.4 BEHAVIORALLY ANCHORED RATING SCALE

Behaviorally anchored rating scales help overcome some of the limitations of standard rating scales. Each point on the scale is accompanied by a behavioral anchor—a summary of an employee behavior that fits that spot on the scale.

**Job:** Specialty store manager
**Dimension:** Inventory control

7 — Always orders in the right quantities and at the right time

6 — Almost always orders at the right time but occasionally orders too much or too little of a particular item

5 — Usually orders at the right time and almost always in the right quantities

4 — Often orders in the right quantities and at the right time

3 — Occasionally orders at the right time but usually not in the right quantities

2 — Occasionally orders in the right quantities but usually not at the right time

1 — Never orders in the right quantities or at the right time

ensure that a valid rating system is developed at the outset and then to train managers in how to use it.

One interesting innovation in performance appraisal used in some organizations today is called 360-degree feedback, in which managers are evaluated by everyone around them— their boss, their peers, and their subordinates. Such a complete and thorough approach provides people with a far richer array of information about their performance than does a conventional appraisal given by just the boss. Of course, such a system also takes considerable time and must be handled so as not to breed fear and mistrust in the workplace.[40]

In this meeting, the manager is sharing the 360-degree feedback he has gathered. This feedback is useful to the employee because it relates to all aspects of her day to day job. She can use that feedback to improve her performance and calibrate her goals.

## Performance Feedback

The last step in most performance appraisal systems is giving feedback to subordinates about their performance. This is usually done in a private meeting between the person being evaluated and his or her boss. The discussion should generally be focused on the facts— the assessed level of performance, how and why that assessment was made, and how it can be improved in the future. Feedback interviews are not easy to conduct. Many managers are uncomfortable with the task, especially if feedback is negative and subordinates are disappointed by what they hear. Properly training managers, however, can help them conduct more effective feedback interviews.[41]

Some firms use a very aggressive approach to terminating people who do not meet expectations. For years General Electric used a system whereby each year the bottom 10 percent of its workforce was terminated and replaced with new employees. Company executives claimed that this approach, although stressful for all employees, helped it to continuously upgrade its workforce. Other firms have started using this same approach. However, both Ford and Goodyear agreed to abandon this approach in response to age discrimination lawsuits.[42] General Electric still uses a modified version of its original system, although it has been modified to provide more flexibility.

**360-degree feedback**
A performance appraisal system in which managers are evaluated by everyone around them—their boss, their peers, and their subordinates

☐ Managers should be familiar with the most common methods for training employees and assessing their performance.

☐ All managers need to understand the advantages and limitations of training and development.

☐ You should understand the strengths and weaknesses of the performance appraisal methods used in your organization

**Manager's Checklist**

# Maintaining Human Resources

After organizations have attracted and developed an effective workforce, they must also make every effort to maintain that workforce. To do so requires effective compensation and benefits as well as career planning.

## Determining Compensation

Compensation is the financial remuneration given by the organization to its employees in exchange for their work. There are three basic forms of compensation. *Wages* are the hourly compensation paid to operating employees. The minimum hourly wage paid in the United States today is $7.25 (though several states have minimum wage levels that exceed this federal minimum). *Salary* refers to compensation paid for total contributions, as opposed to pay based on hours worked. For example, managers earn an annual salary, usually paid monthly. They receive the salary regardless of the number of hours they work. Some firms have started paying all their employees a salary instead of hourly wages. For example, all employees at Chaparral Steel earn a salary, starting at $40,000 a year for entry-level operating employees. Finally, *incentives* represent special compensation opportunities that are usually tied to performance. Sales commissions and bonuses are among the most common incentives.

Compensation is an important and complex part of the organization–employee relationship.[43] Basic compensation is necessary to provide employees with the means to maintain a reasonable standard of living. Beyond this, however, compensation also provides a tangible measure of the value of the individual to the organization. If employees do not earn enough to meet their basic economic goals, they will seek employment elsewhere. Likewise, if they believe that their contributions are undervalued by the organization, they may leave or exhibit poor work habits, low morale, and little commitment to the organization. Thus, designing an effective compensation system is clearly in the organization's best interests.[44]

A good compensation system can help attract qualified applicants, retain present employees, and stimulate high performance at a cost reasonable for one's industry and geographic area. To set up a successful system, management must make decisions about wage levels, the wage structure, and the individual wage determination system. Some firms used the 2009 recession as an opportunity to refine their compensation systems. While many firms reduced their workforces through layoffs, others used targeted salary cuts to avoid layoffs. For instance, at Hewlett-Packard the CEO first cut his own salary by 20 percent. The firm's very top performers kept their same pay levels. But others were given tiered salary cuts ranging from as little as 2.5 percent to as much as 20 percent. A few firms went even further. CareerBuilder.com, for instance, instituted pay cuts for all employees but also told everyone they only had to work half a day on Fridays.[45]

**Wage-Level Decision**   The wage-level decision is a management policy decision about whether the firm wants to pay above, at, or below the going rate for labor in the industry or the geographic area. Most firms choose to pay near the average, although those that cannot afford more pay below average. Large, successful firms may like to cultivate the image of being "wage leaders" by intentionally paying more than average and thus attracting and keeping high-quality employees. Google, IBM, and Microsoft, for example, pay top dollar to get the new employees they want. McDonald's, on the other hand, often pays close to the minimum wage. The level of unemployment in the labor force also affects wage levels. Pay declines when labor is plentiful and increases when labor is scarce.

Once managers make the wage-level decision, they need information to help set actual wage rates. Managers need to know what the maximum, minimum, and average wages are for particular jobs in the appropriate labor market. This information is collected by means of a wage survey. Area wage surveys can be conducted by individual firms or by local HR or business associations. Professional and industry associations often conduct surveys and make the results available to employers.

**Wage Structure Decision**   Wage structures are usually set up through a procedure called job evaluation—an attempt to assess the worth of each job relative to other jobs. At Ben & Jerry's Homemade, company policy once dictated that the highest-paid employee in the firm could not make more than seven times what the lowest-paid employee earned. But this policy had to be modified when the company found that it was simply unable to hire a new CEO

**compensation**
The financial remuneration given by the organization to its employees in exchange for their work

**job evaluation**
An attempt to assess the worth of each job relative to other jobs

without paying more than this amount. The simplest method for creating a wage structure is to rank jobs from those that should be paid the most (for example, the president) to those that should be paid the least (for example, a mail clerk or a janitor).

In a firm with relatively few jobs (like Netflix, for example), this method is quick and practical, but larger firms with thousands of job titles require more sophisticated methods. The next step is setting actual wage rates on the basis of a combination of survey data and the wage structure that results from job evaluation. Jobs of equal value are often grouped into wage grades for ease of administration.

**Individual Wage Decisions** After wage-level and wage structure decisions are made, the individual wage decision must be addressed. This decision concerns how much to pay each employee in a particular job. Although the easiest decision is to pay a single rate for each job, more typically a range of pay rates is associated with each job. For example, the hourly pay range for an individual job might be $10.00 to $15.40 per hour, with different employees earning different rates within the range.

A system is then needed for setting individual rates. This may be done on the basis of seniority (enter the job at $10.00, for example, and increase 50 cents per hour every six months on the job), initial qualifications (inexperienced people start at $10.00; more experienced people start at a higher rate), or merit (raises above the entering rate are given for good performance). Combinations of these bases may also be used. Our A World of Difference feature highlights some of the challenges associated with individual wage rates.

The Internet is also playing a key role in compensation patterns today because both job seekers and current employees can more easily get a sense of what their true market value is. If they can document the claim that their value is higher than what their current employer now pays or is offering, they are in a position to demand a higher salary. Consider the case of one compensation executive who met with a subordinate to discuss her raise. He was surprised when she produced data from five different websites backing up her claim for a bigger raise than he had intended to offer.[46]

## Determining Benefits

Benefits are things of value other than compensation that the organization provides to its workers. (Benefits are sometimes called *indirect compensation*.) The average company spends an amount equal to more than one-third of its cash payroll on employee benefits. Thus an average employee who is paid, say, $60,000 per year averages a bit over $20,000 more per year in benefits.

Benefits come in several forms. Pay for time not worked includes sick leave, vacation, holidays, and unemployment compensation. Insurance benefits often include life and health insurance for employees and their dependents. Workers' compensation is a legally required insurance benefit that provides medical care and disability income for employees injured on the job. Social Security is a government pension plan to which both employers and employees contribute. Many employers also provide a private pension plan to which they and their employees contribute. Employee service benefits include such extras as tuition reimbursement and recreational opportunities.

Some organizations have instituted "cafeteria benefit plans," whereby basic coverage is provided for all employees but employees are then allowed to choose which additional benefits they want (up to a cost limit based on salary). An employee with five children might choose enhanced medical and dental coverage for dependents, a single employee might prefer more vacation time, and an older employee might elect increased pension benefits. Flexible systems are expected to encourage people to stay in the organization and even help the company attract new employees.[47]

In recent years, companies have also started offering more innovative benefits as a way of accommodating different needs. On-site childcare, mortgage assistance, and paid leave programs are interesting new benefits that some firms offer.[48] A good benefits plan

**benefits**
Things of value other than compensation that an organization provides to its workers

## A WORLD OF DIFFERENCE

# The Sin of Wages?

In April 2012, having booked a record profit of $4.9 billion for 2011, and with even better results projected for 2012, Caterpillar, the world's leading maker of engines, turbines, and construction and mining equipment, rewarded top executives with hefty bonuses. As for the blue-collar workforce at its plant in Joliet, Illinois, they were told to prepare for a six-year wage freeze in order to keep the company competitive.

Indeed, as a factor in U.S. economic calculations, meaningful wage increases would appear to be a thing of the past. "For most U.S. workers," reports the Pew Research Center, a Washington D.C. think tank specializing in social issues and demographic trends, "real wages … have been flat or even falling for decades." In January 1973, for example, the average hourly wage for non-management private-sector workers was $4.03. Today, workers need to make $22.41 an hour in order to enjoy the same purchasing power as their 1973 counterparts. In December 2014, however, the average hourly wage for non-management private-sector workers was $20.68. In other words, in terms of *real wages*—wages after inflation has been taken into account—the average hourly wage peaked more than 40 years ago.

It's not that the economy hasn't been generating enough wealth to pay workers. Between 1979 and 2012, U.S. productivity increased by 74.5 percent. Median hourly compensation (wages plus benefits), however, rose by a mere 5 percent, to $12.85. ("Median" means that 50 percent of workers made more and 50 percent less than $12.85.)

A 2013 study conducted by another D.C.-based organization, the Economic Policy Institute (EPI), focuses on the gap between wage and productivity growth in order to analyze economic pressures on the living standards of working families. The findings of the report reflect the effect of economic trends on *wage percentiles*: A worker in the bottom 70th percentile, for example, makes more than 70 percent of the workforce and less than 30 percent of the workforce. During "the Great Recession and its aftermath" (2007–2012), for instance, productivity grew by 7.7 percent while wages declined for the entire bottom

70th percentile. In the previous period (2000–2007), productivity rose by 25 percent while wages for the bottom 70th percentile were either flat or declined. For the entire period (2000–2012), productivity grew by 22.2 percent while wages across the board rose by just 0.8 percent. In other words, the vast majority of U.S. wage earners "experienced a lost decade" in the battle to improve their standard of living.

Since 1979, reports the EPI, while productivity has grown 74.5 percent, wages for workers in the bottom 20th percentile actually declined by 0.4 percent. Meanwhile, 8 out of 10 American workers— those in the bottom 80th percentile—received only a very meager share of the new wealth, as their wages rose by merely 17.5 percent. The "central problem," according to the EPI, is that "the fruits of overall growth have accrued disproportionately to the richest households." Since 2000, according to Pew Research, those at the top of the income distribution have seen real-wage increases of 9.7 percent (as opposed to a decline of 3.7 percent for those in the bottom 10th percentile). During the Great Recession, 65 percent of the country's new wealth was garnered by the richest 1 percent of Americans.

For his part in returning profits of $4.9 billion, Caterpillar CEO Douglas R. Oberhelman received a 60 percent raise, to $16.9 million. The Joliet plant's unionized workforce went out on strike but was ultimately forced to accept a barely sweetened offer from the company. Needless to say, not everyone was happy about it: "We're the people who busted our butts to help them make record profits," said one worker. "We shouldn't be treated like this."

*References:* Steven Greenhouse, "At Caterpillar, Pressing Labor while Business Booms," *New York Times* (July 22, 2012), www.nytimes.com, on January 29, 2015; Drew DeSilver, "For Most Workers, Real Wages Have Barely Budged for Decades," Pew Research Center (October 9, 2014), www.pewresearch.org, on January 29, 2015; Bureau of Labor Statistics, "The Employment Situation—December 2014" (press release), U.S. Department of Labor (January 9, 2015), www.bls.gov, on January 30, 2015; Greenhouse, "Our Economic Pickle," *New York Times* (January 12, 2013), www.nytimes.com, on January 29, 2015; Heidi Shierholz and Lawrence Mishel, "A Decade of Flat Wages: The Key Barrier to Shared Prosperity and a Rising Middle Class," Economic Policy Institute (August 21, 2013), www.epi.org, on January 29, 2015; Greenhouse, "Caterpillar Workers Ratify Deal They Dislike," *New York Times* (August 17, 2012), www.nytimes.com, on January 29, 2015.

may encourage people to join and stay with an organization, but it seldom stimulates high performance, because benefits are tied more to membership in the organization than to performance. To manage their benefits programs effectively, companies should shop carefully, avoid redundant coverage, and provide only those benefits that employees want. Benefits programs should also be explained to employees in clear and straightforward language so that they can use the benefits appropriately and appreciate what the company is providing.

Finally, as a result of economic pressures, some firms have started to reduce employee benefits in the last few years. In 2002, for example, 17 percent of employees in the United States with employer healthcare coverage saw their benefits cut; the 2009 recession led to further reductions. Some employers have also reduced their contributions to employee retirement plans, cut the amount of annual leave they offer to employees, or both.[49] For instance, in 2009 16 major companies announced that they would reduce or eliminate employer contributions to employee retirement plans. Several others followed suit in 2010. Among these were Wells Fargo, Anheuser-Busch, Boise Cascade, Cooper Tire & Rubber, Kimberly-Clark, and Saks.[50] A Prudential survey published in 2013 found that 60 percent of firms surveyed said their companies had eliminated defined benefits plans or closed their defined benefits plan to new employees.[51] On average, companies have cut up to five employee-oriented benefits to reduce spending—401(k) matching, tuition reimbursement, bonuses, and so on. For instance, while Goodyear Tire & Rubber reinstated 401(k) matching for employees, it froze its pension plan to save millions of dollars.[52]

## Career Planning

A final aspect of maintaining human resources is career planning. Few people work in the same jobs their entire careers. Some people change jobs within one organization, others change organizations, and many do both. When these movements are haphazard and poorly conceived, both the individual and the organization suffer. Thus planning career progressions in advance is in everyone's best interests. Of course, planning a 30-year career for a newcomer just joining the organization is difficult. But planning can help map out what areas one is most interested in and help that person see what opportunities are available within the organization.[53]

---

☐ Managers need to know the fundamental components and issues involved in determining compensation in organizations.

☐ You should have a clear understanding of your organization's approach to compensation (including benefits).

**Manager's Checklist** ☑

# Managing Labor Relations

Labor relations is the process of dealing with employees who are represented by a union.[54] At one time, almost a third of the entire U.S. labor force belonged to a labor union. Unions enjoyed their largest membership between 1940 and 1955. Membership began to decline steadily in the mid-1950s though, for several reasons: (1) increased standards of living made union membership seem less important; (2) traditionally unionized industries in the manufacturing sector began to decline; and (3) the globalization of business operations caused many unionized jobs to be lost to foreign workers. This downward trend continued until 2008, when union membership rose by the largest amount in over a quarter century, a gain of 428,000 members (12.4 percent of all U.S. workers).[55] However, union membership again declined in the following few years, dropping to 11.3 percent in 2013.[56] Much of this fluctuation was attributable to fears of job insecurity due to the recession that hit in 2008, but as the economy bottomed out and started to rebound,

**labor relations**
The process of dealing with employees who are represented by a union

Ken Wolter/Shutterstock.com

Labor relations is the process of dealing with employees who are represented by a union. In recent years, though, labor relations experts have had to address issues that go beyond traditional labor unions. Some of these issues relate to highly mobile knowledge workers. Other issues involve immigrant workers who may not always receive the same employment protections as other workers.

membership again declined. Interestingly, while most people associate unions with the manufacturing sector, they are beginning to show up in newer industries as well. For example, workers at Gawker Media, an online publisher of news and blog sites, recently voted to unionize.[57] Managing labor relations is an important part of HRM. However, most large firms have separate labor relations specialists to handle these activities apart from other human resource functions.

## How Employees Form Unions

For employees to form a new local union, several things must occur. First, employees must become interested in having a union. Nonemployees who are professional organizers employed by a national union (such as the Teamsters or United Auto Workers) may generate interest by making speeches and distributing literature outside the workplace. Inside, employees who want a union try to convince other workers of the benefits of a union.

The second step is to collect employees' signatures on authorization cards. These cards state that the signer wishes to vote to determine whether the union will represent him or her. To show the National Labor Relations Board (NLRB) that interest is sufficient to justify holding an election, 30 percent of the employees in the potential bargaining unit must sign these cards. Before an election can be held, however, the bargaining unit must be defined. The bargaining unit consists of all employees who will be eligible to vote in the election and to join and be represented by the union if one is formed.

The election is supervised by an NLRB representative (or, if both parties agree, the American Arbitration Association—a professional association of arbitrators) and is conducted by secret ballot. If a simple majority of those voting (not of all those eligible to vote) votes for the union, then the union becomes certified as the official representative of the bargaining unit.[58] The new union then organizes itself by officially signing up members and electing officers; it will soon be ready to negotiate the first contract. The union-organizing process is diagrammed in Figure 13.5. If workers become disgruntled with their union or if management presents strong evidence that the union is not representing workers appropriately, the NLRB can arrange a decertification election. The results of such an election determine whether the union remains certified.

Organizations usually prefer that employees not be unionized because unions limit management's freedom in many areas. Management may thus wage its own campaign to convince employees to vote against the union. "Unfair labor practices" are often committed at this point. For instance, it is an unfair labor practice for management to promise to give employees a raise (or any other benefit) if the union is defeated. Experts agree that the best way to avoid unionization is to practice good employee relations all the time—not just when threatened by a union election. Providing absolutely fair treatment with clear standards in the areas of pay, promotion, layoffs, and discipline; having a complaint or appeal system for persons who feel unfairly treated; and avoiding any kind of favoritism will help make employees feel that a union is unnecessary. Walmart strives to avoid unionization through these practices.[59]

**collective bargaining**
The process of agreeing on a satisfactory labor contract between management and a union

## Collective Bargaining

The intent of collective bargaining is to agree on a labor contract between management and the union that is satisfactory to both parties. The contract contains agreements about

## FIGURE 13.5  THE UNION-ORGANIZING PROCESS

If employees of an organization want to form a union, the law prescribes a specific set of procedures that both employees and the organization must follow. Assuming that these procedures are followed and the union is approved, the organization must engage in collective bargaining with the new union.

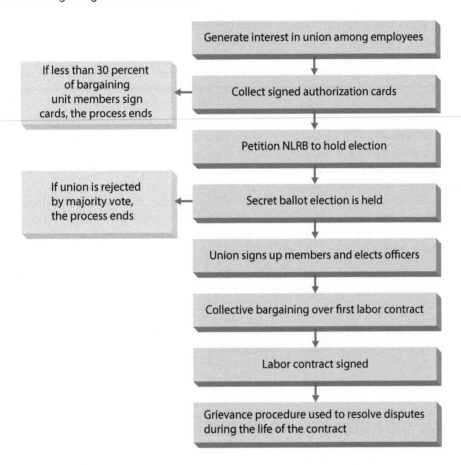

such issues as wages, work hours, job security, promotion, layoffs, discipline, benefits, methods of allocating overtime, vacations, rest periods, and the grievance procedure. The process of bargaining may go on for several weeks, several months, or longer, with representatives of management and the union meeting to make proposals and counterproposals. The resulting agreement must be ratified by the union membership. If it is not approved, the union may strike to put pressure on management, or it may choose not to strike and simply continue negotiating until a more acceptable agreement is reached.

For example, Boeing's machinists' union went on strike a few years ago over issues of job security and the firm's plans to outsource more jobs to foreign factories.[60] Similarly, employees of a Mott's applesauce factory in New York went on a 120-day strike over Dr. Pepper Snapple Group's proposal for wage, pension, and healthcare cuts despite profits being up.[61] For its part, management can also take certain actions if a new contract is not approved. One option is called a lockout—employees are not allowed to work nor do they get paid. The NFL used this measure in 2011 when the players' union would not agree to management's contract proposal. When a final agreement was reached in July 2011, training camps were opened and the players returned to work.

Occasionally circumstances arise that cause management and labor to bargain over changes in existing contracts even before a new contract is needed. This is most likely to happen when unforeseen problems jeopardize the future of the business, and hence the jobs of union members. For example, when General Motors, Ford, and Chrysler were facing financial crisis during the 2009 recession, the United Auto Workers (UAW) agreed to contract concessions with the automakers to help give the firms the flexibility they claimed they needed to restructure their operations. Among others things, for instance, the UAW agreed to allow the companies to delay billions of dollars in payments for healthcare costs for retirees and to eliminate a controversial job banks program that allowed workers to get most of their wages even when they had been laid off.[62]

The grievance procedure is the means by which the contract is enforced. Most of what is in a contract concerns how management will treat employees. When employees feel that they have not been treated fairly under the contract, they file a grievance to correct the problem. The first step in a grievance procedure is for the aggrieved employee to discuss the alleged contract violation with her immediate superior. Often the grievance is resolved at this stage. If the employee still believes that she is being mistreated, however, the grievance can be appealed to the next level. A union official can help an aggrieved employee present her case. If the manager's decision is also unsatisfactory to the employee, additional appeals to successively higher levels are made until, finally, all in-company steps are exhausted. The final step is to submit the grievance to binding arbitration. An arbitrator is a labor law expert who is paid jointly by the union and management. The arbitrator studies the contract, hears both sides of the case, and renders a decision that both parties must obey. The grievance system for resolving disputes about contract enforcement prevents any need to strike during the term of the contract.

---

**Manager's Checklist**

☐ Managers need to know the basic steps employees follow to form a union.

☐ If you work in an organization where unions have a presence you need a clear understanding of how union contracts affect what you can and cannot do.

# New Challenges in the Changing Workplace

As we have seen throughout this chapter, human resource managers face several ongoing challenges in their efforts to keep their organizations staffed with effective workforces. To complicate matters, new challenges arise as the economic and social environments of business change. We conclude this chapter with a look at two of the most important human resource management issues facing business today.

## Managing Knowledge Workers

Employees traditionally added value to organizations because of what they did or because of their experience. In the "information age," however, many employees add value because of what they know.[63]

**The Nature of Knowledge Work** These employees are usually called knowledge workers, and the skill with which they are managed is a major factor in determining which firms will be successful in the future. Knowledge workers, including computer scientists, engineers, and physical scientists, provide special challenges for the HR manager. They tend to work in high-technology firms and are usually experts in some abstract knowledge base. They often like to work independently and tend to identify more strongly with their profession than with any organization—even to the extent of defining performance in terms recognized by other members of their profession.

**grievance procedure**
The means by which a labor contract is enforced

**knowledge workers**
Workers whose contributions to an organization are based on what they know

As the importance of information-driven jobs grows, the need for knowledge workers continues to grow as well. But these employees require extensive and highly specialized training, and not every organization is willing to make the human capital investments necessary to take advantage of these jobs. In fact, even after knowledge workers are on the job, retraining and training updates are critical to prevent their skills from becoming obsolete. It has been suggested, for example, that the "half-life" of a technical education in engineering is about three years. The failure to update such skills will not only result in the loss of competitive advantage but also increase the likelihood that the knowledge worker will go to another firm that is more committed to updating them.

### Knowledge Worker Management and Labor Markets

Even though overall demand for labor has slumped in recent years due to the economic downturn, the demand for knowledge workers remains strong. As a result, organizations that need these workers must introduce regular market adjustments (upward) in order to pay them enough to keep them. This is especially critical in areas in which demand is growing, as even entry-level salaries for these employees are high. Once an employee accepts a job with a firm, the employer faces yet another dilemma. Once hired, workers are more subject to the company's internal labor market, which is not likely to be growing as quickly as the external market for knowledge workers as a whole. Consequently, the longer an employee remains with a firm, the further behind the market his or her pay falls—unless, of course, it is regularly adjusted (upward).

> "The world is not the same as it used to be. Companies pay for skills in an era where brains are more important than brawn, and the forces of automation, globalization, deregulation, and competition have changed what this kind of work is worth in the world."
>
> —JOHN CHALLENGER, CEO OF OUTPLACEMENT FIRM CHALLENGER, GRAY, & CHRISTMAS[64]

Not surprisingly, strong demand for these workers has inspired some fairly extreme measures for attracting them in the first place.[65] High starting salaries and sign-on bonuses are common. BP Exploration was recently paying starting petroleum engineers with undersea platform-drilling knowledge—not experience, just knowledge—salaries in the six figures, plus sign-on bonuses of over $50,000 and immediate profit sharing. Even with these incentives, HR managers complained that, in the Gulf Coast region, they cannot retain specialists because young engineers soon leave to accept sign-on bonuses with competitors.

## Contingent and Temporary Workers

A final contemporary HR issue of note involves the use of contingent or temporary workers.[66] Indeed, recent years have seen an explosion in the use of such workers by organizations. The FBI, for example, routinely employs a cadre of retired agents in various temporary jobs.[67]

**Trends in Contingent and Temporary Employment** In recent years, the number of contingent workers in the workforce has increased dramatically. A contingent worker is a person who works for an organization on something other than a permanent or full-time basis. Categories of contingent workers include independent contractors, on-call workers, temporary employees (usually hired through outside agencies), and contract and leased employees. Another category is part-time workers. The financial services giant Citigroup, for example, makes extensive use of part-time sales agents to pursue new clients. A Staffing Industry Analysts survey estimated that 13 percent of the workforce was classified as contingent workers. However, this is predicted to rise to as much as 40 percent by 2020.[68]

**Managing Contingent and Temporary Workers** Given the widespread use of contingent and temporary workers, HR managers must understand how to use such employees most effectively. In other words, they need to understand how to manage contingent and temporary workers.

One key is careful planning. Even though one of the presumed benefits of using contingent workers is flexibility, it is still important to integrate such workers in a coordinated fashion. Rather than having to call in workers sporadically and with no prior notice, organizations try to bring in specified numbers of workers for well-defined periods of time. The ability to do so comes from careful planning.

A second key is understanding contingent workers and acknowledging both their advantages and their disadvantages. In other words, the organization must recognize what it can and cannot achieve from the use of contingent and temporary workers. Expecting too much from such workers, for example, is a mistake that managers should avoid.

Third, managers must carefully assess the real cost of using contingent workers. We noted previously, for example, that many firms adopt this course of action to save labor costs. The organization should be able to document precisely its labor-cost savings. How much would it be paying people in wages and benefits if they were on permanent staff? How does this cost compare with the amount spent on contingent workers? This difference, however, could be misleading. We also noted, for instance, that contingent workers might be less effective performers than permanent and full-time employees. Comparing employee for employee on a direct-cost basis, therefore, is not necessarily valid. Organizations must learn to adjust the direct differences in labor costs to account for differences in productivity and performance.

Finally, managers must fully understand their own strategies and decide in advance how they intend to manage temporary workers, specifically focusing on how to integrate them into the organization. On a very simplistic level, for example, an organization with a large contingent workforce must make some decisions about the treatment of contingent workers relative to the treatment of permanent, full-time workers. Should contingent workers be invited to the company holiday party? Should they have the same access to such employee benefits as counseling services and childcare? There are no right or wrong answers to such questions. Managers must understand that they need to develop a strategy for integrating contingent workers according to some sound logic and then follow that strategy consistently over time.[69]

Indeed, this last point has become part of a legal battleground in recent years as some workers hired under the rubric of contingent workers have subsequently argued that this has been a title in name only, and that their employers use this title to discriminate against them in various ways. For instance, FedEx relies on over 13,000 "contract" drivers. These individuals wear FedEx uniforms, drive FedEx trucks, and must follow FedEx rules and procedures. However, because the firm has hired them under a different employment agreement than its "regular" employees, it does not provide them with benefits. Groups of these individuals across the country sued FedEx on the grounds that, for all practical purposes, they are employees and should enjoy the same benefits as other drivers. A U.S. district judge in Indiana ruled in favor of FedEx, upholding the drivers' status as independent contractors in 20 of 28 class-action cases. However, the court has ruled against FedEx on at least one claim.[70]

---

 **Manager's Checklist**

☐ Managers need to be aware of the fundamental issues and considerations regarding the use of contingent and temporary employees.

☐ You should be aware of trends and challenges in employment for knowledge workers.

# Summary of Learning Outcomes and Key Points

1. Describe the environmental context of human resource management, including its strategic importance and its relationship with legal and social factors.

   - Human resource management is concerned with attracting, developing, and maintaining the human resources an organization needs.
   - Its environmental context consists of its strategic importance and the legal and social environments that affect human resource management.

2. Discuss how organizations attract human resources, including human resource planning, recruiting, and selection.

   - Attracting human resources is an important part of the HRM function.
   - Human resource planning starts with job analysis and then focuses on forecasting the organization's future need for employees, forecasting the availability of employees both within and outside the organization, and planning programs to ensure that the proper number and type of employees will be available when needed.
   - Recruitment and selection are the processes by which job applicants are attracted, assessed, and hired.
   - Methods for selecting applicants include application blanks, tests, interviews, and assessment centers.
   - Any method used for selection should be properly validated.

3. Describe how organizations develop human resources, including training and development, performance appraisal, and performance feedback.

   - Organizations must also work to develop their human resources.
   - Training and development enable employees to perform their present jobs effectively and to prepare for future jobs.
   - Performance appraisals are important for validating selection devices, assessing the impact of training programs, deciding pay raises and promotions, and determining training needs.

   - Both objective and judgmental methods of appraisal can be applied, and a good system usually includes several methods.
   - The validity of appraisal information is always a concern because it is difficult to accurately evaluate the many aspects of a person's job performance.

4. Discuss how organizations maintain human resources, including the determination of compensation and benefits and career planning.

   - Maintaining human resources is also important.
   - Compensation rates must be fair compared with rates for other jobs within the organization and with rates for the same or similar jobs in other organizations in the labor market.
   - Properly designed incentive or merit pay systems can encourage high performance, and a good benefits program can help attract and retain employees.
   - Career planning is also a major aspect of human resource management.

5. Discuss labor relations, including how employees form unions and the mechanics of collective bargaining.

   - If a majority of a company's nonmanagement employees so desire, they have the right to be represented by a union.
   - Management must engage in collective bargaining with the union in an effort to agree on a contract.
   - While a union contract is in effect, the grievance system is used to settle disputes with management.

6. Describe the key issues associated with managing knowledge and contingent and temporary workers.

   - Two important new challenges in the workplace include
   - the management of knowledge workers
   - issues associated with the use of contingent and temporary workers

# Discussion Questions

## Questions for Review

1. Describe the steps in the process of human resource planning. Explain the relationships between the steps.

2. Describe the common selection methods. Which method or methods are the best predictors of future job performance? Which are the worst? Why?

3. Compare training and development, noting any similarities and differences. What are some commonly used training methods?

4. Define wages and benefits. List different benefits that organizations can offer. What are the three decisions that managers must make to determine compensation and benefits? Explain each decision.

## Questions for Analysis

5. The Family and Medical Leave Act of 1993 is seen as providing much-needed flexibility and security for families and workers. Others think that it places an unnecessary burden on business. Yet another opinion is that the act hurts women, who are more likely to ask for leave, and shuffles them off to a low-paid "mommy track" career path. In your opinion, what are the likely consequences of the act? You can adopt one of the viewpoints expressed above or develop another. Explain your answer.

6. How do you know a selection device is valid? What are the possible consequences of using invalid selection methods? How can an organization ensure that its selection methods are valid?

## Questions for Application

8. Choose three occupations that interest you. (The Labor Department's website has a full list, if you need help choosing.) Then access the Department of Labor, Bureau of Labor Statistics, online *Occupational Outlook Handbook*, at **www.bls.gov/oco**. What are the job prospects like in each of these fields? Based on what you read at the website, do you think you would enjoy any of these occupations? Why or why not?

9. Consider a job that you have held or with which you are familiar. Describe how you think an organization could

7. In a right-to-work state, workers are permitted to decide for themselves whether to join a union. In other states, workers may be required to join a union to obtain certain types of employment. If you live in a right-to-work state, do you agree that the choice to join a union should be made by each worker? If you do not live in a right-to-work state, do you agree that workers should be required to join a union? Finally, if the choice were yours to make, would you join a union? Explain your answers. (*Hint:* Right-to-work states are generally in the South, Midwest, and parts of the West. If you do not know whether you live in a right-to-work state, visit the National Right to Work Legal Defense Foundation website, at **www.nrtw. org/rtws.htm**.)

best provide a realistic job preview for that position. What types of information and experiences should be conveyed to applicants? What techniques should be used to convey the information and experiences?

10. Contact a local organization to determine how that organization evaluates the performance of employees in complex jobs such as middle- or higher-level manager, scientist, lawyer, or market researcher. What problems with performance appraisal can you note?

# Building Effective Decision-Making Skills

## Exercise Overview

Decision-making skills refer to the ability to recognize and define problems and opportunities correctly and then to select an appropriate course of action for solving problems or capitalizing on opportunities. For obvious reasons, these skills should be important to you in making career choices.

## Exercise Background

If you're in the process of making a career choice, you need to have a firm grip on your own abilities, preferences, and limitations. This is particularly true for recent college graduates, who are often preparing to enter career fields that are largely unknown to them. Fortunately, there are many sources of helpful information out there. The Bureau of Labor Statistics, for example, maintains data about occupations, employment prospects, compensation, working conditions, and many other issues of interest to job seekers. Information is available by industry, occupation, employer type, and region.

## Exercise Task

1. Access a summary of the Department of Labor's *National Compensation Survey* at **http://stats.bls.gov/ncs/ocs/sp/ ncbl0449.pdf**. (If the page has moved, search by the survey title.) Find detailed data related to the occupation that you regard as your most likely career choice when you graduate. Then locate detailed data about two other occupations that you might consider—one with a salary that's higher than that of your number-one career choice and one with a salary that's lower.

2. Next, record the hourly salary data for each of your three choices, and then use the hourly salary to project an expected annual income. (*Hint:* Full-time jobs require about 2,000 hours annually.)

3. Based *purely on salary information*, which occupation would be "best" for you?

4. Now go to www.bls.gov/oco and access job descriptions for various occupations. Review the description for each of the three career choices that you've already investigated.

5. Based *purely on job characteristics*, which occupation would be "best" for you?

6. Is there any conflict between your answers to questions 3 and 5? If so, how do you plan to resolve it?

7. Are there any job characteristics that you desire strongly enough to sacrifice compensation in order to get them? What are they? What are the limits, if any, on your willingness to sacrifice pay for these job characteristics?

# Building Effective Technical Skills

## Exercise Overview

Technical skills are necessary to understand or perform the specific kind of work that an organization does. In many organizations, this work includes hiring appropriate people to fill positions. This exercise will help you apply certain technical skills to the process of employee selection.

## Exercise Background

You may choose either of the following exercise variations. We tend to favor Variation 1 because the exercise is usually more useful if you can relate to real job requirements on a personal level.

*Variation 1.* If you currently work or have worked in the past, select two jobs with which you have some familiarity. Try to select one job that entails relatively low levels of skill, responsibility, education, and pay and one job that entails relatively high levels in the same categories.

*Variation 2.* If you've never worked or you're not personally familiar with an array of jobs, assume that you're a manager of a small manufacturing plant. You need to hire people to fill two jobs. One job is for a plant custodian to sweep floors, clean bathrooms, empty trash cans, and so forth. The other job is for an office manager who will supervise a staff of three clerks and secretaries, administer the plant payroll, and coordinate the administrative operations of the plant.

## Exercise Task

Keeping in mind what you've done so far, do the following:

1. Identify the most basic skills needed to perform each of the two jobs effectively.

2. Identify the general indicators or predictors of whether a given person can perform each job.

3. Develop a brief set of interview questions that you might use to determine whether an applicant has the qualifications for each job.

4. How important is it for you, as a manager hiring an employee to perform a job, to possess the technical skills needed to perform the job that you're trying to fill?

# Skill-Building Personal Assessment

## What Do Students Want from Their Jobs?

**Purpose:** This exercise investigates the job values held by college students at your institution. Then it asks the students to speculate about employers' perceptions of college students' job values. This will help you understand how college students can be recruited effectively. It also gives you insight into the difficulties of managing and motivating people with different values and perceptions.

**Introduction:** Employees choose careers that match their job values. Employers try to understand employee values to better recruit, manage, and motivate them. Job values are important therefore, in every HR process, from job advertisements and interviews, to performance appraisals, to compensation planning.

**Instructions:**

1. Complete the following Job Values Survey. Consider what you want from your future career. Using Column 1, rank the 14 job values from 1 to 14, with 1 being the most important to you and 14 being the least important.

2. In your opinion, when potential employers try to attract students, how much importance do they think

students give to each of the values? For Column 2, respond with a 1 (plus) if you think employers would rank it higher than students or with a 2 (minus) if you think employers would rate it lower. This is the employers' perception of students' values, not of their own values.

3. In small groups or a class, compute an average ranking for each value. Then discuss the results.

## Discussion Questions

1. How much variation do you see in the job value rankings in Column 1? That is, are students' values quite different, moderately different, or very similar overall?

2. If there are significant differences between individuals, what impact might these differences have on the recruiting process? On the training process? On the performance evaluation and compensation process?

3. How much variation do you see in the responses for Column 2? That is, does your group or class agree on how employers perceive college students?

4. Is there a large difference between how you think employers perceive college students and your group's or class's reported job values? If there is a large difference, what difficulties might this create for job seekers and potential employers? How might these difficulties be reduced or eliminated?

## Job Values Survey

|  | Column 1 Your Ranking | Column 2 Employer Ranking |
|---|---|---|
| Working conditions | | |
| Working with people | | |
| Employee benefits | | |
| Challenge | | |
| Location of job | | |
| Self-development | | |
| Type of work | | |
| Job title | | |
| Training program | | |
| Advancement | | |
| Salary | | |
| Company reputation | | |
| Job security | | |
| Autonomy on the job | | |

# Management at Work

### The Benefits of the ACA (aka Obamacare)

> "When the government orders people to do something that's costly, it gives them an incentive to push those costs onto someone else."

—*LOS ANGELES TIMES* EDITOR JON HEALEY

In October 2014, Walmart Stores, the nation's largest private employer, announced that, beginning on January 1, 2015, it would no longer offer health-insurance coverage to employees working less than an average of 30 hours per week. The decision affected approximately 30,000 of the firm's 600,000 part-time workers. "Like every company," blogged Sally Wellborn, senior VP of global benefits, "Walmart continues to face rising healthcare costs. This year, the expenses were significant and led us to make some tough decisions."

Asked how much the company would save, Wellborn replied that accountants hadn't yet figured it out, but she reported that Walmart expected to spend $500 million on U.S. healthcare in 2015, up from earlier projections of $330 million. Walmart is hardly alone in cutting part-time employees from health coverage. As of 2013, 62 percent of large retailers had instituted the same policy. Target and Home Depot, for example, had already announced that they would eliminate or sharply curtail coverage in 2015.

According to *Forbes* columnist Rick Ungar, the debate about corporate responsibility for health coverage—indeed, about the entire system of employer-provided coverage in this country—took on both expected and unexpected dimensions with the passage in 2010 of the Patient Protection and Affordable Care Act (ACA—aka Obamacare). Ungar's position in this debate is highly critical of employers like Walmart, whose actions ultimately "stick taxpayers with employee healthcare costs. ... Apparently, Walmart's idea of 'shared responsibility,'" charges Ungar, "is to allow the American taxpayer to pick up the tab for their low-paid workers when these folks avail themselves of Medicaid coverage; meanwhile, Walmart hangs on to all the money they save by blowing off their responsibility to provide healthcare to these workers."

In order to understand not only Ungar's view but opposing views as well, let's focus on two provisions of the ACA:

- As of January 2014, most Americans had to carry health insurance or face a tax penalty.
- Companies with at least 50 employees must offer health coverage to those who work at least 30 hours per week; otherwise, they must pay penalties.

Obviously, this second provision, which went into effect on January 1, 2015, was the immediate catalyst behind Walmart's decision to eliminate healthcare for employees working fewer than 30 hours per week. The first provision, however, is an equally important factor in that decision. According to Walmart, it had underestimated healthcare costs by more than 50 percent because far more employees enrolled for healthcare benefits than it had expected; the company attributed increased enrollments to the ACA requirement that employees carry health insurance or pay a penalty.

So where does that leave the 30,000 employees who lost their employer-provided health insurance on January 1, 2015? Nancy Reynolds, a cashier at a Florida Walmart, contends that "taking away access to healthcare ... is just another example of Walmart manipulating the system to keep workers like me in a state of financial crisis. ... I depend on Walmart's healthcare. I'm not sure what I'm going to do." Some analysts, however, think that people like Reynolds are failing to see a certain silver lining behind their predicament. In fact, it's a position shared by the Obama administration, which wasn't surprised by Walmart's decision. More and more large companies, said White House spokesman Josh Earnest, are cutting healthcare benefits, but workers now have "a legitimate alternative where they can acquire high-quality, affordable healthcare, and that is through the marketplaces that were constructed by the Affordable Care Act."

How does this option work? The ACA established a *Health Insurance Marketplace* consisting of *health insurance exchanges* on which individuals and small businesses can purchase healthcare policies from government-regulated and standardized plans. In addition, many purchasers are eligible for federal subsidies. Amounts vary from state to state because they're based on the cost of the second-lowest *silver plan* in each state—that is, a plan under which the insurer pays 70 percent of covered expenses and the policyholder 30 percent. Let's say, for example, that you're a 40-year-old individual in California who makes $17,235 a year. If you qualify for an ACA subsidy, you'd pay no more than 4 percent of your income ($57 per month). Your subsidy would come to $236 per month, which would save you a considerable portion of the $294 monthly payment charged by the state's second-lowest-cost silver plan. In addition, you'd have no deductible, and you'd pay only $3 for primary care visits. Subsidy amounts vary with income, with anyone earning up to 400 percent of the poverty line being eligible.

"The subsidies are pretty large for the people who get them," says Gary Claxton, VP of the Kaiser Family Foundation, which estimates that 48 percent of Americans in the market for health coverage would qualify. "It may involve some hassle for individual employees," grants *Washington Post* analyst Paul Waldman, "but most of those Walmart workers will likely come out ahead. ... They could be eligible for Medicaid and pay nothing at all for insurance, or get substantial subsidies that would make a private plan extremely affordable."

The contours of the current debate should now come into sharper focus. In particular, the discussion is more complicated than a given employer's financial motives. On the one hand, for example, Ungar argues the position that Walmart is using the ACA as "a tool for ridding itself of the obligation to provide healthcare for many of its associates"; the ACA, charges Ungar, provided "a perfect opportunity for the giant retailer to foist its obligations onto the backs of the American taxpayer." On the other hand, according to Jon Healey, a tech and economics editor at the *Los Angeles Times*, Walmart's move reflects a perfectly logical—and predictable—strategy in light of the ACA requirement that large employers provide healthcare or face penalties. That mandate, says Healey, "is an open invitation for the Walmarts of the world to do what Walmart [did]. It's a lesson some lawmakers seem to have trouble learning: When the government orders people to do something that's costly, it gives them an incentive to push those costs onto someone else."

The *Washington Post*'s Waldman takes this position a step further in arguing that Walmart's decision to act on that incentive is a step in the right direction toward U.S. healthcare reform: "I'm not saying Walmart should get a medal or anything," he writes, "but this is a development that we should welcome. ... The more companies do this, the farther we move away from the system of employer-provided health coverage ... that serves neither employees nor employers very well. ... The most important thing the ACA did was provide health security for everyone. ... Now that everyone can get insurance through the government or through an exchange, there's no reason to keep the middleman of the employer."

## Case Questions

1. What about you? What "things of value" do you want most in a benefits package offered by an employer? If you were offered a "cafeteria benefit plan," what additional or enhanced benefits would you choose? Why?

2. Do you have healthcare? If so, what part of the coverage best satisfies your needs? Do you need any kind of coverage that you can't get or can't afford? Do you think you might be better off if you got your coverage under the Affordable Care Act?

3. In your opinion, what kind of healthcare coverage does the average American worker (and his or her family) need? Is there any level of coverage to which, in your opinion, the average American worker should be entitled at a reasonable cost? What sources should provide the money to pay for this coverage?

4. Person for person, according to *Consumer Reports*, healthcare in the United States costs about twice as much as it does in the rest of the developed world. In 2000, the average family health plan cost U.S. companies $6,438 per worker; by 2013, that figure had reached $16,351. In the same period, average wages increased 20 percent (just barely keeping up with an inflation rate of 18 percent) while the cost of family health coverage went up by 87 percent. "Higher healthcare costs," the report reminds us, "mean higher premiums for everyone."*

   Why do you think healthcare costs are so high in the United States? How are healthcare prices set? What does the former CEO of one giant health maintenance organization mean when he says that healthcare "prices are made up depending on who the payer is"?

*"It's Time to Get Mad about the Outrageous Cost of Healthcare," *Consumer Reports* (September 2014), http://consumerreports.org, on January 27, 2015.

## Case References

Hiroko Tabuchi, "Walmart to End Health Coverage for 30,000 Part-Time Workers," *New York Times* (October 7, 2014), www.nytimes.com, on January 22, 2015; Nathan Layne and Siddharth Cavale, "Wal-Mart Raises Healthcare Costs, Cuts Benefits for Some Part-Timers," Reuters (October 7, 2014), www.reuters.com, on January 22, 2015; Rick Ungar, "Walmart Bails on Obamacare—Sticks Taxpayers with Employee Healthcare Costs," *Forbes* (December 9, 2012), on January 23, 2015; Tami Luhby,

"What You'll Actually Pay for Obamacare," *CNN Money* (August 21, 2013), http://money.cnn.com, on January 26, 2015; Paul Waldman, "How Walmart Is Showing That Obamacare Works," *Washington Post* (October 8, 2014), www.washingtonpost.com, on January 23, 2015; Jon Healey, "Wal-Mart's ACA-Approved Path to Cut Costs: End Part-Timers' Coverage," *Los Angeles Times* (October 7, 2014), www.latimes.com, on January 22, 2015.

## YOU MAKE THE CALL  Elementary, Watson

1. These days, according to more and more experts, "every worker is a knowledge worker." Consider the definition of *knowledge workers* in the text: "workers whose contributions to an organization are based on what they know." In what sense might just about any employee qualify as a "knowledge worker"? For example, what qualifies as "knowledge" in an organization's operational activities (that is, in the work of creating its products and services)? What's the advantage to an organization of regarding all employees as knowledge workers?

2. Review the sections in Chapter 8 entitled "Decision Making Defined" and "Decision-Making Conditions." Why are computers, especially cognitive computing systems, so effective in assisting the decision-making process? In particular, how can they increase the likelihood of good decisions under conditions of *risk* and *uncertainty*?

3. "The overwhelming message," says Geoff Colvin, seems to be that no one is safe. "Technological unemployment … may finally be here. But even if that's true … it will also be true that, as always, technology is making some skills more valuable and others less so. … Which skills will be the winners?" Colvin supplies one at least one answer to his own question: "It just seems common sense that the skills that computers can't acquire—forming emotional bonds, making human judgments—will be valuable." Thomas Davenport agrees: "It's probably not a bad idea," he suggests, "to improve your human-relationship skills."

Think of a few jobs in which the application of "human-relationship skills" is important—even absolutely necessary. Explain why these jobs require more

than just decision-making skills. How about you? Does the job that you want require good human-relationship skills? Do your human-relationship skills need some improvement? What sorts of things can you do to improve them?

4. Science journalist Patrick J. Kiger reports that students of the future are likely to have it a lot easier because digital textbooks equipped with artificial intelligence capabilities will guide them along with the patience and perceptiveness of their favorite kindly professors. Take the newly developed Inquire intelligent biology textbook for the iPad. It allows students to stop and type in a question like "What does a protein do?" and then presents them with a page full of information specific to whatever concept they're stuck on.* Using "What does a protein do?" as a model, think of three questions that you would like to ask this book about topics in this chapter. Explain why you chose the questions that you did and what sort of information you'd find helpful in response to each of your questions.

*"Futurology: Five Ways Society Will Be Affected by Cognitive Technology," *HowStuffWorks* (2015), http://electronics.howstuffworks.com, on January 14, 2015.

# Endnotes

1  Geoff Colvin, "In the Future, Will There Be Any Work Left for People to Do?" *Fortune* (June 16, 2014), http://fortune.com, on January 14, 2015; Larry Greenemeier, "Will IBM's Watson Usher In a New Era of Cognitive Computing?" *Scientific American* (November 13, 2013), www.scientificamerican.com, on January 16, 2015; Thomas H. Davenport, "Cognitive Technology—Replacing or Augmenting Knowledge Workers?" *Wall Street Journal* (June 18, 2014), http://blogs.wsj.com, on January 14, 2015; Marcelo Dascal and Itiel Dror, "The Impact of Cognitive Technologies: Towards a Pragmatic Approach," *Pragmatics & Cognition*, 2005, Vol. 13, No. 3, pp. 451–57, http://cognitiveconsultantsinternational.com, on January 14, 2015; "IBM's Supercomputer Watson to Help Fight Brain Cancer," *BBC News Technology* (March 20, 2014), www.bbc.com, on January 18, 2015.

2  For a complete review of human resource management, see Angelo S. DeNisi and Ricky W. Griffin, *Human Resource Management* (Cincinnati: Cengage Learning, 2011).

3  Patrick Wright and Gary McMahan, "Strategic Human Resources Management: A Review of the Literature," *Journal of Management*, June 1992, pp. 280–319; see also Peter Cappelli, "Talent Management for the Twenty-First Century," *Harvard Business Review*, March 2008, pp. 74–84; and Edward E. Lawler III, "Making Human Capital a Source of Competitive Advantage," *Organizational Dynamics*, January–March 2009, pp. 1–7.

4  "From the Ashes, New Tech Start-Ups Can Bloom," *USA Today*, February 17, 2009, p. 1B.

5  Augustine Lado and Mary Wilson, "Human Resource Systems and Sustained Competitive Advantage: A Competency-Based Perspective," *Academy of Management Review*, 1994, Vol. 19, No. 4, pp. 699–727.

6  David Lepak and Scott Snell, "Examining the Human Resource Architecture: The Relationships among Human Capital, Employment, and Human Resource Configurations," *Journal of Management*, 2002, Vol. 28, No. 4, pp. 517–543. See also Wayne F. Cascio and Herman Aguinis, "Staffing Twenty-First Century Organizations," in James P. Walsh and Arthur P. Brief, *The Academy of Management Annals*, Vol. 2 (London: Routledge, 2008), pp. 133–166.

7  http://www.shrm.org/publications/hrmagazine/editorialcontent/2010/0410/pages/0410grossman3.aspx, accessed on June 8, 2015.

8  "OSHA Claims Company Knowingly Overexposed Workers to Lead," *Advanced Safety and Health*, January 21, 2011.

9  "The Hidden Perils of Layoffs," *BusinessWeek*, March 2, 2009, pp. 52–53.

10  *USA Today*, March 28, 2006, p. 2B.

11  "While Hiring at Most Firms Chills, Wal-Mart's Heats Up," *USA Today*, August 26, 2002, p. 1B.

12  Peter Cappelli, "A Supply Chain Approach to Workforce Planning," *Organizational Dynamics*, January–March 2009, pp. 8–15.

13  "The New Workforce," *BusinessWeek*, March 20, 2000, pp. 64–70.

14  John Beeson, "Succession Planning," *Across the Board*, February 2000, pp. 38–41.

15  "Xerox Names Burns Chief as Mulcahy Retires Early," *Wall Street Journal*, May 22, 2009, pp. B1, B2.

16  http://www.wsj.com/articles/SB10001424052702303395604577434563715828218, accessed on June 8, 2015.

17  "Star Search," *BusinessWeek*, October 10, 2005, pp. 66–78. See also Claudio Fernandez-Aráoz, Boris Groysberg, and Nitin Nohria, "The Definitive Guide to Recruiting in Good Times and Bad," *Harvard Business Review*, May 2009, pp. 74–85; and Brian R. Dineen and Scott M. Soltis, "Recruitment: A Review of Research and Emerging Directions," in Sheldon Zedeck (ed.), *Handbook of Industrial and Organizational Psychology*, Vol. 2: *Selecting and Developing Members for the Organization* (Washington, DC: American Psychological Association, 2010), pp. 43–66.

18  Robert Gatewood, Mary Gowan, and Gary Lautenschlager, "Corporate Image, Recruitment Image, and Initial Job Choice Decisions," *Academy of Management Journal*, 1993, Vol. 36, No. 2, pp. 413–427; see also Karen Holcombe Ehrhart and Jonathan Ziegert, "Why Are Individuals Attracted to Organizations?" *Journal of Management*, 2005, Vol. 31, No. 6, pp. 901–919; and Donald M. Truxillo and Talya N. Bauer, "Applicant Reactions to Organizations and Selection Systems," in Sheldon Zedeck (ed.), *Handbook of Industrial and Organizational Psychology*, Vol. 2, pp. 379–398.

19  "Firms Cook Up New Ways to Keep Workers," *USA Today*, January 18, 2000, p. 1B.

20  "Lean Times Swell Avon's Sales Force," *Wall Street Journal*, October 15, 2008, p. B1.

21  James A. Breaugh and Mary Starke, "Research on Employee Recruiting: So Many Studies, So Many Remaining Questions," *Journal of Management*, 2000, Vol. 26, No. 3, pp. 405–434.

22  See Paul R. Sackett and Filip Lievens, "Personnel Selection," in Susan T. Fiske, Daniel L. Schacter, and Robert Sternberg (eds.), *Annual Review of Psychology 2008* (Palo Alto, CA: Annual Reviews, 2008), pp. 419–450.

23  "Pumping Up Your Past," *Time*, June 10, 2002, p. 96.

24  www.statisticbrain.com/resume-falsification-statistics/; accessed on June 8, 2015.

25  Frank L. Schmidt and John E. Hunter, "Employment Testing: Old Theories and New Research Findings," *American Psychologist*, October 1981, pp. 1128–1137.

26  Robert Liden, Christopher Martin, and Charles Parsons, "Interviewer and Applicant Behaviors in Employment Interviews," *Academy of Management Journal*, 1993, Vol. 36, No. 2, pp. 372–386.

27  Allen I. Huffcutt and Satoris S. Culbertson, "Interviews," in Zedeck, *Handbook of Industrial and Organizational Psychology*, Vol. 2, pp. 185–204.

28  Winfred Arthur Jr. and Eric Anthony Day, "Assessment Centers," in Zedeck, *Handbook of Industrial and Organizational Psychology*, Vol. 2, pp. 205–236.

29  Paul R. Sackett, "Assessment Centers and Content Validity: Some Neglected Issues," *Personnel Psychology*, 1987, Vol. 40, pp. 13–25.

30  Kenneth B. Brown and Traci Sitzmann, "Training and Employee Development for Improved Performance," in Zedeck, *Handbook of Industrial and Organizational Psychology*, Vol. 2, pp. 469–504.

31  "30,000 Trained to Confront Shooters," *USA Today*, December 23, 2015, p. 3A.

32  http://www.entrepreneur.com/article/225967, accessed on June 7, 2015.

33  Renee DeRouin, Barbara Fritzsche, and Eduardo Salas, "E-Learning in Organizations," *Journal of Management*, 2005, Vol. 31, No. 6, pp. 920–940. See Fred Luthans, James B. Avey, and Jaime L. Patera, "Experimental Analysis of a Web-Based Training Intervention to Develop Positive Psychological Capital," *Academy of Management Learning & Education*, 2008, Vol. 7, No. 2, pp. 209–221 for a recent illustration.

34  "'Boeing U': Flying by the Book," *USA Today*, October 6, 1997, pp. 1B, 2B. See also "Is Your Airline Pilot Ready for Surprises?" *Time*, October 13, 2002, p. 72.

35  "The Secret Sauce at In-N-Out Burger," *BusinessWeek*, April 20, 2009, pp. 68–69; "Despite Cutbacks, Firms Invest in Developing Leaders," *Wall Street Journal*, February 9, 2009, p. B4.

36  *Wall Street Journal*, February 9, 2009, p. B4.

37  Jessica L. Wildman, Wendy L. Bedwell, Eduardo Salas, and Kimberly A. Smith-Jentsch, "Performance Measurement at Work: A Multilevel Perspective," in Sheldon Zedeck (ed.), *Handbook of Industrial and Organizational Psychology*, Vol. 1: *Building and Developing the Organization* (Washington, DC: American Psychological Association, 2010), pp. 303–341.

38  See Paul Levy and Jane Williams, "The Social Context of Performance Appraisal: A Review and Framework for the Future," *Journal of Management*, 2004, Vol. 30, No. 6, pp. 881–905. See also Marcus Buckingham and Ashley Goodall, "Reinventing Performance Management," *Harvard Business Review*, April 2015, pp. 40–50.

39  See Michael Hammer, "The 7 Deadly Sins of Performance Measurement (and How to Avoid Them)," *MIT Sloan Management Review*, Spring 2007, pp. 19–30.

40  See Angelo S. DeNisi and Avraham N. Kluger, "Feedback Effectiveness: Can 360-Degree Appraisals Be Improved?" *Academy of Management Executive*, 2000, Vol. 13, No. 1, pp. 129–139.

41  Barry R. Nathan, Allan Mohrman, and John Milliman, "Interpersonal Relations as a Context for the Effects of Appraisal Interviews on Performance and Satisfaction: A Longitudinal Study," *Academy of Management Journal*, June 1991, pp. 352–369.

42  "Goodyear to Stop Labeling 10% of Its Workers as Worst," *USA Today*, September 12, 2002, p. 1B.

43  Joseph J. Martocchio, "Strategic Reward and Compensation Plans," in Zedeck, *Handbook of Industrial and Organizational Psychology*, Vol. 1, pp. 343–372.

44  Jaclyn Fierman, "The Perilous New World of Fair Pay," *Fortune*, June 13, 1994, pp. 57–64. See also "The Best vs. the Rest," *Wall Street Journal*, January 30, 2006, pp. B1, B3.

45  "Pay Cuts Made Palatable," *BusinessWeek*, May 4, 2009, p. 67. See also "The Right Way to Pay," *Forbes*, May 11, 2009, pp. 78–80; and "Do Pay Cuts Pay Off?" *Time*, April 27, 2009, p. 6.

46  Stephanie Armour, "Show Me the Money, More Workers Say," *USA Today*, June 6, 2000, p. 1B.

47  "To Each According to His Needs: Flexible Benefits Plans Gain Favor," *Wall Street Journal*, September 16, 1986, p. 29.

48  "The Future Look of Employee Benefits," *Wall Street Journal*, September 7, 1988, p. 21.

49  See "Companies Chisel Away at Workers' Benefits," *USA Today*, November 18, 2002, pp. 1B, 2B. See also "The Benefits Trap," *BusinessWeek*, July 19, 2004, pp. 64–72.

50  "More Companies Freeze Pensions," *USA Today*, May 11, 2009, p. 1A.

51  www.benefitspro.com/2013/10/18/9-things-to-do-before-terminating-a-pension-plan; accessed on June 9, 2015.

52  "Financially Pinched Companies Snip Employee Benefits," *USA Today*, April 7, 2011.

53  See Sherry E. Sullivan, "The Changing Nature of Careers: A Review and Research Agenda," *Journal of Management*, 1999, Vol. 25, No. 3, pp. 457–484.

54  Barbara Presley Nobel, "Reinventing Labor," *Harvard Business Review*, July–August 1993, pp. 115–125.

55  "Big Gains for Unions," *New York Times*, January 29, 2009, p. C1.

56  Bureau of Labor Statistics, 2015.

57  "Gawkers Staff Vote to Unionize," *USA Today*, June 5, 2015, p. 4B.

58  John A. Fossum, "Labor Relations: Research and Practice in Transition," *Journal of Management*, Summer 1987, pp. 281–300.

59  "How Wal-Mart Keeps Unions at Bay," *BusinessWeek*, October 28, 2002, pp. 94–96.

60  "Outsourcing at Crux of Boeing Strike," *Wall Street Journal*, September 8, 2008, pp. B1, B4.

61  "Was the Mott's Strike 'Victory' Really a Victory?" *Huffington Post*, September 13, 2010; "Mott's Strike Comes to an End," *New York Daily News*, September 13, 2010.

62  "UAW Gives Concessions to Big Three," *Wall Street Journal*, December 4, 2008, pp. B1, B2.

63  Max Boisot, *Knowledge Assets* (Oxford, UK: Oxford University Press, 1998).

64  *USA Today*, March 28, 2006, p. 2B.

65  Thomas Stewart, "In Search of Elusive Tech Workers," *Fortune*, February 16, 1998, pp. 171–172.

66  Elizabeth George and Carmen Kaman Ng, "Nonstandard Workers: Work Arrangements and Outcomes," in Zedeck, *Handbook of Industrial and Organizational Psychology*, Vol. 1, pp. 573–596.

67  "FBI Taps Retiree Experience for Temporary Jobs," *USA Today*, October 3, 2002, p. 1A.

68  "Special Report on Contingent Staffing," *Workforce Management*, October 19, 2009. See also http://http-download.intuit.com/http.intuit/CMO/intuit/futureofsmallbusiness/intuit_2020_report.pdf?_ga=1.4790131.1193111323.1407518315; accessed on June 9, 2015.

69  "When Is a Temp Not a Temp?" *BusinessWeek*, December 7, 1998, pp. 90–92.

70  "Drivers Deliver Trouble to FedEx by Seeking Employee Benefits," *Wall Street Journal*, January 7, 2005, pp. A1, A8; "FedEx Wins Ruling that Contract Drivers Seeking Benefits Aren't Employees," *Bloomberg*, December 13, 2010.

©Markus Pfaff/Shutterstock.com

# 14

# BASIC ELEMENTS OF INDIVIDUAL BEHAVIOR IN ORGANIZATIONS

**After studying this chapter, you should be able to:**

## MANAGEMENT IN ACTION    Engaging with the Company Garbage

> "Once you've seen your garbage up close, it's hard to ignore it."
>
> —SUSTAINABILITY CONSULTANT SHIRA E. NORMAN

Back in 2007, Burt's Bees, a maker of natural personal-care products, found to its dismay that it was creating 40 tons of waste every month. Two years later, the company had reduced that amount to 10 tons through a rigorous program of recycling and composting. It was a start, but at that point, reports CEO John Replogle, "we were stuck and needed to reinvigorate the effort again." The company's *green team*—a group of volunteer employees who oversee efforts to improve the workplace environment—came up with an employee-oriented trash-appreciation exercise. They stockpiled two weeks' worth of company garbage and dumped it in the parking lot. More than 300 employees then donned hazmat suits and waded through the refuse heap to find everything that should have been recycled and everything that could be recycled if there were someplace to send it.[1]

As a result, Burt's was able to cut waste in half and save $25,000 a year in hauling expenses. "We found money in the dumpster," says Replogle. "We've turned our waste stream from a cost center into a profit center." More importantly, adds Replogle, "seeing all that trash in the parking lot translated into a collective 'aha moment,' and we all realized we could do a better job at recycling." In the wake of the dumpster-diving exercise, employee recycling compliance jumped from 80 percent to 98 percent. "Now," reports Replogle, "we have a shared ethos of taking responsibility."

Burt's isn't the only company that's turned dumpster diving into business as usual. Bentley Prince Street, a commercial carpet maker, has been probing its garbage on a monthly basis for more than 15 years. Department-based teams of 20 employees sift through the trash for about 15 minutes looking for recyclable or reusable items. So far, the company has not only saved $50,000 a year in waste hauling, but also earns about $150,000 annually from the sales of recyclables to companies that have commercial uses for them.

"The monetary savings," says sustainability director Judy Pike, "are an important aspect of our program, but equally important is … educating our employees about recycling and sustainability." Bentley Prince

Larry Powell/Shutterstock.com

In order to demonstrate the impact of waste to employees, Burt's Bee, a maker of natural personal-care products, launched an unusual campaign. For two weeks members of its green team sifted through company garbage and piled it all in the parking lot for everyone to see. The piles of garbage provided a vivid illustration of how much waste the company and its employees were generating. Especially dramatic was seeing how much of the garbage consisted of recyclable material.

Street coordinates its employee sustainability efforts through its QUEST initiative (for Quality Utilizing Employee Suggestions and Teamwork), a program through which employee teams determine ways of eliminating waste. Since 1996, QUEST has reduced the firm's water intake by 52 percent, its energy use by 40 percent, its greenhouse emissions by 48 percent, and its waste sent to landfill by 97 percent.

The sustainability success of companies like Burt's Bees and Bentley Prince Street isn't entirely surprising to Hunter Lovins, president of Natural Capital Solutions, a nonprofit specializing in innovations in environmental practices and economic sustainability. "Let's track the logic," she suggests: "Taking care of your workforce, particularly by engaging them in implementing a corporate commitment to sustainability, will drive greater productivity and thus greater profitability."

Lovins's logic tracks as follows: She starts from the premise that satisfied employees are more productive employees, citing studies reporting that unsatisfied workers currently cost the U.S. economy $300 billion per year. Lovins then proceeds to argue that the most satisfied employees are those who are given the opportunity to "make progress in meaningful work." What constitutes "meaningful work"? For that matter, what constitutes "progress"? Lovins suggests that a good measure of both is the extent to which employees put forth *discretionary effort*—the level *above minimum requirements* that people could put forth if they wanted to. "People who believe their jobs are meaningful," says Lovins, "channel their discretionary effort into their work," such as volunteering to dive into dumpsters or serve on waste-elimination teams.

Lovins also believes that work which involves employees in companywide sustainability efforts is "meaningful" to a lot of Americans. "The American workforce," she contends,

> no longer views work solely as a means to a paycheck. To many people, especially the younger generation, their job is an integral part of their lifestyle. ... Ninety-two percent of Millennials say that they want to work for a socially responsible company . ... A 2010 study ... found that 96 percent of Generation Y respondents are highly concerned about the environment and expect that employers will take steps towards becoming more sustainable.

More and more of these people may be able to find the kind of "meaningful" jobs they want because more

and more employers are integrating sustainability programs into their overall business strategies. For many of them, the key to success in the initiative is aligning sustainability goals with broader business goals.

As Burt's Bees puts it, "sustainability is built into our business because it's so good for our business. ... Our sustainability journey has helped to power our growth into a household brand." A 2009 Gallup survey reported that highly "engaged organizations" returned 3.9 times the earnings-per-share growth rate of companies that rated low on engagement. A year later, a survey by Hewitt and Associates, a global human resources consulting firm, found that companies with high levels of employee engagement boasted shareholder return 19 percent above average, while those with lower levels were 44 percent below average. The same study identified social and environmental responsibility as a key factor in driving employee engagement.

How do companies foster employee engagement, particularly when it comes to sustainability programs? First of all, it helps to be genuinely committed to sustainability. A study of employees in the food-processing industry found that "employees' level of organizational commitment is influenced by their perception of their firm's environmental sustainability." More specifically, says Suzanne Tilleman of the University of Montana, engagement is higher when a company turns out a high percentage of organic products and exhibits a *collectivistic identity orientation*—that is, emphasizes companywide contributions to a greater good.

Secondly, organizational commitment is greater when a company fosters a combination of *top-down leadership* and *bottom-up empowerment* in its sustainability practices. At Burt's Bees, for example, if a department fails to pass certain tests for proper recycling, chronic abusers must go through remedial training with the CEO himself. "I'll sit with them and pick through the trash to teach them where everything needs to go," says John Replogle. "It's important because my bonus is tied to [our goal of zero waste], and so is everyone else's." Obviously, Replogle and his management also set such strategic goals as making Burt's Bees a zero-waste company by 2020.

At the same time, the company depends on frontline employees for such ideas as cleaning industrial containers with steam rather than water—an insight that cut water usage for the task by 90 percent. In return, in addition to bonuses tied to companywide sustainability performance, employees receive such

"Eco-benefits" as cash compensation for biking or carpooling to work and buying high-efficiency or hybrid vehicles. Then, of course, there are those paid days for volunteering for activities like dumpster diving. Such activities, says Harvard's Bobbi Thomasin, "are smart

initiatives for showing your people that sustainability is truly important to the organization's central mission." Besides, adds sustainability consultant Shira E. Norman, "once you've seen your garbage up close, it's hard to ignore it."

The people who populate today's business world are characterized by a wide variety of personalities, behaviors, and attitudes. While most people in business have relatively healthy and constructive personalities and behave in ethical and productive ways, there are some who reflect different profiles. Indeed, myriad different and unique characteristics reside in each and every employee and manager. These affect how they feel about the organization, how they will alter their future attitudes about the firm, and how they perform their jobs. These characteristics reflect the basic elements of individual behavior in organizations.

This chapter describes several of these basic elements and is the first of several chapters designed to develop a more complete perspective on the leading function of management. In the next section we investigate the psychological nature of individuals in organizations. The following section introduces the concept of personality and discusses several important personality attributes that can influence behavior in organizations. We then examine individual attitudes and their role in organizations. The role of stress in the workplace is then discussed, followed by a discussion of individual creativity. Finally, we describe a number of basic individual behaviors that are important to organizations.

**psychological contract**
The overall set of expectations held by an individual with respect to what he or she will contribute to the organization and what the organization will provide in return

# Understanding Individuals in Organizations

As a starting point in understanding human behavior in the workplace, we must consider the basic nature of the relationship between individuals and organizations. We must also gain an appreciation of the nature of individual differences.

## The Psychological Contract

Most people have a basic understanding of a contract. Whenever we buy a car or sell a house, for example, both buyer and seller sign a contract that specifies the terms of the agreement. A psychological contract is similar in some ways to a standard legal contract but is less formal and well defined. In particular, a psychological contract is the overall set of expectations held by an individual with respect to what he or she will contribute to the organization and what the organization will provide in return.[2] Thus a psychological contract is not written on paper, nor are all of its terms explicitly negotiated.

A psychological contract refers to the expectations held by an individual regarding what she or he will contribute to the organization and what the organization will provide in return. This manager and subordinate are reviewing the subordinate's goals for the upcoming year and what rewards are most likely to be provided if those goals are met. These agreements are a part of the psychological contract.

Adam Gregor/Shutterstock.com

## FIGURE 14.1  THE PSYCHOLOGICAL CONTRACT

Psychological contracts are the basic assumptions that individuals have about their relationships with their organization. Such contracts are defined in terms of contributions by the person relative to inducements from the organization.

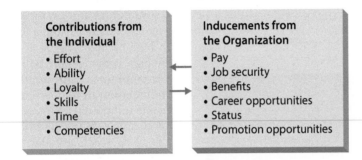

**Contributions from the Individual**
- Effort
- Ability
- Loyalty
- Skills
- Time
- Competencies

**Inducements from the Organization**
- Pay
- Job security
- Benefits
- Career opportunities
- Status
- Promotion opportunities

The essential nature of a psychological contract is illustrated in Figure 14.1. The person makes a variety of contributions to the organization—effort, skills, ability, time, loyalty, and so forth. These contributions presumably satisfy various needs and requirements of the organization. In other words, because the organization may have hired the person because of her skills, it is reasonable for the organization to expect that she will subsequently display those skills in the performance of her job.

In return for these contributions, the organization provides inducements to the person. Some inducements, like pay and career opportunities, are tangible rewards. Others, like job security and status, are more intangible. Just as the contributions available from the individual must satisfy the needs of the organization, the inducements offered by the organization must serve the needs of the individual. Thus, if a person accepts employment with an organization because he thinks he will earn an attractive salary and have an opportunity to advance, he will expect that those rewards will actually be forthcoming.

If both the individual and the organization perceive that the psychological contract is fair and equitable, they will be satisfied with the relationship and will likely continue it. On the other hand, if either party sees an imbalance or inequity in the contract, they may initiate a change. For example, the worker may request a pay raise or promotion, decrease her contributed effort, or look for a better job elsewhere. The organization can also initiate change by requesting that the worker improve his skills through training, transfer him to another job, or terminate his employment altogether.[3]

A basic challenge faced by the organization, then, is to manage psychological contracts. The organization must ensure that it is getting value from its employees. At the same time, it must be sure that it is providing employees with appropriate inducements. If the organization is underpaying its employees for their contributions, for example, they may perform poorly or leave for better jobs elsewhere. On the other hand, if they are being overpaid relative to their contributions, the organization is incurring unnecessary costs.[4]

## The Person–Job Fit

One specific aspect of managing psychological contracts is managing the person–job fit. Person–job fit is the extent to which the contributions made by the individual match the inducements offered by the organization. In theory, each employee has a specific set of needs that he wants fulfilled and a set of job-related behaviors and abilities to contribute. Thus, if the organization can take perfect advantage of those behaviors and abilities and exactly fulfill his needs, it will have achieved a perfect person–job fit.

Of course, such a precise level of person-job fit is seldom achieved. There are several reasons for this. For one thing, organizational selection procedures are imperfect.

**contributions**
What the individual provides to the organization

**inducements**
What the organization provides to the individual

**person–job fit**
The extent to which the contributions made by the individual match the inducements offered by the organization

"Whether someone rock climbs, plays the cello, or enjoys film noir may seem trivial but these leisure pursuits were crucial for assessing someone as a cultural fit."

—LAUREN RIVERA, PROFESSOR AT NORTHWESTERN ON HOW COMPANIES ARE CHANGING THEIR INTERVIEW QUESTIONS[5]

Person-job fit is the extent to which the contributions made by an individual match the inducements offered by the organization. This utility workers is trimming tree branches so they won't interfere with electrical power lines. Some people would find a job such as this interesting and rewarding, while others would be uncomfortable working under these conditions. These feelings contribute to person-job fit.

Organizations can make approximations of employee skill levels when making hiring decisions and can improve them through training. But even simple performance dimensions are often hard to measure in objective and valid ways.

Another reason for imprecise person–job fits is that both people and organizations change. A person who finds a new job stimulating and exciting may find the same job boring and monotonous after a few years of performing it. And when the organization adopts new technology, it changes the skills it needs from its employees. Still another reason for imprecision in the person–job fit is that each individual is unique. Measuring skills and performance is difficult enough. Assessing needs, attitudes, and personality is far more complex. Each of these individual differences serves to make matching individuals with jobs a difficult and complex process.[6]

## The Nature of Individual Differences

**Individual differences** are personal attributes that vary from one person to another. Individual differences may be physical, psychological, or emotional. Taken together, all of the individual differences that characterize any specific person serve to make that person unique from everyone else. Much of the remainder of this chapter is devoted to individual differences. Before proceeding, however, we must also note the importance of the situation in assessing the behavior of individuals.

Are specific differences that characterize a given person good or bad? Do they contribute to or detract from performance? The answer, of course, is that it depends on the circumstances. One person may be very dissatisfied, withdrawn, and negative in one job setting, but very satisfied, outgoing, and positive in another. Working conditions, coworkers, and leadership are all important ingredients.

Thus, whenever an organization tries to assess or account for individual differences among its employees, it must also be sure to consider the situation in which behavior occurs. Individuals who are satisfied or productive workers in one context may prove to be dissatisfied or unproductive workers in another context. Attempting to consider both individual differences and contributions in relation to inducements and contexts, then, is a major challenge for organizations as they try to establish effective psychological contracts with their employees and achieve optimal fits between people and jobs.[7]

**individual differences**
Personal attributes that vary from one person to another

---

**Manager's Checklist**

☐ Managers need to understand the concepts and importance of a psychological contract.

☐ You should also appreciate the importance of person–job fit.

☐ Managers must also remember that no two people are the same.

# Personality and Individual Behavior

Personality traits represent some of the most fundamental sets of individual differences in organizations. Personality is the relatively stable set of psychological attributes that distinguish one person from another.[8] Managers should strive to understand basic personality attributes and the ways they can affect people's behavior in organizational situations, not to mention their perceptions of and attitudes toward the organization.

## The "Big Five" Personality Traits

Psychologists have identified literally thousands of personality traits and dimensions that differentiate one person from another. But in recent years researchers have identified five fundamental personality traits that are especially relevant to organizations. Because these five traits are so important and because they are currently the subject of so much attention, they are now commonly referred to as the "Big Five" personality traits.[9] Figure 14.2 illustrates the Big Five traits.

Agreeableness refers to a person's ability to get along with others. Agreeableness causes some people to be gentle, cooperative, forgiving, understanding, and good-natured in their dealings with others. But it results in others' being irritable, short-tempered, uncooperative, and generally antagonistic toward other people. Although

Agreeableness—a person's ability to get along with others—is one of the "Big Five" personality traits. This man would appear to be very agreeable, given his happy and positive display of emotions.

Pressmaster/Shutterstock.com

## FIGURE 14.2  THE "BIG FIVE" MODEL OF PERSONALITY

The "Big Five" personality model represents an increasingly accepted framework for understanding personality traits in organizational settings. In general, experts tend to agree that personality traits toward the left end of each dimension, as illustrated in this figure, are more positive in organizational settings, whereas traits closer to the right are less positive.

**Agreeableness**
High agreeableness ← → Low agreeableness

**Conscientiousness**
High conscientiousness ← → Low conscientiousness

**Negative Emotionality**
Less negative emotionality ← → More negative emotionality

**Extraversion**
More extraversion ← → More introversion

**Openness**
More openness ← → Less openness

**personality**
The relatively permanent set of psychological and behavioral attributes that distinguish one person from another

**"Big Five" personality traits**
A popular personality framework based on five key traits

**agreeableness**
A person's ability to get along with others

research has not yet fully investigated the effects of agreeableness, it would seem likely that highly agreeable people will be better able to develop good working relationships with coworkers, subordinates, and higher-level managers, whereas less agreeable people will not have particularly good working relationships. This same pattern might also extend to relationships with customers, suppliers, and other key organizational constituents.

Conscientiousness refers to the number of things a person can effectively work on at one time. People who focus on relatively fewer tasks and projects are likely to be organized, systematic, careful, thorough, responsible, and self-disciplined as they work to complete those tasks and projects. Others, however, tend to take on too many tasks and projects and/or to procrastinate and, as a result, are more disorganized, careless, and irresponsible, as well as less thorough and self-disciplined. Research has found that more conscientious people tend to be higher performers than less conscientious people across a variety of different jobs. This pattern seems logical, of course, because more conscientious people will take their jobs seriously and will approach the performance of their jobs in highly responsible fashions.

The third of the Big Five personality dimensions is negative emotionality. People with less negative emotionality will be relatively poised, calm, resilient, and secure. But people with more negative emotionality will be more excitable, insecure, reactive, and subject to extreme mood swings. People with less negative emotionality might be expected to better handle job stress, pressure, and tension. Their stability might also lead them to be seen as more reliable than their less stable counterparts.

Extraversion refers to a person's comfort level with relationships. People who are called "extraverts" are sociable, talkative, assertive, and open to establishing new relationships. Introverts are much less sociable, talkative, and assertive, and less open to establishing new relationships. Research suggests that extraverts tend to be higher overall job performers than introverts and that they are also more likely to be attracted to jobs based on personal relationships, such as sales and marketing positions.

Finally, openness refers to a person's rigidity of beliefs and range of interests. People with high levels of openness are willing to listen to new ideas and to change their own ideas, beliefs, and attitudes as a result of new information. They also tend to have broad interests and to be curious, imaginative, and creative. On the other hand, people with low levels of openness tend to be less receptive to new ideas and less willing to change their minds. Further, they tend to have fewer and narrower interests and to be less curious and creative. People with more openness might be expected to be better performers, owing to their flexibility and the likelihood that they will be better accepted by others in the organization. Openness may also encompass an individual's willingness to accept change. For example, people with high levels of openness may be more receptive to change, whereas people with low levels of openness may be more likely to resist change.

The Big Five framework continues to attract the attention of both researchers and managers. The potential value of this framework is that it encompasses an integrated set of traits that appear to be valid predictors of certain behaviors in certain situations. Thus managers who can develop both an understanding of the framework and the ability to assess these traits in their employees will be in a good position to understand how and why employees behave as they do.[10] On the other hand, managers must also be careful not to overestimate their ability to assess the Big Five traits in others. Even assessment using the most rigorous and valid measures, for instance, is still likely to be somewhat imprecise. Another limitation of the Big Five framework is that it is based primarily on research conducted in the United States. Thus there are unanswered questions as to how accurately it applies to workers in other cultures. And even within the United States, a variety of other factors and traits are also likely to affect behavior in organizations.[11]

## The Myers–Briggs Framework

Another interesting approach to understanding personalities in organizations is the Myers–Briggs framework. This framework, based on the classic work of Carl

**conscientiousness**
The number of things a person can effectively work on at one time

**negative emotionality**
Extent to which a person is poised, calm, resilient, and secure

**extraversion**
A person's comfort level with relationships

**openness**
A person's rigidity of beliefs and range of interests

Jung, differentiates people in terms of four general dimensions. These are defined as follows.

- *Extraversion (E) Versus Introversion (I).* Extraverts get their energy from being around other people, whereas introverts are worn out by others and need solitude to recharge their energy.
- *Sensing (S) Versus Intuition (N).* The sensing type prefers concrete things, whereas intuitives prefer abstract concepts.
- *Thinking (T) Versus Feeling (F).* Thinking individuals base their decisions more on logic and reason, whereas feeling individuals base their decisions more on feelings and emotions.
- *Judging (J) Versus Perceiving (P).* People who are the judging type enjoy completion or being finished, whereas perceiving types enjoy the process and open-ended situations.

To use this framework, people complete a questionnaire designed to measure their personality on each dimension. Higher or lower scores in each of the dimensions are used to classify people into one of 16 different personality categories.

The Myers–Briggs Type Indicator (MBTI) is one popular questionnaire that some organizations use to assess personality types. Indeed, it is among the most popular selection instruments used today, with as many as 2 million people taking it each year. Research suggests that the MBTI is a useful method for determining communication styles and interaction preferences. In terms of personality attributes, however, questions exist about both the validity and the reliability of the MBTI.

## Other Personality Traits at Work

Besides the Big Five and the Myers–Briggs framework, there are several other personality traits that influence behavior in organizations. Among the most important are locus of control, self-efficacy, authoritarianism, Machiavellianism, self-esteem, and risk propensity.

Locus of control is the extent to which people believe that their behavior has a real effect on what happens to them.[12] Some people, for example, believe that if they work hard, they will succeed. They also may believe that people who fail do so because they lack ability or motivation. People who believe that individuals are in control of their lives are said to have an *internal locus of control*. Other people think that fate, chance, luck, or other people's behavior determines what happens to them. For example, an employee who fails to get a promotion may attribute that failure to a politically motivated boss or just bad luck, rather than to her or his own lack of skills or poor performance record. People who think that forces beyond their control dictate what happens to them are said to have an *external locus of control*.

Self-efficacy is a related but subtly different personality characteristic. Self-efficacy is a person's beliefs about his or her capabilities to perform a task.[13] People with high self-efficacy believe that they can perform well on a specific task, whereas people with low self-efficacy tend to doubt their ability to perform a specific task. Although self-assessments of ability contribute to self-efficacy, so, too, does the individual's personality. Some people simply have more self-confidence than do others. This belief in their ability to perform a task effectively results in their being more self-assured and more able to focus their attention on performance.

Another important personality characteristic is authoritarianism, the extent to which one believes that power and status differences are

**locus of control**
The degree to which a person believes that his or her behavior has a direct impact on the consequences of that behavior

**self-efficacy**
An individual's beliefs about her or his capabilities to perform a task

**authoritarianism**
The extent to which a person believes that power and status differences are appropriate within hierarchical social systems like organizations

This employee is explaining to his boss why he deserves a promotion. His high level of self-efficacy is serving him well in this conversation because he is able to highlight his strengths and point to his positive contributions to the latest project.

appropriate within hierarchical social systems like organizations.[14] For example, a person who is highly authoritarian may accept directives or orders from someone with more authority purely because the other person is "the boss." On the other hand, although a person who is not highly authoritarian may still carry out appropriate and reasonable directives from the boss, he or she is also more likely to question things, express disagreement with the boss, and even refuse to carry out orders if they are for some reason objectionable. A highly authoritarian manager may be autocratic and demanding, and highly authoritarian subordinates will be more likely to accept this behavior from their leader. On the other hand, a less authoritarian manager may allow subordinates a bigger role in making decisions, and less authoritarian subordinates will respond positively to this behavior.

Machiavellianism is another important personality trait. This concept is named after Niccolo Machiavelli, a sixteenth-century Italian political philosopher. In his book entitled *The Prince*, Machiavelli explained how the nobility could more easily gain and use power. *Machiavellianism* is now used to describe behavior directed at gaining power and controlling the behavior of others. Research suggests that Machiavellianism is a personality trait that varies from person to person. More Machiavellian individuals tend to be rational and nonemotional, may be willing to lie to attain their personal goals, may put little weight on loyalty and friendship, and may enjoy manipulating others' behavior. Less Machiavellian individuals are more emotional, less willing to lie to succeed, value loyalty and friendship highly, and get little personal pleasure from manipulating others. By all accounts, Dennis Kozlowski, the indicted former CEO of Tyco International who eventually served prison time, had a high degree of Machiavellianism. He apparently came to believe that his position of power in the company gave him the right to do just about anything he wanted with company resources.[15]

Self-esteem is the extent to which a person believes that she is a worthwhile and deserving individual.[16] A person with high self-esteem is more likely to seek high-status jobs, be more confident in her ability to achieve higher levels of performance, and derive greater intrinsic satisfaction from her accomplishments. In contrast, a person with less self-esteem may be more content to remain in a lower-level job, be less confident of his ability, and focus more on extrinsic rewards. Among the major personality dimensions, self-esteem is the one that has been most widely studied in other countries. Although more research is clearly needed, the published evidence does suggest that self-esteem as a personality trait does indeed exist in a variety of countries and that its role in organizations is reasonably important across different cultures.[17]

Risk propensity is the degree to which one is willing to take chances and make risky decisions. A manager with a high risk propensity, for example, might be expected to experiment with new ideas and gamble on new products. She might also lead the organization in new and different directions. This manager might also be a catalyst for innovation. On the other hand, the same person might also jeopardize the continued well-being of the organization if the risky decisions prove to be bad ones. A manager with low risk propensity might lead to a stagnant and overly conservative organization or help the organization successfully weather turbulent and unpredictable times by maintaining stability and calm. Thus the potential consequences of risk propensity to an organization are heavily dependent on that organization's environment.

## Emotional Intelligence

The concept of emotional intelligence has been identified in recent years and provides some interesting insights into personality. Emotional intelligence, or EQ, refers to the extent to which people are self-aware, manage their emotions, motivate themselves, express empathy for others, and possess social skills.[18] These various dimensions can be described as follows:

- *Self-Awareness.* This is the basis for the other components. It refers to a person's capacity for being aware of how they are feeling. In general, more self-awareness allows people to more effectively guide their own lives and behaviors.

**Machiavellianism**
Behavior directed at gaining power and controlling the behavior of others

**self-esteem**
The extent to which a person believes that he or she is a worthwhile and deserving individual

**risk propensity**
The degree to which an individual is willing to take chances and make risky decisions

**emotional intelligence (EQ)**
The extent to which people are self-aware, manage their emotions, motivate themselves, express empathy for others, and possess social skills

- *Managing Emotions.* This refers to a person's capacities to balance anxiety, fear, and anger so that they do not overly interfere with getting things accomplished.
- *Motivating Oneself.* This dimension refers to a person's ability to remain optimistic and to continue striving in the face of setbacks, barriers, and failure.
- *Empathy.* Empathy refers to a person's ability to understand how others are feeling, even without being explicitly told.
- *Social Skill.* This refers to a person's ability to get along with others and to establish positive relationships.

Preliminary research suggests that people with high EQ may perform better than others, especially in jobs that require a high degree of interpersonal interaction and that involve influencing or directing the work of others. Moreover, EQ appears to be something that is not biologically based but can be developed.[19]

---

☐ Managers need to understand personality and the basic personality dimensions most relevant to organizations.

☐ You should also be sufficiently self-aware to understand both your own personality and how your personality affects you at work.

**Manager's Checklist**

---

## Attitudes and Individual Behavior

Another important element of individual behavior in organizations is attitudes. Attitudes are complexes of beliefs and feelings that people have about specific ideas, situations, or other people.[20] Attitudes are important because they are the mechanism through which most people express their feelings. An employee's statement that he feels underpaid by the organization reflects his feelings about his pay. Similarly, when a manager says that she likes the new advertising campaign, she is expressing her feelings about the organization's marketing efforts.

Attitudes have three components. The *affective component* of an attitude reflects feelings and emotions a person has toward a situation. The *cognitive component* of an attitude is derived from knowledge one has about a situation. It is important to note that cognition is subject to individual perceptions (something we discuss more fully later). Thus one person might "know" that a certain political candidate is better than another, whereas someone else might "know" just the opposite. Finally, the *intentional component* of an attitude reflects how one expects to behave toward or in the situation.

To illustrate these three components, consider the case of a manager who places an order for some supplies for his organization from a new office supply firm. Suppose many of the items he orders are out of stock, others are overpriced, and still others arrive damaged. When he calls someone at the supply firm for assistance, he is treated rudely and gets disconnected before his claim is resolved. When asked how he feels about the new office supply firm, he might respond, "I don't

**attitudes**
Complexes of beliefs and feelings that people have about specific ideas, situations, or other people

Attitudes are complexes of beliefs and feelings that people have about specific ideas, situations, or people. This woman has just had a damaged package delivered to her door. She is unhappy with the delivery company for damaging the package and is expressing her feelings to the delivery company representative. She most likely now has a negative attitude toward this delivery company.

like that company [affective component]. They are the worst office supply firm I've ever dealt with [cognitive component]. I'll never do business with them again [intentional component]."

People try to maintain consistency among the three components of their attitudes as well as among all their attitudes. However, circumstances sometimes arise that lead to conflicts. The conflict individuals may experience among their own attitudes is called cognitive dissonance.[21] Say, for example, that a person who has vowed never to work for a big, impersonal corporation intends instead to open her own business and be her own boss. Unfortunately, a series of financial setbacks leads her to have no choice but to take a job with a large company and work for someone else. Thus cognitive dissonance occurs: The affective and cognitive components of the person's attitude conflict with intended behavior. To reduce cognitive dissonance, which is usually an uncomfortable experience for most people, she might tell herself that the situation is only temporary and that she can go back out on her own in the near future. Or she might revise her cognitions and decide that working for a large company is more pleasant than she had expected.

## Work-Related Attitudes

People in organizations form attitudes about many different things. For example, employees are likely to have attitudes about their salaries, promotion possibilities, their bosses, employee benefits, the food in the company cafeteria, and the color of the company softball team uniforms. Of course, some of these attitudes are more important than others. Especially important attitudes are job satisfaction or dissatisfaction and organizational commitment.[22]

**cognitive dissonance**
Caused when an individual has conflicting attitudes

**job satisfaction or dissatisfaction**
An attitude that reflects the extent to which an individual is gratified by or fulfilled in his or her work

### Job Satisfaction or Dissatisfaction
Job satisfaction or dissatisfaction is an attitude that reflects the extent to which an individual is gratified by or fulfilled in his or her work. Extensive research conducted on job satisfaction has indicated that personal factors, such as an individual's needs and aspirations, determine this attitude, along with group and organizational factors, such as relationships with coworkers and supervisors, as well as working conditions, work policies, and compensation.[23]

A satisfied employee also tends to be absent less often, to make positive contributions, and to stay with the organization.[24] In contrast, a dissatisfied employee may be absent more often, may experience stress that disrupts coworkers, and may be continually looking for another job. Contrary to what many managers believe, however, high levels of job satisfaction do not necessarily lead to higher levels of performance. One survey has also indicated that, contrary to popular opinion, Japanese workers are less satisfied with their jobs than their counterparts in the United States.[25]

"How can someone say they're successful if they're not happy doing their work? To me, that's not success."

—NICHOLAS LORE, FOUNDER OF THE ROCKPORT INSTITUTE, A CAREER COACHING FIRM[26]

**organizational commitment**
An attitude that reflects a person's identification with and attachment to the organization itself

**organizational engagement**
The extent to which an employee sees him or herself as part of the organization, actively looks for ways to contribute to the organization, and is involved with the organization in multiple ways

## Organizational Commitment and Engagement

Organizational commitment is an attitude that reflects a person's identification with and attachment to the organization itself. Organizational engagement, similarly, refers to the extent to which an employee sees him or herself as part of the organization, actively looks for ways to contribute to the organization, and is involved with the organization in multiple ways. A person with high levels of commitment and engagement is likely to see herself as a true member of the organization (for example, referring to the organization in personal terms like "We make high-quality products"), to overlook minor sources of dissatisfaction with the organization, and to see herself remaining a member of the organization. In contrast, a person with less organizational commitment and engagement is more likely to see himself as an outsider (for example, referring to the organization in less personal terms like "They don't pay their employees very well"), to express more dissatisfaction about things, and to not see himself as a long-term member of the organization.

Research also suggests that commitment and engagement strengthen with a person's age, years with the organization, sense of job security, and participation in decision making.[27] Employees who feel committed to and engaged with an organization have highly reliable habits, plan a long tenure with the organization, and muster more effort in performance. Although there are few definitive things that organizations can do to create or promote commitment and engagement, there are a few specific guidelines available.[28] For one thing, if the organization treats its employees fairly and provides reasonable rewards and job security, those employees will more likely be satisfied, committed, and engaged. Allowing employees to have a say in how things are done can also promote all three attitudes.[29]

## Affect and Mood in Organizations

Researchers have recently started to focus renewed interest on the affective component of attitudes. Recall from our preceding discussion that the affective component of an attitude reflects our feelings and emotions. Although managers once believed that emotion and feelings varied among people from day to day, research now suggests that, although some short-term fluctuation does indeed occur, there are also underlying stable predispositions toward fairly constant and predictable moods and emotional states.[30]

Some people, for example, tend to have a higher degree of positive affectivity. This means that they are relatively upbeat and optimistic, have an overall sense of well-being, and usually see things in a positive light. Thus they always seem to be in a good mood. It's also recently been proposed that positive affectivity may play a role in entrepreneurial success.[31] Other people, those with more negative affectivity, are just the opposite. They are generally downbeat and pessimistic, and they usually see things in a negative way. They seem to be in a bad mood most of the time.

Of course, as noted above, there can be short-term variations among even the most extreme types. People with a lot of positive affectivity, for example, may still be in a bad mood if they have just received some bad news—being passed over for a promotion, getting extremely negative performance feedback, or being laid off or fired, for instance. Similarly, those with negative affectivity may still be in a good mood—at least for a short time—if they have just been promoted, received very positive performance feedback, or had other good things befall them. After the initial impact of these events wears off, however, those with positive affectivity will generally return to their normal positive mood, whereas those with negative affectivity will gravitate back to their normal bad mood.

**positive affectivity**
A tendency to be relatively upbeat and optimistic, have an overall sense of well-being, see things in a positive light, and seem to be in a good mood

**negative affectivity**
A tendency to be generally downbeat and pessimistic, see things in a negative way, and seem to be in a bad mood

---

☐ Managers should know the three components of an attitude.

☐ Managers should also understand the determinants and consequences of job satisfaction or dissatisfaction, organizational commitment, and organizational engagement.

☐ You should be sufficiently self-aware that you know your own levels of job satisfaction or dissatisfaction, organizational commitment, and organizational engagement and how they affect your behavior.

**Manager's Checklist**

# Perception and Individual Behavior

As noted earlier, an important element of an attitude is the person's perception of the object about which the attitude is formed. Because perception plays a role in a variety of other workplace behaviors, managers need to have a general understanding of basic perceptual processes.[32] The role of attributions is also important.

Selective perception is the process of screening out information that we are uncomfortable with or that contradicts our beliefs. If this manager already has a negative opinion of this worker, he will now become even more negative. But if his assessment has been positive, he may overlook this current incident.

## Basic Perceptual Processes

Perception is the set of processes by which an individual becomes aware of and interprets information about the environment. As shown in Figure 14.3, basic perceptual processes that are particularly relevant to organizations are selective perception and stereotyping.

**Selective Perception**   Selective perception is the process of screening out information that we are uncomfortable with or that contradicts our beliefs. For example, suppose a manager is exceptionally fond of a particular worker. The manager has a very positive attitude about the worker and thinks he is a top performer. One day the manager notices that the worker seems to be goofing off. Selective perception may cause the manager to quickly forget what he observed. Similarly, suppose a manager has formed a very negative image of a particular worker. She thinks this worker is a poor performer and never does a good job. When she happens to observe an example of high performance from the worker, she, too, may not remember it for very long. In one sense, selective perception is beneficial because it allows us to disregard minor bits of information. Of course, this is helpful only if our basic perception is accurate. If selective perception causes us to ignore important information, however, it can become quite detrimental.

**Stereotyping**   Stereotyping is the process of categorizing or labeling people on the basis of a single attribute. Common attributes on which people often stereotype are race, gender, and age.[33] Of course, stereotypes along these lines are inaccurate and can be harmful. For example, suppose a manager forms the stereotype that women can perform only certain tasks and that men are best suited for other tasks. To the extent that this affects the manager's hiring practices, the manager is (1) costing the organization valu-

**perception**
The set of processes by which an individual becomes aware of and interprets information about the environment

**selective perception**
The process of screening out information that we are uncomfortable with or that contradicts our beliefs

**stereotyping**
The process of categorizing or labeling people on the basis of a single attribute

## FIGURE 14.3 PERCEPTUAL PROCESSES

Two of the most basic perceptual processes are selective perception and stereotyping. As shown here, selective perception occurs when we screen out information (represented by the − symbols) that causes us discomfort or that contradicts our beliefs. Stereotyping occurs when we categorize or label people on the basis of a single attribute, illustrated here by color.

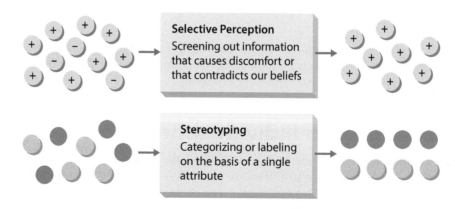

able talent for both sets of jobs, (2) violating federal law, and (3) behaving unethically. On the other hand, certain forms of stereotyping can be useful and efficient. Suppose, for example, that a manager believes that communication skills are important for a particular job and that speech communication majors tend to have exceptionally good communication skills. As a result, whenever he interviews candidates for jobs, he pays especially close attention to speech communication majors. To the extent that communication skills truly predict job performance and that majoring in speech communication does indeed provide those skills, this form of stereotyping can be beneficial.

## Perception and Attribution

Perception is also closely linked with another process called attribution. Attribution is a mechanism through which we observe behavior and then attribute causes to it.[34] The behavior that is observed may be our own or that of others. For example, suppose someone realizes one day that she is working fewer hours than before, that she talks less about her work, and that she calls in sick more often. She might conclude from this that she must have become disenchanted with her job and subsequently decide to quit. Thus she observed her own behavior, attributed a cause to it, and developed what she thought was a consistent response.

More common is attributing cause to the behavior of others. For example, if the manager of the person just described has seen the same behavior, he might form exactly the same attribution. On the other hand, he might instead decide that she has a serious illness, that he is driving her too hard, that she is experiencing too much stress, that she has a drug problem, or that she is having family problems.

The basic framework around which we form attributions is *consensus* (the extent to which other people in the same situation behave the same way), *consistency* (the extent to which the same person behaves in the same way at different times), and *distinctiveness* (the extent to which the same person behaves in the same way in other situations). For example, suppose a manager observes that an employee is late for a meeting. The manager might further realize that he is the only one who is late (low consensus), recall that he is often late for other meetings (high consistency), and subsequently realize that the same employee is sometimes late arriving for work and returning from lunch (low distinctiveness). This pattern of attributions might cause the manager to decide that the person's behavior is something that should be changed. As a result, the manager might meet with the subordinate and establish some punitive consequences for future tardiness.

**attribution**
The process of observing behavior and attributing causes to it

---

☐ Managers should understand perception in general, as well as selective perception and stereotyping in particular.

☐ You need to also appreciate the role of attributions in organizations.

**Manager's Checklist**

# Stress and Individual Behavior

Another important element of behavior in organizations is stress. Stress is a person's response to a strong stimulus.[35] This stimulus is called a *stressor*. Stress generally follows a cycle referred to as the General Adaptation Syndrome, or GAS,[36] shown in Figure 14.4. According to this view, when a person first encounters a stressor, the GAS is initiated, and the first stage, alarm, is activated. He may feel panic, wonder how to cope, and feel helpless. For example, suppose a manager is told to prepare a detailed evaluation of a plan by his firm to buy one of its competitors. His first reaction may be, "How will I ever get this done by tomorrow?"

**stress**
A person's response to a strong stimulus, which is called a stressor

**General Adaptation Syndrome (GAS)**
General cycle of the stress process

---

### FIGURE 14.4 THE GENERAL ADAPTATION SYNDROME

The General Adaptation Syndrome represents the normal process by which we react to stressful events. At stage 1—alarm—we feel panic and alarm, and our level of resistance to stress drops. Stage 2—resistance—represents our efforts to confront and control the stressful circumstance. If we fail, we may eventually reach stage 3—exhaustion—and just give up or quit.

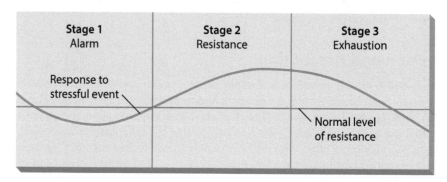

| **Stage 1** Alarm | **Stage 2** Resistance | **Stage 3** Exhaustion |
| --- | --- | --- |

Response to stressful event

Normal level of resistance

**Type A**
Individuals who are extremely competitive, very devoted to work, and have a strong sense of time urgency

**Type B**
Individuals who are less competitive, less devoted to work, and have a weaker sense of time urgency

Stress is a person's response to a strong stimulus. This woman is behind on a major project (a strong stimulus). Her response (stress) is anxiety and worry over her ability to get the project completed.

2xSamara.com/Shutterstock.com

If the stressor is too intense, the person may feel unable to cope and never really try to respond to its demands. In most cases, however, after a short period of alarm, the person gathers some strength and starts to resist the negative effects of the stressor. For example, the manager with the evaluation to write may calm down, call home to say he is working late, roll up his sleeves, order out for coffee, and get to work. Thus, at stage 2 of the GAS, the person is resisting the effects of the stressor.

In many cases, the resistance phase may end the GAS. If the manager can complete the evaluation earlier than expected, he may drop it in his briefcase, smile to himself, and head home tired but satisfied. On the other hand, prolonged exposure to a stressor without resolution may bring on stage 3 of the GAS—exhaustion. At this stage, the person literally gives up and can no longer resist the stressor. The manager, for example, might fall asleep at his desk at 3:00 A.M. and never finish the evaluation.

We should note that stress is not all bad. In the absence of stress, we may experience lethargy and stagnation. An optimal level of stress, on the other hand, can result in motivation and excitement. Too much stress, however, can have negative consequences. It is also important to understand that stress can be caused by "good" as well as "bad" things. Excessive pressure, unreasonable demands on our time, and bad news can all cause stress. But even receiving a bonus and then having to decide what to do with the money can be stressful. So, too, can receiving a promotion, gaining recognition, and similar good things.

One important line of thinking about stress focuses on Type A and Type B personalities.[37] Type A individuals are extremely competitive, very devoted to work, and have a strong sense of time urgency. They are likely to be aggressive, impatient, and very work oriented. They have a lot of drive and want to accomplish as much as possible as quickly as possible. Type B individuals are less competitive, less devoted to work, and have a weaker sense of time urgency. Such people are less likely to experience conflict with others and more likely to have a balanced, relaxed approach to life. They can work at a constant pace without time urgency. Type B people are not necessarily more or less successful than are Type A people, but they are less likely to experience stress.

## Causes and Consequences of Stress

Stress is obviously not a simple phenomenon. Several different things can cause stress, as listed in Figure 14.5. Note that this list includes only work-related conditions. We should keep in mind that stress can also be the result of personal circumstances.[38]

**Causes of Stress**   Work-related stressors fall into one of four categories—task, physical, role, and interpersonal demands. *Task demands* are associated with the task itself. Some occupations are inherently more stressful than others. Having to make fast decisions, decisions with less than complete information, or decisions that have relatively serious consequences are some of the things that can make some jobs stressful. The jobs of surgeon, airline pilot, and stockbroker are relatively more stressful than the jobs of general practitioner, baggage handler, and office receptionist. Although a general practitioner makes important decisions, he is also likely to have time to make a considered diagnosis and fully explore a number of different treatments. But during surgery, the surgeon must make decisions quickly while realizing that the wrong one may endanger her patient's life.

> "Increasing store hours increases the hours that the bad guys can rob you. Darkness to dawn is the highest time of exposure to armed robberies."
>
> — BILL WISE, FORMER MANAGER OF SAFETY AND SECURITY FOR WENDY'S[39]

*Physical demands* are stressors associated with the job setting. Working outdoors in extremely hot or cold temperatures, or even in an improperly heated or cooled office, can lead to stress. Likewise, jobs that have rotating work shifts make it difficult for people to have stable sleep patterns. A poorly designed office—one which, for example, makes it difficult for people to have privacy or promotes too little social interaction—can result in stress, as can poor lighting and inadequate work surfaces. Even more severe are actual threats to health. Examples include jobs like coal mining, poultry processing, and toxic waste handling. Similarly, some jobs carry risks associated with higher incident rates of violence, such as armed robberies. Examples include law enforcement officers, taxi drivers, and convenience store clerks.

*Role demands* can also cause stress. (Roles are discussed more fully in Chapter 18.) A role is a set of expected behaviors associated with a position in a group or organization. Stress can result from either role conflict or role ambiguity that people can experience in groups. For example, an employee who is feeling pressure from her boss to work longer hours or to travel more, while also being asked by her family for more time at home, will almost certainly experience stress as a result of role conflict.[40] Similarly, a new employee experiencing role ambiguity because of poor orientation and training practices by the organization will also suffer from stress. Excessive meetings are also a potential source of stress.[41] While job

## FIGURE 14.5  CAUSES OF WORK STRESS

There are several causes of work stress in organizations. Four general sets of organizational stressors are task demands, physical demands, role demands, and interpersonal demands.

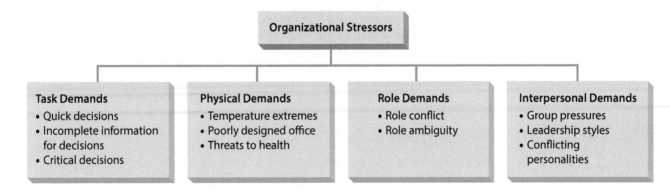

cuts and layoffs during the 2008–2009 recession focused attention on the stress experienced by those losing their jobs (and appropriately so), it's also the case that many of the managers imposing the layoffs experienced stress as well.[42]

*Interpersonal demands* are stressors associated with relationships that confront people in organizations. For example, group pressures regarding restriction of output and norm conformity can lead to stress. Leadership styles may also cause stress. An employee who feels a strong need to participate in decision making may feel stress if his boss refuses to allow such participation. And individuals with conflicting personalities may experience stress if required to work too closely together. For example, a person with an internal locus of control might be frustrated when working with someone who prefers to wait and just let things happen.[43]

> "Some of [the people I laid off] I'd worked with for a very long time. I saw such pain in their faces, but felt I couldn't show my emotions to them.... As soon as I could, I'd close the door, draw the blinds, and have a good sob."
>
> — ALICIA SANERA, HR EXECUTIVE[44]

**Consequences of Stress**   As noted earlier, the results of stress may be positive or negative. The negative consequences may be behavioral, psychological, or medical. Behaviorally, for example, stress may lead to detrimental or harmful actions, such as smoking, alcohol or drug abuse, and overeating. Other stress-induced behaviors are accident proneness, violence toward self or others, and appetite disorders. Substance abuse is also a potential consequence.[45]

As you can see from our *World of Difference* feature, stress can also result in psychological consequences. These can interfere with a person's mental health and well-being. Problems include sleep disturbances, depression, family problems, and sexual dysfunction. Managers are especially prone to sleep disturbances when they experience stress at work.[46] Medical consequences of stress affect an individual's physiological well-being. Heart disease and stroke have been linked to stress, as have headaches, backaches, ulcers and related disorders, and skin conditions such as acne and hives.

Individual stress also has direct consequences for businesses. For an operating employee, stress may translate into poor-quality work and lower productivity. For a manager, it may mean faulty decision making and disruptions in working relationships.[47] Withdrawal behaviors can also result from stress. People who are having difficulties with stress in their jobs are more likely to call in sick or to leave the organization. More subtle forms of withdrawal may also occur. A manager may start missing deadlines, for example, or taking longer lunch breaks. Employees may also withdraw by developing feelings of indifference. The irritation displayed by people under great stress can make them difficult to get along with. Job satisfaction, morale, and commitment can all suffer as a result of excessive levels of stress. So, too, can motivation to perform.

Another consequence of stress is burnout—a feeling of exhaustion that may develop when someone experiences too much stress for an extended period of time. Burnout results in constant fatigue, frustration, and helplessness. Increased rigidity follows, as do a loss of self-confidence and psychological withdrawal. The individual dreads going to work, often puts in longer hours but gets less accomplished than before, and exhibits mental and physical exhaustion. Because of the damaging effects of burnout, some firms are taking steps to help avoid it. For example, British Airways provides all of its employees with training designed to help them recognize the symptoms of burnout and develop strategies for avoiding it.

## Managing Stress

Given the potential consequences of stress, it follows that both people and organizations should be concerned about how to limit its more damaging effects. Numerous ideas and

**burnout**
A feeling of exhaustion that may develop when someone experiences too much stress for an extended period of time

**A WORLD OF DIFFERENCE**

# The Color of Stress

Audrey Murrell, an African American woman, remembers subtle forms of discrimination when she was in school. White classmates, for example, excluded her from study groups and asserted an implicit privilege in using classroom materials before she was allowed a turn. "You're left with this feeling of 'Is it me or is it them?'" says Murrell. "You know it's them, but it's hard to prove because it's not obvious discrimination." As Murrell learned, however, it takes a toll nevertheless, particularly on the emotional, mental, and even physical health of the young people who suffer from it.

As associate professor of business administration and psychology at the University of Pittsburgh's Joseph M. Katz Graduate School of Business, Murrell is also well aware that the same patterns of discrimination often follow African Americans from the classroom to the workplace. "It can lead to a lot of self-doubt and lack of confidence," she says. "Then you're likely to see withdrawal and detaching oneself from the job, which leads to internal bitterness and anger. ... Bias and the way it affects our physical and emotional state has very real consequences."

One of those consequences is stress. African Americans are at higher risk than whites for such conditions as cardiovascular disease and diabetes, and research suggests a connection between differences in the prevalence of such diseases and stress—particularly, stress resulting from racial discrimination. According to the American Psychological Association, *perceived discrimination*—the perception that one has experienced discrimination because of one's race or ethnicity—contributes to high blood pressure and diabetes, such unhealthy behaviors as smoking and alcohol/substance abuse, and mental health disorders among African Americans and other minorities.

Specifically, perceived discrimination is a key factor in what's known as *chronic stress*—that is, long-term stress that results from lingering feelings of despair or hopelessness. When it comes to the workplace, some researchers also distinguish between

*formal* and *interpersonal discrimination*. According to Sabat, Lindsey, and King (2014), *formal discrimination* usually occurs as "formal job discrimination" against individuals in such HR processes as "selection, retention, promotion or termination."

On the other hand, *interpersonal discrimination* occurs in situations that aren't directly related to such "employment outcomes" as being hired or fired. Rather, it occurs in various interpersonal interactions that may be brief or infrequent. It runs the gamut from social distancing (e.g., declining to engage in conversation, ignoring requests for help) to outright threat or harassment. Sabat, Lindsey, and King found that "interpersonal discrimination can lead to high levels of workplace stress due to the fact that it is a more chronic and pervasive form of discrimination than formal discrimination."

In short, racial discrimination and chronic stress go hand in hand. On top of everything else, the situation is even worse for women of color like Audrey Murrell and Philomena Essed, a social psychologist who introduced the concept of *gendered racism* to describe the form of double discrimination—"genderism" plus "racism"—faced by minority women not only in the workplace but in the basic activities of everyday life. Following up on Essed's theory, one team of researchers concluded that "experiences associated with concurrent racism and sexism are substantial sources of stress [among minority women], increasing risk for psychological distress, disorder, and ultimately, thoughts of suicide."

*References:* Michelle K. Massie, "The Stress of Workplace Discrimination," *Monster* (2009), http://career-advice.monster.com, on February 9, 2015; American Psychological Association, "Fact Sheet: Disparities and Health" (2015), www.apa.org, on February 9, 2015; Isaac Sabat, Alex Lindsey, and Eden King, "Antecedents, Outcomes, Prevention and Coping Strategies for Lesbian, Gay, and Bisexual Stress," in Pamela L. Perrewé, Christopher C. Rosen, and Jonathon R.B. Halbesleben (eds.), *The Role of Demographics in Occupational Stress and Well-Being* (Bingley, UK: Emerald Group, 2014), pp. 173–198; American Psychological Association, "Interpersonal Racism: Conceptualization," *Health Psychology* (2015), www.health-pysch. org, on February 18, 2015; Brea L. Perry, Erin L. Pullen, and Carrie B. Oser, "Too Much of a Good Thing? Psychosocial Resources, Gendered Racism, and Suicidal Ideation among Low Socioeconomic Status African American Women," *Social Psychology Quarterly*, 2012, Vol. 75, No. 4, pp. 334–359, www.asanet.org, on February 18, 2015.

approaches have been developed to help manage stress. Some are strategies for individuals; others are strategies for organizations.[48]

One way people manage stress is through exercise. People who exercise regularly feel less tension and stress, are more self-confident, and feel more optimistic. Their better physical condition also makes them less susceptible to many common illnesses. People who do not exercise regularly, on the other hand, tend to feel more stress and are more likely to be depressed. They are also more likely to have heart attacks. And, because of their physical condition, they are more likely to contract illnesses.

Another method people use to manage stress is relaxation. Relaxation allows individuals to adapt to, and therefore better deal with, their stress. Relaxation comes in many forms, such as taking regular vacations and engaging in non-work activities on the weekends. A recent study found that people's attitudes toward a variety of workplace characteristics improved significantly following a weekend when they were able to fully disengage from their work.[49] People can also learn to relax while on the job. For example, some experts recommend that people take regular rest breaks during their normal workday. Google has gone so far as to offer "nap pods" at work where employees can take brief naps during the workday.

People can also use time management to control stress. The idea behind time management is that many daily pressures can be reduced or eliminated if people do a better job of managing time. One approach to time management is to make a list every morning of the things to be done that day. The items on the list are then grouped into three categories: critical activities that must be performed, important activities that should be performed, and optional or trivial things that can be delegated or postponed. The individual performs the items on the list in their order of importance.

Finally, people can manage stress through support groups. A support group can be as simple as a group of family members or friends to enjoy leisure time with. Going out after work with a couple of coworkers to a basketball game or a movie, for example, can help relieve stress built up during the day. Family and friends can help people cope with stress on an ongoing basis and during times of crisis. For example, an employee who has just learned that she did not get the promotion she has been working toward for months may find it helpful to have a good friend to lean on, talk to, or yell at. People also may make use of more elaborate and formal support groups. Community centers or churches, for example, may sponsor support groups for people who have recently gone through a divorce, the death of a loved one, or some other tragedy.

Organizations are also beginning to realize that they should be involved in helping employees cope with stress. One argument for this is that because the business is at least partially responsible for stress, it should also help relieve it. Another is that stress-related insurance claims by employees can cost the organization considerable sums of money. Still another is that workers experiencing lower levels of detrimental stress will be able to function more effectively. AT&T has initiated a series of seminars and workshops to help its employees cope with the stress they face in their jobs. The firm was prompted to develop these seminars for all three of the reasons noted here.

A wellness stress program is a special part of the organization specifically created to help deal with stress. Organizations have adopted stress-management programs, health promotion programs, and other kinds of programs for this purpose. The AT&T seminar program noted earlier is similar to this idea, but true wellness programs are ongoing activities that have a number of different components. They commonly include exercise-related activities as well as classroom instruction programs dealing with smoking cessation, weight reduction, and general stress management. Corning has adopted a stress management program providing workers with resources to help them understand stress and its health effects, as well as how to adopt skills for coping with stress. As part of the program, the company offers various classes in tai chi, biofeedback, meditation, yoga, muscle relaxation, guided imagery, and cognitive restructuring.[50]

Some companies are developing their own programs or using existing programs of this type. Johns Manville, for example, has a gym at its corporate headquarters. Other firms negotiate discounted health club membership rates with local establishments.

For the instructional part of the program, the organization can again either sponsor its own training or perhaps jointly sponsor seminars with a local YMCA, civic organization, or church. Organization-based fitness programs facilitate employee exercise, a very positive consideration, but such programs are also quite costly. Still, more and more companies are developing fitness programs for employees. Similarly, some companies are offering their employees periodic sabbaticals—extended breaks from work that presumably allow people to get revitalized and reenergized. Intel and McDonald's are among the firms offering this benefit.[51]

---

| | |
|---|---|
| ☐ Managers need to understand the nature of stress, especially its primary causes and consequences. | **Manager's Checklist** |
| ☐ You should know if you are more of a Type A or a Type B person. | |

---

# Creativity in Organizations

Creativity is yet another important component of individual behavior in organizations. Creativity is the ability of a person to generate new ideas or to conceive of new perspectives on existing ideas. What makes a person creative? How do people become creative? How does the creative process work? Although psychologists have not yet discovered complete answers to these questions, examining a few general patterns can help us understand the sources of individual creativity within organizations.[52] *Tech Watch* will introduce some of these ideas for you.

**creativity**
The ability of an individual to generate new ideas or to conceive of new perspectives on existing ideas

## The Creative Individual

Numerous researchers have focused their efforts on trying to describe the common attributes of creative people. These attributes generally fall into three categories: background experiences, personal traits, and cognitive abilities.

**Background Experiences and Creativity** Researchers have observed that many creative people were raised in environments in which creativity was nurtured. Mozart was raised in a family of musicians and began composing and performing music at age six. Pierre and Marie Curie, great scientists in their own right, also raised a daughter, Irene, who won the Nobel Prize in chemistry. Thomas Edison's creativity was nurtured by his mother. However, people with background experiences very different from theirs have also been creative. Frederick Douglass was born into slavery in Tuckahoe, Maryland, and had very limited opportunities for education. Nonetheless, his powerful oratory and creative thinking helped lead to the Thirteenth Amendment to the U.S. Constitution, which outlawed slavery in the United States.

**Personal Traits and Creativity** Certain personal traits have also been linked to creativity in individuals. The traits shared by most creative people are openness, an attraction to complexity, high levels of energy, independence and autonomy, strong self-confidence, and a strong belief that one is, in fact, creative. People who possess these traits are more likely to be creative than are those who do not have them.

**Cognitive Abilities and Creativity** Cognitive abilities are an individual's power to think intelligently and to analyze situations and data

Wolfgang Amadeus Mozart is acknowledged as one of the most creative musical composers of all time. He began composing at the age of five and could play both violin and keyboard. Both of his parents were musicians, and they both motivated him to work in the music field and provided a nurturing family to support his passion.

# Picture a Better Mousetrap

In 2009, 25-year-old Kevin Systrom had all the credentials for becoming a high-tech entrepreneur in Silicon Valley—a degree from Stanford, an internship at Twitter, and some job experience at Google. Foursquare, a mobile networking app that let users keep friends posted on their whereabouts, had launched in March 2009, and Systrom decided that he could create a product to compete in the same lucrative space.

He called his app Burbn (he likes bourbon whiskey), which let users "check in" to locations, plan meetings with friends, post pictures, and earn points for hanging around in groups. He brought on a cofounder, a 25-year-old Brazilian-born engineer named Mike Krieger, and in March 2010, the partners set about finding enough money to take on Foursquare, which was already rumored to be worth $100–150 million despite boasting barely a million users. This step in the process, however, turned out to be more frustrating than Systrom and Krieger had bargained for. "Burbn was well liked and had a few passionate daily actives," recalls Krieger, "but it wasn't exactly setting the world on fire. Our attempts at explaining what we were building was often met with blank stares, and we peaked at around 1,000 users."

"We realized the check-in part was a little complicated, but people loved the photo part," says Systrom; unfortunately, however, the whole product "wasn't cool enough" to challenge the market leader (in June 2011, Foursquare raised $50 million on a valuation of $600 million). Whether or not Systrom and Krieger had the makings of a better mousetrap, nobody was beating a path to their door. In fact, David Burkus, author of *The Myths of Creativity: The Truth about How Innovative Companies Generate Great Ideas*, would probably say that Burbn had succumbed to a variation of the "Mousetrap Myth." According to Burkus, that myth—*If you build a better mousetrap, the world will beat a path to your door*—"is really bad advice. We expect a celebration when our product launches or our new work is on display, but this is often not the case. … The world's most common reaction to a new idea isn't to beat a path to our door. It's typically to … ignore the idea."

Creativity, observes Burkus, has an even tougher time in organizational contexts. "The truth is," he writes, "that companies reject the great ideas of their people all the time. … Most companies don't suffer from an idea-generation issue; they suffer from an idea-recognition issue." This organizational habit of mind may also reflect a psychological habit of mind among individuals—namely, a reluctance to embrace risk and innovation.

Fortunately, as we saw in Chapter 9, entrepreneurs like Kevin Systrom and Mike Krieger tend have a greater tolerance for risk and, as Burkus suggests, a better sense of idea recognition, especially when it comes to matching a new product with an emerging market. One day in July 2010, reports Krieger, they realized that

> it was time to try something different — why don't we take the photo updates from Burbn and make them into their own product? … In retrospect, [the idea] may seem "obvious"… but products are defined by a series of decisions and assumptions, and our combination of being photos-first and public-by-default would prove to be a combination that solved an unmet need.

The new idea—Instagram—launched in October 2010, and less than two years later, Facebook bought it for $1 billion.

*References:* Eric Markowitz, "How Instagram Grew from Foursquare Knock-Off to $1 Billion Photo Empire," *Inc.* (April 10, 2012), www.inc.com, on February 27, 2015; Mike Krieger, "How Instagram Worked," *Backchannel* (October 20, 2014), http://medium.com, on February 27, 2015; Megan Garber, "Instagram was First Called 'Burbn,'" *The Atlantic* (July 2, 2014), www.theatlantic.com, on February 27, 2015; David Burkus, "The Myths of Creativity: Building a Better Mousetrap" (book excerpt), *Fast Company* (September 12, 2013), www.fastcompany.com, on February 26, 2015; Paul Sohn, "Interview with David Burkus: *The Myths of Creativity*," *Salt & Light* (November 10, 2013), http://paulsohn.org, on February 26, 2015.

effectively. Intelligence may be a precondition for individual creativity—although most creative people are highly intelligent, not all intelligent people are necessarily creative. Creativity is also linked with the ability to think divergently and convergently. *Divergent thinking* is a skill that allows people to see differences among situations, phenomena, or events. *Convergent thinking* is a skill that allows people to see similarities among situations, phenomena, or events. Creative people are generally very skilled at both divergent and convergent thinking.

Interestingly, Japanese managers have come to question their own creative abilities. The concern is that their emphasis on group harmony may have stifled individual initiative and hampered the development of individual creativity. As a result, many Japanese firms, including Omron Corporation, Fuji Photo, and Shimizu Corporation, have launched training programs intended to boost the creativity of their employees.[53]

## The Creative Process

Although creative people often report that ideas seem to come to them "in a flash," individual creative activity actually tends to progress through a series of stages. Not all creative activity has to follow these four stages, but much of it does.

**Preparation**  The creative process normally begins with a period of *preparation*. To make a creative contribution to business management or business services, a person must usually receive formal training and education in business. Formal education and training are usually the most efficient ways of becoming familiar with this vast amount of research and knowledge. This is one reason for the strong demand for undergraduate and master's level business education. Formal business education can be an effective way for a person to get "up to speed" and begin making creative contributions quickly. Experiences that managers have on the job after their formal training has ended can also contribute to the creative process. In an important sense, the education and training of creative people never really ends. It continues as long as they remain interested in the world and curious about the way things work. Bruce Roth earned a Ph.D. in chemistry and then spent years working in the pharmaceutical industry learning more and more about chemical compounds and how they work in human beings.

**Incubation**  The second phase of the creative process is *incubation*—a period of less intense conscious concentration during which the knowledge and ideas acquired during preparation mature and develop. A curious aspect of incubation is that it is often helped along by pauses in concentrated rational thought. Some creative people rely on physical activity such as jogging or swimming to provide a break from thinking. Others may read or listen to music. Sometimes sleep may even supply the needed pause. Bruce Roth eventually joined Warner-Lambert, an up-and-coming drug company, to help develop medication to lower cholesterol. In his spare time, Roth read mystery novels and hiked in the mountains. He later acknowledged that this was when he did his best thinking. Similarly, twice a year Bill Gates retreats to a secluded wooded cabin to reflect on trends in technology; it is during these weeks, he says, that he develops his sharpest insights into where Microsoft should be heading.[54]

**Insight**  Usually occurring after preparation and incubation, *insight* is a spontaneous breakthrough in which the creative person achieves a new understanding of some problem or situation. Insight represents a coming together of all the scattered thoughts and ideas that were maturing during incubation. It may occur suddenly or develop slowly over time. Insight can be triggered by some external event, such as a new experience or an encounter with new data, which forces the person to think about old issues and problems in new ways, or it can be a completely internal event in which patterns of thought finally coalesce in ways that generate new understanding. One day Bruce Roth was reviewing data from some earlier studies that had found the new drug under development to be no more effective than other drugs already available. But this time he saw some statistical relationships that had not been identified previously. He knew then that he had a major breakthrough on his hands.

**Verification** Once an insight has occurred, *verification* determines the validity or truthfulness of the insight. For many creative ideas, verification includes scientific experiments to determine whether the insight actually leads to the results expected. Verification may also include the development of a product or service prototype. A prototype is one product or a very small number of products built just to see if the ideas behind this new product actually work. Product prototypes are rarely sold to the public but are very valuable in verifying the insights developed in the creative process. Once the new product or service is developed, verification in the marketplace is the ultimate test of the creative idea behind it. Bruce Roth and his colleagues set to work testing the new drug compound and eventually won FDA approval. The drug, named Lipitor, is already the largest-selling pharmaceutical in history. And Pfizer, the firm that bought Warner-Lambert in a hostile takeover, earns more than $10 billion a year on the drug.

### Enhancing Creativity in Organizations

Managers who wish to enhance and promote creativity in their organizations can do so in a variety of ways.[55] One important method for enhancing creativity is to make it a part of the organization's culture, often through explicit goals. Firms that truly want to stress creativity, like 3M and Rubbermaid, for example, state goals that some percentage of future revenues is to be gained from new products. This clearly communicates that creativity and innovation are valued. Best Buy recently picked four groups of salespeople in their 20s and early 30s and asked them to spend 10 weeks living together in a Los Angeles apartment complex (with expenses paid by the company and still earning their normal pay). Their job? Sit around and brainstorm new business ideas that could be rolled out quickly and cheaply.[56]

Another important part of enhancing creativity is to reward creative successes, while being careful not to punish creative failures. Many ideas that seem worthwhile on paper fail to pan out in reality. If the first person to come up with an idea that fails is fired or otherwise punished, others in the organization will become more cautious in their own work. And, as a result, fewer creative ideas will emerge. Steve Jobs encouraged creativity throughout Apple's culture by encouraging debate when discussing new ideas and removing passive aggressive behaviors. Dealing with conflict head-on and embracing the tension spurs new ideas and different angles, and reduces risks.[57]

---

**Manager's Checklist**

☐ Managers need to know the basic elements of creativity and its likely causes.

☐ You should also have a clear understanding of how creativity is valued and fostered in your organization.

## Types of Workplace Behavior

Now that we have looked closely at how individual differences can influence behavior in organizations, let's turn our attention to what we mean by workplace behavior. Workplace behavior is a pattern of action by the members of an organization that directly or indirectly influences organizational effectiveness. Important workplace behaviors include performance and productivity, absenteeism and turnover, and organizational citizenship. Unfortunately, a variety of dysfunctional behaviors can also occur in organizational settings.

### Performance Behaviors

Performance behaviors are the total set of work-related behaviors that the organization expects the person to display. Thus they derive from the psychological contract. For some jobs, performance behaviors can be narrowly defined and easily measured. For example, an

**workplace behavior**
A pattern of action by the members of an organization that directly or indirectly influences organizational effectiveness

**performance behaviors**
The total set of work-related behaviors that the organization expects the person to display

assembly-line worker who sits by a moving conveyor and attaches parts to a product as it passes by has relatively few performance behaviors. He or she is expected to remain at the workstation and correctly attach the parts. Performance can often be assessed quantitatively by counting the percentage of parts correctly attached.

For many other jobs, however, performance behaviors are more diverse and much more difficult to assess. For example, consider the case of a research and development scientist at Merck. The scientist works in a lab trying to find new scientific breakthroughs that have commercial potential. The scientist must apply knowledge learned in graduate school with experience gained from previous research. Intuition and creativity are also important elements. And the desired breakthrough may take months or even years to accomplish. As we discussed in Chapter 13, organizations rely on a number of different methods for evaluating performance. The key, of course, is to match the evaluation mechanism with the job being performed.

## Withdrawal Behaviors

Another important type of work-related behavior is that which results in withdrawal—absenteeism and turnover. Absenteeism occurs when a person does not show up for work. The cause may be legitimate (illness, jury duty, death in the family, and so forth) or feigned (reported as legitimate but actually just an excuse to stay home). When an employee is absent, her or his work does not get done at all, or a substitute must be hired to do it. In either case, the quantity or quality of actual output is likely to suffer. Obviously, some absenteeism is expected. The key concern of organizations is to minimize feigned absenteeism and to reduce legitimate absences as much as possible. High absenteeism may be a symptom of other problems as well, such as job dissatisfaction and low morale.

Turnover occurs when people quit their jobs. An organization usually incurs costs in replacing individuals who have quit, but if turnover involves especially productive people, it is even more costly. Turnover seems to result from a number of factors, including aspects of the job, the organization, the individual, the labor market, and family influences. In general, a poor person–job fit is also a likely cause of turnover.[58] The current high levels of unemployment reduce employee-driven turnover, given that fewer jobs are available. But when unemployment is low (and there are many open jobs) turnover may naturally increase as people seek better opportunities, higher pay, and so forth.

Efforts to directly manage turnover are often fraught with difficulty, even in organizations that concentrate on rewarding good performers. Of course, some turnover is inevitable, and in some cases it may even be desirable. For example, if the organization is trying to cut costs by reducing its staff, having people voluntarily choose to leave is preferable to having to terminate their jobs. And if the people who choose to leave are low performers or express high levels of job dissatisfaction, the organization may also benefit from turnover.

## Organizational Citizenship

Organizational citizenship is the behavior of individuals that makes a positive overall contribution to the organization.[59] Consider, for example, an employee who does work that is acceptable in terms of both quantity and quality. However, she refuses to work overtime, will not help newcomers learn the ropes, and is generally unwilling to make any contribution to the organization beyond the strict performance of her job. Although this person may be seen as a good performer, she is not likely to be seen as a good organizational citizen.

Another employee may exhibit a comparable level of performance. In addition, however, he will always work late when the boss asks him to, will take time to help newcomers learn their way around, and is perceived as being helpful and committed to the organization's success. Although his level of performance may be seen as equal to that of the first worker, he is also likely to be seen as a better organizational citizen.

The determinant of organizational citizenship behaviors is likely to be a complex mosaic of individual, social, and organizational variables. For example, the personality, attitudes,

**absenteeism**
When a person does not show up for work

**turnover**
When people quit their jobs

**organizational citizenship**
The behavior of individuals that makes a positive overall contribution to the organization

and needs of the individual will have to be consistent with citizenship behaviors. Similarly, the social context in which the person works, or the work group, will need to facilitate and promote such behaviors (we discuss group dynamics in Chapter 18). And the organization itself, especially its culture, must be capable of promoting, recognizing, and rewarding these types of behaviors if they are to be maintained. Although the study of organizational citizenship is still in its infancy, preliminary research suggests that it may play a powerful role in organizational effectiveness.[60]

### Dysfunctional Behaviors

Some work-related behaviors are dysfunctional in nature. Dysfunctional behaviors are those that detract from, rather than contribute to, organizational performance.[61] Two of the more common ones, absenteeism and turnover, have been mentioned. But other forms of dysfunctional behavior may be even more costly for an organization. Theft and sabotage, for example, result in direct financial costs for an organization. Sexual and racial harassment also cost an organization, both indirectly (by lowering morale, producing fear, and driving off valuable employees) and directly (through financial liability if the organization responds inappropriately). So, too, can politicized behavior, intentionally misleading others in the organization, spreading malicious rumors, and similar activities. Incivility and rudeness can result in conflict and damage to morale and the organization's culture.[62]

Workplace violence is also a growing concern in some organizations. Violence by disgruntled workers or former workers results in dozens of deaths and injuries each year.[63] The factors that contribute to workplace violence—not to mention the factors involved in increases and decreases—are difficult to pin down. However, many factors appear to contribute to potential violent behavior, including psychological disorders, a feeling of being disrespected by the organization, and a sense of hopelessness.

**dysfunctional behaviors**
Those that detract from, rather than contribute to, organizational performance

---

 **Manager's Checklist**

☐ Managers need to be able to distinguish between performance behaviors, withdrawal behaviors, organizational citizenship, and dysfunctional behaviors.

☐ You should be able to candidly assess your own performance behaviors, withdrawal behaviors, organizational citizenship, and dysfunctional behaviors.

---

# Summary of Learning Outcomes and Key Points

1. Explain the nature of the individual–organization relationship.

   - A basic framework that can be used to facilitate this understanding is the psychological contract—the set of expectations held by people with respect to what they will contribute to the organization and what they expect to get in return.
   - Organizations strive to achieve an optimal person–job fit, but this process is complicated by the existence of individual differences.

2. Define *personality* and describe personality attributes that affect behavior in organizations.

   - Personality is the relatively stable set of psychological and behavioral attributes that distinguish one person from another.

- The "Big Five" personality traits are:
   - agreeableness
   - conscientiousness
   - negative emotionality
   - extraversion
   - openness
- The Myers–Briggs framework can also be a useful mechanism for understanding personality.
- Other important traits are:
   - locus of control
   - self-efficacy
   - authoritarianism
   - Machiavellianism
   - self-esteem
   - risk propensity
- Emotional intelligence, a fairly new concept, may provide additional insights into personality.

3. Discuss individual attitudes in organizations and how they affect behavior.

- Attitudes are based on emotion, knowledge, and intended behavior.
- Whereas personality is relatively stable, some attitudes can be formed and changed easily. Others are more constant.
- Job satisfaction or dissatisfaction, organizational commitment, and organizational engagement are important work-related attitudes.

4. Describe basic perceptual processes and the role of attributions in organizations.

- Perception is the set of processes by which a person becomes aware of and interprets information about the environment.
- Basic perceptual processes include selective perception and stereotyping.
- Perception and attribution are also closely related.

5. Discuss the causes and consequences of stress and describe how it can be managed.

- Stress is a person's response to a strong stimulus.
- The General Adaptation Syndrome outlines the basic stress process.
- Stress can be caused by task, physical, role, and interpersonal demands.

- Consequences of stress include organizational and individual outcomes, as well as burnout.
- Several things can be done to manage stress.

6. Describe creativity and its role in organizations.

- Creativity is the capacity to generate new ideas.
- Creative people tend to have certain profiles of background experiences, personal traits, and cognitive abilities.
- The creative process itself includes preparation, incubation, insight, and verification.

7. Explain how workplace behaviors can directly or indirectly influence organizational effectiveness.

- Workplace behavior is a pattern of action by the members of an organization that directly or indirectly influences organizational effectiveness.
- Performance behaviors are the set of work-related behaviors that the organization expects the person to display to fulfill the psychological contract.
- Basic withdrawal behaviors are absenteeism and turnover.
- Organizational citizenship refers to behavior that makes a positive overall contribution to the organization.
- Dysfunctional behaviors can be very harmful to an organization.

# Discussion Questions

## Questions for Review

1. What is a psychological contract? List the things that might be included in individual contributions. List the things that might be included in organizational inducements.

2. Describe the three components of attitudes and tell how the components are related. What is cognitive dissonance? How do individuals resolve cognitive dissonance?

## Questions for Analysis

5. Organizations are increasing their use of personality tests to screen job applicants. What are the advantages and disadvantages of this approach? What can managers do to avoid some of the potential pitfalls?

6. As a manager, how can you tell that an employee is experiencing job satisfaction? How can you tell that employees are highly committed to the organization? If a worker is not satisfied, what can a manager do to

3. Identify and discuss the steps in the creative process. What can an organization do to increase employees' creativity?

4. Identify and describe several important workplace behaviors.

improve satisfaction? What can a manager do to improve organizational commitment and engagement?

7. Managers cannot pay equal attention to every piece of information, so selective perception is a fact of life. How does selective perception help managers? How does it create difficulties for them? How can managers increase their "good" selective perception and decrease the "bad"?

## Questions for Application

8. Write the psychological contract you have in this class. In other words, what do you contribute, and what

inducements are available? Ask your professor to tell the class about the psychological contract that he or she intended to establish with the students in your class. How does the professor's intended contract compare with the one you wrote? If there are differences, why do you think the differences exist? Share your ideas with the class.

9. Assume that you are going to hire three new employees for the department store you manage. One will sell shoes, one will manage the toy department, and one will work in the stockroom. Identify the basic characteristics you want in each of the people, to achieve a good person–job fit.

10. Describe a time when someone displayed each one of the Big Five personality traits at either a very high or a very low level. For example, tell about someone who appeared to be highly agreeable or highly disagreeable. Then tell about the outcomes that person experienced as a result of displaying that particular personality trait. Do the outcomes seem logical; that is, do positive personality traits usually lead to good outcomes and negative traits to bad ones? Explain your answer.

# Building Effective Interpersonal Skills

## Exercise Overview

Interpersonal skills refer to the ability to communicate with, understand, and motivate individuals and groups. This exercise introduces you to a widely used tool for personality assessment and shows how an understanding of personality can be of use in developing effective interpersonal relationships within organizations.

## Exercise Background

Of the many different ways of interpreting personality, the widely used Myers–Briggs Type Indicator categorizes individual personality types along four dimensions:

1. *Extraversion (E) Versus Introversion (I)*. Extraverts get their energy from being around other people, whereas introverts are worn out by others and need solitude to recharge their energy.

2. *Sensing (S) Versus Intuition (N)*. The sensing type prefers concrete things, whereas the intuitivist prefers abstract concepts.

3. *Thinking (T) Versus Feeling (F)*. Thinking individuals base their decisions more on logic and reason, whereas feeling individuals base their decisions more on feelings and emotions.

4. *Judging (J) Versus Perceiving (P)*. Judging types enjoy completion or being finished, whereas perceiving types enjoy process and open-ended situations.

Using the Myers–Briggs Type Indicator, researchers use survey answers to classify individuals into 16 personality types—all the possible combinations of the four Myers–Briggs dimensions. The resulting personality type is then expressed as a four-character code, such as *ESTP* for *Extravert-Sensing-Thinking-Perceiving*. These four-character codes are then used to describe an individual's preferred way of interacting with others.

## Exercise Task

1. Use a Myers–Briggs assessment form to determine your own personality type. You can find a form at **www. keirsey.com/scripts/newkts.cgi**, a website that also contains additional information about personality type. (*Note:* There are no fees for taking the Temperament Sorter, nor must you agree to receive e-mail.)

2. When you've determined the four-letter code for your personality type, you can get a handout from your instructor which will explain how your personality type affects not only your preferred style of working but your leadership style as well.

3. Conclude by responding to the following questions:
   - How easy is it to measure personality?
   - Do you feel that the online test accurately assessed your personality?
   - Why or why not? Share your assessment results and your responses with the class.

# Building Effective Time-Management Skills

## Exercise Overview

Time-management skills refer to the ability to prioritize tasks, to work efficiently, and to delegate appropriately. Among other reasons, they're important because poor time-management skills may result in stress. This exercise shows you how effective time-management skills can help reduce stress.

## Exercise Background

List several of the major events or expectations that tend to be stressful for you. Common stressors include school (classes, exams), work (finances, schedules), and personal circumstances (friends, romance, family). Try to be as specific as possible and try to identify at least 10 different stressors.

## Exercise Task

Using your list, do each of the following:

1. Evaluate the extent to which poor time-management skills on your part play a role in the way each stressor affects you. Do exams cause stress, for example, because you tend to put off studying?

2. For each stressor that's affected by your time-management habits, develop a strategy for using your time more efficiently.

3. Note the interrelationships among different kinds of stressors to see if they revolve around time-related problems. For example, financial pressures may cause you to work, and work may interfere with school. Can you manage any of these interrelationships more effectively by managing your time more effectively?

4. How do you typically manage the stress in your life? Can you manage stress in a more time-effective manner?

# Skill-Building Personal Assessment

## Understanding your Personality

This self-assessment helps you develop a better understanding of your own personality. It will also give you an appreciation of the complexities involved in trying to measure personality traits.

**Introduction**: Personality traits represent some of the most fundamental individual differences in organizations. Research has identified literally thousands of personality traits and dimensions that differentiate one person from another. But, in recent years, researchers have identified five fundamental personality traits that are especially relevant to organizations. Because these five traits are so important and because they are currently the subject of so much attention, they are now commonly referred to as the "Big Five" personality traits.

**Instructions**: The following survey consists of 15 statements. Answer each statement as candidly as possible by circling the best response. After completing the survey, score your responses.

---

### Big Five Personality Assessment

---

1. How likely are you to make sure other people are happy and comfortable?

| Very Likely | Moderately Likely | Neither Likely Nor Unlikely | Moderately Unlikely | Very Unlikely |
|:---:|:---:|:---:|:---:|:---:|
| 5 | 4 | 3 | 2 | 1 |

2. How likely are you to prepare for things in advance?

| Very Likely | Moderately Likely | Neither Likely Nor Unlikely | Moderately Unlikely | Very Unlikely |
|:---:|:---:|:---:|:---:|:---:|
| 5 | 4 | 3 | 2 | 1 |

3. How likely are you to feel blue or depressed for no real reason?

| Very Likely | Moderately Likely | Neither Likely Nor Unlikely | Moderately Unlikely | Very Unlikely |
|:---:|:---:|:---:|:---:|:---:|
| 5 | 4 | 3 | 2 | 1 |

4. How likely are you to start a conversation with a stranger?

| Very Likely | Moderately Likely | Neither Likely Nor Unlikely | Moderately Unlikely | Very Unlikely |
|:---:|:---:|:---:|:---:|:---:|
| 5 | 4 | 3 | 2 | 1 |

5. How likely are you to use difficult or unusual words?

| Very Likely | Moderately Likely | Neither Likely Nor Unlikely | Moderately Unlikely | Very Unlikely |
|---|---|---|---|---|
| 5 | 4 | 3 | 2 | 1 |

6. How likely are you to forgive someone for a mistake they have made?

| Very Likely | Moderately Likely | Neither Likely Nor Unlikely | Moderately Unlikely | Very Unlikely |
|---|---|---|---|---|
| 5 | 4 | 3 | 2 | 1 |

7. How likely are you to set a schedule and then keep to that schedule?

| Very Likely | Moderately Likely | Neither Likely Nor Unlikely | Moderately Unlikely | Very Unlikely |
|---|---|---|---|---|
| 5 | 4 | 3 | 2 | 1 |

8. How likely are you to feel insecure about something?

| Very Likely | Moderately Likely | Neither Likely Nor Unlikely | Moderately Unlikely | Very Unlikely |
|---|---|---|---|---|
| 5 | 4 | 3 | 2 | 1 |

9. How likely are you to have many different friends at the same time?

| Very Likely | Moderately Likely | Neither Likely Nor Unlikely | Moderately Unlikely | Very Unlikely |
|---|---|---|---|---|
| 5 | 4 | 3 | 2 | 1 |

10. How likely are you to change your mind about something when you learn more about it?

| Very Likely | Moderately Likely | Neither Likely Nor Unlikely | Moderately Unlikely | Very Unlikely |
|---|---|---|---|---|
| 5 | 4 | 3 | 2 | 1 |

11. How likely are you to go along with what other people want to do?

| Very Likely | Moderately Likely | Neither Likely Nor Unlikely | Moderately Unlikely | Very Unlikely |
|---|---|---|---|---|
| 5 | 4 | 3 | 2 | 1 |

12. How likely are you to make a "to do" list and then mark everything off as you get things done?

| Very Likely | Moderately Likely | Neither Likely Nor Unlikely | Moderately Unlikely | Very Unlikely |
|---|---|---|---|---|
| 5 | 4 | 3 | 2 | 1 |

13. How likely are you to feel stressed or worried?

| Very Likely | Moderately Likely | Neither Likely Nor Unlikely | Moderately Unlikely | Very Unlikely |
|---|---|---|---|---|
| 5 | 4 | 3 | 2 | 1 |

14. How likely are you to plan parties or other social events?

| Very Likely | Moderately Likely | Neither Likely Nor Unlikely | Moderately | Very Unlikely |
|---|---|---|---|---|
| 5 | 4 | 3 | 2 | 1 |

15. How likely are you to listen carefully when other people express their opinions?

| Very Likely | Moderately Likely | Neither Likely Nor Unlikely | Moderately Unlikely | Very Unlikely |
|---|---|---|---|---|
| 5 | 4 | 3 | 2 | 1 |

## Discussion Questions

1. How accurately or inaccurately do you think this assessment is describing your personality as you believe it to be?

2. Based on the results of this assessment, what kind of job(s) might you want to seek when you graduate?

3. Do you think it's possible to change one or more of your traits? If so, how might you try to do so?

# Management at Work

### Can't Get No Job Satisfaction?

## "For the most part, the employer contract is dead."

—REBECCA RAY, EXECUTIVE VP, KNOWLEDGE ORGANIZATION, THE CONFERENCE BOARD

*News flash:* American workers aren't happy with rec-room ping pong tables and free massages. Or, to be a little more precise: Such perks aren't enough to make them satisfied with their jobs. According to Gallup's most recent State of the American Workplace Report, a mere 30 percent of U.S. workers are "engaged" in their work. That's up from 28 percent in 2010, but it doesn't amount to much, especially when you consider that more than half of all workers (52 percent) show up every morning but have very little interest in what they do all day. What's worse, the 18 percent that's left are *actively disengaged*—which means, says Gallup CEO Jim Clifton, that "they roam the halls spreading discontent." According to the report, those actively disengaged employees cost the U.S. economy $550 billion a year in lost productivity.

Admittedly, younger workers tend to find workplace perks, such as Google's nap pods and onsite roller-hockey rink, more attractive than their older counterparts. "They're often looking for things they can brag about to their peers," explains Bob Nelson, author of *1,501 Ways to Reward Employees.* But if the boss is a jerk or tasks aren't stimulating, cautions Nelson, "perks aren't going to fix it. You may keep [younger workers] for a while, but at some point, they're going to leave."

Nelson's opinion would seem to be confirmed by another major survey. According to The Conference Board Job Satisfaction report for 2013, while satisfaction among workers aged 25 to 34 came in at 50.5 percent, only 37.8 percent of workers under 25 were satisfied with their jobs—down from 46 percent in 2012 and about 60 percent 20 years earlier. Baby boomers, observes The Conference Board's Linda Barrington, "will compose a quarter of the U.S. workforce [by 2020], and since 1987 we've watched them increasingly losing faith in the workplace." Nelson reports that younger workers tend to leave jobs after about a year, compared to 4.4 years for older employees, and John Gibbons, another Conference Board researcher, notes that 22 percent of all respondents to the survey don't expect to be in their current jobs for more than a year. "These data," he concludes, "throw up a red flag because widespread job dissatisfaction" and the resulting turnover "can impact enterprise-level success." Recent studies indicate, for example, that it can cost an employer from 16 percent to 213 percent of average annual salary to replace every employee who leaves a company.

How do workers become dissatisfied, and what happens when they do? Danielle Lee Novack of Penn State University has created an instructive scenario that we've simplified to fit the needs of our case:*

A woman named Megan has coordinated the onstage portions of dance competitions for three years. From January through June, Megan has to travel to different competition venues, including three weekends per month. This demanding half year is offset by the other six-month period, when her schedule is much more relaxed. Because she likes what she does, she's willing to deal with the unusual schedule, especially as her manager has assured her that, should something important come up on a weekend, she'll try to accommodate Megan. Her manager has recognized her excellent work in each of her three years, and Megan is satisfied with her job responsibilities, coworkers, and salary.

Megan learns in December that her best friend is getting married in June and asks her boss for the wedding weekend off. Despite her promises, her manager refuses to accommodate Megan. Needless to say, Megan is frustrated. As it happens, she's also bothered by her manager's tendency to micromanage subordinates and feels that she has no freedom to make any key decisions on her own. Besides, everything has to be approved before she can act on any of her own initiatives—a situation that's already cost her two promotional partnerships that she'd worked personally to develop. Not only did she receive no recognition for her efforts, but she missed out on two bonuses. Finally, because the company is small and Megan already works directly under a high-ranking manager, she feels that there's no chance for her to advance or take on new responsibilities in the future.

Before long, Megan is resentful about giving up weekends, about her manager's habit of controlling every aspect of every project, and about the feeling that there's little point in trying to excel if she's merely going to be doing the same thing over and over again. In short, Megan is dissatisfied with her job, and she's thinking about finding another one.

A review of both surveys shows that the sources of Megan's dissatisfaction are pretty much the same as those cited by most dissatisfied American workers. At first glance, for example, some people may find it surprising that her pay doesn't figure into Megan's current discontent, but The Conference Board survey found that employees are happier with pay scales than they were in 2005–2007 (at least "marginally").

Not everybody, however, is equally "satisfied" with his or her income. Not surprisingly, The Conference Board says that 64 percent of people earning more than $125,000 are satisfied with their jobs, as are 57.6 percent of those with incomes between $75,000 and $100,000. However, only 24.4 percent of those earning under $15,000 could say the same thing. In the shrinking middle—where Megan no doubt falls—only 32 percent of those making $15,000 to $35,000 and 45 percent of those making $35,000 to $75,000 are satisfied.

Danielle Kurtzleben, however, a former business and economics reporter for *U.S. News and World Report*, observes a contradiction between two survey findings: (1) that "growth in employee compensation has fallen off sharply since the 1980s and 1990s"; and (2) that workers are "not much less satisfied today with their wages than they were 25 years ago." Workers, she cautions, may be more satisfied with *wages* than with total *compensation*, noting that

the deepest levels of dissatisfaction between 1987 and 2013 are in such compensation-related areas as health coverage and sick-leave policies.

In fact, worker satisfaction with compensation plans are at a 10-year low—primarily because such compensation benefits as pension, 401(k), and health plans are fast disappearing. "For the most part," says The Conference Board's Rebecca Ray, "the employer contract is dead." It's a serious matter, she adds, because such benefits have long served to cement long-term employer-employee relationships.

So, according to the Gallup and Conference Board reports, what aspects of their jobs are most workers most dissatisfied with? As it happens, the two areas that received the lowest scores are consistent, whether directly or indirectly, with the sources of Megan's dissatisfaction: According to The Conference Board, only 23.8 percent of workers are satisfied with their employers' promotion policies and only 24.2 percent with their bonus plans. Conversely, the most important drivers of satisfaction include growth potential, recognition, and satisfaction with one's supervisor. It may also be interesting to note that although such areas as promotion policies and bonus plans are typically more important to men, women are significantly less satisfied than men on both counts.

At bottom, the results of both surveys are somewhat paradoxical—and perhaps even misleading. The apparent good news is that, at 47.7 percent, overall job satisfaction in 2013 was up from 47.3 percent in 2012. Obviously, that's very little, and the bad news is that both figures are meaningful only in the context of a 42.6 percent level in 2010—the lowest level ever. The worse news is that recent levels of job satisfaction represent a significant drop from 61.1 percent in 1987, the first year in which The Conference Board began tracking the phenomenon.

## Case Questions

1. What about you? If you're employed, are you (relatively) satisfied or dissatisfied with your job? If you're not working (or haven't yet held down a job), focus on the areas in which you're satisfied or dissatisfied with what you *are* doing (e.g., going to school).

   Following is a table listing 22 factors in job satisfaction *in order of importance* to the U.S. workers surveyed by The Conference Board.† Create your own list of factors *in order of their importance to you at this stage of your life.* Be prepared to discuss the differences between your list and (1) the list that follows and (2) the lists drawn up by various classmates.

| | |
|---|---|
| 1. Growth potential | 12. Wages |
| 2. Communication channels | 13. Training |
| 3. Recognition | 14. People at work |
| 4. Performance review | 15. Family leave |
| 5. Interest in work | 16. Flextime |
| 6. Workload | 17. Bonus |
| 7. Work/life balance | 18. Sick days |
| 8. Supervisor | 19. Vacation |
| 9. Physical environment | 20. Pension |
| 10. Promotion policy | 21. Health coverage |
| 11. Quality of equipment | 22. Commute |

2. What about Megan? First, draw up a list of job-dissatisfaction factors for Megan. Second, regard the following as applicable to Megan's situation:

- She likes the type of work she does and has good relationships with coworkers.
- More than a few of her coworkers are also frustrated by the company's tight supervision and demanding work schedule.
- She is a cheerful and positive person.
- She performs well and gets positive feedback because she looks for solutions to problems rather than dwelling on the negative aspects of things.

What do you think Megan should do? If you think that she should find another job, be prepared to explain why you think it's the best move. If you think that she should try to resolve her frustrations before looking for another job, explain the points that she should try to get across in conversations with her boss.

3. Ilya Pozin, founder of the web-design company Ciplex and contributor to *Inc.* and *Forbes* magazines (and self-confessed "terrible manager"), puts "The Boss Sucks" at the top of his list of "The Top 10 Reasons People Hate Their Jobs." "Do you micromanage?" he asks. "Are you a bad communicator? If you have unhappy employees," Pozin advises,

> the first thing you should look at is your management habits. The next thing to do is actually talk to your employees to get to the bottom of the problem. Brushing off unhappy employees will damage your company. Get to the bottom of their troubles before you lose a valuable employee.‡

Would it be fair to apply this criticism to Megan's manager? What aspects of it apply to her and which do not? Assuming that she has an inkling of Megan's dissatisfaction, how would you advise her to respond to each area of Megan's frustration?

Finally, where did you put "The Boss Sucks" on your list of job-dissatisfaction factors in question 1? Does Pozin's criticism apply to the boss with whom you are or were dissatisfied? What advice would you offer this boss (assuming, of course, that you were in a position to do so)?

4. Gad Levanon, an economist who coauthored The Conference Board report, writes the following:

> Based on macro trends—including a significantly tighter labor market, slowing productivity growth, and more business investment—worker satisfaction should be on the rise. But job dissatisfaction may remain entrenched until we see improvements in worker compensation, which has grown abysmally in recent years despite historically high corporate profits.**

Levanon is expressing an opinion and making a related prediction. Explain his opinion and his prediction in your own words. Do you agree or disagree with this opinion and prediction? In particular, do you expect things to get better economically? Whether you answer yes or no, how do you see your prospects for getting a job that you're satisfied with?

## Case References

Kelli B. Grant, "Americans Hate Their Jobs, Even with Perks," *USA Today* (June 30, 2013), www.usatoday.com, on March 3, 2015; The Conference Board, "U.S. Workers More Satisfied? Just Barely" (press release) (June 18, 2014), www.conference-board.org, on March 4, 2015; Lauren Weber, "U.S. Workers Can't Get No (Job) Satisfaction," *Wall Street Journal* (June 18, 2014), http://blogs.wsj.com, on March 3, 2015; Christina Merhar, "Employee Retention—The Real Cost of Losing an Employee," Zane Benefits (August 28, 2013), www.zanebenefits.com, on March 5, 2015; Danielle Kurtzleben, "Five Reasons US Workers Hate Their Jobs More Than They Used To," *Vox* (June 20, 2014), www.vox.com, on March 4, 2015; Gad Levanon, "New Job Satisfaction Report from The Conference Board," *Human Capital Exchange* (The Conference Board) (June 18, 2014), https://hcexchange.conference-board.org., on March 7, 2015.

*Adapted from Danielle Lee Novack and Karen L. Housell, "Fall 2013 Job Satisfaction Case Study," *Confluence* (November 10, 2013), https://wikispaces.psu.edu, on March 3, 2015.
†Gad Levanon, "The Determinants of Job Satisfaction," The Conference Board (June 25, 2013), www.conference-board.org., on March 7, 2015.
‡"The Top 10 Reasons People Hate Their Jobs," *Linkedin* (July 9, 2013), www.linkedin.com, on March 3, 2015.
**The Conference Board, "U.S. Workers More Satisfied? Just Barely" (press release) (June 18, 2014), www.conference-board.org, on March 4, 2015.

YOU MAKE THE CALL | Engaging with the Company Garbage

1. What about you? *Millennials* and *Generation* Y refer to the same thing—generally speaking, people born between the early 1980s and early 2000s. Does this range of birth years include you? Whether it does or doesn't, how would you characterize your personal attitude toward *sustainability*, especially in the workplace? How does your attitude toward sustainability reflect your attitudes toward such matters as the country's economic future and your own?*

2. Hunter Lovins defines *employee engagement* as "the goal of creating supportive, collaborative, and rewarding work environments." Compare her understanding of employee engagement with the principle of *organizational commitment* as it's characterized in the text. In what sense is developing employee engagement intended to go a step beyond fostering organizational commitment in workplace attitudes?

   Lovins also talks about *employee integration*, by which she means a company's goal of "integrating its sustainability strategies into employee job descriptions and employees' everyday jobs." In your opinion, what sorts of policies and practices would be important in achieving employee integration over and above employee engagement?

3. Again, what about you? Consider the definition of *employee engagement* in question 2. Do you think that you'd be responsive to an employer's efforts to engage you in your job? What kind of values—in terms of both company objectives and employee rewards—would be most likely to engage you? Where would *sustainability* rank among those values? Or do you think that other factors would probably weigh more heavily in your attitude toward your job? What might they be?

4. Some experts report that *employee engagement* "has become the new Holy Grail for many organizations," or that it "has long been the Holy Grail for creating thriving and successful organizations." Robert A. Cooke, however, believes that achieving and optimizing employee engagement is more complicated than it may seem. Cooke, who's CEO of Human Synergistics International, a consultancy specializing in organizational culture and leadership and group and individual behavior, charges that

   *the human capital consulting industry continues to sell the idea that a few sips from the Holy Grail of employee engagement will magically transform organizations and heal whatever ails them. While this is a good start, companies should go beyond this and get to the root of their organizational ills by using a true organizational culture survey to define, activate, and reinforce the behaviors that drive the right kind of engagement and optimize organizational performance.†*

   Review our discussion of *organization culture* in Chapter 3. Discuss the pros and cons of Cooke's statement that "truly understanding how to optimize performance in your organization requires understanding your culture."

*An influential report issued in 2010 says that, if you're a Millennial, you're "confident, self-expressive, liberal, upbeat, and open to change." Although your entry into the working world has been set back by the Great Recession of 2007–2009, you're still "more upbeat than your elders about your own economic futures as well as about the overall state of the nation." You are "less skeptical of government than your elders" and "believe that government should do more to solve problems." There's also a good chance that you have a tattoo.

†Cooke with Richard Sharpe, "Employee Engagement: Is It Really the 'Holy Grail' of HR?" Human Synergistics International (2010), www.humansynergistics.com, on February 25, 2015

# Endnotes

1 Judith Nemes, "Dumpster Diving: From Garbage to Gold," *GreenBiz* (January 9, 2009), www.greenbiz.com, on February 20, 2015; Hunter Lovins, "Employee Engagement Is Key to Sustainable Success," Sustainable Brands (July 5, 2012), www.sustainablebrands.com, on February 18, 2015; Andrea Newell, "Employee Integration: Going Beyond Employee Engagement," *TriplePundit* (June 7, 2012), www.triplepundit.com, on February 18, 2015; Tim Mohin, "How Sustainability Is Driving Employee Engagement and the Bottom Line," *GreenBiz* (September 29, 2011), www.greenbiz.com, on February 18, 2015; Suzanne Tilleman, "Is Employee Organizational Commitment Related to Firm Environmental Sustainability?" *Journal of Small Business and Entrepreneurship*, 2012, Vol. 25, No. 4, pp. 417–431, http://web.a.ebscohost.com, on February 20, 2015; Bobbi

Thomason, "Leadership and the First and Last Mile of Sustainability," *Ivey Business Journal* (September/October 2010), http://iveybusinessjournal.com, on February 19, 2015.

2 Lynn McGarlane Shore and Lois Tetrick, "The Psychological Contract as an Explanatory Framework in the Employment Relationship," in C. L. Cooper and D. M. Rousseau (eds.), *Trends in Organizational Behavior* (London: Wiley, 1994). See also Denise M. Rousseau, "The Individual–Organization Relationship: The Psychological Contract," in Sheldon Zedeck (ed.), *Handbook of Industrial and Organizational Psychology*, Vol. 3: *Maintaining, Expanding, and Contracting the Organization* (Washington, DC: American Psychological Association, 2010), pp. 191–220.

3   For an illustration see Zhen Xiong Chen, Anne Tsui, and Lifeng Zhong, "Reactions to Psychological Contract Breach: A Dual Perspective," *Journal of Organizational Behavior*, 2008, Vol. 29, pp. 527–548.

4   Elizabeth Wolfe Morrison and Sandra L. Robinson, "When Employees Feel Betrayed: A Model of How Psychological Contract Violation Develops," *Academy of Management Review*, January 1997, pp. 226–256.

5   http://www.bloomberg.com/bw/articles/2013-01-03/job-applicants-cultural-fit-can-trump-qualifications; accessed June 15, 2015.

6   See Arne Kalleberg, "The Mismatched Worker: When People Don't Fit Their Jobs," *Academy of Management Perspectives*, 2008, Vol. 22, No. 1, pp. 24–40.

7   Oleksandr S. Chernyshenko, Stephen Stark, and Fritz Drasgow, "Individual Differences: Their Measurement and Validity," in Sheldon Zedeck (ed.), *Handbook of Industrial and Organizational Psychology*, Vol. 2: *Selecting and Developing Members for the Organization* (Washington, DC: American Psychological Association, 2010), pp. 117–141.

8   Lawrence Pervin, "Personality" in Mark Rosenzweig and Lyman Porter (eds.), *Annual Review of Psychology*, Vol. 36 (Palo Alto, CA: Annual Reviews, 1985), pp. 83–114; S. R. Maddi, *Personality Theories: A Comparative Analysis*, 4th ed. (Homewood, IL: Dorsey, 1980); see also Dan P. McAdams and Bradley D. Olson, "Personality Development: Continuity and Change Over the Life Course," in Susan T. Fiske, Daniel L. Schacter, and Robert J. Sternberg (eds.), *Annual Review of Psychology 2010* (Palo Alto, CA: Annual Reviews, 2010), pp. 517–542.

9   L. R. Goldberg, "An Alternative 'Description of Personality': The Big Five Factor Structure," *Journal of Personality and Social Psychology*, 1990, Vol. 59, pp. 1216–1229.

10  Michael K. Mount, Murray R. Barrick, and J. Perkins Strauss, "Validity of Observer Ratings of the Big Five Personality Factors," *Journal of Applied Psychology*, 1994, Vol. 79, no. 2, pp. 272–280; Timothy A. Judge, Joseph J. Martocchio, and Carl J. Thoreson, "Five-Factor Model of Personality and Employee Absence," *Journal of Applied Psychology*, 1997, Vol. 82, No. 5, pp. 745–755.

11  See Robert Renn, David Allen, and Tobias Huning, "Empirical Examination of the Individual-Level Personality-Based Theory of Self-Management Failure," *Journal of Organizational Behavior*, January 2011, pp. 25–43 for a recent extension of the Big Five framework.

12  J. B. Rotter, "Generalized Expectancies for Internal vs. External Control of Reinforcement," *Psychological Monographs*, 1966, Vol. 80, pp. 1–28. See also Simon S. K. Lam and John Schaubroeck, "The Role of Locus of Control in Reactions to Being Promoted and to Being Passed Over: A Quasi Experiment," *Academy of Management Journal*, 2000, Vol. 43, No. 1, pp. 66–78.

13  Marilyn E. Gist and Terence R. Mitchell, "Self-Efficacy: A Theoretical Analysis of Its Determinants and Malleability," *Academy of Management Review*, April 1992, pp. 183–211.

14  T. W. Adorno, E. Frenkel-Brunswick, D. J. Levinson, and R. N. Sanford, *The Authoritarian Personality* (New York: Harper & Row, 1950).

15  "The Rise and Fall of Dennis Kozlowski," *BusinessWeek*, December 23, 2002, pp. 64–77.

16  Jon L. Pierce, Donald G. Gardner, and Larry L. Cummings, "Organization-Based Self-Esteem: Construct Definition, Measurement, and Validation," *Academy of Management Journal*, 1989, Vol. 32, pp. 622–648.

17  Michael Harris Bond and Peter B. Smith, "Cross-Cultural Social and Organizational Psychology," in Janet Spence (ed.), *Annual Review of Psychology*, Vol. 47 (Palo Alto, CA: Annual Reviews, 1996), pp. 205–235.

18  See Daniel Goleman, *Emotional Intelligence: Why It Can Matter More Than IQ* (New York: Bantam, 1995).

19  Daniel Goleman, "Leadership That Gets Results," *Harvard Business Review*, March–April 2000, pp. 78–90. See also Kenneth Law, Chi-Sum Wong, and Lynda Song, "The Construct and Criterion Validity of Emotional Intelligence and Its Potential Utility for Management Studies," *Journal of Applied Psychology*, 2004, Vol. 87, No. 3, pp. 483–496; Joseph C. Rode, Christine H. Mooney, Marne L. Arthaud-Day, Janet P. Near, Timothy T. Baldwin, Robert S. Rubin, and William H. Bommer, "Emotional Intelligence and Individual Performance: Evidence of Direct and Indirect Effects," *Journal of Organizational Behavior*, 2007, Vol. 28, pp. 399–421; and John D. Mayer, Richard D. Roberts, and Sigal G. Barsade, "Human Abilities: Emotional Intelligence," in Susan T. Fiske, Daniel L. Schacter, and Robert Sternberg (eds.), *Annual Review of Psychology 2008* (Palo Alto, CA: Annual Reviews, 2008), pp. 507–536.

20  For a recent review see Gerd Bohner and Nina Dickel, "Attitudes and Attitude Change," in Susan T. Fiske, Daniel L. Schacter, and Shelley Taylor (eds.), *Annual Review of Psychology 2011* (Palo Alto, CA: Annual Reviews, 2011), pp. 391–418.

21  Leon Festinger, *A Theory of Cognitive Dissonance* (Palo Alto, CA: Stanford University Press, 1957).

22  See John J. Clancy, "Is Loyalty Really Dead?" *Across the Board*, June 1999, pp. 14–19.

23  Patricia C. Smith, L. M. Kendall, and Charles Hulin, *The Measurement of Satisfaction in Work and Behavior* (Chicago: Rand-McNally, 1969). See also Steven Currall, Annette Towler, Tomothy Judge, and Laura Kohn, "Pay Satisfaction and Organizational Outcomes," *Personnel Psychology*, 2005, Vol. 58, pp. 613–640.

24  "Companies Are Finding Real Payoffs in Aiding Employee Satisfaction," *Wall Street Journal*, October 11, 2000, p. B1.

25  James R. Lincoln, "Employee Work Attitudes and Management Practice in the U.S. and Japan: Evidence from a Large Comparative Study," *California Management Review*, Fall 1989, pp. 89–106.

26  http://www.nytimes.com/2010/09/12/jobs/12search.html, accessed on June 15, 2015.

27  Richard M. Steers, "Antecedents and Outcomes of Organizational Commitment," *Administrative Science Quarterly*, 1977, Vol. 22, pp. 46–56.

28  See Timothy R. Clark, "Engaging the Disengaged," *HR Magazine*, April 2008, pp. 109–114.

29  Omar N. Solinger, Woody van Olffen, and Robert A. Roe, "Beyond the Three-Component Model of Organizational Commitment," *Journal of Applied Psychology*, 2008, Vol. 93, No. 1, pp. 70–83; see also Steven M. Elias, "Employee Commitment in Times of Change: Assessing the Importance of Attitudes Toward Organizational Change," *Journal of Management*, 2009, Vol. 35, No. 1, pp. 37–55.

30  For research work in this area, see Jennifer M. George and Gareth R. Jones, "The Experience of Mood and Turnover Intentions: Interactive Effects of Value Attainment, Job Satisfaction, and Positive Mood," *Journal of Applied Psychology*, 1996, Vol. 81, No. 3, pp. 318–325; Larry J. Williams, Mark B. Gavin, and Margaret Williams, "Measurement and Nonmeasurement Processes with Negative Affectivity and Employee Attitudes," *Journal of Applied Psychology*, 1996, Vol. 81, No. 1, pp. 88–101.

31  See Robert A. Baron, "The Role of Affect in the Entrepreneurial Process," *Academy of Management Review*, 2008, Vol. 33, No. 2, pp. 328–340.

32  Kathleen Sutcliffe, "What Executives Notice: Accurate Perceptions in Top Management Teams," *Academy of Management Journal*, 1994, Vol. 37, No. 5, pp. 1360–1378.

33  Richard A. Posthuma and Michael A. Campion, "Age Stereotypes in the Workplace: Common Stereotypes, Moderators, and Future Research Directions," *Journal of Management*, 2009, Vol. 35, No. 1, pp. 148–188.

34  For a classic treatment of attribution, see H. H. Kelley, *Attribution in Social Interaction* (Morristown, NJ: General Learning Press, 1971). For a recent application, see Edward C. Tomlinson and Roger C. Mayer, "The Role of Causal Attribution Dimensions in Trust Repair," *Academy of Management Review*, Vol. 34, No. 1, January 2009, pp. 85–104.

35  For an overview of the stress literature, see Frank Landy, James Campbell Quick, and Stanislav Kasl, "Work, Stress, and Well-Being," *International Journal of Stress Management*, 1994, Vol. 1, No. 1, pp. 33–73; see also Mark A. Griffin and Sharon Clarke, "Stress and Well-Being at Work," in Sheldon Zedeck (ed.), *Handbook of Industrial and Organizational Psychology*, Vol. 3: *Maintaining, Expanding, and Contracting the Organization* (Washington, DC: American Psychological Association: Washington, D.C., 2010), pp. 359–397.

36  Hans Selye, *The Stress of Life* (New York: McGraw-Hill, 1976).

37  M. Friedman and R. H. Rosenman, *Type A Behavior and Your Heart* (New York: Knopf, 1974).

38  "Work & Family," *BusinessWeek*, June 28, 1993, pp. 80–88.

39  Quoted in *USA Today*, December 13, 2007, p. 2B.

40  Richard S. DeFrank, Robert Konopaske, and John M. Ivancevich, "Executive Travel Stress: Perils of the Road Warrior," *Academy of Management Executive*, 2000, Vol. 14, No. 2, pp. 58–67.

41  Steven Rogelberg, Desmond Leach, Peter Warr, and Jennifer Burnfield, "'Not Another Meeting!' Are Meeting Time Demands Related to Employee Well Being?" *Journal of Applied Psychology*, 2006, Vol. 91, No. 1, pp. 86–96.

42  "Those Doing Layoffs Can Feel the Pain," *USA Today*, April 23, 2009, p. 5D.

43  Remus Ilies, Michael Johnson, Timothy Judge, and Jessica Keeney, "A Within-Individual Study of Interpersonal Conflict as a Work Stressor: Dispositional and Situational Moderators," *Journal of Organizational Behavior*, January 2011, pp. 44–64.

44  *USA Today*, April 23, 2009, p. 5D.

45  Michael R. Frone, "Are Work Stressors Related to Employee Substance Abuse? The Importance of Temporal Context in Assessments of Alcohol and Illicit Drug Use," *Journal of Applied Psychology*, 2008, Vol. 93, No. 1, pp. 199–296.

46 "Breaking Point," *Newsweek*, March 6, 1995, pp. 56–62. See also "Rising Job Stress Could Affect Bottom Line," *USA Today*, July 28, 2003, p. 18.

47 See Christopher M. Barnes and John R. Hollenbeck, "Sleep Deprivation and Decision-Making Teams: Burning the Midnight Oil or Playing with Fire?" *Academy of Management Review*, Vol. 34, No. 1, January 2009, pp. 56–66.

48 John M. Kelly, "Get a Grip on Stress," *HR Magazine*, February 1997, pp. 51–58; see also Marilyn Macik-Frey, James Campbell Quick, and Debra Nelson, "Advances in Occupational Health: From a Stressful Beginning to a Positive Future," *Journal of Management*, 2007, Vol. 33, No. 6, pp. 809–840.

49 Charlotte Fritz, Sabine Sonnentag, Paul Spector, and Jennifer McInroe, "The Weekend Matters: Relationships Between Stress Recovery and Affective Experiences," *Journal of Organizational Behavior*, November 2010, pp. 1137–1162.

50 "Work Stress: What Are Companies Doing About It?" *AOL Jobs*, August 10, 2010.

51 "Nice Work if You Can Get It," *BusinessWeek*, January 9, 2006, pp. 56–57; see also "Wellness," *Time*, February 23, 2009, pp. 78–79.

52 See Richard W. Woodman, John E. Sawyer, and Ricky W. Griffin, "Toward a Theory of Organizational Creativity," *Academy of Management Review*, April 1993, pp. 293–321. See also Beth A. Hennessey and Teresa M. Amabile, "Creativity," in Susan T. Fiske, Daniel L. Schacter, and Robert J. Sternberg (eds.), *Annual Review of Psychology 2010* (Palo Alto, CA: Annual Reviews, 2010), pp. 569–598; and Jing Zhou and Christina E. Shalley, "Deepening Our Understanding of Creativity in the Workplace: A Review of Different Approaches to Creativity Research," in Sheldon Zedeck (ed.), *Handbook of Industrial and Organizational Psychology*, Vol. 1: *Building and Developing the Organization* (Washington, DC: American Psychological Association, 2010), pp. 275–302.

53 Emily Thornton, "Japan's Struggle to Be Creative," *Fortune*, April 19, 1993, pp. 129–134.

54 "In Secret Hideaway, Bill Gates Ponders Microsoft's Future," *Wall Street Journal*, March 28, 2005, pp. A1, A13.

55 Christina E. Shalley, Lucy L. Gilson, and Terry C. Blum, "Matching Creativity Requirements and the Work Environment: Effects on Satisfaction and Intentions to Leave," *Academy of Management Journal*, 2000, Vol. 43, No. 2, pp. 214–223. See also Filiz Tabak, "Employee Creative Performance: What Makes It Happen?" *Academy of Management Executive*, 1997, Vol. 11, No. 1, pp. 119–122; and Giles Hirst, Daan van Knippenberg, and Jing Zhou, "A Cross-Level Perspective on Employee Creativity: Goal Orientation, Team Learning Behavior, and Individual Creativity," *Academy of Management Journal*, Vol. 52, No. 2, 2009, pp. 280–293.

56 "Real Life Imitates *Real World*," *BusinessWeek*, March 23/30, 2009, p. 42.

57 "Apple's Startup Culture," *Bloomberg Businessweek*, June 14, 2010, pp. 45–46.

58 See Ryan D. Zimmerman, "Understanding the Impact of Personality Traits on Individuals' Turnover Decisions: A Meta-Analytic Path Model," *Personnel Psychology*, 2008, Vol. 61, pp. 309–348.

59 For recent findings regarding this behavior, see Philip M. Podsakoff, Scott B. MacKenzie, Julie Beth Paine, and Daniel G. G. Bacharah, "Organizational Citizenship Behaviors: A Critical Review of the Theoretical and Empirical Literature and Suggestions for Future Research," *Journal of Management*, 2000, Vol. 26, No. 3, pp. 513–563; see also Dennis W. Organ, Philip M. Podsakoff, and Nathan P. Podsakoff, "Expanding the Criterion Domain to Include Organizational Citizenship Behavior: Implications for Employee Selection," in Sheldon Zedeck (ed.), *Handbook of Industrial and Organizational Psychology*, Vol. 2: *Selecting and Developing Members for the Organization* (Washington, DC: American Psychological Association, 2010), pp. 281–323.

60 Dennis W. Organ, "Personality and Organizational Citizenship Behavior," *Journal of Management*, 1994, Vol. 20, No. 2, pp. 465–478; Mary Konovsky and S. Douglas Pugh, "Citizenship Behavior and Social Exchange," *Academy of Management Journal*, 1994, Vol. 37, No. 3, pp. 656–669; and Jacqueline A.-M. Coyle-Shapiro, "A Psychological Contract Perspective on Organizational Citizenship," *Journal of Organizational Behavior*, 2002, Vol. 23, pp. 927–946.

61 Ricky Griffin and Yvette Lopez, "'Bad Behavior' in Organizations: A Review and Typology for Future Research," *Journal of Management*, 2005, Vol. 31, No. 6, pp. 988–1005.

62 For an illustration, see Sandy Lim, Lilia M. Cortina, and Vicki J. Magley, "Personal and Workgroup Incivility: Impact on Work and Health Outcomes," *Journal of Applied Psychology*, 2008, Vol. 93, No. 1, pp. 95–107.

63 See Anne O'Leary-Kelly, Ricky W. Griffin, and David J. Glew, "Organization-Motivated Aggression: A Research Framework," *Academy of Management Review*, January 1996, pp. 225–253. See also Scott C. Douglas, Christian Kiewitz, Mark J. Martinko, Paul Harvey, Younhee Kim, and Jae Uk Chun, "Cognitions, Emotions, and Evaluations: An Elaboration Likelihood Model for Workplace Aggression," *Academy of Management Review*, 2008, Vol. 33, No. 2, p. 425–451; and Laurie J. Barclay and Karl Aquino, "Workplace Aggression and Violence," in Sheldon Zedeck (ed.), *Handbook of Industrial and Organizational Psychology*, Vol. 3: *Maintaining, Expanding, and Contracting the Organization* (Washington, DC: American Psychological Association, 2010), pp. 614–640.

©Markus Pfaff/Shutterstock.com

# MANAGING EMPLOYEE MOTIVATION AND PERFORMANCE

**After studying this chapter, you should be able to:**

1. Characterize the nature of motivation, including its importance and historical perspectives.

2. Identify and describe the major content perspectives on motivation.

3. Identify and describe the major process perspectives on motivation.

4. Describe reinforcement perspectives on motivation.

5. Identify and describe popular motivational strategies.

6. Describe the role of organizational reward systems in motivation.

# MANAGEMENT IN ACTION  Let the Games Begin

"It gives 350 employees a megaphone to stream our content to all of their social networks."

—CORINNE SKLAR, CHIEF MARKETING OFFICER, BLUEWOLF

Bluewolf, a New York-based global consulting agency, specializes in *cloud integration*—providing application programs with which business clients can manage data stored in the "cloud" (i.e., the network of servers known as the Internet). Naturally, one of the firm's chief marketing strategies is informing potential clients about such services as "Cloud Governance"—a suite of tools for helping clients get the most value out of cloud-shared data. Obviously, Bluewolf's sales pitch focuses on its ability to provide highly specialized knowledge, and the company is well aware of the fact that no one has a better understanding of that knowledge than the employees who apply it on a daily basis. In addition, Bluewolf has long been convinced that social media is an effective channel of communication with clients (as well as other stakeholders outside the company).[1]

So, back in 2012, when a marketing team of about 20 people was shouldering the burden of social-media promotion, Bluewolf determined to harness the expertise of the rest of the company's human resources (some 350 people) in the development and promotion of its services. In fact, the goal was to get employees to share their knowledge with coworkers as well as clients. "Internally," says former social programs manager Natasha Oxenburgh, "we looked at how we could get all of our subject-matter experts sharing their knowledge so we could access it to solve [our] business challenges faster. From an external marketing perspective, we asked how we could unlock this knowledge and thought leadership to get it in front of our clients."

Bluewolf already encouraged employees to participate on social networks such as Facebook, Twitter, and Linkedin, as well as the company's internal social network, called Salesforce Chatter. The logical strategy, then, called for motivating employees throughout the company to use social media as a means of showcasing the expertise that they brought to Bluewolf's service offerings. "In light of the social media revolution," recalls marketing manager Ross Warnlof, the "question arose: 'How could we turn this diverse … organization into a unified group of social collaborators?'

"The answer," says Warnlof, "was gamification." In April 2012, Bluewolf teamed with fellow cloud-services provider Bunchball, which specializes in software for designing online games. Bunchball software is geared primarily for *enterprise gamification*—the use of games to improve *customer* loyalty and engagement. What Bluewolf wanted, however, was a program designed chiefly for *social gamification*—the use of games to enhance certain social behaviors, especially sharing. In other words, Bluewolf wanted to

Social media impacts business in many different ways. One major issue is the simple fact that many workers today integrate social media into their everyday lives while employers often seek to limit employee access to social media during normal work hours. Bluewolf, a New York-based consulting company, encourages its employees to engage with social media, in part to showcase their expertise to potential clients and customers.

10 FACE/Shutterstock.com

motivate employees to practice enhanced sharing behaviors in order to achieve a twofold goal:

1. to improve *internal collaboration* by means of social media and
2. to increase the participation of employees as advocates for the company among *external users* of its social media.

Why *gamification*? Because gamification, despite the term itself, is not really about games. It's all about identifying certain behaviors and changing them in order to meet certain goals. The process begins before the game playing does—namely, when an organization examines a set of behaviors and tries to determine how they're actually being applied in an organization. Once the games themselves have been rolled out, they perform a twofold function:

1. They measure certain interactions entailed by the behaviors in question, and
2. They provide "players"—the people who perform those behaviors—with immediate feedback on the way their performance is achieving certain organizational goals.

In the case of Bluewolf, the set of behaviors revolved around employees' use of social media, and the organizational goals centered on employees' expertise-sharing activities.

How does gamification work at Bluewolf? As a preliminary step, the marketing team surveyed employees to find out a few basic facts:

- how active they were on major social networks
- what factors prevented them from being more active
- how they felt about building their "personal brands" through social networks.

Survey responses told the team that employees needed to know more about the possibilities of social media. Consequently, the first part of Bluewolf's three-part #GoingSocial program was designed as a portal through which employees could find tips and videos on how to get started in using social media. "The tips," says Oxenburgh, "explain who [employees] should follow, what groups to join, which content to share." Slide presentations explain "what's in it for them and how to do it" on such social platforms as Pinterest, Facebook, Linkedin, Salesforce, Chatter, and Google+.

The second part of #GoingSocial is a custom-designed feature called "Pack Profiles" (as in *wolf pack*) on which employees publish information about themselves (company affiliations and clients) and their social-media activities (most recent Twitter and blog posts and white papers). Profiles are available not only internally, but to outside users as well—the point, after all, is to showcase employee expertise for current and potential clients. "This is how employees manage their public profiles," explains Oxenburgh, who adds that "it gives them a platform on which to build their own brand"—that is, to "package" or to "market" themselves. Oxenburgh admits that "consulting firms aren't necessarily open" to personal branding, which is a preferred strategy of job seekers, "but we're not worried about employees being poached; we're about creating a workplace where people want to be."

The third part of #GoingSocial is where the games come in. Basically, this part of the program gamifies the process of maintaining "Pack Profiles" by encouraging employees to perform behaviors consistent with the organization's goals. The game function of the system is run by a program called Nitro, which Bunchball created for Salesforce, a platform developed for customer relationship management.

Bluewolf employees can earn badges and points for a range of social-media activities, such as sharing information with colleagues on Salesforce Chatter or sharing knowledge with external users, either by posting content on Twitter, Facebook, or Linkedin or by contributing to the company blog. Employees who accrue enough points can cash them in for tangible rewards, including tickets to industry conferences, flight upgrades, and lunch with the CEO. By shopping at the online rewards store, they can redeem points for limited-edition Patagonia gear and other Bluewolf-branded merchandise.

"It used to be a struggle to get a couple of blogs out of people," says Oxenburgh, but 10 months after #GoingSocial launched, traffic on the company's blog had increased threefold and traffic on its website by 68 percent. "After three years of continual innovation," adds Warnlof, "the program is still facilitating collaboration across the organization to drive business results." Activity on Chatter, for example, is up by 57 percent, social traffic to the website by 45 percent, and social traffic to blogs by 80 percent. "If you think about the content and how this affects us," says Bluewolf's chief marketing officer Corinne Sklar, "it gives 350 employees a megaphone to stream our content to all of their social networks."

As the business world gets increasingly complex, so too are the challenges in motivating people to perform in various ways. For example, 20 years ago no one would have guessed that a business would one day be trying to motivate its employees to use social media more often, yet that is exactly what Bluewolf is striving to do. Regardless of the context, though, much of what managers today worry about is employee motivation, which is the subject of this chapter. We first examine the nature of employee motivation and then explore the major perspectives on motivation. Newly emerging approaches are then discussed. We conclude with a description of rewards and their role in motivation.

# The Nature of Motivation

Motivation is the set of forces that cause people to behave in certain ways.[2] On any given day, an employee may choose to work as hard as possible at a job, work just hard enough to avoid a reprimand, or do as little as possible. The goal for the manager is to maximize the likelihood of the first behavior and minimize the likelihood of the last. This goal becomes all the more important when we understand how important motivation is in the workplace.

## The Importance of Employee Motivation in the Workplace

Individual performance is generally determined by three things: motivation (the desire to do the job), ability (the capability to do the job), and the work environment (the resources needed to do the job). If an employee lacks ability, the manager can provide training or replace the worker. If there is a resource problem, the manager can correct it. But if motivation is the problem, the task for the manager is more challenging.[3] Individual behavior is a complex phenomenon, and the manager may be hard pressed to figure out the precise nature of the problem and how to solve it. Thus motivation is important because of its significance as a determinant of performance and because of its intangible character.[4]

The motivation framework in Figure 15.1 is a good starting point for understanding how motivated behavior occurs. The motivation process begins with a need deficiency. For example, when a worker feels that she is underpaid, she experiences a need for more income. In response, the worker searches for ways to satisfy the need, such as working harder to try to

**motivation**
The set of forces that cause people to behave in certain ways

### FIGURE 15.1  THE MOTIVATION FRAMEWORK

The motivation process progresses through a series of discrete steps. Content, process, and reinforcement perspectives on motivation address different parts of this process.

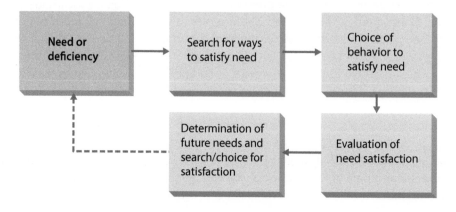

earn a raise or seeking a new job. Next she chooses an option to pursue. After carrying out the chosen option—working harder and putting in more hours for a reasonable period of time, for example—she then evaluates her success. If her hard work results in a pay raise, she probably feels good about things and will continue to work hard. But if no raise is provided, she is likely to try another option.

## Historical Perspectives on Motivation

To appreciate what we know about employee motivation, it is helpful to review earlier approaches. The traditional, human relations, and human resource approaches have each shed partial light on motivation.[5]

**The Traditional Approach** The traditional approach is best represented by the work of Frederick W. Taylor.[6] As noted in Chapter 2, Taylor advocated an incentive pay system. He believed that managers knew more about the jobs being performed than did workers, and he assumed that economic gain was the primary thing that motivated everyone. Other

Frederick Taylor, an early management pioneer, advocated an incentive pay system that would pay workers a set amount of money for each unit of output they produced. One of his earliest projects was studying the craft of brick laying, developing the most efficient steps to perform this job, teaching workers his method, and then paying them based on the number of bricks they laid each hour.

assumptions of the traditional approach were that work is inherently unpleasant for most people and that the money they earn is more important to employees than the nature of the job they are performing. Hence, people could be expected to perform any kind of job if they were paid enough. Although the role of money as a motivating factor cannot be dismissed, proponents of the traditional approach took too narrow a view of the role of monetary compensation and failed to consider other motivational factors.

**The Human Relations Approach** The human relations approach was also summarized in Chapter 2.[7] The human relationists emphasized the role of social processes in the workplace. Their basic assumptions were that employees want to feel useful and important, that employees have strong social needs, and that these needs are more important than money in motivating them. Advocates of the human relations approach advised managers to make workers feel important and allow them a modicum of self-direction and self-control in carrying out routine activities. The illusion of involvement and importance was expected to satisfy workers' basic social needs and result in higher motivation to perform. For example, a manager might allow a work group to participate in making a decision even though he or she had already determined what the decision would be. The symbolic gesture of seeming to

In contrast to the traditional approach, the human relations approach suggests that social process are of paramount importance in employee motivation. Hence, these employees, who appear to like each other and enjoy working together, should presumably be motivated to perform at a high level.

allow participation was expected to enhance motivation, even though no real participation took place.

**The Human Resource Approach** The human resource approach to motivation carries the concepts of needs and motivation one step further. Whereas the human relationists believed that the illusion of contribution and participation would enhance motivation, the human resource view assumes that the contributions themselves are valuable to both individuals and organizations. It assumes that people want to contribute and are able to make genuine contributions. Management's task, then, is to encourage participation and to create a work environment that makes full use of the human resources available. This philosophy guides most contemporary thinking about employee motivation. At Ford, Westinghouse, Texas Instruments, and Hewlett-Packard, for example, work teams are being called on to solve a variety of problems and to make substantive contributions to the organization.

**Manager's Checklist**

☐ Managers need to appreciate the historical perspectives on employee motivation.

☐ You should also be familiar with the various parts of the motivational cycle.

# Content Perspectives on Motivation

Content perspectives on motivation deal with the first part of the motivation process—needs and need deficiencies. More specifically, content perspectives address the question, What factor or factors in the workplace motivate people? Labor leaders often argue that workers can be motivated by more pay, shorter working hours, and improved working conditions. Meanwhile, some experts suggest that motivation can be more effectively enhanced by providing employees with more autonomy and greater responsibility.[8] Both of these views represent content views of motivation. The former asserts that motivation is a function of pay, working hours, and working conditions; the latter suggests that autonomy and responsibility are the causes of motivation. Two widely known content perspectives on motivation are the needs hierarchy and the two-factor theory.

**content perspectives**
Approach to motivation that tries to answer the question, What factor or factors motivate people?

**Maslow's hierarchy of needs**
Suggests that people must satisfy five groups of needs in order—physiological, security, belongingness, esteem, and self-actualization

## The Needs Hierarchy Approach

The needs hierarchy approach has been advanced by many theorists. Needs hierarchies assume that people have different needs that can be arranged in a hierarchy of importance. The two best known are Maslow's hierarchy of needs and the ERG theory.

"Happiness lies not in the mere possession of money; it lies in the joy of achievement, in the thrill of creative effort."

—FRANKLIN D. ROOSEVELT, FORMER U.S. PRESIDENT[10]

**Maslow's Hierarchy of Needs** Abraham Maslow, a human relationist, argued that people are motivated to satisfy five need levels.[9] Maslow's hierarchy of needs is shown in Figure 15.2. At the bottom of the hierarchy are the *physiological needs*—things like food, sex, and air, which represent basic issues of survival and biological function. In organizations, these needs are generally satisfied by adequate wages and the work environment itself, which provides restrooms, adequate lighting, comfortable temperatures, and ventilation.

Next are the *security needs* for a secure physical and emotional environment. Examples include the desire for housing and clothing and the need to be free from worry about money and job security. These needs can be satisfied in the workplace by job continuity (no layoffs), a grievance system (to protect against arbitrary supervisory actions), and an adequate

## FIGURE 15.2  MASLOW'S HIERARCHY OF NEEDS

Maslow's hierarchy suggests that human needs can be classified into five categories and that these categories can be arranged in a hierarchy of importance. A manager should understand that an employee may not be satisfied with only a salary and benefits; he or she may also need challenging job opportunities to experience self-growth and satisfaction.

Source: Adapted from Abraham H. Maslow, "A Theory of Human Motivation," *Psychology Review*, 1943, Vol. 50, pp. 370–396.

insurance and retirement benefit package (for security against illness and provision of income in later life). Even today, however, depressed industries and economic decline can put people out of work and restore the primacy of security needs.

*Belongingness needs* relate to social processes. They include the need for love and affection and the need to be accepted by one's peers. These needs are satisfied for most people by family and community relationships outside of work and by friendships on the job. A manager can help satisfy these needs by allowing social interaction and by making employees feel like part of a team or work group.

*Esteem needs* actually comprise two different sets of needs: the need for a positive self-image and self-respect, and the need for recognition and respect from others. A manager can help address these needs by providing a variety of extrinsic symbols of accomplishment, such as job titles, nice offices, and similar rewards, as appropriate. At a more intrinsic level, the manager can provide challenging job assignments and opportunities for the employee to feel a sense of accomplishment.

At the top of the hierarchy are the *self-actualization needs*. These involve realizing one's potential for continued growth and individual development. The self-actualization

Abraham Maslow suggests that esteem needs play an important role in employee motivation. Esteem needs include the desire to be recognized and respected by others. One avenue for satisfying esteem needs for some individuals is a large and impressive office such as this one.

"I wanted to do something with my life where I felt I was contributing. Somehow, selling more tacos and margaritas than the week before wasn't."

—CATHEY GARDNER, FORMER RESTAURANT MANAGER, ON HER DECISION TO BECOME A NURSE[11]

needs are perhaps the most difficult for a manager to address. In fact, it can be argued that these needs must be met entirely from within the individual. But a manager can help by promoting a culture wherein self-actualization is possible. For instance, a manager could give employees a chance to participate in making decisions about their work and the opportunity to learn new things.

Maslow suggests that the five need categories constitute a hierarchy. A person is motivated first and foremost to satisfy physiological needs. As long as these remain unsatisfied, the person is motivated to fulfill only them. When satisfaction of physiological needs is achieved, they cease to act as primary motivational factors, and the person moves "up" the hierarchy and becomes concerned with security needs. This process continues until the person reaches the self-actualization level. Maslow's concept of the needs hierarchy has a certain intuitive logic and has been accepted by many managers. But research has revealed certain shortcomings and defects in the theory. Some research has found that five levels of need are not always present and that the order of the levels is not always the same as postulated by Maslow.[12] In addition, people from different cultures are likely to have different need categories and hierarchies.

**The ERG Theory** In response to these and similar criticisms, an alternative hierarchy of needs, called the ERG theory of motivation, was developed.[13] This theory collapses the needs hierarchy developed by Maslow into three levels. *Existence needs* correspond to the physiological and security needs. *Relatedness needs* focus on how people relate to their social environment. In Maslow's hierarchy, these would encompass both the need to belong and the need to earn the esteem of others. *Growth needs*, the highest level in this schema, include the needs for self-esteem and self-actualization.

Although the ERG theory assumes that motivated behavior follows a hierarchy in somewhat the same fashion as suggested by Maslow, there are two important differences. First, the ERG theory suggests that more than one level of need can cause motivation at the same time. For example, it suggests that people can be motivated by a desire for money (existence), friendship (relatedness), and the opportunity to learn new skills (growth) all at once. Second, the ERG theory has what has been called a *frustration-regression* element. Thus, if needs remain unsatisfied, the person will become frustrated, regress to a lower level, and begin to pursue those things again. For example, a worker previously motivated by money (existence needs) may have just been awarded a pay raise sufficient to satisfy those needs. Suppose that he then tries to establish more friendships to satisfy relatedness needs. If for some reason he finds that it is impossible to become better friends with others in the workplace, he eventually gets frustrated and regresses to being motivated to earn even more money.

## The Two-Factor Theory

**ERG theory of motivation**
Suggests that people's needs are grouped into three possibly overlapping categories—existence, relatedness, and growth

**two-factor theory of motivation**
Suggests that people's satisfaction and dissatisfaction are influenced by two independent sets of factors—motivation factors and hygiene factors

Another popular content perspective is the two-factor theory of motivation.[14] Frederick Herzberg developed his theory after interviewing 200 accountants and engineers. He asked them to recall occasions when they had been satisfied and motivated and occasions when they had been dissatisfied and unmotivated. Surprisingly, he found that different sets of factors were associated with satisfaction and with dissatisfaction—that is, a person might identify "low pay" as causing dissatisfaction but would not necessarily mention "high pay" as a cause of satisfaction. Instead, different factors—such as recognition or accomplishment—were cited as causing satisfaction and motivation.

This finding led Herzberg to conclude that the traditional view of job satisfaction was incomplete. That view assumed that satisfaction and dissatisfaction are at opposite ends of a single continuum. People might be satisfied, dissatisfied, or somewhere in between. But Herzberg's interviews had identified two different dimensions altogether: one ranging from satisfaction to no satisfaction and the other ranging from dissatisfaction to no dissatisfaction.

## FIGURE 15.3 THE TWO-FACTOR THEORY OF MOTIVATION

The two-factor theory suggests that job satisfaction has two dimensions. A manager who tries to motivate an employee using only hygiene factors, such as pay and good working conditions, will likely not succeed. To motivate employees and produce a high level of satisfaction, managers must also offer factors such as responsibility and the opportunity for advancement (motivation factors).

**Motivation Factors**
- Achievement
- Recognition
- The work itself
- Responsibility
- Advancement and growth

Satisfaction ⟷ No satisfaction

**Hygiene Factors**
- Supervisors
- Working conditions
- Interpersonal relations
- Pay and security
- Company policies and administration

Dissatisfaction ⟷ No dissatisfaction

This perspective, along with several examples of factors that affect each continuum, is shown in Figure 15.3. Note that the factors influencing the satisfaction continuum—called *motivation factors*—are related specifically to the work content. The factors presumed to cause dissatisfaction—called *hygiene factors*—are related to the work environment.

Based on these findings, Herzberg argued that there are two stages in the process of motivating employees. First, managers must ensure that the hygiene factors are not deficient. Pay and security must be appropriate, working conditions must be safe, technical supervision must be acceptable, and so on. By providing hygiene factors at an appropriate level, managers do not stimulate motivation but merely ensure that employees are "not dissatisfied." Employees whom managers try to "satisfy" through hygiene factors alone will usually do just enough to get by. Thus managers should proceed to stage two—giving employees the opportunity to experience motivation factors such as achievement and recognition. The result is predicted to be a high level of satisfaction and motivation. Herzberg also went a step further than most other theorists and described exactly how to use the two-factor theory in the workplace. Specifically, he recommended job enrichment, as discussed in Chapter 10. He argued that jobs should be redesigned to provide higher levels of the motivation factors.

Although widely accepted by many managers, Herzberg's two-factor theory is not without its critics. One criticism is that the findings in Herzberg's initial interviews are subject to different explanations. Another charge is that his sample was not representative of the general population and that subsequent research often failed to uphold the theory.[15] At the present time, Herzberg's theory is not held in high esteem by researchers in the field. The theory has had a major impact on managers, however, and has played a key role in increasing their awareness of motivation and its importance in the workplace.

## Individual Human Needs

In addition to these theories, research has focused on specific individual human needs that are important in organizations. The three most important individual needs are achievement, affiliation, and power.[16]

The **need for achievement**, the best known of the three, is the desire to accomplish a goal or task more effectively than in the past. People with a high need for achievement have a desire to assume personal responsibility, a tendency to set moderately difficult goals, a desire for specific and immediate feedback, and a preoccupation with their task.

**need for achievement**
The desire to accomplish a goal or task more effectively than in the past

The need for achievement is the desire to accomplish a goal or task more effectively than in the past. This woman's need for achievement has motivated her to perform at the highest level possible, and her efforts are being recognized by her boss and acknowledged by her colleagues.

David C. McClelland, the psychologist who first identified this need, argues that only about 10 percent of the U.S. population has a high need for achievement. In contrast, almost one-quarter of the workers in Japan have a high need for achievement.

The need for affiliation is less well understood. Like Maslow's belongingness need, the need for affiliation is a desire for human companionship and acceptance. People with a strong need for affiliation are likely to prefer (and perform better in) a job that entails a lot of social interaction and offers opportunities to make friends. One recent survey found that workers with one or more good friends at work are much more likely to be committed to their work. United Airlines, for instance, allows flight attendants to form their own teams; those who participate tend to form teams with their friends.[17]

The need for power has also received considerable attention as an important ingredient in managerial success. The need for power is the desire to be influential in a group and to control one's environment. Research has shown that people with a strong need for power are likely to be superior performers, have good attendance records, and occupy supervisory positions. One study found that managers as a group tend to have a stronger power motive than the general population and that successful managers tend to have stronger power motives than less successful managers.[18] The need for power might explain why Mark Hurd, the former CEO of Hewlett-Packard, took advantage of his power and role as head of the company in 2010. Hurd was forced to resign after a sexual harassment claim by a female contractor alleging that Hurd had used corporate funds for personal gains in attempts to woo her. The former CEO had submitted personal receipts ranging from $1,000 to $20,000 over a two-year period.[19]

## Implications of the Content Perspectives

**need for affiliation**
The desire for human companionship and acceptance

**need for power**
The desire to be influential in a group and to control one's environment

Managers should remember that Maslow's needs hierarchy, the ERG theory, the two-factor theory, and the needs for achievement, affiliation, and power all provide useful insights into factors that cause motivation. What they do not do is shed much light on the process of motivation. They do not explain why people might be motivated by one factor rather than by another at a given level or how people might go about trying to satisfy their different needs. These questions involve behaviors or actions, goals, and feelings of satisfaction—concepts that are addressed by various process perspectives on motivation.

✔ **Manager's Checklist**

☐ Managers need to remember that needs and need deficiencies are the catalyst in stimulating motivated behavior.

☐ Managers should recognize, however, that different people have different needs.

☐ Finally, you should also remember that any given person's needs change over time.

# Process Perspectives on Motivation

Process perspectives are concerned with how motivation occurs. Rather than attempting to identify motivational stimuli, process perspectives focus on why people choose certain behavioral options to satisfy their needs and how they evaluate their satisfaction after they have attained these goals. Three useful process perspectives on motivation are the expectancy, equity, and goal-setting theories.

## Expectancy Theory

Expectancy theory suggests that motivation depends on two things—how much we want something and how likely we think we are to get it.[20] Assume that you are approaching graduation and looking for a job as a management trainee. You see in the want ads that General Motors is seeking a new vice president with a starting salary of $750,000 per year. Even though you might aspire to have this type of job one day, you will not apply now because you realize that you have very little chance of getting it. The next ad you see is for someone to scrape bubble gum from underneath theater seats for a starting salary of $8 an hour. Even though you could probably get this job, you do not apply because you do not want it. Then you see an ad for a management trainee at a big company, with a starting salary of $55,000. You may apply for this job because you want it and because you think you have a reasonable chance of getting it.

Expectancy theory rests on four basic assumptions. First, it assumes that behavior is determined by a combination of forces in the individual and in the environment. Second, it assumes that people make decisions about their own behavior in organizations. Third, it assumes that different people have different types of needs, desires, and goals. Fourth, it assumes that people make choices from among alternative plans of behavior, based on their perceptions of the extent to which a given behavior will lead to desired outcomes.

Figure 15.4 summarizes the basic expectancy model. The model suggests that motivation leads to effort and that effort, combined with employee ability and environmental factors, results in performance. Performance, in turn, leads to various outcomes, each of which

**process perspectives**
Approaches to motivation that focus on why people choose certain behavioral options to fulfill their needs and how they evaluate their satisfaction after they have attained these goals

**expectancy theory**
Suggests that motivation depends on two things—how much we want something and how likely we think we are to get it

## FIGURE 15.4 THE EXPECTANCY MODEL OF MOTIVATION

The expectancy model of motivation is a complex but relatively accurate portrayal of how motivation occurs. According to this model, a manager must understand what employees want (such as pay, promotions, or status) to begin to motivate them.

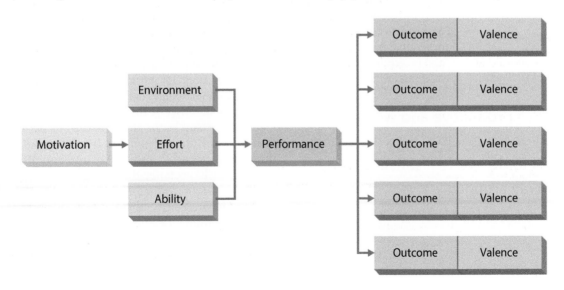

has an associated value, called its *valence*. The most important parts of the expectancy model cannot be shown in the figure, however. These are the individual's expectation that effort will lead to high performance, that performance will lead to outcomes, and that each outcome will have some kind of value.

**Effort-to-Performance Expectancy**  The effort-to-performance expectancy is the individual's perception of the probability that effort will lead to high performance. When the person believes that effort will lead directly to high performance, expectancy will be quite strong (close to 1.00). When the person believes that effort and performance are unrelated, the effort-to-performance expectancy is very weak (close to 0). The belief that effort is somewhat but not strongly related to performance carries with it a moderate expectancy (somewhere between 0 and 1.00).

**Performance-to-Outcome Expectancy**  The performance-to-outcome expectancy is the individual's perception that performance will lead to a specific outcome. For example, if the person believes that high performance *will* result in a pay raise, the performance-to-outcome expectancy is high (approaching 1.00). The person who believes that high performance *may* lead to a pay raise has a moderate expectancy (between 1.00 and 0). The person who believes that performance has no relationship to rewards has a low performance-to-outcome expectancy (close to 0).

**Outcomes and Valences**  Expectancy theory recognizes that a person's behavior results in a variety of outcomes, or consequences, in an organizational setting. A high performer, for example, may get bigger pay raises, faster promotions, and more praise from the boss. On the other hand, she may also be subject to more stress and incur resentment from coworkers. Each of these outcomes also has an associated value, or valence—an index of how much a person values a particular outcome. If the individual wants the outcome, its valence is positive; if the individual does not want the outcome, its valence is negative; and if the individual is indifferent to the outcome, its valence is zero.

It is this part of expectancy theory that goes beyond the content perspectives on motivation. Different people have different needs, and they will try to satisfy these needs in different ways. For an employee who has a high need for achievement and a low need for affiliation, the pay raise and promotions that are outcomes of high performance might have positive valences, the praise and resentment zero valences, and the stress a negative valence. For a different employee, with a low need for achievement and a high need for affiliation, the pay raise, promotions, and praise might all have positive valences, whereas both resentment and stress could have negative valences.

For motivated behavior to occur, three conditions must be met. First, the effort-to-performance expectancy must be greater than 0 (the person must believe that if effort is expended, high performance will result). The performance-to-outcome expectancy must also be greater than 0 (the peson must believe that if high performance is achieved, certain outcomes will follow). And the sum of the valences for the outcomes must be greater than 0. (One or more outcomes may have negative valences if they are more than offset by the positive valences of other outcomes. For example, the attractiveness of a pay raise, a promotion, and praise from the boss may outweigh the unattractiveness of more stress and resentment from coworkers.) Expectancy theory suggests that when these conditions are met, the person is motivated to expend effort.

Starbucks credits its unique stock ownership program with maintaining a dedicated and motivated workforce.

---

**effort-to-performance expectancy**
The individual's perception of the probability that effort will lead to high performance

**performance-to-outcome expectancy**
The individual's perception that performance will lead to a specific outcome

**outcomes**
Consequences of behaviors in an organizational setting, usually rewards

**valence**
An index of how much a person wants a particular outcome; the attractiveness of the outcome to the individual

---

"When we're productive and we've done something good together (and we are recognized for it), we feel satisfied, not the other way around."

—J. RICHARD HACKMAN, RESPECTED ORGANIZATIONAL PSYCHOLOGIST[22]

Based on the fundamental concepts of expectancy theory, Starbucks employees earn stock as a function of their seniority and performance. Thus their hard work helps them earn shares of ownership in the company.[21]

**The Porter-Lawler Extension** An interesting extension of expectancy theory has been proposed by Porter and Lawler.[23] Recall from Chapter 2 that the human relationists assumed that employee satisfaction causes good performance. We also noted that research has not supported such a relationship. Porter and Lawler suggested that there may indeed be a relationship between satisfaction and performance but that it goes in the opposite direction—that is, high performance may lead to high satisfaction. Figure 15.5 summarizes Porter and Lawler's logic. Performance results in rewards for an individual. Some of these are extrinsic (such as pay and promotions); others are intrinsic (such as self-esteem and accomplishment). The person evaluates the equity, or fairness, of the rewards relative to the effort expended and the level of performance attained. If the rewards are perceived to be equitable, the person is satisfied.

## Equity Theory

After needs have stimulated the motivation process and the person has chosen an action that is expected to satisfy those needs, he or she assesses the fairness, or equity, of the resultant outcome. Equity theory contends that people are motivated to seek social equity in the rewards they receive for performance.[24] Equity is an individual's belief that the treatment he or she is receiving is fair relative to the treatment received by others. According to equity theory, outcomes from a job include pay, recognition, promotions, social relationships, and intrinsic rewards. To get these rewards, the individual makes inputs to the job, such as time, experience, effort, education, and loyalty. The theory suggests that people view their

**equity theory**
Suggests that people are motivated to seek social equity in the rewards they receive for performance

---

**FIGURE 15.5** THE PORTER–LAWLER EXTENSION OF EXPECTANCY THEORY

The Porter–Lawler extension of expectancy theory suggests that if performance results in equitable rewards, people will be more satisfied. Thus performance can lead to satisfaction. Managers must therefore be sure that any system of motivation includes rewards that are fair, or equitable, for all.

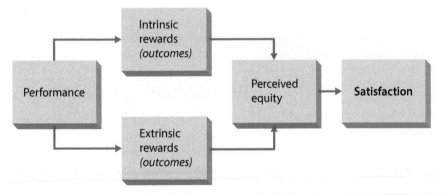

Source: Edward E. Lawler III and Lyman W. Porter, "The Effect of Performance on Job Satisfaction," *Industrial Relations*, October 1967, p. 23. Used with permission of Wiley-Blackwell.

outcomes and inputs as a ratio and then compare it to someone else's ratio. This other "person" may be someone in the work group or some sort of group average or composite. The process of comparison looks like this:

$$\frac{\text{Individual Inputs}}{\text{Individual Outcomes}} = \frac{\text{Other's Inputs}}{\text{Other's Outcomes}}$$

Both the formulation of the ratios and comparisons between them are very subjective and based on individual perceptions. As a result of comparisons, three conditions may result: The person may feel equitably rewarded, underrewarded, or overrewarded. A feeling of equity will result when the two ratios are equal. This may occur even though the other person's outcomes are greater than the individual's own outcomes—provided that the other's inputs are also proportionately greater. Suppose that Mark has a high school education and earns $40,000. He may still feel equitably treated relative to Susan, who earns $60,000, because she has a college degree and more experience.

People who feel underrewarded try to reduce the inequity. Such a person might decrease her inputs by exerting less effort, increase her outcomes by asking for a raise, distort the original ratios by rationalizing, try to get the other person to change her or his outcomes or inputs, leave the situation, or change the object of comparison. An individual may also feel overrewarded relative to another person. This is not likely to be terribly disturbing to most people, but research suggests that some people who experience inequity under these conditions are somewhat motivated to reduce it. Under such a circumstance, the person might increase his inputs by exerting more effort, reduce his outcomes by producing fewer units (if paid on a per-unit basis), distort the original ratios by rationalizing, or try to reduce the inputs or increase the outcomes of the other person.

Managers today may need to pay even greater attention to equity theory and its implications. Many firms, for example, are moving toward performance-based reward systems (discussed later in this chapter) as opposed to standard or across-the-board salary increases. Hence, they must ensure that the bases for rewarding some people more than others are clear and objective. Beyond legal issues such as discrimination, managers need to be sure that they are providing fair rewards and incentives to those who do the best work.[25] Moreover, they must be sensitive to cultural differences that affect how people may perceive and react to equity and inequity.[26]

Luchunyu/Shutterstock.com

Equity is the extent to which an individual feels fairly treated relative to others. The people who work in this open office area should not feel any inequity about their work area, since each team member has a comparable work station. But they may feel inequity if they compare themselves with others who have large private offices.

"People have long memories. They'll remember whether they think they were dealt with equitably."

—WILLIAM CONATY, FORMER DIRECTOR OF HR AT GENERAL ELECTRIC[27]

## Goal-Setting Theory

The goal-setting theory of motivation assumes that behavior is a result of conscious goals and intentions.[28] Therefore, by setting goals for people in the organization, a manager should be able to influence their behavior. Given this premise, the challenge is to develop a thorough understanding of the processes by which people set goals and then work to reach them. In the original version of goal-setting theory, two specific goal characteristics—goal difficulty and goal specificity—were expected to shape performance.

**Goal Difficulty** *Goal difficulty* is the extent to which a goal is challenging and requires effort. If people work to achieve goals, it is reasonable to assume that they will work harder to achieve more difficult goals. But a goal must not be so difficult that it is unattainable. If a new manager asks her sales force to increase sales by 300 percent, the group may become disillusioned. A more realistic but still difficult goal—perhaps a 30 percent increase—would be a better incentive. A substantial body of research supports the importance of goal difficulty. In one study, for example, managers at Weyerhaeuser set difficult goals for truck drivers hauling loads of timber from cutting sites to wood yards. Over a nine-month period, the drivers increased the quantity of wood they delivered by an amount that would have required $250,000 worth of new trucks at the previous per-truck average load.[29]

**Goal Specificity** *Goal specificity* is the clarity and precision of the goal. A goal of "increasing productivity" is not very specific; a goal of "increasing productivity by 3 percent in the next six months" is quite specific. Some goals, such as those involving costs, output, profitability, and growth, are readily amenable to specificity. Other goals, however, such as improving employee job satisfaction, morale, company image and reputation, ethics, and socially responsible behavior, may be much harder to state in specific terms. Like difficulty, specificity has been shown to be consistently related to performance. The study of timber truck drivers just mentioned, for example, also examined goal specificity. The initial loads the truck drivers were carrying were found to be 60 percent of the maximum weight each truck could haul. The managers set a new goal for drivers of 94 percent, which the drivers were soon able to reach. Thus the goal was both specific and difficult.

Because the theory attracted so much widespread interest and research support from researchers and managers alike, an expanded model of the goal-setting process was eventually proposed. The expanded model, shown in Figure 15.6, attempts to capture more fully the complexities of goal setting in organizations.

The expanded theory argues that goal-directed effort is a function of four goal attributes: difficulty and specificity, as already discussed, and acceptance and commitment.

## FIGURE 15.6  THE EXPANDED GOAL-SETTING THEORY OF MOTIVATION

One of the most important emerging theories of motivation is goal-setting theory. This theory suggests that goal difficulty, specificity, acceptance, and commitment combine to determine an individual's goal-directed effort. This effort, when complemented by appropriate organizational support and individual abilities and traits, results in performance. Finally, performance is seen as leading to intrinsic and extrinsic rewards that, in turn, result in employee satisfaction.

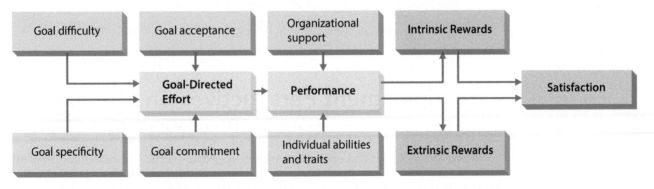

Source: Reprinted from Gary P. Latham and Edwin A. Locke, "A Motivational Technique That Works," *Organizational Dynamics*, Autumn 1979, p. 79, copyright © 1979 with permission from Elsevier Science.

"Your vision is your destination, and small, manageable goals are the motor that will get you there. Without the vision you're on a road to nowhere. Without the goals, you have a destination but no motor. They work in tandem, and you need both."

—DR. FRANK MURTHA, COUNSELING PSYCHOLOGIST[30]

*Goal acceptance* is the extent to which a person accepts a goal as his or her own. *Goal commitment* is the extent to which she or he is personally interested in reaching the goal. The manager who vows to take whatever steps are necessary to cut costs by 10 percent has made a commitment to achieve the goal. Factors that can foster goal acceptance and commitment include participating in the goal-setting process, making goals challenging but realistic, and believing that goal achievement will lead to valued rewards.

The interaction of goal-directed effort, organizational support, and individual abilities and traits determines actual performance. Organizational support is whatever the organization does to help or hinder performance. Positive support might mean making available adequate personnel and a sufficient supply of raw materials; negative support might mean failing to fix damaged equipment. Individual abilities and traits are the skills and other personal characteristics necessary for doing a job. As a result of performance, a person receives various intrinsic and extrinsic rewards, which in turn influence satisfaction. Note that the latter stages of this model are quite similar to the Porter and Lawler expectancy model discussed earlier.[31]

### Implications of the Process Perspectives

Expectancy theory can be useful for managers who are trying to improve the motivation of their subordinates. A series of steps can be followed to implement the basic ideas of the theory. First, figure out the outcomes each employee is likely to want. Second, decide what kinds and levels of performance are needed to meet organizational goals. Then make sure that the desired levels of performance are attainable. Also, make sure that desired outcomes and desired performance are linked. Next, analyze the complete situation for conflicting expectancies and ensure that the rewards are large enough. Finally, make sure the total system is equitable (fair to all). The single most important idea for managers to remember from equity theory is that if rewards are to motivate employees, they must be perceived as being equitable and fair. A second implication is that managers need to consider the nature of the "other" to whom the employee is comparing her- or himself. Goal-setting theory can be used to implement both expectancy and equity theory concepts.

---

**Manager's Checklist**

☐ Managers need to remember that people are motivated both by how much they want a particular outcome and by how likely they think it is that their performance will lead to that outcome.

☐ Managers should also recognize the importance of equity—employees' feeling that they are being treated and rewarded equitably.

☐ You should also understand that goal difficulty and goal specificity can play a major role in motivating employees.

---

**reinforcement theory**
Approach to motivation that argues that behavior that results in rewarding consequences is likely to be repeated, whereas behavior that results in punishing consequences is less likely to be repeated

# Reinforcement Perspectives on Motivation

A third element of the motivational process addresses why some behaviors are maintained over time and why other behaviors change. As we have seen, content perspectives deal with needs, whereas process perspectives explain why people choose various behaviors to satisfy needs and how they evaluate the equity of the rewards they get for those behaviors. Reinforcement perspectives explain the role of those rewards as they cause behavior to change or remain the same over time. Specifically, reinforcement theory argues that behavior that results in rewarding consequences is likely to be repeated, whereas behavior that results in punishing consequences is less likely to be repeated.[32]

## Kinds of Reinforcement in Organizations

There are four basic kinds of reinforcement that can result from behavior—positive reinforcement, avoidance, punishment, and extinction.[33] These are summarized in Table 15.1. Two kinds of reinforcement strengthen or maintain behavior, whereas the other two weaken or decrease behavior.

Positive reinforcement, a method of strengthening behavior, is a reward or a positive outcome after a desired behavior is performed. When a manager observes an employee doing an especially good job and offers praise, the praise serves to positively reinforce the behavior of good work. Other positive reinforcers in organizations include pay raises, promotions, and awards. Employees who work at General Electric's customer service center receive clothing, sporting goods, and even trips to Disney World as rewards for outstanding performance. The other method of strengthening desired behavior is through avoidance. An employee may come to work on time to avoid a reprimand. In this instance, the employee is motivated to perform the behavior of punctuality to avoid an unpleasant consequence that is likely to follow tardiness.

Punishment is used by some managers to weaken undesired behaviors. When an employee is loafing, coming to work late, doing poor work, or interfering with the work of others, the manager might resort to reprimands, discipline, or fines. The logic is that the unpleasant consequence will reduce the likelihood that the employee will choose that particular behavior again. Given the counterproductive side effects of punishment (such as resentment and hostility), though, it is often advisable to use the other kinds of

Positive reinforcement is a reward or other desired outcome. This employee is getting praise and a pat on the back from his boss for finishing an important project. Both serve as positive reinforcement.

*Dmytro Zinkevych/Shutterstock.com*

**positive reinforcement**
A method of strengthening behavior with rewards or positive outcomes after a desired behavior is performed

**avoidance**
Used to strengthen behavior by avoiding unpleasant consequences that would result if the behavior were not performed

**punishment**
Used to weaken undesired behaviors by using negative outcomes or unpleasant consequences when the behavior is performed

---

## TABLE 15.1 ELEMENTS OF REINFORCEMENT THEORY

A manager who wants the best chance of reinforcing a behavior would likely offer the employee a positive reinforcement after a variable number of behaviors (variable-ratio reinforcement). For example, the manager could praise the employee after the third credit card application was received. Additional praise might be offered after the next five applications, then again after the next three, the next seven, the next four, and so on.

### Arrangement of the Reinforcement Contingencies

1. *Positive Reinforcement.* Strengthens behavior by providing a desirable consequence.
2. *Avoidance.* Strengthens behavior by allowing escape from an undesirable consequence.

3. *Punishment.* Weakens behavior by providing an undesirable consequence.
4. *Extinction.* Weakens behavior by ignoring it.

### Schedules for Applying Reinforcement

1. *Fixed-Interval.* Reinforcement is applied at fixed time intervals, regardless of behavior.
2. *Variable-Interval.* Reinforcement is applied at variable time intervals.

1. *Fixed-Ratio.* Reinforcement is applied after a fixed number of behaviors, regardless of time.
2. *Variable-Ratio.* Reinforcement is applied after a variable number of behaviors.

reinforcement if at all possible. Extinction can also be used to weaken behavior, especially behavior that has previously been rewarded. When an employee tells an inappropriate joke and the boss laughs, the laughter reinforces the behavior and the employee may continue to tell inappropriate jokes. By simply ignoring this behavior and not reinforcing it, however, the boss may cause the behavior to subside and eventually become "extinct."

## Providing Reinforcement in Organizations

Not only is the kind of reinforcement important, but so is when or how often it occurs. Various strategies are possible for providing reinforcement. These are also listed in Table 15.1. The fixed-interval schedule provides reinforcement at fixed intervals of time, regardless of behavior. A good example of this schedule is the weekly or monthly paycheck. This method provides the least incentive for good work because employees know they will be paid regularly regardless of their efforts. A variable-interval schedule also uses time as the basis for reinforcement, but the time interval varies from one reinforcement to the next. This schedule is appropriate for praise or other rewards based on visits or inspections. When employees do not know when the boss is going to drop by, they tend to maintain a reasonably high level of effort all the time.

A fixed-ratio schedule gives reinforcement after a fixed number of behaviors, regardless of the time that elapses between behaviors. This results in an even higher level of effort. For example, when Sears is recruiting new credit card customers, salespersons get a small bonus for every fifth application returned from their department. Under this arrangement, motivation will be high because each application gets the person closer to the next bonus. The variable-ratio schedule, the most powerful schedule in terms of maintaining desired behaviors, varies the number of behaviors needed for each reinforcement. A supervisor who praises an employee for her second order, the seventh order after that, the ninth after that, then the fifth, and then the third is using a variable-ratio schedule. The employee is motivated to increase the frequency of the desired behavior because each performance increases the probability of receiving a reward. Of course, a variable-ratio schedule is difficult (if not impossible) to use for formal rewards such as pay because it would be too complicated to keep track of who was rewarded when.

Managers wanting to explicitly use reinforcement theory to motivate their employees generally do so with a technique called behavior modification, or OB Mod.[34] An OB Mod program starts by specifying behaviors that are to be increased (such as producing more units) or decreased (such as coming to work late). These target behaviors are then tied to specific forms or kinds of reinforcement. Although many organizations (such as Procter & Gamble and Ford) have used OB Mod, the best-known application was at Emery Air Freight. Management felt that the containers used to consolidate small shipments into fewer, larger shipments were not being packed efficiently. Through a system of self-monitored feedback and rewards, Emery increased container usage from 45 percent to 95 percent and saved over $3 million during the first three years of the program.[35]

## Implications of the Reinforcement Perspectives

Reinforcement in organizations can be a powerful force for maintaining employee motivation. Of course, for reinforcement to be truly effective, managers need to use it in a manner consistent with the various types and schedules of reinforcement discussed above. In addition, managers must understand that they may be inadvertently motivating undesired or dysfunctional behaviors. For instance, if an employee routinely comes to work late but experiences no consequences, both that worker and others will see that it is all right to be late for work.

**extinction**
Used to weaken undesired behaviors by simply ignoring or not reinforcing them

**fixed-interval schedule**
Provides reinforcement at fixed intervals of time, such as regular weekly paychecks

**variable-interval schedule**
Provides reinforcement at varying intervals of time, such as occasional visits by the supervisor

**fixed-ratio schedule**
Provides reinforcement after a fixed number of behaviors regardless of the time interval involved, such as a bonus for every fifth sale

**variable-ratio schedule**
Provides reinforcement after varying numbers of behaviors are performed, such as the use of complements by a supervisor on an irregular basis

**behavior modification (OB Mod)**
Method for applying the basic elements of reinforcement theory in an organizational setting

# Popular Motivational Strategies

Although the various theories discussed thus far provide a solid explanation for motivation, managers must use various techniques and strategies to actually apply them. Among the most popular motivational strategies today are empowerment and participation and alternative forms of work arrangements. Various forms of performance-based reward systems, discussed in the next section, also reflect efforts to boost motivation and performance.

## Empowerment and Participation

Empowerment and participation represent important methods that managers can use to enhance employee motivation. Empowerment is the process of enabling workers to set their own work goals, make decisions, and solve problems within their sphere of responsibility and authority. Participation is the process of giving employees a voice in making decisions about their own work. Thus empowerment is a somewhat broader concept that promotes participation in a wide variety of areas, including but not limited to work itself, work context, and work environment.[36]

The role of participation and empowerment in motivation can be expressed in terms of both content perspectives and expectancy theory. Employees who participate in decision making may be more committed to executing decisions properly. Furthermore, the successful process of making a decision, executing it, and then seeing the positive consequences can help satisfy one's need for achievement, provide recognition and responsibility, and enhance self-esteem. Simply being asked to participate in organizational decision making also may enhance an employee's self-esteem. In addition, participation should help clarify expectancies; that is, by participating in decision making, employees may better understand the linkage between their performance and the rewards they want most.

Participation and empowerment are popular strategies for improving employee motivation. This manager is giving his team autonomy to make an important decision—that is, he is empowering them.

**Areas of Participation** At one level, employees can participate in addressing questions and making decisions about their own jobs. Instead of just telling them how to do their jobs, for example, managers can ask employees to make their own decisions about how to do them. Based on their own expertise and experience with their tasks, workers might be able to improve their own productivity. In many situations, they might also be well qualified to make decisions about what materials to use, what tools to use, and so forth.

It might also be helpful to let workers make decisions about administrative matters, such as work schedules. If jobs are relatively independent of one another, employees might decide when to change shifts, take breaks, go to lunch, and so forth. A work group or team might also be able to schedule vacations and days off for all of its members.

**empowerment**
The process of enabling workers to set their own work goals, make decisions, and solve problems within their sphere of responsibility and authority

**participation**
The process of giving employees a voice in making decisions about their own work

Furthermore, employees are getting increasing opportunities to participate in broader issues of product quality. Such participation has become a hallmark of successful Japanese and other international firms, and many U.S. companies have followed suit.

**Techniques and Issues in Empowerment** In recent years, many organizations have actively sought ways to extend participation beyond the traditional areas. Simple techniques, such as suggestion boxes and question-and-answer meetings, allow a certain degree of participation, for example. The basic motive has been to better capitalize on the assets and capabilities inherent in all employees. Thus many managers today prefer the term *empowerment* to *participation* because of its more comprehensive character.

One method used to empower workers is the use of work teams. Such teams are collections of employees empowered to plan, organize, direct, and control their own work. Their supervisor, rather than being a traditional "boss," plays more the role of a coach. The other method for empowerment is to change the team's overall method of organizing. The basic pattern is for an organization to eliminate layers from its hierarchy, thereby becoming much more decentralized. Power, responsibility, and authority are delegated as far down the organization as possible, placing control over work squarely in the hands of those who actually do it.[37]

Regardless of the specific technique or method used, however, empowerment will enhance organizational effectiveness only if certain conditions exist. First of all, the organization must be sincere in its efforts to spread power and autonomy to lower levels of the organization. Token efforts to promote participation in only a few areas are not likely to succeed. Second, the organization must be committed to maintaining participation and empowerment. Workers will be resentful if they are given more control, only to later have it reduced or taken away altogether. Third, workers must truly believe that they and their managers are working together in their joint best interests. In some factory settings, for instance, high-performing workers routinely conceal the secrets of their high output. They fear that if management learns those secrets, it will use them to ratchet up performance expectations.[38]

In addition, the organization must be systematic and patient in its efforts to empower workers. Turning over too much control too quickly can spell disaster. And finally, the organization must be prepared to increase its commitment to training. Employees given more freedom in how they work will quite likely need additional training to help them exercise that freedom most effectively.[39]

## Alternative Forms of Work Arrangements

Many organizations today are also experimenting with a variety of alternative work arrangements. These alternative arrangements are generally intended to enhance employee motivation and performance by providing employees with greater flexibility in how and when they work. Among the more popular alternative work arrangements are variable work schedules, flexible work schedules, job sharing, and telecommuting.[40]

**Variable Work Schedules** Although there are many exceptions, of course, the traditional work schedule starts at 8:00 or 9:00 in the morning and ends at 5:00 in the evening, five days a week (and, of course, many managers work additional hours outside of these times). Unfortunately, this schedule makes it difficult to attend to routine personal business—going to the bank, seeing a doctor or dentist for a routine checkup, having a parent–teacher conference, getting an automobile serviced, and so forth. At a surface level, then, employees locked into this sort of arrangement may find it necessary to take a sick day or a vacation day to handle these activities. At a more unconscious level, some people may also feel so powerless and constrained by their job schedule as to feel increased resentment and frustration.

> "These guidelines ... effectively mean that as long as they do their work, our employees can work whenever they want, from wherever they want."
>
> —RICHARD BRANSON, FOUNDER AND CEO, VIRGIN GROUP[41]

To help counter these problems, some businesses have adopted a compressed work schedule, working a full 40-hour week in fewer than the traditional five days.[42] One approach involves working 10 hours a day for four days, leaving an extra day off. Another alternative is for employees to work slightly less than 10 hours a day, but to complete the 40 hours by lunchtime on Friday. And a few firms have tried having employees work 12 hours a day for three days, followed by four days off. Organizations that have used these forms of compressed workweeks include John Hancock, BP Amoco, and Philip Morris. One problem with this schedule is that when employees put in too much time in a single day, they tend to get tired and perform at a lower level later in the day.

A schedule that some organizations today are beginning to use is what they call a "nine-eighty" schedule. Under this arrangement, employees work a traditional schedule one week and a compressed schedule the next, getting every other Friday off. In other words, they work 80 hours (the equivalent of two weeks of full-time work) in nine days. By alternating the regular and compressed schedules across half of its workforce, the organization can be fully staffed at all times, while still giving employees two full days off each month. Shell Oil and BP Amoco Chemicals are two of the firms that currently use this schedule.

**Flexible Work Schedules** Another promising alternative work arrangement is flexible work schedules, sometimes called *flextime*. Flextime gives employees more personal control over the times they work. The workday is broken down into two categories: flexible time and core time. All employees must be at their workstations during core time, but they can choose their own schedules during flexible time. Thus one employee may choose to start work early in the morning and leave in midafternoon, another to start in the late morning and work until late afternoon, and still another to start early in the morning, take a long lunch break, and work until late afternoon.

Organizations that have used the flexible work schedule method for arranging work include Hewlett-Packard, Microsoft, and Texas Instruments.

**Job Sharing** Yet another potentially useful alternative work arrangement is job sharing. In job sharing, two part-time employees share one full-time job. One person may perform the job from 8:00 A.M. to noon and the other from 1:00 P.M. to 5:00 P.M. Job sharing may be desirable for people who want to work only part time or when job markets are tight. For its part, the organization can accommodate the preferences of a broader range of employees and may benefit from the talents of more people.

**Telecommuting** An increasingly popular approach to alternative work arrangements is telecommuting—allowing employees to spend part of their time working offsite, usually at home. By using e-mail, the Internet, and other forms of information technology, many employees can maintain close contact with their organization and still get just as much (or even more) work done at home as they would if they were in the office. The increased power and sophistication of modern communication technology is

**compressed work schedule**
Working a full 40-hour week in fewer than the traditional five days

**flexible work schedule**
Work schedule in which employees have some control over the hours they choose to work; also called flextime

**job sharing**
When two part-time employees share one full-time job

**telecommuting**
Allowing employees to spend part of their time working offsite, usually at home

"I get to sit here and look out my window while I talk to customers [by telecommuting]—and watch the leaves changing, squirrels running around, and kids going off to school."

—WALT SWANSON, AGILENT TECHNOLOGIES CUSTOMER SERVICE REPRESENTATIVE[43]

Telecommuting is a motivational technique that allows employees to spend part of their time working from home or some other alternative workplace. This man is working from his home office.

making telecommuting easier and easier. One recent study found that nearly half of the U.S. workforce (64 million workers) are in jobs that allow for at least partial telecommuting.[44] Nearly half of AT&T's employees have received mobile and remote access technologies that provide them with the flexibility to work from various locations. And 40 percent of IBM's employees currently telecommute. (In the case of IBM, not only are employees more satisfied with the arrangement but the firm has saved close to $2.9 billion in office space needs.)[45]

 **Manager's Checklist**

☐ Managers need to know the role that employee empowerment and participation play in employee motivation.

☐ You should also know the various work schedules used by organizations and how those schedules can affect motivation.

# Using Reward Systems To Motivate Performance

Aside from these types of motivational strategies, an organization's reward system is its most basic tool for managing employee motivation. An organizational reward system is the formal and informal mechanisms by which employee performance is defined, evaluated, and rewarded. Rewards that are tied specifically to performance, of course, have the greatest impact on enhancing both motivation and actual performance.

Performance-based rewards play a number of roles and address a variety of purposes in organizations. The major purposes involve the relationship of rewards to motivation and to performance. Specifically, organizations want employees to perform at relatively high levels and need to make it worth their effort to do so. When rewards are associated with higher levels of performance, employees will presumably be motivated to work harder to achieve those awards. At that point, their own self-interests coincide with the organization's interests. Performance-based rewards are also relevant regarding other employee behaviors, such as retention and citizenship.

### Merit Reward Systems

Merit reward systems are among the most fundamental forms of performance-based rewards.[46] Merit pay generally refers to pay awarded to employees on the basis of the relative value of their contributions to the organization. Employees who make greater contributions are given higher pay than those who make lesser contributions. Merit pay plans, then, are compensation plans that formally base at least some meaningful portion of compensation on merit.

The most general form of merit pay plan is to provide annual salary increases to employees based on their relative merit. Merit, in turn, is usually determined or defined based on the person's performance and overall contributions to the organization. For example, an organization using such a traditional merit pay plan might instruct its supervisors to give all their employees an average pay raise of, say, 4 percent. But the individual supervisor is further instructed to differentiate among high, average, and low performers. Under a simple system, for example, a manager might give the top 25 percent of her employees a 6 percent pay raise, the middle 50 percent a 4 percent or average pay raise, and the bottom 25 percent a 2 percent pay raise.

### Incentive Reward Systems

Incentive reward systems are among the oldest forms of performance-based rewards. For example, some companies were using individual piece-rate incentive plans over 100 years ago.[47]

**reward system**
The formal and informal mechanisms by which employee performance is defined, evaluated, and rewarded

**merit pay**
Pay awarded to employees on the basis of the relative value of their contributions to the organization

**merit pay plan**
Compensation plan that formally bases at least some meaningful portion of compensation on merit

Under a piece-rate incentive plan, the organization pays an employee a certain amount of money for every unit she or he produces. For example, an employee might be paid $1 for every dozen units of product that are successfully completed. But such simplistic systems fail to account for such facts as minimum wage levels and rely very heavily on the assumptions that performance is totally under a worker's control and that the employee does a single task continuously throughout his or her work time. Thus most organizations today that try to use incentive compensation systems use more sophisticated methodologies.

**Incentive Pay Plans**  Generally speaking, *individual incentive plans* reward individual performance on a real-time basis. In other words, rather than increasing a person's base salary at the end of the year, the worker instead receives some level of salary increase or financial reward in conjunction with demonstrated outstanding performance in close proximity to when that performance occurred. Individual incentive systems are most likely to be used in cases in which performance can be objectively assessed in terms of number of units of output or similar measures, rather than on a subjective assessment of performance by a superior. WD-40 Company uses an individual incentive plan that covers almost its entire workforce. The firm's managers credit the incentive plan with motivating its employees to perform at high levels during the 2008–2010 recession in ways that enabled the firm to achieve record profits.[48]

Some variations on a piece-rate system are still fairly popular. Although many of these still resemble the early plans in most ways, a well-known piece-rate system at Lincoln Electric illustrates how an organization can adapt the traditional model to achieve better results. For years, Lincoln's employees were paid individual incentive payments based on their performance. However, the amount of money shared (the incentive pool) was based on the company's profitability. There was also a well-organized system whereby employees could make suggestions for increasing productivity. There was motivation to do this because the employees received one-third of the profits (another third went to the stockholders, and the last share was retained for improvements and seed money). Thus the pool for incentive payments was determined by profitability, and an employee's share of this pool was a function of his or her base pay and rated performance based on the piece-rate system. Lincoln Electric was most famous, however, because of the stories (which were apparently typical) of production workers' receiving a year-end bonus payment that equaled their yearly base pay.[49] In recent years, Lincoln has partially abandoned its famous system for business reasons, but it still serves as a benchmark for other companies seeking innovative piece-rate pay systems.

Perhaps the most common form of individual incentive is *sales commissions* that are paid to people engaged in sales work. For example, sales representatives for consumer products firms and retail sales agents may be compensated under this type of commission system. In general, the person might receive a percentage of the total volume of attained sales as her or his commission for a period of time. Some sales jobs are based entirely on commission, whereas others use a combination of base minimum salary with additional commission as an incentive. Notice that these plans put a considerable amount of the salespersons' earnings "at risk." In other words, although organizations often have drawing accounts to allow the salesperson to live during lean periods (the person then "owes" this money back to the organization), if he or she does not perform well, he or

**piece-rate incentive plan**
Reward system wherein the organization pays an employee a certain amount of money for every unit she or he produces

Sales commissions are among the most common forms of incentive pay plans. This retail sales person, for example, earns a base hourly wage. However, she also earns additional income based on the total volume of sales she generates each week. So, she is incentivized to sell as much merchandise as possible because doing so increases her own pay.

she will not be paid much. The portion of salary based on commission is simply not guaranteed and is paid only if sales reach some target level.

**Other Forms of Incentive**  Occasionally organizations may also use other forms of incentives to motivate people. For example, a nonmonetary incentive, such as additional time off or a special perk, might be a useful incentive. For example, a company might establish a sales contest in which the sales group that attains the highest level of sales increase over a specified period of time will receive an extra week of paid vacation, perhaps even at an arranged place, such as a tropical resort or a ski lodge.[50]

A major advantage of incentives relative to merit systems is that incentives are typically a one-shot reward and do not accumulate by becoming part of the individual's base salary. Stated differently, a person whose outstanding performance entitles him or her to a financial incentive gets the incentive only one time, based on that level of performance. If the person's performance begins to erode in the future, then she or he may receive a lesser incentive or perhaps no incentive in the future. As a consequence, his or her base salary remains the same or is perhaps increased at a relatively moderate pace; he or she receives one-time incentive rewards as recognition for exemplary performance. Furthermore, because these plans, by their very nature, focus on one-time events, it is much easier for the organization to change the focus of the incentive plan. At a simple level, for example, an organization can set up an incentive plan for selling one product during one quarter, but then shift the incentive to a different product the next quarter, as the situation requires. Automobile companies like Ford and GM routinely do this by reducing sales incentives for models that are selling very well and increasing sales incentives for models that are selling below expectations or are about to be discontinued.

## Team and Group Incentive Reward Systems

The merit compensation and incentive compensation systems described in the preceding sections deal primarily with performance-based reward arrangements for individuals. There also exists a different set of performance-based reward programs that are targeted for teams and groups. These programs are particularly important for managers to understand today, given the widespread trends toward team- and group-based methods of work and organization.[51]

**Common Team and Group Reward Systems**  There are two commonly used types of team and group reward systems. One type used in many organizations is an approach called gainsharing. Gainsharing programs are designed to share the cost savings from productivity improvements with employees. The underlying assumption of gainsharing is that employees and the employer have the same goals and thus should appropriately share in incremental economic gains.[52] *Doing Business on Planet Earth* provides an interesting example of an innovative gainsharing program.

In general, organizations that use gainsharing start by measuring team- or group-level productivity. It is important that this measure be valid and reliable and that it truly reflect current levels of performance by the team or group. The team or work group itself is then given the task of trying to lower costs and otherwise improve productivity through any measures that its members develop and its manager approves. Resulting cost savings or productivity gains that the team or group is able to achieve are then quantified and translated into dollar values. A predetermined formula is then used to allocate these dollar savings between the employer and the employees themselves. A typical formula for distributing gainsharing savings is to provide 25 percent to the employees and 75 percent to the company.

One specific type of gainsharing plan is an approach called the Scanlon plan. This approach was developed by Joseph Scanlon in 1927. The Scanlon plan has the same basic strategy as gainsharing plans, in that teams or groups of employees are encouraged to suggest strategies for reducing costs. However, the distribution of these gains is usually tilted much more heavily toward employees, with employees usually receiving between two-thirds and

**gainsharing programs**
Designed to share the cost savings from productivity improvements with employees

**Scanlon plan**
Similar to gainsharing, but the distribution of gains is tilted much more heavily toward employees

# M(otivation) p(er) G(allon)

Drivers for private truck fleets log about 20,000 miles a year. They drive 82 percent of all medium and heavy-duty vehicles in the United States and account for 52 percent of the total miles traveled by commercial motor vehicles (CMVs). "The way these employees drive," says veteran industry journalist Mike Antich, "can either increase or decrease fuel economy and greenhouse gas emissions. If you change driving behavior," Antich argues, "you have a direct impact on the amount of fuel consumed and the amount of emissions produced. Even small increases in mpg" can make a big difference, and Antich points out that fuel-conscious fleet managers have reported up to 30 percent reductions in fuel consumption by changing driver behavior.

How? By motivating drivers to comply with company sustainability policies. Unfortunately, of course, it's not that simple. Most drivers, according to Antich, "want to do the right thing but don't see sustainability as part of their job responsibilities. In fact, the No. 1 reason corporate sustainability programs are not 'sustainable' is driver noncompliance. A successful sustainability initiative," says Antich, "requires developing programs that motivate employees to comply." He goes on to argue that effective motivational programs often involve *gainsharing*—programs designed to share company cost savings with employees.

Again, however, implementing the solution isn't quite as easy as identifying it. Traditionally, observes Antich, gainsharing involves *financial incentives*, but he admits that "in today's cost-constrained business environment, offering financial incentives [may not be] a realistic option." Consequently, many firms have found that *individual recognition* can be an effective alternative to financial incentives: "Repeatedly," says Antich, "respondents to employee surveys rate 'individual recognition' as a key factor that motivates them to want to excel or achieve corporate objectives."

Both scientific studies and the experiences of various companies show that the importance of employee recognition—including financial rewards—should not be underestimated in

sustainability efforts, primarily because the importance of *individual behavior* should not be underestimated. According to a report by Jones Lang LaSalle (JLL), a professional-services and investment-management company, many companies with active efficiency programs are finding that further improvements in sustainability can be achieved only by turning to the people who are responsible for implementing those programs. "The low-hanging fruit has been plucked," JLL's Michael Jordan advises clients. "You now need the participation of humans."

Nussbaum Transportation, for example, has developed a software program called Driver Excelerator, which collects and analyzes fuel-related data from various sources, including electronic control devices for capturing mpg numbers. Using the resulting data, managers award points to drivers of the 230-truck fleet for beating the company's mpg goal. If, for instance, a driver achieves an average quarterly mpg of 8.5 against a goal of 6.5, he or she receives 200 points, which are allotted according to a three-tier system: Bronze pays $0.50 per point, Silver $5.00 per point, and Gold $8.00 per point. Some drivers in the Gold tier earn an extra $1,600 every three months.

Illinois-based Nussbaum was careful to reject an "all-or-nothing" system in which drivers received a bonus for meeting a target and nothing for falling short. "Our experience," says HR director Jeremy Stickling, "shows that that's a big de-motivator" because drivers who miss out tend to blame external circumstances such as weather or load weights. In fact, Nussbaum plans to make mileage-based performance rewards a bigger portion of drivers' base-pay rate. The idea is for drivers to get higher monthly checks instead of big quarterly bonus checks. "Guys want their money now," notes Stickling.

*References:* Mike Antich, "Using 'Gainsharing' to Achieve Sustainability Goals," *Automotive Fleet* (April 2, 2014), www.automotive-fleet.com, on March 16, 2015; Jones Lang LaSalle, "Employee Sustainability Engagement" (2014), www.joneslanglasalle.com, on March 16, 2014; American Transportation Research Institute, "The Role of Truck Drivers in Sustainability" (2012), http://atri-online.org, on March 20, 2014; Aaron Huff, "Performance-Based Pay, Part 1: The Science of Scoring Drivers," *Commercial Carrier Journal* (December 18, 2013), www.ccjdigital.com, on March 21, 2015.

three-fourths of the total cost savings that the plan achieves. Furthermore, the distribution of cost savings resulting from the plan is given not just to the team or group that suggested and developed the ideas, but across the entire organization.

**Other Types of Team and Group Rewards** Although gainsharing and Scanlon-type plans are among the most popular group incentive reward systems, there are other systems that are also used by some organizations. Some companies, for example, have begun to use true incentives at the team or group level. Just as with individual incentives, team or group incentives tie rewards directly to performance increases. And, like individual incentives, team or group incentives are paid as they are earned rather than being added to employees' base salaries. The incentives are distributed at the team or group level, however, rather than at the individual level. In some cases, the distribution may be based on the existing salary of each employee, with incentive bonuses being given on a proportionate basis. In other settings, each member of the team or group receives the same incentive pay.

Some companies also use nonmonetary rewards at the team or group level—most commonly in the form of prizes and awards. For example, a company might designate the particular team in a plant or subunit of the company that achieves the highest level of productivity increase, the highest level of reported customer satisfaction, or a similar index of performance. The reward itself might take the form of additional time off, as described earlier in this chapter, or a tangible award, such as a trophy or plaque. In any event, the idea is that the reward is at the team level and serves as recognition of exemplary performance by the entire team.

There are also other kinds of team- or group-level incentives that go beyond the contributions of a specific work group. These are generally organization-wide kinds of incentives. One longstanding method for this approach is *profit sharing*. In a profit-sharing approach, at the end of the year some portion of the company's profits is paid into a profit-sharing pool that is then distributed to all employees. Either this amount is distributed at that time, or it is put into an escrow account and payment is deferred until the employee retires.

The basic rationale behind profit-sharing systems is that everyone in the organization can expect to benefit when the company does well. But, on the other side of the coin, during bad economic times, when the company is perhaps achieving low or perhaps no profits, then no profit sharing is paid out. This sometimes results in negative reactions from employees, who have perhaps come to feel that profit sharing is really a part of their annual compensation.

*Employee stock ownership plans (ESOPs)* also represent a group-level reward system that some companies use. Under the employee stock ownership plan, employees are gradually given a major stake in ownership of a corporation. The typical form of this plan involves the company's taking out a loan, which is then used to buy a portion of its own stock in the open market. Over time, company profits are then used to pay off this loan. Employees, in turn, receive a claim on ownership of some portion of the stock held by the company, based on their seniority and perhaps on their performance. Eventually, each individual becomes an owner of the company. One recent study found that 20 percent of employees in the private sector (25 million Americans) reported owning stock in their companies, with 10 percent holding stock options.[53]

## Executive Compensation

The top-level executives of most companies have separate compensation programs and plans. These are intended to reward these executives for their performance and for the performance of the organization. *Leading the Way* provides some interesting insights into executive compensation.

**Standard Forms of Executive Compensation** Most senior executives receive their compensation in two forms. One form is a *base salary*. As with the base salary of any staff member or professional member of an organization, the base salary of an executive is a guaranteed amount of money that the person will be paid. For example, in 2014 Hewlett-Packard paid its CEO, Meg Whitman, $1,500,000 in base salary.[54]

Above and beyond this base salary, however, most executives also receive one or more forms of incentive pay. The traditional method of incentive pay for executives is in the form of bonuses. Bonuses, in turn, are usually determined by the performance of the organization. Thus, at the end of the year, some portion of a corporation's profits may be diverted into a bonus pool. Senior executives then receive a bonus expressed as a percentage of this bonus pool. The chief executive officer and president are obviously likely to get a larger percentage bonus than a vice president. The exact distribution of the bonus pool is usually specified ahead of time in the individual's employment contract. Some organizations intentionally leave the distribution unspecified, so that the

Executive compensation is often controversial. Some critics argue that top managers are paid far more than their performance justifies, and they often get paid large salaries even when their organizations perform poorly.

board of directors has the flexibility to give larger rewards to those deemed to be most deserving. HP's Meg Whitman received a cash bonus of $3.97 million in 2014.[55]

**Special Forms of Executive Compensation** Beyond base salary and bonuses, many executives receive other kinds of compensation as well. A form of executive compensation that has received a lot of attention in recent years has been various kinds of stock options. A stock option plan is established to give senior managers the option to buy company stock in the future at a predetermined fixed price. The basic idea underlying stock option plans is that if the executives contribute to higher levels of organizational performance, then the company stock should increase in value. Then the executive will be able to purchase the stock at the predetermined price, which theoretically should be lower than its future market price. The difference then becomes profit for the individual. HP awarded Meg Whitman stock options with a potential value of $12.7 million.[56]

**stock option plan**
Established to give senior managers the option to buy company stock in the future at a predetermined fixed price

Stock options continue to grow in popularity as a means of compensating top managers. Options are seen as a means of aligning the interests of the manager with those of the stockholders, and given that they do not cost the organization much (other than some possible dilution of stock values), they will probably be even more popular in the future. In fact, a recent study by KPMG Peat Marwick indicates that for senior management whose salary exceeds $250,000, stock options represent the largest share of the salary mix (relative to salary and other incentives). Furthermore, when we consider all of top management (annual salary over $750,000), stock options comprise a full 60 percent of their total compensation. And the Peat Marwick report indicates that even among exempt employees at the $35,000-a-year level, stock options represent 13 percent of total compensation.

Top executives often get perquisites, or "perks," in addition to their salary, bonuses, and stock options. Access to corporate planes is a common perk in some companies.

**LEADING THE WAY**

# Compensating for Big Bets

A company's *chief financial officer* (CFO) is responsible for managing its money—or, more specifically, for managing its financial risks. The CFO assesses the risks that a company takes in allocating its financial assets, balancing those risks against potential profitability. The goal is to maximize the company's wealth, especially by maximizing the value of its stock. In short, the CFO is responsible for a company's economic value.

Not surprisingly, CFOs are well paid. The median annual base pay for a CFO in the United States is $317,245 (meaning that 50 percent of CFOs make more and 50 percent less). Base pay, however, accounts for only 58.6 percent of the typical CFO compensation package. Once bonuses and benefits are added to total compensation, CFOs in the 90th percentile (those who earn more than 90 percent of their colleagues) receive total compensation of $949,880. It's a lucrative profession.

As CFO of the investment bank Morgan Stanley, Ruth Porat was in the 90th percentile of the pay scale, and then some. Her base salary in 2013 was $1 million; her bonus came to $3.6 million, plus $5.4 million in stock awards, and with various additional forms of compensation, her total package came to $10.1 million.

Before becoming CFO, Porat was a key player in Morgan Stanley's emergence from the financial crisis of 2007–2008, helping to develop a strategy of focusing on safer ways of making money than trading in securities backed by risky mortgages. She headed the bank's team when the U.S. Treasury Department hired Morgan Stanley to advise it on the bailouts of Fannie Mae and Freddie Mac, two government-sponsored organizations crippled by the mortgage crisis. Between 2010 and 2012, her first two years as CFO, Morgan Stanley's share price doubled, and Porat was widely regarded as "the most powerful woman on Wall Street."

It was big news, then, when Porat left Wall Street for Silicon Valley: In March 2015, the giant tech company Google announced that it had hired Porat away from Morgan Stanley. Her base pay would be $650,000, but she wasn't exactly taking a pay cut: The entire deal was worth more than $70 million in cash and stock, and Porat would actually be making three-and-a-half times what she made at Morgan Stanley.

What does Google expect Porat to be motivated to do? Google isn't exactly teetering on the brink of bankruptcy, but some investors are concerned that advertising income—which accounts for 90 percent of Google's revenues—has slowed and profit margins have declined. Through the end of 2014, the company had missed analysts' projections for five straight quarters. Other observers are nervous about Google's spending on speculative ventures—including self-driving cars, smart glasses, and a balloon-powered wireless network—that have little to do with its core business; they acknowledge that Google needs to diversify its revenue streams but worry about the company's high-risk approach to doing it (while spending too much money in the process).

Porat, of course, is an ideal point person to make the company's case to Wall Street, and many people in the investment business are glad to see a Wall Street veteran take over Google's finances. Clearly, that's one of the main reasons why Google was willing to lay out so much money to get Porat. "I look forward to learning from Ruth," said Google CEO Larry Page, "as we continue to innovate in our core … as well as invest in a thoughtful, disciplined way in our next generation of big bets." The word "disciplined" apparently struck a favorable chord on Wall Street: "Perhaps Google," noted a report from Bank of America Merrill Lynch, "has incentive to cooperate more with the Street."

*References:* "What's the Average Salary of a Chief Financial Officer (CFO)?" *Investopedia* (2015), www.investopedia.com, on April 1, 2015; Stephen Gandel, "Google Is the New Wall Street. Or Is It? New CFO's Pay Tells the Story," *Fortune* (March 26, 2015), http://fortune.com, on March 31, 2015; Nathaniel Popper and Conor Dougherty, "Google Hires Finance Chief Ruth Porat from Morgan Stanley," *New York Times* (March 25, 2015), www.nytimes.com, on April 1, 2015; Jaikumar Vijayan, "Google Antitrust Worries, Growth Slowdown Seen as Temporary Setbacks," *eWeek* (March 31, 2015), www.eweek.com, on March 31, 2015; Jillian D'Onfro, "What Wall Street Wants from Google's New CFO," *Business Insider* (March 25, 2015), www.businessinsider.com, on March 31, 2015.

But events in recent years have raised serious questions about the use of stock options as incentives for executives. For example, several executives at Enron allegedly withheld critical financial information from the markets, cashed in their stock options (while Enron stock was trading at $80 a share), and then watched as the financial information was made public and the stock fell to less than $1 a share. Of course, these actions (if proven) are illegal, but they raise questions in the public's mind about the role of stock options and about the way organizations treat stock options from an accounting perspective. Most organizations have *not* treated stock options as liabilities, even though, when exercised, they are exactly that. There is concern that by not carrying stock options as liabilities, the managers are overstating the value of the company, which, of course, can help raise the stock price. Finally, when stock prices fall below the option price they become essentially worthless.

Aside from stock option plans, other kinds of executive compensation are also used by some companies. Among the more popular are such perquisites as memberships in private clubs, access to company recreational facilities, and similar considerations. Some organizations also make available to senior executives low- or no-interest loans. These are often given to new executives whom the company is hiring from other companies and serve as an incentive for the person to leave his or her current job to join a new organization. HP's Meg Whitman received $1.5 million in other compensation during 2014 for things such as perks, tax reimbursement, and payments for life insurance; she also received an outright award of $4.4 million in stock.[57]

**Criticisms of Executive Compensation** In recent years, executive compensation has come under fire for a variety of reasons. One major reason is that the levels of executive compensation attained by some managers seem simply too large for the average shareholder to understand. It is not uncommon, for instance, for a senior executive of a major corporation to earn total income from his or her job in a given year of well in excess of $1 million. Sometimes the income of chief executive officers can be substantially more than this. Thus, just as the typical person has difficulty comprehending the astronomical salaries paid to some movie stars and sports stars, so, too, would the average person be aghast at the astronomical salaries paid to some senior executives.

Compounding the problem created by perceptions of executive compensation is the fact that there often seems to be little or no relationship between the performance of the organization and the compensation paid to its senior executives.[58] Certainly, if an organization is performing at an especially high level and its stock price is increasing consistently, then most observers would agree that the senior executives responsible for this growth should be entitled to attractive rewards.[59] However, it is more difficult to understand a case in which executives are paid large salaries and other forms of rewards when their company is performing at only a marginal level, yet this is fairly common today. For example, General Electric CEO Jeffrey Immelt recently received stock options increasing his total compensation to $28.5 million from $9.8 million, an increase of 188 percent. However, during that same year shareholder returns fell behind those of similar companies (24.33 percent compared to 32.21 percent).[60]

Finally, we should note that the gap between the earnings of the CEO and the earnings of a typical employee is enormous. First of all, the size of the gap has been increasing in the United States. In 1980 the typical CEO earned 42 times the earnings of an ordinary worker; by 1990 this ratio had increased to 85 times the earnings of an ordinary worker; in 2014 the ratio was 354 times the earnings of a typical worker. In Japan, on the other hand, the CEO-to-worker pay ratio is 67 times; in Germany the ratio is 147 times.[61]

## New Approaches to Performance-Based Rewards

Some organizations have started to recognize that they can leverage the value of the incentives they offer to their employees and to groups in their organization by allowing those individuals and groups to have a say in how rewards are distributed. For example, at the extreme, a company could go so far as to grant salary increase budgets to work groups and then allow the members of those groups themselves to determine how the rewards are going to be allocated among the various members of the group. This strategy would appear to hold considerable promise if everyone understands the performance arrangements that exist in the work group and everyone is committed to being fair and equitable. Unfortunately, it can also create problems if people in a group feel that rewards are not being distributed fairly.[62]

Organizations are also getting increasingly innovative in their incentive programs. For example, some now offer stock options to all their employees, rather than just to top executives. In addition, some firms are looking into ways to purely individualize reward systems. For instance, a firm might offer one employee a paid three-month sabbatical every two years in exchange for a 20 percent reduction in salary. Another employee in the same firm might be offered a 10 percent salary increase in exchange for a 5 percent reduction in company contributions to the person's retirement account. Corning, General Electric, and Microsoft are among the firms closely studying this option.[63]

Regardless of the method used, however, it is also important that managers in an organization effectively communicate what rewards are being distributed and the basis for that distribution. In other words, if incentives are being distributed on the basis of perceived individual contributions to the organization, then members of the organization should be informed of that fact. This will presumably better enable them to understand the basis on which pay increases and other incentives and performance-based rewards have been distributed.

**Manager's Checklist**

☐ Managers need to know the essential elements of merit and incentive reward systems.

☐ You should also be aware of the various issues associated with executive compensation.

# Summary of Learning Outcomes and Key Points

1. Characterize the nature of motivation, including its importance and historical perspectives.

   - Motivation is the set of forces that cause people to behave in certain ways.
   - Motivation is an important consideration for managers because, along with ability and environmental factors, it determines individual performance.
   - Thinking about motivation has evolved from the traditional view through the human relations approach to the human resource view.

2. Identify and describe the major content perspectives on motivation.

   - Content perspectives on motivation are concerned with what factor or factors cause motivation.
   - Popular content theories include Maslow's needs hierarchy, the ERG theory, and Herzberg's two-factor theory.
   - Other important needs are the needs for achievement, affiliation, and power.

3. Identify and describe the major process perspectives on motivation.

   - Process perspectives on motivation deal with how motivation occurs.
   - Expectancy theory suggests that people are motivated to perform if they believe that their effort will result in high performance, that this performance will lead to rewards, and that the positive aspects of the outcomes outweigh the negative aspects.
   - Equity theory is based on the premise that people are motivated to achieve and maintain social equity.
   - Attribution theory is a new process theory.

4. Describe reinforcement perspectives on motivation.

   - The reinforcement perspective focuses on how motivation is maintained.
   - Its basic assumption is that behavior that results in rewarding consequences is likely to be repeated, whereas behavior resulting in negative consequences is less likely to be repeated.

- Reinforcement contingencies can be arranged in the form of positive reinforcement, avoidance, punishment, and extinction, and they can be provided on fixed-interval, variable-interval, fixed-ratio, or variable-ratio schedules.

5. Identify and describe popular motivational strategies.

- Managers use a variety of motivational strategies derived from the various theories of motivation.
- Common strategies include empowerment and participation and alternative forms of work arrangements, such as variable work schedules, flexible work schedules, and telecommuting.

6. Describe the role of organizational reward systems in motivation.

- Reward systems also play a key role in motivating employee performance.
- Popular methods include merit reward systems, incentive reward systems, and team and group incentive reward systems.
- Executive compensation is also intended to serve as motivation for senior managers but has currently come under close scrutiny and criticism.

# Discussion Questions

## Questions for Review

1. Each historical perspective on motivation built on the earlier perspectives and differed from them in some ways. Describe the similarities and differences between the traditional approach and the human relations approach. Then describe the similarities and differences between the human relations approach and the human resource approach.

## Questions for Analysis

5. Choose one theory from the content perspectives and one from the process perspectives. Describe actions that a manager might take to increase worker motivation under each of the theories. What differences do you see between the theories in terms of their implications for managers?

6. Can factors from both the content and the process perspectives be acting on a worker at the same time? Explain

## Questions for Application

8. Think about the worst job you have held. What approach to motivation was used in that organization? Now think about the best job you have held. What approach to motivation was used there? Can you base any conclusions on this limited information? If so, what are they?

9. Interview both a manager and a worker (or administrator and faculty member) from a local organization. What views

2. Compare and contrast content, process, and reinforcement perspectives on motivation.

3. Explain how goal-setting theory works. How is goal setting different from merely asking a worker to "do your best"?

4. Describe some new forms of working arrangements. How do these alternative arrangements increase motivation?

why or why not. Whether you answered yes or no to the previous question, explain the implications for managers.

7. How do rewards increase motivation? What would happen if an organization gave too few rewards? What would happen if it gave too many?

of or approaches to motivation seem to be in use in that organization? Do the manager's views differ from the worker's? If so, how do you explain the differing perceptions?

10. Consider a class you have taken. Using just that one class, offer examples of times when the professor used positive reinforcement, avoidance, punishment, and extinction to manage students' behavior.

# Building Effective Interpersonal Skills

## Exercise Overview

Interpersonal skills refer to your ability to communicate with, understand, and motivate both individuals and groups. This exercise gives you a chance to see whether the factors that

motivate you come primarily from you and your work itself or from factors that are external to you and the nature of your work.

## Exercise Task

Following is a list of 12 factors that contribute to job satisfaction and motivation. To find out how important each factor is to you, select a number from 1 to 5 according to the following scale:

| 5 | 4 | 3 | 2 | 1 |
|---|---|---|---|---|
| Very Important | | Somewhat Important | | Not Important |

1. _____ An interesting job that I enjoy doing
2. _____ A boss who treats everyone the same regardless of the circumstances
3. _____ Getting praise and other recognition and appreciation for my work
4. _____ A job that's routine without much change from day to day
5. _____ Opportunity for advancement
6. _____ A nice title regardless of pay
7. _____ Job responsibility that gives me the freedom to do things my way
8. _____ Good working conditions (e.g., safe environment, convenient cafeteria, etc.)
9. _____ Opportunity to learn new things
10. _____ Emphasis on following rules, regulations, procedures, and policies
11. _____ A job that I can do well and succeed at
12. _____ Job security; a job with one company

### Scoring

Next, the 12 factors are divided into two lists. For each factor, record the number (from 1 to 5) that you put in the blank before it. Then add up each column (each column score should be from 6 to 30 points):

| Motivating factor | Maintenance factor |
|---|---|
| 1. ___ | 2. ___ |
| 3. ___ | 4. ___ |
| 5. ___ | 6. ___ |
| 7. ___ | 8. ___ |
| 9. ___ | 10. ___ |
| 11. ___ | 12. ___ |
| Totals ___ | ___ |

Which factors tend to be more important to you — internal (motivating) or external (maintenance)? *The closer your column score to a total of 30, the more important that factor is to you.*

Adapted from Robert N. Lussier and Christopher F. Achua, *Leadership: Theory, Application, and Skill Development*, 4th ed. (Mason, OH: South-Western Cengage Learning, 2010), pp. 82–84.

# Building Effective Decision-Making Skills

## Exercise Overview

Decision-making skills refer to the ability to recognize and define problems and opportunities correctly and then to select an appropriate course of action for solving problems or capitalizing on opportunities. This exercise allows you to build your decision-making skills while applying goal-setting theory to the task of planning your career.

## Exercise Background

Lee Iacocca started his career at Ford in 1946 in an entry-level engineering job. By 1960 he was a vice president and in charge of the group that designed the Mustang, and 10 years later he was a president of the firm. After being fired from Ford in 1978, he became president at Chrysler and eventually rose to the CEO spot, a job he held until he retired in 1992. What's really remarkable about Iacocca's career arc — at least the upward trajectory — is the fact that he apparently had it all planned out, even before he finished college.

The story goes that, while he was still an undergraduate, Iacocca wrote out a list of all the positions that he'd like to hold during his career. Number one was "engineer at an auto maker," followed by all the career steps that he planned to take until he was a CEO. He also included a timetable for his climb up the corporate ladder. Then he put his list on a three-by-five-inch card that he folded and stowed in his wallet, and we're told that every time he took out that card and looked at it, he gained fresh confidence and drive. He apparently reached the top several years ahead of schedule, but otherwise he followed his career path and timetable faithfully. As you can see, Iacocca used goal-setting theory to motivate himself, and there's no reason why you can't do the same.

## Exercise Task

1. Consider the position that you'd like to hold at the peak of your career. It may be CEO, owner of a chain of clothing stores, partner in a law or accounting firm, or president of a university. Then again, it may be something less lofty. Whatever it is, write it down.

2. Now describe a career path that will lead you toward that goal. It may help to work "backwards"—that is, starting with your final position and working backwards in time to some entry-level job. If you aren't sure about the career path that will lead to your ultimate goal, do some research. Talk to someone in your selected career field, ask an instructor who teaches in it, or go online. The website of the American Institute of Certified Public Accountants, for example, has a section on "Career Resources," which includes information about career paths and position descriptions for accounting.

3. Write down each step in your path on a card or a sheet of paper.

4. If, like Lee Iacocca, you were to carry this piece of paper with you and refer to it often as you pursued your career goals, do you think it would help you achieve them? Why or why not?

# Skill-Building Personal Assessment

## Assessing Your Needs

**Introduction:** Needs are one factor that influences motivation. The following assessment surveys your judgments about some of your personal needs that might be partially shaping your motivation.

**Instructions:** Judge how descriptively accurate each of the following statements is about you. You may find making a decision difficult in some cases, but you should force yourself to make a choice. Record your answers next to each statement according to the following scale:

## Rating Scale

5 Very descriptive of me
4 Fairly descriptive of me
3 Somewhat descriptive of me
2 Not very descriptive of me
1 Not descriptive of me at all

1. _____ I aspire to accomplish difficult tasks and maintain high standards and am willing to work toward distant goals.
2. _____ I enjoy being with friends and people in general and accept people readily.
3. _____ I am easily annoyed and am sometimes willing to hurt people to get my way.
4. _____ I try to break away from restraints or restrictions of any kind.
5. _____ I want to be the center of attention and enjoy having an audience.

6. _____ I speak freely and tend to act on the spur of the moment.
7. _____ I assist others whenever possible, giving sympathy and comfort to those in need.
8. _____ I believe in the saying that "there is a place for everything and everything should be in its place." I dislike clutter.
9. _____ I express my opinions forcefully, enjoy the role of leader, and try to control my environment as much as I can.
10. _____ I want to understand many areas of knowledge and value synthesizing ideas and generalization.

After responding to the questions, reflect on the kinds of jobs and careers most and least likely to help you fulfill these needs.

# Management At Work

## Engaged to Be Motivated

"I don't mind people throwing darts at higher ed, but it doesn't have to take the blame for everything."

—PHILIP D. GARDNER, DIRECTOR, MICHIGAN STATE UNIVERSITYCOLLEGIATE EMPLOYMENT RESEARCH INSTITUTE

*Fact 1*: If you graduate from college, you're more likely to get a full-time job than if you hadn't. *Fact 2*: If you graduate from college, you'll probably enjoy higher lifetime earnings than if you hadn't. *Fact 3*: If you graduate from college, you're *less* likely to be engaged in your work than if you hadn't.

That's right—*less* likely. To be fair, Fact 3 doesn't reflect much of a difference: According to a Gallup survey released in 2013, only 28.3 percent of graduates are "involved in and enthusiastic about" their work, compared to 32.7 percent of people who didn't go beyond high school. Even so, Brandon Busteed of Gallup Education finds the survey results "really stunning. Given that what we all expect out of college is something better," he explains, "you'd think that college graduates are way more engaged in careers than everybody else."

Does the apparent problem lie with colleges or with workplaces? Not surprisingly, the answer is both. Let's start with colleges. First of all, it doesn't appear to make any difference what kind of college a person went to—large or small, public or private, prestigious or mid-tier public: the percentages not only of those engaged at work but of those "thriving" in all areas of personal "well-being" are roughly the same (with graduates of for-profit schools faring not quite as well).

It would appear, then, that colleges of all types are failing to provide the kinds of experiences that result in high levels of workplace engagement. Have you, for example, encountered a professor who cared about you personally, got you excited about learning, or encouraged you to pursue your dreams? If so, you have been "emotionally supported," and your odds of being engaged at work (and of thriving in your well-being) have probably doubled. Have you had a job or internship that let you apply what you've been learning in college, worked on any projects that took a semester or more to complete, or been involved in extracurricular activities? If you've had the advantage of these forms of "experiential and deep learning," you're also twice as likely to be engaged and thriving. Unfortunately, only 14 percent of graduates could answer yes to the first set of criteria and only 6 percent to the second set. As for all six experiences, a mere 3 percent said yes. On individual measures, although 63 percent said that a teacher had fired them up about a subject, only 32 percent had ever worked on a long-term project, and only 22 percent had found mentors who encouraged them.

"It's literally about higher education in general," suggests Busteed. "There's something about the process and the experience that's preventing graduates from getting to a place where they're doing what they're best at." Busteed suspects that, without strong mentorship, college students fail to set clear career paths, and as a result, too many of them fall into one of two traps:

1. getting stuck in jobs for which they're overqualified or
2. resorting to such "fall-back" career paths as law school and investment banking.

"I think we're kind of caught up in preconceived notions of what success should look like," says Busteed, "and it's landing a lot of college graduates in the wrong place." Some educators agree. "The particular value of [the Gallup] survey," says Harold V. Hartley III, senior vice president of the Council of Independent Colleges, "is that it looks at outcomes that are different from the outcomes that we typically look

at—like did you get a job, what's your salary, and those kinds of things."

Not surprisingly, however, many educators are unconvinced that colleges should bear the brunt of the survey's findings. "There's kind of a half-empty, half-full story here," says Alexander McCormick, director of the National Survey of Student Engagement. He points out, for instance, that the survey classifies 55 percent of the respondents as "not engaged" and argues that although these people are not emotionally connected to their workplaces, neither are they dissatisfied with them. Philip D. Gardner, director of Michigan State University's Collegiate Employment Research Institute, adds that the Gallup survey fails to account for differences in individual goals and goal-oriented behavior. Highly educated people, he observes, don't settle into jobs as quickly as most people, and younger workers are less likely to consider work critical to their identities or well-being.

Mark Schneider, vice president of the American Institutes for Research, a nonprofit organization that conducts social-science and behavioral research, contends that the Gallup survey reveals interesting *correlations* (between, for example, college and workplace experiences) but falls short in providing any *causative* explanations. Take, for example, a graduate who reports the following correlation: She had an internship at college and is engaged in her work. What if this graduate was personally motivated to find the internship and is engaged in her work because she brings the same level of personal motivation to her job? The Gallup survey suggests that there is a cause-and-effect relationship between the college experience (the internship) and the workplace experience (engagement). The conclusion, however, does not necessarily follow because personal motivation may be the most significant factor in both experiences.

A critical question, it would seem, remains unaddressed: Which motivational behavior came first—acting on *personal motivation* (such as seeking the experience of the internship) or acting on *learned motivation* (such as applying the lessons learned through the internship to the post-graduation workplace)? Even Busteed admits that the survey's results may suffer from a "chicken-and-egg problem."

Which brings us to the implications of the survey results for business. As we've already seen, the survey is ultimately as much concerned with productivity and motivation in the workplace as with workplace preparation in college. According to Busteed, the survey's findings provide "a formula for something that alters life and career trajectory. ... It's all actionable, by way of who we hire and how we incentivize and reward." The report thus suggests that colleges should do a better job of preparing students to get jobs in workplaces in which they'll be *engaged*—that is, in which they'll be working at something that they're good at and like for organizations that care about their work.

Philip Gardner, for one, thinks that the problem reflects workplace experiences as much as higher-education experiences. "I don't mind people throwing darts at higher ed, but it doesn't have to take the blame for everything," he says, and many researchers and consultants feel that employers should focus more clearly on the *personal motivation* that each individual brings to the workplace. According to The Fortune Group, for instance, which provides personal-development training for businesses, "motivation is internal and personal. Within each person, there has to be that drive or will to succeed, and if it's not there, *no one* can synthetically put it there."

If a company wants to increase "motivation and engagement in the workplace," says the consultancy, it must "create a climate or an environment in which people's natural abilities and internal motivations are allowed to come to the fore." In fact, The Fortune Group operates on the assumption that "employees don't perform because someone or something interferes with their desire or ability to perform." *Task interference*, for example, "could be something the employee *doesn't* have, such as proper resources, tools or training." Another form of interference, *consequence imbalance*, occurs when employees are "doing the right things but aren't getting recognition for it." Like task interference, it should be classified as "mismanagement" because it "creates an imbalance that interferes with people's desire and/or ability to perform."

## Case Questions

1. Consider each of the following *perspectives on motivation*: *needs hierarchy* (including the *ERG theory*), *two-factor theory*, *expectancy theory*, *equity theory*, and *goal-setting theory*. How does each of these perspectives depend upon *learned motivation*? On *personal motivation*?

2. What about you? Which form of motivation—*learned motivation* or *personal motivation*—has played a greater role in your pursuit of your goals, whether in school, at work, or in both areas? Given this assessment of your own experience with motivation, which of the motivational perspectives listed in question 1 is most likely to help you in your work life? Whatever your answers to these questions, be sure to give examples from your own experience.

3. The theory that too few students get the help they need in setting clear career paths suggests that colleges should provide more career counseling. However, according to the National Survey of Student Engagement, only 43 percent of college seniors talked *very often* or *often* about career plans with a faculty member or adviser; 39 percent did *sometimes*, and 17 percent *never* did.*

How about you? Have you sought career advice or counseling from resources available at your school? Do you plan to? Have you sought advice elsewhere? If so, where elsewhere and why elsewhere?

4. The Gallup survey measured levels of engagement by asking respondents whether they *agreed* or *disagreed* with several statements about post-graduation work experiences. Here are six of those statements:

   - I have opportunities to learn and grow.
   - My opinions seem to count.
   - I have the opportunity to do what I do best every day.
   - I have the tools and resources I need to do my job.
   - My supervisor encourages my development.
   - I know what is expected of me.†

   List these six statements *in their order of importance to you as probable factors in your satisfaction with a job*. Be prepared to discuss your priorities.

   [*Note*: One of these statements proved to be the strongest predictor of workplace engagement among all of the statements in the survey. Your instructor can tell you which one it is after you've drawn up and discussed your list.]

*National Survey of Student Engagement, *Promoting Student Learning and Institutional Improvement: Lessons from NSSE at 13: Annual Results 2012* (2012), http://nsse.iub.edu, on March 17, 2015.

†Adapted from Tim Hodges, *Gallup-Purdue Index of Great Jobs and Great Lives* (Gallup Inc., 2014), www.mhec.org, on March 17, 2015.

## Case References

Julie Ray and Stephanie Kafka, "Life in College Matters for Life after College," Gallup Inc. (May 6, 2014), www.gallup.com, on March 9, 2015; Allie Grasgreen, "College Grads Less Engaged in Work Than Those with Less Education, Survey Finds," *Inside Higher Ed* (July 18, 2013), www.inside-highered.com, on March 10, 2015; Ry Rivard, "Gallup Surveys Graduates to Gauge Whether and Why College Is Good for Well-Being," *Inside Higher Ed* (May 6, 2014), www.insidehighered.com, on March 10, 2015; Scott Carlson, "A Caring Professor May Be Key in How a Graduate Thrives," *Chronicle of Higher Education* (May 6, 2014), http://chronicle.com, on March 10, 2015; Grasgreen, "Gallup-Purdue Study Will Measure Graduates' Quality of Life Outcomes," *Inside Higher Ed* (December 17, 2013), www.insidehighered.com, on March 14, 2015; The Fortune Group, "How to Motivate Employees in the Workplace" (2015), www.fortunegroup.com, on March 13, 2015.

## YOU MAKE THE CALL    Let the Games Begin

1. Consider each of the following *perspectives on motivation*: *needs hierarchy* (including the *ERG theory*), *two-factor theory*, and *reinforcement theory*. How would each of these perspectives contribute to an understanding of why *gamification* appears to work as a motivational strategy?

   Note that all but one of these perspectives falls into the *content* category. What about *process perspectives*—*expectancy theory*, *equity theory*, and *goal-setting theory*? Answering the same question with regard to process perspectives would probably prove a little more difficult. Why? In other words, explain what this exercise might tell us about some basic differences between content and process perspectives.

2. Consider gamification in terms of *incentive reward systems*. In what sense, for instance, can a gamification system be regarded as an incentive reward system, whether as an *incentive pay plan* or as some other form of incentive? What, if any, advantages does it have over the various types of incentive reward systems mentioned in the text? What disadvantages does it share?

3. The following table lists two categories of motivation that could be offered to people participating in gaming activities:*

| **Extrinsic Motivation** | **Intrinsic Motivation** |
| --- | --- |
| Earning money | Receiving recognition |
| Earning points/badges/ trophies | Attaining a sense of personal achievement |
| Earning prizes | Earning responsibility |
| Overcoming penalties | Earning power |
| Succeeding in quests | Having fun |
| Advancing on progress bars | Gaining mastery |

- *Extrinsic motivation* occurs when we're motivated to perform a behavior or engage in an activity in order to earn a reward or avoid a punishment.
- *Intrinsic motivation* occurs when we're motivated to perform a behavior or engage in an activity because it's personally rewarding.

   How about you? If your workplace launched a gamification program with rewards similar to those offered by Bluewolf, would you say that you're more likely to be motivated by extrinsic or intrinsic rewards? What extrinsic rewards are you currently working for? What intrinsic rewards?

4. In his list of tips for companies considering gamification, one professional in the motivational field includes the following: "Don't use money as a motivator. Introducing money automatically makes the activity about money—other motivations, such as taking pride in a job well done or collaborating as part of a team, are set aside."[†]

   Certain versions of motivational theory based on *needs* support this contention. Some researchers, for example, say that extrinsic rewards thwart intrinsic motivation because we perceive them as external means of controlling our behavior. Intrinsic rewards, they argue, satisfy our psychological needs for competence and recognition because they provide us—and others—with information about our levels of performance.[‡]

   What do you think? Does your personal experience suggest that this line of thinking is accurate? Do you think of extrinsic rewards as a means of controlling your behavior? How important is feedback about your level of performance? How about recognition for your level of performance? Under what circumstances do you tend to find intrinsic motivation satisfying? Under what circumstances is intrinsic motivation not enough to satisfy you?

---

*Adapted from Stephen Dale, "Gamification: Making Work Fun, or Making Fun of Work?" *Collabor8now* (September 25, 2014), http://collabor8now.com, on March 24, 2015.

†Dale, "Gamification: Making Work Fun, or Making Fun of Work?"

‡Sebastian Deterding, "Gamification Absolved?" Gamification Research Network (August 5, 2014), http://gamification-research.org, on March 23, 2015.

# Endnotes

1  Karen J. Bannan, "Bluewolf Uses Employee Gamification to Increase Social Sharing," *Advertising Age* (June 11, 2012), http://adage.com, on March 24, 2015; Alex Palmer, "Bluewolf Rewards Employees for Going Social," *Incentive Mag* (November 1, 2012), www.incentivemag.com, on March 25, 2015; Srinivas Krishnaswamy, "Enterprise Gamification Case Study—Bluewolf's #GoingSocial Portal," *Learning Pilgrims* (October 14, 2013), https://learningpilgrims.wordpress.com, on March 24, 2015; Stephen Dale, "Gamification: Making Work Fun, or Making Fun of Work?" *Collabor8now* (September 25, 2014), http://collabor8now.com, on March 24, 2015; Charles E. Bess, "Gamification: Driving Behavior Change in the Connected World," *Cutter IT Journal*, 2013, Vol. 6, No 2, www.cutter.com, on March 24, 2015; Ross Warnlof, "Bluewolf Goes Social: Four Keys to Gamification," *Gamification Blog* (October 6, 2014), www.bunchball.com, on March 25, 2015; "Bluewolf #GoingSocial" (Blue Wolf Group LLC, 2015), www.bluewolf.com, on March 29, 2015.

2  Richard M. Steers, Gregory A. Bigley, and Lyman W. Porter, *Motivation and Leadership at Work*, 6th ed. (New York: McGraw-Hill, 1996). See also Maureen L. Ambrose and Carol T. Kulik, "Old Friends, New Faces: Motivation Research in the 1990s," *Journal of Management*, 1999, Vol. 25, No. 3, pp. 231–292; and Edwin Locke and Gary Lartham, "What Should We Do about Motivation Theory? Six Recommendations for the Twenty-First Century," *Academy of Management Review*, 2004, Vol. 29, No. 3, pp. 388–403.

3  See Nigel Nicholson, "How to Motivate Your Problem People," *Harvard Business Review*, January 2003, pp. 57–67. See also Hugo Kehr, "Integrating Implicit Motives, Explicit Motives, and Perceived Abilities: The Compensatory Model of Work Motivation and Volition," *Academy of Management Review*, 2004, Vol. 29, No. 3, pp. 479–499; and James M. Diefendorff and Megan M. Chandler, "Motivating Employees," in Sheldon Zedeck (ed.), *Handbook of Industrial and Organizational Psychology*, Vol. 3: *Maintaining, Expanding, and Contracting the Organization* (Washington, DC: American Psychological Association, 2010), pp. 65–135.

4  See Jeffrey Pfeffer, *The Human Equation* (Cambridge, MA: Harvard Business School Press, 1998); see also Nitin Nohria, Boris Groysberg, and Linda-Eling Lee, "Employee Motivation—A Powerful New Model," *Harvard Business Review*, July–August 2008, pp. 78–89.

5  See Craig Pinder, *Work Motivation in Organizational Behavior* (Upper Saddle River, NJ: Prentice-Hall, 1998).

6  Frederick W. Taylor, *Principles of Scientific Management* (New York: Harper & Brothers, 1911).

7  Elton Mayo, *The Social Problems of an Industrial Civilization* (Cambridge, MA: Harvard University Press, 1945); Fritz J. Rothlisberger and W. J. Dickson, *Management and the Worker* (Cambridge, MA: Harvard University Press, 1939).

8  For a recent discussion of these questions, see Eryn Brown, "So Rich So Young—But Are They Really Happy?" *Fortune*, September 18, 2000, pp. 99–110.

9  Abraham H. Maslow, "A Theory of Human Motivation," *Psychological Review*, 1943, Vol. 50, pp. 370–396; Abraham H. Maslow, *Motivation and Personality* (New York: Harper & Row, 1954). Maslow's most recent work is Abraham H. Maslow and Richard Lowry, *Toward a Psychology of Being* (New York: Wiley, 1999).

10  http://www.nytimes.com/2013/12/15/opinion/sunday/a-formula-for-happiness.html, accessed on June 13, 2015.

11  *USA Today*, August 15, 2004, p. 2B.

12  For a review, see Pinder, *Work Motivation in Organizational Behavior*.

13  Clayton P. Alderfer, *Existence, Relatedness, and Growth* (New York: Free Press, 1972).

14  Frederick Herzberg, Bernard Mausner, and Barbara Snyderman, *The Motivation to Work* (New York: Wiley, 1959); Frederick Herzberg, "One More Time: How Do You Motivate Employees?" *Harvard Business Review*, January–February 1987, pp. 109–120 (reprinted in *Harvard Business Review*, January 2003, pp. 87–98).

15  Robert J. House and Lawrence A. Wigdor, "Herzberg's Dual-Factor Theory of Job Satisfaction and Motivation: A Review of the Evidence and a Criticism," *Personnel Psychology*, Winter 1967, pp. 369–389; Victor H. Vroom, *Work and Motivation* (New York: Wiley, 1964). See also Pinder, *Work Motivation in Organizational Behavior*.

16  David C. McClelland, *The Achieving Society* (Princeton, NJ: Van Nostrand, 1961); David C. McClelland, *Power: The Inner Experience* (New York: Irvington, 1975).

17  "Best Friends Good for Business," *USA Today*, December 1, 2004, pp. 1B, 2B.

18  David McClelland and David H. Burnham, "Power Is the Great Motivator," *Harvard Business Review*, March–April 1976, pp. 100–110 (reprinted in *Harvard Business Review*, January 2003, pp. 117–127).

19  "HP Chief Executive Hurd Resigns after Sexual Harrassment Probe," *Bloomberg Businessweek*, August 7, 2010.

20  Victor H. Vroom, *Work and Motivation* (New York: Wiley, 1964).

21  "Starbucks' Secret Weapon," *Fortune*, September 29, 1997, p. 268.

22  *Harvard Business Review*, May 2009, p. 101.

23  Lyman W. Porter and Edward E. Lawler III, *Managerial Attitudes and Performance* (Homewood, IL: Dorsey, 1968).

24  J. Stacy Adams, "Towards an Understanding of Inequity," *Journal of Abnormal and Social Psychology*, November 1963, pp. 422–436.

25  "The Best vs. the Rest," *Wall Street Journal*, January 30, 2006, pp. B1, B3.

26  Mark C. Bolino and William H. Turnley, "Old Faces, New Places: Equity Theory in Cross-Cultural Contexts," *Journal of Organizational Behavior*, 2008, Vol. 29, pp. 29–50.

27  *BusinessWeek*, June 8, 2009, p. 48.

28  See Edwin A. Locke, "Toward a Theory of Task Performance and Incentives," *Organizational Behavior and Human Performance*, 1968, Vol. 3, pp. 157–189.

29  Gary P. Latham and J. J. Baldes, "The Practical Significance of Locke's Theory of Goal Setting," *Journal of Applied Psychology*, 1975, Vol. 60, pp. 187–191.

30  http://www.entrepreneur.com/article/225356, accessed on June 12, 2015.

31  For a recent extension of goal-setting theory, see Yitzhak Fried and Linda Haynes Slowik, "Enriching Goal-Setting Theory with Time: An Integrated Approach," *Academy of Management Review*, 2004, Vol. 29, No. 3, pp. 404–422.

32  B. F. Skinner, *Beyond Freedom and Dignity* (New York: Knopf, 1971). See also Raymond A. Noe, Michael J. Tews, and Alison McConnell Dachner, "Learner Engagement: A New Perspective for Enhancing Our Understanding of Learner Motivation and Workplace Learning," in James P. Walsh and Arthur P. Brief (eds.), *The Academy of Management Annals 2010* (Philadelphia: Taylor and Francis, 2010), pp. 279–315.

33  Fred Luthans and Robert Kreitner, *Organizational Behavior Modification and Beyond: An Operant and Social Learning Approach* (Glenview, IL: Scott, Foresman, 1985).

34  Ibid.; W. Clay Hamner and Ellen P. Hamner, "Behavior Modification on the Bottom Line," *Organizational Dynamics*, Spring 1976, pp. 2–21.

35  "At Emery Air Freight: Positive Reinforcement Boosts Performance," *Organizational Dynamics*, Winter 1973, pp. 41–50; for a recent update, see Alexander D. Stajkovic and Fred Luthans, "A Meta-Analysis of the Effects of Organizational Behavior Modification on Task Performance, 1975–95," *Academy of Management Journal*, 1997, Vol. 40, No. 5, pp. 1122–1149.

36  David J. Glew, Anne M. O'Leary-Kelly, Ricky W. Griffin, and David D. Van Fleet, "Participation in Organizations: A Preview of the Issues and Proposed Framework for Future Analysis," *Journal of Management*, 1995, Vol. 21, No. 3, pp. 395–421.

37  Robert E. Quinn and Gretchen M. Spreitzer, "The Road to Empowerment: Seven Questions Every Leader Should Consider," *Organizational Dynamics*, Autumn 1997, pp. 37–47.

38  "On Factory Floors, Top Workers Hide Secrets to Success," *Wall Street Journal*, July 1, 2002, pp. A1, A10.

39  Russ Forrester, "Empowerment: Rejuvenating a Potent Idea," *Academy of Management Executive*, 2000, Vol. 14, No. 3, pp. 67–77.

40  Baxter W. Graham, "The Business Argument for Flexibility," *HR Magazine*, May 1996, pp. 104–110.

41  http://www.entrepreneur.com/article/232702, accessed on June 12, 2015.

42  A. R. Cohen and H. Gadon, *Alternative Work Schedules: Integrating Individual and Organizational Needs* (Reading, MA: Addison Wesley, 1978). See also Ellen Ernst Kossek and Jesse S. Michel, "Flexible Work Schedules," in Sheldon Zedeck (ed.), *Handbook of Industrial and Organizational Psychology*, Vol. 1: *Building and Developing the Organization* (Washington, DC: American Psychological Association, 2010), pp. 535–572.

43  *BusinessWeek*, December 12, 2005, p. 79.

44  http://www.globalworkplaceanalytics.com/telecommuting-statistics, accessed on June 15, 2015.

45  "How Telecommuting Lets Workers Mobilize for Sustainability," *GreenBiz.com*, February 17, 2011; "Study: Telecommuting Can Save American Households $1.7 Billion per Year," *SmartPlanet.com*, March 15, 2011.

46  Barry Gerhart, Sara L. Rynes, and Ingrid Smithey Fulmer, "Pay and Performance: Individuals, Groups, and Executives," in James P. Walsh and Arthur P. Brief (eds.), *The Academy of Management Annals 2009* (Philadelphia: Taylor and Francis, 2009), pp. 251–315. See also Joseph J. Martocchio, "Strategic Reward and Compensation Plans," in Sheldon Zedeck (ed.), *Handbook of Industrial and Organizational Psychology*, Vol. 1: *Building and Developing the Organization* (Washington, DC: American Psychological Association, 2010), pp. 343–372.

47 Daniel Wren, *The Evolution of Management Theory*, 4th ed. (New York: Wiley, 1994).

48 Eric Krell, "All for Incentives, Incentives for All," *HR Magazine*, January 2011, pp. 34–38.

49 C. Wiley, "Incentive Plan Pushes Production," *Personnel Journal*, August 1993, p. 91.

50 "When Money Isn't Enough," *Forbes*, November 18, 1996, pp. 154–159.

51 Jacquelyn DeMatteo, Lillian Eby, and Eric Sundstrom, "Team-Based Rewards: Current Empirical Evidence and Directions for Future Research," in L. L. Cummings and Barry Staw (eds.), *Research in Organizational Behavior*, Vol. 20 (Greenwich, CT: JAI, 1998), pp. 141–183.

52 Theresa M. Welbourne and Luis R. Gomez-Mejia, "Gainsharing: A Critical Review and a Future Research Agenda," *Journal of Management*, 1995, Vol. 21, No. 3, pp. 559–609.

53 National Center for Employee Ownership, "A Statistical Profile of Employee Ownership," March 2010.

54 http://www.businessinsider.com/hp-pays-whitman-132-of-her-bonus-2014-2 accessed on June 15, 2015.

55 Ibid.

56 Ibid.

57 Ibid.

58 Harry Barkema and Luis Gomez-Mejia, "Managerial Compensation and Firm Performance: A General Research Framework," *Academy of Management Journal*, 1998, Vol. 41, No. 2, pp. 135–145.

59 Rajiv D. Banker, Seok-Young Lee, Gordon Potter, and Dhinu Srinivasan, "Contextual Analysis of Performance Impacts of Outcome-Based Incentive Compensation," *Academy of Management Journal*, 1996, Vol. 39, No. 4, pp. 920–948.

60 "GE Defends CEO's Pay Package," *The Ledger*, April 11, 2011.

61 "Average Japanese CEO Earns One-Sixth as Much as American CEOs," *thinkprogress.org*, July 8, 2010.

62 Steve Kerr, "The Best-Laid Incentive Plans," *Harvard Business Review*, January 2003, pp. 27–40.

63 "Now It's Getting Personal," *BusinessWeek*, December 15, 2002, pp. 90–92.

©Markus Pfaff/Shutterstock.com

# MANAGING LEADERSHIP AND INFLUENCE PROCESSES

## Learning Outcomes

**After studying this chapter, you should be able to:**

1. Describe the nature of leadership and relate leadership to management.

2. Discuss and evaluate the two generic approaches to leadership.

3. Identify and describe the major situational approaches to leadership.

4. Identify and describe three related approaches to leadership.

5. Describe three emerging approaches to leadership.

6. Discuss political behavior in organizations and how it can be managed.

## MANAGEMENT IN ACTION   Leaders of Oil Repute

"Reputationally, and in every other way, we will be judged by the quality, intensity, speed, and efficacy of our response."

—FORMER BP CHIEF EXECUTIVE TONY HAYWARD

It may come as no surprise that, generally speaking, most oil companies don't have very good reputations. Take BP, the world's sixth-largest oil and gas company. In April 2010, an explosion at its Deepwater Horizon offshore rig poured 300 million gallons of oil into the Gulf of Mexico, polluting 68,000 square miles of open water and devastating economies along 1,100 miles of coastline from Louisiana to Florida. Two months later, BP chief executive Tony Hayward pledged that "we will not rest until we make this right. … Reputationally, and in every other way," he acknowledged, "we will be judged by the quality, intensity, speed, and efficacy of our response."[1]

He was right about the second part of that statement. Within a year of the spill, BP ranked number 59 in Reputation Quotient® on a Harris Poll list of "The 60 Most Visible Companies among the General Public." As of this writing (five years later), BP is still stuck in 59th place.

As a matter of fact, BP was "reputationally" handicapped even before the Gulf disaster. In 2005, an explosion at a Texas refinery killed 15 workers and cost the company $87 million in fines for failing to address safety violations (and a total of $2 billion in compensation damages and lost profits). A year later, when a pipeline leak in Alaska shut down one of the nation's largest oilfields, BP was assessed $20 million in fines. A lawyer for the U.S. Environmental Protection Agency (EPA) called BP "a recurring environmental criminal."

It is ironic that, in 2000, Hayward's predecessor, John Browne, had launched a massive rebranding campaign called "Beyond Petroleum." BP didn't say exactly what "Beyond Petroleum" meant, but when coupled with the company's new logo—a bright green, yellow, and white sunburst—it was undoubtedly meant to suggest that BP was an oil company with a high regard for the planet and a commitment to a future of alternative energy sources. "Our reputation, and therefore our

In 2010 a major oil spill in the Gulf of Mexico resulted in devastating environmental damage and impacted the livelihoods of people all along the Gulf coast. Leaders at BP, the world's six-largest oil company and owner of the oil rig responsible for the leak, did a poor job of making decisions and addressing the key issues following the Deepwater Horizon disaster.

AP Images/Gerald Herbert

future as a business," declared Browne, "depends on each of us, everywhere, every day, taking personal responsibility for the conduct of BP's business." Critics, however, were skeptical. Some characterized the initiative as "greenwashing," and the global environmental organization Greenpeace gave Browne an award for "Best Impression of an Environmentalist." U.S. Senator Diane Feinstein admits that, until the incidents in Texas and Alaska, she had been fooled: "I thought finally there was an oil company that has a sense of conscience. I no longer think that."

How had BP managed to make things even worse, "reputationally" speaking, in the wake of Deepwater Horizon? Mostly by putting its energy into legal maneuvering instead of goodwill building. First, BP challenged the ruling of federal judge Carl Barbier that it had made "profit-driven decisions" amounting to "gross negligence" before the oil spill. It also disputed the government's estimate of the amount of oil spilled into the Gulf and then appealed Barbier's compromise figure. In December 2014, after a two-year legal battle, the U.S. Supreme Court upheld two lower-court rulings that BP had to abide by an agreement to settle cleanup and damage claims determined by a court-appointed administrator. In February 2015, when Barbier finally ruled that BP should pay the maximum fine of $4,300 per barrel (for a total of $9.57 billion), BP challenged the EPA's authority to set the fine and announced that "we are considering all of our legal options."

Citing a poll in which 70 percent of Americans agreed that BP should be fined the maximum amount allowed by law, one Louisiana environmentalist declared that "Americans aren't fooled by ... five years of shenanigans to drag out this court case." It was time, added an EPA official, for BP to "step out of the shadow of lawyers, quit spinning and arguing, and just accept full responsibility."

At this point, it may or may not come as a surprise that, according to a poll conducted by the global consulting firm McKinsey & Co., "senior executives in the energy industry" surpass top managers in most other industries when it comes to "taking an active approach to managing sustainability." Their motivations may reflect bottom-line concerns—McKinsey cites "the potential for regulation and increasing natural-resource constraints"—but their approach to sustainability (and to social responsibility in general) reflects a higher level of commitment.

According to McKinsey, for example, companies are "most engaged with sustainability if ... sustainability is

a top-three priority in their CEOs' agendas [and] is formally embedded in their business practices." Among energy executives, 31 percent list sustainability as a top-three priority (versus 22 percent overall), and 6 percent report that it's number one (versus 3 percent). Forty-three percent of energy executives say that sustainability is built into their business practices (versus 29 percent). "Except among energy companies," adds McKinsey, "reporting practices are relatively poor, considering the impact of sustainability on business [and] ... the role of sustainability in reputation-building efforts."

At the same time, however, 55 percent of corporate leaders report that investing in sustainability helps their companies build reputation, and 36 percent identify reputation building as the number-one reason for investing in sustainability. A report by Ernst & Young (EY), a global professional-services firm, identifies reputation among critical corporate assets that are constantly at risk (placing it in the same class as business continuity and the right to operate). More and more, says EY, "the corporate sustainability conversation" has thus turned to "risk reduction and mitigation," especially corporate policy in disclosing sustainability-related risks to investors and other stakeholders. According to EY, the best measure of corporate disclosure policy is "top management's engagement" in the process. "In order for sustainability to be part and parcel of a company's risk management plan," adds strategic communications specialist Leon Kaye, "buy-in has to start at the board and executive level," where such strategies are formulated.

Finally, research conducted by *MIT Sloan Management Review* and The Boston Consulting Group shows that leadership from the top is crucial among companies that "perceive sustainability issues as significant and thoroughly address them": Seventy percent of these firms reported that sustainability is "permanently on their top-management agenda," as compared to only 39 percent of firms overall. Using criteria that include both "sustainability strategy" and "leadership commitment," the study distinguished between "Walkers"—"companies that 'walk the talk' by identifying and addressing significant sustainability concerns"—and "Talkers" (those who do so "to a far lesser degree"). Among Walkers, 70 percent identified sustainability as "a permanent item on their company's senior management to-do list," as opposed to only 24 percent of Talkers. Two-thirds of Walkers reported strong support from corporate leaders, and 68 percent identified senior management as "the greatest influence on sustainability endeavors."

According to Edward Lawler III, director of the University of Southern California's Center for Effective Organizations, the *MIT Sloan* report shows that

"taking sustainability into account … requires a management reset. … This is only likely to occur if the organization's leadership believes that sustainable performance is critical and that achieving it can only be accomplished with a management approach that focuses on it."

---

This chapter examines leadership in organizations and looks at both effective leaders and less effective ones (like Tony Hayward). We start by characterizing the nature of leadership and discuss the three major approaches to studying leadership—traits, behaviors, and situations. After examining other perspectives on leadership, we conclude by describing another approach to influencing others—political behavior in organizations.

# The Nature of Leadership

In Chapter 15, we described various models and perspectives on employee motivation. From the manager's standpoint, trying to motivate people is an attempt to influence their behavior. In many ways, leadership, too, is an attempt to influence the behavior of others. In this section, we first define leadership, then differentiate it from management, and conclude by relating it to power.

## The Meaning of Leadership

**leadership**
As a process, the use of noncoercive influence to shape the group's or organization's goals, motivate behavior toward the achievement of those goals, and help define group or organizational culture; as a property, the set of characteristics attributed to individuals who are perceived to be leaders

Leadership is both a process and a property.[2] As a process—focusing on what leaders actually do—leadership is the use of noncoercive influence to shape the group or organization's goals, motivate behavior toward the achievement of those goals, and help define group or organizational culture.[3] As a property, leadership is the set of characteristics attributed to individuals who are perceived to be leaders. Thus leaders are (1) people who can influence the behaviors of others without having to rely on force or (2) people whom others accept as leaders.

**leaders**
People who can influence the behaviors of others without having to rely on force; those accepted by others as leaders

## Leadership and Management

From these definitions, it should be clear that leadership and management are related, but they are not the same. A person can be a manager, a leader, both, or neither.[4] Some of the basic distinctions between the two are summarized in Table 16.1. At the left side of the table are four elements that differentiate leadership from management. The two columns show how each element differs when considered from a management and from a leadership point of view. For example, when executing plans, managers focus on monitoring results, comparing them

Management and leadership are not necessarily the same thing. The manager on the left is reviewing financial documents in order to make a decision. These activities are a part of management, but not leadership. However, the manager on the right is engaging in leadership as she is working to motivate her team to meet their new performance expectations.

Dragon Images/Shutterstock.com

Monkey Business Images/Shutterstock.com

---

## TABLE 16.1  DISTINCTIONS BETWEEN MANAGEMENT AND LEADERSHIP

Management and leadership are related, but distinct, constructs. Managers and leaders differ in how they create an agenda, develop a rationale for achieving the agenda, and execute plans, and they differ in the types of outcomes they achieve.

| Activity | Management | Leadership |
|---|---|---|
| Creating an agenda | *Planning and Budgeting* Establishing detailed steps and timetables for achieving needed results; allocating the resources necessary to make those needed results happen | *Establishing Direction* Developing a vision of the future, often the distant future, and strategies for producing the changes needed to achieve that vision |
| Developing a human network for achieving the agenda | *Organizing and Staffing* Establishing some structure for accomplishing plan requirements, staffing that structure with individuals, delegating responsibility and authority for carrying out the plan, providing policies and procedures to help guide people, and creating methods or systems to monitor implementation | *Aligning People* Communicating the direction by words and deeds to everyone whose cooperation may be needed to influence the creation of teams and coalitions that understand the visions and strategies and accept their validity |
| Executing plans | *Controlling and Problem Solving* Monitoring results versus planning in some detail, identifying deviations, and then planning and organizing to solve these problems | *Motivating and Inspiring* Energizing people to overcome major political, bureaucratic, and resource barriers by satisfying very basic, but often unfulfilled, human needs |
| Outcomes | Produces a degree of predictability and order and has the potential to produce consistently major results expected by various stakeholders (for example, for customers, always being on time; for stockholders, being on budget) | Produces change, often to a dramatic degree, and has the potential to produce extremely useful change (for example, new products that customers want, new approaches to labor relations that help make a firm more competitive) |

Source: Reprinted with permission of The Free Press, a division of Simon & Schuster Adult Publishing Group, from *A Force for Change: How Leadership Differs from Management* by John P. Kotter. Copyright © 1990 by John P. Kotter, Inc.

with goals, and correcting deviations. In contrast, the leader focuses on energizing people to overcome bureaucratic hurdles to reach goals.

Organizations need both management and leadership if they are to be effective. Our *Beyond Traditional Business* feature explores this point in more detail. Leadership is necessary to create change, and management is necessary to achieve orderly results. Management in conjunction with leadership can produce orderly change, and leadership in conjunction with management can keep the organization properly aligned with its environment. Indeed, perhaps part of the reason why executive compensation has soared in recent years is the belief that management and leadership skills reflect a critical but rare combination that can lead to organizational success.

## Leadership and Power

To fully understand leadership, it is necessary to understand power. Power is the ability to affect the behavior of others. It is also important to note that one can have power without actually using it. For example, a football coach has the power to bench a player who is not performing up to par. The coach seldom has to use this power because players recognize that the power exists and work hard to keep their starting positions. In organizational settings, there are usually five kinds of power: legitimate, reward, coercive, referent, and expert power.[5]

**Legitimate Power**  Legitimate power is power granted through the organizational hierarchy; it is the power defined by the organization to be accorded to people occupying a particular position. A manager can assign tasks to a subordinate, and a subordinate who refuses

**power**
The ability to affect the behavior of others

**legitimate power**
Power granted through the organizational hierarchy; the power defined by the organization to be accorded to people occupying particular positions

# Underdevelopment in the Nonprofit Sector

A recent study by the consulting firm McKinsey & Co. reveals a curious lack of managerial confidence among leaders of social-sector nonprofits. Only 32 percent, for example, consider themselves "strong" in innovating and implementing organizational strategies. Less than a quarter rate themselves strong on collaboration, and only 20 percent think that they're strong when it comes to surrounding themselves with talented management teams. Even fewer (18 percent) have much confidence that they can achieve the outcomes that they want to achieve.

"The findings," say the authors of the report, "suggest that chronic underinvestment in leadership development within the U.S. social sector, accompanied by 25 percent growth in the number of nonprofit organizations in the past decade, has opened a gap between demands on leaders and their ability to meet those needs." *Leadership development* refers to any program designed to enhance individual and organizational leadership competence. Such programs are fairly common in the for-profit sector but much rarer among nonprofits, which allocate less than 1 percent of annual funding to the task of developing leaders.

According to a survey conducted by the Bridgespan Group, a management consulting firm for nonprofits and philanthropies, only 36 percent of nonprofit leaders say that they're held responsible for leadership development, and only 30 percent are responsible for setting goals for leadership development. While 50 percent report that employees are evaluated for potential as well as performance, just 29 percent have programs for developing individual potential. Only 30 percent have any plans for dealing with a projected leadership deficit in their sector.

That deficit, says Robin Noah, who provides consultant, coaching, and professional-training services to nonprofits, is a product of "both constrained supply and increasing demand." According to the most recent available data, for instance, the number of nonprofits in the United States grew by 25 percent between 2001 and 2011, while the number of for-profits grew by a mere 0.5 percent. During the Great Recession of 2007–2009, while for-profit employment and wages dropped by 8.4 percent and 8 percent, respectively, nonprofit employment went up by 4 percent and wages by 6.5 percent. Noah points out that, judging from a trend begun in 2006, the need for senior managers at nonprofits will have averaged almost 80,000 per year by 2016.

"There's an urgent need for qualified leaders," says Van Evans, a PhD candidate at Indiana University's Center of Philanthropy, "because the sector is expanding while current leaders are retiring. … There is [also] a sense of urgency … to get people with philanthropy and management skills," he adds, because overreliance on untrained senior staff "can undermine the credibility and depress the professionalism of the sector."

A follow-up Bridgespan study identified several areas in which nonprofits should focus their leadership-development efforts: engaging senior leaders in the process, forecasting future needs, and monitoring development programs. "Organizations that are doing well," reports coauthor Preeta Nayak, "make leadership development a part of their everyday business and continuously maintain a vision for what future needs might be. … Nonprofit leaders," she adds, "are not satisfied and realize that there is a gap," but when asked to identify the sources of their dissatisfaction, most answered "time, money, and resource constraint."

*References:* Laura Callinan et al., "What Social-Sector Leaders Need to Succeed," *Insights and Publications* (McKinsey & Co., November 2014), www.mckinsey.com, on April 19, 2015; The Bridgespan Group, *The Nonprofit Sector's Leadership Deficit* (March 2006), www.bridgespan.org, on April 19, 2015; Thomas Betar, "Nonprofit Sector in Need of Qualified Leaders amidst Change," *Deseret News* (Salt Lake City) (August 5, 2012), www.deseretnews.com, on April 17, 2015; Mark Athitakis, "A Crisis of Confidence in Nonprofit Leadership," *Associations Now* (December 15, 2014), http://associationsnow.com, on April 17, 2015; Robin Noah, "The Nonprofit Sector's Leadership Deficit," Executive Coaches of Orange County (November 3, 2014), http://ecofoc.org, on April 17, 2015; The Bridgespan Group, "Nonprofit Leaders Admit to 'Falling Short' on Developing Future Leaders, according to New Bridgespan" (press release), *HR.com* (May 29, 2012), www.hr.com, on April 18, 2015.

to do them can be reprimanded or even fired. Such outcomes stem from the manager's legitimate power as defined and vested in her or him by the organization. Legitimate power, then, is authority. All managers have legitimate power over their subordinates. The mere possession of legitimate power, however, does not by itself make someone a leader. Some subordinates follow only orders that are strictly within the letter of organizational rules and policies. If asked to do something not in their job descriptions, they refuse or do a poor job. The manager of such employees is exercising authority but not leadership.

**Reward Power**  Reward power is the power to give or withhold rewards. Rewards that a manager may control include salary increases, bonuses, promotion recommendations, praise, recognition, and interesting job assignments. In general, the greater the number of rewards a manager controls and the more important the rewards are to subordinates, the greater is the manager's reward power. If the subordinate sees as valuable only the formal organizational rewards provided by the manager, then he or she is not a leader. If the subordinate also wants and appreciates the manager's informal rewards, such as praise, gratitude, and recognition, however, then the manager is also exercising leadership.

**reward power**
The power to give or withhold rewards, such as salary increases, bonuses, promotions, praise, recognition, and interesting job assignments

**coercive power**
The power to force compliance by means of psychological, emotional, or physical threat

**referent power**
The personal power that accrues to someone based on identification, imitation, loyalty, or charisma

**Coercive Power**  Coercive power is the power to force compliance by means of psychological, emotional, or physical threat. In the past, physical coercion in organizations was relatively common. In most organizations today, however, coercion is limited to verbal reprimands, written reprimands, disciplinary layoffs, fines, demotion, and termination. Some managers occasionally go so far as to use verbal abuse, humiliation, and psychological coercion in an attempt to manipulate subordinates. (Of course, most people would agree that these are not appropriate managerial behaviors.) James Dutt, a legendary former CEO of Beatrice Company, once told a subordinate that if his wife and family got in the way of his working a 24-hour day seven days a week, he should get rid of them.[6] Charlie Ergen, founder and chairman of Dish Network, is also known to be an abrasive and hard-nosed leader. Dish is often cited as one of the worst places to work in America.[7] The more punitive the elements under a manager's control and the more important they are to subordinates, the more coercive power the manager possesses. On the other hand, the more a manager uses coercive power, the more likely he is to provoke resentment and hostility and the less likely he is to be seen as a leader.[8]

"[Dish Network's Charlie Ergen's leadership style is] … pounding people into submission."

—FORMER DISH EXECUTIVE[9]

**Referent Power**  Compared with legitimate, reward, and coercive power, which are relatively concrete and grounded in objective facets of organizational life, referent power is abstract. It is based on identification, imitation, loyalty, or charisma. Followers may react favorably because they identify in some way with a leader, who may be like them in personality, background, or attitudes. In other situations, followers might choose to imitate a leader with referent power by wearing the same kind of clothing, working the same hours, or espousing the same management philosophy. Referent power may also take the form of charisma, an intangible attribute of the leader that inspires loyalty and enthusiasm. Thus a manager might have referent power, but it is more likely to be associated with leadership.

Coercive power is the power to force compliance by means of psychological, emotional, or physical threat. This manager is using coercive power by yelling at his assistant. While this may produce immediate results, in the long run it will breed resentment and lead to low morale and turnover.

Expert power is derived from information or expertise. This manager is showing his colleagues how to interpret some complex statistical analyses. At this point, at least, he has expert power.

**Expert Power** Expert power is derived from information or expertise. A manager who knows how to interact with an eccentric but important customer, a scientist who is capable of achieving an important technical breakthrough that no other company has dreamed of, and an administrative assistant who knows how to unravel bureaucratic red tape all have expert power over anyone who needs that information. The more important the information and the fewer the people who have access to it, the greater is the degree of expert power possessed by any one person. In general, people who are both leaders and managers tend to have a lot of expert power.

**Using Power** How does a manager or leader use power? Several methods have been identified.[10] One method is the *legitimate request*, which is based on legitimate power. The manager requests that the subordinate comply because the subordinate recognizes that the organization has given the manager the right to make the request. Most day-to-day interactions between manager and subordinate are of this type. Another use of power is *instrumental compliance*, which is based on the reinforcement theory of motivation. In this form of exchange, a subordinate complies to get the reward the manager controls. Suppose that a manager asks a subordinate to do something outside the range of the subordinate's normal duties, such as working extra hours on the weekend, terminating a relationship with a longstanding buyer, or delivering bad news. The subordinate complies and, as a direct result, reaps praise and a bonus from the manager. The next time the subordinate is asked to perform a similar activity, that subordinate will recognize that compliance will be instrumental in her getting more rewards. Hence the basis of instrumental compliance is clarifying important performance–reward contingencies.

A manager is using *coercion* when she suggests or implies that the subordinate will be punished, fired, or reprimanded if he does do something. *Rational persuasion* occurs when the manager can convince the subordinate that compliance is in the subordinate's best interests. For example, a manager might argue that the subordinate should accept a transfer because it would be good for the subordinate's career. In some ways, rational persuasion is like reward power, except that the manager does not really control the reward.

Still another way a manager can use power is through *personal identification*. A manager who recognizes that she has referent power over a subordinate can shape the behavior of that subordinate by engaging in desired behaviors: The manager consciously becomes a model for the subordinate and exploits personal identification. Sometimes a manager can induce a subordinate to do something consistent with a set of higher ideals or values through *inspirational appeal*. For example, a plea for loyalty represents an inspirational appeal. Referent power plays a role in determining the extent to which an inspirational appeal is successful because its effectiveness depends at least in part on the persuasive abilities of the leader.

A dubious method of using power is through *information distortion*. The manager withholds or distorts information to influence subordinates' behavior. For example, if a manager has agreed to allow everyone to participate in choosing a new group member but subsequently finds one person whom she really prefers, she might withhold some of the credentials of other qualified applicants so that the desired member is selected. This use of power is dangerous. It may be unethical, and if subordinates find out that the manager has deliberately misled them, they will lose their confidence and trust in that manager's leadership.[11]

**expert power**
The personal power that accrues to someone based on the information or expertise they possess

☐ All managers should understand the distinctions between leadership and management.

☐ Managers should also be familiar with the five bases of power.

**Manager's Checklist** ✓

# Generic Approaches To Leadership

Early approaches to the study of leadership adopted what might be called a "universal" or "generic" perspective. Specifically, they assumed that there was one set of answers to the leadership puzzle. One generic approach focused on leadership traits, and the other looked at leadership behavior.

## Leadership Traits

The first organized approach to studying leadership analyzed the personal, psychological, and physical traits of strong leaders. The trait approach assumed that some basic trait or set of traits existed that differentiated leaders from nonleaders. If those traits could be defined, potential leaders could be identified. Researchers thought that leadership traits might include intelligence, assertiveness, above-average height, good vocabulary, attractiveness, self-confidence, and similar attributes.[12]

> "It is wise to persuade people to do things and make them think it was their own idea."
>
> —NELSON MANDELA,
> FORMER PRESIDENT OF SOUTH AFRICA[13]

During the first half of the twentieth century, hundreds of studies were conducted in an attempt to identify important leadership traits. For the most part, the results of the studies were disappointing. For every set of leaders who possessed a common trait, a long list of exceptions was also found, and the list of suggested traits soon grew so long that it had little practical value. Alternative explanations usually existed even for relationships between traits and leadership that initially appeared valid. For example, it was observed that many leaders have good communication skills and are assertive. Rather than those traits being the cause of leadership, however, successful leaders may begin to display those traits after they have achieved a leadership position.

Although most researchers gave up trying to identify traits as predictors of leadership ability, many people still explicitly or implicitly adopt a trait orientation.[14] For example, politicians are all too often elected on the basis of personal appearance, speaking ability, or an aura of self-confidence. In addition, traits like honesty and integrity may very well be fundamental leadership traits that serve an important purpose. Intelligence also seems to play a meaningful role in leadership.[15]

## Leadership Behaviors

Spurred on by their lack of success in identifying useful leadership traits, researchers soon began to investigate other variables, especially the behaviors or actions of leaders. The new hypothesis was that effective leaders somehow behaved differently than less effective leaders. Thus the goal was to develop a fuller understanding of leadership behaviors.

**Michigan Studies**  Researchers at the University of Michigan, led by Rensis Likert, began studying leadership in the late 1940s.[16] Based on

Abraham Lincoln is considered to have been a great leader. Part of this image came from how effectively he made decisions and led the United States during the Civil War. But some people also (erroneously) attributed his leadership to the fact that he was very tall—a physical trait.

Library of Congress Prints and Photographs Division[LC-USZ62-8812]

extensive interviews with both leaders (managers) and followers (subordinates), this research identified two basic forms of leader behavior: job centered and employee centered. Managers using job-centered leader behavior pay close attention to subordinates' work, explain work procedures, and are keenly interested in performance. Managers using employee-centered leader behavior are interested in developing a cohesive work group and ensuring that employees are satisfied with their jobs. Their primary concern is the welfare of subordinates.

The two styles of leader behavior were presumed to be at the ends of a single continuum. Although this suggests that leaders may be extremely job centered, extremely employee centered, or somewhere in between, Likert studied only the two end styles for contrast. He argued that employee-centered leader behavior generally tends to be more effective. We should also note the similarities between Likert's leadership research and his Systems 1 through 4 organization designs (discussed in Chapter 11). Job-centered leader behavior is consistent with the System 1 design (rigid and bureaucratic), whereas employee-centered leader behavior is consistent with the System 4 design (organic and flexible). When Likert advocates moving organizations from System 1 to System 4, he is also advocating a transition from job-centered to employee-centered leader behavior.

**Ohio State Studies**   At about the same time that Likert was beginning his leadership studies at the University of Michigan, a group of researchers at Ohio State University also began studying leadership.[17] The extensive questionnaire surveys conducted during the Ohio State studies also suggested that there are two basic leader behaviors or styles: initiating-structure behavior and consideration behavior. When using initiating-structure behavior, the leader clearly defines the leader–subordinate role so that everyone knows what is expected, establishes formal lines of communication, and determines how tasks will be performed. Leaders using consideration behavior show concern for subordinates and try to establish a warm, friendly, and supportive climate. The behaviors identified at Ohio State are similar to those described at Michigan, but there are important differences. One major difference is that the Ohio State researchers did not interpret leader behavior as being one-dimensional; each behavior was assumed to be independent of the other. Presumably, then, a leader could exhibit varying levels of initiating structure and at the same time varying levels of consideration.

At first, the Ohio State researchers thought that leaders who exhibit high levels of both behaviors would tend to be more effective than other leaders. A study at International Harvester (now Navistar International), however, suggested a more complicated pattern.[18] The researchers found that employees of supervisors who ranked high on initiating structure were high performers but expressed low levels of satisfaction and had a higher absence rate. Conversely, employees of supervisors who ranked high on consideration had low performance ratings but high levels of satisfaction and few absences from work. Later research isolated other variables that make consistent prediction difficult and determined that situational influences also occurred. (This body of research is discussed in the section on situational approaches to leadership.[19])

**Leadership Grid**   Yet another behavioral approach to leadership is the Leadership Grid (formerly called the *Managerial Grid*).[20] The Leadership Grid provides a means for

**job-centered leader behavior**
The behavior of leaders who pay close attention to the job and work procedures involved with that job

**employee-centered leader behavior**
The behavior of leaders who develop cohesive work groups and ensure employee satisfaction

**initiating-structure behavior**
The behavior of leaders who define the leader–subordinate role so that everyone knows what is expected, establish formal lines of communication, and determine how tasks will be performed

**consideration behavior**
The behavior of leaders who show concern for subordinates and attempt to establish a warm, friendly, and supportive climate

Goodluz/Shutterstock.com

Job-centered leader behavior focuses on jobs and work procedures. This manager is exhibiting job-centered behavior as he demonstrates how to perform a task to one of his workers.

evaluating leadership styles and then training managers to move toward an ideal style of behavior. The Leadership Grid is shown in Figure 16.1. The horizontal axis represents concern for production (similar to job-centered and initiating-structure behaviors), and the vertical axis represents concern for people (similar to employee-centered and consideration behaviors). Note the five extremes of managerial behavior: the 1,1 manager (impoverished management), who exhibits minimal concern for both production and people; the 9,1 manager (authority-compliance), who is highly concerned about production but exhibits little concern for people; the 1,9 manager (country club management), who has exactly opposite concerns from the 9,1 manager; the 5,5 manager (middle-of-the-road management), who maintains adequate concern for both people and production; and the 9,9 manager (team management), who exhibits maximum concern for both people and production.

## FIGURE 16.1 THE LEADERSHIP GRID

The Leadership Grid® is a method of evaluating leadership styles. The overall objective of an organization using the Grid is to train its managers using organization development techniques so that they are simultaneously more concerned for both people and production (9,9 style on the Grid).

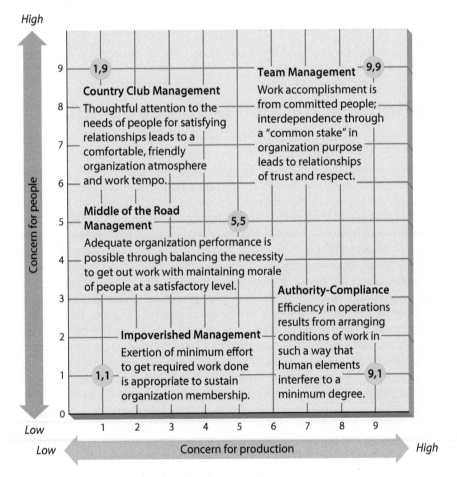

concern for production
The part of the Leadership Grid that deals with the job and task aspects of leader behavior

concern for people
The part of the Leadership Grid that deals with the human aspects of leader behavior

Source: The Leadership Grid figure from *Leadership Dilemmas—Grid Solutions* by Robert R. Blake and Anne Adams McCanse. (Formerly *The Managerial Grid* by Robert R. Blake and Jane S. Mouton.) Houston: Gulf Publishing Company, p. 29. Copyright © 1997 by Grid International, Inc. Reproduced by permission of the owners.

According to this approach, the ideal style of managerial behavior is 9,9. There is a six-phase program to assist managers in achieving this style of behavior. A.G. Edwards, Westinghouse, the FAA, Equicor, and other companies have used the Leadership Grid and reported that it was reasonably successful. However, there is little published scientific evidence regarding its true effectiveness.

The leader-behavior theories have played an important role in the development of contemporary thinking about leadership. In particular, they urge us not to be preoccupied with what leaders are (the trait approach) but to concentrate on what leaders do (their behaviors). Unfortunately, these theories also make universal generic prescriptions about what constitutes effective leadership. When we are dealing with complex social systems composed of complex individuals, however, few, if any, relationships are consistently predictable, and certainly no formulas for success are infallible. Yet the behavior theorists tried to identify consistent relationships between leader behaviors and employee responses in the hope of finding a dependable prescription for effective leadership. As we might expect, they often failed. Other approaches to understanding leadership were therefore needed. The catalyst for these new approaches was the realization that although interpersonal and task-oriented dimensions might be useful for describing the behavior of leaders, they were not useful for predicting or prescribing it. The next step in the evolution of leadership theory was the creation of situational models.

---

 **Manager's Checklist**

☐ Managers should be aware of the basic types of leader behavior identified in the generic approaches to leadership.

☐ You should also be aware of the weaknesses in all of the generic approaches.

## Situational Approaches To Leadership

Situational models assume that appropriate leader behavior varies from one situation to another. The goal of a situational theory, then, is to identify key situational factors and to specify how they interact to determine appropriate leader behavior. Before discussing the major situational theories, we should first discuss an important early model that laid the foundation for subsequent developments. In a 1958 study of the decision-making process, Robert Tannenbaum and Warren H. Schmidt proposed a continuum of leadership behavior. Their model is much like the original Michigan framework.[21] Besides purely job-centered behavior (or "boss-centered" behavior, as they termed it) and employee-centered ("subordinate-centered") behavior, however, they identified several intermediate behaviors that a manager might consider. These are shown on the leadership continuum in Figure 16.2.

This continuum of behavior moves from one extreme, of having the manager make the decision alone, to the other extreme, of having the employees make the decision with minimal guidance. Each point on the continuum is influenced by characteristics of the manager, the subordinates, and the situation. Managerial characteristics include the manager's value system, confidence in subordinates, personal inclinations, and feelings of security. Subordinate characteristics include the subordinates' need for independence, readiness to assume responsibility, tolerance for ambiguity, interest in the problem, understanding of goals, knowledge, experience, and expectations. Situational characteristics that affect decision making include the type of organization, group effectiveness, the problem itself, and time pressures. Although this framework pointed out the importance of situational factors, it was only speculative. It remained for others to develop more comprehensive and integrated theories. In the following sections, we describe four of the most important and widely accepted situational theories of leadership: the LPC theory, the path–goal theory, Vroom's decision tree approach, and the leader–member exchange approach.

## FIGURE 16.2  TANNENBAUM AND SCHMIDT'S LEADERSHIP CONTINUUM

The Tannenbaum and Schmidt leadership continuum was an important precursor to modern situational approaches to leadership. The continuum identifies seven levels of leadership, which range between the extremes of boss-centered and subordinate-centered leadership.

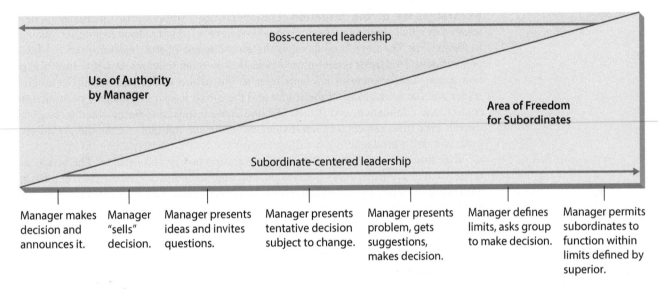

Source: Reprinted by permission of the *Harvard Business Review*. An exhibit from "How to Choose a Leadership Pattern" by Robert Tannenbaum and Warren Schmidt (May–June 1973). Copyright © 1973 by the President and Fellows of Harvard College; all rights reserved.

## LPC Theory

The LPC theory, developed by Fred Fiedler, was the first truly situational theory of leadership.[22] As we will discuss later, LPC stands for least-preferred coworker. Beginning with a combined trait and behavioral approach, Fiedler identified two styles of leadership: task oriented (analogous to job-centered and initiating-structure behavior) and relationship oriented (similar to employee-centered and consideration behavior). He went beyond the earlier behavioral approaches by arguing that the style of behavior is a reflection of the leader's personality and that most personalities fall into one of his two categories—task oriented or relationship oriented by nature. Fiedler measures leadership style by means of a controversial questionnaire called the least-preferred coworker (LPC) measure. To use the measure, a manager or leader is asked to describe the specific person with whom he or she is able to work least well—the LPC—by filling in a set of 16 scales anchored at each end by a positive or negative adjective. For example, 3 of the 16 scales are:

Helpful ____ ____ ____ ____ ____ ____ ____ ____ Frustrating
         8  7  6  5  4  3  2  1

Tense ____ ____ ____ ____ ____ ____ ____ ____ Relaxed
        1  2  3  4  5  6  7  8

Boring ____ ____ ____ ____ ____ ____ ____ ____ Interesting
        1  2  3  4  5  6  7  8

The leader's LPC score is then calculated by adding up the numbers below the line checked on each scale. Note in these three examples that the higher numbers are associated with positive qualities (helpful, relaxed, and interesting), whereas the negative qualities

**LPC theory**
A theory of leadership that suggests that the appropriate style of leadership varies with situational favorableness

**least-preferred coworker (LPC) measure**
The measuring scale that asks leaders to describe the person with whom he or she is able to work least well

(frustrating, tense, and boring) have low point values. A high total score is assumed to reflect a relationship orientation and a low score a task orientation on the part of the leader. The LPC measure is controversial because researchers disagree about its validity. Some question exactly what an LPC measure reflects and whether the score is an index of behavior, personality, or some other factor.[23]

**Favorableness of the Situation**  The underlying assumption of situational models of leadership is that appropriate leader behavior varies from one situation to another. According to Fiedler, the key situational factor is the favorableness of the situation from the leader's point of view. This factor is determined by leader–member relations, task structure, and position power. *Leader–member relations* refer to the nature of the relationship between the leader and the work group. If the leader and the group have a high degree of mutual trust, respect, and confidence, and if they like one another, relations are assumed to be good. If there is little trust, respect, or confidence, and if they do not like one another, relations are poor. Naturally, good relations are more favorable.

*Task structure* is the degree to which the group's task is well defined. The task is structured when it is routine, easily understood, and unambiguous, and when the group has standard procedures and precedents to rely on. An unstructured task is nonroutine, ambiguous, and complex, with no standard procedures or precedents. You can see that high structure is more favorable for the leader, whereas low structure is less favorable. For example, if the task is unstructured, the group will not know what to do, and the leader will have to play a major role in guiding and directing its activities. If the task is structured, the leader will not have to get so involved and can devote time to nonsupervisory activities.

*Position power* is the power vested in the leader's position. If the leader has the power to assign work and to reward and punish employees, position power is assumed to be strong. But if the leader must get job assignments approved by someone else and does not administer rewards and punishment, position power is weak, and it is more difficult to accomplish goals. From the leader's point of view, strong position power is clearly preferable to weak position power. However, position power is not as important as task structure and leader–member relations.

Task structure–the degree to which tasks are clear and well-defined–plays a role in how favorable or unfavorable the situation is for the leader. This job, which involves tracking inventory by scanning bar codes, is relatively structured. Because of this structure, once employees learn their jobs the leader does not need to focus too much on continuing to explain how to do those jobs.

**Favorableness and Leader Style**  Fiedler and his associates conducted many studies linking the favorableness of various situations to leader style and the effectiveness of the group.[24] The results of these studies—and the overall framework of the theory—are shown in Figure 16.3. To interpret the model, look first at the situational factors at the top of the figure. Good or bad leader–member relations, high or low task structure, and strong or weak leader position power can be combined to yield six unique situations. For example, good leader–member relations, high task structure, and strong leader position power (at the far left) are presumed to define the most favorable situation; bad leader–member relations, low task structure, and weak leader power (at the far right) are the least favorable. The other combinations reflect intermediate levels of favorableness.

Below each set of situations are shown the degree of favorableness and the form of leader behavior found to be most strongly associated with effective group performance for those situations.

## FIGURE 16.3  THE LEAST-PREFERRED COWORKER THEORY OF LEADERSHIP

Fiedler's LPC theory of leadership suggests that appropriate leader behavior varies as a function of the favorableness of the situation. Favorableness, in turn, is defined by task structure, leader–member relations, and the leader's position power. According to the LPC theory, the most and least favorable situations call for task-oriented leadership, whereas moderately favorable situations suggest the need for relationship-oriented leadership.

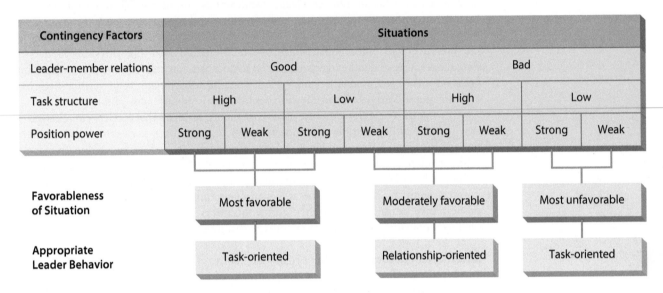

When the situation is most and least favorable, Fiedler found that a task-oriented leader is most effective. When the situation is only moderately favorable, however, a relationship-oriented leader is predicted to be most effective.

**Flexibility of Leader Style**  Fiedler argued that, for any given person, leader style is essentially fixed and cannot be changed; leaders cannot change their behavior to fit a particular situation because it is linked to their personality traits. Thus, when a leader's style and the situation do not match, Fiedler argued that the situation should be changed to fit the leader's style. When leader–member relations are good, task structure low, and position power weak, the leader style that is most likely to be effective is relationship oriented. If the leader is task oriented, a mismatch exists. According to Fiedler, the leader can make the elements of the situation more congruent by structuring the task (by developing guidelines and procedures, for instance) and increasing power (by requesting additional authority or by other means).

Fiedler's contingency theory has been attacked on the grounds that it is not always supported by research, that his findings are subject to other interpretations, that the LPC measure lacks validity, and that his assumptions about the inflexibility of leader behavior are unrealistic.[25] However, Fiedler's theory was one of the first to adopt a situational perspective on leadership. It has helped many managers recognize the important situational factors they must contend with, and it has fostered additional thinking about the situational nature of leadership. Moreover, in recent years Fiedler has tried to address some of the concerns about his theory by revising it and adding such additional elements as cognitive resources.

## Path–Goal Theory

The path–goal theory of leadership—associated most closely with Martin Evans and Robert House—is a direct extension of the expectancy theory of motivation discussed in Chapter 15.[26] Recall that the primary components of expectancy theory included the likelihood of attaining various outcomes and the value associated with those outcomes.

**path–goal theory**
A theory of leadership suggesting that the primary functions of a leader are to make valued or desired rewards available in the workplace and to clarify for the subordinate the kinds of behavior that will lead to those rewards

The path–goal theory of leadership suggests that the primary functions of a leader are to make valued or desired rewards available in the workplace and to clarify for the subordinate the kinds of behavior that will lead to goal accomplishment and valued rewards—that is, the leader should clarify the paths to goal attainment.

**Leader Behavior** The most fully developed version of path–goal theory identifies four kinds of leader behavior. *Directive leader behavior* lets subordinates know what is expected of them, gives guidance and direction, and schedules work. *Supportive leader behavior* is being friendly and approachable, showing concern for subordinates' welfare, and treating team members as equals. *Participative leader behavior* includes consulting with subordinates, soliciting suggestions, and allowing participation in decision making. *Achievement-oriented leader* behavior means setting challenging goals, expecting subordinates to perform at high levels, encouraging subordinates, and showing confidence in subordinates' abilities.

In contrast to Fiedler's theory, path–goal theory assumes that leaders can change their style or behavior to meet the demands of a particular situation. For example, when encountering a new group of subordinates and a new project, the leader may be directive in establishing work procedures and in outlining what needs to be done. Next, the leader may adopt supportive behavior to foster group cohesiveness and a positive climate. As the group becomes familiar with the task and as new problems are encountered, the leader may exhibit participative behavior to enhance group members' motivation. Finally, achievement-oriented behavior may be used to encourage continued high performance.

**Situational Factors** Like other situational theories of leadership, path–goal theory suggests that appropriate leader style depends on situational factors. Path–goal theory focuses on the situational factors of the personal characteristics of subordinates and environmental characteristics of the workplace.

Important personal characteristics include the subordinates' perception of their own abilities and their locus of control. If people perceive that they are lacking in abilities, they may prefer directive leadership to help them understand path–goal relationships better. If they perceive themselves as having a lot of abilities, however, employees may resent directive leadership. Locus of control is a personality trait. People who have an internal locus of control believe that what happens to them is a function of their own efforts and behavior. Those who have an external locus of control assume that fate, luck, or "the system" determines what happens to them. A person with an internal locus of control may prefer participative leadership, whereas a person with an external locus of control may prefer directive leadership. Managers can do little or nothing to influence the personal characteristics of subordinates, but they can shape the environment to take advantage of these personal characteristics by, for example, providing rewards and structuring tasks.

Environmental characteristics include factors outside the subordinates' control. Task structure is one such factor. When structure is high, directive leadership is less effective than when structure is low. Subordinates do not usually need their boss to continually tell them how to do an extremely routine job. The formal authority system is another important environmental characteristic. Again, the higher the degree of formality, the less directive is the leader behavior that will be accepted by subordinates. The nature of the work group also affects appropriate leader behavior. When the work group provides the employee with social support and satisfaction, supportive leader behavior is less critical. When social support and satisfaction cannot be derived from the group, the worker may look to the leader for this support. Greater leadership support may also be an important factor in times of change or under unusually stressful conditions.

The basic path–goal framework as illustrated in Figure 16.4 shows that different leader behaviors affect subordinates' motivation to perform. Personal and environmental characteristics are seen as defining which behaviors lead to which outcomes. The path–goal theory of leadership is a dynamic and incomplete model. The original intent was to state the theory in general terms so that future research could explore a variety of interrelationships and modify the theory.

## FIGURE 16.4 THE PATH-GOAL FRAMEWORK

The path–goal theory of leadership suggests that managers can use four types of leader behavior to clarify subordinates' paths to goal attainment. Personal characteristics of the subordinate and environmental characteristics within the organization both must be taken into account when determining which style of leadership will work best for a particular situation.

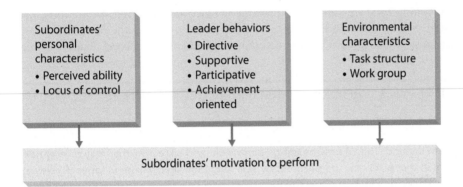

Subordinates'
personal
characteristics
- Perceived ability
- Locus of control

Leader behaviors
- Directive
- Supportive
- Participative
- Achievement oriented

Environmental
characteristics
- Task structure
- Work group

Subordinates' motivation to perform

Research that has been done suggests that the path–goal theory is a reasonably good description of the leadership process and that future investigations along these lines should enable us to discover more about the link between leadership and motivation.[27]

## Vroom's Decision Tree Approach

The third major contemporary approach to leadership is Vroom's decision tree approach. The earliest version of this model was proposed by Victor Vroom and Philip Yetton and later revised and expanded by Vroom and Arthur Jago.[28] Most recently, Vroom has developed yet another refinement of the original model.[29] Like the path–goal theory, this approach attempts to prescribe a leadership style appropriate to a given situation. It also assumes that the same leader may display different leadership styles. But Vroom's approach concerns itself with only a single aspect of leader behavior: subordinate participation in decision making.

**Basic Premises** Vroom's decision tree approach assumes that the degree to which subordinates should be encouraged to participate in decision making depends on the characteristics of the situation. In other words, no one decision-making process is best for all situations. After evaluating a variety of problem attributes (characteristics of the problem or decision), the leader determines an appropriate decision style that specifies the amount of subordinate participation.

Vroom's current formulation suggests that managers use one of two different decision trees.[30] To do so, the manager first assesses the situation in terms of several factors. This assessment involves determining whether the given factor is high or low for the decision that is to be made. For instance, the first factor is decision significance. If the decision is extremely important and

**Vroom's decision tree approach**
Predicts what kinds of situations call for different degrees of group participation

Vroom's decision tree approach focuses on helping leaders decide how much participation to encourage among subordinates when a decision is being made. This leader is actively seeking input from the team in making a decision.

may have a major impact on the organization (such as choosing a location for a new plant), its significance is high. But if the decision is routine and its consequences are not terribly important (selecting a color for the firm's softball team uniforms), its significance is low. This assessment guides the manager through the paths of the decision tree to a recommended course of action. One decision tree is to be used when the manager is interested primarily in making the decision as quickly as possible; the other is to be used when time is less critical and the manager is interested in helping subordinates to improve and develop their own decision-making skills.

The two decision trees are shown in Figures 16.5 and 16.6. The problem attributes (situational factors) are arranged along the top of the decision tree. To use the model, the decision maker starts at the left side of the diagram and assesses the first problem attribute (decision significance). The answer determines the path to the second node on the decision

---

### FIGURE 16.5 VROOM'S TIME-DRIVEN DECISION TREE

This matrix is recommended for situations when time is of the highest importance in making a decision. The matrix operates like a funnel. You start at the left with a specific decision problem in mind. The column headings denote situational factors that may or may not be present in that problem. You progress by selecting high or low (H or L) for each relevant situational factor. Proceed down the funnel, judging only those situational factors for which a judgment is needed, until you reach the recommended process.

| Decision Significance | Importance of Commitment | Leader Expertise | Likelihood of Commitment | Group Support | Group Expertise | Team Competence | |
|---|---|---|---|---|---|---|---|
| H | H | H | H | — | — | — | Decide |
| | | | L | H | H | H | Delegate |
| | | | | | | L | Consult (group) |
| | | | | | L | — | |
| | | | | L | — | — | |
| | | L | H | H | H | H | Facilitate |
| | | | | | | L | Consult (individually) |
| | | | | | L | — | |
| | | | | L | — | — | |
| | | | L | H | H | H | Facilitate |
| | | | | | | L | Consult (group) |
| | | | | | L | — | |
| | | | | L | — | — | |
| | L | H | — | — | — | — | Decide |
| | | L | — | H | H | H | Facilitate |
| | | | | | | L | Consult (individually) |
| | | | | | L | — | |
| | | | | L | — | — | |
| L | H | — | H | — | — | — | Decide |
| | | | L | — | — | H | Delegate |
| | | | | | | L | Facilitate |
| | L | — | — | — | — | — | Decide |

Source: Adapted and reprinted by permission from *Leadership and Decision-Making*, by Victor H. Vroom and Philip W. Yetton, by permission of the University of Pittsburgh Press. Copyright © 1973 by University of Pittsburgh Press.

## FIGURE 16.6 VROOM'S DEVELOPMENT-DRIVEN DECISION TREE

This matrix is to be used when the leader is more interested in developing employees than in making the decision as quickly as possible. Just as with the time-driven tree shown in Figure 16.5, the leader assesses up to seven situational factors. These factors, in turn, funnel the leader to a recommended process for making the decision.

| Decision Significance | Importance of Commitment | Leader Expertise | Likelihood of Commitment | Group Support | Group Expertise | Team Competence | |
|---|---|---|---|---|---|---|---|
| P R O B L E M   S T A T E M E N T | | | | | | | |
| H | H | — | H | H | H | H | Decide |
| | | | | | | L | Facilitate |
| | | | | | L | — | Consult (group) |
| | | | | L | — | — | Consult (group) |
| | | | L | H | H | H | Delegate |
| | | | | | | L | Facilitate |
| | | | | | L | — | Facilitate |
| | | | | L | — | — | Consult (group) |
| | L | — | — | H | H | H | Delegate |
| | | | | | | L | Facilitate |
| | | | | | L | — | Consult (group) |
| | | | | L | — | — | Consult (group) |
| L | H | — | H | — | — | — | Decide |
| | | | L | — | — | — | Delegate |
| | L | — | — | — | — | — | Decide |

Source: Adapted and reprinted by permission from *Leadership and Decision-Making,* by Victor H. Vroom and Philip W. Yetton, by permission of the University of Pittsburgh Press. Copyright © 1973 by University of Pittsburgh Press.

tree, where the next attribute (importance of commitment) is assessed. This process continues until a terminal node is reached. In this way, the manager identifies an effective decision-making style for the situation.

**Decision-Making Styles** The various decision styles reflected at the ends of the tree branches represent different levels of subordinate participation that the manager should ttry to adopt in a given situation. The five styles are defined as follows:

- *Decide.* The manager makes the decision alone and then announces or "sells" it to the group.
- *Consult (individually).* The manager presents the program to group members individually, obtains their suggestions, and then makes the decision.
- *Consult (group).* The manager presents the problem to group members at a meeting, gets their suggestions, and then makes the decision.
- *Facilitate.* The manager presents the problem to the group at a meeting, defines the problem and its boundaries, and then facilitates group member discussion as they make the decision.
- *Delegate.* The manager allows the group to define for itself the exact nature and parameters of the problem and then to develop a solution.

Vroom's decision tree approach represents a very focused but quite complex perspective on leadership. To compensate for this difficulty, Vroom has developed elaborate expert system software to help managers assess a situation accurately and quickly and then to make an appropriate decision regarding employee participation.[31] Many firms, including Halliburton Company, Litton Industries, and Borland International, have provided their managers with training in how to use the various versions of this model.

**Evaluation and Implications**   Because Vroom's current approach is relatively new, it has not been fully scientifically tested. The original model and its subsequent refinement, however, attracted a great deal of attention and generally was supported by research.[32] For example, there is some support for the idea that individuals who make decisions consistent with the predictions of the model are more effective than those who make decisions inconsistent with it. The model therefore appears to be a tool that managers can apply with some confidence in deciding how much subordinates should participate in the decision-making process.

## The Leader–Member Exchange Approach

Because leadership is such an important area, managers and researchers continue to study it. As a result, new ideas, theories, and perspectives are continuously being developed. The leader–member exchange (LMX) model of leadership, conceived by George Graen and Fred Dansereau, stresses the importance of variable relationships between supervisors and each of their subordinates.[33] Each superior–subordinate pair is referred to as a "vertical dyad." The model differs from earlier approaches in that it focuses on the differential relationship leaders often establish with different subordinates. Figure 16.7 shows the basic concepts of the leader–member exchange theory.

The model suggests that supervisors establish a special relationship with a small number of trusted subordinates, referred to as "the in-group." The in-group usually receives special duties requiring responsibility and autonomy; they may also receive special privileges. Subordinates who are not a part of this group are called "the out-group," and they receive less of the supervisor's time and attention. Note in the figure that the leader has a dyadic, or one-to-one, relationship with each of the five subordinates.

Early in his or her interaction with a given subordinate, the supervisor initiates either an in-group or an out-group relationship. It is not clear how a leader selects members of the in-group, but the decision may be based on personal compatibility and subordinates' competence. Research has confirmed the existence of in-groups and out-groups. In addition, studies generally have found that in-group members have a higher level of performance and satisfaction than do out-group members.[34]

---

**FIGURE 16.7**   THE LEADER–MEMBER EXCHANGE (LMX) MODEL

The LMX model suggests that leaders form unique independent relationships with each of their subordinates. As illustrated here, a key factor in the nature of this relationship is whether the individual subordinate is in the leader's out-group or in-group.

**leader–member exchange (LMX) model** Stresses that leaders have different kinds of relationships with different subordinates

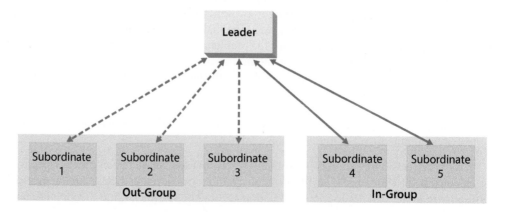

☐ Managers should be familiar with the essential elements of each of the situational approaches to leadership.

☐ You should also have a sense of which situational approach is most useful and least useful for you personally.

☐ Essentially, all managers should know that there is no one set of leadership behaviors that will be universally effective.

# Related Approaches To Leadership

Because of its importance to organizational effectiveness, leadership continues to be the focus of a great deal of research and theory building. New approaches that have attracted much attention are the concepts of substitutes for leadership and transformational leadership.[35]

## Substitutes for Leadership

The concept of substitutes for leadership was developed because existing leadership models and theories do not account for situations in which leadership is not needed.[36] They simply try to specify what kind of leader behavior is appropriate. The substitutes concept, however, identifies situations in which leader behaviors are neutralized or replaced by characteristics of the subordinate, the task, and the organization. For example, when a patient is delivered to a hospital emergency room, the professionals on duty do not wait to be told what to do by a leader. Nurses, doctors, and attendants all go into action without waiting for directive or supportive leader behavior from the emergency room supervisor.

Characteristics of the subordinate that may serve to neutralize leader behavior include ability, experience, need for independence, professional orientation, and indifference toward organizational rewards. For example, employees with a high level of ability and experience may not need to be told what to do. Similarly, a subordinate's strong need for independence may render leader behavior ineffective. Task characteristics that may substitute for leadership include routineness, the availability of feedback, and intrinsic satisfaction. When the job is routine and simple, the subordinate may not need direction. When the task is challenging and intrinsically satisfying, the subordinate may not need or want social support from a leader.

Organizational characteristics that may substitute for leadership include formalization, group cohesion, inflexibility, and a rigid reward structure. Leadership may not be necessary when policies and practices are formal and inflexible, for example. Similarly, a rigid reward system may rob the leader of reward power and thereby decrease the importance of the role. Preliminary research has provided support for the concept of substitutes for leadership.[37]

**substitutes for leadership**
A concept that identifies situations in which leader behaviors are neutralized or replaced by characteristics of subordinates, the task, and the organization

Substitutes for leadership are things that neutralize or replace the need for formal leadership. The professionalism and training of these emergency medical technicians, for example, allows them to respond and carry out their responsibilities without waiting for someone to tell them what to do.

Monkey Business Images/Shutterstock.com

## Charismatic Leadership

The concept of charismatic leadership, like trait theories, assumes that charisma is an individual characteristic of the leader. Charisma is a form of interpersonal attraction that inspires support and acceptance. All else being equal, then, someone with charisma is more likely to be able to influence others than is someone without charisma. For example, a highly charismatic supervisor will be more successful in influencing subordinate behavior than a supervisor who lacks charisma. Thus influence is again a fundamental element of this perspective.

Robert House first proposed a theory of charismatic leadership, based on research findings from a variety of social science disciplines.[38] His theory suggests that charismatic leaders are likely to have a lot of self-confidence, a firm conviction in their beliefs and ideals, and a strong need to influence people. They also tend to communicate high expectations about follower performance and express confidence in followers. Donald Trump is an excellent example of a charismatic leader. Even though he has made his share of mistakes and generally is perceived as only an "average" manager, many people view him as larger than life.

There are three elements of charismatic leadership in organizations that most experts acknowledge today.[39] First, the leader needs to be able to envision the future, set high expectations, and model behaviors consistent with meeting those expectations. Next, the charismatic leader must be able to energize others through a demonstration of personal excitement, personal confidence, and patterns of success. And, finally, the charismatic leader enables others by supporting them, empathizing with them, and expressing confidence in them.[40]

Charismatic leadership ideas are quite popular among managers today and are the subject of numerous books and articles. Unfortunately, few studies have tried to specifically test the meaning and impact of charismatic leadership. There are also lingering ethical issues about charismatic leadership, however, that trouble some people. For instance, President Bill Clinton was a charismatic leader. But some of his critics argued that this very charisma caused his supporters to overlook his flaws and to minimize some of his indiscretions. In contrast, President George W. Bush was not particularly charismatic, and this may have enabled some critics to magnify his shortcomings.

## Transformational Leadership

Another new perspective on leadership has been called by a number of labels: charismatic leadership, inspirational leadership, symbolic leadership, and transformational leadership. We use the term transformational leadership and define it as leadership that goes beyond ordinary expectations by transmitting a sense of mission, stimulating learning experiences, and inspiring new ways of thinking.[41] Because of rapid change and turbulent environments, transformational leaders are increasingly being seen as vital to the success of business.[42]

A widely circulated popular press article once identified seven keys to successful leadership: trusting one's subordinates, developing a vision, keeping cool, encouraging risk, being an expert, inviting dissent, and simplifying things.[43] Although this list was the result of a simplistic survey of the leadership literature, it is nevertheless consistent with the premises underlying transformational leadership. So, too, are recent examples cited as effective leadership. Take the case of 3M. The firm's current CEO is working to make the firm more efficient and profitable while simultaneously keeping its leadership role in new product innovation. He has also changed the reward system, overhauled procedures, and restructured the entire firm. And so far, at least, analysts have applauded these changes.

**charismatic leadership**
Assumes that charisma is an individual characteristic of the leader

**charisma**
A form of interpersonal attraction that inspires support and acceptance

**transformational leadership**
Leadership that goes beyond ordinary expectations by transmitting a sense of mission, stimulating learning experiences, and inspiring new ways of thinking

"Turnaround or growth, it's getting your people focused on the goal that is still the job of leadership."

—ANNE MULCAHY, FORMER CEO OF XEROX[44]

# Emerging Approaches To Leadership

Recently, three potentially very important new approaches to leadership have emerged. One is called "strategic leadership"; the others deal with cross-cultural leadership and ethical leadership.

## Strategic Leadership

Strategic leadership is a new concept that explicitly relates leadership to the role of top management. We define strategic leadership as the ability to understand the complexities of both the organization and its environment and to lead change in the organization in order to achieve and maintain a superior alignment between the organization and its environment. This definition reflects an integration of the leadership concepts covered in this chapter with our discussion of strategic management in Chapter 7.

To be effective as a strategic leader, a manager needs to have a thorough and complete understanding of the organization—its history, its culture, its strengths, and its weaknesses. In addition, the leader needs a firm grasp of the organization's environment. This understanding must encompass current conditions and circumstances as well as significant trends and issues on the horizon. The strategic leader also needs to recognize how the firm is currently aligned with its environment—where it relates effectively and where it relates less effectively with that environment. Finally, looking at environmental trends and issues, the strategic leader works to improve both the current alignment and the future alignment.[45]

Reed Hastings (founder and CEO of Netflix), Indra Nooyi (CEO Pepsico), Hector Ruiz (CEO of Advanced Micro Devices), Michael Dell (founder and CEO of Dell Computer), and Mary Barra (CEO of General Motors) are generally seen today as strong strategic leaders.[46] On the other hand, Ken Lewis (former CEO of Bank of America) and Mike Jeffries (CEO of Abercrombie & Fitch) have recently been cited as less effective strategic leaders.[47]

"[The 3M CEO] … is pulling, pushing, and driving 3M back to its R&D roots. This is a company that prides itself on developing the most iconic products. That all came out of internal innovation, and he wants to make sure that that's not lost."

—ANALYST AT FBR CAPITAL MARKETS[48]

## Cross-Cultural Leadership

Another new approach to leadership is based on cross-cultural issues. In this context, culture is used as a broad concept to encompass both international differences and diversity-based differences within one culture. For instance, when a Japanese firm sends an executive to head the firm's operations in the United States, that person will need to become acclimated to the cultural differences that exist between the two countries and to change his or her leadership style accordingly. Japan is generally characterized by collectivism, whereas the United States is based more on individualism. The Japanese executive, then, will find it necessary to recognize the importance of individual contributions and rewards, as well as the differences in individual and group roles, that exist in Japanese and U.S. businesses.

**strategic leadership**
The ability to understand the complexities of both the organization and its environment and to lead change in the organization in order to achieve and maintain a superior alignment between the organization and its environment

> "Challenges are global ... They require people from every country, every background, every area of expertise, pulling together."
>
> —INDRA KRISHNAMURTHY NOOYI, CEO PEPSICO[49]

Similarly, cross-cultural factors play a growing role in organizations as their workforces become more and more diverse. Most leadership research, for instance, has been conducted on samples or case studies involving white male leaders (until several years ago, most business leaders were white males). But as more females, African Americans, and Latinos achieve leadership positions, it may be necessary to reassess how applicable current theories and models of leadership are when applied to an increasingly diverse pool of leaders. A *World of Difference* looks at some of these issues in more detail.

## Ethical Leadership

Most people have long assumed that top managers are ethical people. But in the wake of recent corporate scandals, faith in top managers has been shaken. Perhaps now more than ever, high standards of ethical conduct are being held up as a prerequisite for effective leadership. More specifically, top managers are being called on to maintain high ethical standards for their own conduct, to exhibit ethical behavior unfailingly, and to hold others in their organizations to the same standards.

> "Reputation is everything."
>
> —KEN CHENAULT, CEO OF AMERICAN EXPRESS[51]

The behaviors of top leaders are being scrutinized more than ever, and those responsible for hiring new leaders for a business are looking more and more closely at the background of those being considered. And the emerging pressures for stronger corporate governance models are likely to further increase commitment to selecting only those individuals with high ethical standards and to hold them more accountable than in the past for both their actions and the consequences of those actions.[50]

---

 **A WORLD OF DIFFERENCE**

# High Tech Does the Math

The good news is that, when it comes to reporting on workforce diversity, tech companies have opted for transparency. In May 2014, for example, Google posted a blog providing detailed information on the gender and ethnic makeup of its entire staff. "We've always been reluctant to publish numbers about the diversity of our workforce," admitted Laszlo Bock, senior VP of People Operations. "We now realize that we were wrong and that it's time to be candid about the issues." Over the next few months, several other tech companies, including Twitter, eBay, LinkedIn, Yahoo, Apple, Microsoft, and Intel, also published their demographic data.

The bad news is that the industrywide labor force is a long way from diverse. According to *Fortune* magazine, the spate of self-disclosures "only confirmed what many people had suspected: White and

Asian men dominate, and everyone else—women, blacks, and Hispanics—is severely lacking." At Google, for instance, only 3 percent of employees are Hispanic and 2 percent black, while 61 percent are white; 70 percent are men and only 30 percent women. Similar breakdowns prevail at Twitter: 70 percent men versus 30 percent women, 59 percent white versus 5 percent Hispanic and black. Likewise, Facebook employs 60 percent men and 31 percent women, with 74 percent white and the usual 5 percent Hispanic and black.

The ethnic numbers don't add up because there's a high percentage of Asians in the tech industry: Asian-Americans represent 34 percent of the workforce at Facebook, 38 percent at LinkedIn, and 39 percent at Yahoo. In particular, Asians account for a significant segment of employees in so-called "tech jobs," such as computer programmers, software developers, and systems analysts. They hold 34 percent of tech jobs at Google, as opposed to 17 percent held by women, who hold 58 percent of non-tech jobs. The numbers are similar at Facebook, where 41 percent of tech employees are Asian and 15 percent female.

At the same time, however, Asians apparently face a "bamboo ceiling" when it comes to attaining leadership positions in the tech industry. The number of Asian-occupied leadership positions at Google, Facebook, and Yahoo is under 20 percent. Ironically, says Chinese-American journalist Brian Fung, "the 'bamboo ceiling' is largely invisible precisely because Asians seem to be doing so well for themselves." For members of groups that aren't doing so well, however—just about everybody but white males— leadership jobs in the tech industry are even harder to come by. According to Google, 90 percent of its "Executive/SR Officials and Managers" are men; at LinkedIn, the number is 80 percent. Between them, the two companies could identify only 12 senior leaders who weren't white or Asian in 2014.

"Like our peers," admits Janet Van Huysse, VP for Diversity and Inclusion at Twitter, "we have a lot of work to do," and she adds that the top management of an organization needs to be as diverse as its customer base because different experiences and value systems broaden a company's strategic horizons and contribute to its bottom line: "It makes good sense," she says,

*that Twitter employees are representative of the vast and varied backgrounds of our users around the world. We also know that it makes good business sense to be more diverse as a workforce—research shows that more diverse teams make better decisions and that companies with women in leadership roles produce better financial results.*

*References:* Laszlo Bock, "Getting to Work on Diversity at Google," *Google Official Blog* (May 28, 2014), http://googleblog.blogspot.com, on April 15, 2015; Maxine Williams, "Building a More Diverse Facebook" (press release) (June 25, 2014), http://newsroom.fb.com, on April 15, 2015; Jena McGregor, "Google Admits It Has a Diversity Problem," *Washington Post* (May 29, 2014), www.washingtonpost.com, on April 13, 2015; J.P. Mangalindan, "How Tech Companies Compare in Employee Diversity," *Fortune* (August 29, 2014), http://fortune.com, on April 13, 2015; Brian Fung, "Tech Companies' Diversity Problems Are Even Worse at the Leadership Level," *Washington Post* (July 24, 2014), www.washingtonpost.com, on April 13, 2015; Max Nisen, "The Emerging Picture of the Tech Industry's Diversity Is Pretty Ugly," *Quartz* (June 18, 2014), http://qz.com, on April 13, 2015; Janet Van Huysse, "Building a Twitter We Can Be Proud Of," *Twitter Blogs* (July 23, 2014), https://blog.twitter.com, on April 15, 2015.

☐ Managers should recognize the growing importance of strategic leadership.

☐ Managers should also know that cross-cultural differences can affect leadership.

☐ You should understand the importance of ethics in leadership.

**Manager's Checklist** ☑

# Political Behavior In Organizations

Another common influence on behavior is politics and political behavior. Political behavior describes activities carried out for the specific purpose of acquiring, developing, and using power and other resources to obtain one's preferred outcomes.[52] Political behavior may be undertaken by managers dealing with their subordinates, subordinates dealing with their managers, and managers and subordinates dealing with others at the same level. In other words, it may be directed upward, downward, or laterally. Decisions ranging from where to locate a manufacturing plant to where to put the company coffee maker are subject to political action. In any situation, individuals may engage in political behavior to further their own ends, to protect themselves from others, to further goals they sincerely believe to be in the organization's best interests, or simply to acquire and exercise power. And power may be sought by individuals, by groups of individuals, or by groups of groups.[53]

**political behavior**
Activities carried out for the specific purpose of acquiring, developing, and using power and other resources to obtain one's preferred outcomes

"In our company, we don't want any politics. If you see or smell anything like politics, kill it."

—DINESH C. PALIWAL CEO
HARMAN INTERNATIONAL INDUSTRIES[54]

Although political behavior is difficult to study because of its sensitive nature, one early survey found that many managers believed that politics influenced salary and hiring decisions in their firm. Many also believed that the incidence of political behavior was greater at the upper levels of their organization and lesser at the lower levels. More than half of the respondents felt that organizational politics was bad, unfair, unhealthy, and irrational, but most suggested that successful executives have to be good politicians and be political to get ahead.[55]

## Common Political Behaviors

Research has identified four basic forms of political behavior widely practiced in organizations.[56] One form is *inducement*, which occurs when a manager offers to give something to someone else in return for that person's support. For example, a product manager might suggest to another product manager that she will put in a good word with his boss if he supports a new marketing plan that she has developed. By most accounts, former WorldCom CEO Bernard Ebbers made frequent use of this tactic to retain his leadership position in the company. For example, he allowed board members to use the corporate jet whenever they wanted and invested heavily in their pet projects.

A second tactic is *persuasion*, which relies on both emotion and logic. An operations manager wanting to construct a new plant on a certain site might persuade others to support his goal on grounds that are objective and logical (it's less expensive; taxes are lower) as well as subjective and personal. Ebbers also used this approach. For instance, when one board member tried to remove him from his position, he worked behind the scenes to persuade the majority of board members to allow him to stay on.

A third political behavior involves the *creation of an obligation*. For example, one manager might support a recommendation made by another manager for a new advertising campaign. Although he might really have no opinion on the new campaign, he might think that by going along, he is incurring a debt from the other manager and will be able to "call in" that debt when he wants to get something done and needs additional support. Ebbers loaned WorldCom board members money, for example, but then forgave the loans in exchange for their continued support.

*Coercion* is the use of force to get one's way. For example, a manager may threaten to withhold support, rewards, or other resources as a way to influence someone else. This, too, was a common tactic used by Ebbers. He reportedly belittled any board member who dared question him, for example. In the words of one former director, "Ebbers treated you like a prince—as long as you never forgot who was king."[57]

**impression management**
A direct and intentional effort by someone to enhance his or her image in the eyes of others

g-stockstudio/Shutterstock.com

Impression management is a direct and intentional effort to enhance how others see us. While there is nothing wrong with wanting to look good and present ourselves in a positive manner, of course, some people take impression management too far and create unrealistic or false impressions.

## Impression Management

Impression management is a subtle form of political behavior that deserves special mention. Impression management is a direct and intentional effort by someone to enhance his or her image in the eyes of others. People engage in impression management for a variety of reasons. For one thing, they may do so to further their own careers. By making themselves look good, they think they are more likely to receive rewards, to be given attractive job assignments, and to receive promotions. They may also engage in impression management to boost their self-esteem. When people have a solid image in an organization, others make them aware of it through compliments, respect, and so forth. Still another reason people use impression management is in an effort to acquire more power and hence more control.

People try to manage how others perceive them through a variety of mechanisms. Appearance is one of the first things people think of. Hence, a person motivated by impression management will pay close attention to choice of attire, selection of language, and use of manners and body posture. People interested in impression management are also likely to jockey for association only with successful projects. By being assigned to high-profile projects led by highly successful managers, a person can begin to link his or her own name with such projects in the minds of others.

Sometimes people too strongly motivated by impression management become obsessed with it and may resort to dishonest or unethical means. For example, some people have been known to take credit for others' work in an effort to make themselves look better. People have also been known to exaggerate or even falsify their personal accomplishments in an effort to build an enhanced image.[58]

> "Every time I turn around, there is someone sticking their head in my office reminding me what they are doing for me."
>
> —TREVOR TRAINA, SILICON VALLEY ENTREPRENEUR[59]

## Managing Political Behavior

By its very nature, political behavior is tricky to approach in a rational and systematic way. But managers can handle political behavior so that it does not do excessive damage.[60] First, managers should be aware that, even if their actions are not politically motivated, others may assume that they are. Second, by providing subordinates with autonomy, responsibility, challenge, and feedback, managers reduce the likelihood of political behavior by subordinates. Third, managers should avoid using power if they want to avoid charges of political motivation. Fourth, managers should get disagreements out in the open so that subordinates will have less opportunity for political behavior by using conflict for their own purposes. Finally, managers should avoid covert activities. Behind-the-scenes activities give the impression of political intent, even if none really exists.[61] Other guidelines include clearly communicating the bases and processes for performance evaluation, tying rewards directly to performance, and minimizing competition among managers for resources.[62]

Of course, these guidelines are much easier to list than they are to implement. The well-informed manager should not assume that political behavior does not exist or, worse yet, attempt to eliminate it by issuing orders or commands. Instead, the manager must recognize that political behavior exists in virtually all organizations and that it cannot be ignored or stamped out. It can, however, be managed in such a way that it will seldom inflict serious damage on the organization. It may even play a useful role in some situations.[63] For example, a manager may be able to use his or her political influence to stimulate a greater sense of social responsibility or to heighten awareness of the ethical implications of a decision.

☐ All managers need to be familiar with the various forms of political behavior in organizations.

☐ You should also recognize impression management and know when it is acceptable behavior and when it is unacceptable behavior.

**Manager's Checklist** ☑

# Summary of Learning Outcomes and Key Points

1. Describe the nature of leadership and relate leadership to management.

   - As a process, leadership is the use of noncoercive influence to shape the group's or organization's goals, motivate behavior toward the achievement of those goals, and help define group or organization culture.
   - As a property, leadership is the set of characteristics attributed to those who are perceived to be leaders.
   - Leadership and management are often related but are also different.
   - Managers and leaders use legitimate, reward, coercive, referent, and expert power.

2. Discuss and evaluate the two generic approaches to leadership.

   - The trait approach to leadership assumed that some basic trait or set of traits differentiated leaders from nonleaders.
   - The leadership behavior approach to leadership assumed that the behavior of effective leaders was somehow different from the behavior of nonleaders.
   - Research at the University of Michigan and Ohio State University identified two basic forms of leadership behavior—one concentrating on work and performance and the other concentrating on employee welfare and support.
   - The Leadership Grid attempts to train managers to exhibit high levels of both forms of behavior.

3. Identify and describe the major situational approaches to leadership.

   - Situational approaches to leadership recognize that appropriate forms of leadership behavior are not universally applicable and attempt to specify situations in which various behaviors are appropriate.
   - The LPC theory suggests that a leader's behaviors should be either task oriented or relationship oriented, depending on the favorableness of the situation.

   - The path–goal theory suggests that directive, supportive, participative, or achievement-oriented leader behaviors may be appropriate, depending on the personal characteristics of subordinates and the environment.
   - Vroom's decision tree approach maintains that leaders should vary the extent to which they allow subordinates to participate in making decisions as a function of problem attributes.
   - The leader–member exchange model focuses on individual relationships between leaders and followers and on in-group versus out-group considerations.

4. Identify and describe three related approaches to leadership.

   - Related leadership perspectives are
   - the concept of substitutes for leadership
   - charismatic leadership
   - the role of transformational leadership in organizations

5. Describe three emerging approaches to leadership.

   - Emerging approaches include
   - strategic leadership
   - cross-cultural leadership
   - ethical leadership

6. Discuss political behavior in organizations and how it can be managed.

   - Political behavior is another influence process frequently used in organizations.
   - Impression management, one especially important form of political behavior, is a direct and intentional effort by someone to enhance his or her image in the eyes of others.
   - Managers can take steps to limit the effects of political behavior.

# Discussion Questions

## Questions for Review

1. What activities do managers perform? What activities do leaders perform? Do organizations need both managers and leaders? Why or why not?

2. What are the situational approaches to leadership? Briefly describe each and compare and contrast their findings.

3. Describe the subordinate's characteristics, leader behaviors, and environmental characteristics used in path–goal theory. How do these factors combine to influence motivation?

4. In your own words, define political behavior. Describe four political tactics and give an example of each.

## Questions for Analysis

5. Even though the trait approach to leadership has no empirical support, it is still widely used. In your opinion, why is this so? In what ways is the use of the trait approach helpful to those who use it? In what ways is it harmful to those who use it?

6. The behavioral theories of leadership claim that an individual's leadership style is fixed. Do you agree or disagree? Give examples to support your position. The behavioral theories also claim that the ideal style is the same in every situation. Do you agree or disagree? Again, give examples.

7. A few universities are experimenting with alternative approaches, such as allowing students to design their own majors, develop a curriculum for that major, choose professors and design courses, or self-direct and self-evaluate their studies. These are examples of substitutes for leadership. Do you think this will lead to better outcomes for students than a traditional approach? Would you personally like to have that type of alternative approach at your school? Explain your answers.

## Questions for Application

8. Consider the following list of leadership situations. For each situation, describe in detail the kinds of power the leader has. If the leader were the same but the situation changed—for example, if you thought of the president as the head of his family rather than of the military—would your answers change? Why?

   - The president of the United States is commander-in-chief of the U.S. military.
   - An airline pilot is in charge of a particular flight.
   - Fans look up to a movie star.
   - Your teacher is the head of your class.

9. Think about a decision that would affect you as a student. Use Vroom's decision tree approach to decide whether the administrator making that decision should involve students in the decision. Which parts of the model seem most important in making that decision? Why?

10. Describe a time when you or someone you know was part of an in-group or an out-group. What was the relationship between each of the groups and the leader? What was the relationship between the members of the two different groups? What was the outcome of the situation for the leader? For the members of the two groups? For the organization?

# Building Effective Interpersonal Skills

## Exercise Overview

Interpersonal skills refer to your ability to communicate with, understand, and motivate both individuals and groups. This exercise asks you to examine the ways in which your attitudes toward work relationships reflect your political behavior in the workplace.

## Exercise Task

Following is a series of 20 statements. To what extent does each statement describe your use—actual or planned—of the described behavior when you're on the job? To address this question, rate your response to each statement according to the following scale:

| 1 | 2 | 3 | 4 | 5 |
|---|---|---|---|---|
| Rarely | Occasionally | | Usually | |

1. _____ I use personal contacts to get jobs and promotions.
2. _____ I try to find out what's going on in every organizational department.
3. _____ I dress the same way as the people in power and develop the same interests (e.g., watch or play sports, join the same clubs, etc.).
4. _____ I purposely seek contacts and network with higher-level managers.
5. _____ If upper management offered me a raise and promotion requiring me to move to a new location, I'd say yes even if I didn't want to move.
6. _____ I get along with everyone, even people regarded as difficult to get along with.
7. _____ I try to make people feel important by complimenting them.
8. _____ I do favors for other people and ask favors in return, and I thank people, often sending thank-you notes.
9. _____ I work at developing a good working relationship with my supervisor.
10. _____ I ask my supervisor and other people for advice.

11.____ When someone opposes me, I still work to maintain a positive working relationship with that person.

12.____ I'm courteous, positive, and pleasant in my relationships with other people.

13.____ When my supervisor makes a mistake, I never point it out publicly.

14.____ I'm more cooperative (I compromise) than competitive (I try to get my own way).

15.____ I tell the truth.

16.____ I avoid saying negative things about my supervisor or other people behind their backs.

17.____ I work at getting people to know me by name and face by continually introducing myself.

18.____ I ask satisfied customers and other people familiar with my work to let my supervisor know how good a job I'm doing.

19.____ I try to win contests and get prizes, pins, and other awards.

20.____ I send notices of my accomplishments to higher-level managers and such outlets as company newsletters.

## Scoring

1. Add up the 20 numbers in the blanks before all the questions. Your total will range between 20 and 100. This number reflects your overall political behavior: *The higher your score, the greater your political behavior.*

2. Record your score here ____ and on the scale that follows:

   20___30___40___50___60___70___80___90___100
   *Nonpolitical*                 *Political*

3. Now you want to determine your use of political power in *four different areas* (e.g., learning organizational culture, being a team player, etc.). To do this, add up your numbers for each of the following *sets of questions* and then divide by 5. You will then have your average score for each area:

   A. *Learning the organizational culture and getting to know the power players:*

      Questions 1–5 total ____ divided by 5 = ____

   B. *Developing good working relationships, especially with your boss:*

      Questions 6–12 total ____ divided by 5 = ____

   C. *Being a loyal, honest team player:*

      Questions 13–16 total ____ divided by 5 = ____

   D. *Gaining recognition:*

      Questions 16–20 total ____ divided by 5 = ____

*The higher your average score for each set of questions, the greater your use of political power in that area. Do you rate about the same in each area, or do you rate more highly in some areas more than others?*

Adapted from Robert N. Lussier and Christopher F. Achua, *Leadership: Theory, Application, and Skill Development,* 4th ed. (Mason, OH: South-Western Cengage Learning, 2010), pp. 120–121.

# Building Effective Conceptual Skills

## Exercise Overview

Conceptual skills require you to think in the abstract. This exercise introduces you to one approach to assessing leadership skills and relating leadership theory to practice.

## Exercise Background

At any given time, there's no shortage of publications offering practical advice on management and leadership. Recent business bestsellers included such titles as *Good to Great,* by Jim Collins; *First, Break All the Rules,* by Marcus Buckingham; and *The 21 Irrefutable Laws of Leadership,* by John C. Maxwell. Some of these books, such as *Winning,* by former General Electric CEO Jack Welch, are written by managers with years of experience. Others are written by consultants, professors, or reporters.

Granted, a lot of these books—okay, most of them—don't have much theoretical foundation, and many are basically compendiums of opinions and suggestions unsupported by scientific evidence. Even so, many touch upon ideas that may well be worth the time it takes a busy manager to read them.

Thus a real issue for contemporary managers is knowing how to analyze what they read in the popular press and how to separate the practical wheat from the pop-culture chaff. This exercise gives you a little practice in doing just that.

### Exercise Task

1. Visit the *Fortune* magazine website at **www.fortune. com/fortune/quizzes/careers/boss_quiz.html**. Take the leadership-assessment quiz devised by management expert Stephen Covey. Then look at Covey's scoring and comments.

2. Review carefully each question and each suggested answer. Do you see any correlation between Covey's questions and the theoretical models of leadership discussed in this chapter? Which model or models do you think Covey is using? What details in his questions, answers, or both led you to that conclusion?

3. Use the Internet to investigate Covey's background, training, and experience. Does the information that you've gathered give you any clues to Covey's attitudes and opinions about leadership? Do you see any connection between Covey's attitudes and the items on his quiz? Explain.

4. Based on what you've learned from this exercise, how confident are you that Covey's quiz is an accurate measure of leadership ability? Explain.

## Skill-Building Personal Assessment

### Managerial Leader Behavior Questionnaire

**Introduction:** Leadership is often seen as consisting of a set of characteristics that is important for managers in an organization to develop. The following assessment surveys the practices or beliefs that you would apply in a management role—that is, your managerial leadership.

**Instructions:** The following statements refer to different ways in which you might behave in a managerial leadership role. For each statement, indicate how you do behave or how you think you would behave. Describing yourself may be difficult in some cases, but you should force yourself to make a selection. Record your answers next to each statement according to the following scale:

**Rating Scale**

   5  Very descriptive of me
   4  Fairly descriptive of me
   3  Somewhat descriptive of me
   2  Not very descriptive of me
   1  Not descriptive of me at all

1. _____ I emphasize the importance of performance and encourage everyone to make a maximum effort.
2. _____ I am friendly, supportive, and considerate toward others.
3. _____ I offer helpful advice to others on how to advance their careers and encourage them to develop their skills.
4. _____ I stimulate enthusiasm for the work of the group and say things to build the group's confidence.
5. _____ I provide appropriate praise and recognition for effective performance and show appreciation for special efforts and contributions.
6. _____ I reward effective performance with tangible benefits.
7. _____ I inform people about their duties and responsibilities, clarify rules and policies, and let people know what is expected of them.
8. _____ Either alone or jointly with others, I set specific and challenging but realistic performance goals.
9. _____ I provide any necessary training and coaching, or arrange for others to do it.
10. _____ I keep everyone informed about decisions, events, and developments that affect their work.
11. _____ I consult with others before making work-related decisions.
12. _____ I delegate responsibility and authority to others and allow them discretion in determining how to do their work.
13. _____ I plan in advance how to efficiently organize and schedule the work.
14. _____ I look for new opportunities for the group to exploit, propose new undertakings, and offer innovative ideas.

15.____ I take prompt and decisive action to deal with serious work-related problems and disturbances.

16.____ I provide subordinates with the supplies, equipment, support services, and other resources necessary to work effectively.

17.____ I keep informed about the activities of the group and check on its performance.

18.____ I keep informed about outside events that have important implications for the group.

19.____ I promote and defend the interests of the group and take appropriate action to obtain necessary resources for the group.

20.____ I emphasize teamwork and try to promote cooperation, cohesiveness, and identification with the group.

21.____ I discourage unnecessary fighting and bickering within the group and help settle conflicts and disagreements in a constructive manner.

22.____ I criticize specific acts that are unacceptable, find positive things to say, and provide an opportunity for people to offer explanations.

23.____ I take appropriate disciplinary action to deal with anyone who violates a rule, disobeys an order, or has consistently poor performance.

Source: Reprinted with permission from David D. Van Fleet and Gary A. Yukl, *Military Leadership: An Organizational Behavior Perspective*, pp. 38–39. © Emerald Group Publishing.

# Management At Work

## A Critique of Practical Leadership

## "Defining the company's purpose is a leader's—and only a leader's—responsibility."

—ARKADI KUHLMANN, FORMER CEO OF ING DIRECT

ING Direct Canada was launched in 1997 by veteran Canadian banker Arkadi Kuhlmann as a subsidiary of ING Groep NV, a global financial-services corporation headquartered in the Netherlands. It was the first test of a new *direct banking* business model featuring no-frills, high-rate savings accounts that could be accessed online only. Doing away with the costs entailed by a network of branches, ING Direct depended instead on a small network of ING Direct Cafes as face-to-face contact points. The motto was "Sip, surf and save": You could hang out over a specialty coffee and use the free Internet and Wi-Fi services, or you could get help from a bank representative to open a savings account paying 4 percent interest—at least twice as much as anything offered by Canada's biggest banks.

Kuhlmann developed the ING Direct strategy, assembled the leadership team, and served as CEO from 1997 to 2000 (being "re-elected" annually by a vote of the company's employees). The bank broke even in just four years and was well on its way to becoming, by 2008, Canada's largest direct bank. An initial investment of US$50 million had been turned into total assets of US$23 billion. And where was Kuhlmann by this time? In 2000, he left to launch ING Direct USA, taking his strategy, his executive team, and his ideas about leadership with him. The new bank hit break-even after just two years, and after just six, it had become the largest online bank in the much bigger U.S. market, with $92.2 billion in assets.

For Kuhlmann, the opportunity to manage ING Direct Canada provided a perfect situation in which to put his ideas about leadership into action. First and foremost, the bank was founded to launch an innovative business model and, in the process, to disrupt the savings end of the banking industry. As it happens, Kuhlmann already believed that "culture-based leadership is necessary in order to adopt innovative business strategies and to unleash the power of disruptive ideas." He was also convinced that "culture-based leadership" had become the most promising approach to launching and operating a company in the contemporary business environment.

According to Kuhlmann, the critical factor in today's business environment is the simple but pervasive fact of change. Nowadays, he says, the forces of competitive pressure change directions more or less constantly and with relatively little warning. As a result, he says,

*companies' life cycles are getting shorter. … Businesses are successful and not successful over shorter lifetimes. … So the world is getting … more short-cycled, but at the same time, we keep hoping for the silver bullet. You want that one spark in the party, that one hit in the company, that one person to stand up and grab it all, and it's tougher than ever before.*

As Kuhlmann sees it, a new company has to hit the ground running with a strategy to innovate and disrupt: If it doesn't, it risks finding itself in a market that's entered yet another cycle—one in which competitors are already innovating its planned innovation.

So how does a company start out—and stay—innovative and disruptive? The key, says Kuhlmann, is identifying a "cause": "A successful company," he argues, "must have a cause that is bigger and broader than the organization itself." What, for example, was the "cause" that Kuhlmann identified for ING Direct? "When we started the bank in 2000," he recalls, "it was a time when instant gratification and spending without regard for one's ability to pay back the money had enveloped America. It was a recipe for disaster, and we believed that the right thing to do was to set off on a crusade to lead Americans back to the old-fashioned values and saving." Having established a cause, a successful leader must then ensure that it's embodied in the company's "vision," which, for Kuhlmann, means what the company intends to do in order "to make a difference" and "make things better," at least in the environment in which it does business. "An effective vision," he maintains, "has to be one that shakes up the status quo and starts a revolution."

All of this is not as abstract as it may seem. "When we started the company," explains Kuhlmann, "we wanted to start with a big idea. Let's go back to some roots and fundamental values: self-reliance, independence, having a grub stake." At the same time, the "big idea" had to be "important and clear" to the new company's prospective customers, and at ING Direct, says Kuhlmann, "that idea was leading Americans back to savings. We saw that there was too much spending going on. Credit cards had become the opium of consumerism. Let's encourage people to save, we decided, and that has been our mission."

What's the difference between *vision* and *mission?* According to Kuhlmann, "vision is aspirational, and mission is how you hold yourself accountable. Our vision was to lead Americans back to saving. Our mission was to simplify financial products." Being accountable, then, means "walking the talk," as Kuhlmann likes to say—in other words, delivering the actual products that will make things better for targeted customers. Thus the product strategy at ING Direct—both for designing and delivering products—focused on simplicity: "Simplifying financial products," explains Kuhlmann,

> was our tactic for helping people save their money. ... Our model was ... a high-volume, low-margin business. We would target the people ... who we thought needed a better value proposition—that is, more affordable savings. We could offer significantly higher rates if we removed costs from our model. Branches are usually a huge cost ... so we didn't have branches and could pass on the savings to our customers. All our services are provided over the telephone and the Internet. We also opened up several ING Cafes to underscore the idea that opening an account should be as easy as buying a cup of coffee.

None of this, Kuhlmann is quick to point out, is feasible without the right kind of leadership—that is, "culture-driven leadership." A company's leader, he argues, "must come up with the mission statement him- or herself. Defining the company's purpose is a leader's—and only a leader's—responsibility. ... The leader must embody the company's cause, and that includes being responsible for defining it." A successful leader strives to be "a person devoted to a cause [rather] than a manager running a company. ... He or she must be identified with the cause."

In turn, a leader must see to it that the cause is the driving force behind the company's *culture*—the set of values that helps employees understand what the company wants to do and how it goes about accomplishing its goals. If a leader doesn't take responsibility for the company's culture, says Kuhlmann, it "gets created on its own. Or you can direct it in a certain way. ... I believe you need to direct the culture—and let the culture direct the business."

Kuhlmann also thinks that directing the culture is the best way to attract and keep committed employees in an age in which career cycles, like environmental cycles, are shorter. Today, he says, "people that are successful and stay ahead are those that gravitate to a culture that is meaningful for them. They're on a mission. It's not a job." Companies can no longer count on employees to perform their jobs simply out of "corporate loyalty and trust. ... I think right now," says Kuhlmann, "the only reason you would follow me—the *only* reason—is that I would voice the attributes of the culture in a way that you would say, 'Yes, that's meaningful to me. I'm connected to that.'"

## Case Questions

1. First, review the definition and discussion of "The Organization's Culture" in Chapter 3. Then address the following question: What effect is a company's culture likely to have on the efforts of management to practice each of the following approaches to leadership: *LPC theory*, *path-goal theory*, the *decision tree approach*, and the *LMX model?*

2. "The way we look at leaders," says Arkadi Kuhlmann, "has changed, and who we follow has become ever more situational." According to one researcher, *situational leadership*

> *evolved from a task-oriented versus people-oriented continuum … representing the extent that the leader focuses on the required tasks or focuses on relations with followers. … Task-oriented leaders define roles for followers, give definite instructions, create organizational patterns, and establish formal communication channels. In contrast, relation-oriented leaders practice concern for others, attempt to reduce emotional conflicts, seek harmonious relations, and regulate equal participation.* *

First, use this definition of situational leadership to get a sharper focus on the discussion of the topic in the text ("Situational Approaches to Leadership"). Then explain how Kuhlmann's concept of "culture-driven leadership" can be understood within the context of situational approaches to leadership.

3. The same researcher that we quoted in question 1 writes that the *transformational leader* convinces followers to transcend their self-interest for the sake of the organization, while elevating "the followers' level of need on Maslow's hierarchy from lower-level concerns for safety and security to higher-level needs for achievement and self-actualization." Over time, four components of transformational leadership emerged: idealized influence, inspirational motivation, intellectual stimulation, and individualized consideration.

First, review the section in the text on "Transformational Leadership" and, if necessary, the discussion in Chapter 15 of "Maslow's Hierarchy of Needs." Then explain how Kuhlmann's concept of "culture-driven leadership" can be understood within the context of the transformational approach to leadership.

4. What about you? In 2011, Kuhlmann published a book entitled *Rock Then Roll: The Secrets of Culture-Driven Leadership*, which gathers some ideas on management collected over more than a decade at ING Direct. "The book," he says, "is really for a younger audience—people who are really looking around and trying to figure out how to make a difference." He adds that

> *a lot of younger people who join us, starting at the entry level at ING Direct, are not totally motivated by money. It's amazing what percentage say, "Wait a minute, I'm committing time. I'm investing my time, and that means a lot to me." They have a little different focus. If you roll back the calendar a couple of decades, it was all about, "How much money am I going to make?" There are still some people like that, but it's amazing how many people really think about the fact that they're investing time.†*

Kuhlmann implies a spectrum of attitudes toward work life running from "How much money am I going to make?" on the one end to "I'm investing time and that means a lot to me" on the other end. Where would you put yourself on this spectrum? Have you pretty much been at the same place for your adult life, or has your attitude shifted to some degree? In any case, explain how you currently feel about the issue that Kuhlmann raises.

*Jim Allen McClesky, "Situational, Transformational, and Transactional Leadership and Leadership Development," *Journal of Business Studies Quarterly*, 2014, Vol. 4, No. 4, pp. 117–130, http://jbsq.org, on April 22, 2015.

†Chris Barth, "Corporate Culture for the Protest Generation," *Forbes* (December 12, 2011), www.forbes.com, on April 23, 2015.

## Case References

Markus Venzin, *Building an International Financial Services Firm: How Successful Companies Design and Execute Cross-Border Strategies* (New York: Oxford University Press, 2009), https://books.google.com, on April 23, 2015; Jeanne Liedtke, Robert Rosen, and Robert Wiltbank, *The Catalyst: How You Can Become an Extraordinary Growth Leader* (New York: Doubleday, 2009), https://books.google.com, on April 23, 2015; Adrian Ryan, *Beating Low Cost Competition: How Premium Brands Can Respond to Cut-Price Rivals* (Hoboken, NJ: John Wiley & Sons, 2009), https://books.google.com, on April 23, 2015; Arkadi Kuhlmann, "Culture-Driven Leadership," *Ivey Business Journal* (March/April 2010), http://iveybusinessjournal.com, on April 22, 2015; Chris Barth, "Corporate Culture for the Protest Generation," *Forbes* (December 12, 2011), www.forbes.com, on April 23, 2015; Robert Reiss, "Creating a New Kind of Savings Bank," *Forbes* (December 1, 2009), www.forbes.com, on April 24, 2015.

## YOU MAKE THE CALL  Leaders of Oil Repute

1. Carefully review the definition of *leadership* as a *process* in the text. Discuss the failure of BP's response to the Deepwater Horizon disaster as a failure of the company's leaders to manage the leadership process. You may want to refer to Table 16.1, "Distinctions between Management and Leadership," particularly the column labeled "Leadership."

2. According to the *MIT Sloan*-Boston Consulting Group study, Walkers focus heavily on both *sustainability strategy* and *leadership commitment*: "Creating a sustainability strategy," says the report, "is a hallmark of Walkers. … Making sustainability a top-management agenda item is also critical."* Review the definitions of *strategy*, *strategy management*, and *effective strategies* in Chapter 7. Referring to these definitions, explain why sustainability strategy and leadership commitment go hand in hand in an organization's sustainability efforts.

3. A former CEO of a major American corporation has the following to say about BP and the Deepwater Horizon disaster:

   *In the aftershock, the world watched BP and its chief executive, Tony Hayward, make blunder after blunder while crude continued to gush. … BP's talk about caring for the environment was for naught, as its actions failed to match its message. … Recently, a BP-sponsored Gulf Coast tourism TV campaign has implied that everything is back to normal. No doubt, substantial reparative progress has been made. But does the latest ad make you feel any better about the offender?†*

   Let's assume that you've been asked to sit on a panel of randomly selected American consumers convened by BP. The company wants to find out what people like you think about its actions in the wake of Deepwater Horizon. How would you answer the question posed at the end of the preceding quote? How would you explain your response?

4. "At this point," says Edward Lawler III,

   *it's hard to be optimistic about companies engaging in the type of redesign that is needed in order for them to become sustainably effective. … There probably will be some companies that change because their CEOs and senior managers feel it's the right thing to do, but unfortunately they are likely to be the exceptions, not the norm. It is likely that in the foreseeable future, sustainability will continue to get some attention in corporations, but it will not be a major focus or a top priority, and as a result corporations will not have a more positive social and environmental impact.‡*

   How about you? Do you agree or disagree? Explain why you are optimistic or pessimistic.

*John Bell, "The Gulf Spill: BP Still Doesn't Get It," *Forbes* (April 20, 2012), www.forbes.com, on April 8, 2015.

†David Kiron et al., "Sustainability's Next Frontier: Walking the Talk on the Sustainability Issues That Matter Most," *MIT Sloan Management Review* (December 16, 2013), http://sloanreview.mit.edu, on April 7, 2015.

‡"Sustainability Must Be a Top Priority," *Forbes* (October 26, 2011), www.forbes.com, on April 6, 2015.

# Endnotes

1 Clifford Krauss, "Oil Spill's Blow to BP's Image May Eclipse Costs," *New York Times* (April 29, 2010), www.nytimes.com, on April 8, 2015; Nelson Schwartz, "Can BP Bounce Back?" *Fortune* (October 31, 2006), http://archive.fortune.com, on April 9, 2015; Jeffrey Sonnenfeld, "The Real Scandal at BP," *Bloomberg Business* (May 13, 2007), on April 9, 2015; Elizabeth van Cleve, "Survey Says Majority of Americans Believe BP Should Pay Maximum Gulf Oil Spill Fines," Restore the Mississippi Delta (February 6, 2015), www.mississippiriverdelta.org, on April 10, 2015; Jennifer Larino, "BP's Oil Spill Settlement Appeal Rejected by U.S. Supreme Court," New Orleans *Times-Picayune* (December 8, 2014), www.nola.com, on April 10, 2015; Larino, "Federal Judge Rejects BP Bid to Lower $13.7 Billion Oil Spill Fine," New Orleans *Times-Picayune* (February 19, 2015), www.nola.com, on April 10, 2015; Sheila Bonini, Stephan Görner, and Alissa Jones, "How Companies Manage Sustainability: McKinsey Global Survey Results" (McKinsey & Co., March 2010), www.mckinsey.com, on April 6, 2015; "Six Growing Trends in Corporate Sustainability: The 'Tone from the Top' for Sustainability Risks" (Ernst & Young Global Ltd., 2015), www.ey.com, on April 6, 2015; Leon Kaye, "Why Sustainability Is Integral to Enterprise Risk Management," *Triple Pundit* (October 15, 2014), www.triplepundit.com, on April 6, 2015; David Kiron et al., "Sustainability's Next Frontier: Walking the Talk on the Sustainability Issues That Matter Most," *MIT Sloan Management Review* (December 16, 2013), http://sloanreview.mit.edu, on April 7, 2015; Edward E. Lawler III, "Sustainability Must Be a Top Priority," *Forbes* (October 26, 2011), www.forbes.com, on April 6, 2015.

2 See Ronald A. Heifetz and Donald L. Laurie, "The Work of Leadership," *Harvard Business Review*, January–February 1997, pp. 124–134. See also Arthur G. Jago, "Leadership: Perspectives in Theory and Research," *Management Science*, March 1982, pp. 315–336; and "The New Leadership," *BusinessWeek*, August 28, 2000, pp. 100–187.

3  Gary A. Yukl, *Leadership in Organizations*, 7th ed. (Upper Saddle River, NJ: Pearson, 2010), p. 5. See also Bruce J. Avolio, Fred O. Walumbwa, and Todd J. Weber, "Leadership: Current Theories, Research, and Future Decisions," in Susan T. Fiske, Daniel L. Schacter, and Robert J. Sternberg (eds.), *Annual Review of Psychology 2009* (Palo Alto, CA: Annual Reviews, 2009), pp. 421–450; and Julian Barling, Amy Christie, and Colette Hoption, "Leadership," in Sheldon Zedeck (ed.), *Handbook of Industrial and Organizational Psychology*, Vol. 1: *Building and Developing the Organization* (Washington, DC: American Psychological Association, 2010), pp. 183–240.

4  John P. Kotter, "What Leaders Really Do," *Harvard Business Review*, May–June 1990, pp. 103–111 (reprinted in *Harvard Business Review*, December 2001, pp. 85–93). See also Daniel Goleman, "Leadership That Gets Results," *Harvard Business Review*, March–April 2000, pp. 78–88; and Keith Grints, *The Arts of Leadership* (Oxford, UK: Oxford University Press, 2000).

5  John R. P. French and Bertram Raven, "The Bases of Social Power," in Dorwin Cartwright (ed.), *Studies in Social Power* (Ann Arbor, MI: University of Michigan Press, 1959), pp. 150–167.

6  Hugh D. Menzies, "The Ten Toughest Bosses," *Fortune*, April 21, 1980, pp. 62–73.

7  "Managament Secrets From the Meanest Company in America," *Bloomberg BusinessWeek*, January 2, 2014, pp. 46–51.

8  Bennett J. Tepper, "Consequences of Abusive Supervision," *Academy of Management Journal*, 2000, Vol. 43, No. 2, pp. 168–190; see also Bennett J. Tepper, "Abusive Supervision in Work Organizations: Review, Synthesis, and Research Agenda," *Journal of Management*, 2007, Vol. 33, No. 3, pp. 261–289.

9  "Managament Secrets From the Meanest Company in America," *Bloomberg BusinessWeek*, January 2, 2014, p. 48.

10  Thomas A. Stewart, "Get with the New Power Game," *Fortune*, January 13, 1997, pp. 58–62.

11  For more information on the bases and uses of power, see Philip M. Podsakoff and Chester A. Schriesheim, "Field Studies of French and Raven's Bases of Power: Critique, Reanalysis, and Suggestions for Future Research," *Psychological Bulletin*, 1985, Vol. 97, pp. 387–411; Robert C. Benfari, Harry E. Wilkinson, and Charles D. Orth, "The Effective Use of Power," *Business Horizons*, May–June 1986, pp. 12–16; and Yukl, *Leadership in Organizations*.

12  Bernard M. Bass, *Bass & Stogdill's Handbook of Leadership*, 3rd ed. (Riverside, NJ: Free Press, 1990).

13  *Time*, July 21, 2008, p. 46.

14  Shelley A. Kirkpatrick and Edwin A. Locke, "Leadership: Do Traits Matter?" *Academy of Management Executive*, May 1991, pp. 48–60. See also Robert J. Sternberg, "Managerial Intelligence: Why IQ Isn't Enough," *Journal of Management*, 1997, Vol. 23, No. 3, pp. 475–493.

15  Timothy Judge, Amy Colbert, and Remus Ilies, "Intelligence and Leadership: A Quantitative Review and Test of Theoretical Propositions," *Journal of Applied Psychology*, 2004, Vol. 89, No. 3, pp. 542–552.

16  Rensis Likert, *New Patterns of Management* (New York: McGraw-Hill, 1961); Rensis Likert, *The Human Organization* (New York: McGraw-Hill, 1967).

17  The Ohio State studies stimulated many articles, monographs, and books. A good overall reference is Ralph M. Stogdill and A. E. Coons (eds.), *Leader Behavior: Its Description and Measurement* (Columbus, OH: Bureau of Business Research, Ohio State University, 1957).

18  Edwin A. Fleishman, E. F. Harris, and H. E. Burt, *Leadership and Supervision in Industry* (Columbus, OH: Bureau of Business Research, Ohio State University, 1955).

19  See Timothy Judge, Ronald Piccolo, and Remus Ilies, "The Forgotten One? The Validity of Consideration and Initiating Structure in Leadership Research," *Journal of Applied Psychology*, 2004, Vol. 89, No. 1, pp. 36–51.

20  Robert R. Blake and Jane S. Mouton, *The Managerial Grid* (Houston: Gulf Publishing, 1964); Robert R. Blake and Jane S. Mouton, *The Versatile Manager: A Grid Profile* (Homewood, IL: Dow Jones-Irwin, 1981).

21  Robert Tannenbaum and Warren H. Schmidt, "How to Choose a Leadership Pattern," *Harvard Business Review*, March–April 1958, pp. 95–101.

22  Fred E. Fiedler, *A Theory of Leadership Effectiveness* (New York: McGraw-Hill, 1967).

23  Chester A. Schriesheim, Bennett J. Tepper, and Linda A. Tetrault, "Least Preferred Co-Worker Score, Situational Control, and Leadership Effectiveness: A Meta-Analysis of Contingency Model Performance Predictions," *Journal of Applied Psychology*, 1994, Vol. 79, No. 4, pp. 561–573.

24  Fiedler, *A Theory of Leadership Effectiveness*; Fred E. Fiedler and M. M. Chemers, *Leadership and Effective Management* (Glenview, IL: Scott, Foresman, 1974).

25  For recent reviews and updates, see Lawrence H. Peters, Darrell D. Hartke, and John T. Pohlmann, "Fiedler's Contingency Theory of Leadership: An Application of the Meta-Analysis Procedures of Schmidt and Hunter," *Psychological Bulletin*, Vol. 97, pp. 274–285; and Fred E. Fiedler, "When to Lead, When to Stand Back," *Psychology Today*, September 1987, pp. 26–27.

26  Martin G. Evans, "The Effects of Supervisory Behavior on the Path-Goal Relationship," *Organizational Behavior and Human Performance*, May 1970, pp. 277–298; Robert J. House and Terence R. Mitchell, "Path-Goal Theory of Leadership," *Journal of Contemporary Business*, Autumn 1974, pp. 81–98. See also Yukl, *Leadership in Organizations*.

27  For a recent review, see J. C. Wofford and Laurie Z. Liska, "Path-Goal Theories of Leadership: A Meta-Analysis," *Journal of Management*, 1993, Vol. 19, No. 4, pp. 857–876.

28  See Victor H. Vroom and Philip H. Yetton, *Leadership and Decision Making* (Pittsburgh: University of Pittsburgh Press, 1973); and Victor H. Vroom and Arthur G. Jago, *The New Leadership* (Englewood Cliffs, NJ: Prentice-Hall, 1988).

29  Victor Vroom, "Leadership and the Decision-Making Process," *Organizational Dynamics*, 2000, Vol. 28, No. 4, pp. 82–94.

30  Vroom and Jago, *The New Leadership*.

31  Ibid.

32  See Madeline E. Heilman, Harvey A. Hornstein, Jack H. Cage, and Judith K. Herschlag, "Reaction to Prescribed Leader Behavior as a Function of Role Perspective: The Case of the Vroom-Yetton Model," *Journal of Applied Psychology*, February 1984, pp. 50–60; R. H. George Field, "A Test of the Vroom-Yetton Normative Model of Leadership," *Journal of Applied Psychology*, February 1982, pp. 523–532.

33  George Graen and J. F. Cashman, "A Role-Making Model of Leadership in Formal Organizations: A Developmental Approach," in J. G. Hunt and L. L. Larson (eds.), *Leadership Frontiers* (Kent, OH: Kent State University Press, 1975), pp. 143–165; Fred Dansereau, George Graen, and W. J. Haga, "A Vertical Dyad Linkage Approach to Leadership Within Formal Organizations: A Longitudinal Investigation of the Role-Making Process," *Organizational Behavior and Human Performance*, 1975, Vol. 15, pp. 46–78.

34  See Kathryn Sherony and Stephen Green, "Coworker Exchange: Relationships Between Coworkers, Leader-Member Exchange, and Work Attitudes," *Journal of Applied Psychology*, 2002, Vol. 87, No. 3, pp. 542–548.

35  See Bruce J. Avolio, Fred O. Walumbwa, and Todd J. Weber, "Leadership: Current Theories, Research, and Future Directions," in Susan T. Fiske, Daniel L. Schacter, and Robert Sternberg (eds.), *Annual Review of Psychology 2009* (Palo Alto, CA: Annual Reviews, 2009), pp. 421–450.

36  Steven Kerr and John M. Jermier, "Substitutes for Leadership: Their Meaning and Measurement," *Organizational Behavior and Human Performance*, December 1978, pp. 375–403.

37  See Charles C. Manz and Henry P. Sims, Jr., "Leading Workers to Lead Themselves: The External Leadership of Self-Managing Work Teams," *Administrative Science Quarterly*, March 1987, pp. 106–129. See also "Living Without a Leader," *Fortune*, March 20, 2000, pp. 218–219.

38  See Robert J. House, "A 1976 Theory of Charismatic Leadership," in J. G. Hunt and L. L. Larson (eds.), *Leadership: The Cutting Edge* (Carbondale, IL: Southern Illinois University Press, 1977), pp. 189–207. See also Jay A. Conger and Rabindra N. Kanungo, "Toward a Behavioral Theory of Charismatic Leadership in Organizational Settings," *Academy of Management Review*, October 1987, pp. 637–647.

39  David A. Nadler and Michael L. Tushman, "Beyond the Charismatic Leader: Leadership and Organizational Change," *California Management Review*, Winter 1990, pp. 77–97.

40  Jane Howell and Boas Shamir, "The Role of Followers in the Charismatic Leadership Process: Relationships and Their Consequences," *Academy of Management Review*, 2005, Vol. 30, No. 1, pp. 96–112.

41  James MacGregor Burns, *Leadership* (New York: Harper & Row, 1978). See also Rajnandini Pillai, Chester A. Schriesheim, and Eric J. Williams, "Fairness Perceptions and Trust as Mediators for Transformational and Transactional Leadership: A Two-Sample Study," *Journal of Management*, 1999, Vol. 25, No. 6, pp. 897–933.

42  Robert Rubin, David Munz, and William Bommer, "Leading from Within: The Effects of Emotion Recognition and Personality on Transformational Leadership Behaviors," *Academy of Management Journal*, 2005, Vol. 48, No. 5, pp. 845–858.

43  Kenneth Labich, "The Seven Keys to Business Leadership," *Fortune*, October 24, 1998, pp. 55–61.

44  *BusinessWeek*, January 10, 2005, p. 62.

45  Dusya Vera and Mary Crossan, "Strategic Leadership and Organizational Learning," *Academy of Management Review*, 2004, Vol. 29, No. 2, pp. 222–240; see also Cynthia A. Montgomery, "Putting Leadership Back into Strategy," *Harvard Business Review*, January 2008, pp. 54-63.

46  "The Best Performing CEOs in the World," *Harvard Business Review*, January–February 2010.

47  "Which of These 9 Grossly Overpaid CEOs Are Worth It?" *seekingalpha.com*, April 20, 2014; "CEO Mike Jeffries Overvalues His Own Brand and Loses His Cool," *About.com*, September 7, 2014; "Leadership Secrets of the Great CEOs," *Bloomberg BusinessWeek*, December 15–December 21, 2014, p. 10.

48  "3M's Buckley Lifts Spending, Fights 'Zombie' Products," *BusinessWeek*, December 22, 2014, pp. 46-47.

49  http://www.foxbusiness.com/business-leaders/2012/04/17/business-leaders-pepsicos-indra-nooyi/, accessed on June 15, 2015.

50  See Kurt Dirks and Donald Ferrin, "Trust in Leadership," *Journal of Applied Psychology*, 2002, Vol. 87, No. 4, pp. 611–628. See also Russell A. Eisenstat, Michael Beer, Nathanial Foote, Tobias Fredberg, and Flemming Norrgren, "The Uncompromising Leader," *Harvard Business Review*, July–August 2008, pp. 51–59.

51  *USA Today*, April 25, 2005, p. 1B.

52  Jeffrey Pfeffer, *Power in Organizations* (Marshfield, MA: Pitman, 1981), p. 7.

53  Gerald R. Ferris and Wayne A. Hochwarter, "Organizational Politics," in Sheldon Zedeck (ed.), *Handbook of Industrial and Organizational Psychology*, Vol. 3: *Maintaining, Expanding, and Contracting the Organization* (Washington, DC: American Psychological Association, 2010), pp. 435–459.

54  http://www.nytimes.com/2013/01/13/business/harmans-chief-on-how-to-reduce-office-politics.html, accessed June 15, 2015.

55  Victor Murray and Jeffrey Gandz, "Games Executives Play: Politics at Work," *Business Horizons*, December 1980, pp. 11–23; Jeffrey Gandz and Victor Murray, "The Experience of Workplace Politics," *Academy of Management Journal*, June 1980, pp. 237–251.

56  Don R. Beeman and Thomas W. Sharkey, "The Use and Abuse of Corporate Power," *Business Horizons*, March–April 1987, pp. 26–30.

57  "How Ebbers Kept the Board in His Pocket," *BusinessWeek*, October 14, 2002, pp. 138–139.

58  See William L. Gardner, "Lessons in Organizational Dramaturgy: The Art of Impression Management," *Organizational Dynamics*, Summer 1992, pp. 51–63; Elizabeth Wolf Morrison and Robert J. Bies, "Impression Management in the Feedback-Seeking Process: A Literature Review and Research Agenda," *Academy of Management Review*, July 1991, pp. 522–541; Mark C. Bolino, K. Michele Kacmar, William H. Turnley, and J. Bruce Gilstrap, "A Multi-Level Review of Impression Management Motives and Behaviors," *Journal of Management*, 2008, Vol. 34, No. 6, pp. 1080–1109.

59  *BusinessWeek*, April 13, 2009, p. 54.

60  See Chad Higgins, Timothy Judge, and Gerald Ferris, "Influence Tactics and Work Outcomes: A Meta-Analysis," *Journal of Organizational Behavior*, 2003, Vol. 24, pp. 89–106; and Gerald R. Ferris, Darren C. Treadway, Pamela L. Perrewe, Robyn L. Brour, Ceasar Douglas, and Sean Lux, "Political Skill in Organizations," *Journal of Management*, 2007, Vol. 33, No. 3, pp. 290–320.

61  Murray and Gandz, "Games Executives Play."

62  Beeman and Sharkey, "The Use and Abuse of Corporate Power."

63  Stefanie Ann Lenway and Kathleen Rehbein, "Leaders, Followers, and Free Riders: An Empirical Test of Variation in Corporate Political Involvement," *Academy of Management Journal*, December 1991, pp. 89

©Markus Pfaff/Shutterstock.com

# 17

# MANAGING INTERPERSONAL RELATIONS AND COMMUNICATION

**Learning Outcomes**

**After studying this chapter, you should be able to:**

1. Describe the interpersonal nature of organizations.

2. Describe the role and importance of communication in the manager's job.

3. Identify the basic forms of communication in organizations.

4. Discuss informal communication, including its various forms and types.

5. Describe how the communication process can be managed to recognize and overcome barriers.

## MANAGEMENT IN ACTION   Buzz Words

"Having nearly 50,000 people all on the same page and moving in the same direction is quite important to me."

—BRUCE BROUSSARD, CEO OF HUMANA

In 2008, Humana, a health insurer based in Louisville, Kentucky, decided that it needed to improve internal communications. In particular, the company wanted to facilitate information sharing among departments, but because the process would by definition cut across existing organizational boundaries, the team charged with implementing the system decided to proceed cautiously. They started by installing a new *social network service* called Yammer in order to build an internal communications network. At the time, Jeff Ross was working with Humana's Enterprise Innovation team. "We wanted to experiment with the idea of enterprise social networking in general," he recalls, "and see if there was something useful in it.[1]

"We let it grow virally for about a year," adds Ross, and when it proved popular among company employees, the team decided to go forward with a full-fledged *enterprise social network* (*ESN*), which is basically an online social network for use in a business context. First, however, they had to sell top management on the idea of an ESN. "At that point," Ross explains, "we were hierarchical, very traditional, top-down. We needed to connect without going through a lot of hoopla." Not surprisingly, the team's chief selling point was the value of an ESN in addressing specific business issues. Fortunately, says Ross, both the issues and the value of an ESN were pretty clear: "We knew that we needed a way to communicate more quickly across business areas to help reduce the duplication of effort that occurs when different departments pursue the same things, such as purchasing, developing products, training, and so forth. We wanted a way to speed up that direct communication across business areas."

Once upper management had bought into the idea, Ross and his team had to select an ESN provider. Naturally, they focused on platforms that would provide a required feature set, including applications for discussions, topic groups, and private messaging. By the end of 2009, they had settled on Socialcast, which, rebranded as "Buzz," was launched in 2010. By 2013, nearly 30,000 of Humana's 50,000 employees were active users. They had created more than 1,200 groups, both business and non-business related, and were generating 6,000 to 7,000 posts per week.

"We have two official purposes for Buzz," reports Ross, who's now Community Manager for Enterprise Social Media. "The first one is to help us accomplish our business objectives, and the second one is to help us establish positive interpersonal relationships around areas of mutual interest." As for the application of the ESN to business objectives, Ross says that "it's up to individuals, teams, and departments to determine how best to use Buzz to accomplish their own business purposes." In practice, he adds, "Buzz provides a 'water-cooler-conversation' experience across the enterprise. Employees use it to avoid long, time-wasting email chains, and new employees can use it to engage rapidly and to accelerate their integration into the company culture. Buzz is also used for ideation to increase efficiencies" (i.e., for brainstorming about ways to save money).

Humana, a large health insurer, is using social media in a variety of different ways to promote wellness and healthy lifestyles.

kstudija/Shutterstock.com

Buzz has proved to be especially useful in facilitating Q&A and feedback from companywide events that Humana calls "Buzz Town Halls." Every quarter, for example, CEO Bruce Broussard hosts a Leadership Meeting for more than 5,000 company managers. A simultaneous Socialcast Town Hall is available to 40,000 employees, who can assess the presentations and post questions that Broussard addresses directly. In a practical sense, says Ross, the value of Socialcast events "is that the Q&A is captured, archived, and available for people to go back at a later date and review." As CEO, Broussard also sees a bigger picture in which the company's strategic objectives are in sync with the activities of the people responsible for achieving them. Asked in one meeting about the cost of the company's ESN, Broussard replied that he didn't know exactly, "but I know that having nearly 50,000 people all on the same page and moving in the same direction is quite important to me."

The CEO is also a regular contributor to a popular topic group dedicated to health and wellness. According to Ross, Broussard, a veteran triathlete, "is very active in terms of conversing about physical fitness, which is important to our company since we're in the health industry. For example, when he's running or biking, he uploads photos and shares his sports activities. Sometimes his conversations are business related, while some are more personal, health-oriented kinds of encouragement."

Broussard's presence on Buzz does more than "humanize" the CEO and furnish him with workplace credibility: It not only reinforces his key role in the development of the company's culture, but also anchors his strategy of sharing the company's culture and mission with the 13.8 million people that Humana insures. Broussard believes that both the healthcare and health-insurance industries are becoming more consumer oriented.

"The discussion," he says, is changing from "worrying about how people are being treated to how you can keep them healthier. … We believe our role in the insurance industry is to shift perceptions and move beyond being simply a provider to empowering our members and helping them live healthy, active, and rewarding lives."

By "members" Broussard means both Humana's employees and its customers. In late 2012, for example, the company launched its "Humana Hope Campaign" with an introductory Town Hall event. Employees were asked to post personal goals for improving their health—physical, emotional, spiritual, or financial—in the coming year. They were also asked to designate individuals to hold them to their goals, typically people outside Humana. Consequently, the campaign helped the company get its story out by means of an external social media campaign. "It was something that resonated," recalls Humana social media strategist Chuck Stephens. "We had people all over the country sending us updates and photos and commenting on their marathon completions or before-and-after photos of weight loss."

Obviously, Humana's social media strategy calls for the integration of internal and external communications. In 2011, Jeff Ross moved the newly launched Buzz ESN from its original home in the IT department to the Digital Marketing Group, which already handled external social media, thus putting both areas of the company's social media in the hands of a single team. He remains convinced, however, that maintaining an ESN needs a "community manager"—that is, someone with a job like his. "Somebody's got to own that baby," he argues, "and be driven to increase awareness and the telling of success stories.… It's not something you tack on to a full time job. It deserves its own role."

Organizations today are continually looking for ways to improve communication among their employees, customers, and other stakeholders. Many, like Humana, are looking to social media platforms and digital technology to take the next step in the evolution of communication. But communication has always been a vital part of managerial work. Indeed, managers around the world agree that communication is one of their most important tasks. It is important for them to communicate with others in order to convey their vision and goals for the organization. And it's important for others to communicate with them so that they will better understand what is going on in their environment and how they and their organization can become more effective.

This chapter is the first of two that focuses on interpersonal processes in organizations. We first establish the interpersonal nature of organizations and then discuss communication, one of the most basic forms of interaction among people. We begin by examining communication in the context of the manager's job. We then identify and discuss forms of interpersonal, group, and organizational communication. After discussing informal means of communication, we describe how organizational communication can be effectively managed. In our next chapter, we discuss other elements of interpersonal relations: group and team processes and conflict.

# The Interpersonal Nature of Organizations

In Chapter 1, we noted how much of a manager's job involves scheduled and unscheduled meetings, telephone calls, e-mail, and related activities. Indeed, a great deal of what all managers do involves interacting with other people, both directly and indirectly and both inside and outside of the organization. The schedule that follows is a typical day for the president of a Houston-based company. He kept a log of his activities for several different days so that you could better appreciate the nature of managerial work.

6:00–6:30 A.M. Read and respond to e-mail from home; scan major news stories online.

7:45–8:15 A.M. Arrive at work; review hardcopy mail sorted by assistant.

8:15–8:30 A.M. Scan digital version of the *Wall Street Journal*; read and respond to e-mail; scan cnn.com for business news and updates.

8:30–9:00 A.M. Meet with labor officials and plant manager to resolve minor labor disputes.

9:00–9:30 A.M. Review internal report; read and respond to new e-mail; read and respond to new text messages.

9:30–10:00 A.M. Meet with two marketing executives to review advertising campaign; instruct them to fax approvals to advertising agency.

10:00–11:30 A.M. Meet with company executive committee to discuss strategy, budgetary issues, and competition (this committee meets weekly).

11:30–12:00 noon. Send several e-mails; read and respond to new e-mail and texts.

12:00–1:15 P.M. Lunch with the financial vice president and two executives from another subsidiary of the parent corporation. Primary topic of discussion is the Houston Rockets basketball team. Place three hands-free phone calls en route to lunch and receive one call en route back to office.

1:15–1:45 P.M. Meet with human resource director and assistant about a recent OSHA inspection; establish a task force to investigate the problems identified and to suggest solutions.

1:45–2:00 P.M. Read and respond to new e-mail and texts.

2:00–2:30 P.M. Skype with four other company presidents.

2:30–3:00 P.M. Meet with financial vice president about a confidential issue that came up at lunch (unscheduled).

3:00–3:30 P.M. Work alone in office; read and respond to new e-mail and texts; send several e-mails and texts.

3:30–4:15 P.M. Meet with a group of sales representatives and the company purchasing agent.

4:15–5:30 P.M. Work alone in office.

5:30–7:00 P.M. Play racquetball at nearby athletic club with marketing vice president.

9:00–9:30 P.M. Read and respond to e-mail and texts from home; send text to assistant about an emergency meeting to be scheduled for the next day.

How did this manager spend his time? He spent most of it working, communicating, and interacting with other people. And this compressed daily schedule does not include several other brief telephone calls, brief conversations with his assistant, and brief conversations with other managers. Clearly, interpersonal relations, communication, and group processes are a pervasive part of all organizations and a vital part of all managerial activities.[2]

## Interpersonal Dynamics

The nature of interpersonal relations in an organization is as varied as the individual members themselves.[3] At one extreme, interpersonal relations can be personal and positive. This occurs when the parties know each other, have mutual respect and affection, and enjoy interacting.

Interpersonal dynamics pervade virtually every facet of organizations. People talk, exchange facial expressions, message, text, or email throughout their work days. In general, interpersonal relations can range from personal and positive to personal and negative or anywhere in between.

"You have to read people quickly to fit into the social network."

—STEPHEN MILES, EXECUTIVE COACH[4]

Two managers who have known each other for years, play golf together on weekends, and are close personal friends will likely interact at work in a positive fashion. At the other extreme, interpersonal dynamics can be personal but negative. This is most likely when the parties dislike each other, do not have mutual respect, and do not enjoy interacting. Suppose a manager has fought openly for years to block the promotion of another manager within the organization. Over the objections of the first manager, however, the other manager eventually gets promoted to the same rank. When the two of them must interact, it will most likely be in a negative manner.

Most interactions fall between these extremes, as members of the organization interact in a professional way focused primarily on goal accomplishment. The interaction deals with the job at hand, is relatively formal and structured, and is task directed. Two managers may respect each other's work and recognize the professional competence that each brings to the job. However, they may also have few common interests and little to talk about besides the job they are doing. These different types of interactions may occur between individuals, between groups, or between individuals and groups, and they can change over time. The two managers in the second scenario, for example, might decide to bury the hatchet and adopt a detached, professional manner. The two managers in the third example could find more common ground than they anticipated and evolve to a personal and positive interaction.

## Outcomes of Interpersonal Behaviors

A variety of things can happen as a result of interpersonal behaviors.[5] Recall from Chapter 15, for example, that many perspectives on motivation suggest that people have social needs. Interpersonal relations in organizations can be a primary source of need satisfaction for many people. For a person with a strong need for affiliation, high-quality interpersonal relations can be an important positive element in the workplace. However, when this same person is confronted with poor-quality working relationships, the effect can be just as great in the other direction.

Interpersonal relations also serve as a solid basis for social support. Suppose that an employee receives a poor performance evaluation or is denied a promotion. Others in the organization can lend support because they share a common frame of reference—an understanding of the causes and consequences of what happened. Good interpersonal relations throughout an organization can also be a source of synergy. People who support one another and who work well together can accomplish much more than people who do not support one another and who do not work well together. Another outcome, implied earlier, is conflict—people may leave an interpersonal exchange feeling angry or hostile. But a common thread is woven through all of these outcomes—communication between people in the organization.[6]

 **Manager's Checklist**

☐ Managers should be aware of the various kinds of interpersonal interactions that can be identified in organizational settings.

☐ You should have an appreciation of how much of your daily life involves interacting with other people.

# Communication and the Manager's Job

As evidenced by the daily log presented earlier, a typical day for a manager includes doing desk work, attending scheduled meetings, placing and receiving telephone calls, reading and answering correspondence (both print and digital), attending unscheduled meetings, and making tours. Most of these activities involve communication. In fact, managers usually spend over half their time on some form of communication. Communication always involves two or more people, so other behavioral processes, such as motivation, leadership, and group and team interactions, all come into play. Top executives must handle communication effectively if they are to be true leaders.[7]

## A Definition of Communication

Imagine three managers working in an office building. The first is all alone but is nevertheless yelling for a subordinate to come help. No one appears, but he continues to yell. The second is talking to a subordinate on a cellphone, but a poor signal causes the subordinate to misunderstand some important numbers being provided by the manager. As a result, the subordinate sends 1,500 crates of eggs to 150 Fifth Street, when he should have sent 150 crates of eggs to 1500 Fifteenth Street. The third manager is talking in her office with a subordinate who clearly hears and understands what is being said. Each of these managers is attempting to communicate, but with different results.

Communication and effective communication are not necessarily the same thing. This man is reading a document, so communication is taking place. At the same time, though, his expression suggests that the communication may not be effective. He may not understand the message, for instance, or he may be angered or confused by it.

Communication is the process of transmitting information from one person to another. Did any of our three managers communicate? The last did, and the first did not. How about the second? In fact, she did communicate. She transmitted information, and information was received. The problem was that the message transmitted and the message received were not the same. The words spoken by the manager were distorted by static and noise. Effective communication, then, is the process of sending a message in such a way that the message received is as close in meaning as possible to the message intended. Although the second manager engaged in communication, it was not effective.

Our definition of effective communication is based on the ideas of meaning and consistency of meaning. Meaning is the idea that the individual who initiates the communication exchange wishes to convey. In effective communication, the meaning is transmitted in such a way that the receiving person understands it. For example, consider these messages:

1. The high today will be only 40 degrees.
2. It will be cold today.
3. Ceteris paribus.
4. Xn1gp bo5cz4ik ab19.

You probably understand the meaning of the first statement. The second statement may seem clear at first, but it is somewhat less clear than the first statement because cold is a relative condition and the word can mean different things to different people. Fewer still understand the third statement, because it is written in Latin. None of you understands the last statement because it is written in a secret code that your author developed as a child.

**communication**
The process of transmitting information from one person to another

**effective communication**
The process of sending a message in such a way that the message received is as close in meaning as possible to the message intended

Andrey_Popov/Shutterstock.com

## The Role of Communication in Management

We noted earlier the variety of activities that fill a manager's day. Meetings, telephone calls, and various kinds of correspondence are all a necessary part of every manager's job—and all clearly involve communication. To better understand the linkages between communication and management, recall the variety of roles that managers must fill. Each of the 10 basic managerial roles discussed in Chapter 1 would be impossible to fill without communication.[8] Interpersonal roles involve interacting with supervisors, subordinates, peers, and others outside the organization. Decisional roles require managers to seek out information to use in making decisions and then communicate those decisions to others. Informational roles focus specifically on acquiring and disseminating information.

Communication also relates directly to the basic management functions of planning, organizing, leading, and controlling. Environmental scanning, integrating planning-time horizons, and decision making, for example, all necessitate communication. Delegation, coordination, and organization change and development also entail communication. Developing reward systems and interacting with subordinates as a part of the leading function would be impossible without some form of communication. And communication is essential to establishing standards, monitoring performance, and taking corrective actions as a part of control. Clearly, then, communication is a pervasive part of virtually all managerial activities.[9]

## The Communication Process

Figure 17.1 illustrates how communication generally takes place between people. The process of communication begins when one person (the sender) wants to transmit a fact, idea, opinion, or other information to someone else (the receiver). This fact, idea, or opinion has meaning to

---

### FIGURE 17.1   THE COMMUNICATION PROCESS

As the figure shows, noise can disrupt the communication process at any step. Managers must therefore understand that a conversation in the next office, a fax machine out of paper, and the receiver's worries may all thwart the manager's best attempts to communicate.

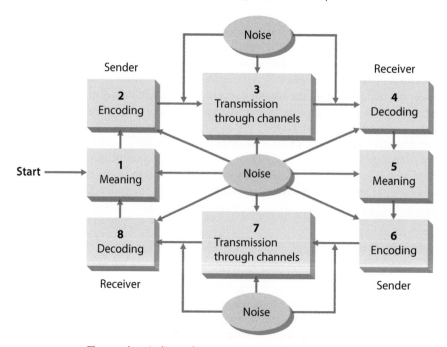

*The numbers indicate the sequence in which steps take place.*

the sender, whether it be simple and concrete or complex and abstract. For example, Linda Porter, a marketing representative at Canon, recently landed a new account and wanted to tell her boss about it. This fact and her motivation to tell her boss represented meaning.

The next step is to encode the meaning into a form appropriate to the situation. The encoding might take the form of words, facial expressions, gestures, or even artistic expressions and physical actions. For example, the Canon representative might have said, "I just landed the Acme account," "We just got some good news from Acme," "I just spoiled Xerox's day," "Acme just made the right decision," or any number of other things. She actually chose the second message. Clearly, the encoding process is influenced by the content of the message, the familiarity of sender and receiver, and other situational factors.

After the message has been encoded, it is transmitted through the appropriate channel or medium. The channel by which this encoded message is being transmitted to you is the printed page. Common channels in organizations include meetings, e-mail or text messages, memos, letters, reports, and telephone calls. Linda Porter might have written her boss a note, sent him an e-mail or text, called him on the telephone, or dropped by his office to convey the news. Because both she and her boss were out of the office when she got the news, she sent him a text.

After the message is received, it is decoded back into a form that has meaning for the receiver. As noted earlier, the consistency of this meaning can vary dramatically. Upon hearing about the Acme deal, the sales manager at Canon might have thought, "This'll mean a big promotion for both of us," "This is great news for the company," or "She's blowing her own horn too much again." His actual feelings were closest to the second statement. In many cases, the meaning prompts a response, and the cycle is continued when a new message is sent by the same steps back to the original sender. The manager might have called the sales representative to offer congratulations, written her a personal note of praise, offered praise in an e-mail or text, or sent a formal letter of acknowledgment. Lin-

da's boss sent her a text and then wrote her a personal note as a follow-up.

"Noise" may disrupt communication anywhere along the way. Noise can be the sound of someone coughing, a truck driving by, or two people talking close at hand. It can also include disruptions such as a letter lost in the mail, a dead telephone line, an interrupted cellphone call, an e-mail misrouted or infected with a virus, a text not being received because of poor service, or one of the participants in a conversation being called away before the communication process is completed. If the note written by Linda's boss had gotten lost, she might have felt unappreciated. As it was, his actions positively reinforced not only her efforts at Acme but also her effort to keep him informed. Another form of noise might be difficulties in understanding messages due to language barriers.

Communication is often a cyclical process involving information passing back and forth between participants. These colleagues are discussing information as they work to solve a problem. They both appear to be actively engaged in the process.

*Monkey Business Images/Shutterstock.com*

---

☐ Managers should recognize the difference between communication and effective communication.

☐ You should also understand the basic elements of the communication process, especially the role of noise.

**Manager's Checklist**

# Forms of Communication in Organizations

Managers need to understand several kinds of communication that are common in organizations today.[10] These include interpersonal communication, communication in networks and teams, organizational communication, and electronic communication.

## Interpersonal Communication

Interpersonal communication generally takes one of two forms: oral and written. As we will see, each has clear strengths and weaknesses.

**Oral Communication** Oral communication takes place in conversations, group discussions, telephone calls, Skype and FaceTime, and other situations in which the spoken word is used to express meaning. Oral communication is so prevalent for several reasons. The primary advantage of oral communication is that it promotes prompt feedback and interchange in the form of verbal questions or agreement, facial expressions, and gestures. Oral communication is also easy (all the sender needs to do is talk), and it can be done with little preparation (though careful preparation is advisable in certain situations). The sender does not need pencil and paper, a printer, or other equipment. In one survey, 55 percent of the executives sampled felt that their own written communication skills were fair or poor, so they chose oral communication to avoid embarrassment![11]

However, oral communication also has drawbacks. It may suffer from problems of inaccuracy if the speaker chooses the wrong words to convey meaning or leaves out pertinent details, if noise disrupts the process, or if the receiver forgets part of the message.[12] In a two-way discussion, there is seldom time for a thoughtful, considered response or for introducing many new facts, and there is no permanent record of what has been said. In addition, although most managers are comfortable talking to people individually or in small groups, fewer enjoy speaking to larger audiences.[13]

**Written Communication** "Putting it in writing" in a letter, report, memorandum, handwritten note, or e-mail or text message can solve many of the problems inherent in oral communication. Nevertheless, and perhaps surprisingly, written communication is not as common as one might imagine, nor is it a mode of communication much respected by managers. Over 80 percent of the managers who responded to one survey indicated that the written communication they received was of fair or poor quality.[14] In a different study, 65 percent of the executives surveyed indicated they preferred to interact with customers, business partners, and vendors with e-mail or text messaging rather than by phone.[15]

The biggest single drawback of traditional forms of written communication is that they inhibit feedback and interchange. When one manager sends another manager a letter, it must be written or dictated, printed, mailed, received, routed, opened, and read. If there is a misunderstanding, it may take several days for it to be recognized, let alone rectified. Although the use of e-mail or texts is, of course, much faster, both sender and receiver must still have access to a computer or other device, and the receiver must open and read the message for it to actually be received. A phone call could settle the whole matter in just a few minutes. Thus written communication often inhibits feedback and interchange and is usually more difficult and time consuming than oral communication.

Of course, written communication offers some advantages. It is often very accurate and provides a permanent record of the exchange. The sender can take the time to collect and assimilate the information and can draft and revise it before it is transmitted. The receiver can take the time to read it carefully and can refer to it repeatedly, as needed. For these reasons, written communication is generally preferable when important details are involved. At times it is important to one or both parties to have a written record available as evidence of exactly what took place. Julie Regan, founder of Toucan-Do, an importing company based in Honolulu, relies heavily on formal business letters in establishing contacts and buying

**oral communication**
Face-to-face conversation, group discussions, telephone calls, and other circumstances in which the spoken word is used to transmit meaning

**written communication**
Memos, letters, reports, notes, and other circumstances in which the written word is used to transmit meaning

merchandise from vendors in Southeast Asia. She believes that such letters give her an opportunity to carefully think through what she wants to say, tailor her message to each person, and avoid later misunderstandings.

**Choosing the Right Form**  Which form of interpersonal communication should the manager use? The best medium will be determined by the situation. Oral communication, e-mail, or text messaging is often preferred when the message is personal, nonroutine, and brief. More formal written communication is usually best when the message is more impersonal, routine, and longer. And, given the prominent role that e-mails have played in several recent court cases, managers should always use discretion when sending messages electronically.[16] For example, private e-mails made public during legal proceedings have played major roles in litigation involving Enron, Tyco, WorldCom, and Morgan Stanley.[17]

The manager can also combine media to capitalize on the advantages of each. For example, a quick phone call to set up a meeting is easy and gets an immediate response. Following up the call with a reminder e-mail, digital meeting invitation, or handwritten note helps ensure that the recipient will remember the meeting, and it provides a record of the meeting's having been called. Digital communication, discussed more fully later, blurs the differences between oral and written communication and can help each be more effective. In some instances, digital communication itself is also the most appropriate way to send a message.

> "I'm not a big e-mailer. I prefer face-to-face whenever possible."
>
> —A. G. LAFLEY, FORMER PROCTER & GAMBLE CHAIRMAN[18]

## Communication in Networks and Work Teams

Although communication among team members in an organization is clearly interpersonal in nature, substantial research also focuses specifically on how people in networks and work teams communicate with one another. A communication network is the pattern through which the members of a group or team communicate. Researchers studying group dynamics have identified several typical networks in groups and teams consisting of three, four, and five members. Representative networks among members of five-member teams are shown in Figure 17.2.[19]

In the wheel pattern, all communication flows through one central person, who is probably the group's leader. In a sense, the wheel is the most centralized network because one person receives and disseminates all information. The Y pattern is slightly less centralized—two people are close to the center. The chain offers a more even flow of information among members, although two people (the ones at each end) interact with only one other person. This path is closed in the circle pattern. Finally, the all-channel network, the most

**communication network**
The pattern through which the members of a group communicate

---

## FIGURE 17.2  TYPES OF COMMUNICATION NETWORKS

Research on communication networks has identified five basic networks for five-person groups. These networks vary in terms of information flow, position of the leader, and effectiveness for different types of tasks. Managers might strive to create centralized networks when group tasks are simple and routine. Alternatively, managers can foster decentralized groups when group tasks are complex and nonroutine.

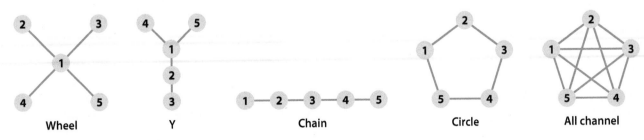

decentralized, allows a free flow of information among all group members. Everyone participates equally, and the group's leader, if there is one, is not likely to have excessive power. Most social media platforms such as Facebook and LinkedIn allow individual users to form groups; these groups, in turn, then communicate like an all-channel network.

Research conducted on networks suggests some interesting connections between the type of network and group performance. For example, when the group's task is relatively simple and routine, centralized networks tend to perform with greatest efficiency and accuracy. The dominant leader facilitates performance by coordinating the flow of information. When a group of accounting clerks is logging incoming invoices and distributing them for payment, for example, one centralized leader can coordinate things efficiently. When the task is complex and nonroutine, such as making a major decision about organizational strategy, decentralized networks tend to be most effective because open channels of communication permit more interaction and a more efficient sharing of relevant information. Managers should recognize the effects of communication networks on group and organizational performance and should try to structure networks appropriately.

## Organizational Communication

Still other forms of communication in organizations are those that flow among and between organizational units or groups. Each of these involves oral or written communication, but each also extends to broad patterns of communication across the organization.[20] As shown in Figure 17.3, two of these forms of communication follow vertical and horizontal linkages in the organization.

**vertical communication**
Communication that flows up and down the organization, usually along formal reporting lines; takes place between managers and their superiors and subordinates and may involve several different levels of the organization

**Vertical Communication** Vertical communication is communication that flows up and down the organization, usually along formal reporting lines—that is, it is the communication that takes place between managers and their superiors and subordinates. Vertical communication may involve only two people, or it may flow through several different organizational levels.

*Upward communication* consists of messages from subordinates to superiors. This flow is usually from subordinates to their direct superior, then to that person's direct superior, and so on up the hierarchy. Occasionally, a message might bypass a particular superior. The typical content of upward communication is requests, information that the lower-level manager

---

## FIGURE 17.3 FORMAL COMMUNICATION IN ORGANIZATIONS

Formal communication in organizations follows official reporting relationships or prescribed channels. For example, vertical communication, shown here with the solid lines, flows between levels in the organization and involves subordinates and their managers. Horizontal communication, shown with dashed lines, flows between people at the same level and is usually used to facilitate coordination.

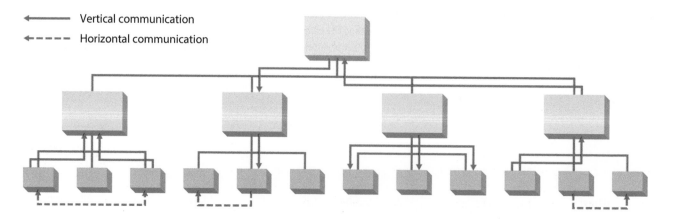

thinks is of importance to the higher-level manager, responses to requests from the higher-level manager, suggestions, complaints, and financial information. Research has shown that upward communication is more subject to distortion than is downward communication. For example, subordinates may tend to withhold or distort information that makes them look bad. The greater the degree of difference in status between superior and subordinate and the greater the degree of distrust, the more likely the subordinate is to suppress or distort information. For instance, subordinates might choose to withhold information about problems from their boss if they think the news will make him angry and if they think they can solve the problem themselves without his ever knowing about it.

*Downward communication* occurs when information flows down the hierarchy from superiors to subordinates. The typical content of these messages is directives on how some-

A lot of communication in organizations is vertical–passing up and down the hierarchy between people at different levels. This manager is explaining a new project to her team. As she discusses what the team will be doing and answers questions from her team members vertical communication is taking place.

thing is to be done, the assignment of new responsibilities, performance feedback, and general information that the higher-level manager thinks will be of value to the lower-level manager. Vertical communication can and usually should be two-way in nature. In other words, give-and-take communication with active feedback is generally likely to be more effective than one-way communication.[21]

**Horizontal Communication** Whereas vertical communication involves a superior and a subordinate, horizontal communication involves colleagues and peers at the same level of the organization. For example, an operations manager might communicate to a marketing manager that inventory levels are running low and that projected delivery dates should be extended by two weeks. Horizontal communication probably occurs more among managers than among nonmanagers.

This type of communication serves a number of purposes. It facilitates coordination among interdependent units. For example, a manager at Motorola was once researching the strategies of Japanese semiconductor firms in Europe. He found a great deal of information that was relevant to his assignment. He also uncovered some additional information that was potentially important to another department, so he passed it along to a colleague in that department, who used it to improve his own operations. Horizontal communication can also be used for joint problem solving, as when two plant managers at Northrop Grumman got together to work out a new method to improve productivity. Finally, horizontal communication plays a major role in work teams with members drawn from several departments.

## Digital Communication

Finally, as already noted, digital communication has become pervasive in organizations today. Both formal information systems and personal information technology have reshaped how managers communicate with one another. Some of the perils of this trend are explored in our *Tech Watch* box.

**Formal Information Systems** Most larger businesses manage at least a portion of their organizational communication through information systems. Some firms go so far as to create a position for a chief information officer, or CIO. General Mills, Xerox, and Burlington

**horizontal communication** Communication that flows laterally within the organization; involves colleagues and peers at the same level of the organization and may involve individuals from several different organizational units

# Thinking (and Talking) on Your Feet

A couple of years ago, MIT psychologist Sherry Turkle contributed an opinion piece to the *New York Times*. In Turkle's opinion, "we live in a technological universe in which … we have sacrificed conversation for mere connection," and it's a habit fraught with psychological and philosophical pitfalls. "We are tempted to think," she argues, "that our little sips of online connection add up to a big gulp of real conversation. But they don't." Why? Because "human relationships are rich; they're messy and demanding. We have learned the habit of cleaning them up with technology. And the move from conversation to connection is part of this [habit]."

Unfortunately, Turkle contends, it's a habit by which "we shortchange ourselves." For one thing, we tend to forget the fact that relationships with other people are inherently complicated matters. "Face-to-face conversation," explains Turkle,

> unfolds slowly. It teaches patience. When we communicate on our digital devices, we learn different habits. As we ramp up the volume and velocity of online connections, we start to expect faster answers. To get these, we ask one another simpler questions; we dumb down our communications, even on the most important matters.

In a practical sense, these new habits fail to engage one of the most significant factors in effective interpersonal communication: the willingness to *listen*. By its very nature, for example, conversation demands responsiveness to the messages—verbal and nonverbal—being sent by another person. We must constantly adjust to the fluidity—the "messiness"—of conversational give and take, and Turkle observes that because conversation requires us to respond to "tone and nuance," we must also "see things from another's point of view." As conversations "tend to play out in person," adds journalist Megan Garber, "they are messy—full of pauses and interruptions and topic changes and assorted awkwardness. But the messiness is what allows for true

exchange. It gives participants the time—and, just as important, the permission—to think and react and glean insights."

According to Paul Barnwell, responding to nuance and tone is a habit—and a skill—that we can ill afford to lose. Barnwell, who teaches Digital Media at a high school specializing in communications and media, wanders if "there is any 21st-century skill more important than being able to sustain a confident, coherent conversation." Unfortunately, he notes,

> kids spend hours each day engaging with ideas and one another through screens, but rarely do they have an opportunity to truly hone their interpersonal communication skills.… Students' reliance on screens for communication is detracting—and distracting—from their engagement in real-time talk.

For example, says Barnwell,

> when it's time to negotiate pay raises and discuss projects with employers, students will have to exude a thoughtful presence and demonstrate the ability to think on their feet. But if the majority of their conversations are based on fragments pinballed back and forth through a screen, how will they develop the ability to truly communicate in person?

Donna Lubrano, of the Newbury College School of Business Management, agrees. More and more businesses, she says, are becoming frustrated by entry-level employees who "lack the ability to speak to customers and present ideas, as well as the communication skills to work in the team environment.… In terms of verbal communication," she adds, "too many students cannot think on their feet."

*References:* Sherry Turkle, "The Flight from Conversation," *New York Times* (April 21, 2012), www.nytimes.com, on May 16, 2015; Megan Garber, "Saving the Lost Art of Conversation," *The Atlantic* (January-February 2014), www.theatlantic.com, on May 16, 2015; Paul Barnwell, "My Students Don't Know How to Have a Conversation," *The Atlantic* (April 2014), www.theatlantic.com, on May 16, 2015; Jamar Ramos, "Communication Breakdown: Interpersonal Skills in the Digital Age," *WorldWideLearn* (May 21, 2014), www.worldwidelearn.com, on May 14, 2015.

Industries all have such a position. The CIO is responsible for determining the information-processing needs and requirements of the organization and then putting in place systems that facilitate smooth and efficient organizational communication.

Part of the CIO's efforts also involves the creation of one or more formal information systems linking all relevant managers, departments, and facilities in the organization. Most enterprise resource planning systems play this role very effectively. In the absence of such a system, a marketing manager, for example, may need to call a warehouse manager to find out how much of a particular product is in stock before promising shipping dates to a customer. An effective formal information system allows the marketing manager to get the information more quickly, and probably more accurately, by plugging directly into a computerized information system.

Digital communication has fundamentally changed how people communicate. These two colleagues, for example, are literally on opposite sides of the world from each other but are able to carry on a conversation just as easily as if they were in the same room.

**Personal Electronic Technology** In recent years, the nature of organizational communication has changed dramatically, mainly because of breakthroughs in personal electronic communication technology, and the future promises even more change. Electronic typewriters and then photocopying machines were early breakthroughs. The photocopier, for example, made it possible for a manager to have a typed report distributed to large numbers of other people in an extremely short time. Personal computers have accelerated the process even more. E-mail networks, the Internet, corporate intranets, social networking sites, wireless communication systems, social media platforms, and other breakthroughs are carrying communication technology even further.

It is also becoming common to have teleconferences in which managers stay at their own locations (such as offices in different cities) but "meet" via Skype, FaceTime, and similar methods. Managers can create messages and deliver them to thousands of colleagues around the world in seconds. Highly detailed information can be retrieved with ease from large electronic databanks. These new technologies are behind the rise of a new version of an old work arrangement—cottage industry. In cottage industry, people work at home (in their "cottage") and periodically bring the products of their labors in to the company. Telecommuting is the label given to a new electronic cottage industry. In telecommuting, people work at home on their computers and transmit their work to their companies digitally.

Mobile phones have made it even easier for managers to communicate with one another. Many now use cellphones to make calls while commuting to and from work, and carry them in their pockets, bags, and briefcases so that they can receive calls regardless of where they are. And other personal computing devices, such as Apple iPhones and iPads, Samsung Android devices, and Microsoft Surface tablets, are further revolutionizing how people communicate with one another. Smartwatches and virtual keyboards are primed to take things to yet the next level.

Psychologists, however, are beginning to associate some problems with these communication advances. For one thing, managers who are seldom in their "real" offices are likely to fall behind in their fields and to be victimized by organizational politics because they are not present to keep in touch with what is going on and to protect themselves. They drop out of the organizational grapevine and miss out on much of the informal communication that takes place. Moreover, the use of digital communication at the expense of face-to-face meetings and conversations makes it hard to build a strong culture, develop solid working relationships, and create a mutually supportive atmosphere of trust and cooperativeness.[22] Finally, digital communication is also opening up new avenues for dysfunctional employee behavior, such as the passing of lewd or offensive materials to others. For example, the *New York Times* once fired almost 10 percent of its workers at one of its branch offices for sending inappropriate e-mails at work.[23]

 **Manager's Checklist**

☐ Managers should be aware of the primary forms of communication that are used by their colleagues.

☐ You should also keep abreast of breakthroughs and new forms of digital communication technologies, as well as being cognizant of the pros and cons of digital communication.

# Informal Communication in Organizations

The forms of organizational communication discussed in the previous section all represent planned and relatively formal communication mechanisms. However, in many cases some of the communication that takes place in an organization transcends these formal channels and instead follows any of several informal methods. Figure 17.4 illustrates many examples of informal communication. Common forms of informal communication in organizations include the grapevine, management by wandering around, and nonverbal communication.

## The Grapevine

**grapevine**
An informal communication network among people in an organization

The grapevine is an informal communication network that can permeate an entire organization. Grapevines are found in all organizations except the very smallest, but they do not always follow the same patterns as, nor do they necessarily coincide with, formal channels of authority and communication. Research has identified several kinds of grapevines.[24] The two most common are illustrated in Figure 17.5. The gossip chain occurs when one person spreads the message to many other people. Each one, in turn, may either keep the

## FIGURE 17.4   INFORMAL COMMUNICATION IN ORGANIZATIONS

Informal communication in organizations may or may not follow official reporting relationships or prescribed channels. It may cross different levels and different departments or work units, and may or may not have anything to do with official organizational business.

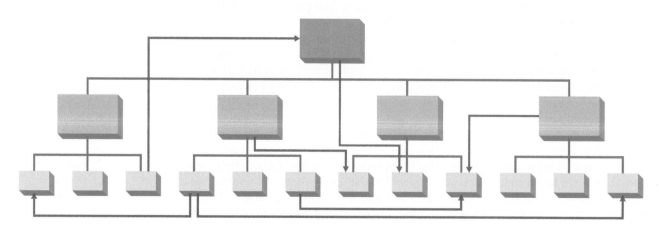

## FIGURE 17.5 COMMON GRAPEVINE CHAINS FOUND IN ORGANIZATIONS

The two most common grapevine chains in organizations are the gossip chain (in which one person communicates messages to many others) and the cluster chain (in which many people pass messages to a few others).

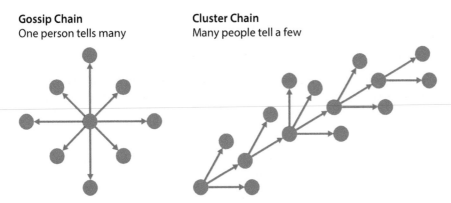

**Gossip Chain**
One person tells many

**Cluster Chain**
Many people tell a few

Source: From Keith Davis and John W. Newstrom, *Human Behavior at Work: Organizational Behavior*, Eighth Edition, 1989. Copyright © 1989 The McGraw-Hill Companies, Inc. Reprinted with permission.

information confidential or pass it on to others. The gossip chain is likely to carry personal information. The other common grapevine is the cluster chain, in which one person passes the information to a selected few individuals. Some of the receivers pass the information to a few other individuals; the rest keep it to themselves.

There is some disagreement about how accurate the information carried by the grapevine is, but research is increasingly finding it to be fairly accurate, especially when the information is based on fact rather than speculation. One study found that the grapevine may be between 75 percent and 95 percent accurate.[26] That same study also found that informal communication is increasing in many organizations for several basic reasons. One contributing factor is the recent increase in merger, acquisition, and takeover activity. Because such activity can greatly affect the people within an organization, it follows that they may spend more time talking about it.[27] The second contributing factor is that as more and more corporations move facilities from inner cities to suburbs, employees tend to talk less and less to others outside the organization and more and more to one another. Yet another contributing factor is simply the widespread availability of information technology that makes it easier than ever before for people to communicate quickly and easily.

More recently, another study looked at the effects of the recent recession and large-scale

"The only way to address uncertainty is to communicate and communicate. And when you think you've just about got to everybody, then communicate some more."

—TERRY LUNDGREN, CHAIRMAN, PRESIDENT AND CEO OF MACY'S[25]

Gossip and the grapevine are a natural part of organizational life. These two people are exchanging secrets. Their conversation may be personal or work-related. It might also be positive and constructive or negative and destructive. Managers need to know that they cannot eliminate gossip but can minimize its dysfunctional consequences by maintaining open and effective formal communication channels.

job losses on informal communication. Over half of the survey participants reported a sharp increase in gossip and rumors in their organizations. The same survey also reported an increase in the amount of eavesdropping in most businesses.[28] Further, in another survey, 32 percent of people claimed to use their work e-mail inappropriately and 48 percent admitted gossiping with other employees through their e-mail.[29] Finally, in another survey conducted in 2015 over half of the participants reported that they had overheard confidential conversations at work.[30]

> "Especially in this climate with job security, any time there's budget talk my ears perk up."
>
> —ANONYMOUS EMPLOYEE WORKING IN A CUBICLE ENVIRONMENT[31]

Attempts to eliminate the grapevine are not likely to succeed, but fortunately the manager does have some control over it. By maintaining open channels of communication and responding vigorously to inaccurate information, the manager can minimize the damage the grapevine can do. The grapevine can actually be an asset. By learning who the key people in the grapevine are, for example, the manager can partially control the information they receive and use the grapevine to sound out employee reactions to new ideas, such as a change in human resource policies or benefit packages. The manager can also get valuable information from the grapevine and use it to improve decision making.[32]

Management by wandering around can be an effective method for managers to communicate with customers and others in the organization. This hotel manager, for instance, is having an impromptu conversation with the hotel restaurant chef. There is a good chance that they will both learn things from their conversation.

## Management by Wandering Around

Another increasingly popular form of informal communication is called, interestingly enough, management by wandering around.[33] The basic idea is that some managers keep in touch with what is going on by wandering around and talking with people—immediate subordinates, subordinates far down the organizational hierarchy, delivery people, customers, or anyone else who is involved with the company in some way. Bill Marriott, for example, frequently visits the kitchens, loading docks, and custodial work areas whenever he tours a Marriott hotel. He claims that, by talking with employees throughout the hotel, he gets new ideas and has a better feel for the entire company. And when American Airlines CEO Doug Parker travels, he makes a point of talking to flight attendants and other passengers to gain continuous insights into how the business can be run more effectively.

**management by wandering around**
An approach to communication that involves the manager's literally wandering around and having spontaneous conversations with others

A related form of organizational communication that really has no specific term is the informal interchange that takes place outside the normal work setting. Employees attending the company picnic, playing on the company softball team, or taking fishing trips together will almost always spend part of their time talking about work. For example, Texas Instruments engineers at TI's Lewisville, Texas, facility often frequent a local bar in town after work. On any given evening, they talk about the Dallas Cowboys, the newest government contract received by the company, the weather, their boss, the company's stock price, local politics, and problems at work. There is no set agenda, and the key topics of discussion vary from group to group and from day to day. Still, the social gatherings serve an important role. They promote a strong culture and enhance understanding of how the organization works.

## Nonverbal Communication

Nonverbal communication is a communication exchange that does not use words or uses words to carry more meaning than the strict definition of the words themselves. Nonverbal communication is a powerful but little-understood form of communication in organizations. It often relies on facial expressions, body movements, physical contact, and gestures. One study found that as much as 55 percent of the content of a message is transmitted by facial expressions and body posture and that another 38 percent derives from inflection and tone. Words themselves account for only 7 percent of the content of the message.[34]

Research has identified three kinds of nonverbal communication practiced by managers—images, settings, and body language.[35] In this context, images are the kinds of words people elect to use. "Damn the torpedoes, full speed ahead" and "Even though there are some potential hazards, we should proceed with this course of action" may convey the same meaning. Yet the person who uses the first expression may be perceived as a maverick, a courageous hero, an individualist, or a reckless and foolhardy adventurer. The person who uses the second might be described as aggressive, forceful, diligent, or narrow minded and resistant to change. At a meeting of Walmart executives, former CEO Lee Scott once announced that "I can tell everyone what color underwear they're wearing." His meaning? There was a political issue dividing the group, and Scott wanted those in attendance to know that he was aware of which executives were on each side of the issue.[36] In short, our choice of words conveys much more than just the strict meaning of the words themselves.

The setting for communication also plays a major role in nonverbal communication. Boundaries, familiarity, the home turf, and other elements of the setting are all important. Much has been written about the symbols of power in organizations. The size and location of an office, the kinds of furniture in the office, and the accessibility of the person in the office all communicate useful information. For example, Donald Trump positions his desk so that it is always between him and a visitor. This keeps him in charge. When he wants a less formal dialogue, he moves around to the front of the desk and sits beside his visitor. Michael Dell of Dell Computer, in contrast, has his desk facing a side window so that, when he turns around to greet a visitor, there is never anything between them.

A third form of nonverbal communication is body language.[38] The distance we stand from someone as we speak has meaning. In the United States, standing very close to someone you are talking to generally signals either familiarity or aggression. The English and Germans stand farther apart than Americans when talking, whereas the Arabs, Japanese, and Mexicans stand closer together.[39] Eye contact is another effective means of nonverbal communication. For example, prolonged eye contact might suggest either hostility or romantic interest. Other kinds of body language include body and hand movement, pauses in speech, and mode of dress.

The manager should be aware of the importance of nonverbal communication and recognize its potential impact. Giving an employee good news about a reward with the wrong

Nonverbal communication often relies on body language—facial expression, posture, gestures, and so forth. This man, for example, is conveying through his crossed arms and demeanor that he is unhappy or impatient.

InesBazdar/Shutterstock.com

> "Make no mistake. I can tell everyone what color underwear they're wearing."
>
> —FORMER WALMART CEO LEE SCOTT, MEANING THAT HE KNEW WHO IN A GROUP OF EXECUTIVES WAS ON HIS SIDE[37]

**nonverbal communication** Any communication exchange that does not use words or uses words to carry more meaning than the strict definition of the words themselves

nonverbal cues can destroy the reinforcement value of the reward. Likewise, reprimanding an employee but providing inconsistent nonverbal cues can limit the effectiveness of the sanctions. The tone of the message, where and how the message is delivered, facial expressions, and gestures can all amplify or weaken the message or change the message altogether.

Emoticons also play a growing role in nonverbal communication. For instance, in a face-to-face conversation we can use a facial expression to indicate that we are kidding or being sarcastic with our words. In an e-mail or text, though, the context clues provided by facial expressions are lost. But now people can attach emoticons—smiling faces, frowning faces, winks, and so forth—to e-mails, texts, or other digital messages to convey additional information.

 **Manager's Checklist**

- ☐ All managers need to understand the three fundamental kinds of informal communication that occur in an organization.

- ☐ Managers should also remember that they cannot eliminate informal communication.

- ☐ You should also understand the role that body language plays in communication.

# Managing Organizational Communication

In view of the importance and pervasiveness of communication in organizations, it is vital for managers to understand how to manage the communication process.[40] Managers should understand how to maximize the potential benefits of communication and minimize the potential problems. We begin our discussion of communication management by considering the factors that might disrupt effective communication and how to deal with them.

## Barriers to Communication

Several factors may disrupt the communication process or serve as barriers to effective communication.[41] As shown in Table 17.1, these may be divided into two classes: individual barriers and organizational barriers.

> "It has taken a lot of work, including cross-cultural understanding and awareness, to help us be productive. The work has paid off. We learned communication was the key. Through communication we discovered our commonalities."
>
> —DEBRA NELSON, ADMINISTRATOR OF EXTERNAL AFFAIRS AT MERCEDES-BENZ U.S. INTERNATIONAL ON GERMAN/AMERICAN INTERACTION AT THEIR TUSCALOOSA, AL PLANT[42]

**Individual Barriers** Several individual barriers may disrupt effective communication. One common problem is conflicting or inconsistent signals. A manager is sending conflicting signals when she says on Monday that things should be done one way, but then prescribes an entirely different procedure on Wednesday. Inconsistent signals are being sent by a manager who says that he has an "open door" policy and wants his subordinates to drop by, but keeps his door closed and becomes irritated whenever someone stops in.

Another barrier is lack of credibility. Credibility problems arise when the sender is not considered a reliable source of information. He may not be trusted or may not be perceived as knowledgeable about the subject at hand. When a politician is caught withholding

## TABLE 17.1  BARRIERS TO EFFECTIVE COMMUNICATION

Many barriers can disrupt effective communication. Some of these barriers involve individual characteristics and processes. Others are functions of the organizational context in which communication is taking place.

| Individual Barriers | Organizational Barriers |
| --- | --- |
| Conflicting or inconsistent signals | Semantics |
| Credibility about the subject | Status or power differences |
| Reluctance to communicate | Different perceptions |
| Poor listening skills | Noise |
| Predispositions about the subject | Overload |
|  | Language differences |

information or when a manager makes a series of bad decisions, the extent to which he or she will be listened to and believed thereafter diminishes. In extreme cases, people may talk about something they obviously know little or nothing about.

Some people are simply reluctant to initiate a communication exchange. This reluctance may occur for a variety of reasons. A manager may be reluctant to tell subordinates about an impending budget cut because he knows they will be unhappy about it. Likewise, a subordinate may be reluctant to transmit information upward for fear of reprisal or because it is felt that such an effort would be futile.

Poor listening habits can be a major barrier to effective communication. Some people are simply poor listeners. When someone is talking to them, they may be daydreaming, looking around, reading, or listening to another conversation. Because they are not concentrating on what is being said, they may not comprehend part or all of the message. They may even think that they really are paying attention, only to realize later that they cannot remember parts of the conversation.

Receivers may also bring certain predispositions to the communication process. They may already have their minds made up, firmly set in a certain way. For example, a manager may have heard that his new boss is unpleasant and hard to work with. When she calls him in for an introductory meeting, he may go into that meeting predisposed to dislike her and discount what she has to say.

> "... a synergy-related headcount adjustment goal."
>
> —WORDING USED IN A NOKIA PRESS RELEASE TO ANNOUNCE THE REDUCTION OF 9,000 JOBS[43]

**Organizational Barriers**  Other barriers to effective communication involve the organizational context in which the communication occurs. Semantics problems arise when words have different meanings for different people. Words and phrases such as *profit, increased output,* and *return on investment* may have positive meanings for managers but less positive meanings for labor.

Communication problems may also arise when people of different power or status try to communicate with each other. The company president may discount a suggestion from an operating employee, thinking, "How can someone at that level help me run my business?" Or, when the president goes out to inspect a new plant, workers may be reluctant to offer suggestions because of their lower status. The marketing vice president may have more power than the human resource vice president and consequently may not pay much attention to a staffing report submitted by the human resource department.

If people perceive a situation differently, they may have difficulty communicating with one another. When two managers observe that a third manager has not spent much time in her office lately, one may believe that she has been to several important meetings, and the other may think she is "hiding out." If they need to talk about her in some official capacity, problems may arise because one has a positive impression and the other a negative impression.

Environmental factors may also disrupt effective communication. As mentioned earlier, noise may affect communication in many ways. If a manager's smartphone loses power or connectivity, communication may be disrupted. Similarly, overload may be a problem when the receiver is being sent more information than he or she can effectively handle. Many managers report getting so many e-mail and text messages each day that they sometimes feel overwhelmed.[44] And when the manager gives a subordinate many jobs on which to work and at the same time the subordinate is being told by family and friends to do other things, overload may result, and communication effectiveness diminishes.

Finally, as businesses become more and more global, different languages can create problems. To counter this problem, some firms are adopting an "official language." For example, when the German chemical firm Hoechst merged with the French firm Rhone-Poulenc, the new company adopted English as its official language. Indeed, English is increasingly becoming the standard business language around the world.[45]

Pressmaster/Shutterstock.com

There are many ways that communication effectiveness can be improved. One of the most powerful ways to be a better communicator is by being a good listener. The man on the left is paying close attention and carefully listening to his colleague on the right. As a result, their conversation will likely end with productive results.

## Improving Communication Effectiveness

Considering how many factors can disrupt communication, it is fortunate that managers can resort to several techniques for improving communication effectiveness.[46] As shown in Table 17.2, these techniques include both individual and organizational skills.

**Individual Skills** The single most important individual skill for improving communication effectiveness is being a good listener.[47] Being a good listener requires that the person be

## TABLE 17.2  OVERCOMING BARRIERS TO COMMUNICATION

Because communication is so important, managers have developed several methods of overcoming barriers to effective communication. Some of these methods involve individual skills, whereas others are based on organizational skills.

| Individual Skills | Organizational Skills |
| --- | --- |
| Develop good listening skills | Follow up |
| Encourage two-way communication | Regulate information flows |
| Be aware of language and meaning | Understand the richness of media |
| Maintain credibility | |
| Be sensitive to receiver's perspective | |
| Be sensitive to sender's perspective | |

prepared to listen, not interrupt the speaker, concentrate on both the words and the meaning being conveyed, be patient, and ask questions as appropriate[48] So important are good listening skills that companies like Delta, IBM, and Boeing conduct programs to train their managers to be better listeners. Figure 17.6 illustrates the characteristics of poor listeners versus good listeners. Our *Leading the Way* feature provides additional insights into the importance of listening.

In addition to being a good listener, several other individual skills can promote effective communication. Feedback, one of the most important, is facilitated by two-way communication. Two-way communication allows the receiver to ask questions, request clarification, and express opinions that let the sender know whether he or she has been understood. In general, the more complicated the message, the more useful two-way communication is. In addition, the sender should be aware of the meanings that different receivers might attach to various words. For example, when addressing stockholders, a manager might use the word *profits* often. When addressing labor leaders, however, she may choose to use *profits* less often.

> "... being a good listener for as long as you can stand it is the most important thing [for a new leader] to do."
>
> —HENRY SCHACHT, FORMER CEO OF LUCENT TECHNOLOGIES[49]

Furthermore, the sender should try to maintain credibility. This can be accomplished by not pretending to be an expert when one is not, by "doing one's homework" and checking facts, and by otherwise being as accurate and honest as possible. The sender should also try to be sensitive to the receiver's perspective. A manager who must tell a subordinate that she has not been recommended for a promotion should recognize that the subordinate will be frustrated and unhappy. The content of the message and its method of delivery should be chosen accordingly. The manager should be primed to accept a reasonable degree of hostility and bitterness without getting angry in return.[50]

Finally, the receiver should also try to be sensitive to the sender's point of view. Suppose that a manager has just received some bad news—for example, that his position is being eliminated next year. Others should understand that he may be disappointed, angry, or even

## FIGURE 17.6  MORE AND LESS EFFECTIVE LISTENING SKILLS

Effective listening skills are a vital part of communication in organizations. There are several barriers that can contribute to poor listening skills in organizations. Fortunately, there are also several practices for improving listening skills.

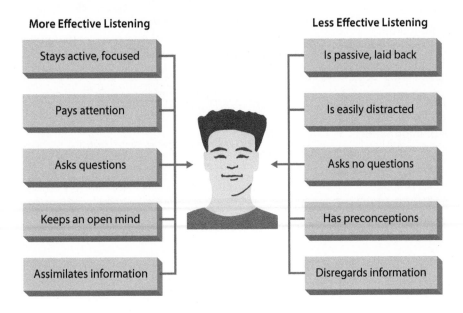

# In Communication We Trust

When James E. Rogers was CEO of the energy company Cinergy, he held regular "listening sessions" in which, among other things, he sought feedback about his own performance, even asking employees at one session to grade him on a scale of *A* to *F*. When fewer than half of his employees gave him an *A*, Rogers started asking open-ended questions about his performance. Ironically, the area in which the most employees suggested improvement was "internal communications."

According to the authors of *Talk, Inc.: How Trusted Leaders Use Conversation to Power Their Organizations*, what Rogers's employees wanted was more "intimacy" in "organizational conversation." "Where conversational intimacy prevails," explain Boris Groysberg of the Harvard Business School and communications consultant Michael Slind,

> those with decision-making authority seek and earn the trust (and hence the careful attention) of those who work under that authority. They do so by cultivating the art of listening to people at all levels of the organization and by learning to speak with employees directly and authentically.

The key factor in conversational intimacy, say Groysberg and Slind, is *trust*: "Where there is no trust," they argue, "there can be no intimacy. … No one will dive into a heartfelt exchange of views with someone who seems to have a hidden agenda or a hostile manner." Research shows that it's a point well taken: One study found that fewer than half of workers trust senior managers, and only 28 percent consider them a credible source of information.

The need for leaders to cultivate trust, says management expert Peter Drucker, accounts for a notable shift in contemporary leadership practice: Organizations, he explains, "are no longer built on force but on trust." He hastens to add that "trust does not necessarily mean that people like each other. It means they understand one another." In today's workplace, says Drucker, a leader's effectiveness in meeting organizational goals depends upon making optimum use of employees' knowledge about the work that's being done (and about how to improve it). Thus "the first secret of effectiveness is to understand the people you work with so that you can make use of their strengths." Communication, therefore, must be a medium of understanding, and it must support the mutual understanding of each party to the conversation.

Groysberg and Slind agree. "The sound of one person talking," they point out, "is obviously not a conversation." Organizational conversation means that "leaders talk *with* employees and not just *to* them." It thus requires *interactivity* as well as intimacy, and employees must have "the institutional support they need to speak up and (where appropriate) talk back."

Not surprisingly, James Rogers is a good case in point. "I think that, as the years have gone on," says Rogers,

> I've really honed my ability to listen and understand everybody's story and to help them build a story around their capabilities—a story that plays to their strengths. … At the end of the day, [employees] have to trust … that you wouldn't be asking them to do this unless you had confidence in them. They have to trust that you see something in them that they may not see completely in themselves.

*References:* Boris Groysberg and Michael Slind, "Leadership Is a Conversation," *Harvard Business Review* (June 2012), https://hbr.org, on May 6, 2015; Kellie Cummings, "Trust, Communication, and Leadership: The Three Laws of Influence," American Society for Training & Development (April 9, 2013), www.td.org, on May 6, 2015; Stephen M.R. Covey, "How the Best Leaders Build Trust," *Leadership Now* (2009), www.leadership.now.com, on May 6, 2015; Adam Bryant, "The C.E.O. as General (and Scout)," *New York Times* (October 10, 2009), www.nytimes.com, on May 7, 2015.

depressed for a while. Thus they might make a special effort not to take too much offense if he snaps at them, and they might look for signals that he needs someone to talk to.[51]

**Organizational Skills**  Three useful organizational skills can also enhance communication effectiveness for both the sender and the receiver—following up, regulating information flow, and understanding the richness of different media. Following up simply involves checking at a later time to be sure that a message has been received and understood. After a manager sends a report to a colleague, she might send a follow-up message a few days later to make sure the report was received. If it was, the manager might ask whether the colleague has any questions about it.

Regulating information flow means that the sender or receiver takes steps to ensure that overload does not occur. For the sender, this could mean not passing too much information through the system at one time. For the receiver, it might mean calling attention to the fact that he is being asked to do too many things at once. Many managers limit the influx of information by periodically weeding out the list of journals and routine reports they receive, or they train their assistant to screen phone calls and visitors. Indeed, some executives now get so much e-mail that they have it routed to an assistant. That person reviews the e-mail, discards those that are not useful (such as "spam"), responds to those that are routine, and passes on to the executive only those that require her or his personal attention.

Both parties should also understand the richness associated with different media. When a manager is going to lay off a subordinate temporarily, the message should be delivered in person. A face-to-face channel of communication gives the manager an opportunity to explain the situation and answer questions. When the purpose of the message is to grant a pay increase, written communication may be appropriate because it can be more objective and precise. The manager could then follow up the written notice with personal congratulations.

---

☐ Managers need to be aware of the primary barriers to communication in organizations.

☐ You should also be aware of how to most effectively overcome those barriers.

 **Manager's Checklist**

---

# Summary of Learning Outcomes and Key Points

1. Describe the interpersonal nature of organizations.

   - Communication is the process of transmitting information from one person to another.
   - Effective communication is the process of sending a message in such a way that the message received is as close in meaning as possible to the message intended.

2. Describe the role and importance of communication in the manager's job.

   - Communication is a pervasive and important part of the manager's world.
   - The communication process consists of a sender's encoding meaning and transmitting it to one or more receivers, who receive the message and decode it into meaning.
   - In two-way communication, the process continues with the roles reversed.
   - Noise can disrupt any part of the overall process.

3. Identify the basic forms of communication in organizations.

   - Several forms of organizational communication exist. Interpersonal communication focuses on communication among a small number of people.
   - Two important forms of interpersonal communication, oral and written, both offer unique advantages and disadvantages.
   - The manager should weigh the pros and cons of each when choosing a medium for communication.
   - Communication networks are recurring patterns of communication among members of a group or work team.
   - Vertical communication between superiors and subordinates may flow upward or downward.
   - Horizontal communication involves peers and colleagues at the same level in the organization.

- Organizations also use information systems to manage communication.
- Electronic communication is having a profound effect on managerial and organizational communication.

4. Discuss informal communication, including its various forms and types.

- There is also a great deal of informal communication in organizations.
- The grapevine is the informal communication network among people in an organization.
- Management by wandering around is also a popular informal method of communication.

- Nonverbal communication includes facial expressions, body movement, physical contact, gestures, and inflection and tone.

5. Describe how the communication process can be managed to recognize and overcome barriers.

- Managing the communication process necessitates recognizing the barriers to effective communication and understanding how to overcome them.
- Barriers can be identified at both the individual and the organizational levels.
- Both individual and organizational skills can be used to overcome these barriers.

# Discussion Questions

## Questions for Review

1. Describe the difference between communication and effective communication. How can a sender verify that a communication was effective? How can a receiver verify that a communication was effective?

2. Which form of interpersonal communication is best for long-term retention? Why? Which form is best for getting across subtle nuances of meaning? Why?

## Questions for Analysis

5. "Personal friendships have no place at work." Do you agree or disagree with this statement, and why?

6. At what points in the communication process can problems occur? Give examples of how noise can interfere with the communication process. What can managers do to reduce problems and noise?

## Questions for Application

8. What forms of communication have you experienced today? What form of communication is involved in a face-to-face conversation with a friend? A telephone call from a customer? A traffic light or crossing signal? A picture of a cigarette in a circle with a slash across it? An area around machinery defined by a yellow line painted on the floor?

9. Keep track of your own activities over the course of a few hours of leisure time to determine what forms of communication you encounter. Which forms were most common? If you had been tracking your communications while at work, how would the list be different? Explain why the differences occur.

10. For each of the following situations, tell which form of communication you would use. Then ask the same

3. What are the similarities and differences of oral and written communication? What kinds of situations call for the use of oral methods? What situations call for written communication?

4. Describe the individual and organizational barriers to effective communication. For each barrier, describe one action that a manager could take to reduce the problems caused by that barrier.

7. How are electronic communication devices and models (smartphones, e-mail, texts, and websites) likely to affect the communication process in the future? Describe both the advantages and the disadvantages of these approaches over traditional communication methods, such as face-to-face conversations, written notes, and phone calls.

question of someone who has been in the workforce for at least 10 years. For any differences that occur, ask the worker to explain why his or her choice is better than yours. Do you agree with his or her assessment? Why or why not?

- Describing complex changes in how healthcare benefits are calculated and administered to every employee of a large firm
- Asking your boss a quick question about how she wants something done
- Telling customers that a new two-for-one promotion is available at your store
- Reprimanding an employee for excessive absences on the job
- Reminding workers that no smoking is allowed in your facility

# Building Effective Technical Skills

### Exercise Overview

Technical skills are necessary to understand or perform the specific kind of work that an organization does. This exercise will help you develop and apply technical skills in using the Internet to gather information for making important decisions.

### Exercise Background

The management of a large retailer wants to leverage the company's enormous purchasing power to buy products in bulk quantities at relatively low prices. The plan calls for individual stores to order specific quantities from a single warehouse and distribution center, and as the company's operations manager, it's your job to identify potential locations for the new facility.

First, you know that you'll need quite a lot of land; the warehouse itself will occupy more than four acres. In addition, because incoming shipments will arrive by both rail and truck, you'll need to be close to railroads and major highways. Land price is important, of course, and the cost of living should be relatively low. Finally, you want relatively mild weather conditions so that shipping disruptions are minimal.

Experience has shown that small to midsize communities work best. Moreover, because the company already maintains warehouses in the West and East, the new one will probably be located in the central or south-central area of the country. Your boss wants you to identify three or four possible sites.

### Exercise Task

With all of this information in mind, do the following:

1. Use the Internet to identify as many as 10 possible locations.

2. Using additional information gathered from the Internet, narrow your set of 10 locations to three or four.

3. Continuing to use the Internet, find out as much as you can about each of the three or four finalists on your list and be ready to discuss the pros and cons of each as they relate to your selection criteria.

# Building Effective Interpersonal Skills

### Exercise Overview

Interpersonal skills refer to the ability to communicate with, understand, and motivate individuals and groups. This in-class demonstration gives you some practice in understanding the roles played by verbal and nonverbal elements in the interaction between two people.

### Exercise Background

Because more than half the information in any face-to-face exchange is conveyed by nonverbal means, body language is a significant factor in any interpersonal communication. Consider, for example, the impact of a yawn or a frown (never mind a shaken fist). At the same time, however, most people pay relatively little conscious attention to the nonverbal elements of an exchange, especially the more subtle ones. And if you misread the complete set of signals that someone is sending you, you're not likely to receive that person's message in the way that's intended.

In this exercise, you'll examine some interactions between two people from which we've eliminated sound; in other words, you'll have only visual clues to help you decipher the meaning of the messages being sent and received. Then you'll be asked to examine those same interactions with both visual and verbal clues intact.

### Exercise Task

1. Observe the silent video segments that your professor shows to the class. For each segment, describe the nature of the relationship and interaction between the two people. What nonverbal clues did you rely on in reaching your conclusions?

2. Next, observe the same video segments with audio included. Describe the interaction again, this time indicating any verbal clues that you relied on.

3. How accurate were your assessments when you had only visual information? Explain why you were or were not accurate in your assessment of the situation.

4. What does this exercise show you about the role of non-verbal factors in interpersonal communication? What advice would you now give managers about the importance of these factors?

# Skill-Building Personal Assessment

### Sex Talk Quiz

**Introduction:** Research shows that men and women sometimes have trouble communicating effectively with one another at work because they have contrasting values and beliefs about differences between the sexes. The following assessment surveys your beliefs and values about each sex.

How much do you know about how men and women communicate? If you think a statement is an accurate description of communication patterns, mark it true. If you think it isn't, mark it false.

1. Men talk more than women.

2. Men are more likely to interrupt women than to interrupt other men.

3. During conversations, women spend more time looking at their partner than men do.

4. Nonverbal messages carry more weight than verbal messages.

5. Female managers communicate with more emotional openness and drama than male managers.

6. Men not only control the content of conversations, they also work harder in keeping conversations going.

7. When people hear generic words, such as "mankind" and "he," they respond inclusively, indicating that the terms apply to both sexes.

8. In classroom communications, male students receive more reprimands and criticism.

9. Women are more likely than men to disclose information about intimate personal concerns.

10. Female speakers are more animated in their style than are males.

11. Women use less personal space than men.

12. When a male speaks, he is listened to more carefully than a female speaker, even when she makes the identical presentation.

13. In general, women speak in a more tentative style than do men.

14. Women are more likely to answer questions that are not addressed to them.

15. There is widespread gender segregation in schools, and it hinders effective classroom communication.

16. Female managers are seen by both male and female subordinates as better communicators than male managers.

17. In classroom communications, teachers are more likely to give verbal praise to female than to male students.

18. In general, men smile more often than women.

# Management at Work

### Standing Up for Warmth

> "Let your body tell you that you're powerful and deserving, and you become more present, enthusiastic, and authentically yourself."
>
> —SOCIAL PSYCHOLOGIST AMY CUDDY

In 2012, Amy Cuddy, a social psychologist who teaches at the Harvard Business School, delivered a presentation at the prestigious TEDGlobal Conference in Edinburgh, Scotland. Her subject was body language and its effect on "the way your life unfolds." TED presentations are offered for free online viewing, and since 2006, they've been watched more than a billion times worldwide. Cuddy's talk has the distinction of being the second-most-watched TED presentation of all time, with nearly 26 million views and counting.* *Time* magazine immediately put Cuddy on its list of "Game Changers," and *Business Insider* ranked her 37th among "50 Women Who Are Changing the World."

What did Cuddy have to say that was so important? Basically, "Smile and sit up straight." The advice, of course, is

---

*You can view the presentation at http://www.ted.com/talks/amy_cuddy_your_body_language_ shapes_who_you_are?language=en. The number-one watched presentation (with more than 33 million views) is Sir Ken Robinson's "How Schools Kill Creativity" (2006).

pretty simple, but the reason why it's good advice is not. Cuddy had research to back her up, and that research had led her to a series of significant insights into the significance of body language. What inspired Cuddy's research? "I noticed in class," she recalls,

*that women tended to make themselves small, holding their wrists, wrapping their arms around themselves. Guys tended to make themselves bigger. They're leaning back, stretching out, draping their arms around chairs. We know from studies of facial feedback that if you smile, you fake yourself into feeling happier. We wondered whether just asking people to spread out would help them feel more powerful.*

So Cuddy and her colleagues invited students into the social-psych laboratory for a few experimental exercises. Participants were asked to spend two minutes alone in a room striking what Cuddy calls "power poses," either "high-power" or "low power." For *high-power poses*, think superhero posture—chest lifted, head held high, arms either raised or propped on the hips. (Cuddy prefers "the Wonder Woman"—hands on hips, legs wide.) *Low-power poses* include putting your hands on your neck and crossing your limbs. In general, says Cuddy, "expansive, open postures reflect high power, whereas contractive, closed postures reflect low power."

Before and after the posing exercises, Cuddy's team recorded participants' levels of two hormones: testosterone, which is known to increase feelings of power and confidence, and cortisol, which is associated with feelings of anxiety and stress. After just two minutes of posing, high-power posers experienced a 20 percent increase in testosterone and a 25 percent drop in cortisol. "Not only do these postures reflect power," explains Cuddy, "they also *produce* it." In addition, high-power posers displayed behavior associated with the exercise of power in the real world—a fact that didn't surprise Cuddy: "Effective leaders," she points out, "have a classic hormone profile: high levels of testosterone, low levels of cortisol. ... When people take over the alpha role, their testosterone rises and their cortisol drops."

The study's findings show not only that our hormonal levels can change, but that we can take the initiative in changing them. The process engages a series of feedback loops. As we've seen, for example, the principle is evident in the effect of a smile: "Feeling happy makes us smile, and smiling makes us happy," observes Cuddy. But what if you don't feel like smiling? "Fake it till you become it," she advises: *Faking* happiness, it seems, has pretty much the same effect as *being* happy. The key is the smile: Using the muscles of your face to communicate nonverbally sends a message to your brain, and as with smiling, so with standing up straight. Thus the purpose of power posing, explains Cuddy, "is to optimize your brain"—to balance your hormones in the way that you want them balanced. "Let your body tell you that you're powerful and deserving," she says, and

when you pass that message along to your brain, "you become more present, enthusiastic, and authentically yourself."

Perhaps even more importantly, adds Cuddy, the feedback that you get from such nonverbal behavior as smiling "is also contagious. We tend to mirror one another's nonverbal expressions and emotions, so when we see someone beaming and emanating genuine warmth, we can't resist smiling ourselves." In addition, such responses typically reflect first impressions and often contribute to snap judgments about people—what Cuddy calls "spontaneous trait inferences." Her research has thus extended to the effect of body language on first impressions, and she's found that there are two critical variables: *warmth* and *competence*. These two factors, she says, account for 90 percent of our evaluations of other people and, more importantly, shape the way we feel about and act toward them.

Unfortunately, projections of both warmth and competence can produce seemingly contradictory behavior in other people. According to Cuddy,

*people judged to be competent but lacking in warmth often elicit envy in others, an emotion involving both respect and resentment that cuts both ways. When we respect someone, we want to cooperate or affiliate ourselves with him or her, but resentment can make that person vulnerable to harsh reprisal. ... On the other hand, people judged as warm but incompetent tend to elicit pity, which also involves a mix of emotions: Compassion moves us to help those we pity, but our lack of respect leads us ultimately to neglect them.*

The first type that Cuddy describes here falls into the category *cold/competent* and the second into the category *warm/incompetent*—two of four categories into which people may fit in Cuddy's warmth/competence matrix. At the extremes are *warm/competent*, which elicits admiration, helping, and cooperation, and *cold/incompetent*, which elicits contempt, neglect, and harassment (and even violence).

As revealing as it is, this matrix raises further questions: Is there any difference between, say, *warm/competent* and *competent/warm*, and, if so, which is optimum, particularly if one's job involves leading other people? According to Cuddy, "putting competence first undermines leadership" because doing so fails to prioritize the most important factor in any relationship—*trust*. "Prioritizing warmth," she says

*helps you connect immediately with those around you, demonstrating that you hear them, understand them, and can be trusted by them. ... In management settings, trust increases information sharing, openness, and cooperation. ... Most important, it provides the opportunity to change people's attitudes and beliefs, not just their outward behavior. That's the sweet spot when it comes to the ability to get people to fully accept your message.*

So, how can you project warmth? First, says Cuddy, "Find the right level. … Aim for a tone that suggests that you're leveling with people—that you're sharing the straight scoop, with no pretense or emotional adornment." Second, "validate feelings": Begin by agreeing with people, letting them know right off that "you hold roughly the same worldview that they do." Last but not least, "Smile—and mean it."

Cuddy hastens to add that coming across effectively is a matter of prioritizing, not of minimizing one trait in favor of the other. The best way to lead, she concludes, "is to combine warmth and strength. … The traits can actually be mutually reinforcing: Feeling a sense of personal strength helps us to be more open, less threatened, and less threatening in stressful situations. When we feel confident and calm, we project authenticity and warmth."

## Case Questions

1. What about you? How do you sit in class? Does Cuddy's description of students' classroom body language seem to apply to you? Specifically, what might you do to improve your classroom body language? How about your body language in other situations?

2. Review the section in the text on "Individual Barriers" to communication. How might Cuddy's analysis of the impressions that we make on people help in understanding these barriers? More specifically, how might that analysis be used in helping to overcome them? Now ask yourself which of these barriers seem to affect your own communication habits. How might Cuddy's analysis help you to understand and deal with the barriers to your own communication habits?

3. Here's a list of Cuddy's four ideal types in the warmth/competence matrix, along with examples of people who, according to her research, tend to fall into each category:

   - warm/competent—fathers
   - warm/incompetent—working mothers
   - cold/competent—Asian students
   - cold/incompetent—economically disadvantaged people

   Bearing in mind that these examples reflect generalized *perceptions* of people, explain why each group falls into its respective category. Add another group to each category. Explain the role played by *stereotyping* in assigning people to each category. Finally, to what extent do you yourself tend to succumb to these generalizations?

4. As we've seen, Cuddy has observed "a gender grade gap" in her MBA classes at Harvard, in which classroom participation accounts for a significant portion of students' grades. "It's competitive—you really have to get in there," she says, and women aren't quite as successful at contributing to discussions as men. Men, she reports, volunteer to answer questions by shooting their arms in the air while women tend toward a polite bent-elbow wave. Women often touch their faces and necks while talking and tend to sit with tightly crossed ankles. "These postures," says Cuddy, "are associated with powerlessness and intimidation and keep people from expressing who they really are."

   Why does this "gender gap" exist in the classroom? Does it help to know that non-white males are often subject to the same disadvantage?

## Case References

Amy Cuddy, "Your Body Language Shapes Who You Are," TEDGlobal 2012 (June 2012), www.ted.com, on May 12, 2015; David Hochman, "Amy Cuddy Takes a Stand," *New York Times* (September 19, 2014), www.nytimes.com, on May 11, 2015; Danielle Venton, "Power Postures Can Make You Feel More Powerful," *Wired* (May 12, 2012), www.wired.com, on May 11, 2015; Craig A. Lambert, "The Psyche on Automatic," *Harvard Magazine* (May-June 2015), http://harvardmagazine.com, on May 11, 2015; Nettra Pan, "One 2-Minute, High-Impact Activity Scientifically Proven to Boost the Success of Your Next Presentation," Business Families Foundation (April 30, 2014), on May 11, 2015; Cuddy, Caroline A. Wilmuth, and Dana R. Carney, "The Benefit of Power Posing before a High-Stakes Social Evaluation," Harvard Business School Working Paper, No. 13-027 (September 2012), http://dash.harvard.edu, on May 12, 2015; Cuddy, Matthew Kohut, and John Neffinger, "Connect, Then Lead," *Harvard Business Review* (July-August 2013), https://hbr.org, on May 11, 2015.

## YOU MAKE THE CALL   Buzz Words

1. Consider *enterprise social networks* (ESNs) in terms of the section in the text on "Organizational Communication." What, for example, might be the effect of communication through an ESN on a company's *vertical communication* flow? On its *horizontal communication* flow? On its *reporting lines*? Take another look at Figure 17.3, which displays in a single flow chart both vertical and horizontal flows of communication. What kinds of adjustments would have to be made in order to accommodate the addition of an ESN to a company's forms of communication? Try your hand at drawing a rough flow chart displaying the possible lines of communication opened up by an ESN.

2. Humana's Jeff Ross has a few words of advice for organizations that want to set up enterprise social networks. First, he says, "be more lenient than heavy handed" in monitoring users' posts. "It is very rare," he adds, "that we have to remove posts. If that happens, it might be because they've violated some HR or solicitation policy." Second, keep guidelines simple: At Humana, he says, "we focus on the 'Buzz Ten Commandments'—a simple list of rules such us 'respecting other people' which is straightforward and easy to understand."*

   Like virtually every company, however, Humana does place certain restrictions on ESN content. What kinds of restrictions do you think are appropriate for ESN usage at a corporation such as Humana? What kinds of restrictions would you regard as too "heavy handed"?

3. According to Ross, "a huge motivator" in setting up Buzz "was just to flatten the organization and … and break down the silos."†

   "Silo" is a word that you'll run across quite often these days when people talk about organization structure and design. What does Ross mean by "silos"? How do "silos" affect organizational communications? Why has Humana—like a lot of companies—set out to "break down the silos"?

4. One recent survey found that employees wanted to engage with senior managers through internal social media: 42 percent, for example, would be willing to talk with line managers or team leaders over Facebook, and 20 percent would be happy to tweet a department head or even the CEO. Twenty percent of managers said that they'd be happy to reciprocate. At the same time, the survey revealed that two-thirds of employees had no involvement in their companies' social media activities, and more than a quarter were not permitted access to their employers' internal communications networks.‡

   Why do you think there's such a disparity between employee attitudes and organizational practice?

*Gloria Lombardi, "Buzzing in Healthcare: Humana's ESN Story," *Simply-Communicate.com* (November 15, 2013), www.simply-communicate.com, on April 30, 2015.

†Ron Miller, "How Humana Got 26,000 Employees to Use an Internal Social Network," *Citeworld* (May 28, 2013), www.citeworld.com, on April 29, 2015

‡Zain Wadee, "Facebook Your Boss: Using Social Media in Internal Communications," *The Guardian* (January 25, 2013), www.theguardian.com, on April 27, 2015.

# Endnotes

1   Gloria Lombardi, "Buzzing in Healthcare: Humana's ESN Story," *Simply-Communicate.com* (November 15, 2013), www.simply-communicate.com, on April 30, 2015; Ron Miller, "How Humana Got 26,000 Employees to Use an Internal Social Network," *Citeworld* (May 28, 2013), www.citeworld.com, on April 29, 2015; Joe McKendrick, "The Buzz at Humana," *Insurance Networking News* (September 3, 2014), www.insurancenetworking.com, on April 30, 2015; Badi Azad, "Humana Employees Buzz'd Over Enterprise Social Network," *Social Business Engine* (August 12, 2014), www.socialbusinessengine.com, on April 30, 2015; John Osborn, "Humana's Bruce Broussard at Industry Confab: Healthcare Is a Mess and We Are All to Blame!" *Forbes* (April 15, 2015), www.forbes.com, on May 4, 2015; VMWare Inc., "Humana: Advancing an Open Culture with Socialcast Town Halls" (2014), www.socialcast.com, on May 5, 2015; Andrea Tortora, "Social Media as a Wellness Engagement Tool," *Cincinnati Business Courier* (November 27, 2013), www.bizjournals.com, on May 4, 2015; Aditi Pai, "Humana Finally Goes Mobile with iOS, Android Apps," *Mobihealthnews* (August 6, 2014), http://mobihealthnews.com, on May 4, 2015.

2   See John J. Gabarro, "The Development of Working Relationships," in Jay W. Lorsch (ed.), *Handbook of Organizational Behavior* (Englewood Cliffs, NJ: Prentice-Hall, 1987), pp. 172–179. See also "Team Efforts, Technology, Add New Reasons to Meet," *USA Today*, December 8, 1997, pp. 1A, 2A.

3   Tara C. Reich and M. Sandy Hershcovis, "Interpersonal Relationships at Work," in Sheldon Zedeck (ed.), *Handbook of Industrial and Organizational Psychology*, Vol. 3: *Maintaining, Expanding, and Contracting the Organization* (Washington, DC: American Psychological Association, 2010), pp. 223–248.

4   *BusinessWeek*, November 29, 2014, p. 17.

5   Martin Kilduff and Daniel J. Brass, "Organizational Social Network Research: Core Ideas and Key Debates," in James P. Walsh and Arthur P. Brief (eds.), *The Academy of Management Annals 2010* (Philadelphia: Taylor and Francis, 2010), pp. 317–358.

6   See C. Gopinath and Thomas E. Becker, "Communication, Procedural Justice, and Employee Attitudes: Relationships under Conditions of Divestiture," *Journal of Management*, 2000, Vol. 26, No. 1, pp. 63–83.

7 Marshall Scott Poole, "Communication," in Sheldon Zedeck (ed.), *Handbook of Industrial and Organizational Psychology*, Vol. 3: *Maintaining, Expanding, and Contracting the Organization* (Washington, DC: American Psychological Association, 2010), pp. 249–270.

8 Ibid.

9 See Batia M. Wiesenfeld, Sumita Charan, and Raghu Garud, "Communication Patterns as Determinants of Organizational Identification in a Virtual Organization," *Organization Science*, 1999, Vol. 10, No. 6, pp. 777–790.

10 Bruce Barry and Ingrid Fulmer, "The Medium and the Message: The Adaptive Use of Communication Media in Dyadic Influence," *Academy of Management Review*, 2004, Vol. 29, No. 2, pp. 272–292.

11 Reid Buckley, "When You Have to Put It to Them," *Across the Board*, October 1999, pp. 44–48.

12 "'Did I Just Say That?!' How to Recover from Foot-in-Mouth," *Wall Street Journal*, June 19, 2012, p. B1.

13 "Executives Who Dread Public Speaking Learn to Keep Their Cool in the Spotlight," *Wall Street Journal*, May 4, 1990, pp. B1, B6.

14 Buckley, "When You Have to Put It to Them."

15 http://images.forbes.com/forbesinsights/StudyPDFs/The_Untethered_Executive.pdf

16 See "Watch What You Put in That Office Email," *BusinessWeek*, September 30, 2012, pp. 114–115.

17 Nicholas Varchaver, "The Perils of E-mail," *Fortune*, February 17, 2003, pp. 96–102; "How a String of E-Mail Came to Haunt CSFB and Star Banker," *Wall Street Journal*, February 28, 2003, pp. A1, A6; "How Morgan Stanley Botched a Big Case by Fumbling Emails," *Wall Street Journal*, May 16, 2014, pp. A1, A10.

18 *Fortune*, December 12, 2005, leadership insert.

19 A. Vavelas, "Communication Patterns in Task-Oriented Groups," *Journal of the Acoustical Society of America*, 1950, Vol. 22, pp. 725–730; Jerry Wofford, Edwin Gerloff, and Robert Cummins, *Organizational Communication* (New York: McGraw-Hill, 1977).

20 Nelson Phillips and John Brown, "Analyzing Communications in and Around Organizations: A Critical Hermeneutic Approach," *Academy of Management Journal*, 1993, Vol. 36, No. 6, pp. 1547–1576.

21 Mary Young and James Post, "How Leading Companies Communicate with Employees," *Organizational Dynamics*, Summer 1993, pp. 31–43.

22 Kristin Byron, "Carrying Too Heavy a Load? The Communication and Miscommunication of Emotion by Email," *Academy of Management Review*, 2008, Vol. 33, No. 2, pp. 309–327.

23 "Those Bawdy E-Mails Were Good for a Laugh—Until the Ax Fell," *Wall Street Journal*, February 4, 2000, pp. A1, A8.

24 Keith Davis, "Management Communication and the Grapevine," *Harvard Business Review*, September–October 1953, pp. 43–49.

25 http://www.mckinsey.com/insights/leading_in_the_21st_century/leadership_lessons_for_hard_times

26 "Spread the Word: Gossip Is Good," *Wall Street Journal*, October 4, 2008, p. B1.

27 See David M. Schweiger and Angelo S. DeNisi, "Communication with Employees Following a Merger: A Longitudinal Field Experiment," *Academy of Management Journal*, March 1991, pp. 110–135.

28 "Job Fears Make Offices All Fears," *Wall Street Journal*, January 20, 2009, p. B7.

29 Institute of Leadership and Management, "32% of People Making Inappropriate Use of Work Emails," April 20, 2013.

30 "Your Secrets Aren't Safe at the Office," *USA Today*, February 27, 2015, p. 2B.

31 *Wall Street Journal*, January 20, 2014, p. B7.

32 Nancy B. Kurland and Lisa Hope Pelled, "Passing the Word: Toward a Model of Gossip and Power in the Workplace," *Academy of Management Review*, 2000, Vol. 25, No. 2, pp. 428–438.

33 See Tom Peters and Nancy Austin, *A Passion for Excellence* (New York: Random House, 1985).

34 Albert Mehrabian, *Non-Verbal Communication* (Chicago: Aldine, 1972).

35 Michael B. McCaskey, "The Hidden Messages Managers Send," *Harvard Business Review*, November–December 1979, pp. 135–148.

36 Suzanne Kapner, "Changing of the Guard at Wal-Mart," *Fortune*, March 2, 2009, pp. 68–76.

37 *Fortune*, March 2, 2009, p. 72.

38 David Givens, "What Body Language Can Tell You That Words Cannot," *U.S. News & World Report*, November 19, 1984, p. 100.

39 Edward J. Hall, *The Hidden Dimension* (New York: Doubleday, 1966).

40 For a detailed discussion of improving communication effectiveness, see Courtland L. Bovee, John V. Thill, and Barbara E. Schatzman, *Business Communication Today*, 7th ed. (Upper Saddle River, NJ: Prentice Hall, 2003).

41 See Otis W. Baskin and Craig E. Aronoff, *Interpersonal Communication in Organizations* (Glenview, IL: Scott, Foresman, 1980).

42 http://www.businessweek.com/adsections/diversity/diversecompet.htm

43 *BusinessWeek*, December 22, 2008, p. 15.

44 See "You Have (Too Much) E-Mail," *USA Today*, March 12, 2004, p. 3B.

45 Justin Fox, "The Triumph of English," *Fortune*, September 17, 2008, pp. 209–212.

46 Joseph Allen and Bennett P. Lientz, *Effective Business Communication* (Santa Monica, CA: Goodyear, 1979).

47 See "Making Silence Your Ally," *Across the Board*, October 1999, p. 11.

48 Boyd A. Vander Houwen, "Less Talking, More Listening," *HR Magazine*, April 1997, pp. 53–58.

49 *Fortune*, January 24, 2015, p. 112.

50 For a discussion of these and related issues, see Eric M. Eisenberg and Marsha G. Witten, "Reconsidering Openness in Organizational Communication," *Academy of Management Review*, July 1987, pp. 417–426.

51 For a recent illustration, see Barbara Kellerman, "When Should a Leader Apologize—And When Not?" *Harvard Business Review*, April 2006, pp. 72–81.

©Markus Pfaff/Shutterstock.com

# MANAGING WORK GROUPS AND TEAMS

## 18

**After studying this chapter, you should be able to:**

## MANAGEMENT IN ACTION  Promoting the Cause of Diversity

"The findings are clear: for groups that value innovation and new ideas, diversity helps."

—KATHERINE W. PHILLIPS,
COLUMBIA UNIVERSITY BUSINESS SCHOOL

In a recent review of the research on workplace diversity, Beryl Nelson, a software-engineering manager at Google, refers to several studies showing that teams "whose members are heterogeneous"—diverse— "have a higher potential for innovation than teams whose members are homogeneous."* According to Nelson, "diverse teams are more effective" in two key respects: "They produce better financial results and results in innovation." She cites, for example, the financial benefits to companies at which women serve in senior positions: Companies in the top quartile— those ranking better than 75 percent of all companies— enjoyed 41 percent greater return on equity and 56 percent greater earnings before taxes. Among

companies with at least three women on their boards of directors, return on equity was 16.7 percent, as opposed to an average of 11.5 percent; return on sales was 16.8 percent, as opposed to an average of 11.5 percent.[1]

Racial diversity also has significant benefits: Studies show that greater racial diversity corresponds to better results in market share, sales revenue, and profits. A study of 366 companies by the consulting firm McKinsey & Co., for example, reveals that for every 10 percent increase in racial diversity among senior executive teams, earnings before taxes increased by 0.8 percent.

Research also indicates that the presence of women contributes to the "collective intelligence and creativity" of teams—and thus to their potential for innovation. One study divided participants into teams of three to five members and assigned each team tasks involving brainstorming, decision making, and problem solving. Individual intelligence tests were given beforehand and used to ensure intellectual equality among teams, which were given collective intelligence scores after

Diversity in groups helps lead to more innovation and collective creativity. Take this group, for example. Diversity is reflected in terms of both gender and ethnicity but not necessarily age. So, we might expect the outcome of their deliberations to be both innovative and creative.

Pressmaster/Shutterstock.com

*This case deals with *cultural* or *social diversity*—diversity in race, ethnicity, or gender. The *Management at Work* case at the end of the chapter focuses on *functional diversity*—diversity in professional or organizational training, experience, or expertise.

they had performed their assigned tasks. There was only one predictor of collective intelligence: the presence of women on a team. All the high-scoring teams were composed of about 50 percent women, while all groups with less gender mix had lower scores. Why did women make a difference? The researchers concluded that higher-scoring teams did a better job of applying the contributions of all members because they displayed better social skills—skills on which, according to additional research, women tend to score more highly.

Note, however, that this study was based on small groups. When we're talking about organizations, as opposed to teams, we're talking about much larger groups, and this difference has an important implication for the study of workplace diversity. One research team, for instance, looked at the top firms on the Standard & Poor's Composite 1500 list in order to see if there was a relationship between the makeup of their top-management teams and their financial results. The researchers concluded that "female representation in top management leads to an increase of $42 million in firm value." Another team analyzed eight years of employee survey data provided by a company with more than 60 offices worldwide. They found that by shifting from an all-male or all-female staff to a staff split 50-50 by gender, an office could increase revenue by 41 percent.

Obviously, large-scale studies like these also suggest a correspondence between greater diversity and better financial performance. But as Katherine W. Phillips of the Columbia University Business School points out, large-scale studies "show only that diversity is *correlated* with better performance, not that it *causes* better performance." Two things may *correlate* with one another simply because we find some reason to associate them, but it doesn't mean that one necessarily *causes* the other. Nelson acknowledges the same drawback in studies of workplace diversity. Many studies, she reminds us, "show a correlation between diverse organizational composition, financial success, and innovation" but demonstrate no "clear causal relationship between diversity and success."

Before going any further, we need to understand what the issue is. The problem has to do with the kinds of conclusions that can be drawn from what Phillips calls "large data-set studies," which involve so many variables that it's difficult to isolate those which indicate cause and effect from those which indicate mere correlation. A firm that enjoys a 41 percent greater return on equity than comparable companies may have given itself a competitive advantage by putting more women in senior positions, but it clearly has additional competitive advantages as well.

Because there are fewer variables involved in smaller-scale studies of teams (as opposed to larger organizations), these studies may reveal a causal relationship that might also be present in larger groups. Phillips thus recommends closer analysis of "diversity in small groups" as a valid means of focusing on possible cause-and-effect relationships between diversity and performance. In fact, she says, "the findings are clear: for groups that value innovation and new ideas, diversity helps."

She cites a study in which she teamed with fellow researchers "to examine the impact of racial diversity on small decision-making groups." The team assembled three-person groups with two different racial compositions—all white and two white members plus one non-white member. Each group had to solve a murder mystery. All groups shared certain common information, but individual members were given important clues that only he or she knew. In order to solve the mystery, each group had to share all of its collective information, including the clues known only to one member. "The groups with racial diversity," reports Phillips, "significantly outperformed the groups with no racial diversity." Why? The researchers concluded that members teamed with "similar others" tended to assume that everyone shared the same information and the same perspective. As a result, all-white groups were less diligent in processing all of their available information—a sure hindrance to creativity and innovation.

Phillips also cites a study designed "to examine the influence of racial and opinion composition in small-group discussions." Groups were given 15 minutes to discuss some relevant social issue (e.g., the death penalty). The researchers created a dissenting opinion on each issue and had one group member present it as part of the discussion. Phillips reports that

> *when a black person presented a dissenting perspective to a group of whites, the perspective was perceived as more novel and led to broader thinking and consideration of alternatives than when a white person introduced that same dissenting perspective. The lesson: when we hear dissent from someone who is different from us, it provokes more thought than when it comes from someone who looks like us.*

Roy Y. J. Chua, an organizational behavior specialist at Harvard, has studied a specific kind of workplace team—multicultural teams. He has found that, for certain types of tasks, culturally diverse teams exhibit greater creativity, mainly because cultural diversity supplies "unique access to a range of knowledge systems." Chua has also discovered, however, that "it's inevitable to have conflict when you bring people from different cultural backgrounds together." Neither teams nor organizations are more creative when the organization suffers from what Chua calls "ambient cultural disharmony"—the effect on individuals and groups of cultural conflict in an organizational environment. If people perceive diversity as a source of conflict, says Chua, they tend to "shut down the search for connections involving ideas from different cultures" and thus miss opportunities for creativity and innovation afforded by diversity of ideas and information.

---

As we noted in Chapter 17, groups and teams are found throughout most organizations. It stands to reason, then, that managers should be interested in making sure those groups and teams are as productive as possible. This chapter's *Management in Action* feature suggests that diversity within groups and teams may be one factor that boosts group and team performance. This chapter is about all of the processes that affect group and team performance. We first introduce basic concepts of group and team dynamics. Subsequent sections explain the characteristics of groups and teams in organizations. We then describe interpersonal and intergroup conflict. Finally, we conclude with a discussion of how conflict can be managed.

**group**
Consists of two or more people who interact regularly to accomplish a common purpose or goal

**functional group**
A permanent group created by the organization to accomplish a number of organizational purposes with an unspecified time horizon

## Groups and Teams in Organizations

Groups are a ubiquitous part of organizational life. They are the basis for much of the work that gets done, and they evolve both inside and outside the normal structural boundaries of the organization. We will define a group as two or more people who interact regularly to accomplish a common purpose or goal.[2] The purpose of a group or team may range from preparing a new advertising campaign, to informally sharing information, to making important decisions, to fulfilling social needs.

A functional group is a permanent group created by the organization. The staff of this hospital emergency room would be considered a functional group comprised of doctors, nurses, and technicians.

### Types of Groups and Teams

In general, three basic kinds of groups are found in organizations—functional groups, informal or interest groups, and task groups and teams.[3] These are illustrated in Figure 18.1.

**Functional Groups** A functional group is a permanent group created by the organization to accomplish a number of organizational purposes with an unspecified time horizon. The advertising department at Target, the management department at Florida Atlantic University, and the nursing staff at the Mayo Clinic are functional groups. The advertising department at Target, for example, seeks to plan effective advertising campaigns, increase sales, run in-store promotions, and develop a unique identity for the company. It is assumed that the functional group will remain in existence after it attains its current objectives; those objectives will be replaced by new ones.

## FIGURE 18.1 TYPES OF GROUPS IN ORGANIZATIONS

Every organization has many different types of groups. In this hypothetical organization, a functional group is shown within the purple area, a cross-functional team within the yellow area, and an informal group within the green area.

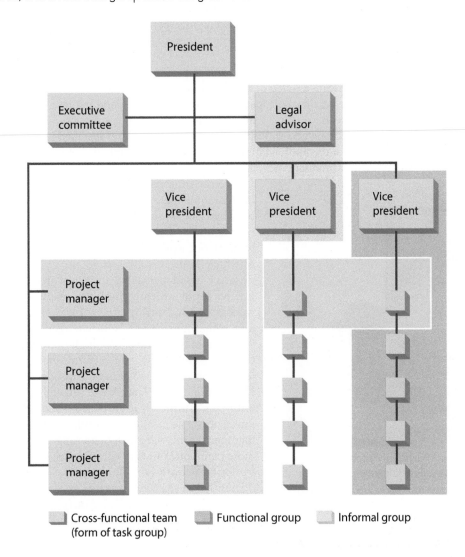

Cross-functional team
(form of task group)   Functional group   Informal group

**Informal or Interest Groups** An informal or interest group is created by its own members for purposes that may or may not be relevant to organizational goals. It also has an unspecified time horizon. A group of employees who lunch together every day may be discussing productivity, money embezzling, or local politics and sports.[4] As long as the group members enjoy eating together, they will probably continue to do so. When lunches cease to be pleasant, they will seek other company or a different activity.

Informal groups can be a powerful force that managers cannot ignore.[5] One writer described how a group of employees at a furniture factory subverted their boss's efforts to increase production. They tacitly agreed to produce a reasonable amount of work but not to work too hard. One man kept a stockpile of completed work hidden as a backup in case he got too far behind. In another example, auto workers described how they left out gaskets and seals and put soft-drink bottles inside doors to cause customer complaints.[6] Of course, informal groups can also be a positive force, as when people work together to help out a

**informal or interest group**
Created by its members for purposes that may or may not be relevant to those of the organization

**task group**
A group created by the organization to accomplish a relatively narrow range of purposes within a stated or implied time horizon

**team**
A group of workers that functions as a unit, often with little or no supervision, to carry out work-related tasks, functions, and activities

**virtual team**
Team comprised of people from remote worksites who work together online

colleague who has suffered a personal tragedy. For example, several instances of this behavior were reported in the wake of the devastating heavy rains and flooding that swept through parts of the Southwest in 2015.

In recent years the Internet has served as a platform for the emergence of more and different kinds of informal or interest groups. As one example, Yahoo! includes a wide array of interest groups that bring together people with common interests. And increasingly, workers who lose their jobs as a result of layoffs are banding together electronically to offer moral support to one another and to facilitate networking as they all look for new jobs.[7]

**Task Groups** A task group is a group created by the organization to accomplish a relatively narrow range of purposes within a stated or implied time horizon. Most committees and task forces are task groups. The organization specifies group membership and assigns a relatively narrow set of goals, such as developing a new product or evaluating a proposed grievance procedure. The time horizon for accomplishing these purposes is either specified (a committee may be asked to make a recommendation within 60 days) or implied (the project team will disband when the new product is developed).

Teams are a special form of task group that have become increasingly popular.[8] In the sense used here, a team is a group of workers that functions as a unit, often with little or no supervision, to carry out work-related tasks, functions, and activities. Table 18.1 lists and defines some of the various types of teams that are being used today. Earlier forms of teams included autonomous work groups and quality circles. Today, teams are also sometimes called "self-managed teams," "cross-functional teams," or "high-performance teams." Many firms today are routinely using teams to carry out most of their daily operations.[9] *Doing Business on Planet Earth* provides several examples. Further, virtual teams—teams comprised of people from remote worksites who work together online—are also becoming more and more common.[10] In fact, virtual connections are sometimes more complex than basic online hookups, and you'd be surprised at what sorts of things well-connected virtual teams can do.

Andrey_Popov/Shutterstock.com

There are many different kinds of groups in organizations today. This virtual group includes members from three different locations. They are interacting together–some in person and some using virtual technology–to review and discuss their unit's performance.

### TABLE 18.1 TYPES OF TEAMS

| | |
|---|---|
| **Problem-solving team** | Most popular type of team; comprises knowledge workers who gather to solve a specific problem and then disband |
| **Management team** | Consists mainly of managers from various functions like sales and production; coordinates work among other teams |
| **Work team** | An increasingly popular type of team; work teams are responsible for the daily work of the organization; when empowered, they are self-managed teams |
| **Virtual team** | A newer type of work team whose members interact in a virtual arena; members enter and leave the network as needed and may take turns serving as leader |
| **Quality circle** | Declining in popularity, quality circles, comprising workers and supervisors, meet intermittently to discuss workplace problems |

**DOING BUSINESS ON PLANET EARTH**

# Cooking Up Sustainability

How much does it cost to cook pasta? It depends on how you do it—and, of course, on how much pasta you want to cook. Olive Garden, for example, cooks a lot of pasta: The Italian-food chain has more than 800 locations worldwide and offers an annual "Never Ending Pasta Bowl" deal in which customers can pack all the pasta they want into their own customized creations. On the other hand, the pasta-cooking process is basically the same one that you use in your own kitchen: bring cold water to a boil, put in the hard pasta, and bring the water to a second boil. Back in 2011, however, Olive Garden tweaked the process by modifying the cold- and hot-water inlet valves on its pasta cookers so that the process uses hot water only. Since then, the chain has saved $2.4 million in energy costs, mostly in the cost of heating and reheating water.

How does a company come up with such sustainable ideas? At Darden Restaurants, Olive Garden's parent corporation, many such ideas originate with in-house Sustainability Teams, which Darden describes as "groups of employees in each restaurant who implement programs to reduce waste and energy and water usage." The company hastens to point out that "they are also responsible for many of the ideas we have used to improve sustainability at our restaurants," and in the spring of 2013, Darden took a step further in seeking out grassroots input by surveying 12,000 employees to gather both feedback on current sustainability efforts and ideas for improvement.

By and large, however, the job of implementing these efforts falls to each restaurant's Sustainability Team, which typically includes three to five members. Individual efforts are important to Darden's overall sustainability strategy because the company has discovered that the regular performance of some basic tasks can make a big difference. Michele Smith, for example, is in charge of thermostats at a Red Lobster outlet.* "When I come to work in the morning," she says, "I make sure all the thermostats are set where they're supposed to be. … It gives me

a chance," she adds, "to feel like I'm helping out and doing something good." Generally speaking, Smith's attitude toward workplace sustainability reflects that of her generation: So-called *millennials*—the roughly one-fourth of Americans born between 1980 and the mid-2000s—are the most sustainability-conscious segment of the population, and according to one recent survey, 80 percent of them want to work for sustainability-conscious companies.

Take Pam Martin, for instance, who is a Sustainability Team member at a Bahama Breeze restaurant. "When I heard about the team," she recalls, "I felt like it was almost a personal obligation … to make sure … our environment is protected and maintained instead of creating a larger carbon footprint. I want to make sure we're doing the most that we can to make sure our impact on the environment is minimal." According to Brandon Tidwell, Manager of Sustainability at Darden, the initiatives that the company launched in 2007 were in part a response to the interest of young employees in stepping up sustainability practices. "The idea of doing more," says Tidwell,

*came out of our millennial workforce. Seventy percent of our employees are 30 and under, and they are very interested in this issue. This millennial generation grew up with environmental education in school, and they want to make a difference in their careers and be actively engaged. They grew up recycling at home and separating their trash, so when they can't do the same thing in the restaurant, it's frustrating for them. They want their workplace to share their same values.*

*References:* Mike Hower, "Here's What's On Olive Garden's Sustainability Menu," *GreenBiz* (October 2, 2014), www.greenbiz.com, on May 22, 2015; Darden Restaurants Inc., "Planet," *Darden Sustainability* (2015), www.darden.com, on May 22, 2015; Sherleen Mahoney, "Leading an Industry while Making a Difference," RFMA *Facilitator* (February-March, 2013), http://c.ymcdn.com, on May 22, 2015; Darden Restaurants Inc., "Reporting Library" (videos), *Darden Sustainability* (2015), www.darden.com, on May 28, 2015; Aarthi Rayapura, "Millennials Most Sustainability-Conscious Generation Yet, But Don't Call Them 'Environmentalists,'" *Sustainable Brands* (March 11, 2014), www.sustainablebrands.com, on May 28, 2015.

*Darden sold Red Lobster in July 2014. The company's other chains include LongHorn Steakhouse and Bahama Breeze.

Organizations create teams for a variety of reasons. For one thing, they give more responsibility for task performance to the workers who are actually performing the tasks. They also empower workers by giving them greater authority and decision-making freedom. In addition, they allow the organization to capitalize on the knowledge and motivation of their workers. Finally, they enable the organization to shed its bureaucracy and to promote flexibility and responsiveness. Ford used teams to design its newest version of the Mustang. Similarly, General Motors used a team to develop its new Chevrolet Volt.

When an organization decides to use teams, it is essentially implementing a major form of organization change, as discussed in Chapter 12. Thus it is important to follow a logical and systematic approach to planning and implementing teams in an existing organization design. It is also important to recognize that resistance may be encountered. This resistance is most likely from first-line managers who will be giving up much of their authority to the team. Many organizations find that they must change the whole management philosophy of such managers away from being supervisors to being coaches or facilitators.[11]

After teams are in place, managers should continue to monitor their contributions and how effectively they are functioning. In the best circumstances, teams will become very cohesive groups with high performance norms. To achieve this state, the manager can use any or all of the techniques described later in this chapter for enhancing cohesiveness. If implemented properly, and with the support of the workers themselves, performance norms will likely be relatively high. In other words, if the change is properly implemented, the team participants will understand the value and potential of teams and the rewards they may expect to get as a result of their contributions. On the other hand, poorly designed and implemented teams will do a less effective job and may detract from organizational effectiveness.[12]

> "If a team can't be fed by two pizzas, it's too large."
>
> —JEFF BEZOS,
> FOUNDER AND CEO OF AMAZON.COM[13]

## Why People Join Groups and Teams

People join groups and teams for a variety of reasons. They join functional groups simply by virtue of joining organizations. People accept employment to earn money or to practice their chosen professions. Once inside the organization, they are assigned to jobs and roles and thus become members of functional groups. People in existing functional groups are told, are asked, or volunteer to serve on committees, task forces, and teams. People join informal or interest groups for a variety of reasons, most of them quite complex.[14] Indeed, the need to be a team player has grown so strong today that many organizations will actively resist hiring someone who does not want to work with others.[15]

**Interpersonal Attraction** One reason why people choose to form informal or interest groups is that they are attracted to one another. Many different factors contribute to interpersonal attraction. When people see a lot of each other, pure proximity increases the likelihood that interpersonal attraction will develop. Attraction is increased when people have similar attitudes, personalities, or economic standings.

**Group Activities** Individuals may also be motivated to join a group because the activities of the group appeal to them. Jogging, playing bridge,

People join groups and teams for many different reasons. For instance, people might join a group in order to participate in social activities such as playing pool, throwing darts, bowling, softball, bridge, and so forth.

Dragon Images/Shutterstock.com

bowling, discussing poetry, playing fantasy football, and flying model airplanes are all activities that some people enjoy. Many of them are more enjoyable to participate in as a member of a group, and most require more than one person. Many large firms like Shell Oil and Apple Computer have a football, softball, or bowling league. A person may join a bowling team, not because of any particular attraction to other group members, but simply because being a member of the group allows that person to participate in a pleasant activity. Of course, if the group's level of interpersonal attraction is very low, a person may choose to forgo the activity rather than join the group.

> "Give us people who are dedicated to making the team work, as opposed to a bunch of talented people with big egos, and we'll win every time."
>
> —JOHN MCCONNELL,
> CEO OF WORTHINGTON INDUSTRIES[16]

**Group Goals**  The goals of a group may also motivate people to join. The Sierra Club, which is dedicated to environmental conservation, is a good example of this kind of interest group. Various fundraising groups are another illustration. Members may or may not be personally attracted to the other fundraisers, and they probably do not enjoy the activity of knocking on doors asking for money, but they join the group because they subscribe to its goal. Workers join unions like the United Auto Workers because they support its goals.

**Need Satisfaction**  Still another reason for joining a group is to satisfy the need for affiliation. New residents in a community may join the Newcomers Club (or similar organization targeted at new residents) partially as a way to meet new people and partially just to be around other people. Likewise, newly divorced people often join support groups as a way to have companionship.

**Instrumental Benefits**  A final reason why people join groups is that membership is sometimes seen as instrumental in providing other benefits to the individual. For example, it is fairly common for college students entering their senior year to join several professional clubs or associations because listing such memberships on a résumé is thought to enhance the chances of getting a good job. Similarly, a manager might join a certain racquet club not because she is attracted to its members (although she might be) and not because of the opportunity to play tennis (although she may enjoy it). The club's goals are not relevant, and her affiliation needs may be satisfied in other ways. However, she may feel that being a member of this club will lead to important and useful business contacts. The racquet club membership is instrumental in establishing those contacts. Membership in civic groups such as the Junior League and Rotary may be solicited for similar reasons.

## Stages of Group and Team Development

Imagine the differences between a collection of five people who have just been brought together to form a group or team and a group or team that has functioned like a well-oiled machine for years. Members of a new group or team are unfamiliar with how they will function together and are tentative in their interactions. In a group or team with considerable experience, members are familiar with one another's strengths and weaknesses and are more secure in their roles in the group. The former group or team is generally considered to be immature; the latter, mature. To progress from the immature phase to the mature phase, a group or team must go through certain stages of development, as shown in Figure 18.2.[17]

The first stage of development is called *forming*. The members of the group or team get acquainted and begin to test which interpersonal behaviors are acceptable and which are unacceptable to the other members. The members are very dependent on others at this point to provide cues about what is acceptable. The basic ground rules for the group or team are established, and a tentative group structure may emerge.[18] At adidas, for example, a

## FIGURE 18.2  STAGES OF GROUP DEVELOPMENT

As groups mature, they tend to evolve through four distinct stages of development. Managers must understand that group members need time to become acquainted, accept one another, develop a group structure, and become comfortable with their roles in the group before they can begin to work directly to accomplish goals.

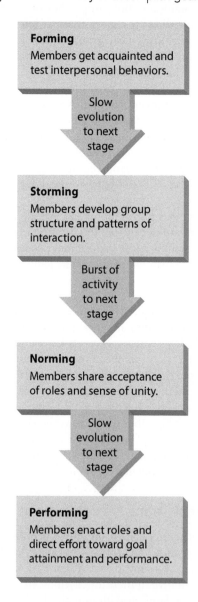

**Forming**
Members get acquainted and test interpersonal behaviors.

Slow evolution to next stage

**Storming**
Members develop group structure and patterns of interaction.

Burst of activity to next stage

**Norming**
Members share acceptance of roles and sense of unity.

Slow evolution to next stage

**Performing**
Members enact roles and direct effort toward goal attainment and performance.

merchandising team was created to handle its sportswear business. The team leader and his members were barely acquainted and had to spend a few weeks getting to know one another.

The second stage of development, often slow to emerge, is *storming*. During this stage, there may be a general lack of unity and uneven interaction patterns. At the same time, some members of the group or team may begin to exert themselves to become recognized as the group leader or at least to play a major role in shaping the group's agenda. In adidas's team, some members advocated a rapid expansion into the marketplace; others argued for a slower entry. The first faction won, with disastrous results. Because of the rush, product quality was poor and deliveries were late. As a result, the team leader was fired and a new manager placed in charge.

The third stage of development, called *norming*, usually begins with a burst of activity. During this stage, each person begins to recognize and accept her or his role and to understand the roles of others. Members also begin to accept one another and to develop a sense of unity. There may also be temporary regressions to the previous stage. For example, the group or team might begin to accept one particular member as the leader. If this person later violates important norms or otherwise jeopardizes his or her claim to leadership, conflict might reemerge as the group rejects this leader and searches for another. Adidas's new leader transferred several people away from the team and set up a new system and structure for managing things. The remaining employees accepted his new approach and settled into doing their jobs.

*Performing*, the final stage of group or team development, is also slow to develop. The team really begins to focus on the problem at hand. The members enact the roles they have accepted, interaction occurs, and the efforts of the group are directed toward goal attainment. The basic structure of the group or team is no longer an issue but has become a mechanism for accomplishing the purpose of the group. Adidas's sportswear business is now growing consistently and has successfully avoided the problems that plagued it at first.

**roles**
The parts individuals play in groups in helping the group reach its goals

---

☐ Managers should be familiar with the basic types of groups and teams.

☐ You should also know the reasons that people choose to join groups.

☐ Managers need to be familiar with the stages of development through which new groups may progress.

**Manager's Checklist**

# Characteristics of Groups and Teams

**role structure**
The set of defined roles and interrelationships among those roles that the group members define and accept

As groups and teams mature and pass through the four basic stages of development, they begin to take on four important characteristics—a role structure, norms, cohesiveness, and informal leadership.[19]

## Role Structures

Each individual in a team has a part, or role, to play in helping the group reach its goals. Some people are leaders, some do the work, some interface with other teams, and so on. Indeed, a person may take on a *task specialist role* (concentrating on getting the group's task accomplished) or a *socioemotional role* (providing social and emotional support to others on the team). A few people, usually the leaders, perform both roles; a few others may do neither. The group's role structure is the set of defined roles and interrelationships among those roles that the group or team members define and accept. Each of us belongs to many groups and therefore plays multiple roles—in work groups, classes, families, and social organizations.[20]

Role structures emerge as a result of role episodes, as shown in Figure 18.3. The process begins with the expected role—what other members of the team expect the individual to do. The expected role gets translated into the sent role—the messages and

This team has just received word from their manager (pictured in the red in the center) that they need to work through lunch (and possibly dinner!) to complete their quarter end report. Clearly her subordinate in the red tie is not pleased with this late information. This is contrary to what the manager told them last quarter when she indicated that no more overtime would be permitted or required. This intrasender conflict is not contributing to a sense of trust and clear communication in this work environment.

---

## FIGURE 18.3 THE DEVELOPMENT OF A ROLE

Roles and role structures within a group generally evolve through a series of role episodes. The first two stages of role development are group processes, as the group members let individuals know what is expected of them. The other two parts are individual processes, as the new group members perceive and enact their roles.

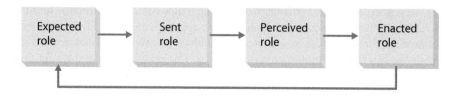

cues that team members use to communicate the expected role to the individual. The perceived role is what the individual perceives the sent role to mean. Finally, the enacted role is what the individual actually does in the role. The enacted role, in turn, influences future expectations of the team. Of course, role episodes seldom unfold this easily. When major disruptions occur, individuals may experience role ambiguity, conflict, or overload.[21]

**role ambiguity**
Arises when the sent role is unclear and the individual does not know what is expected of him or her

**role conflict**
Occurs when the messages and cues composing the sent role are clear but contradictory or mutually exclusive

**Role Ambiguity** Role ambiguity arises when the sent role is unclear. If your instructor tells you to write a term paper but refuses to provide more information, you will probably experience role ambiguity. You do not know what the topic is, how long the paper should be, what format to use, or when the paper is due. In work settings, role ambiguity can stem from poor job descriptions, vague instructions from a supervisor, or unclear cues from coworkers. The result is likely to be a subordinate who does not know what to do. Role ambiguity can be a significant problem for both the individual who must contend with it and the organization that expects the employee to perform.

**Role Conflict** Role conflict occurs when the messages and cues composing the sent role are clear but contradictory or mutually exclusive.[22] One common form is *interrole conflict*—conflict between roles. For example, if a person's boss says that one must work overtime and on weekends to get ahead, and the same person's spouse says that more time is needed at home with the family, conflict may result. In a matrix organization, interrole conflict often arises between the roles one plays in different teams as well as between team roles and one's permanent role in a functional group.

*Intrarole conflict* may occur when the person gets conflicting demands from different sources within the context of the same role. A manager's boss may tell her that she needs to put more pressure on subordinates to follow new work rules. At the same time, her subordinates may indicate that they expect her to get the rules changed. Thus the cues are in conflict, and the manager may be unsure about which course to follow. *Intrasender conflict* occurs when a single source sends clear but contradictory messages. This might arise if the boss says one morning that there can be no

Role conflict is a common occurrence in some organizations. Interrole conflict refers to conflict between roles such as the role of employee and the role of family member. This manager, for instance, is away from his family and interacting with them using his digital device.

bloomua/Shutterstock.com

more overtime for the next month but after lunch tells someone to work late that same evening. *Person–role conflict* results from a discrepancy between the role requirements and the individual's personal values, attitudes, and needs. If a person is told to do something unethical or illegal, or if the work is distasteful (for example, firing a close friend), person–role conflict is likely. Role conflict of all varieties is of particular concern to managers. Research has shown that conflict may occur in a variety of situations and lead to a variety of adverse consequences, including stress, poor performance, and rapid turnover.

**Role Overload**  A final consequence of a weak role structure is role overload, which occurs when expectations for the role exceed the person's capabilities. When a manager gives an employee several major assignments at once, while increasing the person's regular workload, the employee will probably experience role overload. Role overload may also result when one takes on too many roles at one time. For example, a person trying to work extra hard at work, run for election to the school board, serve on a committee in church, coach Little League baseball, maintain an active exercise program, and be a contributing member to her or his family will probably encounter role overload.

In a functional group or team, the manager can take steps to avoid role ambiguity, conflict, and overload. Having clear and reasonable expectations and sending clear and straightforward cues go a long way toward eliminating role ambiguity. Consistent expectations that take into account the employee's other roles and personal value system may minimize role conflict. Role overload can be avoided simply by recognizing the individual's capabilities and limits. In friendship and interest groups, role structures are likely to be less formal; hence, the possibility of role ambiguity, conflict, or overload may not be so great. However, if one or more of these problems does occur, they may be difficult to handle. Because roles in friendship and interest groups are less likely to be partially defined by a formal authority structure or written job descriptions, the person cannot turn to those sources to clarify a role.

> "Some of the worst teams I've ever seen have been those where everybody was a potential CEO."
>
> —DAVID NADLER, CONSULTANT[23]

## Behavioral Norms

Norms are standards of behavior that the group or team accepts for and expects of its members. Most committees, for example, develop norms governing their discussions. A person who talks too much is perceived as doing so to make a good impression or to get his or her own way. Other members may not talk much to this person, may not sit nearby, may glare at the person, and may otherwise "punish" the individual for violating the norm. Norms, then, define the boundaries between acceptable and unacceptable behavior.[24] Some groups develop norms that limit the upper bounds of behavior to "make life easier" for the group—for example, do not make more than two comments in a committee discussion or do not produce any more than you have to. In general, these norms are counterproductive. Other groups may develop norms that limit the lower bounds of behavior—for example, do not come to meetings unless you have read the reports to be discussed or produce as much as you can. These norms tend to reflect motivation, commitment, and high performance. Managers can sometimes use norms for the betterment of the organization. For example, Kodak has successfully used group norms to reduce injuries in some of its plants.[25]

**Norm Generalization**  The norms of one group cannot always be generalized to another group. Some academic departments, for example, have a norm that suggests that faculty members dress up on teaching days. People who fail to observe this norm are "punished" by sarcastic remarks or even formal reprimands. In other departments, the norm may be casual clothes, and the person unfortunate enough to wear dress clothes may be punished just as vehemently. Even within the same work area, similar groups or teams can develop different norms. One team may strive always to produce above its assigned quota; another may maintain productivity just below its quota.

**role overload**
Occurs when expectations for the role exceed the person's ability to perform

**norms**
Standards of behavior that the group accepts for and expects of its members

The norm of one team may be to be friendly and cordial to its supervisor; that of another team may be to remain aloof and distant. Some differences are due primarily to the composition of the teams.

**Norm Variation**   In some cases, there can also be norm variation within a group or team. A common norm is that the least senior member of a group is expected to perform unpleasant or trivial tasks for the rest of the group. These tasks might be to wait on customers who are known to be small tippers (in a restaurant), to deal with complaining customers (in a department store), or to handle the low-commission line of merchandise (in a sales department). Another example is when certain individuals, especially informal leaders, may violate some norms. If the team is going to meet at 8:00 A.M., anyone arriving late will be chastised for holding things up. Occasionally, however, the informal leader may arrive a few minutes late. As long as this does not happen too often, the group probably will not do anything about it.

**Norm Conformity**   Four sets of factors contribute to norm conformity. First, factors associated with the group are important. For example, some groups or teams may exert more pressure for conformity than others. Second, the initial stimulus that prompts behavior can affect conformity. The more ambiguous the stimulus (for example, news that the team is going to be transferred to a new unit), the more pressure there is to conform. Third, individual traits determine the individual's propensity to conform (for example, more intelligent people are often less susceptible to pressure to conform). Finally, situational factors, such as team size and unanimity, influence conformity. As a person learns the group's norms, he can do several different things. The most obvious is to adopt the norms. For example, the new male professor who notices that all the other men in the department dress up to teach can also start wearing a suit. A variation is to try to obey the "spirit" of the norm while retaining individuality. The professor may recognize that the norm is actually to wear a tie; thus he might succeed by wearing a tie with his sport shirt, jeans, and sneakers.

The individual may also ignore the norm. When a person does not conform, several things can happen. At first the group may increase its communication with the deviant person to try to bring her back in line. If this does not work, communication may decline. Over time, the group may begin to exclude the person from its activities and, in effect, ostracize her.

Finally, we need to briefly consider another aspect of norm conformity—socialization. Socialization is generalized norm conformity that occurs as a person makes the transition from being an outsider to being an insider. A newcomer to an organization, for example, gradually begins to learn about such norms as dress, working hours, and interpersonal relations. As the newcomer adopts these norms, she is being socialized into the organizational culture. Some organizations, like Texas Instruments, work to actively manage the socialization process; others leave it to happenstance.

## Cohesiveness

A third important team characteristic is cohesiveness. Cohesiveness is the extent to which members are loyal and committed to the group. In a highly cohesive team, the members work well together, support and trust one another, and are generally effective at achieving their chosen goals.[26] In contrast, a team that lacks cohesiveness is not very coordinated, its members do not necessarily support one another fully, and it may have a difficult time reaching goals. Of particular interest are the factors that increase and reduce cohesiveness and the consequences of team cohesiveness. These are listed in Table 18.2.

**Factors That Increase Cohesiveness**   Five factors can increase the level of cohesiveness in a group or team. One of the strongest is intergroup competition. When two or more groups are

**socialization**
Generalized norm conformity that occurs as a person makes the transition from being an outsider to being an insider in the organization

**cohesiveness**
The extent to which members are loyal and committed to the group; the degree of mutual attractiveness within the group

## TABLE 18.2  FACTORS THAT INFLUENCE GROUP COHESIVENESS

Several different factors can influence the cohesiveness of a group. For example, a manager can establish intergroup competition, assign compatible members to the group, create opportunities for success, establish acceptable goals, and foster interaction to increase cohesiveness. Other factors can be used to decrease cohesiveness.

| Factors That Increase Cohesiveness | Factors That Reduce Cohesiveness |
| --- | --- |
| Intergroup competition | Group size |
| Personal attraction | Disagreement on goals |
| Favorable evaluation | Intragroup competition |
| Agreement on goals | Domination |
| Interaction | Unpleasant experiences |

in direct competition (for example, three sales groups competing for top sales honors or two football teams competing for a conference championship), each group is likely to become more cohesive. Second, just as personal attraction plays a role in causing a group to form, so, too, does attraction seem to enhance cohesiveness. Third, favorable evaluation of the entire group by outsiders can increase cohesiveness. Thus a group's winning a sales contest or a conference title or receiving recognition and praise from a superior tends to increase cohesiveness.

Similarly, if all the members of the group or team agree on their goals, cohesiveness is likely to increase.[27] And the more often members of the group interact with one another, the more likely the group is to become cohesive. A manager who wants to foster a high level of cohesiveness in a team might do well to establish some form of intergroup competition, assign members to the group who are likely to be attracted to one another, provide opportunities for success, establish goals that all members are likely to accept, and allow ample opportunities for interaction.[28]

**Factors That Reduce Cohesiveness**  There are also five factors that are known to reduce team cohesiveness. First of all, cohesiveness tends to decline as a group increases in size. Second, when members of a team disagree on what the goals of the group should be, cohesiveness may decrease. For example, when some members believe the group should maximize output and others think output should be restricted, cohesiveness declines. Third, intragroup competition reduces cohesiveness. When members are competing among themselves, they focus more on their own actions and behaviors than on those of the group.

Fourth, domination by one or more persons in the group or team may cause overall cohesiveness to decline. Other members may feel that they are not being given an opportunity to interact and contribute, and they may become less attracted to the group as a consequence. *Leading the Way* provides more insights into this aspect of group dynamics. Finally, unpleasant experiences that result from group membership may reduce cohesiveness. A sales group that comes in last in a sales contest, an athletic team that sustains a long losing streak, and a work group reprimanded for poor-quality work may all become less cohesive as a result of their unpleasant experiences.

**Consequences of Cohesiveness**  In general, as teams become more cohesive, their members tend to interact more often, conform more to norms, and become more satisfied with the team. Cohesiveness may also influence team performance. However, performance is also influenced by the team's performance norms. Figure 18.4 shows how cohesiveness and performance norms interact to help shape team performance.

**LEADING THE WAY**

# Primed for Power

For a long time, observes industrial/organizational psychologist Liane Davey, we were brought up on the idea that "power is useful in driving performance. You defer to your boss because that's how the hierarchy works. It creates clarity and alignment and keeps things moving." Not surprisingly, then, when bosses function as leaders in group decision-making situations, power encourages them to assume dominant roles. Davey points out, however, that the criteria for successful group performance are no longer what they used to be: "In our innovation economy," she says, "where tasks require creative problem solving, information sharing, and collaboration, we need to get the value of all the members of a team—not just the limited perspective of the boss.

"The research," Davey adds, "bears this out." The research she has in mind was conducted by a team of business professors and reported in an article entitled "When Power Makes Others Speechless: The Negative Impact of Leader Power on Team Performance" (2014). In various experiments, Tost, Gino, and Larrick tested the effect of two variables on team performance: (1) in some cases, they appointed a formal leader, and in others, they did not; (2) in some cases, leaders were "primed" by being asked to recall past exercises of power, and in others, leaders were not primed. In one experiment, teams were asked to solve a murder mystery. The two groups *without formal leaders* were successful 60 percent of the time; the group *with a formal leader primed to feel powerful* had the worst success rate—about 25 percent.

"The problem," says Rick Larrick of Duke University, "is that people who are in a power mindset don't stop to ask what others know and think. And this [habit] is facilitated by formal roles and titles, because it means that those in a less powerful position tend to defer to the person with the higher position." This doesn't mean, however, that leaderless teams are the best way to go. The key factor in team success—or the lack of it—appears to be the way leaders *perceive* their power. "The best teams," Larrick points out, "had leaders who were not reminded of power. This makes sense in that leaders do play an essential role by providing structure to teams. But the structure has to ensure participation. A facilitative leader is one way to create this desirable structure."

As Larrick reminds us, the best success rate in solving the murder mystery—80 percent—was posted by the group *with a formal leader who was not primed to feel powerful ahead of time*. With this team, notes co-researcher Francesca Gino of Harvard, "the leader is sort of stepping back. It's more of what you like to see, where the leader is orchestrating the conversation, but everyone is talking."

In other words, differences in team leadership, response, and performance seem to depend in large part on *perceptions* on the part of both leaders and team members. Leaders, for example, were "primed" to heighten their perception of themselves as powerful: "With the rush that comes with having control," explains Gino, "it's easy for a manager to hog the floor—even feel obligated to play this role." In turn, reports Larrick, when leaders acted on the basis of self-perceived empowerment, team members, who perceived themselves to be "in less powerful positions, tended to defer to the person with the higher position."

"Oftentimes," concludes Gino, "we behave the way we do because we're not aware of the effects of our actions. Bringing this type of awareness to leaders in group decision-making situations could set up a different process whereby they benefit from what others have to offer."

*References:* Liane Davey, "Don't Let Your Voice Be Silenced by Your Boss," *Psychology Today* (February 18, 2014), www.psychologytoday.com, on May 20, 2015; Leigh Plunkett Tost, Francesca Gino, and Richard P. Larrick, "When Power Makes Others Speechless: The Negative Impact of Leader Power on Team Performance" (abstract), *Academy of Management Journal*, 2013, Vol. 56, No. 5, pp. 1465–1486, http://amj.aom.org, on May 20, 2015; Michael Blanding, "Pulpit Bullies: Why Dominating Leaders Kill Teams," *Harvard Business School Working Knowledge* (November 18, 2013), http://hbswk.hbs.edu, on May 18, 2015; Erin Medlyn, "New Research Finds Overbearing Leaders Can Hurt Their Team's Performance," Duke University Fuqua School of Business, October 14, 2013, on May 18, 2015.

## FIGURE 18.4 THE INTERACTION BETWEEN COHESIVENESS AND PERFORMANCE NORMS

Group cohesiveness and performance norms interact to determine group performance. From the manager's perspective, high cohesiveness combined with high performance norms is the best situation, and high cohesiveness with low performance norms is the worst situation. Managers who can influence the level of cohesiveness and performance norms can greatly improve the effectiveness of a work group.

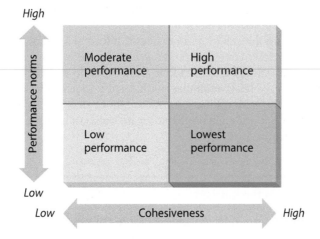

When both cohesiveness and performance norms are high, high performance should result because the team wants to perform at a high level (norms) and its members are working together toward that end (cohesiveness). When norms are high and cohesiveness is low, performance will be moderate. Although the team wants to perform at a high level, its members are not necessarily working well together. When norms are low, performance will be low, regardless of whether group cohesiveness is high or low. The least desirable situation occurs when low performance norms are combined with high cohesiveness. In this case, all team members embrace the standard of restricting performance (owing to the low performance norm), and the group is united in its efforts to maintain that standard (owing to the high cohesiveness). If cohesiveness were low, the manager might be able to raise performance norms by establishing high goals and rewarding goal attainment or by bringing in new group members who are high performers. But a highly cohesive group is likely to resist these interventions.[29]

## Formal and Informal Leadership

Most functional groups and teams have a formal leader—that is, one appointed by the organization or chosen or elected by the members of the group. Because friendship and interest groups are formed by the members themselves, however, any formal leader

This group has just learned that it has exceeded its performance goals for the quarter. As a result, the group will likely become more cohesive and feel a greater commitment to high performance norms in the future.

must be elected or designated by the members. Although some groups do designate such a leader (a softball team may elect a captain, for example), many do not. Moreover, even when a formal leader is designated, the group or team may also look to others for leadership. An informal leader is a person who engages in leadership activities but whose right to do so has not been formally recognized. The formal and the informal leader in any group or team may be the same person, or they may be different people. We noted earlier the distinction between the task specialist and socioemotional roles within groups. An informal leader is likely to be a person capable of carrying out both roles effectively. If the formal leader can fulfill one role but not the other, an informal leader often emerges to supplement the formal leader's functions. If the formal leader can fill neither role, one or more informal leaders may emerge to carry out both sets of functions.

Is informal leadership desirable? In many cases informal leaders are quite powerful because they draw from referent or expert power. When they are working in the best interests of the organization, they can be a tremendous asset. Notable athletes like Ben Roethlisberger and Mia Hamm are classic examples of informal leaders. However, when informal leaders work counter to the goals of the organization, they can cause significant difficulties. Such leaders may lower performance norms, instigate walkouts or wildcat strikes, or otherwise disrupt the organization.

---

**Manager's Checklist**

☐ Identify and describe the fundamental characteristics of groups and teams.

☐ Assume you were assigned to manage a highly cohesive group with low performance norms. What would you do to try to change things?

# Interpersonal and Intergroup Conflict

Of course, when people work together in an organization, things do not always go smoothly. Indeed, conflict is an inevitable element of interpersonal relationships in organizations. In this section, we look at how conflict affects overall performance. We also explore the causes of conflict between individuals, between groups, and between an organization and its environment.

## The Nature of Conflict

Conflict is a disagreement among two or more individuals, groups, or organizations. This disagreement may be relatively superficial or very strong. It may be short-lived or exist for months or even years, and it may be work-related or personal. Conflict may manifest itself in a variety of ways. People may compete with one another, glare at one another, shout, or withdraw. Groups may band together to protect popular members or oust unpopular members. Organizations may seek legal remedies.

Most people assume that conflict is something to be avoided because it connotes antagonism, hostility, unpleasantness, and dissension. Indeed, managers and management theorists have traditionally viewed conflict as a problem to be avoided.[30] In recent years, however, we have come to recognize that, although conflict can be a major problem, certain kinds of conflict may also be beneficial.[31] For example, when two members of a site selection committee disagree over the best location for a new plant, each may be forced to more thoroughly study and defend his or her preferred alternative. As a result of more systematic analysis and discussion, the committee may make a better decision and be better prepared to justify it to others than if everyone had agreed from the outset and accepted an alternative that was perhaps less well analyzed.

As long as conflict is being handled in a cordial and constructive manner, it is probably serving a useful purpose in the organization. On the other hand, when working relationships

**informal leader**
A person who engages in leadership activities but whose right to do so has not been formally recognized by the organization or group

**conflict**
A disagreement among two or more individuals or groups

are being disrupted and the conflict has reached destructive levels, it has likely become dysfunctional and needs to be addressed.[32] We discuss ways of dealing with such conflict later in this chapter.

Figure 18.5 depicts the general relationship between conflict and performance for a group or organization. If there is absolutely no conflict in the group or organization, its members may become complacent and apathetic. As a result, group or organizational performance and innovation may begin to suffer. A moderate level of conflict among group or organizational members, on the other hand, can spark motivation, creativity, innovation, and initiative, and raise performance. Too much conflict, though, can produce such undesirable results as hostility and lack of cooperation, which lower performance. The key for managers is to find and maintain the optimal amount of conflict that fosters performance. Of course, what constitutes optimal conflict varies with both the situation and the people involved.[33]

## Causes of Conflict

Conflict may arise in both interpersonal and intergroup relationships. Occasionally, conflict between individuals and groups may be caused by particular organizational strategies and practices. A third arena for conflict is between an organization and its environment.

**Interpersonal Conflict**  Conflict between two or more people is almost certain to occur in any organization, given the great variety in perceptions, goals, attitudes, and so forth among its members. Bill Gates, founder and CEO of Microsoft, and Kazuhiko Nishi, a former business associate from Japan, once ended a lucrative long-term business relationship because of interpersonal conflict. Nishi accused Gates of becoming too political, while Gates charged that Nishi became too unpredictable and erratic in his behavior.[34]

A frequent source of interpersonal conflict in organizations is what many people call a "personality clash"—when two people distrust each other's motives, dislike each other, or for some other reason simply cannot get along.[35] Conflict may also arise between people who have different beliefs or perceptions about some aspect of their work or their organization. For example, one manager might want the organization to require that all employees use

---

### FIGURE 18.5  THE NATURE OF ORGANIZATIONAL CONFLICT

Either too much or too little conflict can be dysfunctional for an organization. In either case, performance may be low. However, an optimal level of conflict that sparks motivation, creativity, innovation, and initiative can result in higher levels of performance.

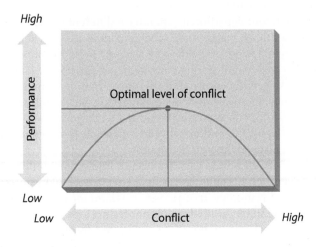

Microsoft Office software, to promote standardization. Another manager might believe that a variety of software packages should be allowed, in order to recognize individuality. Similarly, a male manager may disagree with his female colleague over whether the organization is guilty of discriminating against women in promotion decisions. Conflict can also result from excess competitiveness among individuals. Two people vying for the same job, for example, may resort to political behavior in an effort to gain an advantage. If either competitor sees the other's behavior as inappropriate, accusations are likely to result. Even after the "winner" of the job is determined, such conflict may continue to undermine interpersonal relationships, especially if the reasons given for selecting one candidate are ambiguous or open to alternative explanations. Acer CEO and President Gianfranco Lanci resigned in 2011 due to several months of unresolved conflict with the company's board of directors. Lanci and the board had differing views on organizational growth, customer value creation, brand position enhancement, and resource allocation. Lanci pushed strongly for a move into the mobile segment to compete with Apple's iPad, while the board wanted to maintain its core PC business.[36]

Sometimes, of course, conflicts can't be resolved from within the organization, and when parties—both individuals and companies—are forced to seek resolution outside corporate headquarters, they usually find themselves in a courtroom or the offices of a governmental agency. Once in a great while, conflicts escalate to the point at which they end up in the halls of Congress.

**Intergroup Conflict** Conflict between two or more organizational groups is also quite common. For example, the members of a firm's marketing group may disagree with the production group over product quality and delivery schedules. Two sales groups may disagree over how to meet sales goals, and two groups of managers may have different ideas about how best to allocate organizational resources.

Many intergroup conflicts arise more from organizational causes than from interpersonal causes. In Chapter 11, we described three forms of group interdependence—pooled, sequential, and reciprocal. Just as increased interdependence makes coordination more difficult, it also increases the potential for conflict. For example, recall that in sequential interdependence, work is passed from one unit to another. Intergroup conflict may arise if the first group turns out too much work (the second group will fall behind), too little work (the second group will not meet its own goals), or poor-quality work.

At one JCPenney department store, conflict arose between stockroom employees and sales associates. The sales associates claimed that the stockroom employees were slow in delivering merchandise to the sales floor so that it could be priced and shelved. The stockroom employees, in turn, claimed that the sales associates were not giving them enough lead time to get the merchandise delivered and failed to understand that they had additional duties besides carrying merchandise to the sales floor.

Just like people, different departments often have different goals. Further, these goals may often be incompatible. A marketing goal of maximizing sales, achieved partially by offering many products in a wide variety of sizes, shapes, colors, and models, probably conflicts with a production goal of minimizing costs, achieved partially by long production runs of a few items. Reebok recently confronted this very situation. One group of managers wanted to introduce a new sportswear line as quickly as possible, but other managers wanted to expand more deliberately and cautiously. Because the two groups were not able to reconcile their differences effectively, conflict between the two factions led to quality problems and delivery delays that plagued the firm for months.

Competition for scarce resources can also lead to intergroup conflict. Most organizations—especially universities, hospitals, government agencies, and businesses in depressed industries—have limited resources. In one New England town, for example, the public works department and the library battled over funds from a federal construction grant. The Buick, Pontiac, and Chevrolet divisions of General Motors frequently fought over the right to manufacture various new products developed by the company. This in-fighting was identified as one of many factors that led to GM's recent problems. As part of the solution, the Pontiac brand was eventually discontinued.

**Conflict Between Organization and Environment** Conflict that arises between one organization and another is called *interorganizational conflict.* A moderate amount of inter-organizational conflict resulting from business competition is expected, of course, but sometimes conflict becomes more extreme. For example, Starwood Hotels (owners of Sheraton, Westin, W, and other brands) sued Hilton Hotels Corporation for theft of trade secrets. In an effort to replicate Starwood's successful lifestyle hotels (most notably W), Hilton hired two Starwood executives, Ross Klein and Amar Lalvani, who were ultimately accused of stealing over 100,000 documents from Starwood to use in the development of the new Hilton brand. The suit was recently settled in favor of Starwood, with Hilton being forced to make a $75 million payment to Starwood.[37]

Conflict can also arise between an organization and other elements of its environment. For example, an organization may conflict with a consumer group over claims it makes about its products. McDonald's faced this problem a few years ago when it published nutritional information about its products that omitted details about fat content. A manufacturer might conflict with a governmental agency such as the federal Occupational Safety and Health Administration (OSHA). For example, the firm's management may believe it is in compliance with OSHA regulations, whereas officials from the agency itself believe that the firm is not in compliance. Or a firm might conflict with a supplier over the quality of raw materials. The firm may think the supplier is providing inferior materials, while the supplier thinks the materials are adequate. Finally, individual managers obviously may have disagreements with groups of workers. For example, a manager may think her workers are doing poor-quality work and that they are unmotivated. The workers, on the other hand, may believe they are doing good jobs and that the manager is doing a poor job of leading them.

---

☐  Define conflict and identify its primary causes.

☐  Try to think of a time when you were involved in conflict that had a positive outcome.

**Manager's Checklist** ☑

## Managing Conflict in Organizations

How do managers cope with all this potential conflict? Fortunately, as Table 18.3 shows, there are ways to stimulate conflict for constructive ends, to control conflict before it gets out of hand, and to resolve it if it does. Below we look at ways of managing conflict.[38]

### Stimulating Conflict

In some situations, an organization may stimulate conflict by placing individual employees or groups in competitive situations. Managers can establish sales contests, incentive plans, bonuses, or other competitive stimuli to spark competition. As long as the ground rules are equitable and all participants perceive the contest as fair, the conflict created by the competition is likely to be constructive because each participant will work hard to win (thereby enhancing some aspect of organizational performance).

Another useful method for stimulating conflict is to bring in one or more outsiders who will shake things up and present a new perspective on organizational practices. Outsiders may be new employees, current employees assigned to an existing work group, or consultants or advisors hired on a temporary basis. Of course, this action can also provoke resentment from insiders who feel they were qualified for the position. The Beecham Group, a British company, once hired an executive from the United States for its CEO position,

## TABLE 18.3 METHODS FOR MANAGING CONFLICT

Conflict is a powerful force in organizations and has both negative and positive consequences. Thus managers can draw on several different techniques to stimulate, control, or resolve and eliminate conflict, depending on their unique circumstances.

**Stimulating Conflict**

Increase competition among individuals and teams.

Hire outsiders to shake things up.

Change established procedures.

**Controlling Conflict**

Expand resource base.

Enhance coordination of interdependence.

Set superordinate goals.

Match personalities and work habits of employees.

**Resolving and Eliminating Conflict**

Avoid conflict.

Convince conflicting parties to compromise.

Bring conflicting parties together to confront and negotiate conflict.

expressly to change how the company did business. His arrival brought with it new ways of doing things and a new enthusiasm for competitiveness. Unfortunately, some valued employees also chose to leave Beecham because they resented some of the changes that were made.

Changing established procedures, especially procedures that have outlived their usefulness, can also stimulate conflict. Such actions cause people to reassess how they perform their jobs and whether they perform them correctly. For example, one university president announced that all vacant staff positions could be filled only after written justification had received his approval. Conflict arose between the president and the department heads, who felt they were having to do more paperwork than was necessary. Most requests were approved, but because department heads now had to think through their staffing needs, a few unnecessary positions were appropriately eliminated.

Leaders can use a variety of methods to manage conflict. Some methods focus on stimulating conflict while other techniques help control or resolve conflict. These two managers have been in conflict over a pending decision. However, they have just negotiated an understanding that makes both of them happy and are "sealing the deal" with a handshake.

Wavebreakmedia/Shutterstock.com

## Controlling Conflict

One method of controlling conflict is to expand the resource base. Suppose a top manager receives two budget requests for $100,000 each. If she has only $180,000 to distribute, the stage is set for conflict because each group will believe its proposal is worth funding and will be unhappy if it is not fully funded. If both proposals are indeed worthwhile, it may be possible for the manager to come up with the extra $20,000 from some other source and thereby avoid difficulty.

As noted earlier, pooled, sequential, and reciprocal interdependence can all result in conflict. If managers use an appropriate technique for enhancing coordination, they can reduce the probability that conflict will arise. Techniques for coordination (described in Chapter 11) include making use of the managerial hierarchy, relying on rules and procedures, enlisting liaison people, forming task forces, and integrating departments. At the JCPenney store mentioned earlier, the conflict was addressed by providing salespeople with clearer forms on which to specify the merchandise they needed and in what sequence. If one coordination technique does not have the desired effect, a manager might shift to another one.[39]

Competing goals can also be a source of conflict among individuals and groups. Managers can sometimes focus employee attention on higher-level, or superordinate, goals as a way of eliminating lower-level conflict. When labor unions like the United Auto Workers make wage concessions to ensure the survival of the automobile industry, they are responding to a superordinate goal. Their immediate goal may be higher wages for members, but they realize that, without the automobile industry, their members would not even have jobs.

Finally, managers should try to match the personalities and work habits of employees so as to avoid conflict between individuals. For instance, two valuable subordinates, one a chain smoker and the other a vehement antismoker, probably should not be required to work together in an enclosed space. If conflict does arise between incompatible people, a manager might seek an equitable transfer for one or both of them to other units.

## Resolving and Eliminating Conflict

Despite everyone's best intentions, conflict sometimes flares up. If it is disrupting the workplace, creating too much hostility and tension, or otherwise harming the organization, attempts must be made to resolve it.[40] Some managers who are uncomfortable dealing with conflict choose to avoid the conflict and hope it will go away. Avoidance may sometimes be effective in the short run for some kinds of interpersonal disagreements, but it does little to resolve long-run or chronic conflicts. Even more unadvisable, though, is "smoothing"—minimizing the conflict and telling everyone that things will "get better." Often the conflict only worsens as people continue to brood over it.

Compromise is striking a middle-range position between two extremes. This approach can work if it is used with care, but in most compromise situations, someone wins and someone loses. Budget problems are one of the few areas amenable to compromise because of their objective nature. Assume, for example, that additional resources are not available to the manager mentioned earlier. She has $180,000 to divide, and each of two groups claims to need $100,000. If the manager believes that both projects warrant funding, she can allocate $90,000 to each. The fact that the two groups have at least been treated equally may minimize the potential conflict.

The confrontational approach to conflict resolution—also called *interpersonal problem solving*—consists of bringing the parties together to confront the conflict. The parties discuss the nature of their conflict and try to reach an agreement or a solution. Confrontation requires a reasonable degree of maturity on the part of the participants, and the manager must structure the situation carefully. If handled well, this approach can be an effective means of resolving conflict. In recent years, many organizations have experimented with a technique called *alternative dispute resolution*, using a team of employees to arbitrate conflict in this way.[41] Negotiation, a closely related method, is discussed in our final section.

Regardless of the approach, organizations and their managers should realize that conflict must be addressed if it is to serve constructive purposes and be prevented from bringing about destructive consequences. Conflict is inevitable in organizations, but its effects can be constrained with proper attention. For example, Union Carbide sent 200 of its managers to a three-day workshop on conflict management. The managers engaged in a variety of exercises and discussions to learn with whom they were most likely to come in conflict and how they should try to resolve it. As a result, managers at the firm later reported that hostility and resentment in the organization had been greatly diminished and that people in the firm reported more pleasant working relationships.[42]

## Negotiation

Negotiation is the process in which two or more parties (people or groups) reach agreement on an issue even though they have different preferences regarding that issue. In its simplest form the parties involved may be two individuals who are trying to decide who will pay for lunch. A little more complexity is involved when two people, such as an employee and a manager, sit down to decide on personal performance goals for the next year against which the employee's performance will be measured. Even more complex are the negotiations that take place between labor unions and the management of a company or between two companies as they negotiate the terms of a joint venture. The key issues in such negotiations are that at least two parties are involved, their preferences are different, and they need to reach agreement. Interest in negotiation has grown steadily in recent years.[43] Four primary approaches to negotiation have dominated this study: individual differences, situational characteristics, game theory, and cognitive approaches.

Early psychological approaches concentrated on the personality traits of the negotiators.[44] Traits investigated have included demographic characteristics and personality variables. Demographic characteristics have included age, gender, and race, among others. Personality variables have included risk taking, locus of control, tolerance for ambiguity, self-esteem, authoritarianism, and Machiavellianism. The assumption of this type of research was that the key to successful negotiation was selecting the right person to do the negotiating, one who had the appropriate demographic characteristics or personality. This assumption seemed to make sense because negotiation is such a personal and interactive process. However, the research rarely showed the positive results expected because situational variables negated the effects of the individual differences.[45]

Situational characteristics are the context within which negotiation takes place. They include such things as the types of communication between negotiators, the potential outcomes of the negotiation, the relative power of the parties (both positional and personal), the time frame available for negotiation, the number of people representing each side, and the presence of other parties. Some of this research has contributed to our understanding of the negotiation process. However, the shortcomings of the situational approach are similar to those of the individual characteristics approach. Many situational characteristics are external to the negotiators and beyond their control. Often the negotiators cannot change their relative power positions or the setting within which the negotiation occurs. So, although we have learned a lot from research on the situational issues, we still need to learn much more about the process.

Game theory was developed by economists using mathematical models to predict the outcome of negotiation situations (as illustrated in the Academy Award–winning movie *A Beautiful Mind*). It requires that every alternative and outcome be analyzed with probabilities and numerical outcomes reflecting the preferences for each outcome. In addition, the order in which different parties can make choices and every possible move are predicted, along with associated preferences for outcomes. The outcomes of this approach are exactly what negotiators want: a predictive model of how negotiation should be conducted. One major drawback is that it requires the ability to describe all possible options and outcomes for every possible move in every situation before the negotiation starts. This is often very tedious, if possible at all. Another problem is that this theory assumes that negotiators are rational at all times. Other research in negotiation has shown that negotiators often do not

**negotiation**
The process in which two or more parties (people or groups) reach agreement on an issue even though they have different preferences regarding that issue

act rationally. Therefore, this approach, although elegant in its prescriptions, is usually unworkable in a real negotiation situation.

The fourth approach is the cognitive approach, which recognizes that negotiators often depart from perfect rationality during negotiation; it tries to predict how and when negotiators will make these departures. Howard Raiffa's decision analytic approach focuses on providing advice to negotiators actively involved in negotiation.[46] Bazerman and Neale have added to Raiffa's work by specifying eight ways in which negotiators systematically deviate from rationality.[47] The types of deviations they describe include escalation of commitment to a previously selected course of action, overreliance on readily available information, assuming that the negotiations can produce fixed-sum outcomes, and anchoring negotiation in irrelevant information. These cognitive approaches have advanced the study of negotiation a long way beyond the early individual and situational approaches. Negotiators can use them to attempt to predict in advance how the negotiation might take place.

---

☐ What techniques are available to managers to stimulate, control, and resolve conflict?

☐ What are the primary risks involved if a manager decides to stimulate conflict?

**Manager's Checklist**

# Summary of Learning Outcomes and Key Points

1. Define and identify types of groups and teams in organizations, discuss reasons why people join groups and teams, and list the stages of group and team development.

   - A group is two or more people who interact regularly to accomplish a common purpose or goal.
   - General kinds of groups in organizations are
     o functional groups
     o task groups and teams
     o informal or interest groups
   - A team is a group of workers that functions as a unit, often with little or no supervision, to carry out organizational functions.

2. Identify and discuss four essential characteristics of groups and teams.

   - People join functional groups and teams to pursue a career.
   - Their reasons for joining informal or interest groups include interpersonal attraction, group activities, group goals, need satisfaction, and potential instrumental benefits.
   - The stages of team development include testing and dependence, intragroup conflict and hostility, development of group cohesion, and focusing on the problem at hand.

   - Four important characteristics of teams are role structures, behavioral norms, cohesiveness, and informal leadership.
     o Role structures define task and socioemotional specialists and may be disrupted by role ambiguity, role conflict, or role overload.
     o Norms are standards of behavior for group members.
     o Cohesiveness is the extent to which members are loyal and committed to the team and to one another.
     o Informal leaders are those leaders whom the group members themselves choose to follow.

3. Discuss interpersonal and intergroup conflict in organizations.

   - Conflict is a disagreement between two or more people, groups, or organizations.
   - Too little or too much conflict may hurt performance, but an optimal level of conflict may improve performance.
   - Interpersonal and intergroup conflict in organizations may be caused by personality differences or by particular organizational strategies and practices.

4. Describe how organizations manage conflict.

   • Organizations may encounter conflict with one another and with various elements of the environment.

• Three methods of managing conflict are
  o to stimulate it
  o to control it
  o to resolve and eliminate it

# Discussion Questions

### Questions for Review

1. What is a group? Describe the several different types of groups and indicate the similarities and differences among them. What is the difference between a group and a team?

2. What are the stages of group development? Do all teams develop through all the stages discussed in this chapter? Why or why not? How might the management of a mature team differ from the management of teams that are not yet mature?

3. Describe the development of a role within a group. Tell how each role leads to the next.

4. Describe the causes of conflict in organizations. What can a manager do to control conflict? To resolve and eliminate conflict?

### Questions for Analysis

5. Individuals join groups for a variety of reasons. Most groups contain members who joined for different reasons. What is likely to be the result when members join a group for different reasons? What can a group leader do to reduce the negative impact of a conflict in reasons for joining the group?

6. Consider the case of a developed group, where all members have been socialized. What are the benefits to the individuals of norm conformity? What are the benefits of not conforming to the group's norms? What are the benefits to an organization of conformity? What are the benefits to an organization of nonconformity?

7. Do you think teams are a valuable new management technique that will endure, or are they just a fad that will be replaced with something else in the near future?

### Questions for Application

8. Think of several groups of which you have been a member. Why did you join each? Did each group progress through the stages of development discussed in this chapter? If not, why do you think it did not?

9. Describe the behavioral norms that are in effect in your management class. To what extent are the norms generalized; in other words, how severely are students "punished" for not observing norms? To what extent is there norm variation; that is, are some students able to "get away" with violating norms to which others must conform?

10. Describe a case of interpersonal conflict that you have observed in an organization. Describe a case of intergroup conflict that you have observed. (If you have not observed any, interview a worker or manager to obtain examples.) In each case, was the conflict beneficial or harmful to the organization, and why?

# Building Effective Conceptual Skills

### Exercise Overview

Conceptual skills require you to think in the abstract. This exercise will allow you to practice your conceptual skills as they apply to the activities of work teams in organizations.

### Exercise Background

Business organizations, of course, don't have a monopoly on effective groups. Basketball teams and military squadrons are teams, as is a government policy group such as the president's cabinet, the leadership of a church or civic organization, or even a student committee.

## Exercise Task

1. Use the Internet to identify an example of a real-life team. Be sure to choose one that meets two criteria: (i) it's not part of a for-profit business and (ii) you can argue that it's highly effective.

2. Determine the reasons for the team's effectiveness. (*Hint:* You might look for websites sponsored by the group itself, review online news sources for current articles about it, or enter the group name in a search engine.) Consider team characteristics and activities, such as role structures, norms, cohesiveness, and conflict management.

3. What can a manager learn from the characteristics and activities of this particular team? How might the factors that contribute to this team's success be adopted in a business setting?

# Building Effective Communication Skills

## Exercise Overview

Communication skills refer not only to the ability to convey information and ideas to others but to handle information and ideas received from them. They're essential to effective teamwork because teams depend on the ability of members to send and receive information that's accurate. This exercise invites you to play a game designed to demonstrate how good communication skills can lead to improved teamwork and team performance.

## Exercise Background

You'll play this game in three separate rounds. In round 1, you're on your own. In round 2, you'll work in a small group and share information. You'll also work in a small group in round 3, but this time, you'll have the additional benefit of some suggestions for improving the group's performance. Typically, students find that performance improves over the course of the three rounds. In particular, they find that creativity is enhanced when information is shared.

## Exercise Task

1. Play the "Name Game" that your professor will explain to you. In round 1, work out your answers individually and then report your individual score to the class.

2. For round 2, you'll join a group of three to five students. Work out your answers together and write your group answers on a single sheet of paper. Now allow each group member to look at the answer sheet. If you can do so without being overheard by other groups, have each group member whisper the answers on the sheet to the group. Report your group score to the class.

3. Your professor will then ask the highest-performing individuals and groups to share their methods with the class. At this point, your professor will make some suggestions.

Be sure to consider at least two strategies for improving your score.

4. Now play round 3, working together in the same small groups in which you participated in round 2. Report your group scores to the class.

5. Did average group scores improve upon average individual scores? Why or why not?

6. Did average group scores improve after methods for improvement were discussed at the end of round 2? Why or why not?

7. What has this game taught you about teamwork and effectiveness? Share your thoughts with the class.

# Skill-Building Personal Assessment

## Using Teams

**Introduction:** The use of groups and teams is becoming more common in organizations throughout the world. The following assessment surveys your beliefs about the effective use of teams in work organizations.

**Instructions:** You will agree with some of the statements and disagree with others. In some cases you may find making a decision difficult, but you should force yourself to make a choice. Record your answers next to each statement according to the following scale:

## Rating Scale

4    Strongly agree
3    Somewhat agree
2    Somewhat disagree
1    Strongly disagree

1. _____ Each person in a work team should have a clear assignment so that individual accountability can be maintained.

2. _____ For a team to function effectively, the team must be given complete authority over all aspects of the task.

3. _____ One way to get teams to work is simply to assemble a group of people, tell them in general what needs to be done, and let them work out the details.

4. _____ Once a team gets going, management can turn its attention to other matters.

5. _____ To ensure that a team develops into a cohesive working unit, managers should be especially careful not to intervene in any way during the initial startup period.

6. _____ Training is not critical to a team because the team will develop any needed skills on its own.

7. _____ It's easy to provide teams with the support they need because they are basically self-motivating.

8. _____ Teams need little or no structure to function effectively.

9. _____ Teams should set their own direction, with managers determining the means to the selected end.

10. _____ Teams can be used in any organization.

Source: *Test: adapted from J. Richard Hackman, ed.,* Groups That Work (and Those That Don't), *San Francisco: Jossey-Bass Publishers, 1990, pp. 493–504.*

# Management at Work

An Open Invitation to Innovation

"Any five-year-old has no trouble turning an old blanket and a couple of chairs into an impenetrable fort."

—NINESIGMA CEO ANDY ZYNGA

In 2006, a well-known multinational company hired an innovation consulting firm called NineSigma to draw up a *request for proposal* (RFP) entitled "Nanoparticle Halide Salt: Formulation and Delivery." According to NineSigma CEO Andy Zynga, providing an RFP means "crafting a very precise written needs statement for vetted solution providers who have known expertise in specific areas." In this case, the client was in the market for a chemically designed salt with specific properties—a compound for which its own R&D department didn't have the necessary expertise. So NineSigma, reports Zynga, "marketed" its RFP "to a broad audience of technical experts. Proposals came in from a variety of industries and organization types, including energy and fuels, pharma, and engineering services." The winning proposal was submitted by a team of orthopedics researchers who had created nanoparticles of salt for studies of osteoporosis.

And that's how PepsiCo developed a way to reduce the sodium content of Lay's Classic potato chips without sacrificing the flavor that consumers were used to. This approach to an expanded search for solutions is sometimes called *open innovation,* which Zynga defines as "the process of reaching beyond your team, company, or industry for technologies, solutions, ideas, and knowledge available through global solution-provider networks. ... The rationale," he explains, "is that partnering with outside innovators may lead to something even better and will undoubtedly accelerate the process if a more advanced solution exists elsewhere."

In a very real sense, although it's a "process of reaching beyond your team," open innovation is also an extension of the principle of building teams with a greater diversity of input.* David Feitler, senior program manager at NineSigma, points to a parallel between team building as a means of breaking down *internal* barriers to problem solving and open innovation as a means of breaking down *external* barriers. Feitler explains that another NineSigma client, the Dutch-based multinational paint manufacturer AzkoNobel, was already practicing open innovation as a means of breaching external barriers when it approached NineSigma about improving internal collaboration. The

*This case deals with *functional diversity*—diversity in professional or organizational training, experience, or expertise. The *Management in Action* vignette at the beginning of the chapter focuses on *cultural* or *social diversity*—diversity in race, ethnicity, or gender.

company was divided into 11 autonomous divisions, and it had grown mainly by means of acquisition. As a result, says Feitler, it "had the typical silos, with organizational and geographical boundaries inhibiting the diffusion of knowledge.

"The solution," he reports,

*was to implement the request for proposal process inside the organization, broadly training large numbers of technical staff in the process and more intensively training a core group of "Internal Program Managers" to provide the coaching and guidance required for a well-specified search [for collaborative ideas].*

Two years later, adds Feitler, AzkoNobel had developed a process of assembling "ad hoc SWAT teams" which allows "individuals with challenging problems … to tap into a system that gives them rapid access to colleagues in other divisions and countries."

The idea of "ad hoc SWAT teams," argues Feitler, is consistent with the findings of studies on the role of so called *cross-pollination*—the recombination of previously unrelated ideas—in the diffusion of innovation. In particular, Feitler cites research led by Harvard University's Lee Fleming, who culled data from every U.S. patent granted since 1975. What did Fleming and his team want to find out from all of this data? First, they wanted to know what kind of networks among inventors and researchers had been developed to foster significant cross-pollination. Second, they were interested in how different networks contribute to "creativity," which is commonly defined as the combining of familiar ideas in unexpected ways.

Fleming's team identified two different network models that tend to result in "novel combinations": (1) the *broker*, which revolves around an influential person who's connected to many other people who don't know each other; and (2) the *connector*, which revolves around an influential person who often introduces his collaborators to each other. The researchers found that organizations functioning as brokers were more likely to generate new ideas because they occupied a central position through which information and ideas travel. By the same token, brokers typically found it harder than connectors to get their ideas publicized.

Some related research goes into more practical detail. Gratton and Erickson, for instance, found that cross-pollination "almost always requires the input and expertise of people with disparate views and backgrounds." In other words, *diversity* of expertise and experience is critical, but Gratton and Erickson also concluded that it can "inhibit collaboration": "Diversity," they observe,

*often means that team members are working with people that they know only superficially or have never met before—colleagues drawn from other divisions of the company, perhaps, or even from outside it. We have found that the higher the proportion of strangers on the team and the greater the diversity of background and experience, the less likely the team members are to share knowledge or exhibit other collaborative behaviors.*

In turn, these findings are consistent with Fleming's conclusion that "the evidence linking breakthroughs with multidisciplinary collaborations remains mixed. On average," advises Fleming, "it's more productive to search within established disciplines. Or, when trying to cross-pollinate between fields, the more appropriate approach is to combine areas that have some common ground." Fleming limits the term "breakthrough" to those "very, very few" inventions or innovations that ultimately produce the highest level of value. Thus when it comes to diversity or "multidisciplinary collaboration," the issue is whether "the divergence between collaborators' fields of expertise" is more or less likely to yield a breakthrough. In this respect, the results were in fact mixed. Fleming found, for example, that the greater this divergence, "the lower the *overall* quality" of a team's output. At the same time, however, outputs will vary more widely from useless to extremely valuable, thus making breakthroughs more likely.

Finally, let's go back to NineSigma's Andy Zynga, who attributes the impasse faced by PepsiCo's internal problem solvers to a "cognitive bias" that psychologists call *functional fixedness*. "Any five-year-old," observes Zynga, "has no trouble turning an old blanket and a couple of chairs into an impenetrable fort. But as we get older, knowledge and experience increasingly displace imagination and our ability to see an object for anything other than its original purpose."

Adult-run organizations, Zynga argues, encounter functional fixedness on a much more complex level: "Technologists, engineers, and designers," he says, "not only have their own expertise, they have their own way of applying their expertise. Ironically, the more success they've had with their approach to a solution, the harder it is to imagine a different one." As Zynga sees it, open innovation "replicates the process that a five-year-old goes through to see the potential of a fort in a couple of chairs and a blanket." It's all a matter of making connections between what you want to create and objects—or ideas—that apparently have unrelated applications. "Open innovation practitioners," explains Zynga, "source solutions to specific problems in [an analogous] way—by enabling a connection between a need and potential solutions that reside in unrelated industries."

## Case Questions

1. How good are you at "thinking outside the box"? Are you fixated on functionality? Try solving the following problem before googling the solution.

   You have the three items pictured here: a book of matches, a box of thumbtacks, and a candle.

   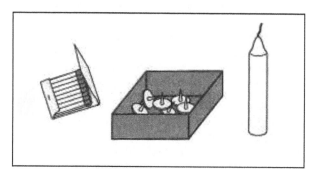

   How can you attach the candle to a wall so that, when it's lit, wax doesn't drip on the floor?[†]

2. Explain the advantages and disadvantages of open innovation and multidisciplinary collaboration in terms of team *cohesion*. What aspects of such teams, for example, may increase cohesiveness? Which aspects may reduce cohesiveness?

3. Consider teams formed for multidisciplinary collaboration or as a result of open innovation in terms of *role structure*. Is role structure, for example, likely to be set or to evolve differently than it usually does in internal functional or task groups? How might the transmission of *sent roles* be more complicated? Is *role ambiguity* likely to be more prevalent? How about *role conflict* (in particular, *intrarole conflict*)?

4. Gratton and Erickson describe two *leadership styles* among leaders of multidisciplinary teams:

   - *relationship-oriented leaders* tend to foster "an environment of trust and goodwill in which people are more likely to share knowledge";
   - *task-oriented leaders* help "to make objectives clear, to create a shared awareness of the dimensions of the task, and to provide monitoring and feedback."

   First of all, ask yourself which of these two leadership styles you're more comfortable with. In other words, if you were assigned to lead a team, which leadership style would you probably bring to the task?

   Now assume that you have been assigned to lead a team of fellow students in drafting a proposed curriculum of required courses for freshmen and sophomores at your college. Naturally, the team consists of students with a broad range of majors. What will probably be your strengths as leader of your group? What will probably be your weaknesses?

   Finally, in trying to determine which style—relationship or task oriented—was most effective in leading collaborative teams, Gratton and Erickson concluded that

   > *an emphasis throughout a project on one style at the expense of the other inevitably hindered the long-term performance of the team. … The most productive, innovative teams were typically led by people who were both task and relationship oriented. What's more, these leaders changed their style during the project.*

   Under what circumstances will you most likely have to change your leadership style in order to keep the group working effectively? Try to be specific in identifying circumstances that might arise over the course of your team project. What do you need to do in order to adjust your style to shifting circumstances?

[†]1. Remove the tacks from the box.
2. Tack the box to the wall.
3. Put the candle in the box.
4. Light the candle.

## Case References

Andy Zynga, "The Cognitive Bias Keeping Us from Innovating," *Harvard Business Review* (June 13, 2013), https://hbr.org, on May 29, 2015; Zynga, "Top Five Open Innovation Myths Debunked," *Wired* (May 15, 2014), http://insights.wired.com, on May 30, 2015; Betsy McKay, "PepsiCo Develops 'Designer Salt' to Chip Away at Sodium Intake," *Wall Street Journal* (March 22, 2010), www.wsj.com, on May 30, 2015; David Feitler, "The Case for Team Diversity Gets Even Better," *Harvard Business Review* (March 27, 2014), https://hbr.org, on May 29, 2015; Lee Fleming, "Breakthroughs and the 'Long Tail' of Innovation," *MIT Sloan Management Review* (Fall 2007), http://sloanreview.mit.edu, on May 31, 2015; Elizabeth Gudrais, "Innovation at the Intersection," *Harvard Magazine* (May-June 2010), http://harvardmagazine.com, on May 31, 2015; Lynda Gratton and Tamara J. Erickson, "Eight Ways to Build Collaborative Teams," *Harvard Business Review* (November 2007), https://hbr.org, on May 29, 2015.

## YOU MAKE THE CALL  Promoting the Cause of Diversity

1. According to Katherine W. Phillips,

   *Research has shown that social diversity in a group can cause discomfort, rougher interactions, a lack of trust, greater perceived interpersonal conflict, lower communication, less cohesion, more concern about disrespect, and other problems. So what is the upside?*[*]

   Provide a cogent answer to Phillips's closing question—that is, one which reflects what you've learned about diversity, group dynamics, workplace teams, and creativity/innovation.

2. Discuss the pros and cons of socially diverse teams in terms of *behavioral norms*. What, for example, is likely to be the extent of *norm variation* in a diverse team? What sorts of variations are likely to affect team performance? How might group leaders deal with such variations? How might they manage variations to the team's benefit? To what extent should group leaders encourage *norm conformity*? What steps can leaders take to encourage conformity?

3. Among "Challenges Faced by Diverse Teams," Beryl Nelson includes *unconscious bias* and *stereotype threat*. We define *stereotyping* in Chapter 14 as "the process of categorizing people on the basis of a single attribute." Nelson explains that stereotypes

   *are learned through cultural messages and stories, comments from family and friends, portrayals in the media, and so forth. Despite our best intentions, they can bias our impressions of, and affect our actions toward, others in our environment. … They shape our expectations of what people should be doing, especially at work… The stereotypes especially relevant in work situations include not only those characteristics that are visible, such as sex, race, weight, and age, but also those not visible but relatively easy to discern, such as educational background and nationality.*[†]

   Nelson also points out that "almost everyone has measurable biases." An ongoing test conducted by Harvard's

   Project Implicit has found, for example, that 70% to 80% of all participants have a bias against women in technology. Findings such as those by Project Implicit indicate the *stereotype threat* to teams composed of diverse members.

   First, explain various ways in which *stereotype threat* can keep a diverse team from being as effective as it could be.

   Second, suggest a few strategies that group and organizational leaders can take to reduce *stereotype threat*.

   Finally, think about your own biases: What biases do you harbor about women (e.g., they don't have an aptitude for math)? About men (e.g., they aren't altruistic or eager to help others)? What biases do you harbor about Asians, African Americans, Hispanics, and older people? Bear in mind, by the way, that even people who are subject to a given bias can actually share it.[‡]

4. *Beware of lurking variables.* In the following two examples, cause-and-effect conclusions have been drawn from evidence of correlation. In each case, the conclusion is false because there is a so-called "lurking variable"—an unstated third variable that affects *both* causes of the correlation. Identify a *probable* lurking variable in each example and explain why each conclusion is false.

   a. When ice cream sales increase, drowning deaths also increase. Therefore, ice cream consumption causes drowning.
   b. A great many people who sleep with their shoes on often wake up with headaches. Therefore, sleeping with one's shoes on causes headaches.

   In the next two examples, matters are complicated because the correlation may work both ways. First, provide both *yes* and *no* answers to the question posed by each statement. Next, identify a *probable* lurking variable in each case and explain why both *yes* and *no* answers are *likely* to be false.

   c. Surveys show that workers who say that they're happy with their jobs tend to be quite productive. Does being happy cause workers to be more productive?
   d. Surveys show that couples who live together before marriage have a higher rate of divorce than couples who don't live together before marriage. Does living together cause divorce?[**]

[*]"How Diversity Makes Us Smarter," *Scientific American* (September 16, 2014), www.scientificamerican.com, on May 29, 2015.
[†]"The Data on Diversity," *Communications of the ACM*, 2014, Vol. 57, No. 11, pp. 86–95, http://cacm.acm.org, on June 2, 2015.
[‡]You can join 8 million other people in taking the Harvard Implicit test at https://implicit.harvard.edu/implicit/.

[**]Lurking variables:
a. seasonal temperature.
b. alcohol consumption.
c. job-skill match.
d. liberal attitudes toward living together and divorce.

# Endnotes

1 Beryl Nelson, "The Data on Diversity," *Communications of the ACM*, 2014, Vol. 57, No. 11, pp. 86–95, http://cacm.acm.org, on June 2, 2015; Katherine W. Phillips, "How Diversity Makes Us Smarter," *Scientific American* (September 16, 2014), www.scientificamerican.com, on May 29, 2015; Vivian Hunt, Dennis Layton, and Sara Prince, "Why Diversity Matters" (McKinsey & Co., *Insights & Publications*, January 2015), www.mckinsey.com, on June 5, 2015; Peter Dizikes, "Study: Workplace Diversity Can Help the Bottom Line," *MIT News* (October 7, 2014), http://newsoffice.mit.edu, on June 5, 2015; Michael Blanding, "Cultural Disharmony Undermines Workplace Creativity," *Harvard Business School Working Knowledge* (December 9, 2013), http://hbswk.hbs.edu, on June 2, 2015; Roy Y. J. Chua, "The Costs of Ambient Social Disharmony: Indirect Intercultural Conflicts in Social Environment Undermine Creativity" (abstract), *Academy of Management Journal*, 2013, Vol. 56, No. 6, pp. 1545–1577, www.hbs.edu, on June 6, 2015.

2 For a review of definitions of groups, see Gregory Moorhead and Ricky W. Griffin, *Organizational Behavior*, 10th ed. (Cincinnati, OH: Cengage Learning, 2012).

3 Dorwin Cartwright and Alvin Zander (eds.), *Group Dynamics: Research and Theory*, 3rd ed. (New York: Harper & Row, 1968).

4 See Willem Verbeke and Stefan Wuyts, "Moving in Social Circles—Social Circle Membership and Performance Implications," *Journal of Organizational Behavior*, 2007, Vol. 28, pp. 357–379 for an interesting extension of these ideas.

5 Rob Cross, Nitin Nohria, and Andrew Parker, "Six Myths about Informal Networks—And How to Overcome Them," *Sloan Management Review*, Spring 2002, pp. 67–77.

6 Robert Schrank, *Ten Thousand Working Days* (Cambridge, MA: MIT Press, 1978); Bill Watson, "Counter Planning on the Shop Floor," in Peter Frost, Vance Mitchell, and Walter Nord (eds.), *Organizational Reality*, 2nd ed. (Glenview, IL: Scott, Foresman, 1982), pp. 286–294.

7 "After Layoffs, More Workers Band Together," *Wall Street Journal*, February 26, 2002, p. B1.

8 Bradley L. Kirkman and Benson Rosen, "Powering Up Teams," *Organizational Dynamics*, Winter 2000, pp. 48–58.

9 John Mathieu, M. Travis Maynard, Tammy Rapp, and Lucy Gibson, "Team Effectiveness 1997–2007: A Review of Recent Advancements and a Glimpse into the Future," *Journal of Management*, 2008, Vol. 34, No. 3, p. 410–476.

10 Arvind Malhotra, Ann Majchrzak, and Benson Rosen, "Leading Virtual Teams," *Academy of Management Perspectives*, 2007, Vol. 21, No. 1, pp. 60–70.

11 "Why Teams Fail," *USA Today*, February 25, 1997, pp. 1B, 2B.

12 Brian Dumaine, "The Trouble with Teams," *Fortune*, September 5, 1994, pp. 86–92. See also Susan G. Cohen and Diane E. Bailey, "What Makes Teams Work: Group Effectiveness Research from the Shop Floor to the Executive Suite," *Journal of Management*, 1997, Vol. 23, No. 3, pp. 239–290; and John Mathieu, Lucy Gilson, and Thomas Ruddy, "Empowerment and Team Effectiveness: An Empirical Test of an Integrated Model," *Journal of Applied Psychology*, 2006, Vol. 91, No. 1, pp. 97–108.

13 *Fortune*, June 12, 2006, p. 122.

14 Marvin E. Shaw, *Group Dynamics: The Psychology of Small Group Behavior*, 4th ed. (New York: McGraw-Hill, 1985).

15 "How to Avoid Hiring the Prima Donnas Who Hate Teamwork," *Wall Street Journal*, February 15, 2000, p. B1.

16 *Fortune*, June 12, 2006, p. 88.

17 See Connie Gersick, "Marking Time: Predictable Transitions in Task Groups," *Academy of Management Journal*, June 1989, pp. 274–309. See also Janis A. Cannon-Bowers and Clint Bowers, "Team Development and Functioning," in Sheldon Zedeck (ed.), *Handbook of Industrial and Organizational Psychology*, Vol. 1: *Building and Developing the Organization* (Washington, DC: American Psychological Association, 2010), pp. 597–650.

18 See Gilad Chen, "Newcomer Adaptation in Teams: Multilevel Antecedents and Outcomes," *Academy of Management Journal*, 2005, Vol. 48, No. 1, pp. 101–116.

19 For a review of other team characteristics, see Michael Campion, Gina Medsker, and A. Catherine Higgs, "Relations Between Work Group Characteristics and Effectiveness: Implications for Designing Effective Work Groups," *Personnel Psychology*, Winter 1993, pp. 823–850.

20 David Katz and Robert L. Kahn, *The Social Psychology of Organizations*, 2nd ed. (New York: Wiley, 1978), pp. 197–221. See also David M. Sluss, Rolf van Dick, and Bryant S. Thompson, "Role Theory in Organizations: A Relational Perspective," in Sheldon Zedeck (ed.), *Handbook of Industrial and Organizational Psychology*, Vol. 1: *Building and Developing the Organization* (Washington, DC: American Psychological Association, 2010), pp. 503–534.

21 See Travis C. Tubre and Judith M. Collins, "Jackson and Schuler (1985) Revisited: A Meta-Analysis of the Relationships Between Role Ambiguity, Role Conflict, and Job Performance," *Journal of Management*, 2000, Vol. 26, No. 1, pp. 155–169.

22 Robert L. Kahn, D. M. Wolfe, R. P. Quinn, J. D. Snoek, and R. A. Rosenthal, *Organizational Stress: Studies in Role Conflict and Role Ambiguity* (New York: Wiley, 1964).

23 *Fortune*, June 12, 2006, p. 88.

24 Daniel C. Feldman, "The Development and Enforcement of Group Norms," *Academy of Management Review*, January 1984, pp. 47–53.

25 "Companies Turn to Peer Pressure to Cut Injuries as Psychologists Join the Battle," *Wall Street Journal*, March 29, 1991, pp. B1, B3.

26 James Wallace Bishop and K. Dow Scott, "How Commitment Affects Team Performance," *HR Magazine*, February 1997, pp. 107–115.

27 Anne O'Leary-Kelly, Joseph Martocchio, and Dwight Frink, "A Review of the Influence of Group Goals on Group Performance," *Academy of Management Journal*, 1994, Vol. 37, No. 5, pp. 1285–1301.

28 See Anat Drach-Zahavy and Anat Freund, "Team Effectiveness Under Stress: A Structural Contingency Approach," *Journal of Organizational Behavior*, 2007, Vol. 28, pp. 423–450 for an interesting application of these ideas.

29 Philip M. Podsakoff, Michael Ahearne, and Scott B. MacKenzie, "Organizational Citizenship Behavior and the Quantity and Quality of Work Group Performance, *Journal of Applied Psychology*, 1997, Vol. 82, No. 2, pp. 262–270.

30 Suzy Wetlaufer, "Common Sense and Conflict," *Harvard Business Review*, January–February 2000, pp. 115–125.

31 Kathleen M. Eisenhardt, Jean L. Kahwajy, and L. J. Bourgeois III, "How Management Teams Can Have a Good Fight," *Harvard Business Review*, July–August 1997, pp. 77–89.

32 Thomas Bergmann and Roger Volkema, "Issues, Behavioral Responses and Consequences in Interpersonal Conflicts," *Journal of Organizational Behavior*, 1994, Vol. 15, pp. 467–471; see also Carsten K. W. De Dreu, "The Virtue and Vice of Workplace Conflict: Food for (Pessimistic) Thought," *Journal of Organizational Behavior*, 2008, Vol. 29, pp. 5–19.

33 Robin Pinkley and Gregory Northcraft, "Conflict Frames of Reference: Implications for Dispute Processes and Outcomes," *Academy of Management Journal*, 1994, Vol. 37, No. 1, pp. 193–205.

34 "How 2 Computer Nuts Transformed Industry before Messy Breakup," *Wall Street Journal*, August 27, 1996, pp. A1, A10.

35 Bruce Barry and Greg L. Stewart, "Composition, Process, and Performance in Self-Managed Groups: The Role of Personality," *Journal of Applied Psychology*, 1997, Vol. 82, No. 1, pp. 62–78.

36 "Acer CEO Resigns Suddenly amid Conflict with Board," *Gadget News Today*, March 31, 2011.

37 "Hilton and Starwood Settle Dispute," *New York Times*, December 22, 2010.

38 See Patrick Nugent, "Managing Conflict: Third-Party Interventions for Managers," *Academy of Management Executive*, 2002, Vol. 16, No. 1, pp. 139–148.

39 Gerardo A. Okhuysen and Beth A. Bechky, "Coordination in Organizations: An Integrative Perspective," in James P. Walsh and Arthur P. Brief (eds.), *The Academy of Management Annals 2009* (Philadelphia: Taylor and Francis, 2009), pp. 463–502.

40 See Kristin J. Behfar, Randall S. Peterson, Elizabeth A. Mannix, and William M. K. Trochim, "The Critical Role of Conflict Resolution in Teams: A Close Look at the Links Between Conflict, Conflict Management Strategies, and Team Outcomes," *Journal of Applied Psychology*, 2008, Vol. 93, No. 1, pp. 170–198.

41 "Solving Conflicts in the Workplace Without Making Losers," *Wall Street Journal*, May 27, 1997, p. B1.

42 "Teaching Business How to Cope with Workplace Conflicts," *BusinessWeek*, February 19, 1990, pp. 136, 139.

43 See Kimberly Wade-Benzoni, Andrew Hoffman, Leigh Thompson, Don Moore, James Gillespie, and Max Bazerman, "Barriers to Resolution in Ideologically

Based Negotiations: The Role of Values and Institutions," *Academy of Management Review*, 2002, Vol. 27, No. 1, pp. 41–57.

44  J. Z. Rubin and B. R. Brown, *The Social Psychology of Bargaining and Negotiation* (New York: Academic Press, 1975).

45  R. J. Lewicki and J. A. Litterer, *Negotiation* (Homewood, IL: Irwin, 1985).

46  Howard Raiffa, *The Art and Science of Negotiation* (Cambridge, MA: Belknap, 1982).

47  K. H. Bazerman and M. A. Neale, *Negotiating Rationally* (New York: Free Press, 1992).

©Markus Pfaff/Shutterstock.com

# 19

# BASIC ELEMENTS OF CONTROL

## Learning Outcomes

**After studying this chapter, you should be able to:**

1. Explain the purpose of control, identify different types of control, and describe the steps in the control process.

2. Identify and explain the three forms of operations control.

3. Describe budgets and other tools for financial control.

4. Identify and distinguish between two opposing forms of structural control.

5. Discuss the relationship between strategy and control, including international strategic control.

6. Identify characteristics of effective control, why people resist control, and how managers can overcome this resistance.

## MANAGEMENT IN ACTION  Metric Tons and Nonfinancial Metrics

"We are well aware that the potential positive impact through our energy and sustainability services to clients can be substantially greater than the environmental impact of our own operations."

—JONES LANG LASALLE

A *Fortune 500* company headquartered in Chicago, Jones Lang LaSalle (JLL) manages property and facilities for clients holding commercial real estate: With 53,000 employees working out of more than 200 offices in 75 countries, JLL oversees 3 billion square feet of property with $47.6 billion in assets. In September 2014, JLL released its 2013 Sustainability Report, entitled *We Are JLL. We Take Responsibility*. As an accounting-related document, the report naturally contains a lot of financial numbers. Between 2007 and 2013, for example, JLL helped U.S. clients reduce greenhouse-gas (GHG) emissions by almost 12 million metric tons, saving them more than $2.5 billion in energy costs. In keeping with this success in saving

clients money, revenue from JLL's Energy and Sustainability Services (ESS) went up 16 percent in 2013. Companywide, revenue in 2013 totaled nearly $4.5 billion, up from $950 million just 10 years earlier.[1]

Unlike the typical financial report, however, JLL's Sustainability Report contains no lengthy tables of accounts and financial results. Rather, it has been prepared in *narrative* form: For the most part, it's written in ordinary language designed to clarify and connect the numbers and to explain the assumptions underlying them. Narrative also permits JLL to explain the factors driving its performance and to show how its various activities are tied to overall corporate strategy. As JLL puts it, "we aimed to reduce the number of metrics, thereby simplifying the message we convey to stakeholders."

Four and a half billion dollars in revenue, for example, is a *financial metric* (a monetary measure), but the metrics in the JLL report aren't simply financial. That 16-percent increase in revenue from ESS, for instance, is a financial metric called *revenue growth rate*, but it also reflects what more and more financial professionals are calling a *key performance indicator (KPI)*—a

Some of these buildings at the World Financial Center in New York City use sustainable energy to stay lit in off-hours, thus impacting both the environment and affecting their firms' overall energy costs.

Drop of Light/Shutterstock.com

measurable value that demonstrates how effectively a company is achieving important business objectives. "The primary reason for including performance indicators in corporate reporting," advises the Big Four accounting firm PricewaterhouseCoopers, "is to enable readers to assess the strategies adopted by the company and their potential to succeed."

In order to understand why revenue growth rate is a KPI for JLL, we thus need a better idea of the company's strategies. Obviously, a company's sustainability report is going to include a discussion of its strategies for *sustainability*—for maintaining a steady level of growth without exhausting resources or causing future ecological damage. The JLL report, for instance, states that the company reduced GHG emissions in its corporate offices by 7 percent per employee from 2012 through 2013. The narrative also provides a detailed explanation of this 7 percent figure:

> In 2013 JLL's total GHG emissions were approximately 52,880 metric tons, up 7% compared with 2012. While our total emissions increased, our business also grew. Our global revenue increased by 13% and the number of corporate office-based employees by 8%. Consequently, our emissions per employee decreased by 7%, to 1.5 metric tons.

The narrative thus reminds readers—primarily JLL stakeholders, including investors—that the metrics of sustainability must be considered in the context of larger strategic goals: While GHG emissions increased because of the operational activities entailed by additional employees, the increase in the company's workforce also reflected growth in business that translated into revenue growth. And that's the message that JLL wants to get across to stakeholders, especially investors.

According to a recent study, U.S.-based institutional investors who consider environmental commitment in their allocation decisions invested almost $2.5 trillion in 2012. The US SIF, a nonprofit association promoting investment in socially responsible companies, reports that "the increased prominence of environmental issues, particularly relating to climate change and carbon emissions," is a key factor in "the near tripling of assets, particularly those held by public funds," available for investment in companies like JLL.

Here's another interesting section from the JLL report:

> We implement green-building practices where possible. Twenty-three of our offices had a

green-building or fit-out certification such as LEED as of 2013. A further 102 offices incorporated green building or fit-out principles but did not obtain a certification. This number is growing (from 15 and 89, respectively, in 2012) as we increase our occupation of green-certified new offices at a higher rate than total offices.

While the statement indicates a sustainability-conscious effort, the data would seem to suggest only modest success. Again, however, the narrative tells a more complete story: JLL typically rents office space in buildings that the company doesn't own, "and as a tenant," explains the report, "JLL has little control over waste practices in the majority of our offices. We manage the waste contract in only 5% of our offices."

Clearly, then, environmental control in its own facilities is not among the premium value drivers of its business that JLL wants to promote among sustainability-conscious investors. What *does* JLL want investors to know about its sustainability efforts? Its Sustainability Report clearly lays out "five focus areas" for those efforts, including "energy and resources," "green buildings," and "client services." In turn, explains JLL, those "five areas of our sustainability strategy cut across two pillars: Services and Operations." We've already looked at JLL's "operational efforts," which it identifies as initiatives "related to our own people and offices." As we've seen, the impact of these efforts is limited.

But what about the efforts that fall under "Services"? "We are well aware," JLL reminds stakeholders, "that the potential positive impact through our energy and sustainability services to clients can be substantially greater than the environmental impact of our own operations." The company's sustainability strategy, therefore, is aimed at *client* outcomes: "An integral part of our Energy and Sustainability Services offering," explains JLL, "is to help clients develop energy management programs that provide measurable savings and results. This approach considers not just how facilities are built, operated, and maintained, but also their location and occupiers' behaviors." In 2012–2013, for instance, JLL's advice allowed clients to save 377 million kilowatt-hours and $39 million in energy costs; in 2013, acting or agreeing to act on JLL's projections, developers planned to avert the release of 18,000 metric tons of $CO_{2e}$—the equivalent of removing 46,300 cars from the road.

Documents like its Sustainability Report are designed to promote what CFO Christie Kelly identifies as "the premium value drivers in JLL's business and how we measure them." In another report, entitled *Sustainability: The Measurement and Reporting Challenge,* the company explains its commitment to the reporting process itself—a process which JLL also regards as critical to its overall sustainability strategy: "Proper measurement and reporting processes," argues the report, "are vital for corporations in order to be accountable and to demonstrate the improvements that they are able to achieve for their stakeholders and the community, while validating their investment in sustainability initiatives."

JLL's Sustainability Report illustrates many of the complexities inherent in the controlling process. Managers must decide where to focus control, what metrics can be used to assess performance, how to interpret those metrics, and what actions to take. As we discussed in Chapter 1, control is one of the four basic managerial functions that provide the organizing framework for this book. This is the first of two chapters devoted to this important area. In the first section of the chapter we explain the purpose of control. We then look at types of control and the steps in the control process. The rest of the chapter examines the four levels of control that most organizations must employ to remain effective: operations, financial, structural, and strategic control. We conclude by discussing the characteristics of effective control, noting why some people resist control and describing what organizations can do to overcome this resistance.

# The Nature of Control

Control is the regulation of organizational activities so that some targeted element of performance remains within acceptable limits. Without this regulation, organizations have no indication of how well they are performing in relation to their goals. Control, like a ship's rudder, keeps the organization moving in the proper direction. At any point in time, it compares where the organization is in terms of performance (financial, productive, or otherwise) to where it is supposed to be. Like a rudder, control provides an organization with a mechanism for adjusting its course if performance falls outside of acceptable boundaries. For example, FedEx has a performance goal of delivering 95 percent of its packages on time. If on-time deliveries fall below 95 percent, control systems will signal the problem to managers, so that they can make necessary adjustments in operations to regain the target level of performance.[2] An organization without effective control procedures is not likely to reach its goals—or, if it does reach them, to know that it has!

## The Purpose of Control

As Figure 19.1 illustrates, control provides an organization with ways to adapt to environmental change, to limit the accumulation of error, to cope with organizational complexity, and to minimize costs. These four functions of control are worth a closer look.

**Adapting to Environmental Change**  In today's complex and turbulent business environment, all organizations must contend with change.[3] If managers could establish goals and achieve them instantaneously, control would not be needed. But between the time a goal is established and the time it is reached, many things can happen in the organization and its environment to disrupt movement toward the goal—or even to change the goal itself. A properly designed control system can help managers anticipate, monitor, and respond to changing circumstances.[4] In contrast, an improperly designed system can result in organizational performance that falls far below acceptable levels.

**control**
The regulation of organizational activities in such a way as to facilitate goal attainment

## FIGURE 19.1  THE PURPOSE OF CONTROL

Control is one of the four basic management functions in organizations. The control function, in turn, has four basic purposes. Properly designed control systems can fulfill each of these purposes.

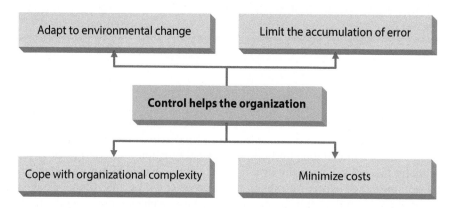

For example, Michigan-based Metalloy, a 60-year-old, family-run metal-casting company, signed a contract to make engine-seal castings for NOK, a big Japanese auto parts maker. Metalloy was satisfied when its first 5,000-unit production run yielded 4,985 acceptable castings and only 15 defective ones. NOK, however, was quite unhappy with this performance and insisted that Metalloy raise its standards. In short, global quality standards in most industries are such that customers demand near-perfection from their suppliers. A properly designed control system can help managers like those at Metalloy stay better attuned to rising standards.

**Limiting the Accumulation of Error**  Small mistakes and errors do not often seriously damage the financial health of an organization. Over time, however, small errors may accumulate and become very serious. For example, Whistler Corporation, a large radar detector manufacturer, was once faced with such rapidly escalating demand that quality essentially became irrelevant. The defect rate rose from 4 percent to 9 percent to 15 percent and eventually reached 25 percent. One day, a manager realized that 100 of the plant's 250 employees were spending all their time fixing defective units and that $2 million worth of inventory was awaiting repair. Had the company adequately controlled quality as it responded to increased demand, the problem would never have reached such proportions. Similarly, a routine quality control inspection of an early prototype of Boeing's 787 Dreamliner revealed that a fastener had not been installed correctly. Closer scrutiny then revealed that literally thousands of fasteners had been installed wrong in every prototype under construction. As a result, the entire project was delayed several months. If the inspection process had been more rigorous to begin with, the error would likely have been found and corrected much earlier, rather than accumulating into a major problem for Boeing.[5]

**Coping with Organizational Complexity**  When a firm purchases only one raw material, produces one product, has a simple organization design, and enjoys constant demand for its product, its managers can maintain control with a very basic and simple system. But a business that produces many products from myriad raw materials and has a large market area, a complicated organization design, and many competitors needs a sophisticated system to maintain adequate control. When large firms merge, the short-term results are often disappointing. The typical reason for this is that the new enterprise is so large and complex that the existing control systems are simply inadequate. Hewlett-Packard and Compaq Computer faced just this problem when HP acquired Compaq and had to address myriad issues to transform the two firms into one. Similarly, when American Airlines and US Airways merged, the entire process took over two years, in large part because of the complexity of each firm.

**Minimizing Costs** When it is practiced effectively, control can also help reduce costs and boost output. For example, Georgia-Pacific Corporation, a large wood-products company, learned of a new technology that could be used to make thinner blades for its saws. The firm's control system was used to calculate the amount of wood that could be saved from each cut made by the thinner blades relative to the costs used to replace the existing blades. The results have been impressive—the wood that is saved annually by the new blades each year fills 800 rail cars. As Georgia-Pacific discovered, effective control systems can eliminate waste, lower labor costs, and improve output per unit of input. Starbucks recently instructed its coffee shops to stop automatically brewing decaffeinated coffee after lunch. Sales of decaf plummet after lunch, and Starbucks realized that baristas were simply pouring most of it down the drain. Now, between noon and early evening they brew decaf only by the cup and only when a customer orders it.[6] A Cadbury chewing gum factory located in Taiwan significantly lowered its operating expenses through the simple replacement of its dehumidifier. Moisture and temperature control are critical to the gum manufacturing process, so Cadbury adopted the new dehumidifying system to reduce these costs. With the system, Cadbury reduced its energy usage by 60 percent and its operating expenses by 50 percent.[7] Similarly, many businesses are cutting back on everything from health insurance coverage to overnight shipping to business lunches for clients in their quest to lower costs.[8]

## Types of Control

The examples of control given thus far have illustrated the regulation of several organizational activities, from producing quality products to coordinating complex organizations. Organizations practice control in a number of different areas and at different levels, and the responsibility for managing control is widespread.

**Areas of Control** Control can focus on any area of an organization. Most organizations define areas of control in terms of the four basic types of resources they use: physical, human, information, and financial.[9] Control of physical resources includes inventory management (stocking neither too few nor too many units in inventory), quality control (maintaining appropriate levels of output quality), and equipment control (supplying the necessary facilities and machinery). Control of human resources includes selection and placement, training and development, performance appraisal, and compensation. Relatedly, organizations also try to control the behavior of their employees—directing them toward higher performance, for example, and away from unethical behaviors.[10] Control of information resources includes sales and marketing forecasting, environmental analysis, public relations, production scheduling, and economic forecasting.[11] Financial control involves managing the organization's debt so that it does not become excessive, ensuring that the firm always has enough cash on hand to meet its obligations but does not have excess cash in a checking account, and that receivables are collected and bills are paid on a timely basis.

In many ways, the control of financial resources is the most important area, because financial resources are related to the control of all the other resources in an organization. Too much inventory leads to storage costs; poor selection of personnel leads to termination and rehiring expenses; inaccurate sales forecasts lead to disruptions in cash flows and other financial effects. Financial issues tend to pervade most control-related activities.

### FIGURE 19.2 LEVELS OF CONTROL

Managers use control at several different levels. The most basic levels of control in organizations are strategic, structural, operations, and financial control. Each level must be managed properly if control is to be most effective.

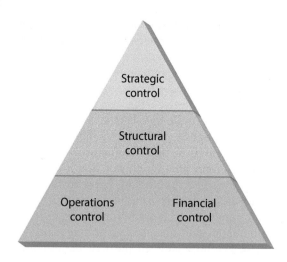

**operations control**
Focuses on the processes the organization uses to transform resources into products or services

**financial control**
Concerned with the organization's financial resources

**structural control**
Concerned with how the elements of the organization's structure are serving their intended purpose

**strategic control**
Focuses on how effectively the organization's strategies are succeeding in helping the organization meet its goals

**controller**
A position in organizations that helps line managers with their control activities

**Levels of Control**  Just as control can be broken down by area, Figure 19.2 shows that it can also be broken down by level within the organizational system. Operations control focuses on the processes the organization uses to transform resources into products or services.[12] Quality control is one type of operations control. Financial control is concerned with the organization's financial resources. Monitoring receivables to make sure customers are paying their bills on time is an example of financial control. Structural control is concerned with how the elements of the organization's structure are serving their intended purpose. Monitoring the administrative ratio to make sure staff expenses do not become excessive is an example of structural control. Finally, strategic control focuses on how effectively the organization's corporate, business, and functional strategies are succeeding in helping the organization meet its goals. For example, if a corporation has been unsuccessful in implementing its strategy of related diversification, its managers need to identify the reasons and either change the strategy or renew their efforts to implement it. We discuss these four levels of control more fully later in this chapter.

**Responsibilities of Control**  Traditionally, managers have been responsible for overseeing the wide array of control systems and concerns in organizations. They decide which types of control the organization will use, and they implement control systems and take actions based on the information provided by control systems. Thus ultimate responsibility for control rests with all managers throughout an organization.

Most larger organizations also have one or more specialized managerial positions called *controllers*. A controller is responsible for helping line managers with their control activities, for coordinating the organization's overall control system, and for gathering and assimilating relevant information. Many businesses that use an H-form or M-form organization design have several controllers: one for the corporation and one for each division. The job of controller is especially important in organizations where control systems are complex.[13]

In addition, some organizations also use operating employees to help maintain effective control. Indeed, employee participation is often used as a vehicle for allowing operating employees an opportunity to help facilitate organizational effectiveness. For example, Whistler Corporation increased employee participation in an effort to turn its quality problems around. As a starting point, the quality control unit, formerly responsible for checking product quality at the end of the assembly process, was eliminated. Next, all operating employees were encouraged to check their own work and told that they would be responsible for correcting their own errors. As a result, Whistler has eliminated its quality problems and is now highly profitable once again.

## Steps in the Control Process

Regardless of the types or levels of control systems an organization needs, there are four fundamental steps in any control process.[14] These are illustrated in Figure 19.3.

**Establishing Standards** The first step in the control process is establishing standards. A control standard is a target against which subsequent performance will be compared.[15] Employees at a Taco Bell fast-food restaurant, for example, work toward the following service standards:

Often issues can be found in a workplace where employees perceive their manager's control measures to be unreasonable. In this photo an irrational manager chastises his subordinates over a minor dip in sales. The employees are trying to explain, with not much success, that the harsh winter conditions negatively affected customer's shopping patterns.

1. A minimum of 95 percent of all customers will be greeted within three minutes of their arrival.
2. Preheated tortilla chips will not sit in the warmer more than 30 minutes before they are served to customers or discarded.
3. Empty tables will be cleaned within five minutes after being vacated.

Standards established for control purposes should be expressed in measurable terms. Note that standard 1 above has a time limit of three minutes and an objective target of 95 percent of all customers. In standard 3, the objective target of "all" empty tables is implied.

**control standard**
A target against which subsequent performance will be compared

## FIGURE 19.3 STEPS IN THE CONTROL PROCESS

Having an effective control system can help ensure that an organization achieves its goals. Implementing a control system, however, is a systematic process that generally proceeds through four interrelated steps.

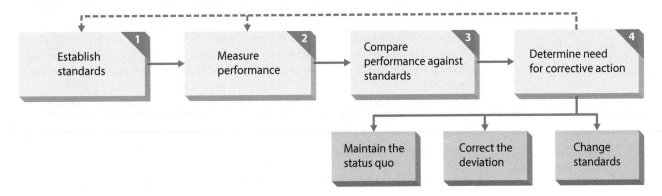

tobkatrina/Shutterstock.com

When Boeing and Airbus are assembling airplanes their managers establish an array of control standards and performance indicators. Maintaining effective control is especially important for massive projects such as these.

Control standards should also be consistent with the organization's goals. Taco Bell has organizational goals involving customer service, food quality, and restaurant cleanliness. A control standard for a retailer like Home Depot should be consistent with its goal of increasing its annual sales volume by 25 percent within five years. A hospital trying to shorten the average hospital stay for a patient will have control standards that reflect current averages. A university reaffirming its commitment to academics might adopt a standard of graduating 80 percent of its student athletes within five years of their enrollment. Control standards can be as narrow or as broad as the level of activity to which they apply and must follow logically from organizational goals and objectives. When Airbus introduced the A380, the world's largest passenger airplane, managers indicated that the firm needed to ship 270 planes in order to break even, and set a goal of delivering 18 per year. Managers also forecast that demand for very large aircraft like the A380 and Boeing's revamped 747 would exceed 1,200 planes during the next 20 years.[16]

A final aspect of establishing standards is to identify performance indicators. Performance indicators are measures of performance that provide information that is directly relevant to what is being controlled. For example, suppose an organization is following a tight schedule in building a new plant. Relevant performance indicators could be buying a site, selecting a building contractor, and ordering equipment. Monthly sales increases are not, however, directly relevant. On the other hand, if control is being focused on revenue, monthly sales increases are relevant, whereas buying land for a new plant is less relevant.

**Measuring Performance**   The second step in the control process is measuring performance. Performance measurement is a constant, ongoing activity for most organizations. For control to be effective, performance measures must be valid. Daily, weekly, and monthly sales figures measure sales performance, and production performance may be expressed in terms of unit cost, product quality, or volume produced. Employees' performance is often measured in terms of quality or quantity of output, but for many jobs, measuring performance is not so straightforward.

A research and development scientist at Merck, for example, may spend years working on a single project before achieving a breakthrough. A manager who takes over a business on the brink of failure may need months or even years to turn things around. Valid performance measurement, however difficult to obtain, is nevertheless vital in maintaining effective control, and performance indicators usually can be developed. The scientist's progress, for example, may be partially assessed by peer review, and the manager's success may be evaluated by her ability to convince creditors that she will eventually be able to restore profitability.

As Airbus completed the design and manufacture of its A380 jumbo jet, managers recognized that delays and cost overruns had changed its breakeven point. New calculations indicated that the company would need to sell 420 planes before it would become profitable. Its annual sales, of course, remained relatively easy to measure.

**Comparing Performance Against Standards**   The third step in the control process is comparing measured performance against established standards. Performance may be higher than, lower than, or identical to the standard. In some cases comparison is easy. The goal of each product manager at General Electric is to make the product either number one or number two (on the basis of total sales) in its market. Because this standard is clear and total sales are easy to calculate, it is relatively simple to determine whether this standard has been met. Sometimes, however, comparisons are less clear-cut. If performance is lower than expected, the question is how much deviation from standards to allow before taking remedial action. For example, is increasing sales by 7.9 percent when the standard was 8 percent close enough?

The timetable for comparing performance to standards depends on a variety of factors, including the importance and complexity of what is being controlled. For longer-run and higher-level standards, annual comparisons may be appropriate. In other circumstances, more frequent comparisons are necessary. For example, a business with a severe cash shortage may need to monitor its on-hand cash reserves daily. In its first year of production, Airbus did indeed deliver 18 A380s, just as it had forecast. Our *Beyond Traditional Business* box provides other insights into the control process in the nonprofit sector.

Taking corrective action is a critical part of the control process. For example, as the end of a sales season approaches most retailers start to cut prices in order to clear inventory. Few people will be looking for sweaters in May (because its getting warmer) or swimsuits in October (because its getting cooler). But they may buy these items anyway if the prices are reduced. This helps the retailer control inventory costs.

**Considering Corrective Action**   The final step in the control process is determining the need for corrective action. Decisions regarding corrective action draw heavily on a manager's analytic and diagnostic skills. For example, as healthcare costs have risen, many firms have sought ways to keep their own expenses in check. Some have reduced benefits; others have opted to pass on higher costs to their employees.[17]

After comparing performance against control standards, one of three actions is appropriate: maintain the status quo (do nothing), correct the deviation, or change the standards. Maintaining the status quo is preferable when performance essentially matches the standards, but it is more likely that some action will be needed to correct a deviation from the standards.

> "Closing underperforming stores is a natural part of business of any smart retailer."
>
> —MARIA SCEPPAGUERICO,
> SPOKESPERSON FOR ANN TAYLOR[18]

Sometimes, performance that is higher than expected may also cause problems for organizations. For example, when highly anticipated new video games or game systems are first introduced, the demand may be so strong that customers are placed on waiting lists. And even some people who are among the first to purchase such products immediately turn around and list them for sale on eBay for an inflated price. The manufacturer may be unable to increase production in the short term, though, and also knows that demand will eventually drop. At the same time, however, the firm would not want to alienate potential customers. Consequently, it may decide to simply reduce its advertising. This may curtail demand a bit and limit customer frustration.

Changing an established standard usually is necessary if it was set too high or too low at the outset. This is apparent if large numbers of employees routinely beat the standard by a wide margin or if no employees ever meet the standard. Also, standards that seemed perfectly appropriate when they were established may need to be adjusted because circumstances have since changed.

# The Intelligent Way to Run a Nonprofit

Opportunity International Network (OI) is a nonprofit specializing in *microfinance*—the practice of making small loans (about $200 on average) to help poor clients in developing countries start up small businesses. Back in 2005, OI's focus was on the victims of a tsunami that struck South Asia in December 2004, killing more than a quarter of a million people and devastating local economies. OI planned to add 10,000 clients in Indonesia and 20,000 in India. Meanwhile, the organization was also committed to adding 11,000 clients in AIDS-ravaged Africa. It also intended to increase its client base from 675,000 to 2 million in the next five years.

Needless to say, the addition of so many loans would entail a lot of additional bookkeeping, and OI's overtaxed IT system was inadequate to the task of managing the extra data. CEO Larry Reed admitted that "when you have a loan for $200 that's paid back weekly, [and it takes] three months before you find out the loan is late, you're behind the curve. ... The ability to manage information—especially to track what's happening with clients [in South Asia]—is very important for us to ramp up the program there."

So OI took steps to gain more control over its data-management process. Key to the project was the assistance of Hyperion Solutions Corp., a California-based company specializing in software for *business performance management*—technology-supported processes for measuring an organization's performance against its strategic goals. Hyperion donated $250,000 worth of tools and services to enhance OI's ability to consolidate and analyze data from various sources, put the resulting information to work in carrying out strategic initiatives, and then measure the success of those initiatives. OI, for example, was able to develop a program for measuring the impact of its initiatives on the lives of its clients and their children.

OI was perhaps ahead of the curve in adopting programs that now tend to fall under the heading of *business intelligence* (*BI*)—software programming that helps organizations evaluate their activities by using various specialized tools, including reporting applications. BI can be particularly valuable to nonprofit organizations, which have traditionally focused their reporting efforts on such broad, strictly quantitative data as number of people served and number of dollars raised.

Today, however, nonprofit decision makers need to evaluate a much wider range of information. Let's say, for example, that a nonprofit sponsors an event through social media. The event may attract a lot of participants (easily quantifiable data), but what the organization really needs to know is whether event participation actually translated into successful fundraising. If so, which social-media message was most effective and through which social media? Are there any strategic lessons for the future to be learned from the answers to these questions?

Nurse-Family Partnerships (NFP), for example, is a nonprofit that arranges for registered nurses to make regular home visits to low-income first-time mothers. Since 2010, NFP has used Efforts to Outcomes (ETO®) BI software to monitor and report program performance. The application tracks program outcomes by sorting thousands of data points for the development of each mother and child. It also permits NFP to monitor numbers of in-person visits and nurses' caseloads and compare the data to evidence-based benchmarks. Ultimately, NFP's BI process not only allows it to monitor program outcomes but to report those outcomes more effectively to its stakeholders, thereby enhancing its ability to secure the funding necessary to maintain programs and outcome levels.

*References:* Heather Havenstein, "Business Intelligence Tools Help Nonprofits Make Loans to Tsunami Victims," *Computerworld* (March 14, 2005), www.computerworld.com, on June 22, 2015; B.J. Cortis, "Business Intelligence Can Drive Nonprofit Sector Decision Making," *Philanthropy Journal* (June 24, 2013), http://philanthropyjournal.blogspot.com, on June 22, 2015; Social Solutions Inc., "Customer Case Study: Nurse Family Partnership" (n.d.), www.social solutions.com, on June 23, 2015; Gil Allouche, "Five Nonprofits Using Big Data to Measure and Improve Effectiveness," *BI Insight* (December 10, 2013), http://businessintelligence.com, on June 22, 2015.

As the 2008–2009 global recession began to take its toll, two major Airbus customers, Qantas and Emirates, indicated that they wanted to defer delivery of some previously ordered A380s. As a result, Airbus found it necessary to reduce its production in 2009 from 18 to only 14. It also indicated that the plane's breakeven point had increased, but would not reveal the new target. In 2011, the devastating tsunami in Japan forced Toyota to adjust its production levels as several of its parts and vehicles were manufactured in the country. As a result, Toyota cut production by 75 percent in its North American plants.[19]

---

☐ All managers should understand the basic purposes of control used in organizations.

☐ Managers need to also be familiar with the various types of control.

☐ You should also know the essential steps in the control process.

**Manager's Checklist** ☑

## Operations Control

One of the four levels of control practiced by most organizations, operations control, is concerned with the processes the organization uses to transform resources into products or services. As Figure 19.4 shows, the three forms of operations control—preliminary, screening, and postaction—occur at different points in relation to the transformation processes used by the organization.

### Preliminary Control

Preliminary control concentrates on the resources—financial, material, human, and information—the organization brings in from the environment. Preliminary control attempts

---

**FIGURE 19.4  FORMS OF OPERATIONS CONTROL**

Most organizations develop multiple control systems that incorporate all three basic forms of control. For example, the publishing company that produced this book screens inputs by hiring only qualified employees, typesetters, and printers (preliminary control). In addition, quality is checked during the transformation process, such as after the manuscript is typeset (screening control), and the outputs—printed and bound books—are checked before they are shipped from the bindery (postaction control).

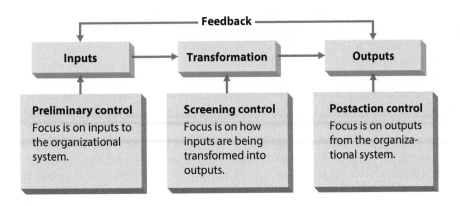

**operations control**
Focuses on the processes the organization uses to transform resources into products or services

**preliminary control**
Attempts to monitor the quality or quantity of financial, physical, human, and information resources before they actually become part of the system

to monitor the quality or quantity of these resources before they enter the organization. Firms like PepsiCo and General Mills hire only college graduates for their management training programs, and even then only after applicants satisfy several interviewers and selection criteria. In this way, they control the quality of the human resources entering the organization. When Sears orders merchandise to be manufactured under its own brand name, it specifies rigid standards of quality, thereby controlling physical inputs. Organizations also control financial and information resources. For example, privately held companies like Toys "R" Us and Mars limit the extent to which outsiders can buy their stock, and television networks verify the accuracy of news stories before they are broadcast.

Screening control focuses on meeting standards for quality or quantity during the production process. This factory makes boots and shoes. At this stage in production the tops and bottoms of the boots have just been attached. This quality control inspector is making sure that the seals meet the quality standards set by the company before the boots move on to the next stage of production.

## Screening Control

Screening control focuses on meeting standards for product or service quality or quantity during the actual transformation process itself. Screening control relies heavily on feedback processes. For example, in a Dell Computer assembly factory, computer system components are checked periodically as each unit is being assembled. This is done to ensure that all the components that have been assembled up to that point are working properly. The periodic quality checks provide feedback to workers so that they know what, if any, corrective actions to take. Because they are useful in identifying the causes of problems, screening controls tend to be used more often than other forms of control.

More and more companies are adopting screening controls because they are an effective way to promote employee participation and catch problems early in the overall transformation process. For example, Corning adopted screening controls for use in manufacturing television glass. In the past, finished television screens were inspected only after they were finished. Unfortunately, over 4 percent of them were later returned by customers because of defects. Now the glass screens are inspected at each step in the production process, rather than at the end, and the return rate from customers has dropped to .03 percent.

## Postaction Control

Postaction control focuses on the outputs of the organization after the transformation process is complete. Corning's old system was postaction control—final inspection after the product was completed. Although Corning abandoned its postaction control system, this still may be an effective method of control, primarily if a product can be manufactured in only one or two steps or if the service is fairly simple and routine. Although postaction control alone may not be as effective as preliminary or screening control, it can provide management with information for future planning. For example, if a quality check of finished goods indicates an unacceptably high defect rate, the production manager knows that he or she must identify the causes and take steps to eliminate them. Postaction control also provides a basis for rewarding employees. Recognizing that an employee has exceeded personal sales goals by a wide margin, for example, may alert the manager that a bonus or promotion is in order.

Most organizations use more than one form of operations control. For example, Honda's preliminary control includes hiring only qualified employees and specifying strict quality standards when ordering parts from other manufacturers. Honda uses numerous screening

**screening control**
Relies heavily on feedback processes during the transformation process

**postaction control**
Monitors the outputs or results of the organization after the transformation process is complete

controls in checking the quality of components during the assembly of cars. A final inspection and test drive as each car rolls off the assembly line is part of the company's postaction control.[20] Indeed, most successful organizations employ a wide variety of techniques to facilitate operations control.

---

☐ Managers should be able to distinguish between preliminary, screening, and postaction control.

☐ You should also understand how the various forms of operations control can be used simultaneously.

**Manager's Checklist** ✓

# Financial Control

Financial control is the control of financial resources as they flow into the organization (revenues, shareholder investments), are held by the organization (working capital, retained earnings), and flow out of the organization (employee wages and salaries, expenses). Businesses must manage their finances so that revenues are sufficient to cover costs and still return a profit to the firm's owners. Not-for-profit organizations such as universities have the same concerns: Their revenues (from tax dollars or tuition) must cover operating expenses and overhead. U.S. automakers Ford and General Motors have had to face the business reality that they have to reduce the costs of paying employees they do not need but whom they are obligated to keep due to long-standing labor agreements. A few years ago Ford offered to cover the full costs of a college education for certain of its employees if they would resign; GM, for its part, offered lump-sum payments of varying amounts to some of its workers in return for their resignations.[21] A complete discussion of financial management is beyond the scope of this book, but we will examine the control provided by budgets and other financial control tools.

## Budgetary Control

A budget is a plan expressed in numerical terms. Organizations establish budgets for work groups, departments, divisions, and the whole organization. The usual time period for a budget is one year, although breakdowns of budgets by the quarter or month are also common. Budgets are generally expressed in financial terms, but they may occasionally be expressed in units of output, time, or other quantifiable factors. When Disney launches the production of a new movie, it creates a budget for how much the movie should cost. Following on the heels of the recent disastrous *Lone Ranger* movie (the movie cost $215 million to make but only earned $90 million at the box office) Disney executives have started scrutinizing budget projects for movies much more carefully.

Because of their quantitative nature, budgets provide yardsticks for measuring performance and facilitate comparisons across departments, between levels in the organization, and from one time period to another. Budgets serve four primary purposes. They help managers coordinate resources and projects (because they use a common denominator, usually dollars). They help define the established standards for control. They provide guidelines about the organization's resources and expectations. Finally, budgets enable the organization to evaluate the performance of managers and organizational units.

**Types of Budgets** Most organizations develop and make use of three different kinds of budgets—financial, operating, and nonmonetary. Table 19.1 summarizes the characteristics of each of these.

A *financial budget* indicates where the organization expects to get its cash for the coming time period and how it plans to use it. Because financial resources are critically important, the

**financial control**
Concerned with the organization's financial resources

**budget**
A plan expressed in numerical terms

## TABLE 19.1 DEVELOPING BUDGETS IN ORGANIZATIONS

Organizations use various types of budgets to help manage their control functions. The three major categories of budgets are financial, operating, and nonmonetary. There are several different types of budgets in each category. To be most effective, each budget must be carefully matched with the specific function being controlled.

| Types of Budgets | What Budget Shows |
| --- | --- |
| Financial Budget | Sources and Uses of Cash |
| Cash flow or cash budget | All sources of cash income and cash expenditures in monthly, weekly, or daily periods |
| Capital expenditures budget | Costs of major assets such as a new plant, machinery, or land |
| Balance sheet budget | Forecast of the organization's assets and liabilities in the event all other budgets are met |
| Operating Budget | Planned Operations in Financial Terms |
| Sales or revenue budget | Income the organization expects to receive from normal operations |
| Expense budget | Anticipated expenses for the organization during the coming time period |
| Profit budget | Anticipated differences between sales or revenues and expenses |
| Nonmonetary Budget | Planned Operations in Nonfinancial Terms |
| Labor budget | Hours of direct labor available for use |
| Space budget | Square feet or meters of space available for various functions |
| Production budget | Number of units to be produced during the coming time period |

organization needs to know where those resources will be coming from and how they are to be used. The financial budget provides answers to both these questions. Usual sources of cash include sales revenue, short- and long-term loans, the sale of assets, and the issuance of new stock.

For years Exxon was very conservative in its capital budgeting. As a result, the firm amassed a huge financial reserve but was overtaken in sales by Royal Dutch/Shell, British Petroleum (now BP), and other oil producers. Executives at Exxon made the decision to use their reserves to help finance the firm's acquisition of Mobil, creating ExxonMobil. The firm's newfound size then allowed it to invest more in exploration, building new refineries, and so forth, and to regain the number-one sales position. Since that time, the firm has become more aggressive in capital budgeting to stay ahead of its European rivals.

An *operating budget* is concerned with planned operations within the organization. It outlines what quantities of products or services the organization intends to create and what resources will be used to create them. Hewlett-Packard creates an operating budget that specifies how many of each model of its personal computers will be produced each quarter.

A *nonmonetary budget* is simply a budget expressed in nonfinancial terms, such as units of output, hours of direct labor, machine hours, or square-foot allocations. Nonmonetary budgets are most commonly used by managers at the lower levels of an organization. For example, a plant manager can schedule work more effectively knowing that he or she has 8,000 labor hours to allocate in a week, rather than trying to determine how to best spend $86,451 in wages in a week.

**Developing Budgets** Traditionally, budgets were developed by top management and the controller and then imposed on lower-level managers. Although some organizations still follow this pattern, many contemporary organizations now allow all managers to participate in the budget process. As a starting point, top management generally issues a call for budget requests, accompanied by an indication of overall patterns the budgets may take. For example, if sales are expected to drop in the next year, managers may be told up front to prepare for cuts in operating budgets.

## FIGURE 19.5 DEVELOPING BUDGETS IN ORGANIZATIONS

Most organizations use the same basic process to develop budgets. Operating units are requested to submit their budget requests to divisions. These divisions, in turn, compile unit budgets and submit their own budgets to the organization. An organizational budget is then compiled for approval by the budget committee, controller, and CEO.

Operating unit budget requests

Division budget requests

Organizational budget
- Prepared by budget committee
- Approved by budget committee, controller, and CEO

As Figure 19.5 shows, the heads of each operating unit typically submit budget requests to the head of their division. An operating unit head might be a department manager in a manufacturing or wholesaling firm or a program director in a social service agency. The division heads might include plant managers, regional sales managers, or college deans. The division head integrates and consolidates the budget requests from operating unit heads into one overall division budget request. A great deal of interaction among managers usually takes place at this stage, as the division head coordinates the budgetary needs of the various departments.

Division budget requests are then forwarded to a budget committee. The budget committee is usually composed of top managers. The committee reviews budget requests from several divisions, and once again, duplications and inconsistencies are corrected. Finally, the budget committee, the controller, and the CEO review and agree on the overall budget for the organization, as well as specific budgets for each operating unit. These decisions are then communicated back to each manager.

**Strengths and Weaknesses of Budgeting** Budgets offer a number of advantages, but they also have weaknesses. On the plus side, budgets facilitate effective control. Placing dollar values on operations enables managers to monitor operations better and pinpoint problem areas. Budgets also facilitate coordination and communication between departments because they express diverse activities in a common denominator (dollars). Budgets help maintain records of organizational performance and are a logical complement to planning. In other words, as managers develop plans, they should simultaneously consider control measures to accompany them. Organizations can use budgets to link plans and control by first developing budgets as part of the plan and then using those budgets as part of control.

On the other hand, some managers apply budgets too rigidly. Budgets are intended to serve as frameworks, but managers sometimes fail to recognize that changing circumstances may warrant budget adjustments. The process of developing budgets can also be very time consuming. Finally, budgets may limit innovation and change. When all available funds are allocated to specific operating budgets, it may be impossible to procure additional funds to take advantage of an unexpected opportunity. Indeed, for these very reasons, some organizations are working to scale back their budgeting systems. Although most organizations are likely to continue to use budgets, the goal is to make them less confining and rigid.

## Other Tools for Financial Control

Although budgets are the most common means of financial control, other useful tools are financial statements, ratio analysis, and financial audits.

**Financial Statements** A financial statement is a profile of some aspect of an organization's financial circumstances. There are commonly accepted and required ways that financial statements must be prepared and presented. The two most basic financial statements prepared and used by virtually all organizations are a balance sheet and an income statement.

The balance sheet lists the assets and liabilities of the organization at a specific point in time, usually the last day of an organization's fiscal year. For example, the balance sheet may summarize the financial condition of an organization on December 31, 2017. Most balance sheets are divided into current assets (assets that are relatively liquid, or easily convertible into cash), fixed assets (assets that are longer term in nature and less liquid), current liabilities (debts and other obligations that must be paid in the near future), long-term liabilities (payable over an extended period of time), and stockholders' equity (the owners' claim against the assets).

Whereas the balance sheet reflects a snapshot profile of an organization's financial position at a single point in time, the income statement summarizes financial performance over a period of time, usually one year. For example, the income statement might be for the period January 1, 2017, through December 31, 2017. The income statement summarizes the firm's revenues less its expenses to report net income (profit or loss) for the period. Information from the balance sheet and income statement is used in computing important financial ratios.

Financial ratios compare different elements of a balance sheet or income statement to one another. Ratio analysis is the calculation of one or more financial ratios to assess some aspect of the financial health of an organization. Organizations use a variety of different financial ratios as part of financial control. For example, *liquidity ratios* indicate how liquid (easily converted into cash) an organization's assets are. *Debt ratios* reflect ability to meet long-term financial obligations. *Return ratios* show managers and investors how much return the organization is generating relative to its assets. *Coverage ratios* help estimate the organization's ability to cover interest expenses on borrowed capital. *Operating ratios* indicate the effectiveness of specific functional areas rather than of the total organization. Walt Disney and Halliburton each rely heavily on financial ratios to keep their financial operations on track.[22]

**Financial Audits** Audits are independent appraisals of an organization's accounting, financial, and operational systems. The two major types of financial audits are the external audit and the internal audit.

*External audits* are financial appraisals conducted by experts who are not employees of the organization. External audits are typically concerned with determining that the organization's accounting procedures and financial statements are compiled in an objective and verifiable fashion. The organization contracts with a certified public accountant (CPA) for this service. The CPA's main objective is to verify for stockholders, the IRS, and other interested parties that the methods by which the organization's financial managers and accountants

---

**financial statement**
A profile of some aspect of an organization's financial circumstances

**balance sheet**
List of assets and liabilities of an organization at a specific point in time

**income statement**
A summary of financial performance over a period of time

**ratio analysis**
The calculation of one or more financial ratios to assess some aspect of the organization's financial health

**audit**
An independent appraisal of an organization's accounting, financial, and operational systems

prepare documents and reports are legal and proper. External audits are so important that publicly held corporations are required by law to have external audits regularly, as assurance to investors that the financial reports are reliable.

Unfortunately, flaws in the auditing process played a major role in the downfall of Enron and several other major firms in the early 2000s. The problem can be traced back partially to the auditing groups' problems with conflicts of interest and eventual loss of objectivity. For instance, Enron was such an important client for its auditing firm, Arthur Andersen, that the auditors started letting the firm take liberties with its accounting systems for fear that if they were too strict, Enron might take its business to another auditing firm. In the aftermath of the resulting scandal, Arthur Andersen was forced to close its doors, Enron became a shell of its former self, executives were indicted, and the entire future of the accounting profession was called into question.[23]

Some organizations are also starting to employ external auditors to review other aspects of their financial operations. For example, some auditing firms now specialize in checking corporate legal bills. An auditor for the Fireman's Fund Insurance Company uncovered several thousands of dollars in legal fee errors. Other auditors are beginning to specialize in real estate, employee benefits, and pension plan investments.

Whereas external audits are conducted by external accountants, an *internal audit* is handled by employees of the organization. Its objective is the same as that of an external audit—to verify the accuracy of financial and accounting procedures used by the organization. Internal audits also examine the efficiency and appropriateness of financial and accounting procedures. Because the staff members who conduct them are a permanent part of the organization, internal audits tend to be more expensive than external audits. But employees, who are more familiar with the organization's practices, may also point out significant aspects of the accounting system besides its technical correctness. Large organizations like Halliburton and Ford have an internal auditing staff that spends all its time conducting audits of different divisions and functional areas of the organization. Smaller organizations may assign accountants to an internal audit group on a temporary or rotating basis.

Satyam Computer Services in India falsely reported profits of over $1 billion when in reality it had only $66 million. The Indian affiliate of PricewaterhouseCoopers, PW India, was in charge of routinely auditing the firm, but failed to follow basic auditing procedures. Rather than confirming the supposed $1 billion cash balances with the banks, PW India relied solely on the information provided by the firm's management. In some cases, auditors failed to follow up on confirmations sent independently by the banks that showed significant differences from the balances reported by management. PW India was eventually fined $7.5 million—the largest penalty ever imposed by India on a foreign accounting firm.[24] Our *Doing Business on Planet Earth* feature presents another perspective on auditing.

☐ Managers should be familiar with the basic kinds of budgets used in their organizations.

☐ You should also understand the budgeting process used in your organization.

☐ All managers should also know how to interpret basic financial statements and understand the meaning of basic financial ratios.

**Manager's Checklist** ✓

# Structural Control

Organizations can create designs for themselves that result in very different approaches to control. Two major forms of structural control, bureaucratic control and decentralized control, represent opposite ends of a continuum, as shown in Figure 19.6.[25] The six dimensions shown in the figure represent perspectives adopted by the two extreme types of structural

**DOING BUSINESS ON PLANET EARTH**

# How Do Investors Rest Assured?

Recall that, in the opening vignette of this chapter, we discussed the Sustainability Report issued in 2014 by the global real estate-management company Jones Lang LaSalle. According to a three-stage model of sustainability reporting developed by the Big Four accounting firm KPMG, JLL would fall into Stage 3—"companies issuing reports that are verified by a third party other than an independent certified public accountant." In accounting parlance, Stage 3 is distinguished by the level of *assurance* provided by an organization—its procedures for ensuring accurate information about the effectiveness of its strategies and operations and its compliance with regulatory requirements. The purpose of assurance is to confirm that reported data and the processes used to gather them are reliable, both for internal users (e.g., decision makers) and external users (e.g., investors).

KPMG explains that "independent assurance ... of an organization's processes, controls, and data helps ensure that the company's sustainability data are reliable and accurate, thereby supporting the credibility of information used in decision making ... and external reporting." Unfortunately, says KPMG, many companies fall short of providing the level of assurance that more and more stakeholders are calling for. "Are your company's customers," asks KPMG, "starting to make decisions based on sustainability data and/or metrics? Does your sustainability data stand up to the same level of scrutiny as your financial data?"

A recent study of 30 Dow Jones companies by Guo and Yang (2014) revealed an "increasing trend of sustainability reporting among publicly traded firms. ... However," add the researchers, "we observed various reporting formats and patterns. ... The lack of uniformity of sustainability reporting and assurance might reduce the comparability, effectiveness, and accuracy of sustainability accounting reporting." In particular, Guo and Yang found substantial variation in assurance practices. 3M, for example, provides "independent

third-party assurance" through Environmental Resources Management, a global consultant on environmental and sustainability issues. The Big Four accounting firm PricewaterhouseCoopers has furnished Alcoa with limited assurance on greenhouse-gas emissions. Microsoft, meanwhile, relies entirely on internal assurance procedures while taking outside feedback into account.

JLL's assurance procedures are also internal. A Global Sustainability Committee, for example, oversees sustainability activities, including reporting, in accordance with the company's Management Policy on Sustainability and Responsible Investing. Granted, JLL seeks to comply with a variety of reporting standards set by outside organizations. It subscribes to the G4 Guidelines established by the Global Reporting Initiative (GRI), an independent standards organization that sets criteria for policies on energy, biodiversity, and emissions. It's also a member of the International Integrated Reporting Council (IIRC), a global coalition of organizations established to promote sustainability accounting.

Note, however, that both the GRI and the IIRC actually set guidelines rather than accredited requirements. The IIRC, for example, suggests that members report information about certain forms of "capital," including "natural" and "social and relationship." JLL CFO Christie Kelly subscribes to the IIRC Framework because it calls for making selected disclosures rather than the publication of a wealth of specific details. It also supports the principle that an organization's managers are the best judges of what it needs to report. "We need to be careful that it's not too much," explains Christie, "and that nonfinancial reporting doesn't take on a life of its own."

*References:* KPMG LLP, *Sustainability Reporting—What You Should Know* (2011), www.kpmg.com, on June 12, 2015; Ying Guo and David C. Yang, "Sustainability Accounting Reporting: A Survey of 30 U.S. Dow Jones Companies," *International Journal of Accounting and Taxation*, 2014, Vol. 2, No. 3, pp. 1–15, http://ijatnet.com, on June 13, 2015; Jones Lang LaSalle Inc., *2013 Sustainability Report* (September 2014), www.jll.com, on June 12, 2015; David M. Katz, "Is Sustainability Reporting Sustainable?" *CFO* (January 27, 2014), http://ww2.cfo.com, on June 12, 2015.

## FIGURE 19.6  ORGANIZATIONAL CONTROL

Organizational control generally falls somewhere between the two extremes of bureaucratic and decentralized control. NBC television uses bureaucratic control, whereas Levi Strauss uses decentralized control.

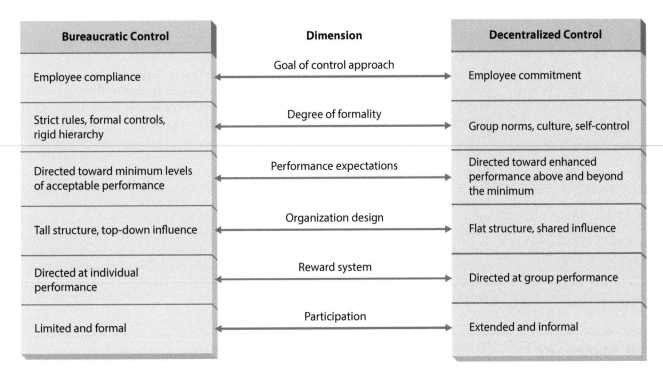

| Bureaucratic Control | Dimension | Decentralized Control |
|---|---|---|
| Employee compliance | Goal of control approach | Employee commitment |
| Strict rules, formal controls, rigid hierarchy | Degree of formality | Group norms, culture, self-control |
| Directed toward minimum levels of acceptable performance | Performance expectations | Directed toward enhanced performance above and beyond the minimum |
| Tall structure, top-down influence | Organization design | Flat structure, shared influence |
| Directed at individual performance | Reward system | Directed at group performance |
| Limited and formal | Participation | Extended and informal |

control. In other words, they have different goals, degrees of formality, performance expectations, organization designs, reward systems, and levels of participation. Although a few organizations fall precisely at one extreme or the other, most tend toward one end but may have specific characteristics of either.

## Bureaucratic Control

Bureaucratic control is an approach to organization design characterized by formal and mechanistic structural arrangements. As the term suggests, it follows the bureaucratic model. The goal of bureaucratic control is employee compliance. Organizations that use it rely on strict rules and a rigid hierarchy, insist that employees meet minimally acceptable levels of performance, and often have a tall structure. They focus their rewards on individual performance and allow only limited and formal employee participation.

NBC Television applies structural controls that reflect many elements of bureaucracy. The organization relies on many rules to regulate employee travel, expense accounts, and other expenses. A new performance appraisal system precisely specifies minimally acceptable levels of performance for everyone. The organization's structure is considerably taller than those of the other major networks, and rewards are based on individual contributions. Perhaps most significantly, many NBC employees have argued that they have too small a voice in how the organization is managed.

In another example, a large oil company recently made the decision to allow employees to wear casual attire to work. But a committee then spent weeks developing a 20-page set of guidelines on what was and was not acceptable. For example, denim pants are not allowed. Similarly, athletic shoes may be worn as long as they are not white. And all shirts must have a collar. Nordstrom, the department store chain, has also moved toward bureaucratic control

**bureaucratic control**
A form of organizational control characterized by formal and mechanistic structural arrangements

of all of its purchasing in an effort to lower costs. Similarly, Home Depot is moving more toward bureaucratic control to cut its costs and more effectively compete with its hard-charging rival, Lowe's.[26]

## Decentralized Control

Decentralized control, in contrast, is an approach to organizational control characterized by informal and organic structural arrangements. As Figure 19.6 shows, its goal is employee commitment to the organization. Accordingly, it relies heavily on group norms and a strong corporate culture, and gives employees the responsibility for controlling themselves. Employees are encouraged to perform beyond minimally acceptable levels. Organizations using this approach are usually relatively flat. They direct rewards at group performance and favor widespread employee participation.

Levi Strauss practices decentralized control. The firm's managers use groups as the basis for work and have created a culture wherein group norms help facilitate high performance. Rewards are subsequently provided to the higher-performing groups and teams. The company's culture also reinforces contributions to the overall team effort, and employees have a strong sense of loyalty to the organization. Levi's has a flat structure, and power is widely shared. Employee participation is encouraged in all areas of operation.[27] Another company that uses this approach is Southwest Airlines. When Southwest made the decision to "go casual," the firm resisted the temptation to develop dress guidelines. Instead, managers decided to allow employees to exercise discretion over their attire and to deal with clearly inappropriate situations on a case-by-case basis.

### Manager's Checklist

☐ Managers need to know the fundamental differences between bureaucratic and decentralized control.

☐ You should also be familiar with the most obvious advantages and disadvantages of bureaucratic versus decentralized control.

# Strategic Control

Given the obvious importance of an organization's strategy, it is also important that the organization assess how effective that strategy is in helping the organization meet its goals.[28] To do this requires that the organization integrate its strategy and control systems. This is especially true for the global organization.

## Integrating Strategy and Control

**decentralized control**
An approach to organizational control based on informal and organic structural arrangements

**strategic control**
Control aimed at ensuring that the organization is maintaining an effective alignment with its environment and moving toward achieving its strategic goals

Strategic control generally focuses on five aspects of organizations—structure, leadership, technology, human resources, and information and operational control systems. For example, an organization should periodically examine its structure to determine whether it is facilitating the attainment of the strategic goals being sought. Suppose a firm using a functional (U-form) design has an established goal of achieving a 20 percent sales growth rate per year, but performance indicators show that it is currently growing at a rate of only 10 percent per year. Detailed analysis might reveal that the current structure is inhibiting growth in some way (for example, by slowing decision making and inhibiting innovation) and that a divisional (M-form) design is more likely to bring about the desired growth (by speeding decision making and promoting innovation).

In this way, strategic control focuses on the extent to which implemented strategy achieves the organization's strategic goals. If, as outlined above, one or more avenues of implementation are inhibiting the attainment of goals, that avenue should be changed. Consequently, the firm might find it necessary to alter its structure, replace key leaders, adopt new technology, modify its human resources, or change its information and operational control systems.

For several years, Pfizer, the world's largest pharmaceutical company, has invested billions of dollars in research and development. But the firm recently acknowledged that it was not getting an adequate return on its investment and announced that it was laying off 800 senior researchers. Pfizer also signaled a strategic reorientation by suggesting it would look for other drug companies to buy in order to acquire new patents and drug formulas.[29] In contrast, 3M is a company that is known for its innovation and product development, with staples like Scotch tape and Post-it notes. The company recently announced that it would increase its R&D spending to 6 percent of sales, hire 60 to 80 additional Ph.D. research scientists, and construct a $150 million R&D lab.

Kohl's department stores essentially redefined how to compete effectively in the mid-tier retailing market and was on trajectory to leave competitors like Sears and Dillard's in its dust. But then the firm inexplicably stopped doing many of the very things that had led to its success—such as keeping abreast of current styles, maintaining low inventories, and keeping its stores neat and clean—and began to stumble. Now, managers are struggling to rejuvenate Kohl's strategic focus and get it back on track.[30]

"Some of the work will be to improve the presentation of our national brands because we know that we have slipped with consumers in their perceptions of Kohl's as a place to get great national brands."

—KEVIN MANSELL, CEO KOHL'S CORPORATION ON 'GETTING THEIR MOJO BACK'[31]

## International Strategic Control

Because they are relatively large firmsoperating in complex markets, global organizations must take an especially pronounced strategic view of their control systems. One very basic question that has to be addressed is whether to manage control from a centralized or a decentralized perspective.[32] Under a centralized system, each organizational unit around the world is responsible for frequently reporting the results of its performance to headquarters. Managers from the home office often visit foreign branches to observe firsthand how the units are functioning.

BP, Unilever, Procter & Gamble, and Sony all use this approach. They believe centralized control is effective because it allows the home office to stay better informed of the performance of foreign units and to maintain more control over how decisions are made. For example, BP discovered that its Australian subsidiary was not billing its customers for charges as quickly as were its competitors. By shortening the billing cycle, BP now receives customer payments five days faster than before. Managers believe that they discovered this oversight only because of a centralized financial control system.

Organizations that use a decentralized control system require foreign branches to report less often and in less detail. For example, each unit may submit summary performance statements on a quarterly basis and provide full statements only once a year. Similarly, visits from the home office are less frequent and less concerned with monitoring and assessing performance. IBM, Ford, and Shell all use this approach. Because Ford practices decentralized control of its design function, European designers have developed several innovative automobile design features. Managers believe that if they had been more centralized, designers would not have had the freedom to develop their new ideas.

☐ Managers should know how strategy and control are most commonly integrated.

☐ Managers should also know in what ways domestic and international control issues are similar and in what ways they differ.

# Managing Control in Organizations

Effective control, whether at the operations, financial, structural, or strategic level, successfully regulates and monitors organizational activities. To use the control process, managers must recognize the characteristics of effective control and understand how to identify and overcome occasional resistance to control.[33]

## Characteristics of Effective Control

Control systems tend to be most effective when they are integrated with planning and when they are flexible, accurate, timely, and objective.

**Integration with Planning** Control should be linked with planning. The more explicit and precise this linkage, the more effective the control system is. The best way to integrate planning and control is to account for control as plans develop. In other words, as goals are set during the planning process, attention should be paid to developing standards that will reflect how well the plan is realized. Managers at Champion Spark Plug Company decided to broaden their product line to include a full range of automotive accessories—a total of 21 new products. As part of this plan, managers decided in advance what level of sales they wanted to realize from each product for each of the next five years. They established these sales goals as standards against which actual sales would be compared. Thus, by accounting for their control system as they developed their plan, managers at Champion did an excellent job of integrating planning and control.

**Flexibility** The control system itself must be flexible enough to accommodate change. Consider, for example, an organization whose diverse product line requires 75 different raw materials. The company's inventory control system must be able to manage and monitor current levels of inventory for all 75 materials. When a change in product line changes the number of raw materials needed, or when the required quantities of the existing materials change, the control system should be flexible enough to handle the revised requirements. The alternative—designing and implementing a new control system—is an avoidable expense. Champion's control system included a mechanism that automatically shipped products to major customers to keep their inventories at predetermined levels. The firm had to adjust this system when one of its biggest customers decided not to stock the full line of Champion products. Because its control system was flexible, though, modifying it for the customer was relatively simple.

**Accuracy** Managers make a surprisingly large number of decisions based on inaccurate information. Field representatives may hedge their sales estimates to make themselves look better. Production managers may hide costs to meet their targets. Human resource managers may overestimate their minority recruiting prospects to meet affirmative action goals. In each case, the information that other managers receive is inaccurate, and the results of inaccurate information may be quite dramatic. If sales projections are inflated, a manager might cut advertising (thinking it is no longer needed) or increase advertising (to further build momentum). Similarly, a production manager unaware of hidden costs may quote a sales price much lower than desirable. Or a human resources manager may speak out publicly on the effectiveness of the company's minority recruiting, only to find out later that these prospects have been overestimated. In each case, the result of inaccurate information is inappropriate managerial action.

**Timeliness**  Timeliness does not necessarily mean quickness. Rather, it describes a control system that provides information as often as is necessary. Because Champion has a wealth of historical data on its sparkplug sales, it does not need information on sparkplugs as often as it needs sales feedback for its newer products. Retail organizations usually need sales results daily so that they can manage cash flow and adjust advertising and promotion. In contrast, they may need information about physical inventory only quarterly or annually. In general, the more uncertain and unstable the circumstances, the more often measurement is needed.

**Objectivity**  The control system should provide information that is as objective as possible. To appreciate this, imagine the task of a manager responsible for control of his organization's human resources. He asks two plant managers to submit reports. One manager notes that morale at his plant is "okay," that grievances are "about where they should be," and that turnover is "under control." The other reports that absenteeism at her plant is running at 4 percent, that 16 grievances have been filed this year (compared with 24 last year), and that turnover is 12 percent. The second report will almost always be more useful than the first. Of course, managers also need to look beyond the numbers when assessing performance. For example, a plant manager may be boosting productivity and profit margins by putting too much pressure on workers and using poor-quality materials. As a result, impressive short-run gains may be overshadowed by longer-run increases in employee turnover and customer complaints.

## Resistance to Control

Managers sometimes make the mistake of assuming that the value of an effective control system is self-evident to employees. This is not always so, however. Many employees resist control, especially if they feel overcontrolled, if they think control is inappropriately focused or rewards inefficiency, or if they are uncomfortable with accountability.

**Overcontrol**  Occasionally, organizations try to control too many things. This becomes especially problematic when the control directly affects employee behavior. An organization that instructs its employees when to come to work, where to park, when to have morning coffee, and when to leave for the day exerts considerable control over people's daily activities. Yet many organizations try to control not only these but other aspects of work behavior as well. Of particular relevance in recent years is some companies' efforts to control their employees' access to private e-mail and the Internet during work hours. Some companies have no policies governing these activities, some attempt to limit it, and some attempt to forbid it altogether.[34]

Troubles arise when employees perceive these attempts to limit their behavior as being unreasonable. A company that tells its employees how to dress, how to arrange their desks, and how to wear their hair may meet with more resistance. Employees at Chrysler who drove non-Chrysler vehicles used to complain because they were forced to park in a distant parking lot. People felt that these efforts to control their personal behavior (what kind of car to drive) were excessive. Managers eventually removed these controls and now allow open parking. Some employees at Abercrombie & Fitch argue that the firm is guilty of overcontrol because of its strict dress and grooming requirements—for example, no necklaces or facial hair for men and only natural nail polish and earrings no larger than a dime for women. Likewise, Enterprise Rent-A-Car has a set of 30 dress-code rules for women and 26 rules for men. The firm was recently sued by one former employee who was fired because of the color of her hair.[35] UBS, the large Swiss bank, had (until recently) a 44-page dress code that prescribed, among other things, that employees should avoid eating garlic and onions (so as to not offend customers), keep their toenails trimmed (so as to not tear their stockings or socks), and wear only skin-colored underwear (so it could remain unseen). Men were instructed in how to knot a tie, and everyone was encouraged to keep their glasses clean. (When the dress code was made public, UBS indicated that it would be making some revisions!)[36]

> "Glasses should always be kept clean. On the one hand this gives you optimal vision, and on the other hand dirty glasses create an appearance of negligence."
>
> —UBS DRESS CODE

**Inappropriate Focus** The control system may be too narrow, or it may focus too much on quantifiable variables and leave no room for analysis or interpretation. A sales standard that encourages high-pressure tactics to maximize short-run sales may do so at the expense of goodwill from long-term customers. Such a standard is too narrow. A university reward system that encourages faculty members to publish large numbers of articles but fails to consider the quality of the work is also inappropriately focused. Employees resist the intent of the control system by focusing their efforts only on the performance indicators being used.

**Rewards for Inefficiency** Imagine two operating departments that are approaching the end of their fiscal years. Department 1 expects to have $25,000 of its budget left over; department 2 is already $10,000 in the red. As a result, department 1 may have its budget cut for the next year ("They had money left, so they obviously got too much to begin with"), and department 2 may get a budget increase ("They obviously haven't been getting enough money"). Thus department 1 is punished for being efficient, and department 2 is rewarded for being inefficient. (No wonder departments commonly hasten to deplete their budgets as the end of the year approaches!) As with inappropriate focus, people resist the intent of this control and behave in ways that run counter to the organization's intent.

**Too Much Accountability** Effective controls allow managers to determine whether employees successfully discharge their responsibilities. If standards are properly set and performance accurately measured, managers know when problems arise and which departments and individuals are responsible. People who do not want to be answerable for their mistakes or who do not want to work as hard as their bosses might therefore resist control. For example, American Express has a system that provides daily information on how many calls each of its customer service representatives handles. If one representative has typically worked at a slower pace and handled fewer calls than other representatives, that person's deficient performance can now more easily be pinpointed.

## Overcoming Resistance to Control

Perhaps the best way to overcome resistance to control is to create effective control to begin with. If control systems are properly integrated with organizational planning and if the controls are flexible, accurate, timely, and objective, the organization will be less likely to overcontrol, to focus on inappropriate standards, or to reward inefficiency. Two other ways to overcome resistance are encouraging employee participation and developing verification procedures.

**Encourage Employee Participation** Chapter 12 noted that participation can help overcome resistance to change. By the same token, when employees are involved with planning and implementing the control system, they are less likely to resist it. For instance, employee participation in planning, decision making, and quality control at the Chevrolet Gear and Axle plant in Detroit resulted in increased employee concern for quality and a greater commitment to meeting standards.

**Develop Verification Procedures**   Multiple standards and information systems provide checks and balances in control and allow the organization to verify the accuracy of performance indicators. Suppose a production manager argues that she failed to meet a certain cost standard because of increased prices of raw materials. A properly designed inventory control system will either support or contradict her explanation. Suppose that an employee who was fired for excessive absences argues that he was not absent "for a long time." An effective human resource control system should have records that support the termination. Resistance to control declines because these verification procedures protect both employees and management. If the production manager's claim about the rising cost of raw materials is supported by the inventory control records, she will not be held solely accountable for failing to meet the cost standard, and some action probably will be taken to lower the cost of raw materials.

---

☐   Managers should know the essential characteristics of effective control.

☐   You should also be familiar with the reasons some people resist control and the best ways to overcome that resistance.

**Manager's Checklist**

# Summary of Learning Outcomes and Key Points

1. **Explain the purpose of control, identify different types of control, and describe the steps in the control process.**

   - Control is the regulation of organizational activities so that some targeted element of performance remains within acceptable limits.
   - Control provides ways to adapt to environmental change, to limit the accumulation of errors, to cope with organizational complexity, and to minimize costs.
   - Control can focus on financial, physical, information, and human resources and includes operations, financial, structural, and strategic levels.
   - Control is the function of managers, the controller, and, increasingly, of operating employees.
   - Steps in the control process are
     o   to establish standards of expected performance
     o   to measure actual performance
     o   to compare performance to the standards
     o   to evaluate the comparison and take appropriate action

2. **Identify and explain the three forms of operations control.**

   - Operations control focuses on the processes the organization uses to transform resources into products or services.

   - Preliminary control is concerned with the resources that serve as inputs to the system.
   - Screening control is concerned with the transformation processes used by the organization.
   - Postaction control is concerned with the outputs of the organization.
   - Most organizations need multiple control systems because no one system can provide adequate control.

3. **Describe budgets and other tools for financial control.**

   - Financial control focuses on controlling the organization's financial resources.
   - The foundation of financial control is budgets, which are plans expressed in numerical terms.
   - Most organizations rely on financial, operating, and nonmonetary budgets.
   - Financial statements, various kinds of ratios, and external and internal audits are also important tools organizations use as part of financial control.

4. **Identify and distinguish between two opposing forms of structural control.**

   - Structural control addresses how well an organization's structural elements serve their intended purpose.

- Two basic forms of structural control are bureaucratic and decentralized control.
- Bureaucratic control is relatively formal and mechanistic.
- Decentralized control is informal and organic.
- Most organizations use a form of organizational control somewhere between total bureaucratic and total decentralized control.

5. Discuss the relationship between strategy and control, including international strategic control.

- Strategic control focuses on how effectively the organization's strategies are succeeding in helping the organization meet its goals.
- The integration of strategy and control is generally achieved through organization structure, leadership, technology, human resources, and information and operational control systems.
- International strategic control is also important for multinational organizations.

- The foundation of international strategic control is whether to practice centralized or decentralized control.

6. Identify characteristics of effective control, why people resist control, and how managers can overcome this resistance.

- One way to increase the effectiveness of control is to fully integrate planning and control.
- The control system should also be as flexible, accurate, timely, and objective as possible.
- Employees may resist organizational controls because of overcontrol, inappropriate focus, rewards for inefficiency, and a desire to avoid accountability.
- Managers can overcome this resistance by improving the effectiveness of controls and by allowing employee participation and developing verification procedures.

# Discussion Questions

## Questions for Review

1. What is the purpose of organizational control? Why is it important?

2. What are the different levels of control? What are the relationships between the different levels?

## Questions for Analysis

5. How can a manager determine whether his or her firm needs improvement in control? If improvement is needed, how can the manager tell what type of control needs improvement (operations, financial, structural, or strategic)? Describe some steps a manager can take to improve each of these types of control.

3. Describe how a budget is created in most organizations. How does a budget help a manager with financial control?

4. Describe the differences between bureaucratic and decentralized control. What are the advantages and disadvantages of each?

6. One company uses strict performance standards. Another has standards that are more flexible. What are the advantages and disadvantages of each system?

7. Are the differences in bureaucratic control and decentralized control related to differences in organization structure? If so, how? If not, why not? (The terms do sound similar to those used to discuss the organizing process.)

## Questions for Application

8. Many organizations today are involving lower-level employees in control. Give at least two examples of specific actions that a lower-level worker could take to help his or her organization better adapt to environmental change. Then do the same for limiting the accumulation of error, coping with organizational complexity, and minimizing costs.

9. Describe ways that the top management team, midlevel managers, and operating employees can participate in

each step of the control process. Do all participate equally in each step, or are some steps better suited for personnel at one level? Explain your answer.

10. Interview a worker to determine which areas and levels of control exist for him or her on the job. Does the worker resist efforts at control? Why or why not?

# Building Effective Time-Management Skills

## Exercise Overview

Not surprisingly, time-management skills—which refer to the ability to prioritize tasks, to work efficiently, and to delegate appropriately—play a major role in performing the control function: Managers can use time-management skills to control their own work activities more effectively. The purpose of this exercise is to demonstrate the relationship between time-management skills and the process of controlling workplace activities.

## Exercise Background

You're a middle manager in a small manufacturing plant. Today is Monday, and you've just returned from a week's vacation. The first thing you discover is that your assistant won't be in today (his aunt died, and he's out of town at the funeral). He did, however, leave you the following note:

*Dear Boss:*
*Sorry about not being here today. I will be back tomorrow. In the meantime, here are some things you need to know:*

*Ms. Glinski [your boss] wants to see you today at 4:00.*

*The shop steward wants to see you as soon as possible about a labor problem.*

*Mr. Bateman [one of your big customers] has a complaint about a recent shipment.*

*Ms. Ferris [one of your major suppliers] wants to discuss a change in delivery schedules.*

*Mr. Prescott from the Chamber of Commerce wants you to attend a breakfast meeting on Wednesday to discuss our expansion plans.*

*The legal office wants to discuss our upcoming OSHA inspection.*

*Human resources wants to know when you can interview someone for the new supervisor's position.*

*Jack Williams, the machinist you fired last month, has been hanging around the parking lot, and his presence is making some employees uncomfortable.*

## Exercise Task

Review the preceding information and then do the following:

1. Prioritize the work that needs to be done by sorting the information into three categories: *very timely*, *moderately timely*, and *less timely*. Then address the following questions.

2. Are *importance* and *timeliness* the same thing?

3. What additional information do you need before you can begin to prioritize all of these demands on your time?

4. How would your approach differ if your assistant were in the office?

# Building Effective Technical Skills

## Exercise Overview

Technical skills are necessary to understand or perform the specific kind of work that an organization does. This exercise allows you to develop the technical skills needed to construct and evaluate the effectiveness of a budget.

## Exercise Background

Although corporate budgets are obviously much more complicated, the basic processes of creating a corporate budget on the one hand and a personal budget on the other share a few important features. Both, for instance, begin with estimations of inflow and outflow. In addition, both compare actual results with estimated results, and both culminate in plans for corrective action.

## Exercise Task

1. Prepare lists of your *estimated* expenditures and income for one month. Remember: You're dealing with budgeted amounts, not the amounts that you actually spend and take in. You're also dealing with figures that represent a typical month or a reasonable minimum. If, for example, you estimate that you spend $200 a month on

groceries, you need to ask yourself whether that's a reasonable amount to spend on groceries for a month. If it's not, perhaps a more typical or reasonable figure is, say, $125.

First, estimate your necessary monthly expenses for tuition, rent, car payments, childcare, food, utilities, and so on. Then estimate your income from all sources, such as wages, allowance, loans, and funds borrowed on credit cards. Calculate both totals.

2. Now write down all of your *actual* expenses and all your *actual* income over the last month. If you don't have exact figures, estimate as closely as you can. Calculate both totals.

3. Compare your *estimates* to your *actual* expenses and actual income. Are there any discrepancies? If so, what caused them?

4. Did you expect to have a surplus or a deficit for the month? Did you actually have a surplus or a deficit? What can you do to make up any deficit or manage any surplus?

5. Do you regularly use a personal budget? If yes, how is it helpful? If no, how might it be helpful?

# Skill-Building Personal Assessment

## Understanding Control

**Introduction**: Control systems must be carefully constructed for all organizations, regardless of their specific goals. The following assessment surveys your ideas about and approaches to control.

**Instructions**: You will agree with some of the statements and disagree with others. In some cases, making a decision may be difficult, but you should force yourself to make a choice. Record your answers next to each statement according to the following scale.

### Rating Scale

4   Strongly agree
3   Somewhat agree
2   Somewhat disagree
1   Strongly disagree

1. _____ Effective controls must be unbending if they are to be used consistently.
2. _____ The most objective form of control is one that uses measures such as stock prices and rate of return on investment (ROI).
3. _____ Control is restrictive and should be avoided if at all possible.
4. _____ Controlling through rules, procedures, and budgets should not be used unless measurable standards are difficult or expensive to develop.
5. _____ Overreliance on measurable control standards is seldom a problem for business organizations.
6. _____ Organizations should encourage the development of individual self-control.
7. _____ Organizations tend to try to establish behavioral controls as the first type of control to be used.
8. _____ The easiest and least costly form of control is output or quantity control.
9. _____ Short-run efficiency and long-run effectiveness result from the use of similar control standards.
10. _____ Controlling by taking into account ROI and using stock prices in making control decisions are ways of ensuring that a business organization is responding to its external market.
11. _____ Self-control should be relied on to replace other forms of control.
12. _____ Controls such as ROI are more appropriate for corporations and business units than for small groups or individuals.
13. _____ Control is unnecessary in a well-managed organization.
14. _____ The use of output or quantity controls can lead to unintended or unfortunate consequences.
15. _____ Standards of control do not depend on which constituency is being considered.
16. _____ Controlling through the use of rules, procedures, and budgets can lead to rigidity and to a loss of creativity in an organization.
17. _____ Different forms of control cannot be used at the same time. An organization must decide how it is going to control and stick to that method.
18. _____ Setting across-the-board output or quantity targets for divisions within a company can lead to destructive results.
19. _____ Control through rules, procedures, and budgets is generally not very costly.
20. _____ Reliance on individual self-control can lead to problems with integration and communication.

# Management at Work

The Law of Cheating

## "Don't go looking for the perfect performance measure. It doesn't exist."

—ROBERT D. BEHN, HARVARD UNIVERSITY,
KENNEDY SCHOOL OF GOVERNMENT

Let's suppose that you're the manager of a factory that manufactures automotive bumpers. When the fourth quarter rolls around, you see that you aren't on track to meet your quota by your year-end deadline. Failure to meet either the quota or the deadline will mean that you won't be getting any bonus or stock options; in fact, your job might be at risk. So you decide to put off regularly scheduled maintenance and repairs for the quarter and produce bumpers at full capacity—a practice called "storming." You meet your quota and deadline, but catching up with maintenance and repairs during the first quarter of the following year reduces your production capacity for three months. Down the line, of course, you'll be facing yet another quota and another deadline, and in order to recoup the resulting loss in production, you'll have to resort to "storming" once again. Obviously, it won't be long before your operations are completely out of control.

Not fair, you say: Your job is constantly on the line because the quotas and deadlines that you have to meet are too demanding. Unfortunately, as any social scientist could tell you, you are a victim of *Campbell's Law*. In 1976, Donald T. Campbell, a social psychologist specializing in research methodology, came to the following conclusion:

> *The more any quantitative social indicator is used for social decision-making, the more subject it will be to corruption pressures and the more apt it will be to distort and corrupt the social processes that it is intended to monitor.*

In other words: Once a measurement (or *metric*) is specified as a key criterion for the success of a process or project, its ability to measure what it's supposed to will almost inevitably be compromised. Why? If the stakes and the cost of failure are too high, people tend to cheat.

Campbell's Law predicted, for example, what actually happened in Atlanta schools beginning in 2005 and culminating in 2015, when 11 former educators were convicted of racketeering charges stemming from a conspiracy to alter student test scores. The original investigation had extended to nearly 180 principals and teachers at more than 40 schools and had resulted in 35 indictments. The educators, it seems, were motivated by increasing pressure to meet official performance standards on which bonuses and even employment status depended, and adherents of Campbell's Law argue that the episode reflects the failure of a misguided control process designed to measure student performance too narrowly. According to one report on the Atlanta episode, the dilemma fostered by high-stakes educational standards is an all-too-clear demonstration of Campbell's original formula for control failure:

> *School districts are increasingly tying teacher pay to performance, and there's no consensus on the best way to measure student proficiency, so high test scores are starting to look a lot like money. What emerges is bad news: a carrot-and-stick approach to a sector of the workforce that many consider to be underpaid.*

We shouldn't be surprised by such responses to impractical performance measures, says Robert D. Behn of Harvard University's Kennedy School of Government: "After all, we have put significant pressure on schools and teachers to improve test scores. … When the pressure becomes personal—when a person's job and income are on the line—some people may resort to cheating. Why do you think all of those professional baseball players used steroids?"

Behn distinguishes between "honest cheating" and "dishonest cheating." Like the tactics used by certain educators in Atlanta, "dishonest cheating is illegal, and you can go to jail for it" (the convicted principals and teachers are facing prison sentences of five to 20 years). On the other hand, such practices as "teaching to the test"—focusing one's efforts on standardized testing to the detriment of other educational activities—are merely "honest cheating": "There is nothing illegal about it. No one goes to jail for it. Still, it illustrates how putting pressure on schools, principals, and teachers to improve on very specific performance measures can produce the distortions about which Campbell worried."

According to Behn and other analysts of the impulse to cheat, a common denominator in both types of "honesty" is the imposition of "very specific performance measures." In business, such measures are often called *key performance indicators (KPIs)*—quantifiable metrics that show how well an organization is achieving its goals. KPIs can help an organization focus on its most effective strategies, but if they aren't conceived or executed properly, KPIs can be misleading. Campbell himself offered the example of a city that sets a strategy to reduce crime, designating the crime rate as a KPI. If the crime rate goes down, can city officials be sure that crime has actually been reduced? Not necessarily: What if police, in order to push down the rate, had adopted new criteria for crimes that must be formally reported or systematically downgraded certain crimes to less serious classifications?

When enforced by such counterstrategic employee behavior, Campbell's Law can sabotage the best-laid plans—as you did when you gamed the process of meeting your quotas and deadlines. You were given a certain amount of discretion in the way you both achieved and reported your results, and you made your decision based on the fact that the stakes and the cost of failure were too high.

Ironically, your employer also gave you incentives to make the decision that you did—literally: In addition to protecting your job, you acted to secure your bonus and stock options. According to EthicalSystems, a nonprofit that compiles research on ethical leadership, conflicts of interest, cheating, and other related issues, extensive research shows that decisions like yours "are frequently distorted by incentives." An example, suggests James Freis Jr., an attorney specializing in financial-industry regulation, "might be a contractor who knows his bonus depends on the fulfillment of certain contracts and so may be tempted to offer a bribe to a foreign official who is responsible for signing off on a license, customs duty, or shipment."

Freis may well have been thinking about the case of Alcatel-Lucent SA, the world's largest supplier of land-line phone networks. In 2010, the company agreed to pay $137 million to settle criminal and civil charges stemming from violations of the U.S. Foreign Corrupt Practices Act. According to the Securities and Exchange Commission, "Alcatel and its subsidiaries failed to detect or investigate numerous red flags suggesting that employees were directing sham consultants to provide gifts and payments to foreign government officials to illegally win business." Managers at Alcatel received the bulk of their pay in the form of stock incentives and bonuses tied to short-term profitability.

The problem, suggests Harvard's Behn, is the practice of pegging high-stakes incentives to narrow win-or-lose KPIs. As Campbell's Law shows, cheating—including the violation of an organization's ethics rules—will probably occur under such circumstances. "So get over it," Behn advises organizational strategists. "Don't go looking for the perfect performance measure. It doesn't exist. Don't waste countless meetings debating whose measure is without defects. All measures have them." Instead, he suggests,

> start with a good measure (or two). Not great, not perfect, just good. From the beginning, try to identify its inadequacies. Recognize what problems the measure might create; then, as you implement your performance strategy, be alert for the emergence of flaws and distortions. When suggesting, adopting, or employing a performance measure, all [managers] should be aware of—and beware of—Campbell's Law.

## Case Questions

1. What about you? Put yourself in the position of the Atlanta educators whose dilemma is described in the case. If there was a real possibility that you'd lose your job because your students performed badly, how would assess your situation and your options? What if there were a real possibility that you'd lose a pay raise and promotion? How about the possibility that you'd be reassigned to a much less desirable school? Be prepared to argue either side of your case.

2. Think about a class that you're taking now or have taken in the past. What *key performance indicator* (KPI) played the most important role in the instructor's evaluation of your performance? What did it tell you about your instructor's strategy for teaching the course? Do you think that it was too narrowly focused or otherwise unreasonable? If so, how do you think your instructor could have improved his performance-evaluation strategy?

3. Again, what about you? After having read this case, have you reconsidered your attitude toward how much control or accountability you'd like to have in a job? If, for example, you're studying to be a teacher, how do you feel about a career goal such as moving up to principal or even multischool administrator? How does your concept of an ideal work/life relationship affect your thinking on the subject?

4. As we saw in Chapter 13, *incentives* "represent special compensation opportunities that are usually tied to performance"—that is, to a certain form of workplace behavior. They can also be tied to other forms of workplace behavior—such as complying with an employer's policies regarding legal and ethical conduct (its so-called *compliance and ethics, or C&E, program*). Incentives can be either "soft" (consisting of nontangible encouragement or recognition) or "hard" (typically consisting of tangible, often monetary rewards).* What "C&E" incentives affect the way you conduct yourself, whether at work or at school? How do they stack up against the incentives to behave in accord with Campbell's Law? Is there any tension between the two sets of incentives? What do you do—or can you do—to resolve any tension as you make decisions affecting your behavior?

---

*Jeffrey M. Kaplan, "The First Word on Compliance Incentives," *The FCPA Blog* (January 19, 2011), www.fcpablog.com, on June 29, 2015.

## Case References

Sam Alexander, "Examples of Campbell's Law," *Xamuel.com* (May 24, 2013), www.xamuel.com, on June 30, 2015; Donald T. Campbell, "Assessing the Impact of Planned Social Change," Occasional Paper Series, #8 (Dartmouth College, December 1976), http://portals.wi.wur.nl, on June 28, 2015; Alia Wong and Terence F. Ross, "When Teachers Cheat," *The Atlantic* (April 2, 2015), www.theatlantic, on June 30, 2015; Robert D. Behn, "Be Aware (and Beware) of Campbell's Law," *Bob Behn's Performance Leadership Report*, 2011, Vol. 9, No. 12, www.hks.harvard.edu, on June 28, 2015; Robert Bloomfield and David Hirshleifer, eds., "Accounting," Ethical Systems (2015), http://ethical systems.org, on June 28, 2015; Deloitte Development LLC, "Global Financial Crime Sparks New Focus on Compliance," *Wall Street Journal* (October 16, 2013), http://deloitte.wsj.com, on June 28, 2015; David Voreacos and Olga Kharif, "Alcatel Lucent to Pay $137 Million in Bribe Probes," *Bloomberg Business* (December 28, 2010), www.bloomberg.com, on June 29, 2015.

## YOU MAKE THE CALL    Metric Tons and Nonfinancial Metrics

1. *"Until recently,"* says David M. Katz, an editor at *Cfo.com, talk of "integrated reporting" and "sustainability" had a high probability of putting a CFO of a U.S.-based company to sleep…. When it came down to it, why should CFOs have cared about inserting such puffery into the nuts-and-bolts world of 10-Ks and proxy statements?*

   It's a good question. Why do so many CFOs now care about providing narrative nonfinancial reports with nonfinancial metrics in addition to traditional financial reports?

2. First of all, explain *sustainability reporting*, particularly as it's practiced by Jones Lang LaSalle, as a function of *control*. Second, review the textbook section on the four "Steps in the Control Process"—*establishing standards, measuring performance, comparing performance against standards*, and *considering corrective action*. As your book says, these steps are "fundamental in any control process." So briefly show how the "Control Process" played a role in producing the results reported by JLL.

   Remember that it won't always be easy to make one-to-one correspondences; it may, for example, take an educated guess to explain JLL's "performance standards" or how closely the company came to meeting them. Feel free to make such guesses, but be prepared to explain why they make sense.

3. The five "Characteristics of Effective Control" discussed in the chapter—*integration with planning, flexibility, accuracy, timeliness*, and *objectivity*—are based largely on the requirements of financial reporting as it's explained throughout the chapter. Using the information that you've been given about JLL's 2013 Sustainability Report, explain how each of these five characteristics can be applied to the requirements of sustainability reporting. Which characteristics are most important in the type of reporting that goes into a sustainability report? Which characteristics are most readily applicable? Which are least readily applicable and may require the most adjustments to make a good fit?

4. "At its heart," says CEO Colin Dyer in JLL's Sustainability Report,

   *sustainability at JLL is about maintaining and expanding our role as a good corporate citizen…. We develop real estate services that anticipate and address our clients' needs while creating positive change in our industry. Together, these will ensure that JLL remains a sustainable enterprise that clients, employees, investors, and other stakeholders can rely on for the long term.*

   In effect, this statement adds another dimension to the definition of *sustainability* as we've used it in the case. It reflects the so-called "triple bottom line" approach to sustainability accounting. According to the American Institute of Certified Public Accountants, the *triple bottom line* consists of: "1) economic viability, 2) social responsibility, and 3) environmental responsibility."[†]

   If we adopt the triple bottom line approach, what does *sustainability* cover in addition to *environmental* resources? In other words, what *else* do companies intend to sustain? Explain how and why the added dimension of sustainability is consistent with the dimension of environmental responsibility.

---

[*]"Is Sustainability Reporting Sustainable?" *Cfo.com* (January 27, 2014), http://ww2.cfo.com, on June 12, 2015.
[†]American Institute of Certified Public Accountants, "Sustainability Accounting and Reporting—FAQ" (2006–2015), www.aicpa.org, on June 16, 2015.

# Endnotes

1 Jones Lang LaSalle Inc., *2013 Sustainability Report* (September 2014), www. jll.com, on June 12, 2015; Jones Lang LaSalle, "JLL Demonstrates Corporate Citizenship and Sustainability Results in Global Sustainability Report" (press release), *Yahoo! Finance* (September 9, 2014), http://finance.yahoo.com, on June 12, 2015; PricewaterhouseCoopers, *Guide to Key Performance Indicators: Communicating the Measures That Matter* (2007), www.pwc.com, on June 15, 2015; Himanshu Sharma, "Understanding Key Performance Indicators (KPIs)— Complete Guide," *Optimize Smart* (May 4, 2015), www.optimizesmart.com, on June 17, 2015; US SIF Foundation, *Report on Sustainable and Responsible Investing Trends in the United States, 2012* (2012), www.ussif.org, on June 15, 2015; Jones Lang LaSalle, *Sustainability: The Measurement and Reporting Challenge* (2008), www.yourbuilding.org, on June 15, 2015.

2 For a complete discussion of how FedEx uses control in its operations, see "The FedEx Edge," *Fortune*, April 3, 2014, pp. 77–84.

3 Thomas A. Stewart, "Welcome to the Revolution," *Fortune*, December 13, 2013, pp. 66–77.

4 William Taylor, "Control in an Age of Chaos," *Harvard Business Review*, November–December 2014, pp. 64–70.

5 "Fastener Woes to Delay Flight of First Boeing 787 Jets," *Wall Street Journal*, November 5, 2008, p. B1.

6 "Starbucks Brews Up New Cost Cuts By Putting Lid on Afternoon Decaf," *Wall Street Journal*, January 28, 2015, p. B1.

7 "Cadbury Factory Cuts Energy 60%, Costs 50% with Dehumidifier," *Environmental Leader*, April 5, 2015.

8 "An Apple a Day," *BusinessWeek*, October 14, 2014, pp. 122–125; "More Business People Say: Let's Not Do Lunch," *USA Today*, December 24, 2014, p. 1B; David Stires, "The Breaking Point," *Fortune*, March 3, 2015, pp. 107–114.

9 Mark Kroll, Peter Wright, Leslie Toombs, and Hadley Leavell, "Form of Control: A Critical Determinant of Acquisition Performance and CEO Rewards," *Strategic Management Journal*, 2007, Vol. 18, No. 2, pp. 85–96.

10 See Donald Lange, "A Multidimensional Conceptualization of Organizational Corruption Control," *Academy of Management Review*, 2008, Vol. 33, No. 3, pp. 710–729 for an example.

11 See Karynne Turner and Mona Makhija, "The Role of Organizational Controls in Managing Knowledge," *Academy of Management Review*, 2006, Vol. 31, No. 1, pp. 197–217.

12 Sim Sitkin, Kathleen Sutcliffe, and Roger Schroeder, "Distinguishing Control from Learning in Total Quality Management: A Contingency Perspective," *Academy of Management Review*, 2012, Vol. 19, No. 3, pp. 537–564.

13 Robert Lusch and Michael Harvey, "The Case for an Off-Balance-Sheet Controller," *Sloan Management Review*, Winter 2009, pp. 101–110.

14 Edward E. Lawler III and John G. Rhode, *Information and Control in Organizations* (Pacific Palisades, CA: Goodyear, 1976).

15 Charles W. L. Hill, "Establishing a Standard: Competitive Strategy and Technological Standards in Winner-Take-All Industries," *Academy of Management Executive*, 2007, Vol. 11, No. 2, pp. 7–16.

16 "Airbus Clips Superjumbo Production," *Wall Street Journal*, May 7, 2014, p. B1.

17 "Shifting Burden Helps Employers Cut Health Costs," *Wall Street Journal*, December 8, 2014, pp. B1, B2. See also "Employees' Health Costs Are Heading North," *USA Today*, December 5, 2014, p. 6B.

18 *USA Today*, April 13, 2013, p. 3B.

19 "Toyota Plans to Reduce Production for 6 Weeks," *New York Times*, April 19, 2011.

20 "An Efficiency Guru Refits Honda to Fight Auto Giants," *Wall Street Journal*, September 15, 2010, p. B1.

21 See "To Shed Idled Workers, Ford Offers to Foot Bill for College," *Wall Street Journal*, January 18, 2006, pp. B1, B3; "GM's Employees Buyout Offer," *Fast Company*, May 2006, p. 58.

22 "Mickey Mouse, CPA," *Forbes*, March 10, 2015, pp. 42–43.

23 Jeremy Kahn, "Do Accountants Have a Future?" *Fortune*, March 3, 2003, pp. 115–117.

24 "Indian Accounting Firm Is Fined $7.5 Million over Fraud at Satyam," *The New York Times*, April 5, 2011.

25 William G. Ouchi, "The Transmission of Control Through Organizational Hierarchy," *Academy of Management Journal*, June 1978, pp. 173–192; Richard E. Walton, "From Control to Commitment in the Workplace," *Harvard Business Review*, March–April 1985, pp. 76–84.

26 "Best Managed Companies in America," *Forbes*, January 9, 2014, p. 118.

27 See "In Bow to Retailers' New Clout, Levi Strauss Makes Alterations," *Wall Street Journal*, June 17, 2005, pp. A1, A15.

28 Peter Lorange, Michael F. Scott Morton, and Sumantra Ghoshal, *Strategic Control* (St. Paul, MN: West, 1986). See also Joseph C. Picken and Gregory G. Dess, "Out of (Strategic) Control," *Organizational Dynamics*, Summer 1997, pp. 35–45.

29 "Pfizer Plans Layoffs in Research," *Wall Street Journal*, January 14, 2014, p. B1.

30 "Kohl's Works to Refill Consumers' Bags," *USA Today*, April 8, 2015, pp. B1, B1.

31 http://fortune.com/2014/09/22/kevin-mansell-kohls/

32 See Hans Mjoen and Stephen Tallman, "Control and Performance in International Joint Ventures," *Organization Science*, May–June 1997, pp. 257–265.

33 Diana Robertson and Erin Anderson, "Control System and Task Environment Effects on Ethical Judgment: An Exploratory Study of Industrial Salespeople," *Organization Science*, November 1993, pp. 617–629.

34 "Workers, Surf at Your Own Risk," *BusinessWeek*, June 12, 2014, pp. 105–106.

35 "Enterprise Takes Idea of Dressed for Success to a New Extreme," *Wall Street Journal*, November 20, 2012, p. B1.

36 "UBS Relaxing Dress Code, Which Set Underwear Standards," *USA Today*, January 25, 2011, p. 1B.

©Markus Pfaff/Shutterstock.com

# 20

# MANAGING OPERATIONS, QUALITY, AND PRODUCTIVITY

**After studying this chapter, you should be able to:**

1. Describe and explain the nature of operations management.

2. Identify and discuss the components involved in designing effective operations systems.

3. Discuss organizational technologies and their role in operations management.

4. Identify and discuss the components involved in implementing operations

systems through supply chain management.

5. Explain the meaning and importance of managing quality and total quality management.

6. Explain the meaning and importance of managing productivity, productivity trends, and ways to improve productivity.

## MANAGEMENT IN ACTION | What to Do When Workers Wonder What Happens Next

"Employee engagement isn't about the free food and nap pods that companies like Google offer."

—*INC.* MAGAZINE EDITOR PAUL KEEGAN

Best Buy, the giant consumer electronics retailer, has been using annual surveys to track levels of *employee engagement* since 2003. Best Buy's strategy calls for providing customers with individualized shopping experiences, and top management realized early on that this strategy depended on the company's most important asset—the employees who engaged with its customers. It also stood to reason that if its customers were motivated by the company's ability to respond to their individual needs, then its employees could be motivated by its willingness to respond to their individual needs as well. In 2003, Best Buy thus launched a fairly radical initiative allowing employees to shape their own jobs and define their own career paths

according to their own needs and talents. In 2010, an independent study concluded that Best Buy had "doubled the rate of increase in employee engagement." In the same year, another study linked increased employee engagement to increased productivity: The researchers found that a 0.1 percent increase in employee engagement at a given store correlated with an annual increase in sales of $100,000.[1]

Findings like those at Best Buy have been confirmed on a much broader scale by a wealth of independent research. In 2012, for example, Gallup examined nearly 50,000 work units (groups of workers assigned to perform specific tasks) across 192 organizations in 34 countries. The purpose of the study was to provide statistical correlations between employee engagement and performance outcomes.* According to Gallup, the study "confirmed the well-established connection between employee engagement and nine performance outcomes" ranging from profitability and customer ratings to absenteeism and workplace theft.

Eddie Sellos (L), who was recently hired by Best Buy, helps customer Guilherme Machado as he shops at the Best Buy store in Miami, Florida. Best Buy strives to engage and reward their employees in an attempt to increase their productivity and customer service.

Joe Raedle/Getty Images

*What's the difference between *engaged* and *disengaged employees*? Gallup's Jim Harter puts it this way: "When you ask people about their intentions during a recession, it's pretty clear that disengaged workers are just waiting around to see what happens. Engaged workers, though, have bought into what the organization is about and are trying to make a difference. This is why they're usually the most productive workers."

Among other things, Gallup found that work units in the top quartile (those that scored better than 75 percent of all organizations in the study) outperformed those in the bottom quartile (those outscored by 75 percent of all organizations) by 10 percent on customer ratings, 22 percent on profitability, and 21 percent on productivity. Units in the top quartile had significantly lower levels of turnover (25–65 percent depending on industrywide turnover rates), absenteeism (37 percent), safety incidents (48 percent), and quality defects (41 percent). Meanwhile, a study by Towers Watson, a global professional services firm, showed that organizations with high employee engagement enjoyed a one-year average increase in operating income of 19 percent and 28 percent growth in earnings per share (EPS); companies with low levels of engagement experienced an average decline of 32 percent in operating income and an 11 percent drop in EPS.

Gallup translated such data into some bottom-line numbers: Actively disengaged employees—about 26 percent of all workers—cost U.S. organizations between $450 billion to $550 billion in lost productivity every year.

It may seem fairly obvious at this point, but according to Gartner, a consulting firm specializing in information technology research, "the positive correlation between employee engagement and organization performance suggests that there is a substantial upside for organizations that focus on enhancing employee engagement." More specifically, however, what do all of these numbers mean for top managers when it comes to implementing changes in practices affecting employee engagement? For one thing, they need to appreciate the numbers. "Many executives and line managers," says Gartner, "still view improving employee engagement as a soft and fuzzy concept," failing to understand "why it's important and what a vital role it plays in driving business success."

The most recent *Harvard Business Review* (HBR) Analytic Services report agrees that "while most executives see a clear need to improve employee engagement, many have yet to develop tangible ways to measure and tackle this goal. However," the report hastens to add, "a growing group of best-in-class companies says that they are gaining competitive advantage through establishing metrics and practices to effectively quantify and improve the impact of their engagement initiatives on overall business performance." In fact, says the report, many companies that have made

employee engagement a high priority "are effectively using metrics … for tying engagement to business performance." When asked which factors they considered most important to business success, leaders tended to give "people-oriented 'soft'" goals: At the top were achieving a high level of customer service, developing more effective communications, and improving employee engagement.

"This is not surprising," observes the report, "as a growing body of research has demonstrated that having a highly engaged workforce not only maximizes a company's investment in human capital and improves productivity, but it can also significantly reduce costs that directly impact the bottom line." But employee engagement, explains an HR executive at the global consumer goods company Newell Rubbermaid,

*is not just a warm, fuzzy thing. It's about giving people the tools they need to succeed in their careers, which in turn drives the outcomes that we're seeking in the marketplace. … When people have the tools they need to succeed, feel good about their personal growth opportunities, and receive the appropriate rewards for their contributions, it's a win-win proposition.*

What are "appropriate rewards"? For one thing, as *Inc.* magazine editor Paul Keegan puts it, employee engagement

*isn't about the free food and nap pods that companies like Google offer. … Most carrot-and-stick motivators don't work in the long term, because people get so fixated on the reward that they lose interest in the activity itself. What we really want in our jobs is autonomy, the chance to get better at what we do, and a purpose that connects us to something larger.*

A survey by Towers Perrin found that workers who consider themselves "highly engaged" feel that their jobs are significantly connected with their employers' goals and practices. Eighty-four percent, for example, believe that they could positively affect product quality, and 68 percent believe that they can positively affect the costs of their jobs or work units.

According to the survey, 72 percent of highly engaged employees also believe that they can positively affect their companies' levels of customer service. In fact, the Gallup survey found that companies with engagement scores in the top quartile averaged

12 percent higher scores on *customer advocacy*—an approach to customer service based on a customer-focused culture. The HBR report states that in the effort to forge a link between employee engagement and productivity, "the two metrics most utilized to measure the outcome of employee-engagement initiatives are employee satisfaction and customer satisfaction." Some best-practice companies, says the HBR report, "are increasingly measuring and monitoring how engagement affects the customer experience" using a measuring technique known as *the*

*service-profit chain*, in which the links can be characterized as follows:

> *Profit and growth are stimulated primarily by customer loyalty. Loyalty is a direct result of customer satisfaction. Satisfaction is largely influenced by the value of services provided to customers. Value is created by satisfied, loyal, and productive employees. Employee satisfaction, in turn, results primarily from high-quality support services and policies that enable employees to deliver results to customers.*

Employee engagement is of growing interest to many managers today. One reason for this interest is the relationship between employee engagement and productivity. Productivity, in turn, has long been important to managers in all organizations. In this chapter, we explore operations management, quality, and productivity. We first introduce operations management and discuss its role in general management and organizational strategy. The next three sections discuss the design of operations systems, organizational technologies, and implementing operations systems. We then introduce and discuss various issues in managing for quality and total quality. Finally, we discuss productivity, which is closely related to quality.

# The Nature of Operations Management

Operations management is at the core of what organizations do as they add value and create products and services. But what exactly are operations? And how are they managed? Operations management is the set of managerial activities used by an organization to transform resource inputs into products and services. When Dell Computer buys electronic components, assembles them into PCs, and then ships them to customers, it is engaging in operations management. When a Pizza Hut employee orders food and paper products and then combines dough, cheese, and tomato paste to create a pizza, he or she is engaging in operations management.

## The Importance of Operations

Operations is an important functional concern for organizations because efficient and effective management of operations goes a long way toward ensuring competitiveness and overall organizational performance, as well as quality and productivity. Inefficient or ineffective operations management, on the other hand, will almost inevitably lead to poorer performance and lower levels of both quality and productivity.

In an economic sense, operations management creates value and utility of one type or another, depending on the nature of the firm's products or services. If the product is a physical good, such as a Harley-Davidson motorcycle, operations creates value and provides form utility by combining many dissimilar inputs (sheet metal, rubber, paint, internal combustion engines, and human skills) to make something (a motorcycle) that is more valuable than the actual cost of the inputs used to create it. The inputs are converted from their incoming

**operations management**
The total set of managerial activities used by an organization to transform resource inputs into products, services, or both

form into a new physical form. This conversion is typical of manufacturing operations and essentially reflects the organization's technology.

In contrast, the operations activities of Delta Airlines create value and provide time and place utility through its services. The airline transports passengers and freight according to agreed-upon departure and arrival places and times. Other service operations, such as a Coors beer distributorship or a Zara retail store, create value and provide place and possession utility by bringing together the customer and products made by others. Although the organizations in these examples produce different kinds of products or services, their operations processes share many important features.[2]

## Manufacturing and Production Operations

Because manufacturing once dominated U.S. industry, the entire area of operations management used to be called "production management." Manufacturing is a form of business that combines and transforms resources into tangible outcomes that are then sold to others. The Goodyear Tire & Rubber Company is a manufacturer because it combines rubber and chemical compounds and uses blending equipment and molding machines to create tires. Broyhill is a manufacturer because it buys wood and metal components, pads, and fabric and then combines them into furniture.

During the 1970s, manufacturing entered a long period of decline in the United States, primarily because of foreign competition. U.S. firms had grown lax and sluggish, and new foreign competitors came onto the scene with better equipment and much higher levels of efficiency. For example, steel companies in the Far East were able to produce high-quality steel for much lower prices than were U.S. companies like Bethlehem Steel and U.S. Steel (now USX Corporation). Faced with a battle for survival, many companies underwent a long and difficult period of change, eliminating waste and transforming themselves into leaner, more efficient and responsive entities. They reduced their workforces dramatically, closed antiquated or unnecessary plants, and modernized their remaining plants. In the last decade, their efforts have started to pay dividends, as U.S. businesses have regained their competitive positions in many different industries. Although manufacturers from other parts of the world are still formidable competitors, and U.S. firms may never again be competitive in some markets, the overall picture is much better than it was just a few years ago. And prospects continue to look bright.[3]

## Service Operations

During the decline of the manufacturing sector, a tremendous growth in the service sector kept the U.S. economy from declining at the same rate. A service organization is one that transforms resources into an intangible output and creates time or place utility for its customers. For example, Merrill Lynch makes stock transactions for its customers, Avis leases cars to its customers, and local hairdressers cut clients' hair. In 1947 the service sector was responsible for less than half of the U.S. gross national product (GNP). By 1975, however, this figure had reached 65 percent. Today the service sector accounts for nearly 80 percent of the private-sector gross domestic product and provides 90 million jobs.[4] Managers in service organizations have come to see that many of the tools, techniques, and methods that are used in a factory are also useful to a service firm. For example, managers of automobile plants and hair salons both have to decide how to design their facilities, identify the best locations for them, determine optimal capacities, make decisions about inventory storage, set procedures for purchasing raw materials, and set standards for productivity and quality.

**manufacturing**
A form of business that combines and transforms resource inputs into tangible outcomes

**service organization**
An organization that transforms resources into an intangible output and creates time or place utility for its customers

### The Role of Operations in Organizational Strategy

It should be clear by this point that operations management is very important to organizations. Beyond its direct impact on such factors as competitiveness, quality, and productivity, it also directly influences the organization's overall level of effectiveness. For example, the deceptively simple strategic decision of whether to stress high quality regardless of cost, lowest possible cost regardless of quality, or some combination of the two has many important implications. A highest-possible-quality strategy will dictate state-of-the-art technology and rigorous control of product design and materials specifications. A combination strategy might call for lower-grade technology and less concern about product design and materials specifications. Just as strategy affects operations management, so, too, does operations management affect strategy. Suppose that a firm decides to upgrade the quality of its products or services. The organization's ability to implement the decision is dependent in part on current production capabilities and other resources. If existing technology will not permit higher-quality work, and if the organization lacks the resources to replace its technology, increasing quality to the desired new standards will be difficult.

**Manager's Checklist**

☐ Managers should be able to distinguish between manufacturing and production operations and service operations.

☐ You should also have a clear understanding of the operations management strategy or strategies in your organization.

A firm's product-service mix is determined in large part by corporate or business strategies. A logical next step is to design operations systems to efficiently produce products to be sold with the desired packaging and sizes. Of course, as shown here, most products are sold in a wide variety of forms and sizes.

**product-service mix**
How many and what kinds of products or services (or both) to offer

# Designing Operations Systems

The problems, challenges, and opportunities faced by operations managers revolve around the acquisition and utilization of resources for conversion. Their goals include both efficiency and effectiveness. A number of issues and decisions must be addressed as operations systems are designed. The most basic ones are product-service mix, capacity, and facilities.

## Determining Product-Service Mix

A natural starting point in designing operations systems is determining the product-service mix. This decision flows from corporate, business, and marketing strategies. Managers have to make a number of decisions about their products and services, starting with how many and what kinds to offer.[5] Procter & Gamble, for example, makes regular, whitening, tartar-control, and various other formulas of Crest toothpaste, offers each in a variety of flavors, and packages them in several different sizes of tubes, pumps, and other dispensers. Similarly, workers at Subway sandwich shops can combine different breads, vegetables, meats, and condiments to create hundreds of different kinds of sandwiches. Decisions also have to be made regarding the level of quality desired, the optimal cost of each product or service, and exactly how each is to be designed. During a review of its manufacturing operations, managers at General Electric figured out how to reduce the number of parts in its industrial circuit breakers from 28,000 to 1,275. This whole process was achieved by carefully analyzing product design and production methods.

## Capacity Decisions

The **capacity** decision involves choosing the amount of products, services, or both that can be produced by the organization. Determining whether to build a factory capable of making 5,000 or 8,000 units per day is a capacity decision. So, too, is deciding whether to build a restaurant with 100 or 150 seats, or a bank with five or 10 teller stations. The capacity decision is truly a high-risk one because of the uncertainties of future product demand and the large monetary stakes involved. An organization that builds capacity exceeding its needs may commit resources (capital investment, space, and so forth) that will never be recovered. Alternatively, an organization can build a facility with a smaller capacity than expected demand. Doing so may result in lost market opportunities, but it may also free capital resources for use elsewhere in the organization.

A major consideration in determining capacity is demand. A company operating with fairly constant monthly demand might build a plant capable of producing an amount each month roughly equivalent to its demand. But if its market is characterized by seasonal fluctuations, building a smaller plant to meet normal demand and then adding extra shifts staffed with temporary workers or paying permanent workers extra to work more hours during peak periods might be the most effective choice. Likewise, a restaurant that needs 150 seats for Saturday night but never needs more than 100 at any other time during the week would probably be foolish to expand to 150 seats. During the rest of the week, it must still pay to light, heat, cool, and clean the excess capacity. Many customer service departments have tried to improve their capacity to deal with customers while also lowering costs by using automated voice prompts to direct callers to the right representative.

Capacity decisions are an important part of operations management. Take this restaurant, for example. Right now many people are waiting for tables. If the restaurant were larger more customers could be seated immediately and the restaurant would generate more revenue. However, during other periods when demand might be lower the restaurant would have unused space and experience higher costs.

## Facilities Decisions

**Facilities** are the physical locations where products or services are created, stored, and distributed. Major decisions pertain to facilities location and facilities layout.

**Location**   Location is the physical positioning or geographic site of facilities and must be determined by the needs and requirements of the organization. A company that relies heavily on railroads for transportation needs to be located close to rail facilities. General Electric decided that it did not need six plants to make circuit breakers, so it invested heavily in automating one plant and closed the other five. Different organizations in the same industry may have different facilities requirements. Benetton uses only one distribution center for the entire world, whereas Walmart has several distribution centers in the United States alone. A retail business must choose its location very carefully to be convenient for consumers.

**capacity**
The amount of products, services, or both that can be produced by an organization

**facilities**
The physical locations where products or services are created, stored, and distributed

**location**
The physical positioning or geographic site of facilities

**Layout**   The choice of physical configuration, or the layout, of facilities is closely related to other operations decisions. The three entirely different layout alternatives shown in Figure 20.1 help demonstrate the importance of the layout decision.

A product layout is appropriate when large quantities of a single product are needed. It makes sense to custom-design a straight-line flow of work for a product when a specific task is performed at each workstation as each unit flows past. Most assembly lines use this format. For example, Dell's personal computer factories use a product layout.

Process layouts are used in operations settings that create or process a variety of products. Auto repair shops and healthcare clinics are good examples. Each car and each person is a separate "product." The needs of each incoming job are diagnosed as it enters the operations system, and the job is routed through the unique sequence of workstations needed to create the desired finished product. In a process layout, each type of conversion task is centralized in a single workstation or department. All welding is done in one designated shop location, and any car that requires welding is moved to that area. This setup is in contrast to the product layout, in which several different workstations may perform welding operations

---

## FIGURE 20.1   APPROACHES TO FACILITIES LAYOUT

When a manufacturer produces large quantities of a product (such as cars or computers), it may arrange its facilities in an assembly line (product layout). In a process layout, the work (such as patients in a hospital or custom pieces of furniture) moves through various workstations. Locomotives and bridges are both manufactured in a fixed-position layout.

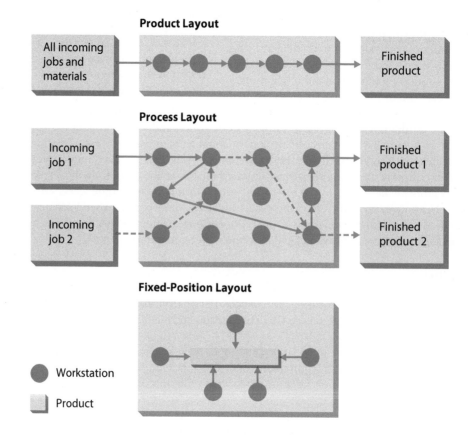

**layout**
The physical configuration of facilities, the arrangement of equipment within facilities, or both

**product layout**
A physical configuration of facilities arranged around the product; used when large quantities of a single product are needed

**process layouts**
A physical configuration of facilities arranged around the process; used in facilities that create or process a variety of products

if the conversion task sequence so dictates. Similarly, in a hospital, all X-rays are done in one location, all surgeries in another, and all physical therapy in yet another. Patients are moved from location to location to get the services they need.

The fixed-position layout is used when the organization is creating a few very large and complex products. Aircraft manufacturers like Boeing and shipbuilders like Newport News use this method. An assembly line capable of moving one of Boeing's new 787 aircraft would require an enormous plant, so instead the airplane itself remains stationary, and people and machines move around it as it is assembled.

The cellular layout is a relatively new approach to facilities design. Cellular layouts are used when families of products can follow similar flow paths. A clothing manufacturer, for example, might create a cell, or designated area, dedicated to making a family of pockets, such as pockets for shirts, coats, blouses, and slacks. Although each kind of pocket is unique, the same basic equipment and methods are used to make all of them. Hence, all pockets might be made in the same area and then delivered directly to different product layout assembly areas where the shirts, coats, blouses, and slacks are actually being assembled.

---

☐ Managers should know the three basic components in designing operations systems.

☐ You should be familiar with the basic decisions that relate to each component in designing operations systems.

**Manager's Checklist** ☑

# Organizational Technologies

One central element of effective operations management is technology. In Chapter 3 we defined technology as the set of processes and systems used by organizations to convert resources into products or services.

## Manufacturing Technology

Numerous forms of manufacturing technology are used in organizations. In Chapter 11 we discussed the research of Joan Woodward. Recall that Woodward identified three forms of technology—unit or small batch, large batch or mass production, and continuous process.[6] Each form of technology was thought to be associated with a specific type of organization structure. Of course, newer forms of technology not considered by Woodward also warrant attention. Two of these are automation and computer-assisted manufacturing.

**Automation**  Automation is the process of designing work so that it can be completely or almost completely performed by machines. Because automated machines operate quickly and make few errors, they increase the amount of work that can be done. Thus automation helps to improve products and services and fosters innovation. Automation is the most recent step in the development of machines and machine-controlling devices. Machine-controlling devices have been around since the 1700s. James Watt, a Scottish engineer, invented a mechanical speed control to regulate the speed of steam engines in 1787. The Jacquard loom, developed by a French inventor, was controlled by paper cards with holes punched in them. Early accounting and computing equipment was controlled by similar punched cards.

Automation relies on feedback, information, sensors, and a control mechanism. Feedback is the flow of information from the machine back to the sensor. Sensors are the parts of the system that gather information and compare it to preset standards. The control mechanism is the device that sends instructions to the automatic machine. Early automatic machines were primitive, and the use of automation was relatively slow to develop. These

---

**fixed-position layout**
A physical configuration of facilities arranged around a single work area; used for the manufacture of large and complex products such as airplanes

**cellular layouts**
A physical configuration of facilities used when families of products can follow similar flow paths

**technology**
The set of processes and systems used by organizations to convert resources into products or services

**automation**
The process of designing work so that it can be completely or almost completely performed by machines

### FIGURE 20.2   A SIMPLE AUTOMATIC CONTROL MECHANISM

All automation includes feedback, information, sensors, and a control mechanism. A simple thermostat is an example of automation. Another example is Benetton's distribution center in Italy. Orders are received, items pulled from stock and packaged for shipment, and invoices prepared and transmitted, with no human intervention.

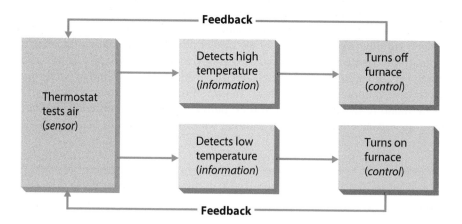

elements are illustrated by the example in Figure 20.2. A thermostat has sensors that monitor air temperature and compare it to a preset value. If the air temperature falls below the preset value, the thermostat sends an electrical signal to the furnace, turning it on. The furnace heats the air. When the sensors detect that the air temperature has reached a value higher than the low preset value, the thermostat stops the furnace. The last step (shutting off the furnace) is known as *feedback*, a critical component of any automated operation.

The big move to automate factories began during World War II. The shortage of skilled workers and the development of high-speed computers combined to bring about a tremendous interest in automation. Programmable automation (the use of computers to control machines) was introduced during this era, far outstripping conventional automation (the use of mechanical or electromechanical devices to control machines). The automobile industry began to use automatic machines for a variety of jobs. In fact, the term *automation* came into use in the 1950s in the automobile industry. The chemical and oil-refining industries also began to use computers to regulate production. During the 1990s, automation became a major element in the manufacture of computers and computer components, such as electronic chips and circuits. It is this computerized, or programmable, automation that presents the greatest opportunities and challenges for management today.

The impact of automation on people in the workplace is complex. In the short term, people whose jobs are automated may find themselves without a job. In the long term, however, more jobs are created than are lost. Nevertheless, not all companies are able to help displaced workers find new jobs, so the human costs are sometimes high. In the coal industry, for instance, automation has been used primarily in mining. The output per miner has risen dramatically from the 1950s on. The demand for coal, however, has decreased, and productivity gains resulting from automation have lessened the need for miners. Consequently, many workers have lost their jobs, and the industry has not been able to absorb them. In contrast, in the electronics industry, the rising demand for products has led to increasing employment opportunities despite the use of automation.[7]

**computer-assisted manufacturing**
A technology that relies on computers to design or manufacture products

**Computer-Assisted Manufacturing** Current extensions of automation generally revolve around computer-assisted manufacturing. Computer-assisted manufacturing is technology that relies on computers to design or manufacture products. One type of computer-assisted manufacturing is *computer-aided design (CAD)*—the use of computers to design parts and complete products and to simulate performance so that prototypes need not be constructed. Boeing uses CAD technology to study hydraulic tubing in its commercial aircraft. Japan's automotive industry uses it to speed up car design. GE used CAD to change the design of circuit breakers, and Benetton uses CAD to design new styles and products. Oneida, the table flatware firm, uses CAD to design new flatware patterns; for example, it can design a new spoon in a single day. CAD is usually combined with *computer-aided manufacturing (CAM)* to ensure that the design moves smoothly to production. The production computer shares the design computer's information and can have machines with the proper settings ready when production is needed. A CAM system is especially useful when reorders come in because the computer can quickly produce the desired product, prepare labels and copies of orders, and send the product out to where it is wanted.

Closely aligned with this approach is *computer-integrated manufacturing (CIM)*. In CIM, CAD and CAM are linked together, and computer networks automatically adjust machine placements and settings to enhance both the complexity and the flexibility of scheduling. In settings that use these technologies, all manufacturing activities are controlled by the computer network. Because the network can access the company's other information systems, CIM is both a powerful and a complex management control tool.

*Flexible manufacturing systems (FMS)* usually have robotic work units or workstations, assembly lines, and robotic carts or some other form of computer-controlled transport system to move material as needed from one part of the system to another. FMS like the one at IBM's manufacturing facility in Lexington, Kentucky, rely on computers to coordinate and integrate automated production and materials-handling facilities. And after it bought Jaguar several years ago, Ford Motor Company used FMS to transform an English factory producing low-cost Ford Escorts into a Jaguar plant making Jaguar luxury cars. Using traditional methods, the plant would have been closed, its workers laid off, and the facility virtually rebuilt from the ground up. But by using FMS, Ford was able to keep the plant open and running continuously while new equipment was being installed and its workers were being retrained in small groups.[8] Ford continues to be a pioneer in FMS as it adjusts plant capabilities to produce pickups, SUVs, or small hybrids depending on fluctuations in demand and supply.[9]

These systems are not without disadvantages, however. For example, because they represent fundamental change, they also generate resistance. Additionally, because of their tremendous complexity, CAD systems are not always reliable. CIM systems are so expensive that they raise the breakeven point for firms using them. This means that the firm must operate at high levels of production and sales to be able to afford the systems.

"Lean isn't good enough anymore. The new reality requires being both lean and flexible."

—DAVID COLE, AUTOMOBILE INDUSTRY EXPERT[10]

**Robotics** Another trend in manufacturing technology is computerized robotics. A robot is any artificial device that can perform functions ordinarily thought to be appropriate for human beings. Robotics refers to the science and technology of the construction, maintenance, and use of robots. The use of industrial robots has steadily increased since 1980 and is expected to continue to increase slowly as more companies recognize the benefits that accrue to users of industrial robots.[11]

Welding was one of the first applications for robots, and it continues to be the area for most applications. A close second is materials handling. Other applications include machine loading and unloading, painting and finishing, assembly, casting, and such machining applications as cutting, grinding, polishing, drilling, sanding, buffing, and deburring. Daimler-Benz, for instance, replaced about 200 welders with 50 robots on an assembly line and increased productivity about 20 percent. The use of robots in inspection work is increasing. They can check for cracks and holes, and they can be equipped with vision systems to perform visual inspections.

**robot**
Any artificial device that is able to perform functions ordinarily thought to be appropriate for human beings

Robots are also beginning to move from the factory floor to other applications. The Dallas police used a robot to apprehend a suspect who had barricaded himself in an apartment building. The robot smashed a window and reached with its mechanical arm into the building. The suspect panicked and ran outside. At the Long Beach Memorial Hospital in California, brain surgeons are assisted by a robot arm that drills into the patient's skull with extreme precision. Some newer applications involve remote work. For example, the use of robot submersibles controlled from the surface can help divers in remote locations. Surveillance robots fitted with microwave sensors can do things that a human guard cannot do, such as "seeing" through nonmetallic walls and in the dark. In other applications, automated farming (called "agrimation") uses robot harvesters to pick fruit from a variety of trees.

> "Neither workers nor robots can reach their productive potential without interacting more closely."
>
> —VOLKER GRÜNENWALD, HEAD OF SYSTEMS INTEGRATION AT PILZ, A GERMAN ENGINEERING FIRM[12]

Robots are also used by small manufacturers. One robot slices carpeting to fit the inside of custom vans in an upholstery shop. Another stretches balloons flat so that they can be spray-painted with slogans at a novelties company. At a jewelry company, a robot holds class rings while they are engraved by a laser. These robots are lighter, faster, stronger, and more intelligent than those used in heavy manufacturing and are the types that more and more organizations will be using in the future.

Hotels are using increasingly sophisticated technology, including apps like Expedia, to enable guests to book reservations and upgrades.

## Service Technology

Service technology is also changing rapidly. And it, too, is moving more and more toward automated systems and procedures. In banking, for example, new technological breakthroughs led to automated teller machines and made it much easier to move funds between accounts or between different banks. Most people now have their paychecks deposited directly into a checking account from which many of their bills are then automatically paid. Electronic banking—where people can access their accounts, move money between accounts, and pay bills—has become commonplace, and many people deposit checks digitally using imaging from their smartphones.

Hotels use increasingly sophisticated technology to accept and record room reservations. People can now, for instance, check in online and stop by the front desk only long enough to pick up their room key. Universities use new technologies to electronically store and provide access to books, scientific journals, government reports, and articles. Hospitals and other healthcare organizations use new forms of service technology to manage patient records, dispatch ambulances and EMTs, and monitor patient vital signs. Restaurants use technology to record and fill customer orders, order food and supplies, and prepare food. If you've ever seen a performance by Cirque du Soleil, you probably have some idea of the role played by technology in its spectacular productions. Given the increased role that service organizations—from restaurants and dry cleaners to hotels and circuses—are playing in today's economy, even more technological innovations are certain to be developed in the years to come.[13]

# Implementing Operations Systems Through Supply Chain Management

After operations systems have been properly designed and technologies developed, they must then be put into use by the organization. Their basic functional purpose is to control transformation processes to ensure that relevant goals are achieved in such areas as quality and costs. Operations management has a number of special purposes within this control framework, including purchasing and inventory management. Indeed, this area of management has become so important in recent years that a new term—*supply chain management*—has been coined. Specifically, supply chain management can be defined as the process of managing operations control, resource acquisition and purchasing, and inventory so as to improve overall efficiency and effectiveness.[14]

## Operations Management as Control

One way of using operations management as control is to coordinate it with other functions. Monsanto Company, for example, established a consumer products division that produces and distributes fertilizers and lawn chemicals. To facilitate control, the operations function was organized as an autonomous profit center. Monsanto finds this effective because its manufacturing division is given the authority to determine not only the costs of creating the product but also the product price and the marketing program.

In terms of overall organizational control, a division like the one used by Monsanto should be held accountable only for the activities over which it has decision-making authority. It would be inappropriate, of course, to make operations accountable for profitability in an organization that stresses sales and market share over quality and productivity. Misplaced accountability results in ineffective organizational control, to say nothing of hostility and conflict. Depending on the strategic role of operations, then, operations managers are accountable for different kinds of results. For example, in an organization using bureaucratic control, accountability will be spelled out in rules and regulations. In a decentralized system, it is likely to be understood and accepted by everyone.

Within operations, managerial control ensures that resources and activities achieve primary goals such as a high percentage of on-time deliveries, low unit-production cost, or high product reliability. Any control system should focus on the elements that are most crucial to goal attainment. For example, firms in which product quality is a major concern (as it is at Rolex) might adopt a screening control system to monitor the product as it is being created. If quantity is a higher priority (as it is at Timex), a postaction system might be used to identify defects at the end of the system without disrupting the manufacturing process itself.

When Boeing started production of its Boeing 787 Dreamliner, the new plane was hailed as the most commercially successful new plane of all time. Airlines around the world pre-ordered over 900 of the planes at a cost of $178 million each before they ever took a test flight, based on its projected fuel efficiency, passenger comfort, low maintenance costs, flexibility, and other major design elements. But the first test flights for the plane were over two years late, largely because of supply chain issues. Boeing subcontracted out the design and assembly of major components of the 787 to firms in Japan, Italy, South Carolina, and Kansas, but did not impose adequate coordination across these various suppliers. As a result,

**supply chain management**
The process of managing operations control, resource acquisition, and inventory so as to improve overall efficiency and effectiveness

subassemblies did not fit together properly, there were numerous quality and delivery issues, and myriad other problems. Clearly, then, poor supply chain management can be disastrous, especially for major new products.[15]

Recent events have also underscored the consequences of disruptions to supply chains. The earthquake and subsequent tsunami that devastated Japan in 2011 caused Japanese automakers in the United States to virtually cease production for several months due to the shortage of parts available from Japanese suppliers. Even U.S. automakers like General Motors and Ford suffered disruptions as well.[16]

## Purchasing Management

Purchasing management, also called *procurement*, is concerned with buying the materials and resources needed to create products and services. In many ways, purchasing is at the very heart of effective supply chain management. The purchasing manager for a retailer like Nordstrom or Sears is responsible for buying the merchandise the store will sell. The purchasing manager for a manufacturer buys raw materials, parts, and machines needed by the organization. Large companies like GE, IBM, and Siemens have large purchasing departments.[17] The manager responsible for purchasing must balance a number of constraints. Buying too much ties up capital and increases storage costs. Buying too little might lead to shortages and high reordering costs. The manager must also make sure that the quality of what is purchased meets the organization's needs, that the supplier is reliable, and that the best financial terms are negotiated.

Many firms have recently changed their approaches to purchasing as a means of lowering costs and improving quality and productivity. In particular, rather than relying on hundreds or even thousands of suppliers, many companies are reducing their numbers of suppliers and negotiating special production–delivery arrangements.[18] For example, the Honda plant in Marysville, Ohio, found a local business owner looking for a new opportunity. They negotiated an agreement whereby the business owner would start a new company to mount car stereo speakers into plastic moldings. He delivers finished goods to the plant three times a day, and Honda buys all he can manufacture. Thus he has a stable sales base, Honda has a local and reliable supplier, and both companies benefit.

## Inventory Management

Inventory control, also called *materials control*, is essential for effective operations management. The four basic kinds of inventories are *raw materials*, *work-in-process*, *finished-goods*, and *in-transit* inventories. As shown in Table 20.1, the sources of control over these inventories are as different as their purposes. Work-in-process inventories, for example, are made up of partially completed products that need further processing; they are controlled by the

**purchasing management**
Buying materials and resources needed to produce products and services

**inventory control**
Managing the organization's raw materials, work in process, finished goods, and products in transit

---

## TABLE 20.1 INVENTORY TYPES, PURPOSES, AND SOURCES OF CONTROL

| Type | Purpose | Source of Control |
|---|---|---|
| Raw materials | Provide the materials needed to make the product | Purchasing models and systems |
| Work in process | Enable overall production to be divided into stages of manageable size | Shop-floor control systems |
| Finished goods | Provide ready supply of products on customer demand and enable long, efficient production runs | High-level production scheduling systems in conjunction with marketing |
| In transit (pipeline) | Distribute products to customers | Transportation and distribution control systems |

shop-floor system. In contrast, the quantities and costs of finished-goods inventories are under the control of the overall production scheduling system, which is determined by high-level planning decisions. In-transit inventories are controlled by the transportation and distribution systems.

Like most other areas of operations management, inventory management has changed notably in recent years. One particularly important breakthrough is the just-in-time (JIT) method. First popularized by the Japanese, the JIT system reduces the organization's investment in storage space for raw materials and in the materials themselves. Historically, manufacturers built large storage areas and filled them with materials, parts, and supplies that would be needed days, weeks, and even months in the future. A manager using the JIT approach orders materials and parts more often and in smaller quantities, thereby reducing investment in both storage space and actual inventory. The ideal arrangement is for materials to arrive just as they are needed—or just in time.[19]

Recall our example about the small firm that assembles stereo speakers for Honda and delivers them three times a day, making it unnecessary for Honda to carry large quantities of the speakers in inventory. In an even more striking example, Johnson Controls makes automobile seats for Mercedes and ships them by small truckloads to a Mercedes plant 75 miles away. Each shipment is scheduled to arrive two hours before it is needed. Clearly, the JIT approach requires high levels of coordination and cooperation between the company and its suppliers. If shipments arrive too early, Mercedes has no place to store them. If they arrive too late, the entire assembly line may have to be shut down, resulting in enormous expense. When properly designed and used, the JIT method controls inventory very effectively.

---

☐ Managers should be familiar with supply chain management and its basic components.

☐ You should also be familiar with your organization's approach to supply chain management.

**Manager's Checklist** ☑

# Managing Total Quality

Quality and productivity have become major determinants of business success or failure today and are central issues in managing organizations. But, as we will see, achieving higher levels of quality is not an easy accomplishment. Simply ordering that quality be improved is about as effective as waving a magic wand.[20] The catalyst for its emergence as a mainstream management concern was foreign business, especially Japanese. And nowhere was it more visible than in the auto industry. During an early energy crisis many people bought Toyotas, Hondas, and Nissans because they were more fuel-efficient than U.S. cars. Consumers soon found, however, that not only were the Japanese cars more fuel-efficient, they were also of higher quality than U.S. cars. Parts fit together better, the trim work was neater, and the cars were more reliable. Thus, after the energy crisis subsided, Japanese cars remained formidable competitors because of their reputation for quality.

> "You cannot copy high quality, and it takes a long time to get a reputation for quality."
>
> —MILLARD "MICKEY" DREXLER, CEO J.CREW[21]

**just-in-time (JIT) method**
An inventory system that has necessary materials arriving as soon as they are needed (just in time) so that the production process is not interrupted

**quality**
The totality of features and characteristics of a product or service that bear on its ability to satisfy stated or implied needs

## The Meaning of Quality

The American Society for Quality Control defines quality as the totality of features and characteristics of a product or service that bear on its ability to satisfy stated or implied needs.[22] Quality has several different attributes. Table 20.2 lists eight basic dimensions that determine

---

## TABLE 20.2   EIGHT DIMENSIONS OF QUALITY

These eight dimensions generally capture the meaning of quality, which is a critically important contributor to organizational success today. Understanding the basic meaning of quality is a good first step toward managing it more effectively.

1. *Performance.* A product's primary operating characteristic; examples are automobile acceleration and a television's picture clarity

2. *Features.* Supplements to a product's basic functioning characteristics, such as power windows on a car

3. *Reliability.* A probability of not malfunctioning during a specified period

4. *Conformance.* The degree to which a product's design and operating characteristics meet established standards

5. *Durability.* A measure of product life

6. *Serviceability.* The speed and ease of repair

7. *Aesthetics.* How a product looks, feels, tastes, and smells

8. *Perceived quality.* As seen by a customer

Source: Reprinted by permission of *Harvard Business Review*. Exhibit from "Competing on the Eight Dimensions of Quality," by David A. Garvin, November/December 1987. Copyright © 1987 by the Harvard Business School Publishing Corporation; all rights reserved.

---

the quality of a particular product or service. For example, a product that has durability and is reliable is of higher quality than a product with less durability and reliability.

Quality is also relative. For example, a Lincoln is a higher-grade car than a Ford Fusion, which, in turn, is a higher-grade car than a Ford Focus. The difference in quality stems from differences in design and other features. The Focus, however, is considered a high-quality car relative to its engineering specifications and price. Likewise, the Fusion and Lincoln may also be high-quality cars, given their standards and prices. Thus quality is both an absolute and a relative concept.

Quality is relevant for both products and services. Although its importance for products like cars and computers was perhaps recognized first, service firms ranging from airlines to restaurants have also come to see that quality is a vitally important determinant of their success or failure. Service quality, as we will discuss later in this chapter, has thus also become a major competitive issue in U.S. industries today.[24] Our *Beyond Traditional Business* feature highlights another venue where quality is of increasing importance.

> "[Porsches] … cost a lot of money. When you spend that kind of money, you expect things to be right."
>
> —LYNN KINZIG, PORSCHE DEALER[23]

### The Importance of Quality

To help underscore the importance of quality, the U.S. government created the Malcolm Baldrige Award, named after the former secretary of commerce who championed quality in U.S. industry. The award, administered by an agency of the Commerce Department, is given annually to firms that achieve major improvements in the quality of their products or services. In other words, the award is based on changes in quality, as opposed to absolute quality. In addition, many other quality awards have been created. For example, the Rochester Institute of Technology and *USA Today* award their Quality Cup award not to entire organizations but to individual teams of workers within organizations. Quality is also an important concern for individual managers and organizations for three very specific reasons: competition, productivity, and costs.[25]

**Malcolm Baldrige Award**
Named after a former secretary of commerce, this prestigious award is given to firms that achieve major quality improvements

**Competition** Quality has become one of the most competitive points in business today. Ford, Daimler, General Motors, and Toyota, for example, each imply that their cars and

**BEYOND TRADITIONAL BUSINESS**

# Reach Out and Give Someone a Quality Touch

Marc Chardon knows that when he talks about the "flight to quality," he has to explain himself. "When I say 'flight to quality,'" he says, "I'm talking about the observable trend of donors deciding to support fewer organizations, consolidating their giving with those that mean the most to them and treat them well. ... I see it happening everywhere," reports Chardon, who was head of Blackbaud, the leading global provider of software and services for nonprofit organizations, until he stepped down in 2013. He adds that when it comes to cultivating and keeping donors, nonprofits need to realize that "surface relationships just don't cut it."

Professional fundraiser Claire Axelrad agrees: "Don't treat your donors like gumballs," she advises nonprofit managers. "Don't stick 'em in your database to save for later." In the current environment, she warns, in which the competition for every charitable dollar is becoming increasingly fierce, they probably won't be there later. Frank Barry, Chardon's onetime colleague at Blackbaud, argues that nonprofits need to devote at least as much energy to retaining the donors they have as they do to prospecting for new donors. "Nearly three out of four new donors," he points out, "leave and *never* come back." Where do they go? "They flee to quality," says Chardon, "to the places where they feel the most connected and the most valued."

From a financial standpoint, the imperative to hold onto donors is particularly pressing. According to Adrian Sargeant, director of the Centre for Sustainable Philanthropy at England's University of Plymouth, it costs a fundraising organization five times as much to attract a new donor as it does to maintain a relationship with an existing donor. The cost of recruiting the new donor will also amount to two or three times more than the value of the donor's first donation. Sargeant's research also indicates that the typical nonprofit will lose 10 to 20 percent of all donors annually, but he hastens to add that "even small improvements in the level of attrition can generate significantly larger improvements in the lifetime value of the fundraising database," with a mere 10 percent improvement in attrition yielding up to a 200 percent increase in database value.

Chardon believes that "donors are just like Amazon customers, expecting service and recognition that nonprofits know who they are and how they are unique." Likewise, Sargeant is convinced that at least "some donors will consciously evaluate the service provided by a nonprofit and compare it to what could be achieved 'in return' for their donations elsewhere." Both argue that donors value certain types of relationships with the nonprofits that they patronize, and Sargeant contends that "donor satisfaction" is "the single greatest driver of loyalty." In turn, he says, donor satisfaction depends in large measure on "delivered service quality."

So, what—in a practical sense—constitutes "service quality" in the mind of a donor? Not surprisingly, it all comes down to "touches"—the contacts that the nonprofit makes with the donor. And according to a 2015 survey by Abila, a provider of software and services to nonprofits, the quality of touches is more important than their quantity (i.e., frequency). Donor communications specialist Lisa Sargent confirms the argument for "rich content" in contacts in her account of the efforts mounted by an unnamed client:

> They created a terrific donor welcome pack and special new donor thank-you; send hand-signed thank-yous promptly and make them as personal as possible; publish a donor-driven, story-focused newsletter four times yearly; invite donors to engage with their organization in ways that don't always include a monetary gift; and continue to invest in a quality donor communications program [which includes] a longer newsletter [about] legacy programs, monthly giving, and major donors.

The organization's donor file, she reports, quintupled between 2008 and 2014, when it broke the 70 percent "retention barrier."

*References:* Marc Chardon, "Nonprofit Trends: Flight to Quality," *Huffington Post* (March 8, 2013), www.huffingtonpost.com, on July 18, 2015; Frank Barry, "One Thing Most Nonprofits Stink At (Donor Retention) and How You Can Change It in 2014," *npEngage* (January 6, 2014), http://npengage.com, on July 18, 2014; Adrian Sargeant, "Donor Retention: What Do We Know and What Can We Do About It?" *Nonprofit Quarterly* (August 15, 2013), http://nonprofitquarterly.org, on July 18, 2015; William Comcowich, "How Nonprofits Can Use Data to Improve Donor Engagement," CyberAlert (April 21, 2015), www.cyberalert.com, on July 18, 2015.

trucks are higher in quality than the cars and trucks of the others. And American, Delta, and United Airlines each claim to provide the best and most reliable service. In the wake of the recent economic recession, many businesses have focused even more attention on service quality as a competitive advantage during lean times. While some firms, for example, cut their staff at customer call centers, others did not. What impact might this have? One study found that cutting four representatives at a call center of three dozen people sent the number of customers put on hold for four minutes from zero to 80. Firms with especially strong reputations for service quality include Amazon.com, USAA (an insurance firm), Lexus, Ritz-Carlton, Ace Hardware, and Apple.[26]

> "During tough times there are plenty of other pressures customers face. We don't want a customer service issue to be what makes them blow a cork."
>
> —JOHN VENHUIZEN, PRESIDENT AND CEO, ACE HARDWARE[27]

**Productivity** Managers have also come to recognize that quality and productivity are related. In the past, many managers thought that they could increase output (productivity) only by decreasing quality. Managers today have learned the hard way that such an assumption is almost always wrong. If a firm installs a meaningful quality enhancement program, three things are likely to result. First, the number of defects is likely to decrease, causing fewer returns from customers. Second, because the number of defects goes down, resources (materials and people) dedicated to reworking flawed output will be decreased. Third, because making employees responsible for quality reduces the need for quality inspectors, the organization can produce more units with fewer resources.

**Costs** Improved quality also lowers costs. Poor quality results in higher returns from customers, high warranty costs, and lawsuits from customers injured by faulty products. Future sales are lost because of disgruntled customers. An organization with quality problems often has to increase inspection expenses just to catch defective products. We noted in Chapter 19, for example, how at one point Whistler Corporation was using 40 percent of its workforce just to fix poorly assembled radar detectors made by the other 60 percent.[28]

## Total Quality Management

Once an organization makes a decision to enhance the quality of its products and services, it must then decide how to implement this decision. The most pervasive approach to managing quality has been called total quality management, or TQM (sometimes called quality assurance)—a real and meaningful effort by an organization to change its whole approach to business in order to make quality a guiding factor in everything the organization does.[29] Figure 20.3 highlights the major ingredients in TQM.

**total quality management (TQM) (quality assurance)**
A strategic commitment by top management to change its whole approach to business in order to make quality a guiding factor in everything it does

**Strategic Commitment** The starting point for TQM is a strategic commitment by top management. Such commitment is important for several reasons. First, the organizational culture must change to recognize that quality is not just an ideal but an objective goal that must be pursued.[30] Second, a decision to pursue the goal of quality carries with it some real costs—for expenditures such as new equipment and facilities. Thus, without a commitment from top management, quality improvement will prove to be just a slogan or gimmick, with little or no real change. Several years ago Porsche had the lowest reliability of any automobile maker in the world. But a major commitment from top

## FIGURE 20.3 TOTAL QUALITY MANAGEMENT

Quality is one of the most important issues facing organizations today. Total quality management, or TQM, is a comprehensive effort to enhance an organization's product or service quality. TQM involves the five basic dimensions shown here. Each is important and must be addressed effectively if the organization expects to truly increase quality.

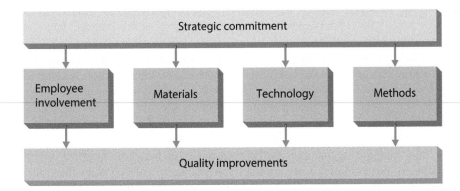

management helped turn the company around. By paying more attention to consumer preferences and using the other methods described below, Porsche shot to the top of global automobile reliability.[31]

**Employee Involvement**   Employee involvement is another critical ingredient in TQM. Virtually all successful quality enhancement programs involve making the person responsible for doing the job responsible for making sure it is done right.[32] By definition, then, employee involvement is a critical component in improving quality. Work teams, discussed in Chapter 18, are common vehicles for increasing employee involvement.

**Technology**   New forms of technology are also useful in TQM programs. Automation and robots, for example, can often make products with higher precision and better consistency than can people. Investing in higher-grade machines capable of doing jobs more precisely and reliably often improves quality. For example, Nokia has achieved notable improvements in product quality by replacing many of its machines with new equipment. Similarly, most U.S. auto and electronics firms make regular investments in new technology to help boost quality.

**Materials**   Another important part of TQM is improving the quality of the materials that organizations use. Suppose that a company that assembles stereos buys chips and circuits from another company. If the chips have a high failure rate, consumers will return defective stereos to the company whose nameplate appears on them, not to the company that made the chips. The stereo firm then loses in two ways: refunds back to customers and a damaged reputation. As a result, many firms have increased the quality requirements they impose on their suppliers as a way of improving the quality of their own products.

**Methods**   Improved methods can improve product and service quality. Methods are operating systems used by the organization during the actual transformation process. American Express Company, for example, has found ways to cut its approval time for new credit cards from three weeks to only two days. This results in improved service quality.

## TQM Tools and Techniques

Beyond the strategic context of quality, managers can also rely on several specific tools and techniques for improving quality. Among the most popular today are value-added analysis, benchmarking, outsourcing, reducing cycle times, ISO 9000:2000 and ISO 14000, statistical quality control, and Six Sigma.

**Value-Added Analysis** Value-added analysis is the comprehensive evaluation of all work activities, materials flows, and paperwork to determine the value that they add for customers. Such an analysis often reveals wasteful or unnecessary activities that can be eliminated without jeopardizing customer service. For example, during a value-added analysis, Hewlett-Packard determined that its contracts were unnecessarily long, confusing, and hard to understand. The firm subsequently cut its standard contract form down from 20 to two pages and experienced an 18 percent increase in its computer sales.

**Benchmarking** Benchmarking is the process of learning how other firms do things in an exceptionally high-quality manner. Some approaches to benchmarking are simple and straightforward. For example, Xerox routinely buys copiers made by other firms and takes them apart to see how they work. This enables the firm to stay abreast of improvements and changes its competitors are using. When Ford was planning the newest version of the Fusion, it identified the 400 features customers identified as being most important to them. It then found the competing cars that did the best job on each feature. Ford's goal was to equal or surpass each of its competitors on those 400 features. Other benchmarking strategies are more indirect. For example, many firms study how Amazon.com manages its online business, how Disney recruits and trains employees, and how FedEx tracks packages for applications they can employ in their own businesses.[33]

**Outsourcing** Another innovation for improving quality is outsourcing. Outsourcing is the process of subcontracting services and operations to other firms that can perform them more cheaply or better. If a business performs each and every one of its own administrative and business services and operations, it is almost certain to be doing at least some of them in an inefficient or low-quality manner. If those areas can be identified and outsourced, the firm will save money and realize a higher-quality service or operation.[34] For example, until recently Eastman Kodak handled all of its own computing operations. Now, however, those operations are subcontracted to IBM, which handles all of Kodak's computing. The result is higher-quality computing systems and operations at Kodak for less money than it was spending before. Firms must be careful in their outsourcing decisions, though, because service or delivery problems can lead to major complications. Boeing's new 787 aircraft, for example, ran several months behind schedule because the firms to which Boeing outsourced some of its production ran late.[35]

**Reducing Cycle Time** Another popular TQM technique is reducing cycle time. Cycle time is the time needed by the organization to develop, make, and distribute products or services.[36] If a business can reduce its cycle time, quality will often improve. A good illustration of the power of cycle time reduction comes from General Electric. At one point the firm needed six plants and three weeks to produce and deliver custom-made industrial circuit breaker boxes. By analyzing and reducing cycle time, the same product can now be delivered in three days, and only a single plant is involved. Table 20.3 identifies a number of basic suggestions that have helped companies reduce the cycle time of their operations. For example, GE found it better to start from scratch with a remodeled plant. GE also wiped out the need for approvals by eliminating most managerial positions and setting up teams as a basis for organizing work. Stressing the importance of the schedule helped Motorola build a new plant and start production of a new product in only 18 months. Samsung used to need 12 to 18 months to design new cellphone models, but can do it now in six months.[37] And Ford is aggressively working on techniques that can shorten the development cycle time for new models.[38]

**value-added analysis**
The comprehensive evaluation of all work activities, materials flows, and paperwork to determine the value that they add for customers

**benchmarking**
The process of learning how other firms do things in an exceptionally high-quality manner

**outsourcing**
Subcontracting services and operations to other firms that can perform them more cheaply or better

**cycle time**
The time needed by the organization to accomplish activities such as developing, making, and distributing products or services

## TABLE 20.3 GUIDELINES FOR INCREASING THE SPEED OF OPERATIONS

Many organizations today are using speed for competitive advantage. Listed in the table are six common guidelines that organizations follow when they want to shorten the time they need to get things accomplished. Although not every manager can do each of these things, most managers can do at least some of them.

1. *Start from scratch.* It is usually easier than trying to do what the organization does now faster.
2. *Minimize the number of approvals needed to do something.* The fewer people who have to approve something, the faster approval will get done.
3. *Use work teams as a basis for organization.* Teamwork and cooperation work better than individual effort and conflict.
4. *Develop and adhere to a schedule.* A properly designed schedule can greatly increase speed.
5. *Do not ignore distribution.* Making something faster is only part of the battle.
6. *Integrate speed into the organization's culture.* If everyone understands the importance of speed, things will naturally get done more quickly.

Source: From *Fortune*, February 13, 1989. Copyright © 1989 Time, Inc. All rights reserved.

**ISO 9000:2000 and ISO 14000** Still another useful technique for improving quality is ISO 9000. ISO 9000:2000 refers to a set of quality standards created by the International Organization for Standardization; the standards were revised and updated in 2000 and then again in 2015. In addition, several substandards and extensions have also been developed. These include:

- ISO 9001:2008 – sets out the requirements of a quality management system
- ISO 9000:2005 – covers the basic concepts and language
- ISO 9004:2009 – focuses on how to make a quality management system more efficient and effective
- ISO 19011:2011 – sets out guidance on internal and external audits of quality management systems

These standards cover such areas as product testing, employee training, record keeping, supplier relations, and repair policies and procedures. Firms that want to meet these standards apply for certification and are audited by a firm chosen by the organization's domestic affiliate (in the United States, this is the American National Standards Institute). These auditors review every aspect of the firm's business operations in relation to the standards. Many firms report that merely preparing for an ISO 9000 audit has been helpful. Many firms today, including General Electric, DuPont, Eastman Kodak, British Telecom, and Philips Electronics, are urging—or in some cases requiring—that their suppliers achieve ISO 9000 certification.[39] All told, more than 163 countries have adopted ISO 9000 as a national standard, and more than 610,000 certificates of compliance have been issued. ISO 14000 is an extension of the same concept to environmental performance. Specifically, ISO 14000 requires that firms document how they are using raw materials more efficiently, managing pollution, and reducing their impact on the environment.

**Statistical Quality Control** Another quality control technique is statistical quality control (SQC). As the term suggests, SQC is concerned primarily with managing quality.[40] Moreover, it is a set of specific statistical techniques that can be used to monitor quality. *Acceptance sampling* involves sampling finished goods to ensure that quality standards have been met. Acceptance sampling is effective only when the correct percentage of products that should be tested (for example, 2, 5, or 25 percent) is determined. This decision is especially important when the test renders the product useless. Batteries, wine, and collapsible steering wheels, for example, are consumed or destroyed during testing. Another SQC method is *in-process sampling*. In-process sampling involves evaluating products during production so that needed changes can be made. The painting department of a furniture

**ISO 9000:2000**
A set of quality standards created by the International Organization for Standardization and revised in 2000

**ISO 14000**
A set of standards for environmental performance

**statistical quality control (SQC)**
A set of specific statistical techniques that can be used to monitor quality; includes acceptance sampling and in-process sampling

Statistical quality control can play a critical role in improving quality. Acceptance sampling is one useful form of statistical quality control. This inspector has just taken a sample of a new liquid detergent. The sample will be tested for quality and adjustments to the detergent ingredients made if needed.

company might periodically check the tint of the paint it is using. The company can then adjust the color as necessary to conform to customer standards. The advantage of in-process sampling is that it allows problems to be detected before they accumulate.

**Six Sigma** Six Sigma was originally developed by Motorola but has now been refined to the point where it can be used by most manufacturing or service organizations. The Six Sigma method tries to eliminate mistakes. Although firms rarely obtain Six Sigma quality, it does provide a challenging target. *Sigma* refers to a standard deviation, so a Six Sigma defect rate is six standard deviations above the mean rate; 1 sigma quality would produce 690,000 errors per million items. Three sigmas is challenging—66,000 errors per million. Six Sigma is obtained when a firm produces a mere 3.4 mistakes per million. Implementing Six Sigma requires making corrections until errors virtually disappear. At General Electric, the technique saved the firm $8 billion in three years. GE is now teaching its customers, including Walmart and Dell, about the approach.

---

**Manager's Checklist**

☐ Managers should know the basic components of total quality management.

☐ You should also be familiar with the common tools used to manage quality.

---

# Managing Productivity

Although the current focus on quality by U.S. companies is a relatively recent phenomenon, managers have been aware of the importance of productivity for years. The stimulus for this attention was a recognition that the gap between productivity in the United States and that in other industrialized countries was narrowing. This section describes the meaning of productivity and underscores its importance. After summarizing recent productivity trends, we suggest ways that organizations can increase their productivity.

## The Meaning of Productivity

In a general sense, productivity is an economic measure of efficiency that summarizes the value of outputs relative to the value of the inputs used to create them.[41] Productivity can be and often is assessed at different levels of analysis and in different forms.

**Levels of Productivity** By level of productivity we mean the units of analysis used to calculate or define productivity. For example, *aggregate productivity* is the total level of productivity achieved by a country. *Industry productivity* is the total productivity achieved by all the firms in a particular industry. *Company productivity*, just as the term suggests, is the level of productivity achieved by an individual company. *Unit* and *individual productivity* refer to the productivity achieved by a unit or department within an organization and the level of productivity attained by a single person.

**productivity**
An economic measure of efficiency that summarizes what is produced relative to resources used to produce it

**Forms of Productivity**   There are many different forms of productivity. *Total factor productivity* is defined by the following formula:

$$\text{Productivity} = \frac{\text{Outputs}}{\text{Inputs}}$$

Total factor productivity is an overall indicator of how well an organization uses all of its resources, such as labor, capital, materials, and energy, to create all of its products and services. The biggest problem with total factor productivity is that all the ingredients must be expressed in the same terms—dollars (it is difficult to add hours of labor to number of units of a raw material in a meaningful way). Total factor productivity also gives little insight into how things can be changed to improve productivity. Consequently, most organizations find it more useful to calculate a partial productivity ratio. Such a ratio uses only one category of resource. For example, labor productivity could be calculated by this simple formula:

$$\text{Labor Productivity} = \frac{\text{Outputs}}{\text{Direct Labor}}$$

This method has two advantages. First, it is not necessary to transform the units of input into some other unit. Second, this method provides managers with specific insights into how changing different resource inputs affects productivity. Suppose that an organization can manufacture 100 units of a particular product with 20 hours of direct labor. The organization's labor productivity index is 100/20, or 5 (5 units per labor hour). Now suppose that worker efficiency is increased (through one of the ways to be discussed later in this chapter) so that the same 20 hours of labor results in the manufacture of 120 units of the product. The labor productivity index increases to 120/20, or 6 (6 units per labor hour), and the firm can see the direct results of a specific managerial action.

## The Importance of Productivity

Managers consider it important that their firm maintain high levels of productivity for a variety of reasons. Firm productivity is a primary determinant of an organization's level of profitability and, ultimately, of its ability to survive. If one organization is more productive than another, it will have more products to sell at lower prices and have more profits to reinvest in other areas. Productivity also partially determines people's standard of living within a particular country. At an economic level, businesses consume resources and produce goods and services. The goods and services created within a country can be used by that country's own citizens or exported for sale in other countries. The more goods and services the businesses within a country can produce, the more goods and services the country's citizens will have. Even goods that are exported result in financial resources flowing back into the home country. Thus the citizens of a highly productive country are likely to have a notably higher standard of living than are the citizens of a country with low productivity.

## Productivity Trends

The United States has one of the highest levels of productivity in the world. Sparked by gains made in other countries, however, U.S. business has begun to focus more attention on productivity.[42] Indeed, this was a primary factor in the decisions made by U.S. businesses to retrench, retool, and become more competitive in the world marketplace. For example, General Electric's dishwasher plant in Louisville cut its inventory requirements by 50 percent, reduced labor costs from 15 percent to only 10 percent of total manufacturing costs, and cut product development time in half. As a result of these kinds of efforts, productivity trends have now leveled out, and U.S. workers are generally maintaining their lead in most industries.[43]

One important factor that has hurt U.S. productivity indices has been the tremendous growth of the service sector in the United States. Although this sector grew, its productivity levels did not. One part of this problem relates to measurement. For example, it is fairly easy to calculate the number of tons of steel produced at a steel mill and divide it by the number of labor hours used; it is more difficult to determine the output of an attorney or a certified public accountant. Still, virtually everyone agrees that improving service-sector productivity is the next major hurdle facing U.S. business.[44]

Figure 20.4 illustrates manufacturing productivity growth from 1970 through 2010 in terms of annual average percentage of increase. As you can see, that growth slowed during the 1970s but began to rise again in the late 1980s. Some experts believe that productivity in both the United States and abroad will continue to improve at even more impressive rates. Their confidence rests on technology's potential ability to improve operations.

## Improving Productivity

How does a business or industry improve its productivity? Suggestions made by experts generally fall into two broad categories: improving operations and increasing employee involvement.

---

### FIGURE 20.4  MANUFACTURING AND SERVICE PRODUCTIVITY GROWTH TRENDS

Both manufacturing productivity and service productivity in the United States continue to grow, although manufacturing productivity is growing at a faster pace. Total productivity, therefore, also continues to grow.

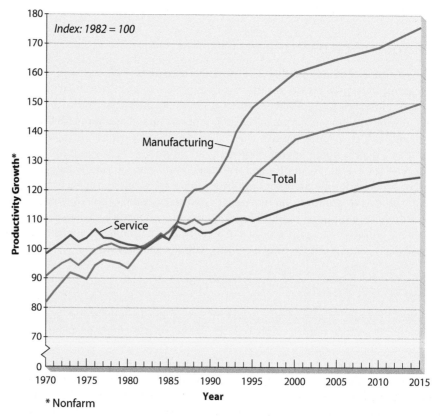

Source: U.S. Bureau of Labor Statistics.

**Improving Operations** One way that firms can improve operations is by spending more on research and development. Research and development (R&D) spending helps identify new products, new uses for existing products, and new methods for making products. Each of these contributes to productivity. For example, Bausch & Lomb almost missed the boat on extended-wear contact lenses because the company had neglected R&D. When it became apparent that its major competitors were almost a year ahead of Bausch & Lomb in developing the new lenses, management made R&D a top-priority concern. As a result, the company made several scientific breakthroughs, shortened the time needed to introduce new products, and greatly enhanced both total sales and profits—and all with a smaller workforce than the company used to employ. Even though other countries are greatly increasing their R&D spending, the United States continues to be the world leader in this area.

Research and development helps identify new products, new uses for existing products, and new methods for making products. Each of these things, in turn, contributes to productivity. The scientists in this R&D lab are working on new chemical compounds which may, in turn, result in new products.

Another way firms can boost productivity through operations is by reassessing and revamping their transformation facilities. We noted earlier how one of GE's modernized plants does a better job than six antiquated ones. Just building a new factory is no guarantee of success, but Maytag, Ford, Caterpillar, and many other businesses have achieved dramatic productivity gains by revamping their production facilities. Further, facilities refinements are not limited to manufacturers. Most McDonald's restaurants now have drive-through windows, and many have moved soft-drink dispensers out to the restaurant floor so that customers can get their own drinks. Each of these moves is an attempt to increase the speed with which customers can be served, and thus to increase productivity.

**Increasing Employee Involvement** The other major thrust in productivity enhancement has been toward employee involvement. We noted earlier that participation can enhance quality. So, too, can it boost productivity. Examples of this involvement are an individual worker's being given a bigger voice in how she does her job, a formal agreement of cooperation between management and labor, and total involvement throughout the organization. GE eliminated most of the supervisors at its one new circuit breaker plant and put control in the hands of workers.

Another method popular in the United States is increasing the flexibility of an organization's workforce by training employees to perform a number of different jobs. Such cross-training allows the firm to function with fewer workers because workers can be transferred easily to areas where they are most needed. For example, at one Motorola plant, 397 of 400 employees learned at least two skills under a similar program.

Rewards are essential to making employee involvement work. Firms must reward people for learning new skills and using them proficiently. At Motorola, for example, workers who master a new skill are assigned for five days to a job requiring them to use that skill. If they perform with no defects, they are moved to a higher pay grade, and then they move back and forth between jobs as they are needed. If there is a performance problem, they receive more training and practice. This approach is fairly new, but preliminary indicators suggest that it can increase productivity significantly. Many unions resist such programs because they threaten job security and reduce a person's identification with one skill or craft. Our *Tech Watch* feature highlights an interesting (and controversial) approach to boosting productivity through increased employee involvement or engagement.

# Is Glassdoor Cracked?

How productive can your company be if your employees aren't "involved" or—if you prefer the term that we use in the *Management in Action* vignette at the beginning of this chapter— "engaged"? Probably not as productive as you'd like. If you accept the calculation of the 2013 Gallup study of the State of the American Workplace that employees who aren't fully engaged cost U.S. companies $450 to $500 billion annually in lost productivity, you can probably assume that your company contributes its share to that flush of fiduciary and commercial money down the macroeconomic toilet.

So, how would you know if your workers weren't involved or engaged (assuming that you can't afford to wait around for long-term productivity statistics)? Obviously, you could simply ask them. You could, for example, borrow its 12-question format from Gallup, which will be happy to tabulate the results for you.

Or you could do what Rob Tarkoff did when he took over as CEO of Lithium Technologies, a San Francisco-based media-software developer—listen in on the social media conversation about your company. Tarkoff discovered that, under his predecessor, Lithium had received six reviews on the job-review site Glassdoor.com, four of which were scathing: "There is not much positive to say about this company," reported one anonymous reviewer. "It's a bad place to work. Stay away!"

Tarkoff decided to accept Glassdoor's sales-pitch invitation to "Join the conversation." He paid Glassdoor $495 a month for an "enhanced profile," which included photos and links to Lithium's company blogs and Facebook and Twitter feeds, plus an elaborately produced video entitled "Why Work for Us?" The campaign worked like a charm. Before long, Lithium was receiving sterling reviews: Working for Lithium, enthused one employee, was "like a thrilling ride with a bright future." In a matter of months, Lithium's Glassdoor

rating had ballooned from a dismal 2.7 to a glittering 4.4 (out of a possible 5), with 61 percent of reviewers testifying that they would recommend the firm to friends. In 2014, Lithium received Glassdoor's own "Best Places to Work Employees' Choice" award.

Not all CEOs, however, are as happy as Tarkoff with the results of their paid Glassdoor profiles. "To me, it's like ransom," says Robb Fujioka, cofounder of tablet maker Fuhu, whose rating remained mired at 2.1 based on 70 reviews. As Fujioka sees it, the problem rests with the questionable validity of Glassdoor's signature reviews: "They should have account representatives to address untrue facts for free," he argues.

Analysts at Workplace Dynamics agree that Glassdoor's statistical reliability is shaky at best: A 2013 study released by the human resources consulting firm charges that Glassdoor reviews represent an average of only 1.6 percent of a company's employees, with "grumpy employees … 5 to 8 times more likely to leave a review on job-review sites than happy employees." On Glassdoor, for example, the 3.2 rating of online lender Quicken Loans, based on 140 reviews, indicated that 46 percent of the firm's employees would not recommend it. Workplace Dynamics, however, surveyed 935 Quicken employees and found that a mere 2 percent would not recommend the company. On a scale of 0 to 90, Quicken's workforce awarded the company a rating of 90.3. The study concluded that "the overall Glassdoor star rating is a very poor indicator of what it is really like to work at a company."

*References:* Samar Birwadker, "The High Cost of Unhappy Employees," LinkedIn (July 17, 2014), www.linkedin.com, on July 13, 2015; Ariana Ayu, "The Enormous Cost of Unhappy Employees," *Inc.com* (August 27, 2014), www.inc.com, on July 13, 2015; Paul Keegan, "The Five New Rules of Employee Engagement," *Inc.* (December 2014/January 2015), www.inc.com, on July 4, 2015; Zoe Henry, "Secrets of a Very Opaque Glassdoor," *Inc.* (December 2014/January 2015), www.inc.com, on July 4, 2015; Workplace Dynamics, "How Good Is Glassdoor?" (March 11, 2013), www.workplacedynamics.com, on July 13, 2015.

☐ Managers should understand the meaning of productivity and know the different levels at which it can be assessed.

☐ You should also be familiar with the basic methods that can improve productivity.

**Manager's Checklist** ✔

# Summary of Learning Outcomes and Key Points

1. Describe and explain the nature of operations management.

   - Operations management is the set of managerial activities that organizations use in creating their products and services.
   - Operations management is important to both manufacturing and service organizations.
   - It plays an important role in an organization's strategy.

2. Identify and discuss the components involved in designing effective operations systems.

   - The starting point in using operations management is designing appropriate operations systems.
   - Key decisions that must be made as part of operations systems design relate to product and service mix, capacity, and facilities.

3. Discuss organizational technologies and their role in operations management.

   - Technology also plays an important role in quality.
   - Automation is especially important today.
   - Numerous computer-aided manufacturing techniques are widely practiced.
   - Robotics is also a growing area.
   - Technology is as relevant to service organizations as to manufacturing organizations.

4. Identify and discuss the components involved in implementing operations systems through supply chain management.

   - After an operations system has been designed and put in place, it must then be implemented.
   - Major areas of interest during the use of operations systems are purchasing and inventory management.
   - Supply chain management is a comprehensive view of managing all of these activities in a more efficient manner.

5. Explain the meaning and importance of managing quality and total quality management.

   - Quality is a major consideration for all managers today.
   - Quality is important because it affects competition, productivity, and costs.
   - Total quality management is a comprehensive, organization-wide effort to enhance quality through a variety of avenues.

6. Explain the meaning and importance of managing productivity, productivity trends, and ways to improve productivity.

   - Productivity is also a major concern to managers.
   - Productivity is a measure of how efficiently an organization is using its resources to create products or services.
   - The United States is a world leader in individual productivity, but firms still work to achieve productivity gains.

# Discussion Questions

## Questions for Review

1. What is the relationship of operations management to overall organizational strategy? Where do productivity and quality fit into that relationship?

2. Describe three basic decisions that must be addressed in the design of operations systems. For each decision, what information do managers need to make that decision?

3. What are some approaches to facilities layout? How do they differ from one another? How are they similar?

4. What is total quality management? What are the major characteristics of TQM?

## Questions for Analysis

5. Is operations management linked most closely to corporate-level, business-level, or functional strategies? Why or in what way?

6. "Automation is bad for the economy because machines will eventually replace almost all human workers, creating high unemployment and poverty." Do you agree or disagree? Explain your answer.

## Questions for Application

8. How can a service organization use techniques from operations management? Give specific examples from your college or university (a provider of educational services).

9. Think of a firm that, in your opinion, provides a high-quality service or product. What attributes of the product or service give you the perception of high quality? Do you think that everyone would agree with your judgment? Why or why not?

7. Some quality gurus claim that high-quality products or services are those that are error free. Others claim that high quality exists when customers' needs are satisfied. Still others claim that high-quality products or services must be innovative. Do you subscribe to one of these views? If not, how would you define quality? Explain how the choice of a definition of quality affects managers' behavior.

10. What advice would you give to the manager of a small local service business, such as a pizza parlor or dry cleaner, about improvements in quality and productivity? Would your advice differ if the small business were a manufacturing company—for example, a T-shirt printing firm? Describe any differences you would expect to see.

# Building Effective Communication Skills

## Exercise Overview

Communication skills refer not only to the ability to convey information and ideas to others but to handle information and ideas received from them. This exercise shows how you can use your communication skills in addressing issues of quality.

## Exercise Background

You're the customer-service manager of a large auto parts distributor. The general manager of a large auto dealer, one of your best customers, has sent the following letter, and it's your job to write a letter in response.

*Dear Customer Service Manager:*

*On the first of last month, ABC Autos submitted a purchase order to your firm. Attached to this letter is a copy of the order. Unfortunately, the parts shipment that we received from you did not contain every item on the order. Further, that fact was not noted on the packing slip that accompanied your shipment, and ABC was charged*

*for the full amount of the order. To resolve the problem, please send the missing items immediately. If you are unable to do so by the end of the week, please cancel the remaining items and refund the overpayment. In the future, if you ship a partial order, please notify us at that time and do not bill for items not shipped.*

*I look forward to your reply and a resolution to my problem.*

> *Sincerely,*
>
> *A. N. Owner, ABC Autos*
> *Attachment: Purchase Order 00001*

## Exercise Task

1. Write an answer to the customer's letter which assumes that you now have the parts available.

2. How would your answer differ if ABC Autos were not a valued customer?

3. How would your answer differ if you found out that the parts were in the original shipment but had been stolen by one of your delivery personnel?

4. How would your answer differ if you found out that the owner of ABC Autos made a mistake and that the order had been filled correctly?

5. Now review your answers to the previous questions. What are the important components of an effective response to a customer quality complaint (setting the tone, expressing an apology, suggesting a solution, and so on)? How did you use these components in your various responses?

# Building Effective Diagnostic Skills

### Exercise Overview

As we noted in this chapter, the quality of a product or service is relative to price and customer expectations. This exercise is designed to show that a manager's diagnostic skills—his or her ability to visualize the most appropriate response to a situation—can be useful in positioning a product's quality relative to price and customer expectations.

### Exercise Background

Think of a recent occasion when you purchased a tangible product—say, clothing, electronic equipment, luggage, or professional supplies—which you subsequently came to feel was of especially high quality. Now think of another product that you regarded as being of appropriate or adequate quality, and then a third product that you judged to be of low or poor quality. (You should now have three separate products in mind.) Next, recall three parallel experiences involving purchases of services. Examples might include an airline, train, or bus trip; a restaurant meal; a haircut; or an oil change for your car. (Again, you should have three examples total.)

Finally, recall three experiences involving both products and services. Perhaps you got some information about a product that you were buying or you returned a defective or broken product for a refund or warranty repair. Were there any instances in which there was an apparent disparity between product and service quality? Did a poor-quality product, for instance, receive surprisingly good service or a high-quality product receive mediocre service?

### Exercise Task

Review your list of nine purchase experiences and then do the following:

1. Assess the extent to which the quality that you associated with each was a function of price and your expectations.

2. Could the quality of each product or service be improved without greatly affecting its price? If so, how?

3. Can high-quality customer service offset adequate or even poor product quality? Can outstanding product quality offset adequate or even poor customer service?

# Skill-Building Personal Assessment

### Defining Quality and Productivity

**Introduction**: *Quality* is a complex term whose meaning has no doubt changed over time. The following assessment surveys your ideas about and approaches to quality.

**Instructions**: You will agree with some of the statements and disagree with others. In some cases, making a decision may be difficult, but you should force yourself to make a choice. Record your answers next to each statement according to the following rating scale:

### Rating Scale

4 Strongly agree
3 Slightly agree
2 Somewhat disagree
1 Strongly disagree

1. _____ Quality refers to a product's or service's ability to fulfill its primary operating characteristics, such as providing a sharp picture for a television set.

2. _____ Quality is an absolute, measurable aspect of a product or service.

3. _____ The concept of quality includes supplemental aspects of a product or service, such as the remote control for a television set.

4. _____ Productivity and quality are inversely related, so that, to get one, you must sacrifice the other.

5. _____ The concept of quality refers to the extent to which a product's design and operating characteristics conform to certain set standards.

6. _____ Productivity refers to what is created relative to what it takes to create it.

7. _____ Quality means that a product will not malfunction during a specified period of time.

8. _____ Quality refers only to products; it is immeasurable for services.

9. _____ The length of time that a product or service will function is what is known as quality.

10. _____ Everyone uses exactly the same definition of quality.
11. _____ Quality refers to the ease and speed with which a product or service can be repaired.
12. _____ Being treated courteously has nothing to do with the quality of anything.
13. _____ How a product looks, feels, tastes, or smells is what is meant by quality.

14. _____ Price, not quality, is what determines the ultimate value of service.
15. _____ Quality refers to what customers think of a product or service.
16. _____ Productivity and quality cannot both increase at the same time.

# Management at Work

### Driving Hard Bargains in Sustainability

## "The guys in the factory in China have no interest whatsoever in sustainability outcomes."

—JONATHAN MAXWELL, CEO OF SUSTAINABLE DEVELOPMENT CAPITAL LTD.

In July of 2011, the southeast Asian nation of Thailand was hit by an unusually severe monsoon season, triggering widespread flooding that killed more than 800 people and affected the lives of 13.6 million. The World Bank estimated economic damages of $45.7 billion, mostly to the country's manufacturing sector. Seven designated industrial zones were inundated by as much as 10 feet of water, and flooding in some areas persisted until January of 2012.

Now cut to your house in December 2011, where the hard drive in your computer has spun its last disk. So you get on your mother's laptop to check hard drive prices. When you last checked a couple of months ago, you could get a Western Digital Green 2TB drive for $79. Imagine your surprise when you find that the same hard drive now goes for $230. Why had Western Digital pumped up its prices to nosebleed altitudes? Because 40 to 45 percent of worldwide hard drive production is located in Thailand, where the flooding reduced production capacity by half.

Needless to say, supply chains are fraught with unpredictable dangers (perhaps especially when climate change is involved), and it may be only partly ironic to cite University of Arkansas logistics expert Matt Waller's observation that "most of the skills and competencies needed to excel in logistics and supply chain management are the same skills and competencies needed to excel at disaster-relief operations."

Supply chain management (SCM), for example, poses a number of critical challenges to companies that have committed themselves to sustainability as a factor in their corporate strategies. Sara A. Greenstein, a senior vice president at U.S. Steel and former head of supply chain and sustainability at Underwriters Laboratories, observes that "as much as 70 percent of product sustainability comes from suppliers,

who can lag significantly behind the curve." Indeed, Greenstein suggests that a sustainability strategy is hardly feasible unless it extends to a firm's supply chain: "The road to creating user-friendly, science-backed, technology-enabled supply chains," she says, "is paved with good sustainability intentions that get foiled by today's dynamic, global complexities. Achieving sustainability of scale requires involvement of the entire supply chain."

MIT's Peter Senge agrees: "You can't possibly source everything sustainably," he says, "unless you engage thousands and thousands of people around the world. You'll need technical innovations, management innovations, process innovations, and cultural innovations." Senge clearly believes that sustainability strategies must begin with a willingness to think differently about business priorities and possibilities. "When someone comes into an organization," he says,

*he or she will ask, "Why do we do it this way?" The answer is often "Just because." Now, 90 percent of those habits may be perfectly okay. But 10 percent are completely dysfunctional, particularly when the world around you is changing. A cool part of sustainability work is uncovering the assumptions that lead people to do things in a way that's out of touch with the company's larger reality.*

Not only sustainability strategy, argues Senge, but all organizational strategy, should be inherently forward looking. Sustainability issues are strategic matters for the simple reason that "they will shape the future of the business." In short, both sustainability and supply-chain strategy should be formulated with a firmer sense of *business continuity*—of how an organization acts to ensure that it continues to function during and after a disaster or some other threat. Senge's understanding of business continuity, however, is broader and reflects the definition of *business continuity management* (BCM) provided by the Business Continuity Institute (BCI): According to the BCI, BCM also "provides a framework for building organizational resilience with the capability of an effective response that safeguards the interests of the organization's key stakeholders, reputation, brand, and value-creating activities." How else, for example, is an organization's BCM strategy supposed to deal with the consequences of global warming, which threaten not only future generations but its own long-term survival?

"This isn't about trying to sell morality in the boardroom," says Jonathan Maxwell, CEO of Sustainable Development Capital Ltd. "It's about providing the ability for businesses to make better decisions to reduce costs, improve productivity, support growth, and make longer-term decisions." According to most proponents of corporate sustainability strategies, the best way to get sustainability on the corporate-strategy (and SCM) agenda is to get it on the "resource-efficiency agenda"—that is, to demonstrate the economic importance of the natural resources on which most organizations depend, such as fuel, water, land, and climate. "Once you have a system to value ecosystem services," says Robert Spencer, sustainability director at the engineering design firm AECOM, "the business case for embedding sustainability will be easier."

As we've seen, however, an organization's commitment to sustainability isn't feasible unless its suppliers buy into its sustainability-oriented SCM strategy. This means that getting the organization's board to implement such a strategy is only half the battle. Generally speaking, says Maxwell, "the guys in the factory in China have no interest whatsoever in sustainability outcomes." For most organizations, however, getting suppliers to implement their sustainability policies is imperative. Neither buyers nor suppliers, of course, can prevent monsoons and floods, but that's why companies develop BCM strategies—to deal with such disruptions in business continuity. In effect, then, by building its sustainability strategy into its BCM strategy, a company can take a proactive approach to supply-chain disruptions. Says Richard Waterer, head of Britain's Marsh Risk Consulting: "You can ... reduce volatility in your business by saying, 'We will not walk consciously into a relationship where we know we're taking on risks that prove to be damaging' to our business continuity."

How can companies avoid walking into potentially volatile supplier relationships—or, better yet, help suppliers to develop sustainability practices that are consistent with their own sustainability strategies? Simon Pringle, head of sustainability at the accounting firm BDO, suggests that companies move from "requesting" certain standards to "requiring" adherence to specific guidelines—telling suppliers that "we've just made a promise, and now you're all going to have to keep that promise." Critics of this approach argue that typical "sustainable procurement guidelines" encourage nothing more than "basic compliance" with existing regulations. Moreover, they contend, once suppliers meet guidelines, they have no incentive to improve their performance.

Proponents of proactive SCM recommend that organizations build stronger measures and more practical activities into their SCM practices. Greenstein, for example, observes that "manufacturers on the leading edge" of sustainable SCM "are pushing their sustainable efforts upstream." The key, she says, is the effective use of "incentives, business leverage, training programs, and progress monitoring to improve suppliers' performance." Best practices involve the collection and analysis of reliable information to understand the business environment of suppliers and to set objectives consistent with environmental conditions; to collaborate with suppliers on meeting those objectives and improving future performance; and to track performance against those goals.

## Case Questions

1. In addition to disruption in the supply of raw materials, supply chain problems can result in damage to the reputation of the buying organization. Think of a hypothetical situation in which this situation could occur, and explain how it could disrupt an organization's *business continuity*. Finally, provide some suggestions to show how the buying organization might avoid future problems by improving its approach to *business continuity management*.

2. Select any two of the following companies and explain how its suppliers can affect the *quality* of its products. In each case, provide two or three concrete examples. (You'll probably want to check company websites in order to make sure that you have a solid idea of what each company does.)

   - Starbucks
   - Ford
   - SmithKline Glaxo
   - Kellogg's
   - GE
   - Johnson & Johnson
   - Nike
   - L'Oréal
   - Walmart
   - Men's Wearhouse

3. Consider the following statement by Jonathan Maxwell, CEO of Sustainable Development Capital Ltd.: "If it's not commercial, it's not sustainable."

   What does Maxwell mean? What, for example, is he saying about the relationship between business priorities and practices on the one hand and the feasibility of effective sustainability priorities and practices on the other?

4. The most recent U.N. Global Compact–Accenture poll of 1,000 CEOs of major companies was released in 2013. Forty-five percent of the CEOs said that they regarded sustainability as

*"very important" to future business success—down from 54 percent in 2010. Nearly 70 percent thought that business was not doing enough to address sustainability challenges, and yet 76 percent felt that their companies were moving quickly and efficiently enough to handle those challenges.\**

How would you account for these numbers—both the contradictions and, perhaps more importantly, the apparent dropoff in concern for sustainability challenges?

*\*Ariel Schwartz, "CEOs No Longer Think Sustainability Is Key to Business Success," Fast Company (September 20, 2013),www.fastcoexist.com, on July 12, 2015.*

### Case References

Craig Scott, "Why Sustainable Supply Chains Make Business Sense," *The Guardian* (October 21, 2013), www.theguardian.com, on July 10, 2015; Woody Leonhard, "Hard-Drive Prices Still Not Back to Pre-Flood Levels," *InfoWorld* (January 30, 2013), www.infoworld.com, on July 11, 2015; "Hurricane Katrina Showed Critical Importance of Logistics and Supply-Chain Management," *University of Arkansas News* (October 6, 2005), http://news. uark.edu, on July 11, 2015; Sara A. Greenstein, "Sustainability Starts with the Supply Chain," *IndustryWeek* (October 29, 2014), www.industryweek. com, on July 10, 2015; Steven Prokesch, "The Sustainable Supply Chain," *Harvard Business Review* (October 2010), https://hbr.org, on July 10, 2015; Sumit Kumar, "Supply Chain Sustainability Needs a Fresh Viewpoint," *TriplePundit* (April 10, 2015), www.triplepundit.com, on July 10, 2015.

---

**YOU MAKE THE CALL** | **What to Do When Workers Wonder What Happens Next**

1. How about you? According to Kevin A. Sheridan, Chief Engagement Officer of HR Solutions International,

   employee engagement *is defined generally as a strong desire to be part of the value an organization creates. Engaged employees exhibit three key characteristics. Namely, they:*

   *Exhibit a strong emotional and intellectual bond with their organization.*
   *Exert discretionary effort that helps the organization realize better outcomes for their organization.*
   *Take co-ownership of their own engagement and commit to improve.\**

   Describe in as much detail as you can the features of the workplace and job that would encourage you to bring all three of these characteristics to your job performance. What seemingly positive factors (e.g., performance recognition awards) don't rank quite as highly in your mind as those that would motivate you to engage in your job?

2. Select any two jobs from the following list and assume for each that you've held it for at least two years:

   - Assistant manager at a restaurant
   - Stock clerk at a large retail outlet
   - Second-grade schoolteacher
   - Driver for a taxi company
   - Foreman of a lawn and landscape crew
   - Assistant librarian at a public library
   - Manager of a beauty salon
   - Custom footwear designer
   - Computer programmer for an applications developer
   - Assistant manager in an automotive repair department

   Based on your (hypothetical) experience in the job, what suggestions for improved productivity could you make, whether for your specific tasks or for company-wide performance?

3. The text explains "Increasing Employee Involvement" as a factor in "Improving Productivity." The discussion there is consistent with the following definition of *employee involvement*:

   Employee involvement *refers to work structures and processes that allow employees to systematically give their input into decisions that affect their own work.*

   "Work structures and processes" refer to such workplace features as continuous improvement teams, structured suggestion systems, and quality of work/life programs.

   Explain in your own words some basic differences between the concepts of *employee involvement* and *employee engagement.*

*\*"Does Employee Involvement Equate to Engagement?" Workforce.com (June 30, 2015), www.workforce.com, on July 9, 2015.*
*†Diane Berry, Lily Mok, and Thomas Otter, CFO Advisory: Employee Engagement Impacts Financial Outcomes and Business Risk (Gartner Inc., March 13, 2013), www.financialexecutives.org, on July 5, 2015.*

4. *A follow-up to question* 3. HCL Technologies, a global IT services company, has introduced a program to drive employee engagement. Components of the program include the following:[†]

- an online Q&A with the CEO
- a reward and recognition portal to provide timely recognition of exemplary employee performance
- a 360-degree feedback process that allows employees to see how well managers are performing
- weekly polls to gather employee feedback on various issues

What are the differences between the goals of a program like this and those of programs that come under the heading of "work structures and processes," such as

- continuous improvement teams
- formal quality of work/life programs
- quality control circles
- flatter organizational structures
- employee problem-solving task forces and teams
- structured suggestion systems?[‡]

[‡]Robert Bullock, "Employee Involvement" (Scontrino-Powell, 2011), www.scontrino-powell, on July 9, 2015.

# Endnotes

1   Susan M. Cantrell and David Smith, *Workforce of One: Revolutionizing Talent Management through Customization* (Dublin, Ireland: Accenture, 2010), pp. 11–14, https://books.google.com, on July 7, 2015; Susan Sorenson, "How Employee Engagement Drives Growth," *Gallup Business Journal* (June 20, 2013), www.gallup.com, on July 7, 2015; Diane Berry, Lily Mok, and Thomas Otter, *CFO Advisory: Employee Engagement Impacts Financial Outcomes and Business Risk* (Gartner Inc., March 13, 2013), www.financialexecutives.org, on July 5, 2015; *The Impact of Employee Engagement on Performance*, Harvard Business School Publishing Analytic Services Report (2013), https://hbr.org, on July 6, 2015; Dan Crim and Gerard Seijts, "What Engages Employees Most; Or, The Ten Cs of Employee Engagement," *Ivey Business Journal* (March-April 2006), http://iveybusinessjournal.com, on July 8, 2015; Paul Keegan, "The Five New Rules of Employee Engagement," *Inc.* (December 2014/January 2015), www.inc.com, on July 4, 2015.

2   Paul M. Swamidass, "Empirical Science: New Frontier in Operations Management Research," *Academy of Management Review*, October 1991, pp. 793–814.

3   See Anil Khurana, "Managing Complex Production Processes," *Sloan Management Review*, Winter 2009, pp. 85–98.

4   Office of Services, International Trade Administration, ita.doc.gov/td/sif on July 5, 2015.

5   For an example, see Robin Cooper and Regine Slagmulder, "Develop Profitable New Products with Target Costing," *Sloan Management Review*, Summer 2009, pp. 23–34.

6   Joan Woodward, *Industrial Organization: Theory and Practice* (London: Oxford University Press, 1965).

7   See "Tight Labor? Tech to the Rescue," *BusinessWeek*, March 20, 2015, pp. 36–37.

8   "New Plant Gets Jaguar in Gear," *USA Today*, November 27, 2000, p. 4B.

9   "Ford Focuses on Flexibility," *USA Today*, February 28, 2015, pp. 1B, 3B.

10   Ibid.

11   "Thinking Machines," *BusinessWeek*, August 7, 2014, pp. 78–86.

12   http://www.economist.com/news/technology-quarterly/21584455-robotics-new-breed-robots-being-designed-collaborate-humans?zid=291&ah=906e69ad01d2ee51960100b7fa502595

13   James Brian Quinn and Martin Neil Baily, "Information Technology: Increasing Productivity in Services," *Academy of Management Executive*, 1994, Vol. 8, No. 3, pp. 28–37.

14   See Charles J. Corbett, Joseph D. Blackburn, and Luk N. Van Wassenhove, "Partnerships to Improve Supply Chains," *Sloan Management Review*, Summer 1999, pp. 71–82; and Jeffrey K. Liker and Yen-Chun Wu, "Japanese Automakers, U.S. Suppliers, and Supply-Chain Superiority," *Sloan Management Review*, Fall 2000, pp. 81–93. See also Mark Pagell and Zhaohui Wu, "Building a More Complete Theory of Sustainable Supply Chain Management Using Case Studies of 10 Exemplars," *Journal of Supply Chain Management*, 2009, Vol. 45, No. 2, pp. 37–56.

15   "Fastener Woes to Delay Flight of First Boeing 787 Jets," *Wall Street Journal*, November 5, 2010.

16   "G.M. Pieces Together Japanese Supply Chain," *New York Times*, May 13, 2011, p. 5.

17   See "Siemens Climbs Back," *BusinessWeek*, June 5, 2014, pp. 79–82.

18   See M. Bensaou, "Portfolios of Buyer-Supplier Relationships," *Sloan Management Review*, Summer 1999, pp. 35–44.

19   "Just-in-Time Manufacturing Is Working Overtime," *BusinessWeek*, November 8, 2007, pp. 36–37.

20   Rhonda Reger, Loren Gustafson, Samuel DeMarie, and John Mullane, "Reframing the Organization: Why Implementing Total Quality Is Easier Said Than Done," *Academy of Management Review*, 1994, Vol. 19, No. 3, pp. 565–584.

21   http://www.fastcompany.com/3007843/creative-conversations/how-jenna-lyons-transformed-jcrew-cult-brand

22   Ross Johnson and William O. Winchell, *Management and Quality* (Milwaukee, WI: American Society for Quality Control, 1989). See also Carol Reeves and David Bednar, "Defining Quality: Alternatives and Implications," *Academy of Management Review*, 1994, Vol. 19, No. 3, pp. 419–445; and C. K. Prahalad and M. S. Krishnan, "The New Meaning of Quality in the Information Age," *Harvard Business Review*, September–October 1999, pp. 109–120.

23   *USA Today*, June 28, 2014, p. B4.

24   "Quality Isn't Just for Widgets," *BusinessWeek*, July 22, 2002, pp. 72–73.

25   W. Edwards Deming, *Out of the Crisis* (Cambridge, MA: MIT Press, 1986).

26   "When Service Means Survival," *BusinessWeek*, March 2, 2015, pp. 26–40.

27   *BusinessWeek*, March 2, 2009, p. 29.

28   Joel Dreyfuss, "Victories in the Quality Crusade," *Fortune*, October 10, 2008, pp. 80–88.

29   Thomas Y. Choi and Orlando C. Behling, "Top Managers and TQM Success: One More Look After All These Years," *Academy of Management Executive*, 1997, Vol. 11, No. 1, pp. 37–48.

30   James Dean and David Bowen, "Management Theory and Total Quality: Improving Research and Practice Through Theory Development," *Academy of Management Review*, 1994, Vol. 19, No. 3, pp. 392–418.

31   See "Porsche Figures Out What Americans Want," *USA Today*, June 28, 2012, p. 4B.

32   Edward E. Lawler, "Total Quality Management and Employee Involvement: Are They Compatible?" *Academy of Management Executive*, 1994, Vol. 8, No. 1, pp. 68–79.

33   Jeremy Main, "How to Steal the Best Ideas Around," *Fortune*, October 19, 2006, pp. 102–106.

34   See James Brian Quinn, "Strategic Outsourcing: Leveraging Knowledge Capabilities," *Sloan Management Review*, Summer 1999, pp. 8–22.

35   "Global Gamble," *Forbes*, April 17, 2006, pp. 78–82.

36   Thomas Robertson, "How to Reduce Market Penetration Cycle Times," *Sloan Management Review*, Fall 1993, pp. 87–96.

37   "Speed Demons," *BusinessWeek*, March 27, 2010, pp. 68–76.

38 "Ford Does Fast Update of Taurus," *USA Today*, April 20, 2011, p. 1B.

39 Ronald Henkoff, "The Hot New Seal of Quality," *Fortune*, June 28, 1993, pp. 116–120. See also Mustafa V. Uzumeri, "ISO 9000 and Other Metastandards: Principles for Management Practice?" *Academy of Management Executive*, 1997, Vol. 11, No. 1, pp. 20–28.

40 Paula C. Morrow, "The Measurement of TQM Principles and Work-Related Outcomes," *Journal of Organizational Behavior*, July 1997, pp. 363–376.

41 John W. Kendrick, *Understanding Productivity: An Introduction to the Dynamics of Productivity Change* (Baltimore, MD: Johns Hopkins University Press, 1977).

42 "Study: USA Losing Competitive Edge," *USA Today*, April 25, 1997, p. 9D.

43 "Why the Productivity Revolution Will Spread," *BusinessWeek*, February 14, 2015, pp. 112–118. See also "Productivity Grows in Spite of Recession," *USA Today*, July 29, 2012, pp. 1B, 2B; and "Productivity's Second Wind," *BusinessWeek*, February 17, 2013, pp. 36–37.

44 Michael van Biema and Bruce Greenwald, "Managing Our Way to Higher Service-Sector Productivity," *Harvard Business Review*, July–August 1997, pp. 87–98.

# NAME INDEX

Note: Tables in the index are referenced by t's and figures by f's.

# ORGANIZATION AND PRODUCT INDEX

Note: Tables in the index are referenced by t's and figures by f's.

Note: Tables in the index are referenced by t's and figures by f's.